Microeconomics

Theory & Applications with Calculus

The Addison-Wesley Series in Economics

Abel/Bernanke/Croushore
Macroeconomics*

Bade/Parkin
Foundations of Economics*

Bierman/Fernandez
Game Theory with Economic Applications

Binger/Hoffman
Microeconomics with Calculus

Boyer
Principles of Transportation Economics

Branson
Macroeconomic Theory and Policy

Bruce
Public Finance and the American Economy

Byrns/Stone
Economics

Carlton/Perloff
Modern Industrial Organization

Caves/Frankel/Jones
World Trade and Payments: An Introduction

Chapman
Environmental Economics: Theory, Application, and Policy

Cooter/Ulen
Law and Economics

Downs
An Economic Theory of Democracy

Ehrenberg/Smith
Modern Labor Economics

Ekelund/Ressler/Tollison
Economics*

Fusfeld
The Age of the Economist

Gerber
International Economics

Ghiara
Learning Economics

Gordon
Macroeconomics

Gregory
Essentials of Economics

Gregory/Stuart
Russian and Soviet Economic Performance and Structure

Hartwick/Olewiler
The Economics of Natural Resource Use

Hoffman/Averett
Woman and the Economy: Family, Work, and Play

Holt
Markets, Games and Strategic Behavior

Hubbard
Money, the Financial System, and the Economy

Hughes/Cain
American Economic History

Husted/Melvin
International Economics

Jehle/Reny
Advanced Microeconomic Theory

Johnson-Lans
A Health Economics Primer

Klein
Mathematical Methods for Economics

Krugman/Obstfeld
International Economics*

Laidler
The Demand for Money

Leeds/von Allmen
The Economics of Sports

Leeds/von Allmen/Schiming
Economics*

Lipsey/Ragan/Storer
Economics*

Melvin
International Money and Finance

Miller
Economics Today*

Miller
Understanding Modern Economics

Miller/Benjamin
The Economics of Macro Issues

Miller/Benjamin/North
The Economics of Public Issues

Mills/Hamilton
Urban Economics

Mishkin
The Economics of Money, Banking, and Financial Markets*

Mishkin
The Economics of Money, Banking, and Financial Markets, Alternate Edition*

Murray
Econometrics: A Modern Introduction

Parkin
Economics*

Perloff
Microeconomics*

Perloff
Microeconomics: Theory and Applications with Calculus

Perman/Common/McGilvray/Ma
Natural Resources and Environmental Economics

Phelps
Health Economics

Riddell/Shackelford/Stamos/ Schneider
Economics: A Tool for Critically Understanding Society

Ritter/Silber/Udell
Principles of Money, Banking, and Financial Markets

Rohlf
Introduction to Economic Reasoning

Ruffin/Gregory
Principles of Economics

Sargent
Rational Expectations and Inflation

Scherer
Industry Structure, Strategy, and Public Policy

Sherman
Market Regulation

Stock/Watson
Introduction to Econometrics

Stock/Watson
Introduction to Econometrics, Brief Edition

Studenmund
Using Econometrics

Tietenberg
Environmental and Natural Resource Economics

Tietenberg
Environmental Economics and Policy

Todaro/Smith
Economic Development

Waldman
Microeconomics

Waldman/Jensen
Industrial Organization: Theory and Practice

Weil
Economic Growth

Williamson
Macroeconomics

*denotes **myeconlab** titles.   **Log onto www.myeconlab.com to learn more**

Microeconomics

Theory & Applications with Calculus

Jeffrey M. Perloff

University of California, Berkeley

PEARSON

Addison
Wesley

Boston   San Francisco   New York
London   Toronto   Sydney   Tokyo   Singapore   Madrid
Mexico City   Munich   Paris   Cape Town   Hong Kong   Montreal

For Lisa

Publisher	**Greg Tobin**
Editor-in-Chief	**Denise Clinton**
Senior Acquisitions Editor	**Adrienne D'Ambrosio**
Development Editor	**Sylvia Mallory**
Assistant Editor	**Margaret Beste**
Managing Editor	**Nancy Fenton**
Senior Production Supervisor	**Meredith Gertz**
Cover Designer	**Regina Hagen Kolenda**
Supplements Editor	**Heather McNally**
Senior Media Producer	**Bethany Tidd**
Senior Marketing Manager	**Roxanne Hoch**
Marketing Assistant	**Ashlee Clevenger**
Senior Prepress Supervisor	**Caroline Fell**
Senior Manufacturing Buyer	**Carol Melville**
Production Coordination, Composition, and Illustrations	**Elm Street Publishing Services, Inc.**
Cover Image	**© Nick Koudis/Getty Images**

ISBN-13: 978-0-321-46858-1
ISBN-10: 0-321-46858-9

If you purchased this book within the United States or Canada you should be aware that it has been wrongfully imported without the approval of the Publisher or the Author.

3 4 5 6 7 8 9 10—DOW—11 10 09 08

Brief Contents

Preface xv

v

Contents

This book is a new type of intermediate microeconomics textbook. Until now, the choice was between books that use calculus to present formal theory dryly and with few, if any, applications to the real world and books that include applications but present theory using only graphs and algebra. This book uses calculus, algebra, and graphs to present microeconomic theory using actual examples, and applies the theory to analyze real-world problems. My purpose is to show students that economic theory has practical, problem-solving uses and is not an empty academic exercise.

This book shows how individuals, policy makers, and firms use microeconomic tools to analyze and resolve problems. For example, students learn that:

- individuals can draw on microeconomic theories when deciding about issues such as whether to invest and whether to sign a contract that pegs prices to the government's measure of inflation;
- policymakers (and voters) can employ microeconomics to predict, before they are enacted, the impact of taxes, regulations, and other measures;
- lawyers and judges use microeconomics in antitrust, discrimination, and contract cases;
- firms apply microeconomic principles to produce at least cost and maximize profit, select strategies, decide whether to buy from a market or to produce internally, and write contracts to provide optimal incentives for employees.

My experience in teaching microeconomics for the departments of economics at MIT, the University of Pennsylvania, and the University of California, Berkeley; the Department of Agricultural and Resource Economics at Berkeley; and the Wharton Business School has convinced me that students prefer this emphasis on real-world issues.

Features

This book differs from most other microeconomics texts in four main ways. First, it uses a mixture of calculus, algebra, and graphs to make economic theory clear. Second, it integrates real-world, "widget-free" examples throughout the exposition, in addition to offering extended applications. Third, it places greater emphasis than other texts on modern theories—such as industrial organization theories, game theory, transaction cost theory, information theory, and contract theory—that are useful in analyzing actual markets. Fourth, it employs a step-by-step approach to demonstrate how to use microeconomic theory to solve problems and analyze policy issues.

CALCULUS

Much of microeconomic theory is based on maximizing behavior. Calculus is particularly helpful in solving maximization problems. Thus this book combines calculus, algebra, graphs, and verbal descriptions to make the theory as clear as possible.

WIDGET-FREE ECONOMICS

To convince students that economics is practical and useful, not just a textbook exercise, this text presents theories using real-world examples rather than made-up analyses of widgets, those nonexistent products beloved by earlier generations of textbook writers. These real economic "stories" are integrated into the formal presentation of many economic theories, discussed in Applications, and analyzed in what-if policy discussions.

INTEGRATED REAL-WORLD EXAMPLES

This book uses real-world examples throughout the narrative to illustrate many basic theories of microeconomics. Students learn the basic model of supply and demand using estimated supply-and-demand curves for Canadian processed pork and U.S. sweetheart roses. They analyze consumer choice by employing typical consumers' estimated indifference curves between beer and wine and mill workers' indifference curves between income and leisure. They learn about production and cost functions using evidence from a U.S. furniture manufacturer. Students see monopoly theory applied to a patented pharmaceutical, Botox. They use oligopoly theories to analyze the rivalry between United Airlines and American Airlines on the Chicago–Los Angeles route and between Coke and Pepsi in the cola industry. They see Apple's monopoly pricing of iPods and learn about multimarket price discrimination through the use of data on how Warner Home Entertainment priced its *Harry Potter and the Prisoner of Azkaban* two-DVD movie set in various countries.

APPLICATIONS

The text also includes many featured Applications to illustrate the versatility of microeconomic theory. The Applications focus on such diverse topics as:

- the derivation of an isoquant for semiconductors, using actual data;
- the measures of the pleasure that consumers get from television;
- the amount by which recipients value Christmas presents relative to the cost to gift givers;
- how auction houses that provide more information achieve higher prices than sellers on eBay;
- whether buying flight insurance makes sense.

Additional Applications are available at **www.aw-bc.com/perloff**.

WHAT-IF POLICY ANALYSIS

In addition, this book uses economic models to probe the likely outcomes of changes in public policies. Students learn how to conduct what-if analyses of policies such as taxes, subsidies, barriers to entry, price floors and ceilings, quotas and tariffs, zoning, pollution controls, and licensing laws. The text analyzes the effects of taxes on virtually every type of market.

 The book also reveals the limits of economic theory for policy analysis. For example, to illustrate why attention to actual institutions is important, the text uses three different models to show how the effects of minimum wages vary across types of markets and institutions. Similarly, the text illustrates that a minimum wage law that is harmful in a competitive market may be desirable in certain noncompetitive markets.

MODERN THEORIES

The first half of the book (Chapters 2–10) examines competitive markets and shows that competition has very desirable properties. The rest of the book (Chapters 11–19) concentrates on imperfectly competitive markets, in which firms have market power, firms and consumers are uncertain about the future and have limited information, and there are externalities and public goods. The book uses behavioral economics to discuss bandwagon effects on monopoly pricing over time and the importance of time-varying discounting in explaining procrastination and in avoiding environmental disasters.

This book goes beyond basic microeconomic theory and looks at theories and applications from many important contemporary fields of economics. Extensive coverage of problems from resource economics, labor economics, international trade, public finance, and industrial organization is featured throughout.

This book also differs from other microeconomics texts by using game theory throughout the second half rather than isolating the topic in a single chapter. Game theory is introduced in Chapter 14, where it is used to study oligopoly quantity and price setting, entry by firms, strategic behavior in multiperiod games (such as collusion and preventing entry), strategic advertising, and auctions. Game theory is employed in later chapters to analyze investing given an uncertain future, pollution (the Coase Theorem), and other topics. Unlike most texts, this book covers pure and mixed strategies and analyzes both normal-form and extensive-form games.

The last two chapters draw from modern contract theory to analyze adverse selection and moral hazard extensively, instead of (as other texts do) mentioning these topics only in passing, if at all. The text covers lemons markets, signaling, preventing shirking, and revealing information (including through contract choice).

STEP-BY-STEP PROBLEM SOLVING

Many instructors report that their biggest challenge in teaching microeconomics is helping students learn to solve new problems. This book is based on the belief that the best way to teach this important skill is to demonstrate problem solving repeatedly and then to give students exercises to do on their own. All the chapters after Chapter 1 provide several Solved Problems that show students how to answer qualitative and quantitative problems using a step-by-step approach. Rather than empty arithmetic exercises demanding no more of students than employing algebra or a memorized mathematical formula, the Solved Problems focus on important economic issues such as analyzing government policies and determining firms' optimal strategies.

One Solved Problem uses game theory to examine the competition between the HD-DVD group and the Blu-ray group. Another shows how a monopolistically competitive airline equilibrium would change if fixed costs (such as fees for landing slots) rise. Others examine why firms charge different prices at factory stores than elsewhere and when markets for lemons exist, among many other topics.

The Solved Problems illustrate how to approach the two sets of formal end-of-chapter exercises. The first set (Questions) can be solved using graphs or verbal arguments; the second set (Problems) requires the use of math. Answers to selected exercises appear at the end of the book, and the solutions to the remaining problems may be found in the *Instructor's Manual*. Select end-of-chapter exercises were written by James Dearden of Lehigh University. These 86 exercises are identified by a **W** that appears at the end of these problems. Each chapter after Chapter 1 includes at least two of Professor Dearden's exercises, and some chapters have as many as six. Many are based on real-world events and are taken from newspapers, and most are multipart exercises. Professor Dearden verbally walks students through the solution for each exercise using slides available on the companion Web site, **www.aw-bc.com/perloff**.

ALTERNATIVE ORGANIZATIONS

Because instructors differ as to the order in which they cover material, this text has been designed for maximum flexibility. The most common approach to teaching microeconomics is to follow the sequence of the chapters in the first half of this book: supply and demand (Chapter 2), consumer theory (Chapters 3, 4, and 5), the theory of the firm (Chapters 6 and 7), and the competitive model (Chapters 8 and 9). Many instructors then cover monopoly (Chapter 11), price discrimination (Chapter 12), oligopoly and monopolistic competition (Chapter 13), game theory (Chapter 14), input markets (Chapter 15), uncertainty (Chapter 16), and externalities (Chapter 17).

A common variant is to present uncertainty (Sections 16.1 through 16.3) immediately after consumer theory. Many instructors like to take up welfare issues between discussions of the competitive model and noncompetitive models, as Chapter 10, on general equilibrium and economic welfare, does. Alternatively, that chapter may be covered at the end of the course. Faculty can assign material on factor markets following the chapters on competition or monopoly. The material in Chapters 13–19 can be presented in a variety of orders, although Chapter 19 should follow Chapter 18 if both are covered, and Section 16.4 should follow Chapter 15.

Many business school courses skip consumer theory (and possibly some aspects of supply and demand) to allow more time for the topics covered in the second half of this book. Business school faculty may want to place particular emphasis on game theory and strategies (Chapter 14), capital markets (Chapter 15), and modern contract theory (Chapters 18 and 19).

Supplements

Excellent supplements for this textbook are available for students and faculty. The *Study Guide*, by Charles F. Mason of the University of Wyoming and Leonie Stone of the State University of New York, Geneseo, provides students with a quick guide to key concepts and formulas, as well as additional Applications, and it walks them through the solution of many problems. Students can then work through a large number of practice problems on their own and check their answers against those in the guide. At the end of each *Study Guide* chapter is a set of exercises suitable for homework assignments. And at the Companion Website, **www.aw-bc.com/perloff**, students will find such varied learning aids as self-assessment chapter quizzes, mini-cases, additional Applications and Solved Problems, and slides with audio solutions to select end-of-chapter problems prepared by James Dearden of Lehigh University.

The *Instructor's Resource Disk* includes the following teaching resources, which are also available online for download at the Instructor Resource Center, **www.aw-bc.com/irc**, on the catalog page for *Microeconomics: Theory and Applications with Calculus*. The *Instructor's Manual,* by Mike Leonard of Kwantlen University College and Oleg V. Pavlov of Worcester Polytechnic Institute, has many useful and creative teaching ideas. It also offers additional Applications, as well as extra problems and answers, and it provides solutions for the end-of-chapter exercises whose answers are not given at the end of this book. The *Test Bank,* by Aaron Finkle of California State University, San Marcos, features many different types of problems of varying levels of complexity, suitable for homework assignments and exams. *The Computerized Test Bank,* offered in TestGen software, provides these test questions in a versatile, editable electronic format. Additionally for instructors, all the text figures and tables are available as full-color *PowerPoint® Presentation* slides.

Acknowledgments

This book grew out of my earlier, noncalculus intermediate microeconomics textbook. In that book, I thank the many faculty members and students who helped me produce it, as well as Jane Tufts, who provided invaluable editorial help. I am very lucky that Sylvia Mallory, who worked on the earlier book, was my development editor on this book as well. Sylvia worked valiantly to improve my writing style and helped to shape and improve every aspect of the book's contents and appearance. Adrienne D'Ambrosio, Senior Acquisitions Editor, worked closely with Sylvia and me in planning the book and was instrumental in every phase of the project.

I have an enormous debt of gratitude to my students at MIT, the University of Pennsylvania, and the University of California, Berkeley, who patiently dealt with my various approaches to teaching them microeconomics and made useful (and generally polite) suggestions. Peter Berck, Ethan Ligon, and Larry Karp, my colleagues at the University of California, Berkeley, made many useful suggestions. Hugo Salgado was incredibly helpful in producing figures, researching many of the Applications, and making constructive comments on the drafts of every chapter.

Many other people were very generous in providing me with data, models, and examples for the various Applications and Solved Problems in this book, including Peter Berck, University of California, Berkeley: exhaustible resources and investments; James Brander, University of British Columbia: American Airlines and United Airlines; Farid Gasmi, Université des Sciences Sociales, Toulouse: Coke and Pepsi; Claudia Goldin, Harvard University: income distribution; Rachel Goodhue, University of California, Davis: incentives; William Greene, New York University: power plants; Nile Hatch, University of Illinois: semiconductors and learning by doing; Charles Hyde, University of Melbourne: demand estimates; Larry Karp, University of California, Berkeley: trade and behavioral economics; Fahad Khalil, University of Washington: contract theory; Jean-Jacques Laffont, Université des Sciences Sociales, Toulouse: Coke and Pepsi; Karl D. Meilke, University of Guelph: pork; Giancarlo Moschini, Iowa State University: pork; Michael Roberts, U.S. Department of Agriculture: exhaustible resources; Peter von Allmen, Moravian College: various Applications; Quang Vuong, Université des Sciences Sociales, Toulouse, and University of Southern California: Coke and Pepsi.

I am grateful to the many teachers of microeconomics who spent untold hours reading and commenting on drafts of the chapters. Many of the best ideas in this book are due to the following reviewers, who provided valuable comments at various stages:

James Brander, *University of British Columbia*
Helle Bunzel, *Iowa State University*
Anoshua Chaudhuri, *San Francisco State University*
Anthony Davies, *Duquesne University*
James Dearden, *Lehigh University*
Wayne Edwards, *University of Alaska, Anchorage*
Patrick M. Emerson, *Oregon State University*
Ron Goettler, *Carnegie Mellon University*
Carrie A. Meyer, *George Mason University*
Joshua B. Miller, *University of Minnesota, Twin Cities*
Alexandre Padilla, *Metropolitan State College of Denver*
Burkhard C. Schipper, *University of California, Davis*
Galina A. Schwartz, *University of California, Berkeley*
Ron S. Warren, Jr., *University of Georgia*
Bruce Wydick, *University of California, San Francisco*

In particular, Jim Brander, Anthony Davies, Jim Dearden, Alexandre Padilla, and Bruce Wydick were participants in an extremely helpful focus group. Jim Dearden, Jim Brander, and Bruce Wydick gave me very insightful advice at many stages. One of my biggest debts is to Jim Dearden, who not only gave me incisive comments on every aspect of my earlier textbook and this one, but also developed and brilliantly executed the idea of writing topical questions with audio slide-show answers—a highly valuable feature in this book. I am also grateful to Ethan Ligon for co-authoring the Calculus Appendix, which follows the last chapter.

In addition, I thank Bob Solow, the world's finest economics teacher, who showed me how to simplify models without losing their essence. I've also learned a great deal over the years about economics and writing from my co-authors on other projects, especially Dennis Carlton (my co-author on *Modern Industrial Organization*), Jackie Persons, Steve Salop, Michael Wachter, Larry Karp, Peter Berck, Amos Golan, George Judge, Ximing Wu, and Dan Rubinfeld (whom I thank for still talking to me despite my decision to write microeconomics textbooks).

It was a pleasure to work with the good people at Addison-Wesley, who were incredibly helpful in producing this book. Denise Clinton, Editor-in-Chief for Economics and Finance, and Adrienne D'Ambrosio signed me to a contract. Meredith Gertz, senior production supervisor, did her usual fine job of supervising the production process and assembling the extended publishing team. Kay Ueno, Director of Development, provided insight and guidance. Gina Hagen Kolenda managed the design of the handsome interior and cover, Joe Vetere, Senior Technical Art Specialist, helped me prepare graphics, and Angel Chavez skillfully prepared the final figures. Heather Johnson and the rest of the staff at Elm Street Publishing Services have my sincere thanks for keeping the project on track and on schedule. I also want to acknowledge, with gratitude, the efforts of Bethany Tidd in developing the Web site and Roxanne Hoch in marketing the entire program. Heather McNally arranged for the supplements, and Margaret Beste, editorial assistant, was very helpful at many stages of the process.

Finally, I thank my family, Mimi Perloff, Jackie Persons, and Lisa Perloff, for their great patience and support during the nearly endless writing process. And I apologize for misusing their names—and those of my other relatives and friends—in this book!

J. M. P.

Chapter 1

Introduction

I've often wondered what goes into a hot dog. Now I know and I wish I didn't.
—William Zinsser

If each of us could get all the food, clothing, and toys we want without working, no one would study economics. Unfortunately, most of the good things in life are scarce—we can't all have as much as we want. Thus scarcity is the mother of economics.

Microeconomics is the study of how individuals and firms make themselves as well off as possible in a world of scarcity, and the consequences of those individual decisions for markets and the entire economy. In studying microeconomics, we examine how individual consumers and firms make decisions and how the interaction of many individual decisions affects markets.

Microeconomics is often called *price theory* to emphasize the important role that prices play in determining market outcomes. Microeconomics explains how the actions of all buyers and sellers determine prices and how prices influence the decisions and actions of individual buyers and sellers.

In this chapter, we discuss three main topics

1. **Microeconomics: The Allocation of Scarce Resources:** Microeconomics is the study of the allocation of scarce resources.

2. **Models:** Economists use models to make testable predictions.

3. **Uses of Microeconomic Models:** Individuals, governments, and firms use microeconomic models and predictions in decision making.

1.1 Microeconomics: The Allocation of Scarce Resources

Individuals and firms allocate their limited resources to make themselves as well off as possible. Consumers pick the mix of goods and services that makes them as happy as possible given their limited wealth. Firms decide which goods to produce, where to produce them, how much to produce to maximize their profits, and how to produce those levels of output at the lowest cost by using more or less of various inputs such as labor, capital, materials, and energy. The owners of a depletable natural resource such as oil decide when to use it. Government decision makers decide which goods and services the government will produce and whether to subsidize, tax, or regulate industries and consumers so as to benefit consumers, firms, or government employees.

TRADE-OFFS

People make trade-offs because they can't have everything. A society faces three key trade-offs:

- **Which goods and services to produce:** If a society produces more cars, it must produce fewer of other goods and services, because there are only so many *resources*—workers, raw materials, capital, and energy—available to produce goods.
- **How to produce:** To produce a given level of output, a firm must use more of one input if it uses less of another input. Cracker and cookie manufacturers switch between palm oil and coconut oil depending on which is less expensive.
- **Who gets the goods and services:** The more of society's goods and services you get, the less someone else gets.

WHO MAKES THE DECISIONS

These three allocation decisions may be made explicitly by the government, or they may reflect the interaction of independent decisions by many individual consumers and firms. In the former Soviet Union, the government told manufacturers how many cars of each type to make and which inputs to use to make them. The government also decided which consumers would get cars.

In most other countries, how many cars of each type are produced and who gets them are determined by how much it costs to make cars of a particular quality in the least expensive way and how much consumers are willing to pay for them. More consumers would own a handcrafted Rolls-Royce and fewer would buy a mass-produced Ford Taurus if a Rolls were not 21 times more expensive than a Taurus.

● APPLICATION

Addressing a Flu Vaccine Shortage[1]

In 2004, the U.S. government expected a record 100 million flu vaccine doses to be available, but one vaccine maker, Chiron, could not ship 46 million doses because of contamination. As a consequence, the government expected a shortage at the traditional price.

In response, government and public health officials urged young, healthy people to forgo getting shots until the sick, elderly, and other high-risk populations such as health care providers and pregnant women were inoculated. When public spirit failed to dissuade enough healthy people from getting the vaccine, federal, state, and local governments restricted access to high-risk populations. Yet ultimately, the Centers for Disease Control and Prevention reported in 2006 that only 29% of the 6.5 million American children with asthma, a group at high risk of influenza complications, received flu shots during the 2004–2005 flu season.

In most markets for non-health-related goods, prices adjust to prevent shortages. In contrast, during the flu shot shortage, governments did not try increasing the price to reduce demand but instead relied on exhortation or formal allocation schemes.

---

[1]Sources for applications appear at the end of the book.

HOW PRICES DETERMINE ALLOCATIONS

> *An Economist's Theory of Reincarnation: If you're good, you come back on a*
> *higher level. Cats come back as dogs, dogs come back as horses, and people—*
> *if they've been real good like George Washington—come back as money.*

Prices link the decisions about *which goods and services to produce, how to produce them,* and *who gets them.* Prices influence the decisions of individual consumers and firms, and the interactions of these decisions by consumers, firms, and the government determine price.

Interactions between consumers and firms take place in a **market,** which is an exchange mechanism that allows buyers to trade with sellers. A market may be a town square where people go to trade food and clothing, or it may be an international telecommunications network over which people buy and sell financial securities. Typically, when we talk about a single market, we are referring to trade in a single good or a group of goods that are closely related, such as soft drinks, movies, novels, or automobiles.

Most of this book concerns how prices are determined within a market. We show that the organization of the market, especially the *number of buyers and sellers* in the market and the *amount of information* they have, helps determine whether the price equals the cost of production. We also show that if there is no market—and hence no market price—serious problems, such as high levels of pollution, result.

● APPLICATION

Twinkie Tax

Many U.S., Canadian, U.K., and Australian jurisdictions are proposing a "Twinkie tax" on fatty and sweet foods to reduce obesity and cholesterol problems, particularly among children. One survey found that 45% of adults would support a 1¢ tax per pound of soft drinks, chips, and butter, with the revenues used to fund health education programs.

Many proponents and opponents of these proposed laws seem unaware that at least 25 states and three cities already impose additional taxes on soft drinks, candy, chewing gum, and snack foods such as potato chips (Chouinard et al., 2006). By 2007, many school districts throughout the United States banned soft drink vending machines. This ban discourages consumption the same way an extremely high tax would.

New taxes will affect *which foods are produced,* as firms offer new low-fat and low-sugar products, and *how fast food is produced,* as manufacturers reformulate their products to lower their tax burden. These taxes will also influence *who gets these goods,* as consumers, especially children, switch to less expensive, untaxed products.

1.2 Models

> *Everything should be made as simple as possible, but not simpler.* —Albert Einstein

To *explain* how individuals and firms allocate resources and how market prices are determined, economists use a **model:** a description of the relationship between two or more economic variables. Economists also use models to *predict* how a change in one variable will affect another variable.

● APPLICATION

Income Threshold Model and China

According to the *income threshold model,* no one who has an income level below a threshold buys a particular *consumer durable,* which is a good, such as a refrigerator or car, that can be used for long periods of time. The theory also holds that almost everyone whose income is above the threshold does buy the durable.

If this theory is correct, the expectation is that as the income of most people in less-developed countries rises above that threshold, consumer durable purchases will go from near zero to large numbers virtually overnight. This prediction is consistent with evidence from Malaysia, where the income threshold for buying a car is about $4,000.

Given similar evidence from other countries, business leaders from around the world believe that this model's predictions apply to present-day China. Incomes have risen rapidly in China and now exceed the threshold levels for many types of durable goods. As a result, the greatest sales boom of consumer durable goods in history may be taking place in China today. Anticipating this boom, foreign companies have greatly increased their investments in durable goods manufacturing plants in China. Annual foreign investments went from $44.2 billion in 2001 to $60.3 billion in 2005. Anticipating this growth potential, even traditional political opponents of the People's Republic—Taiwan, South Korea, and Russia—have invested in China.

SIMPLIFICATIONS BY ASSUMPTION

We stated the income threshold model verbally, but we could have presented it using graphs or mathematics. Regardless of how the model is described, an economic model is a simplification of reality that contains only reality's most important features. Without simplifications, it is difficult to make predictions because the real world is too complex to analyze fully.

By analogy, if the owner's manual accompanying your new DVD recorder had a diagram showing the relationships among all the parts in the DVD, the diagram would be overwhelming and useless. But a diagram that includes a photo of the buttons on the front of the machine, with labels describing the purpose of each, is useful and informative.

Economists make many *assumptions* to simplify their models.[2] When using the income threshold model to explain car-purchasing behavior in Malaysia, we *assume* that factors other than income, such as the color of cars, are irrelevant to the decision to buy cars. Therefore, we ignore the color of cars that are sold in Malaysia when we describe the relationship between average income and the number of cars that consumers want. If this assumption is correct, by ignoring color we make our analysis of the auto market simpler without losing important details. If we're wrong and these ignored issues are important, our predictions may be inaccurate.

Throughout this book, we start with strong assumptions to simplify our models. Later we add complexities. For example, in most of the book, we assume that consumers know the price each firm charges for a product. In many markets, such as the New York Stock Exchange, this assumption is realistic. However, it is not realistic in other markets, such as the market for used automobiles, in which consumers do not know the prices each firm charges. To devise an accurate model for markets in which consumers have limited information, in Chapter 18 we add consumer uncertainty about price into the model.

TESTING THEORIES

Given a choice between two theories, take the one which is funnier. —Blore's Razor

Economic *theory* is the development and use of a model to test *hypotheses,* which are predictions about cause and effect. We are interested in models that make clear, testable predictions, such as "If the price rises, the quantity demanded falls." A theory saying that "People's behavior depends on their tastes, and their tastes change randomly at random intervals" is not very useful because it does not lead to testable predictions.

Economists test theories by checking whether predictions are correct. If a prediction does not come true, economists may reject the theory.[3] Economists use a model until it is refuted by evidence or until a better model is developed.

A good model makes sharp, clear predictions that are consistent with reality. Some very simple models make sharp predictions that are incorrect, and other, more complex models make ambiguous predictions—in which any outcome is possible—that are untestable. The skill in model building is to chart a middle ground.

The purpose of this book is to teach you how to think like an economist, in the sense that you can build testable theories using economic models or apply existing models to new situations. Although economists think alike, in that they develop and use

---

[2]An economist, an engineer, and a physicist are stranded on a deserted island with a can of beans but no can opener. How should they open the can? The engineer proposes hitting the can with a rock. The physicist suggests building a fire under it to build up pressure and burst the can open. The economist thinks for a while and then says, "*Assume* that we have a can opener. . . ."

[3]We can use evidence of whether a theory's predictions are correct to *refute* the theory but not to *prove* it. If a model's prediction is inconsistent with what actually happened, the model must be wrong, so we reject it. Even if the model's prediction is consistent with reality, however, the model's prediction may be correct for the wrong reason. Hence we cannot prove that the model is correct—we can only fail to reject it.

testable models, they often disagree. One may present a logically consistent argument that prices will go up in the next quarter. Another economist, using a different but equally logical theory, may contend that prices will fall in that quarter. If the economists are reasonable, they agree that pure logic alone cannot resolve their dispute. Indeed, they agree that they'll have to use empirical evidence—facts about the real world—to find out which prediction is correct.

MAXIMIZING SUBJECT TO CONSTRAINTS

Although one economist's model may differ from another's, a key assumption in most microeconomic models is that individuals allocate their scarce resources so as to make themselves as well off as possible. Of all the affordable combinations of goods, consumers pick the bundle of goods that gives them the most possible enjoyment. Firms try to maximize their profits given limited resources and existing technology. That resources are limited plays a crucial role in these models. Were it not for scarcity, people could consume unlimited amounts of goods and services, and sellers could become rich beyond limit.

As we show throughout this book, the maximizing behavior of individuals and firms determines society's three main allocation decisions: which goods are produced, how they are produced, and who gets them. For example, diamond-studded pocket combs will be sold only if firms find it profitable to sell them. The firms will make and sell these combs only if consumers value the combs at least as much as it costs the firm to produce them. Consumers will buy the combs only if they get more pleasure from the combs than they would from the other goods they could buy with the same resources.

Thus many of the models that we examine are based on maximizing an objective that is subject to a constraint. Consumers maximize their well-being subject to a budget constraint, which says that their resources limit how many goods they can buy. Firms maximize profits subject to technological and other constraints. Governments may try to maximize the welfare of consumers or firms subject to constraints imposed by limited resources and the behavior of consumers and firms. We cover the formal economic analysis of maximizing behavior in the following chapters and review the underlying mathematics in the appendix at the end of the book.

POSITIVE VERSUS NORMATIVE

The use of models of maximizing behavior sometimes leads to predictions that seem harsh or heartless. For instance, a World Bank economist predicted that if an African government used price controls to keep the price of food low during a drought, food shortages would occur and people would starve. The predicted outcome is awful, but the economist was not heartless. The economist was only making a scientific prediction about the relationship between cause and effect: Price controls (cause) lead to food shortages and starvation (effect).

Such a scientific prediction is known as a **positive statement:** a testable hypothesis about cause and effect. "Positive" does not mean that we are certain about the truth of our statement—it indicates only that we can test the truth of our statement.

If the World Bank economist is correct, should the government control prices? If government policymakers believe the economist's predictions, they'll know that the low prices will help consumers who are lucky enough to be able to buy as much food as they want but hurt both the firms that sell food and the people who cannot buy as much food as they want, some of whom may die. As a result, the government's decision of whether to use price controls turns on whether the government cares more about the winners or the losers. In other words, to decide on its policy, the government makes a value judgment.

Instead of first making a prediction and testing it and then making a value judgment to decide whether to use price controls, government policymakers could make a value judgment directly. The value judgment could be based on the belief that "because people *should* have prepared for the drought, the government *should* not try to help them by keeping food prices low." Alternatively, the judgment could be based on the view that "people *should* be protected against price gouging during a drought, so the government *should* use price controls."

These two statements are *not* scientific predictions. Each is a value judgment or **normative statement:** a conclusion as to whether something is good or bad. A normative statement cannot be tested because a value judgment cannot be refuted by evidence. It is a prescription rather than a prediction. A normative statement concerns what somebody believes *should* happen; a positive statement concerns what *will* happen.

Although a normative conclusion can be drawn without first conducting a positive analysis, a policy debate will be more informed if positive analyses are conducted first.[4] Suppose your normative belief is that the government should help the poor. Should you vote for a candidate who advocates a higher minimum wage (a law that requires firms to pay wages at or above a specified level); a European-style welfare system (guaranteeing health care, housing, and other basic goods and services); an end to our current welfare system; a negative income tax (in which the less income a person has, the more the government gives that person); or job training programs? Positive economic analysis can be used to predict whether these programs will benefit poor people but *not* whether these programs are good or bad. Using these predictions and your value judgment, you decide for whom to vote.

Economists' emphasis on positive analysis has implications for what they study and even their use of language. For example, many economists stress that they study people's *wants* rather than their *needs*. Although people need certain minimum levels of food, shelter, and clothing to survive, most people in developed economies have enough money to buy goods well in excess of the minimum levels necessary to maintain life. Consequently, calling something a "need" in a wealthy country is often a value judgment. You almost certainly have been told by some elder that "you *need* a college education." That person was probably making a value judgment—"you *should* go to college"—rather than a scientific prediction that you will suffer terrible economic deprivation if you do not go to college. We can't test such value judgments, but we can test a hypothesis such as "One-third of the college-age population *wants* to go to college at current prices."

---

[4]Some economists draw the normative conclusion that, as social scientists, we economists *should* restrict ourselves to positive analyses. Others argue that we shouldn't give up our right to make value judgments just like the next person (who happens to be biased, prejudiced, and pigheaded, unlike us).

1.3   Uses of Microeconomic Models

Have you ever imagined a world without hypothetical situations? —Steven Wright

Because microeconomic models *explain* why economic decisions are made and allow us to make *predictions,* they can be very useful for individuals, governments, and firms in making decisions. Throughout this book, we consider examples of how microeconomics aids in actual decision making. Here we briefly look at some uses by individuals and governments.

Individuals use microeconomics to make purchasing and other decisions (Chapters 3–5). For example, we examine how inflation and adjustments for inflation affect individuals in Chapter 5. In Chapter 15, we explore how to determine whether it pays financially to go to college. How to invest in stocks, bonds, and other financial instruments, and whether to buy insurance is covered in Chapter 16. Individuals have to decide whether a used car is a lemon or worth buying (Chapter 18). Whether potential employers regard your college degree as proof of your abilities depends on the fraction of people who have advanced degrees and whether education provides useful training (Chapter 18). Whether you should hire a lawyer by the hour or offer the lawyer a percentage of any winnings depends on the type of case (Chapter 19). Whether you should accept deferred payments can also be analyzed using economics (Chapter 19). Another use of microeconomics is to help citizens make voting decisions on the basis of candidates' views on economic issues.

Your government's elected and appointed officials use (or could use) economic models in many ways. Recent administrations have placed increased emphasis on economic analysis. Today, economic and environmental impact studies are required before many projects can commence. The President's Council of Economic Advisers and other federal economists analyze and advise national government agencies on the likely economic effects of all major policies.

Indeed, a major use of microeconomic models by governments is to predict the probable impact of a policy. In Chapter 2, we show how to predict the likely impact of a tax on the prices consumers pay and on the tax revenues raised. In Chapter 9, we analyze the effects on markets of various international trade policies, such as tariffs and quotas. Chapter 11 considers how San Francisco should set the price for cable car rides and the effects of government regulations on electric utilities. Governments also use economics to decide how best to prevent pollution and global warming (Chapter 17).

Decisions by firms reflect microeconomic analysis. Firms price discriminate or bundle goods to increase their profits (Chapter 12). How American and United Airlines compete on the Chicago-Los Angeles route is predictable using economic analysis (Chapter 13). Indeed, many strategic decisions concerning pricing, setting quantities, advertising, or entry into a market are based on game theory (Chapter 14). When the phone company should replace telephone poles or a mining company should extract depends on interest rates (Chapter 15). Firms decide whether to offer employees deferred payments to ensure hard work (Chapter 19).

Summary

1. **Microeconomics: The Allocation of Scarce Resources:** Microeconomics is the study of the allocation of scarce resources. Consumers, firms, and the government must make allocation decisions. The three key trade-offs a society faces are which goods and services to produce, how to produce them, and who gets them. These decisions are interrelated and depend on the prices that consumers and firms face and on government actions. Market prices affect the decisions of individual consumers and firms, and the interaction of the decisions of individual consumers and firms determines market prices. The organization of the market, especially the number of firms in the market and the information consumers and firms have, plays an important role in determining whether the market price is equal to or higher than the cost of producing an additional unit of output.

2. **Models:** Models based on economic theories are used to predict the future or to answer questions about how some change, such as a tax increase, will affect various sectors of the economy. A good theory is simple to use and makes clear, testable predictions that are not refuted by evidence. Most microeconomic models are based on maximizing behavior. Economists use models to construct *positive* hypotheses concerning how a cause leads to an effect. These positive questions can be tested. In contrast, *normative* statements, which are value judgments, cannot be tested.

3. **Uses of Microeconomic Models:** Individuals, governments, and firms use microeconomic models and predictions to make decisions. For example, to maximize its profits, a firm needs to know consumers' decision-making criteria, the trade-offs between various ways of producing and marketing its product, government regulations, and other factors. For a large company, beliefs about how its rivals will react to its actions play a critical role in how the company forms its business strategies.

Chapter 2

Supply and Demand

Talk is cheap because supply exceeds demand.

When asked "What is the most important thing you know about economics?" many people reply, "Supply equals demand." This statement is a shorthand description of one of the simplest yet most powerful models of economics. The supply-and-demand model describes how consumers and suppliers interact to determine the *quantity* of a good or service sold in a market and the *price* at which it is sold. To use the model, you need to determine three things: buyers' behavior, sellers' behavior, and how buyers' and sellers' actions affect price and quantity. After reading this chapter, you should be able to use the supply-and-demand model to analyze some of the most important policy questions facing your country today, such as those concerning international trade, minimum wages, and price controls on health care.

After reading that grandiose claim, you might ask, "Is that all there is to economics? Can I become an expert economist that fast?" The answer to both questions, of course, is no. In addition, you need to learn the limits of this model and which other models to use when this one does not apply. (You must also learn the economists' secret handshake.)

Even with its limitations, the supply-and-demand model is the most widely used economic model. It provides a good description of how markets function, and it works particularly well in markets that have many buyers and many sellers, such as most agriculture and labor markets. Like all good theories, the supply-and-demand model can be tested—and possibly shown to be false. But in markets where it is applicable, it allows us to make accurate predictions easily.

In this chapter, we examine eight main topics	
	1. **Demand:** The quantity of a good or service that consumers demand depends on price and other factors such as consumers' incomes and the price of related goods.
	2. **Supply:** The quantity of a good or service that firms supply depends on price and other factors such as the cost of inputs that firms use to produce the good or service.
	3. **Market Equilibrium:** The interaction between consumers' demand curve and firms' supply curve determines the market price and quantity of a good or service that is bought and sold.
	4. **Shocking the Equilibrium: Comparative Statics:** Changes in a factor that affect demand (such as consumers' incomes), supply (such as a rise in the price of inputs), or a new government policy (such as a new tax) alter the market price and quantity of a good.
	5. **Elasticities:** Given estimates of summary statistics called elasticities, economists can forecast the effects of changes in taxes and other factors on market price and quantity.

6. **Effects of a Sales Tax:** How a sales tax increase affects the equilibrium price and the quantity of a good and whether the tax falls more heavily on consumers or on suppliers depend on the supply and demand curves.

7. **Quantity Supplied Need Not Equal Quantity Demanded:** If the government regulates the prices in a market, the quantity supplied might not equal the quantity demanded.

8. **When to Use the Supply-and-Demand Model:** The supply-and-demand model applies only to competitive markets.

2.1 Demand

The amount of a good that consumers are *willing* to buy at a given price during a specified time period (such as a day or a year), holding constant the other factors that influence purchases, is the **quantity demanded.** The quantity demanded of a good or service can exceed the quantity *actually* sold. For example, as a promotion, a local store might sell DVDs for $1 each today only. At that low price, you might want to buy 25 DVDs, but because the store has run out of stock, you can buy only 10 DVDs. The quantity you demand is 25—it's the amount you *want*—even though the amount you *actually buy* is only 10.

Potential consumers decide how much of a good or service to buy on the basis of its price, which is expressed as an amount of money per unit of the good (for example, dollars per pound), and many other factors, including consumers' own tastes, information, and income; prices of other goods; and government actions. Before concentrating on the role of price in determining demand, let's look briefly at some of the other factors.

Consumers make purchases based on their *tastes.* Consumers do not purchase foods they dislike, works of art they hate, or clothes they view as unfashionable or uncomfortable. However, advertising may influence people's tastes.

Similarly, *information* (or misinformation) about the uses of a good affects consumers' decisions. A few years ago when many consumers were convinced that oatmeal could lower their cholesterol level, they rushed to grocery stores and bought large quantities of oatmeal. (They even ate some of it until they remembered that they couldn't stand how it tastes.)

The *prices of other goods* also affect consumers' purchase decisions. Before deciding to buy Levi's jeans, you might check the prices of other brands. If the price of a close *substitute*—a product that you view as similar or identical to the one you are considering purchasing—is much lower than the price of Levi's jeans, you may buy that other brand instead. Similarly, the price of a *complement*—a good that you like to consume at the same time as the product you are considering buying—may affect your decision. If you eat pie only with ice cream, the higher the price of ice cream, the less likely you are to buy pie.

Income plays a major role in determining what and how much to purchase. People who suddenly inherit great wealth may purchase a Mercedes or other luxury items and would probably no longer buy do-it-yourself repair kits.

Government rules and regulations affect purchase decisions. Sales taxes increase the price that a consumer must spend on a good, and government-imposed limits on the use of a good may affect demand. If a city's government bans the use of skateboards on its streets, skateboard sales fall.

Other factors may also affect the demand for specific goods. Some people are more likely to buy two-hundred-dollar pairs of shoes if their friends do too. The demand for small, dying evergreen trees is substantially higher in December than in other months.

Although many factors influence demand, economists usually concentrate on how price affects the quantity demanded. The relationship between price and the quantity demanded plays a critical role in determining the market price and quantity in a supply-and-demand analysis. To determine how a change in price affects the quantity demanded, economists must hold constant other factors, such as income and tastes, that affect demand.

THE DEMAND FUNCTION

The **demand function** shows the correspondence between the quantity demanded, price, and other factors that influence purchases. For example, the demand function might be

$$Q = D(p, p_s, p_c, Y), \tag{2.1}$$

where Q is the quantity demanded of a particular good in a given time period, p is its price per unit of the good, p_s is the price per unit of a substitute good (a good that might be consumed instead of this good), p_c is the price per unit of a complementary good (a good that might be consumed jointly with this good, such as cream with coffee), and Y is consumers' income.

An example is the estimated demand function for processed pork in Canada:[1]

$$Q = 171 - 20p + 20p_b + 3p_c + 2Y, \tag{2.2}$$

where Q is the quantity of pork demanded in million kilograms (kg) of dressed cold pork carcass weight per year, p is the price of pork in Canadian dollars per kilogram, p_b is the price of beef (a substitute good) in dollars per kilogram, p_c is the price of chicken (another substitute good) in dollars per kilogram, and Y is the income of consumers in dollars per year. Any other factors that are not explicitly listed in the demand function are assumed to be irrelevant (such as the price of llamas in Peru) or held constant (such as the price of fish).

Usually, we're primarily interested in the relationship between the quantity demanded and the price of the good. That is, we want to know the relationship between the quantity demanded and price, holding all other factors constant. For example, we could set p_b, p_c, and Y at their averages over the period studied: $p_b = \$4$ per kg, $p_c = \$3\frac{1}{3}$ per kg, and $Y = 12.5$ thousand dollars. If we substitute these values

---

[1]Because prices, quantities, and other factors change simultaneously over time, economists use statistical techniques to hold constant the effects of factors other than the price of the good so that they can determine how price affects the quantity demanded. (See Appendix 2 at the end of the chapter.) Moschini and Meilke (1992) used such techniques to estimate the pork demand curve. In Equation 2.2, I've rounded the number slightly for simplicity. As with any estimate, their estimates are probably more accurate in the observed range of pork prices ($1 to $6 per kg) than at very high or very low prices.

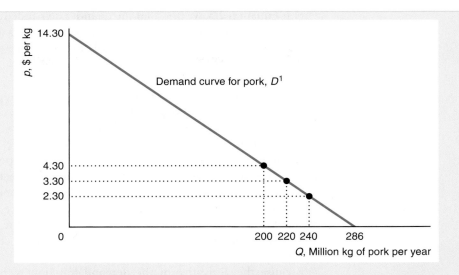

Figure 2.1 A Demand Curve. The estimated demand curve, D^1, for processed pork in Canada (Moschini and Meilke, 1992) shows the relationship between the quantity demanded per year and the price per kg. The downward slope of the demand curve shows that, holding other factors that influence demand constant, consumers demand less of a good when its price is high and more when the price is low. A change in price causes a *movement along the demand curve.*

for p_b, p_c, and Y in Equation 2.2, we can rewrite the quantity demanded as a function of only the price of pork:

$$Q = 171 - 20p + 20p_b + 3p_c + 2Y$$

$$= 171 - 20p + (20 \times 4) + \left(3 \times \frac{1}{3} \right) + (2 \times 12.5) \qquad (2.3)$$

$$= 286 - 20p = D(p).$$

We can graphically show this relationship, $Q = D(p) = 286 - 20p$, between the quantity demanded and price. A **demand curve** is a plot of the demand function that shows the quantity demanded at each possible price, holding constant the other factors that influence purchases. Figure 2.1 shows the estimated demand curve, D^1, for processed pork in Canada. (Although this demand curve is a straight line, demand curves may be smooth curves or wavy lines.) By convention, the vertical axis of the graph measures the price, p, per unit of the good: dollars per kilogram (kg). The horizontal axis measures the quantity, Q, of the good, per physical measure of the good per time period: million kg of dressed cold pork carcass weight per year.

The demand curve, D^1, hits the price (vertical) axis at $14.30, indicating that no quantity is demanded when the price is $14.30 or higher. Using Equation 2.3, if we set $Q = 286 - 20p = 0$, we find that the demand curve hits the price axis at $p = 286/20 = $14.30. The demand curve hits the horizontal quantity axis at 286 million kg—the amount of pork that consumers want if the price is zero. If we set the price equal to zero in Equation 2.3, we find that the quantity demanded is $Q = 286 - (20 \times 0) = 286.$[2] By plugging the particular values for p in the figure into the demand equation, we can determine the corresponding quantities. For example, if $p = \$3.30$, then $Q = 286 - (20 \times 3.30) = 220$.

Effect of a Change in Price on Demand. The demand curve in Figure 2.1 shows that if the price increases from \$3.30 to \$4.30, the quantity consumers demand decreases by 20 units, from 220 to 200. These changes in the quantity demanded in response to changes in price are *movements along the demand curve.* The demand curve is a concise summary of the answers to the question "What happens to the quantity demanded as the price changes, when all other factors are held constant?"

One of the most important empirical findings in economics is the **Law of Demand:** Consumers demand more of a good the lower its price, holding constant tastes, the prices of other goods, and other factors that influence the amount they consume.[3] One way to state the Law of Demand is that the demand curve slopes downward, as in Figure 2.1.

Because the derivative of the demand function with respect to price shows the *movement along the demand curve as we vary price,* another way to state the Law of Demand is that this derivative is negative: A higher price results in a lower quantity demanded. If the demand function is $Q = D(p)$, then the Law of Demand says that $dQ/dp < 0$, where dQ/dp is the derivative of the D function with respect to p. (Unless we state otherwise, we assume that all demand (and other) functions are continuous and differentiable everywhere.) The derivative of the quantity of pork demanded with respect to its price in Equation 2.3 is

$$\frac{dQ}{dp} = -20,$$

which is negative, so the Law of Demand holds.[4] Given $dQ/dp = -20$, a small change in price (measured in dollars per kg) causes a 20-times-larger fall in quantity (measured in million kg per year).

This derivative gives the change in the quantity demanded for an infinitesimal change in price. In general, if we look at a discrete, relatively large increase in price, the change in quantity may not be proportional to the change for a small increase in price. However, here the derivative is a constant that does not vary with price, so the same derivative holds for large as well as for small changes in price.

---

[2]Economists typically do not state the relevant physical and time period measures unless these measures are particularly useful in context. I'll generally follow this convention and refer to the price as, say, \$3.30 (with the "per kg" understood) and the quantity as 220 (with the "million kg per year" understood).

[3]In Chapter 4, we show that the Law of Demand need not hold theoretically; however, available empirical evidence strongly supports the Law of Demand.

[4]We can show the same result using the more general demand function in Equation 2.2, where the demand function has several arguments: price, prices of two substitutes, and income. With several arguments, we need to use a partial derivative with respect to price because we are interested in determining how the quantity demanded changes as the price changes, holding other relevant factors constant. The partial derivative with respect to price is $\partial Q/\partial p = -20 < 0$. Thus using either approach, we find that the quantity demanded falls by 20 times as much as the price rises.

For example, let the price increase from $p_1 = \$3.30$ to $p_2 = \$4.30$. That is, the change in the price $\Delta p = p_2 - p_1 = \$4.30 - \$3.30 = \$1$. (The Δ symbol, the Greek letter capital delta, means "change in" the following variable, so Δp means "change in price.") As Figure 2.1 shows, the corresponding quantities are $Q_1 = 220$ and $Q_2 = 200$. Thus if $\Delta p = \$1$, the change in the quantity demanded is $\Delta Q = Q_2 - Q_1 = 200 - 220 = -20$, or 20 times the change in price.

Because we put price on the vertical axis and quantity on the horizontal axis, the slope of the demand curve is the reciprocal of the derivative of the demand function: slope $= dp/dQ = 1/(dQ/dp)$. In our example, the slope of demand curve D^1 in Figure 2.1 is $dp/dQ = 1/(dQ/dp) = 1/(-20) = -0.05$. We can also calculate the slope in Figure 2.1 using the rise-over-run formula and the numbers we just calculated (because the slope is the same for small and for large changes):

$$\text{slope} = \frac{\text{rise}}{\text{run}} = \frac{\Delta p}{\Delta Q} = \frac{\$1 \text{ per kg}}{-20 \text{ million kg per year}} = -\$0.05 \text{ per million kg per year}.$$

This slope tells us that to sell one more unit (million kg per year) of pork, the price (per kg) must fall by 5¢.

Effects of Changes in Other Factors on Demand Curves. If a demand curve measures the effects of price changes when all other factors that affect demand are held constant, how can we use demand curves to show the effects of a change in one of these other factors, such as the price of beef? One solution is to draw the demand curve in a three-dimensional diagram with the price of pork on one axis, the price of beef on a second axis, and the quantity of pork on the third axis. But just thinking about drawing such a diagram probably makes your head hurt.

Economists use a simpler approach to show the effect on demand of a change in a factor other than the price of the good that affects demand. A change in any factor other than the price of the good itself causes a *shift of the demand curve* rather than a *movement along the demand curve*.

If the price of beef rises while the price of pork remains constant, some people will switch from beef to pork. Suppose that the price of beef rises by 60¢ from $4.00 per kg to $4.60 per kg but that the price of chicken and income remain at their average levels. Using the demand function 2.2, we can calculate the new demand function relating the quantity demanded to only the price:[5]

$$Q = 298 - 20p. \tag{2.4}$$

The higher price of beef causes the entire pork demand curve to shift 12 units to the right from D^1, corresponding to demand function 2.3, to D^2, demand function 2.4, in Figure 2.2. (In the figure, the quantity axis starts at 176 instead of 0 to emphasize the relevant portion of the demand curve.)

Why does the demand function shift by 12 units? Using the demand function 2.2, we find that the partial derivative of the quantity of pork demanded with respect to the

---

[5]Substituting $p_b = \$4.60$ into Equation 2.2 and using the same values as before for p_c and Y, we find that

$$Q = 171 - 20p + 20p_b + 3p_c + 2Y$$

$$= 171 - 20p + (20 \times 4.60) + \left(3 \times 3\tfrac{1}{3}\right) + (2 \times 12.5) = 298 - 20p.$$

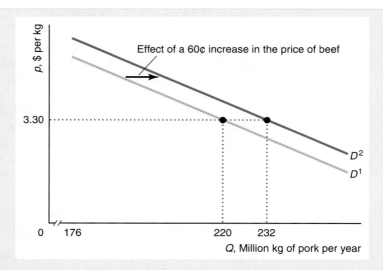

Figure 2.2 A Shift of the Demand Curve. The demand curve for processed pork shifts to the right from D^1 to D^2 as the price of beef rises from $4 to $4.60. As a result of the increase in beef prices, more pork is demanded at any given price.

price of beef is $\partial Q/\partial p_b = 20$. Thus if the price of beef increases by 60¢, the quantity of pork demanded rises by $20 \times 0.6 = 12$ units, holding all other factors constant.

To analyze the effects of a change in some variable on the quantity demanded properly, we must distinguish between a *movement along a demand curve* and a *shift of a demand curve*. A change in the *price of a good* causes a *movement along its demand curve*. A change in *any other factor besides the price of the good* causes a *shift of the demand curve*.

APPLICATION

Sideways Wine

In the Academy Award–winning movie *Sideways,* the lead character, a wine snob, wildly praises pinot noir wine, saying that its flavors are "haunting and brilliant and thrilling and subtle." Bizarrely, the exuberant views of this fictional character apparently caused wine buyers to flock to pinot noir wines, dramatically shifting the U.S. and British demand curves for pinot noir to the right (similar to the shift shown in Figure 2.2).

Between October 2004, when *Sideways* was released in the United States, and January 2005, U.S. sales of pinot noir jumped 16% to record levels (and 34% in California, where the film takes place), while the price remained relatively constant. In contrast, sales of all U.S. table wines rose only 2% in this period. British consumers seemed similarly affected. In the five weeks after the film opened in the United Kingdom, pinot sales increased 20% at Sainsbury's and 10% at Tesco and Oddbins, which ran a *Sideways* promotion.[6]

---

[6]Sources for the applications appear at the back of the book.

SUMMING DEMAND FUNCTIONS

If we know the demand curve for each of two consumers, how do we determine the total demand for the two consumers combined? The total quantity demanded *at a given price* is the sum of the quantity each consumer demands at that price.

We can use the demand functions to determine the total demand of several consumers. Suppose the demand function for Consumer 1 is

$$Q_1 = D^1(p),$$

and the demand function for Consumer 2 is

$$Q_2 = D^2(p).$$

At price is p, Consumer 1 demands Q_1 units, Consumer 2 demands Q_2 units, and the total demand of both consumers is the sum of the quantities each demands separately:

$$Q = Q_1 + Q_2 = D^1(p) + D^2(p).$$

We can generalize this approach to look at the total demand for three or more consumers.

● **APPLICATION**

Aggregating the Demand for Broadband Service

We illustrate how to combine individual demand curves to get a total demand curve graphically using estimated demand curves of broadband (high-speed) Internet service (Duffy-Deno, 2003). The figure shows the demand curve for small firms (1–19 employees), the demand curve for larger firms, and the total demand curve for all firms, which is the horizontal sum of the other two demand curves.

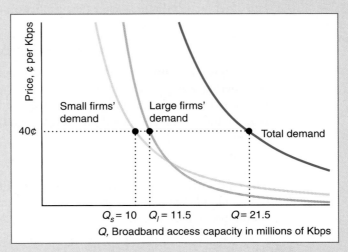

At the current average rate of 40¢ per kilobyte per second (Kbps), the quantity demanded by small firms is $Q_s = 10$ (in millions of Kbps) and the quantity demanded by larger firms is $Q_l = 11.5$. Thus the total quantity demanded at that price is $Q = Q_s + Q_l = 10 + 11.5 = 21.5$.

2.2 Supply

Knowing how much consumers want is not enough, by itself, to tell us the market price and quantity. To determine the market price and quantity, we also need to know how much firms want to supply at any given price.

The **quantity supplied** is the amount of a good that firms *want* to sell during a given time period at a given price, holding constant other factors that influence firms' supply decisions, such as costs and government actions. Firms determine how much of a good to supply on the basis of the price of that good and other factors, including the costs of production and government rules and regulations. Usually, we expect firms to supply more at a higher price. Before concentrating on the role of price in determining supply, we'll briefly consider the role of some of the other factors.

Costs of production affect how much of a good firms want to sell. As a firm's cost falls, it is willing to supply more of the good, all else the same. If the firm's cost exceeds what it can earn from selling the good, the firm sells nothing. Thus factors that affect costs also affect supply. A technological advance that allows a firm to produce a good at a lower cost leads the firm to supply more of that good, all else the same.

Government rules and regulations affect how much firms want to sell or are allowed to sell. Taxes and many government regulations—such as those covering pollution, sanitation, and health insurance—alter the costs of production. Other regulations affect when and how the product can be sold. For instance, the sale of cigarettes and liquor to children is prohibited. Also, most major cities around the world restrict the number of taxicabs.

THE SUPPLY FUNCTION

The **supply function** shows the correspondence between the quantity supplied, price, and other factors that influence the number of units offered for sale. Written generally, the processed pork supply function is

$$Q = S(p, p_h), \tag{2.5}$$

where Q is the quantity of processed pork supplied per year, p is the price of processed pork per kg, and p_h is the price of a hog. The supply function, Equation 2.5, also may be a function of other factors such as wages, but by leaving them out, we are implicitly holding them constant. Based on Moschini and Meilke (1992), the linear pork supply function in Canada is

$$Q = 178 + 40p - 60p_h, \tag{2.6}$$

where quantity is in millions of kg per year and the prices are in Canadian dollars per kg.

If we hold the price of hogs fixed at its typical value of $1.50 per kg, we can rewrite the supply function in Equation 2.6 as[7]

$$Q = 88 + 40p. \tag{2.7}$$

---

[7]If $p_h = \$1.50$, then Equation 2.6 is

$$Q = 178 + 40p - 60p_h = 178 + 40p - (60 \times 1.50) = 88 + 40p.$$

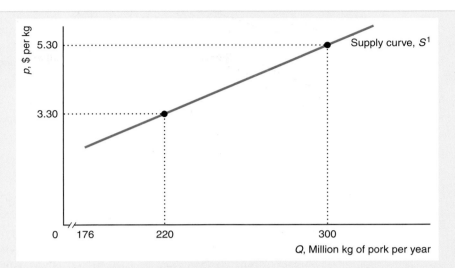

Figure 2.3 A Supply Curve. The estimated supply curve, S^1, for processed pork in Canada (Moschini and Meilke, 1992) shows the relationship between the quantity supplied per year and the price per kg, holding cost and other factors that influence supply constant. The upward slope of this supply curve indicates that firms supply more of this good when its price is high and less when the price is low. An increase in the price of pork causes a *movement along the supply curve*, resulting in a larger quantity of pork supplied.

Corresponding to this supply function is a **supply curve,** which shows the quantity supplied at each possible price, holding constant the other factors that influence firms' supply decisions. Figure 2.3 shows the estimated supply curve, S^1, for processed pork.

Because we hold fixed other variables that may affect the quantity supplied, such as costs and government rules, the supply curve concisely answers the question "What happens to the quantity supplied as the price changes, holding all other factors constant?" As the price of processed pork increases from $3.30 to $5.30, holding other factors (the price of hogs) constant, the quantity of pork supplied increases from 220 to 300 million kg per year, which is a *movement along the supply curve*.

How much does an increase in the price affect the quantity supplied? By differentiating the supply function 2.7 with respect to price, we find that $dQ/dp = 40$. This derivative holds for all values of price, so it holds for both small and large changes in price. That is, the quantity supplied increases by 40 units for each $1 increase in price.

Because this derivative is positive, the supply curve S^1 slopes upward in Figure 2.3. Although the Law of Demand requires that the demand curve slope downward, there is *no* "Law of Supply" that requires the market supply curve to have a particular slope. The market supply curve can be upward sloping, or vertical, horizontal, or downward sloping.

A change in a factor other than price causes a *shift of the supply curve*. If the price of hogs increases by 25¢, the supply function becomes

$$Q = 73 + 40p. \tag{2.8}$$

By comparing this supply function to the original one in Equation 2.7, $Q = 88 + 40p$, we see that the supply curve, S^1, shifts 15 units to the left, to S^2 in Figure 2.4.

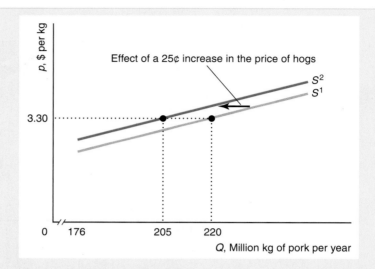

Figure 2.4 A Shift of a Supply Curve. An increase in the price of hogs from $1.50 to $1.75 per kg causes a *shift of the supply curve* from S^1 to S^2. At the price of processed pork of $3.30, the quantity supplied falls from 220 on S^1 to 205 on S^2.

Alternatively, we can determine how far the supply curve shifts by partially differentiating the supply function 2.6 with respect to the price of hogs: $\partial Q/\partial p_h = -60$. This partial derivative holds for all values of p_h and hence for both small and large changes in p_h. Thus a 25¢ increase in the price of hogs causes a $-60 \times 0.25 = -15$ units change in the quantity supplied of pork at any given constant price of pork.

Again, it is important to distinguish between a *movement along a supply curve* and a *shift of the supply curve*. When the price of pork changes, the change in the quantity supplied reflects a *movement along the supply curve*. When costs, government rules, or other variables that affect supply change, the entire *supply curve shifts*.

SUMMING SUPPLY FUNCTIONS

The total supply curve shows the total quantity produced by all suppliers at each possible price. For example, the total supply of rice in Japan is the sum of the domestic and the foreign supply curves of rice.

Suppose that the domestic supply curve (panel a) and foreign supply curve (panel b) of rice in Japan are as Figure 2.5 shows. The total supply curve, S in panel c, is the horizontal sum of the Japanese *domestic* supply curve, S^d, and the *foreign* supply curve, S^f. In the figure, the Japanese and foreign supplies are zero at any price equal to or less than p, so the total supply is zero. At prices above p, the Japanese and foreign supplies are positive, so the total supply is positive. For example, when the price is p^*, the quantity supplied by Japanese firms is Q_d^* (panel a), the quantity supplied by foreign firms is Q_f^* (panel b), and the total quantity supplied is $Q^* = Q_d^* + Q_f^*$ (panel c). Because the total supply curve is the horizontal sum of the domestic and foreign supply curves, the total supply curve is flatter than either of the other two supply curves.

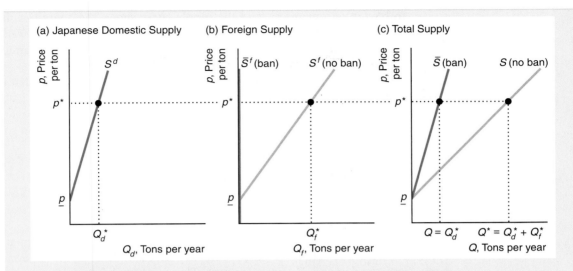

Figure 2.5 Total Supply: The Sum of Domestic and Foreign Supply. If foreigners may sell their rice in Japan, the total Japanese supply of rice, S, is the horizontal sum of the domestic Japanese supply, S^d, and the imported foreign supply, S^f. With a ban on foreign imports, the foreign supply curve, $\overline{S}^f$, is zero at every price, so the total supply curve, $\overline{S}$, is the same as the domestic supply curve, S^d.

EFFECTS OF GOVERNMENT IMPORT POLICIES ON SUPPLY CURVES

We can use this approach for deriving the total supply curve to analyze the effect of government policies on the total supply curve. Traditionally, the Japanese government has banned the importation of foreign rice. We want to determine how much less rice is supplied at any given price to the Japanese market because of this ban.

Without a ban, the foreign supply curve is S^f in panel b of Figure 2.5. A ban on imports eliminates the foreign supply, so the foreign supply curve after the ban is imposed, $\overline{S}^f$, is a vertical line at $Q_f = 0$. The import ban has no effect on the domestic supply curve, S^d, so the supply curve is the same as in panel a.

Because the foreign supply with a ban, $\overline{S}^f$, is zero at every price, the total supply with a ban, $\overline{S}$, in panel c is the same as the Japanese domestic supply, S^d, at any given price. The total supply curve under the ban lies to the left of the total supply curve without a ban, S. Thus the effect of the import ban is to rotate the total supply curve toward the vertical axis.

The limit that a government sets on the quantity of a foreign-produced good that may be imported is called a **quota**. By absolutely banning the importation of rice, the Japanese government sets a quota of zero on rice imports. Sometimes governments set positive quotas, $\overline{Q} > 0$. The foreign firms may supply as much as they want, Q_f, as long as they supply no more than the quota: $Q_f \leq \overline{Q}$.

2.3 Market Equilibrium

The supply and demand curves determine the price and quantity at which goods and services are bought and sold. The demand curve shows the quantities that consumers want to buy at various prices, and the supply curve shows the quantities that firms want to sell at various prices. Unless the price is set so that consumers want to buy exactly the same amount that suppliers want to sell, either some buyers cannot buy as much as they want or some sellers cannot sell as much as they want.

When all traders are able to buy or sell as much as they want, we say that the market is in **equilibrium:** a situation in which no participant wants to change its behavior. A price at which consumers can buy as much as they want and sellers can sell as much as they want is called an *equilibrium price*. The quantity that is bought and sold at the equilibrium price is called the *equilibrium quantity*.

FINDING THE MARKET EQUILIBRIUM

This little piggy went to market . . .

To illustrate how supply and demand curves determine the equilibrium price and quantity, we use our old friend, the processed pork example. Figure 2.6 shows the supply, S, and the demand, D, curves for pork. The supply and demand curves intersect at point e, the market equilibrium, where the equilibrium price is $3.30 and the equilibrium quantity is 220 million kg per year, which is the quantity that firms want to sell and the quantity that consumers want to buy at the equilibrium price.

We can determine the processed pork market equilibrium mathematically using the supply and demand functions, Equations 2.3 and 2.4. We use these two functions to solve for the equilibrium price at which the quantity demanded equals the quantity supplied (the equilibrium quantity).

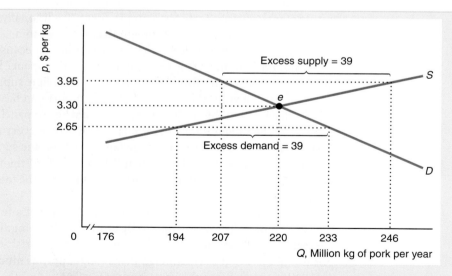

Figure 2.6 Market Equilibrium. The intersection of the supply curve, S, and the demand curve, D, for processed pork determines the market equilibrium point, e, where p = $3.30 per kg and Q = 220 million kg per year. At the lower price of p = $2.65, the quantity supplied is only 194, whereas the quantity demanded is 233, so there is excess demand of 39. At p = $3.95, a price higher than the equilibrium price, there is an excess supply of 39 because the quantity demanded, 207, is less than the quantity supplied, 246. When there is excess demand or supply, market forces drive the price back to the equilibrium price of $3.30.

The demand function, Equation 2.3, shows the relationship between the quantity demanded, Q_d, and the price:

$$Q_d = 286 - 20p.$$

The supply function, Equation 2.4, describes the relationship between the quantity supplied, Q_s, and the price:

$$Q_s = 88 + 40p.$$

We want to find the price at which $Q_d = Q_s = Q$, the equilibrium quantity. Because the left-hand sides of the two equations are equal in equilibrium, $Q_s = Q_d$, the right-hand sides of the two equations must be equal:

$$286 - 20p = 88 + 40p.$$

Adding $20p$ to both sides of this expression and subtracting 88 from both sides, we find that $198 = 60p$. Dividing both sides of this last expression by 60, we learn that the equilibrium price is $p = \$3.30$. We can determine the equilibrium quantity by substituting this equilibrium price, $p = \$3.30$, into either the supply or the demand equation:

$$Q_d = Q_s$$
$$286 - (20 \times 3.30) = 88 + (40 \times 3.30)$$
$$220 = 220.$$

Thus the equilibrium quantity is 220.

FORCES THAT DRIVE THE MARKET TO EQUILIBRIUM

A market equilibrium is not just an abstract concept or a theoretical possibility. We observe markets in equilibrium. Indirect evidence that a market is in equilibrium is that you can buy as much as you want of a good at the market price. You can almost always buy as much as you want of milk, ballpoint pens, and most other goods.

Amazingly, a market equilibrium occurs without any explicit coordination between consumers and firms. In a competitive market such as that for agricultural goods, millions of consumers and thousands of firms make their buying and selling decisions independently. Yet each firm can sell as much as it wants; each consumer can buy as much as he or she wants. It is as though an unseen market force, like an *invisible hand*, directs people to coordinate their activities to achieve a market equilibrium.

What really causes the market to move to an equilibrium? If the price is not at the equilibrium level, consumers or firms have an incentive to change their behavior in a way that will drive the price to the equilibrium level.[8]

If the price were initially lower than the equilibrium price, consumers would want to buy more than suppliers would want to sell. If the price of pork is \$2.65 in Figure 2.6, firms will be willing to supply 194 million kg per year, but consumers will demand 233 million kg. At this price, the market is in *disequilibrium*, meaning that the quantity demanded is not equal to the quantity supplied. There is **excess demand**—the amount by which the quantity demanded exceeds the quantity supplied at a specified price—of 39 (= 233 − 194) million kg per year at a price of \$2.65.

---

[8]Our model of competitive market equilibrium, which occurs at a point in time, does not formally explain how dynamic adjustments occur. The following explanation, though plausible, is just one of a number of possible dynamic adjustment stories that economists have modeled.

Some consumers are lucky enough to be able to buy the pork at $2.65. Other consumers cannot find anyone who is willing to sell them pork at that price. What can they do? Some frustrated consumers may offer to pay suppliers more than $2.65. Alternatively, suppliers, noticing these disappointed consumers, may raise their prices. Such actions by consumers and producers cause the market price to rise. As the price rises, the quantity that firms want to supply increases and the quantity that consumers want to buy decreases. This upward pressure on price continues until it reaches the equilibrium price, $3.30, where there is no excess demand.

If, instead, price is initially above the equilibrium level, suppliers want to sell more than consumers want to buy. For example, at a price of pork of $3.95, suppliers want to sell 246 million kg per year but consumers want to buy only 207 million, as the figure shows. At $3.95, the market is in disequilibrium. There is an **excess supply**—the amount by which the quantity supplied is greater than the quantity demanded at a specified price—of 39 (= 246 − 207) at a price of $3.95. Not all firms can sell as much as they want. Rather than incur storage costs (and possibly have their unsold pork spoil), firms lower the price to attract additional customers. As long as price remains above the equilibrium price, some firms have unsold pork and want to lower the price further. The price falls until it reaches the equilibrium level, $3.30, where there is no excess supply and hence no more pressure to lower the price further.

In summary, at any price other than the equilibrium price, either consumers or suppliers are unable to trade as much as they want. These disappointed people act to change the price, driving the price to the equilibrium level. The equilibrium price is called the *market clearing price* because it removes from the market all frustrated buyers and sellers: There is no excess demand or excess supply at the equilibrium price.

2.4   Shocking the Equilibrium: Comparative Statics

If the variables we hold constant in the demand and supply functions do not change, an equilibrium can persist indefinitely because none of the participants applies pressure to change the price. However, the equilibrium changes if a shock occurs such that one of the variables we were holding constant changes, causing a shift in either the demand curve or the supply curve.

Comparative statics is the method that economists use to analyze how variables controlled by consumers and firms—here, price and quantity—react to a change in *environmental variables* (also called *exogenous variables*), such as prices of substitutes and complements, income, and prices of inputs. The term *comparative statics* literally refers to comparing a *static* equilibrium—an equilibrium at a point in time—from before the change to a static equilibrium after the change. (In contrast, economists may examine a dynamic model, in which the dynamic equilibrium adjusts over time.)

COMPARATIVE STATICS WITH DISCRETE (RELATIVELY LARGE) CHANGES

We can determine the comparative statics properties of an equilibrium by examining the effects of a discrete (relatively large) change in one environmental variable. We can do so by solving for the before- and after-equilibria and comparing them using mathematics or a graph. We illustrate this approach using our beloved pork example. Suppose all the environmental variables remain constant except the price of hogs,

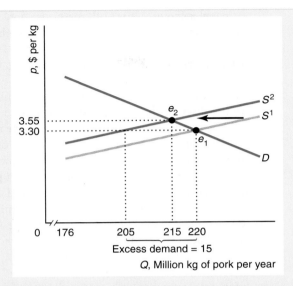

Figure 2.7 The Equilibrium Effect of a Shift of the Supply Curve. A 25¢ increase in the price of hogs causes the supply curve for processed pork to shift to the left from S^1 to S^2, driving the market equilibrium from e_1 to e_2, and the market equilibrium price from \$3.30 to \$3.55.

which increases by 25¢. It is now more expensive to produce pork because the price of a major input, hogs, has increased.

Because the price of hogs is not an argument to the demand function—a change in the price of an input does not affect consumers' desires—the demand curve does not shift. As we have already seen, the increase in the price of hogs causes the supply curve for pork to shift 15 units to the left from S^1 to S^2 in Figure 2.7.

At the original equilibrium price of pork, \$3.30, consumers still want 220 units, but suppliers are now willing to supply only 205, so there is excess demand of 15, as panel a shows. Market pressure forces the price of pork upward until it reaches a new equilibrium at e_2, where the new equilibrium price is \$3.55 and the new equilibrium quantity is 215. Thus the increase in the price of hogs causes the equilibrium price to rise by 25¢ a pound but the equilibrium quantity to fall by 15 units. Here the increase in the price of a factor causes a *shift of the supply curve* and a *movement along the demand curve*.

We can derive the same result by using equations to solve for the equilibrium before the change and after the discrete change in the price of hogs and by comparing the two equations. We have already solved for the original equilibrium, e_1, by setting quantity in the demand function 2.3 equal to the quantity in the supply function 2.7. We obtain the new equilibrium, e_2, by equating the quantity in the demand function 2.3 to that of the new supply function 2.8: $286 - 20p = 73 + 40p$. Simplifying this expression, we find that the new equilibrium price is $p_2 = \$3.55$. Substituting that price into either the demand or the supply function, we learn that the new equilibrium quantity is $Q_2 = 215$, as panel a shows. Thus both methods show that an increase in the price of hogs causes the equilibrium price to rise and the equilibrium quantity to fall.

COMPARATIVE STATICS WITH SMALL CHANGES

Alternatively, we can use calculus to determine the effect of a small change (as opposed to the discrete change we just used) in one environmental variable, holding the other such variables constant. Until now, we have used calculus to examine how an argument of a demand function affects the quantity demanded or how an argument of a supply function affects the quantity supplied. Now, however, we want to know how an environmental variable affects the equilibrium price and quantity that are determined by the intersection of the supply and demand curves.

Our first step is to characterize the equilibrium values as functions of the relevant environmental variables. Suppose that we hold constant all the environmental variables that affect demand so that the demand function is

$$Q = D(p). \tag{2.9}$$

One environmental variable, a, in the supply function changes, causing the supply curve to shift. We write the supply function as

$$Q = S(p, a). \tag{2.10}$$

As before, we determine the equilibrium price by equating the quantities, Q, in Equations 2.9 and 2.10:

$$D(p) = S(p, a). \tag{2.11}$$

The equilibrium equation 2.11 is an example of an *identity*. As a changes, p changes so that this equation continues to hold—the market remains in equilibrium. Thus based on this equation, we can write the equilibrium price as an implicit function of the environmental variable: $p = p(a)$. That is, we can write the equilibrium condition 2.11 as

$$D(p(a)) = S(p(a), a). \tag{2.12}$$

We can characterize how the equilibrium price changes with a by differentiating the equilibrium condition 2.12 with respect to a using the chain rule at the original equilibrium,[9]

$$\frac{dD(p(a))}{dp}\frac{dp}{da} = \frac{\partial S(p(a), a)}{\partial p}\frac{dp}{da} + \frac{\partial S(p(a), a)}{\partial a}. \tag{2.13}$$

Using algebra, we can rearrange Equation 2.13 as

$$\frac{dp}{da} = \frac{\dfrac{\partial S}{\partial a}}{\dfrac{dD}{dp} - \dfrac{\partial S}{\partial p}}, \tag{2.14}$$

where we suppress the arguments of the functions for notational simplicity. Equation 2.14 shows the derivative of $p(a)$ with respect to a.

---

[9]The chain rule is a formula for the derivative of the composite of two functions, such as $f(g(x))$. According to this rule, $df/dx = (df/dg)(dg/dx)$. See the Calculus Appendix.

We know that $dD/dp < 0$ by the Law of Demand. If the supply curve is upward slop-ing, then $\partial S/\partial p$ is positive, so the denominator of Equation 2.14, $dD/dp - \partial S/\partial p$, is neg-ative. Thus dp/da has the same sign as the numerator of Equation 2.14. If $\partial S/\partial a$ is negative, then dp/da is positive: As a increases, the equilibrium price rises. If $\partial S/\partial a$ is positive, an increase in a causes the equilibrium price to fall.

By using either the demand function or the supply function, we can use this result concerning the effect of a on the equilibrium price to determine the effect of a on the equilibrium quantity. For example, we can rewrite the demand function 2.9 as

$$Q = D(p(a)). \tag{2.15}$$

Differentiating the demand function 2.15 with respect to a using the chain rule, we find that

$$\frac{dQ}{da} = \frac{dD}{dp}\frac{dp}{da}. \tag{2.16}$$

Because $\partial D/\partial p < 0$ by the Law of Demand, the sign of dQ/da is the opposite of that of dp/da. That is, as a increases, the equilibrium price moves in the opposite direction of the equilibrium quantity. In Solved Problem 2.1, we use the pork example to illustrate this type of analysis.

SOLVED PROBLEM   **2.1**

How do the equilibrium price and quantity of pork vary as the price of hogs changes if the variables that affect demand are held constant at their typical values? Answer this comparative statics question using calculus. (*Hint:* This problem is of the same form as the more general one we just analyzed. In the pork market, the environmental variable that shifts supply, *a*, is p_h.)

Answer

1. *Solve for the equilibrium price of pork in terms of the price of hogs:* To obtain an expression for the equilibrium similar to Equation 2.14, we equate the right-hand sides of the demand function 2.3 and the supply function 2.6 to obtain

$$286 - 20p = 178 + 40p - 60p_h,$$

or

$$p = 1.8 + p_h. \tag{2.17}$$

(As a check, when p_h equals its typical value, \$1.50, the equilibrium price of pork is $p = \$3.30$ according to Equation 2.17, which is consistent with our ear-lier calculations.)

2. *Use this equilibrium price equation to show how the equilibrium price changes as the price of hogs changes:* Differentiating the equilibrium price expression 2.17 with respect to p_h gives an expression of the form of Equation 2.16:

$$\frac{dp}{dp_h} = 1. \tag{2.18}$$

That is, as the price of hogs increases by 1¢, the equilibrium price of pork increases by 1¢. Because this condition holds for any value of p_h, it also holds for larger changes in the price of hogs. Thus a 25¢ increase in the price of hogs causes a 25¢ increase in the equilibrium price of pork.

3. *Write the pork demand function as in Equation 2.15, and then differentiate it with respect to the price of hogs to show how the equilibrium quantity of pork varies with the price of hogs:* From the pork demand function, Equation 2.3, we can write the quantity demanded as

$$Q = D(p(p_h)) = 286 - 20p(p_h).$$

Differentiating this expression with respect to p_h using the chain rule, we obtain an equation of the form of Equation 2.16 with respect to p_h:

$$\frac{dQ}{dp_h} = \frac{dD}{dp}\frac{dp}{dp_h} = -20 \times 1 = -20. \tag{2.19}$$

That is, as the price of hogs increases by \$1, the equilibrium quantity falls by 20 units.

HOW SHAPES OF DEMAND AND SUPPLY CURVES MATTER

The shapes and positions of the demand and supply curves determine by how much a shock affects the equilibrium price and quantity. We illustrate the importance of the shape of the demand curve by showing how our comparative statics results would change if the processed pork demand curve had a different shape. We continue to use the estimated supply curve of pork and examine what happens if the price of hogs increases by 25¢, causing the supply curve of pork to shift to the left from S^1 to S^2 in panel a of Figure 2.8. In the actual market, the *shift of the supply curve* causes a *movement along the downward-sloping demand curve, D^1,* so the equilibrium quantity falls from 220 to 215 million kg per year, and the equilibrium price rises from \$3.30 to \$3.55 per kg. Thus this supply shock—an increase in the price of hogs—hurts consumers by raising the equilibrium price of pork 25¢ per kg, so customers buy less: 215 instead of 220.

A supply shock would have different effects if the demand curve had a different shape. Suppose that the quantity demanded were not sensitive to a change in the price,

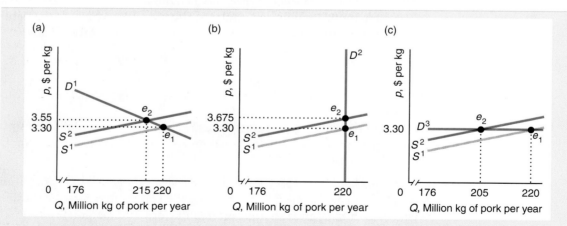

Figure 2.8 The Effect of a Shift of the Supply Curve Depends on the Shape of the Demand Curve. A 25¢ increase in the price of hogs causes the supply curve for processed pork to shift to the left from S^1 to S^2. (a) Given the actual downward-sloping linear demand curve, the equilibrium price rises from \$3.30 to \$3.55 and the equilibrium quantity falls from 220 to 215. (b) If the demand curve were vertical, the supply shock would cause price to rise to \$3.675 while quantity would remain unchanged. (c) If the demand curve were horizontal, the supply shock would not affect price but would cause quantity to fall to 205.

so the same amount is demanded no matter what the price is, as in vertical demand curve D^2 in panel b. A 25¢ increase in the price of hogs again shifts the supply curve from S^1 to S^2. Equilibrium quantity does not change, but the price consumers pay rises by 37.5¢ to $3.675. Thus the amount consumers spend rises by more when the demand curve is vertical instead of downward sloping.

Now suppose that consumers are very sensitive to price, as in the horizontal demand curve, D^3, in panel c. Consumers will buy virtually unlimited quantities of pork at $3.30 per kg (or less), but if the price rises even slightly, they will stop buying pork. Here an increase in the price of hogs has *no* effect on the price consumers pay; however, the equilibrium quantity drops substantially to 205 million kg per year. Thus how much the equilibrium quantity falls and how much the equilibrium price of processed pork rises when the price of hogs increases depend on the shape of the demand curve.

2.5 Elasticities

It is convenient to be able to summarize the responsiveness of one variable to a change in another variable using a summary statistic. In our last example, we wanted to know whether an increase in the price causes a large or a small change in the quantity demanded (that is, whether the demand curve is relatively vertical or relatively horizontal at the current price). We can use summary statistics of the responsiveness of the quantity demanded and the quantity supplied to determine comparative statics properties of the equilibrium. Often, we have reasonable estimates of these summary statistics and can use them to predict what will happen to the equilibrium in a market—that is, to make comparative statistics predictions. Later in this chapter, we will examine how the government can use these summary measures for demand and supply to predict, before it institutes the tax, the effect of a new sales tax on the equilibrium price, firms' revenues, and tax receipts.

Suppose that a variable z (for example, the quantity demanded or the quantity supplied) is a function of a variable x (say, the price of z) and possibly other variables such as y: $z = f(x, y)$. For example, f could be the demand function, where z is the quantity demanded, x is the price, and y is income. We want a summary statistic that describes how much z changes as x changes, holding y constant. An **elasticity** is the percentage change in one variable (here, z) in response to a given percentage change in another variable (here, y), holding other relevant variables (here, y) constant. The elasticity, E, of z with respect to x is

$$E = \frac{\text{percentage change in } z}{\text{percentage change in } x} = \frac{\Delta z/z}{\Delta x/x} = \frac{\partial z}{\partial x}\frac{x}{z}, \tag{2.20}$$

where Δz is the change in z, so $\Delta z/z$ is the percentage change in z. If z changes by 3% when x changes by 1%, then the elasticity E is 3. Thus the elasticity is a pure number (it has no units of measure).[10] As Δx goes to zero, $\Delta z/\Delta x$ goes to the partial derivative $\partial z/\partial x$. Economists usually calculate elasticities only at this limit—that is, for infinitesimal changes in x.

---

[10]Economists use the elasticity rather than the slope, $\partial z/\partial x$, as a summary statistic because the elasticity is a pure number, whereas the slope depends on the units of measurement. For example, if x is a price measured in pennies and we switch to measuring price using dollars, the slope changes, but the elasticity remains unchanged.

DEMAND ELASTICITY

The **price elasticity of demand** (or simply the *demand elasticity* or *elasticity of demand*) is the percentage change in the quantity demanded, Q, in response to a given percentage change in the price, p, at a particular point on the demand curve. The price elasticity of demand (represented by ε, the Greek letter epsilon) is

$$\varepsilon = \frac{\text{percentage change in quantity demanded}}{\text{percentage change in price}} = \frac{\Delta Q/Q}{\Delta p/p} = \frac{\partial Q}{\partial p}\frac{p}{Q}, \quad (2.21)$$

where $\partial Q/\partial p$ is the partial derivative of the demand function with respect to p (that is, holding constant other variables that affect the quantity demanded). For example, if $\varepsilon = -2$, then a 1% increase in the price results in a 2% decrease in the quantity demanded.

We can use Equation 2.12 to calculate the elasticity of demand for a linear demand function (holding fixed other variables that affect demand),

$$Q = a - bp,$$

where a is the quantity demanded when price is zero, $Q = a - (b \times 0) = a$, and $-b$ is the ratio of the fall in quantity to the rise in price: the derivative dQ/dp. The elasticity of demand is

$$\varepsilon = \frac{dQ}{dp}\frac{p}{Q} = -b\frac{p}{Q}. \quad (2.22)$$

For the linear demand function for pork, $Q = a - bp = 286 - 20p$, at the initial equilibrium where $p = \$3.30$ and $Q = 220$, the elasticity of demand is

$$\varepsilon = b\frac{p}{Q} = -20 \times \frac{3.30}{220} = -0.3.$$

The negative sign on the elasticity of demand of pork illustrates the Law of Demand: Less quantity is demanded as the price rises. The elasticity of demand concisely answers the question "How much does quantity demanded fall in response to a 1% increase in price?" A 1% increase in price leads to an $\varepsilon\%$ change in the quantity demanded. At the equilibrium, a 1% increase in the price of pork leads to a -0.3% fall in the quantity of pork demanded: A price increase causes a less than proportionate fall in the quantity of pork demanded.

● APPLICATION

Willingness to Surf

Do you surf the Net for hours and download billions of bits of music? Would you cut back if the price of your Internet service increased? At what price would you give up using the Internet?

Varian (2002) estimated demand curves for connection time by people at a university who paid for access by the minute. He found that the price elasticity of demand was -2.0 for those who used a 128 kilobits per second (Kbps) service and -2.9 for people who connected at 64 Kbps. That is, a 1% increase in the price per minute reduced the connection time used by those with high-speed access by 2% but decreased the connection time by nearly 3% for those with slow phone-line access. Thus high-speed users are less sensitive to connection prices than slow-speed users.

Some recent studies have found that residential users who pay a flat rate (no per-minute charge) for service have a very inelastic demand for dial-up service. That is, few dial-up users will give up their service if the flat fee rises. Residential customers are more sensitive to the flat-fee price of broadband service, with elasticities ranging from −0.75 to −1.5 (Duffy-Deno, 2003). That is, if the price of broadband service increases 10%, between 7.5% and 15% fewer households will use a broadband service.

Elasticities Along the Demand Curve. The elasticity of demand varies along most demand curves. The elasticity of demand is different at every point along a downward-sloping linear demand curve; however, the elasticities are constant along horizontal, vertical, and log-linear demand curves.

On strictly downward-sloping linear demand curves—those that are neither vertical nor horizontal—the elasticity of demand is a more negative number the higher the price. Consequently, even though the slope of the linear demand curve is constant, the elasticity varies along the curve. A 1% increase in price causes a larger percentage fall in quantity near the top (left) of the demand curve than near the bottom (right).

Where a linear demand curve hits the quantity axis ($p = 0$ and $Q = a$), the elasticity of demand is $\varepsilon = -b(0/a) = 0$, according to Equation 2.22. The linear pork demand curve in Figure 2.9 illustrates this pattern. Where the price is zero, a 1% increase in price does not raise the price, so quantity does not change. At a point where the elasticity of demand is zero, the demand curve is said to be *perfectly inelastic*. As a physical analogy, if you try to stretch an inelastic steel rod, the length does not change. The change in the price is the force pulling at demand; if the quantity demanded does not change in response to this pulling, the demand curve is perfectly inelastic.

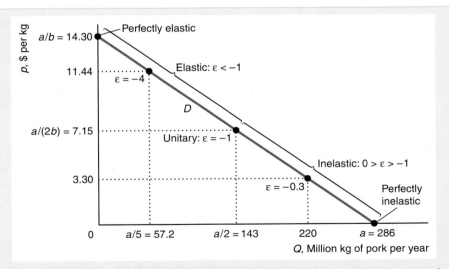

Figure 2.9 Elasticity Along the Linear Pork Demand Curve. With a linear demand curve such as the pork demand curve, the higher the price, the more elastic the demand curve (ε is larger in absolute value—a larger negative number). The demand curve is perfectly inelastic ($\varepsilon = 0$) where the demand curve hits the horizontal axis, is perfectly elastic where the demand curve hits the vertical axis, and has unitary elasticity ($\varepsilon = -1$) at the midpoint of the demand curve.

For quantities between the midpoint of the linear demand curve and the lower end where $Q = a$, the demand elasticity lies between 0 and −1: $0 \, \varepsilon > -1$. A point along the demand curve where the elasticity is between 0 and −1 is *inelastic* (but not perfectly inelastic): A 1% increase in price leads to a fall in quantity of less than 1%. For example, at the original pork equilibrium, $\varepsilon = -0.3$, so a 1% increase in price causes quantity to fall by −0.3%.

At the midpoint of the linear demand curve, $p = a/(2b)$ and $Q = a/2$, so $\varepsilon = -bp/Q = -b[a/(2b)]/(a/2) = -1$.[11] Such an elasticity of demand is called a *unitary elasticity*.

At prices higher than at the midpoint of the demand curve, the elasticity of demand is less than negative one, $\varepsilon < -1$. In this range, the demand curve is called *elastic*: A 1% increase in price causes a more than 1% fall in quantity. A physical analogy is a rubber band that stretches substantially when you pull on it. In the figure where $Q = a/5$, the elasticity is −4, so a 1% increase in price causes a 4% drop in quantity.

As the price rises, the elasticity gets more and more negative, approaching negative infinity. Where the demand curve hits the price axis, it is *perfectly elastic*.[12] At the price a/b where $Q = 0$, a 1% decrease in p causes the quantity demanded to become positive, which is an infinite increase in quantity.

The elasticity of demand varies along most demand curves, not just downward-sloping linear ones. Along a special type of demand curve, called a *constant-elasticity demand curve*, however, the elasticity is the same at every point along the curve. Constant-elasticity demand curves all have the exponential form

$$Q = Ap^{\varepsilon}, \tag{2.23}$$

where A is a positive constant and ε, a negative constant, is the elasticity at every point along this demand curve. By taking natural logarithms of both sides of Equation 2.23, we can rewrite this exponential demand curve as a log-linear demand curve:

$$\ln Q = \ln A + \varepsilon \ln p. \tag{2.24}$$

For example, in the application "Aggregating the Demand for Broadband Service," the estimated demand function for broadband services by large firms is $Q = 16p^{-0.296}$. Here $A = 16$ and $\varepsilon = -0.296$ is the constant elasticity of demand. That is, their demand is inelastic ($0 > \varepsilon > -1$). We can equivalently write the demand function for broadband services by large firms as $\ln Q = \ln 16 - 0.296 \ln p \approx 2.773 - 0.296 \ln p$.

Figure 2.10 shows several constant-elasticity demand curves with different elasticities. Except for the two extreme cases, these curves are convex to the origin. The two extreme cases of these constant-elasticity demand curves are the strictly vertical and the strictly horizontal demand curves. Along the horizontal demand curve, which is horizontal at p^* in Figure 2.10, the elasticity is infinite everywhere. It is also a special case of a linear demand curve with a zero slope ($b = 0$). Along this demand curve, people are willing to buy as much as firms sell at any price less than or equal to p^*. If the price increases even

---

[11]The linear demand curve hits the price axis at $p = a/b$ and the quantity axis at $p = 0$. The midpoint occurs at $p = (a/b - 0)/2 = a/(2b)$. The corresponding quantity is $Q = a - b[a/(2b)] = a/2$.

[12]The linear demand curve hits the price axis at $p = a/b$ and $Q = 0$, so the elasticity is $-bp/0$. As the price approaches a/b, the elasticity approaches negative infinity. An intuition for this convention is provided by looking at a sequence where −1 divided by 1/10 is −10, −1 divided by 1/100 is −100, and so on. The smaller the number we divide by, the more negative the result, which goes to $-\infty$ (negative infinity) in the limit.

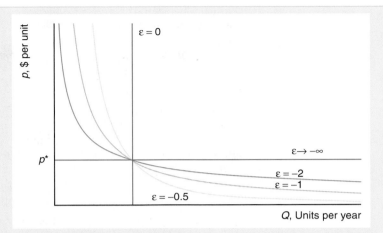

Figure 2.10 Constant Elasticity Demand Curves. These constant elasticity demand curves, $Q = Ap^\varepsilon$, vary with respect to their elasticities. Curves with negative, finite elasticities are convex to the origin. The vertical constant elasticity demand is perfectly inelastic, while the horizontal curve is perfectly elastic.

slightly above p^*, however, demand falls to zero. Thus a small increase in price causes an infinite drop in quantity, which means that the demand curve is perfectly elastic.

Why would a demand curve be horizontal? One reason is that consumers view a good as identical to another good and do not care which one they buy. Suppose that consumers view Washington State apples and Oregon apples as identical. They won't buy Washington apples if these apples sell for more than Oregon apples. Similarly, they won't buy Oregon apples if their price is higher than that of Washington apples. If the two prices are equal, consumers do not care which type of apple they buy. Thus the demand curve for Oregon apples is horizontal at the price of Washington apples.

The other extreme case is a vertical demand curve, which is perfectly inelastic everywhere. Such a demand curve is an extreme case of the linear demand curve with an infinite (vertical) slope. If the price goes up, the quantity demanded is unchanged, $dQ/dp = 0$, so the elasticity of demand must be zero: $(dQ/dp)(p/Q) = 0(p/Q) = 0$.

A demand curve is vertical for *essential goods*—goods that people feel they must have and will pay anything to get. Because Sydney is a diabetic, his demand curve for insulin could be vertical at a day's dose, Q^*. More realistically, he may have a maximum price, p^*, that he can pay, whereupon his demand curve becomes perfectly elastic at that price. Thus his demand curve is vertical at Q^* up to p^* and horizontal at p^*.

SOLVED PROBLEM 2.2

Show that the elasticity of demand is a constant ε if the demand function is exponential, $Q = Ap^\varepsilon$, or, equivalently, log-linear: $\ln Q = \ln A + \varepsilon \ln p$.

Answer

1. *Differentiate the exponential demand curve with respect to price to determine dQ/dp, and substitute that expression into the definition of the elasticity of demand:* Differentiating the demand curve $Q = Ap^\varepsilon$, we find that $dQ/dp = \varepsilon Ap^{\varepsilon-1}$.

Substituting that expression into the elasticity definition, we learn that the elasticity is

$$\frac{dQ}{dp}\frac{p}{Q} = \varepsilon A p^{\varepsilon-1}\frac{p}{Q} = \varepsilon A p^{\varepsilon-1}\frac{p}{Ap^{\varepsilon}} = \varepsilon.$$

Because the elasticity is a constant that does not depend on the particular value of p, it is the same at every point along the demand curve.

2. *Differentiate the log-linear demand curve to determine* dQ/dp, *and substitute that expression into the definition of the elasticity of demand:* Differentiating the log-linear demand curve, $\ln Q = \ln A + \varepsilon \ln p$, with respect to p, we find that $(dQ/dp)/Q = \varepsilon/p$. Multiplying both sides of this equation by p, we again discover that the elasticity is constant:

$$\frac{dQ}{dp}\frac{p}{Q} = \varepsilon\frac{Q}{p}\frac{p}{Q} = \varepsilon.$$

Other Demand Elasticities. We refer to the price elasticity of demand as *the* elasticity of demand. However, there are other demand elasticities that show how the quantity demanded changes in response to changes in variables other than price that affect the quantity demanded. Two such demand elasticities are the income elasticity of demand and the cross-price elasticity of demand.

As income increases, the demand curve shifts. If the demand curve shifts to the right, a larger quantity is demanded at any given price. If instead the demand curve shifts to the left, a smaller quantity is demanded at any given price.

We can measure how sensitive the quantity demanded at a given price is to income by using the **income elasticity of demand** (or *income elasticity*), which is the percentage change in the quantity demanded in response to a given percentage change in income, Y. The income elasticity of demand is

$$\xi = \frac{\text{percentage change in quantity demanded}}{\text{percentage change in income}} = \frac{\Delta Q/Q}{\Delta Y/Y} = \frac{\partial Q}{\partial Y}\frac{Y}{Q},$$

where ξ is the Greek letter xi. If the quantity demanded increases as income rises, the income elasticity of demand is positive. If the quantity demanded does not change as income rises, the income elasticity is zero. Finally, if the quantity demanded falls as income rises, the income elasticity is negative.

By partially differentiating the pork demand function 2.2, $Q = 171 - 20p + 20p_b + 3p_c + 2Y$, with respect to Y, we find that $\partial Q/\partial Y = 2$, so the income elasticity of demand for pork is $\xi = 2Y/Q$. At our original equilibrium, quantity $Q = 220$ and income $Y = 12.5$, so the income elasticity is $2 \times (12.5/220) \approx 0.114$, or about one-ninth. The positive income elasticity shows that an increase in income causes the pork demand curve to shift to the right.

Income elasticities play an important role in our analysis of consumer behavior in Chapter 5. Typically, goods that consumers view as necessities, such as food, have income elasticities near zero. Goods that they consider to be luxuries generally have income elasticities greater than one.

The **cross-price elasticity of demand** is the percentage change in the quantity demanded in response to a given percentage change in the price of another good, p_o. The cross-price elasticity may be calculated as

$$\frac{\text{percentage change in quantity demanded}}{\text{percentage change in price of another good}} = \frac{\Delta Q/Q}{\Delta p_o/p_o} = \frac{\partial Q}{\partial p_o}\frac{p_o}{Q}.$$

When the cross-price elasticity is negative, the goods are complements. If the cross-price elasticity is negative, people buy less of one good when the price of the other, second good increases: The demand curve for the first good shifts to the left. For example, if people like cream in their coffee, as the price of cream rises, they consume less coffee, so the cross-price elasticity of the quantity of coffee with respect to the price of cream is negative.

If the cross-price elasticity is positive, the goods are substitutes.[13] As the price of the second good increases, people buy more of the first good. For example, the quantity demanded of pork increases when the price of beef, p_b, rises. By partially differentiating the pork demand function 2.2, $Q = 171 - 20p + 20p_b + 3p_c + 2Y$, with respect to the price of beef, we find that $\partial Q/\partial p_b = 20$. As a result, the cross-price elasticity between the price of beef and the quantity of pork is $20p_b/Q$. At the original equilibrium where $Q = 220$ million kg per year, and $p_b = \$4$ per kg, the cross-price elasticity is $20 \times (4/220) \approx 0.364$. As the price of beef rises by 1%, the quantity of pork demanded rises by a little more than one-third of 1%.

APPLICATION

Substitution May Save Endangered Species

One reason that many species—including tigers, rhinoceroses, pinnipeds, green turtles, geckos, sea horses, pipefish, and sea cucumbers—are endangered, threatened, or vulnerable to extinction is that certain of their body parts are used as aphrodisiacs in traditional Chinese medicine. Is it possible that consumers will switch from such potions to Viagra, a less expensive and almost certainly more effective alternative treatment, and thereby help save these endangered species?

We cannot directly calculate the cross-price elasticity of demand between Viagra and these endangered species because their trade is illicit and not reported. However, in Asia, harp seal and hooded seal genitalia are also used as aphrodisiacs, and they may be legally traded. Before 1998, Viagra was unavailable (effectively, it had an infinite price). When it became available at about $15 to $20 Canadian per pill, the demand curve for seal sex organs shifted substantially to the left. According to von Hippel and von Hippel (2002, 2004), 30,000 to 50,000 seal organs were sold at between $70 and $100 Canadian in the years just before 1998. In 1998, the price per unit fell to between $15 and $20, and only 20,000 organs were sold. By 1999–2000 (and thereafter), virtually none were sold. This evidence suggests a strong willingness to substitute at current prices: a positive cross-price elasticity between seal organs and the price of Viagra. Thus Viagra can perhaps save more than marriages.

---

[13]*Jargon alert*: Graduate-level textbooks generally call these goods *gross substitutes* (and the goods in the previous example would be called *gross complements*).

SUPPLY ELASTICITY

Just as we can use the elasticity of demand to summarize information about the responsiveness of the quantity demanded to price or other variables, we can use the elasticity of supply to summarize information about the responsiveness of the quantity demanded. The **price elasticity of supply** (or *supply elasticity*) is the percentage change in the quantity supplied in response to a given percentage change in the price. The price elasticity of supply (η, the Greek letter eta) is

$$\eta = \frac{\text{percentage change in quantity supplied}}{\text{percentage change in price}} = \frac{\Delta Q/Q}{\Delta p/p} = \frac{\partial Q}{\partial p}\frac{p}{Q}, \qquad (2.25)$$

where Q is the *quantity supplied*. If $\eta = 2$, a 1% increase in price leads to a 2% increase in the quantity supplied.

The definition of the elasticity of supply, Equation 2.25, is very similar to the definition of the elasticity of demand, Equation 2.21. The key distinction is that the elasticity of supply describes the movement along the *supply* curve as price changes, whereas the elasticity of demand describes the movement along the *demand* curve as price changes. That is, in the numerator, supply elasticity depends on the percentage change in the *quantity supplied*, whereas demand elasticity depends on the percentage change in the *quantity demanded*.

If the supply curve is upward sloping, $\partial p/\partial Q > 0$, the supply elasticity is positive: $\eta > 0$. If the supply curve slopes downward, the supply elasticity is negative: $\eta < 0$. For the pork supply function 2.7, $Q = 88 + 40p$, the elasticity of supply of pork at the original equilibrium, where $p = \$3.30$ and $Q = 220$, is

$$\eta = \frac{dQ}{dp}\frac{p}{Q} = 40 \times \frac{3.30}{220} = 0.6.$$

As the price of pork increases by 1%, the quantity supplied rises by slightly less than two-thirds of a percent.

The elasticity of supply varies along an upward-sloping supply curve. For example, because the elasticity of supply for the pork is $\eta = 40p/Q$, as the ratio p/Q rises, the supply elasticity rises.

At a point on a supply curve where the elasticity of supply is $\eta = 0$, we say that the supply curve is *perfectly inelastic*: The supply does not change as the price rises. If $0 < \eta < 1$, the supply curve is *inelastic* (but not perfectly inelastic): A 1% increase in price causes a less than 1% rise in the quantity supplied. If $\eta > 1$, the supply curve is *elastic*. If η is infinite, the supply curve is *perfectly elastic*.

The supply elasticity does not vary along constant-elasticity supply functions, which are exponential or (equivalently) log-linear: $Q = Bp^{\eta}$ or $\ln Q = \ln B + \eta \ln p$. If η is a positive, finite number, the constant-elasticity supply curve starts at the origin, as Figure 2.11 shows. Two extreme examples of both constant-elasticity of supply curves and linear supply curves are the vertical supply curve and the horizontal supply curve.

A supply curve that is vertical at a quantity, Q^*, is perfectly inelastic. No matter what the price is, firms supply Q^*. An example of inelastic supply is a perishable item such as already picked fresh fruit. If the perishable good is not sold, it quickly becomes worthless. Thus the seller will accept any market price for the good.

A supply curve that is horizontal at a price, p^*, is perfectly elastic. Firms supply as much as the market wants—a potentially unlimited amount—if the price is p^* or

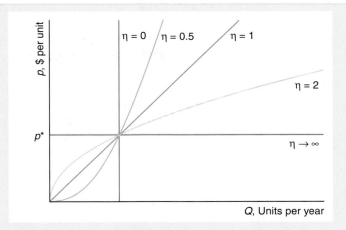

Figure 2.11 Constant Elasticity Supply Curves. Constant elasticity supply curves, $Q = Bp^{\eta}$, with positive, finite elasticities start at the origin. They are concave to the horizontal axis if $1 < \eta < \infty$ and convex if $0 < \eta < 1$. The unitary elasticity supply curve is a straight line through the origin. The vertical constant elasticity supply curve is perfectly inelastic, while the horizontal curve is perfectly elastic.

above. Firms supply nothing at a price below p^*, which does not cover their cost of production.

LONG RUN VERSUS SHORT RUN

Typically, short-run demand or supply elasticities differ substantially from long-run elasticities. The duration of the *short run* depends on the planning horizon—how long it takes consumers or firms to adjust for a particular good.

Demand Elasticities over Time. Two factors that determine whether short-run demand elasticities are larger or smaller than long-run elasticities are ease of substitution and storage opportunities. Often one can substitute between products in the long run but not in the short run.

When oil prices rose rapidly in the 1970s and 1980s because of actions by the Organization of Petroleum Exporting Countries (OPEC), most Western consumers did not greatly alter the amount of oil they demanded. Someone who drove 27 miles to and from work every day in a 1969 Chevy could not easily reduce the amount of gasoline purchased. In the long run, however, this person could buy a smaller car, get a job closer to home, join a car pool, or in other ways reduce the amount of gasoline purchased.

Gallini (1983) estimated long-run demand elasticities that are more elastic than the short-run elasticity for gasoline in Canada. She found that the short-run elasticity is −0.35; the 5-year intermediate-run elasticity is nearly twice as elastic, −0.7; and the 10-year, long-run elasticity is approximately −0.8, which is slightly more elastic. Thus a 1% increase in price lowers the quantity demanded by only about 0.35% in the short run but by more than twice as much, 0.8%, in the long run. Similarly, Grossman and Chaloupka (1998) estimated that a rise in the street price of cocaine has a larger long-run effect than its short-run effect on cocaine consumption by young adults (aged 17–29). The long-run demand elasticity is −1.35, whereas the short-run elasticity is −0.96.

For goods that can be stored easily, short-run demand curves may be more elastic than long-run curves. If frozen orange juice goes on sale this week at your local supermarket, you may buy large quantities and store the extra in your freezer. As a result, you may be more sensitive to price changes for frozen orange juice in the short run than in the long run.

Supply Elasticities over Time. Supply curves too may have different elasticities in the short run than in the long run. If a manufacturing firm wants to increase production in the short run, it can do so by hiring workers to use its machines around the clock, but how much it can expand its output is limited by the fixed size of its manufacturing plant and the number of machines it has. In the long run, however, the firm can build another plant and buy or build more equipment. Thus we would expect this firm's long-run supply elasticity to be greater than its short-run elasticity.

Adelaja (1991) found that the short-run supply elasticity of milk is 0.36, whereas the long-run supply elasticity is 0.51. Thus the long-run quantity response to a 1% increase in price is about 42% [= (0.51 − 0.36)/0.36] more than in the short run.

APPLICATION

Oil Drilling in the Arctic National Wildlife Refuge

We can use information about demand and supply elasticities to answer an important public policy question: Would selling oil from the Arctic National Wildlife Refuge (ANWR) substantially affect the price of oil? Established in 1980, the ANWR covers 20 million acres and is the largest of Alaska's 16 national wildlife refuges. It is believed to contain massive deposits of petroleum. For decades, a debate has raged over whether the ANWR's owners—the citizens of the United States—should keep it undeveloped or permit oil drilling.[14]

In the simplest form of this complex debate, environmentalists stress that drilling would harm the wildlife refuge and pollute the environment, while President George W. Bush and other drilling proponents argue that extracting this oil would substantially reduce the price of petroleum (as well as decrease U.S. dependence on foreign oil and bring in large royalties). Recent spurts in the price of gasoline and the war in Iraq have heightened this intense debate.

The effect of the sale of ANWR oil on the world price of oil is a key element in this debate. We can combine oil production information with supply and demand elasticities to make a "back of the envelope" estimate of the price effects.

---

[14]I am grateful to Robert Whaples, who wrote an earlier version of this analysis. In the following discussion, we assume for simplicity that the oil market is competitive, and use current values of price and quantities even though drilling in the ANWR would not take place for at least a decade.

A number of studies estimate that the long-run elasticity of demand, ε, for oil is about -0.4 and the long-run supply elasticity, η, is about 0.3. Analysts agree less about how much ANWR oil will be produced. The Department of Energy's Energy Information Service (EIS) predicts that production from the ANWR would average about 800,000 barrels per day (the EIS estimates that the ANWR's oil would increase the volume of production by about 0.7% in 2020). That production would be about 1% of the worldwide oil production, which averaged about 82 million barrels per day in 2004 (and was only slightly higher in 2005 and 2006).

A report of the U.S. Department of Energy predicted that ANWR drilling could lower the price of oil by about 50¢ a barrel or 1%, given that the price of a barrel of oil was slightly above $50 at the beginning of 2007. Severin Borenstein, an economist who is the director of the U.C. Energy Institute, concluded that the ANWR might reduce oil prices by up to a few percentage points but that "drilling in ANWR will never noticeably affect gasoline prices."

In the following solved problem, we can make our own calculations of the price effect of drilling in the ANWR. Here and in many of the solved problems in this book, you are asked to determine how a change in a variable or policy affects one or more variables. In this problem, the policy changes from not allowing to permitting drilling in the ANWR, which affects the world's equilibrium price of oil.

SOLVED PROBLEM 2.3

What would be the effect of ANWR production on the world equilibrium price of oil given that $\varepsilon = -0.4$, $\eta = 0.3$, the pre-ANWR daily world production of oil is $Q_1 = 82$ million barrels per day, the pre-ANWR world price is $p_1 = \$50$ per barrel, and daily ANWR production would be 0.8 million barrels per day? For specificity, assume that the supply and demand curves are linear and that the introduction of ANWR oil would cause a parallel shift in the world supply curve to the right by 0.8 million barrels per day.

Answer

1. *Determine the long-run linear demand function that is consistent with pre-ANWR world output and price:* At the original equilibrium, e_1 in the figure, $p_1 = \$50$ and $Q_1 = 82$. There the elasticity of demand is $\varepsilon = (dQ/dp)(p_1/Q_1) = (dQ/dp)(50/82) = -0.4$. Using algebra, we find that dQ/dp equals $-0.4(82/50) = -0.656$, which is the inverse of the slope of the demand curve, D, in the figure. Knowing this slope and that demand equals 82 at $50 per barrel, we can solve for the intercept, because the quantity demanded rises by 0.656 for each dollar by which the price falls. The demand when the price is zero is $82 + (0.656 \times 50) = 114.8$. Thus the equation for the demand curve is $Q = 114.8 - 0.656p$.

2. *Determine the long-run linear supply function that is consistent with pre-ANWR world output and price:* Where S^1 intercepts D at the original equilibrium, e_1, the elasticity of supply is $\eta = (dQ/dp)(p_1/Q_1) = (dQ/dp)(50/82) = 0.3$. Solving, we find that $dQ/dp = 0.3(82/50) = 0.492$. Because the quantity supplied falls by

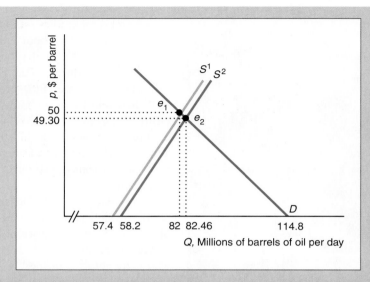

0.492 for each dollar by which the price drops, the quantity supplied when the price is zero is $82 - (0.492 \times 50) = 57.4$. Thus the equation for the pre-ANWR supply curve, S^1 in the figure, is $Q = 57.4 + 0.492p$.

3. *Determine the post-ANWR long-run linear supply function:* The oil pumped from the ANWR would cause a parallel shift in the supply curve, moving S^1 to the right by 0.8 to S^2. That is, the slope remains the same, but the intercept on the quantity axis increases by 0.8. Thus the supply function for S^2 is $Q = 58.2 + 0.492p$.

4. *Use the demand curve and the post-ANWR supply function to calculate the new equilibrium price and quantity:* The new equilibrium, e_2, occurs where S^2 intersects D. Setting the right-hand sides of the demand function and the post-ANWR supply function equal, we obtain an expression in the new price, p_2:

$$58.2 + 0.492p_2 = 114.8 - 0.656p_2.$$

We can solve this expression for the new equilibrium price: $p_2 \approx \$49.30$. That is, the price drops about 70¢, or approximately 1.4%. If we substitute this new price into either the demand curve or the post-ANWR supply curve, we find that the new equilibrium quantity is 82.46 million barrels per day. That is, equilibrium output rises by 0.46 million barrels per day (0.56%), which is only a little more than half of the predicted daily ANWR supply, because other suppliers will decrease their output slightly in response to the lower price.

Comment: Our estimate of a small drop in the world oil price if ANWR oil is sold would not change substantially if our estimates of the elasticities of supply and demand were moderately larger or smaller. The main reason for this result is that the ANWR output would be a very small portion of worldwide supply—the new supply curve is only slightly to the right of the initial supply curve. Thus drilling in the ANWR cannot insulate the American market from international events that roil the oil market. A new war in the Persian Gulf could shift the worldwide supply curve to the left by 3 million barrels a day or more (nearly four times the ANWR production). Such a shock would cause the price of oil to soar whether or not we drill in the ANWR.

2.6 Effects of a Sales Tax

How much a tax affects the equilibrium price and quantity and how much of the tax falls on consumers depends on the elasticities of demand and supply. Knowing only the elasticities of demand and supply, we can make accurate predictions about the effects of a new tax and determine how much of the tax falls on consumers.

In this section, we examine three questions about the effects of a sales tax:

1. What effect does a sales tax have on equilibrium prices and quantity?
2. Is it true, as many people claim, that taxes assessed on producers are *passed along* to consumers? That is, do consumers pay for the entire tax, or do producers pay part of it?
3. Do the equilibrium price and quantity depend on whether the tax is assessed on consumers or on producers?

TWO TYPES OF SALES TAXES

Governments use two types of sales taxes. The most common sales tax is called an *ad valorem* tax by economists and *the* sales tax by real people. For every dollar the consumer spends, the government keeps a fraction, α, which is the *ad valorem* tax rate. Japan's national sales tax is $\alpha = 5\%$. If a consumer in Japan buys a Nintendo Wii for $500, the government collects $\alpha \times \$500 = 5\% \times \$500 = \$25$ in taxes, and the seller receives $(1 - \alpha) \times \$500 = \$475$.[15]

The other type of sales tax is a *specific* or *unit* tax, where a specified dollar amount, τ, is collected per unit of output. The federal government collects $\tau = 18.4\cent$ on each gallon of gas sold in the United States.

EQUILIBRIUM EFFECTS OF A SPECIFIC TAX

To answer our three questions, we must extend the standard supply-and-demand analysis to take taxes into account. Let's start by assuming that the specific tax is assessed on firms at the time of sale. If the consumer pays p for a good, the government takes τ and the seller receives $p - \tau$.

Suppose that the government collects a specific tax of $\tau = \$1.05$ per kg of processed pork from pork producers. Because of the tax, suppliers keep only $p - \tau$ of price p that consumers pay. Thus at every possible price paid by consumers, firms are willing to supply less than when they received the full amount consumers paid. Before the tax, firms were willing to supply 206 million kg per year at a price of $2.95 as the pretax supply curve S^1 in Figure 2.12 shows. After the tax, firms receive only $1.90 if consumers pay $2.95, so they are not willing to supply 206. For firms to be willing to supply 206, they must receive $2.95 after the tax, so consumers must pay $4. As a result, the after-tax supply curve, S^2, is $\tau = \$1.05$ above the original supply curve S^1 at every quantity, as the figure shows.

---

[15]For specificity, we assume that the price firms receive is $p = (1 - \alpha)p^\star$, where $p^\star$ is the price consumers pay and α is the *ad valorem* tax rate on the price consumers pay. However, many governments (including U.S. and Japanese governments) set the *ad valorem* sales tax, β, as an amount added to the price sellers charge, so consumers pay $p^\star = (1 + \beta)p$. By setting α and β appropriately, the taxes are equivalent. Here $p = p^\star/(1 + \beta)$, so $(1 - \alpha) = 1/(1 + \beta)$. For example, if $\beta = \frac{1}{3}$, then $\alpha = \frac{1}{4}$.

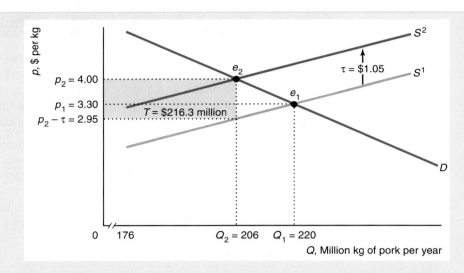

Figure 2.12 Effect of a \$1.05 Specific Tax on the Pork Market Collected from Producers. The specific tax of $\tau = \$1.05$ per kg collected from producers shifts the pretax pork supply curve from S^1 to the posttax supply curve, S^2. The tax causes the equilibrium to shift from e_1 (determined by the intersection of S^1 and D) to e_2 (intersection of S^2 with D). The equilibrium price increases from \$3.30 to \$4.00. Two-thirds of the incidence of the tax falls on consumers, who spend 70¢ more per unit. Producers receive 35¢ less per unit after the tax. The government collects tax revenues of $T = \tau Q_2 = \$216.3$ million per year.

We can use this figure to illustrate the answer to our first question concerning the effects of the tax on the pork market equilibrium. *The specific tax causes the equilibrium price consumers pay to rise, the equilibrium quantity to fall, and the tax revenue to rise.*

The intersection of the pretax pork supply curve S^1 and the pork demand curve D in Figure 2.12 determines the pretax equilibrium, e_1. The equilibrium price is $p_1 = \$3.30$, and the equilibrium quantity is $Q_1 = 220$. The tax shifts the supply curve to S^2, so the after-tax equilibrium is e_2, where consumers pay $p_2 = \$4$, firms receive $p_2 - \$1.05 = \$2.95$, and $Q_2 = 206$. Thus the tax causes the price that consumers pay to increase, $\Delta p = p_2 - p_1 = \$4 - \$3.30 = 70$¢, and the quantity to fall, $\Delta Q = Q_2 - Q_1 = 206 - 220 = -14$.

Although consumers and producers are worse off because of the tax, the government acquires new tax revenue of $T = \tau Q = \$1.05$ per kg $\times$ 206 million kg per year = \$216.3 million per year. The length of the shaded rectangle in the figure is $Q_2 = 206$ million kg per year, and its height is $\tau = \$1.05$ per kg, so the area of the rectangle equals the tax revenue. (The figure shows only part of the length of the rectangle because the horizontal axis starts at 176.)

HOW SPECIFIC TAX EFFECTS DEPEND ON ELASTICITIES

We now turn to our second question: Who is hurt by the tax? To answer this comparative static question, we want to determine how the price that consumers pay and firms receive changes after the tax is imposed.

The government collects a specific or unit tax, τ, from sellers, so sellers receive $p - \tau$ when consumers pay p. We now determine the effect of the tax on the equilibrium.

In the new equilibrium, the price that consumers pay is determined by equality between the demand function and the after-tax supply function,

$$D(p) = S(p - \tau) = 0.$$

Thus the equilibrium price is an implicit function of the specific tax: $p = p(\tau)$. Consequently, the equilibrium condition is

$$D(p(\tau)) = S(p(\tau) - \tau). \tag{2.26}$$

We determine the effect of a small tax on price by differentiating Equation 2.26 with respect to τ:

$$\frac{dD}{dp}\frac{dp}{d\tau} = \frac{dS}{dp}\frac{d(p(\tau) - \tau)}{d\tau} = \frac{dS}{dp}\left(\frac{dp}{d\tau} - 1\right).$$

Rearranging terms, it follows that the change in the price that consumers pay with respect to a change in the tax is

$$\frac{dp}{d\tau} = \frac{\dfrac{dS}{dp}}{\dfrac{dS}{dp} - \dfrac{dD}{dp}}. \tag{2.27}$$

We know that $dD/dp < 0$ from the Law of Demand. If the supply curve slopes upward so that $dS/dp > 0$, then $dp/d\tau > 0$, as Figure 2.12 illustrates. The higher the tax, the greater the price consumers pay. If $dS/dp < 0$, the direction of change is ambiguous: It depends on the relative slopes of the supply and demand curves (the denominator).

By multiplying both the numerator and denominator of the right-hand side of Equation 2.27 by p/Q, we can express this derivative in terms of elasticities,

$$\frac{dp}{d\tau} = \frac{\dfrac{dS}{dp}\dfrac{p}{Q}}{\dfrac{dS}{dp}\dfrac{p}{Q} - \dfrac{dD}{dp}\dfrac{p}{Q}} = \frac{\eta}{\eta - \varepsilon}, \tag{2.28}$$

where the last equality follows because dS/dp and dD/dp are the changes in the quantities supplied and demanded as price changes and the consumer and producer prices are identical when $\tau = 0$.[16] This expression holds for any size change in τ if both the demand and supply curves are linear. For most other shaped curves, the expression holds only for small changes.

We can now answer our second question: Who is hurt by the tax? The **incidence of a tax on consumers** is the share of the tax that falls on consumers. The incidence of the tax that falls on consumers is $dp/d\tau$, the amount by which the price to consumers rises as a fraction of the amount the tax increases. Firms receive $p - \tau$, so the change in the price that firms receive as the tax changes is $d(p - \tau)/d\tau = dp/d\tau - 1$. The *incidence of*

---

[16]To determine the effect on quantity, we can combine the price result from Equation 2.28 with information from either the demand or the supply function. Differentiating the demand function with respect to τ, we know that

$$\frac{dD}{dp}\frac{dp}{d\tau} = \frac{dD}{dp}\frac{\eta}{\eta - \varepsilon},$$

which is negative if the supply curve is upward sloping so that $\eta > 0$.

the tax on firms is the amount by which the price to firms falls: $1 - dp/d\tau$. The sum of the incidence of the tax to consumers and firms is $dp/d\tau + 1 - dp/d\tau = 1$. That is, the increase in price to consumers plus the drop in price to firms equals the tax.

The demand elasticity for pork is $\varepsilon = -0.3$ and the supply elasticity is $\eta = 0.6$, so the incidence of a specific tax on consumers is $dp/d\tau = \eta/(\eta - \varepsilon) = 0.6/[0.6 - (-0.3)] = 0.6/0.9 = 2/3$, and the incidence of the tax on firms is $1 - 2/3 = 1/3$.

Thus a discrete change in the tax of $\Delta\tau = \tau - 0 = \$1.05$ causes the price that consumers pay to rise by $\Delta p = p_2 - p_1 = \$4.00 - \$3.30 = [\eta/(\eta - \varepsilon)]\Delta\tau = 2/3 \times \$1.05 = 70\text{¢}$ and the price to firms to fall by $1/3 \times \$1.05 = 35\text{¢}$, as Figure 2.2 shows. The sum of the increase to consumers plus the loss to firms is $70\text{¢} + 35\text{¢} = \$1.05 = \tau$.

Equation 2.28 shows that, for a given supply elasticity, the more elastic the demand, the less the equilibrium price rises when a tax is imposed. Similarly, for a given demand elasticity, the smaller the supply elasticity, the smaller the increase in the equilibrium price that consumers pay when a tax is imposed. For example, in the pork example, if the supply elasticity were $\eta = 0$ (a perfectly inelastic vertical supply curve), $dp/d\tau = 0/[0 - (-0.3)] = 0$, so none of the incidence of the tax falls on consumers, and the entire incidence of the tax falls on firms.[17]

THE SAME EQUILIBRIUM NO MATTER WHO IS TAXED

Our third question is, "Does the equilibrium or the incidence of the tax depend on whether the tax is collected from producers or consumers?" Surprisingly, in the supply-and-demand model, the equilibrium and the incidence of the tax are the same regardless of whether the government collects the tax from producers or from consumers.

We've already seen that firms are able to pass on some or all of the tax collected from them to consumers. We now show that, if the tax is collected from consumers, they can pass the producers' share back to the firms.

Suppose the specific tax $\tau = \$1.05$ on pork is collected from consumers rather than from producers. Because the government takes τ from each p that consumers spend, producers receive only $p - \tau$. Thus the demand curve as seen by firms shifts downward by \$1.05 from D to D^s in Figure 2.13.

The intersection of D^2 and S determines the after-tax equilibrium, where the equilibrium quantity is Q_2 and the price received by producers is $p_2 - \tau$. The price paid by consumers, p_2 (on the original demand curve D at Q_2), is τ above the price received by producers. We place the after-tax equilibrium, e_2, bullet on the market demand D in Figure 2.11 to show that it is the same as the e_2 in Figure 2.12.

Comparing Figure 2.13 to Figure 2.12, we see that the after-tax equilibrium is the same regardless of whether the tax is imposed on consumers or producers. The price to consumers rises by the same amount, $\Delta p = 70\text{¢}$, and the incidence of the tax, $\Delta p/\Delta\tau = 2/3$, is the same.

A specific tax, regardless of whether the tax is collected from consumers or producers, creates a *wedge* equal to the per-unit tax of τ between the price consumers pay, p, and the price producers receive, $p - \tau$. In short, regardless of whether firms or consumers pay the tax to the government, you can solve tax problems by shifting the supply curve, shifting the demand curve, or inserting a wedge between the supply and demand curves. All three approaches give the same answer.

---

[17]See **www.aw-bc.com/perloff**, Chapter 2, "Incidence of a Tax on Restaurant Meals," for another application.

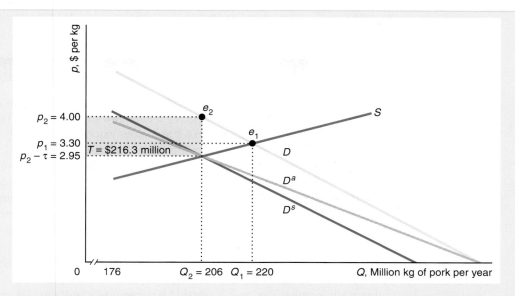

Figure 2.13 Effects of a Specific Tax and of an *Ad Valorem* Tax on Consumers. Without a tax, the demand curve is *D* and the supply curve is *S*. A specific tax of $\tau = \$1.05$ per kg collected from consumers shifts the demand curve to D^s, which is parallel to *D*. The new equilibrium is e_2 on the original demand curve *D*. If instead an *ad valorem* tax of $\alpha = 26.25\%$ is imposed, the demand curve facing firms is D^a. The gap between *D* and D^a, the per-unit tax, is larger at higher prices. The after-tax equilibrium is the same with both of these taxes.

THE SIMILAR EFFECTS OF *AD VALOREM* AND SPECIFIC TAXES

In contrast to specific sales taxes, which are applied to relatively few goods, governments levy *ad valorem* taxes on a wide variety of goods. Most states apply an *ad valorem* sales tax to most goods and services, exempting only a few staples such as food and medicine. There are 6,400 different *ad valorem* sales tax rates across the United States, which can go as high as 8.5% (Besley and Rosen, 1999).

Suppose that the government imposes an *ad valorem* tax of α, instead of a specific tax, on the price that consumers pay for processed pork. We already know that the equilibrium price is $4 with a specific tax of $1.05 per kg. At that price, an *ad valorem* tax of $\alpha = \$1.05/\$4 = 26.25\%$ raises the same amount of tax per unit as a $1.05 specific tax.

It is usually easiest to analyze the effects of an *ad valorem* tax by shifting the demand curve. Figure 2.13 shows how an *ad valorem* tax shifts the processed pork demand curve. The *ad valorem* tax shifts the demand curve to D^a. At any given price p, the gap between *D* and D^a is αp, which is greater at high prices than at low prices. The gap is $1.05 (= 0.2625 \times \$4)$ per unit when the price is $4, and $2.10 when the price is $8.

Imposing an *ad valorem* tax causes the after-tax equilibrium quantity, Q_2, to fall below the original quantity, Q_1, and the after-tax price, p_2, to rise above the original price, p_1. The tax collected per unit of output is $\tau = \alpha p_2$. The incidence of the tax that falls on consumers is the change in price, $\Delta p = (p_2 - p_1)$, divided by the change in the per-unit tax, $\Delta \tau = \alpha p_2 - 0$, that is collected, $\Delta p/(\alpha p_2)$. The incidence of an *ad valorem* tax is generally shared between consumers and producers. Because the *ad valorem* tax of $\alpha = 26.25\%$ has exactly the same impact on the equilibrium pork price and raises the same amount of tax per unit as the $1.05 specific tax, the incidence is the same for both types of taxes.

(As with specific taxes, the incidence of the *ad valorem* tax depends on the elasticities of supply and demand, but we'll spare your having to go through that in detail.)

2.7   Quantity Supplied Need Not Equal Quantity Demanded

In a supply-and-demand model, the quantity supplied does not necessarily equal the quantity demanded because of the way we defined these two concepts. We defined the quantity supplied as the amount firms *want to sell* at a given price, holding constant other factors that affect supply, such as the price of inputs. We defined the quantity demanded as the quantity that consumers *want to buy* at a given price, if other factors that affect demand are held constant. The quantity that firms want to sell and the quantity that consumers want to buy at a given price need not equal the *actual* quantity that is bought and sold.

We could have defined the quantity supplied and the quantity demanded so that they must be equal. If we had defined the quantity supplied as the amount firms *actually* sell at a given price and the quantity demanded as the amount consumers *actually* buy, supply would have to equal demand in all markets because we *defined* the quantity demanded and the quantity supplied as the same quantity.

It is worth emphasizing this distinction because politicians, pundits, and the press are so often confused on this point. Someone insisting that "demand *must* equal supply" must be defining demand and supply as the *actual* quantities sold. Because we define the quantities supplied and demanded in terms of people's *wants* and not *actual* quantities bought and sold, the statement that "supply equals demand" is a theory, not merely a definition.

This theory says that the quantity supplied equals the quantity demanded at the intersection of the supply and demand curves if the government does not intervene. Not all government interventions prevent markets from *clearing* by equilibrating the quantity supplied and the quantity demanded. For example, as we've seen, a government tax affects the equilibrium but does not cause a gap between the quantity demanded and the quantity supplied. However, some government policies do more than merely shift the supply or demand curve.

For example, a government may control price directly. This policy leads to either excess supply or excess demand if the price the government sets differs from the market clearing price. We illustrate this result with two types of price control programs. The government may set a *price ceiling* at $\overline{p}$ so that the price at which goods are sold may be no higher than $\overline{p}$. When the government sets a *price floor* at $\underline{p}$, the price at which goods are sold may not fall below $\underline{p}$.

We can study the effects of such regulations using the supply-and-demand model. Despite the lack of equality between the quantity supplied and the quantity demanded, the supply-and-demand model is useful in analyzing this market because it predicts the excess demand or excess supply that is observed.

PRICE CEILING

Price ceilings have no effect if they are set above the equilibrium price that would be observed in the absence of the price controls. If the government says that firms may charge no more than $\overline{p} = \$5$ per gallon of gas and firms are actually charging $p = \$1$, the government's price control policy is irrelevant. However, if the equilibrium price, p, is above the price ceiling $\overline{p}$, the price that is actually observed in the market is the price ceiling.

The U.S. experience with gasoline illustrates the effects of price controls. In the 1970s, OPEC reduced supplies of oil—which is converted into gasoline—to Western countries. As a result, the total supply curve for gasoline in the United States—the

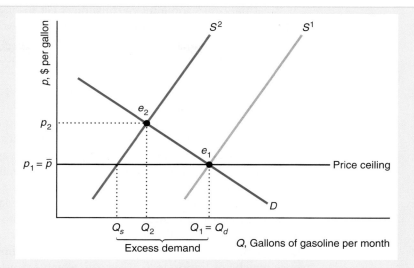

Figure 2.14 Price Ceiling on Gasoline. Supply shifts from S^1 to S^2. Under the government's price control program, gasoline stations may not charge a price above the price ceiling $\bar{p} = p_1$. At that price, producers are willing to supply only Q_s, which is less than the amount $Q_1 = Q_d$ that consumers want to buy. The result is excessive demand, or a shortage of $Q_d - Q_s$.

horizontal sum of domestic and OPEC supply curves—shifted to the left from S^1 to S^2 in Figure 2.14. Because of this shift, the equilibrium price of gasoline would have risen substantially, from p_1 to p_2. In an attempt to protect consumers by keeping gasoline prices from rising, the U.S. government set price ceilings on gasoline in 1973 and 1979.

The government told gas stations that they could charge no more than $\bar{p} = p_1$. Figure 2.14 shows the price ceiling as a solid horizontal line extending from the price axis at $\bar{p}$. The price control is binding because $p_2 > \bar{p}$. The observed price is the price ceiling. At $\bar{p}$, consumers *want* to buy $Q_d = Q_1$ gallons of gasoline, which is the equilibrium quantity they bought before OPEC acted. However, firms supply only Q_s gallons, which is determined by the intersection of the price control line with S^2. As a result of the binding price control, there is excess demand of $Q_d - Q_s$.

Were it not for the price controls, market forces would drive up the market price to p_2, where the excess demand would be eliminated. The government price ceiling prevents this adjustment from occurring. As a result, an enforced price ceiling causes a **shortage:** a persistent excess demand.

At the time of the controls, some government officials falsely contended that the shortages were caused by OPEC's cutting off its supply of oil to the United States. Without the price controls, the new equilibrium would be e_2. In this equilibrium, the price, p_2, is much higher than before, p_1; however, there is no shortage. Moreover, without controls, the quantity sold, Q_2, is greater than the quantity sold under the control program, Q_s.

With a binding price ceiling, the supply-and-demand model predicts an *equilibrium with a shortage*. In this equilibrium, the quantity demanded does not equal the quantity supplied. The reason that we call this situation an equilibrium even though a shortage exists is that no consumers or firms want to act differently, given the law. Without the price controls, consumers facing a shortage would try to get more output by offering to pay more, or firms would raise prices. With effective government price controls, they know that they can't drive up the price, so they live with the shortage.

What happens? Some lucky consumers get to buy Q_s units at the low price of $\bar{p}$. Other potential customers are disappointed: They would like to buy at that price, but they cannot find anyone willing to sell gas to them. With enforced price controls, sellers use criteria other than price to allocate the scarce commodity. They may supply their friends, long-term customers, or people of a certain race, gender, age, or religion. They may sell their goods on a first-come, first-served basis. Or they may limit everyone to only a few gallons.

Another possibility is for firms and customers to evade the price controls. A consumer could go to a gas station owner and say, "Let's not tell anyone, but I'll pay you twice the price the government sets if you'll sell me as much gas as I want." If enough customers and gas station owners behaved that way, no shortage would occur. A study of 92 major U.S. cities during the 1973 gasoline price controls found no gasoline lines in 52 of them. However, in cities such as Chicago, Hartford, New York, Portland, and Tucson, potential customers waited in line at the pump for an hour or more.[18] Deacon and Sonstelie (1989) calculated that for every dollar consumers saved during the 1980 gasoline price controls, they lost $1.16 in waiting time and other factors. This experience may be of importance in Hawaii, which recently suspended gasoline price controls that the state had imposed starting in 2005.

APPLICATION

Zimbabwe Price Controls

During the 2001 presidential campaign, Zimbabwe's government imposed price controls on many basic commodities, including various foods (about a third of citizens' daily consumption), soap, and cement. The controls led to shortages of these goods at retail outlets. Consequently, as the minister of finance and economic development acknowledged, a thriving *black market* or *parallel market* developed, where controls were ignored. Prices on the black market were two to three times higher than the controlled prices.

Cement manufacturers stopped accepting new orders when the price controls were imposed. Dealers quickly shifted existing supplies to the parallel market. Lack of cement crippled the construction industry. By May 2002, the government had nearly doubled the control price of cement in an effort to induce firms to resume selling cement.

In Zimbabwe's sugar industry, as the price controls made sugar significantly cheaper than in the surrounding regions, smuggling to other countries increased. Meanwhile, Zimbabwe suffered from a sugar shortage. Similarly, there was a critical maize shortage—which was exacerbated by other shortsighted policies that caused the quantity of maize produced to fall by 30%. Major supermarkets had no maize meal, sugar, and cooking oil on many days. Bakers scaled back their operations because they could obtain only half as much flour as before the controls. These dire shortages pushed many people to the verge of starvation.

---

[18]See **www.aw-bc.com/perloff,** Chapter 2, "Gas Lines," for a more detailed discussion of the effects of the 1973 and 1979 gasoline price controls.

In 2005, the government announced new price controls on basic food commodities. Food shortages grew worse. More than a third of the populace is malnourished. Only international food aid has kept millions of these people alive. In 2006, the inflation rate (largely prices of non-controlled goods) exceeded 1,000% and the government introduced a new watchdog agency to monitor prices and incomes—a combination likely to exacerbate the situation.

PRICE FLOOR

Governments also commonly use price floors. One of the most important examples of a price floor is the minimum wage in labor markets.

The minimum wage law forbids employers from paying less than a minimum wage, $\underline{w}$. Minimum wage laws date from 1894 in New Zealand, 1909 in the United Kingdom, and 1912 in Massachusetts. The Fair Labor Standards Act of 1938 set a federal U.S. minimum wage of 25¢. The U.S. federal minimum wage is currently $5.15 an hour, but Congress is debating a substantial increase. The statutory monthly minimum wage ranges from the equivalent of 19€ in the Russian Federation to 375€ in Portugal, 1,154€ in France, and 1,466€ in Luxembourg. If the minimum wage binds—exceeds the equilibrium wage, w^*—the minimum wage may cause *unemployment,* which is a persistent excess supply of labor.[19]

For simplicity, suppose that there is a single labor market in which everyone is paid the same wage. Figure 2.15 shows the supply and demand curves for labor services (hours worked). Firms buy hours of labor service—they hire workers. The quantity measure on the horizontal axis is hours worked per year, and the price measure on the vertical axis is the wage per hour.

With no government intervention, the market equilibrium is e, where the wage is w^* and the number of hours worked is L^*. The minimum wage creates a price floor, a horizontal line, at $\underline{w}$. At that wage, the quantity demanded falls to L_d and the quantity supplied rises to L_s. As a result, there is an excess supply or unemployment of $L_s - L_d$. The minimum wage prevents market forces from eliminating this excess supply, so it leads to an equilibrium with unemployment. The original 1938 U.S. minimum wage law caused massive unemployment in Puerto Rico (see **www.aw-bc.com/perloff,** Chapter 2, "Minimum Wage Law in Puerto Rico").

It is ironic that a law designed to help workers by raising their wages may harm some of them by causing them to become unemployed. Such a minimum wage law benefits only those who remain employed.[20]

---

[19]The U.S. Department of Labor maintains at its Web site (**www.dol.gov**) an extensive history of the federal minimum wage law, labor markets, state minimum wage laws, and other information. For European minimum wages, see **www.fedee.com/minwage.html.** Where the minimum wage applies to only some labor markets (Chapter 10) or where only a single firm hires all the workers in a market (Chapter 15), a minimum wage might not cause unemployment. Card and Krueger (1997) provide evidence that recent rises in the minimum wage had negligible (at most) effects on employment in certain low-skill labor markets.

[20]The minimum wage could raise the wage enough that total wage payments, wL, rise despite the fall in demand for labor services. If workers could share the unemployment—everybody works fewer hours than he or she wants—all workers could benefit from the minimum wage. See Problem 40.

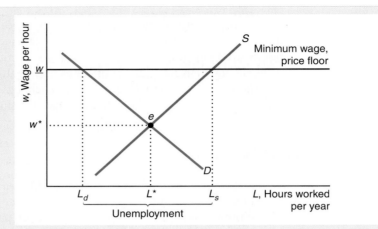

Figure 2.15 Minimum Wage. In the absence of a minimum wage, the equilibrium wage is w^* and the equilibrium number of hours worked is L^*. A minimum wage, $\underline{w}$, set above w^*, leads to unemployment—persistent excess supply—because the quantity demanded, L_d, is less than the quantity supplied, L_s.

2.8 When to Use the Supply-and-Demand Model

As we've seen, supply-and-demand theory can help us to understand and predict real-world events in many markets. Through Chapter 10, we discuss competitive markets in which the supply-and-demand model is a powerful tool for predicting what will happen to market equilibrium if underlying conditions—tastes, incomes, and prices of inputs—change. The types of markets for which the supply-and-demand model is useful are described at length in these chapters, particularly Chapter 8. Briefly, this model is applicable in markets in which:

- **Everyone is a price taker:** Because no consumer or firm is a very large part of the market, no one can affect the market price. Easy entry of firms into the market, which leads to a large number of firms, is usually necessary to ensure that firms are price takers.
- **Firms sell identical products:** Consumers do not prefer one firm's good to another.
- **Everyone has full information about the price and quality of goods:** Consumers know if a firm is charging a price higher than the price others set, and they know if a firm tries to sell them inferior-quality goods.
- **Costs of trading are low:** It is not time consuming, difficult, or expensive for a buyer to find a seller and make a trade or for a seller to find and trade with a buyer.

Markets with these properties are called *perfectly competitive markets*.

Where there are many firms and consumers, no single firm or consumer is a large enough part of the market to affect the price. If you stop buying bread or if one of the many thousands of wheat farmers stops selling the wheat used to make the bread, the price of bread will not change. Consumers and firms are *price takers*: They cannot affect the market price.

In contrast, if there is only one seller of a good or service—a *monopoly* (Chapter 11)—that seller is a *price setter* and can affect the market price. Because demand curves slope downward, a monopoly can increase the price it receives by reducing the amount of a good it supplies. Firms are also price setters in an *oligopoly*—a market with only a small number of firms—or in markets where they sell differentiated products and a consumer prefers one product to another (Chapter 13). In markets with price setters, the market price is usually higher than that predicted by the supply-and-demand model. That doesn't make the model generally wrong. It means only that the supply-and-demand model does not apply to markets with a small number of sellers or buyers. In such markets, we use other models.

If consumers have less information than a firm, the firm can take advantage of consumers by selling them inferior-quality goods or by charging a much higher price than that charged by other firms. In such a market, the observed price is usually higher than that predicted by the supply-and-demand model, the market may not exist at all (consumers and firms cannot reach agreements), or different firms may charge different prices for the same good (Chapter 18).

The supply-and-demand model is also not entirely appropriate in markets in which it is costly to trade with others because the costs of a buyer's finding a seller or of a seller's finding a buyer are high. **Transaction costs** are the expenses of finding a trading partner and making a trade for a good or service other than the price paid for that good or service. These costs include the time and money spent to find someone with whom to trade. When transaction costs are high, trades may not occur; or if they do occur, individual trades may occur at a variety of prices (Chapter 18).

Thus the supply-and-demand model is not appropriate in markets in which there are only one or a few sellers (such as electricity), firms produce differentiated products (such as music CDs), consumers know less than sellers about quality or price (such as used cars), or there are high transaction costs (such as nuclear turbine engines). Markets in which the supply-and-demand model has proved useful include agriculture, finance, labor, construction, services, wholesale, and retail—markets with many firms and consumers and where firms sell identical products.

Summary

1. **Demand:** The quantity of a good or service demanded by consumers depends on their tastes, the price of a good, the price of goods that are substitutes and complements, consumers' income, information, government regulations, and other factors. The *Law of Demand*—which is based on observation—says that *demand curves slope downward*. The higher the price, the less quantity is demanded, holding constant other factors that affect demand. A change in price causes a *movement along the demand curve*. A change in income, tastes, or another factor that affects demand other than price causes a *shift of the demand curve*. To get a total demand curve, we horizontally sum the demand curves of individuals or types of consumers or countries. That is, we add the quantities demanded by each individual at a given price to get the total demanded.

2. **Supply:** The quantity of a good or service supplied by firms depends on the price, the firm's costs, government regulations, and other factors. The market supply curve need not slope upward but usually does. A change in price causes a *movement along the supply curve*. A change in the price of an input or government regulation causes a *shift of the supply curve*. The total supply curve is the horizontal sum of the supply curves for individual firms.

3. **Market Equilibrium:** The intersection of the demand curve and the supply curve determines the equilibrium price and quantity in a market. Market forces—actions of consumers and firms—drive the price and quantity to the equilibrium levels if they are initially too low or too high.

4. **Shocking the Equilibrium: Comparative Statics:** A change in an underlying factor other than price causes a shift of the supply curve or the demand curve, which alters the equilibrium. Comparative statics is the method that economists use to analyze how variables controlled by consumers and firms—such as price and quantity—react to a change in *environmental variables* such as prices of substitutes and complements, income, and prices of inputs.

5. **Elasticities:** An elasticity is the percentage change in a variable in response to a given percentage change in another variable, holding all other relevant variables constant. The elasticity of demand, ε, is the percentage change

in the quantity demanded in response to a given percentage change in price: A 1% increase in price causes the quantity demanded to fall by ε%. Because demand curves slope downward according to the Law of Demand, the elasticity of demand is always negative. The elasticity of supply, η, is the percentage change in the quantity supplied in response to a given percentage change in price. Given estimated elasticities, we can forecast the comparative statics effects of a change in taxes or other variables that affect the equilibrium.

6. **Effects of a Sales Tax:** The two common types of sales taxes are *ad valorem* taxes, by which the government collects a fixed percentage of the price paid per unit, and specific taxes, by which the government collects a fixed amount of money per unit sold. Both types of sales taxes typically raise the equilibrium price and lower the equilibrium quantity. Both usually also raise the price consumers pay and lower the price suppliers receive, so consumers do not bear the full burden or incidence of the tax. The effects on quantity, price, and the incidence of the tax that falls on consumers depend on the demand and supply elasticities. In competitive markets, the effect of a tax on equilibrium quantities, prices, and the incidence of the tax is unaffected by whether the tax is collected from consumers or producers.

7. **Quantity Supplied Need Not Equal Quantity Demanded:** The quantity supplied equals the quantity demanded in a competitive market if the government does not intervene. However, some government policies—such as price floors or ceilings—cause the quantity supplied to be greater or less than the quantity demanded, leading to persistent excesses or shortages.

8. **When to Use the Supply-and-Demand Model:** The supply-and-demand model is a powerful tool to explain what happens in a market or to make predictions about what will happen if an underlying factor in a market changes. However, this model is applicable only in competitive markets, which are markets with many buyers and sellers; identical goods; certainty and full information about price, quantity, quality, incomes, costs, and other market characteristics; and low transaction costs.

Questions

If you ask me anything I don't know, I'm not going to answer. —Yogi Berra

* = *answer at the back of this book;* **W** = *audio-slide show answers by James Dearden at* **www.aw-bc.com/perloff**

*1. Use a supply-and-demand diagram to explain the statement "Talk is cheap because supply exceeds demand." At what price is this comparison being made?

2. The 9/11 terrorist attacks caused the U.S. airline travel demand curve to shift left by an estimated 30% (Ito and Lee, 2005). Use a supply-and-demand diagram to show the likely effect on price and quantity (assuming that the market is competitive). Indicate the magnitude of the likely equilibrium price and quantity effects—for example, would you expect equilibrium quantity to change by about 30%? Show how the answer depends on the shape and location of the supply and demand curves.

3. In 1970, virtually every U.S. funeral involved a casket; however, only 71% did in 2005 as many consumers switched to cremations (Ashley M. Heher, "Rise in Cremations is Forcing Changes," *San Diego Union-Tribune*, March 11, 2006). Government regulations, increasing prices of wood, and other factors drove up the price of burials. Use supply and demand curves to illustrate what happened in the cremation industry. Explain your figure.

4. The Federation of Vegetable Farmers Association of Malaysia reported that a lack of workers caused a 25% drop in production that drove up vegetable prices by 50% to 100% in 2005 ("Vegetable Price Control Sought," **thestar.com.my**, June 6, 2005). Consumers called for price controls on vegetables. Show why the price increased, and predict the effects of a binding price control. **W**

*5. In 2004, as soon as the United States revealed the discovery of a single mad cow in December 2003, more than 40 countries slapped an embargo on U.S. beef. In addition, a few U.S. consumers stopped eating beef. In the three weeks after the discovery, the U.S. price in January 2004 fell by about 15% and the quantity sold increased by 43% over the last week in October 2003. Use supply-and-demand diagrams to explain why these events occurred.

6. The application "Substitution May Save Endangered Species" describes how the equilibrium changed in the market for seal genitalia (used as an aphrodisiac in Asia) when Viagra was introduced. Use a supply-and-demand diagram to illustrate what happened. Show whether the following is possible: A positive quantity is demanded at various prices, yet nothing is sold in the market.

7. In 2002, the U.S. Fish and Wildlife Service proposed banning imports of beluga caviar to protect the beluga sturgeon in the Caspian and Black Seas, whose sturgeon population had fallen 90% in the last two decades. The United States imports 60% of the world's beluga caviar. On the world's legal wholesale market, a kilogram of caviar costs an average of $500, and about $100 million worth is sold per year. What effect would the U.S. ban have

on world prices and quantities? Would such a ban help protect the beluga sturgeon? (In 2005, the service decided not to ban imports.)

8. The prices received by soybean farmers in Brazil, the world's second-largest soybean producer and exporter, tumbled 30%, in part because of China's decision to cut back on imports and in part because of a bumper soybean crop in the United States, the world's leading exporter (Todd Benson, "A Harvest at Peril," *New York Times,* January 6, 2005, C6). In addition, Asian soy rust, a deadly crop fungus, is destroying large quantities of the Brazilian crops.

   a. Use a supply-and-demand diagram to illustrate why Brazilian farmers are receiving lower prices.
   b. If you knew only the *direction* of the shifts in both the supply and the demand curves, could you predict that prices would fall? Why or why not? **W**

9. According to one forecast, half of the country's corn crop in 2008 may be used in producing ethanol (John Donnelly, "Ethanol's Success Story May Have Downside," *Boston Globe,* January 5, 2007). Ethanol production doubled from 2001 to 2005 and may double again by 2008. What effect will this increased use of corn for producing ethanol have on the price of corn and the consumption of corn as food?

10. On January 1, 2005, a three-decades-old system of global quotas that had limited how much China and other countries could ship to the United States and other wealthy nations ended. Over the next four months, U.S. imports of Chinese-made cotton trousers rose by more than 1,505% and their price fell 21% in the first quarter of the year (Tracie Rozhon, "A Tangle in Textiles," *New York Times,* April 21, 2005, C1). The U.S. textile industry demanded quick action, saying that 18 plants had already been forced to close that year and that 16,600 textile and apparel jobs had been lost. The Bush administration reacted to the industry pressure. The United States (and Europe, which faced similar large increases in imports) pressed China to cut back its textile exports, threatening to restore quotas on Chinese exports or to take other actions. Illustrate what happened, and show how the U.S. quota reimposed in May 2005 affected the equilibrium price and quantity in the United States.

11. After Hurricane Katrina damaged a substantial portion of the nation's oil-refining capacity in 2005, the price of gasoline shot up around the country. In 2006, many state and federal elected officials called for price controls. Had they been imposed, what effect would price controls have had? Who would have benefited, and who would have been harmed by the controls? Use a supply-and-demand diagram to illustrate your answers.

*12. Between 1971 and 2006, the United States from time to time imposed quotas or other restrictions on importing steel. Suppose both the domestic supply curve of steel, S^d, and the foreign supply curve of steel for sale in the United States, S^f, are upward-sloping straight lines. How did a quota set by the United States on foreign steel imports of $\overline{Q} > 0$ affect the total American supply curve for steel (domestic and foreign supply combined)?

*13. Given the answer to Question 12, what is the effect of a U.S. quota on steel of $\overline{Q} > 0$ on the equilibrium in the U.S. steel market? (*Hint:* The answer depends on whether the quota binds [is low enough to affect the equilibrium].)

14. Suppose that the demand curve for wheat in each country is inelastic up to some "choke" price p^*—a price so high that nothing is bought—so that the demand curve is vertical at Q^* at prices below p^* and horizontal at p^* (that is, the demand curve forms a box with the axes). If p^* and Q^* vary across countries, what does the world's demand curve look like? Discuss how the elasticity of demand varies with price along the world's demand curve.

15. According to Borjas (2003), immigration into the United States increased the labor supply of working men by 11.0% from 1980 to 2000 and reduced the wage of the average native worker by 3.2%. From these results, can we make any inferences about the elasticity of supply or demand? Which curve (or curves) changed, and why? Draw a supply-and-demand diagram and label the axes to illustrate what happened.

16. The U.S. Bureau of Labor Statistics reports that the average salary for postsecondary economics teachers in the Raleigh-Durham-Chapel Hill metropolitan area, which has many top universities, rose to $105,200 (based on a 52-week work year) in 2003. According to the *Wall Street Journal* (Timothy Aeppel, "Economists Gain Star Power," February 22, 2005, A2), the salary increase resulted from an outward shift in the demand curve for academic economists due to the increased popularity of the economics major, while the supply curve of Ph.D. economists did not shift and the quantity supplied did not change.

   a. If this explanation is correct, what is the short-run price elasticity of supply of academic economists?
   b. If these salaries are expected to remain high, will more people enter doctoral programs in economics? How would such entry affect the long-run price elasticity of supply? **W**

17. According to Agcaoli-Sombilla (1991), the elasticity of demand for rice is −0.47 in Austria; −0.8 in Bangladesh, China, India, Indonesia, and Thailand; −0.25 in Japan; −0.55 in the European Union and the United States; and −0.15 in Vietnam. In which countries is the demand for rice inelastic? In which country is it the least elastic?

18. What effect does a $1 specific tax have on equilibrium price and quantity, and what is the incidence on consumers, if

a. the demand curve is perfectly inelastic?

b. the demand curve is perfectly elastic?

c. the supply curve is perfectly inelastic?

d. the supply curve is perfect elastic?

e. the demand curve is perfectly elastic and the supply curve is perfectly inelastic?

Use graphs and math to explain your answers.

19. On July 1, 1965, the federal *ad valorem* taxes on many goods and services were eliminated. Comparing prices before and after this change, we can determine how much the price fell in response to the tax's elimination. When the tax was in place, the tax per unit on a good that sold for p was αp. If the price fell by αp when the tax was eliminated, consumers must have been bearing the full incidence of the tax. Consequently, consumers got the full benefit of removing the tax from those goods. The entire amount of the tax cut was passed on to consumers for all commodities and services that were studied for which the taxes were collected at the retail level (except admissions and club dues) and for most commodities for which excise taxes were imposed at the manufacturer level, including face powder, sterling silverware, wristwatches, and handbags (Brownlee and Perry, 1967). List the conditions (in terms of the elasticities or shapes of supply or demand curves) that are consistent with 100% pass-through of the taxes. Use graphs to illustrate your answer.

20. Essentially none of the savings from removing the federal *ad valorem* tax were passed on to consumers for motion picture admissions and club dues (Brownlee and Perry, 1967; see Question 19). List the conditions (in terms of the elasticities or shapes of supply or demand curves) that are consistent with 0% pass-through of the taxes. Use graphs to illustrate your answer.

*21. Do you care whether a 15¢ tax per gallon of milk is collected from milk producers or from consumers at the store? Why or why not?

*22. Usury laws place a ceiling on interest rates that lenders such as banks can charge borrowers. Low-income households in states with usury laws have significantly lower levels of consumer credit (loans) than comparable households in states without usury laws (Villegas, 1989). Why? (*Hint:* The interest rate is the price of a loan, and the amount of the loan is the quantity.)

Problems

*23. Using the estimated demand function for processed pork in Canada, Equation 2.2, show how the quantity demanded, Q, at a given price changes as per capita income, Y, increases slightly (that is, calculate the partial derivative of quantity demanded with respect to income). How much does Q change if income rises by $100 a year?

*24. Suppose that the inverse demand function for movies is $p = 120 - Q_1$ for college students and $p = 120 - 2Q_2$ for other town residents. What is the town's total demand function ($Q = Q_1 + Q_2$ as a function of p)? Use a diagram to illustrate your answer.

25. The demand function for movies is $Q_1 = 120 - p$ for college students and $Q_2 = 120 - 2p$ for other town residents. What is the total demand function? Use a diagram to illustrate your answer. (*Hint:* By looking at your diagram, you'll see that some care must be used in writing the demand function.)

26. In the application "Aggregating the Demand for Broadband Service" (based on Duffy-Deno, 2003), the demand function is $Q_s = 15.6p^{-0.563}$ for small firms and $Q_l = 16.0p^{-0.296}$ for larger firms, where price is in cents per kilobyte per second and quantity is in millions of kilobytes per second (Kbps).

a. What is the total demand function for all firms? Suppose that the supply curve for broadband service is horizontal at 40¢ per Kbps (firms will supply as much service as desired at that price).

b. What is the quantity demanded by small firms, large firms, and all firms?

27. In the application "Aggregating the Demand for Broadband Service" (based on Duffy-Deno, 2003), the demand function is $Q_s = 15.6p^{-0.563}$ for small firms and $Q_l = 16.0p^{-0.296}$ for larger ones. As the graph in the application shows, the two demand functions cross. What are the elasticities of demand for small and large firms? Explain.

*28. Green, Howitt, and Russo (2005) estimate the supply and demand curves for California processing tomatoes. The supply function is $\ln Q = 0.2 + 0.55 \ln p$, where Q is the quantity of processing tomatoes in millions of tons per year and p is the price in dollars per ton. The demand function is $\ln Q = 2.6 - 0.2 \ln p + 0.15 \ln p_t$, where p_t is the price of tomato paste (which is what processing tomatoes are used to produce) in dollars per ton. In 2002, $p_t = 110$. What is the demand function for processing tomatoes, where the quantity is solely a function of the price of processing tomatoes? Solve for the equilibrium price and the quantity of processing tomatoes (rounded to two digits after the decimal point). Draw the supply and demand curves (note that they are not straight lines), and label the equilibrium and axes appropriately.

29. The U.S. Tobacco Settlement between the major tobacco companies and 46 states caused the price of cigarettes to jump 45¢ (21%) in November 1998. Levy and Meara

not be preferred to *e*. We can't use the more-is-better property to determine which bundle is preferred because these bundles each contain more of one good and less of the other than *e* does.

INDIFFERENCE CURVES

Suppose we asked Lisa to identify all the bundles that give her the same amount of pleasure as consuming Bundle *e*. Using her answers, we draw curve *I* in panel b of Figure 3.1 through all the bundles she likes as much as *e*. Curve *I* is an **indifference curve:** the set of all bundles of goods that a consumer views as being equally desirable.

Indifference curve *I* includes Bundles *c*, *e*, and *a*, so Lisa is indifferent about consuming Bundles *c*, *e*, and *a*. From this indifference curve, we also know that Lisa prefers *e* (25 pizzas and 15 burritos) to *b* (30 pizzas and 10 burritos). How do we know that? Because Bundle *b* lies below and to the left of Bundle *a*, Lisa prefers Bundle *a* to Bundle *b* by the more-is-better property. Both Bundle *a* and Bundle *e* are on indifference curve *I*, so Lisa likes Bundle *e* as much as Bundle *a*. Because Lisa is indifferent between *e* and *a* and she prefers *a* to *b*, she must prefer *e* to *b* by transitivity.

If we asked Lisa many, many questions, in principle we could draw an entire set of indifference curves through every possible bundle of burritos and pizzas. Lisa's preferences are summarized in an **indifference map** or *preference map*, which is a complete set of indifference curves that summarize a consumer's tastes. Panel c of Figure 3.1 shows three of Lisa's indifference curves, I^1, I^2, and I^3.

The figure shows indifference curves that are continuous (have no gaps). The indifference curves are parallel in the figure, but they need not be. Given our assumptions, all indifference curve maps must have five important properties:

1. Bundles on indifference curves farther from the origin are preferred to those on indifference curves closer to the origin.
2. There is an indifference curve through every possible bundle.
3. Indifference curves cannot cross.
4. Indifference curves slope downward.
5. Indifference curves cannot be thick.

First, we show that bundles on indifference curves farther from the origin are preferred to those on indifference curves closer to the origin. By the more-is-better property, Lisa prefers Bundle *f* to Bundle *e* in panel c of Figure 3.1. She is indifferent among all the bundles on indifference curve I^3 and Bundle *f*, just as she is indifferent among all the bundles, such as Bundle *c* on indifference curve I^2 and Bundle *e*. By the transitivity property, she prefers Bundle *f* to Bundle *e*, which she likes as much as Bundle *c*, so she prefers Bundle *f* to Bundle *c*. By this type of reasoning, she prefers all bundles on I^3 to all bundles on I^2.

Second, we show that there is an indifference curve through every possible bundle as a consequence of the completeness property: The consumer can compare any bundle to another bundle. Compared to a given bundle, some bundles are preferred, some are enjoyed equally, and some are inferior. Connecting the bundles that give the same pleasure produces an indifference curve that includes the given bundle.

Third, we show that indifference curves cannot cross: A given bundle cannot be on two indifference curves. Suppose that two indifference curves crossed at Bundle *e* as in panel a of Figure 3.2. Because Bundles *e* and *a* lie on the same indifference curve I^0, Lisa is indifferent between *e* and *a*. Similarly, she is indifferent between *e* and *b* because

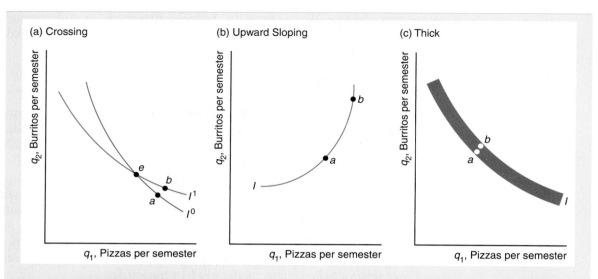

Figure 3.2   Impossible Indifference Curves.
(a) Suppose that the indifference curves cross at Bundle *e*. Lisa is indifferent between *e* and *a* on indifference curve I^0 and between *e* and *b* on I^1. If Lisa is indifferent between *e* and *a* and she is indifferent between *e* and *b*, she must be indifferent between *a* and *b* by transitivity. But *b* has more of both pizzas and burritos than *a*, so she *must* prefer *a* to *b*. Because of this contradiction, indifference curves cannot cross. (b) Suppose that indifference curve *I* slopes upward. The consumer is

indifferent between *b* and *a* because they lie on *I* but prefers *b* to *a* by the more-is-better assumption. Because of this contradiction, indifference curves cannot be upward sloping. (c) Suppose that indifference curve *I* is thick enough to contain both *a* and *b*. The consumer is indifferent between *a* and *b* because both are on *I* but prefers *b* to *a* by the more-is-better assumption because *b* lies above and to the right of *a*. Because of this contradiction, indifference curves cannot be thick.

both are on I^1. By transitivity, if Lisa is indifferent between *e* and *a* and she is indifferent between *e* and *b*, she must be indifferent between *a* and *b*. But that's impossible! Bundle *b* is above and to the right of Bundle *a*, so Lisa *must* prefer *b* to *a* by the more-is-better property. Thus because preferences are transitive and more is better than less, indifference curves cannot cross.

Fourth, we show that indifference curves must be downward sloping. Suppose, to the contrary, that an indifference curve sloped upward, as in panel b of Figure 3.2. The consumer is indifferent between Bundles *a* and *b* because both lie on the same indifference curve, *I*. But the consumer prefers *b* to *a* by the more-is-better property: Bundle *a* lies strictly below and to the left of Bundle *b*. Because of this contradiction—the consumer cannot both be indifferent between *a* and *b* and strictly prefer *b* to *a*—indifference curves cannot be upward sloping.

SOLVED PROBLEM   **3.1**

Can indifference curves be thick?

Answer

Draw an indifference curve that is at least two bundles thick, and show that a preference property is violated: Panel c of Figure 3.2 shows a thick indifference curve, *I*, with two bundles, *a* and *b*, identified. Bundle *b* lies above and to the right of *a*:

Bundle *b* has more of both burritos and pizzas. Thus by the more-is-better property, Bundle *b* must be strictly preferred to Bundle *a*. But the consumer must be
indifferent between *a* and *b* because both bundles are on the same indifference
curve. Because both relationships between *a* and *b* cannot be true, there is a contradiction. Consequently, indifference curves cannot be thick. (We illustrate this
point by drawing indifference curves with very thin lines in our figures.)

3.2 Utility

Underlying our model of consumer behavior is the belief that consumers can compare
various bundles of goods and decide which bundle gives them the greatest pleasure. We
can summarize a consumer's preferences by assigning a numerical value to each possible bundle to reflect the consumer's relative ranking of these bundles.

Following the terminology of Jeremy Bentham, John Stuart Mill, and other nineteenth-
century British utilitarianism economist-philosophers, economists apply the term
utility to this set of numerical values that reflect the relative rankings of various bundles of goods. The statement that "Bonnie prefers Bundle *x* to Bundle *y*" is equivalent
to the statement that "Consuming Bundle *x* gives Bonnie more utility than consuming
Bundle *y*." Bonnie prefers *x* to *y* if Bundle *x* gives Bonnie 10 *utils*—units of utility—
and Bundle *y* gives her 8 utils.

UTILITY FUNCTION

The **utility function** is the relationship between utility measures and every possible
bundle of goods. If we know the utility function, we can summarize the information
in indifference maps succinctly.

Suppose that the utility, *U*, that Lisa gets from pizzas and burritos is

$$U = \sqrt{q_1 q_2}.$$

From this function, we know that the more Lisa consumes of either good, the greater
her utility. Using this function, we can determine whether she would be happier if she
had Bundle *x* with 16 pizzas and 9 burritos or Bundle *y* with 13 of each. The
utility she gets from *x* is $12\,(=\sqrt{16 \times 9})$ utils. The utility she gets from *y* is
$13\,(=\sqrt{13 \times 13})$ utils. Therefore, she prefers *y* to *x*.

The utility function is a concept that economists use to help them think about consumer behavior; utility functions do not exist in any fundamental sense. If you asked
your mother what her utility function is, she would be puzzled—unless, of course, she
is an economist. But if you asked her enough questions about her choices of bundles
of goods, you could construct a function that accurately summarizes her preferences.
For example, by questioning people, Rousseas and Hart (1951) constructed indifference curves between eggs and bacon, and MacCrimmon and Toda (1969) constructed
indifference curves between French pastries and money (which can be used to buy all
other goods).

Typically, consumers can easily answer questions about whether they prefer one
bundle to another, such as "Do you prefer a bundle with one scoop of ice cream and
two pieces of cake to another bundle with two scoops of ice cream and one piece of
cake?" But they have difficulty answering questions about how much more they prefer

one bundle to another because they don't have a measure to describe how their pleasure from two goods or bundles differs. Therefore, we may know a consumer's rank-ordering of bundles, but we are unlikely to know by how much more that consumer prefers one bundle to another.

ORDINAL PREFERENCES

If we know only consumers' relative rankings of bundles, our measure of pleasure is *ordinal* rather than *cardinal*. An ordinal measure is one that tells us the relative ranking of two things but does not tell us how much more one rank is than another.

If a professor assigns only letter grades to an exam, we know that a student who receives a grade of A did better than a student who received a B, but we can't say how much better from that ordinal scale. Nor can we tell whether the difference in performance between an A student and a B student is greater or less than the difference between a B student and a C student.

A cardinal measure is one by which absolute comparisons between ranks may be made. Money is a cardinal measure. If you have $100 and your brother has $50, we know not only that you have more money than your brother but also that you have exactly twice as much money as he does.

Because utility is an ordinal measure, we should not put any weight on the absolute differences between the utility number associated with one bundle and that associated with another. We care only about the relative utility or ranking of the two bundles.

Because preference rankings are ordinal and not cardinal, utility measures are not unique. Let $U(q_1, q_2)$ be the original utility function that assigns numerical values corresponding to any given combination of q_1 and q_2. Let F be an *increasing function* (in jargon: a *positive monotonic transformation*): an order-preserving function that is strictly increasing in the sense that if $x > y$, then $F(x) > F(y)$. By applying this transformation to the original utility function, we obtain a new function, $V(q_1, q_2) = F(U(q_1, q_2))$, which is a utility function with the same ordinal-ranking properties as $U(q_1, q_2)$. Economists often express this idea by using the mellifluous statement that a *utility function is unique only up to a positive monotonic transformation*. As an example, suppose that the transformation is linear: $F(x) = a + bx$, where $b > 0$. Then, $V(q_1, q_2) = a + bU(q_1, q_2)$. The rank-ordering is the same for these utility functions because $V(q_1, q_2) = a + bU(q_1, q_2) > V(q_1^*, q_2^*) = a + bU(q_1^*, q_2^*)$ if and only if $U(q_1, q_2) > U(q_1^*, q_2^*)$.

Thus when we talk about utility numbers, we need to remember that these numbers are not unique and that we place little meaning on the absolute numbers. We care only whether one bundle's utility value is greater than that of another.

UTILITY AND INDIFFERENCE CURVES

We can use Lisa's utility function to construct a three-dimensional diagram that shows how utility varies with changes in the consumption of q_1 and q_2. Imagine that you are standing with your back against a corner of a room. Walking away from the corner along the wall to your left, you are tracing out the q_2 axis: The farther you get from the corner, the more burritos Lisa has. Similarly, starting back at the corner and walking along the wall to your right, you are moving along the q_1 axis. When you stand in the corner, you are leaning against the utility axis, where the two walls meet. The higher the point along your back, the greater Lisa's utility. Because her utility is increasing (more is preferred to less) in both q_1 and q_2, her utility rises as you walk away from the corner (origin) along either wall or into the room, where Lisa has more q_1 or q_2 or both. Lisa's utility or *hill of happiness* rises as you move away from the corner.

What is the relationship between Lisa's utility and one of her indifference curves, those combinations of q_1 and q_2 that give Lisa a particular level of utility? Imagine that the hill of happiness is made of clay. If you were to cut the hill parallel to the floor at a particular height on the wall—a given level of utility—you'd get a smaller hill above the cut. Now suppose that you place that smaller hill directly on the floor and trace the outside edge of the hill. Looking down at the floor, the traced outer edge of the hill represents an indifference curve on the two-dimensional floor. Making other parallel cuts in the hill of happiness, placing the smaller hills on the floor, and tracing their outside edges, you could obtain a map of indifference curves on which each indifference curve reflects a different level of utility.

In short, an indifference curve consists of all those bundles that correspond to a particular utility measure. If Lisa's utility function is $U(q_1, q_2)$, then the expression for one of her indifference curves is

$$\overline{U} = U(q_1, q_2). \tag{3.1}$$

This expression determines all those bundles of q_1 and q_2 that give her $\overline{U}$ utils of pleasure. For example, if the utility function is $U = \sqrt{q_1 q_2}$, then the indifference curve $4 = \overline{U} = \sqrt{q_1 q_2}$ includes any (q_1, q_2) bundles such that $q_1 q_2 = 16$, including the bundles $(4, 4)$, $(2, 8)$, $(8, 2)$, $(1, 16)$, and $(16, 1)$.

WILLINGNESS TO SUBSTITUTE BETWEEN GOODS

To analyze how consumers make choices when faced with limited resources, it is useful to know the slope of an indifference curve at a particular bundle of goods. Economists call the slope at a point of an indifference curve the **marginal rate of substitution** (*MRS*), because it is the maximum amount of one good that a consumer will sacrifice (trade) to obtain one more unit of another good.

Lisa is willing to trade one good for more of another good. The downward slope of her indifference curve in Figure 3.3 shows that Lisa is willing to give up some burritos for more pizzas and vice versa. Because the indifference curve is downward sloping, the *MRS* is a negative number.

We can use calculus to determine the *MRS* at a point on Lisa's indifference curve in Equation (3.1). We will show that the *MRS* depends on how much extra utility Lisa gets from a little more of each good. We call the extra utility that a consumer gets from consuming the last unit of a good the **marginal utility.** Given that Lisa's utility function is $U(q_1, q_2)$, the extra or *marginal utility* that she gets from a little more pizza, holding the quantity of burritos fixed, is

$$\text{marginal utility of pizza} = \frac{\partial U}{\partial q_1} = U_1.$$

Similarly, the marginal utility from more burritos is $U_2 = \partial U / \partial q_2$, where we hold the amount of pizza constant.

We determine the slope of Lisa's indifference curve, the *MRS*, by ascertaining the changes in q_1 and q_2 that leave her utility unchanged, keeping her on her original indifference curve: $\overline{U} = U(q_1, q_2)$. Let $q_2(q_1)$ be the implicit function that shows how much q_2 it takes to keep Lisa's utility at $\overline{U}$ given that she consumes q_1. We want to know how much

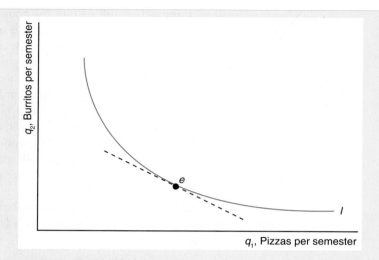

Figure 3.3 Marginal Rate of Substitution. Lisa's marginal rate of substitution, $MRS = dq_2/dq_1$, at Bundle e is the slope of indifference curve I at that point. The marginal rate of substitution, at e is the same as the slope of the line that is tangent to I at e.

q_2 must change if we increase q_1, dq_2/dq_1, given that we require her utility to remain constant. To answer this question, we differentiate $\overline{U} = U(q_1, q_2(q_1))$ with respect to q_1:

$$\frac{d\overline{U}}{dq_1} = 0 = \frac{\partial U(q_1, q_2(q_1))}{\partial q_1} + \frac{\partial U(q_1, q_2(q_1))}{\partial q_2}\frac{dq_2}{dq_1} = U_1 + U_2\frac{dq_2}{dq_1}. \qquad (3.2)$$

Because $\overline{U}$ is a constant, $d\overline{U}/dq_1 = 0$.

Since Lisa derives pleasure from both goods, if we increase one of the goods, we must decrease the other to hold her utility constant and keep her on her indifference curve. Rearranging the terms in Equation (3.2), we find that her marginal rate of substitution is

$$MRS = \frac{dq_2}{dq_1} = -\frac{\partial U/\partial q_1}{\partial U/\partial q_2} = -\frac{U_1}{U_2}. \qquad (3.3)$$

Thus the slope of her indifference curve is the negative of the ratio of her marginal utilities.

We can give a graphical interpretation of the slope of the indifference curve. The slope of her indifference curve I at Bundle e is the same as the slope of the line that is tangent to the indifference curve at that point.

SOLVED PROBLEM   3.2

Suppose that Jackie has what is known as a *Cobb-Douglas utility function:*[8]

$$U = q_1^a q_2^{1-a}, \qquad (3.4)$$

where a is a positive constant, q_1 is the number of music CDs she buys a year, and q_2 is the number of movie DVDs she buys. What is her marginal rate of substitution?

---

[8]The Cobb-Douglas utility function may be written more generally as $U = Aq_1^c q_2^d$. However, we can always transform that utility function into this simpler one through a monotonic transformation: $q_1^a q_2^{1-a} = F(Aq_1^c q_2^d)$, where $F(x) = x^{1/(c + d)}/A$, so that $a = c/(c + d)$.

Answer

1. *Determine Jackie's marginal utilities of CDs and DVDs:* Her marginal utility of CDs is

$$U_1 = aq_1^{a-1}q_2^{1-a} = a\frac{U(q_1, q_2)}{q_1},$$

and her marginal utility of DVDs is

$$U_2 = (1-a)q_1^a q_2^{-a} = (1-a)\frac{U(q_1, q_2)}{q_2}.$$

2. *Express her marginal rate of substitution in terms of her marginal utilities:* Using Equation 3.3, we find that her marginal rate of substitution is

$$MRS = \frac{dq_2}{dq_1} = -\frac{U_1}{U_2} = -\frac{aU/q_1}{(1-a)U/q_2} = -\frac{a}{1-a}\frac{q_2}{q_1}. \tag{3.5}$$

● APPLICATION

MRS Between Music CDs and Movie DVDs

In 2005, a typical owner of a home theater (a television and a DVD player) bought 12 music CDs (q_1) per year and 6 top-20 movie DVDs (q_2) per year. We estimate this average consumer's Cobb-Douglas utility function as

$$U = q_1^{0.6}q_2^{0.4}. \tag{3.6}$$

That is, in the more general Cobb-Douglas equation 3.4, $a = 0.6$.

Continuing our analysis of Solved Problem 3.2, given that Jackie's Cobb-Douglas utility function is that of the typical consumer, we can determine her marginal rate of substitution by substituting $q_1 = 12$, $q_2 = 6$, and $a = 0.6$ into Equation 3.5:

$$MRS = -\frac{a}{1-a}\frac{q_2}{q_1} = -\frac{0.6}{0.4}\frac{6}{12} = -0.75.$$

CURVATURE OF INDIFFERENCE CURVES

Unless the indifference curve is a straight line, the marginal rate of substitution varies along the indifference curve. Because the indifference curve in Figure 3.3 is convex to the origin, as we move to the right along the indifference curve, the *MRS* becomes smaller in absolute value: Lisa will give up fewer burritos to obtain one pizza. This willingness to trade fewer burritos for one more pizza as we move down and to the right along the indifference curve reflects a *diminishing marginal rate of substitution*: The *MRS* approaches zero—becomes flatter or less sloped—as we move down and to the right along an indifference curve.

So far, we have drawn indifference curves as convex to the origin. An indifference curve doesn't have to be convex, but casual observation suggests that most people's

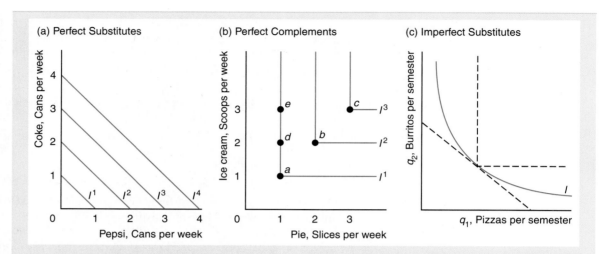

Figure 3.4 Perfect Substitutes, Perfect Complements, Imperfect Substitutes. (a) Ben views Coke and Pepsi as perfect substitutes. His indifference curves are straight, parallel lines with a marginal rate of substitution (slope) of −1. Ben is willing to exchange one can of Coke for one can of Pepsi. (b) Maureen likes pie à la mode but does not like pie or ice cream by itself: She views ice cream and pie as perfect complements. She will not substitute between the two; she consumes them only in equal quantities. (c) Lisa views burritos and pizza as imperfect substitutes. Her indifference curve lies between the extreme cases of perfect substitutes and perfect complements.

indifference curves over commodities are convex. When people have a lot of one good, they are willing to give up a relatively large amount of it to get a good of which they have relatively little. However, after that first trade, they are willing to give up less of the first good to get the same amount more of the second good.

It is hard to imagine that Lisa's indifference curves are *concave* to the origin. If her indifference curve were strictly concave, Lisa would be willing to give up more burritos to get one more pizza, the fewer the burritos she has. Two extreme versions of downward-sloping, convex indifference curves are plausible: straight-line or right-angle indifference curves.

One extreme case is **perfect substitutes,** goods that a consumer is completely indifferent as to which to consume. Because Ben cannot taste any difference between Coca-Cola and Pepsi-Cola, he views them as perfect substitutes: He is indifferent between one additional can of Coke and one additional can of Pepsi. His indifference curves for these two goods are straight, parallel lines with a slope of −1 everywhere along the curve, as in panel a of Figure 3.4. Thus Ben's *MRS* is −1 at every point along these indifference curves. (His marginal utility from each good is identical, so the *MRS* = $-U_1/U_2 = -1$.)

The slope of indifference curves of perfect substitutes need not always be −1; it can be any constant rate. For example, Amos knows from reading the labels that Clorox bleach is twice as strong as a generic brand. As a result, Amos is indifferent between one cup of Clorox and two cups of the generic bleach. Amos's utility function over Clorox, *C*, and the generic bleach, *G*, is

$$U(C, G) = iC + jG,$$ (3.7)

where both goods are measured in cups, $i = 2$, and $j = 1$. His indifference curves are straight lines with a slope or *MRS* of $-i/j = -2$, where the generic bleach is on the vertical axis.[9]

The other extreme case is **perfect complements**: goods that a consumer is interested in consuming only in fixed proportions. Maureen doesn't like apple pie, A, by itself or vanilla ice cream, V, by itself but loves apple pie à la mode: a slice of pie with a scoop of vanilla ice cream on top. Her utility function is

$$U(A, V) = \min(iA, jV), \tag{3.8}$$

where $i = j = 1$ and the min function says that the utility equals the smaller of the two arguments, iA or jV. Her indifference curves have right angles in panel b of Figure 3.4. If she has only one piece of pie, she gets as much pleasure from it and one scoop of ice cream, Bundle a, as from one piece and two scoops, Bundle d, or as from one piece and three scoops, Bundle e. For example, if she were at b, she would be unwilling to give up an extra slice of pie to get, say, two extra scoops of ice cream, as at point e. That is, she won't eat the extra scoops because she does not have pieces of pie to go with the ice cream. The only condition where she doesn't have an excess of either good is when $iA = jV$, or $V/A = i/j = 1$. Therefore, she consumes only bundles like a, b, and c in which pie and ice cream are in fixed (here, equal) proportions, because she is unwilling to substitute more of one good for less of another. (The marginal utility is zero for each good, because increasing that good while holding the other one constant does not increase Maureen's utility.)

The standard-shaped, convex indifference curve in panel c of Figure 3.4 lies between these two extreme examples. Convex indifference curves show that a consumer views two goods as imperfect substitutes. A consumer with a Cobb-Douglas utility function 3.4 has convex indifference curves.

● APPLICATION

Indifference Curves Between Food and Clothing

Using the estimates of Eastwood and Craven (1981), the figure shows the indifference curves of the average U.S. consumer between food consumed at home and clothing. The food and clothing measures are weighted averages of various goods. At relatively low quantities of food and clothing, the indifference curves, such as I^1, are nearly right angles: perfect complements. As we move away from the origin, the indifference curves become flatter: closer to perfect substitutes.

One interpretation of these indifference curves is that there are minimum levels of food and clothing necessary to support life. The consumer cannot trade one good for the other if it means having less than those critical levels. As the consumer obtains more of both goods, however, the consumer is increasingly willing to trade between

---

[9]Sometimes it is difficult to guess which goods are close substitutes. According to Harper's Index 1994, flowers, perfume, and fire extinguishers rank 1, 2, and 3 among Mother's Day gifts that Americans consider "very appropriate."

the two goods. According to Eastwood and Craven's estimates, food and clothing are perfect complements when the consumer has little of either good, and perfect substitutes when the consumer has large quantities of both goods.

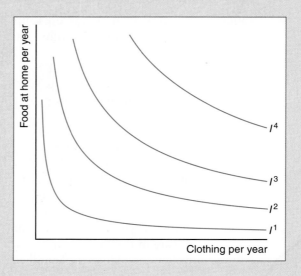

3.3 Budget Constraint

You can't have everything. . . . Where would you put it? —Steven Wright

Knowing an individual's preferences is only the first step in analyzing that person's consumption behavior. Consumers maximize their well-being subject to constraints. The most important constraint most of us face in deciding what to consume is our personal budget constraint.

If we cannot save and borrow, our budget is the income we receive in a given period. If we can save and borrow, we can save money early in life to consume later, such as when we retire; or we can borrow money when we are young and repay those sums later in life. Savings is, in effect, a good that consumers can buy. For simplicity, we assume that each consumer has a fixed amount of money to spend now, so we can use the terms *budget* and *income* interchangeably.

For graphical simplicity, we assume that consumers spend their money on only two goods. If Lisa spends all her budget, Y, on pizza and burritos, then

$$p_1 q_1 + p_2 q_2 = Y, \qquad (3.9)$$

where $p_1 q_1$ is the amount she spends on pizza and $p_2 q_2$ is the amount she spends on burritos. Equation 3.9 is her **budget line** or *budget constraint*: the bundles of goods that can be bought if the entire budget is spent on those goods at given prices.

In Figure 3.5, we plot Lisa's budget line in pizza-burrito space, just as we did with her indifference curves. How many burritos can Lisa buy? Using algebra, we can

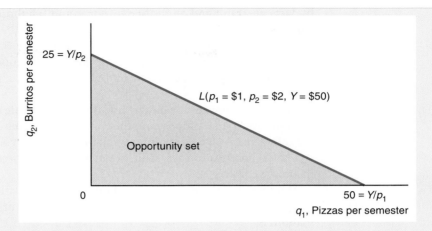

Figure 3.5 Budget Constraint. If $Y = \$50$, $p_1 = \$1$, and $p_2 = \$2$, Lisa can buy any bundle in the opportunity set, the shaded area, including points on the *budget line*, L, which has a slope of $-\frac{1}{2}$.

rewrite her budget constraint, Equation 3.9, as

$$q_2 = \frac{Y - p_1 q_1}{p_2}. \tag{3.10}$$

According to Equation 3.10, she can buy more burritos with a higher income ($dq_2/dY = 1/p_2 > 0$), the purchase of fewer pizzas ($dq_2/dq_1 = -p_1/p_2 < 0$), or a lower price of burritos or pizzas [$dq_2/dp_2 = -(Y - p_1 q_1)/p_2^2 = -q_2/p_2 < 0$, $dq_2/dp_1 = -q_1/p_2 < 0$]. For example, if she has one more dollar of income (Y), she can buy $1/p_2$ more burritos.

If $p_1 = \$1$, $p_2 = \$2$, and $Y = \$50$, Equation 3.10 is

$$q_2 = \frac{\$50 - (\$1 \times q_1)}{\$2} = 25 - \frac{1}{2}q_1.$$

This equation is plotted in Figure 3.5. This budget line shows the combinations of burritos and pizzas that Lisa can buy if she spends all of her $50 on these two goods. As this equation shows, every two pizzas cost Lisa one burrito. How many burritos can she buy if she spends all her money on burritos? By setting $q_1 = 0$ in Equation 3.10, we find that $q_2 = Y/p_2 = \$50/\$2 = 25$. Similarly, if she spends all her money on pizzas, $q_2 = 0$ and $q_1 = Y/p_1 = \$50/\$1 = 50$.

The budget constraint in Figure 3.5 is a smooth, continuous line. Implicitly, Lisa can buy fractional numbers of burritos and pizzas. Is that true? Do you know of a restaurant that will sell you a quarter of a burrito? Probably not. Why, then, don't we draw the opportunity set and the budget constraint as points (bundles) of whole numbers of burritos and pizzas? The reason is that Lisa can buy a burrito at a *rate* of one-half per time period. If Lisa buys one burrito every other week, she buys an average of one-half burrito every week. Thus it is plausible that she could purchase fractional amounts over time, and this diagram concerns her behavior over a semester.

Lisa could, of course, buy any bundle that costs less than $50. The **opportunity set** consists of all the bundles a consumer can buy, including all the bundles inside the budget constraint and on the budget constraint (all those bundles of positive q_1 and q_2 such that $p_1q_1 + p_2q_2 \leq Y$). Lisa's opportunity set is the shaded area in the figure. For example, she could buy 10 burritos and 15 pizzas for $35, which falls inside her budget constraint. However, she can obtain more of the foods she loves by spending all of her budget and picking a bundle on the budget constraint rather than a bundle below the constraint.

We call the slope of the budget line the **marginal rate of transformation** (*MRT*): the trade-off the market imposes on the consumer in terms of the amount of one good the consumer must give up to obtain more of the other good. It is the rate at which Lisa can trade burritos for pizzas in the marketplace, where the prices she pays and her income are fixed.

Holding prices and income constant and differentiating Equation 3.10 with respect to q_1, we find that the slope of the budget constraint, or the marginal rate of transformation, is

$$MRT = \frac{dq_2}{dq_1} = -\frac{p_1}{p_2}. \tag{3.11}$$

Because the price of a pizza is half that of a burrito ($p_1 = \$1$ and $p_2 = \$2$), the marginal rate of transformation that Lisa faces is

$$MRT = -\frac{p_1}{p_2} = -\frac{\$1}{\$2} = -\frac{1}{2}.$$

An extra pizza costs her half an extra burrito—or, equivalently, an extra burrito costs her two pizzas.

3.4   Constrained Consumer Choice

My problem lies in reconciling my gross habits with my net income. —Errol Flynn

Were it not for the budget constraint, consumers who prefer more to less would consume unlimited amounts of at least some goods. Well, they can't have it all! Instead, consumers maximize their well-being subject to their budget constraints. To complete our analysis of consumer behavior, we have to determine the bundle of goods that maximizes well-being subject to the budget constraint. We first take a graphical approach and then use calculus.

THE CONSUMER'S OPTIMAL BUNDLE

Veni, vidi, Visa. (We came, we saw, we went shopping.) —Jan Barrett

We want to determine which bundle within the opportunity set gives the consumer the highest level of utility. That is, we are trying to solve a constrained maximization problem, where a consumer maximizes utility subject to a budget constraint.

To determine which bundle in the opportunity set gives Lisa the highest level of pleasure, we use her indifference curves in panel a of Figure 3.6. We will show that her optimal bundle lies on an indifference curve that touches the budget constraint, L, at only one point (e on I^2)—hence that indifference curve does not cross the constraint.

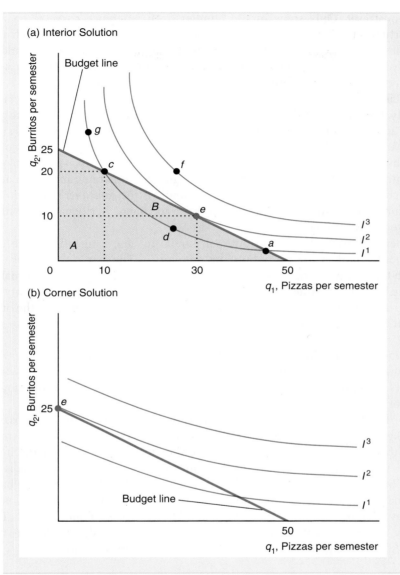

Figure 3.6 Consumer Maximization. (a) *Interior solution:* Lisa's optimal bundle is *e* (10 burritos and 30 pizzas) on indifference curve I^2. Any bundle that is preferred to *e* (such as points on indifference curve I^3) lies outside of the opportunity set—it can't be purchased. Bundles inside the opportunity set, such as *d*, are less desirable than *e*. (b) *Corner solution:* Spenser's indifference curves are relatively flat (he'll give up many pizzas for one more burrito), so his optimal bundle occurs at a corner of the opportunity set at Bundle *e*: 25 burritos and 0 pizzas.

We show this result by rejecting the possibility that the optimal bundle could be located off the budget constraint or that it lies on an indifference curve that intersects the budget constraint.

The optimal bundle must be *on* the budget constraint. Bundles that lie on indifference curves above the constraint, such as those on I^3, are not in the opportunity set. So even though Lisa prefers *f* on indifference curve I^3 to *e* on I^2, *f* is too expensive and she can't purchase it. Although Lisa could buy a bundle inside the budget constraint, she does not want to do so, because more is better than less: For any bundle inside the constraint (such as *d* on I^1), there is another bundle on the constraint with more of at least one of the two goods, and hence she prefers that bundle. Therefore, the optimal bundle must lie on the budget constraint.

Bundles that lie on indifference curves that cross the budget constraint (such as I^1, which crosses the constraint at *a* and *c*) are less desirable than certain other bundles on the constraint. Only some of the bundles on indifference curve I^1 lie within the opportunity set: Bundles a and c and all the points on I^1 between them, such as d, can be purchased. Because I^1 crosses the budget constraint, the bundles between a and c on I^1 lie strictly inside the constraint, so there are bundles in the opportunity set (area $A + B$) that are preferable to these bundles on I^1 and are affordable. By the more-is-better property, Lisa prefers e to d because e has more of both pizzas and burritos than d. By transitivity, Lisa prefers e to a, c, and all the other points on I^1—even those, like g, that Lisa can't afford. Because indifference curve I^1 crosses the budget constraint, area B contains at least one bundle that is preferred to—lies above and to the right of—at least one bundle on the indifference curve.

Thus the optimal bundle must lie on the budget constraint and be on an indifference curve that does not cross it. Such a bundle is the *consumer's optimum*. If Lisa is consuming this bundle, she has no incentive to change her behavior by substituting one good for another.

There are two ways for an optimal bundle to lie on an indifference curve that touches the budget constraint but does not cross it. The first is an *interior solution*, in which the optimal bundle has positive quantities of both goods: The optimal bundle is on the budget line rather than at one end or the other. The other possibility is called a *corner solution*, where the optimal bundle is at one end or the other of the budget line: It is at a corner with one of the axes.

Interior Solution. In panel a of Figure 3.6, Bundle e on indifference curve I^2 is the optimum bundle. It lies in the interior of the budget line away from the corners. Lisa prefers consuming a balanced diet, e, of 10 burritos and 30 pizzas, to eating only one type of food.

For the indifference curve I^2 to touch the budget constraint but not cross it, it must be *tangent* to the budget constraint: The budget constraint and the indifference curve have the same slope at the point e where they touch. The slope of the indifference curve, the marginal rate of substitution, measures the rate at which Lisa is *willing* to trade burritos for pizzas: $MRS = -U_1/U_2$, Equation 3.3. The slope of the budget line, the marginal rate of transformation, measures the rate at which Lisa *can* trade her money for burritos or pizza in the market: $MRT = -p_1/p_2$, Equation 3.11. Thus Lisa's utility is maximized at the bundle where the rate at which she is willing to trade burritos for pizzas equals the rate at which she can trade in the market:

$$MRS = -\frac{U_1}{U_2} = -\frac{p_1}{p_2} = MRT. \qquad (3.12)$$

Rearranging terms, this condition is equivalent to

$$\frac{U_1}{p_1} = \frac{U_2}{p_2}. \qquad (3.13)$$

Equation 3.13 says that U_1/p_1, the marginal utility of pizzas divided by the price of a pizza—the amount of extra utility from pizza per dollar spent on pizza—equals U_2/p_2, the marginal utility of burritos divided by the price of a burrito. Thus Lisa's utility is maximized if the last dollar she spends on pizzas gets her as much extra utility as the last dollar she spends on burritos. If the last dollar spent on pizzas gave Lisa more extra utility than the last dollar spent on burritos, Lisa could increase her happiness by spending more on pizzas and less on burritos. Her cousin Spenser is a different story.

Corner Solution. Spenser's indifference curves in panel b of Figure 3.6 are flatter than Lisa's. His optimal bundle lies on an indifference curve that touches the budget line, *L*, only once, at the upper-left corner of the opportunity set, *e*, where he buys only burritos (25 burritos and 0 pizzas).

Bundle *e* is the optimal bundle because the indifference curve does not cross the constraint into the opportunity set. If it did, another bundle would give Spenser more pleasure.

Spenser's indifference curve is not tangent to his budget line. It would cross the budget line if both the indifference curve and the budget line were continued into the "negative pizza" region of the diagram, on the other side of the burrito axis.

SOLVED PROBLEM   3.3

Nigel, a Brit, and Bob, a Yank, have the same tastes, and both are indifferent between a sport-utility vehicle (SUV) and a luxury sedan. Each has a budget that will allow him to buy and operate one vehicle for a decade. For Nigel, the price of owning and operating an SUV is greater than that for the car. For Bob, an SUV is a relative bargain because he benefits from an SUV tax break. Use an indifference curve–budget line analysis to explain why Nigel buys and operates a car while Bob chooses an SUV.

Answer

1. *Describe their indifference curves:* Because Nigel and Bob view the SUV and the car as perfect substitutes, each has an indifference curve for buying one vehicle that is a straight line with a slope of –1 and that hits each axis at 1 in the figure.

2. *Describe the slopes of their budget lines:* Nigel faces a budget line, L^N, that is flatter than the indifference curve, and Bob faces one, L^B, that is steeper.

3. *Use an indifference curve and a budget line to show why Nigel and Bob make different choices:* As the figure shows, L^N hits the indifference curve, *I*, at 1 on the car axis, e_N, and L^B hits *I* at 1 on the SUV axis, e_B. Thus Nigel buys the relatively inexpensive car and Bob scoops up a relatively cheap SUV.

Comment: If Nigel and Bob were buying a bundle of cars and SUVs for their large families or firms, the analysis would be similar—Bob would buy relatively more SUVs than would Nigel.

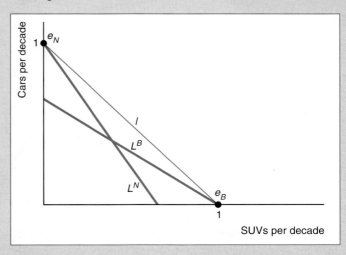

U.S. Versus EU SUVs

If you believe what newspapers report, Americans have a love affair with sport-utility vehicles (SUVs), and Europeans see no reason to drive a vehicle nearly the size of Luxembourg. SUVs are derided as "Chelsea tractors" in England and "Montessori wagons" in Sweden. News stories point to this difference in tastes to explain why SUVs account for less than a twentieth of total car sales in Western Europe but a quarter in the United States. Maybe the narrower European streets or Europeans' greater concern for the environment is the explanation. The analysis in Solved Problem 3.3 provides an alternative explanation: The price of owning and operating an SUV is much lower in the United States than it is in Europe, so people with identical tastes are more likely to buy an SUV in the United States than in Europe.

Higher European gasoline taxes make gas-guzzling SUVs more expensive to operate in Europe than in the United States. In 2005, gas taxes as a percentage of the final gas price were 22% in the United States, 54% in Canada, 85% in Japan, 130% in Spain, 216% in France, and 235% in Britain. After-tax gas prices in Europe can be two to three times that in the United States.

Europeans are calling for taxes against SUVs. The French government is considering raising taxes by up to $3,900 on heavy vehicles while giving discounts on smaller, lighter cars. London's mayor slammed SUV drivers as "complete idiots" and proposed doubling the $9 daily congestion fee for the privilege of driving around the city. A top adviser to the U.K. Department of Transport said that the current average tax on SUVs of £165 ($300) annually is too low and should be raised to three or four times that amount.

In contrast, the U.S. government subsidizes SUV purchases. Under the 2003 Tax Act, people who use a vehicle that weighs more than 6,000 pounds—such as the biggest, baddest SUVs and Hummers—in their business at least 50% of the time could deduct the purchase price up to $100,000 from their taxes. They might get a state tax deduction, too. Originally intended to help self-employed ranchers, farmers, and contractors purchase a heavy pickup truck or van necessary for their businesses, the SUV tax loophole was quickly exploited by accountants, lawyers, and doctors.

When the maximum deduction in this boondoggle was reduced from $100,000 to $25,000 in October 2004 and the price of gas rose, sales plummeted for many brands of SUVs and behemoths such as Hummers. (Sales continued to fall in 2005 and 2006.) The *Boston Globe* concluded that this drop in relative SUV sales proves that U.S. consumers' "tastes are changing again." But a more plausible alternative explanation for the difference in SUVs' share of sales in Europe and the United States (or over time in the United States) is variations in the relative costs of owning and operating SUVs.[10]

---

[10]See **www.aw-bc.com/perloff,** Chapter 3, "Substitution Effects in Canada," which provides a similar example concerning purchases in the United States or in Canada.

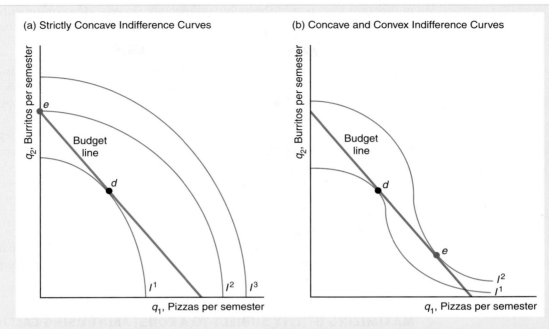

Figure 3.7 **Optimal Bundles on Convex Sections of Indifference Curves.** (a) Indifference curve I^1 is tangent to the budget line at Bundle d, but Bundle e is superior because it lies on a higher indifference curve, I^2. If indifference curves are strictly concave to the origin, the optimal bundle, e, is at a corner. (b) If indifference curves have both concave and convex sections, a bundle such as d, which is tangent to the budget line in the concave portion of indifference curve I^1, cannot be an optimal bundle because there must be a preferable bundle in the convex portion of a higher indifference curve, e on I^2 (or at a corner).

Optimal Bundles on Convex Sections of Indifference Curves. Earlier we argued, on the basis of introspection (and consistent with our assumption of strict convexity of preferences), that most indifference curves are convex to the origin. Now that we know how to determine a consumer's optimal bundle, we can give a more compelling explanation about why we assume that indifference curves are convex. We can show that if indifference curves are smooth, optimal bundles lie either on convex sections of indifference curves or at the point where the budget constraint hits an axis.

Suppose that indifference curves were strictly concave to the origin as in panel a of Figure 3.7. Indifference curve I^1 is tangent to the budget line at d, but that bundle is not optimal. Bundle e on the corner between the budget constraint and the burrito axis is on a higher indifference curve, I^2, than d is. Thus if a consumer had strictly concave indifference curves, the consumer would buy only one good—here, burritos. Similarly, as we saw in Solved Problem 3.3, consumers with straight-line indifference curves buy only the cheapest good. Thus if consumers are to buy more than a single good, indifference curves must have convex sections.

If indifference curves have both concave and convex sections as in panel b of Figure 3.7, the optimal bundle lies in a convex section or at a corner. Bundle d, where a concave section of indifference curve I^1 is tangent to the budget line, cannot be an optimal bundle. Here e is the optimal bundle and is tangent to the budget constraint in the convex portion of the higher indifference curve, I^2. If a consumer buys positive quantities of two goods, the indifference curve is convex and tangent to the budget line at that optimal bundle.

Buying Where More Is Better. A key assumption in our analysis of consumer behavior is that more is preferred to less: Consumers are not satiated. We now show that if both goods are consumed in positive quantities and their prices are positive, more of either good must be preferred to less. Suppose that the opposite were true and that Lisa prefers fewer burritos to more. Because burritos cost her money, she could increase her well-being by reducing the quantity of burritos she consumes until she consumes no burritos—a scenario that violates our assumption that she consumes positive quantities of both goods.[11] Though it is possible that consumers prefer less to more at some large quantities, we do not observe consumers making purchases where that occurs.

In summary, we do not observe consumer optima at bundles where indifference curves are concave or consumers are satiated. Thus we can safely assume that indifference curves are convex and that consumers prefer more to less in the ranges of goods that we actually observe.

MAXIMIZING UTILITY SUBJECT TO A CONSTRAINT USING CALCULUS

The individual choice of garnishment of a burger can be an important point to the consumer in this day when individualism is an increasingly important thing to people.
— Donald N. Smith, president of Burger King

Lisa's objective is to maximize her utility, $U(q_1, q_2)$, subject to (s.t.) her budget constraint:

$$\max_{q_1, q_2} U(q_1, q_2)$$
$$\text{s.t. } Y = p_1 q_1 + p_2 q_2. \tag{3.14}$$

This mathematical statement of her problem shows that her *control variables*—those that she chooses—are q_1 and q_2, which appear under the "max" term in the equation. We assume that Lisa has no control over the prices she faces, p_1 and p_2, or her income, Y.

Because this problem is a constrained maximization, we cannot use the standard unconstrained maximization approach. However, we can transform this problem into one that we can solve. There are at least two approaches that we can use if we know that Lisa buys both goods, so that we are looking for an interior solution: substitution and the Lagrangian method.

---

[11]Similarly, at her optimal bundle, Lisa cannot be *satiated*—indifferent between consuming more or fewer burritos. Suppose that her budget is obtained by working and that Lisa does not like working at the margin. Were it not for the goods she can buy with what she earns, she would not work as many hours as she does. Thus if she were satiated and did not care if she consumed fewer burritos, she would reduce the number of hours she worked, thereby lowering her income, until her optimal bundle occurred at a point where more was preferred to less or where she consumed none.

Substitution. First, we can substitute the budget constraint into the utility function. Using algebra, we can rewrite the budget constraint as $q_1 = (Y - p_2 q_2)/p_1$. If we substitute this expression for q_1 in the utility function, $U(q_1, q_2)$, we can rewrite Lisa's problem as

$$\max_{q_2} \ U\left(\frac{Y - p_2 q_2}{p_1}, q_2\right). \tag{3.15}$$

Equation 3.15 is an unconstrained problem, so we can use standard maximization techniques to solve it. The first-order condition is obtained by setting the derivative of the utility function with respect to q_2 equal to zero:

$$\frac{dU}{dq_2} = \frac{\partial U}{\partial q_1}\frac{dq_1}{dq_2} + \frac{\partial U}{\partial q_2} = \left(-\frac{p_2}{p_1}\right)\frac{\partial U}{\partial q_1} + \frac{\partial U}{\partial q_2} = \left(-\frac{p_2}{p_1}\right)U_1 + U_2 = 0, \tag{3.16}$$

where $\partial U/\partial q_1 = U_1$ is the partial derivative of the utility function with respect to q_1 (the first argument) and dq_1/dq_2 is the derivative of $q_1 = (Y - p_2 q_2)/p_1$ with respect to q_2.

By rearranging these terms in Equation 3.16, we get the same condition for an optimum that we obtained using a graphical approach, Equation 3.12, which is that the marginal rate of substitution equals the marginal rate of transformation:[12]

$$MRS = -\frac{U_1}{U_2} = -\frac{p_1}{p_2} = MRT.$$

To be sure that we have a maximum, we need to check that the second-order conditions hold (see the Calculus Appendix). These conditions hold if the utility function is quasi-concave, which implies that the indifference curves are convex to the origin: The *MRS* is diminishing as we move down and to the right along the curve. If we combine the *MRS* = *MRT* (first-order) condition with the budget constraint, we have two equations in two unknowns, q_1 and q_2, so we can solve for the optimal q_1 and q_2 as functions of prices, p_1 and p_2, and income, Y.

Lagrangian Method. A second approach to solving this constrained maximization problem is to use the Lagrangian method, where we write the equivalent Lagrangian problem as

$$\max_{q_1, q_2, \lambda} \mathscr{L} = U(q_1, q_2) + \lambda(Y - p_1 q_1 - p_2 q_2), \tag{3.17}$$

where λ (the Greek letter lambda) is the Lagrange multiplier. For values of q_1 and q_2 such that the constraint holds, $Y - p_1 q_1 - p_2 q_2 = 0$, so the functions $\mathscr{L}$ and U have the same values. Thus if we look only at values of q_1 and q_2 for which the constraint holds, finding the constrained maximum value of U is the same as finding the critical value of $\mathscr{L}$.

---

[12]Had we substituted for q_2 instead of for q_1 (which you should do to make sure that you understand how to solve this type of problem), we would have obtained the same condition.

The conditions for a critical value of q_1, q_2, and λ—the first-order conditions—for an interior maximization are[13]

$$\frac{\partial \mathcal{L}}{\partial q_1} = \frac{\partial U}{\partial q_1} - \lambda p_1 = U_1 - \lambda p_1 = 0, \qquad (3.18)$$

$$\frac{\partial \mathcal{L}}{\partial q_2} = U_2 - \lambda p_2 = 0, \qquad (3.19)$$

$$\frac{\partial \mathcal{L}}{\partial \lambda} = Y - p_1 q_1 - p_2 q_2 = 0. \qquad (3.20)$$

Equation 3.18 shows that—at the optimal levels of q_1, q_2, and λ—the marginal utility of pizza, $U_1 = \partial U / \partial q_1$, equals its price times λ. Equation 3.19 provides an analogous condition for burritos. Equation 3.20 restates the budget constraint.

These three first-order conditions can be solved for the optimal values of q_1, q_2, and λ. Again, we should check that we have a maximum (see the Calculus Appendix).

What is λ? If we equate Equations 3.19 and 3.18 and rearrange terms, we find that

$$\lambda = \frac{U_1}{p_1} = \frac{U_2}{p_2}. \qquad (3.21)$$

That is, the optimal value of the Lagrangian multiplier, λ, equals the marginal utility of each good divided by its price—or the extra pleasure one gets from the last dollar of expenditure on either good.[14] This optimality condition is the same as the one that we derived using a graphical approach, Equation 3.13.

SOLVED PROBLEM   3.4

If Julia has a Cobb-Douglas utility function $U = q_1^a q_2^{1-a}$, what are her optimal values of q_1 and q_2 in terms of income, prices, and the positive constant a? (*Note*: We can solve this problem using either substitution or the Lagrangian approach. We use the Lagrangian approach here.)

Answer

1. *Show Julia's Lagrangian function and her first-order conditions:* Given that Julia's Lagrangian function is $\mathcal{L} = q_1^a q_2^{1-a} + \lambda(Y - p_1 q_1 - p_2 q_2)$, the first-order conditions for her to maximize her utility subject to the constraint are

$$\mathcal{L}_1 = U_1 - \lambda p_1 = a q_1^{a-1} q_2^{1-a} - \lambda p_1 = a \frac{U}{q_1} - \lambda p_1 = 0, \qquad (3.22)$$

---

[13]To make our presentation as simple as possible, we assume that we have an interior solution, that q_1 and q_2 are infinitely divisible, and that $U(q_1, q_2)$ is continuously differentiable at least twice (so that the second-order condition is well defined). The first-order conditions determine an interior solution in which positive quantities of both goods are consumed. If these conditions do not predict that both quantities are nonnegative, the consumer is at a corner solution. One approach to solving the consumer-maximization problem allowing for a corner solution is to use a Kuhn-Tucker analysis (see the Calculus Appendix).

[14]More generally, the Lagrangian multiplier is often referred to as a *shadow value* that reflects the marginal rate of change in the objective function as the constraint is relaxed (see the Calculus Appendix).

$$\mathcal{L}_2 = U_2 - \lambda p_2 = (1 - a)q_1^a q_2^{-a} - \lambda p_2 = (1 - a)\frac{U}{q_2} - \lambda p_2 = 0, \quad (3.23)$$

$$\mathcal{L}_\lambda = Y - p_1 q_1 - p_2 q_2 = 0. \tag{3.24}$$

2. *Solve these three first-order equations for q_1 and q_2:* By equating the right-hand sides of the first two conditions, we obtain an equation—analogous to Equation 3.21—that depends on q_1 and q_2 but not on λ:

$$(1 - a)p_1 q_1 = ap_2 q_2. \tag{3.25}$$

Equations 3.25 and 3.24 are two equations in q_1 and q_2. Substituting $p_2 q_2 = Y - p_1 q_1$ (from the budget constraint, which is the third first-order condition) into Equation 3.25, we can rewrite this expression as $a(Y - p_1 q_1) = (1 - a)p_1 q_1$. Rearranging terms, we find that

$$q_1 = a\frac{Y}{p_1}. \tag{3.26}$$

Similarly, by substituting $p_1 q_1 = Y - p_2 q_2$ into Equation 3.25 and rearranging, we find that

$$q_2 = (1 - a)\frac{Y}{p_2}. \tag{3.27}$$

Thus we can use our knowledge of the form of the utility function to solve the expression for the q_1 and q_2 that maximize utility in terms of income, prices, and the utility function parameter a. Equations 3.26 and 3.27 are Julia's demand functions for q_1 and q_2, respectively.

SOLVED PROBLEM   3.5

Given that Julia's utility function is $U = q_1^a q_2^{1-a}$, what share of her budget does she spend on q_1 and q_2 in terms of her income, prices, and the positive constant a?

Answer

Use Equations 3.26 and 3.27 to determine her budget shares: The share of her budget that Julia spends on pizza is her expenditure on pizza, $p_1 q_1$, divided by her budget, Y, or $p_1 q_1/Y$. By multiplying both sides of Equation 3.26, $q_1 = aY/p_1$, by p_1, we find that $p_1 q_1/Y = a$. Thus a is both her budget share of pizza and the exponent on the units of pizza in her utility function. Similarly, from Equation 3.27, we find that her budget share of burritos is $p_2 q_2/Y = 1 - a$.

Comment: The Cobb-Douglas functional form was derived to have this property. If an individual has a Cobb-Douglas utility function, we can estimate a and hence the utility function solely from information about the individual's budget shares. Indeed, that is how we obtained our estimate of Jackie's Cobb-Douglas utility function for CDs and DVDs.

APPLICATION

Utility Maximization for Music CDs and Movie DVDs

We return to our typical consumer, Jackie, who has an estimated Cobb-Douglas utility function of $U = q_1^{0.6} q_2^{0.4}$ over music CDs and movie DVDs. The average price of a CD is about $p_1 = \$15$, and the average price of a DVD is roughly $p_2 = \$20$, so her budget constraint for purchasing these entertainment goods is

$$p_1 q_1 + p_2 q_2 = 15q_1 + 20q_2 = 300 = Y,$$

given that Jackie, like the average consumer, spends about $300 per year on these goods.

Using Equations 3.26 and 3.27 from Solved Problem 3.4, we can solve for Jackie's optimal numbers of CDs and DVDs:

$$q_1 = 0.6\frac{Y}{p_1} = 0.6 \times \frac{300}{15} = 12,$$

$$q_2 = 0.4\frac{Y}{p_2} = 0.4 \times \frac{300}{20} = 6.$$

These quantities are the average purchases for 2005. The figure shows that the optimal bundle is e where the indifference curve is tangent to the budget line.

We can use the result in Solved Problem 3.5 to confirm that the budget shares equal the exponents in Jackie's utility function. The share of Jackie's budget devoted to music CDs is $p_1 q_1/Y = (15 \times 12)/300 = 0.6$, which is the exponent on music CDs in her utility function. Similarly, the budget share she allocates to DVDs is $p_2 q_2/Y = (20 \times 6)/300 = 0.4$, which is the DVD exponent.

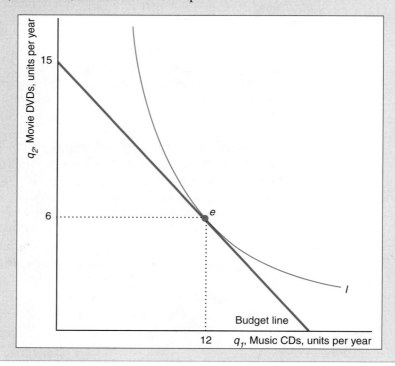

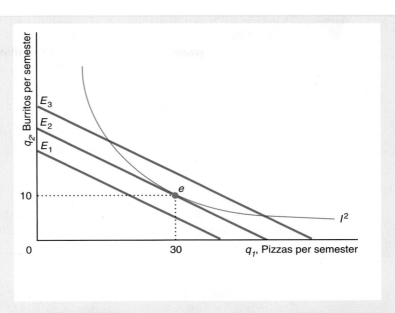

Figure 3.8 Minimizing Expenditure. The lowest expenditure that Lisa can make that will keep her on indifference curve I^2 is E_2. She buys 30 pizzas and 10 burritos.

MINIMIZING EXPENDITURE

Earlier we showed how Lisa chooses quantities of goods so as to maximize her utility subject to a budget constraint. There is a related or *dual* constrained minimization problem where she finds the combination of goods that achieves a particular level of utility for the least expenditure.

In panel a of Figure 3.6, we showed that, given the budget constraint that she faced, Lisa maximized her utility by picking a bundle of $q_1 = 30$ and $q_2 = 10$. She did that by choosing the highest indifference curve, I^2, that touched—was tangent to—the budget constraint.

Now let's consider the alternative problem where we ask how Lisa can make the lowest possible expenditure to maintain her utility at a particular level, $\overline{U}$, which corresponds to indifference curve I^2. Figure 3.8 shows three possible budget lines corresponding to budgets or expenditures of E_1, E_2, and E_3. The lowest of these budget lines with expenditure E_1 lies everywhere below I^2, so Lisa cannot achieve the level of utility on I^2 for such a small expenditure. Both the other budget lines cross I^2; however, the budget line with expenditure E_2 is the least expensive way for her to stay on I^2. The rule for minimizing expenditure while achieving a given level of utility is to choose the lowest expenditure such that the budget line touches—is tangent to—the relevant indifference curve.

The slope of all the expenditure or budget lines is $-p_2/p_1$—see Equation 3.11—which depends only on the market prices and not on income or expenditure. Thus the point of tangency in Figure 3.8 is the same as in panel a of Figure 3.6. Lisa purchases $q_1 = 30$ and $q_2 = 10$ because that is the bundle that minimizes her expenditure conditional on staying on I^2.

Thus solving either of the two problems—maximizing utility subject to a budget constraint or minimizing expenditure subject to maintaining a given level of utility yields the same optimal values. It is sometimes more useful to use the expenditure-minimizing approach because expenditures are observable and utility levels are not.

We can use calculus to solve the expenditure-minimizing problem. Lisa's objective is to minimize her expenditure, E, subject to the constraint that she hold her utility constant at $\overline{U} = U(q_1, q_2)$:

$$\min_{q_1, q_2} E = p_1 q_1 + p_2 q_2$$
$$\text{s.t. } \overline{U} = U(q_1, q_2). \tag{3.28}$$

The solution of this problem is an expression of the minimum expenditure as a function of the prices and the specified utility level:

$$E = E(p_1, p_2, \overline{U}). \tag{3.29}$$

We call this expression the **expenditure function:** the relationship showing the minimal expenditures necessary to achieve a specific utility level for a given set of prices.

SOLVED PROBLEM   3.6

Given that Julia has a Cobb-Douglas utility function $U = q_1^a q_2^{1-a}$, what is her expenditure function?

Answer

1. *Show Julia's Lagrangian function and derive her first-order conditions:* Julia's Lagrangian function is $\mathcal{L} = p_1 q_1 + p_2 q_2 + \lambda(\overline{U} - q_1^a q_2^{1-a})$. The first-order conditions for her to minimize her expenditure subject to remaining on a given indifference curve are obtained by differentiating the Lagrangian with respect to q_1, q_2, and λ and setting each derivative equal to zero:

$$\frac{\partial \mathcal{L}}{\partial q_1} = p_1 - \lambda a q_1^{a-1} q_2^{1-a} = p_1 - \lambda a \frac{U}{q_1} = 0, \tag{3.30}$$

$$\frac{\partial \mathcal{L}}{\partial q_2} = p_2 - \lambda(1-a)q_1^a q_2^{-a} = p_2 - \lambda(1-a)\frac{U}{q_2} = 0, \tag{3.31}$$

$$\frac{\partial \mathcal{L}}{\partial \lambda} = \overline{U} - q_1^a q_2^{1-a} = 0. \tag{3.32}$$

2. *Solve these three first-order equations for q_1 and q_2:* By equating the right-hand sides of the first two conditions, we obtain an equation—analogous to Equation 3.21—that depends on q_1 and q_2 but not on λ: $p_1 q_1/(aU) = p_2 q_2/[(1-a)U]$, or

$$(1-a)p_1 q_1 = ap_2 q_2. \tag{3.33}$$

This condition is the same as Equation 3.25, which we derived in Solved Problem 3.4 when we were maximizing Julia's utility subject to the budget constraint.

Equations 3.33 and 3.32 are two equations in q_1 and q_2. From Equation 3.33, we know that $p_2 q_2 = p_1 q_1(1-a)/a$. If we substitute this expression into the expenditure definition, we find that $E = p_1 q_1 + p_2 q_2 = p_1 q_1 + p_1 q_1(1-a)/a = p_1 q_1/a$. Rearranging terms, we learn that

$$q_1 = a\frac{E}{p_1}. \tag{3.34}$$

Similarly, by substituting $p_1 q_1 = Y - p_2 q_2$ into Equation 3.33 and rearranging, we learn that

$$q_2 = (1 - a)\frac{E}{p_2}. \tag{3.35}$$

By substituting the expressions in Equations 3.34 and 3.35 into the indifference curve expression, Equation 3.32, we observe that

$$\overline{U} = q_1^a q_2^{1-a} = \left(a\frac{E}{p_1}\right)^a \left[(1 - a)\frac{E}{p_2}\right]^{1-a} = E\left(\frac{a}{p_1}\right)^a \left(\frac{1 - a}{p_2}\right)^{1-a}. \tag{3.36}$$

Solving this expression for E, we can write the expenditure function as

$$E = \overline{U}\left(\frac{p_1}{a}\right)^a \left(\frac{p_2}{1 - a}\right)^{1-a}. \tag{3.37}$$

Equation 3.37 shows the minimum expenditure necessary to achieve utility level $\overline{U}$ given prices p_1 and p_2. For example, if $a = 1 - a = \frac{1}{2}$, then $E = 2\overline{U}\sqrt{p_1 p_2}$.

Summary

Consumers maximize their utility (well-being) subject to constraints based on their income and the prices of goods.

1. **Preferences:** To predict consumers' responses to changes in these constraints, economists use a theory about individuals' preferences. One way of summarizing consumers' preferences is with a family of indifference curves. An indifference curve consists of all bundles of goods that give the consumer a particular level of utility. On the basis of observations of consumers' behavior, economists assume that consumers' preferences have three properties: completeness, transitivity, and more is better. Given these three assumptions, indifference curves have the following properties:

   ■ Consumers get more pleasure from bundles on indifference curves the farther from the origin the curves are.
   ■ Indifference curves cannot cross.
   ■ There is an indifference curve through any given bundle.
   ■ Indifference curves have no thickness.
   ■ Indifference curves slope downward.
   ■ Consumers are observed purchasing positive quantities of all relevant goods only where their indifference curves are convex to the origin.

   We also assume that consumers' preferences are continuous, and we use this assumption in our utility function analysis.

2. **Utility:** *Utility* is the set of numerical values that reflect the relative rankings of bundles of goods. Utility is an ordinal measure: By comparing the utility a consumer gets from each of two bundles, we know that the consumer prefers the bundle with the higher utility although we can't tell by how much the consumer prefers that bundle. The utility function is unique only up to a positive monotonic transformation. The marginal utility from a good is the extra utility a person gets from consuming one more unit of that good, holding the consumption of all other goods constant. The rate at which a consumer is willing to substitute Good 1 for Good 2, the marginal rate of substitution, *MRS*, depends on the relative amounts of marginal utility that the consumer gets from each of the two goods.

3. **Budget Constraint:** The amount of goods consumers can buy at given prices is limited by their income. As a result, the greater their income and the lower the prices of goods, the better off consumers are. The rate at which they can exchange Good 1 for Good 2 in the market, the marginal rate of transformation, *MRT*, depends on the relative prices of the two goods.

4. **Constrained Consumer Choice:** Each person picks an affordable bundle of goods to consume so as to maximize his or her pleasure. If an individual consumes both Good 1 and Good 2 (an interior solution), the individual's utility is maximized when the following four equivalent conditions hold:

   ■ The consumer buys the bundle of goods that is on the highest obtainable indifference curve.
   ■ The indifference curve between the two goods is tangent to the budget constraint.
   ■ The consumer's marginal rate of substitution (the slope of the indifference curve) equals the marginal rate of transformation (the slope of the budget line).
   ■ The last dollar spent on Good 1 gives the consumer as much extra utility as the last dollar spent on Good 2.

   However, consumers do not buy some of all possible goods (corner solutions). The last dollar spent on a good that is actually purchased gives ⸺

would a dollar's worth of a good the consumer chose not to buy.

We can use our model where a consumer maximizes his or her utility subject to a budget constraint to predict the consumer's optimal choice of goods as a function of the consumer's income and market prices. The same bundle is chosen if we look at the dual problem of minimizing the consumer's expenditure while holding the consumer's utility fixed.

Questions

* = answer at the back of this book; **W** = audio-slide show answers by James Dearden at **www.aw-bc.com/perloff**

1. Which of the following pairs of goods are complements (people like to consume them together), and which are substitutes (people are willing to trade off one good for the other)? Are the goods that are substitutes likely to be perfect substitutes for some or all consumers?

    a. A popular novel and a gossip magazine
    b. A camera and film
    c. An economics textbook and a mathematics textbook
    d. A Panasonic CD player and a JVC CD player

2. Don is altruistic. Show the possible shape of his indifference curves between charity and all other goods.

*3. Arthur spends his income on bread and chocolate. He views chocolate as a good but is neutral about bread, in that he doesn't care if he consumes it or not. Draw his indifference curve map.

4. Miguel considers tickets to the Houston Grand Opera and to Houston Astros baseball games to be perfect substitutes. Show his preference map. What is his utility function?

*5. Sofia will consume hot dogs only with whipped cream. Show her preference map. What is her utility function?

6. Give as many reasons as you can why economists believe that indifference curves are convex.

7. Fiona requires a minimum level of consumption, a *threshold*, to derive additional utility: $U(X, Z)$ is 0 if $X + Z \le 5$ and is $X + Z$ otherwise. Draw Fiona's indifference curves. Which of our usual assumptions does this example violate?

*8. Gasoline was once less expensive in the United States than in Canada, but now gasoline costs less in Canada than in the United States due to a change in taxes. How will the gasoline-purchasing behavior of a Canadian who lives equally close to gas stations in both countries change? Answer using an indifference curve and budget line diagram.

*9. Governments frequently limit how much of a good a consumer can buy. During emergencies, governments may ration "essential" goods such as water, food, and gasoline rather than let their prices rise. Suppose that the government rations water, setting quotas on how much a consumer can purchase. If a consumer can afford to buy 12 thousand gallons a month but the government restricts purchases to no more than 10 thousand gallons a month, how do the consumer's budget line and opportunity set change?

10. What happens to a consumer's optimal choice of goods if all prices and income double? (*Hint:* What happens to the intercepts of the budget constraint?)

11. Suppose that Boston consumers pay twice as much for avocadoes as they pay for tangerines, whereas San Diego consumers pay half as much for avocadoes as they pay for tangerines. Assuming that consumers maximize their utility, which city's consumers have a higher marginal rate of substitution of avocadoes for tangerines? Explain your answer.

12. Suppose that Solved Problem 3.3 were changed so that Nigel and Bob are buying a bundle of several cars and SUVs for their large families or businesses and have identical tastes, with the usual-shaped indifference curves. Use a figure to discuss how the different slopes of their budget lines affect the bundles of SUVs and cars that each chooses. Can you make any unambiguous statements about the quantity each can buy? Can you make an unambiguous statement if you know that Bob's budget line goes through Nigel's optimal bundle?

13. If a consumer has indifference curves that are convex to the origin but that have a kink in them (similar to the perfect complements example, but the angle at the kink is greater than 90°), how can we determine the optimal bundle? Use a graph to illustrate your answer. Can we use all the conditions that we derived for determining an interior solution?

*14. What is the effect of a 50% income tax on Dale's budget line and opportunity set?

15. Goolsbee (2000) finds that people who live in high sales tax areas are much more likely than other consumers to purchase over the Internet, where they are generally exempt from the sales tax if the firm is located in another state. The National Governors Association (NGA) proposed a uniform tax of 5% on all Internet sales. Goolsbee estimates that the NGA's flat 5% tax would lower the number of online customers by 18% and total sales by 23%. Alternatively, if each state imposed its own taxes (which average 6.33%), the number of buyers would fall

by 24% and spending by 30%. Use an indifference curve–budget line diagram to illustrate the reason for his results.

16. In 2006, Michigan passed legislation that provides greater incentives to drivers who buy ethanol by lowering the state tax on each gallon of ethanol-blended fuel to 12¢,

down from the 19¢ per gallon on regular gas. Show the effects of such a subsidy on a consumer who is indifferent between using ethanol-blended fuel and regular gasoline and on another consumer who views the two types of gasoline as imperfect substitutes.

Problems

17. Elise consumes cans of anchovies, A, and boxes of biscuits, B. Each of her indifference curves reflects strictly diminishing marginal rates of substitution. Where $A = 2$ and $B = 2$, her marginal rate of substitution between cans of anchovies and boxes of biscuits equals -1 ($= MU_A/MU_B$). Will she prefer a bundle with three cans of anchovies and a box of biscuits to a bundle with two of each? Why?

*18. Andy purchases only two goods, apples (a) and kumquats (k). He has an income of $40 and can buy apples at $2 per pound and kumquats at $4 per pound. His utility function is $U(a, k) = 3a + 5k$. What are his marginal utility for apples and his marginal utility for kumquats? What bundle of apples and kumquats should he purchase to maximize his utility? Why?

*19. David's utility function is $U = B + 2Z$. Describe the location of his optimal bundle (if possible) in terms of the relative prices of B and Z.

20. Mark consumes only cookies and books. At his current consumption bundle, his marginal utility from books is 10 and from cookies is 5. Each book costs $10, and each cookie costs $2. Is he maximizing his utility? Explain. If he is not, how can he increase his utility while keeping his total expenditure constant?

*21. Nadia likes spare ribs, R, and fried chicken, C. Her utility function is

$$U = 10R^2C.$$

Her weekly income is $90, which she spends on only ribs and chicken.

a. If she pays $10 for a slab of ribs and $5 for a chicken, what is her optimal consumption bundle? Show her budget line, indifference curve, and optimal bundle, e_1, in a diagram.

b. Suppose the price of chicken doubles to $10. How does her optimal consumption of chicken and ribs change? Show her new budget line and optimal bundle, e_2, in your diagram.

22. Steve's utility function is $U = BC$, where B = veggie burgers per week and C = packs of cigarettes per week. Here $MU_B = C$ and $MU_C = B$. What is his marginal rate of substitution if veggie burgers are on the vertical axis and cigarettes are on the horizontal axis? Steve's income is $120, the price of a veggie burger is $2, and that of a pack

of cigarettes is $1. How many burgers and how many packs of cigarettes does Steve consume to maximize his utility? When a new tax raises the price of a burger to $3, what is his new optimal bundle? Illustrate your answers in a graph.

23. Linda loves buying shoes and going out to dance. Her utility function for pairs of shoes, S, and the number of times she goes dancing per month, T, is $U(S, T) = 2ST$. What are her marginal utility of shoes and her marginal utility of dancing? It costs Linda $50 to buy a new pair of shoes or to spend an evening out dancing. Assume that she has $500 to spend on clothing and dancing.

a. What is the equation for her budget line? Draw it (with T on the vertical axis), and label the slope and intercepts.

b. What is Linda's marginal rate of substitution? Explain.

c. Solve mathematically for her optimal bundle. Show in a diagram how to determine this bundle using indifference curves and a budget line.

24. Diogo has a utility function $U(q_1, q_2) = q_1^{3/4} q_2^{1/4}$, where q_1 is pizza and q_2 is burritos. If the price of burritos, p_2, is $2, the price of pizzas, p_1, is $1, and Y is $100, what is Diogo's optimal bundle?

25. Vasco's utility function is $U = 10q_1q_2^2$. The price of pizza, q_1, is $p_1 = \$5$, the price of burritos, q_2, is $p_2 = \$10$, and his income is $Y = \$150$. What is his optimal consumption bundle? Show it in a graph.

26. If José Maria's utility function is $U(q_1, q_2) = q_1 + Aq_1^a q_2^b + q_2$, what is his marginal utility of q_2? What is his marginal rate of substitution between these two goods?

27. Ann's utility function is $U = q_1q_2/(q_1 + q_2)$. Solve for her optimal values of q_1 and q_2 as function of p_1, p_2, and Y.

*28. Suppose we calculate the MRS at a particular bundle for a consumer whose utility function is $U(q_1, q_2)$. If we use a positive monotonic transformation, F, to obtain a new utility function, $V(q_1, q_2) = F(U(q_1, q_2))$, then this new utility function contains the same information about the consumer's rankings of bundles. Prove that the MRS is the same as with the original utility function.

29. The application "Indifference Curves Between Food and Clothing" postulates that there are minimum levels of food and clothing necessary to support life. Suppose that

the amount of food one has is F, where the minimum level to sustain life is $\underline{F}$, and the amount of clothing is C, where the minimum necessary is $\underline{C}$. We can then modify the Cobb-Douglas utility function to reflect these minimum levels: $U(C, F) = (C - \underline{C})^a(F - \underline{F})^{1-a}$, where $C \geq \underline{C}$ and $F \geq \underline{F}$. Using the approach similar to that in Solved Problem 3.4, derive the optimal amounts of food and clothing as a function of prices and income. To do so, introduce the idea of *extra income*, Y^*, which is the income remaining after paying for the minimum levels of food and clothing: $Y^* = Y - p_C\underline{C} - p_F\underline{F}$. Show that the demand for clothing is $C = \underline{C} + aI^*/p_C$ and that the demand for food is $F = \underline{F} + (1 - a)I^*/p_F$. Derive formulas for the share of income devoted to each good.

30. Use the substitution approach rather than the Lagrangian method in Solved Problem 3.4 to obtain expressions for the optimal levels of q_1 and q_2. (*Hint:* It may help to take logarithms of both sides of the utility expression before you differentiate.)

31. We argued earlier that if all prices and income doubled, we would not expect an individual's choice of an optimal bundle to change. We say that a function $f(X, Y)$ is homogeneous of degree γ if, when we multiply each argument by a constant α, we have $f(\alpha X, \alpha Y) = \alpha^\gamma f(X, Y)$. Thus if a function is homogeneous of degree zero, $f(\alpha X, \alpha Y) = \alpha^0 f(X, Y) = f(X, Y)$, because $\alpha^0 = 1$. Show that optimality conditions that we derived based on the Cobb-Douglas utility function in Solved Problem 3.4 are homogeneous of degree zero. Explain why that result is consistent with our intuition about what happens if we double all prices and income.

32. In 2005, Americans bought 9.1 million home radios for $202 million and 3.8 million home-theater-in-a-box units for $730 million (**www.twice.com/article/CA6319031. html**, March 27, 2006). Suppose that the average consumer has a Cobb-Douglas utility function and buys only

these two goods. Given the results in Solved Problem 3.5, estimate a plausible Cobb-Douglas utility function such that the consumer would allocate income in the proportions actually observed.

*33. The constant elasticity of substitution (CES) utility function is $U(q_1, q_2) = (q_1^\rho + q_2^\rho)^{1/\rho}$, where ρ is a positive constant. Show that there is a positive monotonic transformation such that there is an equivalent utility function (one with the same preference ordering) $U(q_1, q_2) = q_1^\rho + q_2^\rho$.

*34. What is the *MRS* for the CES utility function $U(q_1, q_2) = q_1^\rho + q_2^\rho$?

35. For the CES utility function $U(q_1, q_2) = q_1^\rho + q_2^\rho$, derive the expressions for the optimal levels of q_1 and q_2.

36. Jim spends most of his time in Jazzman's, a coffee shop on the south side of Bethlehem, Pennsylvania. Jim has $12 a week to spend on coffee and muffins. Jazzman's sells muffins for $2 each and coffee for $1.20 per cup. Jim consumes q_c cups of coffee per week and q_m muffins per week. His utility function for coffee and muffins is $U(q_c, q_m) = q_c^{1/2}q_m^{1/2}$.

   a. Draw Jim's budget line.
   b. Use the Lagrange technique to find Jim's optimal bundle.
   c. Now Jazzman's has introduced a frequent-buyer card: For every five cups of coffee purchased at the regular price of $1.20 per cup, Jim receives a free sixth cup. Draw Jim's new budget line. Is Jim's new budget line actually composed of more than one straight line?
   d. With the frequent-buyer card, does Jim consume more coffee? **W**

37. Jen's utility for chocolate, q_1, and coffee, q_2, is $U = q_1^{0.5} + q_2^{0.5}$. Does more money make Jen better off, and does less money reduce her well-being? (*Hint:* To answer the question, derive Jen's expenditure function.) **W**

Chapter 4

Demand

I have enough money to last me the rest of my life, unless I buy something.
—Jackie Mason

Alexx's employer wants to transfer him from the firm's Miami office to its Paris office. Although Alexx likes the idea of living in Paris, he's concerned about the high cost of living there. The firm offers to pay him enough in euros that he can buy the same combination of goods in Paris that he is buying currently in the United States. Does this higher income undercompensate, fully compensate, or overcompensate Alexx for the higher Parisian prices?

When Apple's iPod was virtually the only MP3 player, how much could Apple raise its price above its cost of production? If the government cuts the income tax rate, will tax revenues rise or fall? If the government substantially increases the tax on gasoline, how much of a subsidy would the government have to give poor people to keep them as well off as they were before the tax? The answers to these questions and to many, if not most, important economic questions turn critically on how consumers' demands respond to changes in prices and or in their incomes.

We begin this chapter by extending our analysis of consumer theory to determine the shape of a demand curve for a good by varying the good's price, holding other prices and income constant. Firms use information about the shape of demand curves when setting prices. Governments apply this information in predicting the impact of policies such as taxes and price controls.

We then apply consumer theory to show how an increase in income causes the demand curve to shift. Firms use information about the relationship between income and demand to predict which less-developed countries will substantially increase their demand for the firms' products when incomes rise.

Next we discover that an increase in the price of a good has two effects on demand. First, consumers would buy less of the now relatively more expensive good even if they were compensated with cash for the price increase. Second, consumers' incomes can't buy as much as before because of the higher price, so consumers buy less of at least some goods.

We use the analysis of these two demand effects of a price increase to show why the government's measure of inflation, the Consumer Price Index (CPI), overestimates the amount of inflation. Because of this bias in the CPI, some people gain and some lose from contracts that adjust payment on the basis of the government's inflation index. If you signed a long-term lease for an apartment in which your rent payments increase over time in proportion to the change in the CPI, you lose and your landlord gains from this bias.

Finally, having determined that we can infer a consumer's behavior based on the consumer's preferences, we use a *revealed preference* approach to show the opposite: that we can infer a consumer's preferences if we know the consumer's behavior. Using revealed preferences, we can demonstrate that consumers substitute away from a good when its price rises.

4.1   Deriving Demand Curves

An increase in the price of one good—holding tastes, income, and the price of other goods constant—causes a *movement along the demand curve* (Chapter 2). We use consumer theory to show how a consumer's choice changes as the price changes, thereby tracing out the demand curve.

SYSTEM OF DEMAND EQUATIONS

In Chapter 3, we used calculus to maximize utility subject to a budget constraint. In doing so, we solved for the optimal quantities that a consumer chooses as functions of prices and income. That is, we solved for the consumer's system of demand functions for these goods. For example, Lisa chooses between pizzas, q_1, and burritos, q_2, so her demand functions are of the form

$$q_1 = Z(p_1, p_2, Y),$$

$$q_2 = B(p_1, p_2, Y),$$

where p_1 is the price of pizza, p_2 is the price of burritos, and Y is her income.

In Solved Problem 3.4, we showed that if a consumer has a Cobb-Douglas utility function, $U = q_1^a q_2^{1-a}$, such demand functions are given by Equation 3.26, $q_1 = aY/p_1$, and Equation 3.27, $q_2 = (1 - a)Y/p_2$. Thus the Cobb-Douglas utility function has the unusual property that the demand for each good depends only on its *own price* and not the price of the substitute good.

GRAPHICAL INTERPRETATION

We now examine the properties of this system of demand functions in detail using a graphical approach to construct a demand curve. If we increase a price while holding other prices, tastes, and income constant, we cause the consumer's budget constraint

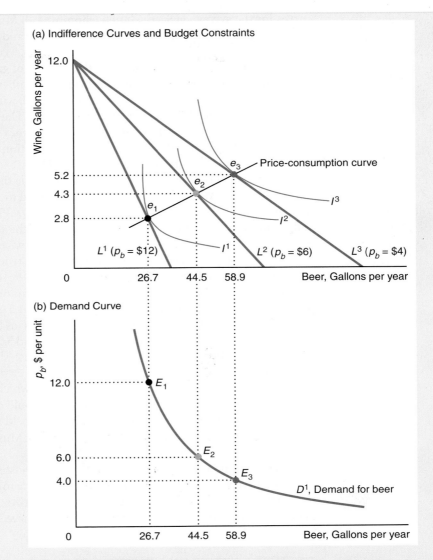

Figure 4.1 Deriving Mimi's Demand Curve. If the price of beer falls, holding the price of wine, the budget, and tastes constant, the typical American consumer, Mimi, buys more beer, according to our estimates. (a) At the actual budget line, L^1, where the price of beer is $12 per unit and the price of wine is $35 per unit, the average consumer's indifference curve I^1 is tangent at Bundle e_1, 26.7 gallons of beer per year and 2.8 gallons of wine per year. If the price of beer falls to $6 per unit, the new budget constraint is L^2, and the average consumer buys 44.5 gallons of beer per year and 4.3 gallons of wine per year. (b) By varying the price of beer, we trace out the Mimi's demand curve for beer. The beer price-quantity combinations E_1, E_2, and E_3 on the demand curve for beer in panel b correspond to optimal Bundles e_1, e_2, and e_3 in panel a.

to rotate, prompting the consumer to choose a new optimal bundle. This change in the quantity demanded is the information we need to draw the demand curve.

We start by estimating a utility function between wine and beer, using data for U.S. consumers. Panel a of Figure 4.1 shows three of the corresponding estimated indifference curves for the average U.S. consumer, whom we call Mimi.[1] These indifference curves are convex to the origin because Mimi views beer and wine as imperfect substitutes (Chapter 3).

The vertical axis in panel a measures the number of gallons of wine Mimi consumes each year, and the horizontal axis measures the number of gallons of beer she drinks per year. Mimi spends $Y = \$419$ per year on beer and wine. The price of beer, p_b, is \$12 per unit, and the price of wine, p_w, is \$35 per unit.[2] The slope of her budget line, L^1, is $-p_b/p_w = -12/35 \approx -\frac{1}{3}$. At those prices, Mimi consumes Bundle e_1, 26.7 gallons of beer per year and 2.8 gallons of wine per year, a combination that is determined by the tangency of indifference curve I^1 and budget line L^1.[3]

If the price of beer is cut in half to \$6 per unit while the price of wine and her budget remain constant, Mimi's budget line rotates outward to L^2. If she were to spend all her money on wine, she could buy the same 12 ($\approx 419/35$) gallons of wine per year as before, so the intercept on the vertical axis of L^2 is the same as for L^1. However, if she were to spend all her money on beer, she could buy twice as much as before (70 instead of 35 gallons of beer), so L^2 hits the horizontal axis twice as far from the origin as L^1. As a result, L^2 has a flatter slope than L^1, about $-\frac{1}{6}$ ($\approx -6/35$).

Because beer is now relatively less expensive, Mimi drinks relatively more beer. She chooses Bundle e_2, 44.5 gallons of beer per year and 4.3 gallons of wine per year, where her indifference curve I^2 is tangent to L^2. If the price of beer falls to \$4 per unit, Mimi consumes Bundle e_3, 58.9 gallons of beer per year and 5.2 gallons of wine per year. The lower the price of beer, the happier Mimi is because she can consume more on the same budget: She is on a higher indifference curve (or perhaps just higher).

Panel a also shows the *price-consumption curve*, which is the line through the equilibrium bundles, such as e_1, e_2, and e_3, that Mimi would consume at each price of beer, when the price of wine and Mimi's budget are held constant. Because the price-consumption curve is upward sloping, we know that Mimi's consumption of both beer and wine increases as the price of beer falls.

We can use the same information in the price-consumption curve to draw Mimi's demand curve, D^1, for beer in panel b. Corresponding to each possible price of beer on the vertical axis of panel b, we record on the horizontal axis the quantity of beer demanded by Mimi from the price-consumption curve.

---

[1]My 92-year-old mother, Mimi, wanted the most degenerate character in the book named after her. She and I hope that you do not consume as much beer or wine as the typical American in this example. ("One reason I don't drink is that I want to know when I am having a good time."— Nancy, Lady Astor.) I estimated the utility function that underlies Figure 4.1 using an almost ideal demand system approach, which is a more flexible, functional form than the Cobb-Douglas, and includes the Cobb-Douglas as a special case.

[2]To ensure that the prices are whole numbers, we state the prices with respect to an unusual unit of measure (not gallons).

[3]These figures are the U.S. average annual per capita consumption of wine and beer. These numbers are startlingly high given that they reflect an average of teetotalers and (apparently very heavy) drinkers. According to a 2006 Organization for Economic Cooperation and Development report, alcohol consumption in liters per capita for people 15 years and older was 8.4 in the United States compared to 4.6 in Mexico, 6.2 in Norway, 6.7 in Iceland, 7.9 in Canada, 8.0 in Italy, 9.2 in New Zealand, 9.7 in the Netherlands, 9.8 in Australia, 10.1 in Germany, 10.7 in Switzerland, 11.4 in Portugal, 11.5 in the United Kingdom, 11.5 in the Czech Republic, 13.6 in Ireland, 14.0 in France, and 15.5 in Luxembourg.

Points E_1, E_2, and E_3 on the demand curve in panel b correspond to Bundles e_1, e_2, and e_3 on the price-consumption curve in panel a. Both e_1 and E_1 show that when the price of beer is \$12, Mimi demands 26.7 gallons of beer per year. When the price falls to \$6 per unit, Mimi increases her consumption to 44.5 gallons of beer, point E_2. The demand curve for beer is downward sloping, as predicted by the Law of Demand.

We can use the relationship between the points in panels a and b to show that Mimi's utility is lower at point E_1 on D^1 than at point E_2. Point E_1 corresponds to Bundle e_1 on indifference curve I^1, whereas E_2 corresponds to Bundle e_2 on indifference curve I^2, which is farther from the origin than I^1, so Mimi's utility is higher at E_2 than at E_1. Mimi is better off at E_2 than at E_1 because the price of beer is lower at E_2, so she can buy more goods with the same budget.

APPLICATION

Going Up in Smoke

I phoned my dad to tell him I had stopped smoking.
He called me a quitter. —Steven Pearl

A tax on cigarettes raises the price of cigarettes, discouraging some people from smoking. Lower-income, minority, and younger populations are more likely than others to quit smoking if the price rises. Several economic studies estimate that the price elasticity of demand is between −0.3 and −0.6 for the U.S. population and between −0.6 and −0.7 for children. When the price of cigarettes in Canada increased 158% from 1979 to 1991 (after adjusting for inflation and including taxes), teenage smoking dropped by 61% and overall smoking fell by 38%.

But what happens to those who continue to smoke heavily? To pay for their now more expensive habit, they have to reduce their expenditures on other goods, such as housing and food. (Similarly, in panel a of Figure 4.1, if the price of beer rises from \$4, budget line L^3, to \$6, budget line L^2, Mimi substantially reduces her consumption of wine as well as beer.)

In 29.1% of poor households, someone smokes. The average low-income family of smokers spends \$1,018 per year on cigarettes, which is 5.1% of their total annual expenditures. That amount is close to what they spend on health care expenditures, \$1,056, and apparel, \$1,138. Smokers spend more on alcohol (1.2% versus 0.5%) and less on food (21.5% versus 22.3%) than nonsmokers. Most strikingly, poor smoking families allocate 36.2% of their expenditures to housing compared to 40.4% for nonsmokers.

Busch et al. (2004) estimate the price elasticity of demand for cigarettes and the cross-price elasticities (see Chapter 2) of other goods when the price of cigarettes rises. They conclude that a 10% increase in the price of cigarettes causes poor smoking families to cut back on cigarettes by 9%, alcohol and transportation by 11%, food by 17%, and health care by 12%. Thus to continue to smoke, these people cut back on many basic goods.

4.2 Effects of an Increase in Income

It is better to be nouveau than never to have been riche at all.

An increase in an individual's income, holding tastes and prices constant, causes a *shift of the demand curve*. An increase in income causes a parallel shift of the budget constraint away from the origin, prompting a consumer to choose a new optimal bundle with more of some or all goods.

HOW INCOME CHANGES SHIFT DEMAND CURVES

We illustrate the relationship between the quantity demanded and income by examining how Mimi's behavior changes when her income rises while the prices of beer and wine remain constant. Figure 4.2 shows three ways of looking at the relationship between income and the quantity demanded. All three diagrams have the same horizontal axis: the quantity of beer consumed per year. In the consumer theory diagram, panel a, the vertical axis is the quantity of wine consumed per year. In the demand curve diagram, panel b, the vertical axis is the price of beer per unit. Finally, in panel c, which directly shows the relationship between income and the quantity of beer demanded, the vertical axis is Mimi's budget, Y.

A rise in Mimi's income causes a parallel shift out of the budget constraint in panel a, which increases Mimi's opportunity set. Her budget constraint L^1 at her original income, $Y = \$419$, is tangent to her indifference curve I^1 at e_1.

As before, Mimi's demand curve for beer is D^1 in panel b. Point E_1 on D^1, which corresponds to point e_1 in panel a, shows how much beer, 26.7 gallons per year, Mimi consumes when the price of beer is \$12 per unit and the price of wine is \$35 per unit.

Now suppose that Mimi's beer and wine budget, Y, increases by roughly 50% to \$628 per year. Her new budget line, L^2 in panel a, is farther from the origin but parallel to her original budget constraint, L^1, because the prices of beer and wine are unchanged. Given this larger budget, Mimi chooses Bundle e_2. The increase in her income causes her demand curve to shift to D^2 in panel b. Holding Y at \$628, we can derive D^2 by varying the price of beer in the same way that we derived D^1 in Figure 4.1. When the price of beer is \$12 per unit, she buys 38.2 gallons of beer per year, E_2 on D^2. Similarly, if Mimi's income increases to \$837 per year, her demand curve shifts to D^3.

The *income-consumption curve* through Bundles e_1, e_2, and e_3 in panel a shows how Mimi's consumption of beer and wine increases as her income rises. As Mimi's income goes up, her consumption of both wine and beer increases.

We can show the relationship between the quantity demanded and income directly rather than by shifting demand curves to illustrate the effect. In panel c, we plot an **Engel curve,** which shows the relationship between the quantity demanded of a single good and income, holding prices constant. Income is on the vertical axis, and the quantity of beer demanded is on the horizontal axis. On Mimi's Engel curve for beer, points E_1^*, E_2^*, and E_3^* correspond to points E_1, E_2, and E_3 in panel b and to e_1, e_2, and e_3 in panel a.

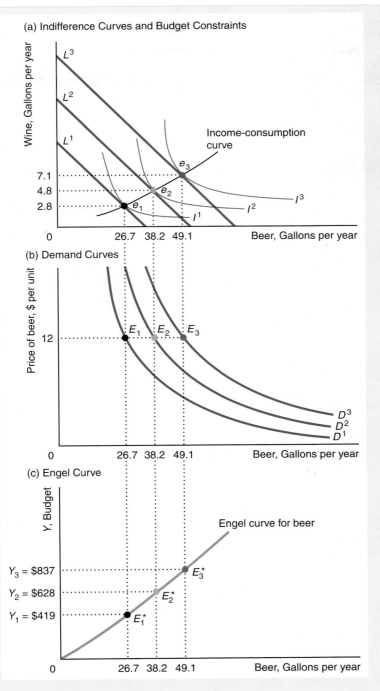

(a) Indifference Curves and Budget Constraints

(b) Demand Curves

(c) Engel Curve

Figure 4.2 Effect of a Budget Increase. As the annual budget for wine and beer, Y, increases from \$419 to \$628 and then to \$837, holding prices constant, the typical consumer buys more of both products, as the upward slope of the income-consumption curve illustrates (a). That the typical consumer buys more beer as income increases is shown by the outward shift of the demand curve for beer (b) and the upward slope of the Engel curve for beer (c).

SOLVED PROBLEM   4.1

Mahdu views Cragmont and Canada Dry ginger ales as perfect substitutes: He is indifferent as to which one he drinks. The price of a 12-ounce can of Cragmont, p, is less than the price of a 12-ounce can of Canada Dry, p^*. What does Mahdu's Engel curve for Cragmont ginger ale look like? How much does his weekly ginger ale budget have to rise for Mahdu to buy one more can of Cragmont ginger ale per week?

Answer

1. *Use indifference curves to derive Mahdu's equilibrium choice:* Because Mahdu views the two brands as perfect substitutes, his indifference curves, such as I^1 and I^2 in panel a of the graphs, are straight lines with a slope of -1 (see Chapter 3). When his income is Y_1, his budget line hits the Canada Dry axis at Y_1/p^* and his Cragmont axis at Y_1/p. Mahdu maximizes his utility by consuming Y_1/p cans of the less expensive Cragmont ginger ale and no Canada Dry (corner solution). As his income rises, say, to Y_2, his budget line shifts outward and is parallel to the original line, with the same slope of $-p/p^*$. Thus at each income level, his budget lines are flatter than his indifference curves, so his equilibria lie along the Cragmont axis.

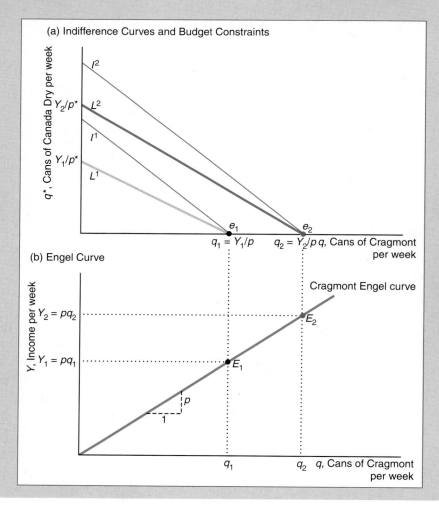

2. *Use the first figure to derive his Engel curve:* Because his entire budget, Y, goes to buying Cragmont, Mahdu buys $q = Y/p$ cans of Cragmont ginger ale. This expression, which shows the relationship between his income and the quantity of Cragmont ginger ale he buys, is Mahdu's Engel curve for Cragmont. The points E_1 and E_2 on the Engel curve in panel b correspond to e_1 and e_2 in panel a. We can rewrite this expression for his Engel curve as $Y = pq$. This relationship is drawn in panel b as a straight line with a slope of p. As q increases by one can ("run"), Y increases by p ("rise"). Because his entire ginger ale budget goes to buy Cragmont, his income needs to rise by only p for him to buy one more can of Cragmont per week.

CONSUMER THEORY AND INCOME ELASTICITIES

Income elasticities tell us how much the quantity demanded changes as income increases. We can use income elasticities to summarize the shape of the Engel curve or the shape of the income-consumption curve. Such knowledge is useful. For example, firms use income elasticities to predict the impact of changes in income taxes on demand for their goods.

Income Elasticity. The *income elasticity of demand* (or *income elasticity*) is the percentage change in the quantity demanded in response to a given percentage change in income, Y (Chapter 2):

$$\xi = \frac{\text{percentage change in quantity demanded}}{\text{percentage change in income}} = \frac{\Delta Q/Q}{\Delta Y/Y} = \frac{\partial Q}{\partial Y}\frac{Y}{Q},$$

where ξ is the Greek letter xi.

Mimi's income elasticity of beer, ξ_b, is 0.88 and that of wine, ξ_w, is 1.38 (based on our estimates for the average American consumer). When her income goes up by 1%, she consumes 0.88% more beer and 1.38% more wine. Thus according to these estimates, as income falls, consumption of beer and wine by the average American falls—contrary to frequent (unsubstantiated) claims in the media that people drink more as their incomes fall during recessions.

Some goods have negative income elasticities: $\xi < 0$. A good is called an **inferior good** if less of it is demanded as income rises. No value judgment is intended by the use of the term *inferior*. An inferior good need not be defective or of low quality. Some of the better-known examples of inferior goods are starchy foods such as potatoes and cassava, which very poor people typically eat in large quantities because they cannot afford meats or other foods. Some economists—apparently seriously—claim that human meat is an inferior good: Only when the price of other foods is very high and people are starving will they turn to cannibalism.

Most goods, like beer and wine, have positive income elasticities. A good is called a **normal good** if as much or more of it is demanded as income rises. Thus a good is a normal good if its income elasticity is greater than or equal to zero: $\xi \geq 0$.

If the quantity demanded of a normal good rises more than in proportion to income, $\xi > 1$, we say it is a *luxury good*. On the other hand, if the quantity demanded

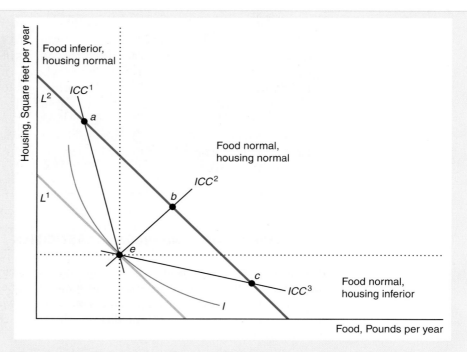

Figure 4.3 Income-Consumption Curves and Income Elasticities. At the initial income, the budget constraint is L^1 and the optimal bundle is *e*. After income rises, the new constraint is L^2. With an upward-sloping income-consumption curve such as ICC^2, both goods are normal. With an income-consumption curve such as ICC^1 that goes through the upper-left section of L^2 (to the left of the vertical dotted line through *e*), housing is normal and food is inferior. With an income-consumption curve such as ICC^3 that cuts L^2 in the lower-right section (below the horizontal dotted line through *e*), food is normal and housing is inferior.

rises less than or in proportion to income ($0 \leq \xi \leq 1$), we say it is a *necessity*. Mimi views beer as a necessity and wine as a luxury.

A good that is inferior for some people may be superior for others. One strange example concerns treating children as a consumption good. Even though people can't buy children in a market, people can decide how many children to have. Willis (1973) estimated the income elasticity for the number of children in a family. He found that children are an inferior good, $\xi = -0.18$, if the wife has relatively little education and the family has average income: These families have fewer children as their income increases. In contrast, children are a normal good, $\xi = 0.044$, in families in which the wife is relatively well educated. For both types of families, the income elasticities are close to zero, so the number of children is not very sensitive to income.

Income-Consumption Curves and Income Elasticities. The shape of the income-consumption curve for two goods tells us the sign of the income elasticities: whether the income elasticities for those goods are positive or negative. To illustrate the relationship between the slope of the income-consumption curve and the sign of income elasticities, we examine Peter's choices of food and housing. Peter purchases Bundle *e* in Figure 4.3 when his budget constraint is L^1. When his income increases so that his budget constraint is L^2, he selects a bundle on L^2. Which bundle he buys depends on his tastes—his indifference curves.

The horizontal and vertical dotted lines through e divide the new budget line, L^2, into three sections. The section where the new optimal bundle is located determines Peter's income elasticities of food and clothing.

Suppose that Peter's indifference curve is tangent to L^2 at a point in the upper-left section of L^2 (to the left of the vertical dotted line that goes through e) such as a. If Peter's income-consumption curve is ICC^1, which goes from e through a, he buys more housing and less food as his income rises. (Although we draw these possible ICC curves as straight lines for simplicity, they may curve in general.) Housing is a normal good, and food is an inferior good.

If instead the new optimal bundle is located in the middle section of L^2 (above the horizontal dotted line and to the right of the vertical dotted line), such as at b, his income-consumption curve ICC^2 through e and b is upward sloping. He buys more of both goods as his income rises, so both food and housing are normal goods.

Finally, suppose that his new optimal bundle is in the bottom-right segment of L^2 (below the horizontal dotted line). If his new optimal bundle is c, his income-consumption curve ICC^3 slopes downward from e through c. As his income rises, Peter consumes more food and less housing, so food is a normal good and housing is an inferior good.

Some Goods Must Be Normal. It is impossible for all goods to be inferior, as Figure 4.3 illustrates. At his original income, Peter faces budget constraint L^1 and buys the combination of food and housing e. When his income goes up, his budget constraint shifts outward to L^2. Depending on his tastes (the shape of his indifference curves), he may buy more housing and less food, such as Bundle a; more of both, such as b; or more food and less housing, such as c. Therefore, either both goods are normal or one good is normal and the other is inferior.

If both goods were inferior, Peter would buy less of both goods as his income rises—which makes no sense. Were he to buy less of both, he would be buying a bundle that lies inside his original budget constraint, L^1. Even at his original, relatively low income, he could have purchased that bundle but chose not to, buying e instead. By the more-is-better assumption of Chapter 3, there is a bundle on the budget constraint that gives Peter more utility than any given bundle inside the constraint.[4]

A good may be normal at some income levels and inferior at others. When Gail was poor and her income increased slightly, she ate meat more frequently, and her meat of choice was hamburger. Thus when her income was low, hamburger was a normal good. As her income increased further, however, she switched from hamburger to steak. Thus at higher incomes, hamburger is an inferior good.

We show Gail's choice between hamburger (horizontal axis) and all other goods (vertical axis) in panel a of Figure 4.4. As Gail's income increases, her budget line shifts outward, from L^1 to L^2, and she buys more hamburger: Bundle e_2 lies to the right of e_1. As her income increases further, shifting her budget line outward to L^3, Gail reduces her consumption of hamburger: Bundle e_3 lies to the left of e_2.

---

[4]Even if an individual does not buy more of the usual goods and services, that person may put the extra money into savings. We can use the consumer theory model to treat savings as a good if we allow for multiple periods. Empirical studies find that savings is a normal good.

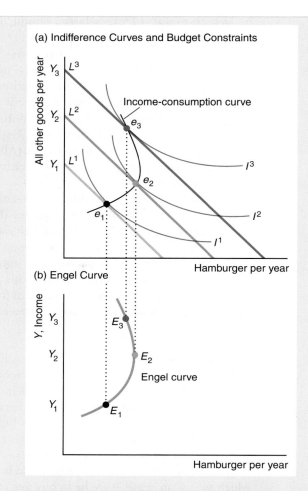

Figure 4.4 A Good That Is Both Inferior and Normal. When she was poor and her income increased, Gail bought more hamburger; however, when she became wealthier and her income rose, she bought less hamburger and more steak. (a) The forward slope of the income-consumption curve from e_1 to e_2 and the backward bend from e_2 to e_3 show this pattern. (b) The forward slope of the Engel curve at low incomes, E_1 to E_2, and the backward bend at higher incomes, E_2 to E_3, also show this pattern.

Gail's Engel curve in panel b captures the same relationship. At low incomes, her Engel curve is upward sloping, indicating that she buys more hamburger as her income rises. At higher incomes, her Engel curve is backward bending.

As their incomes rise, many consumers switch between lower-quality (hamburger) and higher-quality (steak) versions of the same good. This switching behavior explains the pattern of income elasticities across different-quality cars. For example, the income elasticity of demand for a Jetta is 2.1, for an Accord is 2.2, for a BMW 700 Series is 4.4, and for a Jaguar X-Type is 4.5 (Bordley and McDonald, 1993).

● APPLICATION

What to Do with Extra Income

The very rich are different from you and me . . . they have more money.
— Ernest Hemingway

When their incomes rise, how do the rich and the poor spend their extra money? Using the 2003 U.S. Consumer Expenditure Survey, we can compare the ratio of spending by a typical household in the top fifth of the U.S. income distribution to that of a family in the bottom fifth.

The average rich family's overall annual expenditures, $81,731, are 4.4 times those of the poorer family, $18,492. By looking at the table, we can see which goods have a higher or lower ratio than for overall expenditures. The wealthy increase their expenditures on tobacco (on which they spend about the same as the poor), food at home, health care, apparel and services, housing, and education less than in proportion to their overall expenditures. Their spending on food away from home and on alcoholic beverages rises roughly in proportion with their overall expenditures. They spend disproportionately more on entertainment, charitable contributions, insurance, and, especially, pensions and Social Security.

Item	High-Income Expenditures / Low-Income Expenditures
Tobacco	1.2
Food at home	2.1
Health care	2.5
Apparel and services	3.6
Housing	3.7
Education	3.7
Food away from home	4.3
All Items	*4.4*
Alcoholic beverages	4.6
Entertainment	6.4
Cash contributions	7.8
Life and other personal insurance	7.8
Pensions and Social Security	37.8

In all of these fairly aggregate categories, the wealthy spend more than the poor: All of these goods are normal. When all goods are normal, the income-consumption curve is upward sloping, as is ICC^2 in Figure 4.3.

Income elasticities appear to be remarkably similar across time and countries, and broad aggregates of goods are always normal. Ernest Engel, in his 1857 analysis of the budgets of Belgian families, concluded that the share spent on food declined as income increased. Houthhakker (1957), in a paper reviewing 40 budget studies in 30 countries on the hundredth anniversary of Engel's original paper, concluded that the income elasticity of demand for food was 0.6 (that is, the share of food decreases with increases in income), the income elasticity of housing was 0.8, that of clothing was 1.2, and that of everything else was 1.6.

More recently, Reimer and Hertel (2004) compared income elasticities for aggregated goods across most of the countries in the world and found that all are normal. Although the income elasticities generally do not vary substantially across nations, there are a few striking differences. The income elasticity for meat is substantially above 1 in poor countries (1.6 in Tanzania, 1.3 in China) but is only about 0.6 in the richest countries (Japan, the United States, and Switzerland). Similarly, for manufactured goods including electronics, the elasticities are 1.6 in Tanzania, 1.3 in China, and 0.9 in the richest countries.

Weighted Income Elasticities. We just argued by using graphical and verbal reasoning that all goods cannot be inferior. We can derive a stronger result: The weighted sum of a consumer's income elasticities equals one. Firms and governments use this result to make predictions about income effects.

We start with the consumer's budget constraint where there are n goods consumed, p_i is the price, and q_i is the quantity for Good i:

$$p_1 q_1 + p_2 q_2 + \cdots + p_n q_n = Y.$$

By differentiating this equation with respect to income, we obtain

$$p_1 \frac{dq_1}{dY} + p_2 \frac{dq_2}{dY} + \cdots + p_n \frac{dq_n}{dY} = 1.$$

Multiplying and dividing each term by $q_i Y$, we can rewrite this equation as

$$\frac{p_1 q_1}{Y} \frac{dq_1}{dY} \frac{Y}{q_1} + \frac{p_2 q_2}{Y} \frac{dq_2}{dY} \frac{Y}{q_2} + \cdots + \frac{p_n q_n}{Y} \frac{dq_n}{dY} \frac{Y}{q_n} = 1.$$

If we define the budget share of Good i as $\theta_i = p_i q_i / Y$ and note that the income elasticities are $\xi_i = (dq_i/dY)(Y/q_i)$, we can rewrite this expression to show that the weighted sum of the income elasticities equals one:

$$\theta_1 \xi_1 + \theta_2 \xi_2 + \cdots + \theta_n \xi_n = 1. \tag{4.1}$$

This formula is useful in making predictions about income elasticities. If we know the budget share of a good and a little bit about the income elasticities of some goods, we can calculate bounds on other, unknown income elasticities. Being able to obtain bounds on income elasticities is very useful to governments and firms. For example, over the last couple of decades, many Western manufacturing firms, learning that Chinese incomes were rising rapidly, have tried to estimate the income elasticities for their products, to determine whether it is worth building a new plant in China.

SOLVED PROBLEM   4.2

A firm is considering building a plant in a poor country to sell manufactured goods in that country. The firm expects incomes to start rising soon and wants to know the income elasticity for goods other than food. The firm knows that the budget share spent on food is θ and that food is a necessity (its income elasticity, ξ_f, is between 0 and 1). The firm wants to know "How large could the income elasticity on all other goods, ξ_o, be? How small could it be?" What were the bounds on ξ_o for Chinese urban consumers whose θ was 60% in 1983? What are the bounds today when θ is 37%?[5]

Answer

1. *Write Equation 4.1 in terms of ξ_f, ξ_o, and θ, and then use algebra to rewrite this expression with the income elasticity of other goods on the left-hand side:* By substituting ξ_f, ξ_o, and θ into Equation 4.1, we find that

$$\theta\xi_f + (1 - \theta)\xi_o = 1.$$

We can rewrite this expression with the income elasticity of other goods—the number we want to estimate—on the left-hand side:

$$\xi_o = \frac{1 - \theta\xi_f}{1 - \theta}. \tag{4.2}$$

2. *Use Equation 4.2 and the bounds on ξ_f to derive bounds on ξ_o:* Because $\xi_o = (1 - \theta\xi_f)/(1 - \theta)$, ξ_o is smaller the larger ξ_f. Given that food is a necessity, the largest ξ_o can be is $1/(1 - \theta)$, where $\xi_f = 0$. The smallest it can be is $\xi_o = 1$, which occurs if $\xi_f = 1$. [*Note:* If ξ_f equals one, $\xi_o = (1 - \theta)/(1 - \theta) = 1$ regardless of food's budget share, θ.]

3. *Substitute for the two Chinese values of ω to determine the upper bounds:* The upper bound for ξ_o was $1/(1 - \theta) = 1/0.4 = 2.5$ in 1983 and $1/0.63 \approx 1.59$ now.

Comment: The upper bound on the income elasticity of nonfood goods is tighter for the United States than for China because the share of consumption of food in the United States is smaller. The U.S. share of expenditures on food was 22% for welfare recipients and 14% for others in 2001–2002 (Paszkiewicz, 2005). Thus the upper bound on ξ_o is about 1.28 for welfare recipients and 1.16 for others. From Equation 4.2, $\xi_o = (1 - \theta\xi_f)/(1 - \theta) \approx 1.16 - 0.12\xi_f$, for non-welfare recipients. Most estimates of the U.S. ξ_f range between 0.4 and 0.9, so ξ_o must range from about 1.05 to 1.15 for this group.

4.3   Effects of a Price Increase

Holding tastes, other prices, and income constant, an increase in a price of a good has two effects on an individual's demand. One is the **substitution effect:** the change in the quantity of a good that a consumer demands when the good's price rises, holding other prices and the consumer's utility constant. If utility is held constant as the price of the good increases, consumers *substitute* other, now relatively cheaper goods for that one.

---

[5]State Statistical Bureau, *Statistical Yearbook of China*, State Statistical Bureau Publishing House, Beijing, China, various years.

The other effect is the **income effect:** the change in the quantity of a good a consumer demands because of a change in income, holding prices constant. An increase in price reduces a consumer's buying power, effectively reducing the consumer's *income* or opportunity set and causing the consumer to buy less of at least some goods. A doubling of the price of all the goods the consumer buys is equivalent to a drop in the consumer's income to half its original level. Even a rise in the price of only one good reduces a consumer's ability to buy the same amount of all goods as previously. For example, if the price of food increases in a poor country where half or more of the population's income is spent on food, the effective purchasing power of consumers falls substantially.

When a price goes up, the total change in the quantity purchased is the sum of the substitution and income effects. When estimating the effects of a price change on the quantity an individual demands, economists decompose this combined effect into the two separate components. By doing so, they gain extra information that they can use to answer questions about whether inflation measures are accurate, whether an increase in tax rates will raise tax revenue, and what the effects are of government policies that compensate some consumers. For example, President Jimmy Carter, when advocating a tax on gasoline, and President Bill Clinton, when calling for an energy tax, proposed providing an income compensation for poor consumers to offset the harms of the tax. We can use knowledge of the substitution and income effects from a price change of energy to evaluate the effect of these policies.

INCOME AND SUBSTITUTION EFFECTS WITH A NORMAL GOOD

To illustrate the substitution and income effects, we return to Jackie's choice between music CDs and movie DVDs based on our estimate of the average person's Cobb-Douglas utility function (see the application "*MRS* Between Music CDs and Movie DVDs" in Chapter 3). The price of DVDs is $p_2 = \$20$ and the price of CDs is $p_1 = \$15$. Now suppose that the price of CDs rises dramatically to $30, causing Jackie's budget constraint to rotate inward from L^1 to L^2 in Figure 4.5. The new budget constraint, L^2, is twice as steep ($-p_1/p_2 = -30/20 = -1.5$) as L^1 ($-15/20 = -0.75$) because CDs are now twice as expensive as DVDs.

Jackie's opportunity set is smaller, so she must choose between fewer CD-DVD bundles than she could at the lower price. The area between the two budget constraints reflects the decrease in her opportunity set owing to the increase in the price of CDs.

In Chapter 3, we determined that Jackie's demand functions for CDs, q_1, and DVDs, q_2, were

$$q_1 = 0.6\frac{Y}{p_1}, \tag{4.3}$$

$$q_2 = 0.4\frac{Y}{p_2}. \tag{4.4}$$

At the original price of CDs and with an entertainment budget of $300 per year, Jackie chooses Bundle e_1, $q_1 = 0.6 \times 300/15 = 12$ CDs and $q_2 = 0.4 \times 300/20 = 6$ DVDs per year, where her indifference curve I^1 is tangent to her budget constraint L^1. When the price of CDs rises, Jackie's new equilibrium bundle is e_2 (where she buys $q_1 = 0.6 \times 300/30 = 6$ CDs), which occurs where her indifference curve I^2 is tangent to L^2.

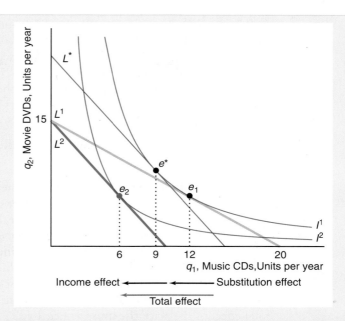

Figure 4.5 Substitution and Income Effects with Normal Goods. An increase in the price of music CDs from \$15 to \$30 causes Jackie's budget line to rotate from L^1 to L^2. The imaginary budget line L^* has the same slope as L^2 and is tangent to indifference curve I^1. The shift of the optimal bundle from e_1 to e_2 is the *total effect* of the price change. The total effect can be decomposed into the *substitution effect*—movement from e_1 to e^*—and the *income effect*—movement from e^* to e_2.

The movement from e_1 to e_2 is the total change in her consumption owing to the rise in the price of CDs. In particular, the *total effect* on Jackie's consumption of CDs from the rise in the price of CDs is that she now buys 6 (= 12 − 6) fewer CDs per year. In the figure, the red arrow pointing to the left and labeled "Total effect" shows this decrease. We can break the total effect into a substitution effect and an income effect.

The substitution effect is the change in the quantity demanded from a *compensated change in the price* of CDs, which occurs when we increase Jackie's income by enough to offset the rise in the price of CDs so that her utility stays constant. To determine the substitution effect, we draw an imaginary budget constraint, L^*, that is parallel to L^2 and tangent to Jackie's original indifference curve, I^1. This imaginary budget constraint, L^*, has the same slope, −1.5, as L^2 because both curves are based on the original, lower price of CDs. For L^* to be tangent to I^1, we need to increase Jackie's budget from \$300 to \$450 to offset the harm of the higher price of CDs. If Jackie's budget constraint were L^*, she would choose Bundle e^*, where she buys $q_1 = 0.6 \times 450/30 = 9$ CDs.

Thus if the price of CDs rises relative to that of DVDs and we hold Jackie's utility constant by raising her income, Jackie's optimal bundle shifts from e_1 to e^*, which is the substitution effect. She buys 3 (= 12 − 9) fewer CDs per year, as the arrow pointing to the left labeled "Substitution effect" shows.

Jackie also faces an income effect. The change in income is due to the change in the price of CDs, which allows Jackie to buy fewer units with her same budget. The parallel shift of the budget constraint from L^* to L^2 captures this effective decrease in income. The movement from e^* to e_2 is the income effect, as the arrow pointing to the left labeled "Income effect" shows. As her budget decreases from \$450 to \$300, Jackie consumes 3 ($= 9 - 6$) fewer CDs per year.

The *total effect* from the price change is the *sum of the substitution and income effects,* as the arrows show. Jackie's total effect (in CDs per year) from a rise in the price of CDs is

$$\text{total effect} = \text{substitution effect} + \text{income effect}$$
$$-6 \quad = \quad -3 \quad + \quad (-3).$$

Because indifference curves are convex to the origin, *the substitution effect is unambiguous:* Less of a good is consumed when its price rises. A consumer always substitutes a less expensive good for a more expensive one, holding utility constant. The substitution effect causes a *movement along an indifference curve.*

The income effect causes a shift to another indifference curve due to a change in the consumer's opportunity set. The direction of the income effect depends on the income elasticity. Because a CD is a normal good for Jackie, her income effect is negative. Thus both Jackie's substitution effect and her income effect go in the same direction, so the total effect of the price rise must be negative.

INCOME AND SUBSTITUTION EFFECTS WITH AN INFERIOR GOOD

If a good is inferior, the income effect goes in the opposite direction from the substitution effect. For most inferior goods, the income effect is smaller than the substitution effect. As a result, the total effect moves in the same direction as the substitution effect, but the total effect is smaller. However, the income effect can more than offset the substitution effect in extreme cases.

A good is called a **Giffen good** if a decrease in its price causes the quantity demanded to fall.[6] Suppose CDs are a Giffen good for Stephen. A price decrease for CDs saves him money that he uses to buy more DVDs. Indeed, he decides to increase his purchase of DVDs even further by reducing his purchase of CDs. Thus the demand curve for a Giffen good has an upward slope! (In the Questions at the end of the chapter, you are asked to draw an example in which you show that the Giffen good effect results from an income effect that more than offsets the substitution effect.)

However, the Law of Demand (Chapter 2) says that demand curves slope downward. You're no doubt wondering how I'm going to worm my way out of this apparent contradiction. I have two explanations. The first is that I claimed that the Law of Demand is an empirical regularity, not a theoretical necessity. Although it's theoretically possible for a demand curve to slope upward, economists have found few, if any, real-world examples of Giffen goods.[7] My second explanation is that the Law of Demand must hold theoretically for compensated demand curves, which we examine next.

---

[6]Robert Giffen, a nineteenth-century British economist, argued that poor people in Ireland increased their consumption of potatoes when the price rose because of a blight. However, more recent studies of the Irish potato famine dispute this observation.

[7]However, Battalio, Kagel, and Kogut (1991) showed in an experiment that quinine water is a Giffen good for lab rats!

COMPENSATED DEMAND CURVE

So far, the demand curves that we have derived graphically and mathematically allow the utility to vary as the price of the good increases. That is, the demand curve reflects both substitution and income effects as the price changes.

As panel a of Figure 4.1 illustrates, Mimi chooses a bundle on a lower indifference curve as the price of beer rises, so her utility level falls. Along her demand curve for beer, we hold other prices, income, and her tastes constant, while allowing her utility to vary. We can observe this type of demand curve by seeing how purchases change as a price increases. It is called *the* demand curve, the Marshallian demand curve (after Alfred Marshall, who popularized this approach), or the *uncompensated demand curve*. (Unless otherwise noted, when we talk about a demand curve, we mean the uncompensated demand curve.)

Alternatively, we could derive a *compensated demand curve,* where we determine how the quantity demanded changes as the price rises, holding utility constant, so that the change in the quantity demanded reflects only pure substitution effects when the price changes. It is called the compensated demand curve because we would have to compensate an individual—give the individual extra income—as the price rises so as to hold the individual's utility constant. The compensated demand curve is also called the Hicksian demand curve, after John Hicks, who introduced the idea.

The compensated demand function for the first good is

$$q_1 = H(p_1, p_2, \overline{U}), \tag{4.5}$$

where we hold utility constant at $\overline{U}$. We cannot observe the compensated demand curve directly because we do not observe utility levels. Because the compensated demand curve reflects only substitution effects, the Law of Demand must hold: A price increase causes the compensated demand for a good to fall.

In Figure 4.6, we derive Jackie's compensated demand function, H, evaluated at her initial indifference curve, I, where her utility is $\overline{U}$. In 2005, the price of CDs was $p_1 = \$15$ and the price of DVDs was $p_2 = \$20$. At those prices, Jackie's budget line, L, has a slope of $-p_1/p_2 = -15/20$ and is tangent to I at e_2 in panel a. At this optimal bundle, she buys 12 CDs. The corresponding point E_2 on her compensated demand curve in panel b shows that she buys 12 CDs when they cost $15 each.

The two blue line segments in panel a show portions of other budget lines where we change p_1 and adjust Jackie's income to keep her on indifference curve I. At the budget line segment in the upper left, the price of CDs is $30, so the budget line's slope is $-30/20$. Her budget is increased enough that the new budget line is tangent to the original indifference curve, I, at e_1. This optimal bundle corresponds to E_1 on her compensated demand curve in panel b. Similarly, when p_1 is $6, we decrease her budget so that this budget line is tangent to her original indifference curve at e_3, which corresponds to E_3 on her compensated demand curve.

Panel b also shows Jackie's uncompensated demand curve: Equation 4.3, $q_1 = 0.6Y/p_1$. Her compensated and uncompensated demand curves *must* cross at the original price, $p_1 = \$15$, where the original budget line, L, is tangent to I along which utility is $\overline{U}$. At that price, and only at that price, both demand curves are derived using the same budget line. The compensated demand curve is steeper than the uncompensated curve around this common point. The reason is that the compensated demand curve reflects only the substitution effect, unlike the uncompensated demand curve, along

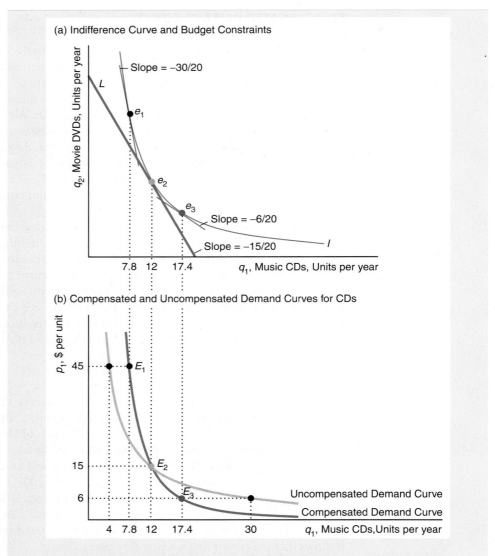

Figure 4.6 **Deriving Jackie's Compensated Demand Curve.** Initially, Jackie's optimal bundle is determined by the tangency of budget line *L* and indifference curve *I* in panel a. If we vary the price of CDs but change her budget so that the new line (segments) are tangent to the same indifference curve, we can determine how the quantity that she demands varies with price, holding her utility constant. Hence, the corresponding quantities in panel b on her compensated demand curve reflect the pure substitution effect of a price change.

which the income effect reinforces the substitution effect (because a CD is a normal good for Jackie).

One way to derive the compensated demand curve is to use the expenditure function, Equation 3.29,

$$E = E(p_1, p_2, \overline{U}),$$

where E is the smallest expenditure that allows the consumer to achieve utility level $\overline{U}$, given market prices. If we differentiate the expenditure function with respect to the price of the first good, we obtain the compensated demand function for that good:[8]

$$\frac{\partial E}{\partial p_1} = H(p_1, p_2, \overline{U}) = q_1. \tag{4.6}$$

Heuristically, Equation 4.6 says that if the price increases by \$1 on each of the q_1 units that the consumer buys, then the minimum expenditure to keep utility constant must increase by \$$q_1$. This expression can also be interpreted as the pure substitution effect on the quantity demanded because we are holding utility constant as we change the price.

SOLVED PROBLEM 4.3

A consumer has a Cobb-Douglas utility function $U = q_1^a q_2^{1-a}$. **Derive the compensated demand function for good q_1. What is Jackie's compensated demand function for CDs = q_1, where $a = 0.6$?**

Answer

1. *Write the formula for the expenditure function for this Cobb-Douglas utility function:* We derived this expenditure function in Solved Problem 3.6, Equation 3.37:

$$E = \overline{U}\left(\frac{p_1}{a}\right)^a \left(\frac{p_2}{1-a}\right)^{1-a}.$$

2. *Differentiate the expenditure function with respect to p_1 to obtain the compensated demand function for q_1:* Based on Equation 4.6, the compensated demand function is

$$q_1 = \frac{\partial E}{\partial p_1} = \overline{U}\left(\frac{a}{1-a}\frac{p_2}{p_1}\right)^{1-a}.$$

3. *Substitute in Jackie's value of a to obtain her expenditure function and compensated demand function for CDs:* Given that her $a = 0.6$, Jackie's expenditure function is

$$E = \overline{U}\left(\frac{p_1}{0.6}\right)^{0.6}\left(\frac{p_2}{0.4}\right)^{0.4} \approx 1.96\overline{U}p_1^{0.6}p_2^{0.4}, \tag{4.7}$$

and her compensated demand function for CDs is

$$q_1 = \overline{U}\left(\frac{0.6}{0.4}\frac{p_2}{p_1}\right)^{0.4} \approx 1.18\overline{U}\left(\frac{p_2}{p_1}\right)^{0.4}. \tag{4.8}$$

---

[8]This result is called Shephard's lemma. As we showed in Solved Problem 3.6, we can use Lagrange's method to derive the expenditure function, where we want to minimize $E = p_1 q_1 + p_2 q_2$ subject to $\overline{U} = U(q_1, q_2)$. The Lagrangian equation is

$$\mathcal{L} = p_1 q_1 + p_2 q_2 + \lambda[\overline{U} - U(q_1, q_2)].$$

According to the envelope theorem (see the Calculus Appendix), at the optimum,

$$\frac{\partial E}{\partial p_1} = \frac{\partial \mathcal{L}}{\partial p_1} = q_1,$$

which is Equation 4.6. It shows that the derivative of the expenditure function with respect to p_1 is q_1, the quantity that the consumer demands.

SLUTSKY EQUATION

We have shown graphically that the total effect from a price change can be decomposed into a substitution effect and an income effect. That same relationship can be derived mathematically. We can use this relationship in a variety of ways. For example, we can apply it to determine how likely a good is to be a Giffen good based on whether it has a large or a small budget share. We can use the relationship to determine the effect of government policies that compensate some consumers.

The usual price elasticity of demand, ε, captures the total effect of a price change—that is, the change along an uncompensated demand curve. We can break this price elasticity of demand into two terms involving elasticities that capture the substitution and income effects. We measure the substitution effect using the pure *substitution elasticity of demand*, ε^*, which is the percentage that the quantity demanded falls for a given percentage increase in price if we compensate the consumer to keep the consumer's utility constant. That is, it is the elasticity of the compensated demand curve. The income effect is the income elasticity, ξ, times the share of the budget spent on that good, θ. This relationship among the price elasticity of demand, ε, the substitution elasticity of demand, ε^*, and the income elasticity of demand, ξ, is the *Slutsky equation* (named after its discoverer, the Russian economist Eugene Slutsky):[9]

$$\begin{array}{ccccc} \text{total effect} & = & \text{substitution effect} & + & \text{income effect} \\ \varepsilon & = & \varepsilon^* & + & (-\theta\xi). \end{array} \quad (4.9)$$

If a consumer spends little on a good, a price change does not affect the consumer's total budget significantly. If the price of garlic triples, your purchasing power is hardly affected (unless perhaps you are a vampire slayer). Thus the total effect, ε, for garlic hardly differs from the substitution effect, ε^*, because the price change has little effect on income.

In Mimi's original equilibrium, e_1 in Figure 4.1, where the price of beer was $12 and Mimi bought 26.7 gallons of beer per year, Mimi spent about three-quarters of her $419 beverage budget on beer: $\theta = 0.76 = (12 \times 26.7)/419$. Her income elasticity is $\xi = 0.88$, her price elasticity is $\varepsilon = -0.76$, and her substitution price elasticity is $\varepsilon^* = -0.09$. Thus Mimi's Slutsky equation is

$$\begin{array}{ccccc} \varepsilon & = & \varepsilon^* & - & \theta\xi \\ -0.76 & \approx & -0.09 & + & 0.76 \times 0.88. \end{array}$$

---

[9]When we derived the compensated demand function, H, we noted that it equals the uncompensated demand function, D, at the initial equilibrium where utility is $\overline{U}$:

$$q_1 = H(p_1, p_2, \overline{U}) = D(p_1, p_2, Y) = D(p_1, p_2, E(p_1, p_2, \overline{U})),$$

where we note that the budget, Y, equals the minimum expenditure needed to achieve that level of utility, as given by the expenditure function. If we differentiate with respect to p_1, we find that

$$\frac{\partial H}{\partial p_1} = \frac{\partial D}{\partial p_1} + \frac{\partial D}{\partial E}\frac{\partial E}{\partial p_1} = \frac{\partial D}{\partial p_1} + \frac{\partial D}{\partial E}q_1,$$

where we know that $\partial E/\partial p_1 = q_1$ from Equation 4.6. Rearranging terms and multiplying all terms by p_1/q_1, and the last term by Y/Y, we obtain

$$\frac{\partial D}{\partial p_1}\frac{p_1}{q_1} = \frac{\partial H}{\partial p_1}\frac{p_1}{q_1} - q_1\frac{\partial D}{\partial E}\frac{p_1}{q_1}\frac{E}{E}.$$

This last expression is the Slutsky equation 4.9, where $\varepsilon = (\partial D/\partial p_1)(p_1/q_1)$, $\varepsilon^* = (\partial H/\partial p_1)(p_1/q_1)$, $\theta = p_1 q_1/E$, and $\xi = (\partial D/\partial E)(p_1/E)$.

Because beer is a normal good for Mimi, the income effect reinforces the substitution effect. Indeed, the size of the total change, $\varepsilon = -0.76$, is due more to the income effect, $-\theta\xi = -0.67$, than to the substitution effect, $\varepsilon^* = -0.09$. If the price of beer rises by 1% but Mimi is given just enough extra income so that her utility remains constant, Mimi would reduce her consumption of beer by less than a tenth of a percent (substitution effect). Without compensation, Mimi reduces her consumption of beer by about three-quarters of a percent (total effect).

Similarly, in Jackie's original equilibrium, e_1 in Figure 4.5, the price of a CD was $15 and Jackie bought 12 CDs per year. She spent $\theta = 0.6$ share of her budget on CDs (Solved Problem 3.5). Her uncompensated demand function, Equation (4.3), is $q_1 = 0.6Y/p_1$, so her price elasticity of demand is $\varepsilon = -1$, and her income elasticity is $\xi = 1$.[10] Her compensated demand function, Equation 4.8, is $q_1 = 1.18\overline{U}(p_2/p_1)^{0.4}$, which has a constant elasticity form. In particular, $\varepsilon^* = -0.4$. Thus her Slutsky equation is

$$
\begin{array}{ccccc}
\varepsilon & = & \varepsilon^* & - & \theta\xi \\
-1 & \approx & -0.4 & - & 0.6 \times 1.
\end{array}
$$

For a Giffen good to have an upward-sloping demand curve, ε must be positive. The substitution elasticity, ε^*, is always negative: Consumers buy less of a good as its price goes up, holding utility constant. Thus for a good to have an upward-sloping demand curve, the income effect, $-\theta\xi$, must be positive and large relative to the substitution effect. The income effect is more likely to be a large positive number if the good is very inferior (that is, ξ is a large negative number, which is not common) and the budget share, θ, is large (closer to one than to zero). One reason we don't see upward-sloping demand curves is that the goods on which consumers spend a large share of their budget, such as housing, are usually normal goods.

SOLVED PROBLEM 4.4

Next to its plant, a manufacturer of dinner plates has an outlet store that sells plates of both first quality (perfect plates) and second quality (plates with slight blemishes). The outlet store sells a relatively large share of seconds. At its regular stores elsewhere, the firm sells many more first-quality plates than second-quality plates. Why? (Assume that consumers' tastes with respect to plates are the same everywhere and that there is a cost, s, of shipping each plate from the factory to the firm's other stores.)

Answer

1. *Determine how the relative prices of plates differ between the two types of stores:* The slope of the budget line that consumers face at the factory outlet store is $-p_1/p_2$, where p_1 is the price of first-quality plates and p_2 is the price of seconds. It costs the same, s, to ship a first-quality plate as a second because they weigh the same and have to be handled in the same way. At all retail stores, the firm adds the cost of shipping to the price it charges at its factory outlet store, so the price of a first-quality plate is $p_1 + s$ and the price of a second is $p_2 + s$. As a result, the slope of the budget line that consumers face at the retail stores is $-(p_1 + s)/(p_2 + s)$. The seconds are relatively less expensive at the factory outlet than they are at the

---

[10]We can equivalently write the demand curve as $\ln q_1 = \ln(0.6) + \ln Y - \ln p_1$, which is a constant-elasticity demand curve. We can find the price elasticity using the method in Solved Problem 2.2. Similarly, differentiating with respect to Y, we find that $(dq_1/dY)/q_1 = 1/Y$. Rearranging terms, we learn that $\xi = (dq_1/dY)(Y/q_1) = 1$.

other stores. For example, if $p_1 = \$2$, $p_2 = \$1$, and $s = \$1$ per plate, the slope of the budget line is -2 at the outlet store and $-3/2$ elsewhere. Thus the first-quality plate costs twice as much as a second at the outlet store but only 1.5 times as much elsewhere.

2. *Use the relative price difference to explain why relatively more seconds are bought at the factory outlet:* Holding a consumer's income and tastes fixed, if the price of seconds rises relative to that of firsts (as we go from the factory outlet to the other retail shops), most consumers will buy relatively more firsts. The substitution effect is unambiguous: Were they compensated so that their utilities were held constant, consumers would unambiguously substitute firsts for seconds. It is possible that the income effect could go in the other direction (if plates are an inferior good); however, as most consumers spend relatively little of their total budget on plates, the income effect is presumably small relative to the substitution effect. Thus we expect relatively fewer seconds to be bought at the retail stores than at the factory outlet.

APPLICATION

Shipping the Good Stuff Away

According to the economic theory discussed in Solved Problem 4.4, we expect that the relatively larger share of higher-quality goods will be shipped, the greater the per-unit shipping fee. Is this theory true, and is the effect large? To answer these questions, Hummels and Skiba (2004) examined shipments between 6,000 country pairs for more than 5,000 goods. They found that doubling per-unit shipping costs results in a 70% to 143% increase in the average price (excluding the cost of shipping) as a larger share of top-quality products is shipped.

The greater the distance between the trading countries, the higher the cost of shipping. Hummels and Skiba speculate that the relatively high quality of Japanese goods is due to that country's relatively great distance to major importers.

4.4 Cost-of-Living Adjustment

In spite of the cost of living, it's still popular. —Kathleen Norris

By knowing both the substitution and income effects, we can answer questions that we could not answer if we knew only the total effect of a price change. One particularly important use of consumer theory is to analyze how accurately the government measures inflation.

Many long-term contracts and government programs include *cost-of-living adjustments* (*COLAs*), which raise prices or incomes in proportion to an index of inflation. Not only business contracts but also rental contracts, alimony payments, salaries, pensions, and Social Security payments are frequently adjusted in this manner over time. We will use consumer theory to show that the cost-of-living measure that governments commonly use overestimates how the true cost of living changes over time. Because of this overestimation, you overpay your landlord if the rent on your apartment rises with this measure.

INFLATION INDEXES

The prices of most goods rise over time. We call the increase in the overall price level *inflation*.

The actual price of a good is called the *nominal price*. The price adjusted for inflation is the *real price*. Because the overall level of prices rises over time, nominal prices usually increase more rapidly than real prices. For example, the nominal price of a McDonald's hamburger rose from 15¢ in 1955 to 98¢ in 2007, a six-and-a-half fold increase. However, the real price of a burger fell because the prices of other goods rose more rapidly than that of a burger.

How do we adjust for inflation to calculate the real price? Governments measure the cost of a standard bundle of goods to compare prices over time. This measure is called the Consumer Price Index (CPI). Each month, the government reports how much it costs to buy the bundle of goods that an average consumer purchased in a *base* year (with the base year changing every few years).

By comparing the cost of buying this bundle over time, we can determine how much the overall price level has increased. In the United States, the CPI was 26.8 in 1955 and 205.4 in March 2007.[11] The cost of buying the bundle of goods increased 766% ($\approx$ 205.4/26.8) from 1955 to 2005.

We can use the CPI to calculate the real price of a hamburger over time. In terms of 2007 dollars, the real price of a hamburger in 1955 was

$$\frac{\text{CPI for 2007}}{\text{CPI for 1955}} \times \text{price of a burger} = \frac{205.4}{26.8} \times 15¢ = \$1.15.$$

If you could have purchased the hamburger in 1955 with 2007 dollars—which are worth less than 1955 dollars—the hamburger would have cost $1.15. The real price in 2007 dollars (and the nominal price) of a hamburger in 2007 was only 98¢. Thus the real price of a hamburger fell by about 15%. If we compared the real prices in both years using 1955 dollars, we would reach the same conclusion that the real price of hamburgers fell by about 15%.

The government collects data on the quantities and prices of 364 individual goods and services, such as housing, dental services, watch and jewelry repairs, college tuition fees, taxi fares, women's hairpieces and wigs, hearing aids, slipcovers and decorative pillows, bananas, pork sausage, and funeral expenses. These prices rise at different rates. If the government merely reported all these price increases separately, most of us

---

[11]The number 205.4 is not an actual dollar amount. Rather, it is the actual dollar cost of buying the bundle divided by a constant. That constant was chosen so that the average expenditure in the period 1982–1984 was 100.

would find this information overwhelming. It is much more convenient to use a single summary statistic, the CPI, which tells us how prices rose *on average*.

We can use an example with only two goods, clothing and food, to show how the CPI is calculated. In the first year, consumers buy C_1 units of clothing and F_1 units of food at prices p_C^1 and p_F^1. We use this bundle of goods, C_1 and F_1, as our base bundle for comparison. In the second year, consumers buy C_2 and F_2 units at prices p_C^2 and p_F^2.

The government knows from its survey of prices each year that the price of clothing in the second year is p_C^2/p_C^1 times as large as the price the previous year and that the price of food is p_F^2/p_F^1 times as large. If the price of clothing was \$1 in the first year and \$2 in the second year, the price of clothing in the second year would be $\frac{2}{1} = 2$ times, or 100%, larger than in the first year.

One way we can average the price increases of each good is to weight them equally. But do we really want to do that? Do we want to give as much weight to the price increase for skateboards as to the price increase for automobiles? An alternative approach is to give a larger weight to the price change of a good as we spend more of our income on that good, its budget share. The CPI takes this approach to weighting, using budget shares.[12]

The CPI for the first year is the amount of income it takes to buy the market basket actually purchased that year:

$$Y_1 = p_C^1 C_1 + p_F^1 F_1. \tag{4.10}$$

The cost of buying the first year's bundle in the second year is

$$Y_2 = p_C^2 C_1 + p_F^2 F_1. \tag{4.11}$$

To calculate the rate of inflation, we determine how much more income it would take to buy the first year's bundle in the second year, which is the ratio of Equation 4.11 to Equation 4.10:

$$\frac{Y_2}{Y_1} = \frac{p_C^2 C_1 + p_F^2 F_1}{p_C^1 C_1 + p_F^1 F_1}.$$

For example, from March 2006 to March 2007, the U.S. CPI rose by $1.028 \approx Y_2/Y_1$ from $Y_1 = 199.8$ to $Y_2 = 205.4$. Thus it cost 2.8% more in 2007 than in 2006 to buy the same bundle of goods.

The ratio Y_2/Y_1 reflects how much prices rise on average. By multiplying and dividing the first term in the numerator by p_C^1 and multiplying and dividing the second term by p_F^1, we find that this index is equivalent to

$$\frac{Y_2}{Y_1} = \frac{\left(\dfrac{p_C^2}{p_C^1}\right) p_C^1 C_1 + \left(\dfrac{p_F^2}{p_F^1}\right) p_F^1 F_1}{Y_1} = \left(\frac{p_C^2}{p_C^1}\right)\theta_C + \left(\frac{p_F^2}{p_F^1}\right)\theta_F,$$

where $\theta_C = p_C^1 C_1/Y_1$ and $\theta_F = p_F^1 F_1/Y_1$ are the budget shares of clothing and food in the first, or base, year. The CPI is a *weighted average* of the price increase for each good, p_C^2/p_C^1 and p_F^2/p_F^1 where the weights are each good's budget share in the base year, θ_C and θ_F.

---

[12]This discussion of the CPI is simplified in a number of ways. Sophisticated adjustments are made to the CPI that are ignored here, including repeated updating of the base year (chaining). See Pollak (1989) and Diewert and Nakamura (1993).

EFFECTS OF INFLATION ADJUSTMENTS

A CPI adjustment of prices in a long-term contract overcompensates for inflation. We use an example involving an employment contract to illustrate the difference between using the CPI to adjust a long-term contract and using a true cost-of-living adjustment, which holds utility constant.

CPI Adjustment. Klaas signed a long-term contract when he was hired. According to the COLA clause in his contract, his employer increases his salary each year by the same percentage by which the CPI increases. If the CPI this year is 5% higher than the CPI last year, Klaas's salary rises automatically by 5% over last year's.

Klaas spends all his money on clothing and food. His budget constraint in the first year is $Y_1 = p_C^1 C + p_F^1 F$, which we rewrite as

$$C = \frac{Y_1}{p_C^1} - \frac{p_F^1}{p_C^1} F.$$

The intercept of the budget constraint, L^1, on the vertical (clothing) axis in Figure 4.7 is Y_1/p_C^1, and the slope of the constraint is $-p_F^1/p_C^1$. The tangency of his indifference curve I^1 and the budget constraint L^1 determine his equilibrium consumption bundle in the first year, e_1, where he purchases C_1 and F_1.

In the second year, his salary rises with the CPI to Y_2, so his budget constraint in that year, L^2, is

$$C = \frac{Y_2}{p_C^2} - \frac{p_F^2}{p_C^2} F.$$

The new constraint, L^2, has a flatter slope, $-p_F^2/p_C^2$, than L^1 because the price of clothing rose more than the price of food. The new constraint goes through the original equilibrium bundle, e_1, because by increasing his salary according to the CPI, the firm ensures that Klaas can buy the same bundle of goods in the second year that he bought in the first year.

He *can* buy the same bundle, but *does* he? The answer is no. His optimal bundle in the second year is e_2, where indifference curve I^2 is tangent to his new budget constraint, L^2. The movement from e_1 to e_2 is the *total effect* from the changes in the real prices of clothing and food. *This adjustment to his income does not keep him on his original indifference curve, I^1.*

Indeed, Klaas is better off in the second year than in the first. The CPI adjustment *overcompensates* for the change in inflation in the sense that his utility increases.

Klaas is better off because the prices of clothing and food did not increase by the same amount. Suppose that the price of clothing and food had both increased by *exactly* the same amount. After a CPI adjustment, Klaas's budget constraint in the second year, L^2, would be exactly the same as in the first year, L^1, so he would choose exactly the same bundle, e_1, in the second year as he chose in the first year.

Because the price of food rose by less than the price of clothing, L^2 is not the same as L^1. Food became cheaper relative to clothing. So by consuming more food and less clothing, Klaas has a higher utility in the second year.

Had clothing become relatively less expensive, Klaas would have raised his utility in the second year by consuming relatively more clothing. Thus it doesn't matter which good becomes relatively less expensive over time for Klaas to benefit from the CPI compensation, it's necessary only for one of the goods to become a relative bargain.

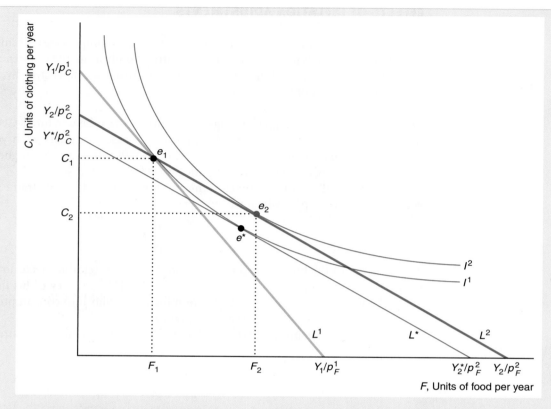

Figure 4.7 CPI Adjustment. In the first year, when Klaas has an income of Y_1, his optimal bundle is e_1, where indifference curve I^1 is tangent to his budget constraint, L^1. In the second year, the price of clothing rises more than the price of food. Because his salary increases in proportion to the CPI, his second-year budget constraint, L^2, goes through e_1, so he can buy the same bundle as in the first year. His new optimal bundle, however, is e_2, where I^2 is tangent to L^2. The CPI adjustment overcompensates Klaas for the increase in prices: He is better off in the second year because his utility is greater on I^2 than on I^1. With a smaller true cost-of-living adjustment, Klaas's budget constraint, L^*, is tangent to I^1 at e^*.

True Cost-of-Living Adjustment. We now know that a CPI adjustment overcompensates for inflation. What we want is a *true cost-of-living index:* an inflation index that holds utility constant over time.

How big an increase in Klaas's salary would leave him exactly as well off in the second year as he was in the first? We can answer this question by applying the same technique we used to identify the substitution and income effects. Suppose that his utility function is $U = 20\sqrt{CF}$, where C is his units of clothing and F is his units of food. We draw an imaginary budget line, L^* in Figure 4.7, that is tangent to I^1 so that Klaas's utility remains constant, but that has the same slope as L^2. The income, Y^*, corresponding to that imaginary budget constraint is the amount that leaves Klaas's utility constant. Had Klaas received Y^* instead of Y_2 in the second year, he would have chosen Bundle e^* instead of e_2. Because e^* is on the same indifference curve, I^1, as e_1, Klaas's utility would be the same in both years.

TABLE 4.1   Cost-of-Living Adjustments

	p_C	p_F	Income, Y	Clothing	Food	Utility, U
First year	$1	$4	$400	200	50	2,000
Second year	$2	$5				
No adjustment			$400	100	40	1,265
CPI adjustment			$650	162.5	65	2,055
True COLA			$632.50	158.1	63.2	2,000

The numerical example in Table 4.1 illustrates how the CPI overcompensates Klaas. Suppose that p_C^1 is $1, p_C^2 is $2, p_F^1 is $4, and p_F^2 is $5. In the first year, Klaas spends his income, Y_1, of $400 on $C_1 = 200$ units of clothing and $F_1 = 50$ units of food and has a utility of 2,000, which is the level of utility on I^1. If his income did not increase in the second year, he would substitute toward the relatively inexpensive food, cutting his consumption of clothing in half but reducing his consumption of food by only a fifth. His utility would fall to 1,265.

If his second-year income increases in proportion to the CPI, he can buy the same bundle, e_1, in the second year as in the first. His second-year income is $Y_2 = $650 $(= p_C^2 C_1 + p_F^2 F_1 = $2 \times 200 + $5 \times 50)$. Klaas is better off if his budget increases to Y_2. He substitutes toward the relatively inexpensive food, buying less clothing than in the first year but buying more food, e_2. His utility rises from 2,000 to approximately 2,055 (the level of utility on I^2).

How much would his income have to rise to leave him only as well off as he was in the first year? If his second-year income is $Y^* \approx 632.50, by appropriate substitution toward food, e^*, he can achieve the same level of utility, 2,000, as in the first year.

We can use the income that just compensates Klaas, Y^*, to construct a true cost-of-living index. In our numerical example, the true cost-of-living index rose 58.1% $[\approx (632.50 - 400)/400]$, while the CPI rose 62.5% $[= (650 - 400)/400]$.

SOLVED PROBLEM   4.5

Alexx doesn't care about where he lives, but he does care about what he eats. Alexx spends all his money on restaurant meals at either American or French restaurants. His firm offers to transfer him from its Miami office to its Paris office, where he will face different prices. The firm will pay him a salary in euros such that he can buy the same bundle of goods in Paris that he is currently buying in Miami.[13] Will Alexx benefit by moving to Paris?

Answer

1. *Show Alexx's optimum bundle in the United States:* Alexx's optimal bundle, *a*, in the United States is determined by the tangency of his indifference curve I^1 and his American budget constraint L^A in the graph.

---

[13]According to Organization Resource Counselors, Inc., 79% of international firms surveyed report that they provide their workers with enough income abroad to maintain their home lifestyle.

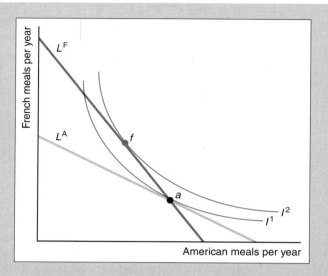

2. *Discuss what happens if prices are higher in France but the relative prices between American and French meals are the same:* If the prices of both French and American meals are *x* times higher in France than in the United States, the relative costs of French and American meals are the same. If the firm raises Alexx's income *x* times, his budget line does not change. Thus if relative prices are the same in Miami and Paris, his budget line and optimal bundle are unchanged, so his level of utility is unchanged.

3. *Show the new optimum if relative prices in France differ from those in the United States:* Alexx's firm adjusts his income so that he can buy the same bundle, *a*, as he bought in the United States, so his new budget line in France, L^F, must go through *a*. Suppose that French meals are relatively less expensive than American meals in Paris. If Alexx spends all his money on French meals, he can buy more in Paris than he could in the United States, and if he spends all his money on American meals, he can buy fewer in Paris than he could in the United States. As a result, L^F hits the vertical axis at a higher point than the L^A line and cuts the L^A line at Bundle *a*. Alexx's new optimal bundle, *f*, is determined by the tangency of I^2 and L^F. Thus if relative prices are different in Paris and Miami, Alexx is better off with the transfer. He was on I^1 and is now on I^2. Alexx could buy his original bundle, *a*, but chooses to substitute toward French meals, which are relatively inexpensive in France, thereby raising his utility.[14]

Comment: The overadjustment here is analogous to the upward bias in the CPI's COLA.

---

[14]A similar issue arises in making cross-country comparisons of income or wealth. See **www.aw-bc .com/perloff,** Chapter 4, "Wealth of Developing Countries."

Size of the CPI Substitution Bias. We have just demonstrated that the CPI has an *upward bias* in the sense that an individual's utility rises if we increase that person's income by the same percentage by which the CPI rises. If we make the CPI adjustment, we are implicitly assuming—incorrectly—that consumers do not substitute toward relatively inexpensive goods when prices change but keep buying the same bundle of goods over time. We call this overcompensation a *substitution bias.*[15]

The CPI calculates the increase in prices as Y_2/Y_1. We can rewrite this expression as

$$\frac{Y_2}{Y_1} = \frac{Y^*}{Y_1}\frac{Y_2}{Y^*}.$$

The first term to the right of the equal sign, Y^*/Y_1, is the increase in the true cost of living. The second term, Y_2/Y^*, reflects the substitution bias in the CPI. It is greater than one because $Y_2 > Y^*$. In the example in Table 4.1, $Y_2/Y^* = 650/632.50 \approx 1.028$, so the CPI overestimates the increase in the cost of living by about 2.8%.

There is no substitution bias if all prices increase at the same rate so that relative prices remain constant. The faster some prices rise relative to others, the more pronounced is the upward bias caused by substitution to now less expensive goods.

● APPLICATION

Fixing the CPI Substitution Bias

Several studies estimate that, due to the substitution bias, the CPI inflation rate is about half a percentage point too high per year. What can be done to correct this bias? One approach is to estimate utility functions for individuals and use those data to calculate a true cost-of-living index. However, given the wide variety of tastes across individuals, as well as various technical estimation problems, this approach is not practical.

A second method is to use a *Paasche* index, which weights prices using the current quantities of goods purchased. In contrast, the CPI (which is also called a *Laspeyres* index) uses quantities from the earlier, base period. A Paasche index is likely to overstate the degree of substitution and thus to understate the change in the cost-of-living index. Hence replacing the traditional Laspeyres index with the Paasche would merely replace an overestimate with an underestimate of the rate of inflation.

A third, compromise approach is to take an average of the Laspeyres and Paasche indexes because the true cost-of-living index lies between these two biased indexes. The most widely touted average is the *Fisher* index, which is the geometric mean of the Laspeyres and Paasche indexes (the square root of their product). If we use the Fisher index, we are implicitly assuming that there is a unitary elasticity of substitution among goods so that the share of consumer expenditures on each item remains constant as relative prices change (in contrast to the Laspeyres approach, where we assume that the quantities remain fixed).

Not everyone agrees that averaging the Laspeyres and Paasche indexes would be an improvement. For example, if people do not substitute, the CPI (Laspeyres)

---

[15]The CPI has other biases as well. For example, see **www.aw-bc.com/perloff**, Chapter 4, "Quality Improvements, New Products, and the CPI."

index is correct and the Fisher index, based on the geometric average, underestimates the rate of inflation.

Nonetheless, in recent years, the Bureau of Labor Statistics (BLS), which calculates the CPI, has made several adjustments to its CPI methodology, including using this averaging approach. Starting in 1999, the BLS replaced the Laspeyres index with a Fisher approach to calculate almost all of its 200 basic indexes (such as "ice cream and related products") within the CPI. It still uses the Laspeyres approach for a few of the categories where it does not expect much substitution, such as utilities (electricity, gas, cable television, and telephones), medical care, and housing, and it uses the Laspeyres method to combine the basic indexes to obtain the final CPI.

Now the BLS updates the CPI weights (the market basket shares of consumption) every two years instead of only every decade or so as the Bureau had done before 2002. More frequent updating reduces the substitution bias in a Laspeyres index because market basket shares are frozen for a shorter period of time. According to the BLS, had it used updated weights between 1989 and 1997, the CPI would have increased by only 31.9% rather than the reported 33.9%. Thus the BLS predicts that this change will reduce the rate of increase in the CPI by approximately 0.2 percentage points per year.

Overestimating the rate of inflation has important implications for U.S. society because Social Security, various retirement plans, welfare, and many other programs include CPI-based cost-of-living adjustments. According to one estimate, the bias in the CPI alone makes it the fourth-largest "federal program" after Social Security, health care, and defense. For example, the U.S. Postal Service (USPS) has a CPI-based COLA in its union contracts. In 2007, a typical employee earned about $43,000 a year, including benefits. A substitution bias of half a percent a year costs the USPS nearly $215 per employee. Because the USPS has about 804,750 employees, the bias costs the USPS over $173 million per year—and benefits its employees by the same amount.

4.5 Revealed Preferences

We have seen that we can infer a consumer's behavior from that person's preferences. We can also do the opposite: We can infer a consumer's preferences if we know the consumer's behavior. If we observe a consumer's choice at many different prices and income levels, we can derive the consumer's indifference curves using the *theory of revealed preferences* (Samuelson, 1947). We can also use this theory to demonstrate the substitution effect. Economists can use this approach to estimate demand curves merely by observing choices consumers make over time.

RECOVERING PREFERENCES

The basic assumption of the theory of revealed preference is that a consumer chooses bundles to maximize utility subject to a budget constraint: The consumer chooses the best bundle that the consumer can afford. We also assume that the consumer's indifference curve is convex to the origin so that the consumer picks a unique bundle on any budget constraint.

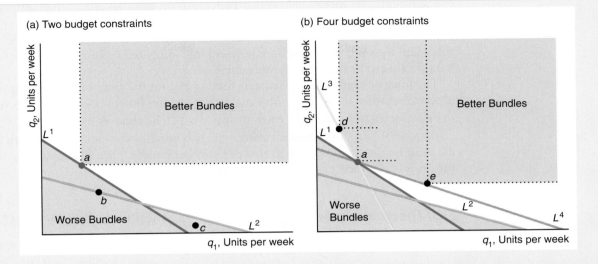

Figure 4.8 Revealed Preference. (a) Linda chooses Bundle *a* on budget constraint L^1, so she prefers it to *b*, which costs less. On L^2, she chooses *b*, so she prefers it to *c*, which costs less. Thus, by transitivity, Linda prefers *a* to *c* or any other of the *worse bundles*. By the more-is-better property, she prefers the bundles in the shaded area above and to the right of *a*. (b) With more budget lines and choices, we learn more about the *better bundles*. Linda's indifference curve through *a* must lie in the white area between the worse and better bundles.

If such a consumer chooses a more expensive bundle of goods, *a*, over a less expensive bundle, *b*, then we say that the consumer *prefers* Bundle *a* to *b*. In panel a of Figure 4.8, when Linda's budget constraint is L^1, she chooses Bundle *a*, showing that she prefers *a* to *b*, which costs less than *a* because it lies strictly within the opportunity set.

If the consumer prefers Bundle *a* to *b* and Bundle *b* to *c*, then a rational consumer must prefer Bundle *a* to *c* because the consumer's preferences are transitive. In panel a, Linda chooses Bundle *a* over *b* when the budget line is L^1, and she picks Bundle *b* over *c* when the constraint is L^2; so, by transitivity, Linda prefers *a* to *c*. We say that Bundle *a* is *revealed to be preferred* to Bundle *c* if Linda chooses *a* over *c* directly or if we learn indirectly that Linda prefers *a* to *b* and *b* to *c*. We know that Linda prefers *a* to any other bundle in the shaded area, labeled "Worse bundles," by a sequence of direct or indirect comparisons. By the more-is-better property (Chapter 3), Linda prefers bundles in the area above and to the right of *a*. Thus the indifference curve through *a* must lie within the white area between the worse and better bundles.

If we learn that Linda chooses *d* when faced with budget line L^3 and *e* given L^4 as panel b shows, we can expand her *better bundle* area. We know that her indifference curve through *a* must lie in the white area between the better and worse bundle areas. Thus if we observe a large number of choices, we can determine the shape of her indifference curves, which summarizes her preferences.

SUBSTITUTION EFFECT

One of the clearest and most important results from consumer theory is that the substitution effect is negative: The Law of Demand holds for compensated demand curves. This result stems from utility maximization, given that indifference curves are convex to the origin. The theory of revealed preference provides an alternative justification without appealing to unobservable indifference curves or utility functions.

Suppose that Steven is indifferent between Bundle a, which consists of M_a electronic songs and C_a candy bars, and Bundle b, with M_b songs and C_b candy bars. That is, the bundles are on the same indifference curve.

The price of candy bars, C, remains fixed at p_C, but the price of songs changes. We observe that when the price for M is p_M^a, Steven chooses Bundle a—that is, a is revealed to be preferred to b. Similarly, when the price is p_M^b, he chooses b over a.

Because Steven is indifferent between the two bundles, the cost of the chosen bundle must be less than or equal to that of the other bundle. Thus if he chooses a when the price is p_M^a, then $p_M^a M_a + p_C C_a \le p_M^a M_b + p_C C_b$, or

$$p_M^a(M_a - M_b) + p_C(C_a - C_b) \le 0. \tag{4.12}$$

And, if he chooses b when the price is p_M^b, then $p_M^b M_b + p_C C_b \le p_M^b M_a + p_C C_a$, or

$$p_M^b(M_b - M_a) + p_C(C_b - C_a) \le 0. \tag{4.13}$$

Adding Equations (4.12) and (4.13) together, we learn that

$$\left(p_M^a - p_M^b\right)(M_a - M_b) \le 0. \tag{4.14}$$

Equation 4.14 shows that the product of the difference in prices times the difference in quantities of music purchased is nonpositive. That result can be true only if the price and the quantity move in opposite directions: When the price rises, the quantity falls. Thus we were able to derive the substitution effect result without using utility functions or making any assumption about the curvature of indifference curves.

Summary

1. **Deriving Demand Curves:** Individual demand curves can be derived by using the information about tastes contained in a consumer's indifference curve map. Varying the price of one good, holding other prices and income constant, we find how the quantity demanded varies with that price, which is the information we need to draw the demand curve. Consumers' tastes, which are captured by the indifference curves, determine the shape of the demand curve.

2. **Effects of an Increase in Income:** The entire demand curve shifts as a consumer's income rises. By varying income as we hold prices constant, we show how quantity demanded shifts with income. An Engel curve summarizes the relationship between income and quantity demanded, holding prices constant.

3. **Effects of a Price Increase:** An increase in the price of a good causes both a substitution effect and an income effect. The substitution effect is the amount by which a consumer's demand for the good changes as a result of a price increase when we compensate the consumer for the price increase by raising the individual's income by just enough that his or her utility does not change. The substitution effect is unambiguous: A compensated rise in a good's price always causes consumers to buy less of that good. The income effect shows how a consumer's demand for a good changes as the consumer's income falls. The price rise lowers the consumer's opportunities because the consumer can now buy less than before with the same income. The income effect can be positive or negative. If a good is normal (income elasticity is positive), the income effect is negative.

4. **Cost-of-Living Adjustment:** The government's major index of inflation, the Consumer Price Index, overestimates inflation by ignoring the substitution effect. Though on average small, the substitution bias may be substantial for particular individuals and firms.

5. **Revealed Preference:** If we observe a consumer's choice at various prices and income levels, we can infer the consumer's preferences: the shape of the consumer's indifference curves. We can also use the theory of revealed preference to show that a consumer substitutes away from a good as its price rises.

Questions

*1. Don spends his money on food and on operas. Food is an inferior good for Don. Does he view an opera performance as an inferior or a normal good? Why? In a diagram, show a possible income-consumption curve for Don.

2. Under what conditions does the income effect reinforce the substitution effect? Under what conditions does it have an offsetting effect? If the income effect more than offsets the substitution effect for a good, what do we call that good?

3. Michelle spends all her money on food and clothing. When the price of clothing decreases, she buys more clothing.
   a. Does the substitution effect cause her to buy more or less clothing? Explain. (If the direction of the effect is ambiguous, say so.)
   b. Does the income effect cause her to buy more or less clothing? Explain. (If the direction of the effect is ambiguous, say so.)

*4. Alix consumes only coffee and coffee cake and consumes them only together (they are perfect complements). If we calculate a CPI using only these two goods, by how much will this CPI differ from the true cost-of-living index?

5. Are relatively more high-quality navel oranges sold in California or in New York? Why?

*6. Draw a figure to illustrate the verbal answer given in Solved Problem 4.4. Use math and a figure to show how adding an *ad valorem* tax changes the analysis. (See the application "Shipping the Good Stuff Away.")

7. During his first year at school, Ximing buys eight new college textbooks at a cost of $50 each. Used books cost $30 each. When the bookstore announces a 20% price increase in new texts and a 10% increase in used texts for the next year, Ximing's father offers him $80 extra. Is Ximing better off, the same, or worse off after the price change? Why?

8. Jean views coffee and cream as perfect complements. In the first year, Jean picks an optimal bundle of coffee and cream, e_1. In the second year, inflation occurs, the prices of coffee and cream change by different amounts, and Jean receives a cost-of-living adjustment (COLA) based on the consumer price index (CPI) for these two goods. After the price changes and she receives the COLA, her new optimal bundle is e_2. Show the two equilibria in a figure. Is she better off, worse off, or equally well off at e_2 compared to e_1? Explain why.

9. Ann's only income is her annual college scholarship, which she spends exclusively on gallons of ice cream and books.

Last year when ice cream cost $10 and used books cost $20, Ann spent her $250 scholarship on 5 gallons of ice cream and 10 books. This year, the price of ice cream rose to $15 and the price of books increased to $25. So that Ann can afford the same bundle of ice cream and books that she bought last year, her college raised her scholarship to $325. Ann has the usual-shaped indifference curves. Will Ann change the amount of ice cream and books that she buys this year? If so, explain how and why. Will Ann be better off, as well off, or worse off this year than last year? Why?

10. The *Economist* magazine publishes the Big Mac Index for various countries, based on the price of a Big Mac hamburger at McDonald's over time. Under what circumstances would people find this index to be as useful as or more useful than the consumer price index in measuring how their true cost of living changes over time?

11. Illustrate that the Paasche cost-of-living index (see the application "Fixing the CPI Substitution Bias") underestimates the rate of inflation when compared to the true cost-of-living index.

12. In Spenser's state, a sales tax of 10% is applied to clothing but not to food. Using indifference curves, show the effect of this tax on Spenser's choice between food and clothing.

13. Minnesota customers of Earthlink, Inc., a high-speed Internet service provider, who get broadband access from a cable modem pay no tax, but Earthlink customers who use telephone digital subscriber lines pay $3.10 a month in state and local taxes and other surcharges (Matt Richtel, "Cable or Phone? Difference Can Be Taxing," *New York Times*, April 5, 2004, C1, C6). Suppose that, were it not for the tax, Earthlink would set its prices for the two services so that Sven would be indifferent between using cable or phone service. Describe his indifference curves. Given the tax, Earthlink raises its price for the phone service but not its cable service. Use a figure to show how Sven chooses between the two services.

14. Ralph usually buys one pizza and two colas from the local pizzeria. The pizzeria announces a special: All pizzas after the first one are half-price. Show the original and the new budget constraints. What can you say about the bundle Ralph will choose when faced with the new constraint?

15. The local swimming pool charges nonmembers $10 per visit. If you join the pool, you can swim for $5 per visit, but you have to pay an annual fee of F. Use an indifference curve diagram to find the value of F such that you are indifferent between joining and not joining. Suppose that the pool charged you exactly F. Would you go to the pool more or fewer times than if you did not join? For simplicity, assume that the price of all other goods is $1.

16. In Solved Problem 4.5, suppose that French meals are relatively more expensive than American meals in Paris, so the L^F budget line cuts the L^A budget line from below rather than from above as in the solved problem's figure. Show that the conclusion that Alexx is better off after his move still holds. Explain the logic behind the following statement: "The analysis holds as long as the relative prices differ in the two cities. Whether both prices, one price, or neither price in Paris is higher than in Miami is irrelevant to the analysis."

17. Guerdon eats eggs and toast for breakfast and insists on having three pieces of toast for every two eggs he eats. Derive his utility function. If the price of eggs increases but we compensate Guerdon to make him just as "happy" as he was before the price change, what happens to his consumption of eggs? Draw a graph and explain your diagram. Does the change in his consumption reflect a substitution or an income effect?

Problems

18. Because people dislike commuting to work, homes closer to employment centers tend to be more expensive. The price of a home in a given employment center is $60 per day. The daily rental price for housing drops by $2.50 per mile for each mile a house is farther from the employment center. The price of gasoline per mile of the commute is p_g (which is less than $2.50). Thus the net cost of traveling an extra mile to work is $p_g - 2.5$. Lan chooses the distance she lives from the job center, D (where D is at most 50 miles), and all other goods. The price of A is $1 per unit. Lan's utility function is $U = (50 - D)^{0.5}A^{0.5}$, and her income is Y, which for technical reasons is between $60 and $110.

   a. Is D an economic bad (the opposite of a good)? To answer this question, find $\partial U/\partial D$.
   b. Draw Lan's budget constraint.
   c. Use the Lagrange method to derive Lan's demands for A and D.
   d. Show that, as the price of gasoline increases, Lan chooses to live closer to the employment center. That is, show that $\partial D^*/\partial p_G < 0$.
   e. Show that, as Lan's income increases, she chooses to live closer to the employment center. Reportedly, increases in gasoline prices hit the poor especially hard because they live father from their jobs, consume more gasoline in commuting, and spend a greater fraction of their income on gasoline (Ball, "For Many Low-Income Workers, High Gasoline Prices Take a Toll," *Wall Street Journal*, July 12, 2004, A1). Demonstrate that as Lan's income decreases, she spends more per day on gasoline. That is, show that $\partial D^*/\partial Y < 0$. **W**

19. Recent research by economists Cutler, Glaeser, and Shapiro (2003) on Americans' increasing obesity points to improved technology in the preparation of tasty and more caloric foods as a possible explanation of weight gain. Before World War II, people rarely prepared french fries at home because of the significant amount of peeling, cutting, and cooking required. Today french fries are prepared in factories using low-cost labor, shipped frozen, and then simply reheated in homes. Paul consumes two goods: potatoes and leisure, N. The number of potatoes Paul consumes does not vary, but their tastiness, T, does. For each extra unit of tastiness, he must spend p_t hours in the kitchen. Thus Paul's time constraint is $N + p_tT = 24$. Paul's utility function is $U = TN^{1/2}$.

   a. What is Paul's marginal rate of substitution, MU_T/MU_N?
   b. What is the marginal rate of transformation, p_T/p_N?
   c. What is Paul's optimal choice (T^*, N^*)?
   d. With a decrease in the price of taste (the ability to produce a given level of tastiness faster), does Paul consume more taste (and hence gain weight) or spend more of his time in leisure? Does a decrease in the price of taste contribute to weight gain? **W**

20. According to the U.S. Consumer Expenditure Survey for 2003, low-income Americans spend 37% of their income on housing. What are the limits on their income elasticity of housing if all other goods are collectively normal? Given that they spend 1.6% on books and other reading material, what are the limits on their income elasticity of housing if all other goods are collectively normal?

*21. Redraw Figure 4.1 using Jackie's utility function for CDs and DVDs: $U = q_1^{0.6}q_2^{0.4}$. Explain the shape of the price-consumption curve.

22. In Solved Problem 4.1, Mahdu is indifferent between Canada Dry and Cragmont ginger ale. Derive his demand curve for Cragmont ginger ale graphically and mathematically.

23. Guerdon always puts bananas on his cereal—the two goods are perfect complements. Derive his demand curve for cereal graphically and mathematically.

*24. Madeline views Coke and Pepsi as perfect substitutes. Derive her demand curve for Coke graphically and mathematically. (*Hints:* See Solved Problem 4.1. The quantity of Coke consumed where the budget line hits the Coke axis is Y/p_c, where p_c = the price of Coke.)

25. Derive and plot Olivia's demand curve for pie if she eats pie only à la mode and does not eat either pie or ice cream alone (she views pie and ice cream as perfect complements).

How much does her weekly budget have to rise for her to buy one more piece of pie per week?

*26. Given Jackie's estimated Cobb-Douglas utility function $U = q_1^{0.6} q_2^{0.4}$ for CDs, q_1, and DVDs, q_2, derive her Engel curve for CDs. Illustrate in a figure.

27. Ryan has a constant elasticity of substitution (CES) utility function $U = q_1^\rho + q_2^\rho$. Derive his Engel curve.

28. Derive Ryan's demand curve for q_1, given his CES utility function $U = q_1^\rho + q_2^\rho$.

29. Rui's utility function is $U = q_1 + q_1 q_2 + q_2$.

   a. What is her expenditure function?
   b. Derive her uncompensated demand curve for q_1.
   c. Derive her compensated demand curve for q_1.

30. Philip's utility function is $U = \ln q_1 + q_2$. Derive his demand curves. Discuss how the demand curves depend on income. (*Hint*: The quantity demanded cannot be completely independent of income: You cannot buy goods if you have no income.)

31. David consumes two things: gasoline (G) and bread (B). David's utility function is $U(G, B) = 10G^{0.25}B^{0.75}$.

   a. Use the Lagrange technique to solve for David's optimal choices of gasoline and bread as a function of the price of gasoline, p_G, the price of bread, p_B, and his income, Y.
   b. With recent increases in the price of gasoline, does David reduce his consumption of gasoline?
   c. For David, how does $\partial G/\partial p_G$ depend on his income? That is, how does David's change in gasoline consumption due to an increase in the price of gasoline depend on his income level? To answer these questions, find the cross-partial derivate, $\partial^2 G/(\partial p_G \partial Y)$. **W**

Chapter 5

Consumer Welfare and Policy Analysis

The welfare of the people is the ultimate law. —Cicero

The U.S. government and many other governments around the world provide child-care subsidies to poor parents so that they can work and better provide for themselves and their children. But does a price subsidy of this kind offer the most benefit to families? Or would a comparable amount of unrestricted cash or direct provision of child-care services benefit poor families more?

To answer these types of questions, we will first use consumer theory to develop various measures of consumer welfare. We will then examine how several types of government policies affect consumer well-being. Finally, we will use consumer theory to study individuals' labor supply and analyze the impact of income taxes.

In this chapter, we examine five main topics

1. **Consumer Welfare:** The degree to which a consumer is helped or harmed by a change in the equilibrium price can be measured by using information from a consumer's demand curve or utility function.

2. **Expenditure Function and Consumer Welfare:** We can use the expenditure function to calculate how much more money we would have to give a consumer to offset the harm from a price increase.

3. **Market Consumer Surplus:** The market consumer surplus—the sum of the welfare effect across all consumers—can be measured using the market demand curve.

4. **Effects of Government Policies on Consumer Welfare:** We use our consumer welfare measures to determine the degree to which consumers are helped or harmed by quotas, food stamps, and child-care subsidies.

5. **Deriving Labor Supply Curves:** We derive a worker's labor supply curve using the worker's demand curve for leisure. We use the labor supply curve to determine how a reduction in the income tax rate affects consumer welfare, labor supply, and tax revenues.

5.1 Consumer Welfare

Economists and policymakers want to know how much consumers are helped or harmed by shocks that affect the equilibrium price and quantity. Prices change when new inventions reduce costs or when a government imposes a tax or subsidy. Quantities change when a government sets a quota. To determine how these changes affect consumers, we need a measure of consumers' welfare.

If we knew a consumer's utility function, we could directly answer the question of how an event affects a consumer's welfare. If the price of beef increases, the budget line of someone who eats beef rotates inward, so the consumer is on a lower indifference curve at the new equilibrium. If we knew the levels of utility associated with the original indifference curve and the new indifference curve, we could measure the impact of the tax in terms of the change in the utility level.

However, this approach is not practical for a couple of reasons. First, we rarely, if ever, know individuals' utility functions. Second, even if we had utility measures for various consumers, we would have no obvious way to compare the measures. One person might say that he gets 1,000 utils (units of utility) from the same bundle that another consumer says gives her 872 utils of pleasure. The first person is not necessarily happier—he may just be using a different scale.

As a result, *we measure consumer welfare in terms of dollars.* Instead of asking the rather silly question "How many utils would you lose if your daily commute increased by 15 minutes?" we could ask, "How much would you pay to avoid having your daily commute grow a quarter of an hour longer?" or "How much would it cost you in forgone earnings if your daily commute were 15 minutes longer?" It is more practical to compare dollars rather than utils across people.

In this section, we first examine *consumer surplus,* the most widely used measure of consumer welfare. Consumer surplus is relatively easy to calculate using the uncompensated demand function and is a good but not exact measure of the true value. We then discuss approaches that provide exact values using compensated demand functions and examine how close consumer surplus comes to the exact values.

MEASURING CONSUMER WELFARE

Consumer welfare from a good is the benefit a consumer gets from consuming that good in excess of the cost of the good. How much pleasure do you get from a good above and beyond its price? If you buy a good for exactly what it's worth to you, you are indifferent between making that transaction and not making it. Frequently, however, you buy things that are worth more to you than what they cost. Imagine that you've played tennis in the hot sun and are very thirsty. You can buy a soft drink from a vending machine for 75¢, but you'd be willing to pay much more because you are so thirsty. As a result, you're much better off making this purchase than not.

If we can measure how much more you'd be willing to pay than you actually paid, we'd know how much you gained from this transaction. Luckily for us, the demand curve or (the equivalent) inverse demand curve contains the information we need to make this measurement.[1]

---

[1]We have referred interchangeably to the plotted curve as the *demand curve,* which plots quantity demanded as a function of price, $Q = D(p)$, and as the *inverse demand curve,* which plots price as a function of the quantity demanded, $p = p(Q)$, because they show the same relationship between price and quantity demanded. In this chapter, when we conduct consumer surplus analyses where we discuss the area under the curve, we will distinguish between the two terms. If we are referring to "the area under the curve" that lies between the curve and the quantity axis, we will refer to the *inverse demand curve* (which plots price against the quantity demanded). If we are discussing the *demand curve,* we are talking about the area between the curve and the price axis. If making a distinction is not critical to the discussion, we will generally call it the demand curve.

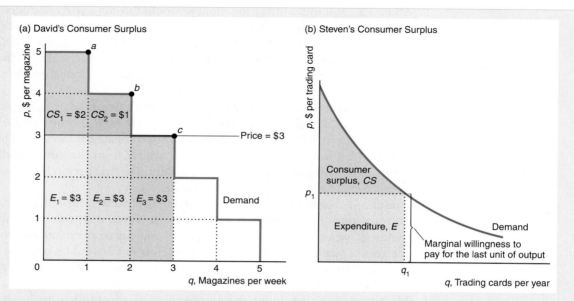

Figure 5.1 Consumer Surplus. (a) David's demand curve for magazines has a steplike shape. When the price is $3, he buys three magazines, point *c*. David's marginal value for the first magazine is $5, areas $CS_1 + E_1$, and his expenditure is $3, area E_1, so his consumer surplus is $CS_1 = \$2$. His consumer surplus is $1 for the second magazine, area CS_2, and is $0 for the third (he is indifferent between buying and not buying it). Thus his total consumer surplus is the blue shaded area $CS_1 + CS_2 + CS_3 = \$3$, and his total expenditure is the tan shaded area $E_1 + E_2 + E_3 = \$9$. (b) Steven's willingness to pay for trading cards is the height of his smooth demand curve. At price p_1, Steven's expenditure is $E\ (= p_1 q_1)$, his consumer surplus is CS, and the total value he places on consuming q_1 trading cards per year is $CS + E$.

Marginal Willingness to Pay. To develop a welfare measure based on the inverse demand curve, we need to know what information is contained in an inverse demand curve. The inverse demand curve reflects a consumer's *marginal willingness to pay*: the maximum amount a consumer will spend for an extra unit. The consumer's marginal willingness to pay is the *marginal value* the consumer places on the last unit of output.

David's inverse demand curve for magazines per week in Figure 5.1 indicates his marginal willingness to buy various numbers of magazines. David places a marginal value of $5 on the first magazine. As a result, if the price of a magazine is $5, David buys one magazine, point *a* on the inverse demand curve. His marginal willingness to buy a second magazine is $4, so if the price falls to $4, he buys two magazines, *b*. His marginal willingness to buy three magazines is $3, so if the price of magazines is $3, he buys three magazines, *c*.

APPLICATION

Willingness to Pay on eBay

People differ in their willingness to pay for a given item. We can determine individuals' willingness to pay for one Homer and Marge Simpson wedding cake topper on the basis of how much they bid in an eBay auction in July 2005. As we show in Chapter 14, an individual's best strategy is to bid his or her *willingness to pay*: the maximum value that the bidder places on the item. From what eBay reports, we know the maximum bid of each person except the winner: eBay uses a *second-price*

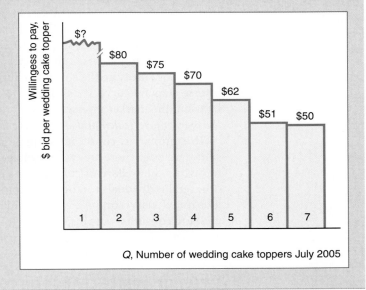

auction, where the winner pays the second-highest amount bid (plus a small increment—in the case of the cake topper, $1). In the figure, bids are arranged from highest to lowest. Because each bar on the graph indicates one cake topper, the figure shows how many units could have been sold to this group of bidders at various prices. That is, it is the market inverse demand curve.

Consumer Surplus. The monetary difference between what a consumer is willing to pay for the quantity of the good purchased and what the good actually costs is called **consumer surplus** (*CS*). Consumer surplus is a dollar-value measure of the extra pleasure the consumer receives from the transaction beyond its price.

David's consumer surplus from each additional magazine is his marginal willingness to pay minus what he pays to obtain the magazine. His marginal willingness to pay for the first magazine, $5, is area $CS_1 + E_1$. If the price is $3, his expenditure to obtain the magazine is area $E_1 = \$3$. Thus his consumer surplus on the first magazine is area $CS_1 = (CS_1 + E_1) - E_1 = \$5 - \$3 = \$2$. Because his marginal willingness to pay for the second magazine is $4, his consumer surplus for the second magazine is the smaller area, $CS_2 = \$1$. His marginal willingness to pay for the third magazine is $3, which equals what he must pay to obtain it, so his consumer surplus is zero, $CS_3 = \$0$. He is indifferent between buying and not buying the third magazine.

At a price of $3, David buys three magazines. His total consumer surplus from the three magazines he buys is the sum of the consumer surplus he gets from each of these magazines: $CS_1 + CS_2 + CS_3 = \$2 + \$1 + \$0 = \$3$. This total consumer surplus of $3 is the extra amount that David is willing to spend for the right to buy three magazines at $3 each. Thus *an individual's consumer surplus is the area under the inverse demand curve and above the market price up to the quantity the consumer buys.*

David is unwilling to buy a fourth magazine unless the price drops to $2 or less. If David's mother gives him a fourth magazine as a gift, the marginal value that David puts on that fourth magazine, $2, is less than what it cost his mother, $3.

We can determine consumer surplus for smooth inverse demand curves in the same way as we did with David's unusual stairlike inverse demand curve. Steven has a smooth demand curve for baseball trading cards, panel b of Figure 5.1. The height of this inverse demand curve measures his willingness to pay for one more card. This willingness varies with the number of cards he buys in a year. The total value he places on obtaining q_1 cards per year is the area under the inverse demand curve up to q_1, the areas *CS* and *E*. Area *E* is his actual expenditure on q_1 cards. Because the price is p_1, his expenditure is p_1q_1. Steven's consumer surplus from consuming q_1 trading cards is the value of consuming those cards, areas *CS* and *E*, minus his actual expenditures *E* to obtain them, or *CS*. Thus his consumer surplus, *CS*, is the area under the inverse demand curve and above the horizontal line at the price p_1 up to the quantity he buys, q_1.

Just as we measure the consumer surplus for an individual by using that individual's inverse demand curve, we measure the consumer surplus of all consumers in a market by using the market inverse demand curve. *Market consumer surplus is the area under the market inverse demand curve above the market price up to the quantity consumers buy.*

To summarize, consumer surplus is a practical and convenient measure of consumer welfare. There are two advantages to using consumer surplus rather than utility to discuss the welfare of consumers. First, the dollar-denominated consumer surplus of several individuals can be easily compared or combined, whereas the utility of various individuals cannot be easily compared or combined. Second, it is relatively easy to measure consumer surplus, whereas it is difficult to get a meaningful measure of utility directly. To calculate consumer surplus, all we have to do is measure the area under an inverse demand curve.

EFFECT OF A PRICE CHANGE ON CONSUMER SURPLUS

If the price of a good rises, purchasers of that good lose consumer surplus. To illustrate this loss, we return to Jackie's estimated Cobb-Douglas utility, $U = q_1^{0.6}q_2^{0.4}$, between music CDs, q_1, and movie DVDs, q_2 (Chapters 3 and 4). At the initial price $p_1 = \$15$, she bought 12 CDs.

Suppose that a government tax or high production costs cause the price of CDs, p_1, to rise from \$15 to \$20. She now buys $q_1 = 180/20 = 9$ CDs. In Figure 5.2, she loses consumer surplus, ΔCS, equal to area $A + B$: the area between \$15 and \$20 on the price axis to the left of her uncompensated demand curve. Due to the price rise, she now buys 12 CDs. For the 12 CDs that she originally bought, she now pays \$5 less than before, area $A = \$45$. In addition, she loses surplus from no longer consuming the last 3 ($= 12 - 9$) CDs, area B.[2]

SOLVED PROBLEM   5.1

> **What is the exact change in Jackie's consumer surplus, $A + B$, in Figure 5.2? How large is area B?**
>
> **Answer**
>
> 1. *State Jackie's uncompensated demand function of CDs given her initial budget:* From Chapters 3 and 4, we know that her demand function for CDs is $q_1 = 0.6Y/p_1 = 180/p_1$.

---

[2]If we replace the curved demand curve with a straight line, we slightly overestimate area *B* as the area is a triangle: $\frac{1}{2} \times 5 \times 3 = 7.5$. We calculate the exact amount in Solved Problem 5.1.

2. *Integrate between $15 and $20 to the left of Jackie's uncompensated demand curve for CDs:* Her lost consumer surplus is

$$\Delta CS = -\int_{15}^{20} \frac{180}{p_1} dp_1 = -180 \ln p_1 \Big|_{15}^{20}$$
$$= -180(\ln 20 - \ln 15) \approx -180 \times 0.2877 \approx -51.79,$$

where we put a minus sign in front of the integrated area because the price increased, causing a loss of consumer surplus.

3. *Determine the size of B residually:* Because $-\Delta CS =$ area $A + B$ and area $A = \$45$ [$= (\$20 - \$15) \times 9$], we know that area B is $\$6.79$ (= $\$51.79 - \$45$).

Comment: A 33% increase in price causes Jackie's consumer surplus to fall by $51.79, which is 29% of the $180 she spends on CDs.

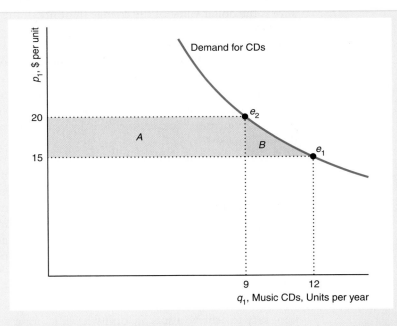

Figure 5.2 Change in Consumer Surplus. As the price increases from 15 to 20, Jackie loses consumer surplus equal to areas $A + B$.

APPLICATION

Bruce Springsteen's Gift to His Fans

In 2002, the $75 that Bruce Springsteen and the E Street Band charged for their concerts was well below the market clearing price. When the tickets went on sale at the Bradley Center in Milwaukee, 9,000 tickets sold in the first 10 minutes and virtually all were gone after 20 minutes.

Some tickets were available from scalpers and ticket brokers and on the Internet at higher prices. One Web site offered tickets for the concert at the American Airlines Center in Dallas for $540 to $1,015. According to a survey, the average price of a resold ticket for the concert at the First Union Center in Philadelphia was $280. Mr. Springsteen said that he set the price relatively low to give value to his fans (in addition, he may have helped to promote his new album). Assuming that he could have sold all the tickets at $280, he gave almost $3 million of consumer surplus to his Philadelphia fans—double the ticket revenue for that concert.

5.2   Expenditure Function and Consumer Welfare

Our desired consumer surplus measure is the income that we would have to give a consumer to offset the harm of an increase in price. That is, it is the extra income we would have to provide so that the consumer's utility did not change. Equivalently, this measure is the dollar value of the change in utility in the absence of compensation.

So far, we have measured the effect of a price increase by a change in consumer surplus using an uncompensated demand curve, which provides an inexact measure. An uncompensated demand curve does not hold a consumer's utility constant as the price changes. Along an uncompensated demand curve, as the price rises, the change in the quantity that the consumer buys reflects both a substitution and an income effect (Chapter 4). Economists frequently use the uncompensated demand curve to calculate consumer surplus because they usually have estimates of only the uncompensated demand curve.

However, if economists have an estimated compensated demand curve, they can calculate the desired pure income effect measure. Indeed, a compensated demand curve is constructed to answer the question of how much less a consumer would purchase in response to a price increase if the consumer is given extra income to offset the price increase so as to hold the consumer's utility constant. That is, along a compensated demand curve, as the price rises, the change in quantity reflects a pure substitution effect. The corresponding amount of income compensation is the measure we seek.

Luckily, we already have a means to calculate the relevant income compensation: the expenditure function, Equation 3.29, which contains the same information as the compensated demand curve.[3] The expenditure function is the minimal expenditure necessary to achieve a specific utility level, $\overline{U}$, for a given set of prices,

$$E = E(p_1, p_2, \overline{U}).   \tag{5.1}$$

Thus we can evaluate the consumer surplus loss of a price increase from p_1 to p_1^* as the difference between the expenditures at these two prices:

$$\text{welfare change} = E(p_1, p_2, \overline{U}) - E(p_1^*, p_2, \overline{U}).   \tag{5.2}$$

In Equation 5.2, an increase in the price causes a drop in welfare.

---

[3]In Chapter 4, we showed that the compensated demand function for q_1 is the partial derivative of the expenditure function with respect to p_1: $q_1 = \partial E(p_1, p_2, \overline{U})/\partial p_1$. Thus if we integrate with respect to price to the left of the compensated demand function, we get the expenditure function.

However, to use this approach, we have to decide which level of utility, $\overline{U}$, to use. We could use the level of utility corresponding to the original indifference curve or the level on the indifference curve of the optimum after the price change. We call the first of these measures the *compensating variation* and the second one the *equivalent variation*.

Compensating variation (CV) is the amount of money one would have to give a consumer to offset completely the harm from a price increase—to keep the consumer on the original indifference curve. This measure of the welfare harm of a price increase is called the compensating variation because we give money to the consumer: We compensate him or her.

Equivalent variation (EV) is the amount of money one would have to take from a consumer to harm the consumer by as much as the price increase. This measure is the same—equivalent—harm as that of the price increase: It moves the consumer to the new indifference curve.

INDIFFERENCE CURVE ANALYSIS

We can use indifference curves to determine CV and EV effects of an increase in price. Again, we use the example based on Jackie's estimated utility function where she chooses between music CDs and movie DVDs. Figure 5.3 is very similar to the ones we've previously used; however, we make one change for graphical convenience. The actual price of a DVD is $20, but we normalize the units so that the price equals a dollar. That is, each dollar buys 1/20th of a DVD. This change is only an accounting convention and doesn't change the actual figure.

The units and price of CDs remain unchanged. Initially, Jackie pays $p_1 = \$15$ for a CD. Her original budget constraint is L^a and has a slope of $-p_1 = -15$. The budget constraint is tangent to indifference curve I at her optimal bundle, a, where she buys 12 CDs.

Now the price of CDs rises to $p_1^* = 20$, so that Jackie's budget line rotates to L^b and has a slope of -20. The new budget line is tangent to indifference curve I^* at her new optimal bundle, b, where she buys 9 CDs. Jackie is worse off because of the price increase: She is on a lower indifference curve I^* (utility level $\overline{U}^*$) instead of on I (utility level $\overline{U}$).

Compensating Variation. The amount of money that would fully compensate Jackie for a price increase is the compensating variation, CV. Suppose that after the price increases to $20, Jackie is given enough extra income, CV, so that her utility remains at $\overline{U}$. At this new income, $Y + CV$, Jackie's budget line is L^{CV}, which has the same slope, -20, as L^a. After the price change and this income compensation, she buys Bundle c.

How large is CV? Because the price of a DVD is now $1 per unit (a twentieth of a DVD), the before-compensation budget line, L^b, hits the DVD axis at $Y = \$300$, and the after-compensation budget line, L^{CV}, hits at $Y + CV$. Thus the gap between the two intercepts is CV.

This analysis is the same one we engaged in to determine the substitution and income effects of a price change. The compensating variation measure is the income (CV) involved in the income effect (the movement from b to c).

Equivalent Variation. The amount of income that, if taken from Jackie, would lower her utility by the same amount as the price increase from $15 to $20 is the equivalent variation, EV. The increase in price harms Jackie by as much as a loss of income equal

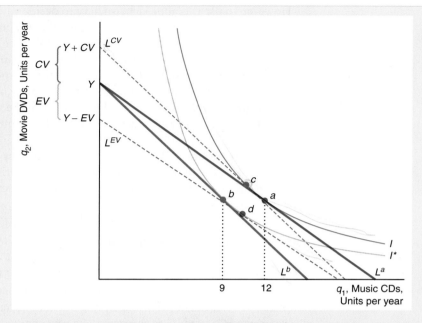

Figure 5.3 Compensating Variation and Equivalent Variation. At the initial price, Jackie's budget constraint, L^a, is tangent to her initial indifference curve I at a, where she buys 12 CDs. After the price of CDs rises, her new budget constraint, L^b, is tangent to her indifference curve I^* at b, where she buys 9 CDs. If we choose units so that the price of DVDs is \$1, L^b hits the vertical axis at Y. If Jackie were given CV extra income to offset the price increase, her budget line would be L^{CV} (which is parallel to L^b), and she would be tangent to her original indifference curve, I, at point c. The budget line L^{CV} hits the vertical axis at $Y + CV$, so the difference between where this budget line and the L^b line strike the vertical axis equals CV. Similarly, at the original price, if we removed income equal to EV, her budget line would shift down to L^{EV}, and Jackie would choose bundle d on I^*. Thus taking EV from her harms her as much as the price increase. The gap between where L^b and L^{EV} touch the vertical axis equals EV.

to EV would if the price remained at \$15. That is, Jackie's income would have to fall by enough to shift the original budget constraint, L^a, down to L^{EV}, where it is tangent to I^* at Bundle d. Because the price of DVDs is \$1, EV is the distance between the intercept of L and that of L^{EV} on the DVD axis. The key distinction between these two measures is that the equivalent variation is calculated by using the new, lower utility level, whereas the compensating variation is based on the original utility level.

● **APPLICATION**

Compensating Variation for Television

How much do you value watching television? Fewer than one in four (23%) Americans say that they would be willing to "give up watching absolutely all types of television" for the rest of their lives in exchange for \$25,000. Almost half (46%) say that they'd refuse to give up TV for anything under \$1 million. One in four Americans wouldn't give it up for \$1 million. Indeed, one-quarter of those who earn under \$20,000 a year wouldn't give up TV for \$1 million—more than they will earn in 50 years.

Thus if you ask how much consumer surplus people receive from television, you will get many implausibly high answers. For this reason, economists typically calculate consumer surplus by using estimated inverse demand curves, which are based on actual observed behavior, or by conducting surveys that ask consumers to choose between relatively similar bundles of goods. A more focused survey of families in Great Britain and Northern Ireland in 2000 found that they were willing to pay £10.40 ($15.60) per month to keep their current, limited television service (BBC1, BB2, ITV, Channel 4, and Channel 5) and that they received £2 ($3) per month of consumer surplus.

COMPARING THE THREE WELFARE MEASURES

Economists usually think of the change in consumer surplus as an approximation to the pure income effect measures: compensating variation and equivalent variation. We now compare in a single graph the three measures of the consumer welfare harm of price increases. Which consumer welfare measure is larger depends on the income elasticity. If the good is normal (as a CD is for Jackie), $|CV| > |\Delta CS| > |EV|$. With an inferior good, $|CV| < |\Delta CS| < |EV|$.

An Example. To illustrate the relative size of the three measures, we return to Jackie's estimated Cobb-Douglas utility, where a government tax causes the price of CDs, p_1, to increase from $15 to $20, so she now buys 9 rather than 12 CDs.

In Figure 5.4, her lost consumer surplus, ΔCS, is areas $A + B$: the area between $15 and $20 on the price axis to the left of her uncompensated demand curve.

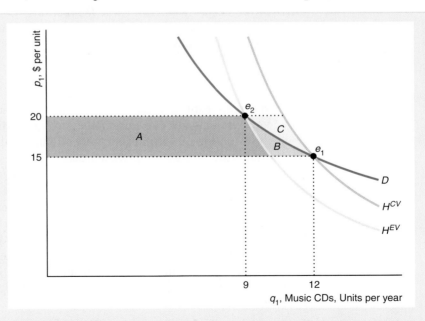

Figure 5.4 Compare *CV, EV,* and ΔCS. When the price rises from $15 to $20, Jackie loses consumer surplus, ΔCS, equal to $A + B$. Using her compensated demand curve at her initial utility level, H^{CV}, an increase of income or compensating variation, CV, equal to area $A + B + C$ would offset the harm from the price increase. Based on her compensated demand curve at the new utility level, H^{EV}, Jackie's loss from the price increase is equal to a loss of income of $EV =$ area A.

Her compensating variation is $A + B + C$, which is the area between $15 and $20 to the left of the compensated demand curve corresponding to the original utility level, H^{CV}. This amount of money is just large enough to offset the harm of the higher price so that Jackie would remain on the initial indifference curve. Finally, her equivalent variation is $A + B + C$, which is the area between $15 and $20 to the left of the compensated demand curve corresponding to the new, lower utility level, H^{EV}. Losing this amount of money would harm Jackie as much as would the price increase.

We can calculate CV and EV as the change in Jackie's expenditure function as the price rises.[4] We hold the price of DVDs constant at $p_2 = \$20$. Substituting this price into Equation 4.7, we know that Jackie's expenditure function is

$$E = \overline{U}\left(\frac{p_1}{0.6}\right)^{0.6}\left(\frac{p_2}{0.4}\right)^{0.4} \approx 1.96\overline{U}p_1^{0.6}p_2^{0.4} \approx 6.50\overline{U}p_1^{0.6}. \tag{5.3}$$

At Jackie's initial optimum where $q_1 = 12$ and $q_2 = 6$, her utility is $\overline{U} = 12^{0.6}6^{0.4} \approx 9.09$. Thus the expenditure function at the original equilibrium is $E \approx 59.08p_1^{0.6}$. At the new equilibrium, the utility level $\overline{U}^* = 9^{0.6}6^{0.4} \approx 7.65$, so the new expenditure function is $E^* \approx 49.72p_1^{0.6}$. Thus

$$CV = E(15) - E(20) = 59.08(15^{0.6} - 20^{0.6}) \approx 59.08 \times (-0.96) \approx -56.52, \tag{5.4}$$

$$EV = E^*(15) - E^*(20) = 49.72(15^{0.6} - 20^{0.6}) \approx 49.72 \times (-0.96) \approx -47.56. \tag{5.5}$$

As Figure 5.4 shows, Jackie's equivalent variation, $EV = -\$47.56$, is a smaller loss than her consumer surplus loss, $\Delta CS = -\$51.79$, which is a smaller loss than her compensating variation, $CV = -\$56.52$.

Little Difference Between the Three Measures. Although the three measures of welfare could in principle differ substantially, for most goods they do not. According to the Slutsky equation (Chapter 4),

$$\varepsilon = \varepsilon^* - \theta\xi,$$

the uncompensated elasticity of demand, ε, equals the compensated elasticity of demand (pure substitution elasticity), ε^*, minus the budget share of the good, θ, times the income elasticity, ξ. The smaller the income elasticity or the smaller the budget share, the closer the substitution elasticity is to the total elasticity, and the closer are the compensated and the uncompensated demand curves. Thus the smaller the income elasticity or budget share, the closer the three welfare measures are to each other.

Because the budget share of most goods is small, these three measures are virtually identical. Even for aggregate goods on which consumers spend a relatively large share of their budget, these differences tend to be small. Table 5.1 gives estimates of these three measures for various goods based on an estimated system of U.S. demand curves. For each good, the table shows the income elasticity, the budget share, the ratio of compensating variation to the change in consumer surplus, $CV/\Delta CS$, and the ratio of the equivalent variation to the change in consumer surplus, $EV/\Delta CS$, for a 50% increase in price.

---

[4]Alternatively, we can integrate to the left of the relevant compensated demand curve, as we did with the uncompensated demand curve to get our consumer surplus measure. These two methods are identical.

TABLE 5.1   Welfare Measures

	Income Elasticity, ξ	Budget Share	$\frac{EV}{\Delta CS}$	$\frac{CV}{\Delta CS}$
Alcohol & tobacco	0.39	4	99%	100.4%
Food	0.46	17	97	103
Clothing	0.88	8	97	102
Utilities	1.00	4	98	101
Transportation	1.04	8	97	103
Medical	1.37	9	95	104
Housing	1.38	15	93	107

Source: Calculations based on Blanciforti (1982).

The three welfare measures for alcohol and tobacco, which have the smallest income elasticity and budget share, are virtually identical. Because housing has the largest income elasticity and budget share, it has a relatively large gap between the measures. However, even for housing, the difference between the change in uncompensated consumer surplus and either of the compensating consumer surplus measures is only 7%.

Willig (1976) showed theoretically that the three measures vary little for small price changes regardless of the size of the income effect. Indeed, for the seven goods in the table, if the price change were only 10%—instead of the 50% in the table—the differences between *CV* or *EV* and ΔCS are a small fraction of a percentage point for all goods except housing, where the difference is only about 1%.

Thus the three measures of welfare give very similar answers even for aggregate goods. As a result, economists frequently use the change in consumer surplus, which is relatively easy to calculate because it is based on the uncompensated demand curve.

5.3   Market Consumer Surplus

A change in total consumer surplus captures the effects of a shock on all consumers in a market. Because the market demand curve is the (horizontal) sum of the individual demand curves, the market consumer surplus is the sum of each individual's consumer surplus, as we illustrated in the application "Willingness to Pay on eBay."

We first measure the effect of a price increase on market consumer surplus using an estimated market demand curve for sweetheart and hybrid tea roses sold in the United States.[5] We then discuss which markets are likely to have the greatest loss of consumer surplus due to a price increase.

LOSS OF MARKET CONSUMER SURPLUS FROM A HIGHER PRICE

Suppose that a new tax causes the (wholesale) price of roses to rise from the original equilibrium price of 30¢ to 32¢ per rose stem, a shift along the market inverse demand

[5] I estimated this model using data from the *Statistical Abstract of United States*, *Floriculture Crops*, *Floriculture and Environmental Horticulture Products* and **usda.mannlib.cornell.edu/data-sets/crops/95917/sb917.txt**. The prices are in real 1991 dollars.

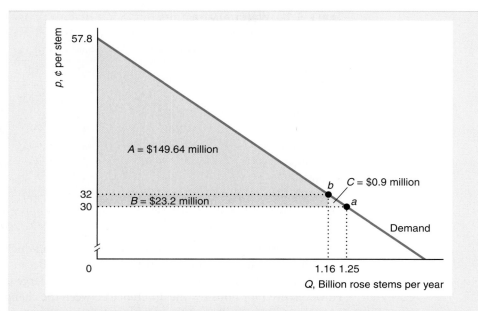

Figure 5.5 Fall in Market Consumer Surplus as the Price of Roses Rises. As the price of roses rises 2¢ per stem from 30¢ per stem, the quantity demanded decreases from 1.25 to 1.16 billion stems per year. The loss in consumer surplus from the higher price, areas *B* and *C*, is $24.1 million per year.

curve in Figure 5.5. The consumer surplus is area $A + B + C = \$173.74$ million per year at a price of 30¢, and it is only area $A = \$149.64$ million at a price of 32¢.[6] Thus the loss in consumer surplus from the increase in the price is $B + C = \$24.1$ million per year.

MARKETS IN WHICH CONSUMER SURPLUS LOSSES ARE LARGE

In general, as the price increases, consumer surplus falls more (1) the greater the initial revenues spent on the good and (2) the less elastic the demand curve.[7] More is

---

[6]The height of triangle *A* is 25.8¢ = 57.8¢ − 32¢ per stem and the base is 1.16 billion stems per year, so its area is $\frac{1}{2} \times \$0.258 \times 1.16$ billion = $149.64 million per year. The area of rectangle *B* is $\$0.02 \times 1.16$ billion = $23.2 million. The area of triangle *C* is $\frac{1}{2} \times \$0.02 \times 0.09$ billion = $0.9 million.

[7]If the demand curve is linear, as in Figure 5.5, the lost consumer surplus, area $B + C$, equals the sum of the area of a rectangle, $Q\Delta p$, with length Q and height Δp, plus the area of a triangle, $\frac{1}{2}\Delta Q\Delta p$, of length ΔQ and height Δp. For small changes in price, we can approximate any demand curve with a straight line, so $\Delta CS = Q\Delta p + \frac{1}{2}\Delta Q\Delta p$ is a reasonable approximation to the true change in consumer surplus (a rectangle plus a triangle). We can rewrite this expression for ΔCS as

$$\Delta p\left(Q + \frac{1}{2}\Delta Q\right) = Q\Delta p\left[1 + \frac{1}{2}\left(\frac{\Delta Q}{Q}\frac{p}{\Delta p}\right)\frac{\Delta p}{p}\right]$$

$$= (pQ)\frac{\Delta p}{p}\left(1 + \frac{1}{2}\varepsilon\frac{\Delta p}{p}\right)$$

$$= Rx\left(1 + \frac{1}{2}\varepsilon x\right),$$

where $x = \Delta p/p$ is the percentage increase in the price, $R (= pQ)$ is the total revenue from the sale of good Q, and ε is the elasticity of demand. This equation is used to calculate the last column in Table 5.2.

TABLE 5.2   Effect of a 10% Increase in Price on Consumer Surplus (Revenue and Consumer Surplus in Billions of 2004 Dollars)

	Revenue	Elasticity of Demand, ε	Change in Consumer Surplus, ΔCS
Medical	1,392	−0.604	−135
Housing	1,239	−0.633	−120
Food	604	−0.245	−60
Clothing	327	−0.405	−32
Transportation	302	−0.461	−29
Utilities	178	−0.448	−17
Alcohol and tobacco	176	−0.162	−17

Sources: Revenues are from National Income and Product Accounts (NIPA), **www.econstats.com/nipa/ NIPA2u_2_4_5U_.htm;** elasticities are based on Blanciforti (1982).

spent on a good when its demand curve is farther to the right so that areas like *A*, *B*, and *C* in Figure 5.5 are larger. The larger *B* + *C* is, the greater is the drop in consumer surplus from a given percentage increase in price. Similarly, the less elastic a demand curve is (the closer it is to vertical), the less willing consumers are to give up the good, so consumers do not cut their consumption much as the price increases, and hence they suffer a greater consumer surplus loss.

Higher prices cause greater consumer surplus loss in some markets than in others. Consumers would benefit if policymakers, before imposing a tax, considered in which market the tax would be likely to harm consumers the most.

We can use estimates of demand curves to predict for which good a price increase causes the greatest loss of consumer surplus. Table 5.2 shows the consumer surplus loss in billions of 2004 dollars from a 10% increase in the price of various goods. The table shows that the larger the loss in consumer surplus, the larger the initial revenue (price times quantity) that is spent on a good. A 10% increase in price causes a much greater loss of consumer surplus if the increase is imposed on medical services, $135 billion, than if the increase is imposed on alcohol and tobacco, $17 billion, because much more is spent on medical services.

At first glance, the relationship between elasticities of demand and the loss in consumer surplus in Table 5.2 looks backward: A given percent change in prices has a larger effect on consumer surplus for the relatively elastic demand curves. However, this relationship is coincidental: The large-revenue goods happen to have relatively elastic demand curves. The effect of a price change depends on both revenue and the demand elasticity. In this table, the relative size of the revenues is more important than the relative elasticities.

If we could hold revenue constant and vary the elasticity, we would find that consumer surplus loss from a price increase is larger as the demand curve becomes less elastic. If the demand curve for alcohol and tobacco were 10 times more elastic, −1.62, while the revenue stayed the same—that is, the demand curve became flatter at the initial price and quantity—the consumer surplus loss would be nearly $1 million less.

SOLVED PROBLEM   **5.2**

Suppose that two linear demand curves go through the initial equilibrium, e_1. One demand curve is less elastic than the other at e_1. For which demand curve will a price increase cause the larger consumer surplus loss?

Answer

1. *Draw the two demand curves, and indicate which one is less elastic at the initial equilibrium:* Two demand curves cross at e_1 in the diagram. The steeper demand curve is less elastic at e_1.[8]

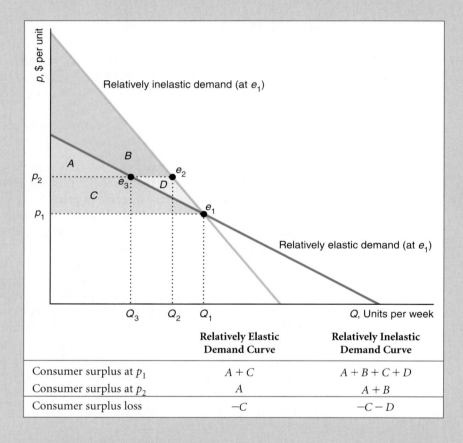

	Relatively Elastic Demand Curve	Relatively Inelastic Demand Curve
Consumer surplus at p_1	$A + C$	$A + B + C + D$
Consumer surplus at p_2	A	$A + B$
Consumer surplus loss	$-C$	$-C - D$

2. *Illustrate that a price increase causes a larger consumer surplus loss with the less elastic demand curve:* If the price rises from p_1 to p_2, the consumer surplus falls by only $-C$ with the relatively elastic demand curve and by $-C - D$ with the relatively inelastic demand curve.

---

[8]As we discussed in Chapter 2, the price elasticity of demand, $\varepsilon = (dQ/dp)(p/Q)$, equals 1 over the slope of the demand curve, dp/dQ, times the ratio of the price to the quantity. At the point of intersection, where both demand curves have the same price, p_1, and the same quantity, Q_1, the steeper the demand curve, the lower the elasticity of demand.

5.4 Effects of Government Policies on Consumer Welfare

The various consumer welfare measures are used to answer questions about the effect on consumers of government programs and other events that shift consumers' budget constraints. If the government imposes a quota, which reduces the number of units that a consumer buys, or provides a consumer with quantities of a good—in this section, we use the example of food transfers—the government creates a kink in the consumer's budget constraint. In contrast, if the government subsidizes the price of a good or provides cash to the consumer—we look at both types of child-care subsidies—it causes a rotation or a parallel shift of the budget line.

QUOTAS

Consumers' welfare is reduced if they cannot buy as many units of a good as they want. As a promotion, firms often sell a good at an unusually low price but limit the number of units that one can purchase. Governments, too, frequently limit how much of a good one can buy by setting a quota.

During emergencies, for example, governments may ration "essential" goods such as food and gasoline rather than let these goods' prices rise. In 2005, Spain, Thailand, and parts of Washington State restricted water supplies during severe droughts. Shanghai, China, rationed power in 2005. Also in 2005, legislation was proposed in the United States and Britain to limit energy use. Under the U.K. proposal, known as Domestic Tradable Quotas, individuals would be issued a "carbon card" from which points would be deducted every time the cardholder purchased fossil fuel—for example, when filling up a gas tank or taking a flight. In 2006 and 2007, many nations discussed rationing bird flu vaccines.

To illustrate the effect of a quota, we return to Jackie's decision about how many CDs and DVDs to purchase. As Figure 5.6 shows, before the quota is imposed, Jackie's downward-sloping budget constraint consists of two line segments, L^1 and L^2. Her optimal bundle e_1, where she purchases 12 CDs and 6 DVDs per year, occurs where L^2 is tangent to I^1.

Now suppose that a government (or her mother) limits Jackie's purchases to no more than 8 CDs per year. Her new budget constraint is the same as the original one up to 8 CDs, L^1, and then becomes vertical at 8 CDs. She loses part of the original opportunity set: the shaded triangle determined by the vertical line at 8 CDs, L^2, and the horizontal axis. Now her best option is to purchase Bundle e_2—8 CDs and 9 DVDs—which is the point where the highest indifference curve, I^2, touches the new constraint. However, I^2 is not tangent to the budget constraint. Thus with a quota, a consumer may have an interior solution where she buys some of all the goods, but the tangency condition does not hold because the limit causes a kink in the budget constraint (as in the corner solution in Chapter 3).

The quota harms Jackie because she is now on indifference curve I^2, which is below her original indifference curve, I^1. To determine by how much she is harmed, we can calculate the equivalent variation: the amount of money we would have to take from Jackie to harm her as much as the quota does. We draw a budget line, L^3, that is parallel to L^2 but that just barely touches I^2. The difference between the expenditure on the original budget line and the new expenditure is Jackie's equivalent variation.

As we know, Jackie's original expenditure is \$300. We can use her expenditure function, Equation 5.3, $E \approx 6.50 \, \overline{U} p_1^{0.6}$, to determine the expenditure on L^3. Substituting

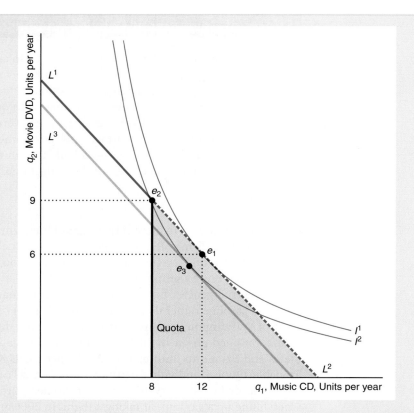

Figure 5.6 Quota. Originally, Jackie faces a budget constraint of the line segments L^1 and L^2 and buys 12 CDs and 6 DVDs at e_1 on indifference curve I^1. When a quota limits purchases of CDs to 8 per year (vertical line at 8), the L^2 segment is no longer available and the shaded triangle is lost from the opportunity set. The best that Jackie can do now is to purchase e_2 on indifference curve I^2. The equivalent variation would be if Jackie did not face a quota but lost EV amount of her budget so that her budget constraint is L^3, which is tangent to indifference curve I^3 at e_3.

$p_1 = \$15$ and her utility on I^2 at e_2, $\overline{U} = 8^{0.6}9^{0.4} \approx 8.39$, into her expenditure function, we find that her expenditure on L^3 is nearly \$277. Thus Jackie's equivalent variation is \$13 ($= \$300 - \$277$).

FOOD STAMPS

> *I've known what it is to be hungry, but I always went right to a restaurant.*
> —Ring Lardner

We can use the theory of consumer choice to analyze whether poor people are better off receiving food or a comparable amount of cash. Currently, federal, state, and local governments work together to provide a food subsidy for poor Americans. Nearly 11% of U.S. households worry about having enough money to buy food, and 3.3% report that they suffer from inadequate food (Sullivan and Choi, 2002). Households that meet income, asset, and employment eligibility requirements receive coupons—food stamps—that they can use to purchase food from retail stores. The U.S. Food Stamp

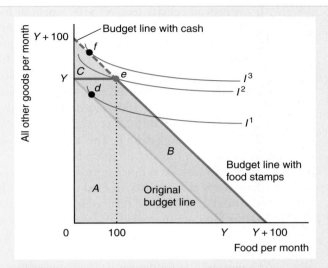

Figure 5.7 Food Stamps Versus Cash. The lighter line shows the original budget line of an individual with Y income per month. The heavier line shows the budget constraint with $100 worth of food stamps. The budget constraint with a grant of $100 in cash is a line between Y + 100 on both axes. The opportunity set increases by area B with food stamps but by B + C with cash. An individual with these indifference curves consumes Bundle d (with less than 100 units of food) with no subsidy, e (Y units of all other goods and 100 units of food) with food stamps, and f (more than Y units of all other goods and less than 100 units of food) with a cash subsidy. This individual's utility is greater with a cash subsidy than with food stamps.

Program is one of the nation's largest social welfare programs, with expenditures of $33.1 billion for nearly 29.1 million people in 2006.

Since the food stamp programs started in the early 1960s, economists, nutritionists, and policymakers have debated "cashing out" food stamps by providing checks or cash instead of coupons that can be spent only on food. Legally, food stamps may not be sold, though a black market for them exists. Because of technological advances in electronic fund transfers, switching from food stamps to a cash program would lower administrative costs and reduce losses due to fraud and theft.

Would a switch to a comparable cash subsidy increase the well-being of food stamp recipients? Would the recipients spend less on food and more on other goods?

Why Cash Is Preferred to Food Stamps. Poor people who receive cash have more choices than those who receive a comparable amount of food stamps. With food stamps, only extra food can be obtained. With cash, either food or other goods can be purchased. As a result, a cash grant increases a recipient's opportunity set by more than food stamps of the same value do.

In Figure 5.7, we made the price of a unit of food and the price of all other goods both $1, by choosing the units for each such that $1 buys one unit of each. Felicity has a monthly income of Y, so her budget line hits both axes at Y. Her opportunity set is area A.

If Felicity receives a subsidy of $100 in cash per month, her new monthly income is Y + $100. Her new budget constraint with cash hits both axes at Y + 100 and is parallel to the original budget constraint. Her opportunity set increases by B + C to A + B + C.

If instead Felicity receives $100 worth of food stamps, her food stamp budget constraint has a kink. Because the food stamps can be spent only on food, the budget constraint shifts 100 units to the right for any quantity of other goods up to Y units. For example, if Felicity buys only food, now $Y + 100$ units of food can be purchased. If she buys only other goods with the original Y income, she can get Y units of other goods plus 100 units of food. Because the food stamps cannot be turned into other goods, Felicity can't buy $Y + 100$ units of other goods, as she could under a cash transfer program. The food stamps opportunity set is area $A + B$, which is larger than the presubsidy opportunity set by B. The opportunity set with food stamps is smaller than that with the cash transfer program by C.

Felicity benefits as much from cash or an equivalent amount of food stamps if she would have spent at least $100 on food if given cash. In other words, she is indifferent between cash and food stamps if her indifference curve is tangent to the downward-sloping section of the food stamp budget constraint. Here the equivalent variation is $100.

Conversely, if she would not spend at least $100 on food if given cash, she prefers receiving cash to food stamps. If she has the indifference curves in Figure 5.7, she prefers cash to food stamps. She chooses Bundle e (Y units of all other goods and 100 units of food) given food stamps but Bundle f (more than Y units of all other goods and less than 100 units of food) if given cash. She is on a higher indifference curve, I^2 rather than I^1, if given cash rather than food stamps. If we draw a budget line with the same slope as the original one (-1) that is tangent to I^2, we can calculate the equivalent variation as the difference between the expenditure on that budget line and the original one. The equivalent variation is less than $100.

● **APPLICATION**

Food Stamps

If recipients of food stamps received cash instead of the stamps, their utility would remain the same or rise, some recipients would consume less food and more of other goods, potential recipients would be more likely to participate, and the administrative costs of these welfare programs would fall.

Whitmore (2002) finds that a sizable minority of food stamp recipients would be better off if they were given cash instead of an equivalent value in food stamps. She estimates that between 20% and 30% of food stamp recipients would spend less on food than their food stamp benefit amount if they received cash instead of stamps, and therefore would be better off with cash. Of those who would trade their food stamps for cash, the average food stamp recipient values the stamps at 80% of their face value (the average price on the underground market is only 65%, however). Thus across all such recipients, $500 million is wasted by giving food stamps rather than cash.

According to a review of statistical analyses (Fraker, 1990), an additional dollar of income causes an average low-income household to increase its food expenditures by 5¢ to 10¢, and an additional dollar of food stamps leads to a 20¢ to 45¢

increase in food expenditures. Based on her statistical study of the types of food that recipients consume, Whitmore (2002) concludes that giving cash would not lower their nutrition and might reduce their odds of obesity. Recipients of food stamps increase their food expenditures by around 30% on average (Levedahl, 2002), while cash payments have virtually no effect on food expenditures (Fraker et al., 1995).

It is also possible that the stigma of using food stamps may discourage participation in food stamp programs. Only 54% of families with children and incomes below the poverty line participated in the U.S. Food Stamp Program in 1999 (Winicki, 2001). To make participating easier and to reduce the stigma associated with presenting food stamps at a grocery store, the federal government required that by 2005, all states replace "food stamps" with ATM-like cards such as that shown in the photo. Using these cards instead of stamps also reduces administrative costs by half in some states.

Why We Give Food Stamps. Two groups in particular object to giving cash instead of food stamps: some policymakers, because they fear that cash might be spent on booze or drugs, and some nutritionists, who worry that poor people will spend the money on housing or other goods and get too little nutrition. In response, many economists argue that poor people are the best judges of how to spend their scarce resources. The question of whether it is desirable to let poor people choose what to consume is normative (a question of values), and economic theory cannot answer it. How poor people will change their behavior, however, is a positive (scientific) question, one that we *can* analyze. Experiments to date find that cash recipients consume slightly lower levels of food but receive at least adequate levels of nutrients and that they prefer receiving cash.

Given that recipients are as well off or better off receiving cash as they are receiving food stamps, why do we have programs that provide food stamps instead of programs that provide cash? The introduction to a report by the U.S. Department of Agriculture's Food and Nutrition Service, which administers the food stamp program (Fasciano et al., 1993, p. 6), offers this explanation:

> From the perspective of recipient households, cash is more efficient than coupons in that it permits each household to allocate its resources as it sees fit. . . . But in a more general sense, recipients' welfare clearly depends on public support for the program. And what evidence we have suggests that taxpayers are more comfortable providing in-kind, rather than cash, benefits and may consequently be more generous in their support of a coupon-based program. The question of which benefit form best promotes the welfare of financially needy households is thus more complex than it might appear.

Child-Care Subsidies. Child-care subsidies allow poor parents to work and better provide for themselves and their children. Child care is a major burden for the poor and may prevent poor mothers from working.[9] In the United States, child-care expenses for children under the age of 5 absorb 25% of the earnings for families with annual incomes under $14,400 but only 6% for families with incomes of $54,000 or more.

A 1996 U.S. welfare law, the Personal Responsibility and Work Opportunity Reconciliation Act (PRWORA), sought to facilitate the transition from welfare to work and to help keep low-income parents employed. Up to 30% of the funding came from the major welfare program, Temporary Assistance for Needy Families (TANF), which provides relatively unrestricted lump-sum funds to poor families. Passed during the Clinton administration, PRWORA aimed to double the number of children from poor families receiving federal child care between 1997 and 2003.

Under the Bush administration, Congress has reauthorized this program twice. The amount spent on child care rose from $10.4 billion in 2001 to $12.3 billion in 2003, but has fallen since then to $11.9 billion in 2004 and to $11.7 billion in 2005, while the average number of children served has remained essentially constant over this period.[10]

Child-care programs vary substantially across states in their generosity and in the form of the subsidy. A family's maximum child-care fee is currently 85% of the cost of care in Nevada and 70% in Louisiana; $72.50 per week in Alabama; 10% of gross income in Maine; and $153 per month plus $5 per month for each extra child in Mississippi. The reimbursement rate for infants and toddlers is $2.51 per hour in Kansas, $16 per day in Kentucky, and $125 per week in Minnesota. Some states provide an *ad valorem* subsidy, while others use a specific subsidy (Chapter 2) to lower the hourly rate that a poor family pays for day care.

Instead of subsidizing the price of child care, the government, under the major welfare program, can provide an unrestricted lump-sum payment that could be spent on day care or on all other goods, such as food and housing. (We ignore a third alternative, that of providing child-care services directly, because our analysis would be the same as for food stamps.)

Would a price subsidy or a lump-sum subsidy provide greater benefit to recipients for a given government expenditure? Which program increases the demand for day-care services by more? Which approach benefits poor families most? Which inflicts on other consumers a lower cost of day care?

To answer these questions, we use an indifference curve–budget line analysis where a poor family chooses between hours of day care per day, Q, and all other goods per day (with a price of $1 per unit). Given that its initial budget constraint is L^o, a poor family chooses Bundle e_1 on indifference curve I^1. The family consumes Q_1 hours of day care services in Figure 5.8.

If the government gives a day care price subsidy, which lowers the daily price of day care, the new budget line L^{PS} rotates out along the day care axis. Now the family consumes Bundle e_2 on higher indifference curve I^2. The family consumes more hours of day care, Q_2, because day care is now less expensive and is a normal good.

---

[9]The increased employment of mothers outside the home has led to a steep rise in the use of child care over the past several decades. In the United States, 6 out of 10 mothers work today—twice the rate in 1970. Six out of 10 children under the age of 6 are in child care, as are 45% of children under age 1. Eight of 10 employed mothers with children under age 6 are likely to have some form of nonparental child-care arrangement.

[10]Center for Law and Social Policy, **www.clasp.org/publications/ccdbgparticipation_2005.pdf.**

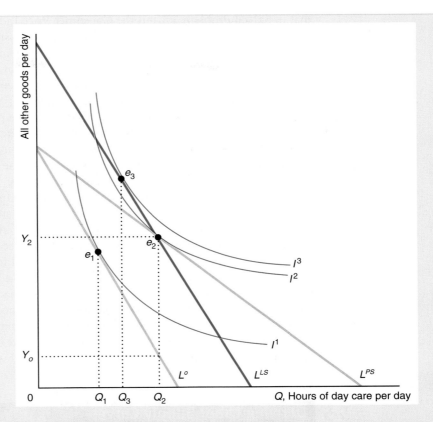

Figure 5.8 Child-Care Subsidies. Given the initial budget constraint L^o, the family obtains Q_1 hours of day care per day. If the government subsidizes the price of day care, the budget line rotates out to L^{PS} and the family consumes Q_2 hours of day care. Conditional of obtaining Q_2 hours of day care, the family could have spent Y_o on other goods originally, but it can now buy Y_2 amount. If the government gives the family $Y_2 - Y_o$ instead of the price subsidy, the family's budget constraint is L^{LS}, and it buys only Q_3 hours of day care. The family is better off with the lump sum than with the price subsidy because it is on indifference curve I^3 rather than I^2.

One way to measure the value of the subsidy that the family receives is to calculate the equivalent variation. Given that the family consumes Q_2 hours of day care, the family could have consumed Y_o other goods with the original budget constraint and Y_2 with the price-subsidy budget constraint. Given that Y_2 is the family's remaining income after paying for child care, the family buys Y_2 units of all other goods. That is, $Y_2 - Y_o$ is the extra amount of money that the family spends on other goods.

If, instead of receiving a day care price subsidy, the family were to receive a lump-sum payment of $Y_2 - Y_o$, taxpayers' costs for the two programs would be the same. The family's budget constraint after receiving a lump-sum payment, L^{LS}, has the same slope as the original budget constraint, L^o, because the relative prices of day care and all other goods are the same as originally. This budget constraint must go through e_2 because the family has just enough money to buy that bundle. However, the family will be better off if it buys Bundle e_3 on indifference curve I^3 (the reasoning is the same as that in Solved Problem 4.5 and the Consumer Price Index analysis in Figure 5.7). The family consumes less day care with the lump-sum subsidy: Q_3 rather than Q_2.

Thus the lump-sum payment of $Y_2 - Y_o$ is slightly more than the equivalent variation of the price subsidy. (If we draw a budget line that is parallel to L^o but tangent to I^2, then the equivalent variation is the difference between the intersection of that budget line with the vertical axis and the intersection of L^o with the vertical axis.)

Poor families prefer the lump-sum payment to the price subsidy because indifference curve I^3 is above I^2. Taxpayers should be indifferent between the two programs because they both cost the same. The day care industry prefers the price subsidy because the demand curve for its service is farther to the right: At any given price, more child care is demanded by poor families who receive a price subsidy rather than a lump-sum subsidy. In Question 13 at the end of the chapter, you are asked to show that parents who do not receive subsidies prefer the lump-sum approach.

Given that most of the directly affected groups should prefer lump-sum payments to price subsidies, why are price subsidies so heavily used? One possible explanation is that the day care industry has very effectively lobbied for price supports, but there is little evidence that occurred. Second, politicians might believe that poor families will not make intelligent choices about day care, so politicians might see price subsidies as a way of getting such families to consume relatively more (or better-quality) day care than they would otherwise choose. Third, politicians may prefer that poor people consume more day care so that poor people can work more hours, thereby increasing society's wealth. Fourth, politicians may not understand this analysis.

5.5   Deriving Labor Supply Curves

Throughout Chapters 4 and 5, we've used consumer theory to examine consumers' demand behavior. Perhaps surprisingly, we can also apply the consumer theory model to derive the supply curve of labor. We do so by using consumer theory to obtain a demand curve for leisure time and then using that demand curve to derive the supply curve of hours spent working. We use our labor supply model to analyze the consumer welfare and other effects of income taxes.

LABOR-LEISURE CHOICE

The human race is faced with a cruel choice: work or daytime television.

People choose between working to earn money to buy goods and services and consuming *leisure*: all their time spent not working for pay. In addition to sleeping, eating, and playing, leisure—or more accurately nonwork, N—includes time spent cooking meals and fixing things around the house.

Hugo spends his total income, Y, on various goods. For simplicity, we assume that the price of these goods is $1 per unit, so he buys Y goods. His utility, U, depends on how many goods, Y, and how much leisure, N, he consumes:

$$U = U(Y, N). \tag{5.6}$$

He faces an hours-worked constraint and an income constraint. The number of hours he works per day, H, equals 24 minus the hours he spends on leisure:

$$H = 24 - N. \tag{5.7}$$

The total income, Y, that Hugo has to spend on goods equals his earned income—his wage times the number of hours he works, wH—and his unearned income, Y^*, such as from an inheritance or a gift from his parents:

$$Y = wH + Y^*. \tag{5.8}$$

Using consumer theory, we can determine Hugo's demand curve for leisure once we know the price of leisure. What does it cost you to watch TV or go to school or do anything other than work for an hour? It costs you the wage, w, you could have earned from an hour's work: The price of leisure is forgone earnings. The higher your wage, the more an hour of leisure costs you. For this reason, taking an afternoon off costs a lawyer who earns \$250 an hour much more than it costs a fast-food server who earns the minimum wage.

Panel a of Figure 5.9 shows Hugo's choice between leisure and goods. The vertical axis shows how many goods, Y, Hugo buys. The horizontal axis shows both hours of leisure, N, which are measured from left to right, and hours of work, H, which are measured from right to left. Hugo maximizes his utility given the *two* constraints he faces. First, he faces a time constraint, which is a vertical line at 24 hours of leisure. There are only 24 hours in a day; all the money in the world won't buy him more hours in a day. Second, Hugo faces a budget constraint. Because Hugo has no unearned income, his initial budget constraint, L^1, is $Y = w_1 H = w_1(24 - N)$. The slope of his budget constraint is $-w_1$, because each extra hour of leisure he consumes costs him w_1 goods.

Hugo picks his optimal hours of leisure, $N_1 = 16$, so he is on the highest indifference curve, I^1, that touches his budget constraint. He works $H_1 = 24 - N_1 = 8$ hours per day and earns an income of $Y_1 = w_1 H_1 = 8w_1$.

We derive Hugo's demand curve for leisure using the same method by which we derived Mimi's demand curve for beer in Chapter 4. We raise the price of leisure—the wage—in panel a of Figure 5.9 to trace out Hugo's demand curve for leisure in panel b. As the wage increases from w_1 to w_2, leisure becomes more expensive, and Hugo demands less of it.

We can also solve this problem using calculus. Hugo maximizes his utility, Equation 5.6, subject to the time constraint, Equation 5.7, and the income constraint, Equation 5.8. Although we can analyze this problem using Lagrangian techniques, it is easier to do so by substitution. By substituting Equations 5.7 and 5.8 into Equation 5.6, we can convert this constrained problem into an unconstrained maximization problem where Hugo maximizes his utility through his choice of how many hours to work per day:

$$\max_{H} U = U(Y, N) = U(wH, 24 - H). \tag{5.9}$$

By using the chain rule of differentiation, we find that the first-order condition for an interior maximum to the problem in Equation 5.9 is

$$\frac{\partial U}{\partial Y}\frac{dY}{dH} + \frac{\partial U}{\partial N}\frac{dN}{dH} = U_Y w - U_N = 0, \tag{5.10}$$

where $U_Y = \partial U/\partial Y$ is the marginal utility of goods or income and $U_N = \partial U/\partial N$ is the marginal utility of leisure.[11] That is, Hugo sets his marginal rate of substitution of

---

[11]The second-order condition for an interior maximum is

$$\frac{\partial^2 U}{\partial Y^2}w^2 - 2\frac{\partial^2 U}{\partial Y \partial N}w + \frac{\partial^2 U}{\partial N^2} < 0.$$

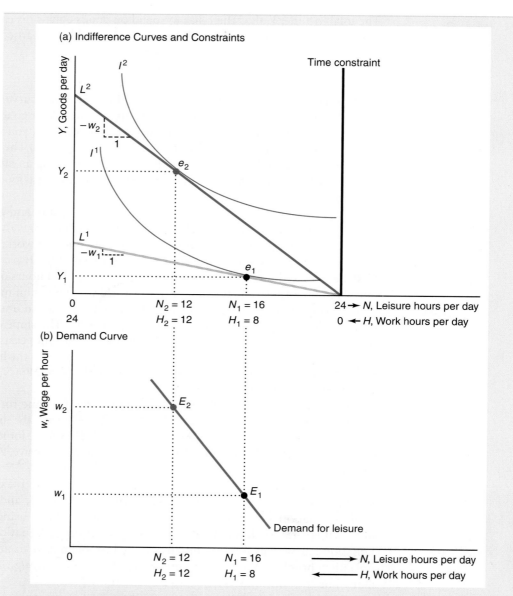

Figure 5.9 Demand for Leisure. (a) Hugo chooses between leisure, N, and other goods, Y, subject to a time constraint (vertical line at 24 hours) and a budget constraint, L^1, which is $Y = w_1 H = w_1 \times (24 - N)$, with a slope of $-w_1$. The tangency of his indifference curve, I^1, with his budget constraint, L^1, determines his optimal bundle, e_1, where he has $N_1 = 16$ hours of leisure and works $H_1 = 24 - N_1 = 8$ hours. If his wage rises from w_1 to w_2, Hugo shifts from optimal bundle e_1 to e_2. (b) Bundles e_1 and e_2 correspond to E_1 and E_2 on his leisure demand curve.

income for leisure, $MRS = -U_N/U_Y$, equal to his marginal rate of transformation of income for leisure, $MRT = -w$, in the market:

$$MRS = -\frac{U_N}{U_Y} = -w = MRT. \tag{5.11}$$

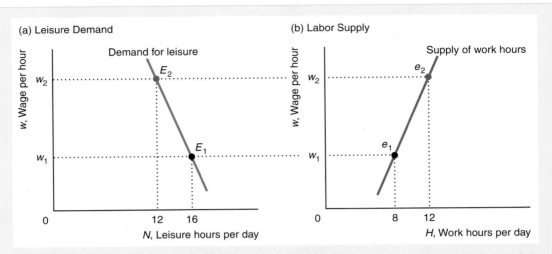

(a) Leisure Demand

(b) Labor Supply

Figure 5.10 Supply Curve of Labor. (a) Hugo's demand for leisure is downward sloping. (b) At any given wage, the number of hours that Hugo works, H, and the number of hours of leisure, N, that he consumes add to 24. Thus his supply curve for hours worked, which equals 24 hours minus the number of hours of leisure he demands, is upward sloping.

Equivalently, the last dollar's worth of leisure, U_N/w, equals the marginal utility from the last dollar's worth of good's, U_Y.

By subtracting Hugo's demand for leisure at each wage—his demand curve for leisure in panel a of Figure 5.10—from 24, we construct his labor supply curve—the hours he is willing to work as a function of the wage, $H(w)$—in panel b. His supply curve for hours worked is the mirror image of the demand curve for leisure: For every extra hour of leisure that Hugo consumes, he works one hour less.

SOLVED PROBLEM 5.3

If Sofia has a Cobb-Douglas utility function, $U = (wH)^a(24 - H)^{1-a}$, what is her labor supply function? What is the supply function if $a = \frac{1}{3}$?

Answer

1. *To find the values that maximize her utility, set the derivative of Sofia's utility function with respect to H equal to zero:* This first-order condition is $aw(wH)^{a-1}(24 - H)^{1-a} - (1 - a)(wH)^a(24 - H)^{-a} = 0$. Simplifying, we find that $H = 24a$. Thus Sofia works a fixed number of hours regardless of the wage.

2. *Substitute in the value $a = \frac{1}{3}$ to obtain the specific hours-worked function:* Given that $a = \frac{1}{3}$, she works 8 hours a day whether the wage is 50¢ or $500 per hour.

INCOME AND SUBSTITUTION EFFECTS

An increase in the wage causes both income and substitution effects, which alter an individual's demand for leisure and supply of hours worked. The *total effect* of an

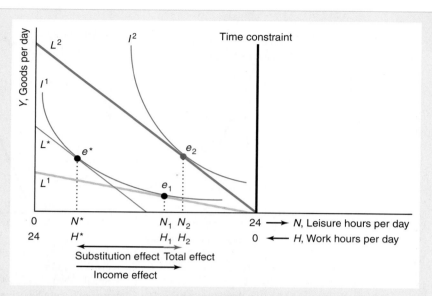

Figure 5.11 Income and Substitution Effects of a Wage Change. A wage change causes both a substitution and an income effect. As the wage rises, Hugo's optimal bundle changes from e_1 to e_2. The movement from e_1 to e^* is the substitution effect, the movement from e^* to e_2 is the income effect, and the movement from e_1 to e_2 is the total effect. The compensating variation is $Y^* - Y_2$.

increase in Hugo's wage from w_1 to w_2 is the movement from e_1 to e_2 in Figure 5.11. Hugo works $H_2 - H_1$ fewer hours and consumes $N_2 - N_1$ more hours of leisure.

By drawing an imaginary budget constraint, L^*, that is tangent to Hugo's original indifference curve and has the slope of the new wage, we can divide the total effect into substitution and income effects. The *substitution effect*, the movement from e_1 to e^*, must be negative: A compensating wage increase causes Hugo to consume fewer hours of leisure, N^*, and to work more hours, H^*.

As the wage rises, if Hugo works the same number of hours as before, he has a higher income. The *income effect* is the movement from e^* to e_2. Because leisure is a normal good for Hugo, as his income rises, he consumes more leisure. When leisure is a normal good, the substitution and income effects work in opposite directions, so whether leisure demand increases or not depends on which effect is larger. Hugo's income effect dominates the substitution effect, so the total effect for leisure is positive: $N_2 > N_1$. Hugo works fewer hours as the wage rises, so his labor supply curve is backward bending.

If leisure is an inferior good, both the substitution effect and the income effect work in the same direction, and hours of leisure definitely fall. As a result, if leisure is an inferior good, a wage increase unambiguously causes the hours worked to rise.

In Figure 5.11, by removing $Y^* - Y_2$ income from Hugo, we could completely offset the benefit of the wage increase by keeping him on indifference curve I^1. Thus $Y^* - Y_2$ is the compensating variation.

SOLVED PROBLEM 5.4

Enrico receives a no-strings-attached scholarship that pays him an extra Y^* per day. How does this scholarship affect the number of hours he wants to work? Does his utility increase?

Answer

1. *Show his consumer equilibrium without unearned income:* When Enrico had no unearned income, his budget constraint, L^1 in the graphs, hit the hours-leisure axis at 0 hours and had a slope of $-w$.

2. *Show how the unearned income affects his budget constraint:* The extra income causes a parallel upward shift of Y^*. His new budget constraint, L^2, has the same slope as before because his wage does not change. The extra income cannot buy Enrico more time, of course, so L^2 cannot extend to the right of the time constraint. As a result, L^2 is vertical at 0 hours up to Y^*: His income is Y^* if he works no hours. Above Y^*, L^2 slants toward the goods axis with a slope of $-w$.

3. *Show that the relative position of the new to the original equilibrium depends on his tastes:* The change in the number of hours he works depends on Enrico's tastes. Panels a and b show two possible sets of indifference curves. In both diagrams, when facing budget constraint L^1, Enrico chooses to work H_1 hours. In panel a, leisure is a normal good, so as his income rises, Enrico consumes more leisure than originally: He moves from Bundle e_1 to Bundle e_2. In panel b, he views leisure as an inferior good and consumes fewer hours of leisure than originally: He moves from e_1 to e_3. (Another possibility is that the number of hours he works is unaffected by the extra unearned income.)

4. *Discuss how his utility changes:* Regardless of his tastes, Enrico has more income in the new equilibrium and is on a higher indifference curve after receiving the scholarship. In short, he believes that more money is better than less.

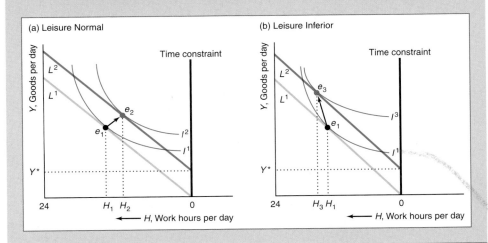

Leisure-Income Choices of Textile Workers

Dunn (1977, 1978, 1979), using data obtained by questioning southern cotton mill workers and examining their behavior, determined their indifference curves, which we can use to examine income and substitution effects. A typical worker's indifference curves are close to right angles (see the graph), indicating that leisure and all other goods are nearly perfect complements: The worker is relatively unwilling to substitute goods for leisure.

At the original wage, $2.09 per hour, the budget constraint is L^1 and a typical worker chooses to work 42.4 hours per week (assuming that there are 100 total hours to be allocated between work and leisure), Bundle e_1. An increase in the wage of $1 per hour causes the budget constraint to rotate outward to L^2. An uncompensated increase in the wage increases the demand for leisure and reduces the hours worked to 29.5 per week, Bundle e_2. Thus workers' labor supply curves are backward bending: Workers decrease their hours as their wage rises. An increase in the wage from $2.09 to $3.09 leads to weekly earnings rising only from $88.69 to $91.18 because of the offsetting reduction in the hours worked.

What would happen if, when the wage increased, workers' incomes were reduced so that they remained on the original indifference curve, I^1? That is, what is the substitution effect for this $1 wage increase? The imaginary budget constraint L^* is parallel to L^2 but tangent to indifference curve I^1 at e^*. Thus the substitution effect—the movement from e_1 to e^*—due to a compensating wage increase is an increase in weekly hours by half an hour a week to 42.9 hours. The income effect (the movement from e^* to e_2) is to work 13.4 ($= 29.5 - 42.9$) fewer hours a week.

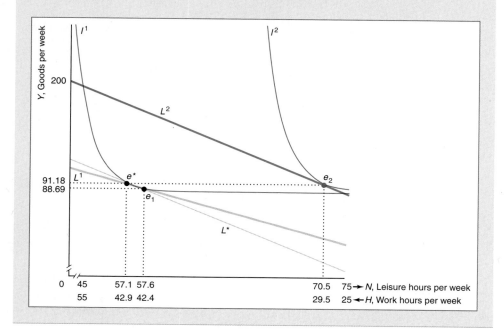

SHAPE OF THE LABOR SUPPLY CURVE

Whether the labor supply curve slopes upward, bends backward, or has sections with both properties depends on the income elasticity of leisure. Suppose that a worker views leisure as an inferior good at low wages and a normal good at high wages. As the wage increases, the demand for leisure first falls and then rises, and the hours supplied to the market first rise and then fall. (Alternatively, the labor supply curve may slope upward and then backward even if leisure is normal at all wages: At low wages, the substitution effect—work more hours—dominates the income effect—work fewer hours—while the opposite occurs at higher wages.)

The budget line rotates upward from L^1 to L^2 as the wage rises in panel a of Figure 5.12. Because leisure is an inferior good at low incomes, in the new optimal bundle, e_2, this worker consumes less leisure and buys more goods than at the original bundle, e_1.

At higher incomes, however, leisure is a normal good. At an even higher wage, the new equilibrium is e_3 on budget line L^3, where the quantity of leisure demanded is higher and the number of hours worked is lower. Thus the corresponding supply curve for labor slopes upward at low wages and bends backward at higher wages in panel b.

Do labor supply curves slope upward or backward? Economic theory alone cannot answer this question, as both forward-sloping and backward-bending supply curves are *theoretically* possible. Empirical research is necessary to resolve this question.

Most studies (Killingsworth, 1983; MaCurdy et al., 1990) find that the labor supply curves for British and American men are virtually vertical because both the income and the substitution effects are about zero. Studies find that wives' labor supply curves are also virtually vertical: slightly backward bending in Canada and the United States and slightly forward sloping in the United Kingdom and Germany. In contrast, studies of the labor supply of single women find relatively large positive supply elasticities of 4.0 and even higher. Thus only single women tend to work substantially more hours when their wages rise.

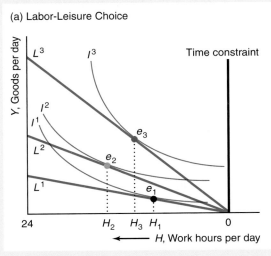
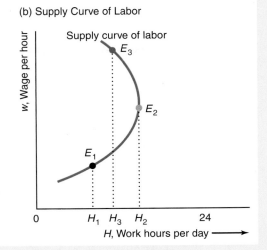
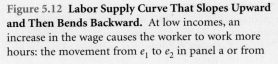

Figure 5.12 Labor Supply Curve That Slopes Upward and Then Bends Backward. At low incomes, an increase in the wage causes the worker to work more hours: the movement from e_1 to e_2 in panel a or from E_1 to E_2 in panel b. At higher incomes, an increase in the wage causes the worker to work fewer hours: the movement from e_2 to e_3 or from E_2 to E_3.

● APPLICATION

Winning the Good Life

Would you stop working if you won a lottery jackpot or inherited a large sum? Economists want to know how unearned income affects labor supply because this question plays a crucial role in many government debates on taxes and welfare. For example, some legislators oppose negative income tax and welfare programs because they claim that giving money to poor people will stop them from working. Is that assertion true?

We could clearly answer this question if we could observe the behavior of a large group of people, only some of whom were randomly selected to receive varying large payments of unearned income each year for decades. Luckily for us, governments conduct such experiments by running lotteries.

Imbens et al. (2001) compared the winners of major prizes and others who played the Massachusetts Megabucks lottery. Major prizes ranged from $22,000 to $9.7 million, with an average of $1.1 million, and were paid in yearly installments over two decades.

A typical player in this lottery earned $16,100. The average winner received $55,200 in prize money per year and chose to work slightly fewer hours so that his or her labor earnings fell by $1,877 per year. That is, winners increased their consumption and savings but did not substantially decrease how much they worked.

For every dollar of unearned income, winners reduced their work effort and hence their labor earnings by 11¢ on average. Men and women, big and very big prize winners, and people of all education levels behaved the same. However, there were differences by age of the winner and by income groups. People ages 55 to 65 reduced their effort by about a third more than younger people did, presumably because they decided to retire early. Most striking, people with no earnings in the year before winning the lottery tended to increase their labor earnings after winning.

INCOME TAX RATES AND LABOR SUPPLY

The wages of sin are death, but by the time taxes are taken out, it's just sort of a tired feeling.
                                                              —Paula Poundstone

Why do we care about the shape of labor supply curves? One reason is that we can tell from the shape of the labor supply curve whether an increase in the income tax rate— a percent of earnings—will cause a substantial reduction in the hours of work.[12] Taxes on earnings are an unattractive way of collecting money for the government if supply curves are upward sloping, because the taxes cause people to work fewer hours, reducing the amount of goods that society produces and raising less tax revenue than if the supply curve were vertical or backward bending. On the other hand, if supply curves are

---

[12]Although taxes are ancient, the income tax is a relatively recent invention. William Pitt the Younger introduced the British income tax (10% on annual incomes above £60) in 1798 to finance the war with Napoleon. The U.S. Congress followed suit in 1861, using the income taxes (3% on annual incomes over $800) to pay for the Civil War.

backward bending, a small increase in the tax rate increases tax revenue *and* boosts total production—but reduces leisure.

Although unwilling to emulate Lady Godiva's tax-fighting technique—allegedly, her husband, Leofric, the Earl of Mercia, agreed to eliminate taxes if she rode naked through the Coventry marketplace—various U.S. presidents have advocated tax cuts. Presidents John Kennedy, Ronald Reagan, and George W. Bush argued that cutting the marginal tax rate (the percentage of the last dollar earned that the government takes in taxes) would stimulate people to work longer and produce more, both desirable effects. President Reagan claimed that tax receipts would increase due to the additional work.

Because tax rates have changed substantially over time, we have a natural experiment to test this hypothesis. The Kennedy tax cuts lowered the top personal marginal tax rate from 91% to 70%. Due to the Reagan tax cuts, the maximum rate fell to 50% in 1982–1986, 38.5% in 1987, and 28% in 1988–1990. The rate rose to 31% in 1991–1992 and to 39.6% in 1993–2000. The Bush administration's Tax Relief Act of 2001 reduced this rate to 38.6% for 2001–2003, 37.6% for 2004–2005, and 35% for 2006 and thereafter.

Many other countries' central governments have also lowered their top marginal tax rates in recent years. For example, Japan's rate fell from 88% in 1986 to 65% in 1994 and to 50% in 1999.

In 2005, according to the Organization for Economic Cooperation and Development (OECD), the highest marginal tax rate in OECD (relatively developed) countries ranges from 12% in Switzerland to 50% in Belgium (which had a 71% rate in 1988). The top federal rate in the United States is 35% (however, state and local taxes raise the marginal rate substantially for most workers); in other countries the rates are 25% in Sweden (87% in 1979), 27% in Iceland, 29% in Canada, 37% in Japan, 39% in New Zealand, 40% in the United Kingdom, 47% in Australia, and 52% in the Netherlands (72% in 1988).

If the tax does not affect the pretax wage, the effect of imposing a tax rate of $\tau = 0.28$ is to reduce the effective wage from w to $(1 - \tau)w = 0.72w$.[13] The tax reduces the after-tax wage by 28%, so a worker's budget constraint rotates downward, similar to rotating the budget constraint downward from L^2 to L^1, in Figure 5.12.

As we discussed, if the budget constraint rotates downward, the hours of work may increase or decrease, depending on whether leisure is a normal or an inferior good. The worker in panel b of Figure 5.12 has a labor supply curve that at first slopes upward and then bends backward. If the worker's wage is very high, the worker is in the backward-bending section of the labor supply curve.

If so, the relationship between the marginal tax rate, τ, and tax revenue, τwH, is bell-shaped, as in Figure 5.13. At a zero tax rate, a small increase in the tax rate *must* increase the tax revenue, because no revenue was collected when the tax rate was zero.

---

[13]Under a progressive income tax system, the marginal tax rate increases with income. The average tax rate differs from the marginal tax rate. In 2004, people in the top 1% of income had a marginal rate of 37.6% but an average rate of 19.7%. Suppose that the marginal tax rate is 20% on the first $10,000 earned and 30% on the second $10,000. Someone who earned $20,000 would pay $2,000 (= 0.2 × $10,000) on the first $10,000 of earnings and $3,000 on the next $10,000. That taxpayer's average tax rate is 25% (= ($2,000 + $3,000)/$20,000). For simplicity in the following analysis, we assume that the marginal tax rate is a constant, τ, so the average tax rate is also τ. To see your marginal and average tax rates, use the calculator at **www.smartmoney.com/tax/filing/index.cfm?story=taxbracket**.

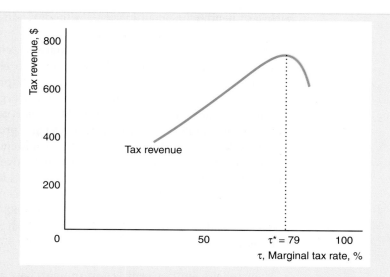

Figure 5.13 Relationship of Tax Revenue to Tax Rates. At marginal tax rates below τ^*, an increase in the rate leads to larger tax collections. At rates above τ^*, however, an increase in the marginal rate decreases tax revenue. These calculations (Fullerton, 1982, Table 1, p. 15) are based on the assumption that the labor supply elasticity with respect to the after-tax wage is 0.15 and that the labor demand curve is horizontal.

However, if the tax rate rises a little more, tax revenue must rise even higher, for two reasons. First, the government collects a larger percentage of every dollar earned because the tax rate is higher. Second, employees work more hours as the tax rate rises because workers are in the backward-bending section of their labor supply curves.

As the tax rate rises far enough, however, the workers are in the upward-sloping section of their labor supply curves. In that section, an increase in the tax rate reduces the number of hours worked. When the tax rate rises high enough, the reduction in hours worked more than offsets the gain from the higher rate, so tax revenue falls.

It makes little sense for a government to operate at very high marginal tax rates in the downward-sloping portion of this bell-shaped curve. The government could get more output *and* more tax revenue by cutting the marginal tax rate.

What is the effect on tax revenue of an increase in the income tax rate? To answer this question, we let τ be the constant marginal income tax rate and w be the worker's wage, so that for every w a worker is paid, the government receives τw. (We ignore unearned income and the possibility that the tax rate varies with income.)

Suppose the government collects τ share of the wage. If w is the worker's wage, then the government takes τw, and the worker's after-tax wage is $\omega = (1 - \tau)w$. The government's tax revenue, T, is

$$T = \tau w H[(1 - \tau)w] = \tau w H(\omega), \qquad (5.12)$$

where $H(\omega)$ is the hours of labor that a worker supplies given the after-tax wage ω.

By differentiating Equation 5.12 with respect to τ, we can show how revenue changes as the tax rate increases:

$$\frac{dT}{d\tau} = wH(\omega) - \tau w^2 \frac{dH}{d\omega}. \qquad (5.13)$$

Thus a change in the tax rate has two effects. First, the government collects more revenue because of the higher tax rate: A 1-unit increase in τ causes tax revenue to increase by $wH(\omega)$, the amount that the worker earns. Second, the change in the tax alters the hours worked. As the rate goes up, before-tax labor earnings, $wH(\omega)$, decrease if the labor supply is upward sloping, $dH/d\omega > 0$, which reduces tax revenue by $\tau w^2 dH/d\omega$.

The government can raise tax revenues by lowering the tax rate if the economy is on the downward sloping part of the tax revenue curve to the right of τ^* in Figure 5.13. For tax revenue to decrease when the tax rate increases (or to rise when the tax rate decreases), we need $dT/d\tau = wH - \tau w^2 dH/d\omega < 0$. Using algebra, we can rewrite this condition as

$$\frac{1}{\tau} < \frac{dH}{d\omega} \frac{\omega}{H(\omega)}.$$

If we multiply both sides of this expression by $(1 - \tau)$, we obtain the condition that

$$\frac{1 - \tau}{\tau} < \frac{dH}{d\omega} \frac{w}{H(\omega)} = \eta, \qquad (5.14)$$

where $\eta = [dH/d\omega][\omega/H(\omega)]$ is the elasticity of supply of hours of work with respect to after-tax wages, ω.

Thus for tax revenue to fall from a small increase in the tax rate, the elasticity of supply of labor must be greater than $(1 - \tau)/\tau$. In the United States in 2006, a single person making between \$30,651 and \$74,200 faced a marginal tax rate of $\tau = 25\%$. For a small increase in this rate to lower tax revenue, such a person's η had to be greater than 3 ($= 0.75/0.25$), which was not likely. On the other hand, in countries with very high tax rates, this condition might be met. For example, if $\tau = 90\%$, the condition is met if the elasticity of supply is greater than $1/9$.

APPLICATION

Tax Revenues and Tax Cuts

The marginal tax rate, τ^*, that maximizes tax revenue is very high for the United States: Estimates range from 79% (Fullerton, 1982) to 85% (Stuart, 1984). Thus the Kennedy-era tax cuts from 91% to 70% raised tax revenue and increased the work effort of top-income-bracket workers, but the Reagan tax cut (in which the actual rate was only about half that of τ^*) and the Bush tax cut had the opposite effect. Goolsbee (2000) examined the effect of higher taxes on corporate executives and found that even this extremely high-income group has little long-run response to tax changes. Fullerton and Gan (2004) estimated that the 2001 Bush tax cut caused almost no change in expected working hours of married women between the ages of 25 and 55 and lowered their tax revenue by an average of \$843 per person.

Heijman and van Ophem (2005) reported the typical marginal tax rate (including all taxes, not just income taxes) and their simulations of τ^* for various countries:

	Sweden	France	Ireland	Spain	Switzerland	U.K.	Japan
Marginal tax rate	65	47	41	37	35	26	24
Optimal tax rate	58	59	57	59	58	54	54

According to their calculations, τ^* is above the actual marginal tax rate in all countries except Sweden. In Japan and the United Kingdom, τ^* is twice the actual marginal rate. Thus in these countries, small tax rate increases would raise total tax revenue.

Summary

1. **Consumer Welfare:** The pleasure a consumer receives from a good in excess of its cost is called *consumer surplus*. Consumer surplus equals the area under the consumer's demand curve above the market price up to the quantity that the consumer buys. The degree to which consumers are harmed by an increase in price is measured by the change in consumer surplus.

2. **Expenditure Function and Consumer Welfare:** Consumer surplus, which does not hold a consumer's utility constant, reflects both substitution and income effects. In contrast, we can use the expenditure function to determine how much of a change in income is necessary to offset a change in price so as to hold a consumer's utility constant, reflecting a pure *income effect*. *Compensating variation* is the amount of money one would have to give a consumer to offset completely the harm from a price increase—to keep the consumer on the original indifference curve. *Equivalent variation* is the amount of money one would have to take from a consumer to harm the consumer by as much as the price increase would. Typically, the change in consumer surplus due to a price rise, compensating variation, or equivalent variation is a very similar measure.

3. **Market Consumer Surplus:** The market consumer surplus—the sum of the welfare effect across all consumers—is the area under the market inverse demand curve above the market price. It is larger, the more revenue that is spent on the good and the less elastic the demand curve is.

4. **Effects of Government Policies on Consumer Welfare:** A pure income transfer benefits consumers more or harms them less than quotas, food stamps, and child-care price subsidies do. Quotas and food stamps create a kink in the budget constraint, so a consumer's optimal bundle may be at the kink where the indifference curve is not tangent to the budget line, which leads to additional welfare harms.

5. **Deriving Labor Supply Curves:** Using consumer theory, we can derive the daily demand curve for leisure, which is time spent on activities other than work. By subtracting the demand curve for leisure from 24 hours, we obtain the daily labor supply curve, which shows how the number of hours worked varies with the wage. Depending on whether leisure is an inferior good or a normal good, the supply curve of labor may be upward sloping or backward bending. The shape of the supply curve for labor determines the effect of a tax cut. Empirical evidence based on this theory shows why tax cuts since the 1980s have failed to increase tax revenue collections as predicted by the Reagan administration.

Questions

* = answer at the back of this book; **W** *= audio-slide show answers by James Dearden at* **www.aw-bc.com/perloff**

1. In the "Compensating Variation for Television" application, people are asked how much they would be willing to pay to watch television or how much they'd have to be paid never to watch again. Graph what is being measured. What alternative question could have been asked that would have provided more details on the value consumers place on watching an extra hour of television?

2. Use a graph to show what his fans received according to the "Bruce Springsteen's Gift to His Fans" application.

3. What happens to the budget line if the government applies a specific tax of $1 per gallon on gasoline but does not tax other goods? What happens to the budget line if the tax applies only to purchases of gasoline in excess of 10 gallons per week?

4. Max chooses between water and all other goods. If he spends all his money on water, he can buy 12 thousand gallons per week. At current prices, his optimal bundle is e_1. Show in a diagram. During a drought, the government limits the number of gallons per week that he may purchase to 10 thousand. Using diagrams, discuss under which conditions his new optimal bundle, e_2, will be the same as e_1. If the two bundles differ, can you state where e_2 must be located?

5. Since 1979, low-income recipients have been given food stamps. Before 1979, however, people bought food stamps at a subsidized rate. For example, to get $1 worth of food stamps, a household paid about 15¢ (the exact amount varied by household characteristics and other factors). Show the budget constraint facing an individual if that individual may buy up to $100 per month in food stamps at 15¢ per each $1 coupon.

6. Is a poor person more likely to benefit from $100 a month worth of food stamps (that can be used only to buy food) or $100 a month worth of clothing stamps (that can be used only to buy clothing)? Why?

7. If a relatively wealthy person spends more on food than a poor person before receiving food stamps, is the wealthy person less likely than the poor person to have a tangency at a point like f in Figure 5.7?

8. Is a wealthy person more likely than a poor person to prefer to receive a government payment of $100 in cash to $100 worth of food stamps? Why or why not?

9. Federal housing assistance programs provide allowances that can be spent only on housing. Several empirical studies find that recipients increase their nonhousing expenditures by 10% to 20% (cited in Harkness and Newman, 2003). Show that recipients might—but do not necessarily—increase their spending on nonhousing, depending on their tastes.

10. Federal housing and food stamp subsidy programs are two of the largest in-kind transfer programs for the poor. In President George W. Bush's proposed 2006 budget, the Food Stamp Program (FSP) provided approximately $33.1 billion in benefits and the housing program added another $38.4 billion. Many poor people are eligible for both programs: 30% of housing assistance recipients also used food stamps, and 38% of FSP participants also received housing assistance (Harkness and Newman, 2003). Suppose Jill's income is $500 a month, which she spends on food and housing. The prices of food and housing are each $1 per unit. Draw her budget line. If she receives $100 in food stamps and $200 in a housing subsidy (which she can spend only on housing), how do her budget line and opportunity set change?

11. In 2002, the Supreme Court ruled that school voucher programs do not violate the Establishment Clause of the First Amendment, provided that parents, not the state, direct where the money goes. Educational vouchers are increasingly used in various parts of the United States. Suppose that the government offers poor people a $5,000 education voucher that can be used only to pay for education. Doreen would be better off with $5,000 in cash than with the educational voucher. In a graph, determine the cash value, V, Doreen places on the education voucher (that is, the amount of cash that would leave her as well off as with the educational voucher). Show how much education and "all other goods" she would consume with the educational voucher or with a cash payment of V.

12. A poor person who has an income of $1,000 receives $100 worth of food stamps. Draw the budget constraint if the food stamp recipient can sell these coupons on the black market for less than their face value.

13. Show how much an individual's opportunity set increases if the government gives food stamps rather than sells them at subsidized rates.

*14. How do parents who do not receive subsidies feel about the two child-care programs analyzed in Figure 5.8? (*Hint:* Use a supply-and-demand analysis from Chapter 2.)

*15. How could the government set a smaller lump-sum subsidy that would make poor parents as well off as the hourly child-care subsidy yet cost less? Given the tastes shown in Figure 5.8, what would be the effect on the number of hours of child-care service that these parents buy? Are you calculating a compensating variation or an equivalent variation (given that the original family is initially at e_1 in the figure)?

16. Under a welfare plan, poor people are given a lump-sum payment of L. If they accept this welfare payment, they must pay a high tax, $\tau = \frac{1}{2}$, on anything they earn. If they do not accept the welfare payment, they do not have to pay a tax on their earnings. Show that whether an individual accepts welfare depends on the individual's tastes.

17. If an individual's labor supply curve slopes forward at low wages and bends backward at high wages, is leisure a Giffen good? If so, at high or low wage rates?

18. Bessie, who can currently work as many hours as she wants at a wage of w, chooses to work 10 hours a day. Her boss decides to limit the number of hours that she can work to 8 hours per day. Show how her budget constraint and choice of hours change. Is she unambiguously worse off as a result of this change? Why or why not?

19. Suppose that Roy could choose how many hours to work at a wage of w and chose to work seven hours a day.

The employer now offers him time-and-a-half wages (1.5w) for every hour he works beyond a minimum of eight hours per day. Show how his budget constraint changes. Will he choose to work more than seven hours a day?

20. Jerome moonlights: He holds down two jobs. The higher-paying job pays w, but he can work at most eight hours. The other job pays w^*, but he can work as many hours as he wants. Show how Jerome determines how many hours to work.

21. Suppose that the job in the previous question with no restriction on hours was the higher-paying job. How do Jerome's budget constraint and behavior change?

22. Taxes during the fourteenth century were very progressive. The 1377 poll tax on the Duke of Lancaster was 520 times the tax on a peasant. A poll tax is a lump-sum (fixed amount) tax per person, which is independent of the hours a person works or earns. Use a graph to show the effect of a poll tax on the labor-leisure decision. Does knowing that the tax was progressive tell us whether a nobleman or a peasant—assuming they have identical tastes—worked more hours?

23. Today most developed countries have progressive income taxes. Under such a taxation program, is the marginal tax higher than, equal to, or lower than the average tax?

24. Several political leaders, including some recent candidates for the presidency, have proposed a flat income tax, where the marginal tax rate is constant.

    a. Show that if each person is allowed a "personal deduction" where the first $10,000 is untaxed, the flat tax can be a progressive tax.

    b. Proponents of the flat tax claim that it will stimulate production (relative to the current progressive income tax where marginal rates increase with income). Discuss the merits of their claim.

25. Inheritance taxes are older than income taxes. Caesar Augustus instituted a 5% tax on all inheritances (except gifts to children and spouses) to provide retirement funds for the military. During the George W. Bush administration, congressional Republicans and Democrats have vociferously debated the wisdom of cutting income taxes and inheritance taxes (which the Republicans call the death tax) to stimulate the economy by inducing people to work harder. Presumably the government cares about a tax's effect on work effort and tax revenues.

    a. Suppose George views leisure as a normal good. He works at a job that pays w an hour. Use a labor-leisure analysis to compare the effects on the hours he works from a marginal tax rate on his wage, τ, or a lump-sum tax (a tax collected regardless of the number of hours he works), T. If the per-hour tax is used, he works 10 hours and earns $10w(1 - \tau)$. The government sets $T = 10w\tau$, so that it earns the same from either tax.

    b. Now suppose that the government wants to raise a given amount of revenue through taxation by imposing either an inheritance tax or an income (wage) tax. Which is likely to reduce George's hours of work more, and why?

*26. Can a flat tax (constant marginal tax rate) be a progressive tax (rich people pay a higher average tax rate than poor people)? Explain your answer.

*27. Prescott (2004) argued that U.S. employees work 50% more than do German, French, and Italian employees because European employees face lower marginal tax rates. Assuming that workers in all four countries have the same tastes toward leisure and goods, must it necessarily be true that U.S. employees work longer hours? Use graphs to illustrate your answer, and explain why it is true or is not true. Does Prescott's evidence indicate anything about the relative sizes of the substitution and income effects? Why or why not?

*28. Originally, Julia could work as many hours as she wanted at a wage of w. She chose to work 12 hours per day. Then her employer told her that, in the future, she may work as many hours as she wants up to a maximum of eight hours (and she can find no additional part-time job). How does her optimal choice between leisure and goods change? Does this change hurt her?

Problems

29. Using calculus, show the effect of a change in the wage on the amount of leisure that an individual wants to consume.

30. Cynthia buys gasoline and other goods. The government considers imposing a lump-sum tax, L dollars per person, or a tax on gasoline of τ dollars per gallon. If L and τ are such that either tax will raise the same amount of tax revenue from Cynthia, which tax does she prefer and why? Show your answer using a graph or calculus.

31. Suppose that Joe's wage varies with the hours he works: $w(H) = \alpha H, \alpha > 0$. Use both a graph and calculus to show how the number of hours he chooses to work depends on his tastes.

32. Jim's utility function is $U(q_1, q_2) = \min(q_1, q_2)$. The price of each good is $1, and his monthly income is $2,000. His firm wants him to relocate in another city where the price of q_2 is $2, but the price of q_1 and his

income remain constant. Obviously, Jim would be worse off due to the move. What would be his equivalent variation or compensating variation?

33. Jane's utility function is $U(q_1, q_2) = q_1 + q_2$. The price of each good is $1, and her monthly income is $2,000. Her firm wants her to relocate in another city where the price of q_2 is $2, but the price of q_1 and her income remain constant. What would be her equivalent variation or compensating variation?

34. Compare the welfare effects on a consumer between a lump-sum tax and an equal *ad valorem* (percentage) tax on all goods that raise the same amount of tax revenue.

35. Use the numbers for the alcohol and tobacco category from Table 5.2 to draw a figure that illustrates the roles that the revenue and the elasticity of demand play in determining the loss of consumer surplus due to an increase in price. Indicate how the various areas of your figure correspond to the equation derived in footnote 7.

36. Suppose that the inverse market demand for an upcoming Bruce Springsteen concert at Philadelphia's 20,000-seat Wachovia Center is $p = 1,000 - 0.04Q$. Mr. Springsteen and his promoters consider whether to auction the tickets to the concert. The auction works as follows: An auctioneer orders the bids from highest to lowest, and the price of each ticket equals the 20,000th highest bid. The tickets go to the highest bidders. In the auction, assume that each person bids his or her willingness to pay.

a. What is the price of the tickets? What is the market consumer surplus?

b. Instead, suppose that Mr. Springsteen, for the benefit of his fans, decides to sell each ticket for $100. Based on the demand function, there are 22,500 people who are willing to pay $100 or more. So, not everyone who wants to see the concert at the $100 price can purchase a ticket. Of these 22,500 people, suppose that each of the 20,000 people who actually acquires a ticket has a lower willingness to pay than each of the 2,500 people who do not. What is the consumer surplus?

c. Suppose Bruce Springsteen's objective in choosing whether to auction the tickets or to set a price of $100 is to maximize the market consumer surplus. Which does he choose: an auction or a $100 ticket price? **W**

37. Joe won $365,000 a year for life in the state lottery. Use a labor-leisure choice analysis to answer the following questions:

a. Show how Joe's lottery winnings affect the position of his budget line.

b. Joe's utility function for goods per day (Y) and hours of leisure per day (N) is $U = Y + 240N^{0.5}$. After winning the lottery, does Joe continue to work the same number of hours each day? What is the income effect of Joe's lottery gains on the amount of goods he buys per day? **W**

Chapter 6

Firms and Production

Hard work never killed anybody, but why take a chance? —Charlie McCarthy

The Ghirardelli Chocolate Company converts chocolate and other inputs into an output of 144,000 wrapped chocolate bars and 340,000 wrapped chocolate squares a day. The material inputs include chocolate, other food products, and various paper goods for wrapping and boxing the candy. The labor inputs include chefs, assembly-line workers, and various mechanics and other technicians. The capital inputs are the manufacturing plant, the land on which the plant is located, conveyor belts, molds, wrapping machines, and various other types of equipment.

Over time, Ghirardelli has changed how it produces its finished product, increasing the ratio of machines to workers. Several years ago, to minimize employees' risk of repetitive motion injuries, the company spent $300,000 on robots, which pack the wrapped chocolate and put it on pallets. The use of robotic arms resulted in greatly reduced downtime, increased production, and improved working conditions.

In this chapter we look at the types of decisions that the owners of firms have to make. First, a decision must be made as to how a firm is owned and managed. Ghirardelli, for example, is a corporation—it is not owned by an individual or partners—and is run by professional managers. Second, the firm must decide how to produce. Ghirardelli now uses relatively more machines and robots and fewer workers than in the past. Third, if a firm wants to expand output, it must decide how to do so in both the short run and the long run. In the short run, Ghirardelli can expand output by extending the workweek to six or seven days and using extra materials. To expand output more, Ghirardelli would have to install more equipment (such as extra robotic arms), hire more workers, and eventually build a new plant, all of which take time. Fourth, given its ability to change its output level, a firm must determine how large to grow. Ghirardelli determines its current investments on the basis of its beliefs about demand and costs in the future.

This chapter examines the nature of a firm and how a firm chooses its inputs so as to produce efficiently. Chapter 7 considers how the firm chooses the least costly among all possible efficient production processes. Then Chapter 8 combines this information about costs with information about revenues to determine how a firm selects the output level that maximizes profit.

By using robotic equipment to pack finished, wrapped chocolate, the Ghirardelli Chocolate Company benefits from reduced downtime and increased production.

The main lesson of this chapter and the next is that firms are not black boxes that mysteriously transform inputs (such as labor, capital, and material) into outputs. Economic theory explains how firms make decisions about production processes, types of inputs to use, and the volume of output to produce.

In this chapter, we examine six main topics	
	1. **The Ownership and Management of Firms:** Decisions must be made as to how a firm is owned and run.
	2. **Production:** A firm converts inputs into outputs using one of possibly many available technologies.
	3. **Short-Run Production: One Variable and One Fixed Input:** In the short run, only some inputs can be varied, so the firm changes its output by adjusting its variable inputs.
	4. **Long-Run Production: Two Variable Inputs:** The firm has more flexibility in how it produces and how it changes its output level in the long run when all factors can be varied.
	5. **Returns to Scale:** How the ratio of output to input varies with the size of the firm is an important factor in determining a firm's size.
	6. **Productivity and Technical Change:** The amount of output that can be produced with a given amount of inputs varies across firms and over time.

6.1 The Ownership and Management of Firms

A **firm** is an organization that converts *inputs* such as labor, materials, and capital into *outputs,* the goods and services that it sells. U.S. Steel combines iron ore, machinery, and labor to create steel. A local restaurant buys raw food, cooks it, and serves it. A landscape designer hires gardeners and machines, buys trees and shrubs, transports them to a customer's home, and supervises the work.

Most goods and services produced in Western countries are produced by firms. In the United States, firms produce 79% of national production (U.S. gross domestic product); the government, 10%; nonprofit institutions (such as some universities and hospitals), 5%; and households, 7% (*Survey of Current Business,* 2006). In developing countries, the government's share of total national production can be much higher, reaching 37% in Ghana, 38% in Zambia, 40% in Sudan, and 90% in Algeria, although it is as low as 3% in Bangladesh, Paraguay, and Nepal (United Nations, *Industry and Development: Global Report 1992/93*). This book focuses on production by for-profit firms rather than by nonprofit organizations and governments.

THE OWNERSHIP OF FIRMS

In most countries, for-profit firms have one of three legal forms: sole proprietorships, partnerships, and corporations.

Sole proprietorships are firms owned and run by a single individual.

Partnerships are businesses jointly owned and controlled by two or more people. The owners operate under a partnership agreement. If any partner leaves, the partnership agreement ends. For the firm to continue to operate, a new partnership agreement must be written.

Corporations are owned by *shareholders* in proportion to the number of shares of stock they hold. The shareholders elect a board of directors who run the firm. In turn, the board of directors usually hires managers who make short-term decisions and long-term plans.

Corporations differ from the other two forms of ownership in terms of personal liability for the debts of the firm. Sole proprietors and partners are personally responsible for the debts of their firms. All of an owner's personal wealth—not just that invested in the firm—is at risk if the business becomes bankrupt and is unable to pay its bills. Even the assets of partners who are not responsible for the failure can be taken to cover the firm's debts.

Corporations have **limited liability:** The personal assets of the corporate owners cannot be taken to pay a corporation's debts if it goes into bankruptcy. Because of the limited liability of corporations, the most that shareholders can lose if the firm goes bankrupt is the amount they paid for their stock, which becomes worthless if the corporation fails. Sole proprietors have unlimited liability—that is, even their personal assets can be taken to pay the firm's debts. Partners share liability: Even the assets of partners who are not responsible for the failure can be taken to cover the firm's debts. General partners can manage the firm but have unlimited liability. Limited partners are prohibited from managing but are liable only to the extent of their investment in the business.[1]

In the United States, 84% of business sales are made by corporations, even though only 20% of all firms are corporations. Nearly 72% of all firms are sole proprietorships. However, sole proprietorships tend to be small, so they are responsible for only 4% of all sales. Partnerships account for 8% of all firms and make 11% of sales (*Statistical Abstract of the United States,* 2004–2005).

THE MANAGEMENT OF FIRMS

In a small firm, the owner usually manages the firm's operations. In larger firms, typically corporations and larger partnerships, a manager or team of managers usually runs the company. In such firms, owners, managers, and lower-level supervisors are all decision makers.

As revelations about Enron and WorldCom illustrate, the various decision makers may have conflicting objectives. What is in the best interest of the owners may not be what is in the best interest of managers or other employees. For example, a manager may want a fancy office, a company car, a company jet, and other perks, but the owner would likely oppose those drains on profit.

The owner replaces the manager if the manager pursues personal objectives rather than the firm's objectives. In a corporation, the board of directors is supposed to ensure that managers do not stray. If the manager and the board of directors run the firm badly, the shareholders can fire both or directly change some policies through votes at the corporation's annual meeting for shareholders. Until Chapter 19, we'll

---

[1]Due to changes in corporate and tax laws over the last decade, *limited liability companies* (LLCs) have become common in the United States. Owners are liable only to the extent of their investment (as in a corporation) and can play an active role in management (as in a partnership or sole proprietorship). When an owner leaves, the LLC does not have to dissolve, whereas a partnership ends.

ignore the potential conflict between managers and owners and assume that the owner *is* the manager of the firm and makes all the decisions.

WHAT OWNERS WANT

Economists usually assume that a firm's owners try to maximize profit. Presumably, most people invest in a firm to make money—lots of money, they hope. They want the firm to earn a positive profit rather than suffer a loss (a negative profit). A firm's **profit,** π, is the difference between its revenue, R, which is what it earns from selling the good, and its cost, C, which is what it pays for labor, materials, and other inputs:

$$\pi = R - C. \tag{6.1}$$

Typically, revenue is p, the price, times q, the firm's quantity: $R = pq$. (For simplicity, we will assume that the firm produces only one product.)

In reality, some owners have other objectives, such as having as big a firm as possible or a fancy office or keeping risks low. However, Chapter 8 shows that a competitive firm is likely to be driven out of business if it doesn't maximize profits.

To maximize profits, a firm must produce as efficiently as possible. A firm engages in **efficient production** (achieves **technological efficiency**) if it cannot produce its current level of output with fewer inputs, given existing knowledge about technology and the organization of production. Equivalently, the firm produces efficiently if, given the quantity of inputs used, no more output could be produced using existing knowledge.

If the firm does not produce efficiently, it cannot be maximizing profit—so efficient production is a *necessary condition* for profit maximization. Even if a firm efficiently produces a given level of output, it is not maximizing profit if that output level is too high or too low or if it is using excessively expensive inputs. Thus efficient production alone is not a *sufficient condition* to ensure that a firm's profit is maximized.

A firm may use engineers and other experts to determine the most efficient ways to produce with a known method or technology. However, this knowledge does not indicate which of the many technologies, each of which uses different combinations of inputs, allows for production at the lowest cost or with the highest possible profit. How to produce at the lowest cost is an economic decision that the firm's manager typically makes (Chapter 7).

6.2 Production

A firm uses a *technology* or *production process* to transform *inputs* or *factors of production* into *outputs*. Firms use many types of inputs, most of which fall into three broad categories:

- **Capital services (K):** Use of long-lived inputs such as land, buildings (factories, stores), and equipment (machines, trucks)
- **Labor services (L):** Work performed by managers, skilled workers (architects, economists, engineers, plumbers), and less-skilled workers (custodians, construction laborers, assembly-line workers)
- **Materials (M):** Raw goods (oil, water, wheat) and processed products (aluminum, plastic, paper, steel) that are typically consumed in making, or incorporated in, the final product

We typically refer to *capital services* as *capital* and *labor services* as *labor* for brevity. The output can be a *service* such as an automobile tune-up by a mechanic, or a *physical product* such as a computer chip or a potato chip.

PRODUCTION FUNCTIONS

Firms can transform inputs into outputs in many different ways. Candy-manufacturing companies differ in the skills of their workforce and the amount of equipment they use. While all employ a chef, a manager, and relatively unskilled workers, some candy firms also use skilled technicians and modern equipment. In small candy companies, the relatively unskilled workers shape the candy, decorate it, package it, and box it by hand. In slightly larger firms, the relatively unskilled workers use conveyor belts and other equipment that was invented decades ago. In modern large-scale plants, the relatively unskilled laborers work with robots and other state-of-the-art machines that skilled technicians maintain. Before deciding which production process to use, a firm needs to consider its various options.

The various ways that a firm can transform inputs into output are summarized in the **production function:** the relationship between the quantities of inputs used and the *maximum* quantity of output that can be produced, given current knowledge about technology and organization. The production function for a firm that uses only labor and capital is

$$q = f(L, K), \tag{6.2}$$

where q units of output (wrapped candy bars) are produced using L units of labor services (days of work by relatively unskilled assembly-line workers) and K units of capital (the number of conveyor belts).

The production function shows only the *maximum* amount of output that can be produced from given levels of labor and capital, because the production function includes only efficient production processes. A profit-maximizing firm is not interested in production processes that are inefficient and waste inputs: Why would the firm want to use two workers to do a job that one worker can perform as efficiently?

TIME AND THE VARIABILITY OF INPUTS

A firm can more easily adjust its inputs in the long run than in the short run. Typically, a firm can vary the amount of materials and of relatively unskilled labor it uses comparatively quickly. However, it needs more time to find and hire skilled workers, order new equipment, or build a new manufacturing plant.

The more time a firm has to adjust its inputs, the more factors of production it can alter. The **short run** is a period of time so brief that at least one factor of production cannot be varied practically. A factor that a firm cannot vary practically in the short run is called a **fixed input.** In contrast, a **variable input** is a factor of production whose quantity the firm can change readily during the relevant time period. The **long run** is a lengthy enough period of time that all inputs can be varied. There are no fixed inputs in the long run—all factors of production are variable inputs.

Suppose that a painting company gets more work than usual one day. Even if it wanted to do so, the firm does not have time to buy or rent an extra truck and buy another compressor to run a power sprayer; these inputs are fixed in the short run. To get the work done that afternoon, the firm uses the company's one truck to drop off a temporary worker, equipped with only a brush and a can of paint, at the last job. In the long run, however, the firm can adjust all its inputs. If the firm wants to paint more houses every day, it hires more full-time workers, gets a second truck, purchases more compressors to run the power sprayers, and buys a computer to keep track of all its projects.

How long it takes for all inputs to be variable depends on the factors a firm uses. For a janitorial service whose only major input is workers, the long run is a very brief period of time. In contrast, an automobile manufacturer may need many years to build a new manufacturing plant or to design and construct a new type of machine. A pistachio farmer needs the better part of a decade before newly planted trees yield a substantial crop of nuts.

For many firms over a short period, say a month, materials and often labor are variable inputs. However, labor is not always a variable input. Finding additional highly skilled workers may take substantial time. Similarly, capital may be a variable or a fixed input. A firm can rent small capital assets (trucks and personal computers) quickly, but it may take the firm years to obtain larger capital assets (buildings and large, specialized pieces of equipment).

To illustrate the greater flexibility that a firm has in the long run than in the short run, we examine the production function in Equation 6.2, in which output is a function of only labor and capital. We look first at the short-run and then at the long-run production process.

6.3 Short-Run Production: One Variable and One Fixed Input

In the short run, we assume that capital is a fixed input and that labor is a variable input, so the firm can increase output only by increasing the amount of labor it uses. In the short run, the firm's production function is

$$q = f(L, \overline{K}), \tag{6.3}$$

where q is output, L is workers, and $\overline{K}$ is the fixed number of units of capital. The short-run production function is also referred to as the **total product of labor**—the amount of output (or *total product*) that a given amount of labor can produce.

The exact relationship between *output* or *total product* and *labor* is given by Equation 6.3. The **marginal product of labor** (MP_L) is the change in total output resulting from using an extra unit of labor, holding other factors (capital) constant. The marginal product of labor is the partial derivative of the production function with respect to labor,

$$MP_L = \frac{\partial q}{\partial L} = \frac{\partial f(L, K)}{\partial L}.$$

The **average product of labor** (AP_L) is the ratio of output to the number of workers used to produce that output,[2]

$$AP_L = \frac{q}{L}.$$

---

[2]*Jargon alert:* Some economists call the MP_L the marginal physical product of labor and the AP_L the average physical product of labor.

SOLVED PROBLEM   **6.1**

A computer assembly firm's production function is $q = 0.1LK + 3L^2K - 0.1L^3K$. What is its short-run production function if capital is fixed at $\overline{K} = 10$? Give the formulas for its marginal product of labor and its average product of labor. Draw two figures, one above the other. In the top figure, show the relationship between output (total product) and labor. In the bottom figure, show the MP_L and AP_L curves. Is this production function valid for all values of labor?

Answer

1. *Write the formula for the short-run production function by replacing K in the production function with its fixed short-run value:* To obtain a production function of the form of Equation 6.3, set capital in the production function equal to 10:

$$q = L + 30L^2 - L^3.$$

2. *Determine the MP_L by differentiating the short-run production function with respect to labor:* The marginal product of labor is[3]

$$MP_L = \frac{dq}{dL} = \frac{d(L + 30L^2 - L^3)}{dL} = 1 + 60L - 3L^2.$$

3. *Determine the AP_L by dividing the short-run production function by labor:* The average product of labor is

$$AP_L = \frac{q}{L} = \frac{L + 30L^2 - L^3}{L} = 1 + 30L - L^2.$$

4. *Draw the requested figures by plotting the short-run production function, MP_L, and AP_L equations:* Figure 6.1 shows how the total product of labor, marginal product of labor, and average product of labor vary with the number of workers.

5. *Show that the production function equation does not hold for all values of labor by noting that, beyond a certain level, extra workers lower output:* In the figure, the total product curve to the right of $L = 20$ appears as a dashed line to indicate that this section is not part of the true production function. Because output falls—the curve decreases—as the firm uses more than 20 workers, a rational firm would never use more than 20 workers. From the definition of a production function, we want the *maximum* quantity of output that can be produced from the given inputs, so if the firm had more than 20 workers, it could increase its output by sending the extra ones home. (The portions of the MP_L and AP_L curves beyond 20 workers also appear as dashed lines because they correspond to irrelevant sections of the short-run production function equation.)

INTERPRETATION OF GRAPHS

Figure 6.1 shows how the total product of labor (computers assembled), the average product of labor, and the marginal product of labor vary with the number of workers. The figures are smooth curves because the firm can hire a "fraction of a worker" by

---

[3]Because the short-run production function is solely a function of labor, $MP_L = dq/dL$. An alternative way to derive the MP_L is to differentiate the production function with respect to labor and then set capital equal to 10: $MP_L = \partial q/\partial L = \partial(0.1LK + 3L^2K - 0.1L^3K)/\partial L = 0.1K + 6LK - 0.3L^2K$. Evaluating at $\overline{K} = 10$, we obtain $MP_L = 1 + 60L - 30L^2$.

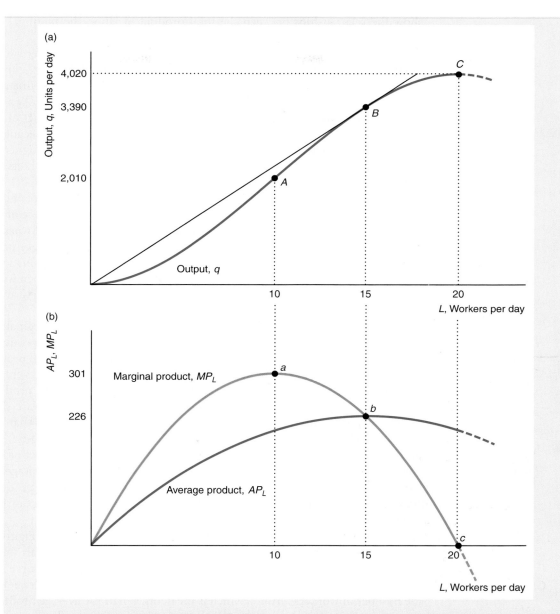

Figure 6.1 Production Relationships with Variable Labor. (a) The short-run total product of labor curve, $q = L + 30L^2 - L^3$, shows how much output, q, can be assembled with 10 units of capital, which is fixed in the short run. Where extra workers reduce the amount of output produced, the total product curve is a dashed line, which indicates that such production is inefficient production and not part of the production function. The slope of the line from the origin to point B is the average product of labor for 15 workers. (b) The marginal product of labor, MP_L, equals the average product of labor, AP_L, at the peak of the average product curve where the firm employs 15 workers.

employing a worker for a fraction of a day. The total product of labor curve in panel a shows that output rises with labor until the firm employs 20 workers.

Panel b illustrates how the average product of labor and the marginal product of labor vary with the number of workers. By lining up the two panels vertically, we can show the relationships between the total product of labor, the marginal product of labor, and the average product of labor curves.

In most production processes—and as Figure 6.1 shows—the average product of labor first rises and then falls as labor increases. For example, the AP_L curve may initially rise because it helps to have more than two hands when assembling a computer. One worker holds a part in place while another worker bolts it down. As a result, output increases more than in proportion to labor, so the average product of labor rises. Similarly, output may initially rise more than in proportion to labor because of greater specialization of activities. With greater specialization, workers are assigned to tasks at which they are particularly adept, and time is saved by not having workers move from task to task.

However, as the number of workers rises further, output may not increase by as much per worker because workers have to wait to use a particular piece of equipment or because they get in each other's way. In Figure 6.1, as the number of workers exceeds 15, total output increases less than in proportion to labor, so the average product falls.

The three curves are geometrically related. First we use panel b to illustrate the relationship between the average and marginal product of labor curves. Then we use panels a and b to show the relationship between the total product of labor curve and the other two curves.

The average product of labor curve slopes upward where the marginal product of labor curve is above it and slopes downward where the marginal product curve is below it. If an extra worker adds more output—that worker's marginal product—than the average product of the initial workers, the extra worker raises the average product. As panel b shows, when there are fewer than 15 workers, the marginal product curve is above the average product curve, so the average product curve is upward sloping.

Similarly, if the marginal product of labor for a new worker is less than the former average product of labor, the average product of labor falls. In the figure, the average product of labor falls beyond 15 workers. Because the average product of labor curve rises when the marginal product of labor curve is above it and the average product of labor falls when the marginal product of labor is below it, the average product of labor curve reaches a peak, point *b* in panel b, where the marginal product of labor curve crosses it.[4]

We can determine the average product of labor curve, panel b of Figure 6.1, using the total product of labor curve, panel a. The AP_L for L workers equals the slope of a straight line from the origin to a point on the total product of labor curve for L workers in panel a. The slope ("rise over run") of this line equals output ("rise") divided by the number of workers ("run"), which is the definition of the average product of labor.

---

[4]We can use calculus to prove that the MP_L curve intersects the AP_L at its peak. Because capital is fixed, we can write the production function solely in terms of labor: $q = f(L)$. In the figure, $MP_L = dq/dL = df/dL > 0$ and $d^2f/dL^2 < 0$. A necessary condition to identify the amount of labor where the average product of labor curve, $AP_L = q/L = f(L)/L$, reaches a maximum is that the derivative of AP_L with respect to L equals zero:

$$\frac{dAP_L}{dL} = \left(\frac{dq}{dL} - \frac{q}{L}\right)\frac{1}{L} = 0.$$

(At the L determined by this first-order condition, AP_L is maximized if the second-order condition is negative: $d^2AP_L/dL^2 = d^2f/dL^2 < 0$.) By rearranging this equation, we learn that $MP_L = dq/dL = q/L = AP_L$, so the MP_L curve hits the AP_L curve at its peak.

For example, the slope of the straight line drawn from the origin to point B ($L = 15$, $q = 3{,}390$) is 226, which is the height of the AP_L curve in panel b when $L = 15$.

The marginal product of labor also has a geometric interpretation in terms of the total product curve. The slope of the total product curve at a given point, dq/dL, equals the MP_L. That is, the MP_L equals the slope of a straight line that is tangent to the total output curve for a given number of workers. For example, at point C in panel a where there are 20 workers, the line tangent to the total product curve is flat, so the MP_L is zero: A little extra labor has no effect on output. The total product curve is upward sloping when there are fewer than 20 workers, so the MP_L is positive. If the firm is foolish enough to hire more than 20 workers, the total product curve slopes downward (dashed line), so the MP_L would be negative: Extra workers lower output. Again, this portion of the MP_L curve is not part of the production function.

When there are 15 workers, the average product of labor equals the marginal product of labor. The reason is that the line from the origin to point B in panel a is tangent to the total product curve, so the slope of that line, 226, is the marginal product of labor and the average product of labor at point b in panel b.

SOLVED PROBLEM 6.2

> Tian and Wan (2000) estimated the production function for rice in China as a function of labor, fertilizer, and other inputs such as seed, draft animals, and equipment. Holding the other inputs besides labor fixed, the total product of labor is $\ln q = 4.63 + 1.29 \ln L - 0.2(\ln L)^2$. What is the marginal product of labor? What is the relationship of the marginal product of labor to the average product of labor? What is the elasticity of output with respect to labor?
>
> ### Answer
>
> 1. *Totally differentiate the short-run production function to obtain the marginal product of labor:* Differentiating $\ln q = 4.63 + 1.29 \ln L - 0.2(\ln L)^2$ with respect to q and L, we obtain
>
> $$\frac{dq/dL}{q} = \frac{1.29 - 0.4 \ln L}{L}.$$
>
> By rearranging terms, we find that the $MP_L = dq/dL = (q/L)(1.29 - 0.4 \ln L)$.
>
> 2. *Determine the relationship between MP_L and AP_L using the expression for MP_L:* Using the definition for $AP_L = q/L$, we can rewrite the expression we just derived for the marginal product of labor as $MP_L = AP_L(1.29 - 0.4 \ln L)$. That is, $MP_L/AP_L = (1.29 - 0.4 \ln L)$, so MP_L is $(1.29 - 0.4 \ln L)$ times as large as AP_L.
>
> 3. *Show that the elasticity of output with respect to labor is the ratio of the marginal product of labor to the average product of labor and make use of the equation relating the MP_L to the AP_L:* Given the general definition of an elasticity, the elasticity of output produced with respect to labor is $(dq/dL)(L/q)$. By substituting into this expression the definitions of $MP_L = dq/dL$ and $AP_L = q/L$, we find that the elasticity of output with respect to labor is $(dq/dL)(L/q) = MP_L/AP_L = 1.29 - 0.4 \ln L$.

LAW OF DIMINISHING MARGINAL RETURNS

Next to *supply equals demand,* probably the most commonly used phrase of economic jargon is the *law of diminishing marginal returns.* This "law" determines the shapes of the total product and marginal product of labor curves as a firm uses more and more labor. As with the "law" of supply and demand, this "law" is not theoretically necessary but is an empirical regularity.

The *law of diminishing marginal returns* (or *diminishing marginal product*) holds that, *if a firm keeps increasing an input, holding all other inputs and technology constant, the corresponding increases in output will become smaller eventually.* That is, if only one input is increased, *the marginal product of that input will diminish eventually.* The marginal product of labor diminishes if $\partial MP_L/\partial L = \partial(\partial q/\partial L)/\partial L = \partial^2 q/\partial L^2 = \partial^2 f(L, K)/\partial L^2 < 0$. That is, the marginal product falls with increased labor if the second partial derivative of the production function with respect to labor is negative.

Panel b of Figure 6.1 illustrates diminishing marginal product of labor. At low levels of labor, the marginal product of labor rises with the number of workers. However, when the number of workers exceeds 10, each additional worker reduces the marginal product of labor.

Unfortunately, many people, when attempting to cite this empirical regularity, overstate it. Instead of talking about "diminishing *marginal* returns," they talk about "diminishing returns." The two phrases have different meanings. Where there are "diminishing marginal returns," the MP_L curve is falling—beyond 10 workers in panel b of Figure 6.1—but it may be positive, as the solid MP_L curve between 10 and 20 workers shows. With "diminishing returns," extra labor causes *output* to fall. There are diminishing total returns for more than 20 workers, and consequently the MP_L is negative, as the dashed MP_L line in panel b shows.

Thus saying that there are diminishing returns is much stronger than saying that there are diminishing marginal returns. We often observe firms producing where there are diminishing marginal returns to labor, but we never see a well-run firm operating where there are diminishing total returns. Such a firm could produce more output by using fewer inputs.

A second common misinterpretation of this law is claiming that marginal products must fall as we increase an input without requiring that technology and other inputs stay constant. If we increase labor while simultaneously increasing other factors or adopting superior technologies, the marginal product of labor may rise indefinitely. Thomas Malthus provided the most famous example of this fallacy (as well as the reason economics is referred to as the "dismal science").

● **APPLICATION**

Malthus and the Green Revolution

In 1798, Thomas Malthus—a clergyman and professor of modern history and political economy—predicted that population (if unchecked) would grow more rapidly than food production because the quantity of land was fixed. The problem, he believed, was that the fixed amount of land would lead to diminishing marginal product of labor, so output would rise less than in proportion to the increase in farmworkers. Malthus grimly concluded that mass starvation would result. Brander and Taylor (1998) argue that such a disaster may have occurred on Easter Island around 500 years ago.

Since Malthus's day, world population has increased nearly 800%. Why haven't we starved to death? The simple explanation is that fewer workers using less land can produce much more food today than was possible when Malthus was alive. Two hundred years ago, most of the population had to work in agriculture to prevent starvation. Today, less than 2% of the U.S. population works in agriculture, and the share of land devoted to farming is constantly falling. Yet U.S. food production has grown faster than the U.S. population. Since World War II, world population has doubled but food production has tripled.

Two key factors (in addition to birth control) are responsible for the rapid increase in food production per capita in most countries. First, agricultural technology—such as disease-resistant seeds and better land management practices—has improved substantially, so more output can be produced with the same inputs. Second, although the amounts of land and labor used have remained constant or fallen in most countries in recent years, the use of other inputs such as fertilizer and tractors has increased significantly, so output per acre of land has risen.

In the last three decades of the twentieth century, U.S. farm productivity rose at an average of 4.5% a year, about triple the rate of improvement of nonfarm business productivity. For example, although the nation's dairy herd had shrunk to about three-fourths its size in the late 1960s, milk production increased by more than a third. By 2002, one in seven U.S. farms was experimenting with robotic milking systems.

In 1850, it took more than 80 hours of labor to produce 100 bushels of corn. Introducing mechanical power cut the labor required in half. Labor needs were again cut in half by the introduction of hybrid seed and chemical fertilizers, and then in half again by the advent of herbicides and pesticides. Biotechnology, with

the 1996 introduction of herbicide-tolerant and insect-resistant crops, has reduced the labor requirement to about two hours of labor. (See **www.aw-bc.com/perloff,** Chapter 6, "Does that Compute Down on the Farm?")

Of course, the risk of starvation is more severe in developing countries. Luckily, one man decided to defeat the threat of Malthusian disaster personally. Do you know anyone who saved a life? A hundred lives? Do you know the name of the man who probably saved the most lives in history? According to some estimates, Norman Borlaug and his fellow scientists prevented a *billion deaths* with their green revolution, which resulted in a spectacular increase in wheat, rice, and maize production in the developing world.

Starting in Mexico, they developed new seeds and new approaches involving fertilizer, tractors, irrigation, soil treatments, and anything else that would increase production—anything. (Hear Dr. Borlaug's story in his own words: **webcast .berkeley.edu/events/details.html?event_id=86.**)

In the late 1960s, Dr. Borlaug and his colleagues brought the techniques they developed in Mexico to India and Pakistan because of the risk of mass starvation there. The results were stunning. Pakistan's wheat crop in 1968 soared to 146% of the 1965 pre–green revolution crop. By 1970, it was 183% of the 1965 crop. The comparable outputs for India were 134% and 163%.

In 2002, Dr. Borlaug explained why Malthus was wrong:

> Biotechnology helps farmers produce higher yields on less land. This is a very environmentally favorable benefit. For example, the world's grain output in 1950 was 692 million tons. Forty years or so later, the world's farmers used about the same amount of acreage but they harvested 1.9 billion tons—a 170% increase! We would have needed an additional 1.8 billion hectares of land, instead of the 600 million used, had the global cereal harvest of 1950 prevailed in 1999 using the same conventional farming methods.

However, as Dr. Borlaug noted in his 1970 Nobel Prize speech, superior science is not the complete answer to preventing starvation. A sound economic system is needed, too. It is the lack of a sound economic system that has doomed many Africans. Per capita food production has fallen in parts of Africa over the past two decades. Worse, in several recent years, mass starvation has plagued some African countries. Although droughts have contributed, these tragedies appear to be primarily due to political problems such as wars and the breakdown of economic production and distribution systems. If these economic and political problems cannot be solved, Malthus may prove to be right for the wrong reason.

6.4   Long-Run Production: Two Variable Inputs

Eternity is a terrible thought. I mean, where's it going to end? —Tom Stoppard

We started our analysis of production functions by looking at a short-run production function in which one input, capital, was fixed, and the other, labor, was variable. In the long run, however, both of these inputs are variable. With both factors variable, a firm can usually produce a given level of output by using a great deal of labor and very little capital, a great deal of capital and very little labor, or moderate amounts of both. That is, the firm can substitute one input for another while continuing to produce the same level of output, in much the same way that a consumer can maintain a given level of utility by substituting one good for another.

Typically, a firm can produce in a number of different ways, some of which require more labor than others. For example, a lumberyard can produce 200 planks an hour with 10 workers using hand saws, with 4 workers using handheld power saws, or with 2 workers using bench power saws.

We can illustrate the basic idea using an estimated Cobb-Douglas production function.[5] The Cobb-Douglas production function has the same functional form as the Cobb-Douglas utility function, which we studied in Chapters 3–5. Hsieh (1995) estimated that a Cobb-Douglas production function for a U.S. electronic and other electric equipment firm is

$$q = L^{0.5}K^{0.5}, \tag{6.4}$$

where L is labor (workers) per day and K is capital services per day.[6] From inspection, there is a variety of combinations of labor and capital that will produce the same level of output.

ISOQUANTS

We can summarize the possible combinations of inputs that will produce a given level of output using an **isoquant**, which is a curve that shows the efficient combinations of labor and capital that can produce a single (*iso*) level of output (*quantity*). If the production function is $q = f(L, K)$, then the equation for an isoquant where output is held constant at $\bar{q}$ is

$$\bar{q} = f(L, K). \tag{6.5}$$

For our particular production function, Equation 6.4, the isoquant is $\bar{q} = L^{0.5}K^{0.5}$.

Figure 6.2 shows an isoquant for $q = 6$, $q = 9$, and $q = 12$, which are three of the many possible isoquants. The isoquants show the flexibility that a firm has in producing a given level of output. These isoquants are smooth curves because the firm can use fractional units of each input.

There are many combinations of labor and capital, (L, K), that will produce 6 units of output, including (1, 36), (2, 18), (3, 12), (4, 9), (6, 6), (9, 4), (12, 3), (18, 2), and (36, 1). Figure 6.2 shows some of these combinations as points *a* through *f* on the $q = 6$ isoquant.

Properties of Isoquants. Isoquants have most of the same properties as indifference curves. The main difference between indifference curves and isoquants is that an isoquant holds quantity constant, whereas an indifference curve holds utility constant. The quantities associated with isoquants have cardinal properties (for example, an output of 12 is twice as much as an output of 6), while the utilities associated with indifference curves have only ordinal properties (for example, 12 utils are associated with more pleasure than 6, but not necessarily twice as much pleasure).

We now consider four major properties of isoquants. Most of these properties result from firms' producing efficiently.

First, *the farther an isoquant is from the origin, the greater the level of output*. That is, the more inputs a firm uses, the more output it gets if it produces efficiently. At point *e*

---

[5]The Cobb-Douglas production function (named after its inventors, Charles W. Cobb, a mathematician, and Paul H. Douglas, an economist and U.S. senator) is probably the most commonly estimated production function.

[6]Hsieh (1995) actually estimated a function of the form $q = AL^{0.5}K^{0.5}$. Because capital, K, includes various types of machines, and output, q, reflects different types of printed matter, their units cannot be described by any common terms. By redefining a unit of output as $1/A$, we can write the production function as in Equation 6.4.

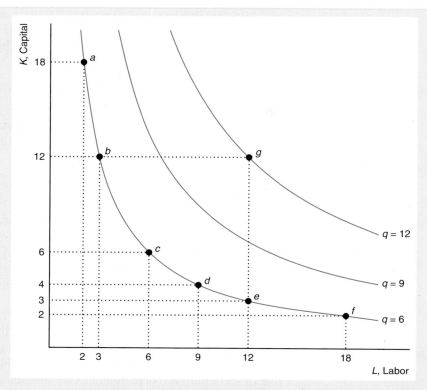

Figure 6.2 Family of Isoquants for a U.S. Electronics Manufacturing Firm. These isoquants for a U.S. electronic and other electric equipment firm (Hsieh, 1995) show the combinations of labor and capital that produce various levels of output. Isoquants farther from the origin correspond to higher levels of output. Points *a, b, c, d, e,* and *f* are various combinations of labor and capital that the firm can use to produce *q* = 6 units of output. If the firm holds capital constant at 12 and increases labor from 3 (point *b*) to 12 (point *g*), the firm shifts from operating on the *q* = 6 isoquant to producing on the *q* = 12 isoquant.

in Figure 6.2, the electronics firm is producing 6 units of output with 12 workers and 3 units of capital. If the firm holds the number of workers constant and adds 9 more units of capital, it produces at point *g*. Point *g* must be on an isoquant with a higher level of output—here, 12 units—if the firm is producing efficiently and not wasting the extra labor.

Second, *isoquants do not cross.* Such intersections are inconsistent with the requirement that the firm always produce efficiently. For example, if the *q* = 15 and *q* = 20 isoquants crossed, the firm could produce at either output level with the same combination of labor and capital. The firm must be producing inefficiently if it produces *q* = 15 when it could produce *q* = 20. Thus that labor-capital combination should not lie on the *q* = 15 isoquant, which should include only efficient combinations of inputs. So efficiency requires that isoquants do not cross.

Third, *isoquants slope downward.* If an isoquant sloped upward, the firm could produce the same level of output with relatively few inputs or relatively many inputs. Producing with relatively many inputs would be inefficient. Consequently, because isoquants show only efficient production, an upward-sloping isoquant is impossible.

Fourth, *isoquants must be thin.* This result follows from virtually the same argument we just used to show that isoquants slope downward.

Shape of Isoquants. The curvature of an isoquant shows how readily a firm can substitute one input for another. The two extreme cases are production processes in which inputs are perfect substitutes or those in which inputs cannot be substituted for each other.

If the inputs are perfect substitutes, each isoquant is a straight line. Suppose either potatoes from Maine, x, or potatoes from Idaho, y, both of which are measured in pounds per day, can be used to produce potato salad, q, measured in pounds. This technology has a *linear production function,*

$$q = x + y.$$

One pound of potato salad can be produced by using 1 pound of Idaho potatoes and no Maine potatoes, 1 pound of Maine potatoes and no Idahoes, or $^1/_2$ pound of each type of potato. The isoquant for $q = 1$ pound of potato salad is $1 = x + y$, or $y = 1 - x$. The slope of this straight-line isoquant is -1. Panel a of Figure 6.3 shows the $q = 1, 2$, and 3 isoquants.

Sometimes it is impossible to substitute one input for the other: Inputs must be used in fixed proportions. Such a technology is called a *fixed-proportions production function.* For example, the inputs needed to produce a 12-ounce box of cereal, q, are

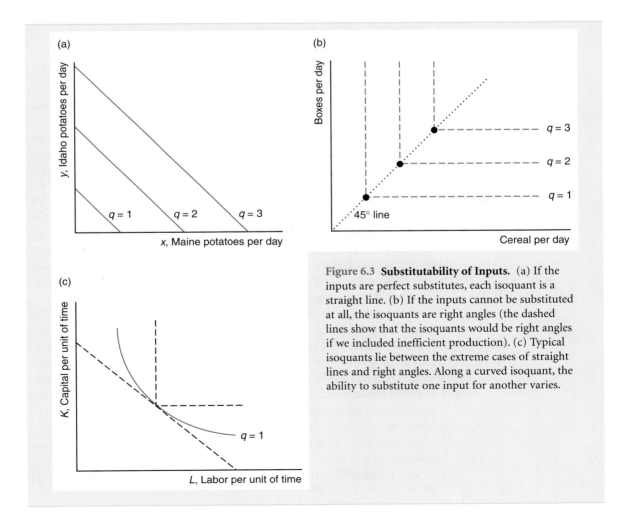

Figure 6.3 Substitutability of Inputs. (a) If the inputs are perfect substitutes, each isoquant is a straight line. (b) If the inputs cannot be substituted at all, the isoquants are right angles (the dashed lines show that the isoquants would be right angles if we included inefficient production). (c) Typical isoquants lie between the extreme cases of straight lines and right angles. Along a curved isoquant, the ability to substitute one input for another varies.

cereal (in 12-ounce units per day), g, and cardboard boxes (boxes per day), b. This fixed-proportions production function is

$$q = \min(g, b),$$

where the min function means "the minimum number of g or b." For example, if the firm has $g = 4$ units of cereal and $b = 3$ boxes, it can produce only $q = 3$ boxes of cereal. Thus in panel b of Figure 6.3, the only efficient points of production are the large dots along the 45° line, where the firm uses equal quantities of both inputs. Dashed lines show that the isoquants would be right angles if isoquants could include inefficient production processes.

Other production processes allow imperfect substitution between inputs. These isoquants are convex (so the middle of the isoquant is closer to the origin than it would be if the isoquant were a straight line). They do not have the same slope at every point, unlike the straight-line isoquants. Most isoquants are smooth, slope downward, curve away from the origin, and lie between the extreme cases of straight lines (perfect substitutes) and right angles (nonsubstitutes), as panel c of Figure 6.3 illustrates.

APPLICATION

A Semiconductor Integrated Circuit Isoquant

We can show why isoquants curve away from the origin by deriving an isoquant for semiconductor integrated circuits (ICs, or "chips"). ICs—the "brains" of computers and other electronic devices—are made by building up layers of conductive and insulating materials on silicon wafers. Each wafer contains many ICs, which are subsequently cut into individual chips, called *dice*.

Semiconductor manufacturers ("fabs") buy the silicon wafers and then use labor and capital to produce the chips. A semiconductor IC's several layers of conductive and insulating materials are arranged in patterns that define the function of the chip.

During the manufacture of ICs, a track moves a wafer into a machine, where the wafer is spun and a light-sensitive liquid called photoresist is applied to its whole surface; the photoresist is then hardened. The wafer advances along the track to a point where photolithography is used to define patterns in the photoresist. In photolithography, light transfers a pattern from a template, called a photomask, to the photoresist, which is then "developed" like film, creating a pattern by removing the resist from certain areas. A subsequent process then can either add to or etch away those areas not protected by the resist.

In a repetition of this entire procedure, additional layers are created on the wafer. Because the conducting and insulating patterns in each layer interact with those in the previous layers, the patterns must line up correctly.

To align layers properly, firms use combinations of labor and equipment. In the least capital-intensive technology, employees use machines called *aligners*. Operators look through microscopes and line up the layers by hand and then expose the entire surface. An operator running an aligner can produce 250 layers a day, or 25 ten-layer chips.

A second, more capital-intensive technology uses machines called *steppers*. The stepper picks a spot on the wafer, automatically aligns the layers, and then exposes that area to light. Then the machine moves—*steps* to other sections—lining up and

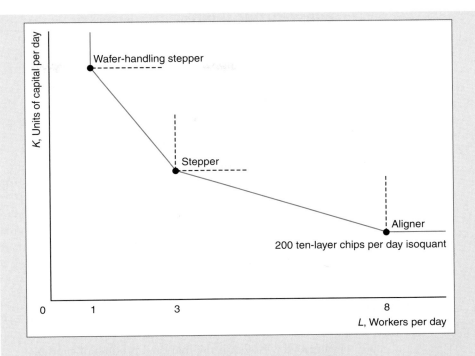

exposing each area in turn until the entire surface has been aligned and exposed. This technology requires less labor: A single worker can run two steppers and produce 500 layers, or 50 ten-layer chips, per day.

A third, even more capital-intensive technology uses a stepper with wafer-handling equipment, which reduces the amount of labor even more. By linking the tracks directly to a stepper and automating the chip transfer process, human handling can be greatly reduced. A single worker can run four steppers with wafer-handling equipment and produce 1,000 layers, or 100 ten-layer chips, per day.

Only steppers can be used if the chip requires line widths of 1 micrometer or less. We show an isoquant for producing 200 ten-layer chips that have lines that are more than 1 micrometer wide, for which any of the three technologies can be used.

All three technologies use labor and capital in fixed proportions. Producing 200 chips takes 8 workers and 8 aligners, 3 workers and 6 steppers, or 1 worker and 4 steppers with wafer-handling capabilities. The accompanying graph shows the three right-angle isoquants corresponding to each of these three technologies.

Some fabs, however, employ a combination of these technologies; some workers use one type of machine while others use different types. By doing so, the fabs can produce using intermediate combinations of labor and capital, as the solid-line, kinked isoquant illustrates. The firm does *not* use a combination of the aligner and the wafer-handling stepper technologies because those combinations are less efficient than using the plain stepper (the line connecting the aligner and wafer-handling stepper technologies is farther from the origin than the lines between those technologies and the plain stepper technology).

New processes are constantly being invented. As they are introduced, the isoquant will have more and more kinks (one for each new process) and will begin to resemble the smooth, usual-shaped isoquants we've been drawing.

SUBSTITUTING INPUTS

The slope of an isoquant shows the ability of a firm to replace one input with another while holding output constant. The slope of an isoquant is called the *marginal rate of technical substitution (MRTS)*:

$$MRTS = \frac{\text{change in capital}}{\text{change in labor}} = \frac{\Delta K}{\Delta L} = \frac{dK}{dL}.$$

The **marginal rate of technical substitution** tells us how many units of capital the firm can replace with an extra unit of labor while holding output constant. Because isoquants slope downward, the *MRTS* is negative.

To determine the slope at a point on an isoquant, we totally differentiate the isoquant, $\bar{q} = f(L, K)$, with respect to L and K. Along the isoquant, we can write capital as an implicit function of labor: $K(L)$. That is, for a given quantity of labor, there is a level of capital such that $\bar{q}$ units are produced. Differentiating with respect to labor (and realizing that output does not change along the isoquant as we change labor), we have

$$\frac{d\bar{q}}{dL} = 0 = \frac{\partial f}{\partial L} + \frac{\partial f}{\partial K}\frac{dK}{dL} = MP_L + MP_K \frac{dK}{dL}, \tag{6.6}$$

where $MP_K = \partial f/\partial K$ is the marginal product of capital.

There is an appealing intuition behind Equation 6.6. As we move down and to the right along an isoquant (such as the ones in Figure 6.2), we increase the amount of labor slightly, so we must decrease the amount of capital to stay on the same isoquant. A little extra labor produces MP_L amount of extra output, the marginal product of labor. For example, if the MP_L is 2 and the firm hires one extra worker, its output rises by 2 units. Similarly, a little extra capital increases output by MP_K, so the change in output due to the drop in capital in response to the increase in labor is $MP_K \times dK/dL$. If we are to stay on the same isoquant—that is, hold output constant—these two effects must offset each other: $MP_L = -MP_K \times dK/dL$.

By rearranging Equation 6.6, we find that the marginal rate of technical substitution, which is the change in capital relative to the change in labor, equals the negative of the ratio of the marginal products:

$$MRTS = \frac{dK}{dL} = -\frac{MP_L}{MP_K}. \tag{6.7}$$

SOLVED PROBLEM 6.3

What is the marginal rate of technical substitution for a general Cobb-Douglas production function, $q = AL^aK^b$?

Answer

1. *Calculate the marginal products of labor and capital by differentiating the Cobb-Douglas production function first with respect to labor and then with respect to capital:* The marginal product of labor is $MP_L = \partial q/\partial L = aAL^{a-1}K^b = aq/L$, and the marginal product of capital is $MP_K = \partial q/\partial K = bAL^aK^{b-1} = bq/K$.

2. *Substitute the expression for MP_L and MP_K into Equation 6.7 to determine the MRTS:* Making the indicated substitutions,

$$MRTS = -\frac{MP_L}{MP_K} = -\frac{a\dfrac{q}{L}}{b\dfrac{q}{K}} = -\frac{a}{b}\frac{K}{L}. \qquad (6.8)$$

Thus the *MRTS* for a Cobb-Douglas production function is a constant, $-a/b$, times the capital-labor ratio, K/L.

DIMINISHING MARGINAL RATES OF TECHNICAL SUBSTITUTION

We can illustrate how the *MRTS* changes along an isoquant using the estimated $q = 6 = L^{0.5}K^{0.5}$ isoquant for an electronics firm from Figure 6.2, which is reproduced in Figure 6.4. The slope along this isoquant is $MRTS = -K/L$, because $a = b = 0.5$ in Equation 6.8.

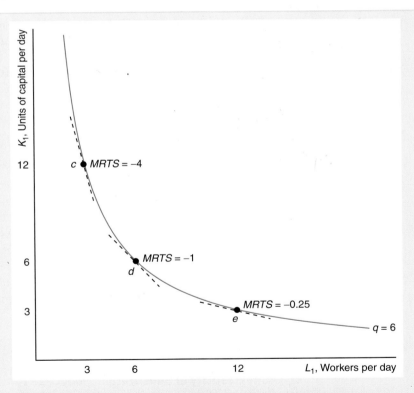

Figure 6.4 How the Marginal Rate of Technical Substitution Varies Along an Isoquant.
Moving from point *c* to *d*, a U.S. electronics firm (Hsieh, 1995) can produce the same amount of output, $q = 6$, using six fewer units of capital, $\Delta K = -6$, if it uses three more workers. The slope of the isoquant, the *MRTS*, at a point is the same as the slope of the dashed tangent line. The *MRTS* goes from -4 at point *c* to -1 at *d* to -0.25 at *e*. Thus as we move down and to the right, the isoquant becomes flatter: The slope gets closer to zero. Because it curves away from the origin, this isoquant exhibits a diminishing marginal rate of technical substitution: With each extra worker, the firm reduces capital by a smaller amount as the ratio of capital to labor falls.

At point *c* in Figure 6.4, where $K = 12$ and $L = 3$, the *MRTS* = −4. The dashed line that is tangent to the isoquant at that point has the same slope. In contrast, the *MRTS* = −1 at *d* ($K = 6$, $L = 6$), and the *MRTS* = −0.25 at *e* ($K = 3$, $L = 12$). Thus as we move down and to the right along this curved isoquant, the slope becomes flatter—the slope gets closer to zero—because the ratio *K/L* grows closer to zero.

The curvature of the isoquant away from the origin reflects *diminishing marginal rates of technical substitution*. The more labor the firm has, the harder it is to replace the remaining capital with labor, so the *MRTS* falls as the isoquant becomes flatter.

In the special case in which isoquants are straight lines, isoquants do not exhibit diminishing marginal rates of technical substitution because neither input becomes more valuable in the production process: The inputs remain perfect substitutes. In our earlier example of producing potato salad using Idaho or Maine potatoes, the *MRTS* is −1 at every point along the isoquant: 1 pound of Idaho potatoes always can be replaced by 1 pound of Maine potatoes. In the other special case of fixed proportions, where isoquants are right angles (or, perhaps more accurately, single points), no substitution is possible.

THE ELASTICITY OF SUBSTITUTION

We've just seen that the marginal rate of technical substitution, the slope of the isoquant at a single point, varies as we move along a curved isoquant. It is useful to have a measure of this curvature, which reflects the ease with which a firm can substitute capital for labor. The best-known measure of the ease of substitution is the **elasticity of substitution**, σ (the Greek letter sigma), which is the percentage change in the capital-labor ratio divided by the percentage change in the *MRTS*:

$$\sigma = \frac{\dfrac{d(K/L)}{K/L}}{\dfrac{dMRTS}{MRTS}} = \frac{d(K/L)}{dMRTS}\frac{MRTS}{K/L}. \tag{6.9}$$

This measure tells us how the input factor ratio changes as the slope of the isoquant changes. If the elasticity is large—a small change in the slope results in a big increase in the factor ratio—the isoquant is relatively flat. As the elasticity falls, the isoquant becomes more curved. As we move along the isoquant, both *K/L* and the absolute value of the *MRTS* change in the same direction (see Figure 6.4), so the elasticity is positive.

Both the factor ratio, *K/L*, and the absolute value of the *MRTS*, |*MRTS*|, are positive numbers, so the logarithm of each is meaningful. It is often helpful to write the elasticity of substitution as a logarithmic derivative:[7]

$$\sigma = \frac{d \ln (K/L)}{d \ln |MRTS|}. \tag{6.10}$$

Constant Elasticity of Substitution Production Function. In general, the elasticity of substitution varies along an isoquant. An exception is the *constant elasticity of substitution* (CES) production function,

$$q = (aL^\rho + bK^\rho)^{d/\rho}, \tag{6.11}$$

---

[7] By totally differentiating, we find that $d \ln (K/L) = d(K/L)/(K/L)$ and $d \ln |MRTS| = dMRTS/MRTS$, so $[d \ln (K/L)]/[d \ln |MRTS|] = [d(K/L)/dMRTS][MRTS/(K/L)] = \sigma$.

where ρ is a positive constant. For simplicity, we assume that $a = b = d = 1$, so

$$q = (L^{\rho} + K^{\rho})^{1/\rho}. \tag{6.12}$$

The marginal rate of technical substitution for a CES isoquant is[8]

$$MRTS = -\left(\frac{L}{K}\right)^{\rho - 1}. \tag{6.13}$$

That is, the *MRTS* varies with the labor-capital ratio. At every point on a CES isoquant, the constant elasticity of substitutions is[9]

$$\sigma = \frac{1}{1 - \rho}. \tag{6.14}$$

The linear, fixed-proportion, and Cobb-Douglas production functions are special cases of the constant elasticity production function.

Linear Production Function. Setting $\rho = 1$ in Equation 6.12, we get the linear production function $q = L + K$. At every point along a linear isoquant, the elasticity of substitution, $\sigma = 1/(1 - \rho) = 1/0$, is infinite: The two inputs are perfect substitutes for each other.

Cobb-Douglas Production Function. As ρ approaches zero, the CES isoquants approach the Cobb-Douglas isoquants, and hence the CES production function approaches the Cobb-Douglas production function. According to Equation 6.13, the CES $MRTS = -K/L$. Similarly, setting $a = b$ in Equation 6.8, we find that the Cobb-Douglas *MRTS* is the same. The elasticity of substitution is $\sigma = 1/(1 - \rho) = 1/1 = 1$ at every point along a Cobb-Douglas isoquant.

Fixed-Proportion Production Function. As ρ approaches negative infinity, this production function approaches the fixed-proportion production function, which has right-angle isoquants (or, more accurately, single-point isoquants).[10] The elasticity of substitution is $\sigma = 1/(-\infty) = 0$: Substitution between the inputs is impossible.

SOLVED PROBLEM 6.4

What is the elasticity of substitution for the general Cobb-Douglas production function, $q = AL^aK^b$? (Comment: We just showed that the elasticity of substitution is one for a Cobb-Douglas where $a = b$. We want to know if that result holds for the more general Cobb-Douglas.)

Answer

1. *Using the formula for the marginal rate of technical substitution, determine* $d(K/L)/dMRTS$ *and* $MRTS/(K/L)$, *which are needed for the elasticity of substitution formula:* The marginal rate of technical substitution of a general Cobb-Douglas

---

[8]Using the chain rule, we know that the $MP_L = (1/\rho)(L^{\rho} + K^{\rho})^{1/\rho - 1}\rho L^{\rho - 1} = (L^{\rho} + K^{\rho})^{1/\rho - 1}L^{\rho - 1}$. Similarly, the $MP_K = (L^{\rho} + K^{\rho})^{1/\rho - 1}K^{\rho - 1}$. Thus the $MRTS = -MP_L/MP_K = (L/K)^{\rho - 1}$.

[9]From the *MRTS* equation 6.13, we know that $L/K = |MRTS|^{1/(1 - \rho)}$. Taking logarithms of both sides of this expression, we find that $\ln(L/K) = [1/(1 - \rho)]\ln|MRTS|$. Using the logarithmic derivative of the elasticity of substitution, Equation 6.10, we find that $\sigma = (d \ln K/L)/(d \ln |MRTS|) = 1/(1 - \rho)$.

[10]We show that as ρ approaches $-\infty$, the CES isoquant approaches the right-angle, fixed-proportions isoquant. According to Equation 6.13, the $MRTS = -(L/K)^{-\infty}$. Thus the *MRTS* is zero if $L > K$, and the *MRTS* goes to infinity if $K > L$.

production function, Equation 6.8, is $MRTS = -(a/b)(K/L)$. Rearranging these terms:

$$\frac{K}{L} = -\frac{b}{a}MRTS. \tag{6.15}$$

Differentiating Equation 6.15, we find that $d(K/L)/dMRTS = -b/a$. By rearranging the terms in Equation 6.15, we also know that $MRTS/(K/L) = -a/b$.

2. *Substitute the two expressions from Step 1 into the elasticity of substitution formula and simplify:* The elasticity of substitution for a Cobb-Douglas production function is

$$\sigma = \frac{d(K/L)}{dMRTS}\frac{MRTS}{K/L} = \left(-\frac{b}{a}\right)\left(-\frac{a}{b}\right) = 1. \tag{6.16}$$

6.5 Returns to Scale

So far, the discussion has examined the effects of increasing one input while holding the other input constant (the shift from one isoquant to another) or decreasing the other input by an offsetting amount (the movement along an isoquant). We now turn to the question of *how much output changes if a firm increases all its inputs proportionately.* The answer to this question helps a firm determine its *scale* or size in the long run.

In the long run, a firm can increase its output by building a second plant and staffing it with the same number of workers as in the first plant. The firm's decision about whether to build a second plant partly depends on whether its output increases less than in proportion, in proportion, or more than in proportion to its inputs.

CONSTANT, INCREASING, AND DECREASING RETURNS TO SCALE

If, when all inputs are increased by a certain percentage, output increases by that same percentage, the production function is said to exhibit **constant returns to scale** (*CRS*). A firm's production process has constant returns to scale if, when the firm doubles its inputs—builds an identical second plant and uses the same amount of labor and equipment as in the first plant—it doubles its output: $f(2L, 2K) = 2f(L, K)$. [More generally, a production function is said to be homogeneous of degree γ if $f(xL, xK) = x^\gamma f(L, K)$, where x is a positive constant, so constant returns to scale is homogeneity of degree one.]

We can check whether the linear potato salad production function has constant returns to scale. If a firm uses x_1 pounds of Idaho potatoes and y_1 pounds of Maine potatoes, it produces $q_1 = x_1 + y_1$ pounds of potato salad. If it doubles both inputs, using $x_2 = 2x_1$ Idaho and $y_2 = 2y_1$ Maine potatoes, it doubles its output:

$$q_2 = x_2 + y_2 = 2x_1 + 2y_1 = 2q_1.$$

Thus the potato salad production function exhibits constant returns to scale.

If output rises more than in proportion to an equal percentage increase in all inputs, the production function is said to exhibit **increasing returns to scale** (*IRS*). A technology exhibits increasing returns to scale if doubling inputs more than doubles the output: $f(2L, 2K) > 2f(L, K)$.

Why might a production function have increasing returns to scale? One reason is that, although it could duplicate a small factory and double its output, the firm might be able to more than double its output by building a single large plant, allowing for greater specialization of labor or capital. In the two smaller plants, workers have to perform many unrelated tasks such as operating, maintaining, and fixing the machines they use. In the large plant, some workers may specialize in maintaining and fixing machines, thereby increasing efficiency. Similarly, a firm may use specialized equipment in a large plant but not in a small one.

If output rises less than in proportion to an equal percentage increase in all inputs, the production function exhibits **decreasing returns to scale** (*DRS*). A technology exhibits decreasing returns to scale if doubling inputs causes output to rise less than in proportion: $f(2L, 2K) < 2f(L, K)$.

One reason for decreasing returns to scale is that the difficulty of organizing, coordinating, and integrating activities increases with firm size. An owner may be able to manage one plant well but may have trouble running two plants. In some sense, the owner's difficulties in running a larger firm may reflect our failure to take into account some factor such as management in our production function. When the firm increases the various inputs, it does not increase the management input in proportion. If so, the "decreasing returns to scale" is really due to a fixed input. Another reason is that large teams of workers may not function as well as small teams in which each individual takes greater personal responsibility.

SOLVED PROBLEM **6.5**

Under what conditions does a general Cobb-Douglas production function, $q = AL^aK^b$, exhibit decreasing, constant, or increasing returns to scale?

Answer

1. *Show how output changes if both inputs are doubled:* If the firm initially uses L and K amounts of inputs, it produces

$$q_1 = AL^aK^b.$$

When the firm doubles the amount of both labor and capital it uses, it produces

$$q^2 = A(2L)^a(2K)^b = 2^{a+b}AL^aK^b.$$

Thus its output increases by

$$\frac{q_2}{q_1} = \frac{2^{a+b}AL^aK^b}{AL^aK^b} = 2^{a+b} \equiv 2^\gamma,$$

where $\gamma \equiv a + b$.

2. *Give a rule for determining the returns to scale:* The Cobb-Douglas production function parameter γ determines the returns to scale. The production function has decreasing returns to scale if $\gamma < 1$, constant returns to scale if $\gamma = 1$, and increasing returns to scale if $\gamma > 1$. For example, if $\gamma = 1$, doubling inputs doubles output, $q_2/q_1 = 2^\gamma = 2^1 = 2$, so the production function exhibits constant returns to scale.

APPLICATION

Returns to Scale in U.S. Manufacturing

Increasing, constant, and decreasing returns to scale are commonly observed. The table shows estimates of Cobb-Douglas production functions and rates of returns in various U.S. manufacturing industries (based on Hsieh, 1995). The returns to scale measure in the table, γ, is an elasticity. It represents the percentage change in output for a 1% increase in all the inputs. Because the estimated returns to scale measure for an electronics firm is virtually 1, a 1% increase in the inputs causes a 1% increase in output. Thus an electronics firm's production function exhibits constant returns to scale.

	Labor, a	Capital, b	Scale, $\gamma = a + b$
Decreasing Returns to Scale			
Tobacco products	0.18	0.33	0.51
Food and kindred products	0.43	0.48	0.91
Transportation equipment	0.44	0.48	0.92
Constant Returns to Scale			
Apparel and other textile products	0.70	0.31	1.01
Furniture and fixtures	0.62	0.40	1.02
Electronic and other electric equipment	0.49	0.53	1.02
Increasing Returns to Scale			
Paper and allied products	0.44	0.65	1.09
Petroleum and coal products	0.30	0.88	1.18
Primary metal	0.51	0.73	1.24

The estimated returns to scale measure for a tobacco firm is 0.51: A 1% increase in inputs causes output to rise by 0.51%. Because output rises less than in proportion to the inputs, the tobacco production function exhibits decreasing returns to scale. In contrast, firms that manufacture primary metals have increasing returns to scale production functions, in which a 1% increase in all inputs causes output to rise by 1.24%.

The accompanying graphs use isoquants to illustrate the returns to scale for the electronics, tobacco, and primary metal firms. We measure the units of labor, capital, and output so that, for all three firms, 100 units of labor and 100 units of capital produce 100 units of output on the $q = 100$ isoquant in the three panels. For the constant returns to scale electronics firm, panel a, if both labor and capital are doubled from 100 to 200 units, output doubles to 200 ($= 100 \times 2^1$, multiplying the original output by the rate of increase using Equation 6.5).

That same doubling of inputs causes output to rise to only 142 ($\approx 100 \times 2^{0.51}$) for the tobacco firm, panel b. Because output rises less than in proportion to inputs, the production function has decreasing returns to scale. If the

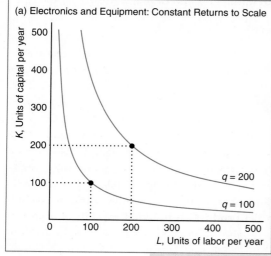

(a) Electronics and Equipment: Constant Returns to Scale

K, Units of capital per year

L, Units of labor per year

$q = 200$

$q = 100$

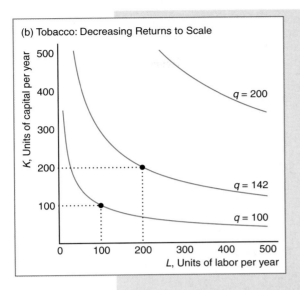

(b) Tobacco: Decreasing Returns to Scale

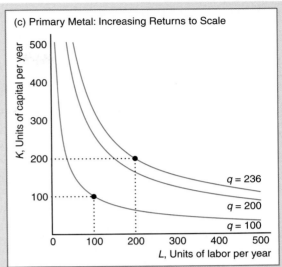

(c) Primary Metal: Increasing Returns to Scale

primary metal firm doubles its inputs, panel c, its output more than doubles, to 236 ($\approx 100 \times 2^{1.24}$), so the production function has increasing returns to scale.

These graphs illustrate that the spacing of the isoquant determines the returns to scale. The closer together the $q = 100$ and $q = 200$ isoquants, the greater the returns to scale.

The returns to scale in these industries are estimated to be the same at all levels of output. A production function's returns to scale may vary, however, as the scale of the firm changes.

VARYING RETURNS TO SCALE

Many production functions have increasing returns to scale for small amounts of output, constant returns for moderate amounts of output, and decreasing returns for large amounts of output. When a firm is small, increasing labor and capital allows for gains from cooperation between workers and greater specialization of workers and equipment—*returns to specialization*—so there are increasing returns to scale. As the firm grows, returns to scale are eventually exhausted. There are no more returns to specialization, so the production process has constant returns to scale. If the firm continues to grow, the owner starts having difficulty managing everyone, so the firm suffers from decreasing returns to scale.

Figure 6.5 shows such a pattern. Again, the spacing of the isoquants reflects the returns to scale. Initially, the firm has one worker and one piece of equipment, point *a*, and produces 1 unit of output on the $q = 1$ isoquant. If the firm doubles its inputs, it produces at *b*, where $L = 2$ and $K = 2$, which lies on the dashed line through the origin and point *a*. Output more than doubles to $q = 3$, so the production function exhibits increasing returns to scale in this range. Another doubling of inputs to *c* causes output to double to 6 units, so the production function has constant returns to scale in this range. Another doubling of inputs to *d* causes output to increase by only a third, to $q = 8$, so the production function has decreasing returns to scale in this range.

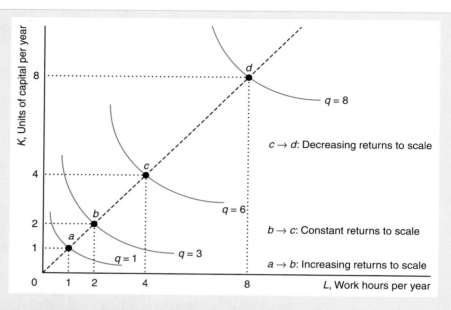

Figure 6.5 Varying Scale Economies. This production function exhibits varying returns to scale. Initially, the firm uses one worker and one unit of capital, point *a*. It repeatedly doubles these inputs to points *b*, *c*, and *d*, which lie along the dashed line. The first time the inputs are doubled, *a* to *b*, output more than doubles from $q = 1$ to $q = 3$, so the production function has increasing returns to scale. The next doubling, *b* to *c*, causes a proportionate increase in output, constant returns to scale. At the last doubling, from *c* to *d*, the production function exhibits decreasing returns to scale.

6.6 Productivity and Technical Change

Because firms may use different technologies and different methods of organizing production, the amount of output that one firm produces from a given amount of inputs may differ from that produced by another firm. Moreover, after a technical or managerial innovation, a firm can produce more today from a given amount of inputs than it could in the past.

RELATIVE PRODUCTIVITY

This chapter has assumed that firms produce efficiently. A firm must produce efficiently if it is to maximize its profit. Even if each firm in a market produces as efficiently as possible, however, firms may not be equally *productive,* in the sense that one firm can produce more than another from a given amount of inputs.

A firm may be more productive than others if its manager knows a better way to organize production or if it is the only firm with access to a new invention. Union-mandated work rules, government regulations, other institutional restrictions, or racial or gender discrimination that affect only some firms may lower the relative productivity of those firms.

We can measure the *relative productivity* of a firm by expressing the firm's actual output, q, as a percentage of the output that the most productive firm in the industry could have produced, q^*, from the same amount of inputs: $100q/q^*$. The most productive firm in an industry has a relative productivity measure of 100% ($= 100q^*/q^*$ percent).

Caves and Barton (1990) reported that the average productivity of firms across U.S. manufacturing industries ranges from 63% to 99%. That is, in the manufacturing industry with the most diverse firms, the average firm produces slightly less than two-thirds as much as the most productive firm, whereas in the manufacturing industry with the most homogeneous firms, all firms are nearly equally productive.

Differences in productivity across markets may be due to differences in the degree of competition. In competitive markets, in which many firms can enter and exit the market easily, less productive firms lose money and are driven out of business, so the firms that are actually producing are equally productive (as Chapter 8 shows). In a less competitive oligopoly market, with few firms and no possibility of entry by new firms, a less productive firm may be able to survive, so firms with varying levels of productivity are observed.

In communist and other government-managed economies in which firms are not required to maximize profits, inefficient firms may survive. For example, a study of productivity in 48 medium-size, machine-building state enterprises in China (Kalirajan and Obwona, 1994) found that the productivity measure ranges from 21% to 100%, with an average of 55%.

INNOVATIONS

> *Maximum number of miles that Ford's most fuel-efficient 2003 car could drive on a gallon of gas: 36. Maximum number its 1912 Model T could: 35.*
>
> —Harper's Index 2003

In its production process, a firm tries to use the best available technological and managerial knowledge. An advance in knowledge that allows more output to be produced with the same level of inputs is called **technical progress.** The invention of new products is a form of technical innovation. The use of robotic arms increases the number of automobiles produced with a given amount of labor and raw materials. Better *management or organization of the production process* similarly allows the firm to produce more output from given levels of inputs.

Technical Progress. A technological innovation changes the production process. Last year a firm produced

$$q_1 = f(L, K)$$

units of output using L units of labor services and K units of capital service. Due to a new invention that the firm uses, this year's production function differs from last year's, so the firm produces 10% more output with the same inputs:

$$q_2 = 1.1f(L, K).$$

This firm has experienced *neutral technical change,* in which it can produce more output using the same ratio of inputs. For example, a technical innovation in the form of a new printing press allows more output to be produced using the same ratio of inputs as before: one worker to one printing press.

Table 6.1   Annual Percentage Rates of Neutral Productivity Growth for Computer and Related Capital Goods

	1990–1995	1995–2002
Australia	1.4	1.5
Canada	0.4	1.0
France	0.8	1.4
Japan	0.8	0.6
United Kingdom	1.2	0.9*
United States	0.8	1.3

*United Kingdom rate is for 1995–2001.

Source: OECD Productivity Database, December 17, 2004.

Many empirical studies find that systematic neutral technical progress occurs over time. In these studies, the production function is

$$q = A(t)f(L, K), \tag{6.17}$$

where $A(t)$ is a function of time, t, that shows how much output grows over time for any given mix of inputs. Table 6.1 shows estimates of the annual rate at which computer and related goods output grew for given levels of inputs in several countries. According to this estimate, the U.S. computer production function, Equation 6.17, is $q = e^{0.017t}f(L, K)$, so that output grows at a 1.7% rate per year.

Nonneutral technical changes are innovations that alter the proportion in which inputs are used. If a printing press that required two people to operate is replaced by a press that can be run by a single worker, the technical change is *labor saving*. The ratio of labor to the other inputs used to produce a given level of output falls after the innovation.[11] Similarly, the ratio of output to labor, the average product of labor, rises.

Organizational Change. Organizational changes may also alter the production function and increase the amount of output produced by a given amount of inputs. Organizational innovations have been very important in automobile manufacturing.

In the early 1900s, Henry Ford revolutionized mass production through two organizational innovations. First, he introduced interchangeable parts, which cut the time required to install parts because workers no longer had to file or machine individually made parts to get them to fit. Second, Ford introduced a conveyor belt and an assembly line to his production process. Before Ford, workers walked around the car, and each worker performed many assembly activities. In Ford's plant, each worker specialized in a single activity such as attaching the right rear fender to the chassis. A conveyor belt moved the car at a constant speed from worker to worker along the assembly line. Because his workers gained proficiency from specializing in only a few activities and because the conveyor belts reduced the number of movements workers had to make, Ford could produce more automobiles with the same number of workers. By the early 1920s, Ford had cut the cost of a car by more than two-thirds and had increased production from fewer than a thousand cars per year to two million per year.

---

[11]See **www.aw-bc.com/perloff**, Chapter 6, "More Productive Death" and "Rolls Royce."

● APPLICATION

Dell Computer's Organizational Innovations

Michael Dell, the president of Dell Computer, has become rich by innovating in organizational practices rather than by producing the most technologically advanced computers. Dell Computer is probably the world's most efficient personal computer manufacturer due in large part to two organizational innovations: building to order and just-in-time delivery. Dell made its name by selling directly to customers and allowing them to specify the features they want on their personal computer. It has adopted and extended the use of just-in-time inventories, a practice developed by Toyota and other Japanese auto manufacturers. Upon getting an order, Dell uses the Internet to tell its suppliers which parts it needs, and receives delivery within an hour and a half. As Michael Dell writes, "Keep your friends close, and your suppliers closer." Its just-in-time strategy virtually eliminates the need for Dell to maintain any inventory of parts and finished products.

Twelve years ago, Dell had 30 days of parts in inventory, and its main competitors still maintain 12–16 weeks of inventory. In 2005, Dell had just two hours' worth of inventories at its plant in Limerick, Ireland. Consequently, Dell has eliminated warehouses in its factories, cutting the number of buildings it needs in each factory from two to one.

To streamline its manufacturing further, the company uses special hydraulic tools, conveyor belts, and tracks, slashing human intervention in half. Workers snap computer components into place, rarely having to use screwdrivers. Every screw and every sticker they remove by design from a machine saves four seconds of assembly time. Building a PC in 1999 took 2 workers 14 minutes but in 2004 took a single worker roughly 5 minutes. On average, slightly over 25 computers were built per Dell employee in 2000 compared to over 75 in 2004.

Summary

1. **The Ownership and Management of Firms:** Firms are sole proprietorships, partnerships, or corporations. In smaller firms (particularly sole proprietorships and partnerships), the owners usually run the company. In large firms (such as most corporations), the owners hire managers to run the firms. Owners want to maximize profits. If managers have different objectives than owners, owners must keep a close watch over managers to ensure that profits are maximized.

2. **Production:** Inputs, or factors of production—labor, capital, and materials—are combined to produce output using the current state of knowledge about technology and management. To maximize profits, a firm must produce as efficiently as possible: It must get the maximum amount of output from the inputs it uses, given existing knowledge. A firm may have access to many efficient production processes that use different combinations of inputs to produce a given level of output. New technologies or new forms of organization can increase the amount of output that can be produced from a given combination of inputs. A production function shows how much output can be produced efficiently from various levels of inputs. A firm can vary all its inputs in the long run but only some of its inputs in the short run.

3. **Short-Run Production: One Variable and One Fixed Input:** In the short run, a firm cannot adjust the quantity of some inputs, such as capital. The firm varies its output by adjusting its variable inputs, such as labor. If all factors

are fixed except labor, and a firm that was using very little labor increases its use of labor, its output may rise more than in proportion to the increase in labor because of greater specialization of workers. Eventually, however, as more workers are hired, the workers get in each other's way or wait to share equipment, so output increases by smaller and smaller amounts. This latter phenomenon is described by the law of diminishing marginal returns: The marginal product of an input—the extra output from the last unit of input—eventually decreases as more of that input is used, holding other inputs fixed.

4. **Long-Run Production: Two Variable Inputs:** In the long run, when all inputs are variable, firms can substitute between inputs. An isoquant shows the combinations of inputs that can produce a given level of output. The marginal rate of technical substitution is the slope of the isoquant. Usually, the more of one input the firm uses, the more difficult it is to substitute that input for another input. That is, there are diminishing marginal rates of technical substitution as the firm uses more of one input. The elasticity of substitution reflects the ease of replacing one input with another in the production process, or, equivalently, the curvature of an isoquant.

5. **Returns to Scale:** If, when a firm increases all inputs in proportion, its output increases by the same proportion, the production process is said to exhibit constant returns to scale. If output increases less than in proportion to inputs, the production process has decreasing returns to scale; if it increases more than in proportion, it has increasing returns to scale. All three types of returns to scale are commonly seen in actual industries. Many production processes exhibit first increasing, then constant, and finally decreasing returns to scale as the size of the firm increases.

6. **Productivity and Technical Change:** Although all firms in an industry produce efficiently, given what they know and what institutional and other constraints they face, some firms may be more productive than others: They can produce more output from a given bundle of inputs. Due to innovations such as technical progress and new methods of organizing production, a firm can produce more today than it could in the past from the same bundle of inputs. Such innovations change the production function.

Questions

* = *answer at the back of this book;* W = *audio-slide show answers by James Dearden at* **www.aw-bc.com/perloff**

*1. If each extra worker produces an extra unit of output, how do the total product of labor, the average product of labor, and the marginal product of labor vary with labor?

2. Each extra worker produces an extra unit of output, up to six workers. After six, no additional output is produced. Draw the total product of labor, average product of labor, and marginal product of labor curves.

3. What are the differences between an isoquant and an indifference curve?

4. Why must isoquants be thin?

5. Suppose that a firm has a fixed-proportions production function in which one unit of output is produced using one worker and two units of capital. If the firm has an extra worker and no more capital, it still can produce only one unit of output. Similarly, one more unit of capital does the firm no good.

   a. Draw the isoquants for this production function.
   b. Draw the total product, average product, and marginal product of labor curves (you will probably want to use two diagrams) for this production function.

*6. To produce a recorded CD, $q = 1$, a firm uses one blank disc, $D = 1$, and the services of a recording machine, $M = 1$, for one hour. Draw an isoquant for this production process. Explain the reason for its shape.

7. Michelle's business produces ceramic cups using labor, clay, and a kiln. She can manufacture 25 cups a day with one worker and 35 with two workers. Does her production process illustrate *diminishing returns to scale* or *diminishing marginal returns to scale*? What is a plausible explanation for why output does not increase proportionately with the number of workers?

8. The production function at Ginko's Copy Shop is $q = 1,000 \times \min(L, 3K)$, where q is the number of copies per hour, q, L is the number of workers, and K is the number of copy machines. As an example, if $L = 2$ and $K = 1$, then $\min(L, 3K) = 3$, and $q = 3,000$.

   a. Draw the isoquants for this production function.
   b. Draw the total product, average product, and marginal product of labor curves for this production function for some fixed level of capital.

9. Why might we expect the law of diminishing marginal product to hold?

*10. Mark launders his white clothes using the production function $q = B + 2G$, where B is the number of cups of Clorox bleach and G is the number of cups of a generic bleach that is half as potent. Draw an isoquant. What is the marginal product of B? What is the marginal rate of technical substitution at each point on an isoquant?

11. To speed relief to isolated South Asian communities that were devastated by the December 2004 tsunami, the U.S. government doubled the number of helicopters from 45 to 90 in early 2005. Navy Admiral Thomas Fargo, head of the U.S. Pacific Command, was asked if doubling the number of helicopters would "produce twice as much [relief]." He predicted, "Maybe pretty close to twice as

much." (Vicky O'Hara, *All Things Considered,* National Public Radio, January 4, 2005, **www.npr.org/dmg/dmg .php?prgCode=ATC&showDate=04-Jan-2005&segNum= 10&NPRMediaPref=WM&getAd=1**). Identify the outputs and inputs and describe the production process. Is the admiral discussing a production process with nearly constant returns to scale, or is he referring to another property of the production process?

12. Ginko's Print Shop can use any one of three fixed-proportion technologies. Each involves one printer and one worker. Describe the possible shapes of the firm's isoquant. (*Hint:* Review the discussion in the application "A Semiconductor Integrated Circuit Isoquant.")

13. From the ninth century B.C. until the proliferation of gunpowder in the fifteenth century A.D., the ultimate weapon of mass destruction was the catapult (John N. Wilford, "How Catapults Married Science, Politics and War," *New York Times,* February 24, 2004, D3). As early as the fourth century B.C., rulers set up research and development laboratories to support military technology. Research on improving the catapult was by trial and error until about 200 B.C., when the engineer Philo of Byzantium reported that, by using mathematics, it was determined that each part of the catapult was proportional to the size of the object it was designed to propel. For example, the weight and length of the projectile was proportional to the size of the torsion springs (bundles of sinews or ropes that were tightly twisted to store enormous power). Mathematicians devised precise reference tables of specifications for builders and soldiers on the firing line. The Romans had catapults capable of delivering 60-pound boulders at least 500 feet. (Legend has it that Archimedes' catapults used stones that were three times heavier than those boulders.) If the output of the production process is measured as the weight of a delivered projectile, how does the amount of capital needed vary with output? If the amount of labor to operate the catapult did not vary substantially with the projectile's size, what can you say about the marginal productivity of capital and scale economies?

14. Until the mid-eighteenth century when spinning became mechanized, cotton was an expensive and relatively unimportant textile (Virginia Postrel, "What Separates Rich Nations from Poor Nations?" *New York Times,* January 1,

2004). Where it used to take an Indian hand-spinner 50,000 hours to hand-spin 100 pounds of cotton, an operator of a 1760s-era hand-operated cotton mule spinning machine could produce 100 pounds of stronger thread in 300 hours. When the self-acting mule spinner automated the process after 1825, the time dropped to 135 hours, and cotton became an inexpensive, common cloth. Was this technological progress neutral? In a figure, show how these technological changes affected isoquants.

15. Draw a circle in a diagram with labor services on one axis and capital services on the other. This circle represents all the combinations of labor and capital that produce 100 units of output. Now draw the isoquant for 100 units of output. (*Hint:* Remember that the isoquant includes only the efficient combinations of labor and capital.)

16. In a manufacturing plant, workers use a specialized machine to produce belts. A new machine is invented that is labor saving. With the new machine, the firm can use fewer workers and still produce the same number of belts as it did using the old machine. In the long run, both labor and capital (the machine) are variable. From what you know, what is the effect of this invention on the AP_L, MP_L, and returns to scale? If you require more information to answer this question, specify what else you need to know.

17. Show in a diagram that a production function can have diminishing marginal returns to a factor and constant returns to scale.

18. If a firm lays off workers during a recession, how will the firm's marginal product of labor change?

*19. During recessions, American firms lay off a larger proportion of their workers than Japanese firms do. (It has been claimed that Japanese firms continue to produce at high levels and store the output or sell it at relatively low prices during recessions.) Assuming that the production function remains unchanged over a period that is long enough to include many recessions and expansions, would you expect the average product of labor to be higher in Japan or in the United States? Why or why not?

20. Does it follow that, because we observe that the average product of labor is higher for Firm 1 than for Firm 2, Firm 1 is more productive in the sense that it can produce more output from a given amount of inputs? Why or why not?

Problems

21. By studying, Will can produce a higher grade, G_W, on an upcoming economics exam. His production function depends on the number of hours he studies marginal analysis problems, A, and the number of hours he studies supply and demand problems, R. Specifically, $G_W = 2.5A^{0.36}R^{0.64}$. His roommate David's grade production function is $G_D = 2.5A^{0.25}R^{0.75}$.

a. What is Will's marginal productivity of studying supply and demand problems? What is David's?

b. What is Will's marginal rate of technical substitution between studying the two types of problems? What is David's?

c. Is it possible that Will and David have different marginal productivity functions but the same marginal rate of technical substitution functions? Explain. **W**

*22. Suppose that the production function is $q = L^{3/4}K^{1/4}$.

    a. What is the average product of labor, holding capital fixed at $\overline{K}$?

    b. What is the marginal product of labor?

    c. Does this production function have increasing, constant, or decreasing returns to scale?

23. What is the production function if L and K are perfect substitutes and each unit of q requires 1 unit of L or 1 unit of K (or a combination of these inputs that adds to 1)?

*24. At $L = 4$ and $K = 4$, the marginal product of labor is 2 and the marginal product of capital is 3. What is the marginal rate of technical substitution?

25. In the short run, a firm cannot vary its capital, $K = 2$, but it can vary its labor, L. It produces output q. Explain why the firm will or will not experience diminishing marginal returns to labor in the short run if its production function is:

    a. $q = 10L + K$

    b. $q = L^{1/2}K^{1/2}$

26. Under what conditions do the following production functions exhibit decreasing, constant, or increasing returns to scale?

    a. $q = L + K$, a linear production function

    b. $q = AL^aK^b$, a general Cobb-Douglas production function

    c. $q = L + L^aK^b + K$

    d. $q = (aL^\rho + bK^\rho)^{d/\rho}$, a general CES production function

*27. Firm 1 and Firm 2 use the same type of production function, but Firm 1 is only 90% as productive as Firm 2. That is, the production function of Firm 2 is $q_2 = f(L, K)$, and the production function of Firm 1 is $q_1 = 0.9f(L, K)$. At a particular level of inputs, how does the marginal product of labor differ between the firms?

28. Is it possible that a firm's production function exhibits increasing returns to scale while exhibiting diminishing marginal productivity of each of its inputs? To answer this question, calculate the marginal productivities of capital and labor for the production of electronics and equipment, tobacco, and primary metal using the information listed in the "Returns to Scale in U.S. Manufacturing" application. **W**

*29. The production function for the automotive and parts industry is $q = L^{0.27}K^{0.16}M^{0.61}$, where M is energy and materials (based loosely on Klein, 2003). What kind of returns to scale does this production function exhibit? What is the marginal product of energy and materials?

30. A production function is said to be homogeneous of degree γ if $f(xL, xK) = x^\gamma f(L, K)$, where x is a positive constant. That is, the production function has the same returns to scale for every combination of inputs. For such a production function, show that the marginal product of labor and marginal product of capital functions are homogeneous of degree $\gamma - 1$.

31. Show that with a constant returns to scale production function, the *MRTS* between labor and capital depends only on the K/L ratio and not on the scale of production. (*Hint*: Use your result from Problem 30.)

32. Prove Euler's theorem that, if $f(L, K)$ is homogeneous of degree γ (see Problem 30), then $L(\partial f/\partial L) + K(\partial f/\partial K) = \gamma f(L, K)$. Given this result, what can you conclude if a production function has constant returns to scale? Express your results in terms of the marginal products of labor and capital.

33. Show that $f(L, K) = (aL^\rho + bK^\rho)^{1/\rho}$, a CES production function, can be written as $f(L, K) = B(\rho)[cL^\rho + (1 - c) \times K^\rho]^{1/\rho}$.

34. Ben's swim coach estimates that his time, t, in the 100-yard butterfly at a big upcoming meet as a function of the number of yards he swims per week, y, is $t = 47 + 7e^{-0.00005y}$. Based on this production function, his coach also estimates that if Ben swims 20,000 yards per week, his time will be 49.57 seconds, and he will finish in tenth place. If he swims 40,000 yards per week, his time will be 47.94 seconds, and he will come in third. If he swims 60,000 yards per week, his time will be 47.34 seconds, and he will win the meet.

    a. Use calculus to determine Ben's marginal productivity of time given the number of yards he practices. Is there diminishing marginal productivity of practice yards?

    b. In terms of Ben's place in the big meet, what is his marginal productivity of the number of yards he practices? Is there diminishing marginal productivity of practice yards? **W**

35. In recent years, professional sports teams have used sabermetrics (the application of statistics to measuring player productivity) to study the productivity of professional baseball players. Sabermetrics is now being used to study the contributions of individual players to the productivity of their teams. (See Allen St. John, "An NBA MBA," *Wall Street Journal*, Nov. 3, 2006, p. W5.)

    a. In the CES basketball production function, $q = (a_1L_1^\rho + \cdots + a_nL_n^\rho)^{d/\rho}$, q is the number of points per game that a team scores, and L_i is the number of minutes in a game that player i is on the court. According to sabermetric analyses, a player's productivity depends on how the player and the other four on the court interact. What is the plausible range of values of the ρ parameter?

    b. In the CES baseball production function, $q = (a_1L_1^\rho + \cdots + a_nL_n^\rho)^{d/\rho}$, q is the number of team hits per game, and L_i is the number of times that player i bats is a game. The statisticians who study player contributions contend that in baseball, a player's batting contribution is independent of his teammates' productivity. What is the value of the ρ parameter given this statistical evidence? Now suppose that q represents the number of team *runs* per game in the CES production function. What is the range of values of the ρ parameter? **W**

Costs

An economist is a person who, when invited to give a talk at a banquet,
tells the audience there's no such thing as a free lunch.

A semiconductor manufacturer can produce a chip by using many pieces of equipment and relatively few workers' labor or by using many workers and relatively few machines. How does the firm make its choice?

The firm uses a two-step procedure to determine how to produce a certain amount of output efficiently. It first determines which production processes are *technologically efficient* so that it can produce the desired level of output with the least amount of inputs. As we saw in Chapter 6, the firm uses engineering and other information to determine its production function, which summarizes the many technologically efficient production processes available.

The firm's second step is to select the technologically efficient production process that is also **economically efficient,** minimizing the cost of producing a specified amount of output. To determine which process minimizes its cost of production, the firm uses information about the production function and the cost of inputs.

By reducing its cost of producing a given level of output, a firm can increase its profit. Any profit-maximizing competitive, monopolistic, or oligopolistic firm minimizes its cost of production.

1. **Measuring Costs:** Economists count both explicit costs and implicit (opportunity) costs.

2. **Short-Run Costs:** To minimize its costs in the short run, a firm adjusts its variable factors (such as labor), but it cannot adjust its fixed factors (such as capital).

3. **Long-Run Costs:** In the long run, a firm adjusts all its inputs because usually all inputs are variable.

4. **Lower Costs in the Long Run:** Long-run cost is as low as or lower than short-run cost because the firm has more flexibility in the long run, technological progress occurs, and workers and managers learn from experience.

5. **Cost of Producing Multiple Goods:** If the firm produces several goods simultaneously, the cost of each may depend on the quantity of all the goods produced.

In this chapter, we examine five main topics

Businesspeople and economists need to understand the relationship between the costs of inputs and production to determine the least costly way to produce. Economists have an additional reason for wanting to know about costs. As we'll see in later chapters, the relationship between output and costs plays an important role in determining the nature of a market—how many firms are in the market and how high price is relative to cost.

7.1 Measuring Costs

How much would it cost you to stand at the wrong end of a shooting gallery?
—S. J. Perelman

To show how a firm's cost varies with its output, we first have to measure costs. Business people and economists often measure costs differently.

ECONOMIC COST

Economists include all relevant costs. To run a firm profitably, a manager acts like an economist and considers all relevant costs. However, this same manager may direct the firm's accountant or bookkeeper to measure costs in ways that are consistent with tax laws and other laws so as to make the firm's financial statement look good to stockholders or to minimize the firm's taxes this year.[1]

Economists consider both explicit costs and implicit costs. *Explicit costs* are a firm's direct, out-of-pocket payments for inputs to its production process during a given time period such as a year. These costs include production workers' wages, managers' salaries, and payments for materials. However, firms use inputs that may not have an explicit price. These *implicit costs* include the value of the working time of the firm's owner and the value of other resources used but not purchased in a given period.

The **economic cost** or **opportunity cost** is the value of the best alternative use of a resource. The economic or opportunity cost includes both explicit and implicit costs. If a firm purchases and uses an input immediately, that input's opportunity cost is the amount the firm pays for it. If the firm uses an input from its inventory, the firm's opportunity cost is not necessarily the price it paid for the input years ago. Rather, the opportunity cost is what the firm could buy or sell that input for today.[2]

The classic example of an implicit opportunity cost is captured in the phrase "There's no such thing as a free lunch." Suppose that your parents offer to take you to lunch tomorrow. You know that they'll pay for the meal, but you also know that this lunch will not really be free for you. Your opportunity cost for the lunch is the best alternative use of your time. Presumably, the best alternative use of your time is studying this textbook, but other possible alternatives include working at a job and watching TV. Often such an opportunity cost is substantial.

If you start your own firm, you should be very concerned about opportunity costs. Suppose that your explicit cost is $40,000, including the rent for your work space, the cost of materials, and the wage payments to your employees. Because you do not pay yourself a salary—instead, you keep any profit at the year's end—the explicit cost does not include the value of your time. According to an economist, your firm's full economic cost is the sum of the explicit cost plus the opportunity value of your time. If the highest wage you could have earned working for some other firm is $25,000, your full economic cost is $65,000.

In deciding whether to continue running your firm or to work for someone else, you must consider both explicit and opportunity costs. If your annual revenue is $60,000 after you pay your explicit cost of $40,000, you keep $20,000 at the end of the year.

---

[1]Similarly, see **www.aw-bc.com/perloff**, Chapter 7, "Tax Rules."

[2]See **www.aw-bc.com/perloff**, Chapter 7, "Cost of Caring for Parents."

The opportunity cost of your time, $25,000, exceeds $20,000, so you can earn more working for someone else. (What are you giving up to study opportunity costs?)

Waiting for the Doctor

In Britain and Canada, taxes pay for public health care. However, taxes do not cover the full cost of medical care. To contain costs, providers ration health care, in part by having patients wait for treatment. People who are forced to wait are less likely to request treatment because some diseases clear up on their own during the wait—and some patients die while waiting. Many patients suffer or cannot work while waiting for treatment. Doctors estimate that 41% of all patients and 88% of cardiology patients have difficulty carrying on their work or daily duties as a result of their medical conditions.

Do people wait for long? In 2004, waiting times in England and Scotland were 5 months to repair a slipped disc or a hernia, 8 months for cataract surgery, 11 months for a hip replacement, and 12 months for a knee replacement. When Rachel King suffered from incapacitating dizziness and could not work after she was run over by a car, she was told that she would have to wait up to 80 weeks for a Health Service MRI brain scan (but that she could get one done privately in 2 weeks).

In Canada, the waiting time between referral from a general practitioner and treatment averaged 18 weeks across all 12 specialties and 10 provinces surveyed in 2005. Waiting times in Saskatchewan, Canada, was 23 months for knee replacement surgery and 11 months for cataract surgery in 2006. In Newfoundland in 2004, the wait for a mammogram averaged 14 months (compared to weeks in other provinces). As of 2007, the average waiting time for a specialist to start cancer treatment on a patient in Britain is close to the government target of 62 days.

Are the costs of waiting large? Dudley Lusted, chief economist at PPP Healthcare, estimated that the economic cost to British employers due to working days lost while employees wait for treatment (after the first four weeks' absence) is £1.5 billion.

What are the opportunity costs to individuals? Bishai and Lang (2000) estimated the value that people place on a one-month reduction in waiting time for cataract surgery at $128 per patient in Canada, $160 in Denmark, and $243 in Barcelona, Spain.

According to Professor Carole Propper of Bristol University, the average cost of anxiety and limitations on activity across diseases is £5 a day. Thus given that the collective British wait for treatment (beyond an initial four weeks) is 1,065,000 years, the cost to individuals is about £19.4 billion.

Most important, there are additional major health benefits from earlier treatment. For example, a New Zealand study found that twice as many women avoid recurrences of breast cancer when they have treatment in the first 8 weeks after discovery rather than in the typical 9 to 16 weeks after discovery.

CAPITAL COSTS

Determining the opportunity cost of capital, such as land or equipment, requires special considerations. Capital is a **durable good:** a product that is usable for years. Two problems may arise in measuring the cost of capital. The first concerns how to allocate the initial purchase cost over time. The second is what to do if the value of the capital changes over time.

Allocating Capital Costs over Time. Capital may be rented or purchased. For example, a firm may rent a truck for $200 a month or buy it outright for $18,000.

If the firm rents the truck, the rental payment is the relevant opportunity cost. By using the rental rate, we avoid the two measurement problems. The truck is rented period by period, so the firm does not have to worry about how to allocate the purchase cost of a truck over time. Moreover, the rental rate adjusts if the cost of a new truck changes over time.

Suppose, however, that the firm buys the truck. The firm's bookkeeper may *expense* the cost by recording the full $18,000 when the purchase is made, or may *amortize* the cost by spreading the $18,000 over the life of the truck according to an arbitrary rule set by the relevant government authority, such as the Internal Revenue Service (IRS). If the IRS approves of several approaches to amortizing expenses, a bookkeeper or an accountant may use whichever arbitrary rule minimizes the firm's taxes.

An economist amortizes the cost of the truck on the basis of its opportunity cost at each moment of time, which is the amount that the firm could charge others to rent the truck. That is, regardless of whether the firm buys or rents the truck, an economist views the opportunity cost of this capital good as a rent per time period: the amount the firm will receive if it rents its truck to others at the going rental rate.[3] If the value of an older truck is less than that of a newer one, the rental rate for the truck falls over time.

Actual and Historical Costs. Not only may the rental rate for a piece of capital fall over time as the capital ages, but it may also change because of shifts in supply and demand in the market for capital goods or for other reasons. A piece of capital may be worth much more or much less today than when it was purchased.

To maximize its profit, a firm must properly measure the cost of a piece of capital—its current opportunity cost of the capital good—and not what the firm paid for it—its historical cost. Suppose that a firm paid $30,000 for a piece of land that it can resell for only $20,000. Also suppose that it uses the land itself and that the current value of the land to the firm is only $19,000. Should the firm use the land or sell it? As any child can tell the firm, there's no point in crying over spilled milk. The firm should ignore how much it paid for the land in making its decision. Because the value of the land to the firm, $19,000, is less than the opportunity cost of the land, $20,000, the firm can make more by selling the land.

The firm's current opportunity cost of capital may be less than what it paid if the firm cannot resell the capital. A firm that bought a specialized piece of equipment that has no alternative use cannot resell the equipment. Because the equipment has no alternative use, the historical cost of buying that capital is a **sunk cost:** an expenditure that cannot be recovered. Because this equipment has no alternative use, the current or opportunity cost of the capital is zero. In short, when determining the rental value of capital, economists use the opportunity value and ignore the historical price.

---

[3]If trucks cannot be rented, an economist calculates an implicit rental rate for trucks that takes account both explicit and opportunity costs. If the firm could sell the truck for $5,000, the opportunity cost of keeping the truck is the interest that could be earned on $5,000 (Chapter 15). In addition, the firm incurs direct maintenance costs and the opportunity cost due to *depreciation:* the drop in value from wear and tear.

● **APPLICATION**

Swarthmore College's Cost of Capital

Many nonprofit institutions such as universities and governmental agencies are notorious for ignoring the implicit cost of their capital. When setting tuition and making other plans, Swarthmore College in Pennsylvania estimates its annual cost at $40,000 per student, based on the cost of salaries, academic and general institutional support, food, maintenance of and additions to the physical plant, and other annual expenses such as student aid. This cost calculation is a gross underestimate, however, because it ignores the opportunity cost of the campus—the amount the college could earn by renting out its land and buildings. Including that opportunity cost of its land and buildings raises its true economic cost to about $50,000 annually per student.

7.2 **Short-Run Costs**

To make profit-maximizing decisions, a firm needs to know how its cost varies with output. A firm's cost rises as the firm increases its output. A firm cannot vary some of its inputs, such as capital, in the short run (Chapter 6). As a result, it is usually more costly for a firm to increase output in the short run than in the long run when all inputs can be varied. In this section, we look at the cost of increasing output in the short run.

SHORT-RUN COST MEASURES

We start by using a numerical example to illustrate the basic cost concepts. We then examine the graphic relationship between these concepts.

Cost Levels. To produce a given level of output in the short run, a firm incurs costs for both its fixed and variable inputs. A firm's **fixed cost** (F) is its production expense that does not vary with output. The fixed cost includes the cost of inputs that the firm cannot practically adjust in the short run, such as land, a plant, large machines, and other capital goods. The fixed cost for a capital good that a firm owns and uses is the opportunity cost of not renting the good to someone else.

A firm's **variable cost** (VC) is the production expense that changes with the quantity of output produced. The variable cost is the cost of the variable inputs—the inputs the firm can adjust to alter its output level, such as labor and materials.

A firm's **cost** (or **total cost,** C) is the sum of a firm's variable cost and fixed cost:

$$C = VC + F.$$

Because variable cost changes with the level of output, total cost also varies with the level of output.

To decide how much to produce, a firm uses measures of marginal and average costs. We derive four such measures using the fixed cost, the variable cost, and the total cost.

Marginal Cost. A firm's **marginal cost** (*MC*) is the amount by which a firm's cost changes if the firm produces one more unit of output. The marginal cost is

$$MC = \frac{dC(q)}{dq}. \tag{7.1}$$

Because only variable cost changes with output, we can also define marginal cost as the change in variable cost from a small increase in output,

$$MC = \frac{dVC(q)}{dq},$$

where $VC(q)$ is the firm's variable cost function. Chapter 8 will show that a firm uses its marginal cost to decide whether changing its output level pays off.

Average Cost. Firms use three average cost measures. The **average fixed cost** (*AFC*) is the fixed cost divided by the units of output produced: $AFC = F/q$. The average fixed cost falls as output rises because the fixed cost is spread over more units: $dAFC/dq = -F/q^2 < 0$. It approaches zero as the output level grows very large.

The **average variable cost** (*AVC*) is the variable cost divided by the units of output produced: $AVC = VC/q$. Because the variable cost increases with output, the average variable cost may either increase or decrease as output rises. As Chapter 8 shows, a firm uses the average variable cost to determine whether to shut down operations when demand is low.

The **average cost** (*AC*)—or average total cost—is the total cost divided by the units of output produced: $AC = C/q$. Because total cost equals variable cost plus fixed cost, $C = VC + F$, when we divide both sides of the equation by q, we learn that

$$AC = \frac{C}{q} = \frac{VC}{q} + \frac{F}{q} = AVC + AFC. \tag{7.2}$$

That is, the average cost is the sum of the average variable cost and the average fixed cost. A firm uses its average cost to determine if it is making a profit.

SOLVED PROBLEM   7.1

A manufacturing plant has a short-run cost function of $C(q) = 100q - 4q^2 + 0.2q^3 + 450$. What is the firm's short-run fixed cost and variable cost function? Derive the formulas for its marginal cost, average fixed cost, average variable cost, and average cost. Draw two figures, one above the other. In the top figure, show the fixed cost, variable cost, and total cost curves. In the bottom figure, show the corresponding marginal cost curve and three average cost curves.

Answer

1. *Identify the fixed cost as the part of the short-run cost function that does not vary with output, q, and the remaining part of the cost function as the variable cost function:* The fixed cost is $F = 450$, the only part that does not vary with q. The variable cost function, $VC(q) = 100q - 4q^2 + 0.2q^3$, is the part of the cost function that varies with q.

2. *Determine the marginal cost by differentiating the short-run cost function (or variable cost function) with respect to output:* Differentiating, we find that

$$MC = \frac{dC(q)}{dq} = \frac{d(100q - 4q^2 + 0.2q^3 + 450)}{dq} = 100 - 8q + 0.6q^2.$$

3. *Calculate the three average cost functions using the definitions:* By definition,

$$AFC = \frac{F}{q} = \frac{450}{q};$$

$$AVC = \frac{V(q)}{q} = \frac{100q - 4q^2 + 0.2q^3}{q} = 100 - 4q + 0.2q^2;$$

$$AC = \frac{C(q)}{q} = \frac{100q - 4q^2 + 0.2q^3 + 450}{q}$$

$$= 100 - 4q + 0.2q^2 + \frac{450}{q} = AVC + AFC.$$

4. *Use these cost, marginal cost, and average cost functions to plot the specified figures:* Figure 7.1 shows these plots.

SHORT-RUN COST CURVES

We illustrate the relationship between output and the various cost measures using the example in Solved Problem 7.1. Panel a of Figure 7.1 shows the variable cost, fixed cost, and total cost curves. The fixed cost, which does not vary with output, is a horizontal line at $450. The variable cost curve is zero when output is zero and rises as output increases. The total cost curve, which is the vertical sum of the variable cost curve and the fixed cost line, is $450 higher than the variable cost curve at every output level, so the variable cost and total cost curves are parallel.

Panel b shows the average fixed cost, average variable cost, average cost, and marginal cost curves. The average fixed cost curve falls as output increases. It approaches zero as output gets large because the fixed cost is spread over many units of output. The average cost curve is the vertical sum of the average fixed cost and average variable cost curves. For example, at 10 units of output, the average variable cost is 80 and the average fixed cost is 45, so the average cost is 125.

The marginal cost curve cuts the U-shaped average cost and the average variable cost curves at their minimums.[4] The average cost (or average variable cost) curve rises where the marginal cost curve is above it and falls where the marginal cost curve is below it, so the marginal cost curve must cut the average cost curve at its

---

[4]To determine the output level q where the average cost curve, $AC(q)$, reaches its minimum, we set the derivative of average cost with respect to q equal to zero:

$$\frac{dAC(q)}{dq} = \frac{d[C(q)/1]}{dq} = \left[\frac{dC(q)}{dq} - \frac{C(q)}{q}\right]\frac{1}{q} = 0.$$

This condition holds at the output q where $dC(q)/dq = C(q)/q$, or $MC = AC$. If the second-order condition holds at that q, the average cost curve reaches its minimum at that quantity. The second-order condition requires that the average cost curve be falling to the left of this quantity and rising to the right. Similarly, $dAVC/dq = d[VC(q)/q]/dq = [dVC/dq - VC(q)/q](1/q) = 0$, so $MC = AVC$ at the minimum of the average variable cost curve.

Figure 7.1 Short-Run Cost Curves.
(a) Because the total cost differs from the variable cost by the fixed cost, $F = \$450$, the cost curve, C, is parallel to the variable cost curve, VC.
(b) The marginal cost curve, MC, cuts the average variable cost, AVC, and average cost, AC, curves at their minimums. The height of the AC curve at point a equals the slope of the line from the origin to the cost curve at A. The height of the AVC at b equals the slope of the line from the origin to the variable cost curve at B. The height of the marginal cost is the slope of either the C or VC curve at that quantity.

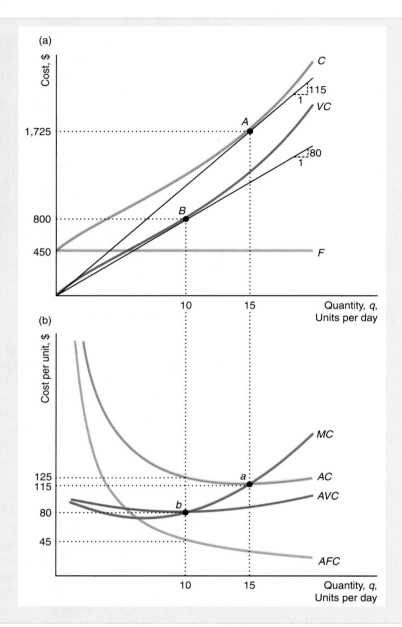

minimum (by the same type of reasoning used in Chapter 6 where we discussed average and marginal products).

PRODUCTION FUNCTIONS AND THE SHAPE OF COST CURVES

The production function determines the shape of a firm's cost curves. The production function shows the amount of inputs needed to produce a given level of output. The firm calculates its cost by multiplying the quantity of each input by its price and summing.

If a firm produces output using capital and labor and its capital is fixed in the short run, the firm's variable cost is its cost of labor. Its labor cost is the wage per hour, w, times the number of hours of labor, L, employed by the firm: $VC = wL$.

If input prices are constant, the production function determines the shape of the variable cost curve. We can write the short-run production function as $q = f(L, \overline{K}) = g(L)$ because capital does not vary. By inverting, we know that the amount of labor we need to produce any given amount of output is $L = g^{-1}(q)$. If the wage of labor is w, the variable cost function is $V(q) = wL = wg^{-1}(q)$. Similarly, the cost function is $C(q) = V(q) + F/q = wg^{-1}(q) + F/q$.

In the short run, when the firm's capital is fixed, the only way the firm can increase its output is to use more labor. If the firm increases its labor enough, it reaches the point of *diminishing marginal returns to labor,* where each extra worker increases output by a smaller amount. Because the variable cost function is the inverse short-run production function, its properties are determined by the short-run production function. If the production function exhibits diminishing marginal returns, then the variable cost rises more than in proportion as output increases.

Because the production function determines the shape of the variable cost curve, it also determines the shape of the marginal, average variable, and average cost curves. We now examine the shape of each of these cost curves in detail because in making decisions, firms rely more on these per-unit cost measures than on total variable cost.

Shape of the Marginal Cost Curve. The marginal cost is the change in variable cost as output increases by one unit: $MC = dVC/dq$. In the short run, capital is fixed, so the only way a firm can produce more output is to use extra labor. The extra labor required to produce one more unit of output is $dL/dq = 1/MP_L$. The extra labor costs the firm w per unit, so the firm's cost rises by $w(dL/dq)$. As a result, the firm's marginal cost is

$$MC = \frac{dV(q)}{dq} = w\frac{dL}{dq}.$$

The marginal cost equals the wage times the extra labor necessary to produce one more unit of output.

How do we know how much extra labor is needed to produce one more unit of output? That information comes from the production function. The marginal product of labor—the amount of extra output produced by another unit of labor, holding other inputs fixed—is $MP_L = dq/dL$. Thus the extra labor needed to produce one more unit of output, dL/dq, is $1/MP_L$, so the firm's marginal cost is

$$MC = \frac{w}{MP_L}. \tag{7.3}$$

Equation 7.3 says that the marginal cost equals the wage divided by the marginal product of labor. If it takes four extra hours of labor services to produce one more unit of output, the marginal product of an hour of labor is $\frac{1}{4}$. Given a wage of $5 an hour, the marginal cost of one more unit of output is $5 divided by $\frac{1}{4}$, or $20.

Equation 7.3 shows that the marginal cost moves in the direction opposite to that of the marginal product of labor. At low levels of labor, the marginal product of labor commonly rises with additional labor because extra workers help the original workers and they collectively can make better use of the firm's equipment (Chapter 6). As the marginal product of labor rises, the marginal cost falls.

Eventually, however, as the number of workers increases, workers must share the fixed amount of equipment and may get in each other's way, so the marginal cost curve slopes upward because of diminishing marginal returns to labor. Thus the marginal cost first falls and then rises, as panel b of Figure 7.1 illustrates.

Shape of the Average Cost Curve. By determining the shape of the variable cost curve, diminishing marginal returns to labor also determine the shape of the average variable cost curve. The average variable cost is the variable cost divided by output: $AVC = VC/q$. For the firm we've been examining, whose only variable input is labor, variable cost is wL, so average variable cost is

$$AVC = \frac{VC}{q} = \frac{wL}{q}.$$

Because the average product of labor is q/L, average variable cost is the wage divided by the average product of labor:

$$AVC = \frac{w}{AP_L}. \tag{7.4}$$

With a constant wage, the average variable cost moves in the opposite direction of the average product of labor in Equation 7.4. As we saw in Chapter 6, the average product of labor tends to rise and then fall, so the average cost tends to fall and then rise, as in panel b of Figure 7.1.

The average cost curve is the vertical sum of the average variable cost curve and the average fixed cost curve, as in panel b. If the average variable cost curve is U-shaped, adding the strictly falling average fixed cost makes the average cost fall more steeply than the average variable cost curve at low output levels. At high output levels, the average cost and average variable cost curves differ by ever smaller amounts, as the average fixed cost, F/q, approaches zero. Thus the average cost curve is also U-shaped.

● APPLICATION

Short-Run Cost Curves for a Furniture Manufacturer

We can derive the various short-run cost curves for a typical furniture firm using its Cobb-Douglas production function (as estimated by Hsieh, 1995) and the prices of the inputs, which we assume are $w = \$24$ and $r = \$8$. The figure shows that the short-run average cost curve for this firm is U-shaped, even though its average variable cost is strictly upward sloping. The graph shows the firm's various short-run cost curves where the firm's capital is fixed at $\overline{K} = 100$.

Given that the rental rate of a unit of capital is $8, the fixed cost, F, is $800 ($= \$8 \times \overline{K}$). The figure shows that the average fixed cost, $AFC = F/q = 800/q$, falls as output, q, increases.

We can use the production function to derive the variable cost. The estimated production function is

$$q = 1.52L^{0.6}K^{0.4}, \tag{7.5}$$

where labor, L, is measured in hours and K is the number of units of capital. We start by determining how output and labor are related. Setting capital, $K = \overline{K} = 100$ units in the production function, we find that the output produced in the short run is solely a function of labor:

$$q = 1.52L^{0.6}100^{0.4} \approx 9.59L^{0.6}.$$

Rearranging this expression, we can write the number of workers per year, L, needed to produce q units of output, as a function solely of output:

$$L(q) = \left(\frac{q}{1.52 \times 100^{0.4}}\right)^{1/0.6} \approx 0.023q^{1.67}.$$

Now that we know how labor and output are related, we can calculate variable cost directly. The only variable input is labor, so if the wage is $w = \$24$, the firm's variable cost is $VC(q) = wL(q) = 24L(q)$. Substituting for $L(q)$, we see how variable cost varies with output:

$$V(q) = 24L(q) = 24\left(\frac{q}{1.52 \times 100^{0.4}}\right)^{1/0.6} \approx 0.55q^{1.67}.$$

Using this expression for variable cost, we can construct the other cost measures.

We obtain the average variable cost as a function of output, $AVC(q)$, by dividing both sides of this last equation by q:

$$AVC(q) = \frac{V(q)}{q} = \frac{24L(q)}{q} \approx 24\left(\frac{0.023q^{1.67}}{q}\right) = 0.55q^{0.67}.$$

As the figure shows, the average variable cost is strictly increasing.

To obtain the equation for marginal cost as a function of output, we differentiate the variable cost, $V(q)$, with respect to output:

$$MC(q) = \frac{dV(q)}{dq} \approx \frac{d(0.55q^{1.67})}{dq} = 1.67 \times 0.55q^{0.67} \approx 0.92q^{0.67}.$$

The firm's average fixed cost (AFC) curve falls as output increases. The firm's average variable cost (AVC) curve is strictly increasing. The average cost (AC) curve is the vertical sum of the average variable cost and average fixed cost curves. Because the average fixed cost curve falls with output and the average variable cost curve rises with output, the average cost curve is U-shaped. The firm's marginal cost curve lies above the rising average variable cost curve for all positive quantities of output and cuts the average cost curve at its minimum at $q = 100$.

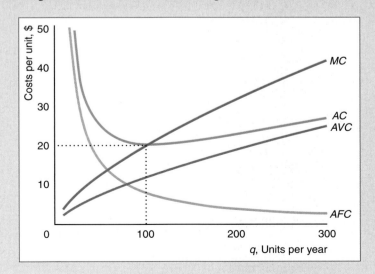

EFFECTS OF TAXES ON COSTS

Taxes applied to a firm shift some or all of the marginal and average cost curves. For example, suppose that the government collects a specific tax of $10 per unit of output. This specific tax, which varies with output, affects the firm's variable cost but not its fixed cost. As a result, it affects the firm's average cost, average variable cost, and marginal cost curves but not its average fixed cost curve.

At every quantity, the average variable cost and the average cost rise by the full amount of the tax. Thus the firm's after-tax average variable cost, AVC^a, is its average variable cost of production—the before-tax average variable cost, AVC^b—plus the tax per unit, $10: $AVC^a = AVC^b + \$10$.

The average cost equals the average variable cost plus the average fixed cost. For example, in the last application, the furniture firm's before-tax average cost is $AC^b = AVC + AFC = 0.55q^{0.67} + 800/q$. Because the tax increases average variable cost by $10 and does not affect the average fixed cost, the tax increases average cost by $10: $AC^a = AC^b + 10 = 0.55q^{0.67} + 800/q + 10$. The tax also increases the firm's marginal cost by $10 per unit. The furniture firm's pre-tax marginal cost is $MC^b = 0.92q^{0.67}$, so its after-tax marginal cost is $MC^a = 0.92q^{0.67} + 10$.

Figure 7.2 shows these shifts in the marginal and average cost curves. The new marginal cost curve and average cost curve are parallel to the old ones: $10 higher at each quantity. At first, it may not look like the shift of the average cost curve is parallel, but you can convince yourself that it is a parallel shift by using a ruler.

Similarly, we can analyze the effect of a franchise tax on costs. A franchise tax—also called a business license fee—is a lump sum that a firm pays for the right to operate a business. For example, an $800-per-year tax is levied "for the privilege of doing business

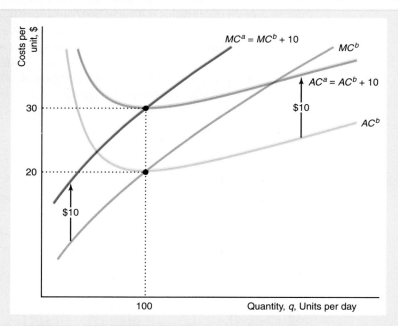

Figure 7.2 Effect of a Specific Tax on Furniture Firm's Cost Curves. A specific tax of $10 per unit shifts both the marginal cost and average cost curves upward by $10. Because of the parallel upward shift of the average cost curve, the minimum of both the before-tax average cost curve, AC^b, and the after-tax average cost curve, AC^a, occurs at the same output, 100 units.

in California." A three-year license to sell hot dogs in front of New York City's Metropolitan Museum of Art costs $900,600. These taxes do not vary with output, so they affect firms' fixed costs only—not their variable costs—as the following solved problem illustrates.

SOLVED PROBLEM 7.2

What is the effect of a lump-sum franchise tax $\mathcal{L}$ on the quantity at which a firm's after-tax average cost curve reaches its minimum, given that the firm's before-tax average cost curve is U-shaped?

Answer

1. *Determine the average tax per unit of output:* Because the franchise tax is a lump-sum payment that does not vary with output, the more the firm produces, the less tax it pays per unit. The tax per unit is $\mathcal{L}/q$. (The lump-sum is a fixed cost, so the tax per unit is calculated the same way as we do to obtain the average fixed cost.) If the firm sells only 1 unit, its cost is $\mathcal{L}$; however, if it sells 100 units, its tax payment per unit is only $\mathcal{L}/100$.

2. *Show how the tax per unit affects the average cost:* The firm's after-tax average cost, AC^a, is the sum of its before-tax average cost, AC^b, and its average tax payment per unit, $\mathcal{L}/q$. Because the average tax payment per unit falls with output, the gap between the after-tax average cost curve and the before-tax average cost curve also falls with output, as shown on the graph.

3. *Determine the effect of the tax on the marginal cost curve:* Because the franchise tax does not vary with output, it does not affect the marginal cost curve.

4. *Compare the minimum points of the two average cost curves:* The marginal cost curve crosses both average cost curves from below at their minimum points. Because the after-tax average cost curve lies above the before-tax average cost curve, the quantity, q_a, at which the after-tax average cost curve reaches its minimum, is larger than the quantity q_b at which the before-tax average cost curve achieves a minimum.

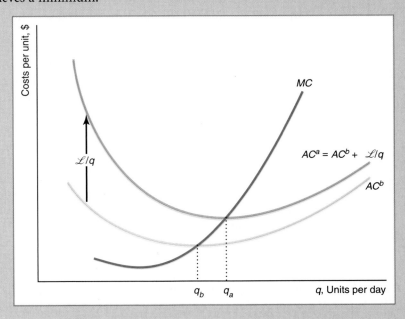

SHORT-RUN COST SUMMARY

We have examined three cost-level curves—total cost, fixed cost, and variable cost—and four cost-per-unit curves—average cost, average fixed cost, average variable cost, and marginal cost. Understanding the shapes of these curves and the relationships among them is crucial to understanding the analysis of a firm's behavior in the rest of this book. The following four basic concepts capture most of what you need to know about the shapes and the relationships among the curves:

- In the short run, the cost associated with inputs that cannot be adjusted is fixed, while the cost from inputs that can be adjusted is variable.
- Given constant input prices, the shapes of the cost, variable cost, marginal cost, and average cost curves are determined by the production function.
- Where there are diminishing marginal returns to a variable input, the variable cost and cost curves become relatively steep as output increases, so the average cost, average variable cost, and marginal cost curves rise with output.
- Both the average cost curve and the average variable cost curve fall when marginal cost is below them and rise when marginal cost is above them, so the marginal cost curve cuts both of these average cost curves at their minimum points.

7.3 Long-Run Costs

In the long run, a firm adjusts all its inputs so that its cost of production is as low as possible. The firm can change its plant size, design and build new machines, and otherwise adjust inputs that were fixed in the short run.

Although firms may incur fixed costs in the long run, these fixed costs are *avoidable* (rather than *sunk,* as in the short run). The rent of *F* per month that a restaurant pays is a fixed cost because it does not vary with the number of meals (output) served. In the short run, this fixed cost is sunk: The firm must pay *F* even if the restaurant does not operate. In the long run, this fixed cost is avoidable: The firm does not have to pay this rent if it shuts down. The long run is determined by the length of the rental contract, during which time the firm is obligated to pay rent.

The examples throughout this chapter assume that all inputs can be varied in the long run, so there are no long-run fixed costs ($F = 0$). As a result, the long-run total cost equals the long-run variable cost: $C = VC$. Thus our firm is concerned about only three cost concepts in the long run—total cost, average cost, and marginal cost—instead of the seven cost concepts that it considers in the short run.

To produce a given quantity of output at minimum cost, our firm uses information about the production function and the price of labor and capital. In the long run, the firm chooses how much labor and capital to use, whereas in the short run, when capital is fixed, it chooses only how much labor to use. As a consequence, the firm's long-run cost is lower than its short-run cost of production if it has to use the "wrong" level of capital in the short run. This section shows how a firm determines the cost-minimizing combinations of inputs in the long run.

INPUT CHOICE

A firm can produce a given level of output using many different *technologically efficient* combinations of inputs, as summarized by an isoquant (Chapter 6). From among the technologically efficient combinations of inputs, a firm wants to choose the particular bundle with the lowest cost of production, which is the *economically efficient* combination of inputs. To do so, the firm combines information about technology from the isoquant with information about the cost of labor and capital.

We now show how information about cost can be summarized in an *isocost line*. Then we show how a firm can combine the information in isoquant and isocost lines to determine the economically efficient combination of inputs.

Isocost Line. The cost of producing a given level of output depends on the price of labor and capital. The firm hires L hours of labor services at a wage of w per hour, so its labor cost is wL. The firm rents K hours of machine services at a rental rate of r per hour, so its capital cost is rK. (If the firm owns the capital, r is the implicit rental rate.) The firm's total cost is the sum of its labor and capital costs:

$$C = wL + rK. \tag{7.6}$$

The firm can hire as much labor and capital as it wants at these constant input prices.

The firm can use many combinations of labor and capital that cost the same amount. These combinations of labor and capital are plotted on an **isocost line,** which indicates all the combinations of inputs that require the same (*iso*) total expenditure (*cost*). Along an isocost line, cost is fixed at a particular level, $\overline{C}$, so by setting cost at $\overline{C}$ in Equation 7.6, we can write the equation for the $\overline{C}$ isocost line as

$$\overline{C} = wL + rK. \tag{7.7}$$

Figure 7.3 shows three isocost lines for the furniture manufacturer where the fixed cost is $\overline{C} = \$1,000$, $\$2,000$, or $\$3,000$; $w = \$24$ per hour; and $r = \$8$ per hour.

Using algebra, we can rewrite Equation 7.7 to show how much capital the firm can buy if it spends a total of $\overline{C}$ and purchases L units of labor:

$$K = \frac{\overline{C}}{r} - \frac{w}{r}L. \tag{7.8}$$

The equation for the isocost lines in the figure is $K = \overline{C}/8 - (24/8)L = \overline{C}/8 - 3L$. We can use Equation 7.8 to derive three properties of isocost lines.

First, where the isocost lines hit the capital and labor axes depends on the firm's cost, $\overline{C}$, and the input prices. The $\overline{C}$ isocost line intersects the capital axis where the firm is using only capital. Setting $L = 0$ in Equation 7.8, we find that the firm buys $K = \overline{C}/r$ units of capital. Similarly, the intersection of the isocost line with the labor axis is at $\overline{C}/w$, which is the amount of labor the firm hires if it uses only labor.

Second, isocosts that are farther from the origin have higher costs than those that are closer to the origin. Because the isocost lines intersect the capital axis at $\overline{C}/r$ and the labor axis at $\overline{C}/w$, an increase in the cost shifts these intersections with the axes proportionately outward.

Third, the slope of each isocost line is the same. By differentiating Equation 7.8, we find that the slope of any isocost line is

$$\frac{dK}{dL} = -\frac{w}{r}.$$

Thus the slope of the isocost line depends on the relative prices of the inputs. Because all isocost lines are based on the same relative prices, they all have the same slope, so they are parallel.

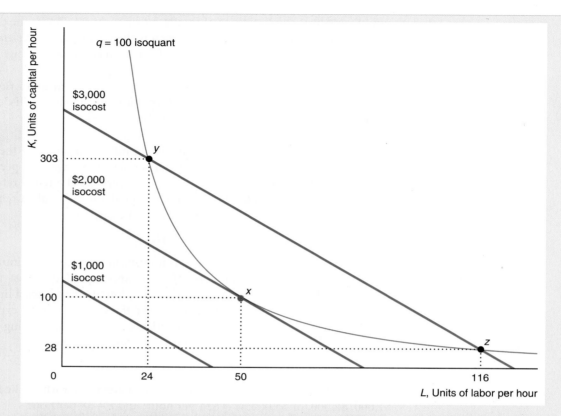

Figure 7.3 Cost Minimization. The furniture manufacturer minimizes its cost of producing 100 units of output by producing at x ($L = 50$ and $K = 100$). This cost-minimizing combination of inputs is determined by the tangency between the $q = 100$ isoquant and the lowest isocost line, $2,000, that touches that isoquant. At x, the isocost is tangent to the isoquant, so the slope of the isocost, $-w/r = -3$, equals the slope of the isoquant, which is the negative of the marginal rate of technical substitution. That is, the rate at which the firm can trade capital for labor in the input markets equals the rate at which it can substitute capital for labor in the production process.

The role of the isocost line in the firm's decision making is similar to the role of the budget line in a consumer's decision making. Both an isocost line and a budget line are straight lines whose slopes depend on relative prices. There is an important difference between them, however. The consumer has a single budget line determined by the consumer's income. The firm faces many isocost lines, each of which corresponds to a different level of expenditures the firm might make. A firm may incur a relatively low cost by producing relatively little output with few inputs, or it may incur a relatively high cost by producing a relatively large quantity.

Minimizing Cost. By combining the information about costs that is contained in the isocost lines with information about efficient production that is summarized by an isoquant, a firm chooses the lowest-cost way to produce a given level of output. We examine how our furniture manufacturer picks the combination of labor and capital that minimizes its cost of producing 100 units of output. Figure 7.3 shows the isoquant for 100 units of output and the isocost lines where the rental rate of a unit of capital is $8 per hour and the wage rate is $24 per hour.

The firm can choose any of three equivalent approaches to minimize its cost:

- **Lowest-isocost rule:** Pick the bundle of inputs where the lowest isocost line touches the isoquant.
- **Tangency rule:** Pick the bundle of inputs where the isoquant is tangent to the isocost line.
- **Last-dollar rule:** Pick the bundle of inputs where the last dollar spent on one input gives as much extra output as the last dollar spent on any other input.

Using the *lowest-isocost rule,* the firm minimizes its cost by using the combination of inputs on the isoquant that is on the lowest isocost line that touches the isoquant. The lowest possible isoquant that will allow the furniture manufacturer to produce 100 units of output is tangent to the $2,000 isocost line. This isocost line touches the isoquant at the bundle of inputs x, where the firm uses $L = 50$ workers and $K = 100$ units of capital.

How do we know that x is the least costly way to produce 100 units of output? We need to demonstrate that other practical combinations of input produce fewer than 100 units or produce 100 units at greater cost.

If the firm spent less than $2,000, it could not produce 100 units of output. Each combination of inputs on the $1,000 isocost line lies below the isoquant, so the firm cannot produce 100 units of output for $1,000.

The firm can produce 100 units of output using other combinations of inputs besides x; however, using these other bundles of inputs is more expensive. For example, the firm can produce 100 units of output using the combinations y ($L = 24, K = 303$) or z ($L = 116, K = 28$). Both these combinations, however, cost the firm $3,000.

If an isocost line crosses the isoquant twice, as the $3,000 isocost line does, there must be another lower isocost line that also touches the isoquant. The lowest possible isocost line that touches the isoquant, the $2,000 isocost line, is tangent to the isoquant at a single bundle, x. Thus the firm may use the *tangency rule:* The firm chooses the input bundle where the relevant isoquant is tangent to an isocost line to produce a given level of output at the lowest cost.

We can interpret this tangency or cost minimization condition in two ways. At the point of tangency, the slope of the isoquant equals the slope of the isocost. As we saw in Chapter 6, the slope of the isoquant is the marginal rate of technical substitution (*MRTS*). The slope of the isocost is the negative of the ratio of the wage to the cost of capital, $-w/r$. Thus to minimize its cost of producing a given level of output, a firm chooses its inputs so that the marginal rate of technical substitution equals the negative of the relative input prices:

$$MRTS = -\frac{w}{r}. \tag{7.9}$$

The firm chooses inputs so that the rate at which it can substitute capital for labor in the production process, the *MRTS*, exactly equals the rate at which it can trade capital for labor in input markets, $-w/r$.

Using Equation 6.8 where $a = 0.6$ and $b = 0.4$, we know that the furniture manufacturer's marginal rate of technical substitution is $-1.5K/L$. At $K = 100$ and $L = 50$, its *MRTS* is -3, which equals the negative of the ratio of the input prices that it faces, $-w/r = -24/8 = -3$. In contrast, at y, the isocost cuts the isoquant so that the slopes are not equal. At y, the $MRTS$ is -18.9375, which is greater than the ratio of the input price, 3. Because the slopes are not equal at y, the firm can produce the same output at lower cost. As the figure shows, the cost of producing at y is $3,000, whereas the cost of producing at x is only $2,000.

We can interpret the condition in Equation 7.9 in another way. Chapter 6 showed that the marginal rate of technical substitution equals the negative of the ratio of the marginal product of labor to that of capital: $MRTS = -MP_L/MP_K$. Thus the cost-minimizing condition in Equation 7.9 is (taking the absolute value of both sides)

$$\frac{MP_L}{MP_K} = \frac{w}{r}. \tag{7.10}$$

This expression may be rewritten as

$$\frac{MP_L}{w} = \frac{MP_K}{r}. \tag{7.11}$$

Equation 7.11 states the *last-dollar rule:* Cost is minimized if inputs are chosen so that the last dollar spent on labor adds as much extra output as the last dollar spent on capital.

Because the furniture manufacturer's production function is $q = 1.52L^{0.6}K^{0.4}$, Equation 7.5, its marginal product of labor is $MP_L = 0.6 \times 1.52L^{0.6-1}K^{0.4} = 0.6q/L$, and its marginal product of capital is $MP_K = 0.4q/K$. At Bundle x, the furniture firm's marginal product of labor is 1.2 ($= 0.6 \times 100/50$) and its marginal product of capital is 0.4. The last dollar spent on labor gets the firm

$$\frac{MP_L}{w} = \frac{1.2}{24} = 0.05$$

more output. Spending its last dollar on capital, the firm produces

$$\frac{MP_K}{r} = \frac{0.4}{8} = 0.05$$

extra output. Thus spending one more dollar on labor at x gets the firm as much extra output as spending the same amount on capital. Equation 7.11 holds, so the firm is minimizing its cost of producing 100 units of output.

If instead the firm produced at y, where it is using more capital and less labor, its MP_L is 2.5 ($= 0.6 \times 100/24$) and its MP_K is approximately 0.13 ($\approx 0.4 \times 100/303$). As a result, the last dollar spent on labor gets $MP_L/w \approx 0.1$ more unit of output, whereas the last dollar spent on capital gets only a fourth as much extra output, $MP_K/r \approx 0.017$. At y, if the firm shifts one dollar from capital to labor, output falls by 0.017 because there is less capital and increases by 0.1 because there is more labor, for a net gain of 0.083 more output at the same cost. The firm should shift even more resources from capital to labor—thereby increasing the marginal product of capital and decreasing the marginal product of labor—until Equation 7.10 holds with equality at x.

To summarize, there are three equivalent rules that the firm can use to determine the lowest-cost combination of inputs to produce a given level of output when isoquants are smooth: the lowest-isocost rule; the tangency rule, Equations 7.9 and 7.10; and the last-dollar rule, Equation 7.11. If the isoquant is not smooth, the lowest-cost method of production cannot be determined by using the tangency rule or the last-dollar rule. The lowest-isocost rule always works—even when isoquants are not smooth—as **www.aw-bc.com/perloff**, Chapter 7, "Rice Milling on Java," illustrates.

Using Calculus to Minimize Cost. Formally, the firm is minimizing its cost, Equation 7.6, subject to the information in the production function contained in the isoquant expression: $\bar{q} = f(L, K)$. The corresponding Lagrangian problem is

$$\min_{L, K, \lambda} \mathscr{L} = wL + rK + \lambda[\bar{q} - f(L, K)]. \tag{7.12}$$

Assuming that we have an interior solution where both L and K are positive, the first-order conditions are

$$\frac{\partial \mathscr{L}}{\partial L} = w - \lambda \frac{\partial f}{\partial L} = 0, \tag{7.13}$$

$$\frac{\partial \mathscr{L}}{\partial K} = r - \lambda \frac{\partial f}{\partial K} = 0, \tag{7.14}$$

$$\frac{\partial \mathscr{L}}{\partial \lambda} = \bar{q} - f(L, K) = 0. \tag{7.15}$$

Dividing Equation 7.13 by Equation 7.14 and rearranging terms, we obtain the same expression as in Equation 7.10:

$$\frac{w}{r} = \frac{\dfrac{\partial f}{\partial L}}{\dfrac{\partial f}{\partial K}} = \frac{MP_L}{MP_K}. \tag{7.16}$$

That is, we find that cost is minimized where the factor price ratio equals the ratio of the marginal products.[5]

Maximizing Output. We could equivalently examine the dual problem of maximizing output for a given level of cost. (In a similar pair of problems in Chapter 3, we examined maximizing utility for a given budget constraint and minimizing expenditure for a given level of utility.) Here the Lagrangian problem is

$$\max_{L, K, \lambda} \mathscr{L} = f(L, K) + \lambda(\overline{C} - wL - rK). \tag{7.17}$$

Assuming that we have an interior solution where both L and K are positive, the first-order conditions are

$$\frac{\partial \mathscr{L}}{\partial L} = \frac{\partial f}{\partial L} - \lambda w = 0, \tag{7.18}$$

$$\frac{\partial \mathscr{L}}{\partial K} = \frac{\partial f}{\partial K} - \lambda r = 0, \tag{7.19}$$

---

[5]Using Equations 7.13, 7.14, and 7.16, we find that $\lambda = w/MP_L = r/MP_K$. That is, the Lagrangian multiplier, λ, equals the ratio of the input price to the marginal product for each factor. As we already know, the input price divided by the factor's marginal product equals the marginal cost. Thus the Lagrangian multiplier equals the marginal cost of production: It measures how much the cost increases if we produce one more unit of output.

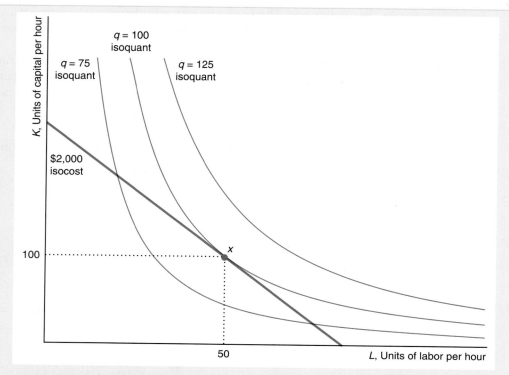

Figure 7.4 Output Maximization. The furniture manufacturer maximizes its production at a cost of $2,000 by producing 100 units of output at x using $L = 50$ and $K = 100$. The $q = 100$ isoquant is the highest one that touches the $2,000 isocost line. The firm operates where the $q = 100$ isoquant is tangent to the $2,000 isocost line.

$$\frac{\partial \mathscr{L}}{\partial \lambda} = \overline{C} - wL - rK = 0. \tag{7.20}$$

By examining the ratio of the first two conditions, Equations 7.18 and 7.19, we obtain the same condition as when we minimized cost by holding output constant: $MP_L/MP_K = (\partial f/\partial L)/(\partial f/\partial K) = w/r$. That is, at the maximum, the slope of the isoquant equals the slope of the isocost line. Figure 7.4 shows that the firm maximizes its output for a given level of cost by operating where the highest feasible isoquant, $q = 100$, is tangent to the $2,000 isocost line.

Factor Price Changes. Once the furniture manufacturer determines the lowest-cost combination of inputs to produce a given level of output, it uses that method as long as the input prices remain constant. How should the firm change its behavior if the cost of one of the factors changes? Suppose that the wage falls from $24 to $8 but that the rental rate of capital stays constant at $8.

The firm minimizes its new cost by substituting away from the now relatively more expensive input, capital, toward the now relatively less expensive input, labor. The change in the wage does not affect technological efficiency, so it does not affect the isoquant in Figure 7.5. Because of the wage decrease, the new isocost lines have a flatter slope, $-w/r = -8/8 = -1$, than the original isocost lines, $-w/r = -24/8 = -3$.

The relatively steep original isocost line is tangent to the 100-unit isoquant at Bundle x ($L = 50$, $K = 100$). The new, flatter isocost line is tangent to the isoquant at

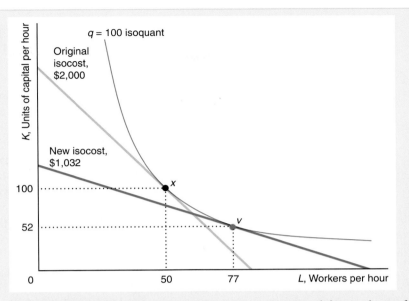

Figure 7.5 Change in Factor Price. Originally, the wage was $24 and the rental rate of capital was $8, so the lowest isocost line ($2,000) was tangent to the $q = 100$ isoquant at x ($L = 50, K = 100$). When the wage fell to $8, the isocost lines became flatter: Labor became relatively less expensive than capital. The slope of the isocost lines falls from $-w/r = -24/8 = -3$ to $-8/8 = -1$. The new lowest isocost line ($1,032) is tangent at v ($L = 77, K = 52$). Thus when the wage falls, the firm uses more labor and less capital to produce a given level of output, and the cost of production falls from $2,000 to $1,032.

Bundle v ($L = 77, K = 52$). Thus the firm uses more labor and less capital as labor becomes relatively less expensive. Moreover, the firm's cost of producing 100 units falls from $2,000 to $1,032 because of the decrease in the wage. This example illustrates that a change in the relative prices of inputs affects the mix of inputs that a firm uses.

Formally, we know from Equation 7.10 that the ratio of the factor prices equals the ratio of the marginal products: $w/r = MP_L/MP_K$. As we've already determined, this expression is $w/r = 1.5K/L$ for the furniture firm. Holding r fixed for a small change in w, the change in the factor ratio is $d(K/L)/dw = 1/(1.5r)$. For the furniture manufacturer, where $r = 8$, $d(K/L)/dw = 1/12 \approx 0.083$. Because this derivative is positive, a small change in the wage leads to a higher capital-labor ratio because the firm substitutes some relatively less expensive capital for labor.

APPLICATION

The Internet and Outsourcing

To start a children's pajama business, Philip Chigos, 26, and Mary Domenico, 25, are designing garments, choosing fabrics, and searching for low-cost workers in China and Mexico from a basement office in their San Francisco apartment. Increasingly, such mom-and-pop operations are sending their clothing, jewelry, and programming work to Sri Lanka, China, India, Mexico, and Eastern Europe.

A firm *outsources* if it retains others to provide services that the firm had previously performed itself. Firms have always used outsourcing. For example, a restaurant buys goods such as butter and flour or finished products such as bread and pies from other firms or contracts with another firm to provide cleaning services. A firm outsources if others can produce a good or service for less than the firm's own cost. Though all domestic firms face the same factor prices, some firms can produce at lower cost than others because they specialize in a good or service.

Newspaper writers and politicians have been wringing their hands about outsourcing to other countries. The different factor prices that foreign firms face may allow them to produce at lower cost.

In the past, outsourcing to other countries was not practical because of the high costs of finding partners abroad and communicating with them, as well as the high transportation costs of quickly sending goods vast distances. The Internet and other communication technologies have made outsourcing abroad much easier. Without the Internet and modern telecommunications, small U.S. firms wouldn't be able to find foreign suppliers in countries they will never visit. But by using e-mail, fax, and phone, they can inexpensively communicate with foreign factories, transmit images and design specifications, and track inventory.

Mr. Chigos used the Internet to find potential Chinese and Mexican manufacturers for the pajamas that Ms. Domenico designed. Hiring foreign workers is crucial to their nascent enterprise. Mr. Chigos claims, "We'd love it to say 'made in the U.S.A.' and use American textiles and production." However, if they did so, their cost would rise 4 to 10 times, and "We didn't want to sell our pajamas for $120." One benefit of easy access to cheap manufacturing, Chigos said, is that more American entrepreneurs may be able to turn an idea into a product.

The would-be pajama tycoons plan to outsource to U.S. firms as well. They will use a Richmond, California, freight management company to receive the shipments, check the merchandise's quality, and ship it to customers. They will market their clothes on the Internet and through boutique retailers. Indeed, their business will be entirely virtual: They have no manufacturing plant, storefront, or warehouse. As Mr. Chigos notes, "With the technology available today, we'll never touch the product."

Thus lower communication and transportation costs have made foreign outsourcing feasible by lowering transaction costs. Ultimately, however, such outsourcing occurs because the costs of production are lower abroad.

If relative factor prices (and hence slopes of isocost lines) are different abroad than at home, a firm with smooth isoquants uses a different factor mix when producing abroad, as Figure 7.5 illustrates. However, if isoquants are not smooth curves, the firm does not necessarily use a different factor mix. Solved Problem 7.3 shows that small differences in factor prices may not induce the firm to change technologies or factor mixes if isoquants have kinks. In Problem 32 at the end of the chapter, you are asked to show that, if all foreign factor prices are proportionally lower than domestic prices, the firm will use the same technology as at home. Problems 33–35 ask you to show what happens in the typical case with smooth isoquants.

SOLVED PROBLEM   7.3

A U.S. semiconductor manufacturing company plans to move its production abroad. (According to the Semiconductor Industry Association, worldwide semiconductor billings from the Americas dropped from 33% in 1998 to 17% in 2005.) Its technologies are described in the application "A Semiconductor Integrated Circuit Isoquant" (Chapter 6).

The firm currently produces using a wafer-handling stepper. The cost of equipment is the same everywhere; however, the wage is lower abroad. Will the firm necessarily use a different technology when it produces abroad? Why might it use a different technology?

Answer

1. *Show the isoquant and the relevant domestic isoquant:* The figure shows the same isoquant as in Chapter 6. We are told there that the firm produces at home using the wafer-handling stepper technology, so its C^1 isocost must hit the isoquant at that technology. Because the isoquant is not smooth, the C^1 isoquant could have any of several different slopes.

2. *State what happens to the slope of the isocost line if the firm produces abroad:* The firm's new isocost line will be flatter than the C^1 isocost. The slope of the isocost is $-w/r$, where w is the wage and r is the rental cost of the machine. Thus the smaller w is, the less steeply sloped the isocost curve.

3. *Show that a flatter isocost might but does not necessarily hit the isoquant at a different technology:* Because the isoquant has kinks, a small change in the relative input prices does not necessarily induce a change in technique. The C^2 and C^3 isocost curves are both flatter than the C^1 isocost. If the wage drops just slightly, so that the C^2 isocost is only slightly flatter, the firm still uses the capital-intensive wafer-handling stepper technology. However, with a larger drop in the wage, the much flatter C^3 isocost curve hits the isoquant at the stepper technology (if it were even flatter, it could hit at the aligner technology).

Comment: The firm's cost will drop due to the lower wage even if it uses the same technology: $C^2 < C^1$. However, if the wage is low enough that it can shift to a more labor-intensive technology, its costs will be even lower: $C^3 < C^2$. If the isoquant were smooth (without kinks), any change in relative factor costs would induce the firm to change the technology (labor-capital ratio) that it uses.

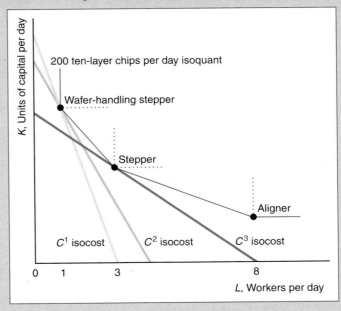

HOW LONG-RUN COST VARIES WITH OUTPUT

We now know how a firm determines the cost-minimizing output for any given level of output. By repeating this analysis for different output levels, the firm determines how its cost varies with output.

Expansion Path. Panel a of Figure 7.6 shows the relationship between the lowest-cost factor combinations and various levels of output for the furniture manufacturer when input prices are held constant at $w = \$24$ and $r = \$8$. The curve through the tangency points is the long-run **expansion path**: the cost-minimizing combination of labor and capital for each output level. The lowest-cost way to produce 100 units of output is to use the labor and capital combination x ($L = 50$ and $K = 100$), which lies on the $2,000 isocost line. Similarly, the lowest-cost way to produce 200 units is to use z, which is on the $4,000 isocost line. The expansion path for the furniture manufacturer is a straight line through the origin and x, y, and z, which has a slope of 2: At any given output level, the firm uses twice as much capital as labor. (In general, the expansion path need not be a straight line but can curve up or down as input use increases.)

SOLVED PROBLEM   7.4

> **What is the expansion path function for a constant-returns-to-scale Cobb-Douglas production function $q = AL^a K^{1-a}$? Show the special cases for the furniture firm: $q = 1.52L^{0.6}K^{0.4}$.**
>
> **Answer**
>
> *Use the tangency condition between the isocost and isoquant that determines the factor ratio when the firm is minimizing cost to derive the expansion path:* Because the marginal product of labor is $MP_L = aq/L$ and the marginal product of capital is $MP_K = (1 - a)q/K$, the tangency condition is
>
> $$\frac{w}{r} = \frac{aq/L}{(1-a)q/K} = \frac{a}{1-a}\frac{K}{L}.$$
>
> Using algebra to rearrange this expression, we obtain the expansion path formula that we would use to plot an expansion path:
>
> $$K = \frac{(1-a)}{a}\frac{w}{r}L. \tag{7.21}$$
>
> For the furniture firm in panel a of Figure 7.6, the expansion path, Equation 7.6, is $K = (0.4/0.6)(24/8)L = 2L$.

Long-Run Cost Function. The furniture manufacturer's expansion path contains the same information as its long-run cost function, $C(q)$, which shows the relationship between the cost of production and output. As the expansion path plot in Figure 7.6 shows, to produce q units of output takes $K = q$ units of capital and $L = q/2$ units of labor. Thus the long-run cost of producing q units of output is

$$C(q) = wL + rK = wq/2 + rq = (w/2 + r)q = (24/2 + 8)q = 20q.$$

That is, the long-run cost function corresponding to this expansion path is $C(q) = 20q$. This cost function is consistent with the expansion path in panel a: $C(100) = \$2,000$ at x on the expansion path, $C(150) = \$3,000$ at y, and $C(200) = \$4,000$ at z.

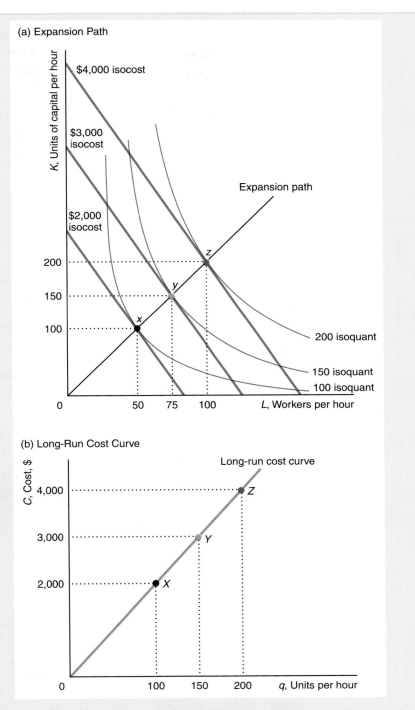

Figure 7.6 Expansion Path and Long-Run Cost Curve. (a) The curve through the tangency points between isocost lines and isoquants, such as *x*, *y*, and *z*, is called the expansion path. The points on the expansion path are the cost-minimizing combinations of labor and capital for each output level. (b) The furniture manufacturer's expansion path shows the same relationship between long-run cost and output as the long-run cost curve.

Panel b of Figure 7.6 plots this long-run cost curve. Points X, Y, and Z on the cost curve correspond to points x, y, and z on the expansion path. For example, the $2,000 isocost line hits the $q = 100$ isoquant at x, which is the lowest-cost combination of labor and capital that can produce 100 units of output. Similarly, X on the long-run cost curve is at $2,000 and 100 units of output. Consistent with the expansion path, the cost curve shows that as output doubles, cost doubles.

Solving for the cost function from the production function is not always easy. However, a cost function is relatively simple to derive from the production function if the production function is homogeneous of degree γ: $q = f(xL^*, xK^*) = x^\gamma f(L^*, K^*)$, where x is a positive constant and L^* and K^* are particular values of labor and capital. That is, the production function has the same returns to scale for any given combination of inputs. Important examples of such production functions include the Cobb-Douglas ($q = AL^a K^b$, $\gamma = a + b$), constant elasticity of substitution (CES), linear, and fixed-proportions production functions (see Chapter 6).

We know that a firm's cost identity is $C = wL + rK$, Equation 7.6. Were we to double the inputs, we would double the cost, or more generally: $C = (wL^* + rK^*)x = \theta x$, where $\theta = wL^* + rK^*$. Solving the production function for x, we know that $x = q^{1/\gamma}$. Substituting that expression in the cost identity, we find that the cost function for any homogeneous of degree γ production function is $C = \theta q^{1/\gamma}$. The constant in this cost function depends on factor prices and two constants, L^* and K^*. We would prefer to express the constant in terms of only the factor prices and parameters. We can do so by noting that the fix chooses the cost-minimizing pair of labor and capital, as summarized in the expansion path equation. In the following Solved Problem, you are asked to do so for a Cobb-Douglas that is homogeneous of degree one.

SOLVED PROBLEM   7.5

Derive the long-run cost as a function of only output and factor prices for a Cobb-Douglas production function $q = AL^a K^{1-a}$. Show the special case for the furniture firm: $q = 1.52L^{0.6}K^{0.4}$.

Answer

1. *Combine the cost identity, Equation 7.6, with the expansion path equation 7.21, which contains information on how the cost-minimizing factor ratio varies with factor prices, to derive expressions for the inputs as a function of cost and factor prices:* From the expansion path, we know that $rK = wL(1 - a)/a$. Substituting for rK in the cost identity gives $C = wL + wL(1 - a)/a$. Simplifying shows that $L = aC/w$. Repeating this process to solve for K, we find that $K = aC/r$.

2. *To derive the cost function, substitute these expressions of labor and capital into the production function:* By combining this information with the production function, we can get a relationship between cost and output. By substituting, we find that

$$q = A\left(\frac{aC}{w}\right)^a \left[\frac{(1 - a)C}{r}\right]^{1-a}. \tag{7.22}$$

We can rewrite Equation 7.22 as $C = q\theta$, where $\theta = w^a r^{1-a}/[Aa^a(1 - a)^{1-a}]$.

> 3. *To derive the long-run cost function for the furniture firm, substitute the parameter values into* $C = q\theta$: For the furniture firm, $C = q24^{0.6}8^{0.4}/(1.52 \times 0.6^{0.6}0.4^{0.4}) \approx 20q$.

THE SHAPE OF LONG-RUN COST CURVES

The shapes of the average cost and marginal cost curves depend on the shape of the long-run cost curve. The relationships among total, marginal, and average costs are the same for the long-run cost function and the short-run cost function. For example, if the long-run average cost curve is U-shaped, the long-run marginal cost curve cuts it at its minimum.

The long-run average cost curve may be U-shaped, but the reason for this shape differs from those reasons given for the short-run average cost curve being U-shaped. A key reason the short-run average cost is initially downward sloping is that the average fixed cost curve is downward sloping: Spreading the fixed cost over more units of output lowers the average fixed cost per unit. Because there are no fixed costs in the long run, fixed costs cannot explain the initial downward slope of the long-run average cost curve.

A major reason why the short-run average cost curve slopes upward at higher levels of output is diminishing marginal returns. In the long run, however, all factors can be varied, so diminishing marginal returns do not explain the upward slope of a long-run average cost curve.

As with the short-run curves, the shape of the long-run curves is ultimately determined by the production function relationship between output and inputs. In the long run, returns to scale play a major role in determining the shape of the average cost curve and the other cost curves. As Chapter 6 discussed, increasing all inputs in proportion may cause output to increase more than in proportion (increasing returns to scale) at low levels of output, in proportion (constant returns to scale) at intermediate levels of output, and less than in proportion (decreasing returns to scale) at high levels of output. If a production function has this returns-to-scale pattern and the prices of inputs are constant, the long-run average cost curve must be U-shaped.

A cost function is said to exhibit **economies of scale** if the average cost of production falls as output expands, as we would expect in the range where the production function had increasing returns to scale. In the range where the production function has constant returns to scale, the average cost remains constant, so the cost function has *no economies of scale*. Finally, in the range where the production function has decreasing returns to scale, average cost increases. A firm suffers from **diseconomies of scale** if average cost rises when output increases.

Returns to scale in the production function are a sufficient but not necessary condition for economies of scale in the average cost curve. In the long run, a firm may change the ratio of capital to labor that it uses as it expands output. As a result, the firm could have economies of scale in costs without increasing returns to scale in production or could have diseconomies of scale in costs without decreasing returns to scale in production.

Table 7.1   Shape of Average Cost Curves in Canadian Manufacturing

Scale Economies	Share of Manufacturing Industries, %
Economies of scale: Initially downward-sloping *AC*	57
Everywhere downward-sloping *AC*	18
L-shaped *AC* (downward sloping, then flat)	31
U-shaped *AC*	8
No economies of scale: Flat *AC*	23
Diseconomies of scale: Upward-sloping *AC*	14

Source: Robidoux and Lester (1992).

Consider a firm that has constant returns to scale in production at every output level. At small levels of output, the firm uses a large number of workers and commonly available tools. At large levels of output, the firm designs and builds its own specialized equipment and uses relatively few workers, thereby lowering its average cost. Such a firm has economies of scale in cost despite having constant returns to scale in production.

Average cost curves can have many different shapes. In competitive markets, firms typically have U-shaped average cost curves. In noncompetitive markets, average cost curves may be U-shaped, L-shaped (average cost at first falls rapidly and then levels off as output increases), downward sloping everywhere, or upward sloping everywhere— or they may have other shapes. The shapes of the average cost curves indicate whether the production process has economies or diseconomies of scale.

Table 7.1 summarizes the shapes of average cost curves of firms in various Canadian manufacturing industries (as estimated by Robidoux and Lester, 1992). The table shows that U-shaped average cost curves are the exception rather than the rule in Canadian manufacturing and that nearly one-third of these average cost curves are L-shaped. Cement firms provide an example of such a cost curve.

Some of these apparently L-shaped average cost curves may be part of a U-shaped curve with long, flat bottoms, where we don't observe any firm producing enough to exhibit diseconomies of scale.

APPLICATION

Innovations and Economies of Scale

Before the introduction of robotic assembly lines in the tire industry, firms had to produce large runs of identical products to take advantage of economies of scale and thereby keep their per-unit costs low. A traditional plant might be half a mile in length and be designed to produce popular models in batches of a thousand or more. To change to a different model, workers in traditional plants labored for eight hours or more to switch molds and set up the machinery.

In contrast, in its modern plant in Rome, Georgia, Pirelli Tire uses its modular integrated robotized system (MIRS) to produce small batches of a large number of products without driving up the cost per tire. A MIRS production unit has a dozen robots feeding a group of rubber-extruding and ply-laying machines. MIRS fabricates tires around metal drums that the robotic arms powerfully grip. The robots hand the tire-in-progress to extruding machinery at various angles, where strips of rubber and reinforcing materials are built up to form the tire's structure. One MIRS system can simultaneously build 12 different tire models. At the end of the process, robots load the unfinished tires into molds that emboss the tread pattern and sidewall lettering. By being able to produce as needed, Pirelli avoids the inventory cost of storing large quantities of expensive raw materials and finished tires.

Because Pirelli can practically produce as few as four tires at a time, it can build some wild variations. "We make tires for ultra-big bling-bling wheels in small numbers, but they are quite profitable," brags Gaetano Mannino, the president of Pirelli Tire North America.

ESTIMATING COST CURVES VERSUS INTROSPECTION

Economists use statistical methods to estimate a cost function. However, sometimes we can infer the shape by casual observation and deductive reasoning.

For example, in the good old days, the Good Humor Company sent out herds of ice-cream trucks to purvey its products. It seems likely that the company's production process had fixed proportions and constant returns to scale: If it wanted to sell more, Good Humor dispatched one more truck and one more driver. Drivers and trucks are almost certainly nonsubstitutable inputs (the isoquants are right angles). If the cost of a driver is w per day, the rental cost is r per day, and q is the quantity of ice cream sold in a day, then the cost function is $C = (w + r)q$.

Such deductive reasoning can lead one astray, as I once discovered. A water heater manufacturing firm provided me with many years of data on the inputs it used and the amount of output it produced. I also talked to the company's engineers about the production process and toured the plant (which resembled a scene from Dante's *Inferno*, with deafening noise levels and flames everywhere).

A water heater consists of an outside cylinder of metal, a liner, an electronic control unit, hundreds of tiny parts, and a couple of rods that slow corrosion. Workers cut out the metal for the cylinder, weld it together, and add the other parts. "OK," I said to myself, "this production process must be one of fixed proportions because the firm needs one of everything to produce a water heater. How could you substitute a cylinder for an electronic control unit? How could you substitute labor for metal?"

I then used statistical techniques to estimate the production and cost functions. Following the usual procedure, I did not assume that I knew the exact form of the functions. Rather, I allowed the data to "tell" me the type of production and cost functions. To my surprise, the estimates indicated that the production process was not one of fixed proportions. Rather, the firm could readily substitute between labor and capital.

"Surely I've made a mistake," I said to the plant manager after describing these results.

"No," he said, "that's correct. There's a great deal of substitutability between labor and metal."

"How can they be substitutes?"

"Easy," he said. "We can use a lot of labor and waste very little metal by cutting out exactly what we want and being very careful. Or we can use relatively little labor, cut quickly, and waste more metal. When the cost of labor is relatively high, we waste more metal. When the cost of metal is relatively high, we cut more carefully." This practice, as the manager explained, minimizes the firm's cost.

7.4 Lower Costs in the Long Run

In its long-run planning, a firm chooses a plant size and makes other investments so as to minimize its long-run cost on the basis of how many units it produces. Once it chooses its plant size and equipment, these inputs are fixed in the short run. Thus the firm's long-run decision determines its short-run cost. Because the firm cannot vary its capital in the short run but can vary it in the long run, its short-run cost is at least as high as long-run cost and is higher if the "wrong" level of capital is used in the short run.

LONG-RUN AVERAGE COST AS THE ENVELOPE OF SHORT-RUN AVERAGE COST CURVES

As a result, the long-run average cost is always equal to or below the short-run average cost. Panel a of Figure 7.7 shows a firm with a U-shaped long-run average cost curve. Suppose initially that the firm has only three possible plant sizes. The firm's short-run average cost curve is $SRAC^1$ for the smallest possible plant. The average cost of producing q_1 units of output using this plant, point a on $SRAC^1$, is $10. If instead the plant used the next larger plant size, its cost of producing q_1 units of output, point b on $SRAC^2$, would be $12. Thus if the firm knows that it will produce only q_1 units of output, it minimizes its average cost by using the smaller plant. If it expects to be producing q_2, its average cost is lower on the $SRAC^2$ curve, point e, than on the $SRAC^1$ curve, point d.

In the long run, the firm chooses the plant size that minimizes its cost of production, so it selects the plant size that has the lowest average cost for each possible output level. At q_1, it opts for the small plant, whereas at q_2, it uses the medium plant. Thus the long-run average cost curve is the solid, scalloped section of the three short-run cost curves.

But if there are many possible plant sizes, the long-run average curve, $LRAC$, is smooth and U-shaped. The $LRAC$ includes one point from each possible short-run average cost curve. This point, however, is not necessarily the minimum point from a short-run curve. For example, the $LRAC$ includes point a on $SRAC^1$ and not the curve's minimum point, c. A small plant operating at minimum average cost cannot produce at as low an average cost as a slightly larger plant that is taking advantage of economies of scale.

Panel b of Figure 7.7 shows the relationship between short-run and long-run average cost curves for the furniture manufacturer. Because this production function has constant returns to scale, doubling both inputs doubles output, so the long-run average cost, $LRAC$, is constant at $20, as we saw earlier. If capital is fixed at 200 units, the firm's short-run average cost curve is $SRAC^1$. If the firm produces 200 units of output, its short-run and long-run average costs are equal. At any other output, its short-run cost is higher than its long-run cost.

The short-run marginal cost curves, $SRMC^1$ and $SRMC^2$, are upward sloping and equal the corresponding U-shaped short-run average cost curves, $SRAC^1$ and $SRAC^2$, only at their minimum points, $20. In contrast, because the long-run average cost is horizontal at $20, the long-run marginal cost curve, $LRMC$, is horizontal at $20. Thus the long-run marginal cost curve is not the envelope of the short-run marginal cost curves.

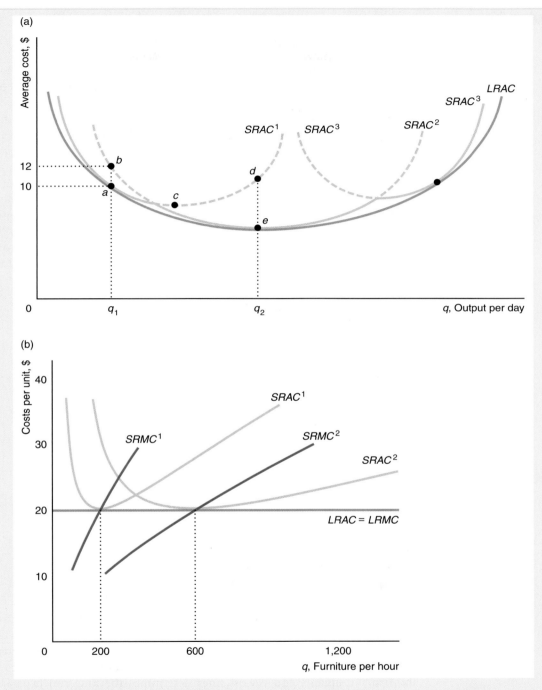

Figure 7.7 Long-Run Average Cost as the Envelope of Short-Run Average Cost Curves. (a) If there are only three possible plant sizes, with short-run average costs $SRAC^1$, $SRAC^2$, and $SRAC^3$, the long-run average cost curve is the solid, scalloped portion of the three short-run curves. *LRAC* is the smooth and U-shaped long-run average cost curve if there are many possible short-run average cost curves. (b) Because the furniture firm's production function has constant returns to scale, its long-run average cost and marginal cost curves are horizontal.

Choosing an Ink-Jet or a Laser Printer

You decide to buy a printer for your college assignments. You need to print in black and white. In 2007 you can buy a personal laser printer for $150 or an ink-jet printer for $75 that prints 15 pages a minute at 1,200 dots per inch.

If you buy the ink jet, you save $75 right off the bat. The laser printer costs less per page to operate, however. The cost of ink and paper is about 4¢ per page for a laser compared to about 7¢ per page for an ink jet. That means that the average cost per page of operating a laser ($150/$q$ + 0.04, where q is the number of pages) is less than that of an ink jet ($75/$q$ + 0.07) after q reaches about 2,500 pages.

The graph shows the short-run average cost curves for the laser printer and the ink-jet printer. The lower-cost choice is the ink-jet printer if you're printing fewer than 2,500 pages and the laser printer if you're printing more.

So should you buy the laser printer? If you print more than 2,500 pages over its lifetime, the laser is less expensive to own and operate than the ink jet. If the printers last two years and you print 25 or more pages per week, then the laser printer is cost effective.

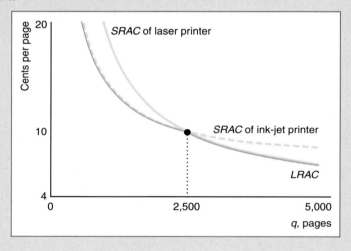

SHORT-RUN AND LONG-RUN EXPANSION PATHS

Long-run cost is lower than short-run cost because a firm has more flexibility in the long run. To show the advantage of flexibility, we can compare the short-run and long-run expansion paths, which correspond to the short-run and long-run cost curves.

The furniture manufacturer has greater flexibility in the long run. The tangency of the firm's isoquants and isocost lines determines the long-run expansion path in Figure 7.8. The firm expands output by increasing both its labor and its capital, so its long-run expansion path is upward sloping. To increase its output from 100 to 200 units (that is, move from x to z), it doubles its capital from 100 to 200 units and its labor from 50 to 100 workers. Its cost increases from $2,000 to $4,000.

In the short run, the firm cannot increase its capital, which is fixed at 100 units. The firm can increase its output only by using more labor, so its short-run expansion path is horizontal at $K = 100$. To expand its output from 100 to 200 units (move from x to y),

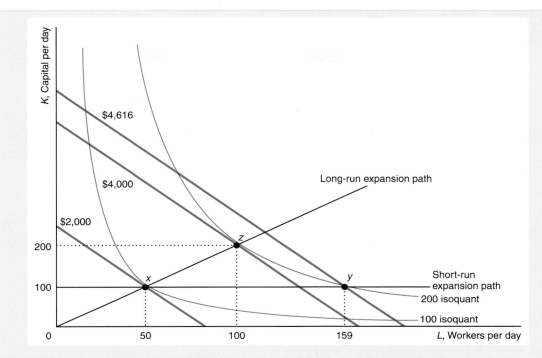

Figure 7.8 Long-Run and Short-Run Expansion Paths. In the long run, the furniture manufacturer increases its output by using more of both inputs, so its long-run expansion path is upward sloping. In the short run, the firm cannot vary its capital, so its short-run expansion path is horizontal at the fixed level of output. That is, it increases its output by increasing the amount of labor it uses. Expanding output from 100 to 200 raises the furniture firm's long-run cost from $2,000 to $4,000 but raises its short-run cost from $2,000 to $4,616.

the firm must increase its labor from 50 to 159 workers, and its cost rises from $2,000 to $4,616. Doubling output increases long-run cost by a factor of 2 and short-run cost by approximately 2.3.

HOW LEARNING BY DOING LOWERS COSTS

Two reasons why long-run cost is lower than short-run cost are that firms have more flexibility in the long run and that technological progress (Chapter 6) may lower cost over time. A third reason is the benefits of **learning by doing:** the productive skills and knowledge of better ways to produce that workers and managers gain from experience.

In some firms, learning by doing is a function of the time since the product was introduced. In other firms, learning by doing is a function of *cumulative output:* the total number of units of output produced since the product was introduced. Learning is connected to cumulative output if workers become increasingly adept the more times they perform a task. As a consequence, workers become more productive if they make many units over a short period than if they produce a few units over a longer period. For example, the average labor cost of producing an Intel Pentium central processing unit or CPU (panel a of Figure 7.9) fell with cumulative output (based on Salgado, 2007).

If a firm is operating in the economies of scale section of its average cost curve, expanding output lowers its cost for two reasons: Its average cost falls today because of

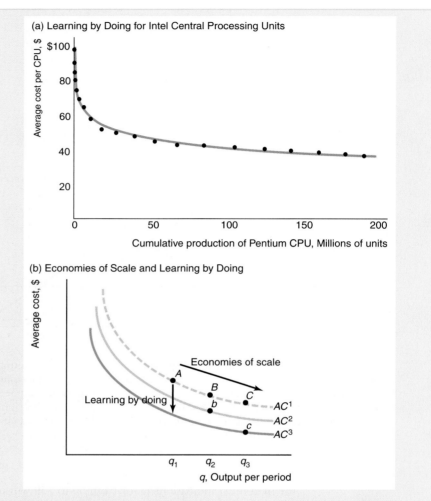

Figure 7.9 Learning by Doing. (a) As Intel produces more cumulative central processing units (CPUs), the average cost of production per unit falls (Salgado, 2007). The horizontal axis measures the cumulative production. (b) In the short run, extra production reduces a firm's average cost owing to economies of scale: Because $q_1 < q_2 < q_3$, A is higher than B, which is higher than C. In the long run, extra production reduces average cost because of learning by doing. To produce q_2 this period costs B on AC^1, but to produce that same output in the next period would cost only b on AC^2. If the firm produces q_3 instead of q_2 in this period, its average cost in the next period is AC^3 instead of AC^2 because of additional learning by doing. Thus, extra output in this period lowers the firm's cost in two ways: It lowers average cost in this period due to economies of scale and lowers average cost for any given output level in the next period due to learning by doing.

economies of scale; and for any given level of output, its average cost is lower in the next period due to learning by doing.

In panel b of Figure 7.9, the firm is currently producing q_1 units of output at point A on average cost curve AC^1. If it expands its output to q_2, its average cost falls in this period to point B because of economies of scale. The learning by doing in this period results in a lower average cost, AC^2, in the next period. If the firm continues to produce q_2 units of output in the next period, its average cost falls to point b on AC^2.

If the firm expands to q_3 instead of expanding output to q_2 in this period, its average cost is even lower in this period (point C on AC^1) due to even more economies of scale. Moreover, its average cost in the next period is even lower, AC^3, due to the extra experience in this period. If the firm continues to produce q_3 in the next period, its average cost is point c on AC^3. Thus all else the same, if learning by doing depends on cumulative output, firms have an incentive to produce more in the short run than they otherwise would to lower their costs in the future.

● **APPLICATION**

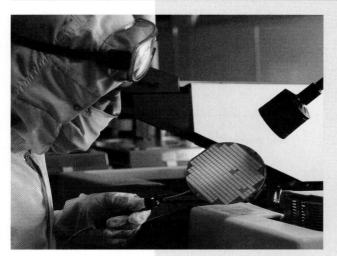

Learning by Doing in Computer Chips

The cost of producing a computer memory chip falls substantially due to learning by doing. There are several different types of MOS (metal oxide on silicon) memory chips: EPROM (erasable programmable read-only memory), DRAM (dynamic random-access memory), and fast SRAM (static random-access memory). From one generation to another, EPROM's storage capacity doubles, whereas the storage capacity of DRAM and SRAM increases by a factor of 4. Like clockwork, a new EPROM generation appears every 18 months; a new DRAM, every three years.

Gruber (1992) finds that the average cost of EPROM chips falls with cumulative output but does not decrease over time or with the scale of production. With each doubling in the cumulative output of an EPROM chip, its average cost falls by 22%. This effect may encourage firms to produce more EPROM chips in the first few months after a new generation is introduced than they would without learning by doing. By doing so, the firm gains experience more rapidly, and consequently its average cost falls more rapidly.

Irwin and Klenow (1994) find an average 20% learning curve effect on cumulative output for DRAMs. Chung (2001) reports 17% learning for 64K DRAM and 9% for 256K DRAM in Korea.

Although the type and speed of learning by doing vary across chips, they are the same across generations of the same chip. Thus firms know that they can count on their costs falling and build these predictable cost reductions into their planning over time.

7.5 Cost of Producing Multiple Goods

Few firms produce only a single good—we have discussed single-output firms only for simplicity. If a firm produces two or more goods, the cost of one good may depend on the output level of the other.

Outputs are linked if a single input is used to produce both of them. For example, mutton and wool both come from sheep, cattle provide beef and hides, and oil supplies both heating fuel and gasoline. It is less expensive to produce beef and hides together than separately. If the goods are produced together, a single steer yields one unit of beef

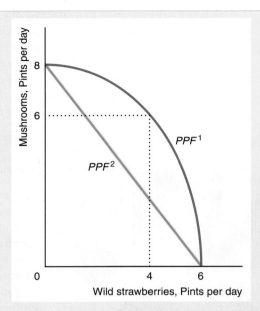

Figure 7.10 Joint Production. If there are economies of scope, the production possibility frontier is bowed away from the origin, PPF^1. If instead the production possibility frontier is a straight line, PPF^2, the cost of producing both goods does not fall if they are produced together.

and one hide. If beef and hides are produced separately (throwing away the unused good), the same amount of output requires two steers and more labor.

We say that there are **economies of scope** if it is less expensive to produce goods jointly than separately (Panzar and Willig, 1977, 1981). A measure of the degree to which there are economies of *scope* (*SC*) is

$$SC = \frac{C(q_1, 0) + C(0, q_2) - C(q_1, q_2)}{C(q_1, q_2)},$$

where $C(q_1, 0)$ is the cost of producing q_1 units of the first good by itself, $C(0, q_2)$ is the cost of producing q_2 units of the second good, and $C(q_1, q_2)$ is the cost of producing both goods together. If the cost of producing the two goods separately, $C(q_1, 0) + C(0, q_2)$, is the same as the cost of producing them together, $C(q_1, q_2)$, then *SC* is zero. If it is cheaper to produce the goods jointly, *SC* is positive. If *SC* is negative, there are diseconomies of scope, and the two goods should be produced separately.

To illustrate this idea, suppose that Laura spends one day collecting mushrooms and wild strawberries in the woods. Her **production possibility frontier**—the maximum amount of outputs (mushrooms and strawberries) that can be produced from a fixed amount of input (Laura's effort during one day)—is PPF^1 in Figure 7.10. The production possibility frontier summarizes the trade-off Laura faces: She picks fewer mushrooms if she collects more strawberries in a day.

If Laura spends all day collecting only mushrooms, she picks 8 pints; if she spends all day picking strawberries, she collects 6 pints. If she picks some of each, however, she can harvest more total pints: 6 pints of mushrooms and 4 pints of strawberries. The product possibility frontier is concave (the middle of the curve is farther from the origin than it would be if it were a straight line) because of the diminishing marginal returns to collecting only one of the two goods. If she collects only mushrooms, she must walk past wild strawberries without picking them. As a result, she has to walk farther if she collects only mushrooms than if she picks both. Thus there are economies of scope in jointly collecting mushrooms and strawberries.

If instead the production possibility frontier were a straight line, the cost of producing the two goods jointly would not be lower. Suppose, for example, that mushrooms grow in one section of the woods and strawberries in another section. In that case, Laura can collect only mushrooms without passing any strawberries. That production possibility frontier is a straight line, PPF^2 in Figure 7.10. By allocating her time between the two sections of the woods, Laura can collect any combination of mushrooms and strawberries by spending part of her day in one section of the woods and part in the other.

A number of empirical studies show that some processes have economies of scope, others have none, and some have diseconomies of scope. Ida and Kuwahara (2004) found substantial economies of scope ($SC = 0.2$) between producing and transmitting electricity in Japan.

Friedlaender, Winston, and Wang (1983) determined that for American automobile manufacturers, it is 25% less expensive ($SC = 0.25$) to produce large cars together with small cars and trucks than to produce large cars separately and small cars and trucks together. However, there are no economies of scope from producing trucks together with small and large cars. Producing trucks separately from cars is efficient.

Kim (1987) found substantial diseconomies of scope in using railroads to transport freight and passengers together. It is 41% less expensive ($SC = -0.41$) to transport passengers and freight separately than together. In the early 1970s, passenger service in the United States was transferred from the private railroad companies to Amtrak, and the services are now separate. Kim's estimates suggest that this separation is cost effective.

Summary

From all available technologically efficient production processes, a firm chooses the one that is economically efficient. The economically efficient production process is the technologically efficient process for which the cost of producing a given quantity of output is lowest, or the one that produces the most output for a given cost.

1. **Measuring Costs:** The economic or opportunity cost of a good is the value of its next best alternative use. Economic cost includes both explicit and implicit costs.

2. **Short-Run Costs:** In the short run, a firm can vary the costs of the factors that it can adjust, but the costs of other factors are fixed. The firm's average fixed cost falls as its output rises. If a firm has a short-run average cost curve that is U-shaped, its marginal cost curve is below the average cost curve when average cost is falling and above the average cost curve when it is rising, so the marginal cost curve cuts the average cost curve at its minimum.

3. **Long-Run Costs:** In the long run, all factors can be varied, so all costs are variable. As a result, average cost and average variable cost are identical. A firm chooses the combination of inputs it uses to minimize its cost. To produce a given output level, it chooses the lowest isocost line that touches the relevant isoquant, which is tangent to the isoquant. Equivalently, to minimize cost, the firm adjusts inputs until the last dollar spent on any input increases output by as much as the last dollar spent on any other input. If the firm calculates the cost of producing every possible output level given current input prices, it knows its cost function: Cost is a function of the input prices and the output level. If the firm's average cost falls as output expands, it has economies of scale. If the firm's average cost rises as output expands, it has diseconomies of scale.

4. **Lower Costs in the Long Run:** The firm can always do in the long run what it does in the short run, so its long-run cost can never be greater than its short-run cost. Because some factors are fixed in the short run, the firm, to expand output, must greatly increase its use of other factors, a relatively costly choice. In the long run, the firm can adjust all factors, a process that keeps its cost down. Long-run

cost may also be lower than short-run cost if technological progress or learning by doing occurs.

5. **Cost of Producing Multiple Goods:** If it is less expensive for a firm to produce two goods jointly rather than separately, there are economies of scope. If there are diseconomies of scope, it is less expensive to produce the goods separately.

Questions

*= answer at the back of this book; W = audio-slide show answers by James Dearden at **www.aw-bc.com/perloff**

*1. "There are certain fixed costs when you own a plane," [Andre] Agassi explained during a break in the action at the Volvo/San Francisco tennis tournament, "so the more you fly it, the more economic sense it makes. . . . The first flight after I bought it, I took some friends to Palm Springs for lunch." (Ostler, Scott, "Andre Even Flies like a Champ," *San Francisco Chronicle*, February 8, 1993, C1.) Discuss whether Agassi's analysis is reasonable.

2. The only variable input a janitorial service firm uses to clean offices is workers who are paid a wage, w, of $8 an hour. Each worker can clean four offices in an hour. Use math to determine the variable cost, the average variable cost, and the marginal cost of cleaning one more office. Draw a diagram like Figure 7.1 to show the variable cost, average variable cost, and marginal cost curves.

*3. A firm builds shipping crates out of wood. How does the cost of producing a 1-cubic-foot crate (each side is 1 foot square) compare to the cost of building an 8-cubic-foot crate if wood costs $1 per square foot and the firm has no labor or other costs? More generally, how does cost vary with volume?

*4. You have 60 minutes to complete an exam with two questions. You want to maximize your score. Toward the end of the exam, the more time you spend on either question, the fewer extra points per minute you get for that question. How should you allocate your time between the two questions? (*Hint:* Think about producing an output of a score on the exam using inputs of time spent on each of the problems. Then use Equation 7.6.)

5. Boxes of cereal are produced by using a fixed-proportion production function: One box and one unit (8 ounces) of cereal produce one box of cereal. What is the expansion path?

6. Suppose that your firm's production function has constant returns to scale. What is the long-run expansion path?

7. The production process of the firm you manage uses labor and capital services. How does the long-run expansion path change when the wage increases while the rental rate of capital stays constant?

8. A U-shaped long-run average cost curve is the envelope of U-shaped short-run average cost curves. On what part of the curve (downward sloping, flat, or upward sloping) does a short-run curve touch the long-run curve? (*Hint:* Your answer should depend on where the two curves touch on the long-run curve.)

9. Suppose that the government subsidizes the cost of workers by paying for 25% of the wage (the rate offered by the U.S. government in the late 1970s under the New Jobs Tax Credit program). What effect will this subsidy have on the firm's choice of labor and capital to produce a given level of output?

10. Suppose in Solved Problem 7.2 that the government charges the firm a franchise tax each year instead of only once. Describe the effect of this tax on the marginal cost, average variable cost, short-run average cost, and long-run average cost curves.

11. Over the last century, department stores and supermarkets have largely replaced smaller specialty stores, as consumers have found it more efficient to go to one rather than to many stores. Consumers incur a transaction cost (or search cost) to shop, primarily the opportunity cost of their time. This transaction cost includes a fixed cost of traveling to and from the store and a variable cost that rises with the number of different types of items the consumer tries to find on the shelves. By going to a supermarket that carries meat, fruit, vegetables, and other items, consumers can avoid some of the fixed transaction costs of traveling to a separate butcher shop, produce mart, and so forth. Use math or figures to explain why a shopper's average costs are lower when buying at a single supermarket than when buying from many stores. (*Hint:* Define the goods as the items purchased and brought home.)

*12. The all-American baseball is made using cork from Portugal, rubber from Malaysia, yarn from Australia, and leather from France, and it is stitched (108 stitches exactly) by workers in Costa Rica. To assemble a baseball takes one unit each of these inputs. Ultimately, the finished product must be shipped to its final destination—say, Cooperstown, New York. The materials used cost the same anywhere. Labor costs are lower in Costa Rica than in a possible alternative manufacturing site in Georgia, but shipping costs from Costa Rica are higher. What production function is used? What is the cost function? What can you conclude about shipping costs if it is less expensive to produce baseballs in Costa Rica than in Georgia?

13. The Bouncing Ball Ping Pong Co. sells table tennis sets, which include two paddles and one net. What is the firm's long-run expansion path if it incurs no costs other than what it pays for paddles and nets, which it buys at market prices? How does its expansion path depend on the relative prices of paddles and nets?

*14. A bottling company uses two inputs to produce bottles of the soft drink Sludge: bottling machines, K, and workers, L. The isoquants have the usual smooth shape. The machine costs $1,000 per day to run; the workers earn $200 per day. At the current level of production, the marginal product of the machine is an additional 200 bottles per day, and the marginal product of labor is 50 more bottles per day. Is this firm producing at minimum cost? If it is minimizing cost, explain why. If it is not minimizing cost, explain how the firm should change the ratio of inputs it uses to lower its cost. (*Hint:* Examine the conditions for minimizing cost: Equations 7.10 and 7.11.)

15. Rosenberg (2004) reports the invention of a new machine that serves as a mobile station for receiving and accumulating packed flats of strawberries close to where they are picked, reducing workers' time and burden of carrying full flats of strawberries. A machine-assisted crew of 15 pickers produces as much output, q^*, as that of an unaided crew of 25 workers. In a 6-day, 50-hour workweek, the machine replaces 500 worker-hours. At an hourly wage cost of $10, a machine saves $5,000 per week in labor costs, or $130,000 over a 26-week harvesting season. The cost of machine operation and maintenance expressed as a daily rental is $200, or $1,200 for a six-day week. Thus the net savings equal $3,800 per week, or $98,800 for 26 weeks.

   a. Draw the q^* isoquant assuming that only two technologies are available (pure labor and labor-machine). Label the isoquant and axes as thoroughly as possible.

   b. Add an isocost line to show which technology the firm chooses (be sure to measure wage and rental costs on a comparable time basis).

   c. Draw the corresponding cost curves (with and without the machine), assuming constant returns to scale, and label the curves and the axes as thoroughly as possible.

16. In February 2003, Circuit City Stores, Inc., replaced skilled sales representatives who earn up to $54,000 per year with relatively unskilled workers who earn $14 to $18 per hour (Carlos Tejada and Gary McWilliams, "New Recipe for Cost Savings: Replace Highly Paid Workers," *Wall Street Journal*, June 11, 2003). Suppose that sales representatives sell one specific Sony high-definition TV model. Let q represent the number of TVs sold per hour, s the number of skilled sales reps per hour, and u the number of unskilled reps per hour. Working eight hours per day, each skilled worker sells six TVs per day, and each unskilled worker sells four. The wage rate of the skilled workers is $w_s = \$26$ per hour, and the wage rate of the unskilled workers is $w_u = \$16$ per hour.

   a. Show the isoquant for $q = 4$ with both skilled and unskilled sales representatives. Are they substitutes?

   b. Draw a representative isocost for $c = \$104$ per hour.

   c. Using an isocost-isoquant diagram, identify the cost-minimizing number of skilled and unskilled reps to sell $q = 4$ TVs per hour. **W**

17. Many corporations allow CEOs to use the firm's corporate jet for personal travel. The Internal Revenue Service (IRS) requires that the firm report personal use of its corporate jet as taxable executive income, and the Securities and Exchange Commission (SEC) requires that publicly traded corporations report the value of this benefit to shareholders. An important issue is the determination of the value of this benefit. The *Wall Street Journal* (Mark Maremont, "Amid Crackdown, the Jet Perk Suddenly Looks a Lot Pricier," May 25, 2005, A1) reports three valuation techniques. The IRS values a CEO's personal flight at or below the price of a first-class ticket. The SEC values the flight at the "incremental" cost of the flight: the additional costs to the corporation of the flight. The third alternative is the market value of chartering an aircraft. Of the three methods, the first-class ticket is least expensive and the chartered flight is most expensive.

   a. What factors (such as fuel) determine the marginal explicit cost to a corporation of an executive's personal flight? Does any one of the three valuation methods correctly determine the marginal explicit cost?

   b. What is the marginal opportunity cost to the corporation of an executive's personal flight? **W**

18. In 1796, Gottfried Christoph Härtel, a German music publisher, calculated the cost of printing music using an engraved plate technology and used these estimated cost functions to make production decisions. Härtel figured that the fixed cost of printing a musical page—the cost of engraving the plates—was 900 pfennings. The marginal cost of each additional copy of the page was 5 pfennings (Scherer, 2001).

   a. Graph the total cost, average total cost, average variable cost, and marginal cost functions.

   b. Is there a cost advantage to having only one music publisher print a given composition? Why?

   c. Härtel used his data to do the following type of analysis: Suppose he expected to sell exactly 300 copies of a composition at 15 pfennings per page of the composition. What is the greatest amount the publisher would be willing to pay the composer per page of the composition? **W**

*19. In Solved Problem 7.3, show that there are a wage and a cost of capital services such that the firm is indifferent between using the wafer-handling stepper technology and the stepper technology. How does this wage/cost of capital ratio compare to those in the C^2 and C^3 isocosts?

20. What can you say about Laura's economies of scope if her time is valued at $5 an hour and her production possibility frontier is PPF^1 in Figure 7.10?

Problems

21. Give the formulas for and plot AFC, MC, AVC, and AC if the cost function is

    a. $C = 10 + 10q$
    b. $C = 10 + q^2$
    c. $C = 10 + 10q - 4q^2 + q^3$

22. The short-run cost function of a U.S. furniture manufacturer ("Short-Run Cost Curves for a Furniture Manufacturer" application) is approximately $C(q) = 0.55q^{1.67} + 800/q$. At what positive quantity does the average cost function reach its minimum? If a $400 lump-sum tax is applied to the firm, at what positive quantity is the after-tax average cost minimized? (*Hint*: See Solved Problem 7.2.)

*23. What is the long-run cost function if the production function is $q = L + K$?

24. Gail works in a flower shop, where she produces 10 floral arrangements per hour. She is paid $10 an hour for the first eight hours she works and $15 an hour for each additional hour she works. What is the firm's cost function? What are its AC, AVC, and MC functions? Draw the AC, AVC, and MC curves.

25. A firm's cost curve is $C = F + 10q - bq^2 + q^3$, where $b > 0$.

    a. For what values of b are cost, average cost, and average variable cost positive? (From now on, assume that all these measures of cost are positive at every output level.)
    b. What is the shape of the AC curve? At what output level is the AC minimized?
    c. At what output levels does the MC curve cross the AC and the AVC curves?
    d. Use calculus to show that the MC curve must cross the AVC at its minimum point.

26. A firm has two plants that produce identical output. The cost functions are $C_1 = 10q - 4q^2 + q^3$ and $C_2 = 10q - 2q^2 + q^3$.

    a. At what output levels does the average cost curve of each plant reach its minimum?
    b. If the firm wants to produce 4 units of output, how much should it produce in each plant?

27. For a Cobb-Douglas production function, how does the expansion path change if the wage increases while the rental rate of capital stays the same?

28. A firm has a Cobb-Douglas production function, $Q = AL^aK^b$, where $a + b < 1$. On the basis of this information, what properties does its cost function have?

*29. A firm's average cost is $AC = \alpha q^\beta$, where $\alpha > 0$. How can you interpret α? (*Hint*: Suppose that $q = 1$.) What sign must β have if there is learning by doing? What happens to average cost as q gets large? Draw the average cost curve as a function of output for a particular set of α and β.

30. A U.S. chemical firm has a production function of $q = 10L^{0.32}K^{0.56}$ (Hsieh, 1995). It faces factor prices of $w = 10$ and $r = 20$. What are its short-run marginal and average variable cost curves?

31. A glass manufacturer's production function is $q = 10L^{1/2}K^{1/2}$ (Hsieh, 1995). Suppose that its wage, w, is $1 per hour and that the rental cost of capital, r, is $4.

    a. Draw an accurate figure showing how the glass firm minimizes its cost of production.
    b. What is the equation of the (long-run) expansion path for a glass firm? Illustrate in a graph.
    c. Derive the long-run total cost curve equation as a function of q.

32. If it manufactures at home, a firm faces input prices for labor and capital of $\hat{w}$ and $\hat{r}$ and produces $\hat{q}$ units of output using $\hat{L}$ units of labor and $\hat{K}$ units of capital. Abroad, the wage and cost of capital are half as much as at home. If the firm manufactures abroad, will it change the amount of labor and capital it uses to produce $\hat{q}$? What happens to its cost of producing $\hat{q}$?

33. A U.S. electronics firm is considering moving its production to a plant in Mexico. Its production function is $q = L^{1/2}K^{1/2}$ (based on Hsieh, 1995). The U.S. factor prices are $w = r = 10$. In Mexico, the wage is half that in the United States, but the firm faces the same cost of capital: $w^* = 5$ and $r^* = r = 10$. What are L and K, and what is the cost of producing $q = 100$ units in both countries?

*34. A U.S. electronics firm is considering moving its production to a plant in Asia. Its production function is $q = L^{1/2}K^{1/2}$ (based on Hsieh, 1995). In the United States, $w = 10 = r$. At its Asian plant, the firm will pay a 10% lower wage and a 10% higher cost of capital: $w^* = 10/1.1$ and $r^* = 1.1 \times 10 = 11$. What are L and K, and what is the cost of producing $q = 100$ units in both countries? What would the cost of production be in Asia if the firm had to use the same factor quantities as in the United States?

35. A U.S. apparel manufacturer is considering moving its production abroad. Its production function is $q = L^{0.7}K^{0.3}$ (based on Hsieh, 1995). In the United States, $w = 7$ and $r = 3$. At its Asian plant, the firm will pay a 50% lower wage and a 50% higher cost of capital: $w = 10/1.1$ and $r = 1.1 \times 10 = 11$. What are L and K, and what is the cost of producing $q = 100$ units in both countries? What would the cost of production be in Asia if the firm had to use the same factor quantities as in the United States?

36. A production function is homogeneous of degree γ and involves three inputs, L, K, and M (materials). The

corresponding factor prices are w, r, and e. Derive the long-run cost curve.

37. Equation 7.22 gives the long-run cost function of a firm with a constant-returns-to-scale Cobb-Douglas production function. Show how, for a given output level, cost changes as the wage, w, increases. Explain why.

38. Derive the long-run cost function for the constant elasticity of substitution production function, Equation 6.12, $q = (L^\rho + K^\rho)^{1/\rho}$.

39. Consider a water heater manufacturing company. The number of water heaters manufactured per day, q, is a function of the number of workers per day, L, and the number of square feet of sheet metal per day, S. Specifically, its (general) CES production function is $q = (L^{-2} + S^{-2}/40)^{-1/2}$. The hourly wage rate is \$20, and the price per square foot of sheet metal is 50¢.

   a. What is the marginal productivity of labor? What is the marginal productivity of capital?
   b. What is the formula needed to draw the expansion path? Draw the expansion path.

   c. Derive the long-run cost function.
   d. Suppose the price of sheet metal increases to 25¢. Draw the new expansion path. Associated with the 50% decrease in the price of sheet metal (50¢ to 25¢), discuss the magnitude of the shift in the expansion path. **W**

40. Swim coach Rob teaches athletes how to swim freestyle while keeping their hips raised. Let q represent the number of swimmers that learn the technique, and let h represent the number of hours of individual training Rob provides in which the swimmers focus on their hips. The team's production function is $q = h^{1/2}$. Rob is paid \$150 per hour of practice.

   a. What is the cost function $C(q)$? What is the marginal cost function $m(q)$?
   b. Now suppose that Rob has learned a new method to teach swimmers how to swim with their hips raised. His new team production function is $q = h^{3/4}$. What is the cost function? What is the marginal cost function?
   c. Compare the marginal cost functions of parts a and b. **W**

Chapter 8

Competitive Firms and Markets

The love of money is the root of all virtue. — George Bernard Shaw

One of the major questions that firms face is "How much should we produce?" To pick a level of output that maximizes its profit, a firm must consider its cost function and how much it can sell at a given price. The amount the firm thinks it can sell depends in turn on the market demand of consumers and the firm's beliefs about how other firms in the market will behave. The behavior of firms depends on the **market structure:** the number of firms in the market, the ease with which firms can enter and leave the market, and the ability of firms to differentiate their products from those of their rivals.

In this chapter, we look at a competitive market structure, one in which many firms produce identical products and firms can easily enter and exit the market. Because each firm produces a small share of the total market output and its product is identical to that of other firms, each firm is a *price taker*, meaning that the firm cannot raise its price above the market price. If a firm were to try to do so, it would be unable to sell any of its output because consumers would buy the good at a lower price from the other firms in the market. The market price summarizes everything that a firm needs to know about the demand of consumers *and* the behavior of its rivals. Thus a competitive firm can ignore the specific behavior of individual rivals in deciding how much to produce.[1]

In this chapter, we examine four main topics	
	1. **Competition:** A competitive firm is a price taker, and as such, it faces a horizontal demand curve.
	2. **Profit Maximization:** To maximize profit, any firm must make two decisions: how much to produce and whether to produce at all.
	3. **Competition in the Short Run:** Variable costs determine a profit-maximizing, competitive firm's supply curve; the market supply curve; and, with the market demand curve, the competitive equilibrium in the short run.
	4. **Competition in the Long Run:** Firm supply, market supply, and competitive equilibrium are different in the long run than in the short run because firms can vary inputs that were fixed in the short run and new firms can enter the market.

---

[1]In contrast, in a market with a small number of firms, each firm must consider the behavior of each of its rivals, as we discuss in Chapter 13.

8.1 Competition

Competition is a common market structure with very desirable properties, so it is useful to compare other market structures to competition. In this section, we examine the properties of competitive firms and markets.

PRICE TAKING

When most people talk about "competitive firms," they mean firms that are rivals for the same customers. By this interpretation, any market that has more than one firm is competitive. However, to an economist, only some of these multifirm markets are competitive.

Economists say that a market is competitive if each firm in the market is a *price taker:* a firm that cannot significantly affect the market price for its output or the prices at which it buys its inputs. If any one of the more than 107,000 soybean farms in the United States were to stop producing soybeans or to double its production, the market price of soybeans would not change appreciably. Similarly, by stopping production or doubling its production, a soybean farm would have little or no effect on the price for soybean seeds, fertilizer, and other inputs.

Why would a competitive firm be a price taker? It has no choice. The firm *has* to be a price taker if it faces a demand curve that is horizontal at the market price. If the demand curve is horizontal at the market price, the firm can sell as much as it wants at that price, so it has no incentive to lower its price. Similarly, the firm cannot increase the price at which it sells by restricting its output because it faces an infinitely elastic demand (see Chapter 2): A small increase in price results in its demand falling to zero.

WHY A FIRM'S DEMAND CURVE IS HORIZONTAL

Firms are likely to be price takers in markets that have some or all of four properties:

- Consumers believe that all firms in the market sell *identical products*.
- Firms *freely enter and exit* the market.
- *Buyers and sellers know the prices* charged by firms.
- *Transaction costs*—the expenses of finding a trading partner and making a trade for a good or service other than the price paid for that good or service—*are low*.

When the products of all firms are seen as perfect substitutes, no firm can sell its product if it charges more than other firms because no consumer is willing to pay a premium for that product. Consumers don't ask which farm grew a Granny Smith apple because they view apples as *homogeneous* or *undifferentiated* products. In contrast, consumers who know that the characteristics of a Jaguar and a Civic differ substantially view automobiles as *heterogeneous* or *differentiated* products. If some customers prefer one firm's product to those of other firms, the firm's demand curve has a downward slope. One firm can charge more than other firms without losing all its customers.

No firm can raise its price above the market price if other firms are able and eager to undercut another firm's high price to attract more customers. Even in markets with only a few firms, if other firms can quickly and easily enter, a firm cannot raise its price without other firms' entering the market and undercutting its price. Moreover, ease of entry may cause the number of firms in a market to be large. The more firms there are in a market, the less the effect of a change in one firm's output on total market output and hence on the market price. If one of the 107,000 soybean growers drops out of the market, market supply falls by only 0.00093% (assuming that the firms are of equal size), so the market price is unaffected.

If buyers know the prices that other firms charge—the market price—a firm cannot raise its price without losing its customers. In contrast, if consumers do not know the prices that other firms charge, a firm can charge more than other firms without losing all its customers, so its demand curve is downward sloping.

If transaction costs are low, it is easy for a customer to buy from a rival firm if the customer's usual supplier raises its price. Transaction costs are low if buyers and sellers do not have to spend time and money finding each other or hiring lawyers to write contracts in order to make a trade. In some markets, buyers and sellers are brought together in a single room, so transaction costs are virtually zero. For example, transaction costs are very low at the four flower auctions in Amsterdam that the Bloemenveiling Aalsmeer, FloraHolland, Veiling Oost Nederland, and Veiling Vleuten cooperatives hold daily for 10,000 sellers who ship 16,000 types of flowers and plants from Zimbabwe, Colombia, Israel, Thailand, and Europe to 5,000 buyers around the world, with over 100,000 transaction per day—60% of world trade.[2]

We call a market in which all these conditions hold a *perfectly competitive market*. In such a market, if a firm raised its price above the market price, the firm would be unable to make any sales. Its former customers would know that other firms sell an identical product at a lower price. These customers can easily find those other firms and buy from them without incurring extra transaction costs. If firms that are currently in the market cannot meet the demand of this firm's former customers, new firms can quickly and easily enter the market. Thus firms in such a market must be price takers.

The market for wheat is an example of an almost perfectly competitive market. It is a market in which many farmers produce identical products and transaction costs are negligible. Wheat is sold in a formal exchange or market such as the Chicago Commodity Exchange. Using a formal exchange, buyers and sellers can easily place buy or sell orders in person, over the telephone, or electronically, so transaction costs are negligible. No time is wasted in finding someone who wants to trade, and the transactions are made virtually instantaneously without much paperwork. Moreover, every buyer and seller in the market knows the market prices, quantities, and qualities of wheat available at any moment.

Even if some of these conditions are violated, firms and consumers may still be price takers. For example, even if the entry of new firms is limited but the market has a very large number of firms, each of which can produce much more than its current output at about the same cost, firms are price takers. If one of these firms tries to raise its price, it will be unable to sell to consumers because other firms will expand their output if necessary to meet demand. A firm's demand curve is essentially horizontal as long as there are many firms in the market.

---

[2]In contrast, if transaction (including search) costs are high, it is less likely that the customer will buy from a rival firm, so the higher the transaction costs, the more likely that a firm's demand curve is downward sloping. For example, because finding a new competent auto mechanic may be very time consuming or may involve traveling a considerable distance, some consumers will continue to use their current auto repair shop even if it charges more than other firms (see Chapter 18).

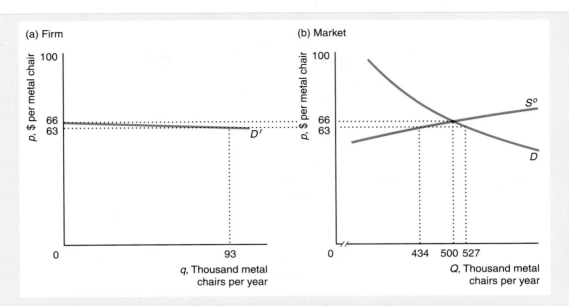

Figure 8.1 Residual Demand Curve. The residual demand curve, $D^r(p)$, that a single office furniture manufacturing firm faces is the market demand, $D(p)$, minus the supply of the other firms in the market, $S^o(p)$. The residual demand curve is much flatter than the market demand curve.

DERIVATION OF A COMPETITIVE FIRM'S DEMAND CURVE

Are the demand curves faced by individual competitive firms actually flat? To answer this question, we use a modified supply-and-demand diagram to derive the demand curve that an individual firm faces.

The demand curve that an individual firm faces is called the **residual demand curve:** the market demand that is not met by other sellers at any given price. The firm's residual demand function, $D^r(p)$, shows the quantity demanded from the firm at price p. A firm sells only to people who have not already purchased the good from another seller. We can determine how much demand is left for a particular firm at each possible price using the market demand curve and the supply curve for all *other* firms in the market. The quantity the market demands is a function of the price: $Q = D(p)$. The supply curve of the other firms is $S^o(p)$. The residual demand function equals the market demand function, $D(p)$, minus the supply function of all other firms:

$$D^r(p) = D(p) - S^o(p). \tag{8.1}$$

At prices so high that the amount supplied by other firms, $S^o(p)$, is greater than the quantity demanded by the market, $D(p)$, the residual quantity demanded, $D^r(p)$, is zero.

In Figure 8.1, we derive the residual demand for a Canadian manufacturing firm that produces metal chairs. Panel b shows the market demand curve, D, and the supply of all but one manufacturing firm, S^o.[3] At $p = \$66$ per chair, the supply of other firms, 500 units (one unit being 1,000 metal chairs) per year, exactly equals the market

---

[3]The figure uses constant elasticity demand and supply curves. The elasticity of supply, 3.1, is based on the estimated cost function from Robidoux and Lester (1988) for Canadian office furniture manufacturers. I estimate that the elasticity of demand is −1.1, using data from Statistics Canada, *Office Furniture Manufacturers.*

demand (panel b), so the residual quantity demanded of the remaining firm (panel a) is zero.

At prices below \$66, the other chair firms are not willing to supply as much as the market demands. At $p = \$63$, for example, the market demand is 527 units, but other firms want to supply only 434 units. As a result, the residual quantity demanded from the individual firm at $p = \$63$ is 93 (= 527 − 434) units. Thus the residual demand curve at any given price is the horizontal difference between the market demand curve and the supply curve of the other firms.

The residual demand curve that the firm faces, panel a, is much flatter than the market demand curve, panel b. As a result, the elasticity of the residual demand curve is much higher than the market elasticity.

If there are n identical firms in the market, the elasticity of demand, ε_i, facing Firm i is

$$\varepsilon_i = n\varepsilon - (n - 1)\eta_o, \tag{8.2}$$

where ε is the market elasticity of demand (a negative number), η_o is the elasticity of supply of each of the other firms (typically a positive number), and $n - 1$ is the number of other firms.[4]

There are $n = 78$ firms manufacturing metal chairs in Canada. If they are identical, the elasticity of demand facing a single firm is

$$\varepsilon_i = n\varepsilon - (n - 1)\eta_o = [78 \times (-1.1)] - (77 \times 3.1) = -85.8 - 238.7 = -324.5.$$

That is, a typical firm faces a residual demand elasticity, −324.5, that's nearly 300 times the market elasticity, −1.1. If a firm raises its price by one-tenth of a percent, the quantity it could sell would fall by nearly one-third. Therefore, the competitive model assumption that this firm faces a horizontal demand curve with an infinite price elasticity is not much of an exaggeration.

As Equation 8.2 shows, a firm's residual demand curve is more elastic the more firms, n, in the market, the more elastic the market demand, ε, and the larger the elasticity of supply of the other firms, η_o. If the supply curve slopes upward, the residual demand elasticity, ε_i, must be at least as elastic as $n\varepsilon$ (because the second term makes the estimate only more elastic), so using $n\varepsilon$ as an approximation is conservative. For example, even though the market elasticity of demand for soybeans is very inelastic, about −0.2, because there are roughly 107,000 soybean farms, the residual demand facing a single firm must be at least $n\varepsilon = 107,000 \times (-0.2) = -21,400$, which is extremely elastic.

---

[4]To derive Equation 8.2, we start by differentiating the residual demand function, Equation 8.1, with respect to p:

$$\frac{dD^r}{dp} = \frac{dD}{dp} - \frac{dS^o}{dp}.$$

Because the n firms in the market are identical, each firm produces $q = Q/n$, where Q is total output. The output produced by the other firms is $Q_o = (n - 1)q$. Multiplying both sides of the last expression by p/q and multiplying and dividing the first term on the right-hand side by Q/Q and the second term by Q_o/Q_o, this expression may be rewritten as

$$\frac{dD^r}{dp}\frac{p}{q} = \frac{dD}{dp}\frac{p}{Q}\frac{Q}{q} - \frac{dS^o}{dp}\frac{p}{Q_o}\frac{Q_o}{q},$$

where $q = D^r(p)$, $Q = D(p)$, and $Q_o = S^o(p)$. This expression can be rewritten as Equation 8.2 by noting that $Q/q = n$, $Q_o/q = (n - 1)$, $(dD^r/dp)(p/q) = \varepsilon_i$, $(dD/dp)(p/Q) = \varepsilon$, and $(dS^o/dp)(p/Q_o) = \eta_o$.

WHY PERFECT COMPETITION IS IMPORTANT

To summarize, perfect competition takes place in markets in which firms are price takers because products are homogeneous, firms enter and exit the market freely, buyers and sellers know the prices charged by firms, and transaction costs are low.[5]

Perfectly competitive markets are important for two reasons. First, many markets can be reasonably described as competitive. Many agricultural and other commodity markets, stock exchanges, retail and wholesale markets, building construction markets, and other markets have many or all of the properties of a perfectly competitive market. The competitive supply-and-demand model works well enough in these markets that it accurately predicts the effects of changes in taxes, costs, incomes, and other factors on market equilibrium.

Second, a perfectly competitive market has many desirable properties. Economists use this model as the ideal against which real-world markets are compared. Throughout the rest of this book, we consider that society as a whole is worse off if the properties of the perfectly competitive market fail to hold. From this point on, for brevity, we use the phrase *competitive market* to mean a *perfectly competitive market* unless we explicitly note an imperfection.

8.2 Profit Maximization

"Too caustic?" To hell with the cost. If it's a good picture, we'll make it. — Samuel Goldwyn

Economists usually assume that *all* firms—not just competitive firms—want to maximize their profits. One reason is that many businesspeople say that their objective is to maximize profits. A second reason is that firms—especially competitive firms—that do not maximize profit are likely to lose money and be driven out of business. In this section, we examine how any type of firm—not just a competitive firm—maximizes its profit.

PROFIT

A firm's *profit*, π, is the difference between a firm's revenues, R, and its cost, C: $\pi = R - C$. If profit is negative, $\pi < 0$, the firm makes a *loss*.

Economists and businesspeople often measure profit differently. Because both economists and businesspeople measure revenue the same way—revenue is price times quantity—the difference in their profit measures is due to the way they measure costs (see Chapter 7). Some businesses use only explicit costs: a firm's out-of-pocket expenditures on inputs such as workers' wage payments, payments for materials, and payments for energy. *Economic cost* includes both explicit and implicit costs. Economic cost is the *opportunity cost*: the value of the best alternative use of any asset the firm employs.

Economic profit is revenue minus economic cost. Because explicit cost is less than economic cost, *business profit*—based on only explicit cost—is often larger than economic profit. The reason that this distinction is important is that a firm may make a costly mistake if it mismeasures profit by ignoring relevant opportunity costs.

---

[5]In addition, economists often require that a perfectly competitive market has no externalities such as pollution (see Chapter 17).

A couple of examples illustrate the difference between the two profit measures and the importance of this distinction. First, let's return to the scenario in Chapter 7 in which you start your own firm.[6] You have to pay explicit costs such as workers' wages and the price of materials. Like many owners, you do not pay yourself a salary. Instead, you take home a business profit of $20,000 per year.

Economists (well-known spoilsports) argue that your profit is less than $20,000. Economic profit is business profit minus any additional opportunity cost. Suppose that you could have earned $25,000 a year working for someone else instead of running your own business. The opportunity cost of your time working in your business is $25,000—your forgone salary. So even though your firm made a business profit of $20,000, you had an economic loss (negative economic profit) of $5,000. Put another way, the price of being your own boss is $5,000.

By looking at only the business profit and ignoring opportunity cost, you conclude that running your business is profitable. However, if you consider economic profit, you realize that working for others maximizes your income.

Similarly, when a firm decides whether to invest in a new venture, it must consider its next best alternative use of its funds. A firm that is considering setting up a new branch in Tucson must consider all the alternatives—placing the branch in Santa Fe, putting the money that the branch would cost in the bank where it earns interest, and so on. If the best alternative use of the money is to put it in the bank and earn $10,000 per year in interest, the firm should build the new branch in Tucson only if it expects to make $10,000 or more per year in business profits. That is, the firm should create a Tucson branch only if its economic profit from the new branch is zero or positive. If its economic profit is zero, then it is earning the same return on its investment as it would from putting the money into its next best alternative, the bank. From this point on, when we use the term *profit*, we mean *economic profit* unless we specifically refer to business profit.

● APPLICATION

Breaking Even on Christmas Trees

On the day after Thanksgiving each year, Tom Ruffino begins selling Christmas trees in Lake Grove, New York. The table summarizes his seasonal explicit costs.

Fixed Costs	
Permit	$300
Security (guard patrol to prevent theft when the lot is closed)	360
Insurance	700
Electricity	1,000
Lot rental (undeveloped land across from a major shopping mall)	2,500
Miscellaneous (fences, lot cleanup, snow removal)	2,000
Total fixed costs:	$6,860
Variable Costs	
Labor (two full-time employees at $12 an hour for 50 hours a week, plus some part-time workers)	$5,500
Trees (1,500 trees bought from a Canadian tree farm at $11.50 each)	17,250
Shipping (1,500 trees at $2 each)	3,000
Total variable costs:	$25,750
Total accounting costs:	$32,610

---

[6]Michael Dell started a mail-order computer company while he was in college. Today, his company is the world's largest personal computer company. In 2006, *Forbes* listed Mr. Dell as the fourth-richest man in the United States with $18 billion.

Mr. Ruffino sells trees for 29 days at the market price of $25 each. To break even, he has to sell an average of 45 trees per day, so his average cost is $25. If he can sell an average of 52 trees per day (1,508 trees total), he makes an accounting profit of $5,090 for the season.

To calculate his economic profit, he has to subtract his forgone earnings at another job and the interest he would have earned on the money he paid at the beginning of the month (on his fixed costs and the price of the trees, $27,110) if he had invested that money elsewhere, such as in a bank, for a month. Although the forgone interest is small, his alternative earnings could be a large proportion of his business profit.

TWO STEPS TO MAXIMIZING PROFIT

Any firm (not just a competitive firm) uses a two-step process to maximize profit. Because both revenue and cost vary with output, a firm's profit varies with its output level. Its profit function is

$$\pi(q) = R(q) - C(q). \tag{8.3}$$

To maximize its profit, a firm must answer two questions:

- **Output decision:** If the firm produces, what output level, q^*, maximizes its profit or minimizes its loss?
- **Shutdown decision:** Is it more profitable to produce q^* or to shut down and produce no output?

We use the profit curve in Figure 8.2 to illustrate these two basic decisions. This firm makes losses at very low and very high output levels and makes positive profits at moderate output levels. The profit curve first rises and then falls, reaching a maximum profit

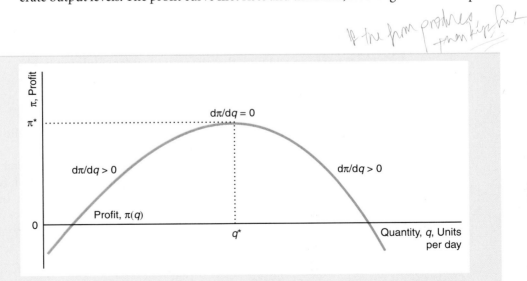

Figure 8.2 Maximizing Profit. By setting its output at q^*, the firm maximizes its profit at π^*, where $d\pi/dq = 0$.

of π^* when its output is q^*. Because the firm makes a positive profit at that output, it chooses to produce q^* units of output.

Output Rules. A firm can use one of three equivalent rules to choose how much output to produce. All types of firms maximize profit using the same rules.

The most straightforward rule is:

Output Rule 1: The firm sets its output where its profit is maximized.

The profit curve in Figure 8.2 is maximized at π^* when output is q^*. If the firm knows its entire profit curve, it can immediately set its output to maximize its profit.

Even if the firm does not know the exact shape of its profit curve, it may be able to find the maximum by experimenting: The firm slightly increases its output. If profit increases, the firm increases the output more. The firm keeps increasing output until profit does not change. At that output, the firm is at the peak of the profit curve. If profit falls when the firm first increases its output, the firm tries decreasing its output. It keeps decreasing its output until it reaches the peak of the profit curve.

What the firm is doing is experimentally determining the slope of the profit curve. The slope of the profit curve is the firm's **marginal profit:** the change in the profit the firm gets from selling one more unit of output, $d\pi/dq$. In the figure, the marginal profit or slope is positive when output is less than q^*, zero when output is q^*, and negative when output is greater than q^*.

Thus:

Output Rule 2: A firm sets its output where its marginal profit is zero.

We obtain this result formally using the first-order condition for a profit maximum. We set the derivative of the profit function, Equation 8.3, with respect to quantity equal to zero:

$$\frac{d\pi(q^*)}{dq} = 0. \tag{8.4}$$

Equation 8.4 states that a necessary condition for profit to be maximized is that the quantity be set at q^* where the firm's marginal profit with respect to quantity equals zero.

Equation 8.4 is a necessary condition for profit to be maximized. Sufficiency requires, in addition, that the second-order condition hold:

$$\frac{d^2\pi(q^*)}{dq^2} < 0. \tag{8.5}$$

That is, for profit to be maximized at q^*, when we increase the output beyond q^*, the marginal profit must decline.

Because profit is a function of revenue and cost, we can state this last condition in one additional way. We can obtain another necessary condition for profit maximization by setting the derivative of $\pi(q) = R(q) - C(q)$ with respect to output equal to zero:

$$\frac{d\pi(q^*)}{dq} = \frac{dR(q^*)}{dq} - \frac{dC(q^*)}{dq} = MR(q^*) - MC(q^*) = 0. \tag{8.6}$$

The derivative of cost with respect to output, $dC(q)/dq = MC(q)$, is its marginal cost (Chapter 7). The firm's **marginal revenue,** *MR,* is the change in revenue it gets from selling one more unit of output: dR/dq. Equation 8.6 says that a necessary condition for profit to be maximized is that the firm set its quantity at q^* where the difference between the firm's marginal revenue and its marginal cost is zero. Thus a third, equivalent rule is:

   Output Rule 3: A firm sets its output where its marginal revenue equals its marginal cost,

$$MR(q^*) = MC(q^*). \tag{8.7}$$

For profit to be maximized at q^*, the second-order condition must hold:

$$\frac{d^2\pi(q^*)}{dq^2} = \frac{d^2R(q^*)}{dq^2} - \frac{d^2C(q^*)}{dq^2} = \frac{dMR(q^*)}{dq} - \frac{dMC(q^*)}{dq} < 0. \tag{8.8}$$

That is, for profit to be maximized at q^*, the slope of the marginal revenue curve, dMR/dq, must be less than the slope of the marginal cost curve, dMC/dq.

Shutdown Rule. The firm chooses to produce q^* if it can make a profit. But even if the firm is maximizing its profit at q^*, it does not necessarily follow that the firm is making a positive profit. If the firm is making a loss, does it shut down? The answer, surprisingly, is "It depends." The general rule, which holds for all types of firms in both the short run and in the long run, is:

   Shutdown Rule 1: The firm shuts down only if it can reduce its loss by doing so.

In the short run, the firm has variable and sunk fixed costs (Chapter 7). By shutting down, it can eliminate the variable cost, such as labor and materials, but not the sunk fixed cost, the amount it paid for its factory and equipment. By shutting down, the firm stops receiving revenue and stops paying the avoidable costs, but it is still stuck with its fixed cost. Thus it pays the firm to shut down only if its revenue is less than its avoidable cost.

Suppose that the firm's revenue is $R = \$2,000$, its variable cost is $VC = \$1,000$, and its fixed cost is $F = \$3,000$, which is the price it paid for a machine that it cannot resell or use for any other purpose. This firm is making a short-run loss:

$$\pi = R - VC - F = \$2,000 - \$1,000 - \$3,000 = -\$2,000.$$

If the firm shuts down, it loses its fixed cost, $\$3,000$, so it is better off operating. Its revenue more than covers its avoidable, variable cost and offsets some of the fixed cost.

However, if its revenue is only $\$500$, its loss is $\$3,500$, which is greater than the loss from the fixed cost alone, $\$3,000$. Because its revenue is less than its avoidable, variable cost, the firm reduces its loss by shutting down.

In conclusion, the firm compares its revenue to its variable cost only when deciding whether to stop operating. Because the fixed cost is *sunk*—the expense cannot be avoided by stopping operations (Chapter 7)—the firm pays this cost whether it shuts down or not. Thus the sunk fixed cost is irrelevant to the shutdown decision.[7]

In the long run, all costs are avoidable because the firm can eliminate them all by shutting down. Thus in the long run, where the firm can avoid all losses by not operating,

---

[7]We usually assume that fixed cost is sunk. However, if a firm can sell its capital for as much as it paid, its fixed cost is avoidable and should be taken into account when the firm is considering whether to shut down. A firm with a fully avoidable fixed cost always shuts down if it makes a short-run loss. If a firm buys a specialized piece of machinery for $\$1,000$ that can be used only in its business but can be sold for scrap metal for $\$100$, then $\$100$ of the fixed cost is avoidable and $\$900$ is sunk. Only the avoidable portion of fixed cost is relevant for the shutdown decision.

it pays to shut down if the firm faces any loss at all. As a result, we can restate the shut-down rule as:

   Shutdown Rule 2: The firm shuts down only if its revenue is less than its avoidable cost. This rule holds for all types of firms in both the short run and the long run.

8.3   Competition in the Short Run

Having considered how firms maximize profit in general, we now examine the profit-maximizing behavior of competitive firms. In this section, we focus on the short run; in Section 8.4, we look at the long run. In doing so, we pay careful attention to a firm's shutdown decision.

SHORT-RUN COMPETITIVE PROFIT MAXIMIZATION

A competitive firm, like other firms, first determines the output at which it maximizes its profit (or minimizes its loss). Second, it decides whether to produce or to shut down.

Short-Run Output Decision. We've already seen that *any* firm maximizes its profit at the output where its marginal profit is zero or, equivalently, where its marginal cost equals its marginal revenue. *Because it faces a horizontal demand curve, a competitive firm can sell as many units of output as it wants at the market price,* p. Thus a competitive firm's revenue, $R(q) = pq$, increases by p if it sells one more unit of output, so its marginal revenue is p: $MR = d(pq)/dq = p$. A competitive firm maximizes its profit by choosing its output such that

$$\frac{d\pi(q^\star)}{dq} = \frac{dR(q^\star)}{dq} - \frac{dC(q^\star)}{dq} = p - MC(q^\star) = 0. \tag{8.9}$$

That is, because a competitive firm's marginal revenue equals the market price, a profit-maximizing competitive firm produces the amount of output $q^\star$ at which its marginal cost equals the market price: $MC(q^\star) = p$.

   For the quantity determined by Equation 8.9 to maximize profit, the second-order condition must hold: $d^2\pi(q^\star)/dq^2 = dp/dq - dMC(q^\star)/dq < 0$. Because the firm's marginal revenue, p, does not vary with q, $dp/dq = 0$. Thus the second-order condition requires that the second derivative of the cost function (the first derivative of the marginal cost function) with respect to quantity evaluated at the profit-maximizing quantity is positive:

$$\frac{dMC(q^\star)}{dq} > 0. \tag{8.10}$$

That is, the marginal cost curve is upward sloping at $q^\star$.

   To illustrate how a competitive firm maximizes its profit, we examine a typical Canadian lime manufacturing firm (based on the estimates of the variable cost function by Robidoux and Lester, 1988). Lime is a nonmetallic mineral used in mortars, plasters, cements, bleaching powders, steel, paper, glass, and other products. The lime plant's estimated cost curve, C, in panel a of Figure 8.3 rises less rapidly with output at

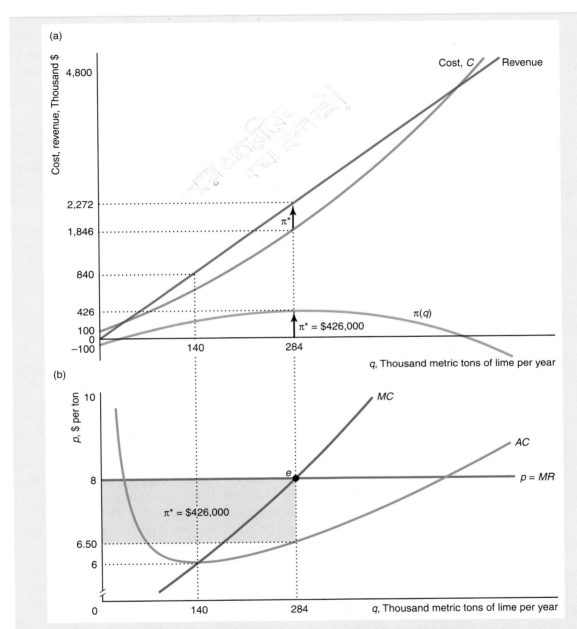

Figure 8.3 **How a Competitive Firm Maximizes Profit.**
(a) A competitive lime manufacturing firm produces 284 units of lime so as to maximize its profit at $\pi^* = \$426,000$ (Robidoux and Lester, 1988). (b) The firm's profit is maximized where its marginal revenue, *MR*, which is the market price, $p = \$8$, equals its marginal cost, *MC*.

low quantities than at higher quantities.[8] If the market price of lime is $p = 8$, the competitive firm faces a horizontal demand curve at 8 (panel b), so the revenue curve, $R = pq = 8q$, in panel a is an upward-sloping straight line with a slope of 8.

---

[8]In the figure, we assume that the minimum of the average variable cost curve is $5 at 50,000 metric tons of output. Based on information from Statistics Canada, we set the fixed cost so that the average cost is $6 at 140,000 tons.

By producing 284 units (where a unit is 1,000 metric tons), the firm maximizes its profit at $\pi^* = \$426,000$, which is the height of the profit curve and the difference between the revenue and cost curves at that quantity in panel a. At the competitive firm's profit-maximizing output, determined by Equation 8.9, its marginal cost equals the market price of \$8 at point e in panel b.

Point e is the competitive firm's equilibrium. Were the firm to produce less than the equilibrium quantity, 284 units, the market price would be above its marginal cost. As a result, the firm could increase its profit by expanding output because the firm earns more on the next ton, $p = 8$, than it costs to produce it, $MC < 8$. If the firm were to produce more than 284 units, so that market price was below its marginal cost, $MC > 8$, the firm could increase its profit by reducing its output. Thus the firm does not want to change the quantity that it sells only if it is producing where its marginal cost equals the market price.

The firm's maximum profit, $\pi^* = \$426,000$, is the shaded rectangle in panel b. The length of the rectangle is the number of units sold, $q = 284$ units. The height of the rectangle is the firm's average profit, which is the difference between the market price, or average revenue, and its average cost:

$$\frac{\pi}{q} = \frac{R}{q} - \frac{C}{q} = \frac{pq}{q} - \frac{C}{q} = p - AC. \tag{8.11}$$

Here the average profit per unit is $p - AC(284) = \$8 - \$6.50 = \$1.50$.

As panel b illustrates, the firm chooses its output level to maximize its total profit rather than its profit per ton. By producing 140 units, where its average cost is minimized at \$6, the firm could maximize its average profit at \$2. Although the firm gives up 50¢ in profit per ton when it produces 284 units instead of 140 units, it more than makes up for that by selling an extra 144 units. The firm's profit is \$146,000 higher at 284 units than at 140 units.

Using the $MC = p$ rule, a firm can decide how much to alter its output in response to a change in its cost due to a new tax. For example, only one of the many lime plants in Canada is in the province of Manitoba. If that province taxes that lime firm, the Manitoba firm is the only one in the lime market affected by the tax, so the tax will not affect market price. Solved Problem 8.1 shows how a profit-maximizing competitive firm would react to a tax that affected it alone.

SOLVED PROBLEM   **8.1**

If a specific tax of τ is collected from only one competitive firm, how should that firm change its output level to maximize its profit, and how does its maximum profit change? Answer using both calculus and a graph.

Answer

1. *Use calculus to find the firm's profit-maximizing output before the tax is imposed:* The firm's before-tax profit function is $\pi = pq - C(q)$. According to its first-order condition for a profit maximum, it sets its output at q_1 where $d\pi(q_1)/dq = p - dC(q_1)/dq = 0$, or $p = MC(q_1)$. As the figure shows, the firm maximizes its profit at e_1, where its marginal cost curve crosses the market price line.

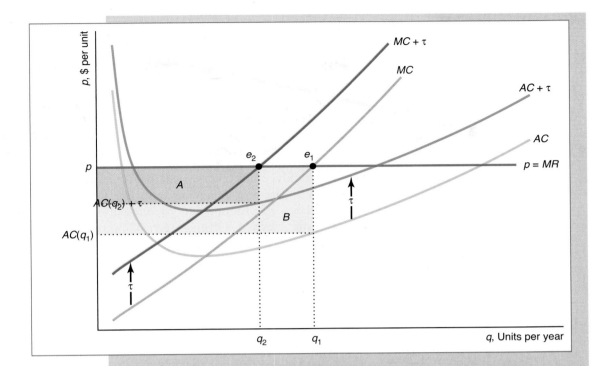

2. *Use calculus to find the firm's profit-maximizing output after the tax is imposed:*
The after-tax profit is $\overline{\pi} = pq - C(q) - \tau q$. The firm maximizes its profit at q_2
where

$$\frac{d\overline{\pi}(q_2)}{dq} = p - \frac{dC(q_2)}{dq} - \tau = 0, \tag{8.12}$$

or $p = MC(q_2) + \tau$. (When $\tau = 0$, we obtain the same result as in our before-tax
analysis.) The figure shows that the firm's after-tax marginal cost curve shifts
from MC to $MC + \tau$. Because the firm is a price taker and the tax is applied to
only this one firm, its marginal revenue before and after the tax is the market
price, p. In the figure, the firm's new maximum is at e_2.

3. *Use comparative statics to determine how a change in the tax rate affects output:*
Given the first-order condition, Equation 8.12, we can write the optimal quantity as a function of the tax rate: $q(\tau)$. Differentiating the first-order condition
with respect to τ, we obtain:

$$-\frac{d^2C}{dq^2}\frac{dq}{d\tau} - 1 = -\frac{dMC}{dq}\frac{dq}{d\tau} - 1 = 0.$$

The second-order condition for a profit maximum, Equation 8.10, requires that
dMC/dq be negative, so

$$\frac{dq}{d\tau} = -\frac{1}{dMC/dq} < 0. \tag{8.13}$$

At $\tau = 0$, the firm chooses q_1. As τ increases, the firm reduces its output from q_1
to q_2. The figure shows that the tax shifts up the firm's after-tax marginal cost

curve by τ, so it produces less. (*Note:* The figure shows a relatively large change in tax, whereas the calculus analysis examines a marginal change.)

4. *Show that the profit must fall, using the definition of a maximum or showing that profit falls at every output:* Because the firm's before-tax profit is maximized at q_1, when the firm reduces its output in response to the tax, its before-tax profit falls: $\pi(q_2) < \pi(q_1)$. Because its after-tax profit is lower than its before-tax profit, $\bar{p}(q_2) = \pi(q_2) - \tau q_2 < \pi(q_2)$, its profit must fall after the tax: $\bar{p}(q_2) < \pi(q_1)$.

We can also show this result by noting that the market price is constant but that the firm's average cost curve shifts up by τ (see Chapter 7), so the firm's profit at every output level falls. The firm sells fewer units (because of the increase in marginal cost) and makes less profit per unit (because of the increase in average cost). The after-tax profit is area $A = \bar{\bar{\pi}}(q_2) = [p - AC(q_2) - \tau]q_2$, and the before-tax profit is area $A + B = \pi(q_1) = [p - AC(q_1)]q_1$, so profit falls by area B due to the tax.

Short-Run Shutdown Decision. Does the competitive lime firm operate or shut down? At the market price of $8 in Figure 8.3, the lime firm is making an economic profit, so it chooses to operate.

If the market price falls below $6, which is the minimum of the average cost curve, the price does not cover average cost, so average profit, Equation 8.11, is negative, and the firm makes a loss. (A firm cannot "lose a little on every sale but make it up on volume.") The firm shuts down only if doing so reduces or eliminates its loss. This shutdown may be temporary: When the market price rises, the firm resumes producing.

The firm can gain by shutting down only if its revenue is less than its short-run variable cost:

$$pq < VC(q). \tag{8.14}$$

By dividing both sides of Equation 8.14 by output, we can write this condition as

$$p < \frac{VC(q)}{q} = AVC. \tag{8.15}$$

A competitive firm shuts down if the market price is less than the minimum of its short-run average variable cost curve.

We illustrate this rule in Figure 8.4 using the Canadian lime firm's cost curves. The minimum of the average variable cost, point *a*, is $5 at 50 units (one unit again being 1,000 metric tons). If the market price is less than $5 per ton, the firm shuts down. The firm stops hiring labor, buying materials, and paying for energy, thereby avoiding these variable costs. If the market price rises above $5, the firm starts operating again.

In this figure, the market price is $5.50 per ton. Because the minimum of the firm's average cost, $6 (point *b*), is more than $5.50, the firm loses money if it produces.

If the firm produces, it sells 100 units at *e*, where its marginal cost curve intersects its demand curve, which is horizontal at $5.50. By operating, the firm loses area *A*,

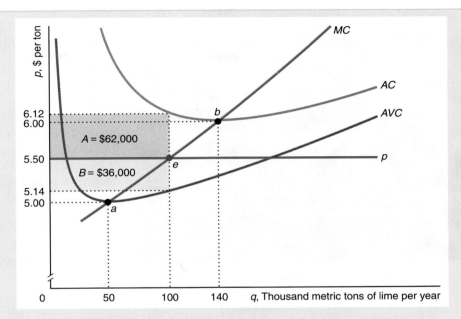

Figure 8.4 The Short-Run Shutdown Decision. The competitive lime manufacturing plant operates if price is above the minimum of the average variable cost curve, point *a*, at $5. With a market price of $5.50, the firm produces 100 units because that price is above $AVC(100) = \$5.14$, so the firm more than covers its out-of-pocket, variable costs. At that price, the firm makes a loss of area $A = \$62,000$ because the price is less than the average cost of $6.12. If it shuts down, its loss is its fixed cost, area $A + B = \$98,000$. Thus the firm does not shut down.

or $62,000. The length of *A* is 100 units, and the height is the average loss per ton, or 62¢, which equals the price of $5.50 minus the average cost at 100 units of $6.12.

The firm is better off producing than shutting down. If the firm shuts down, it has no revenue or variable cost, so its loss is the fixed cost, $98,000, which equals area $A + B$. The length of this box is 100 units, and its height is the lost average fixed cost of 98¢, which is the difference between the average variable cost and the average cost at 100 units.

The firm saves area $B = \$36,000$ by producing rather than shutting down. This amount is the money left over from the revenue after paying for the variable cost, which helps cover part of the fixed cost. Thus even if $p < AC$ so that the firm is making a loss, the firm continues to operate if $p > AVC$ so that it is more than covering its variable costs.

In summary, a competitive firm uses a two-step decision-making process to maximize its profit. First, the competitive firm determines the output that maximizes its profit or minimizes its loss when its marginal cost equals the market price (which is its marginal revenue): $MC = p$. Second, the firm chooses to produce that quantity unless it would lose more by operating than by shutting down. The firm shuts down only if the market price is less than the minimum of its average variable cost, $p < AVC$.

● **APPLICATION**

Oil Sands Shutdowns

Oil wells often shut down when prices drop. In 1998–1999, 74,000 of the 136,000 oil wells in the United States were temporarily shut down or permanently abandoned. At the time, Terry Smith, the general manager of Tidelands Oil Production Company, who had shut down 327 of his company's 834 wells, said that he would operate these wells again when the price of oil rose above $10 a barrel—his minimum average variable cost.

Getting oil from oil wells is relatively easy. It is harder and more costly to obtain oil from other sources, so firms that use those alternative sources have higher shutdown points.

Canada has an important alternative source of oil. You probably know that Saudi Arabia has the most (259 billion barrels) "proven" crude oil reserves of any country in the world. But did you know that Canada has the second-largest known reserves, 180 billion barrels?[9] Canada's reserves far exceed Iraq's third-place 113 billion (and the Arctic National Wildlife Refuge's estimated 10 billion). You rarely see discussions of Canada's vast oil reserves in newspapers because 97% of those reserves are oil sands covering an area the size of Florida.

Oil sands are a mixture of heavy petroleum (bitumen), water, and sandstone. Producing oil from oil sands is extremely expensive and polluting. To liberate four barrels of crude from the sands, a processor must burn the equivalent of a fifth barrel. With the technology available in 2007, two tons of sand yield a single barrel (42 gallons) of oil and produce more greenhouse gas emissions than do four cars operating for a day. Today's limited production draws from the one-fifth of the oil sand deposits that lie close enough to the surface to allow strip mining. Going after deeper deposits will be even more expensive.

The first large oil sands mining began in the 1960s, but as oil prices often were less than the $25-per-barrel average variable cost of recovering crude from the sand, production was often halted. Today, a barrel of oil sells for more than $50 and technological improvements have lowered the average variable cost to $18 a barrel, so firms are producing. Because they expect oil prices to remain high, virtually every large U.S. oil firm and one Chinese firm have Canadian oil sands projects, and their planned investments over the next decade exceed $25 billion.

---

[9]According to some estimates as of 2006, oil shale deposits in Colorado and neighboring areas of Utah and Wyoming contain 800 billion recoverable barrels (the equivalent of 40 years of U.S. oil consumption). Oil shale is much more difficult to extract and to transform into crude oil than are oil sands. Indeed, it is not clear when or whether it will be profitable to extract this oil.

SHORT-RUN FIRM SUPPLY CURVE

We just analyzed how a competitive firm chooses its output for a given market price so as to maximize its profit. By repeating this analysis at different possible market prices, we learn how the amount the competitive firm supplies varies with the market price, thereby deriving the firm's short-run supply curve.

Tracing Out the Short-Run Supply Curve. As the market price increases from $p_1 = \$5$ to $p_2 = \$6$ to $p_3 = \$7$ to $p_4 = \$8$, the lime firm increases its output from 50 to 140 to 215 to 285 units per year, as Figure 8.5 shows. The equilibrium at each market price, e_1 through e_4, is determined by the intersection of the relevant demand curve—market price line—and the firm's marginal cost curve. That is, as the market price increases, the equilibria trace out the marginal cost curve.

If the price falls below the firm's minimum average variable cost of $5, the firm shuts down. Thus *the competitive firm's short-run supply curve is its marginal cost curve above its minimum average variable cost.*

The firm's short-run supply curve, S, is a thick line in the figure. At prices above $5, the short-run supply curve is the same as the marginal cost curve. The supply is zero when price is less than the minimum of the *AVC* curve of $5. (From now on, for simplicity, the graphs will not show the supply curve at prices below the minimum *AVC*.)

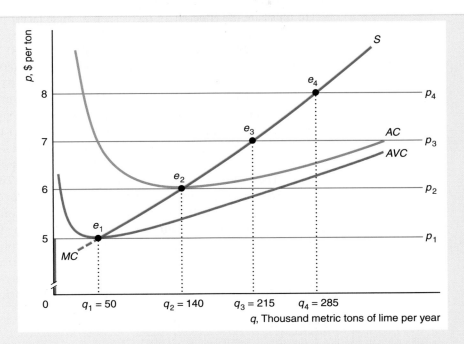

Figure 8.5 How the Profit-Maximizing Quantity Varies with Price. As the market price increases, the lime manufacturing firm produces more output. The change in the price traces out the marginal cost curve of the firm.

SOLVED PROBLEM   8.2

> Given that a competitive firm's short-run cost function is $C(q) = 100q - 4q^2 + 0.2q^3 + 450$, what is the firm's short-run supply curve? If the price is $p = 115$, how much output does the firm supply?
>
> **Answer**
>
> 1. *Determine the firm's supply curve by determining for which output levels the firm's marginal cost is greater than its minimum average variable cost:* The firm's supply curve is its marginal cost above its minimum average variable cost. From Solved Problem 7.1, we know that $MC(q) = dC(q)/dq 100 - 8q + 0.6q^2$ and $AVC(q) = VC(q)/q = 100 - 4q + 0.2q^2$. We also know that the marginal cost cuts the average variable cost at its minimum (Chapter 7), so we can solve for the q where the AVC reaches its minimum by equating the AVC and MC functions: $A\overline{V}C = 100 - 4q + 0.2q^2 = 100 - 8q + 0.6q^2 = MC$. Solving, the minimum is $q = 10$ (see Figure 7.1). Thus the supply curve is the MC curve for output greater than or equal to 10.
>
> 2. *Determine the quantity where $p = MC = 115$:* The firm operates where price equals marginal cost. At $p = 115$, the firm produces the quantity q such that $115 = MC = 100 - 8q + 0.6q^2$, or $q = 15$ (see Figure 7.1).

Factor Prices and the Short-Run Firm Supply Curve. An increase in factor prices causes the production costs of a firm to rise, shifting the firm's supply curve to the left. If all factor prices double, it costs the firm twice as much as before to produce a given level of output. If only one factor price rises, costs rise less than in proportion.

To illustrate the effect of an increase in a single factor price on supply, we examine a typical Canadian vegetable oil mill (based on the estimates of the variable cost function for vegetable oil mills by Robidoux and Lester, 1988). This firm uses vegetable oil seed to produce canola and soybean oils, which customers use in commercial baking and soap making, as lubricants, and for other purposes. At the initial factor prices, the oil mill's average variable cost curve, AVC^1, reaches its minimum of $7 at 100 units (where one unit is 100 metric tons) of vegetable oil, as in Figure 8.6. As a result, the firm's initial short-run supply curve, S^1, is the initial marginal cost curve, MC^1, above $7.

If the wage, the price of energy, or the price of oil seeds increases, the oil mill's cost of production rises. The mill cannot substitute between oil seeds and other factors of production. The cost of oil seeds is 95% of the variable cost. Thus if the price of raw materials increases by 25%, variable cost rises by 95% × 25%, or 23.75%. This increase in the price of oil seeds causes the marginal cost curve to shift from MC^1 to MC^2 and the average variable cost curve to shift from AVC^1 to AVC^2 in the figure. As a result, the mill's short-run supply curve shifts upward from S^1 to S^2. The price increase causes the shutdown price to rise from $7 per unit to $8.66. At a market price of $12 per unit, at the original factor prices, the mill produces 178 units. After the increase in the price of vegetable oil seeds, the mill produces only 145 units if the market price remains constant.

SHORT-RUN MARKET SUPPLY CURVE

The market supply curve is the horizontal sum of the supply curves of all the individual firms in the market (see Chapter 2). In the short run, the maximum number of firms in a market, n, is fixed because new firms need time to enter the market. If all the firms in a competitive market are identical, each firm's supply curve is identical, so the

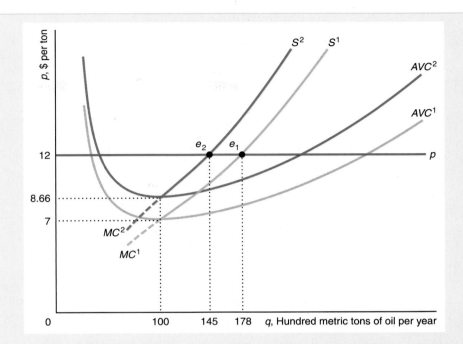

Figure 8.6 Effect of an Increase in the Cost of Materials on the Vegetable Oil Supply Curve.
Materials are 95% of variable costs, so when the price of materials rises by 25%, variable costs
rise by 23.75% (95% of 25%). As a result, the supply curve of a vegetable oil mill shifts upward
from S^1 to S^2. If the market price is $12, the quantity supplied falls from 178 to 145 units.

market supply at any price is n times the supply of an individual firm. Where firms
have different shutdown prices, the market supply reflects a different number of firms
at various prices even in the short run. We examine competitive markets first with
firms that have identical costs and then with firms that have different costs.

Short-Run Market Supply with Identical Firms. To illustrate how to construct a short-
run market supply curve, we suppose that the lime manufacturing market has $n = 5$
competitive firms with identical cost curves. Panel a of Figure 8.7 plots the short-run
supply curve, S^1, of a typical firm—the MC curve above the minimum AVC—where
the horizontal axis shows the firm's output, q, per year. Panel b illustrates the competitive market supply curve, the dark line S^5, where the horizontal axis is market output,
Q, per year. The price axis is the same in the two panels.

   If the market price is less than $5 per ton, no firm supplies any output, so the mar-
ket supply is zero. At $5, each firm is willing to supply $q = 50$ units, as in panel a.
Consequently, the market supply is $Q = 5q = 250$ units in panel b. At $6 per ton, each
firm supplies 140 units, so the market supply is 700 (= 5 × 140) units.

   Suppose, however, that there were fewer than five firms in the short run. The light-
colored lines in panel b show the market supply curves for various other numbers of
firms. The market supply curve is S^1 if there is one price-taking firm, S^2 with two firms,
S^3 with three firms, and S^4 with four firms. The market supply curve flattens as the
number of firms in the market increases because the market supply curve is the horizontal sum of more and more upward-sloping firm supply curves. As the number of
firms grows very large, the market supply curve approaches a horizontal line at $5.

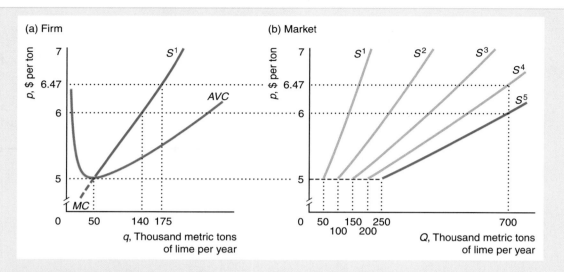

Figure 8.7 Short-Run Market Supply with Five Identical Lime Firms. (a) The short-run supply curve, S^1, for a typical lime manufacturing firm is its *MC* above the minimum of its *AVC*. (b) The market supply curve, S^5, is the horizontal sum of the supply curves of each of the five identical firms. The curve S^4 shows what the market supply curve would be if there were only four firms in the market.

Thus *the more identical firms producing at a given price, the flatter (more elastic) the short-run market supply curve at that price.* As a result, the more firms in the market, the less the price has to increase for the short-run market supply to increase substantially. Consumers pay $6 per ton to obtain 700 units of lime if there are five firms but must pay $6.47 per ton to obtain that much with only four firms.

Short-Run Market Supply with Firms That Differ. If the firms in a competitive market have different minimum average variable costs, not all firms produce at every price, a situation that affects the shape of the short-run market supply curve. Suppose that the only two firms in the lime market are our typical lime firm with a supply curve of S^1 and another firm with a higher marginal and minimum average cost with the supply curve of S^2 in Figure 8.8. The first firm produces at a market price of $5 or above, whereas the second firm does not produce unless the price is $6 or more. At $5, the first firm produces 50 units, so the quantity on the market supply curve, *S*, is 50 units. Between $5 and $6, only the first firm produces, so the market supply, *S*, is the same as the first firm's supply, S^1. At and above $6, both firms produce, so the market supply curve is the horizontal summation of their two individual supply curves. For example, at $7, the first firm produces 215 units, and the second firm supplies 100 units, so the market supply is 315 units.

As with the identical firms, where both firms are producing, the market supply curve is flatter than that of either firm. Because the second firm does not produce at as low a price as the first firm, the short-run market supply curve has a steeper slope (less elastic supply) at relatively low prices than it would if the firms were identical.

Where firms differ, only the low-cost firm supplies goods at relatively low prices. As the price rises, the other, higher-cost firm starts supplying, creating a stairlike market supply curve. The more suppliers there are with differing costs, the more steps there are in the market supply curve. As price rises and more firms are supplying goods, the

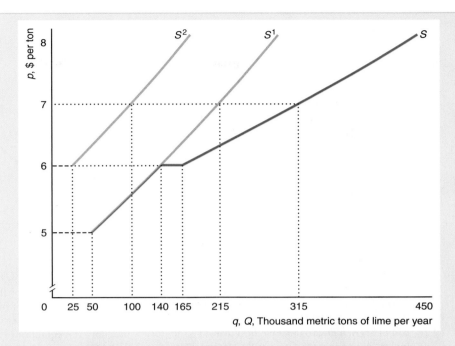

Figure 8.8 Short-Run Market Supply with Two Different Lime Firms. The supply curve S^1 is the same as for the typical lime firm in Figure 8.7. A second firm has an *MC* that lies to the left of the original firm's cost curve and a higher minimum of its *AVC*. Thus its supply curve, S^2, lies above and to the left of the original firm's supply curve, S^1. The market supply curve, *S*, is the horizontal sum of the two supply curves. When prices are high enough for both firms to produce, at $6 and above, the market supply curve is flatter than the supply curve of either individual firm.

market supply curve flattens, so it takes a smaller increase in price to increase supply by a given amount. Stated the other way, the more that firms differ in costs, the steeper the market supply curve at low prices. Differences in costs are one explanation for why some market supply curves are upward sloping.

SHORT-RUN COMPETITIVE EQUILIBRIUM

By combining the short-run market supply curve and the market demand curve, we can determine the short-run competitive equilibrium. We examine first how to determine the equilibrium in the lime market and then how the equilibrium changes when firms are taxed.

Short-Run Equilibrium in the Lime Market. Suppose that there were five identical firms in the short-run equilibrium in the lime manufacturing industry. Panel a of Figure 8.9 shows the short-run cost curves and the supply curve, S^1, for a typical firm, and panel b shows the corresponding short-run competitive market supply curve, *S*.

In panel b, the initial demand curve D^1 intersects the market supply curve at E_1, the market equilibrium. The equilibrium quantity is $Q_1 = 1,075$ units of lime per year, and the equilibrium market price is $7.

In panel a, each competitive firm faces a horizontal demand curve at the equilibrium price of $7. Each price-taking firm chooses its output where its marginal cost curve intersects the horizontal demand curve at e_1. Because each firm is maximizing its

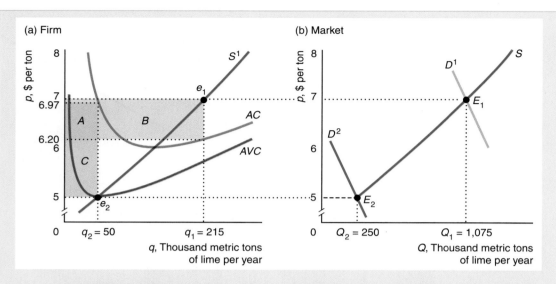

Figure 8.9   Short-Run Competitive Equilibrium in the Lime Market. (a) The short-run supply curve is the marginal cost above the minimum average variable cost of $5. At a price of $5, each firm makes a short-run loss of $(p − AC)q = (\$5 − \$6.97) \times 50{,}000 = −\$98{,}500$, area $A + C$. At a price of $7, the short-run profit of a typical lime firm is $(p − AC)q = (\$7 − \$6.20) \times 215{,}000 =$ $172,000, area $A + B$. (b) If there are five firms in the lime market in the short run, so that the market supply is S, and if the market demand curve is D^1, then the short-run equilibrium is E_1, the market price is $7, and market output is $Q_1 = 1{,}075$ units. If the demand curve shifts to D^2, the market equilibrium is $p = \$5$ and $Q_2 = 250$ units.

profit at e_1, no firm wants to change its behavior, so e_1 is each firm's equilibrium. In panel a, each firm makes a short-run profit of area $A + B = \$172{,}000$, which is the average profit per ton, $p − AC = \$7 − \$6.20 = 80$¢, times the firm's output, $q_1 = 215$ units. The equilibrium market output, Q_1, is the number of firms, n, times the equilibrium output of each firm: $Q_1 = nq_1 = 5 \times 215$ units $= 1{,}075$ units (panel b).

Now suppose that the demand curve shifts to D^2. The new market equilibrium is E_2, where the price is only $5. At that price, each firm produces $q = 50$ units, and market output is $Q = 250$ units. In panel a, each firm loses $98,500, area $A + C$, because it makes an average per ton of $(p − AC) = (\$5 − \$6.97) = −\$1.97$ and it sells $q_2 = 50$ units. However, such a firm does not shut down because price equals the firm's average variable cost, so the firm is able to cover its out-of-pocket expenses.

SOLVED PROBLEM   **8.3**

What is the effect, on the short-run equilibrium, of a specific tax of τ per unit that is collected from all n identical firms in a market? What is the incidence of the tax?

Answer

1. *Show how the tax shifts a typical firm's marginal cost and average cost curves and hence its supply curve:* In Solved Problem 8.1, we showed that such a tax causes the marginal cost curve, the average cost curve, and (hence) the minimum average cost of the firm to shift up by τ, as illustrated in panel a of the figure. As a result, the short-run supply curve of the firm, labeled $S^1 + \tau$, shifts up by τ from the pretax supply curve, S^1.

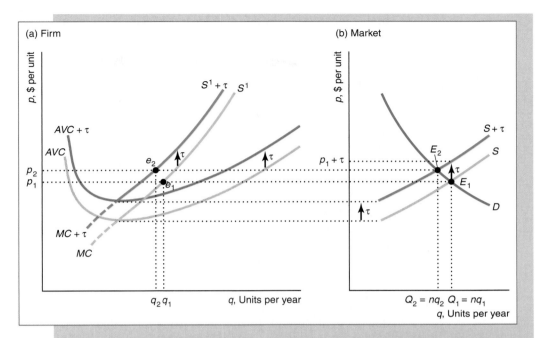

2. *Show how the market supply curve shifts:* The market supply curve is the sum of all the individual firm's supply curves, so it too shifts up by τ, from S to $S + \tau$ in panel b of the figure.

3. *Determine how the short-run market equilibrium changes:* The pretax short-run market equilibrium is E_1, where the downward-sloping market demand curve D intersects S in panel b. In that equilibrium, price is p_1 and quantity is Q_1, which equals n (the number of firms) times the quantity q_1 that a typical firm produces at p_1. The after-tax short-run market equilibrium, E_2, determined by the intersection of D and the after-tax supply curve, $S + \tau$, occurs at p_2 and Q_2. Because the after-tax price p_2 is above the after-tax minimum average variable cost, all the firms continue to produce, but they produce less than before: $q_2 < q_1$. Consequently the equilibrium quantity falls from $Q_1 = nq_1$ to $Q_2 = nq_2$.

4. *Discuss the incidence of the tax:* The equilibrium price increases, but by less than the full amount of the tax: $p_2 < p_1 + \tau$. The incidence of the tax is shared between consumers and producers because both the supply and the demand curves are sloped (Chapter 2).[10]

8.4 Competition in the Long Run

I think there is a world market for about five computers.
— Thomas J. Watson, IBM chairman, 1943

In the long run, competitive firms can vary inputs that were fixed in the short run, so the long-run firm and market supply curves differ from the short-run curves. After

---

[10]See Chapter 2 for the calculus analysis of the incidence of a specific tax in a competitive market.

briefly looking at how a firm determines its long-run supply curve so as to maximize its profit, we examine the relationship between short-run and long-run market supply curves and competitive equilibria.

LONG-RUN COMPETITIVE PROFIT MAXIMIZATION

A firm's two profit-maximizing decisions—how much to produce and whether to produce at all—are simpler in the long run than in the short run. In the long run, typically all costs are variable, so the firm does not have to consider whether fixed costs are sunk or avoidable.

Long-Run Output Decision. The firm chooses the quantity that maximizes its profit using the same rules as in the short run. The firm picks the quantity that maximizes long-run profit, which is the difference between revenue and long-run cost. Equivalently, it operates where long-run marginal profit is zero and where marginal revenue equals long-run marginal cost.

Long-Run Shutdown Decision. After determining the output level, q^*, that maximizes its profit or minimizes its loss, the firm decides whether to produce or shut down. The firm shuts down if its revenue is less than its avoidable or variable cost. In the long run, however, all costs are variable. As a result, in the long run, the firm shuts down if it would make an economic loss by operating.

LONG-RUN FIRM SUPPLY CURVE

A firm's long-run supply curve is its long-run marginal cost curve above the minimum of its long-run average cost curve (because all costs are variable in the long run). The firm is free to choose its capital in the long run, so the firm's long-run supply curve may differ substantially from its short-run supply curve.

The firm chooses a plant size to maximize its long-run economic profit in light of its beliefs about the future. If its forecast is wrong, it may be stuck with a plant that is too small or too large for its level of production in the short run. The firm acts to correct this mistake in plant size in the long run.

The firm in Figure 8.10 has different short- and long-run cost curves. In the short run, the firm uses a plant that is smaller than the optimal long-run size if the price is $35. The firm produces 50 units of output per year in the short run, where its short-run marginal cost, $SRMC$, equals the price, and makes a short-run profit equal to area A. The firm's short-run supply curve, S^{SR}, is its short-run marginal cost above the minimum, $20, of its short-run average variable cost, $SRAVC$.

If the firm expects the price to remain at $35, it builds a larger plant in the long run. Using the larger plant, the firm produces 110 units per year, where its long-run marginal cost, $LRMC$, equals the market price. It expects to make a long-run profit, area $A + B$, which is greater than its short-run profit by area B because it sells 60 more units and its equilibrium long-run average cost, $LRAC = \$25$, is lower than its short-run average cost in equilibrium, $28.

The firm does not operate at a loss in the long run when all inputs are variable. It shuts down if the market price falls below the firm's minimum long-run average cost of $24. Thus the competitive firm's long-run supply curve is its long-run marginal cost curve above $24.

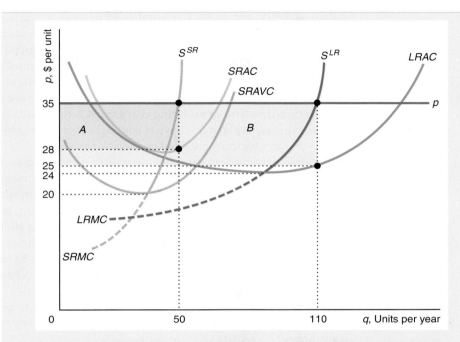

Figure 8.10 The Short-Run and Long-Run Supply Curves. The firm's long-run supply curve, S^{LR}, is zero below its minimum average cost of $24 and equals the long-run marginal cost, *LRMC*, at higher prices. The firm produces more in the long run than in the short run, 110 units instead of 50 units, and earns a higher profit, area $A + B$, instead of just area A.

LONG-RUN MARKET SUPPLY CURVE

The competitive market supply curve is the horizontal sum of the supply curves of the individual firms in both the short run and the long run. Because the maximum number of firms in the market is fixed in the short run, we add the supply curves of a known number of firms to obtain the short-run market supply curve. The only way for the market to supply more output in the short run is for existing firms to produce more.

In the long run, firms can enter or leave the market. Thus before we can add all the relevant firm supply curves to obtain the long-run market supply curve, we need to determine how many firms are in the market at each possible market price.

To construct the long-run market supply curve properly, we also have to determine how input prices vary with output. As the market expands or contracts substantially, changes in factor prices may shift firms' cost and supply curves. If so, we need to determine how such shifts in factor prices affect firm supply curves so that we can properly construct the market supply curve. The effect of changes in input prices is greater in the long run than in the short run because market output can change more dramatically in the long run.

We now look in detail at how entry and changing factor prices affect long-run market supply. We first derive the long-run market supply curve, assuming that the price of inputs remains constant as market output increases, so as to isolate the role of entry. We then examine how the market supply curve is affected if the price of inputs changes as market output rises.

Role of Entry and Exit. The number of firms in a market in the long run is determined by the *entry* and *exit* of firms. In the long run, each firm decides whether to enter or exit, depending on whether it can make a long-run profit.

In many markets, firms face barriers to entry or must incur significant costs to enter. For example, many city governments limit the number of cab drivers, creating an insurmountable barrier that prevents additional firms from entering. And in some markets, a new firm considering entry must hire consultants to determine the profit opportunities, pay lawyers to write contracts, and incur other expenses. Typically, such costs of entry (or exit) are fixed costs.

Even if existing firms are making positive profits, no entry occurs in the short run if entering firms need time to find a location, build a new plant, and hire workers. In the long run, firms enter the market if they can make profits by so doing. The costs of entry are often lower, and hence the profits from entering are higher, if a firm takes its time to enter. As a result, firms may enter markets long after profit opportunities first appear. For example, Starbucks announced that it planned to enter the Puerto Rican and Spanish markets in 2002 but that it would take up to two years to build its initial 11 to 16 stores in each market. By May 2007, Starbucks had 22 stores in Puerto Rico and 61 stores in Spain.

In contrast, firms usually react faster to losses than to potential profits. We expect firms to shut down or exit the market quickly in the short run when price is below average variable cost.

In markets without barriers or fixed costs to entry, firms can freely enter and exit. For example, many construction firms, which have no capital and provide only labor services, engage in *hit-and-run* entry and exit: They enter the market whenever they can make a profit and exit whenever they can't. These firms may enter and exit markets several times a year.

In such markets, a shift of the market demand curve to the right entices firms to enter. For example, if there were no government regulations, the market for taxicabs would have free entry and exit. Car owners could enter or exit the market virtually instantaneously. If the demand curve for cab rides shifted to the right, the market price would rise, and existing cab drivers would make unusually high profits in the short run. Seeing these profits, other car owners would enter the market, causing the market supply curve to shift to the right and the market price to fall. Entry occurs until the last firm to enter—the *marginal firm*—makes zero long-run profit.

Similarly, if the demand curve shifts to the left so that the market price drops, firms suffer losses. Firms with minimum average costs above the new, lower market price exit the market. Firms continue to leave the market until the next firm considering leaving, the marginal firm, is again earning a zero long-run profit.

Thus in a market with free entry and exit:

- A firm enters the market if it can make a long-run profit, $\pi > 0$.
- A firm exits the market to avoid a long-run loss, $\pi < 0$.

If firms in a market are making zero long-run profit, they are indifferent between staying in the market and exiting. We presume that if they are already in the market, they stay in the market when they are making zero long-run profit.

Most transportation markets are thought to have free entry and exit unless governments regulate them. Relatively few airline, trucking, or shipping firms may serve a particular route, but they face extensive potential entry. Other firms can and will quickly enter and serve a route if a profit opportunity appears. Entrants shift their

TABLE 8.1   Average Annual Entry and Exit Rates in Selected U.S. Industries, 1989–1996

Industry	Entry Rate, %	Exit Rate, %
Total economy	10	8
Agriculture, hunting, forestry, and fishing	11	8
Construction	11	9
Services	10	8
Mining and quarrying	8	9
Total manufacturing	8	7
Textile products, leather, and footwear	12	12
Wood products	10	9
Paper products, printing, and publishing	8	8
Food products, beverages, and tobacco	8	7
Chemical, rubber, plastics, and fuel products	8	6
Electricity, gas, and water supply	4	3

Source: Calculations based on data from the OECD Firm-Level Data Project, **www.oecd.org,** as of 2005.

highly mobile equipment from less profitable routes to more profitable ones. See **www. aw-bc.com/perloff,** Chapter 8, "Threat of Entry in Shipping."

Evidence on Ease of Entry and Exit. Entry and exit are relatively difficult in many manufacturing and mining industries as well as in government-regulated industries such as public utilities and insurance. In contrast, firms can enter and exit easily in many agriculture, construction, wholesale and retail trade, and service industries.

Table 8.1 lists the average annual entry rate (percentage of firms that enter per year relative to total firms) and exit rate for various U.S. industries. Rates range from a low of 4% for entry and 3% for exit in the highly regulated electricity, gas, and water public utility sector to a high of 12% for both entry and exit in the relatively competitive textile products, leather, and footwear industry. Industries with high entry rates tend to have high exit rates. That is, entry and exit barriers are likely to be related.

Long-Run Market Supply with Identical Firms and Free Entry. The *long-run market supply curve is flat* at the minimum long-run average cost *if firms can freely enter and exit* the market, an unlimited number of *firms have identical costs,* and *input prices are constant.* This result follows from our reasoning about the short-run supply curve, in which we showed that the market supply curve was flatter, the more firms there were in the market. With many firms in the market in the long run, the market supply curve is effectively flat. ("Many" is 10 firms in the vegetable oil market.)

The long-run supply curve of a typical vegetable oil mill, S^1 in panel a of Figure 8.11, is the long-run marginal cost curve above a minimum long-run average cost of $10. Because each firm shuts down if the market price is below $10, the long-run market supply curve is zero at a price below $10. If the price rises above $10, firms are making positive profits, so new firms enter, expanding market output until profits are driven to zero, where price is again $10. The long-run market supply curve in panel b is a horizontal line at the minimum long-run average cost of the typical firm, $10. At a price of $10, each firm produces $q = 150$ units (where one unit equals 100 metric tons). Thus the total output produced by n firms in the market is $Q = nq = n \times 150$ units. Extra market output is obtained by new firms entering the market.

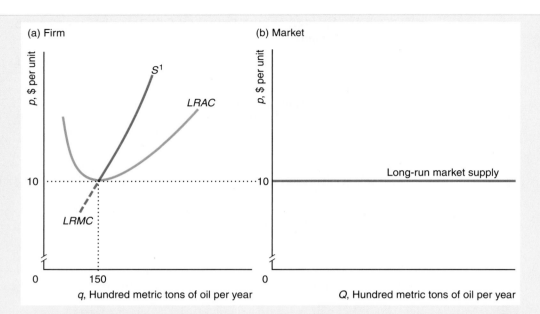

Figure 8.11 Long-Run Firm and Market Supply with Identical Vegetable Oil Firms. (a) The long-run supply curve of a typical vegetable oil mill, S^1, is the long-run marginal cost curve above the minimum average cost of $10. (b) The long-run market supply curve is horizontal at the minimum of the long-run minimum average cost of a typical firm. Each firm produces 150 units, so market output is $150n$, where n is the number of firms.

In summary, the long-run market supply curve is horizontal if the market has free entry and exit, an unlimited number of firms have identical costs, and input prices are constant. When these strong assumptions do not hold, the long-run market supply curve has a slope, as we now show.

Long-Run Market Supply when Entry Is Limited. If the number of firms in a market is limited in the long run, the market supply curve slopes upward. The number of firms is limited if the government restricts that number, if firms need a scarce resource, or if entry is costly. An example of a scarce resource is the limited number of lots on which a luxury beachfront hotel can be built in Miami. High entry costs restrict the number of firms in a market because firms enter only if the long-run economic profit is greater than the cost of entering.

The only way to get more output if the number of firms is limited is for existing firms to produce more. Because individual firms' supply curves slope upward, the long-run market supply curve is also upward sloping. The reasoning is the same as in the short run, as panel b of Figure 8.7 illustrates, given that no more than five firms can enter. The market supply curve is the upward-sloping S^5 curve, which is the horizontal sum of the five firms' upward-sloping marginal cost curves above minimum average cost.

Long-Run Market Supply when Firms Differ. A second reason why some long-run market supply curves slope upward is that firms differ. Because firms with relatively low minimum long-run average costs are willing to enter the market at lower prices than others, an upward-sloping long-run market supply curve results.

The long-run supply curve is upward sloping because of differences in costs across firms *only* if the amount that lower-cost firms can produce is limited. If there were an unlimited number of the lowest-cost firms, we would never observe any higher-cost firms producing. Effectively, then, the only firms in the market would have the same low costs of production.

● APPLICATION

Upward-Sloping Long-Run Supply Curve for Cotton

Many countries produce cotton. Production costs differ among countries because of differences in the quality of land, rainfall, the costs of irrigation and labor, and other factors.

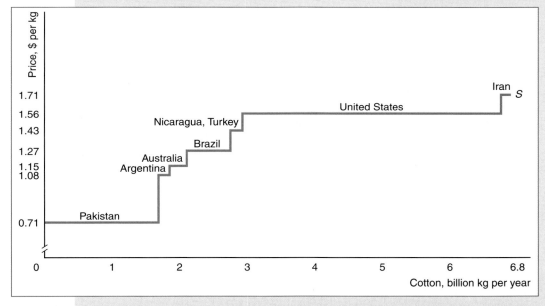

The length of each steplike segment of the long-run supply curve of cotton in the graph is the quantity produced by the named country. The amount that the low-cost countries can produce must be limited, or we would not observe production by the higher-cost countries.

The height of each segment of the supply curve is the typical minimum average cost of production in that country. The average cost of production in Pakistan is less than half that in Iran. The supply curve has a steplike appearance because we are using an average of the estimate average cost in each country, which is a single number. If we knew the individual firms' supply curves in each of these countries, the market supply curve would have a smoother shape.

As the market price rises, the number of countries producing rises. At market prices below $1.08 per kilogram, only Pakistan produces. If the market price is below $1.50, the United States and Iran do not produce. If the price increases to $1.56, the United States supplies a large amount of cotton. In this range of the supply curve, supply is very elastic. For Iran to produce, the price has to rise to $1.71. Price increases in that range result in only a relatively small increase in supply. Thus the supply curve is relatively inelastic at prices above $1.56.

Long-Run Market Supply when Input Prices Vary with Output. A third reason why market supply curves may slope is nonconstant input prices. In markets in which factor prices rise or fall when output increases, the long-run supply curve slopes even if firms have identical costs and can freely enter and exit.

If the market buys a relatively small share of the total amount of a factor of production that is sold, then, as market output expands, the price of the factor is unlikely to be affected. For example, dentists do not hire enough receptionists to affect the market wage for receptionists.

In contrast, if the market buys most of the total sales of a factor, then the price of that input is more likely to vary with market output. As jet plane manufacturers expand and buy more jet engines, the price of these engines rises because the jet plane manufacturers are the sole purchaser of these engines.

To produce more goods, firms must use more inputs. If the prices of some or all inputs rise when more inputs are purchased, the cost of producing the final good also rises. We call a market in which input prices rise with output an *increasing-cost market*. Few steelworkers have no fear of heights and are willing to construct tall buildings, so their supply curve is steeply upward sloping. As more skyscrapers are built at one time, the demand curve for these workers shifts to the right, driving up their wage.

We assume that all firms in a market have the same cost curves and that input prices rise as market output expands. We use the cost curves of a representative firm in panel a of Figure 8.12 to derive the upward-sloping market supply curve in panel b.

When input prices are relatively low, each identical firm has the same long-run marginal cost curve, MC^1, and average cost curve, AC^1, in panel a. A typical firm produces at minimum average cost, e_1, and sells q_1 units of output. The market supply is

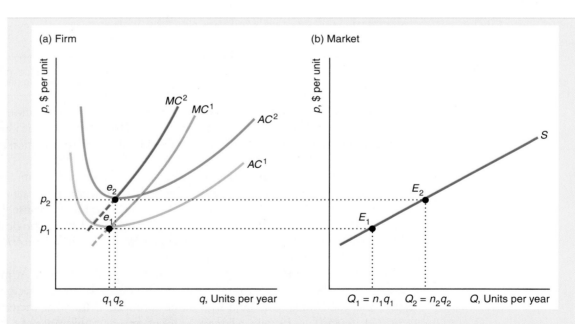

Figure 8.12 Long-Run Market Supply in an Increasing-Cost Market. (a) At a relatively low market output, Q_1, the firm's long-run marginal and average cost curves are MC^1 and AC^1. At the higher market quantity Q_2, the cost curves shift upward to MC^2 and AC^2 because of the higher input prices. Given identical firms, each firm produces at minimum average cost, such as points e_1 and e_2. (b) Long-run market supply, S, is upward sloping.

Q_1 in panel b when the market price is p_1. The n_1 firms collectively sell $Q_1 = n_1q_1$ units of output, which is point E_1 on the market supply curve in panel b.

If the market demand curve shifts outward, the market price rises to p_2, new firms enter, and market output rises to Q_2, causing input prices to rise. As a result, the marginal cost curve shifts from MC^1 to MC^2, and the average cost curve rises from AC^1 to AC^2. The typical firm produces at a higher minimum average cost, e_2. At this higher price, there are n_2 firms in the market, so market output is $Q_2 = n_2q_2$ at point E_2 on the market supply curve.

Thus in both an increasing-cost market and a *constant-cost market*—in which input prices remain constant as output increases—firms produce at minimum average cost in the long run. The difference is that the minimum average cost rises as market output increases in an increasing-cost market, whereas minimum average cost is constant in a constant-cost market. In conclusion, *the long-run supply curve is upward sloping in an increasing-cost market and flat in a constant-cost market.*

In a *decreasing-cost market,* as market output rises, at least some factor prices fall. As a result, *in a decreasing-cost market, the long-run market supply curve is downward sloping.*

Increasing returns to scale may cause factor prices to fall. For example, when DVD drives were first introduced, relatively few were manufactured, at relatively high costs. Both because of the price and the lack of DVDs, there was much less demand for DVD drives than there is today. As demand for DVD drives increased, it became practical to automate more of the production process so that drives could be produced at a lower average cost. The decrease in the price of these drives lowers the cost of personal computers.

To summarize, theory tells us that competitive long-run market supply curves may be flat, upward sloping, or downward sloping. If all firms are identical in a market in which firms can freely enter and input prices are constant, the long-run market supply curve is flat. If entry is limited, firms differ in costs, or input prices rise with output, the long-run supply curve is upward sloping. Finally, if input prices fall with market output, the long-run supply curve is downward sloping. (See **www.aw-bc.com/perloff,** Chapter 8, "Slope of Long-Run Market Supply Curves.")

Long-Run Market Supply Curve with Trade. Cotton, oil, and many other goods are traded on world markets. The world equilibrium price and quantity for a good are determined by the intersection of the world supply curve—the horizontal sum of the supply curves of each producing country—and the world demand curve—the horizontal sum of the demand curves of each consuming country.

A country that imports a good has a supply curve that is the horizontal sum of its domestic industry's supply curve and the import supply curve. The domestic supply curve is the competitive long-run supply curve that we have just derived. However, we need to determine the import supply curve.

The country imports the world's **residual supply curve:** the quantity that the market supplies that is not consumed by other demanders at any given price.[11] The country's import supply function is its residual supply function, $S^r(p)$, which is the quantity supplied to this country at price p. Because the country buys only that part of the world supply, $S(p)$, that is not consumed by any *other* demander elsewhere in the

---

[11]*Jargon alert:* It is traditional to use the expression *excess supply* when discussing international trade and *residual supply* otherwise, though the terms are equivalent.

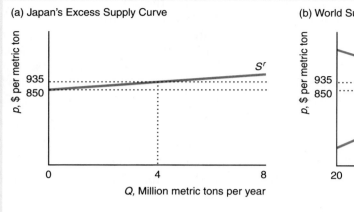

Figure 8.13 Excess or Residual Supply Curve. Japan's excess supply curve, S^r, for cotton is the horizontal differ-ence between the world's supply curve, S, and the demand curve of the other countries in the world, D^o.

world, $D^o(p)$, its residual supply function is

$$S^r(p) = S(p) - D^o(p). \tag{8.16}$$

At prices so low that $D^o(p)$ is greater than $S(p)$, the residual supply, $S^r(p)$, is zero.

In Figure 8.13, we derive Japan's residual supply curve for cotton in panel a using the world supply curve, S, and the demand curve of the rest of the world, D^o, in panel b. The scales differ for the quantity axes in the two panels. At a price of $850 per metric ton, the demand in other countries exhausts world supply (D^o intersects S at 32 million metric tons per year), so there is no residual supply for Japan. At a much higher price, $935, Japan's excess supply, 4 million metric tons, is the difference between the world supply, 30 million tons, and the quantity demanded elsewhere, 34 million tons. As the figure illustrates, the residual supply curve facing Japan is much closer to horizontal than is the world supply curve.

The elasticity of residual supply, η_r, facing a given country is[12]

$$\eta_r = \frac{\eta}{\theta} - \frac{1 - \theta}{\theta} \varepsilon_o, \tag{8.17}$$

where η is the market supply elasticity, ε_o is the demand elasticity of the other countries, and $\theta = Q_r/Q$ is the importing country's share of the world's output.

If a country imports a small fraction of the world's supply, we expect it to face a nearly perfectly elastic, horizontal residual supply curve. On the other hand, a relatively large consumer of the good might face an upward-sloping residual supply curve.

We can illustrate this difference for cotton, where $\eta = 0.5$ and $\varepsilon = -0.7$ (Green et al., 2005). The United States imports only $\theta = 0.1\%$ of the world's cotton, so its residual supply elasticity is

$$\eta_r = \frac{\eta}{0.001} - \frac{0.999}{0.001}\varepsilon_o$$

$$= 1,000\eta - 999\varepsilon_o$$

$$= (1,000 \times 0.5) - [999 \times (-0.7)] = 1,199.3,$$

---

[12]The derivation of this equation is similar to that of Equation 8.2. See Problem 36.

which is 2,398.6 times more elastic than the world's supply elasticity. Canada's import share is 10 times larger, $\theta = 1\%$, so its residual supply elasticity is "only" 119.3. Nonetheless, its residual supply curve is nearly horizontal: A 1% increase in its price would induce imports to more than double, rising by 119.3%. Even Japan's $\theta = 2.5\%$ leads to a relatively elastic $\eta_r = 46.4$. In contrast, China imports 18.5% of the world's cotton, so its residual supply elasticity is 5.8. Even though its residual supply elasticity is more than 11 times larger than the world's elasticity, it is still small enough that its excess supply curve is upward sloping.

Thus, if a country is "small"—imports a small share of the world's output—then it faces a horizontal import supply curve at the world equilibrium price. If its domestic supply curve is everywhere above the world price, then it only imports and faces a horizontal demand curve. If some portion of its upward-sloping domestic supply curve is below the world price, then its total supply curve is the upward-sloping domestic supply curve up to the world price and is horizontal at the world price (Chapter 9 shows such a supply curve for oil).

This analysis of trade applies to trade within a country too. The following application shows that it can be used to look at trade across geographic areas or jurisdictions such as states.

APPLICATION

Special Blends and Gasoline Supply Curves

You can't buy the gasoline sold in Milwaukee elsewhere in Wisconsin. Houston gas isn't the same as western Texas gas. California, Minnesota, and Nevada and most of America's biggest cities use one or more of 17 specialized blends, while the rest of the country uses regular gas. Because special blends usually are designed to cut air pollution, they are more likely to be used in areas with serious pollution problems.

The number of working U.S. refineries has dropped from 324 in 1981 to 144 in 2005. Many of these refiners produce regular gasoline, which is sold throughout most of the country. Wholesalers are willing to ship regular gas across state lines in response to slightly higher prices in neighboring states. If the price rises slightly in New Hampshire, firms will quickly send gasoline from Vermont or Maine to New Hampshire. As a consequence, the residual supply curve for regular gasoline for a given state is close to horizontal.

In contrast, gasoline is usually not imported into jurisdictions that require special blends. Few refiners produce any given special blend. Only 13 of the 22 California refineries can produce California's special low-polluting blend of gasoline, California Reformulated Gasoline (CaRFG). Because refineries require expensive upgrades to produce a new kind of gas, they generally do not switch from producing one type to producing another type of gas. Thus even if the price of gasoline starts rising in California, wholesalers in other states do not send gasoline to California, because they cannot legally sell regular gasoline in California and it would cost too much to start producing CaRFG.

As a result, the supply curve for California's special blend is eventually upward sloping. At relatively small quantities, refineries can produce more gasoline without incurring higher costs, so California's supply curve in this region is relatively flat. However, to produce much larger quantities of gasoline, refiners have to run their plants around the clock and convert a larger fraction of each gallon of oil into gasoline, incurring higher costs of production. Thus they are willing to sell larger quantities in this range only at a higher price, so the supply curve slopes upward.

When the refineries reach capacity, no matter how high the price gets, firms cannot produce more gasoline (at least until new refineries go online), so the supply curve becomes vertical. California normally operates in the steeply upward-sloping section of its supply curve. In 2003, the 14.8 billion gallons consumed nearly equaled refiners' 15-billion-gallon maximum capacity.

SOLVED PROBLEM 8.4

In the short run, what happens to the competitive market price of gasoline if the demand curve in a state shifts to the right as more people move to the state or start driving gas-hogging SUVs? In your answer, distinguish between areas in which regular gasoline is sold and jurisdictions that require special blends.

Answer

1. *Show the effect of a shift of the demand curve in areas that use regular gasoline:* In an area that uses regular gasoline, the supply curve is horizontal, as panel a of the figure shows. Thus as the demand curve shifts to the right from D^1 to D^2, the equilibrium shifts along the supply curve from e_1 to e_2, and the price remains at p_1.

2. *Show the effects of both a small and a large shift of the demand curve in a jurisdiction that uses a special blend:* The supply curve in panel b is drawn as described in the previous application. If the demand curve shifts slightly to the right from D^1 to D^2, the price remains unchanged at p_1 because the demand curve continues to intersect the supply curve in the flat region. However, if the demand curve shifts farther to the right to D^3, then the new intersection is in the upward-sloping section of the supply curve and the price increases to p_2. Consequently, unforeseen "jumps" in demand are more likely to cause a *price spike*—a large increase in price—in jurisdictions that use special blends.[13]

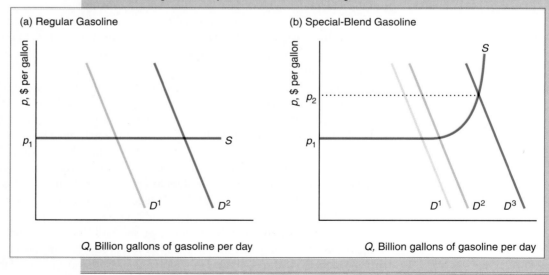

(a) Regular Gasoline (b) Special-Blend Gasoline

Q, Billion gallons of gasoline per day

---

[13]The gasoline wholesale market may not be completely competitive, especially in areas where special blends are used. Moreover, gas can be stored. Hence price differences across jurisdictions may be due to other factors as well. See Borenstein et al. (2004).

LONG-RUN COMPETITIVE EQUILIBRIUM

The intersection of the long-run market supply and demand curves determines the long-run competitive equilibrium. With identical firms, constant input prices, and free entry and exit, the long-run competitive market supply is horizontal at minimum long-run average cost, so the equilibrium price equals long-run average cost. A shift in the demand curve affects only the equilibrium quantity and not the equilibrium price, which remains constant at minimum long-run average cost.

The market supply curve is different in the short run than in the long run, so the long-run competitive equilibrium differs from the short-run equilibrium. The relationship between the short- and long-run equilibria depends on where the market demand curve crosses the short- and long-run market supply curves. Figure 8.14 illustrates this point using the short- and long-run supply curves for the vegetable oil mill market.

The short-run firm supply curve for a typical firm in panel a is the marginal cost above the minimum of the average variable cost, $7. At a price of $7, each firm produces 100 units, so the 20 firms in the market in the short run collectively supply 2,000 ($= 20 \times 100$) units of oil in panel b. At higher prices, the short-run market supply curve slopes upward because it is the horizontal summation of the firm's upward-sloping marginal cost curves.

We assume that the firms use the same size plant in the short run and the long run so that the minimum average cost is $10 in both the short run and the long run. Because all firms have the same costs and can enter freely, the long-run market supply curve is flat at the minimum average cost, $10, in panel b. At prices between $7 and $10, firms supply goods at a loss in the short run but not in the long run.

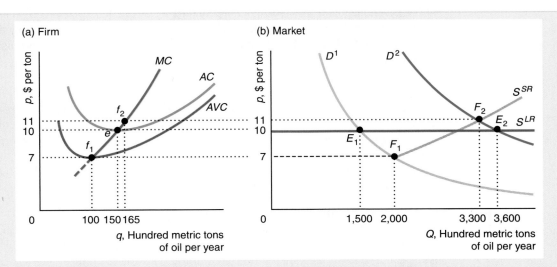

Figure 8.14 The Short-Run and Long-Run Equilibria for Vegetable Oil. (a) A typical vegetable oil mill is willing to produce 100 units of oil at a price of $7, 150 units at $10, or 165 units at $11. (b) The short-run market supply curve, S^{SR}, is the horizontal sum of 20 individual firms' short-run marginal cost curves above minimum average variable cost, $7. The long-run market supply curve, S^{LR}, is horizontal at the minimum average cost, $10. If the demand curve is D^1 in the short-run equilibrium, F_1, 20 firms sell 2,000 units of oil at $7. In the long-run equilibrium, E_1, 10 firms sell 1,500 units at $10. If demand is D^2, the short-run equilibrium is F_2 ($11, 3,300 units, 20 firms) and the long-run equilibrium is E_2 ($10, 3,600 units, 24 firms).

If the market demand curve is D^1, the short-run market equilibrium, F_1, is below and to the right of the long-run market equilibrium, E_1. This relationship is reversed if the market demand curve is D^2.[14]

In the short run, if the demand is as low as D^1, the market price in the short-run equilibrium, F_1, is $7. At that price, each of the 20 firms produces 100 units, at f_1 in panel a. The firms lose money because the price of $7 is below average cost at 100 units. These losses drive some of the firms out of the market in the long run, so market output falls and the market price rises. In the long-run equilibrium, E_1, price is $10, and each firm produces 150 units, e, and breaks even. As the market demands only 1,500 units, only 10 (= 1,500/150) firms produce, so half the firms that produced in the short run exit the market.[15] Thus with the D^1 demand curve, price rises and output falls in the long run.

If demand expands to D^2 in the short run, each of the 20 firms expands its output to 165 units, f_2, and the price rises to $11, where the firms make profits: The price of $11 is above the average cost at 165 units. These profits attract entry in the long run, and the price falls. In the long-run equilibrium, each firm produces 150 units, e, and 3,600 units are sold by the market, E_2, by 24 (= 3,600/150) firms. Thus with the D^2 demand curve, price falls and output rises in the long run.

Because firms may enter and exit in the long run, taxes can have a counterintuitive effect on the competitive equilibrium. For example, as Solved Problem 8.5 shows, a lump-sum franchise tax causes the competitive equilibrium output of a firm to increase even though market output falls.

SOLVED PROBLEM   8.5

If the government starts collecting a lump-sum franchise tax of $\mathcal{L}$ each year from each identical firm in a competitive market with free entry and exit and an unlimited number of potential firms, how do the long-run market and firm equilibria change? Answer using a graph. (In Problem 38, you are asked for a calculus solution.)

Answer

1. *Show that the franchise tax causes the minimum long-run average cost to rise:* Panel a shows a typical firm's cost curves, while panel b shows the market equilibrium. In panel a, a lump-sum franchise tax shifts the typical firm's average cost curve upward from AC^1 to $AC^2 = AC^1 + \mathcal{L}/q$ but does not affect the marginal cost (see Solved Problem 7.2). As a result, the minimum average cost rises from e_1 to e_2.

2. *Show that the shift in the minimum average cost causes the market supply curve to shift upward, equilibrium quantity to fall, and equilibrium price to rise:* The long-run market supply is horizontal at minimum average cost. Thus the market supply curve shifts upward by the same amount as the minimum average cost

---

[14]Using data from *Statistics Canada*, I estimated that the elasticity of demand for vegetable oil is -0.8. Both D^1 and D^2 are constant -0.8 elasticity demand curves, but the demand at any price on D^2 is 2.4 times that on D^1.

[15]How do we know which firms leave? If the firms are identical, the theory says nothing about which ones leave and which ones stay. The firms that leave make zero economic profit, and those that stay make zero economic profit, so firms are indifferent as to whether they stay or exit.

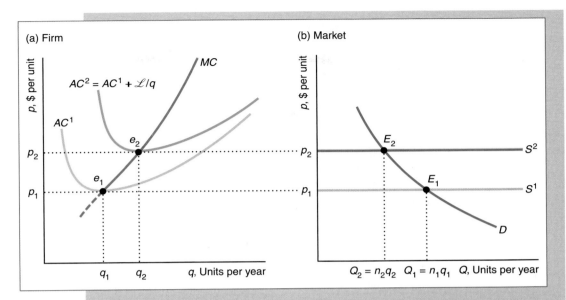

(a) Firm

(b) Market

increases in panel b. With a downward-sloping market demand curve, the new equilibrium, E_2, has a lower quantity, $Q_2 < Q_1$, and higher price, $p_2 > p_1$, than the original equilibrium, E_1.

3. Show that the increase in the equilibrium price causes the output of an individual firm to rise: Because the market price rises, the quantity that a firm produces rises from q_1 to q_2. Thus if the firm remains in the market, it will produce more.

4. Use the market quantity and individual firm quantity to determine how the number of firms changes: At the initial equilibrium, the number of firms was $n_1 = Q_1/q_1$. The new equilibrium number of firms, $n_2 = Q_2/q_2$, must be smaller than n_1 because $Q_2 < Q_1$ and $q_2 > q_1$. Thus there are fewer firms but each remaining firm produces more output at the new equilibrium.

Summary

1. **Competition:** Competitive firms are price takers that cannot influence market price. Markets are likely to be competitive if all firms in the market sell identical products, firms can enter and exit the market freely, buyers and sellers know the prices charged by firms, and transaction costs are low. A competitive firm faces a horizontal demand curve at the market price.

2. **Profit Maximization:** Most firms maximize economic profit, which is revenue minus economic cost (explicit and implicit costs). Because business profit, which is revenue minus only explicit cost, does not include implicit cost, economic profit tends to be less than business profit.

A firm earning zero economic profit is making as much as it could if its resources were devoted to their best alternative uses. To maximize profit, all firms (not just competitive firms) must make two decisions. First, the firm must determine the quantity at which its profit is highest. Profit is maximized when marginal profit is zero or, equivalently, when marginal revenue equals marginal cost. Second, the firm must decide whether to produce at all.

3. **Competition in the Short Run:** Because a competitive firm is a price taker, its marginal revenue equals the market price. As a result, a competitive firm maximizes its profit by setting its output so that its short-run marginal

cost equals the market price. The firm shuts down if the market price is less than its minimum average variable cost. Thus a profit-maximizing competitive firm's short-run supply curve is its marginal cost curve above its minimum average variable cost. The short-run market supply curve, which is the sum of the supply curves of the fixed number of firms producing in the short run, is flat at low output levels and upward sloping at larger levels. The short-run competitive equilibrium is determined by the intersection of the market demand curve and the short-run market supply curve. The effect of an increase in demand depends on whether demand intersects the market supply in the flat or upward-sloping section.

4. **Competition in the Long Run:** In the long run, a competitive firm sets its output where the market price equals its long-run marginal cost. It shuts down if the market price is less than the minimum of its average long-run cost

because all costs are variable in the long run. Consequently, the competitive firm's supply curve is its long-run marginal cost above its minimum long-run average cost. The long-run supply curve of a firm may have a different slope than the short-run curve because the firm can vary its fixed factors in the long run. The long-run market supply curve is the horizontal sum of the supply curves of all the firms in the market. If all firms are identical, entry and exit are easy, and input prices are constant, the long-run market supply curve is flat at minimum average cost. If firms differ, entry is difficult or costly, or input prices vary with output, the long-run market supply curve has an upward slope. The long-run market supply curve slopes upward if input prices increase with output and slopes downward if input prices decrease with output. The long-run market equilibrium price and quantity are different from the short-run price and quantity.

Questions

* = *answer at the back of this book;* W = *audio-slide show answers by James Dearden at* **www.aw-bc.com/perloff**

1. Should a competitive firm ever produce when it is losing money? Why or why not?

*2. A competitive firm's bookkeeper, upon reviewing the firm's books, finds that the firm spent twice as much on its plant, a fixed cost, as the firm's manager had previously thought. Should the manager change the output level because of this new information? How does this new information affect profit?

*3. Many marginal cost curves are U-shaped. As a result, it is possible that the marginal cost curve hits the demand or price line at two output levels. Which is the profit-maximizing output? Why?

4. Within the last couple of years, virtually every U.S. food company seemed to "Atkinize," introducing low-carbohydrate foods by removing sugar and starch. In 1999, few food or beverage products were marketed as "no-carb" or "low-carb." In 2003, some 500 products carried such labels, and by 2004, more than 3,000 products made such a claim (Melanie Warner, "Is the Low-Carb Boom Over?" *New York Times,* December 5, 2004, 3.1 and 3.9). But low-carb product sales rose only 6% in the 13 weeks ending September 24, 2004, compared to double-digit gains in the corresponding period in 2003 and triple-digit gains in the beginning of 2004. By 2005, low-carb products were disappearing rapidly. Assume that food firms can be properly viewed as being competitive. Use side-by-side firm and market diagrams to show why firms quickly entered and then quickly exited the low-carb market. Did the

firms go wrong by introducing so many low-carb products? (Answer in terms of fixed costs and expectations about demand.)

5. The war in Iraq has caused Defense Department purchases from contractors to soar (Todd Wallack, "Business Booms for Bay Area Contractors: $5.5 Billion Flowed from the Defense Dept. to Local Firms Last Year," *San Francisco Chronicle,* March 18, 2004: A1, A15), including firms as diverse as ice-cream vendors and armored vehicle manufacturers. Use side-by-side firm-market diagrams to show the effects (number of firms, price, output, profits) of such a shift in demand in one such industry in both the short run and the long run. Explain how your answer depends on whether the shift in demand is expected to be temporary or permanent.

6. The Internet is affecting holiday shipping. In years past, the busiest shipping period was Thanksgiving week. Now, as people have become comfortable with e-commerce, they put off purchases to the last minute and are more likely to have their purchases shipped to them (rather than to purchase locally). In December 2004, FedEx handled a 40% increase in packages over the previous year (Pia Sakar, "Shippers Snowed Under," *San Francisco Chronicle,* December 21, 2004: D1, D8). FedEx, along with Amazon.com and other e-commerce firms, had to hire extra workers during this period, and many regular workers logged substantial overtime hours (up to 60 a week).

a. Are a firm's marginal and average costs likely to rise or fall with this extra business? (Discuss economies of scale and the slopes of marginal and average cost curves.)

b. Use side-by-side firm-market diagrams to show the effects on the number of firms, equilibrium price and output, and profits of such a seasonal shift in demand for e-retailers in both the short run and the long run. Explain your reasoning.

7. Carol Skonberg, a housewife and part-time piano teacher, thought she was filling a crying need with her wineglass jewelry (Eve Tahmincioglu, "Even the Best Ideas Don't Sell Themselves," *New York Times*, October 9, 2003, C9). Her Wine Jewels are sterling silver charms of elephants, palm trees, and other subjects that hook on wineglass stems so that people don't lose their drinks at parties. In 2000, her first year, she signed up 90 stores in Texas to carry her charms. Then almost overnight, orders disappeared as rival companies offered similar products—with names such as Wine Charms, Stemmies, and That Wine Is Mine—at lower prices. Ellen Petti started That Wine Is Mine in 1999. She set up a national network of sales representatives and got the product in national catalogs. Her company's sales surged from $250,000 the first year to $6 million in 2001, before falling to $4.5 million in 2002, when she sold the company. Tina Matte's firm started selling Stemmies in late 2000, making $90,000 in its first year, before sales fell to $75,000 the following year. Assume that this market is competitive and use side-by-side firm and market diagrams to show what happened to prices, quantities, number of firms, and profit as this market evolved over a couple of years. (*Hint:* Consider the possibility that firms' cost functions differ.)

8. Dairy farms can produce Grade A milk, which meets the highest sanitation standards designed for the fluid market, or Grade B milk, which meets the lower sanitation standards designed for the cheese, butter, and nonfluid markets (Caputo and Paris, 2005). Substantial additional physical and human capital is necessary to produce Grade A rather than Grade B milk. From 1949 to 1999, the share of Grade A milk produced in the United States rose from 57% to 97%, as most dairy farms adopted the necessary technology. Use graphs to explain why Caputo and Paris conclude that "the rising relative price of Grade A milk gave dairy farmers the incentive to adopt the technology for Grade A milk production since such adoption resulted in higher future expected profits than did Grade B milk production."

*9. For Red Delicious apple farmers in Washington, 2001 was a terrible year (Linda Ashton, "Bumper Crop a Bummer for Struggling Apple Farmers," *San Francisco Chronicle*, January 9, 2001: C7). The average price for Red Delicious apples was $10.61 per box, well below the shutdown level of $13.23. Many farmers did not pick the apples off their trees. Other farmers bulldozed their trees, getting out of the Red Delicious business for good, removing 25,000 acres from production. Why did some farmers choose not to pick apples, and others to bulldoze their trees? (*Hint:* Consider the average variable cost and expectations about future prices.)

10. According to the "Oil Sands Shutdowns" application, the minimum average variable cost of processing oil sands dropped from $25 a barrel in the 1960s to $18 today due to technological advances. In a figure, show how this change affects the supply curve of a typical competitive firm and the supply curve of all the firms producing oil from oil sands.

11. The African country Lesotho gains most of its export earnings—90% in 2004—from its garment and textile factories. Your T-shirts from Wal-Mart and fleece sweats from J. C. Penney probably were made in Lesotho. In 2005, the demand curve for Lesotho products shifted downward precipitously due to increased Chinese supply with the end of textile quotas on China and the resulting increase in Chinese exports and the plunge of the U.S. dollar exchange rate against China's currency. Lesotho's garment factories had to sell roughly $55 worth of clothing in the United States to cover a factory worker's monthly wage in 2002, but they had to sell an average of $109 to $115 in 2005. Consequently, in the first quarter of 2005, 6 of Lesotho's 50 clothes factories shut down, as the world price plummeted below their minimum average variable cost. These shutdowns eliminated 5,800 of the 50,000 garment jobs. Layoffs at other factories have eliminated another 6,000. Since 2002, Lesotho has lost an estimated 30,000 textile jobs.

a. What is the shape of the demand curve facing Lesotho textile factories, and why? (*Hint:* They are price takers in the world market.)

b. Use figures to show how the increase in Chinese exports affected the demand curve the Lesotho factories face.

c. Discuss how the change in the exchange rate affected their demand curve, and explain why.

d. Use figures to explain why the factories have temporarily or permanently shut down. How does a factory decide whether to shut down temporarily or permanently?

12. Chinese art factories are flooding the world's generic art market (Keith Bradsher, "Own Original Chinese Copies of Real Western Art!" *New York Times*, July 15, 2005). The value of bulk shipments of Chinese paintings to the United States nearly tripled from slightly over $10 million in 1996 to $30.5 million in 2004 (and early 2005 sales were up 50% from the corresponding period in 2004). A typical artist earns less than $200 a month, plus modest room and board, or $360 a month without food and housing. Using a steplike supply function (similar to the one in the "Upward-Sloping Long-Run Supply Curve for Cotton" application), show how the entry of the Chinese affects

the world supply curve and how this change affects the equilibrium (including who produces art). Explain.

13. Cheap handheld video cameras have revolutionized the hard-core pornography market. Previously, making movies required expensive equipment and some technical expertise. Now anyone with a couple thousand dollars and a moderately steady hand can buy and use a video camera to make a movie. Consequently, many new firms have entered the market, and the supply curve of porn movies has slithered substantially to the right. Whereas only 1,000 to 2,000 video porn titles were released annually in the United States from 1986 to 1991, that number grew to nearly 10,000 by 1999 ("Branded Flesh," *Economist,* August 14, 1999: 56). Use a side-by-side diagram to illustrate how this technological innovation affected the long-run supply curve and the equilibrium in this market.

14. In June 2005, Eastman Kodak announced that it would no longer produce black-and-white photographic paper—the type used to develop photographs by a traditional darkroom process. Kodak based its decision on the substitution of digital photography for traditional photography. In making its exit decision, did Kodak compare the price of its paper and average variable cost (at its optimal output)? Alternatively, did Kodak compare the price of its paper and average total cost (again, at its optimal output)? **W**

15. During the winter of 2004–2005, wholesale gasoline prices rose rapidly. Although retail gasoline prices increased, retailers' profit per gallon fell. The difference between price and average variable cost for self-service regular gasoline averaged 7.7¢ a gallon in the first quarter of 2005 compared with 9.1¢ for all of 2004. Further, many gasoline retailers exited the market (Thaddeus Herrick, "Pumping Profits from Gas Sales Is Tough to Do," *Wall Street Journal,* May 25, 2005, B1).

    a. Show how an increase in wholesale gasoline prices affects the individual retailer's marginal cost and supply curves.
    b. Show how shifts in the individual retailer's supply curves affect the market supply curve.
    c. Show and explain why an $x per gallon increase in wholesale gasoline prices results in a retail market price increase that is less than $x.
    d. Identify the effect of wholesale gasoline price increases on the profit margins of an individual gasoline retailer.
    e. Why has the increase in wholesale gasoline prices prompted many gasoline retailers to exit the market? **W**

16. When natural gas prices rose in the first half of 2004, producers considered using natural gas fields that once had been passed over because of the high costs of extracting the gas (Russell Gold, "Natural Gas Is Likely to Stay Pricey," *Wall Street Journal,* June 14, 2004: A2).

    a. Show in a figure what this statement implies about the shape of the natural gas extraction cost function.

    b. Use the cost function you drew in part a to show how an increase in the market price of natural gas affects the amount of gas that a competitive firm extracts. Show the change in the firm's equilibrium profit. **W**

17. In late 2004 and early 2005, the price of raw coffee beans jumped as much as 50% from the previous year. In response, the price of roasted coffee rose about 14%. Why would firms increase the price less than in proportion to the rise in the cost of raw beans?

18. Fierce storms in October 2004 caused TomatoFest Organic Heirlooms Farm to end its tomato harvest two weeks early. According to Gary Ibsen, a partner in this small business (Carlyn Said, "Tomatoes in Trouble," *San Francisco Chronicle,* October 29, 2004: C1, C2), TomatoFest lost about 20,000 pounds of tomatoes that would have sold for about $38,000; however, because he did not have to hire pickers and rent trucks during these two weeks, his net loss was about $20,000. In calculating the revenue lost, he used the post-storm price, which was double the pre-storm price. Assume that TomatoFest's experience was typical of that of many small tomato farms.

    a. Draw a diagram for a typical farm next to one for the market to show what happened as a result of the storm.
    b. Did TomatoFest suffer an economic loss? What extra information (if any) do you need to answer this question? How do you define "economic loss" in this situation?

19. If we plot a firm's profit against the number of vacation days taken by its owner, Julia, we find that profit first rises with vacation days (a few days of vacation improve Julia's effectiveness as a manager the rest of the year) but eventually falls as she takes more vacation days. Use a diagram to determine whether Julia takes the number of vacation days that maximizes profit given that she has usual-shaped indifference curves between profit and vacation days. Explain.

20. The "Upward-Sloping Long-Run Supply Curve for Cotton" application shows a supply curve for cotton. Discuss the equilibrium if the world demand curve crosses this supply curve in either (a) a flat section labeled "Brazil" or (b) the vertical section to its right. What do farms in the United States do?

21. Mercedes-Benz of San Francisco advertises on the radio that it has been owned and operated by the same family in the same location for 44 years (as of 2006). It then makes two claims: first, that because it has owned this land for 44 years, it has lower overhead than other nearby auto dealers, and second, because of its lower overhead, it charges a lower price on its cars. Discuss the logic of these claims.

22. In Solved Problem 8.5, would it make a difference to the analysis whether the franchise tax were collected annually or only once when the firm starts operation? How would each of these franchise taxes affect the firm's long-run supply curve? Explain your answer.

23. Answer Solved Problem 8.5 for the short run rather than for the long run. (*Hint:* The answer depends on where the demand curve intersects the original short-run supply curve.)

24. A San Francisco supervisor called for a tax on plastic grocery store bags collected from the stores (Suzanne Herel, "Grocery Store Bag Fee Lacks Public Support; Supervisors Ponder Lower Charge, Other Ways to Reduce Use," *San Francisco Chronicle*, May 13, 2005: B1, B4). He said that he had never intended that this surcharge be passed on to consumers. Does such a tax affect marginal cost? By how much? How much of the tax would store likely pass on to consumers? In 2007, San Francisco's Board of Supervisors instead banned plastic bags. Compare the grocery store equilibrium with a tax and a ban.

*25. What is the effect on firm and market equilibrium of the U.S. law requiring a firm to give its workers six months' notice before it can shut down its plant?

26. Redraw Figure 8.10 to show the situation where the short-run plant size is too large, relative to the optimal long-run plant size.

27. Is it true that the long-run supply curve for a good is horizontal only if the long-run supply curves of all factors are horizontal? Explain.

28. Navel oranges are grown in California and Arizona. If Arizona starts collecting a specific tax per orange from its firms, what happens to the long-run market supply curve? (*Hint:* You may assume that all firms initially have the same costs. Your answer may depend on whether unlimited entry occurs.)

29. Americans bought 33 million real Christmas trees and 40 million artificial trees in 1994. The number of tree producers had fallen by about a third over the previous 10 years, to about 2,000 in 1994, due to artificial tree sales. That year, trees sold for an average of $26.50, about 50¢ more than the previous year. Retailers' average cost was $20. In 1998, 33 million trees sold for an average of $29.25. Use graphs to illustrate this information.

30. Bribes paid by Swiss companies to foreign officials, which had been tax deductible since 1946, are no longer deductible as of 1999. Use economic models from this chapter and Chapter 7 to show the likely effects of this ban on the bribing behavior of Swiss firms.

31. To reduce pollution, the California Air Resources Board in 1996 required the reformulation of gasoline sold in California. In 1999, a series of disasters at California refineries substantially cut the supply of gasoline and contributed to large price increases. Environmentalists and California refiners (who had sunk large investments to produce the reformulated gasoline) opposed imports from other states, which would have kept prices down. To minimize fluctuations in prices in California, Severin Borenstein and Steven Stoft suggest setting a 15¢ surcharge on sellers of standard gasoline. In normal times, none of this gasoline would be sold, because it costs only 8¢ to 12¢ more to produce the California version. However, when disasters trigger a large shift in the supply curve of gasoline, firms could profitably import standard gasoline and keep the price in California from rising more than about 15¢ above prices in the rest of the United States. Use figures to evaluate Borenstein and Stoft's proposal.

Problems

32. If the cost function for John's Shoe Repair is $C(q) = 100 + 10q - q^2 + \frac{1}{3}q^3$, what is the firm's marginal cost function? What is its profit-maximizing condition if the market price is p? What is its supply curve?

*33. If a competitive firm's cost function is $C(q) = a + bq + cq^2 + dq^3$, where a, b, c, and d are constants, what is the firm's marginal cost function? What is the firm's profit-maximizing condition?

34. Each firm in a competitive market has a cost function of $C = 16 + q^2$. The market demand function is $Q = 24 - p$. Determine the long-run equilibrium price, quantity per firm, market quantity, and number of firms.

*35. The finding that the average real price of abortions has remained relatively constant over the last 25 years suggests that the supply curve is horizontal. Medoff (1997) estimated that the price elasticity of demand for abortions ranges from −0.70 to −0.99. By how much would the market price of abortions and the number of abortions change if a lump-sum tax is assessed on abortion clinics that raises their minimum average cost by 10%? Use a figure to illustrate your answer.

*36. Derive the residual supply elasticity Equation 8.17. What is the formula if there are n identical countries?

*37. As of 2005, the federal specific tax on gasoline is 18.4¢ per gallon, and the average state specific tax is 20.2¢, ranging from 7.5¢ in Georgia to 25¢ in Connecticut (down from 38¢ in 1996). A statistical study (Chouinard and Perloff, 2004) finds that the incidence (Chapter 2) of the federal specific tax on consumers is substantially lower than that from state specific taxes. When the federal specific tax increases by 1¢, the retail price rises by about $\frac{1}{2}$¢: Retail consumers bear half the tax incidence. In contrast, when a state that uses regular gasoline increases its specific tax by 1¢, the incidence of the tax falls almost entirely on consumers: The retail price rises by nearly 1¢.

a. What are the incidences of the federal and state specific gasoline taxes on firms?

b. Explain why the incidence on consumers differs between a federal and a state specific gasoline tax, assuming that the market is competitive. (*Hint:* Consider the residual supply curve facing a state compared to the supply curve facing the nation.)

c. Using the residual supply Equation 8.17, estimate how much more elastic is the residual supply elasticity to one state than is the national supply elasticity. (For simplicity, assume that all 50 states are identical.)

*38. Answer Solved Problem 8.5 using calculus. (*Note:* This comparative statics problem is difficult because you will need to solve two or three equations simultaneously, and hence you probably need to use matrix techniques.)

39. What is the effect of an *ad valorem* tax of α (the share of the price that goes to the government) on a competitive firm's profit-maximizing output?

40. Consider the Christmas tree seller in the application "Breaking Even on Christmas Trees." Suppose that the seller's cost function is $C = 6,860 + (p_T + t + 7/12)q + 37/27,000,000q^3$, where p_T is the wholesale price of each tree and t is the shipping price per tree. Suppose $p_T = \$11.50$ and $t = \$2.00$.

a. What is the seller's marginal cost function?

b. What is the shutdown price?

c. What is the seller's short-run supply function?

d. If the seller's supply curve is $S(q, t)$, what is $\partial(q, t)/\partial t$? Evaluate it at $p_T = \$11.50$ and $t = \$2.00$. **W**

41. Joey operates a lemonade stand. His cost of the lemons, sugar, and water per 8 oz. glass is 15¢. Joey's fixed cost is $180. Joey sells five glasses of lemonade per hour that he operates.

a. When he was eight years old, Joey had a near zero opportunity cost of time. What was Joey's total cost function? What was his marginal cost function? What was his shutdown price?

b. Joey has aged and is now 17. If he were not selling lemonade, he would be working six hours per day at $6 per hour; and then would be spending the remainder of the day with his friends. Joey's total value of the time he spends with his friends, t, is $6t + t^2$. What is Joey's total cost function? What is his marginal cost function, $MC(q)$? What is his shutdown price?

c. Compare the shutdown prices of 8-year-old and 17-year-old Joey. **W**

Properties and Applications of the Competitive Model

No more good must be attempted than the public can bear. —Thomas Jefferson

In 2004, the World Trade Organization (WTO), which referees global trade disputes, ruled that the European Union, Japan, Canada, and other U.S. trading partners could slap $150 million per year in retaliatory trade sanctions on U.S. exports until the United States eliminated the Byrd amendment. The Byrd amendment allowed the United States to fine foreign countries that were believed to be dumping their products in the United States at below the true costs, and to turn the fines over to the allegedly harmed U.S. firms. Two years later in 2006, to prevent a trade war, Europe, the United States, and Canada called on the WTO to set up an adjudication tribunal to rule against China on its tariff (import tax) on auto parts imports.

How do such trade conflicts and government actions affect consumers and producers? This chapter shows how the competitive model can answer this type of question. One of the major strengths of the competitive market model is that it can predict how trade wars, changes in government policies, global warming, and major cost-saving discoveries affect consumers and producers.

We start by examining the properties of a competitive market and then consider how government actions and other shocks affect the market and its properties. We concentrate on two main properties of such a market. First, firms in a competitive equilibrium generally make zero (economic) profit. Second, competition maximizes a measure of societal welfare. To most people, the term *welfare* refers to the government's payments to the poor. However, no such meaning is implied when economists employ the term. Economists use *welfare* to refer to the well-being of various groups such as consumers and producers. They call an analysis of the impact of a change on various groups' well-being a study of *welfare economics*. The chapter introduces a measure, *producer surplus*, that is closely related to profit and that economists frequently employ to determine whether firms gain or lose when the equilibrium of a competitive market changes. The sum of producer surplus and *consumer surplus* (Chapter 5) equals the measure of welfare that we use in this chapter. By predicting the effects of a proposed policy on consumer surplus, producer surplus, and welfare, economists can advise policymakers as to who will benefit, who will lose, and what the net effect of this policy will be. To decide whether to adopt a particular policy, policymakers can combine these predictions with their normative views (values), such as whether they are more interested in helping the group that gains or the group that loses.

1. **Zero Profit for Competitive Firms in the Long Run:** In the long-run competitive market equilibrium, profit-maximizing firms break even, so firms that do not try to maximize profits lose money and leave the market.

In this chapter, we examine six main topics

2. **Producer Welfare:** How much producers gain or lose from a change in the equilibrium price can be measured by using information from the marginal cost curve or by measuring the change in profits.

3. **How Competition Maximizes Welfare:** Competition maximizes a measure of social welfare based on consumer and producer welfare.

4. **Policies That Shift Supply Curves:** Government policies that limit the number of firms in competitive markets harm consumers and lower welfare.

5. **Policies That Create a Wedge Between Supply and Demand Curves:** Government policies such as taxes, price ceilings, price floors, and tariffs that create a wedge between the supply and demand curves reduce the equilibrium quantity, raise the equilibrium price to consumers, and lower welfare.

6. **Comparing Both Types of Policies: Trade:** Policies that limit supply (such as quotas or bans on imports) or create a wedge between supply and demand (such as tariffs, which are taxes on imports) have different welfare effects when both policies reduce imports by equal amounts.

9.1 Zero Profit for Competitive Firms in the Long Run

Competitive firms earn zero profit in the long run whether or not entry is completely free. As a consequence, competitive firms must maximize profit.

ZERO LONG-RUN PROFIT WITH FREE ENTRY

The long-run supply curve is horizontal if firms are free to enter the market, firms have identical cost, and input prices are constant. All firms in the market are operating at minimum long-run average cost. That is, they are indifferent between shutting down or not shutting down because they are earning zero profit.

One implication of the shutdown rule is that firms are willing to operate in the long run even if they are making zero profit. This conclusion may seem strange unless you remember that we are talking about *economic profit,* which is revenue minus opportunity cost. Because opportunity cost includes the value of the next best investment, at a zero long-run economic profit, firms are earning the normal business profit that they could earn by investing elsewhere in the economy.

For example, if a firm's owner had not built the plant the firm uses to produce, the owner could have spent that money on another business or put the money in a bank. The opportunity cost of the current plant, then, is the forgone profit from what the owner could have earned by investing the money elsewhere.

The five-year after-tax accounting return on capital across all firms is 10.5%, indicating that the typical firm earned a business profit of 10.5¢ for every dollar it invested in capital (*Forbes*). These firms were earning roughly zero economic profit but positive business profit.

Because business cost does not include all opportunity costs, business profit is larger than economic profit. Thus *a profit-maximizing firm may stay in business if it earns zero long-run economic profit, but the firm shuts down if it earns zero long-run business profit.*

ZERO LONG-RUN PROFIT WHEN ENTRY IS LIMITED

In some markets, firms cannot enter in response to long-run profit opportunities. The number of firms in these markets may be limited because the supply of an input is limited. For example, only so much land is suitable for mining uranium, and only a few people have the superior skills needed to play professional basketball.

One might think that firms could make positive long-run economic profits in such markets; however, that's not true. The reason firms earn zero economic profits is that firms bidding for the scarce input drive its price up until the firms' profits are zero.

Suppose that the number of acres suitable for growing tomatoes is limited. Figure 9.1 shows a typical farm's average cost curve if the rental cost of land is zero (the average cost curve includes only the farm's costs of labor, capital, materials, and energy—not land). At the market price p^*, the firm produces q^* bushels of tomatoes and makes a profit of π^*, the shaded rectangle in the figure.

Thus if the owner of the land does not charge rent, the farmer makes a profit. Unfortunately for the farmer, the landowner rents the land for π^*, so the farmer actually earns zero profit. Why does the landowner charge that much? The reason is that π^* is the opportunity cost of the land: The land is worth π^* to other potential farmers. These farmers will bid against each other to rent this land until the rent is driven up to π^*.

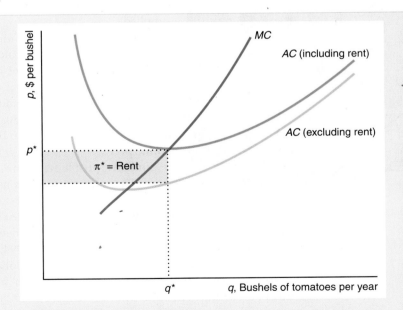

Figure 9.1 Rent. If farmers did not have to pay rent for their farms, a farmer with relatively high-quality land would earn a positive long-run profit of π^*. Due to competitive bidding for this land, however, the rent equals π^*, so the landlord reaps all the benefits of the superior land, and the farmer earns a zero long-run economic profit.

This rent is a fixed cost to the farmer because it does not vary with the amount of output. Thus the rent affects the farm's average cost curve but not its marginal cost curve.

As a result, if the farm produces at all, it produces q^*, where its marginal cost equals the market price, no matter what rent is charged. The higher average cost curve in the figure includes a rent equal to π^*. The minimum point of this average cost curve is p^* at q^* bushels of tomatoes, so the farmer earns zero economic profit.

If the demand curve shifts to the left so that the market price falls, the farmer will make short-run losses. In the long run, the rental price of the land will fall enough that, once again, each farm earns zero economic profit.

Does it make a difference whether farmers own or rent the land? Not really. The opportunity cost to a farmer who owns superior land is the amount for which that land could be rented in a competitive land market. Thus the economic profit of both owned and rented land is zero at the long-run equilibrium.

Good-quality land is not the only scarce resource. The price of any fixed factor will be bid up in the same way so that economic profit for the firm is zero in the long run.

Similarly, the government may require that a firm have a license to operate and then limit the number of licenses. The price of the license gets bid up by potential entrants, driving profit to zero. For example, the license fee is $326,000 a year for the hot dog stand on the north side of the steps of the Metropolitan Museum of Art in New York City.

A scarce input—whether its fixed factor is a person with high ability or land—earns an extra opportunity value. This extra opportunity value is called a **rent:** a payment to the owner of an input beyond the minimum necessary for the factor to be supplied.

Bonnie manages a store for the salary of $30,000, which is what a typical manager is paid. Because she's a superior manager, however, the firm earns an economic profit of $50,000 a year. Other firms, seeing what a good job Bonnie is doing, offer her a higher salary. The bidding for her services drives her salary up to $80,000: her $30,000 base salary plus the $50,000 rent. After paying this rent to Bonnie, the store makes zero economic profit.

Similarly, people with unusual abilities can earn staggering rents. Though no law stops anyone from trying to become a professional entertainer, most of us do not have enough talent that others will pay to watch us perform. By the time Cher ended (one hopes) her four-year-long "Never Can Say Goodbye" tour at the Hollywood Bowl on April 30, 2005, she had sold nearly $200 million worth of tickets. In 1994, the Rolling Stones' concert tour grossed $121.2 million ($159 million in May 2005 dollars). To put these receipts in perspective, these amounts exceed many small nations' 2005 gross domestic product (the value of total output in millions of U.S. dollars): $132 million (U.S. dollars) in Anguilla (population: 13,638); $76 million, Kiribati (105,432); $144 million, Marshall Islands (56,417); $60 million, Nauru (13,287); $145 million, Palau (20,579); $57 million, São Tomé and Príncipe (193,413); and $15 million, Tuvalu (11,810).

In short, if some firms in a market make short-run economic profits due to a scarce input, the other firms in the market bid for that input. This bidding drives up the price of the factor until all firms earn zero long-run profits. In such a market, the supply curve is flat because all firms have the same minimum long-run average cost.

THE NEED TO MAXIMIZE PROFIT

The worst crime against working people is a company which fails to operate at a profit.
—Samuel Gompers, first president of the American Federation of Labor

In a competitive market with identical firms and free entry, if most firms are profit-maximizing, profits are driven to zero at the long-run equilibrium. Any firm that does not maximize profit—that is, any firm that sets its output so that its marginal cost exceeds the market price or that fails to use the most cost-efficient methods of production—will lose money. Thus *to survive in a competitive market, a firm must maximize its profit.*

9.2 Producer Welfare

Economists often use a measure that is closely related to profit when evaluating the effects of policies on firms' welfare. We developed a measure of consumer welfare—consumer surplus—in Chapter 5. A firm's gain from participating in the market is measured by its **producer surplus** (*PS*), which is the difference between the amount for which a good sells and the minimum amount necessary for the seller to be willing to produce the good. The minimum amount that a seller must receive to be willing to produce is the firm's avoidable production cost (the shutdown rule discussed in Chapter 8).

MEASURING PRODUCER SURPLUS USING A SUPPLY CURVE

To determine a competitive firm's producer surplus, we use its supply curve: its marginal cost curve above its minimum average variable cost (Chapter 8). The firm's supply curve in panel a of Figure 9.2 looks like a staircase. The marginal cost of producing the first unit is $MC_1 = \$1$, which is the area under the marginal cost curve between 0 and 1. The marginal cost of producing the second unit is $MC_2 = \$2$, and so on. The variable cost, *VC*, of producing 4 units is the sum of the marginal costs for the first 4 units: $VC = MC_1 + MC_2 + MC_3 + MC_4 = \$1 + \$2 + \$3 + \$4 = \$10$.

If the market price, *p*, is $4, the firm's revenue from the sale of the first unit exceeds its cost by $PS_1 = p - MC_1 = \$4 - \$1 = \$3$, which is its producer surplus on the first unit. The firm's producer surplus is $2 on the second unit and $1 on the third unit. On the fourth unit, the price equals marginal cost, so the firm just breaks even. As a result, the firm's total producer surplus, *PS*, from selling 4 units at $4 each is the sum of its producer surplus on these 4 units: $PS = PS_1 + PS_2 + PS_3 + PS_4 = \$3 + \$2 + \$1 + \$0 = \$6$.[1] Graphically, the total producer surplus is the area above the supply curve and below the market price up to the quantity actually produced. This same reasoning holds when the firm's supply curve is smooth, as in panel b.

---

[1]The firm is indifferent between producing the fourth unit or not. Its producer surplus would be the same if it produced only three units, because its marginal producer surplus from the fourth unit is zero.

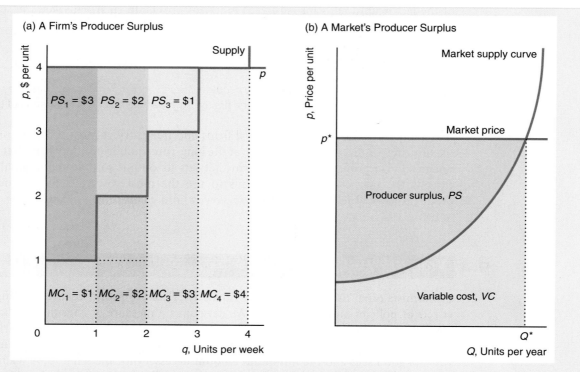

Figure 9.2 Producer Surplus. (a) The firm's producer surplus, $6, is the area below the market price, $4, and above the marginal cost (supply curve) up to the quantity sold, 4. The area under the marginal cost curve up to the number of units actually produced is the variable cost of production.

(b) The market producer surplus is the area above the supply curve and below the line at the market price, p^*, up to the quantity produced, Q^*. The area below the supply curve and to the left of the quantity produced by the market, Q^*, is the variable cost of producing that level of output.

The producer surplus is found by integrating the difference between the firm's demand function—the straight line at p—and its marginal cost function, $MC(q)$, up to the quantity produced, q^* (here $q^* = 4$ units):[2]

$$PS = \int_0^{q^*} [p - MC(q)]dq = pq^* - VC(q^*) = R(q^*) - VC(q^*), \qquad (9.1)$$

where $R = pq^*$ is revenue. In panel a of Figure 9.2, revenue is $R = \$4 \times 4 = \$16$ and variable cost is $VC = \$10$, so producer surplus is $PS = \$6$.

Producer surplus is closely related to profit. Profit is revenue minus total cost, C, which equals variable cost plus fixed cost, F:

$$\pi = R - C = R - (VC + F). \qquad (9.2)$$

---

[2]As we noted in Chapter 7, the marginal cost can be obtained by differentiating with respect to output either the variable cost function, $VC(q)$, or the total cost function, $C(q) = VC(q) + F$, because F is a constant. When we integrate under the marginal cost function, we obtain the variable cost function (that is, we cannot recover the constant fixed cost).

Thus the difference between producer surplus, Equation 9.1, and profit, Equation 9.2, is fixed cost, $PS - \pi = F$. If the fixed cost is zero (as often occurs in the long run), producer surplus equals profit.[3]

Another interpretation of producer surplus is as a gain to trade. In the short run, if the firm produces and sells its good—that is, if the firm trades—it earns a profit of $\pi = R - VC - F$. If the firm shuts down—does not trade—it loses its fixed cost of $-F$. Thus producer surplus equals the profit from trading minus the loss (fixed costs) it incurs from not trading:

$$PS = (R - VC - F) - (-F) = R - VC.$$

USING PRODUCER SURPLUS

Even in the short run, we can use producer surplus to study the effects of any shock that does not affect the fixed cost of firms, such as a change in the price of a substitute or an input. Such shocks change profit by exactly the same amount as they change producer surplus because fixed costs do not change.

A major advantage of producer surplus is that we can use it to measure the effect of a shock on *all* the firms in a market without having to measure the profit of each firm in the market separately. We can calculate market producer surplus using the market supply curve in the same way that we calculate a firm's producer surplus using its supply curve. The market producer surplus in panel b of Figure 9.2 is the area above the supply curve and below the market price line at p^* up to the quantity sold, Q^*. The market supply curve is the horizontal sum of the marginal cost curves of each of the firms (Chapter 8).

SOLVED PROBLEM 9.1

Green et al. (2005) estimate the inverse supply curve for California processed tomatoes as $p = 0.693Q^{1.82}$, where Q is the quantity of processing tomatoes in millions of tons per year and p is the price in dollars per ton. If the price falls from $60 (where the quantity supplied is about 11.6) to $50 (where the quantity supplied is approximately 10.5), how does producer surplus change? Illustrate in a figure. Show that you can obtain a good approximation using rectangles and triangles. (Round results to the nearest tenth.)

Answer

1. *Calculate the producer surplus at each price (or corresponding quantity) and take the difference to determine how producer surplus changes:* When price is $60, the producer surplus is

$$PS_1 = \int_0^{11.6} (60 - 0.693Q^{1.82})\,dQ = 60Q - \frac{0.693}{2.82}Q^{2.82}\Big|_0^{11.6} \approx 449.3.$$

---

[3]Even though each competitive firm makes zero profit in the long run, owners of scarce resources used in that market may earn rents, as we discussed in Section 9.1. Thus owners of scarce resources may receive positive producer surplus in the long run.

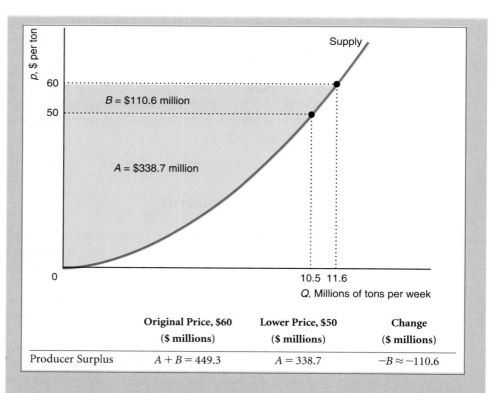

	Original Price, $60 ($ millions)	Lower Price, $50 ($ millions)	Change ($ millions)
Producer Surplus	$A + B = 449.3$	$A = 338.7$	$-B \approx -110.6$

The producer surplus at the new price is $PS_2 = \int_0^{10.5}\left(50 - 0.693Q^{1.82}\right)dQ \approx$ 338.7. Thus the change in producer surplus is $\Delta PS = PS_2 - PS_1 \approx -110.6$.

2. *At each price, the producer surplus is the area above the supply curve below the price up to the quantity sold:* In the figure, area A corresponds to PS_2 because it is the area above the supply curve, below the price of $50, up to the quantity 10.5. Similarly, PS_1 is the sum of areas A and B, so the loss in producer surplus, ΔPS, is area B.

3. *Approximate area B as the sum of a rectangle and a triangle:* Area B consists of a rectangle with a height of 10 ($= 60 - 50$) and a length of 10.5 and a shape that's nearly a triangle with a height of 10 and a width of 1.1 ($= 11.6 - 10.5$). The sum of the areas of the rectangle and the triangle is $(10 \times 10.5) + (1/2 \times 10 \times 1.1) = 110.5$, which is close to the value, 110.6, that we obtained by integrating.

9.3 How Competition Maximizes Welfare

How should we measure society's welfare? There are many reasonable answers to this question. One commonly used measure of the welfare of society, W, is the sum of consumer surplus (Chapter 5) plus producer surplus:

$$W = CS + PS.$$

This measure implicitly weights the well-being of consumers and producers equally. By using this measure, we are making a value judgment that the well-being of consumers and that of producers are equally important.

Not everyone agrees that society should try to maximize this measure of welfare. Groups of producers argue for legislation that helps them even if it hurts consumers by more than the producers gain—as though only producer surplus matters. Similarly, some consumer advocates argue that we should care only about consumers, so social welfare should include only consumer surplus.

In this chapter, we use the consumer surplus plus producer surplus measure of welfare (and postpone a further discussion of other welfare concepts until the next chapter). One of the most striking results in economics is that competitive markets maximize this measure of welfare. If either less or more output than the competitive level is produced, welfare falls.

WHY PRODUCING LESS THAN THE COMPETITIVE OUTPUT LOWERS WELFARE

Producing less than the competitive output lowers welfare. At the competitive equilibrium in Figure 9.3, e_1, where output is Q_1 and price is p_1, consumer surplus equals area $CS_1 = A + B + C$, producer surplus is $PS_1 = D + E$, and total welfare is $W_1 = A + B + C +$

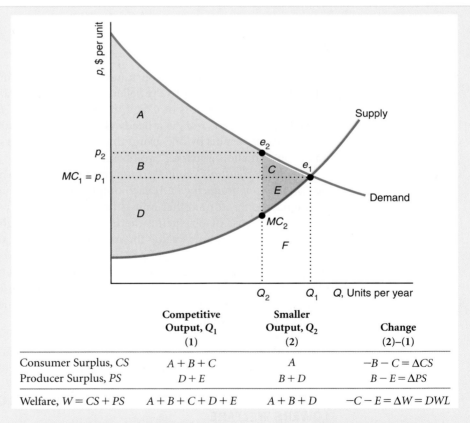

	Competitive Output, Q_1 (1)	Smaller Output, Q_2 (2)	Change (2)–(1)
Consumer Surplus, CS	$A + B + C$	A	$-B - C = \Delta CS$
Producer Surplus, PS	$D + E$	$B + D$	$B - E = \Delta PS$
Welfare, $W = CS + PS$	$A + B + C + D + E$	$A + B + D$	$-C - E = \Delta W = DWL$

Figure 9.3 **Why Reducing Output from the Competitive Level Lowers Welfare.** Reducing output from the competitive level, Q_1, to Q_2 causes price to increase from p_1 to p_2. Consumers suffer: Consumer surplus is now A, a fall of $\Delta CS = -B - C$. Producers may gain or lose: Producer surplus is now $B + D$, a change of $\Delta PS = B - E$. Overall, welfare falls by $\Delta W = -C - E$, which is a deadweight loss (*DWL*) to society.

$D + E$. If output is reduced to Q_2 so that price rises to p_2 at e_2, consumer surplus is $CS_2 = A$, producer surplus is $PS_2 = B + D$, and welfare is $W_2 = A + B + D$.

The change in consumer surplus is

$$\Delta CS = CS_2 - CS_1 = A - (A + B + C) = -B - C.$$

Consumers lose B because they have to pay $p_2 - p_1$ more than at the competitive price for the Q_2 units they buy. Consumers lose C because they buy only Q_2 rather than Q_1 at the higher price.

The change in producer surplus is

$$\Delta PS = PS_2 - PS_1 = (B + D) - (D + E) = B - E.$$

Producers gain B because they now sell Q_2 units at p_2 rather than at p_1. They lose E because they sell $Q_2 - Q_1$ fewer units.

The change in welfare is

$$
\begin{aligned}
\Delta W &= W_2 - W_1 \\
&= (CS_2 + PS_2) - (CS_2 + PS_2) \\
&= (CS_2 - CS_1) + (PS_2 - PS_1) \\
&= \Delta CS + \Delta PS \\
&= (-B - C) + (B - E) \\
&= -C - E.
\end{aligned}
$$

The area B is a transfer from consumers to producers—the extra amount consumers pay for the Q_2 units goes to the sellers—so it does not affect welfare. Welfare drops because the consumer loss of C and the producer loss of E benefit no one. This drop in welfare, $\Delta W = -C - E$, is a **deadweight loss** (*DWL*): the net reduction in welfare from a loss of surplus by one group that is not offset by a gain to another group from an action that alters a market equilibrium.

The deadweight loss results because consumers value extra output by more than the marginal cost of producing it. At each output between Q_2 and Q_1, consumers' marginal willingness to pay for another unit—the height of the demand curve—is greater than the marginal cost of producing the next unit—the height of the supply curve. For example, at e_2, consumers value the next unit of output at p_2, which is much greater than the marginal cost, MC_2, of producing it. Increasing output from Q_2 to Q_1 raises firms' variable cost by area F, the area under the marginal cost (supply) curve between Q_2 and Q_1. Consumers value this extra output by the area under the demand curve between Q_2 and Q_1, area $C + E + F$. Thus consumers value the extra output by $C + E$ more than it costs to produce it.

Society would be better off producing and consuming extra units of this good than spending this amount on other goods. In short, *the deadweight loss is the opportunity cost of giving up some of this good to buy more of another good.*

WHY PRODUCING MORE THAN THE COMPETITIVE OUTPUT LOWERS WELFARE

Increasing output beyond the competitive level also decreases welfare because the cost of producing this extra output exceeds the value consumers place on it. Figure 9.4 shows the effect of increasing output from the competitive level Q_1 to Q_2 and letting the price fall to p_2, point e_2 on the demand curve, so consumers buy the extra output.

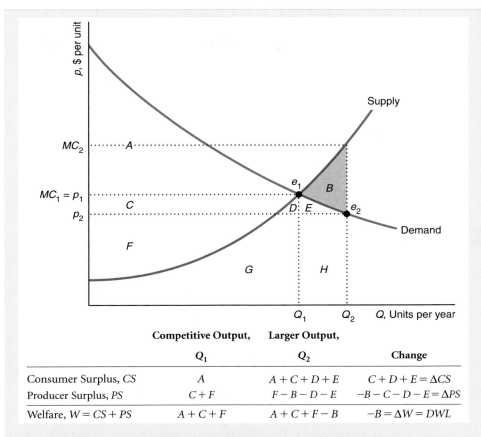

	Competitive Output, Q_1	Larger Output, Q_2	Change
Consumer Surplus, CS	A	$A + C + D + E$	$C + D + E = \Delta CS$
Producer Surplus, PS	$C + F$	$F - B - D - E$	$-B - C - D - E = \Delta PS$
Welfare, $W = CS + PS$	$A + C + F$	$A + C + F - B$	$-B = \Delta W = DWL$

Figure 9.4 Why Increasing Output from the Competitive Level Lowers Welfare. Increasing output from the competitive level, Q_1, to Q_2 lowers the price from p_1 to p_2. Consumer surplus rises by $C + D + E$, producer surplus falls by $B + C + D + E$, and welfare falls by B, which is a deadweight loss to society.

Because price falls from p_1 to p_2, consumer surplus rises by

$$\Delta CS = C + D + E,$$

which is the area between p_2 and p_1 to the left of the demand curve. At the original price, p_1, producer surplus was $C + F$. The cost of producing the larger output is the area under the supply curve up to Q_2, $B + D + E + G + H$. The firms sell this quantity for only $p_2 Q_2$, area $F + G + H$. Thus the new producer surplus is $F - B - D - E$. As a result, the increase in output causes producer surplus to fall by

$$\Delta PS = -B - C - D - E.$$

Because producers lose more than consumers gain, the deadweight loss is

$$\Delta W = \Delta CS + \Delta PS = (C + D + E) + (-B - C - D - E) = -B.$$

A net loss occurs because consumers value the $Q_2 - Q_1$ extra output by only $E + H$, which is less than the extra cost, $B + E + H$, of producing it. The new price, p_2, is less than the marginal cost, MC_2, of producing Q_2. Too much is being produced.

The reason that competition maximizes welfare is that price equals marginal cost at the competitive equilibrium. At the competitive equilibrium, demand equals supply, which ensures that price equals marginal cost. When price equals marginal cost, consumers value the last unit of output by exactly the amount that it costs to produce it. If consumers value the last unit by more than the marginal cost of production, welfare rises if more is produced. Similarly, if consumers value the last unit by less than its marginal cost, welfare is higher at a lower level of production.

A **market failure** is inefficient production or consumption, often because a price exceeds marginal cost. In the next application, we show that the surplus for the recipient of a gift is often less than the giver's cost, and hence is inefficient.

● **APPLICATION**

Deadweight Loss of Christmas Presents

Just how much did you enjoy the expensive woolen socks with the dancing purple teddy bears that your Aunt Fern gave you last Christmas? Often the cost of a gift exceeds the value that the recipient places on it.

Only 10% to 15% of holiday gifts are money. A gift of cash typically gives at least as much pleasure to the recipient as a gift that costs the same but can't be exchanged for cash. (So what if giving cash is tacky?) Of course, it's possible that a gift can give more pleasure to the recipient than it cost the giver—but how often does that happen to you?

An "efficient" gift is one that the recipient values as much as the gift cost the giver. The difference between the price of the gift and its value to the recipient is a deadweight loss to society. Joel Waldfogel (1993) asked Yale undergraduates just how large this deadweight loss is. He estimated that the deadweight loss is between 10% and 33% of the value of gifts. Waldfogel (2004) found that consumers value their own purchases at 10% to 18% more, per dollar spent, than items received as gifts. He found that gifts from friends and "significant others" are most efficient, while noncash gifts from members of the extended family are least efficient (one-third of the value is lost). Luckily, grandparents, aunts, and uncles are most likely to give cash.

Given holiday expenditures of about $40 billion per year in the United States, he concluded that a conservative estimate of the deadweight loss of Christmas, Hanukkah, and other holidays with gift-giving rituals is between a tenth and a third as large as estimates of the deadweight loss from inefficient income taxation.

People sometimes deal with a lame present by "regifting" it. Some families have been passing the same fruitcake among family members for decades. According to a survey just before Christmas in 2004, 33% of women and 19% of men admitted that they pass on an unwanted gift to someone else (and 28% of respondents said that they would not admit it if asked whether they had done so).

The question remains why people don't give cash instead of presents. If the reason is that they get pleasure from picking the "perfect" gift, the deadweight loss that adjusts for the pleasure of the giver is lower than these calculations suggest. (Bah, humbug!)

9.4　Policies That Shift Supply Curves

> *I don't make jokes. I just watch the government and report the facts.* —Will Rogers

One of the main reasons that economists developed welfare tools was to predict the impact of government programs that alter a competitive equilibrium. Virtually all government actions affect a competitive equilibrium in one of two ways. Some government policies, such as limits on the number of firms in a market, shift the supply or demand curve. Others, such as sales taxes, create a wedge or gap between price and marginal cost so that they are not equal, even though they were in the original competitive equilibrium.

These government interventions move us from an unconstrained competitive equilibrium to a new, constrained competitive equilibrium. Because welfare was maximized at the initial competitive equilibrium, the examples of government-induced changes that we consider here lower welfare. In later chapters, we examine markets in which government intervention may raise welfare because welfare was not maximized initially.

Although government policies may cause either the supply curve or the demand curve to shift, we concentrate on policies that limit supply because they are frequently used and have clear-cut effects. The two most common types of government policies that shift the supply curve are limits on the number of firms in a market and quotas or other limits on the amount of output that firms may produce. We study restrictions on entry and exit of firms in this section and examine quotas later in the chapter.

Government policies that cause a decrease in supply at each possible price (that is, shift the supply curve to the left) lead to fewer purchases by consumers at higher prices, an outcome that lowers consumer surplus and welfare. Welfare falls when governments restrict the consumption of competitive products that we all agree are *goods*, such as food and medical services. In contrast, if most of society wants to discourage the use of certain products, such as hallucinogenic drugs and poisons, policies that restrict consumption may increase some measures of society's welfare.

Governments, other organizations, and social pressures limit the number of firms in at least three ways. The number of firms is restricted explicitly in some markets such as the one for taxi service. In other markets, some members of society are barred from owning firms or performing certain jobs or services. In yet other markets, the number of firms is controlled indirectly by raising the cost of entry.

RESTRICTING THE NUMBER OF FIRMS

A limit on the number of firms causes the supply curve to shift to the left. As a result, the equilibrium price rises and the equilibrium quantity falls. Consumers are harmed: They do not buy as much as they would at lower prices. Firms that are in the market when the limits are first imposed benefit from higher profits.

To illustrate these results, we examine the regulation of taxicabs. Countries throughout the world regulate taxicabs. Many American cities limit the number of taxicabs. To operate a cab in these cities legally, you must possess a city-issued permit, which may be a piece of paper or a medallion.

Two explanations are given for such regulation. First, using permits to limit the number of cabs raises the earnings of permit owners—usually taxi fleet owners—who lobby city officials for such restrictions. Second, some city officials contend that limiting cabs allows for better regulation of cabbies' behavior and protection of consumers. (However, it would seem possible that cities could directly regulate behavior and not restrict the number of cabs.)

Whatever the justification for such regulation, the limit on the number of cabs raises the market prices. If the city does not limit entry, a virtually unlimited number of potential taxi drivers with identical costs can enter freely.

Panel a of Figure 9.5 shows a typical taxi owner's marginal cost curve, MC, and average cost curve, AC^1. The MC curve slopes upward because a typical cabbie's opportunity cost of working more hours increases as the cabbie works longer hours (drives more customers). An outward shift of the demand curve is met by new firms entering, so the long-run supply curve of taxi rides, S^1 in panel b, is horizontal at the minimum of AC^1 (Chapter 8). For the market demand curve in the figure, the equilibrium is E_1, where the equilibrium price, p_1, equals the minimum of AC^1 of a typical cab. The total number of rides is $Q_1 = n_1 q_1$, where n_1 is the equilibrium number of cabs and q_1 is the number of rides per month provided by a typical cab.

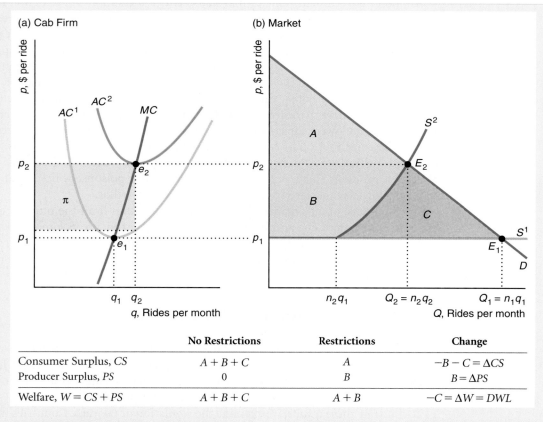

	No Restrictions	Restrictions	Change
Consumer Surplus, CS	$A + B + C$	A	$-B - C = \Delta CS$
Producer Surplus, PS	0	B	$B = \Delta PS$
Welfare, $W = CS + PS$	$A + B + C$	$A + B$	$-C = \Delta W = DWL$

Figure 9.5 Effect of a Restriction on the Number of Cabs. A restriction on the number of cabs causes the supply curve to shift from S^1 to S^2 in the short run and the equilibrium to change from E_1 to E_2. The resulting lost surplus, C, is a deadweight loss to society. In the long run, the unusual profit, π, created by the restriction becomes a rent to the owner of the license. As the license owner increases the charge for using the license, the average cost curve rises to AC^2, so the cab driver earns a zero long-run profit. That is, the producer surplus goes to the permit holder, not to the cab driver.

Consumer surplus, $A + B + C$, is the area under the market demand curve above p_1 up to Q_1. There is no producer surplus because the supply curve is horizontal at the market price, which equals marginal and average cost. Thus welfare is the same as consumer surplus.

Legislation limits the number of permits to operate cabs to $n_2 < n_1$. The market supply curve, S^2, is the horizontal sum of the marginal cost curves above minimum average cost of the n_2 firms in the market. For the market to produce more than $n_2 q_1$ rides, the price must rise to induce the n_2 firms to supply more.

With the same demand curve as before, the equilibrium market price rises to p_2. At this higher price, each licensed cab firm produces more than before by operating longer hours, $q_2 > q_1$, but the total number of rides, $Q_2 = n_2 q_2$, falls because there are fewer cabs, n_2. Consumer surplus is A, producer surplus is B, and welfare is $A + B$.

Thus because of the higher fares (prices) under a permit system, consumer surplus falls by

$$\Delta CS = -B - C.$$

The producer surplus of the lucky permit owners rises by

$$\Delta PS = B.$$

As a result, total welfare falls,

$$\Delta W = \Delta CS + \Delta PS = (-B - C) + B = -C,$$

which is a deadweight loss.

By preventing other potential cab firms from entering the market, limiting cab permits creates economic profit, the area labeled π in panel a, for permit owners. In many cities, these permits can be sold or rented, so the owner of the scarce resource, the permit, can capture the unusual profit, or rent. The rent for the permit or the implicit rent paid by the owner of a permit causes the cab driver's average cost to rise to AC^2. Because the rent allows the use of the cab for a certain period of time, it is a fixed cost that is unrelated to output. As a result, it does not affect the marginal cost.

Cab drivers earn zero economic profits because the market price, p_2, equals their average cost, the minimum of AC^2. The producer surplus, B, created by the limits on entry goes to the original owners of the permits rather than to the current cab drivers. Thus the permit owners are the *only* ones who benefit from the restrictions, and their gains are less than the losses to others. If the government collected the rents each year in the form of an annual license, then these rents could be distributed to all citizens instead of to just a few lucky permit owners.

In many cities, the rents and welfare effects that result from these laws are large. The size of the loss to consumers and the benefit to permit holders depend on how severely a city limits the number of cabs.

APPLICATION

Cab Fare

Too bad the only people who know how to run the country are busy driving cabs and cutting hair. —George Burns

Limiting the number of cabs has large effects in cities around the world. Some cities regulate the number of cabs much more strictly than others. Tokyo has five

times as many cabs as New York City. San Francisco, which limits cabs, has only a tenth as many cabs as Washington, D.C., which has fewer people but does not restrict the number of cabs. The number of residents per cab is 757 in Detroit, 748 in San Francisco, 538 in Dallas, 533 in Baltimore, 350 in Boston, 301 in New Orleans, and 203 in Honolulu.

In San Francisco, permit holders lease their permits for up to $3,500 a month to taxi companies, which own only about a quarter of all permits. Thus each permit is worth up to $42,000 a year. This rent is the extra producer surplus of the lucky permit holders that would be eliminated if anyone could supply taxi services.

In 1937, when New York City started regulating the number of cabs, all 11,787 cab owners could buy a permit, called a medallion, for $10. Because New York City allows these medallions to be sold, medallion holders do not have to operate a cab to benefit from the restriction on the number of cabs. A holder can sell a medallion for an amount that captures the unusually high future profits from the limit on the number of cabs. The number of medallions has hardly increased to only 12,779 in 2006 and another 308 in 2007 for hybrid-electric or "green" taxicabs. Because the number of users of cabs has increased substantially, this limit has become more binding over time, so the price of a medallion has soared. In a 2004 auction, a license sold for $344,400. In 2005, New York City auctioned an extra 300 taxi permits to the tune of $90 million. The cumulative value of New York City taxi licenses was $3.3 billion—nearly equal to the $3.6 billion insured value of the World Trade Center. The average winning bid for a green taxi medallion in 2007 was $514,328, so the value continues to soar.

Medallion systems in other cities have also generated large medallion values: for example, $250,000 in Boston and $55,000 in Chicago as of mid-2003. Taxi licenses usually sell for £25,000 ($44,400) in the United Kingdom and for more than $100,000 in Rome as of 2005.

Cab drivers do not make unusual returns. New York City cab drivers who lease medallions earn as little as $50 to $115 a day. In Boston, cabbies average 72 hours a week driving someone else's taxi, to net maybe $550.

A 1984 study for the U.S. Department of Transportation estimated consumers' annual extra cost from restrictions on the number of taxicabs throughout the United States at nearly $1.9 billion (in 2005 dollars). The total lost consumer surplus is even greater because this amount does not include lost waiting time and other inconveniences associated with having fewer taxis. Movements toward liberalizing entry into taxi markets started in the United States in the 1980s and in Sweden, Ireland, the Netherlands, and the United Kingdom in the 1990s, but tight regulation remains common throughout the world.

RAISING ENTRY AND EXIT COSTS

Instead of directly restricting the number of firms that may enter a market, governments and other organizations may raise the cost of entering, thereby indirectly restricting that number. Similarly, raising the cost of exiting a market discourages some firms from entering.

Entry Barriers. If its cost will be greater than that of firms already in the market, a potential firm might not enter a market even if existing firms are making a profit. Any cost that falls only on potential entrants and not on current firms discourages entry. A long-run **barrier to entry** is an explicit restriction or a cost that applies only to potential new firms—existing firms are not subject to the restriction or do not bear the cost.

At the time they entered, incumbent firms had to pay many of the costs of entering a market that new entrants incur, such as the fixed costs of building plants, buying equipment, and advertising a new product. For example, the fixed cost to McDonald's and other fast-food chains of opening a new fast-food restaurant is about $2 million. These fixed costs are *costs of entry* but are *not* barriers to entry because they apply equally to incumbents and entrants. Costs incurred by both incumbents and entrants do not discourage potential firms from entering a market if existing firms are making money. Potential entrants know that they will do as well as existing firms once they are in business, so they are willing to enter as long as profit opportunities exist.

Large sunk costs can be barriers to entry under two conditions. First, if capital markets do not work well so that new firms have difficulty raising money, new firms may be unable to enter profitable markets. Second, if a firm must incur a large *sunk* cost, which makes the loss if it exits great, the firm may be reluctant to enter a market in which it is uncertain of success.

Exit Barriers. Some markets have barriers that make it difficult (though typically not impossible) for a firm to exit by going out of business. In the short run, exit barriers can keep the number of firms in a market relatively high. In the long run, exit barriers may limit the number of firms in a market.

Why do exit barriers limit the number of firms in a market? Suppose that you are considering starting a construction firm with no capital or other fixed factors. The firm's only input is labor. You know that there is relatively little demand for construction during business downturns and in the winter. To avoid paying workers when business is slack, you plan to shut down during those periods. If you can avoid losses by shutting down during those periods, you enter this market if your expected economic profits during good periods are zero or positive.

A law that requires you to give your workers six months' warning before laying them off prevents you from shutting down quickly. You know that you'll regularly suffer losses during business downturns because you'll have to pay your workers for up to six months during periods when you have nothing for them to do. Knowing that you'll incur these regular losses, you are less inclined to enter the market. Unless the economic profits during good periods are much higher than zero—high enough to offset your losses—you will not enter the market. See "Job Termination Laws," in Chapter 9 of **www.ac-bc.com/perloff.**

If exit barriers limit the number of firms, the same analysis that we used to examine entry barriers applies. Thus exit barriers may raise prices, lower consumer surplus, and reduce welfare.

9.5 | Policies That Create a Wedge Between Supply and Demand Curves

The most common government policies that create a wedge between supply and demand curves are sales taxes (or subsidies) and price controls. Because these policies create a gap between marginal cost and price, either too little or too much is produced. For example, a tax causes price to exceed marginal cost—that is, consumers value the good more than it costs to produce it—with the result that consumer surplus, producer surplus, and welfare fall (although tax revenue rises).

WELFARE EFFECTS OF A SALES TAX

A new sales tax causes the price that consumers pay to rise (Chapter 2), resulting in a loss of consumer surplus, $\Delta CS < 0$, and the price that firms receive to fall, resulting in a drop in producer surplus, $\Delta PS < 0$. However, the new tax provides the government with new tax revenue, $\Delta T = T > 0$, if tax revenue was zero before this new tax.

Assuming that the government does something useful with the tax revenue, we should include tax revenue in our definition of welfare:

$$W = CS + PS + T.$$

As a result, the change in welfare is

$$\Delta W = \Delta CS + \Delta PS + \Delta T.$$

Even when we include tax revenue in our welfare measure, a specific tax must lower welfare in, for example, the competitive market for tea roses. We show the welfare loss from a specific tax of $\tau = 11¢$ per rose stem in Figure 9.6. (In the following analysis, we use the estimated rose demand curve, our earlier calculations concerning the consumer surplus from Chapter 5, and an estimated supply curve.)

Without the tax, the intersection of the demand curve, D, and the supply curve, S, determines the competitive equilibrium, e_1, at a price of 30¢ per stem and a quantity of 1.25 billion rose stems per year. Consumer surplus is $A + B + C$; producer surplus is $D + E + F$; tax revenue is zero; and there is no deadweight loss.

The specific tax shifts the effective supply curve up by 11¢, creating an 11¢ wedge or differential between the price consumers pay, 32¢, and the price producers receive, $32¢ - \tau = 21¢$. Equilibrium output falls from 1.25 to 1.16 billion stems per year.

The extra 2¢ per stem that buyers pay causes consumer surplus to fall by $B + C = \$24.1$ million per year, as we showed earlier. Due to the 9¢ drop in the price firms receive, they lose producer surplus of $D + E = \$108.45$ million per year (Solved Problem 9.1). The government gains tax revenue of $\tau Q = 11¢$ per stem $\times$ 1.16 billion stems per year $= \$127.6$ million per year, area $B + D$.

The combined loss of consumer surplus and producer surplus is only partially offset by the government's gain in tax revenue, so welfare drops:

$$\Delta W = \Delta CS + \Delta PS + \Delta T = -\$24.1 - \$108.45 + \$127.6 = -\$4.95 \text{ million per year.}$$

This deadweight loss is area $C + E$.

Why does society suffer a deadweight loss? The reason is that the tax lowers output from the competitive level where welfare is maximized. An equivalent explanation for this inefficiency or loss to society is that the tax puts a wedge between price and marginal cost. At the new equilibrium, buyers are willing to pay 32¢ for one more rose

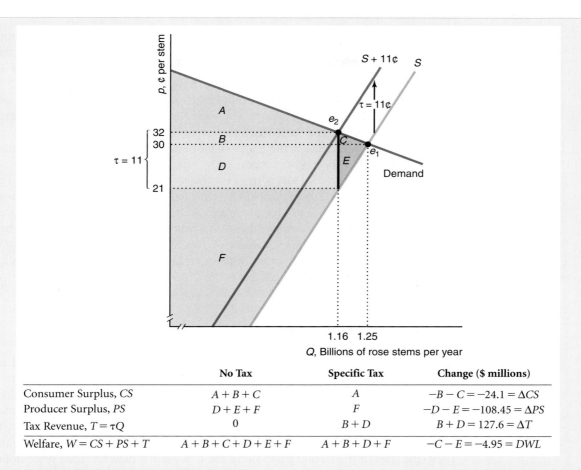

	No Tax	Specific Tax	Change ($ millions)
Consumer Surplus, CS	$A + B + C$	A	$-B - C = -24.1 = \Delta CS$
Producer Surplus, PS	$D + E + F$	F	$-D - E = -108.45 = \Delta PS$
Tax Revenue, $T = \tau Q$	0	$B + D$	$B + D = 127.6 = \Delta T$
Welfare, $W = CS + PS + T$	$A + B + C + D + E + F$	$A + B + D + F$	$-C - E = -4.95 = DWL$

Figure 9.6 Welfare Effects of a Specific Tax on Roses. The $\tau = 11¢$ specific tax on roses creates an 11¢ per stem wedge between the price customers pay, 32¢, and the price producers receive, 21¢. Tax revenue is $T = \tau Q = \$127.6$ million per year. The deadweight loss to society is $C + E = \$4.95$ million per year.

stem, while the marginal cost to firms is only 21¢ (= the price minus τ). Shouldn't at least one more rose be produced if consumers are willing to pay nearly a third more than the cost of producing it? That's what our welfare study indicates.

● APPLICATION

Deadweight Loss from Wireless Taxes

Federal, state, and local government taxes and fees on cell phone and other wireless services create deadweight loss by raising costs to consumers and reducing the quantity demanded. These fees vary substantially across jurisdictions. The median state tax is 10%, and the median combined state and federal tax is 14.5%, which corresponds to a yearly payment of about $91. California and Florida have even higher state taxes of 21%, so their combined taxes are 25.5%, or $185 per year (and New York's is nearly as high). Overall, governments raise about $4.8 billion in wireless taxes.

The marginal cost of supplying a minute of wireless service is constant at about 5¢. If this market is competitive, the market supply curve is horizontal, producer surplus is zero, and the entire incidence of the tax is on consumers (see Chapter 2). Thus a tax inflicts consumer surplus loss but not producer surplus loss.

Hausman (2000) estimated the deadweight loss (efficiency cost) to the economy from taxes to be about $2.6 billion.[4] For every $1 raised in tax revenue, the average efficiency cost is 53¢, and the loss in high-tax states is about 70¢. Moreover, for every additional tax dollar raised, the marginal efficiency cost is 72¢ for the typical state and about 93¢ for the high-tax states.

The wireless efficiency loss is large relative to that imposed by other taxes. For example, estimates of the marginal efficiency loss per dollar of income tax range from 26¢ to 41¢. One reason for the relatively large wireless efficiency losses is that the price elasticity of mobile telephones is about −0.7, which is more elastic than that for other telecommunications services (see Solved Problem 5.2). In contrast, a tax on landlines creates almost no deadweight loss because the price elasticity for local landline phone service is virtually zero (−0.005).

WELFARE EFFECTS OF A PRICE FLOOR

In some markets, the government sets a *price floor*, or minimum price, which is the lowest price a consumer can legally pay for the good. For example, in most countries, the government creates price floors under at least some agricultural prices to guarantee producers that they will receive at least a price of $\underline{p}$ for their good. If the market price is above $\underline{p}$, the support program is irrelevant. If the market price is below $\underline{p}$, however, the government buys as much output as necessary to drive the price up to $\underline{p}$. Since 1929 (the start of the Great Depression), the U.S. government has used price floors or similar programs to keep the prices of many agricultural products above the price that competition would determine in unregulated markets.

My favorite program is the wool and mohair subsidy. The U.S. government instituted wool price supports after the Korean War to ensure "strategic supplies" for uniforms. Congress later added mohair subsidies, even though mohair has no military use. In some years, the mohair subsidy exceeded the amount consumers paid for mohair, and the subsidies on wool and mohair reached a fifth of a billion dollars over the first half-century of support. No doubt the Clinton-era end of these subsidies in 1995 endangered national security. Thanks to Senator Phil Gramm, a well-known fiscal conservative, and other patriots (primarily from Texas, where much mohair is produced), the subsidy was resurrected in 2000.[5] Representative Lamar Smith took vehement exception to people who questioned the need to subsidize mohair: "Mohair is popular! I have a mohair sweater! It's my favorite one!" The 2006 budget called for $11 million for wool and mohair with a loan rate of $4.20 per pound.

---

[4]We can analyze the consumer surplus loss from taxes in both competitive and noncompetitive markets similarly. Hausman took account of higher than competitive pretax prices in his analysis of the wireless market.

[5]As U.S. Representative Lynn Martin said, "No matter what your religion, you should try to become a government program, for then you will have everlasting life."

We now show the effect of a price support using estimated supply and demand curves for the soybean market (Holt, 1992). The intersection of the market demand curve and the market supply curve in Figure 9.7 determines the competitive equilibrium, e, in the absence of a price support program, where the equilibrium price is $p_1 = 4.59 per bushel and the equilibrium quantity is $Q_1 = 2.1$ billion bushels per year.

With a price support on soybeans of $\underline{p} = 5.00 per bushel and the government's pledge to buy as much output as farmers want to sell, quantity sold is $Q_s = 2.2$ billion bushels.[6] At $\underline{p}$, consumers buy less output, $Q_d = 1.9$ billion bushels, than the Q_1 they would have bought at the market-determined price p_1. As a result, consumer surplus falls by $B + C = 864 million. The government buys $Q_g = Q_s - Q_d \approx 0.3$ billion bushels per year, which is the excess supply, at a cost of $T = \underline{p} \times Q_g = C + D + F + G = 1.283 billion.

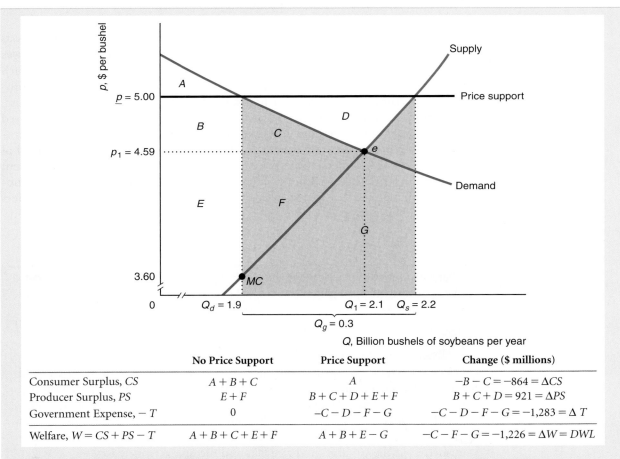

	No Price Support	Price Support	Change ($ millions)
Consumer Surplus, CS	$A + B + C$	A	$-B - C = -864 = \Delta CS$
Producer Surplus, PS	$E + F$	$B + C + D + E + F$	$B + C + D = 921 = \Delta PS$
Government Expense, $-T$	0	$-C - D - F - G$	$-C - D - F - G = -1,283 = \Delta T$
Welfare, $W = CS + PS - T$	$A + B + C + E + F$	$A + B + E - G$	$-C - F - G = -1,226 = \Delta W = DWL$

Figure 9.7 Effect of Price Supports in Soybeans. Without government price supports, the equilibrium is e, where $p_1 = 4.59 per bushel and $Q_1 = 2.1$ billion bushels of soybeans per year (based on estimates in Holt, 1992). With the price support at $\underline{p} = 5.00 per bushel, output sold increases to Q_s and consumer purchases fall to Q_d, so the government must buy $Q_g = Q_s - Q_d$ at a cost of $1.283 billion per year. The deadweight loss is $C + F + G = 1.226 billion per year, not counting storage and administrative costs.

---

[6]In 1985, the period Holt studied, the price support was $5.02. The 2002 farm bill set the support at $5.80 for 2002–2007.

The government cannot resell the output domestically, because if it tried to do so, it would succeed only in driving down the price consumers pay. Instead, the government stores the output or sends it abroad.

Although farmers gain producer surplus of $B + C + D = \$921$ million, this program is an inefficient way to transfer money to them. Assuming that the government's purchases have no alternative use, the change in welfare is $\Delta W = \Delta CS + \Delta PS - T = -C - F - G = -\$1.226$ billion per year.[7] This deadweight loss reflects two distortions in this market:

- **Excess production:** More output is produced than is consumed, so Q_g is stored, destroyed, or shipped abroad.
- **Inefficiency in consumption:** At the quantity they actually buy, Q_d, consumers are willing to pay $5 for the last bushel of soybeans, which is more than the marginal cost, $MC = \$3.60$, of producing that bushel.

Alternative Price Support. Because of price supports, the U.S. government was buying and storing large quantities of grains and other foods, much of which was allowed to spoil. As a consequence since 1938, the government has limited how much farmers can produce. Because there is uncertainty about how much a farmer will produce, the government sets quotas, or limits, on the amount of land farmers can use, thereby restricting their output. See **www.aw-bc.com/perloff,** Chapter 9, Solved Problem 2. Today, the government uses an alternative subsidy program. The government sets a support price, $\underline{p}$. Farmers decide how much to grow, and they sell all of their produce to consumers at the price, p, that clears the market. The government then gives the farmers a *deficiency* payment equal to the difference between the support and actual prices, $\underline{p} - p$, for every unit sold so that farmers receive the support price on their entire crop.

SOLVED PROBLEM   9.2

What are the effects in the soybean market of a $5-per-bushel price support using a deficiency payment on the equilibrium price and quantity, consumer surplus, producer surplus, and deadweight loss?

Answer

1. *Describe how the program affects the equilibrium price and quantity:* Without a price support, the equilibrium is e_1 in the figure, where the price is $p_1 = \$4.59$ and the quantity is 2.1 billion bushels per year. With a support price of $5 per bushel, the new equilibrium is e_2. Farmers produce at the quantity where the price support line hits their supply curve at 2.2 billion bushels. The equilibrium price is the height of the demand curve at 2.2 billion bushels, or approximately $4.39 per bushel. Thus the equilibrium price falls and the quantity increases.

2. *Show the welfare effects:* Because the price consumers pay drops from p_1 to p_2, consumer surplus rises by area $D + E$. Producers now receive $\underline{p}$ instead of p_1,

---

[7]This measure of deadweight loss underestimates the true loss. The government also pays storage and administration costs. In 2005, the U.S. Department of Agriculture, which runs farm support programs, had 109,832 employees, or one worker for every eight farms that received assistance (although many of these employees have other job responsibilities).

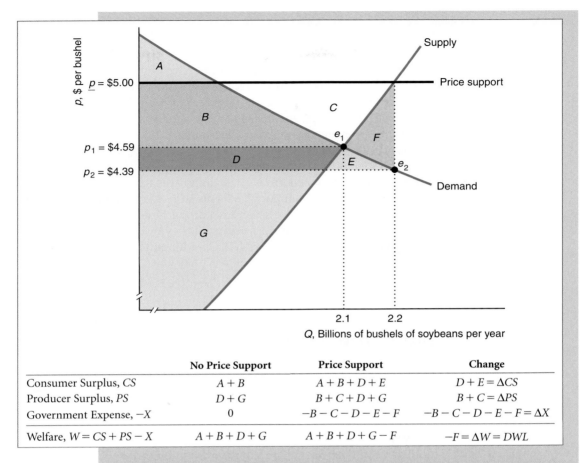

	No Price Support	Price Support	Change
Consumer Surplus, CS	$A + B$	$A + B + D + E$	$D + E = \Delta CS$
Producer Surplus, PS	$D + G$	$B + C + D + G$	$B + C = \Delta PS$
Government Expense, $-X$	0	$-B - C - D - E - F$	$-B - C - D - E - F = \Delta X$
Welfare, $W = CS + PS - X$	$A + B + D + G$	$A + B + D + G - F$	$-F = \Delta W = DWL$

so their producer surplus rises by $B + C$. Government payments are the difference between the support price, $\underline{p} = \$5$, and the price consumers pay, $p_2 = \$4.39$, times the number of units sold, 2.2 billion bushels per year, or the rectangle $B + C + D + E + F$. Because government expenditures exceed the gains to consumers and producers, welfare falls by the deadweight loss triangle F.[8]

Who Benefits. Presumably, the purpose of these programs is to help poor farmers, not to hurt consumers and taxpayers. However, the lion's share of American farm subsidies goes to large agricultural corporations, not to poor farmers. Three-quarters of U.S. farms have sales of less than $50,000 per year, yet these farms received only 16% of the total direct government payments for agriculture in 2003. In contrast, farms with over half a million dollars in annual sales are only 3.5% of all farms, yet they received 29% of all direct government payments. Farms with over a quarter of a million dollars in sales (top 8% of all farms) received 50% of the payments.

---

[8]Compared to the soybean price support program in Figure 9.6, the deficiency payment approach results in a smaller deadweight loss (less than a tenth of the original one) and lower government expenditures (though the expenditures need not be smaller in general).

● **APPLICATION**

Giving Money to Farmers

Virtually every country in the world showers its farmers with subsidies. For example, EU sugar producers receive three times the world price of sugar.

Farmers in developed countries received $280 billion in direct agricultural producer support payments (subsidies) in 2005 (OECD, 2006). These payments are a large percentage of actual sales in many countries, averaging 29% in developed countries, and ranging from 68% in Switzerland, 64% in Norway, 560% in Japan, 32% in the European Union, 21% in Canada, 16% in the United States; but the payment shares are only 5% in Australia and 3% in New Zealand.

Total agricultural support payments were $110 billion in the United States. About 1% of the U.S. gross domestic product goes to support agriculture. Each adult in the United States pays about $500 a year to support agriculture. Did you get full value for your money? (Cargill, Monsanto, and Archer Daniels Midland thank you.)

WELFARE EFFECTS OF A PRICE CEILING

In some markets, the government sets a *price ceiling:* the highest price that a firm can legally charge. If the government sets the ceiling below the pre-control competitive price, consumers demand more than the pre-control equilibrium quantity and firms supply less than that quantity (Chapter 2). Producer surplus must fall because firms receive a lower price and sell fewer units.

Because of the price ceiling, consumers can buy the good at a lower price but cannot buy as much of it as they would like. Because less is sold than at the pre-control equilibrium, there is deadweight loss: Consumers value the good more than the marginal cost of producing extra units.

In the 1970s, the U.S. government used price controls to keep gasoline prices below the market price (Chapter 2). This policy led to long lines at gas stations and large deadweight losses. Frech and Lee (1987) estimated that the loss in consumer surplus in California in 2006 dollars was $2.2 billion during the December 1973 to March 1974 price controls and $1.5 billion during the May 1979 to July 1979 controls.

SOLVED PROBLEM   9.3

What is the effect on the equilibrium and welfare if the government sets a price ceiling, $\bar{p}$, below the unregulated competitive equilibrium price?

Answer

1. *Show the initial unregulated equilibrium:* The intersection of the demand curve and the supply curve determines the unregulated, competitive equilibrium e_1, where the equilibrium quantity is Q_1.

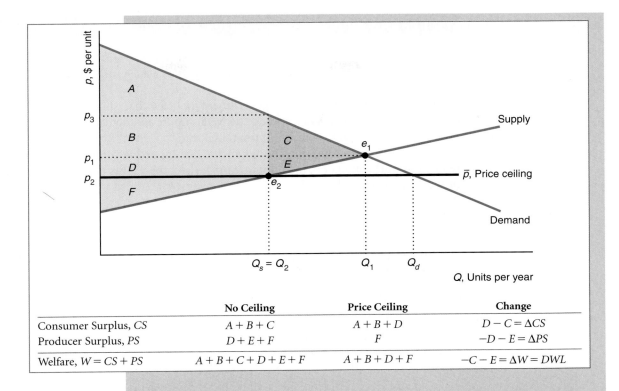

	No Ceiling	Price Ceiling	Change
Consumer Surplus, CS	$A + B + C$	$A + B + D$	$D - C = \Delta CS$
Producer Surplus, PS	$D + E + F$	F	$-D - E = \Delta PS$
Welfare, $W = CS + PS$	$A + B + C + D + E + F$	$A + B + D + F$	$-C - E = \Delta W = DWL$

2. *Show how the equilibrium changes with the price ceiling:* Because the price ceiling, $\bar{p}$, is set below the equilibrium price of p_1, the ceiling binds. At this lower price, consumer demand increases to Q_d while the quantity that firms are willing to supply falls to Q_s, so only $Q_s = Q_2$ units are sold at the new equilibrium, e_2. Thus the price control causes the equilibrium quantity and price to fall, but consumers have excess demand of $Q_d - Q_s$.

3. *Describe the welfare effects:* Because consumers are able to buy Q_s units at a lower price than before the controls, they gain area D. Consumers lose consumer surplus of C, however, because they can purchase only Q_s instead of Q_1 units of output. Thus consumers gain net consumer surplus of $D - C$. Because they sell fewer units at a lower price, firms lose producer surplus $-D - E$. Part of this loss, D, is transferred to consumers because of lower prices, but the rest, E, is a loss to society. The deadweight loss to society is at least $\Delta W = \Delta CS + \Delta PS = -C - E$.

Comment: This measure of the deadweight loss may *underestimate* the true loss. Because consumers want to buy more units than are sold, they may spend time searching for a store that has units for sale. This (unsuccessful) search activity is wasteful and hence a deadweight loss to society. (Strangely, such wasteful search does not occur if the good is efficiently but inequitably distributed to people of one race or one gender, people in the military, or attractive people, or if it is based on some other known discriminatory criterion.) Another possible inefficiency is that consumers who buy the good may value it less than those who are unable to find a unit to purchase. For example, someone might purchase the good who values it at p_2, while someone who values it at p_3 cannot find any to buy.

9.6   Comparing Both Types of Policies: Trade

Traditionally, most of Australia's imports come from overseas.
—Keppel Enderbery, former Australian cabinet minister

We have examined examples of government policies that shift supply or demand curves and policies that create a wedge between supply and demand. Governments use both types of policies to control international trade.

Allowing imports of foreign goods benefits the importing country. If a government reduces imports of a good, the domestic price rises; the profits of domestic firms that produce the good increase, but domestic consumers are hurt. Our analysis will show that the loss to consumers exceeds the gain to producers.

The government of the (potentially) importing country can use one of four trade (import) policies:

- **Allow free trade:** Any firm can sell in the importing country without restrictions.
- **Ban all imports:** The government sets a quota of zero on imports.
- **Set a positive quota:** The government limits imports to $\overline{Q}$.
- **Set a tariff:** The government imposes a tax called a **tariff** (or a *duty*) only on imported goods.

We compare welfare under free trade to welfare under bans and quotas, which change the supply curve, and to welfare under tariffs, which create a wedge between supply and demand.

To illustrate the differences in welfare under these various policies, we examine the U.S. market for crude oil. We also assume, for the sake of simplicity, that transportation costs are zero and that the supply curve of the potentially imported good is horizontal at the world price p^*. Given these two assumptions, the importing country, the United States, can buy as much of this good as it wants at p^* per unit: It is a price taker in the world market because its demand is too small to influence the world price.

FREE TRADE VERSUS A BAN ON IMPORTS

No nation was ever ruined by trade. —Benjamin Franklin

Preventing imports raises the domestic market price, as we illustrated in Chapter 2 for the Japan rice market. We now compare the equilibrium with and without free trade in the U.S. oil market.

The estimated U.S. daily demand function for oil is[9]

$$Q = D(p) = 35.4p^{-0.37}, \tag{9.3}$$

and the U.S. daily domestic supply function is

$$Q = S(p) = 3.35p^{0.33}. \tag{9.4}$$

Although the estimated U.S. domestic supply curve, S^a, in Figure 9.8 is upward sloping, the foreign supply curve is horizontal at the world price of $14.70. The total U.S.

---

[9]These short-run, constant-elasticity supply and demand equations for crude oil in 1988 are based on the short-run supply and demand elasticities reported in Anderson and Metzger (1991).

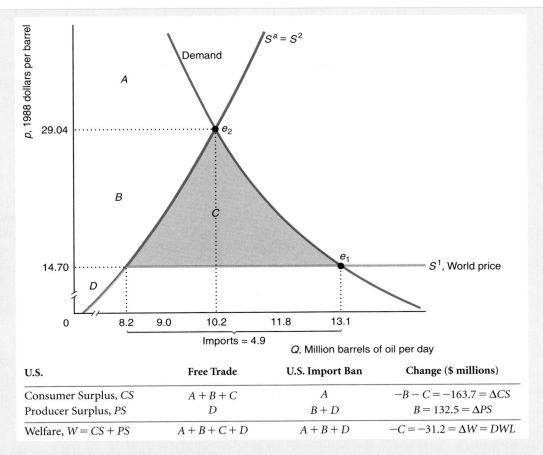

U.S.	Free Trade	U.S. Import Ban	Change ($ millions)
Consumer Surplus, CS	$A + B + C$	A	$-B - C = -163.7 = \Delta CS$
Producer Surplus, PS	D	$B + D$	$B = 132.5 = \Delta PS$
Welfare, $W = CS + PS$	$A + B + C + D$	$A + B + D$	$-C = -31.2 = \Delta W = DWL$

Figure 9.8 Loss from Eliminating Free Trade. Because the supply curve that foreigners face is horizontal at the world price of $14.70, the total U.S. supply curve of crude oil is S^1 when there is free trade. The free-trade equilibrium is e_1. With a ban on imports, the equilibrium e_2 occurs where the domestic supply curve, $S^a = S^2$, intersects D. The ban increases producer surplus by $B = 132.5 million per day and decreases consumer surplus by $B + C = 163.7 million per day, so the deadweight loss is $C = 31.2 million per day or $11.4 billion per year.

supply curve, S^1, is the horizontal sum of the domestic supply curve and the foreign supply curve. Thus S^1 is the same as the upward-sloping domestic supply curve for prices below $14.70 and is horizontal at $14.70. Under free trade, the United States imports crude oil if its domestic price in the absence of imports would exceed the world price, $14.70 per barrel.

The free-trade equilibrium, e_1, is determined by the intersection of S^1 and the demand curve, where the U.S. price equals the world price, $14.70. Substituting $p = 14.70 into demand function 9.3, we find that the equilibrium quantity is about 13.1 [$\approx 35.4(14.70)^{-0.37}$] million barrels per day. At the equilibrium price of $14.70, domestic supply is about 8.2, so imports are 4.9 (= 13.1 − 8.2). U.S. consumer surplus is $A + B + C$, U.S. producer surplus is D, and U.S. welfare is $A + B + C + D$. Throughout our discussion of trade, we ignore welfare effects in other countries.

If imports are banned, the total U.S. supply curve, S^2, is the American domestic supply curve, S^a. The equilibrium is at e_2, where S^2 intersects the demand curve. The new equilibrium price is $29.04, and the new equilibrium quantity, 10.2 million barrels per day, is produced domestically.[10] Consumer surplus is A, producer surplus is $B + D$, and welfare is $A + B + D$.

The ban helps producers but harms consumers. Because of the higher price, domestic firms gain producer surplus of $\Delta PS = B$. The change in consumer surplus is $\Delta CS = -B - C$. Does the ban help the United States? The change in total welfare, ΔW, is the difference between the gain to producers and the loss to consumers, $\Delta W = \Delta PS + \Delta CS = -C$, so the ban hurts society.

SOLVED PROBLEM   9.4

Based on the estimates of the U.S. daily oil demand function 9.3 and the supply function 9.4, use calculus to determine the changes in producer surplus, consumer surplus, and welfare from eliminating free trade. (Round results to the nearest tenth.)

Answer

1. *Integrate with respect to price between the free-trade and no-trade prices to obtain the change in producer surplus:* If imports are banned, the gain in domestic producer surplus is the area to the left of the domestic supply curve between the free-trade price, $14.70, and the price with the ban, $29.04, which is area B in Figure 9.8.[11] Integrating, we find that

$$\Delta PS = \int_{14.70}^{29.04} S(p)\,dp = \int_{14.70}^{29.04} 3.35p^{0.33}\,dp$$

$$= \frac{3.35}{1.33}p^{1.33}\bigg|_{14.70}^{29.04} \approx 2.52(29.04^{1.33} - 14.70^{1.33}) \approx 132.5.$$

2. *Integrate with respect to price between the free-trade and no-trade prices to obtain the change in consumer surplus:* The lost consumer surplus is found by integrating to the left of the demand curve between the relevant prices:

$$\Delta CS = -\int_{14.70}^{29.04} D(p)\,dp = -\int_{14.70}^{29.04} 35.41p^{-0.37}\,dp = -163.7.$$

3. *To determine the change in welfare, sum the changes in consumer surplus and producer surplus:* The change in welfare is $\Delta W = \Delta CS + \Delta PS = -163.7 + 132.5 = -\$31.2$ million per day or $-\$11.4$ billion per year. This deadweight loss is 24% of the gain to producers: Consumers lose $1.24 for every $1 that producers gain from a ban.

---

[10]In equilibrium, the right-hand sides of Equations 9.3 and 9.4 are equal: $35.4p^{-0.37} = 3.35p^{0.33}$. By dividing both sides by $p^{-0.37}$ and 3.35, we find that $p^{0.7} \approx 10.57$. Raising both sides of this expression to the $1/0.7 = 1.43$ power shows that the no-trade equilibrium price is about $29.04. Substituting this price into Equation 9.3 or 9.4 gives us the equilibrium quantity, which is about 10.2.

[11]Earlier we noted that we can also calculate the producer surplus by integrating below the price, above the supply (or marginal cost) function, up to the relevant quantity.

FREE TRADE VERSUS A TARIFF

> *TARIFF, n. A scale of taxes on imports, designed to protect the domestic producer against the greed of his customers.*
> —Ambrose Bierce

There are two common types of tariffs: *specific tariffs* (τ dollars per unit) and *ad valorem tariffs* (α percent of the sales price). In recent years, tariffs have been applied throughout the world, most commonly to agricultural products.[12] American policy-makers have frequently debated the optimal tariff on crude oil as a way to raise revenue or to reduce "dependence" on foreign oil.

You may be asking yourself, "Why should we study tariffs if we've already looked at taxes? Isn't a tariff just another tax?" Good point! Tariffs are just taxes. If only imported goods were sold, the effect of a tariff in the importing country would be the same as for a sales tax. We study tariffs separately because a tariff is applied only to imported goods, so it affects domestic and foreign producers differently.

Because tariffs are applied only to imported goods, all else the same, they do not raise as much tax revenue or affect equilibrium quantities as much as taxes applied to all goods in a market. De Melo and Tarr (1992) found that almost five times more tax revenue would be generated by a 15% additional *ad valorem* tax on petroleum products ($34.6 billion) than by a 25% additional import tariff on oil and gas ($7.3 billion).

To illustrate the effect of a tariff, suppose that the government imposes a specific tariff of $\tau = \$5$ per barrel of crude oil. Given this tariff, firms will not import oil into the United States unless the U.S. price is at least $5 above the world price, $14.70. The tariff creates a wedge between the world price and the American price. This tariff causes the total supply curve to shift from S^1 to S^3 in Figure 9.9. Given that the world's excess supply curve to the United States is horizontal at $14.70, a tariff shifts this supply curve upward so that it is horizontal at $19.70. As a result, the total U.S. supply curve with the tariff, S^3, equals the domestic supply curve for prices below $19.70 and is horizontal at $19.70.

The new equilibrium, e_3, occurs where S^3 intersects the demand curve. At this equilibrium, price is $19.70 and quantity is 11.8 million barrels of oil per day. At this higher price, domestic firms supply 9.0 million barrels, so imports are 2.8 ($= 11.8 - 9.0$).

The tariff *protects* American producers from foreign competition. The larger the tariff, the less oil imported, hence the higher the price that domestic firms can charge. (With a large enough tariff, nothing is imported, and the price rises to the no-trade level, $29.04.) With a tariff of $5, domestic firms' producer surplus increases by area $B = \$42.8$ million per day.

Because of the rise in the price from $14.70 to $19.70, consumer surplus falls by $61.9 million per day. The government receives tariff revenues, T, equal to area $D = \$14$ million per day, which is $\tau = \$5$ times the quantity imported, 2.8.

---

[12]After World War II, most trading nations signed the General Agreement on Tariffs and Trade (GATT), which limited their ability to subsidize exports or limit imports using quotas and tariffs. The rules prohibited most export subsidies and import quotas, except when imports threatened "market disruption" (a term that unfortunately was not defined). The GATT also required that any new tariff be offset by a reduction in other tariffs to compensate the exporting country. Modifications of the GATT and agreements negotiated by its successor, the World Trade Organization, have reduced or eliminated many tariffs.

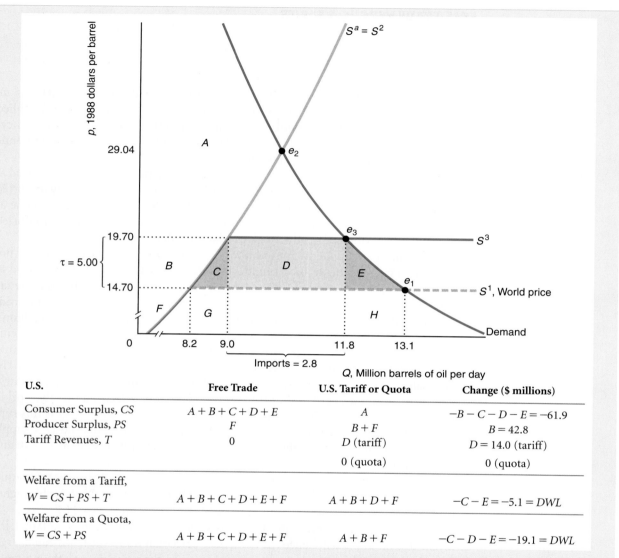

U.S.	Free Trade	U.S. Tariff or Quota	Change ($ millions)
Consumer Surplus, CS	$A + B + C + D + E$	A	$-B - C - D - E = -61.9$
Producer Surplus, PS	F	$B + F$	$B = 42.8$
Tariff Revenues, T	0	D (tariff)	$D = 14.0$ (tariff)
		0 (quota)	0 (quota)
Welfare from a Tariff, $W = CS + PS + T$	$A + B + C + D + E + F$	$A + B + D + F$	$-C - E = -5.1 = DWL$
Welfare from a Quota, $W = CS + PS$	$A + B + C + D + E + F$	$A + B + F$	$-C - D - E = -19.1 = DWL$

Figure 9.9 Effect of a Tariff (or Quota). A tariff of $\tau = \$5$ per barrel of oil imported or a quota of $\overline{Q} = 2.8$ drives the U.S. price of crude oil to \$19.70, which is \$5 more than the world price. Under the tariff, the equilibrium, e_3, is determined by the intersection of the S_3 total U.S. supply curve and the D demand curve. Under the quota, e_3 is determined by a quantity wedge of 2.8 million barrels per day between the quantity demanded, 9.0 million barrels per day, and the quantity supplied, 11.8 million barrels per day. Compared to free trade, producers gain $B = \$42.8$ million per day and consumers lose $B + C + D + E = \$61.9$ million per day from the tariff or quota. The deadweight loss under the quota is $C + D + E = \$19.1$ million per day. With a tariff, the government's tariff revenue increases by $D = \$14$ million a day, so the deadweight loss is only $C + E = \$5.1$ million per day.

The deadweight loss is $C + E = \$5.1$ million per day, or nearly \$1.9 billion per year.[13] This deadweight loss is almost 12% of the gain to producers. Consumers lose

---

[13]If the foreign supply is horizontal, welfare in the importing country *must* fall. However, if the foreign supply is upward sloping, welfare in the importing country may rise.

$1.45 for each $1 that domestic producers gain. Because the tariff does not completely eliminate imports, the welfare loss is smaller than it would be if all imports were banned.

We can interpret the two components of this deadweight loss. First, C is the loss from producing 9.0 million barrels per day instead of 8.2 million barrels per day. Domestic firms produce this extra output because the tariff drives up the price from $14.70 to $19.70. The cost of producing this extra 0.8 million barrels of oil per day domestically is $C + G$, the area under the domestic supply curve, S^a, between 8.2 and 9.0. Had Americans bought this oil at the world price, the cost would have been only $G = \$11.8$ million per day. Thus C is the extra cost of producing the extra 0.8 million barrels of oil per day domestically instead of importing it.

Second, E is a *consumption distortion loss* from American consumers' buying too little oil, 11.8 instead of 13.1 million barrels, because the price rose from $14.70 to $19.70, owing to the tariff. American consumers value this extra output as $E + H$, the area under their demand curve between 11.8 and 13.1, whereas the value in international markets is only H, the area below the line at $14.70 between 11.8 and 13.1. Thus E is the difference between the value at world prices and the value American consumers place on this extra 1.3 million barrels per day.

SOLVED PROBLEM 9.5

Based on the estimates of the U.S. daily oil demand function 9.3 and supply function 9.4 and the preceding discussion, use calculus to determine the change in equilibrium quantity, the amount supplied by domestic firms, and their producer surplus from a marginal increase in a tariff, evaluated where the tariff is initially zero.

Answer

1. *Discuss what effect the tariff has on the U.S. equilibrium quantity and on the domestic supply of oil at the free-trade equilibrium:* Without the tariff, the U.S. supply curve of oil is horizontal at a price of $14.70 ($S^1$ in Figure 9.9), and the equilibrium is determined by the intersection of this horizontal supply curve with the demand curve. With a new, small tariff of τ, the U.S. supply curve is horizontal at $\$14.70 + \tau$, and the new equilibrium quantity is determined by substituting $p = 14.70 + \tau$ into the demand function 9.3: $Q = 35.4(14.70 + \tau)^{-0.67}$. The domestic supply is determined by substituting $\$14.70 + \tau$ into the U.S. supply function 9.4: $Q = 3.35(\$14.70 + \tau)^{0.33}$. Evaluated at $\tau = 0$, the equilibrium quantity remains 13.1 and the domestic supply is still 8.2 million barrels of oil per day.

2. *Differentiate the expression for producer surplus with respect to τ and evaluate at $\tau = 0$:* The producer surplus is the area below $14.70 and to the left of the supply curve (area $B + F$ in Figure 9.9):

$$PS = \int_0^{14.70 + \tau} S(p)\,dp = \int_0^{14.70 + \tau} 3.35p^{0.33}\,dp.$$

To see how a change in τ affects producer surplus, we differentiate PS with respect to τ:[14]

$$\frac{dPS}{d\tau} = \frac{d}{d\tau} \int_0^{14.70 + \tau} S(p)dp = S(14.70 + \tau)$$

$$= \frac{d}{d\tau} \int_0^{14.70 + \tau} 3.35p^{0.33}\,dp = 3.35(14.70 + \tau)^{0.33}.$$

If we evaluate this expression at $\tau = 0$, we find that $dPS/d\tau = S(14.70) = 3.35(14.70)^{0.33} \approx 8.2$ million. That is, the change in producer surplus is $dPS = S(14.70 + \tau)d\tau$. If $\tau = 1$¢, then the change in producer surplus is about $82,000. (Problem 37 asks about the effect of a change of τ on deadweight loss.)

FREE TRADE VERSUS A QUOTA

The effect of a positive quota is similar to that of a tariff. If the government limits imports to $\overline{Q} = 2.8$ million barrels per day, the quota is binding because 4.9 million barrels per day would be imported under free trade. Given this binding quota, at the equilibrium price, the quantity demanded minus the quantity supplied by domestic producers equals 2.8 million barrels per day. In Figure 9.9 where the price is $19.70, the gap between the quantity demanded, 11.8 million barrels per day, and the quantity supplied, 9.0 million barrels per day, is 2.8 million barrels per day. Thus a quota on imports of 2.8 million barrels leads to the same equilibrium, e_3, as a tariff of $5.

The gain to domestic producers, B, and the loss to consumers, $C + E$, are the same as those with a tariff. However, unlike with a tariff, the government does not receive any revenue when it uses a quota (unless the government sells import licenses). Area D may go to foreign exporters. As a result, the deadweight loss from the quota, $19.1 million per day, or $7.0 billion per year, is greater than under the tariff. This deadweight loss is nearly half (45%) of the gains to producers.

Thus the importing country fares better using a tariff than setting a quota that reduces imports by the same amount. Consumers and domestic firms do as well under the two policies, but the government gains tariff revenues, D, only when the tariff is used.

RENT SEEKING

Given that tariffs and quotas hurt the importing country, why do the Japanese, U.S., and other governments impose tariffs, quotas, or other trade barriers? The reason is

---

[14]We are using Leibniz's rule for differentiating a definite integral. According to Leibniz's rule,

$$\frac{d}{d\tau} \int_{a(\tau)}^{b(\tau)} f(\tau, p)dp = \int_{a(\tau)}^{b(\tau)} \frac{\partial f(\tau, p)}{\partial \tau}dp + f[\tau, b(\tau)]\frac{db(\tau)}{d\tau} - f[\tau, a(\tau)]\frac{da(\tau)}{d\tau}.$$

In our problem, neither a nor b are functions of τ.

TABLE 9.1   Welfare Cost of Trade Barriers (millions of 2005 dollars)

Industry	DWL	ΔPS	Government Revenues	ΔCS
Meat products	−31	2,595	75	−2,702
Dairy products[a]	−16,931	30,916	1,160	−45,340
Sugar confectionery[a]	−1,057	4,849	308	−6,211
Grain mill products	−11	1,262	11	−1,178
Fats and oils	−147	2,617	5	−2,770
Beverages	−10	1,210	162	−1,381
Tobacco	−226	4,225	105	−4,555
All food and tobacco	**−14,917**	**53,972**	**2,189**	**−71,075**

[a]Import quotas were the primary instrument of protection.

Notes: As estimated, $\Delta CS = DWL - \Delta PS -$ government revenue. Dollar amounts were adjusted using the Consumer Price Index.

Source: Lopez and Pagoulatos (1994).

that domestic producers stand to make large gains from such government actions; hence it pays for them to organize and lobby the government to enact these trade policies. Although consumers as a whole suffer large losses, the loss to any one consumer is usually small. Moreover, consumers rarely organize to lobby the government about trade issues. Thus in most countries, producers are often able to convince (cajole, influence, or bribe) legislators or government officials to aid them, even though consumers suffer more-than-offsetting losses.

If domestic producers can talk the government into a tariff, quota, or other policy that reduces imports, they gain extra producer surplus (rents), such as area *B* in Figures 9.7 and 9.8. Economists call efforts and expenditures to gain a rent or a profit from government actions **rent seeking.** If producers or other interest groups bribe legislators to influence policy, the bribe is a transfer of income and hence does not increase deadweight loss (except to the degree that a harmful policy is chosen). However, if this rent-seeking behavior—such as hiring lobbyists and engaging in advertising to influence legislators—uses up resources, the deadweight loss from tariffs and quotas understates the true loss to society. The domestic producers may spend an amount up to the gain in producer surplus to influence the government.[15]

Indeed, some economists argue that the government revenues from tariffs are completely offset by administrative costs and rent-seeking behavior. If so (and if the tariffs and quotas do not affect world prices), the loss to society from tariffs and quotas is the entire change in consumer surplus, such as area *B + C* in Figure 9.8 and area *B + C + D + E* in Figure 9.9.

Lopez and Pagoulatos (1994) estimated the deadweight loss and the additional losses due to rent-seeking activities in the United States in food and tobacco products. Table 9.1 summarizes their estimates for several industries in 2005 dollars. They estimated that the deadweight loss is $15 billion, which is 2.6% of the domestic consumption of these products. The largest deadweight losses were in dairy products and sugar manufacturing, which primarily use import quotas to raise domestic prices. The overall gain in

---

[15]This argument was made in Tullock (1967) and Posner (1975). Fisher (1985) and Varian (1989) argued that the expenditure is typically less than the producer surplus.

producer surplus is $54 billion, or 9.5% of domestic consumption. The government obtained $2 billion in tariff revenues, or 0.4% of consumption. If all of producer surplus and government revenues were expended in rent-seeking behavior and other wasteful activities, the total loss is $71 billion, or 12.5% of consumption, which is 4.75 times larger than the deadweight loss alone. In other words, the loss to society is somewhere between the deadweight loss of $15 billion and $71 billion.

Summary

1. **Zero Profit for Competitive Firms in the Long Run:** Although firms may make profits or losses in the short run, they earn zero economic profit in the long run. If necessary, the prices of scarce inputs adjust to ensure that competitive firms make zero long-run profit. Because profit-maximizing firms just break even in the long run, firms that do not try to maximize profits will lose money. Competitive firms must maximize profit to survive.

2. **Producer Welfare:** A firm's gain from trading is measured by its producer surplus. Producer surplus is the largest amount of money that could be taken from a firm's revenue and still leave the firm willing to produce. That is, the producer surplus is the amount that the firm is paid minus its variable cost of production, which is profit in the long run. It is the area below the price and above the supply curve up to the quantity that the firm sells. The effect of a change in a price on a supplier is measured by the change in producer surplus.

3. **How Competition Maximizes Welfare:** One standard measure of welfare is the sum of consumer surplus and producer surplus. The more price is above marginal cost, the lower this measure of welfare. In the competitive equilibrium, in which price equals marginal cost, welfare is maximized.

4. **Policies That Shift Supply Curves:** Governments frequently limit the number of firms in a market directly, by licensing them, or indirectly, by raising the costs of entry to new firms or by raising the cost of exiting. A reduction in the number of firms in a competitive market raises price, hurts consumers, helps producing firms, and lowers the standard measure of welfare. This reduction in welfare is a deadweight loss: The gain to producers is less than the loss to consumers.

5. **Policies That Create a Wedge Between Supply and Demand:** Taxes, price ceilings, and price floors create a gap between the price consumers pay and the price firms receive. These policies force price above marginal cost, which raises the price to consumers and lowers the amount consumed. The wedge between price and marginal cost results in a deadweight loss: The loss of consumer surplus and producer surplus is not offset by increased taxes or by benefits to other groups.

6. **Comparing Both Types of Policies: Trade:** A government may use either a quantity restriction such as a quota, which shifts the supply curve, or a tariff, which creates a wedge, to reduce imports or achieve other goals. These policies may have different welfare implications. A tariff that reduces imports by the same amount as a quota has the same harms—a larger loss of consumer surplus than increased domestic producer surplus—but has a partially offsetting benefit—increased tariff revenues for the government. Rent-seeking activities are attempts by firms or individuals to influence a government to adopt a policy that favors them. By using resources, rent seeking exacerbates the welfare loss beyond the deadweight loss caused by the policy itself. In a perfectly competitive market, government policies frequently lower welfare. As later chapters show, however, in markets that are not perfectly competitive, government policies may increase welfare.

Questions

*= answer at the back of this book; **W** = audio-slide show answers by James Dearden at **www.aw-bc.com/perloff**

1. How would the quantitative effect of a specific tax on welfare change as demand becomes more elastic? As it becomes less elastic? (*Hint:* See Solved Problem 5.2.)

2. What were the welfare effects (who gained, who lost, what was the deadweight loss) of the gasoline price controls described in Chapter 2? Add the relevant areas to a drawing like Figure 2.14.

3. Use an indifference curve diagram (gift goods on one axis and all other goods on the other) to illustrate that one is better off receiving cash than a gift. (*Hint:* See the discussion of gifts in this chapter and the discussion of food stamps in Chapter 5.) Relate your analysis to the "Deadweight Loss of Christmas Presents" application.

*4. What is the long-run welfare effect of a profit tax (the government collects a specified percentage of a firm's profit) assessed on each competitive firm in a market?

5. What is the welfare effect of an *ad valorem* sales tax, α, assessed on each competitive firm in a market?

6. What are the welfare effects of a binding minimum wage? Use a graphical approach to show what happens if all workers are identical. Then describe in writing what is likely to happen to workers who differ by experience, education, age, gender, and race.

*7. What is the welfare effect of a lump-sum tax, $\mathscr{L}$, assessed on each competitive firm in a market? (*Hint:* See Chapter 8.)

8. In 2002, Los Angeles imposed a ban on new billboards. Owners of existing billboards did not oppose the ban. Why? What are the implications of the ban for producer surplus, consumer surplus, and welfare? Who are the producers and consumers in your analysis? How else does the ban affect welfare in Los Angeles?

9. The government wants to drive the price of soybeans above the equilibrium price, p_1, to p_2. It offers growers a payment of x to reduce their output from Q_1 (the equilibrium level) to Q_2, which is the quantity demanded by consumers at p_2. Show in a figure how large x must be for growers to reduce output to this level. What are the effects of this program on consumers, farmers, and total welfare? Compare this approach to (a) offering a price support of p_2, (b) offering a price support and a quota set at Q_1, and (c) offering a price support and a quota set at Q_2.

10. The park service wants to restrict the number of visitors to Yellowstone National Park to Q^*, which is fewer than the current volume. It considers two policies: (a) raising the price of admissions and (b) setting a quota. Compare the effects of these two policies on consumer surplus and welfare. Use a graph to show which policy is superior by your criterion.

11. By 1996, the world price for raw sugar, 11.75¢ per pound, was about half the domestic price, 22.5¢ per pound, because of quotas and tariffs on sugar imports. As a consequence, American-made corn sweetener, which costs 12¢ a pound to make, can be profitably sold. Archer Daniels Midland made an estimated profit of $290 million in 1994 from selling corn sweetener. The U.S. Commerce Department says that the quotas and price supports reduce American welfare by about $3 billion a year. If so, each dollar of Archer Daniels Midland's profit costs Americans about $10. Model the effects of a quota on sugar in both the sugar and corn sweetener markets.

12. A government is considering a quota and a tariff, both of which will reduce imports by the same amount. Why might the government prefer one of these policies to the other?

13. Given that the world supply curve is horizontal at the world price for a given good, can a subsidy on imports raise welfare in the importing country? Explain your answer.

14. Canada has 20% of the world's known freshwater resources, yet many Canadians believe that the country has little or none to spare. Over the years, U.S. and Canadian firms have struck deals to export bulk shipments of water to drought-afflicted U.S. cities and towns. Provincial leaders have blocked these deals in British Columbia and Ontario. Use graphs to show the likely outcome of such barriers to exports on the price and quantity of water used in Canada and in the United States if markets for water are competitive. Show the effects on consumer and producer surplus in both countries.

15. A mayor wants to help renters in her city. She considers two policies that will benefit renters equally. One policy is a *rent control*, which places a price ceiling, $\bar{p}$, on rents. The other is a government housing subsidy of s dollars per month that lowers the amount renters pay (to $\bar{p}$). Who benefits and who loses from these policies? Compare the two policies' effects on the quantity of housing consumed, consumer surplus, producer surplus, government expenditure, and deadweight loss. Does the comparison of deadweight loss depend on the elasticities of supply and demand? (*Hint:* Consider extreme cases.) If so, how?

16. The U.S. Supreme Court ruled in May 2005 that people can buy wine directly from out-of-state vineyards. In the 5–4 decision, the Court held that state laws requiring people to buy directly from wine retailers located in the state violate the Constitution's commerce clause.

    a. Suppose the market for wine in New York is perfectly competitive both before and after the Supreme Court decision. Use the analysis of Section 9.6 to evaluate the effect of the Court's decision on the price of wine in New York.

    b. Evaluate the increase in New York consumer surplus.

    c. How does the increase in consumer surplus depend on the price elasticity of supply and demand? **W**

17. Ethanol, which is distilled from corn, is blended into gasoline (allegedly) to make the gasoline burn cleaner and to increase the supply of fuel. Given that ethanol is a close substitute for gasoline, its price in a competitive market would be closely tied to the price of gasoline. However, ethanol usually costs more to make than gasoline, so its usage depends on federal incentives and clean-air legislation mandates for oil companies to produce cleaner fuels.

    a. Suppose that without federal clean-air legislation mandates, ethanol and gasoline are perfect substitutes. Derive the wholesale-market demand function for ethanol. How does this market demand function depend on the price of gasoline?

    b. Suppose that federal clean-air legislation mandates that at least 5% of automobile fuel must contain ethanol. Derive the wholesale-market demand function for ethanol.

    c. Compare the wholesale-market demand functions of parts a and b.

d. Suppose that for any refining plant output, q gallons per day, the marginal cost of ethanol refining, $MC_e(q)$, is greater than the marginal cost of gasoline refining, $MC_g(q)$. Compare the wholesale-market supply functions of ethanol and gasoline. Show that if the wholesale price of gasoline is sufficiently low, federal mandates are needed to ensure that ethanol is produced, but that if the price of gasoline is sufficiently high, federal mandates are not needed. **W**

18. Government policies affect who gets the scarce water in the western United States and how that water is used. In 2004, farmers in California's Central Valley paid as little as $10 per acre-foot, while in urban San Jose, California, a water agency shelled out $80 an acre-foot. Price differentials between agricultural and other uses can persist only if the groups cannot trade. Critics argue that eliminating the agricultural subsidy would encourage farmers to conserve water. The California Department of Water Resources estimates that doubling water prices would reduce agricultural water use by roughly 30% (Jim Carlton, "Is Water Too Cheap?" *Wall Street Journal*, March 17, 2004, B1). Further, farmers would use water more efficiently. [An alternative approach is to allow farmers to sell their (cheap) water in a competitive market—an approach some areas are using.]

   a. Based on the data in this description, what is the price elasticity of demand for water?
   b. What is the relationship between the price elasticity of demand for water and the effect of a price increase on water conservation? **W**

19. Google, Yahoo!, and other Internet search companies charge advertisers for each click on their ads (which sends the browser to the advertiser's Web site). Per-click advertising fees present an opportunity for "click fraud," an industry term describing someone (say, a rival firm or a hacker) clicking on a Web-search ad with ill intent. If the advertiser can demonstrate that a click was fraudulent, the search company does not bill for that click. A market for click-fraud detectives has developed to fight click fraud. The market demand for the detectives depends on the amount of fraud they can catch, which reduces the firm's advertising bill. Let p_C denote the per-click fee, n denote the number of clicks per month an advertiser generates, and X be the fraction of clicks that are fraudulent. Let Z represent the fraction of fraudulent clicks that a detective can prove are fraudulent.

   a. Show how much money the advertiser can save by hiring a click-fraud detective in terms of p_C, n, X, and Z. What is the advertiser's willingness to pay for the detective services?
   b. Suppose there are 500 advertisers with the following attributes: $p_C = \$5$, $n = 700$, $X = 0.2$, and $Z = 0.8$. There are 200 advertisers with the attributes $p_C = \$9$, $n = 600$,

$X = 0.3$, and $Z = 0.8$. Finally, there are 300 advertisers with the attributes $p_C = \$12$, $n = 100$, $X = 0.1$, and $Z = 0.7$. Draw the inverse market demand curve for click-fraud detectives. [*Hint:* The demand curve is a "step" function (see Figure 9.2a).]

   c. Suppose the market supply curve for click-fraud detective services is perfectly price elastic with an intercept of $500 on the price axis. What is the consumer surplus to the advertisers? **W**

20. There are many possible ways to limit the number of cabs in a city. The most common method is an explicit quota using a medallion that is kept forever and can be resold. One alternative is to charge a high license fee each year, which is equivalent to the city's issuing a medallion or license that lasts only a year. A third option is to charge a daily tax on taxicabs. Using figures, compare and contrast the equilibrium under each of these approaches. Discuss who wins and who loses from each plan, considering consumers, drivers, the city, and (if relevant) medallion owners.

21. Although 23 states barred the sale of self-service gasoline in 1968, most removed the bans by the mid-1970s. By 1992, self-service outlets sold nearly 80% of all U.S. gas, and only New Jersey and Oregon continued to ban self-service sales. Using predicted values for self-service sales for New Jersey and Oregon, Johnson and Romeo (2000) estimated that the ban in those two states raised the price of gasoline by approximately 3¢ to 5¢ per gallon. Why did the ban affect the price? Illustrate using a figure and explain. Show the welfare effects in your figure. Use a table to show who gains or loses.

22. The U.S. Department of Agriculture's (USDA) minimum general recommendation is five servings of fruits and vegetables a day. Jetter et al. (2004) estimated that if consumers followed that guideline, the equilibrium price and quantity of most fruits and vegetables would increase substantially. For example, the price of salad would rise 7.2%, output would increase 3.5%, and growers' revenues would jump 7.3% (presumably, health benefits would occur, too). Use a diagram to illustrate as many of these effects as possible and to show how consumer surplus and producer surplus change. Discuss how to calculate the consumer surplus (given that the USDA's recommendation shifts consumers' tastes or behavior).

23. After Mexico signed the North American Free Trade Agreement (NAFTA) with the United States in 1994, corn imports from the United States doubled within a year, and today U.S. imports are nearly one-third of the corn consumed in Mexico. According to Oxfam (2003), the price of Mexican corn has fallen more than 70% since NAFTA took effect. Part of the reason for this flow south of our border is that the U.S. government subsidizes corn production to the tune of $10 billion a year. According to Oxfam, the

2002 U.S. cost of production was $3.08 per bushel, but the export price was $2.69 per bushel, with the difference reflecting an export subsidy of 39¢ per bushel. The U.S. exported 5.3 metric tons. Use graphs to show the effect of such a subsidy on the welfare of various groups and on government expenditures in the United States and Mexico.

24. In 2004 the Bush administration made a preliminary ruling that China and Vietnam were dumping shrimp in the United States at below their costs, and proposed duties as high as 112%. Suppose that China and Vietnam were subsidizing their shrimp fishers. Show in a diagram who gains and who loses in the United States (compared to the equilibrium in which those nations do not subsidize their shrimp fishers). Currently, the United States imposes a 10.17% antidumping duty (essentially a tariff) on shrimp from these and several other countries. Use your diagram to show how the large tariff would affect government revenues and the welfare of consumers and producers.

25. The United States not only subsidizes producers of cotton (in several ways, including a water subsidy and a price support) but also pays $1.7 billion to U.S. agribusiness and manufacturers to buy American cotton. It has paid $100 million each to Allenberg Cotton and Dunavant Enterprises and large amounts to more than 300 other firms (Elizabeth Becker, "U.S. Subsidizes Companies to Buy Subsidized Cotton," *New York Times*, November 4, 2003: C1, C2). Assume for simplicity that specific subsidies (dollars per unit) are used. Use a diagram to show how applying both subsidies changes the equilibrium from the no-subsidy case. Show who gains and who loses.

26. Using the information in the "Deadweight Loss from Wireless Taxes" application, draw graphs to illustrate why the tax on landlines creates almost no deadweight loss whereas the tax on cell phones creates more substantial deadweight loss.

27. During the Napoleonic Wars, Britain blockaded North America, seizing U.S. vessels and cargo and impressing sailors. At President Thomas Jefferson's request, Congress imposed a nearly complete—perhaps 80%—embargo on international commerce from December 1807 to March 1809. Just before the embargo, exports were about 13% of the U.S. gross national product (GNP). Due to the embargo, U.S. consumers could not find acceptable substitutes for manufactured goods from Europe, and producers could not sell farm produce and other goods for as much as in Europe. According to Irwin (2005), the welfare cost of the embargo was at least 8% of the GNP in 1807. Use graphs to show the effects of the embargo on a market for an exported good and one for an imported good. Show the change in equilibria and the welfare effects on consumers and firms.

28. Show that if the importing country faces an upward-sloping foreign supply curve (excess supply curve), a tariff may raise welfare in the importing country.

*29. Suppose that the government gives rose producers a specific subsidy of $s = 11$¢ per stem (Figure 9.6 shows the original demand and supply curves). What is the effect of the subsidy on the equilibrium prices and quantity, consumer surplus, producer surplus, government expenditures, welfare, and deadweight loss? (*Hint:* A subsidy is a negative tax, so we can use the same approach of shifting a supply curve as we would use with a tax.)

Problems

*30. If the inverse demand function for toasters is $p = 60 - Q$, what is the consumer surplus if price is 30?

31. If the inverse demand function for radios is $p = a - bQ$, what is the consumer surplus if price is $a/2$?

32. If the supply function is $Q = Ap^\eta$, what is the producer surplus if price is $p^\star$?

33. If the inverse demand function for books is $p = 60 - Q$ and the supply function is $Q = p$, what is the initial equilibrium? What is the welfare effect of a specific tax of $\tau = \$2$?

*34. Suppose that the demand curve for wheat is $Q = 100 - 10p$ and that the supply curve is $Q = 10p$. The government imposes a price support at $\underline{p} = 6$ using a deficiency payment program.

   a. What are the quantity supplied, the price that clears the market, and the deficiency payment?

   b. What effect does this program have on consumer surplus, producer surplus, welfare, and deadweight loss?

35. Suppose that the demand curve for wheat is $Q = 100 - 10p$ and that the supply curve is $Q = 10p$. The government imposes a specific tax of $\tau = 1$ per unit.

   a. How do the equilibrium price and quantity change?

   b. What effect does this tax have on consumer surplus, producer surplus, government revenue, welfare, and deadweight loss?

36. Suppose that the demand curve for wheat is $Q = 100 - 10p$ and that the supply curve is $Q = 10p$. The government imposes a price ceiling of $\bar{p} = 3$.

   a. Describe how the equilibrium changes.

   b. What effect does this ceiling have on consumer surplus, producer surplus, and deadweight loss?

*37. Based on the estimates of the U.S. daily oil demand function 9.3 and supply function 9.4, use calculus to determine the change in deadweight loss from a marginal increase in a tariff, evaluated where the tariff is initially zero. (*Hint:* You are being asked to determine how an area similar to that of $C + E$ in Figure 9.9 changes when a small tariff is initially applied.)

38. Suppose that the inverse market demand for silicone replacement tips for Sony EX71 earbud headphones is $p = p_N - 0.1Q$, where p is the price per pair of replacement tips, p_N is the price of a new pair of headphones, and Q is the number of tips per week. Suppose that the inverse supply function of the replacement tips is $p = 2 + 0.012Q$.

a. Find the effect of a change in the price of a new pair of headphones on the equilibrium price of replacement tips at the equilibrium, dp/dp_N.

b. If $p_N = \$30$, what are the equilibrium p and Q? What is the consumer surplus? What is the producer surplus? **W**

39. Suppose that the market demand for 32-oz. wide mouth Nalgene bottles is $Q = 50{,}000p^{-1.076}$, where Q is the quantity of bottles per week and p is the price per bottle. The market supply is $Q = 0.01p^{7.208}$. What is the equilibrium price and quantity? What is the consumer surplus? What is the producer surplus? **W**

Chapter 10

General Equilibrium and Economic Welfare

Capitalism is the astounding belief that the most wickedest of men will do the most wickedest of things for the greatest good of everyone. —John Maynard Keynes

A change in government policies, a natural disaster, or other shocks often affect equilibrium price and quantity in more than one market. Determining the effects of such a change requires examining the interrelationships among markets. In this chapter, we extend our analysis of equilibrium in a single market to equilibrium in all markets.

We also examine how a society decides whether a particular equilibrium (or change in equilibrium) in all markets is desirable. To do so, society must answer two questions: "Is the equilibrium efficient?" and "Is the equilibrium equitable?"

For an equilibrium to be efficient, both consumption and production must be efficient. Production is efficient only if it is impossible to produce more output at current cost given current knowledge (Chapter 6). Consumption is efficient only if goods cannot be reallocated among people so that at least someone is better off and no one is harmed. This chapter shows how we determine whether consumption is efficient.

Whether an equilibrium is efficient is a scientific question. It is possible that all members of society could agree on how to answer scientific questions concerning efficiency.

To determine whether an equilibrium is equitable, however, society must make a value judgment as to whether each member of society has his or her "fair" or "just" share of all the goods and services. A common view in individualistic cultures is that each person is the best—and possibly, the only legitimate—judge of his or her own welfare. Nonetheless, to make social choices about events that affect more than one person, we have to make interpersonal comparisons, through which we decide whether one person's gain is more or less important than another person's loss. For example, we showed that a price ceiling lowers a measure of total welfare where the value judgment that the well-being of consumers, consumer surplus, and the well-being of the owners of firms, producer surplus, are weighted equally (Chapter 9). People of goodwill—and others—may disagree greatly about questions of equity.

As a first step in studying welfare issues, many economists use a narrow value criterion, called the *Pareto principle* (after the Italian economist Vilfredo Pareto), to rank different allocations of goods and services for which no interpersonal comparisons need to be made. According to this principle, a change that makes one person better off without harming anyone else is desirable. An allocation is **Pareto efficient** if any possible reallocation would harm at least one person.

Presumably, you agree that any government policy that makes all members of society better off is desirable. Do you also agree that a policy that makes some members better off without harming others is desirable? What about a policy that helps one group more than it hurts another group? Or how about a policy that hurts another group more than it helps your group? It is very unlikely that all members of society will agree on how to answer these questions—much less agree on the answers.

The efficiency and equity questions arise even in small social units such as your family. Suppose that your family has gathered together in November and everyone wants pumpkin pie. How much pie you get will depend on the answer to efficiency and equity questions such as "How can we make the pie as large as possible with available resources?" and "How should we divide the pie?" It will probably be easier to get agreement about how to make the largest possible pie than about how to divide it equitably.

So far in this book, aside from Chapter 9's welfare analysis, we have used economic theory to answer the scientific efficiency question. We have concentrated on that question because the equity question requires a value judgment. (Strangely, most members of our society seem to believe that economists are no better at making value judgments than anyone else.)

In this chapter, we examine various views on equity, focusing on five main topics	1. **General Equilibrium:** The welfare analysis in Chapter 9 (involving gains and losses in consumer and producer surplus) changes when a shift in government policy or some other shock affects several markets at once.
	2. **General-Equilibrium Exchange Economy: Trading Between Two People:** When two people have goods but cannot produce more goods, both parties benefit from mutually agreeable trades.
	3. **Competitive Exchange:** The competitive equilibrium has two desirable properties: Any competitive equilibrium is Pareto efficient, and any Pareto-efficient allocation can be obtained by using competition, given an appropriate income distribution.
	4. **Production and Trading:** The benefits from trade continue to hold when production is introduced.
	5. **Efficiency and Equity:** Because there are many Pareto-efficient allocations, a society uses its views about equity to choose among them.

10.1 General Equilibrium

So far we have used a **partial-equilibrium analysis:** an examination of equilibrium and changes in equilibrium in one market in isolation. In a partial-equilibrium analysis in which we hold the prices and quantities of other goods fixed, we implicitly ignore the possibility that events in this market affect other markets' equilibrium prices and quantities.

When stated this baldly, partial-equilibrium analysis sounds foolish, but it need not be. Suppose that the government puts a specific tax on the price of hula hoops. If the tax is sizable, it will dramatically affect sales of hula hoops. However, even a very large tax on hula hoops is unlikely to affect the markets for automobiles, doctors' services, or orange juice. It is even unlikely to affect the demand for other toys greatly. Thus a partial-equilibrium analysis of the effect of such a tax should serve us well. Studying all markets simultaneously to analyze this tax would be unnecessary at best and confusing at worst.

Sometimes, however, we need to use a **general-equilibrium analysis:** the study of how equilibrium is determined in all markets simultaneously. For example, the discovery of a major oil deposit in a small country raises the income of its citizens, and the increased income affects all of that country's markets. Economists sometimes model many markets in an economy and solve for the general equilibrium in all of them simultaneously.

Frequently, economists look at equilibrium in several—but not all—markets simultaneously. We would expect a tax on comic books to affect the price of comic books, which in turn would affect the price of video games because video games are substitutes for comics. But we would not expect this tax on comics to have a measurable effect on the demand for washing machines. It is therefore reasonable to conduct a "general-equilibrium" analysis of the effects of a tax on comics by looking only at the markets for comics, video games, and a few other closely related markets such as those for movies and trading cards.

Markets are closely related if an increase in the price in one market causes the demand or supply curve in another market to shift measurably. Suppose that a tax on coffee causes the price of coffee to rise. The rise in the price of coffee causes the demand curve for tea to shift outward (more tea is demanded at any given price of tea) because tea and coffee are substitutes. The price increase in coffee also causes the demand curve for cream to shift inward because coffee and cream are complements.

Similarly, supply curves in different markets may be related. If a farmer produces both corn and soybeans, an increase in the price of corn will affect the relative amounts of both crops that the farmer chooses to produce.

Markets may also be linked if the output of one market is an input in another market. A shock that raises the price of computer chips will also raise the price of computers.

Thus an event in one market may have a *spillover effect* on other, related markets for a number of reasons. Indeed, a single event may start a chain reaction of spillover effects that reverberates back and forth between markets.

COMPETITIVE EQUILIBRIUM IN TWO INTERRELATED MARKETS

Suppose that the demand functions for Good 1, Q_1, and Good 2, Q_2, depend on both prices, p_1 and p_2,

$$Q_1 = D_1(p_1, p_2),$$
$$Q_2 = D_2(p_1, p_2),$$

but that the supply function for each good depends only on the good's own price,

$$Q_1 = S_1(p_1),$$
$$Q_2 = S_2(p_2).$$

To solve for the equilibrium p_1, p_2, Q_1, and Q_2, we need to solve these four equations in four unknowns simultaneously. Doing so is straightforward with linear equations.

Suppose that the demand functions are linear,

$$Q_1 = a_1 - b_1 p_1 + c_1 p_2, \tag{10.1}$$

$$Q_2 = a_2 - b_2 p_2 + c_2 p_1, \tag{10.2}$$

as are the supply functions,

$$Q_1 = d_1 + e_1 p_1, \tag{10.3}$$

$$Q_2 = d_2 + e_2 p_2, \tag{10.4}$$

where all the coefficients are positive numbers.

Equating the quantity demanded and supplied for both markets—setting the right-hand side of Equation 10.1 equal to the right-hand side of Equation 10.3, and similarly for Equations 10.2 and 10.4—we obtain

$$a_1 - b_1 p_1 + c_1 p_2 = d_1 + e_1 p_1, \tag{10.5}$$

$$a_2 - b_2 p_2 + c_2 p_1 = d_2 + e_2 p_2. \tag{10.6}$$

We now have two equations, 10.5 and 10.6, in two unknowns, p_1 and p_2, to solve. The solutions of these two equations are:

$$p_1 = \frac{(b_2 + e_2)(a_1 - d_1) + c_1(a_2 - d_2)}{(b_1 + e_1)(b_2 + e_2) - c_1 c_2}, \tag{10.7}$$

$$p_2 = \frac{(b_1 + e_1)(a_2 - d_2) + c_2(a_1 - d_1)}{(b_1 + e_1)(b_2 + e_2) - c_1 c_2}. \tag{10.8}$$

Substituting these values for p_1 and p_2 in the demand functions 10.1 and 10.2 or in the supply functions 10.3 and 10.4, we obtain expressions for Q_1 and Q_2. Thus by simultaneously solving the demand and supply curves for related markets, we can determine the equilibrium price and quantities in both markets.

● APPLICATION

Partial-Equilibrium Versus General-Equilibrium Analysis in Corn and Soy Markets

Consumers and producers substitute between corn and soybeans, so the demand and supply curves in these two markets are related according to the estimates of Holt (1992). The quantity of corn demanded and the quantity of soybeans demanded both depend on the price of corn, the price of soybeans, and other variables. Similarly, the quantities of corn and soybeans supplied depend on their relative prices.

A shock in one market affects both markets. Given actual supply and demand curves for corn and soybeans, the original equilibrium price of corn is $2.15 per bushel, and the quantity is 8.44 billion bushels per year; and the equilibrium price of soybeans is $4.12 per bushel, and the quantity is 2.07 billion bushels per year (see the first row of the table).[1] Now suppose that a scare about the safety of corn causes a parallel shift to the left of the foreign demand curve for American corn so that at the original price, the export of corn falls by 10%.

If we were conducting a partial-equilibrium analysis, we would examine the new corn equilibrium, where the new U.S. corn demand curve intersects the corn supply curve. The second row of the table shows the partial equilibrium effects on the corn equilibrium holding other prices (such as the price of soybeans) constant.

---

[1]Until recently, the corn and soybean markets were subject to price controls (Chapter 9). However, we use the estimated demand and supply curves to determine what would happen in these markets without price controls.

In a general-equilibrium analysis, we consider how this shock to the corn market affects the soybean market, and how the changed soybean price in turn affects the corn market. The third row of the table shows the new general equilibrium in both markets.

Equilibria	Corn		Soybeans	
	Price	Quantity	Price	Quantity
Original equilibria	2.15	8.44	4.12	2.07
New partial equilibrium	1.917	8.227		
New general equilibria	1.905	8.263	3.82	2.05

Suppose that we were interested only in the effect of the shift in the foreign corn demand curve on the corn market. Could we rely on a partial-equilibrium analysis? According to a partial-equilibrium analysis, the price of corn falls 10.8% to $1.917. In contrast, in the general-equilibrium analysis, the price falls 11.4% to $1.905, which is 1.2¢ less per bushel. That is, the partial-equilibrium analysis underestimates the price effect by 0.6 percentage point. Similarly, the fall in quantity is 2.5% according to the partial-equilibrium analysis and only 2.1% according to the general-equilibrium analysis. Thus in this market, the biases from using a partial-equilibrium analysis are small. See **www.aw-bc.com/perloff,** Chapter 10, "Sin Taxes," for an example where the bias from using a partial-equilibrium analysis instead of a general-equilibrium analysis is large.

MINIMUM WAGES WITH INCOMPLETE COVERAGE

We used a partial-equilibrium analysis in Chapter 2 to examine the effects of a minimum wage law that holds throughout the entire labor market. The minimum wage causes the quantity of labor demanded to be less than the quantity of labor supplied. Workers who lose their jobs cannot find work elsewhere and become unemployed.

The story changes substantially, however, if the minimum wage law covers workers in only some sectors of the economy, as we show using a general-equilibrium analysis. This analysis is relevant because the U.S. minimum wage law has not covered all workers historically.

When a minimum wage is applied to a covered sector of the economy, the increase in the wage causes the quantity of labor demanded in that sector to fall. Workers who are displaced from jobs in the covered sector move to the uncovered sector, driving down the wage in that sector. When the U.S. minimum wage law was first passed in 1938, some economists joked that its purpose was to maintain family farms: The law drove workers out of manufacturing and other covered industries into agriculture, which the law did not cover.

Figure 10.1 shows the effect of a minimum wage law when coverage is incomplete. The total demand curve, D in panel c, is the horizontal sum of the demand curve for labor services in the covered sector, D^c in panel a, and the demand curve in the uncovered sector, D^u in panel b. In the absence of a minimum wage law, the wage in both sectors is w_1, which is determined by the intersection of the total demand curve, D, and the total supply curve, S. At that wage, L_c^1 annual hours of work are hired in the covered

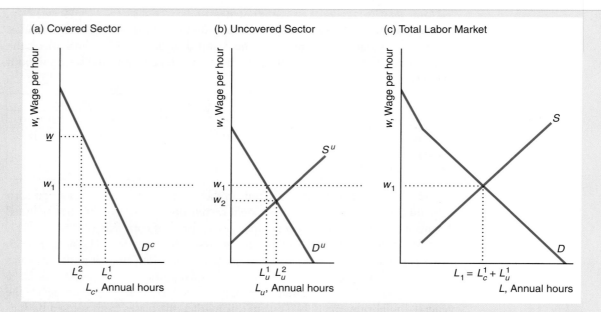

Figure 10.1 Minimum Wage with Incomplete Coverage. In the absence of a minimum wage, the equilibrium wage is w_1. Applying a minimum wage, $\underline{w}$, to only one sector causes the quantity of labor services demanded in the covered sector to fall. The extra labor moves to the uncovered sector, driving the wage there down to w_2.

sector, L_u^1 annual hours are hired in the uncovered sector, and $L_1 = L_c^1 + L_u^1$ total annual hours of work are performed.

If a minimum wage of $\underline{w}$ is set in only the covered sector, employment in that sector falls to L_c^2. To determine the wage and level of employment in the uncovered sector, we first need to determine how much labor service is available to that sector.

Anyone unable to find work in the covered sector goes to the uncovered sector. The supply curve of labor to the uncovered sector in panel b is a *residual supply curve:* the quantity the market supplies that is not met by demanders in other sectors at any given wage (see Chapter 8). With a binding minimum wage in the covered sector, the residual supply function in the uncovered sector is[2]

$$S^u(w) = S(w) - D^c(\underline{w}).$$

Thus the residual supply to the uncovered sector, $S^u(w)$, is the total supply, $S(w)$, at any given wage w minus the amount of labor used in the covered sector, $L_c^2 = D^c(\underline{w})$.

The intersection of D^u and S^u determines w_2, the new wage in the uncovered sector, and L_u^2, the new level of employment.[3] This general-equilibrium analysis shows that a

---

[2]If there is no minimum wage, the residual supply curve for the uncovered sector is $S^u(w) = S(w) - D^c(w)$.

[3]This analysis is incomplete if the minimum wage causes the price of goods in the covered sector to rise relative to those in the uncovered sector, which in turn causes the demands for labor in those two sectors, D^c and D^u, to shift. Ignoring that possibility is reasonable if labor costs are a small fraction of total costs (hence the effect of the minimum wage is minimal on total costs) or if the demands for the final goods are relatively price insensitive.

minimum wage causes employment to drop in the covered sector, employment to rise (by a smaller amount) in the uncovered sector, and the wage in the uncovered sector to fall below the original competitive level. Thus a minimum wage law with only partial coverage affects wage levels and employment levels in various sectors but need not create unemployment.

When the U.S. minimum wage was first passed in 1938, only 56% of workers were employed in covered firms (see **www.aw-bc.com/perloff,** Chapter 10, "U.S. Minimum Wage Laws and Teenagers"). Today, many state minimum wages provide incomplete coverage.

By 2007, more than 130 U.S. cities and counties enacted living-wage laws, a new type of minimum wage legislation where the minimum is high enough to allow a fully employed person to live above the poverty level in a given locale. Living-wage laws provide incomplete coverage, typically extending only to the employees of a government or to firms that contract with that government (see **www.aw-bc.com/perloff,** Chapter 10, "Living Wage Laws").

SOLVED PROBLEM 10.1

After the government starts taxing the cost of labor by τ per hour in a covered sector only, the wage that workers in both the covered and the uncovered sectors receive is w, but the wage paid by firms in the covered sector is $w + \tau$. What effect does the subsidy have on wages, total employment, and employment in the covered and uncovered sectors of the economy?

Answer

1. *Determine the original equilibrium:* In panel c of the diagram, the intersection of the total demand curve, D^1, and the total supply curve of labor, S, determines the original equilibrium, e_1, where the wage is w_1 and total employment is L_1. The total demand curve is the horizontal sum of the demand curves in the covered, D_1^c, and uncovered, D^u, sectors.

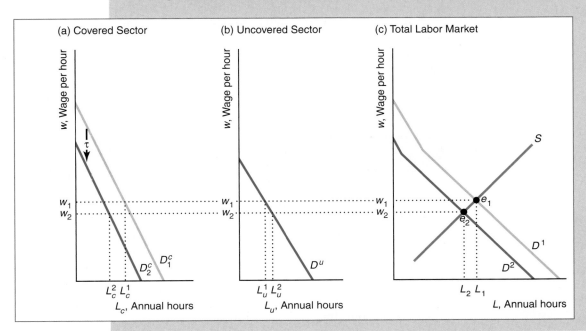

2. *Show the shift in the demand for labor in the covered sector and the resulting shift in the total demand curve:* The tax causes the demand curve for labor in the covered sector to shift downward from D_1^c to D_2^c in panel a. As a result, the total demand curve shifts inward to D^2 in panel c.

3. *Determine the equilibrium wage using the total demand and supply curves; then determine employment in the two sectors:* Workers shift between sectors until the new wage is equal in both sectors at w_2, which is determined by the intersection of the new total demand curve, D^2, and the total supply curve, S. Employment in the two sectors is L_2^c and L_2^u.

4. *Compare the equilibria:* The tax causes the wage, total employment, and employment in the covered sector to fall and employment in the uncovered sector to rise.

● APPLICATION

Urban Flight

Philadelphia and some other cities tax wages, while suburban areas do not (or they set much lower rates). Philadelphia collects a wage tax from residents whether or not they work in the city and from nonresidents who work in the city. Unfortunately for Philadelphia, this approach drives people and jobs from the city to the suburbs. To offset such job losses, Philadelphia has enacted a gradual wage tax reduction program. During the program's first five years, the wage tax on the city's workers declined from a high of 4.96% in 1983–1995 to 4.5635% in 2000, 4.4625% in 2003, and 4.331% in 2005.

The consulting firm Econsult (2003) conducted a study for Philadelphia and estimated that if the city were to lower the wage tax by 0.4175 percentage points, 30,500 more people would work in the city. Local wage tax cuts are more effective than a national cut because employers generally cannot leave the country to avoid a tax, but they can move a few miles out of a city. As Crawford et al. (2004) noted, much more growth is taking place on the suburban side of City Line Avenue, which runs along Philadelphia's border, than on the city side.

10.2   General-Equilibrium Exchange Economy: Trading Between Two People

In Chapter 9, we learned that tariffs, quotas, and other restrictions on trade usually harm both importing and exporting nations. The reason is that both parties to a voluntary trade benefit from that trade; otherwise, they would not have traded. In this section, we use a general-equilibrium model to show that free trade is Pareto efficient: After all voluntary trades have occurred, we cannot reallocate goods so as to make one person better off without harming another person. Our analysis demonstrates that trade between two people has this Pareto property and that the same property holds when many people trade using a competitive market.

ENDOWMENTS

Suppose that Jane and Denise live near each other in the wilds of Massachusetts. A snowstorm strikes, isolating them from the rest of the world. They must either trade with each other or consume only what they have at hand.

Collectively, they have 50 cords of firewood and 80 candy bars and no way of producing more of either good. Jane's **endowment**—her initial allocation of goods—is 30 cords of firewood and 20 candy bars. Denise's endowment is 20 (= 50 − 30) cords of firewood and 60 (= 80 − 20) candy bars. So Jane has relatively more wood, and Denise has relatively more candy.

We show these endowments in Figure 10.2. Panels a and b are typical indifference curve diagrams (Chapter 3) in which we measure cords of firewood on the vertical axis

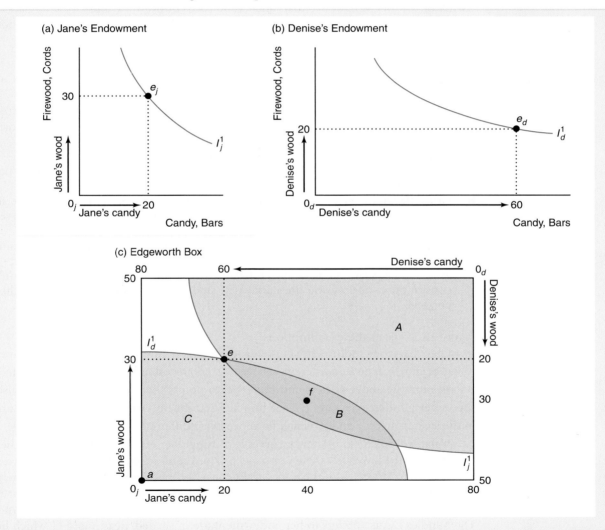

Figure 10.2 Endowments in an Edgeworth Box.
(a) Jane's endowment is e_j; she has 20 candy bars and 30 cords of firewood. She is indifferent between that bundle and the others that lie on her indifference curve I_j^1. (b) Denise is indifferent between her endowment, e_d (60 candy bars and 20 cords of wood), and the other bundles on I_d^1. (c) Their endowments are at e in the Edgeworth box formed by combining panels a and b. Jane prefers bundles in A and B to e. Denise prefers bundles in B and C to e. Thus both prefer any bundle in area B to e.

and candy bars on the horizontal axis. Jane's endowment is e_j (30 cords of firewood and 20 candy bars) in panel a, and Denise's endowment is e_d in panel b. Both panels show the indifference curve through the endowment.

If we take Denise's diagram, rotate it, and put it on Jane's diagram, we obtain the box in panel c. This type of figure, called an *Edgeworth box* (after the English economist Francis Ysidro Edgeworth), illustrates trade between two people with fixed endowments of two goods. We use this Edgeworth box to illustrate a general-equilibrium model in which we examine simultaneous trade in firewood and in candy.

The height of the Edgeworth box represents 50 cords of firewood, and the length represents 80 candy bars, which are the combined endowments of Jane and Denise. Bundle e shows both endowments. Measuring from Jane's origin, 0_j, at the lower-left corner of the diagram, we see that Jane has 30 cords of firewood and 20 candy bars at endowment e. Similarly, measuring from Denise's origin, 0_d, at the upper-right corner, we see that Denise has 60 candy bars and 20 cords of firewood at e.

MUTUALLY BENEFICIAL TRADES

Should Jane and Denise trade? The answer depends on their tastes, which are summarized by their indifference curves. We make four assumptions about their tastes and behavior:

- **Utility maximization:** Each person *maximizes* her *utility.*
- **Usual-shaped indifference curves:** Each person's indifference curves have the usual convex shape.
- **Nonsatiation:** Each person has strictly positive *marginal utility* for each good, so each person wants as much of the good as possible (that is, neither person is ever satiated).
- **No interdependence:** Neither person's utility depends on the other's consumption (that is, neither person gets pleasure or displeasure from the other's consumption), and neither person's consumption harms the other person (that is, one person's consumption of firewood does not cause smoke pollution that bothers the other person).

Figure 10.2 reflects these assumptions.

In panel a, Jane's indifference curve, I_j^1, through her endowment point, e_j, is convex to her origin, 0_j. Jane is indifferent between e_j and any other bundle on I_j^1. She prefers bundles that lie above I_j^1 to e_j and prefers e_j to points that lie below I_j^1. Panel c also shows her indifference curve I_j^1. The bundles that Jane prefers to her endowment are in the shaded areas A and B, which lie above her indifference curve I_j^1.

Similarly, Denise's indifference curve, I_d^1, through her endowment is convex to her origin, 0_d, in the lower-left corner of panel b. This indifference curve, I_d^1, is still convex to 0_d in panel c, but 0_d is in the upper-right corner of the Edgeworth box. (It may help to turn this book around when viewing Denise's indifference curves in an Edgeworth box. Then again, possibly many points will be clearer if the book is held upside down.) The bundles Denise prefers to her endowment are in shaded areas B and C, which lie on the other side of her indifference curve I_d^1 from her origin 0_d (above I_d^1 if you turn the book upside down).

At endowment *e* in panel c, Jane and Denise can both benefit from a trade. Jane prefers bundles in *A* and *B* to *e*, and Denise prefers bundles in *B* and *C* to *e*, so *both* prefer bundles in area *B* to their endowment at *e*.

Suppose that they trade, reallocating goods from Bundle *e* to Bundle *f*. Jane gives up 10 cords of firewood for 20 more candy bars, and Denise gives up 20 candy bars for 10 more cords of wood. As Figure 10.3 illustrates, both gain from such a trade. Jane's indifference curve I_j^2 through allocation *f* lies above her indifference curve I_j^1 through allocation *e*, so she is better off at *f* than at *e*. Similarly, Denise's indifference curve I_d^2 through *f* lies above (if you hold the book upside down) her indifference curve I_d^1 through *e*, so she also benefits from the trade.

Now that they've traded to Bundle *f*, do Jane and Denise want to make further trades? To answer this question, we can repeat our analysis. Jane prefers all bundles above I_j^2, her indifference curve through *f*. Denise prefers all bundles above (when the book is held upside down) I_d^2 to *f*. However, there are no bundles that both prefer because I_j^2 and I_d^2 are tangent at *f*. Neither Jane nor Denise wants to trade from *f* to a bundle such as *e*, which is below both of their indifference curves. Jane would love to trade from *f* to *c*, which is on her higher indifference curve I_j^3, but such a trade would

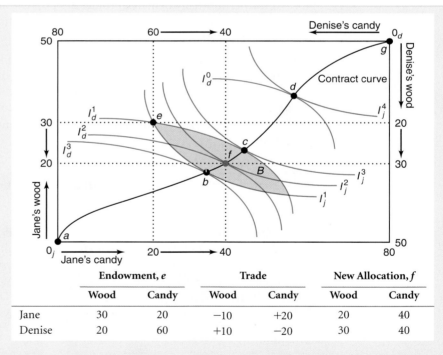

	Endowment, *e*		Trade		New Allocation, *f*	
	Wood	Candy	Wood	Candy	Wood	Candy
Jane	30	20	−10	+20	20	40
Denise	20	60	+10	−20	30	40

Figure 10.3 Contract Curve. The contract curve contains all the Pareto-efficient allocations. Any bundle for which Jane's indifference curve is tangent to Denise's indifference curve lies on the contract curve, because no further trade is possible, so we can't reallocate goods to make one of them better off without harming the other. Starting at an endowment of *e*, Jane and Denise will trade to a bundle on the contract curve in area *B*: bundles between *b* and *c*. The table shows how they would trade to Bundle *f*.

make Denise worse off because this bundle is on a lower indifference curve, I_d^1. Similarly, Denise prefers b to f, but Jane does not. Thus *any* move from f harms at least one of them.

The reason no further trade is possible at a bundle like f is that Jane's marginal rate of substitution (the slope of her indifference curve), MRS_j, between wood and candy equals Denise's marginal rate of substitution, MRS_d. Jane's MRS_j is $-\frac{1}{2}$: She is willing to trade one cord of wood for two candy bars. Because Denise's indifference curve is tangent to Jane's, Denise's MRS_d must also be $-\frac{1}{2}$. When they both want to trade wood for candy at the same rate, they can't agree on further trades.

In contrast, at a bundle such as e where their indifference curves are not tangent, MRS_j does not equal MRS_d. Denise's MRS_d is $-\frac{1}{3}$, and Jane's MRS_j is -2. Denise is willing to give up one cord of wood for three more candy bars or to sacrifice three candy bars for one more cord of wood. If Denise offers Jane three candy bars for one cord of wood, Jane will accept because she is willing to give up one cord of wood for two candy bars. This example illustrates that trades are possible where indifference curves intersect, because marginal rates of substitution are unequal.

To summarize, we can make four equivalent statements about allocation f:

1. The indifference curves of the two parties are tangent at f.
2. The parties' marginal rates of substitution are equal at f.
3. No further mutually beneficial trades are possible at f.
4. The allocation at f is Pareto efficient: One party cannot be made better off without harming the other.

Indifference curves are also tangent at Bundles b, c, and d, so these allocations, like f, are Pareto efficient. By connecting all such bundles, we draw the **contract curve:** the set of all Pareto-efficient bundles. The reason for this name is that only at these points are the parties unwilling to engage in further trades, or contracts—these allocations are the final contracts. A move from any bundle on the contract curve must harm at least one person.

SOLVED PROBLEM   10.2

Are allocations a and g in Figure 10.3 part of the contract curve?

Answer

By showing that no mutually beneficial trades are possible at those points, demonstrate that those bundles are Pareto efficient: The allocation at which Jane has everything, g, is on the contract curve because no mutually beneficial trade is possible: Denise has no goods to trade with Jane. As a consequence, we cannot make Denise better off without taking goods from Jane. Similarly, when Denise has everything, a, we can make Jane better off only by taking wood or candy from Denise and giving it to Jane.

DERIVING THE CONTRACT CURVE

We can use calculus to derive the contract curve. We want to specify conditions where we make one individual as well off as possible without harming the other person.

Let Denise's utility function be $U_d(q_{d1}, q_{d2})$, where q_{d1} is the amount of candy and q_{d2} is the amount of wood belonging to Denise. Similarly, Jane's utility function is

$U_j(q_{j1}, q_{j2})$. We want to determine the bundle that maximizes Jane's well-being, $U_j(q_{j1}, q_{j2})$, given that we hold Denise's utility constant at $\overline{U}_d = U_d(q_{d1}, q_{d2})$.

For example, in Figure 10.3, we take Denise's indifference curve I_d^2, along which her utility is $\overline{U}_d$, and ask what bundle places Jane on her highest indifference curve subject to Denise's being on I_d^2. That is, I_d^2 is the constraint (analogous to the budget line in earlier chapters) that Jane faces, and we pick a bundle on the highest one of Jane's indifference curves that touches I_d^2. As we already know, at Bundle f, Denise is on I_d^2 and Jane is on the highest feasible indifference curve, I_j^2.

Using a Lagrangian multiplier, λ, we can pose the problem as

$$\max_{q_{j1}, q_{j2}, \lambda} \mathcal{L} = U_j(q_{j1}, q_{j2}) + \lambda[U_d(q_1 - q_{j1}, q_2 - q_{j2}) - \overline{U}_d], \qquad (10.9)$$

where $q_1 = q_{d1} + q_{j1}$ is the total amount of candy available and q_2 is the total amount of wood. The first-order conditions are

$$\frac{\partial \mathcal{L}}{\partial q_{j1}} = \frac{\partial U_j}{\partial q_{j1}} - \lambda \frac{\partial U_d}{\partial q_{j1}} = 0, \qquad (10.10)$$

$$\frac{\partial \mathcal{L}}{\partial q_{j2}} = \frac{\partial U_j}{\partial q_{j2}} - \lambda \frac{\partial U_d}{\partial q_{j2}} = 0, \qquad (10.11)$$

$$\frac{\partial \mathcal{L}}{\partial \lambda} = U_d(q_1 - q_{j1}, q_2 - q_{j2}) - \overline{U}_d = 0. \qquad (10.12)$$

If we equate the right-hand sides of Equations 10.10 and 10.11, we find that

$$MRS_j = \frac{\partial U_j / \partial q_{j1}}{\partial U_j / \partial q_{j2}} = \frac{\partial U_d / \partial q_{d1}}{\partial U_d / \partial q_{d2}} = MRS_d. \qquad (10.13)$$

That is, Jane's marginal rate of substitution equals Denise's marginal rate of substitution at an optimal bundle. In geometric terms, this condition says that Jane's indifference curve is tangent to Denise's indifference curve along the contract curve.

SOLVED PROBLEM   10.3

In a pure exchange economy with two goods, *G* and *H*, the two traders, Amos and Elise, have Cobb-Douglas utility functions. Amos's utility is $U_a = (G_a)^\alpha (H_a)^{1-\alpha}$, and Elise's is $U_e = (G_e)^\beta (H_e)^{1-\beta}$. Between them, Amos and Elise own 100 units of *G* and 50 units of *H*. Thus if Amos has G_a and H_a, Elise has $G_e = 100 - G_a$ and $H_e = 50 - H_a$. Solve for their contract curve. Solve for the contract curve if $\alpha = \beta$.

Answer

1. *Use Equation 10.13 and the information about their endowments to determine the necessary condition for Amos and Elise's contract curve:* From Solved Problem 3.2, we know that Amos's marginal rate of substitution is $MRS_a = [\alpha/(1-\alpha)]H_a/G_a$ and that Elise's is $MRS_e = [\beta/(1-\beta)]H_e/G_e$. From Equation 10.13, we know that these marginal rates of substitution are equal along the contract curve: $MRS_a = MRS_e$. Equating the right-hand sides of the expressions for MRS_a and MRS_e and

using the information about the endowments and some algebra, we can write the (quadratic) formula for the contract curve in terms of Amos's goods as

$$(\beta - \alpha)G_aH_a + \beta(\alpha - 1)50G_a + \alpha(1 - \beta)100H_a = 0.$$

2. *Substitute in $\alpha = \beta$ and solve:* If $\alpha = \beta$, then $(\beta^2 - \beta)50G_a + (\beta - \beta^2)100H_a = 0$. Dividing by $(\beta^2 - \beta)$ and using algebra, we conclude that the contract curve is a straight line: $G_a/H_a = 2$.

BARGAINING ABILITY

For every allocation off the contract curve, there are allocations on the contract curve that benefit at least one person. If they start at endowment e, Jane and Denise should trade until they reach a point on the contract curve between Bundles b and c in Figure 10.3. All the allocations in area B are better for one or both of them. However, if they trade to any allocation in B that is not on the contract curve, further beneficial trades are possible because their indifference curves intersect at that allocation.

Where will they end up on the contract curve between b and c? That depends on who is better at bargaining. Suppose that Jane is better at bargaining. Jane knows that the more she gets, the worse off Denise will be and that Denise will not agree to any trade that makes her worse off than she is at e. Thus the best trade Jane can make is one that leaves Denise only as well off as at e, which are the bundles on I_d^1. If Jane could pick any point she wanted along I_d^1, she would choose the bundle on her highest possible indifference curve, Bundle c, where I_j^3 is just tangent to I_d^1. After this trade, Denise is no better off than before, but Jane is much happier. By similar reasoning, if Denise is better at bargaining, the final allocation will be at b.

10.3   Competitive Exchange

Most trading throughout the world occurs without one-on-one bargaining between people. When you go to the store to buy a bottle of shampoo, you read its posted price and then decide whether to buy it. You've probably never tried to bargain with the store's clerk over the price of shampoo: You're a price taker in the shampoo market.

If we don't know much about how Jane and Denise bargain, all we can say is that they will trade to some allocation on the contract curve. If we know the exact trading process they use, however, we can apply that process to determine the final allocation. In particular, we can examine the competitive trading process to determine the competitive equilibrium in a pure exchange economy.

In Chapter 9, we used a partial-equilibrium approach to show that one measure of welfare, W, is maximized in a competitive market in which many voluntary trades occur. We now use a general-equilibrium model to show that a competitive market has two desirable properties:

■ **The competitive equilibrium is efficient:** Competition results in a Pareto-efficient allocation—no one can be made better off without making someone worse off—in all markets.

■ **Any efficient allocations can be achieved by competition:** All possible efficient allocations can be obtained by competitive exchange, given an appropriate initial allocation of goods.

Economists call these results the *First Theorem of Welfare Economics* and the *Second Theorem of Welfare Economics,* respectively. These results hold under fairly weak conditions.

COMPETITIVE EQUILIBRIUM

When two people trade, they are unlikely to view themselves as price takers. However, if there were a large number of people with tastes and endowments like Jane's and a large number with tastes and endowments like Denise's, each person would be a price taker in the two goods. We can use an Edgeworth box to examine how such price takers would trade.

Because they can trade only two goods, each person needs to consider only the relative price of the two goods when deciding whether to trade. If the price of a cord of wood, p_w, is \$2, and the price of a candy bar, p_c, is \$1, then a candy bar costs half as much as a cord of wood: $p_c/p_w = \frac{1}{2}$. An individual can sell one cord of wood and use that money to buy two candy bars.

At the initial allocation, *e*, Jane has goods worth \$80 = (\$2 per cord × 30 cords of firewood) + (\$1 per candy bar × 20 candy bars). At these prices, Jane could keep her endowment or trade to an allocation with 40 cords of firewood and no candy, 80 candy bars and no firewood, or any combination in between, as the price line (budget line) in panel a of Figure 10.4 shows. The price line is all the combinations of goods that Jane could get by trading, given her endowment. The price line goes through point *e* and has a slope of $-p_c/p_w = -\frac{1}{2}$.

Given the price line, what bundle of goods will Jane choose? She wants to maximize her utility by picking the bundle where one of her indifference curves, I_j^2, is tangent to her budget or price line. Denise wants to maximize her utility by choosing a bundle in the same way.

In a competitive market, prices adjust until the quantity supplied equals the quantity demanded. An auctioneer could help determine the equilibrium by calling out relative prices and asking how much is demanded and how much is offered for sale at those prices. If demand does not equal supply, the auctioneer calls out another relative price. When demand equals supply, the transactions occur and the auction stops. At some ports, fishing boats sell their catch to fish wholesalers at a daily auction run in this manner.

Panel a of Figure 10.4 shows that, when candy costs half as much as wood, the quantity demanded of each good equals the quantity supplied. Jane (and every person like her) wants to sell 10 cords of firewood and use that money to buy 20 additional candy bars. Similarly, Denise (and everyone like her) wants to sell 20 candy bars and buy 10 cords of wood. Thus the quantity of wood sold equals the quantity of wood bought, and the quantity of candy demanded equals the quantity of candy supplied. We can see in the figure that the quantities demanded equal the quantities supplied because the optimal bundle for both types of consumers is the same, Bundle *f*.

At any other price ratio, the quantity demanded of each good would not equal the quantity supplied. For example, if the price of candy remained constant at $p_c = \$1$ per bar but the price of wood fell to $p_w = \$1.33$ per cord, the price line would be steeper,

Figure 10.4 Competitive Equilibrium. The initial endowment is *e*. (a) If, along the price line facing Jane and Denise, $p_w = \$2$ and $p_c = \$1$, they trade to point *f*, where Jane's indifference curve, I_j^2, is tangent to the price line and to Denise's indifference curve, I_d^2. (b) No other price line results in an equilibrium. If $p_w = \$1.33$ and $p_c = \$1$, Denise wants to buy 12 (= 32 − 20) cords of firewood at these prices, but Jane wants to sell only 8 (= 30 − 22) cords. Similarly, Jane wants to buy 10 (= 30 − 20) candy bars, but Denise wants to sell 17 (= 60 − 43). Thus these prices are not consistent with a competitive equilibrium.

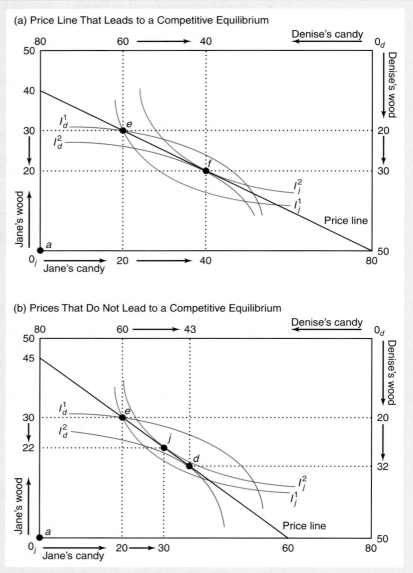

(a) Price Line That Leads to a Competitive Equilibrium

(b) Prices That Do Not Lead to a Competitive Equilibrium

with a slope of $-p_c/p_w = -1/1.33 = -3/4$ in panel b. At these prices, Jane wants to trade to Bundle *j* and Denise wants to trade to Bundle *d*. Because Jane wants to buy 10 extra candy bars but Denise wants to sell 17 extra candy bars, the quantity supplied does not equal the quantity demanded, so this price ratio does not result in a competitive equilibrium when the endowment is *e*.

SOLVED PROBLEM 10.4

Continuing with the example in Solved Problem 10.3—a pure exchange economy with two goods, *G* and *H*, and two traders, Amos and Elise, with Cobb-Douglas utility functions $U_a = (G_a)^\alpha(H_a)^{1-\alpha}$ and $U_e = (G_e)^\beta(H_e)^{1-\beta}$, respectively—what are the competitive equilibrium prices? (*Note:* We can solve only for the relative prices. Let the price of *G* be *p* and normalize the price of *H* to equal 1.)

Answer

1. *Determine their demand curves:* If G_a and H_a are Amos's endowment, then his income is $Y_a = pG_a + H_a$ and Elise's income is $Y_e = p(100 - G_a) + (50 - H_a)$. Using Equations 3.26 and 3.27 for a Cobb-Douglas utility function, we know that Amos's demand functions are $G_a = \alpha Y_a/p$ and $H_a = (1 - \alpha)Y_a/1$. Similarly, Elise's demands are $G_e = \beta Y_e/p$ and $H_e = (1 - \beta)Y_e/1$.

2. *To determine the competitive equilibrium price, equate the demand and supply curves:* The sum of their demands for *G* equals the supply: $G_a + G_e = 100$. Rearranging the terms in this expression and then substituting for G_e and H_e, we find that the equilibrium price of *G* is

$$p = \frac{\alpha H_a + \beta H_e}{100 - \alpha G_a + \beta G_e} = \frac{50\beta + (\alpha - \beta)H_a}{100(1 - \beta) + (\beta - \alpha)G_a}.$$

THE EFFICIENCY OF COMPETITION

In a competitive equilibrium, the indifference curves of both types of consumers are tangent at the same bundle on the price line. As a result, the slope (*MRS*) of each person's indifference curve equals the slope of the price line, so the slopes of the indifference curves are equal:

$$MRS_j = -\frac{p_c}{p_w} = MRS_d. \tag{10.14}$$

The marginal rates of substitution are equal among consumers in the competitive equilibrium, so the competitive equilibrium must lie on the contract curve. Thus we have demonstrated the First Theorem of Welfare Economics:

> *Any competitive equilibrium is Pareto efficient.*

The intuition for this result is that people (who face the same prices) make all the voluntary trades they want in a competitive market. Because no additional voluntary trades can occur, there is no way to make someone better off without making someone else worse off in a competitive equilibrium. (If an involuntary trade occurs, at least one person is made worse off. A person who steals goods from another person—an involuntary exchange—gains at the expense of the victim.)

OBTAINING ANY EFFICIENT ALLOCATION USING COMPETITION

Of the many possible Pareto-efficient allocations, the government may want to choose one. Can it achieve that allocation using the competitive market mechanism?

Our previous example illustrates that the competitive equilibrium depends on the endowment: the initial distribution of wealth. For example, if the initial endowment were *a* in panel a of Figure 10.4—where Denise has everything and Jane has nothing—the competitive equilibrium would be *a* because no trades would be possible.

Thus for competition to lead to a particular allocation—say, *f*—the trading must start at an appropriate endowment. If the consumers' endowment is *f*, a Pareto-efficient point, their indifference curves are tangent at *f*, so no further trades occur. That is, *f* is a competitive equilibrium.

Many other endowments will also result in a competitive equilibrium at *f*. Panel a of Figure 10.4 shows that the resulting competitive equilibrium is *f* if the endowment is *e*. In that figure, a price line goes through both *e* and *f*. If the endowment is any bundle along this price line—not just *e* or *f*—then the competitive equilibrium is *f*, because only at *f* are the indifference curves tangent.

To summarize, any Pareto-efficient bundle *x* can be obtained as a competitive equilibrium if the initial endowment is *x*. That allocation can also be obtained as a competitive equilibrium if the endowment lies on a price line through *x*, where the slope of the price line equals the marginal rate of substitution of the indifference curves that are tangent at *x*. Thus we have demonstrated the Second Theorem of Welfare Economics:

> *Any Pareto-efficient equilibrium can be obtained by competition, given an appropriate endowment.*

The first welfare theorem tells us that society can achieve efficiency by allowing competition. The second welfare theorem adds that society can obtain the particular efficient allocation it prefers, based on its value judgments about equity, by appropriately redistributing endowments (income).

10.4 Production and Trading

So far our discussion has been based on a pure exchange economy with no production. We now examine an economy in which a fixed amount of a single input can be used to produce two different goods.

COMPARATIVE ADVANTAGE

Jane and Denise can produce candy or chop firewood using their own labor. However, they differ as to how much of each good they produce from a day's work.

Production Possibility Frontier. Jane can produce either 3 candy bars or 6 cords of firewood in a day. By splitting her time between the two activities, she can produce various combinations of the two goods. If *t* is the fraction of a day she spends making candy and $1 - t$ is the fraction she spends cutting wood, she produces $3t$ candy bars and $6(1 - t)$ cords of wood.

By varying *t* between 0 and 1, we trace out the line in panel a of Figure 10.5. This line is Jane's *production possibility frontier* (*PPF^j*; Chapter 7), which shows the maximum combinations of wood and candy that she can produce from a given amount of input. If Jane works all day using the best available technology (such as a sharp ax), she achieves *efficiency in production* and produces combinations of goods on *PPF^j*. If she

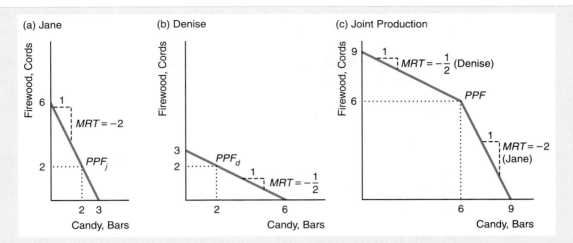

Figure 10.5 Comparative Advantage and Production Possibility Frontiers. (a) Jane's production possibility frontier, PPF^j, shows that in a day, she can produce 6 cords of firewood or 3 candy bars or any combination of the two. Her marginal rate of transformation (MRT) is -2. (b) Denise's production possibility frontier, PPF^d, has an MRT of $-\frac{1}{2}$. (c) Their joint production possibility frontier, PPF, has a kink at 6 cords of firewood (produced by Jane) and 6 candy bars (produced by Denise) and is concave to the origin.

sits around part of the day or does not use the best technology, she produces an inefficient combination of wood and candy that lies inside PPF^j.

Marginal Rate of Transformation. The slope of the production possibility frontier is the *marginal rate of transformation* (MRT).[4] The marginal rate of transformation tells us how much more wood can be produced if the production of candy is reduced by one bar. Because Jane's PPF^j is a straight line with a slope of -2, her MRT is -2 at every allocation.

Denise can produce up to 3 cords of wood or 6 candy bars in a day. Panel b shows her production possibility function, PPF^d, with an $MRT = -\frac{1}{2}$. Thus with a day's work, Denise can produce relatively more candy, and Jane can produce relatively more wood, as reflected by their differing marginal rates of transformation.

The marginal rate of transformation shows how much it costs to produce one good in terms of the forgone production of the other good. Someone with the ability to produce a good at a lower opportunity cost than someone else has a **comparative advantage** in producing that good. Denise has a comparative advantage in producing candy (she forgoes less in wood production to produce a given amount of candy), and Jane has a comparative advantage in producing wood.

By combining their outputs, they have the joint production possibility frontier PPF in panel c. If Denise and Jane spend all their time producing wood, Denise produces

---

[4]In Chapter 3, we called the slope of a consumer's budget line the marginal rate of transformation. For a price-taking consumer who obtains goods by buying them, the budget line plays the same role as the production possibility frontier for someone who produces the two goods.

3 cords and Jane produces 6 cords for a total of 9, which is where the joint *PPF* hits the wood axis. Similarly, if they both produce candy, they can jointly produce 9 bars. If Denise specializes in making candy and Jane specializes in cutting wood, they produce 6 candy bars and 6 cords of wood, a combination that appears at the kink in the *PPF*.

If they choose to produce a relatively large quantity of candy and a relatively small amount of wood, Denise produces only candy and Jane produces some candy and some wood. Jane chops the wood because that is her comparative advantage. The marginal rate of transformation in the lower portion of the *PPF* is Jane's, -2, because only she produces both candy and wood.

Similarly, if they produce little candy, Jane produces only wood and Denise produces some wood and some candy, so the marginal rate of transformation in the higher portion of the *PPF* is Denise's, $-\frac{1}{2}$. In short, the *PPF* has a kink at 6 cords of wood and 6 candy bars and is concave (bowed away from the origin).

Benefits of Trade. Because of the difference in their marginal rates of transformation, Jane and Denise can benefit from a trade. Suppose that Jane and Denise like to consume wood and candy in equal proportions. If they do not trade, each produces 2 candy bars and 2 cords of wood in a day. If they agree to trade, Denise, who excels at making candy, spends all day producing 6 candy bars. Similarly, Jane, who has a comparative advantage at chopping wood, produces 6 cords of wood. If they split this production equally, they can each have 3 cords of wood and 3 candy bars—50% more than without trade.

They do better if they trade because each person uses her comparative advantage. Without trade, if Denise wants an extra cord of wood, she must give up two candy bars. Producing an extra cord of wood costs Jane only half a candy bar in forgone production. Denise is willing to trade up to two candy bars for a cord of wood, and Jane is willing to trade the wood as long as she gets at least half a candy bar. Thus there is room for a mutually beneficial trade.

SOLVED PROBLEM   **10.5**

How does the joint production possibility frontier in panel c of Figure 10.5 change if Jane and Denise can also trade with Harvey, who can produce 5 cords of wood, 5 candy bars, or any linear combination of wood and candy in a day?

Answer

1. *Describe each person's individual production possibility frontier:* Panels a and b of Figure 10.5 show the production possibility frontiers of Jane and Denise. Harvey's production possibility frontier is a straight line that hits the firewood axis at 5 cords and the candy axis at 5 candy bars.

2. *Draw the joint PPF by starting at the quantity on the horizontal axis that is produced if everyone specializes in candy and then connecting the individual production possibility frontiers in order of comparative advantage in chopping wood:* If all three produce candy, they make 14 candy bars (on the horizontal axis of the accompanying graph). Jane has a comparative advantage at chopping wood over Harvey and Denise, and Harvey has a comparative advantage over Denise. Thus Jane's production possibility frontier is the first frontier (starting at the lower right), then comes Harvey's, and then Denise's. The resulting *PPF* is concave to the origin. (If we change the order of the individual frontiers, the resulting

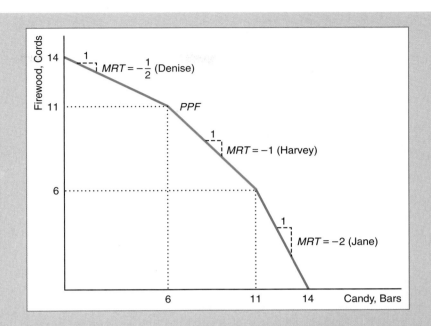

kinked line lies inside the *PPF*. Thus the new line cannot be the joint production possibility frontier, which shows the maximum possible production from the available labor inputs.)

The Number of Producers. When there are only two ways of producing wood and candy—Denise's and Jane's methods with different marginal rates of transformation—the joint production possibility frontier has a single kink (panel c of Figure 10.5). If another method of production with a different marginal rate of transformation—Harvey's—is added, the joint production possibility frontier has two kinks (as in Solved Problem 10.5).

If many people can produce candy and firewood with different marginal rates of transformation, the joint production possibility frontier has even more kinks. As the number of people becomes very large, the *PPF* becomes a smooth curve that is concave to the origin, as in Figure 10.6.

Because the *PPF* is concave, the marginal rate of transformation decreases (in absolute value) as we move up the *PPF*. The *PPF* has a flatter slope at a, where the $MRT = -\frac{1}{2}$, than at b, where the $MRT = -1$. At a, giving up a candy bar leads to half a cord more wood production. In contrast, at b, where relatively more candy is produced, giving up producing a candy bar frees enough resources that an additional cord of wood can be produced.

The marginal rate of transformation along this smooth *PPF* tells us about the marginal cost of producing one good relative to the marginal cost of producing the other good. The marginal rate of transformation equals the negative of the ratio of the marginal cost of producing candy, MC_c, and wood, MC_w (Equation 10.14):

$$MRS_j = -\frac{p_c}{p_w} = MRS_d.$$

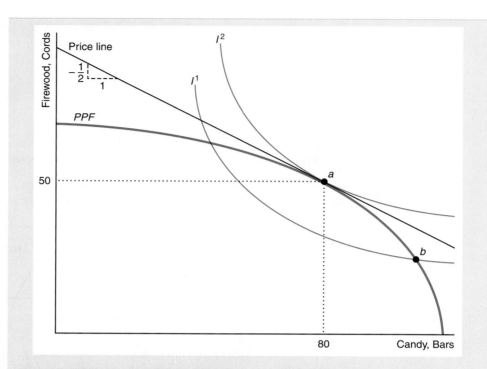

Figure 10.6 Optimal Product Mix. The optimal product mix, *a*, could be determined by max-imizing an individual's utility by picking the allocation for which an indifference curve is tan-gent to the production possibility frontier. It could also be determined by picking the allocation where the relative competitive price, p_c/p_f, equals the slope of the *PPF*.

Suppose that at point *a* in Figure 10.6, a person's marginal cost of producing an extra candy bar is $1, and the marginal cost of producing an additional cord of fire-wood is $2. As a result, the person can produce one extra candy bar or half a cord of wood at a cost of $1. The marginal rate of transformation is the negative of the ratio of the marginal costs, $-(\$1/\$2) = -\frac{1}{2}$. To produce one more candy bar, the person must give up producing half a cord of wood.

EFFICIENT PRODUCT MIX

Which combination of products along the *PPF* does society choose? If a single person were to decide on the product mix, that person would pick the allocation of wood and candy along the *PPF* that maximized his or her utility. A person with the indifference curves in Figure 10.6 would pick Allocation *a*, which is the point where the *PPF* touches indifference curve I^2.

Because I^2 is tangent to the *PPF* at *a*, that person's marginal rate of substitution (the slope of indifference curve I^2) equals the marginal rate of transformation (the slope of the *PPF*). The marginal rate of substitution, *MRS*, tells us how much a consumer is willing to give up of one good to get another. The marginal rate of transformation, *MRT*, tells us how much of one good we need to give up to be able to produce more of another good.

If the *MRS* does not equal the *MRT*, the consumer will be happier with a different product mix. At Allocation *b*, the indifference curve I^1 intersects the *PPF*, so the *MRS* does not equal the *MRT*. At *b*, the consumer is willing to give up one candy bar to get a third of a cord of wood ($MRS = -\frac{1}{3}$), but firms can produce one cord of wood for every candy bar not produced ($MRT = -1$). Thus at *b*, too little wood is being produced. If the firms increase wood production, the *MRS* will fall and the *MRT* will rise until they are equal at *a*, where $MRS = MRT = -\frac{1}{2}$.

We can extend this reasoning to look at the product mix choice of all consumers simultaneously. Each consumer's marginal rate of substitution must equal the economy's marginal rate of transformation, *MRS* = *MRT*, if the economy is to produce the optimal mix of goods for each consumer. How can we ensure that this condition holds for all consumers? One way is to use the competitive market.

COMPETITION

Each price-taking consumer picks a bundle of goods so that the consumer's marginal rate of substitution equals the slope of the consumer's price line (the negative of the relative prices):

$$MRS = -\frac{p_c}{p_w}. \tag{10.15}$$

Thus if all consumers face the same relative prices in the competitive equilibrium, all consumers will buy a bundle where their marginal rates of substitution are equal (Equation 10.14). Because all consumers have the same marginal rates of substitution, no further trades can occur. Thus the competitive equilibrium achieves *consumption efficiency*: It is impossible to redistribute goods among consumers to make one consumer better off without harming another consumer. That is, the competitive equilibrium lies on the contract curve.

If candy and wood are sold by competitive firms, each firm sells a quantity of candy for which its price equals its marginal cost,

$$p_c = MC_c, \tag{10.16}$$

and a quantity of wood for which its price and marginal cost are equal,

$$p_w = MC_w. \tag{10.17}$$

Taking the ratio of Equations 10.16 and 10.17, we find that in competition, $p_c/p_w = MC_c/MC_w$. From Equation 10.14, we know that the marginal rate of transformation equals $-MC_c/MC_w$, so

$$MRT = -\frac{p_c}{p_w}. \tag{10.18}$$

We can illustrate why firms want to produce where Equation 10.18 holds. Suppose that a firm were producing at *b* in Figure 10.6, where its *MRT* is −1, and that $p_c = \$1$ and $p_w = \$2$, so $-p_c/p_w = -\frac{1}{2}$. If the firm reduces its output by one candy bar, it loses $1 in candy sales but makes $2 more from selling the extra cord of wood, for a net gain of $1. Thus at *b*, where the $MRT < -p_c/p_w$, the firm should reduce its output of candy and increase its output of wood. In contrast, if the firm is producing at *a*, where the $MRT = -p_c/p_w = -\frac{1}{2}$, it has no incentive to change its behavior: The gain from producing a little more wood exactly offsets the loss from producing a little less candy.

Combining Equations 10.3 and 10.6, we find that in the competitive equilibrium, the *MRS* equals the ratio of relative prices, which equal the *MRT*:

$$MRS = -\frac{p_c}{p_w} = MRT.$$

Because competition ensures that the *MRS* equals the *MRT*, a competitive equilibrium achieves an *efficient product mix:* The rate at which firms can transform one good into another equals the rate at which consumers are willing to substitute between the goods, as reflected by their willingness to pay for the two goods.

By combining the production possibility frontier and an Edgeworth box, we can show the competitive equilibrium in both production and consumption. Suppose that firms produce 50 cords of firewood and 80 candy bars at *a* in Figure 10.7. The size of the Edgeworth box—the maximum amount of wood and candy available to consumers—is determined by point *a* on the *PPF*.

The prices consumers pay must equal the prices producers receive, so the price lines that consumers and producers face must have the same slope of $-p_c/p_w$. In equilibrium, the price lines are tangent to each consumer's indifference curve at *f* and to the *PPF* at *a*.

In this competitive equilibrium, supply equals demand in all markets. Consumers buy the mix of goods at *f*. Consumers like Jane, whose origin, 0_j, is at the lower-left corner, consume 20 cords of firewood and 40 candy bars. Consumers like Denise, whose origin is *a* at the upper right of the Edgeworth box, consume 30 (= 50 − 20) cords of firewood and 40 (= 80 − 40) candy bars.

Figure 10.7
Competitive Equilibrium. At the competitive equilibrium, the relative prices that firms and consumers face are the same (the price lines are parallel), so the $MRS = -p_c/p_w = MRT$.

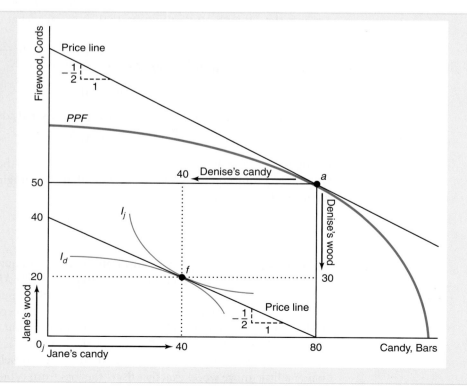

The two key results concerning competition still hold in an economy with production. First, a competitive equilibrium is Pareto efficient, achieving efficiency in consumption and in output mix.[5] Second, any particular Pareto-efficient allocation between consumers can be obtained through competition, given that the government chooses an appropriate endowment.

10.5 Efficiency and Equity

How well the various people in a society live depends on how the society deals with efficiency (the size of the pie) and equity (the way the pie is divided). The actual outcome depends on individual choices and on government actions.

ROLE OF THE GOVERNMENT

By altering the efficiency with which goods are produced and distributed and the endowment of resources, governments help determine how much is produced and how goods are allocated. By redistributing endowments or by refusing to do so, governments, at least implicitly, are making value judgments about which members of society should get relatively more of society's goodies.

Virtually every government program, tax, or action redistributes wealth. Proceeds from a British lottery, played mostly by lower-income people, subsidize the Royal Opera House at Covent Garden, thereby transferring funds to the "rich toffs" who attend operas. Agricultural price support programs (Chapter 9) redistribute wealth to farmers from other taxpayers. Income taxes and food stamp programs (Chapter 5) redistribute income from better-off taxpayers to the poor.

◉ APPLICATION

Wealth Distribution in the United States

Since the United States was founded, changes in the economy have altered the share of the nation's wealth that is concentrated in the hands of the richest 1% of Americans (see the figure). An array of social changes—sometimes occurring during or after wars and often codified into new laws—have led to new equilibria and new distributions of wealth. For example, the emancipation of slaves in 1863 transferred vast wealth—the labor of the former slaves—from rich southern landowners to the poor freed slaves. Anti-immigration laws have helped the domestic poor, because immigrant labor is typically a substitute for low-skilled domestic labor, and have hurt the middle and upper classes because low-skilled immigrant labor is a complement to capital and high-skilled labor.

Q9

---

[5]Although we have not shown it here, competitive firms choose factor combinations so that their marginal rates of technical substitution between inputs equal the negative of the ratios of the relative factor prices (see Chapter 7). That is, competition also results in *efficiency in production:* Firms could not produce more of one good without producing less of another good.

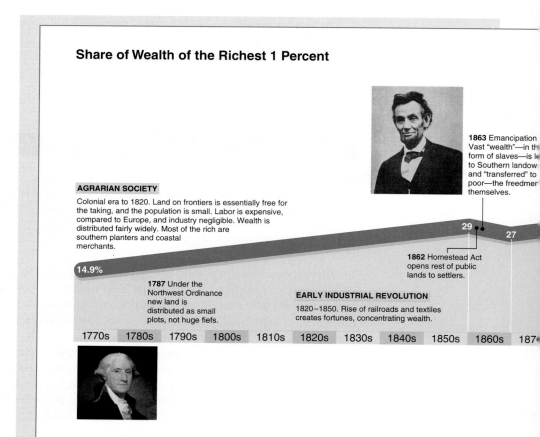

Share of Wealth of the Richest 1 Percent

AGRARIAN SOCIETY

Colonial era to 1820. Land on frontiers is essentially free for the taking, and the population is small. Labor is expensive, compared to Europe, and industry negligible. Wealth is distributed fairly widely. Most of the rich are southern planters and coastal merchants.

1863 Emancipation Vast "wealth"—in th form of slaves—is le to Southern landow and "transferred" to poor—the freedmer themselves.

29

27

14.9%

1787 Under the Northwest Ordinance new land is distributed as small plots, not huge fiefs.

1862 Homestead Act opens rest of public lands to settlers.

EARLY INDUSTRIAL REVOLUTION

1820–1850. Rise of railroads and textiles creates fortunes, concentrating wealth.

| 1770s | 1780s | 1790s | 1800s | 1810s | 1820s | 1830s | 1840s | 1850s | 1860s | 187 |

The share of wealth held by the richest 1% generally increased until the Great Depression and then declined through the mid-1970s, when the trend reversed dramatically.[6] The share of income earned by the top 0.1% of the U.S. population doubled to 7.4% from 1980 to 2002. In 2001, roughly a third of total wealth was held by the wealthiest 1% of the populace, a third by the next highest 9%, and the remaining third by the poorest 90%. As of 2004, 2.5 million Americans, or almost 1% of the population over the age of 15, had more than $1 million each in financial assets such as stocks, bonds, and bank accounts.

One reason for the increased concentration of wealth in recent decades is that the top income tax rate fell from 70% to less than 30% at the beginning of the Reagan administration, shifting more of the tax burden to the middle class. The top federal tax rate rose under the Clinton administration but then fell under the Bush administration.

The federal government transfers 5% of total national household income from the rich to the poor: 2% through cash assistance such as general welfare programs and 3% through in-kind transfers such as food stamps and school lunch programs.

---

[6]According to *Forbes,* the wealth of Bill Gates, the wealthiest American, was $50 billion in 2006 (down from $85 billion in 1999). His wealth is 1/266th of the U.S. gross domestic product (down from 1/109th in 1999). (CNNMoney.com in 2006 reported that Mr. Gates does not enjoy being the world's richest man because of the attention it brings him.)

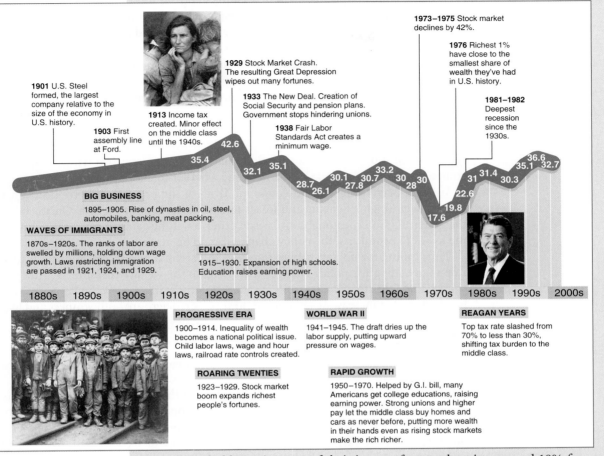

1901 U.S. Steel formed, the largest company relative to the size of the economy in U.S. history.

1903 First assembly line at Ford.

1913 Income tax created. Minor effect on the middle class until the 1940s.

1929 Stock Market Crash. The resulting Great Depression wipes out many fortunes.

1933 The New Deal. Creation of Social Security and pension plans. Government stops hindering unions.

1938 Fair Labor Standards Act creates a minimum wage.

1973–1975 Stock market declines by 42%.

1976 Richest 1% have close to the smallest share of wealth they've had in U.S. history.

1981–1982 Deepest recession since the 1930s.

42.6 · 35.4 · 32.1 · 35.1 · 28.7 · 26.1 · 30.1 · 27.8 · 30.7 · 33.2 · 30 · 28 · 30 · 31 · 22.6 · 19.8 · 17.6 · 31.4 · 30.3 · 36.6 · 35.1 · 32.7

BIG BUSINESS

1895–1905. Rise of dynasties in oil, steel, automobiles, banking, meat packing.

WAVES OF IMMIGRANTS

1870s–1920s. The ranks of labor are swelled by millions, holding down wage growth. Laws restricting immigration are passed in 1921, 1924, and 1929.

EDUCATION

1915–1930. Expansion of high schools. Education raises earning power.

1880s · 1890s · 1900s · 1910s · 1920s · 1930s · 1940s · 1950s · 1960s · 1970s · 1980s · 1990s · 2000s

PROGRESSIVE ERA

1900–1914. Inequality of wealth becomes a national political issue. Child labor laws, wage and hour laws, railroad rate controls created.

ROARING TWENTIES

1923–1929. Stock market boom expands richest people's fortunes.

WORLD WAR II

1941–1945. The draft dries up the labor supply, putting upward pressure on wages.

RAPID GROWTH

1950–1970. Helped by G.I. bill, many Americans get college educations, raising earning power. Strong unions and higher pay let the middle class buy homes and cars as never before, putting more wealth in their hands even as rising stock markets make the rich richer.

REAGAN YEARS

Top tax rate slashed from 70% to less than 30%, shifting tax burden to the middle class.

Poor households receive 26% of their income from cash assistance and 18% from in-kind assistance.

The U.S. government gives only 0.1% of its gross national product to poor nations. In contrast, Britain gives 0.26%, and the Netherlands gives 0.8%.

EFFICIENCY

Many economists and political leaders make the value judgment that governments *should* use the Pareto principle, preferring allocations by which someone is made better off if no one else is harmed. That is, they believe that governments should allow voluntary trades, encourage competition, and otherwise try to prevent problems that reduce efficiency.

We can use the Pareto principle to rank allocations or government policies that alter allocations. The Pareto criterion ranks allocation *x* over allocation *y* if some people are better off at *x* and no one else is harmed. If that condition is met, we say that *x* is *Pareto superior* to *y*.

The Pareto principle cannot always be used to compare allocations. Because there are many possible Pareto-efficient allocations, however, a value judgment based on interpersonal comparisons must be made to choose between the allocations. Issues of interpersonal comparisons often arise when we evaluate various government policies. If both allocation *x* and allocation *y* are Pareto efficient, we cannot use this criterion to rank them. For example, if Denise has all the goods in x and Jane has all the goods in y, then we cannot rank these allocations using the Pareto rule.

Suppose that when a country ends a ban on imports and allows free trade, domestic consumers benefit by many times more than domestic producers suffer. Nonetheless, this policy change does not meet the Pareto efficiency criterion that someone be made better off without anyone suffering. However, the government could adopt a more complex policy that meets the Pareto criterion. Because consumers benefit by more than producers suffer, the government could take enough of the free-trade gains from consumers to compensate the producers so that no one is harmed and some people benefit.

The government rarely uses policies by which winners subsidize losers, however. If such subsidization does not occur, additional value judgments involving interpersonal comparisons must be made before deciding whether to adopt a policy.

We have been using a welfare measure, $W =$ consumer surplus + producer surplus, that equally weights benefits and losses to consumers and producers. On the basis of that particular interpersonal comparison criterion, if the gains to consumers outweigh the losses to producers, the policy change should be made.

Thus calling for policy changes that lead to Pareto-superior allocations is a weaker rule than calling for policy changes that increase the welfare measure W. Any policy change that leads to a Pareto-superior allocation must increase W; however, some policy changes that increase W are not Pareto superior: There are both winners and losers.

EQUITY

All animals are equal, but some animals are more equal than others. —George Orwell

If we are unwilling to use the Pareto principle or if that criterion does not allow us to rank the relevant allocations, we must make additional value judgments to rank these allocations. A way to summarize these value judgments is to use a *social welfare function* that combines various consumers' utilities to provide a collective ranking of allocations. Loosely speaking, a social welfare function is a utility function for society.

We illustrate the use of a social welfare function using the pure exchange economy in which Jane and Denise trade wood and candy. There are many possible Pareto-efficient allocations along the contract curve in Figure 10.3. Jane and Denise's utility levels vary along the contract curve. Figure 10.8 shows the *utility possibility frontier (UPF)*: the set of utility levels corresponding to the Pareto-efficient allocations along the contract curve. Point a in panel a corresponds to the end of the contract curve at which Denise has all the goods, and c corresponds to the allocation at which Jane has all the goods.

The curves labeled W^1, W^2, and W^3 in panel a are *isowelfare curves* based on the social welfare function. These curves are similar to indifference curves for individuals. They summarize all the allocations with identical levels of welfare. Society maximizes its welfare at point b.

Who decides on the welfare function? In most countries, government leaders make decisions about which allocations are most desirable. These officials may believe that transferring money from wealthy people to poor people raises welfare, or vice versa. When government officials choose a particular allocation, they are implicitly or explicitly judging which consumers are relatively deserving and hence should receive more goods than others.

Voting. In a democracy, important government policies that determine the allocation of goods are made by voting. Such democratic decision making is often difficult

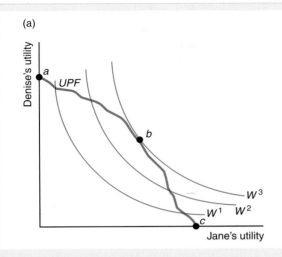

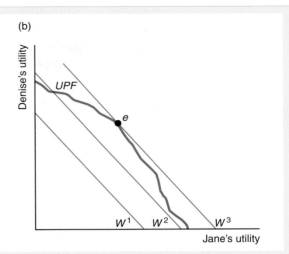

Figure 10.8 Welfare Maximization. Society maximizes welfare by choosing the allocation for which the highest possible isowelfare curve touches the utility possibility frontier, *UPF*. (a) The isowelfare curves have the shape of a typical indifference curve. (b) The isowelfare lines have a slope of −1, indicating that the utilities of both people are treated equally at the margin.

because people fundamentally disagree on how issues should be resolved and which groups of people should be favored.

In Chapter 3, we assumed that consumers could rank-order all bundles of goods in terms of their preferences (completeness) and that their rank over goods was transitive.[7] Suppose now that people have preferences over the allocations of goods among consumers. One possibility, as we assumed earlier, is that individuals care only about how many goods they receive—they do not care about how much others have. Another possibility is that because of envy, charity, pity, love, or other interpersonal feelings, individuals do care about how much everyone has.[8]

Let *a* be a particular allocation of goods that describes how much of each good an individual has. Each person can rank this allocation relative to Allocation *b*. For instance, individuals know whether they prefer an allocation by which everyone has equal amounts of all goods to another allocation by which people who work hard—or those of a particular skin color or religion—have relatively more goods than others.

Through voting, individuals express their rankings. One possible voting system requires that before the vote is taken, everyone agrees to be bound by the outcome in the sense that if a majority of people prefer Allocation *a* to Allocation *b*, then *a* is *socially preferred* to *b*.

Using majority voting to determine which allocations are preferred by society sounds reasonable, doesn't it? Such a system might work well. For example, if all

---

[7]The transitivity (or *rationality*) assumption is that a consumer's preference over bundles is consistent in the sense that if the consumer weakly prefers Bundle *a* to Bundle *b* and weakly prefers Bundle *b* to Bundle *c*, then the consumer weakly prefers Bundle *a* to Bundle *c*.

[8]To an economist, love is nothing more than interdependent utility functions. Thus it's a mystery how each successive generation of economists is produced.

TABLE 10.1   Preferences over Allocations of Three People

	Individual 1	Individual 2	Individual 3
First choice	*a*	*b*	*c*
Second choice	*b*	*c*	*a*
Third choice	*c*	*a*	*b*

individuals have the same transitive preferences, the social ordering has the same transitive ranking as that of each individual.

Unfortunately, sometimes voting does not work well, and the resulting social ordering of allocations is not transitive. To illustrate this possibility, suppose that three people have the transitive preferences in Table 10.1. Individual 1 prefers Allocation *a* to Allocation *b* to Allocation *c*. The other two individuals have different preferred orderings. Two out of three of these individuals prefer *a* to *b*; two out of three prefer *b* to *c*; and two out of three prefer *c* to *a*. Thus voting leads to nontransitive preferences, even though the preferences of each individual are transitive. As a result, there is no clearly defined socially preferred outcome. A majority of people prefers some other allocation to any particular allocation. Compared to Allocation *a*, a majority prefers *c*. Similarly, a majority prefers *b* over *c*, and a majority prefers *a* over *b*.

If people have this type of ranking of allocations, the chosen allocation will depend crucially on the order in which the vote is taken. Suppose that these three people first vote on whether they prefer *a* or *b* and then compare the winner to *c*. Because a majority prefers *a* to *b* in the first vote, they will compare *a* to *c* in the second vote, and *c* will be chosen. If instead they first compare *c* to *a* and the winner to *b*, then *b* will be chosen. Thus the outcome depends on the political skill of various factions in determining the order of voting.

Similar problems arise with other types of voting schemes. Kenneth Arrow (1951), who received a Nobel Prize in economics in part for his work on social decision making, proved a startling and depressing result about democratic voting. This result is often referred to as Arrow's Impossibility Theorem. Arrow suggested that a socially desirable decision-making system, or social welfare function, should satisfy the following criteria:

- Social preferences should be complete (Chapter 4) and transitive, like individual preferences.
- If everyone prefers Allocation *a* to Allocation *b*, *a* should be socially preferred to *b*.
- Society's ranking of *a* and *b* should depend only on individuals' ordering of these two allocations, not on how they rank other alternatives.
- Dictatorship is not allowed; social preferences must not reflect the preferences of only a single individual.

Although each of these criteria seems reasonable—indeed, innocuous—Arrow proved that it is impossible to find a social decision-making rule that *always* satisfies all of these criteria. His result indicates that *democratic decision making* may fail—not that *democracy* must fail. After all, if everyone agrees on a ranking, these four criteria are satisfied.

If society is willing to give up one of these criteria, a democratic decision-making rule can guarantee that the other three criteria are met. For example, if we give up the third criterion, often referred to as the *independence of irrelevant alternatives,* certain complicated voting schemes in which individuals rank their preferences can meet the other criteria.

How You Vote Matters

The 15 members of a city council must decide whether to build a new road (R), repair the high school (H), or install new streetlights (L). Each councilor lists the options in order of preference. Six favor L to H to R; five prefer R to H to L; and four desire H over R over L.

One of the proponents of installing streetlights suggests a plurality vote where everyone casts a single vote for his or her favorite project. Plurality voting would result in six votes for L, five for R, and four for H, so streetlights would win.

"Not so fast," responds a council member who favors roads. Given that H was the least favorite first choice, he suggests a runoff between L and R. Since the four members whose first choice was H prefer R to L, roads would win by nine votes to six.

A supporter of schools is horrified by these self-serving approaches to voting. She calls for pairwise comparisons. A majority of 10 would choose H over R, and nine would prefer H to L. Consequently, although the high school gets the least number of first-place votes, it has the broadest appeal in pairwise comparisons.

Finally, suppose the council uses a voting method developed by Jean-Charles de Borda in 1770 (to elect members to the Academy of Sciences in Paris), where, in an n-person race, a person's first choice gets n votes, the second choice gets $n - 1$, and so forth. (This method has been used in Australia.) Here H gets 34 votes, R receives 29, and L trails with 27, and so the high school project is backed. Thus the outcome of an election or other vote may depend on the voting procedures used.[9]

Social Welfare Functions. How would you rank a given set of allocations if you were asked to vote? Philosophers, economists, newspaper columnists, politicians, radio talk-show hosts, and other deep thinkers have suggested various rules by which society might decide among various possible allocations. All these systems answer the question of which individuals' preferences should be given more weight in society's decision making. Determining how much weight to give to the preferences of various members of society is usually the key step in determining a social welfare function.

Probably the simplest and most egalitarian rule is that every member of society should receive exactly the same bundle of goods. If no further trading is allowed, this rule results in complete equality in the allocation of goods.

Jeremy Bentham (1748–1832) and his followers (including John Stuart Mill), the utilitarian philosophers, suggested that society should maximize the sum of the utilities of all members of society. Their social welfare function is the sum of the utilities of every member of society. The utilities of all people in society are given equal weight.[10] If U_i is the utility

---

[9]Cambridge, Massachusetts; Davis, California; Oakland, Minneapolis; and Pierce County, Washington have adopted "instant runoff" or "proportional representation" voting in city and county elections in which voters rank the candidates—effectively voting on several options at once (Nancy Vogel, "'Instant Runoff' Voting Touted, *Los Angeles Times*, December 25, 2006, **www.latimes.com/news/local/la-me-voting25dec25,1,404720.story?ctrack=1&cset=true**).

[10]It is difficult to compare utilities across individuals because the scaling of utilities across individuals is arbitrary (Chapter 3). A rule that avoids this utility comparison is to maximize a welfare measure that equally weights consumer surplus and producer surplus, which are denominated in dollars.

of Individual i and there are n people, the utilitarian welfare function is

$$W = U_1 + U_2 + \cdots + U_n.$$

However, this social welfare function may not lead to an egalitarian distribution of goods. Indeed, under this system, an allocation is judged superior, all else the same, if people who get the most pleasure from consuming certain goods are given more of those goods.

Panel b of Figure 10.8 shows some isowelfare lines corresponding to the utilitarian welfare function. These lines have a slope of -1 because the utilities of both parties are weighted equally. In the figure, welfare is maximized at e.

A generalization of the utilitarian approach assigns different weights to various individuals' utilities. If the weight assigned to Individual i is α_i, this generalized utilitarian welfare function is

$$W = \alpha_1 U_1 + \alpha_2 U_2 + \cdots + \alpha_n U_n.$$

Society could give greater weight to adults, hardworking people, or those who meet other criteria. Under South Africa's former apartheid system, the utilities of people with white skin were given more weight than those of people with other skin colors.

John Rawls (1971), a philosopher at Harvard University, believed that society should maximize the well-being of the worst-off member of society, the person with the lowest level of utility. In the social welfare function, all the weight should be placed on the utility of the person with the lowest utility level. The Rawlsian welfare function is

$$W = \min(U_1, U_2, \ldots, U_n).$$

Rawls's rule leads to a relatively egalitarian distribution of goods.

One final rule, frequently espoused by various members of Congress and by wealthy landowners in less-developed countries, is to maintain the status quo. Proponents of this rule believe that the current allocation is the best possible allocation, and they argue against any reallocation of resources from one individual to another. Under this rule, the final allocation is likely to be very unequal. Why else would the wealthy want it?

All of these rules or social welfare functions reflect value judgments in which interpersonal comparisons are made. Because each reflects value judgments, we cannot compare them on scientific grounds.

EFFICIENCY VERSUS EQUITY

Given a particular social welfare function, *society might prefer an inefficient allocation to an efficient one.* We can show this result by comparing two allocations. In Allocation a, you have everything and everyone else has nothing. This allocation is Pareto efficient: It is impossible to make others better off without harm to you. In Allocation b, everyone has an equal amount of all goods. Allocation b is not Pareto efficient: I would be willing to trade all my zucchini for just about anything else. Despite Allocation b's inefficiency, most people probably prefer b to a.

Although society might prefer an inefficient Allocation b to an efficient Allocation a, according to most social welfare functions, society would prefer some efficient allocation to b. Suppose that Allocation c is the competitive equilibrium that would be obtained if people were allowed to trade starting from Endowment b, in which everyone has an equal share of all goods. By the utilitarian social welfare functions, Allocation *b* might be socially preferred to Allocation *a*, but Allocation *c* is certainly socially preferred to *b* (ruling out envy and similar interpersonal feelings). After all, if everyone is as well off or better off in Allocation *c* than in *b*, *c* must be better than *b* regardless of weights on individuals' utilities. According to the egalitarian rule, however, *b* is preferred to *c* because only strict equality matters. Thus by most, but not all, of the well-known social welfare functions, *there is an efficient allocation that is socially preferred to an inefficient allocation.*

Competitive equilibrium may not be very equitable even though it is Pareto efficient. Consequently, societies that believe in equity may tax the rich to give to the poor. If the money taken from the rich is given directly to the poor, society moves from one Pareto-efficient allocation to another.

Sometimes, however, in an attempt to achieve greater equity, efficiency is reduced. For example, advocates for the poor argue that providing public housing to the destitute leads to an allocation that is superior to the original competitive equilibrium. This reallocation is not efficient: The poor view themselves as better off receiving an amount of money equal to what the government spends on public housing. They could spend the money on the type of housing they like—rather than the type the government provides—or they could spend some of the money on food or other goods.[11]

Unfortunately, there is frequently a conflict between a society's goal of efficiency and its goal of achieving an equitable allocation. Even when the government redistributes money from one group to another, there are significant costs to this redistribution. If tax collectors and other government bureaucrats could be put to work producing rather than redistributing, total output would increase. Similarly, income taxes discourage people from working as hard as they otherwise would (Chapter 5). Nonetheless, probably few people believe that the status quo is optimal and that the government should engage in no redistribution at all (though some members of Congress vote for tax laws as though they believe that we should redistribute from the poor to the rich).

THEORY OF THE SECOND BEST

Many politicians and media pundits—influenced by the basic logic of the argument that competition maximizes efficiency and our usual welfare measure—argue that we should eliminate any distortion (such as tariffs and quotas). However, care must be taken in making this argument. The argument holds if we eliminate *all* distortions, but it does not necessarily hold if we eliminate only some of the distortions.

Consider a competitive economy with no distortions. It is a *first-best equilibrium* in which any distortion will reduce efficiency. If a single distortion arises—such as one caused by a ban on trade—and that distortion is eliminated, efficiency must rise as the economy reverts to the first-best equilibrium (see Chapter 9). Everyone can gain—welfare rises—if losers (such as producers who lose the benefits of a ban on trade) are compensated.

However, according to the Theory of the Second Best (Lipsey and Lancaster, 1956), if an economy has at least two market distortions, correcting one of them may either

---

[11]Letting the poor decide how to spend their income is efficient by our definition, even if they spend it on "sin goods" such as cigarettes, liquor, or illicit drugs. A similar argument was made regarding food stamps in Chapter 5.

increase or decrease welfare. For example, if a small country has a ban on trade and a subsidy on one good, permitting free trade may not raise efficiency.

Suppose that a wheat-producing country is a price taker on the world wheat market, where the world price is p_w. As we saw in Chapter 9, the country's total welfare is greater if it permits rather than bans free trade. Panel a of Figure 10.9 shows the gain to trade in the usual case. The domestic supply curve, S, is upward sloping, but the home country can import as much as it wants at the world price, p_w. In the free-trade equilibrium, e_1, the equilibrium quantity is Q_1 and the equilibrium price is the world price, p_w. With a ban on imports, the equilibrium is e_2, quantity falls to Q_2, and price rises to p_2. Consequently, the deadweight loss from the ban is area D.

Now suppose that the home government subsidizes its agricultural sector with a payment of s per unit of output. The subsidy creates a distortion: excess production (Chapter 9). The per-unit subsidy s causes the supply curve to shift down from S to S^* in panel b of Figure 10.9. If there is a ban on trade, the equilibrium is at e_3, with a larger quantity, Q_3, than in the original free-trade equilibrium and a lower consumer price, p_3. Because the true marginal cost (the height of the S curve at Q_3) is above the consumer price, there is deadweight loss.

If free trade is permitted, the Theory of the Second Best tells us that welfare does not necessarily rise, because the country still has the subsidy distortion. The free-trade equilibrium is e_4. Firms sell all their quantity, Q_4, at the world price, with Q_1 going to domestic consumers and $Q_4 - Q_1$ to consumers elsewhere. The private gain to trade—ignoring the government's cost of providing the subsidy—is area $A + B$ (see the discussion of Figure 9.9). However, the expansion of domestic output increases the

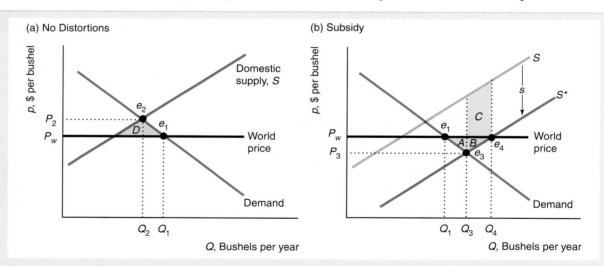

Figure 10.9 Welfare Effect of Trade with and Without a Subsidy. Whether permitting trade raises welfare (consumer surplus plus producer surplus) depends on whether the economy has distortions. (a) If the only distortion is a trade ban, eliminating it must raise welfare. With free trade, the supply curve is the sum of the domestic supply curve and the world supply curve, which is horizontal at the world price, p_w. The equilibrium is e_1 where the supply curve intersects the domestic demand curve. In contrast, without trade, the equilibrium is e_2, where the domestic supply curve intersects the domestic demand curve. The deadweight loss from the ban is area D. (b) With a subsidy, the domestic supply curve shifts to S^*. The equilibrium with a trade ban is e_3 and the free-trade equilibrium is e_4. The gain to trade (ignoring the government's subsidy cost) is area $A +$ B. The expansion of domestic output increases the government's subsidy cost by area $B + C$. Welfare falls because area C is greater than area A.

government's cost of the subsidy by area $B + C$ (the height of this area is the distance between the two supply curves, which is the subsidy, s, and the length is the extra output sold). Thus if area C is greater than area A, there is a net welfare loss from permitting trade. As the diagram is drawn, C is greater than A, so allowing trade lowers welfare, given that the subsidy is provided.

Does it follow from this argument that the country should prohibit free trade? No: To maximize efficiency, the country should allow free trade and eliminate the subsidy. However, unless winners compensate losers, not everyone will benefit.

Summary

1. **General Equilibrium:** A shock to one market may have a spillover effect in another market. A general-equilibrium analysis takes account of the direct effects of a shock in one market and the spillover effects in other markets. In contrast, a partial-equilibrium analysis looks only at one market and ignores such spillover effects. The partial-equilibrium and general-equilibrium effects can differ.

2. **General-Equilibrium Exchange Economy: Trading Between Two People:** If people make all the trades they want, the resulting equilibrium will be Pareto efficient: That is, by moving from this equilibrium, we cannot make one person better off without harming another person. At a Pareto-efficient equilibrium, the marginal rates of substitution between people are equal because their indifference curves are tangent.

3. **Competitive Exchange:** Competition, in which all traders are price takers, leads to an allocation in which the ratio of relative prices equals the marginal rates of substitution of each person. Thus every competitive equilibrium is Pareto efficient. Moreover, any Pareto-efficient equilibrium can be obtained by competition, given an appropriate endowment.

4. **Production and Trading:** When one person can produce more of one good and another person can produce more of another good using the same inputs, trading can result in greater combined production.

5. **Efficiency and Equity:** The Pareto efficiency criterion reflects a value judgment that a change from one allocation to another is desirable if it makes someone better off without harming anyone else. This criterion does not allow all allocations to be ranked, because some people may be better off with one allocation and others may be better off with another allocation. Nor does majority voting necessarily allow society to produce a consensus, transitive ordering of allocations. Economists, philosophers, and others have proposed many criteria for ranking allocations, as summarized in welfare functions. Society may use a welfare function to choose among Pareto-efficient (or other) allocations. If an economy suffers from multiple distortions, correcting only one of them may not raise welfare.

Questions

*= answer at the back of this book; **W** = audio-slide show answers by James Dearden at **www.aw-bc.com/perloff**

*1. What is the effect of a subsidy of s per hour on labor in only one sector of the economy on the equilibrium wage, total employment, and employment in the covered and uncovered sectors?

2. Philadelphia collects an *ad valorem* tax of 4.331% on its residents' earnings (see the "Urban Flight" application), unlike the surrounding areas. Show the effect of this tax on the equilibrium wage, total employment, employment in Philadelphia, and employment in the surrounding areas.

3. A central city imposes a rent control law that places a binding ceiling on the rent that can be charged for an apartment. The suburbs of this city do not have rent control. What happens to the rental prices in the suburbs and to the equilibrium number of apartments in the total metropolitan area, in the city, and in the suburbs? (For simplicity, you may assume that people are indifferent as to whether they live in the city or in the suburbs.)

4. Initially, all workers are paid a wage of w_1 per hour. The government taxes the cost of labor by t per hour only in the "covered" sector of the economy. That is, if the wage workers receive in the covered sector is w_2 per hour, firms

pay $w_2 + t$ per hour. Show how the wages in the covered and uncovered sectors are determined in the post-tax equilibrium. Compared to the pre-tax equilibrium, what happens to total employment, L, employment in the covered sector, L_c, and employment in the uncovered sector, L_u?

5. Suppose that the government gives a fixed subsidy of T per firm in one sector of the economy to encourage firms to hire more workers. What is the effect on the equilibrium wage, total employment, and employment in the covered and uncovered sectors?

6. Competitive firms located in Africa sell their output only in Europe and the United States (which do not produce the good themselves). The industry's supply curve is upward sloping. Europe puts a tariff of t per unit on the good, but the United States does not. What is the effect of the tariff on the total quantity of the good sold, the quantity sold in Europe, the quantity sold in the United States, and equilibrium price(s)?

7. Peaches are sold in a competitive market. There are two types of demanders: consumers who eat fresh peaches and canners. If the government places a binding price ceiling only on peaches sold directly to consumers, what happens to prices and quantities of peaches sold for each use?

8. Initially, electricity is sold in New York and in other states at a competitive single price. Now suppose that New York restricts the quantity of electricity that its citizens can buy. Show what happens to the price of electricity and the quantities sold in New York and elsewhere.

9. A competitive industry with an upward-sloping supply curve sells Q_h of its product in its home country and Q_f in a foreign country, so the total quantity it sells is $Q = Q_h + Q_f$. No one else produces this product. There is no cost of shipping. Determine the equilibrium price and quantity in each country. Now the foreign government imposes a binding quota, Q ($< Q_f$ at the original price). What happens to prices and quantities in both the home and the foreign market?

10. Initially, Michael has 10 candy bars and 5 cookies, and Tony has 5 candy bars and 10 cookies. After trading, Michael has 12 candy bars and 3 cookies. In an Edgeworth box, label the initial allocation A and the new allocation B. Draw some indifference curves that are consistent with this trade being optimal for both Michael and Tony.

*11. Pat and Chris can spend their nonleisure time working either in the marketplace or at home (preparing dinner, taking care of children, doing repairs). In the marketplace, Pat earns a higher wage, $w_p = \$20$, than Chris, $w_c = \$10$. Discuss how living together is likely to affect how much each of them works in the marketplace. In particular, discuss what effect marriage would have on their individual and combined budget constraints and their labor-leisure choices (see Chapter 5). In your discussion, take into account the theory of comparative advantage.

12. The two people in a pure exchange economy have identical utility functions. Will they ever want to trade? Why or why not?

13. Two people trade two goods that they cannot produce. Suppose that one consumer's indifference curves are bowed away from the origin—the usual type of curves—but the other's are concave to the origin. In an Edgeworth box, show that a point of tangency between the two consumers' indifference curves is not a Pareto-efficient bundle. (Identify another allocation that Pareto dominates.)

14. If Jane and Denise have identical, linear production possibility frontiers, are there gains to trade? Explain.

15. Suppose that Britain can produce 10 units of cloth or 5 units of food per day (or any linear combination) with available resources and that Greece can produce 2 units of food per day or 1 unit of cloth (or any combination). Britain has an *absolute* advantage over Greece in producing both goods. Does it still make sense for these countries to trade? Explain.

16. Give an example of a social welfare function that leads to the egalitarian allocation that everyone should be given exactly the same bundle of goods.

*17. In panel c of Figure 10.5, the joint production possibility frontier is concave to the origin. When the two individual production possibility frontiers are combined, however, the resulting *PPF* could have been drawn so that it was convex to the origin. How do we know which of these two ways of drawing the *PPF* to use?

18. Suppose that society used the "opposite" of a Rawlsian welfare function: It tried to maximize the well-being of the best-off member of society. Write this welfare function. What allocation maximizes welfare in this society?

Problems

19. Mexico and the United States can both produce food and toys. Mexico has 100 workers and the United States has 300 workers. If they do not trade, the United States consumes 10 units of food and 10 toys, and Mexico consumes 5 units of food and 1 toy. The following table shows how many workers are necessary to produce each good:

	Mexico	United States
Workers per pound of food	10	10
Workers per toy	50	20

a. In the absence of trade, how many units of food and toys can the United States produce? How many can Mexico produce?
b. Which country has a comparative advantage in producing food? In producing toys?
c. Draw the production possibility for each country and show where the two produce without trade. Label the axes accurately.
d. Draw the production possibility frontier with trade.
e. Show that both countries can benefit from trade.

20. Adrienne and Stephen consume pizza, Z, and cola, C. Adrienne's utility function is $U_A = Z_A C_A$, and Stephen's is $U_A = Z_S^{0.5} C_S^{0.5}$. Their endowments are $Z_A = 10$, $C_A = 20$, $Z_S = 20$, and $C_S = 10$.

a. What are the marginal rates of substitution for each person?
b. What is the formula for the contract curve? Draw an Edgeworth box and indicate the contract curve.

21. The demand curve in Sector 1 of the labor market is $L_1 = a - bw$. The demand curve in Sector 2 is $L_2 = c - dw$. The supply curve of labor for the entire market is $L = e + fw$. In equilibrium, $L_1 + L_2 = L$.

a. Solve for the equilibrium with no minimum wage.
b. Solve for the equilibrium at which the minimum wage is w in Sector 1 ("the covered sector") only.
c. Solve for the equilibrium at which the minimum wage w applies to the entire labor market.

22. The demand functions for Q_1 and Q_2 are

$$Q_1 = 10 - 2p_1 + p_2,$$
$$Q_2 = 10 - 2p_2 + p_1,$$

and there are five units of each good. What is the general equilibrium?

23. The demand for two goods depends on the prices of Good 1 and Good 2, p_1 and p_2,

$$Q_1 = 15 - 3p_1 + p_2,$$
$$Q_2 = 6 - 2p_2 + p_1,$$

but each supply curve depends only on its own price:

$$Q_1 = 2 + p_1,$$
$$Q_2 = 1 + p_2.$$

Solve for the equilibrium: p_1, p_2, Q_1, and Q_2.

24. In a pure exchange economy with two goods, G and H, the two traders have Cobb-Douglas utility functions. Suppose that Tony's utility function is $U_t = G_t H_t$ and that Margaret's utility function is $U_m = G_m (H_m)^2$. Between them, they own 100 units of G and 50 units of H. Solve for their contract curve.

25. Continuing with Problem 24, determine p, the competitive price of G, where the price of H is normalized to equal one.

26. The market demand for medical checkups per day, Q_F, is $Q_F = 25(198 + n_C/20,000 - p_F)$, where n_C is the number of patients per day who are at least 40 years old, and p_F is the price of a checkup. The market demand for the number of dental checkups per day, Q_T, is $Q_T = 100(150 - p_T)/3$, where p_T represents the price of a dental checkup. The long-run market supply of medical checkups is $Q_F = 50p_F - 10p_T$. The long-run market supply of dentists is $Q_T = 50p_T - 10p_F$. The supplies are linked because people decide whether to be doctors and dentists on the basis of relative earnings.

a. If $n_C = 40,000$, what is the equilibrium number of medical and dental checkups? What are the equilibrium prices? How would an increase in n_C affect the equilibrium prices? Determine dp_F/dn_C and dp_T/dn_C.
b. Suppose that, instead of determining the price of medical checkups by a market process, large health insurance companies set their reimbursement rates, effectively determining all medical prices. A medical doctor receives $35 per checkup from the insurance company, and patients pay only $10. How many checkups do doctors offer collectively? What is the equilibrium quantity and price of dental checkups?
c. What is the effect of a shift from a competitive medical checkup market to insurance-company-dictated medical-doctor payments on the equilibrium salaries of dentists? **W**

27. A society consists of two people with utilities U_1 and U_2, and the social welfare function is $W = \alpha_1 U_1 + \alpha_2 U_2$. Draw a utility possibilities frontier similar to the ones in Figure 10.8. Use calculus to show that where social welfare is maximized, as α_1/α_2 increases, Person 1 benefits, and Person 2 is harmed. **W**

Chapter 11

Monopoly

Monopoly: one parrot.

A **monopoly** is the only supplier of a good for which there is no close substitute. Monopolies have been common since ancient times. In the fifth century B.C., the Greek philosopher Thales gained control of most of the olive presses during a year of exceptionally productive harvests. Similarly, the ancient Egyptian pharaohs controlled the sale of food. In England, until Parliament limited the practice in 1624, kings granted monopoly rights called royal charters or patents to court favorites. Today, virtually every country grants a *patent*—an exclusive right to sell that lasts for a limited period of time—to an inventor of a new product, process, substance, or design. Until 1999, the U.S. government gave one company the right to be the sole registrar of Internet domain names.

Consumers hate monopolies, which charge them high prices. A monopoly can *set* its price—it is not a price taker like a competitive firm is. A monopoly's output is the market output, and the demand curve a monopoly faces is the market demand curve. Because the market demand curve is downward sloping, the monopoly (unlike a competitive firm) doesn't lose all its sales if it raises its price. As a consequence, the monopoly sets its price above marginal cost to maximize its profit. Consumers buy less at this high monopoly price than they would at the competitive price, which equals marginal cost.

In this chapter, we examine eight main topics	1. **Monopoly Profit Maximization:** Like all firms, a monopoly maximizes its profit by setting its price or output so that its marginal revenue equals its marginal cost.
	2. **Market Power:** How much the monopoly's price is above its marginal cost depends on the shape of the demand curve that the monopoly faces.
	3. **Welfare Effects of Monopoly:** By setting its price above marginal cost, a monopoly creates a deadweight loss.
	4. **Taxes and Monopoly:** Specific and *ad valorem* taxes increase the deadweight loss due to monopoly, may have consumer incidences in excess of 100%, and affect welfare differently from each other.
	5. **Cost Advantages That Create Monopolies:** A firm can use a cost advantage over other firms (due, say, to control of a key input or to economies of scale) to become a monopoly.
	6. **Government Actions That Create Monopolies:** Governments create monopolies by establishing government monopoly firms, limiting entry of other firms to create a private monopoly, and issuing patents, which are temporary monopoly rights.

7. **Government Actions That Reduce Market Power:** The welfare loss of a monopoly can be reduced or eliminated if the government regulates the price the monopoly charges or allows other firms to enter the market.

8. **Monopoly Decisions over Time:** If its current sales affect a monopoly's future demand curve, a monopoly that maximizes its long-run profit may choose not to maximize its short-run profit.

11.1 Monopoly Profit Maximization

Competitive firms and monopolies alike maximize their profits using a two-step procedure (Chapter 8). First, the firm determines the output at which it makes the highest possible profit. Second, the firm decides whether to produce at that output level or to shut down, using the rules described in Chapter 8.

For a competitive firm, we distinguished between a lowercase q, which represented a firm's output, and an uppercase Q, which reflected the market quantity. Because a monopoly sells the entire market quantity, we use Q to indicate both the monopoly's quantity and the market quantity.

THE NECESSARY CONDITION FOR PROFIT MAXIMIZATION

A monopoly's first step is to pick its optimal output level. A monopoly, like any firm (Chapter 8), maximizes its profit by operating where its marginal revenue equals its marginal cost, as we now show formally.

A monopoly's profit function is $\pi(Q) = R(Q) - C(Q)$, where $R(Q)$ is its revenue function and $C(Q)$ is its cost function. The necessary condition for the monopoly to maximize its profit is found by choosing that output Q^* such that the derivative of its profit function with respect to output equals zero:

$$\frac{d\pi(Q^*)}{dQ} = \frac{dR(Q^*)}{dQ} - \frac{dC(Q^*)}{dQ} = 0, \tag{11.1}$$

where $dR/dQ = MR$ is its marginal revenue function (Chapter 8) and $dC/dQ = MC$ is its marginal cost function (Chapter 7). Thus Equation 11.1 requires the monopoly to choose that output level Q^* such that *its marginal revenue equals its marginal cost:* $MR(Q^*) = MC(Q^*)$.

The sufficient condition for a profit maximum requires that the second derivative of the profit function with respect to output be negative,

$$\frac{d^2\pi(Q^*)}{dQ^2} = \frac{d^2R(Q^*)}{dQ^2} - \frac{d^2C(Q^*)}{dQ^2} < 0, \tag{11.2}$$

where d^2R/dQ^2 is the second derivative of the revenue function with respect to Q and d^2C/dQ^2 is the second derivative of the cost function. By definition, $d^2R/dQ^2 = dMR/dQ$ is the slope of its marginal revenue curve. Similarly, $d^2C/dQ^2 = dMC/dQ$ is the slope of the marginal cost curve. Thus Equation 11.2 requires that the slope of the marginal revenue curve be less than that of the marginal cost curve: $d^2R/dQ^2 < d^2C/dQ^2$ or $dMR/dQ < dMC/dQ$. Typically this condition is met because the marginal cost curve is frequently constant or increasing with output $(dMC/dQ \geq 0)$ and the monopoly's marginal revenue curve is downward sloping $(dMR/dQ < 0)$, as we will now show.

MARGINAL REVENUE AND THE DEMAND CURVES

A firm's marginal revenue curve depends on its demand curve. We will demonstrate that a monopoly's marginal revenue curve is downward sloping and lies below its demand curve at any positive quantity because its demand curve is downward sloping. The following reasoning applies to any firm that faces a downward-sloping demand curve—not just to a monopoly.

The monopoly's inverse demand function shows the price it receives for selling a given quantity: $p(Q)$. That price, $p(Q)$, is the monopoly's *average revenue* for a given quantity, Q. Its revenue function is its average revenue or price times the number of units it sells: $R(Q) = p(Q)Q$.

Using the product rule of differentiation, we can write the monopoly's marginal revenue function as

$$MR(Q) = \frac{dR(Q)}{dQ} = \frac{dp(Q)Q}{dQ} = p(Q)\frac{dQ}{dQ} + \frac{dp(Q)}{dQ}Q. \qquad (11.3)$$

The first term on the right-hand side of Equation 11.3 is the price or average revenue. The second term is the slope of the demand curve, $dp(Q)/dQ$, times the number of units sold. Because the monopoly's inverse demand curve slopes downward, $dp(Q)/dQ < 0$, this second term is negative. (In contrast, a competitive firm's inverse demand curve has a slope of zero because it is horizontal, so the second term is zero, and the competitive firm's marginal revenue equals the market price, as we saw in Chapter 8.)

Thus at a given positive quantity, a monopoly's marginal revenue is less than its price or average revenue by $[dp(Q)/dp]Q$. That is, *a monopoly's marginal revenue curve lies below its inverse demand curve at any positive quantity.*

Figure 11.1 illustrates the reason a monopoly's marginal revenue is less than its price. The monopoly, which is initially selling Q units at p_1, can sell one extra unit—$Q + 1$ total units—only if it lowers its price to p_2.

The monopoly's initial revenue is $R_1 = p_1 Q = A + C$. When it sells the extra unit, its revenue is $R_2 = p_2(Q + 1) = A + B$. Thus its marginal revenue from selling one additional unit is

$$MR = R_2 - R_1 = (A + B) - (A + C) = B - C.$$

The monopoly sells the extra unit of output at the new price, p_2, so it gains extra revenue from that last unit of $B = p_2 \times 1 = p_2$, which corresponds to the $p(Q)$ term in Equation 11.3. Because it had to lower its price, the monopoly loses the difference between the new price and the original price, $\Delta p = (p_2 - p_1)$, on the Q units it originally sold, $C = \Delta pQ$, which corresponds to the $(dp/dQ)Q$ term in Equation 11.3. Thus the monopoly's marginal revenue, $B - C = p_2 - C$, is less than the price it charges by an amount equal to area C.

In general, the relationship between the marginal revenue and demand curves depends on the shape of the demand curve. For all linear demand curves, the relationship between the marginal revenue and demand curve is the same.

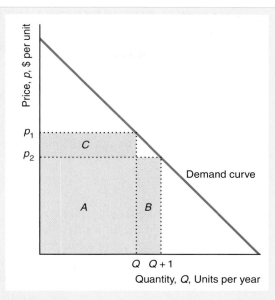

Figure 11.1 Average and Marginal Revenue. The demand curve shows the average revenue or price per unit of output sold. The monopoly's marginal revenue is less than the price p_2 by area C (the revenue lost due to a lower price on the Q units originally sold). The monopoly's initial revenue is $R_1 = p_1 Q = A + C$. If it sells one more unit, its revenue is $R_2 = p_2(Q + 1) = A + B = A + p_2$. Thus its marginal revenue (if one extra unit is a very small increase in its output) is $MR = R_2 - R_1 = B - C = p_2 - C$, which is less than p_2.

SOLVED PROBLEM 11.1

Show that if a monopoly's inverse demand curve is linear, its marginal revenue curve is also linear, has twice the slope of the inverse demand curve, intersects the vertical axis at the same point as the inverse demand curve, and intersects the horizontal axis at half the distance as does the inverse demand curve.

Answer

1. *Write a general formula for any downward-sloping linear inverse demand curve:* Any linear demand curve can be written as $p(Q) = a - bQ$, where a and b are positive constants.

2. *Derive the monopoly's revenue function and then derive its marginal revenue function by differentiating the revenue function with respect to its output:* The monopoly's revenue function is $R = p(Q)Q = aQ - bQ^2$. The marginal revenue function is the derivative of the revenue function with respect to quantity: $MR(Q) = dR/dQ = a - 2bQ$.

3. *Describe the properties of the marginal revenue function relative to those of the inverse demand function:* Both the marginal revenue function and the inverse demand functions are linear. Both hit the vertical (price) axis at a: $MR(0) = a - (2b \times 0) = a$ and $p(0) = a - (b \times 0) = a$. The slope of the marginal revenue curve, $dMR/dQ = -2b$, is twice the slope of the inverse demand curve $dp(Q)/dQ = -b$. Consequently, the MR curve hits the quantity axis at half the distance of the demand curve: $MR = 0 = a - 2bQ$, where $Q = a/(2b)$, and $p = 0 = a - bQ$, where $Q = a/b$.

MARGINAL REVENUE CURVE AND THE PRICE ELASTICITY OF DEMAND

The marginal revenue at any given quantity depends on the inverse demand curve's height (the price) and the elasticity of demand. From Chapter 2, we know that the price elasticity of demand is $\varepsilon = (dQ/dp)/(p/Q) < 0$, which tells us the percentage by which quantity demanded falls as the price increases by 1%.

According to Equation 11.3, $MR = p + (dp/dQ)/Q$. By multiplying and dividing the second term by p, rearranging terms, and substituting using the definition of the elasticity of demand, we can write marginal revenue in terms of the elasticity of demand:

$$MR = p + \frac{dp}{dQ}Q = p + p\frac{dp}{dQ}\frac{Q}{p} = p\left[1 + \frac{1}{(dQ/dp)(p/Q)}\right] = p\left(1 + \frac{1}{\varepsilon}\right). \quad (11.4)$$

According to Equation 11.4, marginal revenue is closer to price as demand becomes more elastic. In the limit where $\varepsilon \to -\infty$, a monopoly faces a perfectly elastic demand curve (similar to that of a competitive firm), and its marginal revenue equals its price.

In Figure 11.2, we illustrate the relationship between the marginal revenue and the price elasticity of demand for a particular linear inverse demand function,

$$p(Q) = 24 - Q. \quad (11.5)$$

Its corresponding demand function is $Q(p) = 24 - p$. The slope of this demand function is $dQ/dp = -1$, so the elasticity of demand at a given output level is $\varepsilon = (dQ/dp)(p/Q) = -p/Q = -(24 - Q)/Q = 1 - 24/Q$.

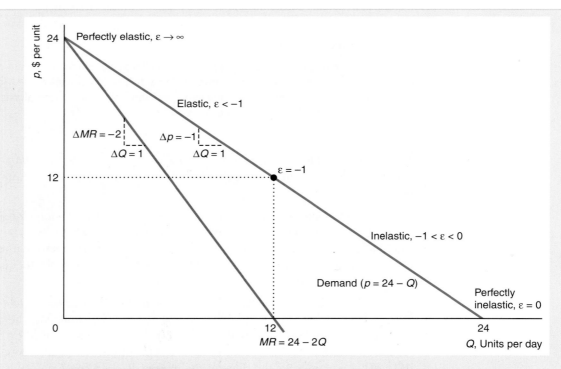

Figure 11.2 Elasticity of Demand and Total, Average, and Marginal Revenue. The demand curve (or average revenue curve), $p = 24 - Q$, lies above the marginal revenue curve, $MR = 24 - 2Q$. Where the marginal revenue equals zero, $Q = 12$, and the elasticity of demand is $\varepsilon = -1$.

From the results of Solved Problem 11.1, the monopoly's marginal revenue function is

$$MR(Q) = 24 - 2Q. \tag{11.6}$$

Where the demand curve hits the price axis ($Q = 0$), the demand curve is perfectly elastic, so the marginal revenue equals price: $MR = p$. At the midpoint of any linear demand curve, the demand elasticity is unitary (see Chapter 2), $\varepsilon = -1$, so the marginal revenue is zero: $MR = p[1 + 1/(-1)] = 0$. In our example at the midpoint of the demand curve where $Q = 12$, the elasticity is $\varepsilon = 1 - 12/24 = -1$, and the marginal revenue is $MR = 24 - (2 \times 12) = 0$. To the right of the midpoint of the demand curve, the demand curve is inelastic, $-1 < \varepsilon \leq 0$, so the marginal revenue is negative.

AN EXAMPLE OF MONOPOLY PROFIT MAXIMIZATION

In Chapter 8, we found that any type of firm maximizes its profit by selling its output such that its marginal cost equals its marginal revenue. We now examine how a monopoly maximizes its profit using an example with the linear inverse demand function in Equation 11.5, $p(Q) = 24 - Q$, and a quadratic short-run cost function,

$$C(Q) = VC(Q) + F = Q^2 + 12, \tag{11.7}$$

where the monopoly's variable cost is $VC(Q) = Q^2$ and its fixed cost is $F = 12$ (see Chapter 7). The firm's marginal cost function is

$$MC(Q) = \frac{dC(Q)}{dQ} = 2Q. \tag{11.8}$$

The average variable cost is $AVC = Q^2/Q = Q$, so it is a straight line through the origin with a slope of 1. The average cost is $AC = C/Q = (Q^2 + 12)/Q = Q + 12/Q$, which is U-shaped. Panel a of Figure 11.3 shows the MC, AVC, and AC curves.

The Profit-Maximizing Output. The firm's highest possible profit is obtained by producing at the quantity Q^* where its marginal revenue equals its marginal cost function:

$$MR(Q^*) = 24 - 2Q^* = 2Q^* = MC(Q^*).$$

Solving this expression, we find that $Q^* = 6$. Panel a of Figure 11.3 shows that the monopoly's marginal revenue and marginal cost curves intersect at $Q^* = 6$.

Panel b shows the corresponding profit and revenue curves. The profit curve reaches its maximum at 6 units of output, where marginal profit—the slope of the profit curve—is zero. Because *marginal profit is marginal revenue minus marginal cost* (Chapter 8), marginal profit is zero where the marginal revenue curve intersects the marginal cost curve at 6 units in panel a. The height of the demand curve at the profit-maximizing quantity is $p = 18$. Thus the monopoly maximizes its profit at point e, where it sells 6 units per day at a price of 18 per unit.

Why does the monopoly maximize its profit by producing 6 units where its marginal revenue equals its marginal cost? At smaller quantities, the monopoly's marginal revenue is greater than its marginal cost, so its marginal profit is positive. By increasing its output slightly, it raises its profit. Similarly, at quantities greater than 6 units, the monopoly's marginal cost is greater than its marginal revenue, so it can increase its profit by reducing its output slightly.

The profit-maximizing quantity is smaller than the revenue-maximizing quantity. The revenue curve reaches its maximum at $Q = 12$, where the slope of the revenue curve, the marginal revenue, is zero (panel a). In contrast, the profit curve reaches its maximum at $Q = 6$, where marginal revenue equals marginal cost. Because marginal

Figure 11.3 Maximizing Profit. (a) At $Q = 6$, where marginal revenue, MR, equals marginal cost, MC, profit is maximized. The rectangle showing the maximum profit \$60 is average profit per unit, $p - AC = \$18 - \$8 = \$10$, times the number of units, 6. (b) Profit is maximized at a smaller quantity, $Q = 6$ (where marginal revenue equals marginal cost), than revenue is maximized, $Q = 12$ (where marginal revenue is zero).

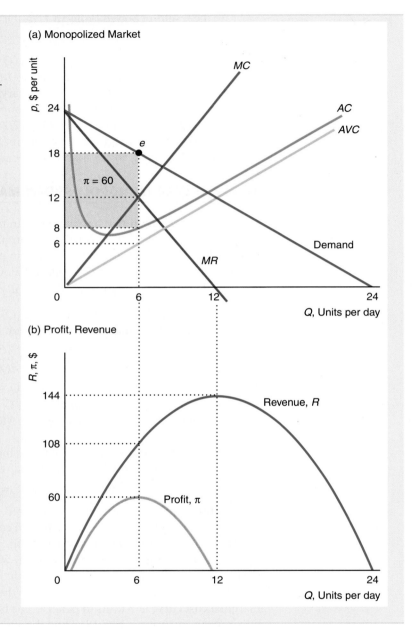

cost is positive, marginal revenue must be positive when profit is maximized. Given that the marginal revenue curve has a negative slope, marginal revenue is positive at a smaller quantity than where it equals zero. Thus the profit curve must reach a maximum at a smaller quantity, 6, than the revenue curve, 12.

As we already know, marginal revenue equals zero at the quantity where the demand curve has a unitary elasticity. Because a linear demand curve is more elastic at smaller quantities, *monopoly profit is maximized in the elastic portion of the demand curve.* (Here profit is maximized at $Q = 6$ where the elasticity of demand is -3.) Equivalently, *a monopoly never operates in the inelastic portion of its demand curve.*

APPLICATION

Cable Cars and Profit Maximization

Since San Francisco's cable car system started operating in 1873, it has been one of the city's main tourist attractions. In mid-2005, the cash-strapped Municipal Railway raised the one-way fare by two-thirds from $3 to $5. Not surprisingly, the number of riders dropped substantially, and many in the city called for a rate reduction.

The rate increase prompted many locals to switch to buses or other forms of transportation, but most tourists have a relatively inelastic demand curve for cable car rides. Frank Bernstein of Arizona, who visited San Francisco with his wife, two children, and mother-in-law, said that there was no way they would visit San Francisco without riding a cable car: "That's what you do when you're here." But the $50 cost for his family to ride a cable car from the Powell Street turnaround to Fisherman's Wharf and back "is a lot of money for our family. We'll do it once, but we won't do it again."

If the city ran the cable car system like a profit-maximizing monopoly, the decision to raise fares would be clearer. The 67% rate hike resulted in a 23% increase in revenue to $9,045,792 in the 2005–2006 fiscal year. For a reduction in rides (output) to raise revenue, the city must have been operating in the inelastic portion of its demand curve ($\varepsilon > -1$) where $MR = p(1 + 1/\varepsilon) < 0$ prior to the fare increase. With fewer riders, costs stay constant or fall (if the city chooses to run fewer than its traditional 40 cars). Thus its profit must increase.

However, the city may not be interested in maximizing its profit on the cable cars. Mayor Gavin Newsom said that having fewer riders "was my biggest fear when we raised the fare. I think we're right at the cusp of losing visitors who come to San Francisco and want to enjoy a ride on a cable car." The mayor believes that enjoyable and inexpensive cable car rides help attract tourists to the city, thereby benefiting many local businesses.[1] Newsom observed, "Cable cars are so fundamental to the lifeblood of the city, and they represent so much more than the revenue they bring in." Thus he is considering whether to run the cable cars at a price below the profit-maximizing level.

The Shutdown Decision. Should the monopoly produce this output level or shut down? In the short run, the monopoly shuts down if the monopoly-optimal price is less than its average variable cost. In our short-run example in Figure 11.3 at the profit-maximizing output, the average variable cost is $AVC(6) = 6$, which is less than the price, $p(6) = 18$, so the firm chooses to produce. Equivalently, the firm's revenue, $R(6) = p(6)6 = (24 - 6)6 = 108$, exceeds its variable (or avoidable) cost, $VC(6) = 6^2 = 36$, so the firm chooses to produce.

---

[1]That is, the mayor believes that cable cars provide a positive externality; see Chapter 17.

Indeed, the monopoly makes a positive profit. Because its profit is $\pi = p(Q)Q - C(Q)$, its average profit is $\pi/Q = p(Q) - C(Q)/Q = p(Q) - AC$. Thus its average profit (and hence profit) is positive only if price is above the average cost. At $Q^\star = 6$, its average cost, $AC(6) = 8$, is above its price, $p(6) = 18$. Its profit is $\pi = 60$, which is the shaded rectangle with a height equal to the average profit per unit, $p(6) - AC(6) = 18 - 8 = 10$, and a width of 6 units.

CHOOSING PRICE OR QUANTITY

Unlike a competitive firm, a monopoly can adjust its price, so it has the choice of setting its price *or* its quantity to maximize its profit. (A competitive firm must set its quantity to maximize profit because it cannot affect market price.)

The monopoly is constrained by the market demand curve. Because the demand curve slopes downward, the monopoly faces a trade-off between a higher price and a lower quantity or a lower price and a higher quantity. The monopoly chooses the point on the demand curve that maximizes its profit. Unfortunately for the monopoly, it cannot set both its quantity and its price and thereby pick a point that is above the demand curve. If it could do so, the monopoly would choose an extremely high price and an extremely high output level and would become exceedingly wealthy.

If the monopoly sets its price, the demand curve determines how much output it sells. If the monopoly picks an output level, the demand curve determines the price. Because the monopoly wants to operate at the price and output at which its profit is maximized, it chooses the same profit-maximizing solution whether it sets the price or the output. In this chapter, we assume that the monopoly sets the quantity.

EFFECTS OF A SHIFT OF THE DEMAND CURVE

Shifts in the demand curve or marginal cost curve affect the monopoly optimum and can have a wider variety of effects in a monopolized market than in a competitive market. In a competitive market, the effect of a shift in demand on a competitive firm's output depends only on the marginal cost curve (Chapter 8). In contrast, the effect of a shift in demand on a monopoly's output depends on the marginal cost curve and the demand curve.

A competitive firm's marginal cost curve tells us everything we need to know about the amount that the firm will supply at any given market price. The competitive firm's supply curve is its upward-sloping marginal cost curve above its minimum average variable cost. A competitive firm's supply behavior does not depend on the shape of the market demand curve because the firm always faces a horizontal residual demand curve at the market price. Thus if you know a competitive firm's marginal cost curve, you can predict how much that firm will produce at any given market price.

In contrast, a monopoly's output decision depends on its marginal cost curve and its demand curve. Unlike a competitive firm, *a monopoly does not have a supply curve.* Knowing the monopoly's marginal cost curve is not enough for us to predict how much a monopoly will sell at any given price.

Figure 11.4 illustrates that the relationship between price and quantity is unique in a competitive market but not in a monopoly market. If the market is competitive, the initial equilibrium is e_1 in panel a, where the original demand curve D^1 intersects the supply curve, MC, which is the sum of the marginal cost curves of a large number of competitive firms. When the demand curve shifts to D^2, the new competitive equilibrium,

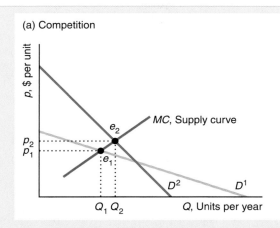
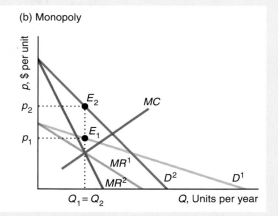

Figure 11.4 Effects of a Shift of the Demand Curve.
(a) A shift of the demand curve from D^1 to D^2 causes the competitive equilibrium to move from e_1 to e_2 along the supply curve (the horizontal sum of the marginal cost curves of all the competitive firms). Because the competitive equilibrium lies on the supply curve, each quantity corresponds to only one possible equilibrium price. (b) With a monopoly, this same shift of demand causes the monopoly optimum to change from E_1 to E_2. The monopoly quantity stays the same, but the monopoly price rises. Thus a shift in demand does not map out a unique relationship between price and quantity in a monopolized market: The same quantity, $Q_1 = Q_2$, is associated with two different prices, p_1 and p_2.

e_2, has a higher price and quantity. A shift of the demand curve maps out competitive equilibria along the marginal cost curve, so for every equilibrium quantity, there is a single corresponding equilibrium price.

Panel b shows the corresponding situation with a monopoly. As demand shifts from D^1 to D^2, the monopoly optimum shifts from E_1 to E_2, so the price rises but the quantity stays constant, $Q_1 = Q_2$. Thus *a given quantity can correspond to more than one monopoly-optimal price*. A shift in the demand curve may cause the monopoly-optimal price to stay constant and the quantity to change, or both price and quantity to change.

11.2   Market Power

What determines how high a price a monopoly can charge? A monopoly has **market power:** the ability of a firm to charge a price above marginal cost and earn a positive profit. In this section, we examine the factors that determine how much above its marginal cost a monopoly sets its price.

MARKET POWER AND THE SHAPE OF THE DEMAND CURVE

The degree to which the monopoly raises its price above its marginal cost depends on the shape of the demand curve at the profit-maximizing quantity. If the monopoly faces a highly elastic—nearly flat—demand curve at the profit-maximizing quantity, it would lose substantial sales if it raised its price by even a small amount. Conversely, if the demand curve is not very elastic (is relatively steep) at that quantity, the monopoly would lose fewer sales from raising its price by the same amount.

TABLE 11.1   Elasticity of Demand, Price, and Marginal Cost

	Elasticity of Demand, ε	Price/Marginal Cost Ratio, $p/MC = 1/[1 + (1/\varepsilon)]$	Lerner Index, $(p - MC)/p = -1/\varepsilon$
←more elastic less elastic→	−1.01	101	0.99
	−1.1	11	0.91
	−2	2	0.50
	−3	1.5	0.33
	−5	1.25	0.20
	−10	1.11	0.10
	−100	1.01	0.01
	$-\infty$	1	0

We can derive the relationship between market power and the elasticity of demand at the profit-maximizing quantity using the expression for marginal revenue in Equation 11.4 and the firm's profit-maximizing condition that marginal revenue equals marginal cost:

$$MR = p\left(1 + \frac{1}{\varepsilon}\right) = MC. \tag{11.9}$$

By rearranging terms, we can rewrite Equation 11.9 as

$$\frac{p}{MC} = \frac{1}{1 + (1/\varepsilon)}. \tag{11.10}$$

According to Equation 11.10, the ratio of the price to marginal cost depends *only* on the elasticity of demand at the profit-maximizing quantity.

In our linear demand example in panel a of Figure 11.3, the elasticity of demand is $\varepsilon = -3$ at the monopoly optimum where $Q^* = 6$. As a result, the ratio of price to marginal cost is $p/MC = 1/[1 + 1/(-3)] = 1.5$, or $p = 1.5MC$. The profit-maximizing price, $18, in panel a is 1.5 times the marginal cost of $12.

Table 11.1 illustrates how the ratio of price to marginal cost varies with the elasticity of demand. When the elasticity is −1.01, which is only slightly elastic, the monopoly's profit-maximizing price is 101 times larger than its marginal cost: $p/MC = 1/[1 + 1/(-1.01)] \approx 101$. As the elasticity of demand approaches negative infinity (becomes perfectly elastic), $1/\varepsilon$ approaches zero, so the ratio of price to marginal cost shrinks to $p/MC = 1$.

This table illustrates that not all monopolies can set high prices. A monopoly that faces a horizontal, perfectly elastic demand curve sets its price equal to its marginal cost—just like a price-taking competitive firm. If this monopoly were to raise its price, it would lose all its sales, so it maximizes its profit by setting its price equal to its marginal cost.

The more elastic the demand curve, the less a monopoly can raise its price without losing sales. All else the same, the more close substitutes for the monopoly's good there are, the more elastic the demand the monopoly faces. For example, Addison-Wesley has the monopoly right to produce and sell this textbook. Many other publishers, however, have the rights to produce and sell similar microeconomics textbooks (although you wouldn't like them as much). The demand Addison-Wesley faces is much more

elastic than it would be if no substitutes were available. If you think this textbook is expensive, imagine the cost if no substitutes were published!

LERNER INDEX

Another way to show how the elasticity of demand affects a monopoly's price relative to its marginal cost is to look at the firm's **Lerner Index** (or *price markup*):[2] the ratio of the difference between price and marginal cost to the price: $(p - MC)/p$. This measure is zero for a competitive firm because a competitive firm cannot raise its price above its marginal cost. The greater the difference between price and marginal cost, the larger the Lerner Index and the greater the monopoly's ability to set price above marginal cost.

If the firm is maximizing its profit, we can express the Lerner Index in terms of the elasticity of demand by rearranging Equation 11.10:

$$\frac{p - MC}{p} = -\frac{1}{\varepsilon}. \tag{11.11}$$

Because $MC \geq 0$ and $p \geq MC$, $0 \leq p - MC \leq p$ and the Lerner Index ranges from 0 to 1 for a profit-maximizing firm.[3] Equation 11.11 confirms that a competitive firm has a Lerner Index of zero because its demand curve is perfectly elastic. As Table 11.1 illustrates, the Lerner Index for a monopoly increases as the demand becomes less elastic. If $\varepsilon = -5$, the monopoly's markup (Lerner Index) is $1/5 = 0.2$; if $\varepsilon = -2$, the markup is $1/2 = 0.5$; and if $\varepsilon = -1.01$, the markup is 0.99. Monopolies that face demand curves that are only slightly elastic set prices that are multiples of their marginal cost and have Lerner Indexes close to 1.

APPLICATION

Apple's iPod

Apple introduced its iPod on October 23, 2001. Although the iPod was not the first hard-drive music player, it was the most elegant one to date. Endowed with a tiny hard drive, it was about a quarter the size of its competitors, fit in one's pocket, and weighed only 6.5 ounces. Moreover, it was the only player to use a high-speed FireWire interface to transfer files, and it held a thousand songs. Perhaps most importantly, the iPod offered an intuitive interface and an attractive white case with unusual ear buds.

From the start, people have loved the iPod. Even at its extremely high price of $399, Apple had a virtual monopoly for half a decade. In 2004, the iPod had 96% of the hard-drive player market (if one includes the 3.6% share of iPods produced by Hewlett-Packard under license from Apple). Even by the beginning of 2007, Apple claimed that its share was 72%.

---

[2]This index is named after its inventor, Abba Lerner.

[3]For the Lerner Index to be above 1, ε would have to be a negative fraction, indicating that the demand curve was inelastic at the monopoly optimum. However, a profit-maximizing monopoly never operates in the inelastic portion of its demand curve.

To keep ahead of potential competitors, Apple has introduced subsequent generations of iPods in quick succession (although it always sells its top-of-the-line model for $399). Its iTunes proprietary media player software and its iTunes Music Store help Apple maintain its stranglehold on the market for paid-for-music downloads with an 85% share in 2006. At the iTunes Music Store, users can easily download tracks for 99¢, burn them to a CD, play them using iTunes, or sync them with their MP3 player. However, iTunes supports copying music to the iPod and not from it, and songs purchased from the iTunes Music Store are copy protected with Apple's FairPlay digital rights management scheme, which prevents iTunes customers from using the purchased music on portable digital music players other than the Apple iPod. Consequently, some current owners of iPods and iTunes are hesitant to switch to potential competitors because they would have to learn new software and might be unable to transfer some of their previously purchased songs to the new equipment.

SOLVED PROBLEM   11.2

Apple's constant marginal cost of producing its top-of-the-line iPod is $200, its fixed cost is $736 million, and its inverse demand function is $p = 600 - 25Q$, where Q is units measured in millions.[4] What is Apple's average cost function? Assuming that Apple is maximizing short-run monopoly profit, what is its marginal revenue function? What are its profit-maximizing price and quantity, profit, and Lerner Index? What is the elasticity of demand at the profit-maximizing level? Show Apple's profit-maximizing solution in a figure.

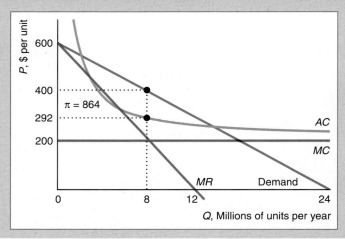

[4]The marginal cost estimate comes from **www.eetimes.com/news/latest/showArticle.jhtml? articleID=18306938**. Although we assume that the marginal cost curve is constant, there is some evidence from Apple's other lines that it might be downward sloping. The quantity in 2004 is from In-Stat market research, **www.tomshardware.com/hardnews/20050621_123943.html**. We assumed that the company's gross profit margin for 2004, **www.apple.com/pr/library/ 2004/oct/13results.html**, held for the iPod line and used that to calculate the fixed cost. We derived the linear demand curve by assuming Apple maximizes profit and using the information on price, marginal cost, and quantity. Assuming that Apple maximizes its short-run profit may not be completely realistic, as we discuss in the last section of this chapter.

Answer

1. *Derive the average cost function using the information about Apple's marginal and fixed costs:* Given that Apple's marginal cost is constant, its average variable cost equals its marginal cost, $200. Its average fixed cost is its fixed cost divided by the quantity produced, $736/Q$. Thus its average cost is $AC = 200 + 736/Q$.

2. *Derive Apple's marginal revenue function using the information about its demand function:* Because the inverse demand function is $p = 600 - 25Q$, Apple's revenue function is $R = 600Q - 25Q^2$, so $MR = dR/dQ = 600 - 50Q$.

3. *Derive Apple's profit-maximizing price and quantity by equating the marginal revenue and marginal cost functions and solving:* Apple maximizes its profit where

$$MR = 600 - 50Q = 200 = MC.$$

Solving this equation for the profit-maximizing output, we find that $Q = 8$ million units. By substituting this quantity into the inverse demand equation, we determine that the profit-maximizing price is $p = 400 per unit, as the figure shows.

4. *Calculate Apple's profit using the profit-maximizing price and quantity and the average cost:* The firm's profit is $\pi = (p - AC)Q = [400 - (200 + 736/8)]8 = 864 million. The figure shows that the profit is a rectangle with a height of $(p - AC)$ and a length of Q.

5. *Determine the Lerner Index by substituting into the Lerner definition:* Apple's Lerner Index is $(p - MC)/p = (400 - 200)/400 = 1/2$.

6. *Use Equation 11.11 to infer the elasticity:* According to that equation, a profit-maximizing monopoly operates where $(p - MC)/p = -1/\varepsilon$. Substituting into this expression from the previous step, we learn that $1/2 = -1/\varepsilon$, or $\varepsilon = -2$.

SOURCES OF MARKET POWER

When will a monopoly face a relatively elastic demand curve and hence have little market power? Ultimately, the elasticity of demand of the market demand curve depends on consumers' tastes and options. The more consumers want a good—the more willing they are to pay "virtually anything" for it—the less elastic is the demand curve.

All else the same, the demand curve that a firm (not necessarily a monopoly) faces becomes more elastic as *better substitutes* for the firm's product are introduced, as *more firms* enter the market selling the same product, or as firms that provide the same service *locate closer* to this firm. The demand curves for Xerox, the U.S. Postal Service, and McDonald's have become more elastic in recent decades for these three reasons.

When Xerox started selling its plain-paper copier, no other firm sold a close substitute. Other companies' machines produced copies on special slick paper that yellowed quickly. As other firms developed plain-paper copiers, the demand curve that Xerox faced became more elastic.

The U.S. Postal Service (USPS) has a monopoly in first-class mail service. Today, phone calls, faxes, and e-mail are excellent substitutes for many types of first-class mail.

The USPS had a monopoly in overnight-delivery services until 1979. Today FedEx, United Parcel Service (UPS), and many other firms compete with the USPS to provide overnight deliveries. Because of this increased competition, the USPS's share of business and personal correspondence fell from 77% in 1988 to 59% in 1996, and its overnight-mail market fell to 4%.[5] Thus over time the demand curves that the USPS has faced for first-class mail and overnight services have shifted downward and become more elastic.

As you drive down a highway, you may notice that McDonald's restaurants are spaced a fixed number of miles apart. The purpose of this spacing is to reduce the likelihood that two McDonald's outlets will compete for the same customer. Although McDonald's can prevent its own restaurants from competing with each other, it cannot prevent Wendy's or Burger King from locating near its restaurants. As other fast-food restaurants open near a McDonald's, that restaurant faces a more elastic demand.

What happens as a profit-maximizing monopoly faces more elastic demand? It has to lower its price. See **www.aw-bc.com/perloff**, Chapter 11, "Airport Monopolies," for an illustration of how a monopoly adjusts its price as it changes its beliefs about the elasticity of demand that it faces.

11.3   Welfare Effects of Monopoly

Welfare, W, defined as the sum of consumer surplus, CS, and producer surplus, PS, is lower under monopoly than it is under competition. Chapter 9 showed that competition maximizes welfare because price equals marginal cost. By setting its price above its marginal cost, a monopoly causes consumers to buy less than the competitive level of the good, so a deadweight loss to society occurs.

We illustrate this loss using our linear example. If the monopoly were to act like a competitive market and operate where its inverse demand curve, Equation 11.5, intersects its marginal cost (supply) curve, Equation 11.8,

$$p = 24 - Q = 2Q = MC,$$

it would sell $Q_c = 8$ units of output at a price of $16, as Figure 11.5 shows. At this competitive price, consumer surplus is area $A + B + C$ and producer surplus is area $D + E$.

If the firm acts like a monopoly and operates where its marginal revenue equals its marginal cost, only 6 units are sold at the monopoly price of $18, and consumer surplus is only A. Part of the lost consumer surplus, B, goes to the monopoly; but the rest, C, is lost.

By charging the monopoly price of $18 instead of the competitive price of $16, the monopoly receives $2 more per unit and earns an extra profit of area $B = \$12$ on the $Q_m = 6$ units it sells. The monopoly loses area E, however, because it sells less than the competitive output. Consequently, the monopoly's producer surplus increases by $B - E$ over the competitive level. We know that its producer surplus increases, $B - E > 0$, because the monopoly had the option of producing at the competitive level and chose not to do so.

Social welfare with a monopoly is lower than with a competitive industry. The deadweight loss of monopoly is $-C - E$, which represents the consumer surplus and producer

---

[5]Peter Passell, "Battered by Its Rivals," *New York Times*, May 15, 1997:C1. However, 2007 reports indicated that its share of the overnight market rose over the last couple of years.

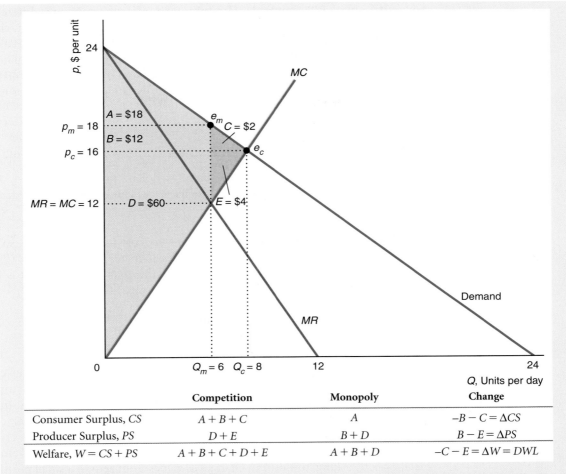

	Competition	Monopoly	Change
Consumer Surplus, *CS*	$A + B + C$	A	$-B - C = \Delta CS$
Producer Surplus, *PS*	$D + E$	$B + D$	$B - E = \Delta PS$
Welfare, $W = CS + PS$	$A + B + C + D + E$	$A + B + D$	$-C - E = \Delta W = DWL$

Figure 11.5 Deadweight Loss of Monopoly. A competitive market would produce $Q_c = 8$ at $p_c = \$16$, where the demand curve intersects the marginal cost (supply) curve. A monopoly produces only $Q_m = 6$ at $p_m = \$18$, where the marginal revenue curve intersects the marginal cost curve. Under monopoly, consumer surplus is A, producer surplus is $B + D$, and the lost welfare or deadweight loss of monopoly is $-C - E$.

surplus lost because less than the competitive output is produced. As in the analysis of a tax in Chapter 9, the deadweight loss is due to the gap between price and marginal cost at the monopoly output. At $Q_m = 6$, the price, $18, is above the marginal cost, $12, so consumers are willing to pay more for the last unit of output than it costs to produce it.

11.4 Taxes and Monopoly

Monopolies may face specific taxes (the government charges τ dollars per unit) or *ad valorem* taxes (the government collects αp per unit of output, where α is the tax rate, a fraction, and p is the price it charges consumers). Either type of tax raises the price that consumers pay and lowers welfare—the same effect as when a tax is applied to a competitive market (Chapter 2). However, taxes affect a monopoly differently than they affect a competitive industry in two ways. First, the tax incidence on consumers can exceed 100% in a monopoly market but not in a competitive market. Second, if tax rates α and τ are set so that the after-tax output is the same with either an *ad valorem* or a specific tax, the government raises the same amount of tax revenue from either tax in a competitive market (Chapter 2), but more by using an *ad valorem* tax with a monopoly.

EFFECTS OF A SPECIFIC TAX

If the government imposes a specific tax of τ dollars per unit on a monopoly, the monopoly will reduce its output and raise its price. The incidence of the tax on consumers may exceed 100%.

Comparative Statics. The monopoly's before-tax cost function is $C(Q)$, so its after-tax cost function is $C(Q) + \tau Q$. The monopoly's after-tax profit is $R(Q) - C(Q) - \tau Q$. A necessary condition for the monopoly to maximize its after-tax profit is found by equating the derivative of its after-tax profit to zero:

$$\frac{dR(Q)}{dQ} - \frac{dC(Q)}{dQ} - \tau = 0, \tag{11.12}$$

where dR/dQ is its marginal revenue and $dC/dQ + \tau$ is its after-tax marginal cost. That is, the monopoly equals its marginal revenue with its relevant (after-tax) marginal cost. At $\tau = 0$, this condition gives the before-tax necessary condition for profit maximization, Equation 11.1. The sufficient condition is the same as the before-tax condition 11.2, $d^2R/dQ^2 - d^2C/dQ^2 < 0$, because $d\tau/dQ = 0$.

We can use comparative statics techniques to determine the effect of imposing a specific tax by asking how output changes as τ goes from zero to a small positive value. Based on the necessary condition 11.2, we can write the monopoly's optimal quantity as a function of the tax: $Q(\tau)$. Differentiating the necessary condition with respect to τ, we find that

$$\frac{d^2R}{dQ^2}\frac{dQ}{d\tau} - \frac{d^2C}{dQ^2}\frac{dQ}{d\tau} - 1 = 0,$$

or

$$\frac{dQ}{d\tau} = \frac{1}{\dfrac{d^2R}{dQ^2} - \dfrac{d^2C}{dQ^2}}. \tag{11.13}$$

The denominator is the left-hand side of the sufficiency condition 11.2, so we know that the denominator of Equation 11.13 is negative and hence $dQ/d\tau < 0$. That is, as the specific tax rises, the monopoly reduces its output. Because its demand curve is downward sloping, when the monopoly lowers its output, it raises its price by $dp(Q(\tau))/d\tau = (dp/dQ)(dQ/d\tau) > 0$.

Tax Incidence on Consumers. In a competitive market, the incidence of a specific or *ad valorem* tax on consumers is less than or equal to 100% of the tax, and the incidence

on consumers plus the incidence on suppliers is 100% (Chapter 2). In contrast in a monopoly market, the incidence of a specific tax falling on consumers can exceed 100%: The price consumers pay may rise by an amount greater than the tax.

To demonstrate this possibility, we suppose that a monopoly's marginal cost is constant at m and that its demand curve has a constant elasticity of ε, so its inverse demand function is $p = Q^{1/\varepsilon}$. Consequently, the monopoly's revenue function is $R = pQ = Q^{1+1/\varepsilon}$. The monopoly's marginal revenue is $MR = dQ^{1+1/\varepsilon}/dQ = (1 + 1/\varepsilon)Q^{1/\varepsilon}$.

To maximize its profit, the monopoly equates its after-tax marginal cost, $m + \tau$, with its marginal revenue function:

$$m + \tau = (1 + 1/\varepsilon)Q^{1/\varepsilon}.$$

Solving this equation for the profit-maximizing output, the monopoly produces $Q = [(m + \tau)/(1 + 1/\varepsilon)]\varepsilon$. The monopoly substitutes that value of Q into its inverse demand function to choose the price it sets:

$$p = \frac{m + \tau}{1 + 1/\varepsilon}. \tag{11.14}$$

To determine the effect of a change in the tax on the price that consumers pay, we differentiate Equation 11.14 with respect to the tax: $dp/d\tau = 1/(1 + 1/\varepsilon)$. We know that $dp/d\tau$ is greater than one because $\varepsilon < -1$ (a monopoly never operates in the inelastic portion of its demand curve). Thus the incidence of the tax that falls on consumers exceeds 100%. However, for other types of demand curves, the tax incidence on consumers may be less than 100%, as the following Solved Problem shows.

SOLVED PROBLEM 11.3

If the government imposes a specific tax of $\tau = \$8$ per unit on the monopoly in the linear example in Figure 11.3, how does the monopoly change its profit-maximizing quantity and price? Use a figure to show how the tax affects tax revenue, consumer surplus, producer surplus, welfare, and deadweight loss. What is the incidence of the tax on consumers?

Answer

1. *Determine how imposing the tax affects the monopoly's optimum quantity by equating marginal revenue and after-tax marginal cost, and substitute the optimum quantity into the inverse demand function to find the profit-maximizing price:* The monopoly's marginal revenue, Equation 11.6, is $MR = 24 - 2Q$. Its before-tax marginal cost, Equation 11.8, is $2Q$, so its after-tax marginal cost is $MC = 2Q + 8$. The monopoly picks the output, Q^*, that equates its marginal revenue and its after-tax marginal cost: $24 - 2Q^* = 2Q^* + 8$. Solving, we find that $Q^* = 4$. Because the monopoly's inverse demand function 11.5 is $p = 24 - Q$, it charges $p^* = 24 - 4 = 20$.

The graph shows that the intersection of the marginal revenue curve, MR, and the before-tax marginal cost curve, MC^1, determines the before-tax monopoly's optimum quantity, $Q_1 = 6$. At the before-tax optimum, e_1, the price is $p_1 = \$18$. The specific tax causes the monopoly's before-tax marginal cost curve, $MC^1 = 2Q$, to shift upward by \$8 to $MC^2 = MC^1 + 8 = 2Q + 8$. After the tax is applied, the monopoly operates where $MR = 24 - 2Q = 2Q + 8 = MC^2$. In the after-tax monopoly optimum, e_2, the quantity is $Q_2 = 4$ and the price is $p_2 = \$20$. Thus output falls by $\Delta Q = 2$ units and the price increases by $\Delta p = \$2$.

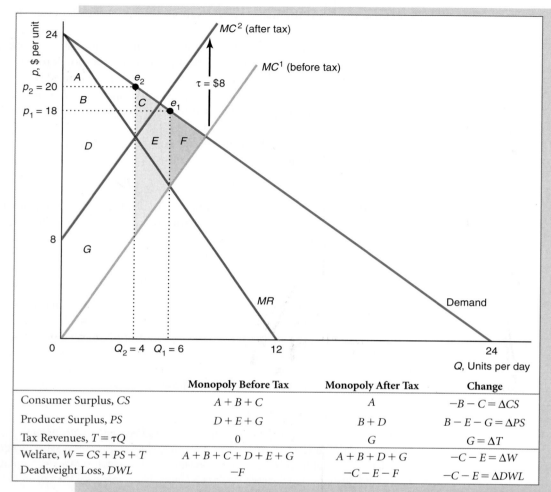

	Monopoly Before Tax	Monopoly After Tax	Change
Consumer Surplus, CS	$A + B + C$	A	$-B - C = \Delta CS$
Producer Surplus, PS	$D + E + G$	$B + D$	$B - E - G = \Delta PS$
Tax Revenues, $T = \tau Q$	0	G	$G = \Delta T$
Welfare, $W = CS + PS + T$	$A + B + C + D + E + G$	$A + B + D + G$	$-C - E = \Delta W$
Deadweight Loss, DWL	$-F$	$-C - E - F$	$-C - E = \Delta DWL$

2. *Show the change in tax revenue and the various welfare measures:* In the figure, area G is the tax revenue collected by the government, $\tau Q = \$32$, because its height is the distance between the two marginal cost curves, $\tau = \$8$, and its length is the output the monopoly produces after the tax is imposed, $Q = 4$. The tax reduces consumer and producer surplus and increases the deadweight loss. Consumer surplus falls by area $B + C$ from $A + B + C$ to A. The monopoly's producer surplus drops from $D + E + G$ to $B + D$, so its net decrease is $B - E - G$. We know that producer surplus falls because (a) the monopoly could have produced this reduced output level in the absence of the tax but did not because it was not the profit-maximizing output, so its before-tax profit falls, and (b) the monopoly must now pay taxes. The before-tax deadweight loss due to monopoly pricing was $-F$. The after-tax deadweight loss is $-C - E - F$, so the increase in deadweight loss (or loss in welfare) due to the tax is $-C - E$.

3. *Calculate the incidence of the tax:* Because the tax goes from $0 to $8, the change in the tax is $\Delta \tau = \$8$. The incidence of the tax on consumers is $\Delta p / \Delta \tau = \$2/\$8 = \frac{1}{4}$. That is, the monopoly absorbs $6 of the tax and passes on only $2.

from imitation. According to a survey of 650 research and development managers of U.S. firms (Levin, Klevorick, Nelson, and Winter, 1987), secrecy is more commonly used than patents to prevent duplication of new or improved processes by other firms but is less commonly used to protect new products.

NATURAL MONOPOLY

A market has a **natural monopoly** if one firm can produce the total output of the market at lower cost than several firms could. If the cost for any firm to produce q is $C(q)$, the condition for a natural monopoly is

$$C(Q) < C(q_1) + C(q_2) + \cdots + C(q_n), \tag{11.15}$$

where $Q = q_1 + q_2 + \cdots + q_n$ is the sum of the output of any $n \geq 2$ firms and where the condition holds for all output levels that could be demanded by the market. With a natural monopoly, it is more efficient to have only one firm produce than to have more than one firm produce.[10] Believing that they are natural monopolies, governments frequently grant monopoly rights to *public utilities* to provide essential goods or services such as water, gas, electric power, and mail delivery.

Suppose that a public utility has economies of scale (Chapter 7) at all levels of output, so its average cost curve falls as output increases for any observed level of output. If all potential firms have the same strictly declining average cost curve, this market has a natural monopoly, as we now consider.[11]

A company that supplies water to homes incurs a high fixed cost, F, to build a plant and connect houses to the plant. The firm's marginal cost, m, of supplying water is constant, so its marginal cost curve is horizontal and its average cost, $AC = m + F/Q$, declines as output rises. (The iPod cost function in Solved Problem 11.2 has this functional form.)

Figure 11.7 shows such marginal and average cost curves where $m = \$10$ and $F = \$60$. If the market output is 12 units per day, one firm produces that output at an average cost of $15, or a total cost of $180 (= 15×12). If two firms each produce 6 units, the average cost is $20, and the cost of producing the market output is $240 (= 20×12), which is greater than the cost with a single firm.

If the two firms were to divide the total production in any other way, their costs of production would still exceed the cost of a single firm (as the following Solved Problem asks you to prove). The reason is that the marginal cost per unit is the same no matter how many firms produce, but each additional firm adds a fixed cost, which raises the

---

[10]A natural monopoly is the most efficient market structure only in the sense that the single firm produces at lowest cost. However, society's welfare may be greater with more than one firm in the industry producing at higher cost, because competition drives down the price from the monopoly level. A solution that allows society to maximize welfare is for the government to allow only one firm to produce and where the government regulates that firm to force it to charge a price equal to marginal cost (as we discuss later in this chapter).

[11]A firm may be a natural monopoly even if its cost curve does not fall at all levels of output. If a U-shaped average cost curve reaches its minimum at 100 units of output, it may be less costly for only one firm to produce an output of 101 units even though its average cost curve is rising at that output. Thus a cost function with economies of scale everywhere is a sufficient but not a necessary condition for a natural monopoly.

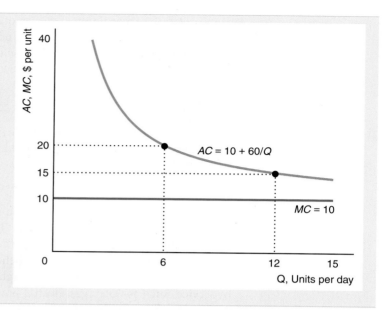

Figure 11.7 Natural Monopoly. This natural monopoly has a strictly declining average cost.

cost of producing a given quantity. If only one firm provides water, the cost of building a second plant and a second set of pipes is avoided.

SOLVED PROBLEM 11.4

A firm that delivers Q units of water to households has a total cost of $C(Q) = mQ + F$. If any entrant would have the same cost, does this market have a natural monopoly?

Answer

Determine whether costs rise if two firms produce a given quantity: Let q_1 be the output of Firm 1 and q_2 be the output of Firm 2. The combined cost of these two firms producing $Q = q_1 + q_2$ is

$$C(q_1) + C(q_2) = (mq_1 + F) + (mq_2 + F) = m(q_1 + q_2) + 2F = mQ + 2F.$$

If a single firm produces Q, its cost is $C(Q) = mQ + F$. Thus the cost of producing any given Q is greater with two firms than with one firm, so this market has a natural monopoly.

APPLICATION

Electric Power Utilities

According to the estimates of Christensen and Greene (1976), the average cost curve for U.S. electric-power-producing firms in 1970 was U-shaped, reaching its minimum at 33 billion kilowatt-hours (kWh) per year (see graph). Thus whether an electric power utility was a natural monopoly depended on the demand it faced.

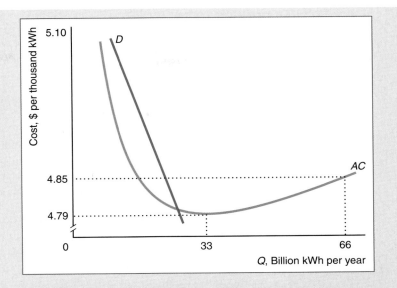

For example, if the demand curve for an electric utility were *D* on the graph, the quantity demanded would be less than 33 billion kWh per year at any price, so the electric utility would operate in the strictly declining section of its average cost curve and would be a natural monopoly. In 1970, most electric companies were operating in regions of substantial economies of scale. Newport Electric produced only 0.5 billion kWh per year, and Iowa Southern Utilities produced 1.3 billion kWh per year.

A few of these firms operated in the upward-sloping section of the average cost curve and were not natural monopolies. The largest electric utility in 1970, Southern, produced 54 billion kWh per year. It was not a natural monopoly because two firms could have produced that quantity at 3¢ less per thousand kWh than a single firm could have. As the graph shows, two firms producing 33 billion kWh each had an average cost of $4.79 per thousand kWh, while one firm producing 66 billion kWh had an average cost of $4.85, or 6¢ more per thousand kWh.

11.6 Government Actions That Create Monopolies

I think it's wrong that only one company makes the game Monopoly. —Steven Wright

Governments create many monopolies. Sometimes governments own and manage monopolies. In the United States, as in most other countries, the postal service is a government monopoly. Indeed, the U.S. Constitution explicitly grants the government the right to establish a postal service. Many local governments own and operate public utility monopolies that provide garbage collection, electricity, water, gas, phone services, and other utilities.

Frequently, however, governments create monopolies by preventing competing firms from entering a market. For example, when a government grants a patent, it limits entry and allows the patent-holding firm to earn a monopoly profit from an invention—a reward for developing the new product.

BARRIERS TO ENTRY

By preventing other firms from entering a market, governments create monopolies. Governments typically create monopolies in one of three ways: by making it difficult for new firms to obtain a license to operate, by granting a firm the rights to be a monopoly, or by auctioning the rights to be a monopoly.

Licenses to Operate. Frequently, firms need government licenses to operate. If a government makes it difficult for new firms to obtain licenses, the first firm may maintain its monopoly. Until recently, many U.S. cities required new hospitals or other inpatient establishments to demonstrate the need for a new facility by securing a certificate of need, which allowed them to enter the market.

Grants of Monopoly Rights. Government grants of monopoly rights have been common for public utilities. Instead of running a public utility itself, a government gives a private company the monopoly rights to operate the utility. A government may capture some of the monopoly's profits by charging a high rent to the monopoly. Alternatively, government officials may capture the rents for monopoly rights by means of bribes.

Auctions of Monopoly Rights. Governments around the world have privatized many state-owned monopolies in the past several decades. By selling its monopolies to private firms, a government can capture the future value of monopoly earnings.[12]

PATENTS

If a firm cannot prevent imitation by keeping its discovery secret, it may obtain government protection to prevent other firms from duplicating its discovery and entering the market. Virtually all countries provide such protection through a **patent:** an exclusive right granted to the inventor to sell a new and useful product, process, substance, or design for a fixed period of time. A patent grants an inventor the right to be the monopoly provider of the good for a number of years.

Patent Length. The length of a patent varies across countries. The U.S. Constitution explicitly gives the government the right to grant authors and inventors exclusive rights to their writings (copyrights) and to their discoveries (patents) for limited periods of time. Traditionally, U.S. patents lasted 17 years from the date they were *granted*, but the United States agreed in 1995 to change its patent law as part of a GATT agreement. Now U.S. patents last for 20 years after the date the inventor *files* for patent protection. The length of protection is likely to be shorter under the new rules because it frequently takes more than three years after filing to obtain final approval of a patent.

Patents Stimulate Research. A firm with a patent monopoly sets a high price that results in deadweight loss. Why, then, do governments grant patent monopolies? The main reason is that inventive activity would fall if there were no patent monopolies or

---

[12]See **www.aw-bc.com/perloff**, Chapter 11, "Government Sales of Monopolies." However, for political or other reasons, governments frequently sell at a lower price that does not capture all future profits. (See **www.aw-bc.com/perloff**, Chapter 11, "Iceland's Government Creates Genetic Monopoly.")

other incentives to inventors. The costs of developing a new drug or new computer chip are often hundreds of millions or even billions of dollars. If anyone could copy a new drug or computer chip and compete with the inventor, few individuals or firms would undertake the costly research. Thus the government is explicitly trading off the long-run benefits of additional inventions against the shorter-term harms of monopoly pricing during the period of patent protection.

APPLICATION

Botox Patent Monopoly

Ophthalmologist Dr. Alan Scott turned the deadly poison botulinum toxin into a miracle drug to treat two eye conditions: strabismus, which affects about 4% of children, and blepharospasm, an uncontrollable closure of the eyes. Blepharospasm left about 25,000 Americans functionally blind before Scott's discovery. His patented drug, Botox, is sold by Allergan, Inc.

Dr. Scott has been amused to see several of the unintended beneficiaries of his research at the annual Academy Awards. Even before it was explicitly approved for cosmetic use, many doctors were injecting Botox into the facial muscles of actors, models, and others to smooth out their wrinkles. (The drug paralyzes the muscles, so those injected with it also lose their ability to frown or smile—and, some would say, to act.) The treatment is only temporary, lasting up to 120 days, so repeated injections are necessary. Allergan had expected to sell $400 million worth of Botox in 2002. However, in April of that year, the Federal Food and Drug Administration approved the use of Botox for cosmetic purposes. The FDA ruling allows the company to advertise the drug widely.

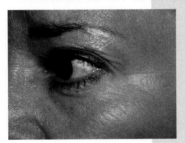

Consequently, Allergan had Botox sales of $800 million in 2004, and approximately $1 billion in 2005. Allergan has a near-monopoly in the treatment of wrinkles, although plastic surgery, as well as injections of collagen, Restylane, hyaluronic acid, and other fillers, provide limited competition. Between 2002 and 2004, the number of facelifts dropped 3% to about 114,000, according to the American Society of Plastic Surgeons, while the number of Botox injections skyrocketed 166%. Indeed, Botox injections rose 388% from 2000 to 2005.

Dr. Scott says that he can produce a vial of Botox in his lab for about $25. Allergan then sells the potion to doctors for about $400. Assuming that the firm is setting its price to maximize its short-run profit, we can rearrange Equation 11.9 to determine the elasticity of demand for Botox:

$$\varepsilon = -\frac{p}{p - MC} = -\frac{400}{400 - 25} \approx -1.067.$$

Thus the demand that Allergan faces is only slightly elastic: A 1% increase in price causes quantity to fall by only a little more than 1%.

If we assume that the demand curve is linear and that the elasticity of demand is −1.067 at the 2002 monopoly optimum, e_m (1 million vials sold at $400 each, producing revenue of $400 million), then Allergan's inverse demand function is

$$p = 775 - 375Q.$$

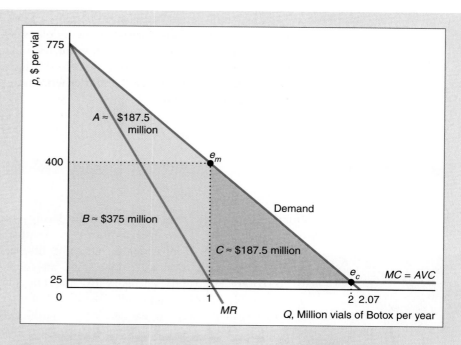

This demand curve (see the graph) has a slope of −375 and hits the price axis at $775 and the quantity axis at about 2.07 million vials per year. The corresponding marginal revenue curve,

$$MR = 775 - 750Q,$$

strikes the price axis at $775 and has twice the slope, −750, as the demand curve.

The intersection of the marginal revenue and marginal cost curves,

$$MR = 775 - 750Q = 25 = MC,$$

determines the monopoly equilibrium at the profit-maximizing quantity of 1 million vials per year and at a price of $400 per vial.

Were the company to sell Botox at a price equal to its marginal cost of $25 (as a competitive industry would), consumer surplus would equal area $A + B + C = \$750$ million per year. At the higher monopoly price of $400, the consumer surplus is $A = \$187.5$ million. Compared to the competitive solution, e_c, buyers lose consumer surplus of $B + C = \$562.5$ million per year. Part of this loss, $B = \$375$ million per year, is transferred from consumers to Allergan. The rest, $C = \$187.5$ million per year, is the deadweight loss from monopoly pricing. Allergan's profit is its producer surplus, B, minus its fixed costs.

Alternatives to Patents. Instead of using patents to spur research, the government could give research grants or offer prizes. Rather than trying these alternative approaches, Congress has modified the patent system. In the 1960s and 1970s, the effective life of a patent on a drug shrank because of the additional time it took to get FDA approval to sell the drug. By 1978, the average drug had patent protection for fewer than 10 years. The Drug Price Competition and Patent Term Restoration Act of 1984 restored up to three years of the part of the patent life that was lost while the firm demonstrated efficacy and safety to the FDA. At the same time, the Act made it easier for generic products to enter at the end of the patent period. Thus the law aimed both to encourage the development of new drugs by increasing the reward—the monopoly period—and to stimulate price competition at the end of the period.

APPLICATION

Internet and Other Pirates: Protecting Intellectual Property Rights

A patent grants its owner the exclusive or monopoly right to sell a new and useful product, process, substance, or design for a fixed period. Similarly, a copyright gives its owner the exclusive production, publication, or sales rights to artistic, dramatic, literary, or musical works. The main purpose of providing these intellectual property rights is to encourage research and artistic creativity.

However, patents and copyrights are of little value to their owners if these rights are not enforced. Protecting intellectual property such as music and computer software from unauthorized copying has proved increasingly difficult over the past several years. The growth of piracy over the Internet has threatened traditional copyright protection for books, music, and films. Authors, artists, and publishers are no longer assured of being paid for their work.

Many users download music, movies, and books over the Internet without paying for them. Condemning these actions as piracy, music and software publishers have sued Napster and other firms that facilitate copying, and have instituted copy protection schemes. These attempts to prevent copying have had only limited success. In China, illegal copies of movies, music, and software openly sell for a fraction—one-fifth for many new DVDs—of the price of the original.

Worldwide use of music-sharing services such as Napster, KaZaA, and others has flourished, particularly before a series of lawsuits by publishers in 2003. Lawsuits and the threat of them initially discouraged some downloading in the United States. According to one survey, the share of computer users who employed file-sharing programs to download music fell from 29% in the spring of 2003 to 14% by late 2003. Since then, the number of global file-sharing users has doubled. The U.S. Supreme Court ruled in June 2005 that Internet file-trading networks such as Grokster and Morpheus could be held liable when their users copy music, movies, and other protected works without permission, so more U.S. prosecutions are likely. In 2006, China signed an agreement with the Motion Picture Association of America and other industry groups to protect movies, television programs, software, and literary works from piracy via the Internet in China.

The Business Software Alliance's 2006 annual survey (for 2005) claims that legal software is the exception in many developing countries. It reports that the rate of software piracy is 90% in Vietnam and Zimbabwe, 88% in China, 87% in Indonesia,

54% in the Asia-Pacific region, 36% in Europe, and "only" 22% in North America, which has the toughest penalties for illegal software usage. The Alliance says that $60 billion worth of PC software is sold legally in developed countries, while $22 billion is pirated. The corresponding figures for emerging countries are $6 billion and $12 billion. However, these piracy loss numbers may be overestimates because they are based on list prices. Moreover, consumers who use pirated copies of a work may eventually decide to purchase legitimate copies of it or other related works. Thus the effect of piracy on legitimate demand is still an empirical question.

In the short run, artists and producers are harmed by piracy. If consumers benefit by being able to buy music or software for less or by stealing it, the overall short-run welfare effect of piracy is ambiguous. For example, in the extreme case where downloaders would not have bought the product, piracy raises welfare and harms no one.

Rob and Waldfogel (2004) surveyed college students at the University of Pennsylvania and elsewhere. They found that each album download reduces purchases by at least 0.2 of an album. Students reported downloading almost as many albums as they purchased and admitted that, if downloading had not been possible, they would have purchased 26% of the albums they downloaded. Among Penn undergrads, the researchers found that downloading reduced their personal expenditures on hit albums from $126 to $100 but raised their per capita consumer surplus by $70. Thus for this group, the increase in consumer surplus more than offset the loss in revenues.

Regardless of the short-run welfare effects, the more serious harm occurs in the long run. Reduced copyright and patent protection lowers the drive to create or to innovate.

11.7 Government Actions That Reduce Market Power

Some governments take actions to reduce or eliminate monopolies' market power so as to reduce the prices that consumers must pay. Most Western countries have laws forbidding a firm from driving other firms out of the market so as to monopolize it. Many governments either regulate monopolies—especially those that the government has created—or destroy monopolies by breaking them up into smaller, independent firms or encouraging other firms to enter the market.

REGULATING MONOPOLIES

Governments limit monopolies' market power in a number of ways. Most utilities, for example, are subject to direct regulation. One method that governments use to limit the harms of monopoly is to place a ceiling on the price that a monopoly charges.

Optimal Price Regulation. In some markets, the government can eliminate the deadweight loss of monopoly by requiring that a monopoly charge no more than the competitive price. We use our earlier linear example to illustrate this type of regulation in Figure 11.8.

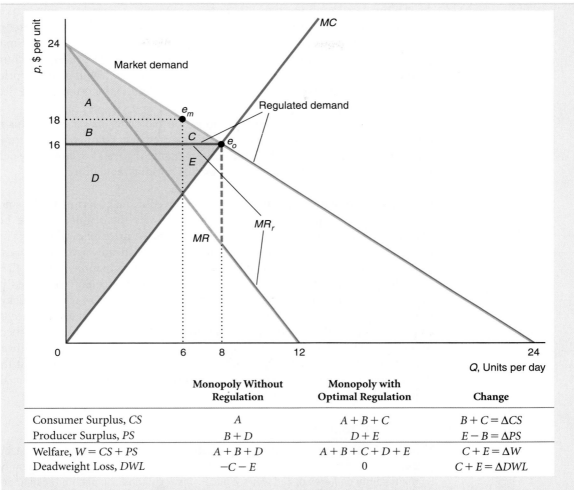

	Monopoly Without Regulation	Monopoly with Optimal Regulation	Change
Consumer Surplus, CS	A	$A + B + C$	$B + C = \Delta CS$
Producer Surplus, PS	$B + D$	$D + E$	$E - B = \Delta PS$
Welfare, $W = CS + PS$	$A + B + D$	$A + B + C + D + E$	$C + E = \Delta W$
Deadweight Loss, DWL	$-C - E$	0	$C + E = \Delta DWL$

Figure 11.8 Optimal Price Regulation. If the government sets a price ceiling at $16, where the monopoly's marginal cost curve hits the demand curve, the new demand curve that the monopoly faces has a kink at 8 units, and the corresponding marginal revenue curve, MR_r, "jumps" at that quantity. The regulated monopoly sets its output where $MR_r = MC$, selling the same quantity, 8 units, at the same price, $16, as a competitive industry would. The regulation eliminates the monopoly deadweight loss, $C + E$. Consumer surplus, $A + B + C$, and producer surplus, $D + E$, are the same as under competition.

If the government doesn't regulate the profit-maximizing monopoly, the monopoly optimum is e_m, at which 6 units are sold at the monopoly price of $18. Suppose that the government sets a ceiling price of $16, the price at which the marginal cost curve intersects the market demand curve. Because the monopoly cannot charge more than $16 per unit, the monopoly's regulated demand curve is horizontal at $16 (up to 8 units) and is the same as the market demand curve at lower prices. The marginal revenue curve corresponding to the regulated demand curve, MR_r, is horizontal where the regulated demand curve is horizontal (up to 8 units) and equals the marginal revenue curve, MR, corresponding to the market demand curve at larger quantities.

The regulated monopoly sets its output at 8 units, where MR_r equals its marginal cost, MC, and charges the maximum permitted price of $16. The regulated firm still makes a profit because its average cost is less than $16 at 8 units. The optimally regulated monopoly optimum, e_o, is the same as the competitive equilibrium, where marginal cost (supply) equals the market demand curve.[13] Thus setting a price ceiling where the MC curve and market demand curve intersect eliminates the deadweight loss of monopoly.

How do we know that this regulation is optimal? The answer is that this regulated outcome is the same as would occur if this market were competitive, where welfare is maximized (Chapter 9). As the table accompanying Figure 11.8 shows, the deadweight loss of monopoly, $C + E$, is eliminated by this optimal regulation.

Nonoptimal Price Regulation. Welfare is reduced if the government does not set the price optimally. Suppose that the government sets the regulated price below the optimal level, which is $16 in our example. If it sets the price below the firm's minimum average cost, the firm shuts down. If that happens, the deadweight loss equals the sum of the consumer plus producer surplus under optimal regulation, $A + B + C + D + E$.

If the government sets the price ceiling below the optimally regulated price but high enough so that the firm does not shut down, consumers who are lucky enough to buy the good are better off because they can buy goods at a lower price than they could with optimal regulation. Some customers, however, are frustrated because the monopoly will not sell them the good, as we show next. There is a deadweight loss because less output is sold than with optimal regulation. (Question 10 at the end of the chapter asks you to determine the effects of a regulated price that is above the optimal level.)

SOLVED PROBLEM   11.5

Suppose that the government sets a price, p_2, that is below the socially optimal level, p_1, but above the monopoly's minimum average cost. How do the price, the quantity sold, the quantity demanded, and welfare under this regulation compare to those under optimal regulation?

Answer

1. *Describe the optimally regulated outcome:* With optimal regulation, e_1, the price is set at p_1, where the market demand curve intersects the monopoly's marginal cost curve on the accompanying graph. The optimally regulated monopoly sells Q_1 units.

2. *Describe the outcome when the government regulates the price at* p_2: Where the market demand is above p_2, the regulated demand curve for the monopoly is horizontal at p_2 (up to Q_d). The corresponding marginal revenue curve, MR_r, is horizontal where the regulated demand curve is horizontal and equals the marginal revenue curve corresponding to the market demand curve, MR, where the regulated demand curve is downward sloping. The monopoly maximizes its

---

[13]The monopoly produces at e_o only if the regulated price is greater than its average variable cost. Here the regulated price, $16, exceeds the average variable cost at 8 units of $8. Indeed, the firm makes a profit because the average cost at 8 units is $9.50.

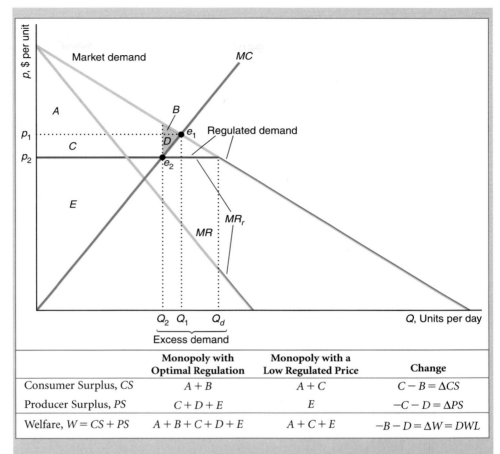

	Monopoly with Optimal Regulation	Monopoly with a Low Regulated Price	Change
Consumer Surplus, CS	$A + B$	$A + C$	$C - B = \Delta CS$
Producer Surplus, PS	$C + D + E$	E	$-C - D = \Delta PS$
Welfare, $W = CS + PS$	$A + B + C + D + E$	$A + C + E$	$-B - D = \Delta W = DWL$

profit by selling Q_2 units at p_2. The new regulated monopoly optimum is e_2, where MR_r intersects MC. The firm does not shut down when regulated as long as its average variable cost at Q_2 is less than p_2.

3. *Compare the outcomes:* The quantity that the monopoly sells falls from Q_1 to Q_2 when the government lowers its price ceiling from p_1 to p_2. At that lower price, consumers want to buy Q_d, so there is excess demand equal to $Q_d - Q_2$. Compared to optimal regulation, welfare is lower by at least $B + D$.

Comment: The welfare loss is greater if unlucky consumers waste time trying to buy the good unsuccessfully or if goods are not allocated optimally among consumers. A consumer who values the good at only p_2 may be lucky enough to buy it, while a consumer who values the good at p_1 or more may not be able to obtain it.

Problems in Regulating. Governments often fail to regulate monopolies optimally. For example, because government regulatory agencies do not know the actual demand and marginal cost curves or because they cannot offer a subsidy, they may set the price at the wrong level. Moreover, regulated firms may bribe or otherwise influence government regulators to help the firms rather than society as a whole.

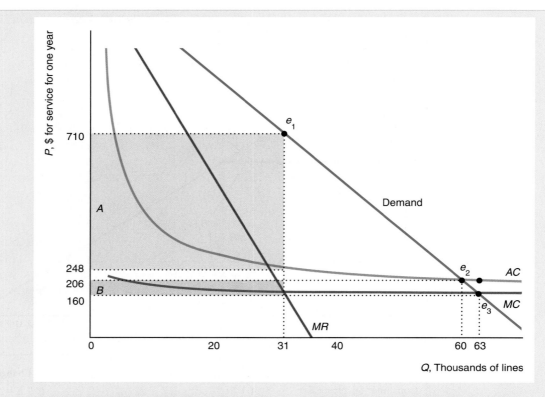

Figure 11.9 Regulating a Telephone Utility. If the phone utility is an unregulated profit-maximizing monopoly, e_1, it provides 31,000 telephone lines at $710 each annually and makes a profit of $14,322,000, equal to area A. The government may regulate the price so that the utility breaks even, e_2. Alternatively, the government may regulate the utility to behave like a price taker, e_3. If so, the government must subsidize the utility by area $B = \$2,583,000$ to keep it from shutting down.

Because of limited information about the demand and marginal cost curves, governments may set a price ceiling above or below the competitive level. Moreover, a regulatory agency may have to set the price higher than is optimal because it cannot offer a subsidy.

If the regulatory agency were to set the price equal to a natural monopoly's marginal cost, the price would be below the firm's average cost. The monopoly would threaten to shut down unless the regulatory agency subsidized it or raised the price.

To illustrate this problem, we calculate how setting the price too low would affect a phone monopoly in Macon, Georgia (before the deregulation in 1995 that allowed additional firms into the market).[14] In the absence of regulation and in light of the curves in Figure 11.9, this firm maximizes its profit by operating where its marginal cost equals its marginal revenue, e_1, where it provides 31,000 telephone lines at

---

[14]This example is based on Gasmi et al. (2002, Appendix A). We approximate their exponential demand curve with a linear demand curve, where both curves have a price elasticity of demand of −0.2 at point e_2.

$710 each annually. Because its average cost at that quantity is $248, its profit is ($710 − $248)31,000 = $14,322,000, area *A*.

Alternatively, the government may regulate the utility to behave like a price taker, e_3. The firm would lose money if it faced a price ceiling of $160 annually, where the demand curve intersects the marginal cost curve at 63,000 lines. At that quantity, its average cost is $204, so it loses ($204 − $160)63,000 = $2,722,000, area *B*.

Typically, it is politically infeasible for a government regulatory agency to subsidize a firm. Instead, the agency might set the price at $248, where the demand curve intersects the average cost curve and the monopoly breaks even. There is still a deadweight loss because that price is above marginal cost, but the deadweight loss is smaller than it would be if the monopoly were unregulated. The government may regulate the price so that the utility breaks even, e_2. If so, the government must subsidize the utility by area *B* = $2,772,000 to keep it from shutting down.

Unfortunately, regulation is often ineffective when regulators are *captured:* influenced by the firms they regulate. Typically, this influence is more subtle than an outright bribe. Many American regulators worked in the industry before they became regulators and hence are sympathetic to those firms. For many other regulators, the reverse is true: They aspire to obtain good jobs in the industry eventually, so they do not want to offend potential employers. And some regulators, relying on industry experts for their information, may be misled or at least heavily influenced by the industry. For example, the California Public Utilities Commission urged telephone and cable companies to negotiate among themselves as to how they wanted to open local phone markets to competition by 1997. Arguing that these influences are inherent, some economists contend that price and other types of regulation are unlikely to result in efficiency.

INCREASING COMPETITION

Encouraging competition is an alternative to regulation as a means of reducing the harms of monopoly. When a government has created a monopoly by preventing entry, it can quickly reduce the monopoly's market power by allowing other firms to enter. As new firms enter the market, the former monopoly must lower its price to compete, so welfare rises. Many governments are actively encouraging entry into telephone, electricity, and other utility markets that were formerly monopolized.

Similarly, a government may end a ban on imports so that a domestic monopoly faces competition from foreign firms. If costs for the domestic firm are the same as costs for the foreign firms and there are many foreign firms, the former monopoly becomes just one of many competitive firms. As the market becomes competitive, consumers pay the competitive price, and the deadweight loss of monopoly is eliminated.

Governments around the world are increasing competition in previously monopolized markets. For example, many U.S. and European governments are forcing former telephone and energy monopolies to compete. See **www.aw-bc.com/perloff**, Chapter 11, "Ending the Monopoly in Telephone Service" and "Deregulating Energy."

Similarly, under pressure from the World Trade Organization, many countries are reducing or eliminating barriers that protected domestic monopolies. The entry of foreign competitive firms into a market can create a new, more competitive market structure. For example, see **www.aw-bc.com/perloff**, Chapter 11, "Dominant Firm and Competitive Fringe."

Creating and Destroying an Auto Monopoly

In the early 1980s, Mahathir Mohamad, Malaysia's prime minister, fulfilled his dream and created a national car. Putting the Islamic star-and-crescent badge on the front of what was even then an aging Mitsubishi Lancer, Mahathir called the vehicle the Proton Saga. By 1986, the Saga hit the road. Today, Protons are about two-thirds of all of the cars in Malaysia.

The government aided the company by having taxpayers foot the bill for building its plants (about $2 billion). More important, it set import tariffs of between 140% and 300% that served as a major barrier to entry for foreign-made cars. Such barriers were necessary for the Proton to survive because the car's production costs were nearly three times those of Japanese and Korean competitors (partially because Proton production lacked economies of scale).

More recently, the government has undermined this monopoly. It created a second national car, the Perodua, to add variety for consumers. It also introduced a locally assembled multipurpose vehicle sold by Naza Kia Sdn, the Malaysian distributor of South Korea's Kia Motors Corp. Most important, the government reduced the trade barrier. Under the Association of Southeast Asia Nations (ASEAN) Free Trade Area rules, Malaysia slashed its tariff on cars imported from ASEAN countries from 190% to 20% in 2005 and will cut it to 5% by 2008. Partially offsetting this change, the Malaysian government hiked excise duties on all cars sold in Malaysia. Although Proton must pay those duties, it receives a 50% rebate. Nonetheless, Proton's share of the market fell from 65% a couple of years before to 44% in 2005.

11.8 Monopoly Decisions over Time

We have examined how a monopoly behaves in the current period, ignoring the future. For many markets, this kind of analysis is appropriate. However, in some markets, decisions today affect demand or cost in a future period. In such markets, the monopoly may maximize its long-run profit by making a decision today that does not maximize its short-run profit. For example, frequently a firm introduces a product—such as a new candy bar—by initially charging a low price or by giving away free samples so that customers learn about its quality and provide word-of-mouth publicity. We now consider an important reason why consumers' demand in the future may depend on a monopoly's actions in the present.

NETWORK EXTERNALITIES

The number of customers a firm has today may affect the demand curve it faces in the future. A good has a **network externality** if one person's demand depends on the consumption of a good by others.[15] If a good has a *positive* network externality, its value to a consumer grows as the number of units sold increases.

---

[15]In Chapter 17, we discuss the more general case of an externality, which occurs when a person's well-being or a firm's production capability is directly affected by the actions of other consumers or firms rather than indirectly through changes in prices. The following discussion on network externalities is based on Liebenstein (1950), Rohlfs (1974), Katz and Shapiro (1994), Economides (1996), Shapiro and Varian (1999), and Rohlfs (2001).

The telephone provides a classic example of a positive network externality. When the phone was introduced, potential adopters had no reason to get phone service unless their family and friends did. Why buy a phone if there's no one to call? For Bell's phone network to succeed, it had to achieve a *critical mass* of users—enough adopters that others wanted to join. Had it failed to achieve this critical mass, demand would have withered and the network would have died. Similarly, the market for fax machines grew very slowly until a critical mass was achieved where many end users had them.

Direct Size Effect. Many industries exhibit positive network externalities where the customer gets a *direct* benefit from a larger network. The larger an ATM network such as the Plus network, the greater the odds that you will find an ATM when you want one, so the more likely it is that you will want to use that network. The more people who use a particular computer operating system, the more attractive it is to someone who wants to exchange files or programs with other users.

Behavioral Economics. These examples of the direct effect of network externalities depend on the size of the network because customers want to interact with each other. However, sometimes consumers' behavior depends on beliefs or tastes that can be explained by psychological and sociological theories. These explanations are the focus of a subfield of economics called *behavioral economics*.

One alternative explanation for a direct network externality effect is based on tastes. Harvey Liebenstein (1950) suggested that consumers sometimes want a good because "everyone else has it." A fad or other popularity-based explanation for a positive network externality is called a **bandwagon effect:** A person places greater value on a good as more and more other people possess it.[16] The success of the iPod today may be partially due to its early popularity. Ugg boots may be another example of a bandwagon effect.

The opposite of the bandwagon effect (positive network externality), is a negative network externality called a **snob effect:** A person places greater value on a good as fewer and fewer other people possess it. Some people prefer an original painting by an unknown artist to a lithograph by a star because no one else can possess that painting. (As Yogi Berra said, "Nobody goes there anymore; it's too crowded.")

Indirect Effect. In some markets, positive network externalities are indirect and stem from complementary goods that are offered when a product has a critical mass of users. Why buy a particular computer if no software programs for it are available? The more extra devices and software that work with a particular computer, the more people want to buy that computer; but these extra devices are available only if a critical mass of customers buys the computer. Similarly, the more people who drive diesel-powered cars, the more likely it is that gas stations will sell diesel fuel; and the more stations that sell the fuel, the more likely it is that someone will want to drive a diesel car. As a final example, once a critical mass of customers has broadband Internet service, more services will provide downloadable music and movies, and more high-definition Web pages will become available; and once those killer apps appear, more people will sign up for broadband service.

---

[16]*Jargon alert:* Some economists use *bandwagon effect* to mean any positive network externality—not just those that are based on popularity.

NETWORK EXTERNALITIES AS AN EXPLANATION FOR MONOPOLIES

Because of the need for a critical mass of customers in a market with a positive network externality, we frequently see only one large firm surviving, as in the case of eBay. Several online auctions started a few years ago, including eBay and Yahoo!. However, all else the same, sellers want to use the site that has the most potential buyers, and buyers want the largest choice of sellers. Thus after eBay reached a critical mass, it grew rapidly, its rivals lost customers, and eventually eBay became a virtual monopoly.

Visa's ad campaign tells consumers that Visa cards are accepted "everywhere you want to be," including at stores that "don't take American Express." One could view its ad campaign as an attempt to convince consumers that its card has a critical mass and therefore that everyone should switch to it.

But having obtained a monopoly, a firm does not necessarily keep it. History is filled with examples where one product knocks off another: "The king is dead; long live the king." Google replaced Yahoo! as the predominant search engine. Explorer displaced Netscape as the big-dog browser (and Firefox lurks in the wings). Levi Strauss is no longer the fashion leader among the jeans set.

A TWO-PERIOD MONOPOLY MODEL

A monopoly may be able to solve the chicken-and-egg problem of getting a critical mass for its product by initially selling the product at a low introductory price. By so doing, the firm maximizes its long-run profit but not its short-run profit.

Suppose that a monopoly sells its good—say, root-beer-scented jeans—for only two periods (after that, the demand goes to zero as a new craze hits the market). If the monopoly sells less than a critical quantity of output, Q, in the first period, its second-period demand curve lies close to the price axis. However, if the good is a success in the first period—at least Q units are sold—the second-period demand curve shifts substantially to the right.

If the monopoly maximizes its short-run profit in the first period, it charges p^* and sells Q^* units, which is fewer than Q. To sell Q units, it would have to lower its first-period price to $\underline{p} < p^*$, which would reduce its first-period profit from π^* to $\underline{\pi}$.

In the second period, the monopoly maximizes its profit given its second-period demand curve. If the monopoly sold only Q^* units in the first period, it earns a relatively low second-period profit of π_l. However, if it sold Q units in the first period, it makes a relatively high second-period profit, π_h.

Should the monopoly charge a low introductory price in the first period? Its objective is to maximize its long-run profit: the sum of its profit in the two periods.[17] It maximizes its long-run profit by charging a low introductory price in the first period if the extra profit in the second period, $\pi_h - \pi_l$, from achieving a critical mass in the first period is greater than its forgone profit in the first period, $\pi^* - \underline{\pi}$. This policy must pay for some firms: A Google search found 1.2 million Web pages touting introductory prices.

---

[17]In Chapter 15, we discuss why firms place lower value on profit in the future than on profit today and how a firm can compare profit in the future to profit today. For now, we assume that the monopoly places equal value on profit in either period.

Summary

1. **Monopoly Profit Maximization:** Like any firm, a monopoly—a single seller—maximizes its profit by setting its output so that its marginal revenue equals its marginal cost. The monopoly makes a positive profit if its average cost is less than the price at the profit-maximizing output. Because a monopoly does not have a supply curve, the effect of a shift in demand on a monopoly's output depends on the shapes of both its marginal cost curve and its demand curve. As a monopoly's demand curve shifts, price and output may change in the same direction or in different directions.

2. **Market Power:** Market power is the ability of a firm to charge a price above marginal cost and earn a positive profit. The more elastic the demand the monopoly faces at the quantity at which it maximizes its profit, the closer its price to its marginal cost and the closer the Lerner Index or price markup, $(p - MC)/p$, is to zero, which is the competitive level.

3. **Welfare Effects of Monopoly:** Because a monopoly's price is above its marginal cost, too little output is produced, and society suffers a deadweight loss. The monopoly makes higher profit than it would if it acted as a price taker. Consumers are worse off, buying less output at a higher price.

4. **Taxes and Monopoly:** A specific or an *ad valorem* tax exacerbates the deadweight loss of a monopoly by further reducing sales and driving up the price to consumers. Unlike in a competitive market, the tax incidence on consumers can exceed 100% in a monopoly market. In a monopoly, the welfare losses from an *ad valorem* tax are less than from a specific tax that reduces output by the same amount (unlike in a competitive market where both taxes reduce welfare by the same amount).

5. **Cost Advantages That Create Monopolies:** A firm may be a monopoly if it controls a key input, has superior knowledge about producing or distributing a good, or has substantial economies of scale. In markets with substantial economies of scale, the single seller is called a natural monopoly because total production costs would rise if more than one firm produced.

6. **Government Actions That Create Monopolies:** Governments may establish government-owned and -operated monopolies. They may also create private-monopolies by establishing barriers to entry that prevent other firms from competing. Governments grant patents, which give inventors monopoly rights for a limited period of time.

7. **Government Actions That Reduce Market Power:** A government can eliminate the welfare harm of a monopoly by forcing the firm to set its price at the competitive level. If the government sets the price at a different level or otherwise regulates nonoptimally, welfare at the regulated monopoly optimum is lower than in the competitive equilibrium. A government can eliminate or reduce the harms of monopoly by allowing or facilitating entry.

8. **Monopoly Decisions over Time:** If a good has a positive network externality so that its value to a consumer grows as the number of units sold increases, then current sales affect a monopoly's future demand curve. A monopoly may maximize its long-run profit—its profit over time—by setting a low introductory price in the first period that it sells the good and then later raising its price as its product's popularity ensures large future sales at a higher price. Consequently, the monopoly is not maximizing its short-run profit in the first period but is maximizing the sum of its profits over all periods.

Questions

* = answer at the back of this book; **W** *= audio-slide show answers by James Dearden at* **www.aw-bc.com/perloff**

1. Show that after a shift in the demand curve, a monopoly's price may remain constant but its output may rise.

2. What is the effect of a franchise (lump-sum) tax on a monopoly? (*Hint:* Consider the possibility that the firm may shut down.)

3. When is a monopoly unlikely to be profitable? (*Hint:* Discuss the relationship between market demand and average cost.)

4. A monopoly has a constant marginal cost of production of $1 per unit and a fixed cost of $10. Draw the firm's *MC*, *AVC*, and *AC* curves. Add a downward-sloping demand curve, and show the profit-maximizing quantity and price. Indicate the profit as an area on your diagram. Show the deadweight loss.

*5. Can a firm be a natural monopoly if it has a U-shaped average cost curve? Why or why not?

6. Can a firm operating in the upward-sloping portion of its average cost curve be a natural monopoly? Explain.

7. Using the information in the "Electric Power Utilities" application, if a utility produced 34 billion kWh per year—which is on the upward-sloping section of the average cost curve—would it be a natural monopoly? Explain.

8. Show why a monopoly may operate in the upward- or downward-sloping section of its long-run average cost curve but a competitive firm will operate only in the upward-sloping section.

9. When will a monopoly set its price equal to its marginal cost?

10. Describe the effects on output and welfare if the government regulates a monopoly so that it may not charge a price above $\bar{p}$, which lies between the unregulated monopoly price and the optimally regulated price (determined by the intersection of the firm's marginal cost and the market demand curve).

11. Suppose that many similar price-taking consumers (such as Denise in Chapter 10) have a single good (candy bars). Jane has a monopoly in wood, so she can set prices. Assume that no production is possible. Using an Edgeworth box, illustrate the monopoly optimum and show that it does not lie on the contract curve (that is, isn't Pareto efficient).

12. A monopoly drug company produces a lifesaving medicine at a constant cost of $10 per dose. The demand for this medicine is perfectly inelastic at prices less than or equal to the $100 (per day) income of the 100 patients who need to take this drug daily. At a higher price, nothing is bought. Show the equilibrium price and quantity and the consumer and producer surplus in a graph. Now the government imposes a price ceiling of $30. Show how the equilibrium, consumer surplus, and producer surplus change. What is the deadweight loss, if any, from this price control?

13. The price of wholesale milk dropped by 30.3% in 1999 as the Pennsylvania Milk Marketing Board lowered the regulated price. The price to consumers fell by substantially less than 30.3% in Philadelphia. Why? (*Hint:* Show that a monopoly will not necessarily lower its price by the same percentage as its constant marginal cost drops.)

14. Today, drug companies spend large sums to determine additional uses for their existing drugs. For example, GlaxoWellcome PLC, a pharmaceutical giant, learned that its drug bupropion hydrochloride is more effective than the nicotine patch for helping people quit smoking. That drug is now sold as Zyban, but it was introduced in 1997 as an antidepressant, Wellbutrin. Projected 1999 sales were $250 million for Zyban and $590 million for Wellbutrin. Using a graph, show the demand curves for Wellbutrin and Zyban and the aggregate demand for this drug, bupropion hydrochloride. On the graph, indicate the quantity of pills sold for each use and total use at the current price. Why does Glaxo, the monopoly producer, set the same price, $1.16 a pill, for both drugs?

15. Once the copyright runs out on a book or musical composition, the work can legally be placed on the Internet for anyone to download. However, the U.S. Congress recently extended the copyright law to 95 years after the original publication. But in Australia and Europe, the copyright holds for only 50 years. Thus an Australian Web site could post *Gone With the Wind,* a 1936 novel, or Elvis Presley's 1954 single "That's All Right," while a U.S. site could not. Obviously, this legal nicety won't stop American fans from downloading from Australian or European sites. Discuss how limiting the length of a copyright would affect the pricing used by the publisher of a novel.

16. Are major-league baseball clubs profit-maximizing monopolies? Some observers of this market have contended that baseball club owners want to maximize attendance or revenue. Alexander (2001) says that one test of whether a firm is a profit-maximizing monopoly is to check whether the firm is operating in the elastic portion of its demand curve, which, according to his analysis, is true. Why is that a relevant test? What would the elasticity be if a baseball club were maximizing revenue?

17. Hotels tend to charge a lot for phone calls made from guests' rooms. Cell phones endangered this nice little "monopoly" business to the point that average telephone profit per available room at hotels in the United States fell from $637 in 2000 to $152 in 2003 (Christopher Elliott, "Mystery of the Cellphone That Doesn't Work at the Hotel," *New York Times,* September 7, 2004: C6). But now many travelers complain that their cell phones don't work in hotels. Although hotels deny that they are doing anything as nefarious as blocking signals, Netline Communications Technologies in Tel Aviv says that it has sold hundreds of cell phone jammers to hotels around the world. A Federal Communications Commission rule prohibits cell phone jammers, but the rule is unenforced. By one estimate, a device that could block all cell phone transmissions would cost $25,000 for a small hotel and $35,000 to $50,000 for a big chain hotel. Assume that the blocker lasts for one year. Under what conditions (in terms of profit per room, number of rooms, and so forth) would it pay for a hotel to install a jammer, assuming the law permits it? Explain your answer.

18. Bleyer Industries Inc., the only U.S. manufacturer of plastic Easter eggs, manufactured 250 million eggs each year. Over the past seven years, imports from China have cut into its business. In 2005, Bleyer filed for bankruptcy because the Chinese firms could produce the eggs at much lower costs ("U.S. Plastic Egg Industry a Shell of Its Former Self," *San Francisco Chronicle,* January 14, 2005). Use graphs to show how a competitive import industry could drive a monopoly out of business.

19. Draw an example of a monopoly with a linear demand curve and a constant marginal cost curve.

   a. Show the profit-maximizing price and output, p^* and Q^*, and identify the areas of consumer surplus, producer surplus, and deadweight loss. Also show the quantity, Q_c, that would be produced if the monopoly were to act like a price taker.

b. Now suppose that the demand curve is a smooth concave-to-the-origin curve (whose ends hit the axes) that is tangent to the original demand curve at the point (Q^*, p^*). Explain why the monopoly equilibrium will be the same as with the linear demand curve. Show how much output the firm would produce if it acted like a price taker. Show how the welfare areas change.

c. Repeat the exercises in part b if the demand curve is a smooth convex-to-the-origin curve (whose ends hit the axes) that is tangent to the original demand curve at the point (Q^*, p^*).

20. A country has a monopoly that is protected by a specific tariff, τ, on imported goods. The monopoly's profit-maximizing price is p^*. The world price of the good is p_w, which is less than p^*. Because the price of imported goods with the tariff is $p_w + \tau$, no foreign goods are imported.

Under WTO pressure the government removes the tariff so that the supply of foreign goods to the country's consumers is horizontal at p_w. Show how much the former monopoly produces and what price it charges. Show who gains and who loses from removing the tariff. (*Hint:* Look at the effect of government price regulation on a monopoly's demand curve in Section 11.7.)

21. A monopoly chocolate manufacturer faces two types of consumers. The larger group, the hoi polloi, loves desserts and has a relatively flat, linear demand curve for chocolate. The smaller group, the snobs, is interested in buying chocolate only if the hoi polloi do not buy it. Given that the hoi polloi do not buy the chocolate, the snobs have a relatively steep, linear demand curve. Show the monopoly's possible outcomes—high price and low quantity, or low price and high quantity—and explain the condition under which the monopoly chooses to cater to the snobs rather than to the hoi polloi.

Problems

*22. Show that the elasticity of demand is unitary at the midpoint of a linear inverse demand function and hence that a monopoly will not operate to the right of this midpoint.

23. The inverse demand curve that a monopoly faces is

$$p = 100 - Q.$$

The firm's cost curve is $C(Q) = 10 + 5Q$. What is the profit-maximizing solution? How does your answer change if $C(Q) = 100 + 5Q$?

24. The inverse demand curve that a monopoly faces is

$$p = 10Q^{-1/2}.$$

The firm's cost curve is $C(Q) = 5Q$. What is the profit-maximizing solution?

25. If the inverse demand function facing a monopoly is $P(Q)$ and its cost function is $C(Q)$, show the effect of a specific tax, τ, on the monopoly's profit-maximizing output. How does imposing τ affect its profit?

26. In the "Botox Patent Monopoly" application, consumer surplus, area A, equals the deadweight loss, area C. Show that this equality is a result of the linear demand and constant marginal cost assumptions.

27. Based on the information in the "Botox Patent Monopoly" application, what would happen to the equilibrium price and quantity if the government had collected a specific tax of $75 per vial of Botox? What welfare effects would such a tax have?

28. Based on the information in the "Botox Patent Monopoly" application, what would happen to the equilibrium

price and quantity if the government had set a price ceiling of $200 per vial of Botox? What welfare effects would such a tax have?

29. The Commonwealth of Pennsylvania is the monopoly retailer of wine in that state. Suppose that Quaker Cabernet has no close substitutes and that the statewide inverse demand function for this wine is $p = 5 - 0.001Q$. The state purchases the wine on the wholesale market for $2 per bottle, and the state-operated liquor stores incur no other expenses to sell this wine.

a. What are the state's profit-maximizing price and quantity?

b. Neighboring New Jersey permits private retailers to sell wine. They face the same statewide demand curve as in Pennsylvania. No interstate wine trade is permitted. Suppose the New Jersey market for Quaker Cabernet is perfectly competitive. What are the equilibrium price and quantity?

c. New Jersey taxes wine sales. While the retailers pay the taxes on wine sales, they may pass on some or all of these taxes to consumers by raising prices. Identify the specific tax (tax per bottle sold) for which New Jersey's equilibrium market price and quantity equal the Pennsylvania monopoly price and quantity. Given the quantity tax, show that New Jersey's tax revenue equals Pennsylvania's profit. **W**

30. Suppose that all iPod owners consider only two options for downloading music to their MP3 players: purchasing songs from iTunes or copying songs from friends' CDs. With these two options, suppose the weekly inverse market

demand for the Rolling Stones' song "Satisfaction" is $p = 1.98 - 0.00198Q$. The marginal cost to Apple Inc. of downloading a song is zero.

a. What is Apple's optimal price of "Satisfaction"? How many downloads of "Satisfaction" does Apple sell each week?

b. Now suppose that Apple sells a version of the iPod equipped with software in which songs played on the iPod must be downloaded from iTunes. For this iPod, the inverse market demand for "Satisfaction" is $p = 2.58 - 0.0129Q$. What is Apple's optimal price of downloads of "Satisfaction" for this new player? How many downloads of "Satisfaction" does Apple sell each week? **W**

31. In addition to the hard-drive-based iPod, Apple produces a flash-based audio player. Its 512MB iPod Shuffle (which does not have a hard drive) sold for $99 in 2005. According to iSuppli, Apple's per-unit cost of manufacturing the Shuffle is $45.37 (Brian Dipert, "Song Wars: Striking Back Against the iPod Empire," **www.reed-electronics.com**, June 9, 2005). What is Apple's price/marginal cost ratio? What is its Lerner Index? If we assume (possibly incorrectly) that Apple acts like a short-run profit-maximizing monopoly in pricing its iPod Shuffle, what elasticity of demand does Apple believe it faces?

*32. Humana hospitals in 1991 charged very high prices relative to their marginal costs. For example, Humana's Suburban Hospital in Louisville, Kentucky, charged patients $44.90 for a container of saline solution (salt water) that cost the hospital 81¢ (Douglas Frantz, "Congress Probes Hospital Costs—$9 Tylenols, $118 Heat Pads," *San Francisco Chronicle*, October 18, 1991: A2). Calculate the hospital's price/marginal cost ratio, its Lerner Index, and the demand elasticity, ε, that it faces for saline solution (assuming that it maximizes its profit).

33. According to the California Nurses Association, Tenet Healthcare hospitals mark up drugs substantially. At Tenet's Sierra Vista Regional Medical Center, drug prices are 1,840.80% of the hospital's costs (Chuck Squatriglia and Tyche Hendricks, "Tenet Hiked Drug Prices, Study Finds More Than Double U.S. Average," *San Francisco Chronicle*, November 24, 2002: A1, A10). Assuming Tenet is maximizing its profit, what is the elasticity of demand that Tenet believes it faces? What is its Lerner Index for drugs?

34. According to one estimate, the parts for a Segway Human Transporter—which has five gyroscopes, two tilt sensors, dual redundant motors, and 10 microprocessors and can travel up to 12.5 mph—cost at least $1,500 (Eric A. Taub, "Segway Transporter Slow to Catch On," *San Francisco Chronicle*, August 11, 2003: E4). Suppose that a Segway's marginal cost is $2,000. Given that the Segway's price is $5,000, calculate the firm's price/marginal cost ratio, its

Lerner Index, and the elasticity of demand it believes it faces (assuming that it is trying to maximize its short-run profit).

35. In 2005, Apple introduced the Mac mini G4, a miniature computer that weighs only 2.9 pounds but comes fully loaded with lots of memory and a large hard disk drive. According to one estimate, the cost of production was $258 (Toni Duboise, "Low-cost Apple Mini Packs Punch, but BYO Peripherals," **www.eetimes.com**), while its suggested price was $499. Although other firms produce computers, the Mac is viewed as a different product by aficionados. What is Apple's price/marginal cost ratio? What is its Lerner Index? If we assume that Apple is a profit-maximizing monopoly, what elasticity of demand does it believe it faces for this tiny computer?

36. The U.S. Postal Service (USPS) has a constitutionally guaranteed monopoly on first-class mail. It currently charges 37¢ for a stamp, which is probably not the profit-maximizing price, as the alleged USPS goal is to break even rather than to turn a profit. Following the postal services in Australia, Britain, Canada, Switzerland, and Ireland, the USPS allowed Stamps.com to sell a sheet of twenty 37¢ stamps with a photo of your dog, your mommy, or whatever for $16.99 (that's 84.95¢ per stamp, or a nearly 230% markup). Stamps.com keeps the extra profit beyond the 37¢ it pays the USPS (Mary Fitzgerald, "Customized Stamps May Lick Postal Service's Finance Woes," *Boston Sunday Globe*, September 12, 2004: A23). What is the firm's Lerner Index? If Stamps.com is a profit-maximizing monopoly, what elasticity of demand does it face for a customized stamp?

*37. Only Indian tribes can run casinos in California. These casinos are spread around the state so that each is a monopoly in its local community. California Governor Arnold Schwarzenegger negotiated with the state's tribes, getting them to agree to transfer a fraction of their profits to the state in exchange for concessions (Dan Morain and Evan Halper, "Casino Deals Said to Be Near," *Los Angeles Times*, June 16, 2004:1). In 2004, he started with a proposal that the state get 25% of casino profits and then dropped the level to 15%. He announced a deal with two tribes at 10% in 2005. How does a profit tax affect a monopoly's output and price? How would a monopoly change its behavior if the profit tax were 10% rather than 25%? (*Hint:* You may assume that the profit tax refers to the tribe's economic profit.)

38. In 1996, Florida voted on (and rejected) a 1¢-per-pound excise tax on refined cane sugar in the Florida Everglades Agricultural Area. Swinton and Thomas (2001) used linear supply and demand curves (based on elasticities estimated by Marks, 1993) to calculate the incidence from this tax given that the market is competitive. Their inverse demand curve was $p = 1.787 - 0.0004641Q$, and their

inverse supply curve was $p = -0.4896 + 0.00020165Q$. Calculate the incidence of the tax that falls on consumers (Chapter 3) for a competitive market. If producers joined together to form a monopoly, and the supply curve is actually the monopoly's marginal cost curve, what is the incidence of the tax? (*Hint:* The incidence that falls on consumers is the difference between the equilibrium price with and without the tax divided by the tax. You should find that the incidence is 70% in a competitive market and 41% with a monopoly.)

39. A monopoly manufactures its product in two factories with marginal cost functions $MC_1(Q_1)$ and $MC_2(Q_2)$, where Q_1 is the quantity produced in the first factory and Q_2 is the quantity manufactured in the second factory. The monopoly's total output is $Q = Q_1 + Q_2$. Use a graph (or math) to determine how much total output the monopoly produces and how much it produces at each factory. (*Hint:* Consider the cases where the factories have constant marginal costs—not necessarily equal costs—and where they have upward-sloping marginal cost curves.)

40. A monopoly sells music CDs. It has a constant marginal and average cost of 20. It faces two groups of potential customers: honest and dishonest people. The dishonest and the honest consumers' demand functions are the same: $p = 120 - Q$.

   a. If it is not possible for the dishonest customers to steal the music, what are the monopoly's profit-maximizing price and quantity? What is its profit? What are the consumer surplus, producer surplus, and welfare?

   b. Answer the same questions as in part a if the dishonest customers can pirate the music.

   c. How do consumer surplus, producer surplus, and welfare change if piracy occurs?

*41. A monopoly produces a good with a network externality at a constant marginal and average cost of 2. In the first period, its inverse demand curve is $p = 10 - Q$. In the second period, its demand is $p = 10 - Q$ unless it sells at least $Q = 8$ units in the first period. If it meets or exceeds this target, then the demand curve rotates out by β (that is, it sells β times as many units for any given price), so that its

inverse demand curve is $p = 10 - Q/\beta$. The monopoly knows that it can sell no output after the second period. The monopoly's objective is to maximize the sum of its profits over the two periods. In the first period, should the monopoly set the output that maximizes its profit in that period? How does your answer depend on β? (*Hint:* See the discussion of the two-period monopoly model in Section 11.8 of this chapter.)

42. A monopoly's production function is Cobb-Douglas, $Q = L^{0.5}K^{0.5}$, where L is labor and K is capital. The demand function is $p = 100 - Q$. The wage, w, is $1 per hour, and the rental cost of capital, r, is $4.

   a. What is the equation of the (long-run) expansion path? Illustrate in a graph.

   b. Derive the long-run total cost curve equation as a function of q.

   c. What quantity maximizes this firm's profit?

   d. Find the optimal input combination that produces the profit-maximizing quantity. Illustrate with a graph.

43. Suppose that the inverse demand function for a monopolist's product is $p = 9 - Q/20$. Its cost function is $C = 10 + 10Q - 4Q^2 + 2/3Q^3$.

   a. Draw marginal revenue and marginal cost curves. At what outputs does marginal revenue equal marginal cost?

   b. What is the profit-maximizing output? Check the second-order condition, $d^2\pi/dQ^2$, at the monopoly optimum. **W**

44. Suppose that the inverse demand for San Francisco cable car rides is $p = 10 - Q/1,000$, where p is the price per ride and Q is the number of rides per day.

   a. Suppose the objective of San Francisco's Municipal Authority (the cable car operator) is to maximize is its revenues. What is the revenue-maximizing price?

   b. The city of San Francisco calculates that the city's businesses benefit from tourists and habitants alike riding on the city's cable cars by $4 per ride. Suppose the city's objective is to maximize the sum of the cable car revenues and the economic impact. What is the optimal price? **W**

Chapter 12

Pricing and Advertising

Everything is worth what its purchaser will pay for it. —Publilius Syrus (first century B.C.)

Why does Disneyland charge local residents $154 for one-year admissions but out-of-towners $239? Why are airlines' fares substantially less if you book in advance? Why are some goods, including computers and software, sold bundled together at a single price? To answer these questions, we need to examine how monopolies and other noncompetitive firms set prices.

Monopolies and other noncompetitive firms often can use information about individual consumers' demand curves to increase their profits. Instead of setting a single price, such firms use **nonuniform pricing:** charging consumers different prices for the same product or charging a single customer a price that depends on the number of units the customer buys. By replacing a single price with nonuniform pricing, the firm raises its profit.

Why is it that a monopoly can earn a higher profit from using a nonuniform pricing scheme than from setting a single price? A monopoly that uses nonuniform prices can capture some or all of the consumer surplus and deadweight loss that results if the monopoly sets a single price. As we saw in Chapter 11, a monopoly that sets a high single price sells only to the customers who value the good the most, and those customers retain some consumer surplus. The monopoly loses sales to other customers who value the good less than the single price. These lost sales are a *deadweight loss*: the value of these potential sales in excess of the cost of producing the good. But a monopoly that uses nonuniform pricing captures additional consumer surplus by raising the price for customers who value the good the most. By lowering the good's price for other customers, the monopoly makes additional sales, thereby converting into profit what would otherwise be deadweight loss.

This chapter examines several types of nonuniform pricing, including price discrimination, two-part tariffs, and tie-in sales. Through **price discrimination,** the most common form of nonuniform pricing, a firm charges consumers different prices for the same good. For example, many magazines price discriminate by charging college students less for subscriptions than they charge older adults. If a popular magazine were to start setting a high price for everyone, many student subscribers—who are sensitive to price increases (have relatively elastic demands)—would cancel their subscriptions. If, on the other hand, the magazine were to let everyone pay the student price, it would gain few additional subscriptions because most potential older adult subscribers are relatively insensitive to the price, and it would earn less from those older adults who are willing to pay the higher price. Thus the magazine makes more profit by price discriminating.

Some noncompetitive firms that cannot practically price discriminate use other forms of nonuniform pricing to increase profits. One such method is for a firm to charge a *two-part tariff*, where a customer pays one fee for the right to buy the good and another price for each unit purchased. For example, health club members pay an annual fee to join the club and then an additional amount each time they use the facilities.

In another type of nonuniform pricing, the *tie-in sale*, a customer may buy one good only if he or she also agrees to buy another good or service. Vacation package deals, for example, may include airfare and a hotel room for a single price. Some restaurants provide only full-course dinners, where a single price buys an appetizer, an entrée, and dessert. A firm may sell copiers under the condition that customers agree to buy all future copier service and supplies from the firm.

A monopoly may also increase its profit by advertising. A monopoly (or another firm with market power) may advertise to shift its demand curve so as to raises its profit, taking into account the cost of advertising.

In this chapter, we examine seven main topics	1. **Why and How Firms Price Discriminate:** A firm can increase its profit by price discriminating if it has market power, can identify which customers are more price sensitive than others, and can prevent customers who pay low prices from reselling to those who pay high prices.
	2. **Perfect Price Discrimination:** If a monopoly can charge the maximum that each customer is willing to pay for each unit of output, the monopoly captures all potential consumer surplus and sells the efficient (competitive) level of output.
	3. **Quantity Discrimination:** Some firms profit by charging different prices for large purchases and for small ones, which is a form of price discrimination.
	4. **Multimarket Price Discrimination:** Firms that cannot perfectly price discriminate may charge a group of consumers with relatively elastic demands a lower price than they charge other groups of consumers.
	5. **Two-Part Tariffs:** By charging consumers a fee for the right to buy any number of units and a price per unit, firms earn higher profits than they do by charging a single price per unit.
	6. **Tie-In Sales:** By requiring a customer to buy a second good or service along with the first, firms make higher profits than they do by selling the goods or services separately.
	7. **Advertising:** A monopoly advertises to shift its demand curve and to increase its profit.

12.1 Why and How Firms Price Discriminate

Until now, we have examined how a monopoly sets its price if it charges all its customers the same price. However, many noncompetitive firms increase their profits by charging *nonuniform prices,* which vary across customers. We start with the most common form of nonuniform pricing: price discrimination.

WHY PRICE DISCRIMINATION PAYS

For almost any good or service, some consumers are willing to pay more than others. A firm that sets a single price faces a trade-off between charging consumers who really want the good as much as they are willing to pay and charging a low enough price that the firm does not lose sales to less enthusiastic customers. As a result, the firm usually sets an intermediate price. A price-discriminating firm that varies its prices across customers avoids this trade-off.

There are two reasons a firm earns a higher profit from price discrimination than from uniform pricing. First, a price-discriminating firm charges a higher price to customers who are willing to pay more than the uniform price, capturing some or all of their consumer surplus—the difference between what a good is worth to a consumer and what the consumer pays—under uniform pricing. Second, a price-discriminating firm sells to some people who are not willing to pay as much as the uniform price.

WHO CAN PRICE DISCRIMINATE

Not all firms can price discriminate. For a firm to price discriminate successfully, three conditions must be met.

First, a firm must have *market power,* or else it cannot charge any consumer more than the competitive price. A monopoly, an oligopoly firm, a monopolistically competitive firm, or a cartel may be able to price discriminate. A competitive firm cannot price discriminate.

Second, consumers must *differ* in their sensitivity to price (demand elasticities), and a firm must be able to *identify* how consumers differ in this sensitivity.[1] The movie theater owner knows that college students and older adults differ in their willingness to pay for a ticket, and Disneyland strategists know that tourists and "townies" differ in their willingness to pay for admission. In both cases, the firms can identify members of these two groups by using driver's licenses or other forms of identification. Similarly, if a firm knows that each individual's demand curve slopes downward, it may charge each customer a higher price for the first unit of a good than it charges for subsequent units.

Third, a firm must be able to *prevent or limit resales* to higher-price-paying customers from customers whom the firm charges relatively low prices. Price discrimination is ineffective if resales are easy, because ease of reselling would inhibit the firm's ability to make higher-price sales. The movie theater owner can charge different prices because older adults enter the theater as soon as they buy their tickets, and thus do not have time to resell them.

Except for competitive firms, the first two conditions—market power and ability to identify groups with different price sensitivities—frequently hold. Usually, the biggest obstacle to price discrimination is a firm's inability to prevent resales. In some markets, however, resales are inherently difficult or impossible, firms can take actions that prevent resales, or government actions or laws prevent resales.

PREVENTING RESALES

Resales are difficult or impossible for most *services* and when *transaction costs are high.* If a plumber charges you less than he charges your neighbor for clearing a pipe, you cannot make a deal with your neighbor to resell this service. The higher the transaction costs a consumer must incur to resell a good, the less likely it is that resales will occur. Suppose that you are able to buy a jar of pickles for $1 less than the usual price. Could you practically find and sell this jar to someone, or would the transaction costs

---

[1]Even if consumers are identical, price discrimination is possible if each consumer has a downward-sloping demand curve for the monopoly's product. To price discriminate over the units purchased by a consumer, the monopoly has to know how the elasticity of demand varies with the number of units purchased.

be prohibitive? The more valuable a product or the more widely consumed it is, the more likely it is that transaction costs are low enough that resales occur.

Some firms act to raise transaction costs or otherwise make resales difficult. If your college requires that someone with a student ticket show a student identification card with a picture on it before being admitted to a sporting event, you'll find it difficult to resell your low-price tickets to nonstudents, who must pay higher prices. When students at some universities buy computers at lower-than-usual prices, they must sign a contract that forbids them to resell the computer.

Similarly, a firm can prevent resales by *vertically integrating:* participating in more than one successive stage of the production and distribution chain for a good or service. Alcoa, the former aluminum monopoly, wanted to sell aluminum ingots to producers of aluminum wire at a lower price than it set for producers of aluminum aircraft parts. If Alcoa did so, however, the wire producers could easily resell their ingots. By starting its own wire production firm, Alcoa prevented such resales and was able to charge high prices to firms that manufactured aircraft parts (Perry, 1980).

Governments frequently establish policies to promote price discrimination and to prevent resales. For example, U.S. federal and some state governments require that milk producers, under penalty of law, price discriminate by selling milk at a higher price for fresh use than for processing (cheese, ice cream), and forbid resales. Government *tariffs* (taxes on imports) limit resales by making it expensive to buy goods in a low-price country and resell them in a high-price country. In some cases, laws prevent such reselling explicitly. Under U.S. trade laws, certain brand-name perfumes may not be sold in the United States except by their manufacturers.

● APPLICATION

Disneyland Pricing

Disneyland, in southern California, is a well-run operation that rarely misses a trick when it comes to increasing profits. (Indeed, Disneyland mints money: When you enter the park, you can exchange U.S. currency for Disney dollars, which can be spent only in the park.)[2]

In 2007, Disneyland charged most adults $122 for a park-hopper ticket (good for both Disneyland and Disney's California Adventure park) for two days but charged southern Californians only $83. This policy of giving locals discounts makes sense if visitors from afar are willing to pay more than locals and if Disneyland can prevent locals from selling discount tickets to nonlocals. Imagine a Midwesterner who's never been to

---

[2]According to **www.babycenter.com**, it costs $832,056 to raise a child from cradle through college. Parents can cut that total in half, however: They don't *have* to take their kids to Disneyland.

Disneyland before and wants to visit. Travel accounts for most of the trip's cost, so an extra $5 for entrance to Disneyland makes little percentage difference in the total cost of a visit and hence does not greatly affect that person's decision whether to go. In contrast, for a local who has gone to Disneyland many times and for whom the entrance price is a larger share of the total cost of the visit, a slightly higher price might prevent a visit.

Charging both groups the same price is not in Disney's best interest. If Disney were to charge the higher price to everyone, many locals would stay away. If Disney were to use the lower price for everyone, it would be charging nonresidents much less than they are willing to pay.

By setting different prices for the two groups, Disney increases its profit if it can prevent the locals from selling discount tickets to others. Disney prevents resales by checking a purchaser's driver's license and requiring that the ticket be used for same-day entrance.

NOT ALL PRICE DIFFERENCES ARE PRICE DISCRIMINATION

Not every seller who charges consumers different prices is price discriminating. Hotels charge newlyweds more for bridal suites. Is that price discrimination? Some hotel managers say no. They contend that honeymooners, more so than other customers, steal mementos, so the price differential reflects an actual cost differential.

The price for a year's worth of issues of *TV Guide* magazine is $103.48 at the newsstand, $37.95 with a standard subscription, and $32.25 through a college student subscription. The difference between the newsstand cost and the standard subscription cost reflects, at least in part, the higher cost of selling at a newsstand rather than mailing the magazine directly to customers, so this price difference does not reflect pure price discrimination. But the price difference between the standard subscription rate and the college student rate reflects pure price discrimination because the two subscriptions are identical in every respect except the price.

TYPES OF PRICE DISCRIMINATION

There are three main types of price discrimination. With **perfect price discrimination**—also called *first-degree price discrimination*—the firm sells each unit at the maximum amount any customer is willing to pay for it, so prices differ across customers, and a given customer may pay more for some units than for others.

With **quantity discrimination** (*second-degree price discrimination*), the firm charges a different price for large quantities than for small quantities, but all customers who buy a given quantity pay the same price. With **multimarket price discrimination** (*third-degree price discrimination*), the firm charges different groups of customers different prices but charges a given customer the same price for every unit of output sold. Typically, not all customers pay different prices—the firm sets different prices only for a few groups of customers. Because this last type of discrimination is the most common, the term *price discrimination* is often used to mean *multimarket price discrimination*.

In addition to price discriminating, many firms use other, more complicated types of nonuniform pricing. Later in this chapter, we examine two other frequently used nonuniform pricing methods—two-part tariffs and tie-in sales—that are similar to quantity discrimination.

12.2 Perfect Price Discrimination

If a firm with market power knows exactly how much each customer is willing to pay for each unit of its good and it can prevent resales, the firm charges each person his or her **reservation price:** the maximum amount a person would be willing to pay for a unit of output. Such an all-knowing firm *perfectly price discriminates.* By selling each unit of its output to the customer who values it the most at the maximum price that person is willing to pay, the perfectly price-discriminating monopoly captures all possible consumer surplus. For example, the managers of the Suez Canal set tolls on an individual basis, taking into account many factors such as weather and each ship's alternative routes.

We first analyze how a firm uses its information about consumers to perfectly price discriminate. We then compare the perfectly price-discriminating monopoly to competition and single-price monopoly. By showing that the same quantity is produced as would be produced by a competitive market and that the last unit of output sells for the marginal cost, we demonstrate that perfect price discrimination is efficient. We then illustrate how the perfect price discrimination equilibrium differs from single-price monopoly by using the Botox application from Chapter 11. Finally, we discuss how firms obtain the information they need to perfectly price discriminate.

HOW A FIRM PERFECTLY PRICE DISCRIMINATES

Suppose that a monopoly has market power, can prevent resales, and has enough information to perfectly price discriminate. The monopoly sells each unit at its reservation price, which is the height of the demand curve: the maximum price consumers will pay for a given amount of output.

Graphical Analysis. Figure 12.1 illustrates how a perfectly price-discriminating firm maximizes its profit. The figure shows that the first customer is willing to pay $6 for a unit, the next customer is willing to pay $5, and so forth. This perfectly price-discriminating firm sells its first unit of output for $6. Having sold the first unit, the firm can get, at most, $5 for its second unit. The firm must drop its price by $1 for each successive unit it sells.

A perfectly price-discriminating monopoly's marginal revenue is the same as its price. As the figure shows, the firm's marginal revenue is $MR_1 = \$6$ on the first unit, $MR_2 = \$5$ on the second unit, and $MR_3 = \$4$ on the third unit. As a result, *the firm's marginal revenue curve is its demand curve.*

This firm has a constant marginal cost of $4 per unit. It pays for the firm to produce the first unit because the firm sells that unit for $6, so its marginal revenue exceeds its marginal cost by $2. Similarly, the firm certainly wants to sell the second unit for $5, which also exceeds its marginal cost. The firm breaks even when it sells the third unit for $4. The firm is unwilling to sell more than 3 units because its marginal cost would exceed its marginal revenue on all successive units. Thus like any profit-maximizing firm, a perfectly price-discriminating firm produces at point *e,* where its marginal revenue curve intersects its marginal cost curve. (If you find it upsetting that the firm is

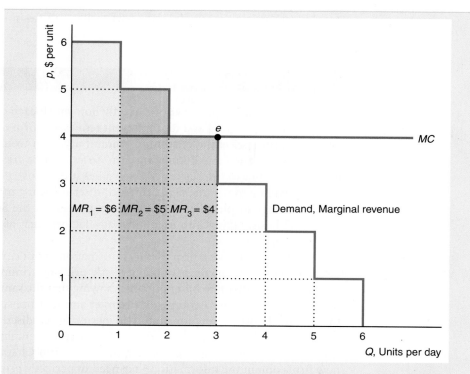

Figure 12.1 Perfect Price Discrimination. The monopoly can charge $6 for the first unit, $5 for the second, and $4 for the third, as the demand curve shows. Its marginal revenue is $MR_1 = \$6$ for the first unit, $MR_2 = \$5$ for the second unit, and $MR_3 = \$4$ for the third unit. Thus the demand curve is also the marginal revenue curve. Because the firm's marginal and average cost is $4 per unit, it is unwilling to sell at a price below $4, so it sells 3 units, point *e*, and breaks even on the last unit.

indifferent between producing 2 and 3 units, assume that the firm's marginal cost is $3.99, so it definitely wants to produce 3 units.)

This perfectly price-discriminating firm earns revenues of $MR_1 + MR_2 + MR_3 = \$6 + \$5 + \$4 = \$15$, which is the area under its marginal revenue curve up to the number of units, 3, it sells. If the firm has no fixed cost, its cost of producing 3 units is $12 = \$4 \times 3$, so its profit is $3.

The same type of analysis can be used with the usual, smooth demand curve. In Figure 12.2, a perfectly price-discriminating monopoly sells each unit at its reservation price, which is the height of the demand curve. As a result, the firm's marginal revenue curve, MR_d, is the same as its demand curve. The firm sells the first unit for p_1 to the consumer who will pay the most for the good. The firm's marginal cost for that unit is MC_1, so it makes $p_1 - MC_1$ on that unit. The firm receives a lower price and has a higher marginal cost for each successive unit. It sells Q_d units, where its marginal revenue curve, MR_d, intersects the marginal cost curve, MC. The last unit sells for p_e, so the monopoly just covers its marginal cost on the last unit. The firm is unwilling to sell additional units because its marginal revenue would be less than the marginal cost of producing them.

The perfectly price-discriminating monopoly's total producer surplus on the Q_d units it sells is the area below its demand curve and above its marginal cost curve, $A + B + C + D + E$. Its profit is the producer surplus minus its fixed cost, if any.

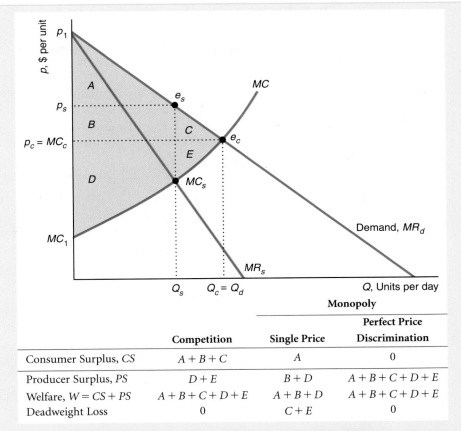

		Monopoly	
		Single Price	**Perfect Price Discrimination**
	Competition		
Consumer Surplus, CS	$A + B + C$	A	0
Producer Surplus, PS	$D + E$	$B + D$	$A + B + C + D + E$
Welfare, $W = CS + PS$	$A + B + C + D + E$	$A + B + D$	$A + B + C + D + E$
Deadweight Loss	0	$C + E$	0

Figure 12.2 Competitive, Single-Price, and Perfect Discrimination Equilibria. In the competitive market equilibrium, e_c, price is p_c, quantity is Q_c, consumer surplus is $A + B + C$, producer surplus is $D + E$, and there is no deadweight loss. In the single-price monopoly equilibrium, e_s, price is p_s, quantity is Q_s, consumer surplus falls to A, producer surplus is $B + D$, and deadweight loss is $C + E$. In the perfect discrimination equilibrium, the monopoly sells each unit at the customer's reservation price on the demand curve. It sells Q_d $(= Q_c)$ units, where the last unit is sold at its marginal cost. Customers have no consumer surplus, but there is no deadweight loss.

Calculus Analysis. A perfectly price-discriminating monopoly charges each customer the reservation price $p = D(Q)$, where $D(Q)$ is the inverse demand function and Q is total output. The discriminating monopoly's revenue, R, is the area under the demand curve up to the quantity, Q, it sells,

$$R = \int_0^Q D(z)\,\mathrm{d}z,$$

where z is a placeholder for quantity. Its objective is to maximize its profit through its choice of Q:

$$\max_Q \pi = \int_0^Q D(z)\,\mathrm{d}z - C(Q). \tag{12.1}$$

Its first-order condition for a maximum is found by differentiating Equation 12.1 to obtain

$$\frac{d\pi}{dQ} = D(Q) - \frac{dC(Q)}{dQ} = 0. \tag{12.2}$$

According to Equation 12.2, the discriminating monopoly sells units up to the quantity, Q, where the reservation price for the last unit, $D(Q)$, equals its marginal cost, $dC(Q)/dQ$. (This quantity is Q_d in Figure 12.2.)

For this solution to maximize profits, the second-order condition must hold:

$$\frac{d^2\pi}{dQ^2} = \frac{dD(Q)}{dQ} - \frac{d^2C(Q)}{dQ^2} < 0.$$

Given that the demand curve has a negative slope, the second-order condition holds if the demand curve has a greater (absolute) slope than the marginal cost curve.

The perfectly price-discriminating monopoly's profit is

$$\pi = \int_0^Q D(z)dz - C(Q).$$

For example, if $D(Q) = a - bQ$,

$$\pi = \int_0^Q (a - bz)dz - C(Q) = aQ - \frac{b}{2}Q^2 - C(Q). \tag{12.3}$$

The monopoly finds the output that maximizes the profit by setting the derivative of the profit in Equation 12.3 equal to zero:

$$a - bQ - \frac{dC(Q)}{dQ} = 0.$$

By rearranging terms, we find that $D(Q) = a - bQ = dC(Q)/dQ = MC$, as in Equation 12.2. Thus the monopoly produces the quantity at which the demand curve hits the marginal cost curve.

● APPLICATION

Amazon Is Watching You

Amazon, a giant among e-commerce vendors, collects an enormous amount of information about its 23 million customers' tastes and willingness to buy. If you've shopped at Amazon, you've probably noticed that its Web site greets you by name (thanks to a *cookie* it leaves on your computer, which provides information about you to Amazon's Web site).

In 2000, the firm decided to use this information to engage in *dynamic pricing*, where the price it charges its customers today depends on these customers' actions in the recent past—including what they bought, how much they paid, and whether they paid for high-speed shipping—and personal data such as where they live. Several Amazon customers discovered this practice. One man reported on the

Web site DVDTalk.com that he had bought Julie Taylor's *Titus* for $24.49. The next week, he returned to Amazon and saw that the price had jumped to $26.24. As an experiment, he removed the cookie that identified him, and found that the price dropped to $22.74.

Presumably, Amazon reasoned that a returning customer was less likely to compare prices across Web sites than a new customer, and was pricing accordingly. Other DVDTalk.com visitors reported that regular Amazon customers were charged 3% to 5% more than new customers.

Amazon announced that its pricing variations stopped as soon as it started receiving complaints from DVDTalk members. It claimed that the variations were random and designed only to determine price elasticities. A spokesperson explained, "This was a pure and simple price test. This was not dynamic pricing. We don't do that and have no plans ever to do that." Right. An Amazon customer service representative called it dynamic pricing in an e-mail to a DVDTalk member, allowing that dynamic pricing was a common practice among firms. A 2003 experiment, **www.managingchange.com/dynamic/survey/analysis.htm**, suggests that Amazon did not continue to use dynamic pricing; however, in 2007, a *Los Angeles Times* reporter experienced what might be dynamic pricing.

PERFECT PRICE DISCRIMINATION: EFFICIENT BUT HARMFUL TO CONSUMERS

A perfect price discrimination equilibrium is efficient and maximizes total welfare, where welfare is defined as the sum of consumer surplus and producer surplus. As such, this equilibrium has more in common with a competitive equilibrium than with a single-price-monopoly equilibrium.

If the market in Figure 12.2 is competitive, the intersection of the demand curve and the marginal cost curve, MC, determines the competitive equilibrium at e_c, where price is p_c and quantity is Q_c. Consumer surplus is $A + B + C$, producer surplus is $D + E$, and there is no deadweight loss. The market is efficient because the price, p_c, equals the marginal cost, MC_c.

With a single-price monopoly (which charges all its customers the same price because it cannot distinguish among them), the intersection of the MC curve and the single-price monopoly's marginal revenue curve, MC_s, determines the output, Q_s. The monopoly operates at e_s, where it charges p_s. The deadweight loss from monopoly is $C + E$. This efficiency loss is due to the monopoly's charging a price, p_s, that is above its marginal cost, MC_s, so less is sold than in a competitive market.

Again, the perfectly price-discriminating monopoly's total producer surplus on the Q_d units it sells is the area below its demand curve and above its marginal cost curve, $A + B + C + D + E$. Consumers receive no consumer surplus because each consumer pays his or her reservation price. The perfectly price-discriminating monopoly's equilibrium has *no deadweight loss* because the last unit is sold at a price, p_c, that equals the marginal cost, MC_c, as in a competitive market. Thus both a perfect price discrimination equilibrium and a competitive equilibrium are efficient.

The perfect price discrimination equilibrium differs from the competitive equilibrium in two ways. First, in the competitive equilibrium, everyone is charged a price equal to the equilibrium marginal cost, $p_c = MC_c$; however, in the perfect price discrimination equilibrium, only the last unit is sold at that price. The other units are sold at customers' reservation prices, which are greater than p_c. Second, consumers receive some welfare (consumer surplus, $A + B + C$) in a competitive market, whereas a perfectly price-discriminating monopoly captures all the welfare. Thus perfect price discrimination does not reduce efficiency—the output and total welfare are the same as under competition—but it does redistribute income away from consumers: Consumers are much better off under competition.

Is a single-price or perfectly price-discriminating monopoly better for consumers? The perfect price discrimination equilibrium is more efficient than the single-price monopoly equilibrium because more output is produced. A single-price monopoly, however, takes less consumer surplus from consumers than a perfectly price-discriminating monopoly. Consumers who put a very high value on the good are better off under single-price monopoly, where they have consumer surplus, than with perfect price discrimination, where they have none. Consumers with lower reservation prices who purchase from the perfectly price-discriminating monopoly but not from the single-price monopoly have no consumer surplus in either case. All the social gain from the extra output goes to the perfectly price-discriminating firm. Consumer surplus is greatest with competition, lower with single-price monopoly, and eliminated by perfect price discrimination.

◯ APPLICATION

Botox Revisited

We illustrate how perfect price discrimination differs from competition and single-price monopoly using the "Botox Patent Monopoly" application from Chapter 11. The graph shows a linear demand curve for Botox and a constant marginal cost (and average variable cost) of $25 per vial. If the market had been competitive (that is, the price equaled marginal cost at e_c), consumer surplus would have been area $A + B + C = \$750$ million per year, and there would have been no producer surplus or deadweight loss. In the single-price monopoly equilibrium, e_s, the Botox vials sell for $400, and 1 million vials are sold. The corresponding consumer surplus is triangle $A = \$187.5$ million per year, producer surplus is rectangle $B = \$375$ million, and the deadweight loss is triangle $C = \$187.5$ million.

If Allergan, the manufacturer of Botox, could perfectly price discriminate, its producer surplus would double to $A + B + C = \$750$ million per year, and consumers would obtain no consumer surplus. The marginal consumer would pay the marginal cost of $25, the same as in a competitive market.

Allergan's inability to perfectly price discriminate costs the company and society dearly. The profit of the single-price monopoly, $B = \$375$ million per day, is lower than that of a perfectly price-discriminating monopoly by $A + C = \$375$ million per year. Similarly, society's welfare under single-price monopoly is lower than from perfect price discrimination by the deadweight loss, C, of $187.5 million per year.

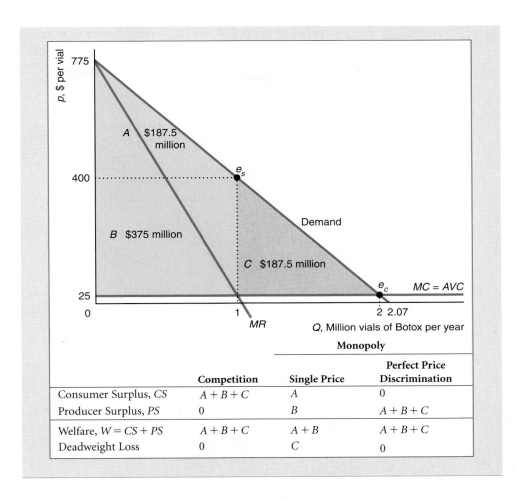

	Competition	Monopoly	
		Single Price	Perfect Price Discrimination
Consumer Surplus, CS	$A + B + C$	A	0
Producer Surplus, PS	0	B	$A + B + C$
Welfare, $W = CS + PS$	$A + B + C$	$A + B$	$A + B + C$
Deadweight Loss	0	C	0

TRANSACTION COSTS AND PERFECT PRICE DISCRIMINATION

Although some firms come close to perfect price discrimination, many more firms set a single price or use another nonuniform pricing method. Transaction costs are a major reason these firms do not perfectly price discriminate: It is too difficult or costly to gather information about each customer's price sensitivity. Recent advances in computer technologies, however, have lowered these costs, allowing hotels, car- and truck-rental companies, cruise lines, and airlines to price discriminate more often.

Private colleges request and receive financial information from students, which allows the schools to nearly perfectly price discriminate. The schools give partial scholarships as a means of reducing tuition to relatively poor students.

Many auto dealerships try to increase their profit by perfectly price discriminating, charging each customer the most that the customer is willing to pay. These firms hire salespeople to ascertain potential customers' willingness to pay for a car and to bargain with them. Not all car companies believe that it pays to price discriminate in this way, however. General Motor's Saturn line, for example, charges all customers the same price, on the reasoning that the transaction costs (including wages of salespeople) of such information gathering and bargaining exceed the benefits to the firm of charging customers differential prices.

Many other firms believe that, taking the transaction costs into account, it pays to use quantity discrimination, multimarket price discrimination, or other nonuniform pricing methods rather than try to perfectly price discriminate. We now turn to these alternative approaches.

SOLVED PROBLEM   12.1

Competitive firms are the customers of a union, which is the monopoly supplier of labor services. Show the union's "producer surplus" if it perfectly price discriminates. Then suppose that the union makes the firms a take-it-or-leave-it offer: They must guarantee to hire a minimum of H^* hours of work at a wage of w^*, or they can hire no one. Show that by setting w^* and H^* appropriately, the union can achieve the same outcome as if it could perfectly price discriminate.

Answer

1. *Show the outcome and welfare areas if the union can perfectly price discriminate:* The figure shows the labor supply curve if the market were competitive. The union views this curve as its marginal cost curve. For each successive hour of labor service, the union sets the wage equal to the height of the demand curve and sells H^* total hours of labor services (see the discussion of Figure 12.2). Its producer surplus equals the total welfare: $A + B$.

2. *Show that the firms will agree to hire H^* at w^*, and that the union will capture all of the surplus:* If the union gives the firms a take-it-or-leave-it offer of hiring H^* hours at w^* or of hiring no one, the firms will accept the offer because area C is the same size as area A in the figure. At a wage of w^*, the firms have "consumer surplus" (the amount they are willing to pay above the wage for a given amount of labor services) of A for the first $\overline{H}$ hours of work, but they have negative consumer surplus of C for the remaining $H^* - \overline{H}$ hours of work. Thus they have no consumer surplus overall, so they are indifferent between hiring the workers or not. The union's producer surplus is $B + C$, which equals its surplus if it perfectly

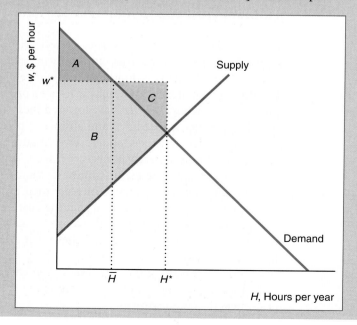

price discriminated: $A + B$. Similarly, the number of hours of labor service provided, H^*, is the same under both pricing schemes.

Unions That Have It All

Most unions act as a single-price monopoly of labor services. They set a wage and allow their customers to determine how many units of labor services to purchase. However, a few unions set both wages and a minimum number of work hours that employers must provide. Such contracts are common only in the transportation industry (excluding railroads and airplanes).

The International Longshore and Warehouse Union (ILWU) negotiates with the companies represented by the Pacific Maritime Association. The 10,500 union workers at West Coast ports handle $300 billion worth of goods per year. The registered union workers earn at least $80,000 (and some estimates set the figure at $100,000) per year with benefits and other perks worth about $42,000. The union contract in effect through 2008 guarantees a weekly income for each worker (it effectively sets the minimum number of hours). However, the number of dockworkers has shrunk over the years as firms have automated to become more efficient. Consequently, the union has insisted that the lost positions be replaced with new clerical positions.

12.3 Quantity Discrimination

Many firms are unable to determine which customers have the highest reservation prices. Firms may know, however, that most customers are willing to pay more for the first unit than for successive units—in other words, that the typical customer's demand curve is downward sloping. Such firms can price discriminate by letting the price that each customer pays vary with the number of units the customer buys. Here the price varies only with quantity: All customers pay the same price for a given quantity.

Not all quantity discounts are a form of price discrimination. Some reflect the reduction in a firm's cost with large-quantity sales. For example, the cost per ounce of selling a soft drink in a large cup is less than that of selling it in a smaller cup; the cost of cups varies little with size, and the cost of pouring and serving is the same. A restaurant offering quantity discounts on drinks may be passing on actual cost savings to larger purchasers rather than price discriminating. However, if the quantity discount is not due to cost differences, the firm is engaging in quantity discrimination. Moreover, a firm may quantity discriminate by charging customers who make large purchases more per unit than those who make small purchases.

Many utilities use *block-pricing* schedules, by which they charge one price for the first few units (a *block*) of usage and a different price for subsequent blocks. Both declining-block and increasing-block pricing are common.

The utility monopoly in Figure 12.3 faces a linear demand curve for each (identical) customer. The demand curve hits the vertical axis at $90 and the horizontal axis at 90 units. The monopoly has a constant marginal and average cost of $m = \$30$. Panel a

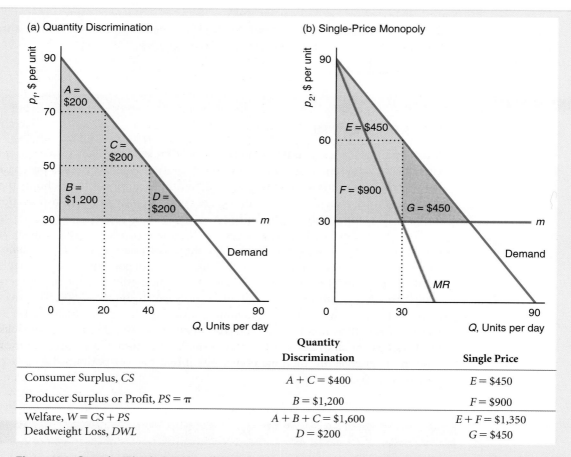

	Quantity Discrimination	Single Price
Consumer Surplus, CS	$A + C = \$400$	$E = \$450$
Producer Surplus or Profit, $PS = \pi$	$B = \$1,200$	$F = \$900$
Welfare, $W = CS + PS$	$A + B + C = \$1,600$	$E + F = \$1,350$
Deadweight Loss, DWL	$D = \$200$	$G = \$450$

Figure 12.3 Quantity Discrimination. If this monopoly engages in quantity discounting, it makes a larger profit (producer surplus) than it does if it sets a single price, and welfare is greater. (a) With quantity discounting, profit is $B = \$1,200$ and welfare is $A + B + C = \$1,600$. (b) If it sets a single price (so that its marginal revenue equals its marginal cost), the monopoly's profit is $F = \$900$, and welfare is $E + F = \$1,350$.

shows how this monopoly maximizes its profit if it can quantity discriminate by setting two prices. The firm uses declining-block prices to maximize its profit.

The utility monopoly faces an inverse demand curve $p = 90 - Q$, and its marginal and average cost is $m = 30$. Consequently, the quantity-discounting utility's profit is

$$\pi = p(Q_1)Q_1 + p(Q_2)(Q_2 - Q_1) - mQ_2$$
$$= (90 - Q_1)Q_1 + (90 - Q_2)(Q_2 - Q_1) - 30Q_2,$$

where Q_1 is the largest quantity for which the first-block rate, $p_1 = 90 - Q_1$, is charged and Q_2 is the total quantity that a consumer purchases. The utility chooses Q_1 and Q_2 to maximize its profit. It sets the derivative of profit with respect to Q_1 equal to zero, $d\pi/dQ_1 = Q_2 - 2Q_1 = 0$, and the derivative of profit with respect to Q_2 equal to zero, $d\pi/dQ_2 = Q_1 - 2Q_2 + 60 = 0$. By solving these two equations simultaneously, the utility determines its profit-maximizing quantities, $Q_1 = 20$ and $Q_2 = 40$. The corresponding block prices are $p_1 = 90 - 20 = 70$ and $p_2 = 50$. That is, the monopoly charges a price of $70 on any quantity between 1 and 20—the first block—and $50 on any units beyond the first 20—the second block. (The point that determines the first block, $70 and 20 units, lies on the demand curve.) Given each consumer's demand curve, a consumer who decides to buy 40 units pays $1,400 (= $70 × 20) for the first block and $1,000 (= $50 × 20) for the second block.

If the monopoly can set only a single price (panel b), it produces where its marginal revenue equals its marginal cost, selling 30 units at $60 per unit. Thus by quantity discriminating instead of using a single price, the utility sells more units, 40 instead of 30, and makes a higher profit, $B = \$1,200$ instead of $F = \$900$. With quantity discounting, consumer surplus is lower, $A + C = \$400$ instead of $E = \$450$; welfare (consumer surplus plus producer surplus) is higher, $A + B + C = \$1,600$ instead of $E + F = \$1,350$; and deadweight loss is lower, $D = \$200$ instead of $G = \$450$. Thus in this example, the firm and society are better off with quantity discounting, but consumers as a group suffer.

The more block prices that the monopoly can set, the closer the monopoly can get to perfect price discrimination. The deadweight loss results from the monopoly's setting a price above marginal cost so that too few units are sold. The more prices the monopoly sets, the lower the last price and hence the closer it is to marginal cost.

12.4   Multimarket Price Discrimination

Typically, a firm does not know the reservation price for each of its customers. But the firm may know which groups of customers are likely to have higher reservation prices than others. The most common method of multimarket price discrimination is to divide potential customers into two or more groups and to set a different price for each group. All units of the good sold to customers within a group are sold at a single price. As with perfect price discrimination, to engage in multimarket price discrimination, a firm must have market power, be able to identify groups with different demands, and prevent resales.

For example, first-run movie theaters with market power charge older citizens a lower ticket price than they charge younger adults because seniors typically are not willing to pay as much as many other adults to see a movie. By admitting people as soon as they demonstrate their age and buy tickets, the theater prevents resales.

MULTIMARKET PRICE DISCRIMINATION WITH TWO GROUPS

Suppose that a monopoly can divide its customers into two (or more) groups—for example, consumers in each of two countries. It sells Q_1 to the first group and earns revenues of $R_1(Q_1)$, and it sells Q_2 units to the second group and earns $R_2(Q_2)$. Its cost of producing total output $Q = Q_1 + Q_2$ units is $C(Q)$. The monopoly can maximize its profit through its choice of prices or quantities to each group. We examine its problem when it chooses quantities:

$$\max_{Q_1, Q_2} \pi = R_1(Q_1) + R_2(Q_2) - C(Q_1 + Q_2). \tag{12.4}$$

The first-order conditions corresponding to Equation 12.4 are obtained by differentiating with respect to Q_1 and Q_2 and setting the partial derivative equal to zero:

$$\frac{\partial \pi}{\partial Q_1} = \frac{dR_1(Q_1)}{dQ_1} - \frac{dC(Q)}{dQ} \frac{\partial Q}{\partial Q_1} = 0, \tag{12.5}$$

$$\frac{\partial \pi}{\partial Q_2} = \frac{dR_2(Q_2)}{dQ_2} - \frac{dC(Q)}{dQ} \frac{\partial Q}{\partial Q_2} = 0. \tag{12.6}$$

Equation 12.5 says that the marginal revenue from sales to the first group, $MR^1 = dR_1(Q_1)/dQ_1$, should equal the marginal cost of producing the last unit of total output, $MC = dC(Q)/dQ$, because $\partial Q/\partial Q_1 = 1$. Similarly, Equation 12.6 shows that the marginal revenue from the second group, MR^2, should also equal the marginal cost. By combining Equations 12.5 and 12.6, we find that the two marginal revenues are equal where the monopoly is profit maximizing:

$$MR^1 = MC = MR^2. \tag{12.7}$$

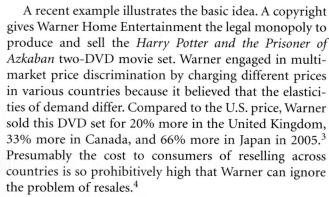

A recent example illustrates the basic idea. A copyright gives Warner Home Entertainment the legal monopoly to produce and sell the *Harry Potter and the Prisoner of Azkaban* two-DVD movie set. Warner engaged in multimarket price discrimination by charging different prices in various countries because it believed that the elasticities of demand differ. Compared to the U.S. price, Warner sold this DVD set for 20% more in the United Kingdom, 33% more in Canada, and 66% more in Japan in 2005.[3] Presumably the cost to consumers of reselling across countries is so prohibitively high that Warner can ignore the problem of resales.[4]

For simplicity, we consider how Warner prices just in the United States and the United Kingdom. Warner charges its American consumers p_A for Q_A units, so its revenue is $p_A Q_A$. If Warner has the same constant marginal and average cost, m, in both countries, its profit (ignoring any sunk development cost and other fixed costs) from selling the DVD sets is $\pi_A = p_A Q_A - m Q_A$, where $m Q_A$ is its cost of producing Q_A units. Warner wants to maximize its combined profit, π, which is the sum of its American and British profits, π_A and π_B:

$$\pi = \pi_A + \pi_B = (p_A Q_A - m Q_A) + (p_B Q_B - m Q_B).$$

How should Warner set its prices p_A and p_B—or, equivalently, Q_A and Q_B—so that it maximizes its combined profit? Because its marginal cost is the same to both sets of customers, we can use our understanding of a single-price monopoly's behavior to answer this question. A multimarket-price-discriminating monopoly with a constant marginal cost maximizes its total profit by maximizing its profit from each group separately. Warner sets its quantities so that the marginal revenue for each group equals the common marginal cost, m, which is about $1 per unit.

Warner released the *Azkaban* DVD set in November 2004. Figure 12.4 uses sales data through the end of that year. In panel a, Warner equates its marginal revenue to its

---

[3]Sources of information and data for this section include **www.timewarner.com**, Amazon Web sites for each country, **www.ukfilmcouncil.org.uk**, **www.dvdexclusive.com**, and **www.leesmovieinfo.com**.

[4]Why don't customers in higher-price countries order the DVDs from a low-price country using Amazon or other Internet vendors? Explanations include consumers' lack of an Internet connection, their ignorance, higher shipping costs (although the price differentials slightly exceed this cost), language differences in the DVDs, region encoding (fears of incompatibilities), desire for quick delivery, and legal restrictions.

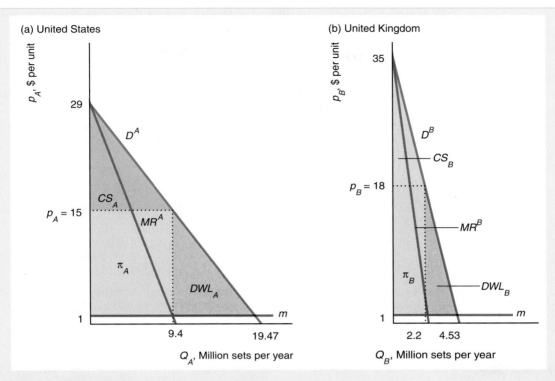

Figure 12.4 Multimarket Pricing of *Harry Potter* DVD. Warner Home Entertainment, the monopoly producer of the *Harry Potter and the Prisoner of Azkaban* DVD set, charges more in the United Kingdom, $p_B = \$18$, than in the United States, $p_A = \$15$, because the elasticity of demand is greater in the United States. Warner sets the quantity independently in each country where its relevant marginal revenue equals its common, constant marginal cost, $m = \$1$. As a result, it maximizes its profit by equating the two marginal revenues: $MR^A = 1 = MR^B$.

marginal cost, $MR^A = m = \$1$, at $Q_A = 9.4$ million sets. The resulting price is $p_A = \$15$ per set. In panel b, $MR^B = m = \$1$ at $Q_B = 2.2$ million sets and the price is $p_B = \$18$ per set.

This price-setting rule must be profit maximizing if the firm does not want to change its price to either group. Would the monopoly want to lower its price and sell more output in the United States? If it did, its marginal revenue would be below its marginal cost, so this change would reduce its profit. Similarly, if the monopoly sold less output in the United States, its marginal revenue would be above its marginal cost, which would reduce its profit. The same arguments can be made about its pricing in Britain. Thus the price-discriminating monopoly maximizes its profit by operating where its marginal revenue for each country equals its common marginal cost.

Because the monopoly equates the marginal revenue for each group to its common marginal cost, $MC = m$, the marginal revenues for the two countries are equal, $MR^A = m = MR^B$, as in Equation 12.7. We can use this equation to determine how the prices to the two groups vary with the price elasticities of demand at the profit-maximizing outputs. Each marginal revenue is a function of the corresponding price and the price elasticity of demand: $MR^A = p_A(1 + 1/\varepsilon_A)$, where ε_A is the price elasticity of demand for U.S. consumers, and $MR^B = p_B(1 + 1/\varepsilon_B)$, where ε_B is the price elasticity of demand for British consumers. Rewriting the equation using these expressions for marginal revenue, we find that

$$MR^A = p_A\left(1 + \frac{1}{\varepsilon_A}\right) = m = p_B\left(1 + \frac{1}{\varepsilon_B}\right) = MR^B. \qquad (12.8)$$

If $m = \$1$, $p_A = \$15$, and $p_B = \$18$ in Equation 12.8, Warner must believe that $\varepsilon_A = -15/14 \approx -1.07$ and $\varepsilon_B = -18/17 \approx -1.06$.[5]

By rearranging Equation 12.8, we learn that the ratio of prices in the two countries depends only on demand elasticities in those countries:

$$\frac{p_B}{p_A} = \frac{1 + 1/\varepsilon_A}{1 + 1/\varepsilon_B}. \qquad (12.9)$$

Substituting the prices and the demand elasticities into Equation 12.9, we determine that

$$\frac{p_B}{p_A} = \frac{\$18}{\$15} = 1.2 = \frac{1 + 1/(-15/14)}{1 + 1/(-18/17)} = \frac{1 + 1/\varepsilon_A}{1 + 1/\varepsilon_B}.$$

Thus because Warner believes that the British demand curve is less elastic at its profit-maximizing prices, it charges British consumers 20% more than U.S. customers.

● **APPLICATION**

Smuggling Prescription Drugs into the United States

A federal law forbids citizens of the United States from importing pharmaceuticals from Canada and other countries, but many U.S. citizens, city governments, and state governments openly flout this law. U.S. senior citizens have taken well-publicized bus trips across the Canadian and Mexican borders to buy their drugs at lower prices; and many Canadian, Mexican, and other Internet sites offer to ship drugs to U.S. customers. In a 2004 poll, two-thirds of Americans favored making importation of drugs easier. (European countries permit such imports.)

A U.S. citizen's incentive to import is great, as the prices of many popular drugs are substantially lower in virtually every other country. The antidepression drug Zoloft sells for one-third the U.S. price in Mexico and about one-half in Luxembourg and Austria. U.S. citizens paid an average of 81% more for brand-name drugs than buyers in Canada and six Western European countries, according to a 2004 Boston University study. Citizens in the United States pay 75% more than residents of Canada, which sets its prices at the median level of the countries it surveys.

However, most U.S. citizens are not buying outside the country. According to Espicom, the U.S. expenditures on pharmaceuticals were $270 billion in 2004, of

---

[5]Rearranging the left side of Equation 12.8, we can obtain expressions that are of the form of the Lerner Index, Equation 11.11, which we can use to solve for the elasticity of demand. For example, $(p_A - m)/p_A = (15 - 1)/15 = -1/\varepsilon_A$, so $\varepsilon_A = -15/14$.

which Canadian drug Internet imports were only $1.2 billion. Thus the ban appears to be relatively effective.

The Bush administration opposes changing the importation law. The U.S. Food and Drug Administration (FDA) has raised the specter that imported brand-name drugs are not as safe as those purchased in the United States, although the FDA has not identified a single American injured by defective imported drugs.

Not surprisingly, U.S. pharmaceutical companies support the FDA's opposition to imports. They fear the possibility of resales, by which the drugs they sell at lower prices in other countries will then be shipped to the United States. Resales would drive down the drug firms' U.S. prices. The lower prices in other countries may reflect price discrimination by pharmaceutical firms, more competition due to differences in patent laws, price regulation by governments, or other causes.

GlaxoSmithKline, Pfizer, and other drug companies are trying to reduce imports by cutting off Canadian pharmacies that ship south of the border. Wyeth and AstraZeneca watch Canadian pharmacies and wholesale customers for spikes in sales volume that could indicate exports, and then restrict supplies to the Canadian pharmacies.

To date, the FDA has not enforced restrictions on purchases by individuals. Many states, including Minnesota, North Dakota, New Hampshire, Rhode Island, and Wisconsin, as well as many local governments, have provided Web site information about Canadian sources and plan to import the drugs. However, starting in 2003, the FDA sent threatening letters to various state attorneys general advising that state agencies that import Canadian prescription drugs violate federal law—a practice the agency continued in 2007 (**www.fda.gov/importeddrugs**). In 2003, the FDA completed a sting operation targeting the supplier of Canadian drugs to the employee insurance program of the city of Springfield, Massachusetts, which had reported that it could save $4–$9 million a year by ordering drugs through Canada. The FDA also acted to close a Canadian drugstore chain that ships drugs to the United States (Rx Depot has 85 stores in 26 states and operates other stores in Canada under the name Rx of Canada).

The interesting question is not why many Democrats, Republicans, seniors, and most other U.S. citizens favor permitting such imports, but whether Canadians should oppose them. The following solved problem addresses these questions.

SOLVED PROBLEM 12.2

A monopoly drug producer with a constant marginal cost of $m = 1$ sells in only two countries and faces a linear demand curve of $Q_1 = 12 − 2p_1$ in Country 1 and $Q_2 = 9 − p_2$ in Country 2. What price does the monopoly charge in each country? What quantity does it sell in each? What profit does it earn in each country with and without a ban against shipments between the countries?

Answer

If resales across borders are banned so that price discrimination is possible:
1. *Determine the profit-maximizing price that the monopoly sets in each country by setting the relevant marginal revenue equal to the marginal cost:* If the monopoly can price discriminate, it sets a monopoly price independently in each country (as in Section 11.1). By rearranging the demand function for Country 1, we find

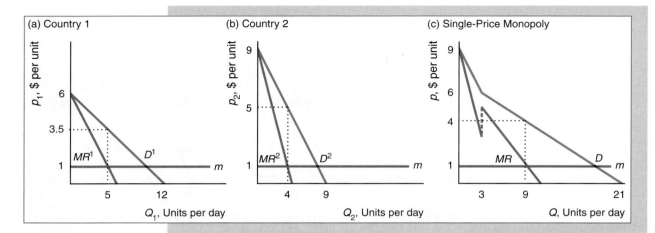

that the inverse demand function is $p_1 = 6 - 1/2Q_1$ for quantities less than 6, and zero otherwise, as panel a in the figure shows. Because revenue is $R^1 = 6Q_1 - 1/2(Q_1)^2$, the marginal revenue curve is twice as steeply sloped as the linear inverse demand curve: $MR^1 = dR^1/dQ_1 = 6 - Q_1$. The monopoly maximizes its profit where its marginal revenue equals its marginal cost,

$$MR^1 = 6 - Q_1 = 1 = m.$$

Solving, we find that its profit-maximizing output is $Q_1 = 5$. Substituting this expression back into the monopoly's inverse demand curve, we learn that its profit-maximizing price is $p_1 = 3.50$—see panel a. In Country 2, the inverse demand curve is $p_2 = 9 - Q_2$, so the monopoly chooses Q_2 such that $MR^2 = 9 - 2Q_2 = 1 = m$. Thus it maximizes its profit in Country 2 where $Q_2 = 4$ and $p_2 = 5$, as panel b shows.

2. *Calculate the profits:* The monopoly's profit in each country is the output times the difference between the price and its constant average cost, 1. The monopoly's profit in Country 1 is $\pi_1 = (3.50 - 1)5 = 12.50$. Its profit in Country 2 is $\pi_2 = (5 - 1)4 = 16$. Thus its total profit is $\pi = \pi_1 + \pi_2 = 12.50 + 16 = 28.50$.

If imports are permitted so that price discrimination is impossible:
3. *Derive the total demand curve:* If the monopoly cannot price discriminate, it charges the same price, p, in both countries. We can determine the aggregate demand curve it faces by horizontally summing the demand curves in each country at a given price (see Chapter 2). The total demand curve, D, in panel c is the horizontal sum of the demand curves for each of the two countries in panels a and b. Because no drugs are sold in Country 1 at prices above $p = 6$, the total demand curve equals Country 2's demand curve (panel b) at prices above 6. The total demand curve is the horizontal sum of the two countries' demand curves (panels a and b) at lower prices: $Q = (12 - 2p) + (9 - p) = 21 - 3p$, where $Q = q_1 + q_2$ is the total quantity that the monopoly sells. Thus the total demand curve has a kink where $p = 6$ and $Q = 3$.

4. *Determine the marginal revenue curve corresponding to the total demand curve:* Because the total demand curve has a kink at $Q = 3$, the corresponding marginal revenue curve has two sections at either side of $Q = 3$. At quantities smaller than 3, the marginal revenue curve is the same as that of Country 2. At larger quantities,

higher than the plan-ahead rate). The expected absolute difference in fares between two passengers on the same route is 36% of the airline's average ticket price.

Reverse Auctions Priceline.com and other online merchants use a name-your-own-price or "reverse" auction to identify price-sensitive customers. A customer enters a relatively low-price bid for a good or service, such as airline tickets. Then merchants decide whether to accept that bid or not. To prevent their less price-sensitive customers from using those methods, airlines force successful Priceline bidders to be flexible: to fly at off hours, to make one or more connections, and to accept any type of aircraft. Similarly, when bidding on groceries, a customer must list "one or two brands you like." As Jay Walker, Priceline's founder explained, "The manufacturers would rather not give you a discount, of course, but if you prove that you're willing to switch brands, they're willing to pay to keep you."

SOLVED PROBLEM 12.3

A monopoly producer with a constant marginal cost of $m = 20$ sells in two countries and can prevent reselling between the two countries. The inverse linear demand curve is $p_1 = 100 - Q_1$ in Country 1 and $p_2 = 100 - 2Q_2$ in Country 2. What price does the monopoly charge in each country? What quantity does it sell in each country? Does it price discriminate? Why or why not?

Answer

1. *Determine the profit-maximizing price and quantity that the monopoly sets in each country by setting the relevant marginal revenue equal to the marginal cost:* In Country 1, the inverse demand curve is $p_1 = 100 - Q_1$, so the revenue function is $R^1 = 100Q_1 - (Q_1)^2$, and hence the marginal revenue function is $MR^1 = dR^1/dQ_1 = 100 - 2Q_1$. It equates its marginal revenue to its marginal cost to determine its profit-maximizing quantity: $100 - 2Q_1 = 20$. Solving, the monopoly sets $Q_1 = 40$. Substituting this quantity into its inverse demand function, we learn that the monopoly's price is $p_1 = 100 - 40 = 60$. Similarly, in Country 2, the inverse demand curve is $p_2 = 100 - 2Q_2$, so the revenue function is $R^2 = 100Q_2 - 2(Q_2)^2$, and hence the marginal revenue function is $MR^2 = dR^2/dQ_2 = 100 - 4Q_2$. Equating marginal revenue and marginal cost, $100 - 4Q_2 = 20$, and solving, the monopoly sets $Q_2 = 20$ in Country 2. Its price is $p_2 = 100 - (2 \times 20) = 60$. Thus the monopoly sells twice as much in Country 1 as in Country 2 but charges the same price in both countries.

2. *Explain, by solving for a general linear inverse demand function, why the monopoly does not price discriminate:* Although the firm has market power, can prevent reselling, and faces consumers in the two countries with different demand functions, it does not pay for the monopoly to price discriminate. Consider the monopoly's problem with a general linear inverse demand function: $p = a - bQ$. Here revenue is $R = aQ - bQ^2$, so $MR = dR/dQ = a - 2bQ$. Equating marginal revenue and marginal cost, $a - 2bQ = m$, and solving for Q, we find that $Q = (a - m)/(2b)$. Consequently, the price is $p = a - b(a - m)/(2b) = (a - m)/2$. Thus the price depends only on the inverse demand function's intercept on the vertical axis, a, and not on its slope, b. Because both inverse demand functions in this example have the same vertical intercept—they differ only in their slopes—the monopoly

> sets the same equilibrium price in both countries. In equilibrium, the elasticity of demand is the same in both countries (Problem 38 asks you to show this result). Thus while the monopoly could price discriminate, it chooses not to do so.

WELFARE EFFECTS OF MULTIMARKET PRICE DISCRIMINATION

Multimarket price discrimination results in inefficient production and consumption. As a result, welfare under multimarket price discrimination is lower than it is under competition or perfect price discrimination. Welfare may be lower or higher with multimarket price discrimination than with a single-price monopoly, however.

Multimarket Price Discrimination Versus Competition. Consumer surplus is greater and more output is produced with competition (or perfect price discrimination) than with multimarket price discrimination. In Figure 12.4, consumer surplus with multimarket price discrimination is CS_A (for American consumers in panel a) and CS_B (for British consumers in panel b). Under competition, consumer surplus is the area below the demand curve and above the marginal cost curve: $CS_A + \pi_A + DWL_A$ in panel a and $CS_B + \pi_B + DWL_B$ in panel b.

Thus multimarket price discrimination transfers some of the competitive consumer surplus, π_1 and π_2, to the monopoly as additional profit and causes the deadweight loss, DWL_1 and DWL_2, of some of the rest of the competitive consumer surplus. The deadweight loss is due to the multimarket-price-discriminating monopoly's charging prices above marginal cost, which results in reduced production from the optimal competitive level.

Multimarket Price Discrimination Versus Single-Price Monopoly. From theory alone, it is impossible to tell whether welfare is higher if the monopoly uses multimarket price discrimination or if it sets a single price. Both types of monopolies set price above marginal cost, so too little is produced relative to competition. Output may rise as the firm starts discriminating if groups that did not buy when the firm charged a single price start buying.

The closer the multimarket-price-discriminating monopoly comes to perfect price discrimination (say, by dividing its customers into many groups rather than just two), the more output it produces, so the less the production inefficiency there is. However, unless a multimarket-price-discriminating monopoly sells significantly more output than it would if it had to set a single price, welfare is likely to be lower with discrimination because of consumption inefficiency and time wasted shopping. These two inefficiencies do not occur with a monopoly that charges all consumers the same price. As a result, consumers place the same marginal value (the single sales price) on the good, so they have no incentive to trade with each other. Similarly, if everyone pays the same price, consumers have no incentive to search for lower prices.

12.5   Two-Part Tariffs

We now turn to two other forms of second-degree price discrimination: *two-part tariffs* in this section and *tie-in sales* in Section 12.6. Both are similar to the type of second-degree price discrimination we examined earlier because the average price per unit varies with the number of units that consumers buy.

With a **two-part tariff,** the firm charges a consumer a lump-sum fee (the first tariff) for the right to buy as many units of the good as the consumer wants at a specified price (the second tariff). Because of the lump-sum fee, consumers pay more per unit if they buy a small number of goods than if they buy a larger number.

To get telephone service, you may pay a monthly connection fee and a price per minute of use. Some car-rental firms charge a per-day fee and a price per mile driven. When they returned to Oakland from exile in Los Angeles, the Oakland Raiders charged fans a fee of $250 to $4,000 for a *personal seat license* (PSL), which gave the fan the right to buy season tickets for the next 11 years at a ticket price per game ranging between $40 and $60.

To profit from two-part tariffs, a firm must have market power, know how demand differs across customers or with the quantity that a single customer buys, and successfully prevent resales. We now examine two results. First we consider how a firm uses a two-part tariff to extract consumer surplus (as in our previous price discrimination examples). Second we see how, if the firm cannot vary its two-part tariff across its customers, its profit is greater the more similar the demand curves of its customers are.

We illustrate these two points for a monopoly that knows its customers' demand curves. We start by examining the monopoly's two-part tariff where all its customers have identical demand curves, and then we look at one where its customers' demand curves differ.

A TWO-PART TARIFF WITH IDENTICAL CONSUMERS

If all the monopoly's customers are identical, a monopoly that knows its customers' demand curve can set a two-part tariff that has the same two properties as the perfect price discrimination equilibrium. First, the efficient quantity, Q_1, is sold because the price of the last unit equals marginal cost. Second, all consumer surplus is transferred from consumers to the firm.

Suppose that the monopoly has a constant marginal and average cost of $m = \$10$ (no fixed cost) and that every consumer has the demand curve D^1 in panel a of Figure 12.5. To maximize its profit, the monopoly charges a price, p, equal to the constant marginal and average cost, $m = \$10$, and just breaks even on each unit sold. By setting price equal to marginal cost, it maximizes the *potential consumer surplus:* the consumer surplus if no lump-sum fee is charged. It charges the largest possible lump-sum fee, $\mathscr{L}$, which is the potential consumer surplus $A_1 + B_1 + C_1 = \$2,450$. Thus its profit is $2,450 times the number of customers.

If the firm charged a higher per-unit price, it would sell fewer units and hence make a smaller profit. For example, if the monopoly charges $p = \$20$, it sells 60 units, making a profit from its unit sales of $B_1 = (\$20 - \$10)60 = \$600$. It must lower its fee to equal the new potential consumer surplus of $A_1 = \$1,800$, so its total profit per customer is only $2,400. It loses area $C_1 = \$50$ by charging the higher price. Similarly, if the monopoly charged a lower per-unit price, its profit would be lower: It would sell too many units and make a loss on each unit because its price would be below its marginal cost.

Because the monopoly knows the demand curve, it could instead perfectly price discriminate by charging each customer a different price for each unit purchased: the price along the demand curve. Thus this knowledgeable monopoly can capture all potential consumer surplus either by perfectly price discriminating or by setting its optimal two-part tariff.

If the monopoly does not know its customers' demand curve, it must guess how high a lump-sum fee to set. This fee will almost certainly be less than the potential consumer surplus. If the firm sets its fee above the potential consumer surplus, it loses all its customers.

A TWO-PART TARIFF WITH NONIDENTICAL CONSUMERS

Now suppose that there are two customers, Consumer 1 and Consumer 2, with demand curves D^1 and D^2 in panels a and b of Figure 12.5. If the monopoly knows each customer's demand curve and can prevent resales, it can capture all the consumer surplus by varying its two-part tariffs across customers. However, if the monopoly is unable to distinguish among the types of customers or cannot charge consumers different prices, efficiency and profitability fall.

Suppose that the monopoly knows its customers' demand curves. By charging each customer $p = m = \$10$ per unit, the monopoly makes no profit per unit but sells the number of units that maximizes the potential consumer surplus. The monopoly then captures all this potential consumer surplus by charging Consumer 1 a lump-sum fee of $\mathscr{L}_1 = A_1 + B_1 + C_1 = \$2,450$ and Consumer 2 a fee of $\mathscr{L}_2 = A_2 + B_2 + C_2 = \$4,050$. The monopoly's total profit is $\mathscr{L}_1 + \mathscr{L}_2 = \$6,500$. By doing so, the monopoly maximizes its total profit by capturing the maximum potential consumer surplus from both customers.

Now suppose that the monopoly has to charge each consumer the same lump-sum fee, $\mathscr{L}$, and the same per-unit price, p. For example, because of legal restrictions, a telephone

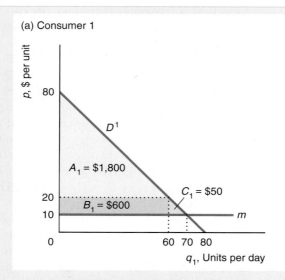

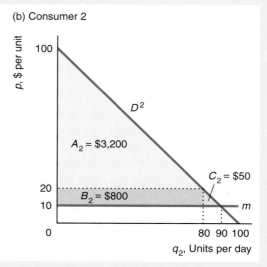

(a) Consumer 1

(b) Consumer 2

Figure 12.5 Two-Part Tariff. If all consumers have the demand curve in panel a, a monopoly can capture all the consumer surplus with a two-part tariff by which it charges a price, p, equal to the marginal cost, $m = \$10$, for each item and a lump-sum membership fee of $\mathscr{L} = A_1 + B_1 + C_1 = \$2,450$. Now suppose that the monopoly has two customers, Consumer 1 in panel a and Consumer 2 in panel b. If the monopoly can treat its customers differently, it maximizes its profit by setting $p = m = \$10$ and charging Consumer 1 a fee equal to its potential consumer surplus, $A_1 + B_1 + C_1 = \$2,450$, and Consumer 2 a fee of $A_2 + B_2 + C_2 = \$4,050$, for a total profit of $\$6,500$. If the monopoly must charge all customers the same price, it maximizes its profit at $\$5,000$ by setting $p = \$20$ and charging both customers a lump-sum fee equal to the potential consumer surplus of Consumer 1, $\mathscr{L} = A_1 = \$1,800$.

company charges all residential customers the same monthly fee and the same fee per call, even though the company knows that consumers' demands vary. As with multimarket price discrimination, the monopoly does not capture all the consumer surplus.

The monopoly charges a lump-sum fee, $\mathcal{L}$, equal to either the potential consumer surplus of Consumer 1, CS_1, or of Consumer 2, CS_2. Because CS_2 is greater than CS_1, both customers buy if the monopoly charges $\mathcal{L} = CS_1$, whereas only Consumer 2 buys if the monopoly charges $\mathcal{L} = CS_2$. The monopoly sets the lower or higher lump-sum fee depending on which produces the greater profit.

Any other lump-sum fee would lower its profit. The monopoly has no customers if it charges more than $\mathcal{L} = CS_2$. If it charges between CS_1 and CS_2, it loses money on Consumer 2 compared to what it could earn by charging CS_2, and it still does not sell to Consumer 1. By charging less than $\mathcal{L} = CS_1$, it earns less per customer and does not gain any additional customers.

In our example in Figure 12.5, the demand curves for Consumers 1 and 2 are $q_1 = 80 - p$ and $q_2 = 100 - p$. The consumer surplus for Consumer 1 is $CS_1 = \frac{1}{2}(80 - p)q_1 = \frac{1}{2}(80 - p)^2$. Similarly, $CS_2 = \frac{1}{2}(100 - p)^2$. If the monopoly charges the lower fee, $\mathcal{L} = CS_1$, it sells to both consumers and its profit is

$$\pi = 2\mathcal{L} + (p - m)(q_1 + q_2) = (80 - p)^2 + (p - 10)(180 - 2p).$$

Setting the derivative of π with respect to p equal to zero, we find that the profit-maximizing price is $p = 20$. The monopoly charges a fee of $\mathcal{L} = CS_1 = \$1,800$ and makes a profit of \$5,000. If the monopoly charges the higher fee, $\mathcal{L} = CS_2$, it sells only to Consumer 2, and its profit is

$$\pi = \mathcal{L} + (p - m)q_2 = 1/2(100 - p)^2 + (p - 10)(100 - p).$$

The monopoly's profit-maximizing price is $p = 10$, and its profit is $\mathcal{L} = CS_2 = \$4,050$. The monopoly hence makes more by setting $\mathcal{L} = CS_1$ and selling to both customers.

Thus the monopoly maximizes its profit by setting the lower lump-sum fee and charging a price $p = \$20$, which is above marginal cost. Consumer 1 buys 60 units, and Consumer 2 buys 80 units. The monopoly makes $(p - m) = (\$20 - \$10) = \$10$ on each unit, so it earns $B_1 + B_2 = \$600 + \$800 = \$1,400$ from the units it sells. In addition, it gets a fee from both consumers equal to the consumer surplus of Consumer 1, $A_1 = \$1,800$. Thus its total profit is $2 \times \$1,800 + \$1,400 = \$5,000$, which is \$1,500 less than if it could set different lump-sum fees for each customer. Consumer 1 has no consumer surplus, but Consumer 2 enjoys a consumer surplus of \$1,400 (= \$3,200 - \$1,800).

Why does the monopoly charge a price above marginal cost when using a two-part tariff? By raising its price, the monopoly earns more per unit from both types of customers but lowers its customers' potential consumer surplus. Thus if the monopoly can capture each customer's potential surplus by charging different lump-sum fees, it sets its price equal to marginal cost. However, if the monopoly cannot capture all the potential consumer surplus because it must charge everyone the same lump-sum fee, the increase in profit from Customer 2 due to the higher price more than offsets the reduction in the lump-sum fee (the potential consumer surplus of Customer 1).[8]

---

[8]If the monopoly lowers its price from \$20 to the marginal cost of \$10, it loses B_1 from Customer 1, but it can raise its lump-sum fee from A_1 to $A_1 + B_1 + C_1$, so its total profit from Customer 1 increases by $C_1 = \$50$. The lump-sum fee it collects from Customer 2 also rises by $B_1 + C_1 = \$650$, but its profit from unit sales falls by $B_2 = \$800$, so its total profit decreases by \$150. The loss from Customer 2, −\$150, more than offsets the gain from Customer 1, \$50. Thus the monopoly makes \$100 more by charging a price of \$20 rather than \$10. For another application, see **www.aw-bc.com/perloff**, Chapter 12, "Warehouse Stores."

12.6   Tie-In Sales

Another type of nonuniform pricing is a **tie-in sale,** in which customers can buy one product only if they agree to purchase another product as well. There are two forms of tie-in sales.

The first type is a **requirement tie-in sale,** in which customers who buy one product from a firm are required to make all their purchases of another product from that firm. Some firms sell durable machines such as copiers under the condition that customers buy copier services and supplies from them in the future. Because the amount of services and supplies that each customer buys differs, the per-unit price of copiers varies across customers.

The second type of tie-in sale is **bundling** (or a *package tie-in sale*), in which two goods are combined so that customers cannot buy either good separately. For example, a Whirlpool refrigerator is sold with shelves, and a Hewlett-Packard ink-jet printer comes in a box that includes both black and color printer cartridges.

Most tie-in sales increase efficiency by lowering transaction costs. Indeed, tie-ins for efficiency purposes are so common that we hardly think about them. Presumably, no one would want to buy a shirt without buttons, so selling shirts with buttons attached lowers transaction costs. Because virtually everyone wants certain basic software, most companies sell computers with that software already installed. Firms also often use tie-in sales to increase profits, as we now consider.

REQUIREMENT TIE-IN SALES

Frequently, a firm cannot tell which customers are going to use its product the most and hence are willing to pay the most for the good. These firms may be able to use a requirement tie-in sale to identify heavy users of the product and charge them more.

APPLICATION

IBM

In the 1930s, IBM increased its profit by using a requirement tie-in. IBM produced card punch machines, sorters, and tabulating machines (precursors of modern computers) that computed by using punched cards. Rather than selling its card punch machines, IBM leased them under the condition that the lease would terminate if any card not manufactured by IBM were used. (By leasing the equipment, IBM avoided resale problems and forced customers to buy cards from it.) IBM charged customers more per card than other firms would have charged. If we think of the extra payment per card as part of the cost of using the machine, this requirement tie-in resulted in heavy users' paying more for the machines than others did. This tie-in was profitable because heavy users were willing to pay more.[9]

---

[9]The U.S. Supreme Court held that IBM's actions violated antitrust laws because they lessened competition in the (potential) market for tabulating cards. IBM's defense was that its requirement was designed to protect its reputation. IBM claimed that badly made tabulating cards might cause its machines to malfunction and that consumers would falsely blame IBM's equipment. The Court did not accept IBM's argument. The Court apparently did not understand—or at least care about—the price discrimination aspect of IBM's actions.

BUNDLING

Firms that sell two or more goods may use bundling to raise profits. Bundling allows firms that cannot directly price discriminate to charge customers different prices. Whether bundling is profitable depends on customers' tastes and a firm's ability to prevent resales.

Imagine that you are in charge of selling season tickets for the local football team. Your stadium can hold all your potential customers, so the marginal cost of selling one more ticket is zero.

Should you bundle tickets for preseason (exhibition) and regular-season games, or should you sell books of tickets for the preseason and the regular season separately?[10] To answer this question, you have to determine how the fans differ in their desires to see preseason and regular-season games.

For simplicity, suppose that there are two customers (or types of customers). Both of these football fans are so fanatical that they are willing to pay to see preseason exhibition games: There's no accounting for tastes!

Whether you should bundle depends on your customers' tastes. It does not pay to bundle in panel a of Table 12.1, in which Fan 1 is willing to pay more for both regular and preseason tickets than Fan 2. Bundling does pay in panel b, in which Fan 1 is willing to pay more for regular-season but less for exhibition tickets than Fan 2.

To determine whether it pays to bundle, we have to calculate the profit-maximizing unbundled and bundled prices. We start by calculating the profit-maximizing unbundled prices in panel a. If you charge $2,000 for the regular-season tickets, you earn only $2,000 because Fan 2 won't buy tickets. It is more profitable to charge $1,400, sell tickets to both customers, and earn $2,800 for the regular season. By similar reasoning, the

Table 12.1 Bundling of Tickets to Football Games

(a) *Unprofitable Bundle*	Regular Season	Preseason	Bundle
Fan 1	$2,000	$500	$2,500
Fan 2	$1,400	$100	$1,500
Profit-maximizing price	$1,400	$500	$1,500
(b) *Profitable Bundle*	Regular Season	Preseason	Bundle
Fan 1	$1,700	$300	$2,000
Fan 2	$1,500	$500	$2,000
Profit-maximizing price	$1,500	$300	$2,000

---

[10]We assume that you don't want to sell tickets to each game separately. One reason for selling only season tickets is to reduce transaction costs. A second explanation is the same type of bundling argument that we discuss in this section.

profit-maximizing price for the exhibition tickets is $500, at which you sell only to Fan 1 and earn $500. As a result, you earn $3,300 (= $2,800 + $500) if you do not bundle.

If you bundle and charge $2,500, you sell only to Fan 1. Your better option if you bundle is to set a bundle price of $1,500 and sell to both fans, earning $3,000. Nonetheless, you earn $300 more if you sell the tickets separately than if you bundle.

In this first example, in which it does not pay to bundle, the customer who values the regular-season tickets the most also values the preseason tickets the most. In contrast, in panel b, the fan who values the regular-season tickets more values the exhibition season tickets less than the other fan does. Here your profit is higher if you bundle. If you sell the tickets separately, you charge $1,500 for regular-season tickets, earning $3,000 from the two customers, and $300 for preseason tickets, earning $600, for a total of $3,600. By selling a bundle of tickets for all games at $2,000 each, you earn $4,000. Thus you earn $400 more by bundling than by selling the tickets separately.

By bundling, you can charge the fans different prices for the two components of the bundle. Fan 1 is paying $1,700 for regular-season tickets and $300 for exhibition tickets, while Fan 2 is paying $1,500 and $500, respectively.[11] If you could perfectly price discriminate, you would charge each consumer his or her reservation price for the preseason and regular-season tickets and would make the same amount as you do by bundling.

These examples illustrate that bundling a pair of goods pays only if their demands are *negatively correlated:* Customers who are willing to pay relatively more for regular-season tickets are not willing to pay as much as others for preseason tickets, and vice versa. When a good or service is sold to different people, the price is determined by the purchaser with the *lowest* reservation price. If reservation prices differ substantially across consumers, a monopoly has to charge a relatively low price to make many sales. By bundling when demands are negatively correlated, the monopoly reduces the dispersion in reservation prices, so that it can charge more and still sell to a large number of customers.

12.7   Advertising

In addition to setting its price or quantity, a monopoly has to make other decisions, one of the most important of which is how much to advertise. Advertising is only one way to promote a product. Other promotional activities include providing free samples and using sales agents. Some promotional tactics are subtle. For example, grocery stores place sugary breakfast cereals on lower shelves so that they are at children's eye level. According to a survey of 27 supermarkets nationwide by the Center for Science in the Public Interest, the average position of 10 child-appealing brands (44% sugar) was on the next-to-bottom shelf, while the average position of 10 adult brands (10% sugar) was on the next-to-top shelf.

A successful promotional campaign shifts the monopoly's demand curve by changing consumers' tastes or informing consumers about new products. The monopoly

---

[11]As with price discrimination, you have to prevent resales for bundling to increase your profit. Someone could make a $198 profit by purchasing the bundle for $2,000, selling Fan 1 the regular-season tickets for $1,699, and selling Fan 2 the preseason tickets for $499. Each fan would prefer attending only one type of game at those prices to paying $2,000 for the bundle.

may be able to change the tastes of some consumers by telling them that a famous athlete or performer uses the product. Children and teenagers are frequently the targets of such advertising. (See **www.aw-bc.com/perloff**, Chapter 14, "Smoking Gun Evidence?" for a discussion of cigarette advertising aimed at youths.) If the advertising convinces some consumers that they can't live without the product, the monopoly's demand curve may shift outward and become less elastic at the new equilibrium, at which the firm charges a higher price for its product. If the firm informs potential consumers about a new use for the product—for example, "Vaseline petroleum jelly protects lips from chapping"—demand at each price increases.

The Decision Whether to Advertise. Even if advertising succeeds in shifting demand, it may not pay for the firm to advertise. If advertising shifts demand outward or makes it less elastic, the firm's *gross profit,* which ignores the cost of advertising, must rise. The firm undertakes this advertising campaign, however, only if it expects its *net profit* (gross profit minus the cost of advertising) to increase.

To illustrate a monopoly's decision making, in Figure 12.6 we examine Coke's analysis of how much to advertise. For simplicity, we model Coke as a monopoly (by ignoring Pepsi and other brands). We use the estimated demand curve for Coke, which takes into account its advertising, from Gasmi, Laffont, and Vuong (1992). If Coke does not

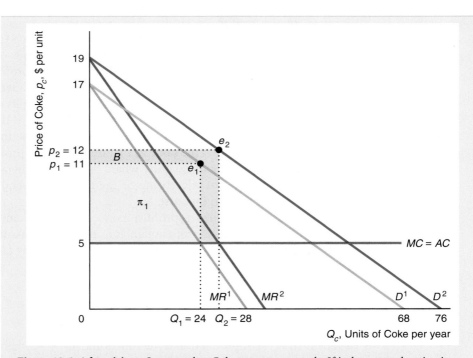

Figure 12.6 Advertising. Suppose that Coke were a monopoly. If it does not advertise, its demand curve is D^1. At its actual level of advertising, its demand curve is D^2. Advertising increases Coke's gross profit (ignoring the cost of advertising) from π_1 to $\pi_2 = \pi_1 + B$. Thus if the cost of advertising is less than the benefits from advertising, B, Coke's net profit (gross profit minus the cost of advertising) rises.

advertise, it faces the demand curve D^1. If Coke advertises at its current level, its demand curve shifts from D^1 to D^2.

Coke's marginal cost, MC, is constant and equals its average cost, AC, at $5 per unit (10 cases). Before advertising, Coke chooses its output, $Q_1 = 24$ million units, where its marginal cost equals its marginal revenue, MR^1, based on its demand curve, D^1. The profit-maximizing equilibrium is e_1, and the monopoly charges a price of $p_1 = \$11$. The monopoly's profit, π_1, is a box whose height is the difference between the price and the average cost, $6 (= \$11 - \$5)$ per unit, and whose length is the quantity, 24 units (tens of millions of cases of 12-ounce cans).

After its advertising campaign (involving dancing polar bears or whatever) shifts its demand curve to D^2, Coke chooses a higher quantity, $Q_2 = 28$, where the MR^2 and MC curves intersect. In this new equilibrium, e_2, Coke charges $p_2 = \$12$. Despite this higher price, Coke sells more Coke after advertising because of the outward shift of its demand curve.

As a consequence, Coke's gross profit rises more than 36%. Coke's new gross profit is the rectangle $\pi_1 + B$, where the height of the rectangle is the new price minus the average cost, $7, and the length is the quantity, 28. Thus the benefit, B, to Coke from advertising at this level is the increase in its gross profit. If its cost of advertising is less than B, its net profit rises, and it pays for Coke to advertise at this level rather than not to advertise at all.

How Much to Advertise. In general, how much should a monopoly advertise to maximize its net profit? To answer this question, we consider what happens if the monopoly raises or lowers its advertising expenditures by $1, which is its marginal cost of an additional unit of advertising. If a monopoly spends one more dollar on advertising and its gross profit rises by more than $1, its net profit rises, so the extra advertising pays. In contrast, the monopoly should reduce its advertising if the last dollar of advertising raises its gross profit by less than $1, causing its net profit to fall. Thus the monopoly's level of advertising maximizes its net profit if the last dollar of advertising increases its gross profit by $1. In short, the rule for setting the profit-maximizing amount of advertising is the same as that for setting the profit-maximizing amount of output: Set advertising or quantity where the marginal benefit (the extra gross profit from one more unit of advertising or the marginal revenue from one more unit of output) equals its marginal cost.

Formally, to maximize its profit, a monopoly sets its quantity, Q, and level of advertising, A, to maximize its profit. Again, for simplicity, we assume that advertising affects only current sales, so the demand function the monopoly faces is

$$p = p(Q, A).$$

As a result, the firm's revenue is

$$R = p(Q, A)Q = R(Q, A).$$

The firm's cost of production is the function $C(Q) + A$, where $C(Q)$ is the cost of manufacturing Q units and A is the cost of advertising because each unit of advertising costs $1 (by choosing the units of measure appropriately).

The monopoly maximizes its profit through its choice of quantity and advertising:

$$\max_{Q, A} \pi = R(Q, A) - C(Q) - A. \tag{12.10}$$

Its necessary (first-order) conditions are found by differentiating the profit function in Equation 12.10 with respect to Q and A in turn:

$$\frac{\partial \pi(Q, A)}{\partial Q} = \frac{\partial R(Q, A)}{\partial Q} - \frac{dC(Q)}{dQ} = 0, \qquad (12.11)$$

$$\frac{\partial \pi(Q, A)}{\partial A} = \frac{\partial R(Q, A)}{\partial A} - 1 = 0. \qquad (12.12)$$

The profit-maximizing output and advertising levels are the Q^* and A^* that simultaneously satisfy Equations 12.11 and 12.12. Equation 12.11 says that output should be chosen so that the marginal revenue from one more unit of output, $\partial R/\partial Q$, equals the marginal cost, dC/dQ. According to Equation 12.12, the monopoly advertises to the point where its marginal revenue or marginal benefit from the last unit of advertising, $\partial R/\partial A$, equals the marginal cost of the last unit of advertising, \$1.

APPLICATION

Magazine Advertising

Virtually all magazines carry ads—a rare exception is *Consumer Reports*. All else the same, advertisers pay more per ad, the larger a magazine's circulation. Consequently, a magazine may drop its subscription price to boost its circulation and in turn to increase its advertising revenue. Adjusting subscription prices is the key to increasing sales for most magazines. In 2005, eight out of nine magazines were obtained through a subscription, while only one in nine was bought at a newsstand.

In the second half of the twentieth century, total magazine circulation grew substantially. However, for the past decade, the total number of magazines sold has been relatively constant, at 360 million copies in both 1994 and 2005. (Yet newsstand sales continue to fall. In the first half of 2006, newsstands sold 49.7 million fewer copies of magazines, a 4% drop.)

Over this period, subscription prices fell while advertising revenue rose, so the share of revenue from advertising rose. The average price of subscriptions fell from \$28.51 in 1994 (\$36.34 in 2004 dollars) to \$25.93 in 2004. Magazine advertising pages rose 30% from 180,589 in 1994 to 234,428 in 2004, while advertising revenue (in 2004 dollars) jumped 96% from \$10.9 billion to \$21.3 billion.[12] The percentage of advertising to overall consumer magazine revenue rose from 50.3% in 1996 to 56.8% in 2001 and to 67.4% in 2004. One exception to the trend of dropping magazine prices to increase advertising revenue is *Time* magazine, which, at the end of 2006 raised its price by \$1 to \$4.95 and reduced the number of copies guaranteed to advertisers.

---

[12]Magazine advertising is 17% of total advertising in all media. This share is exceeded only by newspapers (20%) and network television (18%) and far exceeds Internet advertising (6%).

SOLVED PROBLEM   12.4

A magazine on costumes for dogs, *Canine Haute Couture*, has a monopoly: It has no close substitutes. The magazine's price for an ad is aQ, where a is the price per unit of circulation and Q is the number of subscriptions. The n firms that produce costumes for dogs are each willing to place one ad per issue as long as the magazine charges no more than aQ.

That is, a is determined by the advertising market. The magazine's inverse demand curve for subscriptions is $p(Q)$, where p is the price of a subscription. The magazine's marginal cost per subscription is constant at m (primarily printing, paper, and mailing), and its fixed cost is F (office space and payments to its editorial staff, authors, and photographers). Use a figure and calculus to show how the magazine determines its profit-maximizing quantity.

Answer

1. *Write the monopoly's profit:* The magazine's profit is

$$\pi = p(Q)Q + naQ - mQ - F,$$

where $p(Q)Q$ is the revenue the magazine receives from its subscribers, naQ is the advertising revenue, and mQ is its variable cost.

2. *Graphically show how the advertising shifts the demand curve:* We can think of the advertising revenue, naQ, as being much like a specific (per-unit) subsidy or negative tax, where na is the specific subsidy per subscription. Thus the advertising revenue shifts up the demand curve as a subsidy would. In the figure, the curves D^1 and MR^1 are the demand curve for magazines and the corresponding marginal revenue curve if no advertising were sold. The curves D^2 and MR^2 are the corresponding curves including advertising. Demand curve D^2 lies na units above D^1.

3. *Derive the monopoly's first-order condition:* The monopoly maximizes its profit by setting the optimal quantity (the only variable within its control). It sets the derivative of the profit function with respect to Q equal to zero:

$$\pi_Q = p(Q^\star) + p_Q(Q^\star)Q^\star + na - m = 0.$$

The magazine's marginal revenue in the absence of advertising is $p(Q) + p_Q(Q)Q$, and its advertising revenue from the marginal subscription is na, so $p(Q) + p_Q(Q)Q + na$ is its marginal revenue, MR. The magazine equates this marginal revenue to its marginal cost, m, to determine its profit-maximizing output, $Q^\star$.

4. *Use a graph to illustrate the role of advertising in determining the optimal output level:* As the figure shows, in the absence of advertising, the monopoly's optimum is determined by where its marginal revenue curve MR_1 (which corresponds to D^1) hits its marginal cost curve at m. It sells Q_1 subscriptions at a subscription price of p_1. With advertising, the monopoly operates where MR_2 (which corresponds to D^2) intersects its marginal cost curve. It provides Q_2 (= $Q^\star$ in our calculus solution) subscriptions at a price of p_2, which is the height of D^1 (the no-advertising demand curve) at that quantity. The firm receives $p^\star = p_2 + na$ per subscription.

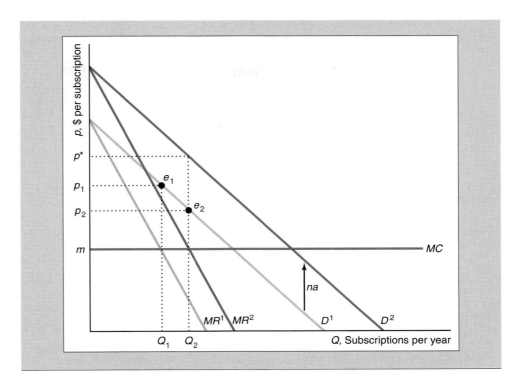

Summary

1. **Why and How Firms Price Discriminate:** A firm can price discriminate if it has market power, knows which customers will pay more for each unit of output, and can prevent customers who pay low prices from reselling to those who pay high prices. A firm earns a higher profit from price discrimination than from uniform pricing because (a) the firm captures some or all of the consumer surplus of customers who are willing to pay more than the uniform price and (b) the firm sells to some people who would not buy at the uniform price.

2. **Perfect Price Discrimination:** To perfectly price discriminate, a firm must know the maximum amount each customer is willing to pay for each unit of output. If a firm charges customers the maximum that each is willing to pay for each unit of output, the monopoly captures all potential consumer surplus and sells the efficient (competitive) level of output. Compared to competition, total welfare is the same, consumers are worse off, and firms are better off under perfect price discrimination.

3. **Quantity Discrimination:** Some firms charge customers different prices depending on how many units they purchase. If consumers who want more water have less elastic demands, a water utility can increase its profit by using declining-block pricing, in which the price for the first few gallons of water is higher than that for additional gallons.

4. **Multimarket Price Discrimination:** A firm that does not have enough information to perfectly price discriminate may know the relative elasticities of demand of groups of its customers. Such a profit-maximizing firm charges groups of consumers prices in proportion to their elasticities of demand, the group of consumers with the least elastic demand paying the highest price. Welfare is less under multimarket price discrimination than under competition or perfect price discrimination but may be greater or less than that under single-price monopoly.

5. **Two-Part Tariffs:** By charging consumers one fee for the right to buy and a separate price per unit, firms may earn higher profits than if they charge only for each unit sold. If a firm knows its customers' demand curves, it can use two-part tariffs (instead of perfect price discrimination) to capture all the consumer surplus. Even if the firm does

not know each customer's demand curve or cannot vary the two-part tariffs across customers, it can use a two-part tariff to make a larger profit than it could get if it set a single price.

6. **Tie-In Sales:** A firm may increase its profit by using a tie-in sale that allows customers to buy one product only if they also purchase another product. In a requirement tie-in sale, customers who buy one good must make all of

their purchases of another good or service from that firm. With bundling (a package tie-in sale), a firm sells only a bundle of two goods together. Prices differ across customers under both types of tie-in sales.

7. **Advertising:** A monopoly advertises or engages in other promotional activities to shift its demand curve to the right or to make it less elastic so as to raise its profit net of its advertising expenses.

Questions

* = answer at the back of this book; **W** = audio-slide show answers by James Dearden at **www.aw-bc.com/perloff**

1. Alexx's monopoly currently sells its product at a single price. What conditions must be met so that he can profitably price discriminate?

*2. Spenser's Superior Stoves advertises a one-day sale on electric stoves. The ad specifies that no phone orders will be accepted and that the purchaser must transport the stove. Why does the firm include these restrictions?

*3. Many colleges provide students from low-income families with scholarships, subsidized loans, and other programs so that they pay lower tuitions than students from high-income families. Explain why universities behave this way.

4. In 2002, seven pharmaceutical companies announced a plan to provide low-income elderly people with a card guaranteeing them discounts of 20% or more on dozens of prescription medicines. Why did the firms institute this program?

5. Disneyland price discriminates by charging lower entry fees for children than adults and for local residents than for other visitors. Why does it not have a resales problem?

6. The 2002 production run of 25,000 new Thunderbirds included only 2,000 cars for Canada. Yet potential buyers besieged Ford dealers there. Many buyers hoped to make a quick profit by reselling the cars in the United States. Reselling was relatively easy, and shipping costs were comparatively low. When the Thunderbird with the optional hardtop first became available at the end of 2001, Canadians paid $56,550 Cdn. for the vehicle, while U.S. customers spent up to $73,000 Cdn. in the United States. Why? Why would a Canadian want to ship a T-Bird south? Why did Ford require Canadian dealers to sign an agreement with Ford that prohibited moving vehicles to the United States?

7. As described in the "Amazon Is Watching You" application, some Amazon customers contended that Amazon

used a dynamic pricing approach, where the price offered depended on a customer's past purchases. What type of price discrimination is this?

8. On August 2, 2005, Hertz charged $141.06 a day to rent a Taurus in New York City but only $66.68 a day in Miami. Is this price discrimination? Why or why not?

9. College students once could buy a computer at a substantial discount through a campus buying program. The discounts largely disappeared in the late 1990s, when PC companies dropped their prices. "The industry's margins just got too thin to allow for those [college discounts]," said the president of Educause, a group that promotes and surveys using technology on campus (David LaGesse, "A PC Choice: Dorm or Quad?" *U.S. News & World Report,* May 5, 2003: 64). Using the concepts and terminology discussed in this chapter, explain why shrinking profit margins are associated with the reduction or elimination of student discounts.

10. Ticketmaster Corp. used an Internet auction to sell tickets for a Sting concert (Leslie Walker, "Auctions Could Set Ticket Prices for Future Events," *San Francisco Chronicle,* October 13, 2003: E5).

   a. The floor seats were auctioned in a uniform price format where all winning bidders paid the same amount: the lowest bid ($90) at which all the seats were sold. Is this price discrimination? If so, what type?

   b. Suppose, instead, that each ticket was sold at the bid price to the highest bidder. Is this price discrimination? If so, what type?

11. Using the information in the "Botox Revisited" application, determine how much Allergan loses by being a single-price monopoly rather than a perfectly price-discriminating monopoly. Explain your answer.

12. Consider a third pricing scheme that the union in Solved Problem 12.1 might use: It sets a wage, w^*, and lets the firms hire as many workers as they want (that is, the union does not set a minimum number of hours), but requires a lump-sum contribution to each worker's retirement fund.

What is such a pricing scheme called? Can the union achieve the same outcome as it would if it perfectly price discriminated? (*Hint:* It could set the wage where the supply curve hits the demand curve.) Does your answer depend on whether the union workers are identical?

13. A firm is a natural monopoly (see Chapter 11). Its marginal cost curve is flat, and its average cost curve is downward sloping (because it has a fixed cost). The firm can perfectly price discriminate.

    a. In a graph, show how much the monopoly produces, Q^*. Will it produce to where price equals its marginal cost?

    b. Show graphically (and explain) what its profit is.

14. Are all the customers of the quantity-discriminating monopoly in panel a of Figure 12.3 worse off than they would be if the firm set a single price (panel b)? Why or why not?

15. A monopoly has a marginal cost of zero and faces two groups of consumers. At first, the monopoly could not prevent resales, so it maximized its profit by charging everyone the same price, $p = \$5$. No one from the first group chose to purchase. Now the monopoly can prevent resales, so it decides to price discriminate. Will total output expand? Why or why not? What happens to profit and consumer surplus?

16. Each week, a department store places a different item of clothing on sale. Give an explanation based on price discrimination for why the store conducts such regular sales.

17. Does a monopoly's ability to price discriminate between two groups of consumers depend on its marginal cost curve? Why or why not? [Consider two cases: (a) the marginal cost is so high that the monopoly is uninterested in selling to one group; (b) the marginal cost is low enough that the monopoly wants to sell to both groups.]

18. A monopoly sells two products, of which consumers want only one. Assuming that it can prevent resales, can the monopoly increase its profit by bundling them, forcing consumers to buy both goods? Explain.

19. How would the analysis in Solved Problem 12.2 change if $m = 7$ or if $m = 4$? (*Hint:* Where $m = 4$, the marginal cost curve crosses the *MR* curve three times—if we include the vertical section. The single-price monopoly will choose one of these three points where its profit is maximized.)

20. Abbott Laboratories, the patent holder of the anti-AIDS drug Norvir, raised the price from $1.71 to $8.57 a day in 2003 (Lauran Neergaard, "No Price Rollback on Costly AIDS Drug," *San Francisco Chronicle*, August 5, 2004: A4). The price was increased in the United States only when low doses of Norvir are used to boost the effects of other anti-HIV medicines—not in Abbott's own Kaletra, a medicine that includes Norvir. Why did Abbott raise one price but not others?

21. In the spring of 2005, General Motors shifted its auto discounting policy to regionally targeted rebates, in which GM offers varying discounts to different parts of the United States. Suppose that GM dealers offer all consumers in a given region the same posted price for a specific model (which is GM's pricing policy for its Saturn automobiles). Assume that it is unprofitable for a consumer to purchase an automobile in a low-price area and then to resell it in a high-price area.

    a. What form of price discrimination is GM's new policy?

    b. What is the relationship between a region's price and its price elasticity of demand?

    c. GM also eliminated a high-profile discount program "in an apparent effort to damp consumer expectation of big price cuts" (Lee Hawkins Jr., "GM Alters U.S. Discount Program with a Region-Specific Strategy," *Wall Street Journal,* March 7, 2005: A2). How do expected future prices of an automobile affect the current demand? Is a national discount program that is targeted to reduce slumping sales a form of price discrimination? Explain. **W**

22. In the 2003 Major League Baseball season, the New York Mets began charging fans up to twice as much to attend games involving the cross-town Yankees or other popular teams than less popular or less competitive teams. Other professional teams have adopted the same pricing strategy. While the Yankees increased the prices of popular games, they dropped the price of upper-deck seats for some weekday games against weak opponents.

    a. A Mets-Yankees game is more popular than a Mets-Marlins game. Is the Mets' policy of charging fans more to see the New York Yankees than the Florida Marlins a form of price discrimination? If so, which type?

    b. What is the effect on the quantity of tickets demanded for the Yankees-Mets games if the Mets drop the price of the cheap seats for unpopular games? How do the Mets take this effect into account when setting ticket prices? In answering the question, assume that the Mets choose two ticket prices—one for the Mets-Yankees game and the other for the Mets-Marlins game—to maximize the sum of revenues of the two games. **W**

23. Grocery stores often set consumer-specific prices by issuing frequent-buyer cards to willing customers and collecting information on their purchases. Grocery chains can use that data to offer customized discount coupons to individuals.

    a. Which type of price discrimination—first-degree, second-degree, or third-degree—are these personalized discounts?

    b. How should a grocery store use past-purchase data to set individualized prices to maximize its profit? (*Hint:* Refer to a customer's price elasticity of demand.) **W**

24. The publisher Reed Elsevier uses what economists call a mixed-bundling pricing strategy. The publisher sells a

university access to a bundle of 930 of its journals for $1.7 million for one year. It also offers the journals separately at individual prices. Because Elsevier offers the journals online (with password access), universities can track how often their students and faculty access journals and then cancel those journals that are seldom read. Suppose that a publisher offers a university only three journals—*A*, *B*, and *C*—at the unbundled, individual annual subscription prices of $p_A = \$1,600$, $p_B = \$800$, and $p_C = \$1,500$. Suppose a university's willingness to pay for each of the journals is $v_A = \$2,000$, $v_B = \$1,100$, and $v_C = \$1,400$.

a. If the publisher offers the journals only at the individual subscription prices, to which journals does the university subscribe?

b. Given these individual prices, what is the highest price that the university is willing to pay for the three journals bundled together?

c. Now suppose that the publisher offers the same deal to a second university with willingness to pay $v_A = \$1,800$, $v_B = \$100$, and $v_C = \$2,100$. With the two universities, calculate the revenue-maximizing individual and bundle prices. **W**

25. To promote her platinum-selling CD *Feels Like Home* in 2005, singer Norah Jones toured the country for live performances. However, she sold an average of only two-thirds of the tickets available for each show, T^* (Robert Levine, "The Trick of Making a Hot Ticket Pay," *New York Times,* June 6, 2005: C1, C4).

a. Suppose that the local promoter is the monopoly provider of each concert. Each concert hall has a fixed number of seats. Assume that the promoter's cost is independent of the number of people who attend the concert (Ms. Jones received a guaranteed payment). Graph the promoter's marginal cost curve for the concert hall, where the number of tickets sold is on the horizontal axis. Be sure to show T^*.

b. If the monopoly can charge a single market price, does the concert's failure to sell out prove that the monopoly set too high a price? Explain.

c. Would your answer in part b be the same if the monopoly can perfectly price discriminate? Use a graph to explain.

26. According to a report from the Foundation for Taxpayer and Consumer Rights, gasoline costs more than $5 a gallon in Europe because taxes are higher there than in the United States, where pump prices are only half as much as in Europe. However, the amount per gallon net of taxes that U.S. consumers pay is higher than that paid by Europeans (24¢ per gallon net of taxes). The report concludes that "U.S. motorists are essentially subsidizing European drivers, who pay more for taxes but substantially less into oil company profits" (Tom Doggett, "US Drivers Subsidize European Pump Prices," *Reuters,* August 31, 2006). Given that oil companies have market power and can price discriminate across countries, is it reasonable to conclude that U.S. consumers are subsidizing Europeans? Explain your answer.

27. Why are newsstand prices higher than subscription prices for a magazine?

Problems

*28. Suppose that the union in Solved Problem 12.1 faces a demand curve of $H = 100 - w$ and that the labor supply curve is $H = w - 20$ (for $w \geq 20$). Solve for w^*, H^*, and $\overline{H}$.

*29. A patent gave Sony a legal monopoly to produce a robot dog called Aibo ("eye-BO"). The Chihuahua-size pooch robot can sit, beg, chase balls, dance, and play an electronic tune. When Sony started selling the toy in July 1999, it announced that it would sell 3,000 Aibo robots in Japan for about $2,000 each and a limited litter of 2,000 in the United States for $2,500 each. Suppose that Sony's marginal cost of producing Aibos is $500. Its inverse demand curve is $p_J = 3,500 - \frac{1}{2}Q_J$ in Japan and $p_A = 4,500 - Q_A$ in the United States. Solve for the equilibrium prices and quantities (assuming that U.S. customers cannot buy robots from Japan). Show how the profit-maximizing price ratio depends on the elasticities of demand in the two countries. What are the deadweight losses in each country, and in which is the loss from monopoly pricing greater?

*30. A monopoly sells its good in the U.S. and Japanese markets. The American inverse demand function is $p_A = 100 - Q_A$, and the Japanese inverse demand function is $p_J = 80 - 2Q_J$, where both prices, p_A and p_J, are measured in dollars. The firm's marginal cost of production is $m = 20$ in both countries. If the firm can prevent resales, what price will it charge in both markets? [*Hint:* The monopoly determines its optimal (monopoly) price in each country separately because customers cannot resell the good.]

31. Warner Home Entertainment sells the *Harry Potter and the Prisoner of Azkaban* two-DVD movie set around the world. Warner charges 33% more in Canada and 66% more in Japan than in the United States. Using the information about Warner's marginal cost and U.S. sales in Section 12.4, determine what the elasticities of demand must be in Canada and in Japan if Warner is profit maximizing.

*32. Warner Home Entertainment sells the *Harry Potter and the Prisoner of Azkaban* two-DVD movie set in China for about $3, which is only one-fifth the U.S. price, and has sold nearly 100,000 units. The price is extremely low in China because Chinese consumers are less wealthy than those in the other countries and because (lower-quality) pirated versions are available in China for 72¢–$1.20, compared to the roughly $3 required for the legal version (Jin Baicheng, "Powerful Ally Joins Government in War on Piracy," *China Daily,* March 11, 2005: 13). Assuming a marginal cost of $1, what is the Chinese elasticity of demand? Derive the demand function for China and illustrate Warner's policy in China using a figure similar to panel a in Figure 12.4.

33. In panel b of Figure 12.3, the single-price monopoly faces a demand curve of $p = 90 - Q$ and a constant marginal (and average) cost of $m = \$30$. Find the profit-maximizing quantity (or price) using math (Chapter 11). Determine the profit, consumer surplus, welfare, and deadweight loss.

34. Suppose that the quantity-discriminating monopoly in panel a of Figure 12.3 can set three prices, depending on the quantity a consumer purchases. The firm's profit is

$$\pi = p_1 Q_1 + p_2(Q_2 - Q_1) + p_3(Q_3 - Q_2) - mQ_3,$$

where p_1 is the high price charged on the first Q_1 units (first block), p_2 is a lower price charged on the next $Q_2 - Q_1$ units, p_3 is the lowest price charged on the $Q_3 - Q_2$ remaining units, Q_3 is the total number of units actually purchased, and $m = \$30$ is the firm's constant marginal and average cost. Use calculus to determine the profit-maximizing p_1, p_2, and p_3.

35. In the quantity-discrimination analysis in panel a of Figure 12.3, suppose that the monopoly can make consumers a take-it-or-leave-it offer (similar to the union in Solved Problem 12.1).

   a. Suppose the monopoly sets a price, p^*, and a minimum quantity, Q^*, that a consumer must pay to be able to purchase any units at all. What price and minimum quantity should it set to achieve the same outcome as it would if it perfectly price discriminated?
   b. Now suppose that the monopolist charges a price of $90 for the first 30 units and a price of $30 for all subsequent units, but requires that a consumer buy at least 30 units to be allowed to buy any units. Compare this outcome to the one in part a and to the perfectly price-discriminating outcome.

36. A monopoly sells its good in the United States, where the elasticity of demand is −2, and in Japan, where the elasticity of demand is −5. Its marginal cost is $10. At what price does the monopoly sell its good in each country if resales are impossible?

37. A monopoly sells in two countries, and resales between the countries are impossible. The demand curves in the countries are

$$p_1 = 100 - Q_1,$$
$$p_2 = 120 - 2Q_2.$$

The monopoly's marginal cost is $m = 30$. Solve for the equilibrium price in each country.

38. Show that the equilibrium elasticities in the two countries must be equal in Solved Problem 12.3.

39. Using math, show why a two-part tariff causes customers who purchase few units to pay more per unit than customers who buy more units.

40. Show how a change in the advertising rate a affects the optimal number of subscriptions in Solved Problem 12.4.

41. Canada subsidizes Canadian magazines to offset the invasion of foreign (primarily U.S.) magazines, which take 90% of the country's sales. The Canada Magazine Fund provides a lump-sum subsidy to various magazines to "maintain a Canadian presence against the overwhelming presence of foreign magazines." Eligibility is based on high levels of investment in Canadian editorial content and reliance on advertising revenues. What effect will a lump-sum subsidy have on the number of subscriptions sold?

42. Show how a monopoly would solve for its optimal price and advertising level if it sets price instead of quantity.

43. The demand a monopoly faces is

$$p = 100 - Q + A^{1/2},$$

where Q is its quantity, p is its price, and A is its level of advertising. Its marginal cost of production is 10, and its cost of a unit of advertising is 1. What is the firm's profit equation? Solve for the firm's profit-maximizing price, quantity, and level of advertising.

44. What is the monopoly's profit-maximizing output, Q, and level of advertising, A, if it faces a demand curve of $p = a - bQ + cA^{\alpha}$, its constant marginal cost of producing output is m, and the cost of a unit of advertising is $1?

45. For every dollar spent on advertising pharmaceuticals, revenue increases by about $4.20 (CNN, December 17, 2004). If this number is accurate and the firms are operating rationally, what (if anything) can we infer about marginal production and distribution costs?

46. Knoebels Amusement Park in Elysburg, Pennsylvania, charges a lump-sum fee, $\mathscr{L}$, to enter its Crystal Pool. It also charges p per trip down a slide on the pool's water slides. Suppose that 400 teenagers visit the park, each of whom has a demand function of $q_1 = 5 - p$, and that 400 seniors also visit, each of whom has a demand function of $q_2 = 4 - p$. Knoebels's objective is to set $\mathscr{L}$ and p so as to maximize its profit given that it has no (non-sunk) cost and must charge both groups the same prices. What are the optimal $\mathscr{L}$ and p? **W**

47. Hershey Park sells tickets at the gate and at local municipal offices. There are two groups of people. Suppose that the demand function for people who purchase tickets at the gate is $Q_G = 10,000 - 100p_G$ and that the demand function for people who purchase tickets at municipal offices is $Q_G = 9,000 - 100p_G$. The marginal cost of each patron is 5.

   a. Suppose that Hershey Park cannot successfully segment the two markets. What are the profit-maximizing price and quantity? What is its maximum possible profit?

   b. Suppose that the people who purchase tickets at one location would never consider purchasing them at the other and that Hershey Park can successfully price discriminate. What are the profit-maximizing price and quantity? What is its maximum possible profit? **W**

Oligopoly and Monopolistic Competition

Anyone can win unless there happens to be a second entry. —George Ade

Three firms, Nintendo, Microsoft, and Sony, dominate the \$13 billion U.S. video game market. Each firm's profit depends on the actions it takes and on those of its rivals. At the beginning of 2007, only months after it introduced its new wireless Wii game console, Nintendo was selling as many Wii's as the Microsoft Xbox 360 and the Sony PlayStation 3 combined—despite the superior graphics of the other two consoles. One of the major reasons for its success was that Wii sold for \$250, much below PlayStation's \$599 price tag and Xbox 360's \$399. To compete, both its rivals had to consider cutting their prices substantially.[1]

The video game market is an **oligopoly**: a small group of firms in a market with substantial barriers to entry. Because relatively few firms compete in such a market, each can influence the price, and hence each affects rival firms. The need to consider the behavior of rival firms makes an oligopoly firm's profit maximization decision more difficult than that of a monopoly or a competitive firm. A monopoly has no rivals, and a competitive firm ignores the behavior of individual rivals—it considers only the market price and its own costs in choosing its profit-maximizing output.

An oligopoly firm that ignores or inaccurately predicts its rivals' behavior is likely to suffer a loss of profit. For example, as its rivals produce more cars, the price that Ford can get for its cars falls. If Ford underestimates how many cars its rivals will produce, Ford may produce too many automobiles and lose money.

Oligopolistic firms may act independently or may coordinate their actions. A group of firms that explicitly agree (collude) to coordinate their activities is called a **cartel**. These firms may agree on how much each firm will sell or on a common price. By cooperating and behaving like a monopoly, the members of a cartel collectively earn the monopoly profit—the maximum possible profit. In most developed countries, cartels are generally illegal.

If oligopolistic firms do not collude, they earn lower profits. Yet because there are relatively few firms in the market, oligopolistic firms that act independently may earn positive economic profits in the long run, unlike competitive firms.

In an oligopolistic market, one or more barriers to entry keep the number of firms small. In a market with no barriers to entry, firms enter the market until profits are driven to zero. In perfectly competitive markets, enough entry occurs that firms face a horizontal demand curve and are price takers. However, in other markets, even after entry has driven profits to zero, each firm faces a downward-sloping demand curve. Because of this slope, the firm can charge a price above its marginal cost, creating a

---

[1]Elizabeth Millard, "Nintendo Wii Outsells Xbox 360 and PlayStation 3," *Sci-Tech Today*, March 16, 2007; and Pia Sarkar, "Low Price, Unique Controller Make Nintendo Most Popular," *San Francisco Chronicle*, March 17, 2007.

market failure: inefficient (too little) consumption (Chapter 9). **Monopolistic competition** is a market structure in which firms have market power (the ability to raise price profitably above marginal cost) but no additional firm can enter and earn a positive profit.

In this chapter, we examine cartelized, oligopolistic, and monopolistically competitive markets in which firms set quantities or prices. As we saw in Chapter 11, the monopoly equilibrium is the same whether a monopoly sets price or quantity. Similarly, if colluding oligopolies sell identical products, the cartel equilibrium is the same whether they set price or quantity. However, the oligopolistic and monopolistically competitive equilibria differ if firms set prices instead of quantities.

In this chapter, we examine eight main topics	1. **Market Structures:** The number of firms, price, profits, and other properties of markets vary depending on whether the market is monopolistic, oligopolistic, monopolistically competitive, or competitive.
	2. **Cartels:** If firms successfully coordinate their actions, they can collectively behave like a monopoly.
	3. **Noncooperative Oligopoly:** There are many different models of oligopoly in which firms act without colluding, in which the equilibrium price and quantity range between competition at one extreme and monopoly at the other.
	4. **Cournot Oligopoly Model:** In a Cournot model, in which firms simultaneously set their output levels without colluding, market output and firms' profits lie between the competitive and monopoly levels.
	5. **Stackelberg Oligopoly Model:** In a Stackelberg model, in which a *leader* firm chooses its output level before follower rival firms choose their output levels, market output is greater than if all firms choose their output simultaneously, and the leader makes a higher profit than the other firms.
	6. **Comparison of Collusive, Cournot, Stackelberg, and Competitive Equilibria:** Total market output declines from the competitive level to the Stackelberg level to the Cournot level and reaches a minimum with monopoly or collusion.
	7. **Bertrand Oligopoly Model:** In a Bertrand model, in which firms simultaneously set their prices without colluding, the equilibrium depends critically on the degree of product differentiation.
	8. **Monopolistic Competition:** When firms can freely enter the market but face downward-sloping demand curves in equilibrium, firms charge prices above marginal cost but make no profit.

13.1   Market Structures

Markets differ according to the number of firms in the market, the ease with which firms may enter and leave the market, and the ability of firms in a market to differentiate their products from those of their rivals. Table 13.1 lists the characteristics and properties of monopoly, oligopoly, monopolistic competition, and competition. For each of these market structures, we assume that the firms face many price-taking buyers.

TABLE 13.1 Properties of Monopoly, Oligopoly, Monopolistic Competition, and Competition

	Monopoly	Oligopoly	Monopolistic Competition	Competition
1. Profit maximization condition	$MR = MC$	$MR = MC$	$MR = MC$	$p = MR = MC$
2. Ability to set price	Price setter	Price setter	Price setter	Price taker
3. Market power	$p > MC$	$p > MC$	$p > MC$	$p = MC$
4. Entry conditions	No entry	Limited entry	Free entry	Free entry
5. Number of firms	1	Few	Few or many	Many
6. Long-run profit	≥ 0	≥ 0	0	0
7. Strategy dependent on individual rival firms' behavior	No (has no rivals)	Yes	Yes	No (cares about market price only)
8. Products	May be differentiated	May be differentiated	May be differentiated	Undifferentiated
9. Example	Local natural gas utility	Automobile manufacturers	Plumbers in a small town	Apple farmers

Regardless of market structures, a firm maximizes its profit by setting quantity so that marginal revenue equals marginal cost (row 1 of Table 13.1). The four market structures differ in terms of the market power of firms (ability to set price above marginal cost), ease of entry of new firms, and strategic behavior on the part of firms (taking account of rivals' actions). Monopolies, oligopolies, and monopolistically competitive firms are price setters rather than price takers (row 2) because they face downward-sloping demand curves. As a consequence, market failures occur in each of these market structures because price is above marginal revenue and hence is above marginal cost (row 3). In contrast, a competitive firm faces a horizontal demand curve, so its price equals its marginal cost.

A monopoly or an oligopoly does not fear entry (row 4) because of insurmountable barriers to entry such as government licenses and patents. These impediments to entry restrict the number of firms so that there is only one firm (*mono*) in a monopoly, and, usually, only a few (*oligo*) firms in an oligopoly (row 5). The key difference between oligopolistic and monopolistically competitive markets is that the number of firms is fixed in an oligopolistic market and firms are free to enter or exit in a a monopolistically competitive market.

In both competitive and monopolistically competitive markets, entry occurs until no new firm can profitably enter (so the marginal firm earns zero profit, row 6). Monopolistically competitive markets have fewer firms than perfectly competitive markets do. Because they have relatively few rivals and hence are large relative to the market, each monopolistically competitive firm faces a downward-sloping demand curve.

Oligopolistic and monopolistically competitive firms pay attention to rival firms' behavior, in contrast to monopolistic or competitive firms (row 7). A monopoly has no rivals. A competitive firm ignores the behavior of individual rivals in choosing its output because the market price tells the firm everything it needs to know about its competitors.

Oligopolistic and monopolistically competitive firms may produce differentiated products (row 8). For example, Camry and Taurus automobiles differ in size, weight, and various other dimensions. In contrast, competitive apple farmers sell undifferentiated (homogeneous) products.

13.2   Cartels

Oligopolistic firms have an incentive to collude so as to increase their profits. However, because firms can make even more money by cheating on the cartel, firms do not always collude successfully.

WHY CARTELS SUCCEED OR FAIL

> *A thing worth having is a thing worth cheating for.* —W. C. Fields

Firms have an incentive to form a cartel in which each firm reduces its output, which leads to higher prices and higher profits for individual firms and the firms collectively. As Adam Smith observed more than two centuries ago, "People of the same trade seldom meet together, even for merriment and diversion, but the conversation ends in a conspiracy against the public, or some contrivance to raise prices." Luckily for consumers' pocketbooks, cartels often fail because a government forbids them and because each firm in a cartel has an incentive to cheat on the cartel agreement by producing extra output. We now consider why cartels form, what laws prohibit cartels, why cartel members have an incentive to deviate from the cartel agreement, and why some cartels succeed where others fail.

Why Cartels Form. A cartel forms if members of the cartel believe that they can raise their profits by coordinating their actions. Although cartels usually involve oligopolies, cartels may form in a market that would otherwise be competitive.

If a competitive firm is maximizing its profit, why should joining a cartel increase its profit? The answer involves a subtle argument. When a competitive firm chooses its profit-maximizing output level, it considers how varying its output affects its own profit only. The firm ignores the effect that changing its output level has on other firms' profits. A cartel, by contrast, takes into account how changes in any one firm's output affect the profits of all members of the cartel.

If a competitive firm lowers its output, it raises the market price very slightly—so slightly that the firm ignores the effect not only on other firms' profits but also on its own. If all the identical competitive firms in an industry lower their output by this same amount, however, the market price will change noticeably. Recognizing this effect of collective action, a cartel chooses to produce a smaller market output than is produced by a competitive market.

Figure 13.1 illustrates this difference between a competitive market and a cartel. There are n firms in this market, and no further entry is possible. Panel a shows the marginal and average cost curves of a typical firm. If all firms are price takers, the market supply curve, S, is the horizontal sum of the individual marginal cost curves above minimum average cost, as shown in panel b. At the competitive price, p_c, each price-taking firm produces q_c units of output (where MC intersects the line at p_c in panel a). The market output is $Q_c = nq_c$ (where S intersects the market demand curve in panel b).

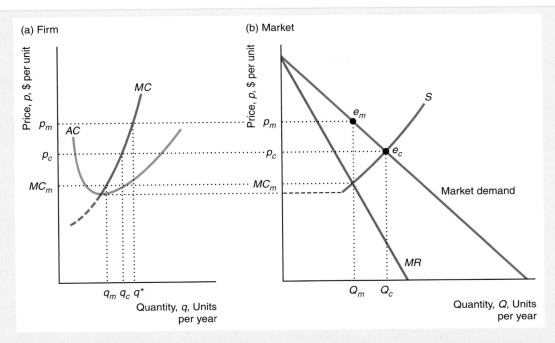

Figure 13.1 Competition Versus Cartel. (a) The marginal cost and average cost of one of the n firms in the market are shown. A competitive firm produces q_c units of output, whereas a cartel member produces $q_m < q_c$. At the cartel price, p_m, each cartel member has an incentive to increase its output from q_m to q^* (where the dotted line at p_m intersects the MC curve). (b) The competitive equilibrium, e_c, has more output and a lower price than the cartel equilibrium, e_m.

Now suppose that the firms form a cartel. Should they reduce their output? At the competitive output, the cartel's marginal cost (which is the competitive industry supply curve, S in panel b) is greater than its marginal revenue, so the cartel's profit rises if it reduces output. The cartel's collective profit rises until output is reduced by enough that its marginal revenue equals its marginal cost at Q_m, the monopoly output. If the profit of the cartel increases, the profit of each of the n members of the cartel also increases. To achieve the cartel output level, each firm must reduce its output to $q_m = Q_m/n$, as panel a shows.

Why must the firms form a cartel to achieve these higher profits? A competitive firm produces q_c, where its marginal cost equals the market price. If only one firm reduces its output, it loses profit because it sells fewer units at essentially the same price. By getting all the firms to lower their output together, the cartel raises the market price and hence individual firms' profits. The less elastic the market demand curve that the potential cartel faces, all else the same, the higher the price the cartel sets (Chapter 11) and the greater the benefit from cartelizing. If the penalty for forming an illegal cartel is relatively low, some unscrupulous businesspeople may succumb to the lure of extra profits and join.

Laws Against Cartels. In the late nineteenth century, cartels (or, as they were called then, *trusts*) were legal and common in the United States. Oil, railroad, sugar, and tobacco trusts raised prices substantially above competitive levels.[2]

In response to the trusts' high prices, the U.S. Congress passed the Sherman Antitrust Act in 1890 and the Federal Trade Commission Act of 1914, which prohibit firms from *explicitly* agreeing to take actions that reduce competition. In particular, cartels that are formed for the purpose of jointly setting price are strictly prohibited. By imposing penalties on firms caught colluding, these antitrust laws reduce the probability that cartels form. Virtually all industrialized nations have *antitrust laws*—or, as they are known in other countries, *competition policies*—that limit or forbid some or all cartels. In 2006, the U.S. Department of Justice, quoting the Supreme Court that collusion is the "supreme evil of antitrust," stated that prosecuting cartels was its "top enforcement priority."

However, cartels persist despite these laws for three reasons. First, international cartels and cartels within certain countries operate legally. Second, some illegal cartels operate believing that they can avoid detection or that the punishment will be insignificant. Third, some firms are able to coordinate their activities without explicitly colluding and thereby running afoul of competition laws.

Some international cartels that are organized by countries rather than by firms are legal. The Organization of Petroleum Exporting Countries (OPEC) is an international cartel that was formed in 1960 by five major oil-exporting countries: Iran, Iraq, Kuwait, Saudi Arabia, and Venezuela. In 1971, OPEC members agreed to take an active role in setting oil prices.

Many illegal cartels flout the competition laws in major industrial countries. These firms apparently believe that they are unlikely to get caught or that the punishments they face are so negligible that it pays to collude anyway. Small fines fail to discourage cartel behavior. In a cartel case involving the $9 billion American carpet industry, a firm with $150 million in annual sales agreed with the U.S. Justice Department to plead guilty and pay a fine of $150,000. It is hard to imagine that a fine of one-tenth of 1% of annual sales significantly deters cartel behavior.

Even larger fines fail to discourage repeated collusion. In 1996, Archer Daniels Midland (ADM) paid to settle three civil price-fixing-related cases: $35 million in a case involving citric acid (used in many consumer products), $30 million to shareholders as compensation for lost stock value after the citric acid price-fixing scandal became public, and $25 million in a lysine (a feed additive) case. ADM paid a $100 million fine in a federal criminal case for fixing the price of lysine and citric acid in 1996 and settled a fructose corn syrup price-fixing case for $400 million in 2004.

American antitrust laws use evidence of conspiracy (such as explicit agreements) rather than the economic effect of monopoly to determine guilt. Charging monopoly-level prices is not necessarily illegal—only the "bad behavior" of explicitly agreeing to raise prices is against the law. As a result, some groups of firms charge monopoly-level prices without violating the competition laws. These firms may *tacitly collude* without

---

[2]Nineteenth-century and early twentieth-century robber barons who made fortunes due to these cartels include John Jacob Astor (real estate, fur), Andrew Carnegie (railroads, steel), Henry Clay Frick (steel), Jay Gould (finance, railroads), Mark Hopkins (railroads), J. P. Morgan (banking), John D. Rockefeller (oil), Leland Stanford (railroads), and Cornelius Vanderbilt (railroads, shipping).

meeting by signaling to each other through their actions. Although the firms' actions may not be illegal, they behave much like cartels. For example, MacAvoy (1995) concluded that the major U.S. long-distance telephone companies tacitly colluded; as a result, each firm's Lerner Index (Chapter 11), $(p - MC)/p$, exceeded 60%, which is well above the competitive level, 0%. (See **www.aw-bc.com/perloff**, Chapter 13, "Tacit Collusion in Long-Distance Service.")

Over the past dozen years, the European Commission has been pursuing antitrust (competition) cases under laws that are similar to U.S. statutes. Recently the European Commission, the DOJ, and the FTC have become increasingly aggressive, prosecuting many more cases. Following the lead of the United States, which imposes both civil and criminal penalties, the British government introduced legislation in 2002 to criminalize certain cartel-related conduct. The European Union uses only civil penalties, but its fines have increased dramatically, as have U.S. fines.

In 1993, the DOJ introduced the Corporate Leniency Program, guaranteeing that whistle-blowing participants in cartels will receive immunity from federal prosecution. As a consequence, the DOJ has caught, prosecuted, and fined several gigantic cartels (see **www.aw-bc.com/perloff**, Chapter 13, "Vitamin Price Fixing"). In 2002, the European Commission adopted a similar policy. In 2004, Japan started more aggressively pursuing antitrust cases.

APPLICATION

Catwalk Cartel

Being thin, rich, and beautiful doesn't make you immune to exploitation. Some of the world's most successful models charged 10 of New York's top modeling agencies—including Wilhelmina, Ford, Next, IMG, and Elite—with operating a sleazy cartel that cut their commissions by millions of dollars.

Carolyn Fears—a 5'11" redheaded former model who had earned up to $200,000 a year—initiated the suit when she learned that her agency not only charged her a 20% commission every time she was booked, but also extracted a 20% commission from her employers (mostly magazines). Her class-action lawsuit alleged that the agencies collectively fixed commissions for Claudia Schiffer, Heidi Klum, Gisele Bundchen, and thousands of other models over many years.

The agencies had formed an industry group, International Model Managers Association, Inc. (IMMA), which held repeated meetings. Monique Pillard, an executive at Elite Model Management, fired off a memo concerning one IMMA meeting, in which she "made a point . . . that we are all committing suicide, if we do not stick together. Pauline's agreed with me but as usual, Bill Weinberg [of Wilhelmina] cautioned me about price fixing. . . . Ha! Ha! Ha! . . . the usual (expletive)." As the trial judge, Harold Baer, Jr., observed, while "Wilhelmina objects to the outward discussion of price fixing, it is plausible from Pillard's reaction that Wilhelmina's objection was to the dissemination of information, not to the underlying price-fixing agreement."

The models argue that the association was little more than a front for helping agency heads keep track of each other's pricing policies. Documents show that, shortly after association meetings, the agencies uniformly raised their commission rates from 10% to 15% and then to 20%. For example, at a meeting before the last increase, an Elite executive gave his competitors a heads-up—but had not informed his clients—that Elite planned to raise its commissions to 20%. He said that at Elite, "we were also favorable to letting everyone know as much as possible about our pricing policies."

The trial started in 2004. Most of the parties settled in 2005. IMG alone paid the models $11 million.

Why Cartels Fail. Many cartels fail even without legal intervention. *Cartels fail if noncartel members can supply consumers with large quantities of goods.* For example, copper producers formed an international cartel that controlled only about a third of the noncommunist world's copper production and faced additional competition from firms that recycle copper from scrap materials. Because of this competition from noncartel members, the cartel was not successful in raising copper prices and keeping them high.

In addition, *each member of a cartel has an incentive to cheat on the cartel agreement.* The owner of a firm may reason, "I joined the cartel to encourage others to reduce their output and increase profits for everyone. I can make more, however, if I cheat on the cartel agreement by producing extra output. I can get away with cheating if the other firms can't tell who's producing the extra output because I'm just one of many firms and because I'll hardly affect the market price." By this reasoning, it is in each firm's best interest for all *other* firms to honor the cartel agreement—thus driving up the market price—while it ignores the agreement and makes extra profitable sales at the high price.

Figure 13.1 illustrates why firms want to cheat. At the cartel output, q_m in panel a, each cartel member's marginal cost is MC_m. The marginal revenue of a firm that violates the agreement is p_m because it is acting like a price taker with respect to the market price. Because the firm's marginal revenue (price) is above its marginal cost, the firm wants to increase its output. If the firm decides to violate the cartel agreement, it maximizes its profit by increasing its output to q^*, where its marginal cost equals p_m. As more and more firms leave the cartel, the cartel price falls. Eventually, if enough firms quit, the cartel collapses.

MAINTAINING CARTELS

To keep firms from violating the cartel agreement, the cartel must be able to detect cheating and punish violators. Further, the members of the cartel must keep their illegal behavior hidden from customers and government agencies.

Detection and Enforcement. Cartels use various techniques to detect cheating. Some cartels, for example, give members the right to inspect each other's books. Some rely on governments to report bids on government contracts so that the firms in the cartel can learn if a member bids below the agreed-on price. Cartels may also divide the market by region or by customers, making it more likely that a firm that steals another firm's customers is detected, as in the case of a two-country mercury cartel (1928–1972) that allocated the Americas to Spain and Europe to Italy. Another option is for a cartel to turn to industry organizations that collect data on market share by firm. A cheating cartel's market share would rise, tipping off the other firms that it cheated.

You perhaps have seen "low price" ads in which local retail stores guarantee to meet or beat the prices of any competitors. These ads may in fact be a way for the firm to induce its customers to report cheating by other firms on a cartel agreement (Salop, 1986).

Various methods are used to enforce cartel agreements. For example, GE and Westinghouse, the two major sellers of large steam-turbine generators, included "most-favored-nation clauses" (more accurately, most-favored-customer clauses) in their contracts. These contracts stated that the seller would not offer a lower price to any other current or future buyer without offering the same price decrease to that buyer. This type of rebate clause creates a penalty for cheating on the cartel: If either company cheats by cutting prices, it has to lower prices to all previous buyers as well. Threats of violence are another means of enforcing a cartel agreement (see **www.aw-bc.com/perloff**, Chapter 13, "Bad Bakers").

Government Support. Sometimes governments help create and enforce cartels, exempting them from antitrust laws. For example, U.S., European, and other governments signed an agreement in 1944 to establish a cartel to fix prices for international airline flights and prevent competition.[3]

Professional baseball teams have been exempted from some U.S. antitrust laws since 1922. As a result, they can use the courts to help enforce certain aspects of their cartel agreement. Major-league clubs are able to avoid competing for young athletes by means of a draft and contracts, limited geographic competition between teams, joint negotiations for television and other rights, and acting collectively in many other ways.

Barriers to Entry. Barriers to entry that limit the number of firms help the cartel detect and punish cheating. The fewer the firms in a market, the more likely it is that other firms will know if a given firm cheats and the easier it is to impose penalties. Cartels with a large number of firms are relatively rare, except those involving professional associations. Hay and Kelley (1974) examined Department of Justice price-fixing cases from 1963 to 1972 and found that only 6.5% involved 50 or more conspirators, the average number of firms was 7.25, and 48% involved 6 or fewer firms.

When new firms enter their market, cartels frequently fail. For example, when only Italy and Spain sold mercury, they were able to establish and maintain a stable cartel. When a larger group of countries joined them, their attempts to cartelize the world mercury market repeatedly failed (MacKie-Mason and Pindyck, 1986).

APPLICATION

Bail Bonds

The state of Connecticut sets a maximum fee that bail-bond businesses can charge for posting a given-size bond (Ayres and Waldfogel, 1994). The bail-bond fee is set at virtually the maximum amount allowed by law in cities with only one active firm (Plainville, 99% of the maximum; Stamford, 99%; and Wallingford, 99%). The price is as high in cities with a duopoly (Ansonia, 99.6%; Meriden, 98%; and New London, 98%). In cities with 3 or more firms, however, the price falls well below the maximum permitted price. The fees are only 54% of the maximum in Norwalk with 3 firms, 64% in New Haven with 8 firms, and 78% in Bridgeport with 10 firms. The explanation may be the rising difficulty of maintaining a cartel or tacit collusion as the number of firms increases.

---

[3]The European Court of Justice struck down the central provisions of aviation treaties among the United States and eight other countries in 2002. The European Commission plans to try to negotiate new treaties.

MERGERS

If antitrust or competition laws prevent firms from colluding, firms may try to merge instead. Recognizing this potential problem, U.S. laws restrict the ability of firms to merge if the effect would be anticompetitive. Whether the Department of Justice or the Federal Trade Commission challenges a proposed merger turns on a large number of issues. Similarly, for the last 12 years, the European Commission has been actively reviewing and blocking mergers. With only one exception (in 2002), none of the Commission's decisions have been rejected by the courts. One reason governments limit mergers is that all the firms in a market could combine and form a monopoly.

Would it be a good idea to ban all mergers? No, because some mergers result in more efficient production. Formerly separate firms may become more efficient because of greater scale, the sharing of trade secrets, or the closure of duplicative retail outlets. For example, when Chase and Chemical banks merged, they closed or combined seven branches in Manhattan that were located within two blocks of other branches. Thus whether a merger raises or lowers welfare depends on which of its two offsetting effects—reducing competition and increasing efficiency—is larger.

● APPLICATION

Airline Mergers: Market Power Versus Flight Frequency

Airline mergers illustrate both the anticompetitive and efficiency effects. When duopoly airlines merge, the resulting monopoly may raise its price—due to its greater market power—and change its flight schedule. Consumers value both low prices and frequent, convenient flights. If the duopoly firms had similar departure times for their flights, the monopoly could schedule fewer but more convenient flights that would reduce costly travel delays for consumers.

Richard (2003) empirically examined United Airlines' and American Airlines' routes out of Chicago's O'Hare Airport. He concluded that airline mergers reduce passenger volume and cause consumer surplus to fall 20% on average, taking account of schedules. However, in one in nine markets, a gain from better schedules would increase consumer surplus by 19%.

13.3 Noncooperative Oligopoly

How do oligopolistic firms behave if they do not collude? Although there is only one model of competition and only one model of monopoly, there are many models of noncooperative oligopolistic behavior that have many possible equilibrium prices and quantities.

Which model is appropriate to use depends on the characteristics of the market, such as the type of *actions* firms take—such as set quantity or price—and whether firms act simultaneously or sequentially. We examine the three best-known oligopoly models in turn. In the *Cournot model,* firms simultaneously choose quantities without colluding. In the *Stackelberg model,* a leader firm chooses its quantity and then the other, follower firms independently choose their quantities. In the *Bertrand model,* firms simultaneously and independently choose prices.

To illustrate these models as simply and as clearly as possible, we start by making three restrictive assumptions, which we will later relax. First, we initially assume that all firms are identical in the sense that they have the same cost functions and produce identical, *undifferentiated* products. We show how the market outcomes change if costs differ or if consumers believe that the products differ across firms.

Second, we initially illustrate each of these oligopoly models for a **duopoly:** an oligopoly with two (*duo*) firms. Each of these models can be applied to markets with many firms. The Cournot and Stackelberg outcomes vary, whereas the Bertrand market outcome with undifferentiated goods does not vary, as the number of firms increases.

Third, we assume that the market lasts for only one period. Consequently, each firm chooses its quantity or price only once. In the next chapter, we examine markets that last for more than one period.

To compare market outcomes under the various models, we need to be able to characterize the oligopoly equilibrium. In Chapter 2, we defined an *equilibrium* as a situation in which no one wants to change his or her behavior. For a competitive market to be in equilibrium, no firm wants to change its output level given what the other firms are producing. Because oligopolistic firms may take many possible actions (such as setting price or quantity or choosing a level of advertising), the oligopoly equilibrium rule needs to refer to firms' behavior more generally than just setting output.

John Nash (1951), a Nobel Prize–winning economist and mathematician, defined an equilibrium concept that has wide applicability, including to oligopoly models. We will give a general definition of a Nash equilibrium in the next chapter. In this chapter, we use a special case of that definition that is appropriate for the single-period oligopoly models in which the only action that a firm can take is to set either its quantity or its price: A set of actions that the firms take is a *Nash equilibrium* if, holding the actions of all other firms constant, no firm can obtain a higher profit by choosing a different action.

13.4 Cournot Oligopoly Model

The French economist and mathematician Antoine-Augustin Cournot introduced the first formal model of oligopoly in 1838. Cournot explained how oligopoly firms behave if they simultaneously choose how much they produce. The firms act independently and have imperfect information about their rivals, so each firm must choose its output level before knowing what the other firms will choose. The quantity that one firm produces directly affects the profits of the other firms because the market price depends on total output. Thus in choosing its strategy to maximize its profit, each firm takes into account its beliefs about the output its rivals will sell. Cournot introduced an equilibrium concept that is the same as the Nash definition in which the action that firms take is to choose quantities.

We look at equilibrium in a market that lasts for only one period. Initially, we make four assumptions: (1) there are two firms and no other firms can enter the market, (2) the firms have identical costs, (3) they sell identical products, and (4) the firms set their quantities simultaneously. Later we relax each of these assumptions in turn and examine how the equilibrium changes.

COURNOT MODEL OF AN AIRLINE MARKET

To illustrate the basic idea of the Cournot model, we turn to an actual market, where American Airlines and United Airlines compete for customers on flights between Chicago and Los Angeles.[4] The total number of passengers flown by these two firms, Q, is the sum of the number of passengers flown on American, q_A, and those flown on United, q_U. We assume that no other companies can enter this market because they cannot obtain landing rights at both airports.[5]

How many passengers does each airline firm choose to carry? To answer this question, we determine the Nash equilibrium for this model. This Nash equilibrium, in which firms choose quantities, is also called a **Cournot equilibrium** or **Nash-Cournot equilibrium** (or *Nash-in-quantities equilibrium*): a set of quantities chosen by firms such that, holding the quantities of all other firms constant, no firm can obtain a higher profit by choosing a different quantity.

To determine the Cournot equilibrium, we need to establish how each firm chooses its quantity. We start by using the total demand curve for the Chicago–Los Angeles route and a firm's belief about how much its rival will sell to determine its *residual demand curve:* the market demand that is not met by other sellers at any given price (Chapter 8). Next we examine how a firm uses its residual demand curve to determine its best response: the output level that maximizes its profit given its belief about how much its rival will produce. Finally, we use the information contained in the firms' best-response functions to determine the Nash-Cournot equilibrium quantities.

The quantity that each firm chooses depends on the residual demand curve it faces and its marginal cost. American Airlines' profit-maximizing output depends on how many passengers it believes United will fly.

Our estimated airline market demand function is linear,

$$Q = 339 - p, \tag{13.1}$$

where price, p, is the dollar cost of a one-way flight, and total quantity of the two airlines combined, Q, is measured in thousands of passengers flying one way per quarter. Panels a and b of Figure 13.2 show that this market demand curve, D, is a straight line that hits the price axis at $339 and the quantity axis at 339 units (thousands of passengers) per quarter. Each airline has a constant marginal cost, MC, and average cost, AC, of $147 per passenger per flight. Using only this information and our economic model, we can determine the Nash-Cournot equilibrium quantities for the two airlines.

Figure 13.2 illustrates two possibilities. If American Airlines were a monopoly, it wouldn't have to worry about United Airlines' actions. American's demand would be the market demand curve, D in panel a. To maximize its profit, American would set its output so that its marginal revenue curve, MR, intersected its marginal cost curve, MC, which is constant at $147 per passenger. Panel a shows that the monopoly output is 96 units (thousands of passengers) per quarter and that the monopoly price is $243 per passenger (one way).

---

[4]This example is based on Brander and Zhang (1990). They reported data for economy and discount passengers taking direct flights between the two cities in the third quarter of 1985. In calculating the profits, we assume that Brander and Zhang's estimate of the firms' constant marginal cost is the same as the firms' relevant long-run average cost.

[5]With the end of deregulation, existing firms were given the right to buy, sell, or rent landing slots. However, by controlling landing slots, existing firms can make entry difficult.

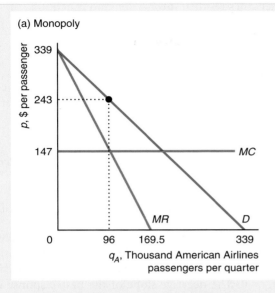

(a) Monopoly

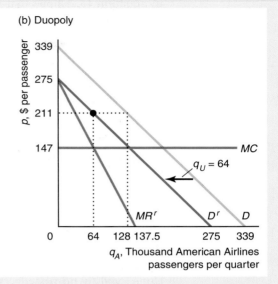

(b) Duopoly

Figure 13.2 American Airlines' Profit-Maximizing Output. (a) If American is a monopoly, it picks its profit-maximizing output, $q_A = 96$ units (thousand passengers) per quarter, so that its marginal revenue, MR, equals its marginal cost, MC. (b) If American believes that United will fly $q_U = 64$ units per quarter, its residual demand curve, D^r, is the market demand curve, D, minus q_U. American maximizes its profit at $q_A = 64$, where its marginal revenue, MR^r, equals MC.

But because American competes with United, American must take account of United's behavior when choosing its profit-maximizing output. American's demand is not the entire market demand. Rather, American is concerned with its residual demand curve. In general, if the market demand function is $D(p)$, and the supply of other firms is $S^o(p)$, then the residual demand function, $D^r(p)$, is

$$D^r(p) = D(p) - S^o(p).$$

Thus if United flies q_U passengers regardless of the price, American transports only the residual demand, $Q = D(p)$, minus the q_U passengers, so $q_A = Q - q_U$. The residual demand that American faces is

$$q_A = Q(p) - q_U = (339 - p) - q_U. \tag{13.2}$$

In panel b, American believes that United will fly $q_U = 64$, so American's residual demand curve, D^r, is the market demand curve, D, moved to the left by $q_U = 64$. For example, if the price is $211, the total number of passengers who want to fly is $Q = 128$. If United transports $q_U = 64$, American flies $Q - q_U = 128 - 64 = 64 = q_A$.

What is American's best-response, profit-maximizing output if its managers believe that United will fly q_U passengers? *American can think of itself as having a monopoly with respect to the people who don't fly on United,* which its residual demand curve, D^r, shows. We will use our analysis based on the residual demand curve to derive American's *best-response function*, $q_A = B_A(q_U)$, which shows American's best-response or profit-maximizing output, q_A, as a function of United's output, q_U.[6]

To maximize its profit, American sets its output so that its marginal revenue corresponding to this residual demand, MR^r, equals its marginal cost. Rearranging the terms

---

[6]*Jargon alert:* Some economists refer to the *best-response function* as the *reaction function*.

in Equation 13.2 shows that American's residual inverse demand function is

$$p = 339 - q_A - q_U. \tag{13.3}$$

Consequently, its revenue function based on its residual demand function is

$$R^r(q_A) = pq_A = (339 - q_A - q_U)q_A = 339q_A - (q_A)^2 - q_Uq_A.$$

American views its revenue as a function solely of its own output, $R^r(q_A)$, because American treats United's quantity as a constant. Thus American's marginal revenue is

$$MR^r = \frac{dR^r(q_A)}{dq_A} = 339 - 2q_A - q_U. \tag{13.4}$$

Equating its marginal revenue with its marginal cost, $147, American derives its best-response function, $MR^r = 339 - 2q_A - q_U = 147 = MC$, or

$$q_A = 96 - \frac{1}{2}q_U = B_A(q_U). \tag{13.5}$$

Figure 13.3 plots American Airlines' best-response function, Equation 13.5, which shows how many tickets American sells for each possible q_U. As the best-response curve shows, American sells the monopoly number of tickets, 96, if American thinks United will fly no passengers, $q_U = 0$. The negative slope of the best-response curve shows that American sells fewer tickets the more people American thinks that United will fly. American sells $q_A = 64$ if it thinks q_U will be 64. American shuts down, $q_A = 0$, if it thinks q_U will be 192 or more, because operating wouldn't be profitable.

We can derive United's best-response function, $q_U = B_U(q_A)$, similarly. Given that the two firms have identical marginal costs and face the same market demand function, United's best-response function is the same as American's with the quantity subscripts reversed:

$$q_U = 96 - \frac{1}{2}q_A = B_U(q_A). \tag{13.6}$$

We obtain the Nash-Cournot equilibrium quantities by solving Equation 13.5 and 13.6 simultaneously for q_A and q_U.[7] This solution is the point where the firms' best-response curves intersect at $q_A = q_U = 64$. In a Nash-Cournot equilibrium, neither firm wants to change its output level given that the other firm is producing the equilibrium quantity. If American expects United to sell $q_U = 64$, American wants to sell $q_A = 64$. Because this point is on its best-response curve, American doesn't want to change its output from 64. Similarly, if United expects American to sell $q_A = 64$, United doesn't want to change q_U from 64. Thus this pair of outputs is a Nash equilibrium: Given its correct belief about its rival's output, each firm is maximizing its profit, and neither firm wants to change its output.

Any pair of quantities other than the pair at an intersection of the best-response functions is *not* a Nash-Cournot equilibrium. If either firm is not on its best-response curve, it wants to change its output to increase its profit. For example, the output pair $q_A = 96$ and $q_U = 0$ is not a Nash-Cournot equilibrium. American is perfectly happy producing the monopoly output if United doesn't operate at all: American is on its best-response curve. United, however, would not be happy with this outcome because it is not on United's best-response curve. As its best-response curve shows, if it knows

---

[7]For example, we can substitute for q_U in Equation 13.5 using Equation 13.6 to obtain an equation in only q_A. Then we can substitute that value of q_A in Equation 13.6 to obtain q_U. Alternatively, because the firms are identical, $q_A = q_U = q$, so we can replace both q_A and q_U with q in either best-response function and solve for q.

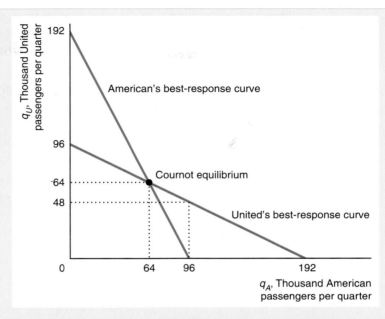

Figure 13.3 American's and United's Best-Response Curves. The best-response curves show the output that each firm picks to maximize its profit, given its belief about its rival's output. The Cournot equilibrium occurs at the intersection of the best-response curves.

that American will sell $q_A = 96$, United maximizes its profit by selling $q_U = 48$. Only if $q_A = q_U = 64$ does neither firm want to change its action. Based on statistical tests, Brander and Zhang (1990) reported that they could not reject the hypothesis that the Cournot model is consistent with American's and United's behavior.[8]

THE COURNOT EQUILIBRIUM WITH TWO OR MORE FIRMS

We've seen that the price to consumers is lower if two firms set output independently than if there is one firm (or the firms collude). The price to consumers is even lower if there are more than two firms acting independently in the market. We now examine how the Nash-Cournot equilibrium varies with the number of firms. We first solve the problem for general demand and marginal cost functions for n firms. Then we solve using a linear inverse demand function and a constant marginal cost and apply that analysis to our airline example.

General Case. If output is homogeneous, the market inverse demand function is $p(Q)$, where Q, the total market output, is the sum of the output of each of the n firms: $Q = q_1 + q_2 + \cdots + q_n$. Each of the n identical firms has the same cost function, $C(q_i)$. To analyze a Cournot market of identical firms, we first examine the behavior of a representative firm. Firm 1 wants to maximize its profit through its choice of q_1:

$$\max_{q_1} \pi_1(q_1, q_2, \ldots, q_n) = q_1 p(q_1 + q_2 + \cdots + q_n) - C(q_1) = q_1 p(Q) - C(q_1). \quad (13.7)$$

---

[8]Because the model described here is a simplified version of the Brander and Zhang (1990) model, the predicted output levels, $q_A = q_U = 64$, differ slightly from theirs. Nonetheless, our predictions are very close to the actual observed outcome, $q_A = 65.9$ and $q_U = 62.7$.

Firm 1 views the outputs of the other firms as fixed, so $q_2, q_3, \ldots, q_n$ are constants. Firm 1's first-order condition is the derivative of its profit with respect to q_1 set equal to zero:

$$\frac{\partial \pi}{\partial q_1} = p(Q) + q_1 \frac{dp(Q)}{dQ} \frac{\partial Q}{\partial q_1} - \frac{dC(q_1)}{dq_1} = 0. \tag{13.8}$$

Given that the other firms' outputs are constants, $dQ/dq_1 = d(q_1 + q_2 + \cdots + q_n)/dq_1 = 1$. Making this substitution and rearranging terms, we see that the firm's first-order condition implies that Firm 1 equates is marginal revenue and its marginal cost:

$$MR = p(Q) + q_1 \frac{dp(Q)}{dQ} = \frac{dC(q_1)}{dq_1} = MC. \tag{13.9}$$

Equation 13.9 gives the firm's best-response function, allowing the firm to calculate its optimal q_1 for any given set of outputs of other firms. We can write Firm 1's best-response function as a function of the other firm's output levels: $p(q_1 + q_2 + \cdots + q_n) + q_1(dp/dQ) - dC(q_1)/dq_1 = 0$. Thus for any given set of $q_2, \ldots, q_n$, the firm can solve for the profit-maximizing q_1 using this expression.

Solving the best-response functions for all the firms simultaneously, we obtain the Nash-Cournot equilibrium quantities $q_1, q_2, \ldots, q_n$. Because all the firms are identical, in equilibrium $q_1 = q_2 = \cdots = q_n = q$.

The marginal revenue expression can be rewritten as $p[1 + (q/p)(dp/dQ)]$. Multiplying and dividing the last term by n, noting that $Q = nq$ (given that all firms are identical), and observing that the market elasticity of demand, ε, is defined as $(dQ/dp)(p/Q)$, we can rewrite the first-order conditions, such as Equation 13.9, as

$$p\left(1 + \frac{1}{n\varepsilon}\right) = \frac{dC(q)}{dq}. \tag{13.10}$$

The left-hand side of Equation 13.10 expresses the firm's marginal revenue in terms of the elasticity of demand of its residual demand curve, $n\varepsilon$, which is the number of firms, n, times the market demand elasticity, ε. Holding ε constant, the more firms there are, the more elastic the residual demand curve, and hence the closer a firm's marginal revenue is to the price.

We can rearrange Equation 13.10 to obtain an expression for the Lerner Index, $(p - MC)/p$, in terms of the market demand elasticity and the number of firms:

$$\frac{p - MC}{p} = -\frac{1}{n\varepsilon}. \tag{13.11}$$

The larger the Lerner Index, the greater the firm's market power. As Equation 13.11 shows, if we hold the market elasticity constant and increase the number of firms, the Lerner Index falls. As n approaches ∞, the elasticity facing any one firm approaches $-\infty$, so the Lerner Index approaches 0 and the market is competitive.

Linear Case. We cannot explicitly solve for a firm's best-response function or the Nash-Cournot equilibrium given general functional forms, but we can if we specify particular functions. Suppose that the inverse market demand function is linear,

$$p = a - bQ,$$

and that each firm's marginal cost is m, a constant, and it has no fixed cost.

For this linear model, we can rewrite Firm 1's objective, Equation 13.7, as

$$\max_{q_1} \pi_1(q_1) = q_1[a - b(q_1 + q_2 + \cdots + q_n)] - mq_1. \tag{13.12}$$

Firm 1's first-order condition, Equation 13.9, to maximize its profit is

$$MR = a - b(2q_1 + q_2 + \cdots + q_n) = m = MC. \tag{13.13}$$

Because all firms have the same cost function, $q_2 = q_3 = \cdots = q_n \equiv q$ in equilibrium. Substituting these equalities into Equation 13.13, we find that the first firm's best-response function, B_1, is

$$q_1 = B_1(q_2, q_3, \ldots, q_n) = \frac{a - m}{2b} - \frac{n - 1}{2}q. \tag{13.14}$$

The right-hand sides of the other firms' best-response functions are identical.

All these best-response functions must hold simultaneously. The intersection of the best-response functions determines the Nash-Cournot equilibrium. Given that all the firms are identical, all choose the same output level in equilibrium. Thus we can solve for the equilibrium by setting $q_1 = q$ in Equation 13.14 and rearranging terms to obtain

$$q = \frac{a - m}{(n + 1)b}. \tag{13.15}$$

Total market output, $Q = nq$, equals $n(a - m)/[(n + 1)b]$. The corresponding price is obtained by substituting this expression for market output into the demand function:

$$p = \frac{a + nm}{n + 1}. \tag{13.16}$$

Setting $n = 1$ in Equations 13.15 and 13.16 yields the monopoly quantity and price. As n becomes large, each firm's quantity approaches zero, total output approaches $(a - m)/b$, and price approaches m, which are the competitive levels.[9] The Lerner Index is

$$\frac{p - MC}{p} = \frac{a - m}{a + nm}. \tag{13.17}$$

As n grows large, the denominator in Equation 13.17 goes to ∞, so the Lerner Index goes to 0 and there is no market power.

Airline Example. We can illustrate these results using our airline example, where $a = 339$, $b = 1$, $m = 147$, and $n = 2$. Suppose that additional airlines with an identical marginal cost of $m = \$147$ were to fly between Chicago and Los Angeles. Table 13.2 shows how the Cournot equilibrium price and the Lerner Index vary with the number of firms. Using the equations for the general linear model, we know that each firm's Nash-Cournot equilibrium quantity is $q = (339 - 147)/(n + 1) = 192/(n + 1)$ and the Nash-Cournot equilibrium price is $p = (339 + 147n)/(n + 1)$.

As we already know, if there were only one firm, it would produce the monopoly quantity, 96, at the monopoly price, \$243. We also know that each duopoly firm's output is 64, so market output is 128 and price is \$211. The duopoly market elasticity is $\varepsilon = 1.65$, so the residual demand elasticity that each duopoly firm faces is twice as large as the market elasticity, $2\varepsilon = -3.3$.

---

[9]As the number of firms goes to infinity, the Cournot equilibrium goes to perfect competition only if average cost is nondecreasing (Ruffin, 1971).

TABLE 13.2   Cournot Equilibrium Varies with the Number of Firms

Number of Firms, n	Firm Output, q	Market Output, Q	Price, p	Market Elasticity, ε	Residual Demand Elasticity, $n\varepsilon$	Lerner Index, $(p - m)/p = -1/(n\varepsilon)$
1	96	96	243	−2.53	−2.53	0.40
2	64	128	211	−1.65	−3.30	0.30
3	48	144	195	−1.35	−4.06	0.25
4	38.4	154	185.40	−1.21	−4.83	0.21
5	32	160	179	−1.12	−5.59	0.18
10	17.5	175	164.45	−0.94	−9.42	0.11
50	3.8	188	150.76	−0.80	−40.05	0.02
100	1.9	190	148.90	−0.78	−78.33	0.01
200	1.0	191	147.96	−0.77	−154.89	0.01

As the number of firms increases, each firm's output falls toward zero, but total output approaches 192, the quantity on the market demand curve where price equals the marginal cost of $147. Although the market elasticity of demand falls as the number of firms grows, the residual demand curve for each firm becomes increasingly horizontal (perfectly elastic). As a result, the price approaches the marginal cost, $147. Similarly, as the number of firms increases, the Lerner Index approaches the price-taking level of zero.

The table shows that having extra firms in the market benefits consumers. When the number of firms rises from 1 to 4, the price falls by a quarter and the Lerner Index is cut nearly in half. At 10 firms, the price is one-third less than the monopoly level, and the Lerner Index is a quarter of the monopoly level.

THE COURNOT MODEL WITH NONIDENTICAL FIRMS

For simplicity, we initially assumed that the firms were essentially identical: All firms had identical costs and produced identical products. However, costs often vary across firms, and firms often differentiate the products they produce from those of their rivals.

Unequal Costs. In the Cournot model, the firm sets its output so as to equate its marginal revenue to its marginal cost, as specified by its first-order condition. If firms' marginal costs vary, then so will the firms' first-order conditions and hence their best-response functions. In the resulting Nash-Cournot equilibrium, the relatively low-cost firm produces more, as Solved Problem 13.1 illustrates. However, as long as the products are not differentiated, the firms charge the same price.

SOLVED PROBLEM   13.1

If the inverse market demand function facing a duopoly is $p = a - bQ$, what are the Nash-Cournot equilibrium quantities if the marginal cost of Firm 1 is m and that of Firm 2 is $m + x$, where $x > 0$? Which firm produces more and which has the higher profit?

Answer

1. *Determine each firm's best-response function:* Firm 1's profit is the same as in Equation 13.12 where $n = 2$: $\pi_1 = [a - b(q_1 + q_2)]q_1 - mq_1$. Consequently, its

best-response function is the same as Equation 13.14,

$$q_1 = \frac{a - m - bq_2}{2b}. \tag{13.18}$$

Firm 2's profit is the same as in Equation 13.12 except that m is replaced by $m + x$:
$\pi_2 = q_2[a - b(q_1 + q_2)] - (m + x)q_2$. Setting the derivative of Firm 2's profit with
respect to q_2 (holding q_1 fixed) equal to zero, and rearranging terms, we find that
the first-order condition for Firm 1 to maximize its profit is $MR_2 = a - b(2q_2 + q_1) = m + x = MC_2$. Rearranging this expression shows that Firm 2's best-
response function is

$$q_2 = \frac{a - (m + x) - bq_1}{2b}. \tag{13.19}$$

2. Use the best-response functions to solve for the Nash-Cournot equilibrium: To
determine the equilibrium, we solve Equations 13.18 and 13.19 simultaneously
for q_1 and q_2:[10]

$$q_1 = \frac{a - m + x}{3b}, \tag{13.20}$$

$$q_2 = \frac{a - m - 2x}{3b}. \tag{13.21}$$

*3. Use the Nash-Cournot equilibrium quantity equations to determine which firm
produces more:* By inspection, $q_1 = [a - m + x]/[3b] > q_2 = [a - m - 2x]/[3b]$. As
x increases, q_1 increases by $dq_1/dx = 1/[3b]$ and q_2 falls by $dq_2/dx = -2/[3b]$.

*4. Substitute the Nash-Cournot equilibrium quantity equations into the profit func-
tions to determine which firm has a higher profit:* The low-cost firm has the higher
profit. Using Equations 13.20 and 13.21, $q_1 + q_2 = (2a - 2m - x)/(3b)$.
Substituting this expression and the expression for q_1 from Equation 13.20 into
the profit function for Firm 1, we find that $\pi_1 = [a - m - b(q_1 + q_2)]q_1 = [a - m - (2a - 2m - x)/3](a - m + x)/(3b) = (a - m + x)^2/[9b]$ and, by similar reasoning,
$\pi_2 = (a - m - 2x)^2/[9b]$. Thus

$$\pi_1 = \frac{(a - m + x)^2}{9b} > \frac{(a - m - 2x)^2}{9b} = \pi_2.$$

Differentiated Products. Firms differentiate their products to increase their profits. A
firm can charge a higher price if differentiation causes its residual demand curve to
become less elastic. Whether the differentiation is related to a nonslip handle or a

---

[10]By substituting the expression for q_1 from Equation 13.18 into Equation 13.19, we obtain

$$q_2 = \left[a - m - x - b\left(\frac{a - m - bq_2}{2b}\right)\right]/(2b).$$

Solving for q_2, we derive Equation 13.21. Substituting that expression into Equation 13.18 and
simplifying, we get Equation 13.20.

sneaker pump, if a firm can convince some customers that its branded product is superior in some way, it can charge a higher price than it could if it sold plain or generic products.

For example, after Heinz introduced funny-color ketchup—Blastin' Green, Funky Purple, and Stellar Blue—its share of all ketchup rose substantially, from 50% in 1999 to more than 60% by 2005. (Contrary to my wife's views, my purchases did not make a very major contribution to this increase.) However, its Kool Blue french fries were less successful.

If consumers think products differ, the Nash-Cournot quantities and prices will differ across firms. Each firm faces a different inverse demand function and hence charges a different price. For example, suppose that Firm 1's inverse demand function is $p_1 = a - b_1 q_1 - b_2 q_2$, where $b_1 > b_2$ if consumers believe that Good 1 is different from Good 2 and $b_1 = b_2 = b$ if the goods are identical. Given that consumers view the products as differentiated and Firm 2 faces a similar inverse demand function, we replace the single market demand with these individual demand functions in the Cournot model. Solved Problem 13.2 shows how to solve for the Nash-Cournot equilibrium in an actual market.

SOLVED PROBLEM   13.2

Intel and Advanced Micro Devices (AMD) are the only two firms that produce central processing units (CPUs), which are the brains of personal computers. Both because the products differ physically and because Intel's "Intel Inside" advertising campaign has convinced some consumers' of its superiority, consumers view the CPUs as imperfect substitutes. Consequently, the two firms' inverse demand functions differ:

$$p_A = 197 - 15.1q_A - 0.3q_I, \tag{13.22}$$

$$p_I = 490 - 10q_I - 6q_A, \tag{13.23}$$

where price is dollars per CPU, quantity is in millions of CPUs, the subscript I indicates Intel, and the subscript A represents AMD.[11] Each firm faces a constant marginal cost of $m = \$40$ per unit. (For simplicity, we will assume there are no fixed costs.) Solve for the Nash-Cournot equilibrium quantities and prices.

Answer

1. *Determine each firm's best-response function:* Substituting the inverse demand equations 13.22 and 13.23 into the definition of profit, we learn that the firms'

---

[11]I thank Hugo Salgado for estimating these inverse demand functions for me and for providing evidence that this market is well described by a Nash-Cournot equilibrium.

profit functions are

$$\pi_A = (p_A - m)q_A = (157 - 15.1q_A - 0.3q_I)q_A, \tag{13.24}$$

$$\pi_I = (p_I - m)q_I = (450 - 10q_I - 6q_A)q_I. \tag{13.25}$$

The first-order conditions are $\partial\pi_A/\partial q_A = 157 - 30.2q_A - 0.3q_I$ and $\partial\pi_I/\partial q_I = 450 - 20q_I - 6q_A$. Rearranging these expressions, we obtain the best-response functions:

$$q_A = \frac{157 - 0.3q_I}{30.2}, \tag{13.26}$$

$$q_I = \frac{450 - 6q_A}{20}. \tag{13.27}$$

2. *Use the best-response functions to solve for the Nash-Cournot equilibrium:* Solving the system of best-response functions 13.26 and 13.27, we find that the Nash-Cournot equilibrium quantities are $q_A = 15,025/3,011 \approx 5$ million CPUs, and $q_I = 63,240/3,011 \approx 21$ million CPUs. Substituting these values into the inverse demand functions, we obtain the corresponding prices: $p_A = \$115.20$ and $p_I = \$250$ per CPU.

● APPLICATION

Air Ticket Prices and Rivalry

Because costs vary across competing airlines and consumers prefer one airline to another, airlines often have unequal market shares. The markup of price over marginal cost is much greater on routes in which one airline carries most of the passengers than it is on other routes. Unfortunately for consumers, a single firm is the only carrier or the dominant carrier on 58% of all U.S. domestic routes (Weiher et al., 2002).

The first column of the table identifies the market structure for U.S. air routes. The last column shows the share of routes. A single firm (monopoly) serves 18% of all routes. Duopolies control 19% of the routes, three-firm markets are 16%, four-firm markets are 13%, and five or more firms fly on 35% of the routes.

Although nearly two-thirds of all routes have three or more carriers, one or two firms dominate virtually all routes. We call a carrier a *dominant firm* if it has at least 60% of ticket sales by value but is not a monopoly. We call two carriers a *dominant pair* if they collectively have at least 60% of the market but neither firm is a dominant firm and three or more firms fly this route. All but 0.1% of routes have a monopoly (18%), a dominant firm (40%), or a dominant pair (42%).

The first row of the table shows that the price is slightly more than double (2.1 times) marginal cost on average across all U.S. routes and market structures. (This average price includes "free" frequent-flier tickets and other below-cost tickets.)

Type of Market	Lerner Index, $(p - MC)/p$	Share of All Routes (%)
All market types	0.52	100
Dominant firm	0.68	40
Dominant pair	0.17	42
One firm (monopoly)	0.70	18
Two firms (duopoly)	0.55	19
Dominant firm	0.57	14
No dominant firm	0.33	5
Three firms	0.44	16
Dominant firm	0.47	9
No dominant firm	0.23	7
Four firms	0.44	13
Dominant firm	0.55	6
Dominant pair	0.23	7
No dominant firm or pair	0.52	~0
Five or more firms	0.23	35
Dominant firm	0.71	11
Dominant pair	0.29	23
No dominant firm or pair	0.09	0.1

The price is 3.3 times marginal cost for monopolies and 3.1 times marginal cost for dominant firms. In contrast, over the sample period, the average price is only 1.2 times marginal cost for dominant pairs.

The markup of price over marginal cost depends much more on whether there is a dominant firm or dominant pair than on the total number of firms in the market. If there is a dominant pair, whether there are four or five firms, the price is between 1.3 times marginal cost for a four-firm route and 1.4 times marginal cost for a route with five or more firms. If there is a dominant firm, price is 2.3 times marginal cost on duopoly routes, 1.9 times on three-firm routes, 2.2 times on four-firm routes, and 3.5 times on routes with five or more firms.

Thus preventing a single firm from dominating a route may substantially lower prices. Even if two firms dominate the market, the markup of price over marginal cost is substantially lower than if a single firm dominates.

13.5   Stackelberg Oligopoly Model

In the Cournot model, both firms announce their output decisions simultaneously. In contrast, suppose that one of the firms, called the *leader*, can set its output before its rival, the *follower*, sets its output. This type of situation where one firm acts before the other arises naturally if one firm enters a market before the other.

Would the firm that acts first have an advantage? The German economist Heinrich von Stackelberg showed how to modify the Cournot model to answer this question.

Unlike in the Cournot model where both firms choose output at the same time, the Stackelberg leader, Firm 1, sets its output before the follower, Firm 2, chooses a quantity.

How does the leader decide to set its output? The leader realizes that once it sets its output, the rival firm will use its Cournot best-response curve to select a best-response output. Thus the leader predicts what the follower will do before the follower acts. Using this knowledge, the leader manipulates the follower, thereby benefiting at the follower's expense.

CALCULUS SOLUTION: AIRLINE EXAMPLE

We can use calculus to derive the Stackelberg equilibrium. We'll use the linear example, $p = a - bQ$, with two firms with identical marginal costs, m, so that we can solve for an explicit solution.

Because Firm 1, the Stackelberg leader, chooses its output first, it knows that Firm 2, the follower, will choose its output using its best-response function. Using Equation 13.14 and setting $n = 2$, we know that Firm 2's best-response function, B_2, is

$$q_2 = B_2(q_1) = \frac{a - m}{2b} - \frac{1}{2}q_1. \tag{13.28}$$

The market price depends on the output of both firms, $p(q_1 + q_2)$. Consequently, the Stackelberg leader's profit is a function of its own and the follower's output: $\pi_1(q_1 + q_2) = p(q_1 + q_2)q_1 - mq_1$. By replacing the follower's output with the follower's best-response function, we can write the leader's profit function as $\pi_1(q_1 + R_2(q_1))$, so the leader's profit depends only on its own output. Thus the Stackelberg leader's objective is

$$\max_{q_1} \pi_1(q_1, B_2(q_1)) = q_1\left[a - b\left(q_1 + \frac{a - m}{2b} - \frac{1}{2}q_1\right)\right] - mq_1. \tag{13.29}$$

The leader's first-order condition is derived by setting the derivative of its profit with respect to q_1 equal to zero: $a - 2bq_1 - (a - m)/2 + bq_1 - m = 0$. Solving this expression for q_1, we find that the profit-maximizing output of the leader is

$$q_1 = \frac{a - m}{2b}. \tag{13.30}$$

Substituting the expression for q_1 in Equation 13.30 into the follower's best-response function 13.28 gives the equilibrium output of the follower:

$$q_2 = \frac{a - m}{4b}.$$

Thus with a linear demand curve and constant marginal cost, the leader produces twice as much as the follower.[12]

We can use this analysis to ask what would happen in our airline example if American Airlines can act before United Airlines, so that American is a Stackelberg leader and United is a Stackelberg follower. Replacing the parameters in our linear analysis with those for the airlines, $a = 339$, $b = 1$, $m = 147$, and $n = 2$, we find that American's output is $q_1 = (339 - 147)/2 = 96$, and United's output is $q_2 = (339 - 147)/4 = 48$.

---

[12]Here the leader produces the same quantity as a monopoly would, and the follower produces the same quantity as it would in the cartel equilibrium. These relationships are due to the linear demand curve and the constant marginal cost—they do not hold more generally.

GRAPHICAL SOLUTION: AIRLINES EXAMPLE

We can illustrate this airline analysis using graphs. American, the Stackelberg leader, uses its residual demand curve to determine its profit-maximizing output. American knows that when it sets q_A, United will use its Cournot best-response function to pick its best-response q_U. Thus American's residual demand curve, D^r (panel a of Figure 13.4), is the market demand curve, D (panel a), minus the output United will produce as summarized by United's best-response curve (panel b). For example, if American sets $q_A = 192$, United's best response is $q_U = 0$ (as shown by United's best-response curve in panel b). As a result, the residual demand curve and the market demand curve are identical at $q_A = 192$ (panel a).

Similarly, if American set $q_A = 0$, United would choose $q_U = 96$, so the residual demand at $q_A = 0$ is 96 less than demand. The residual demand curve hits the vertical axis, where $q_A = 0$, at $p = \$243$, which is 96 units to the left of demand at that price. When $q_A = 96$, $q_U = 48$, so the residual demand at $q_A = 96$ is 48 units to the left of the demand.

American chooses its profit-maximizing output, $q_A = 96$, where its marginal revenue curve that corresponds to the residual demand curve, MR^r, equals its marginal cost, \$147. At $q_A = 96$, the price, which is the height of the residual demand curve, is \$195. Total demand at \$195 is $Q = 144$. At that price, United produces $q_U = Q - q_A = 48$, its best response to American's output of $q_A = 96$. Thus in this Stackelberg equilibrium, the leader produces twice as much as the follower, as Figure 13.4 shows.

WHY MOVING SEQUENTIALLY IS ESSENTIAL

Why don't we get the Stackelberg equilibrium when both firms move simultaneously? Why doesn't American announce that it will produce the Stackelberg leader's output to induce United to produce the Stackelberg follower's output level? The answer is that when the firms move simultaneously, United doesn't view American's warning that it will produce a large quantity as a *credible threat*.

If United believed that threat, it would indeed produce the Stackelberg follower's output level. But United doesn't believe the threat because it is not in American's best interest to produce that large a quantity of output. If American produced the leader's level of output and United produced the Cournot level, American's profit would be lower than if it too produced the Cournot level. Because American cannot be sure that United will believe its threat and reduce its output, American will produce the Cournot output level.

Indeed, each firm may make the same threat and announce that it wants to be the leader. Because neither firm can be sure that the other will be intimidated and produce the smaller quantity, both produce the Cournot output level. In contrast, when one firm moves first, its threat to produce a large quantity is credible because it has already *committed* to producing the larger quantity, thereby carrying out its threat.

STRATEGIC TRADE POLICY: AN APPLICATION OF THE STACKELBERG MODEL

Suppose that two identical firms in two different countries compete in a world market. Both firms act simultaneously, so neither firm can make itself the Stackelberg leader. However, a government may intervene to make its firm a Stackelberg leader. For example,

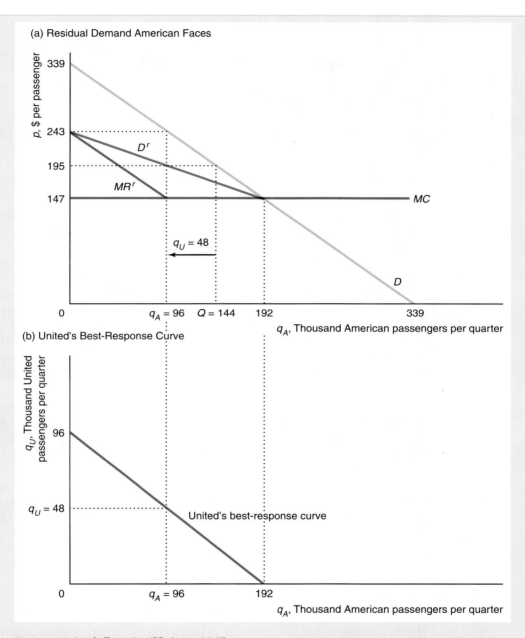

Figure 13.4 Stackelberg Equilibrium. (a) The residual demand that the Stackelberg leader faces is the market demand minus the quantity produced by the follower, q_U, given the leader's quantity, q_A. The leader chooses $q_A = 96$ so that its marginal revenue, MR^r, equals its marginal cost. The total output, $Q = 144$, is the sum of the output of the two firms. (b) The quantity that the follower produces is its best response to the leader's output, as given by its Cournot best-response curve.

the Japanese and French governments often help their domestic firms compete with international rivals; occasionally, so do the U.S., British, Canadian, and many other governments. If only one government intervenes, it can make its domestic firm's threat to produce a large quantity of output credible, causing foreign rivals to produce the Stackelberg follower's level of output (Spencer and Brander, 1983).

We have already conducted a similar analysis. In Solved Problem 13.1, we showed that a firm with a lower marginal cost would produce more than its higher cost rival in a Nash-Cournot equilibrium. Thus a government can subsidy its domestic firm to make it a more fearsome rival to the unsubsidized firm.

Government Subsidy for an Airline. We now modify our airline example to illustrate how one country's government can aid its firm. Suppose that United Airlines were based in one country and American Airlines in another. Initially, United and American are in a Nash-Cournot equilibrium. Each firm has a marginal cost of $147 and flies 64 thousand passengers (64 units) per quarter at a price of $211.

Now suppose that United's government gives United a $48-per-passenger subsidy but the other government doesn't help American. As a result, American's marginal cost remains at $147, but United's marginal cost after the subsidy is only $99.

The firms continue to act as in the Cournot model, but the playing field is no longer level.[13] How does the Nash-Cournot equilibrium change? Your intuition probably tells you that United's output increases relative to that of American, as we now show.

United still acts at the same time as American, so United behaves like any Cournot firm and determines its best-response curve. United's best response to any given American output is the output at which its marginal revenue corresponding to its residual demand, MR^r, equals its marginal cost. The subsidy does not affect United's MR^r curve, but it lowers its MC curve, so United produces more output for any given American output after the cost falls.

Panel a of Figure 13.5 illustrates this reasoning. United's residual demand, D^r, lies 64 units to the left of the market demand, D, if American produces 64. The MR^r curve intersects the original marginal cost, $MC^1 = \$147$, at 64 and the new marginal cost, $MC^2 = \$99$, at 88. Thus if we hold American's output constant at 64, United produces more as its marginal cost falls.

Because this reasoning applies for any level of output American picks, United's best-response curve in panel b shifts outward as its after-subsidy marginal cost falls. United sets the marginal revenue that corresponds to its residual demand curve, MR_U, equal to its new, lower marginal cost, MC:

$$MR_U = 339 - 2q_U - q_A = 99 = MC.$$

Thus United's best-response function is

$$q_U = 120 - \frac{1}{2}q_A.$$

This best-response function calls for United to provide more output for any given q_A than in the original best-response function, Equation 13.6, where $q_U = 96 - \frac{1}{2}q_A$.

As a result, the Nash-Cournot equilibrium shifts from the original e_1, at which both firms sold 64, to e_2, at which United sells 96 and American sells 48. Thus the $48 subsidy to United causes it to sell the Stackelberg leader quantity and American to sell the Stackelberg follower quantity. The subsidy works by convincing American that United will produce large quantities of output.

---

[13]Don't you think that anyone who uses the phrase "level playing field" should have to pay a fine?

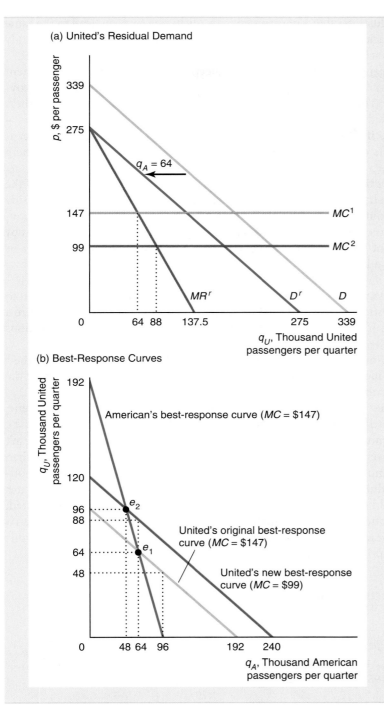

Figure 13.5 Effect of a Government Subsidy on a Cournot Equilibrium. (a) A government subsidy that lowers United's marginal cost from $MC^1 = \$147$ to $MC^2 = \$99$ causes United's best-response output to American's $q_A = 64$ to rise from $q_U = 64$ to 88. (b) If both airlines' marginal costs are $147, the Cournot equilibrium is e_1. If United's marginal cost falls to $99, its best-response function shifts outward. It now sells more tickets in response to any given American output than previously. At the new Cournot equilibrium, e_2, United sells $q_U = 96$, while American sells only $q_A = 48$.

Using the market demand curve, Equation 13.1, we find that the market price drops from $211 to $195, benefiting consumers. United's profit increases from $4.1 million to $9.2 million, while American's profit falls to $2.3 million. Consequently, United Airlines and consumers gain and American Airlines and taxpayers lose from the drop in United's marginal cost.

This example illustrates that a government subsidy to one firm *can* lead to the same outcome as in a Stackelberg equilibrium. Would a government *want* to give the subsidy that leads to the Stackelberg outcome?

The answer depends on the government's objective. Suppose that the government is interested in maximizing its domestic firm's profit net of (not including) the government's subsidy. The subsidy is a transfer from some citizens (taxpayers) to others (the owners of United). We assume that the government does not care about consumers—as is certainly true if they live in another country. Given this objective, the government maximizes its objective by setting the subsidy so as to achieve the Stackelberg equilibrium.

Table 13.3 shows the effects of various subsidies and a tax (a negative subsidy). If the subsidy is zero, we have the usual Cournot equilibrium. A $48-per-passenger subsidy leads to the same outcome as in the Stackelberg equilibrium and maximizes the government's welfare measure. At a larger subsidy, such as $60, United's profit rises, but by less than the cost of the subsidy to the government. Similarly, at smaller subsidies or taxes, welfare is also lower.

Problems with Government Intervention. Thus in theory, a government may want to subsidize its domestic firm to make it produce the same output as it would if it were a Stackelberg leader. If such subsidies are to work as desired, however, five conditions must hold.

First, the government must be able to set its subsidy before the firms choose their output levels. The idea behind this intervention is that one firm cannot act before the other, but its government can act first.

Second, the other government must not retaliate. If both governments intervene, both countries may lose, as Solved Problem 13.3 illustrates.

Third, the government's actions must be credible. If the foreign firm's country doesn't believe that the government actually will subsidize its domestic firm, the foreign firm produces the Cournot level. Countries have difficulty in committing to long-term policies. For example, during the 1996 Republican presidential primaries, many candidates said that they would reverse President Bill Clinton's trade policies if they were elected. The 2004 Democratic presidential candidates promised to change President George W. Bush's trade policies. Similarly, the major candidates for the 2008 election have conflicting views on optimal trade policies.

TABLE 13.3   Effects of a Subsidy Given to United Airlines

Subsidy,	United			American	
s	q_U	π_U	Welfare, $\pi_U - sq_U$	q_A	π_A
60	104	$10.8	$4.58	44	$1.9
48	96	$9.2	$4.61	48	$2.3
30	84	$7.1	$4.50	54	$2.9
0	64	$4.1	$4.10	64	$4.1
−30	44	$1.9	$3.30	74	$5.5

Notes: The subsidy is in dollars per passenger (and is a tax if negative).

Output units are in thousands of passengers per quarter.

Profits and welfare (defined as United's profits minus the subsidy) are in millions of dollars per quarter.

Fourth, the government must know enough about how firms behave to intervene appropriately. If it doesn't know the demand function and the costs of all firms, the government may set its subsidy at the wrong level.

Fifth, the government must know how the firms will behave. If their behavior is inconsistent with that in the Cournot model, the government would have to intervene in a different way.

Many economists who analyze strategic trade policies strongly oppose them because they are difficult to implement and mean-spirited, "beggar thy neighbor" policies. If only one government intervenes, another country's firm is harmed. If both governments intervene, both countries may suffer. For these reasons, the General Agreement on Tariffs and Trade and the World Trade Organization have forbidden the use of virtually all explicit export subsidies.

APPLICATION

Government Aircraft Subsidies

Governments consistently intervene in aircraft manufacturing markets. France, Germany, Spain, and the United Kingdom own and heavily subsidize Airbus, which competes in the widebody aircraft market with the U.S. firm Boeing. The U.S. government decries the European subsidies to Airbus while directing lucrative military contracts to Boeing that the Europeans view as implicit subsidies. In 1992, the governments signed a U.S.–EU agreement on trade in civil aircraft that limits government subsidies (including a maximum direct subsidy limit of 33% of development costs and various limits on variable costs).

Irwin and Pavcnik (2004) found that aircraft prices increased by about 3.7% after the 1992 agreement. This price hike is consistent with a 5% increase in firms' marginal costs after the subsidy cuts.

As of 2007, Washington and the European Union continue to trade counter-complaints in front of the World Trade Organization. Each again charged the other with illegally subsidizing its aircraft manufacturer. And the cycle of subsidies, charges, agreements, and new subsidies continues.

SOLVED PROBLEM 13.3

In our duopoly, linear demand, constant marginal cost example, what happens to each firm's best-response function and the Nash-Cournot equilibrium quantities if governments give each firm a specific subsidy of s (> 0) per unit of output? Illustrate your result with a figure showing how the best-response curves shift.

Answer

1. *Modify the original Cournot best-response functions and equilibrium conditions to allow for the possibility that the firms receive a per-unit subsidy:* A per-unit subsidy reduces a firm's after-subsidy marginal cost. Thus we can use the same equations we derived for the Cournot model for $n = 2$ where we replace the original marginal cost m by $m - s$. The best-response function for Firm i (for $i = 1$ or 2), formerly Equation 13.14, becomes

$$q_i = \frac{a - m + s}{2b} - \frac{1}{2} q. \tag{13.31}$$

Similarly, the equilibrium output expression, formerly Equation 13.15, becomes

$$q = \frac{a - m + s}{3b}.$$ (13.32)

If $s = 0$, Equations 13.31 and 13.32 are the original, before-subsidy best-response function and equilibrium quantity function, respectively.

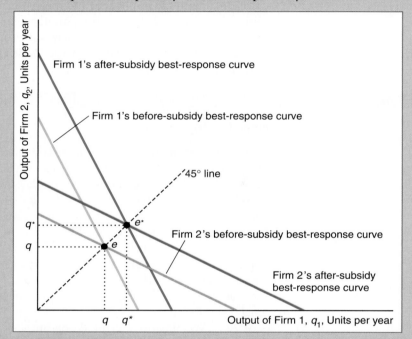

2. *Show how the best-response curves shift in response to the subsidy by differentiating the best-response function with respect to the subsidy:* Differentiating Equation 13.31 with respect to s, we find that $dq_i/ds = 1/(2b) > 0$. That is, if the other firm were to continue to produce q units of output, Firm i's best-response quantity would increase by $1/(2b)$. (In the airline example, where $b = 1$, a \$1 subsidy would cause Firm i to increase its best-response output by 1/2 unit, or 500 passengers per quarter.) Consequently, each firm's new best-response curve is parallel to the original curve and lies $1/(2b)$ units farther from the origin, as the figure shows.

3. *By differentiating the equilibrium conditions, show how the Nash-Cournot equilibrium changes as the subsidy increases:* Differentiating Equation 13.32 with respect to s, we find that $dq/ds = 1/(3b) > 0$. That is, if both firms receive the subsidy, equilibrium output for both firms rises by $1/(3b)$. In the figure, the equilibrium without the subsidy is e, where each firm produces $q = (a - m)/(3b)$, and the equilibrium with the subsidy is e^*, where each firm produces $q^* = (a - m + s)/(3b)$. (In the airline example, a \$1 subsidy would cause the equilibrium output to rise by a third of a unit, or about 333 passengers per quarter.)

Comment: In the subsidized equilibrium, the firms produce more than in the Cournot equilibrium, so both firms earn less. Thus the subsidies hurt both countries.

13.6 Comparison of Collusive, Cournot, Stackelberg, and Competitive Equilibria

In Table 13.4, we compare the Cournot and Stackelberg equilibria to the collusive and competitive equilibria for the airline example. The table demonstrates that the Cournot and Stackelberg equilibrium quantities, prices, and profits lie between those for the competitive and collusive equilibria.

How would American and United behave if they colluded? They would maximize joint profits by producing the monopoly output, 96 units, at the monopoly price, $243 per passenger (panel a of Figure 13.2). If the airlines colluded, they could split the monopoly quantity in many ways. American could act as a monopoly and serve all the passengers, $q_A = 96$ and $q_U = 0$, and possibly give United some of the profits. Or they could reverse roles so that United served everyone: $q_A = 0$ and $q_U = 96$. Or the two airlines could share the passengers in any combination such that the sum of the airlines' passengers equals the monopoly quantity:

$$q_A + q_U = 96. \tag{13.33}$$

Panel a of Figure 13.6 shows the possible collusive output combinations in Equation 13.33 as a line labeled "Contract curve." Collusive firms could write a contract in which they agree to produce at any of the points along this curve. In the figure, we assume that the collusive firms split the market equally so that $q_A = q_U = 48$.

If the firms were to act as price takers, they would each produce where their residual demand curve intersects their marginal cost curve, so price would equal marginal cost of $147. The price-taking equilibrium is $q_A = q_U = 96$.

The cartel profits are the highest-possible level of profits that the firms can earn. The contract curve shows how the firms split the total monopoly-level profit. Panel b of Figure 13.6 shows the profit possibility frontier, which corresponds to the contract curve. At the upper left of the profit possibility frontier, United is a monopoly and earns

TABLE 13.4 Comparison of Airline Market Structures

	Monopoly	Cartel	Cournot	Stackelberg	Price Taking
q_A	96	48	64	96	96
q_U	0	48	64	48	96
$Q = q_A + q_U$	96	96	128	144	192
p	$243	$243	$211	$195	$147
π_A	$9.2	$4.6	$4.1	$4.6	$0
π_U	$0	$4.6	$4.1	$2.3	$0
Total profit $\Pi = \pi_A + \pi_U$	$9.2	$9.2	$8.2	$6.9	$0
Consumer surplus, CS	$4.6	$4.6	$8.2	$10.4	$18.4
Welfare, $W = CS + \Pi$	$13.8	$13.8	$16.4	$17.3	$18.4
Deadweight loss, DWL	$4.6	$4.6	$2.0	$1.2	$0

Notes: Passengers are in thousands per quarter.

Price is in dollars per passenger.

Profits, consumer surplus, welfare, and deadweight loss are in millions of dollars per quarter.

Figure 13.6 Duopoly Equilibria. (a) The intersection of the best-response curves determines the Cournot equilibrium. The possible cartel equilibria lie on the contract curve. If the firms act as price takers, each firm produces where its residual demand equals its marginal cost. (b) The highest possible profit for the two firms combined is given by the profit possibility frontier. It reflects all the possible collusive equilibria, including the one indicated where the firms split the market equally. All equilibria except collusive ones lie within the profit possibility frontier.

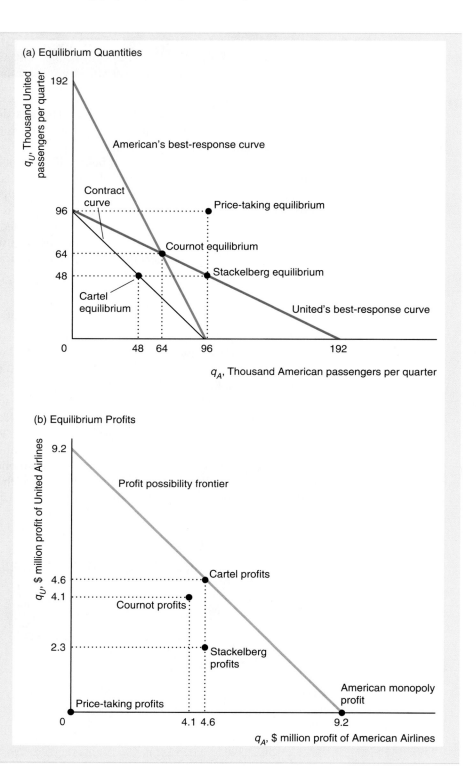

(a) Equilibrium Quantities

q_U, Thousand United passengers per quarter

American's best-response curve

Contract curve

Price-taking equilibrium

Cournot equilibrium

Stackelberg equilibrium

Cartel equilibrium

United's best-response curve

q_A, Thousand American passengers per quarter

(b) Equilibrium Profits

q_U, $ million profit of United Airlines

Profit possibility frontier

Cartel profits

Cournot profits

Stackelberg profits

Price-taking profits

American monopoly profit

q_A, $ million profit of American Airlines

the entire monopoly profit of approximately $9.2 million per quarter.[14] At the lower right, American earns the entire monopoly profit. At points in between, they split the profit. Where they split the profit equally, each earns approximately $4.6 million.

In contrast, if the firms act independently, each earns the Cournot profit of approximately $4.1 million. Because the Cournot price, $211, is lower than the cartel price, $243, consumers are better off if the firms act independently than if they collude. The Stackelberg leader earns $4.6 million, which is more than it could earn in a Cournot outcome, $4.1 million. Total Stackelberg profit, $6.9 million, is less than total Cournot profit, $8.2 million, because the Stackelberg follower, earning $2.3 million, is much worse off than in the Cournot equilibrium.

Table 13.4 also shows how welfare measures vary with market structure. As we did in Chapter 9, we define welfare as consumer surplus plus producer surplus, which is the sum of the two firms' profits in our example.

At one extreme, if one firm has a monopoly or if the two firms form a cartel and split the market equally, total output is relatively low, price is high, consumer surplus and welfare are low, and deadweight loss is high. At the other extreme, if American and United act as price takers, output is relatively high, price is low, consumer surplus and welfare are high, and society does not suffer a deadweight loss.

The duopoly Cournot and Stackelberg equilibria (in the table, American is the leader) lie between the extreme cases of monopoly or cartel and price taking. The Stackelberg equilibrium is closer to the price-taking equilibrium than the Cournot equilibrium in terms of total output, price, consumer surplus, welfare, and deadweight loss.

We showed that the Cournot equilibrium approaches the price-taking equilibrium as the number of firms grows. Similarly, we can show that the Stackelberg equilibrium approaches the price-taking equilibrium as the number of Stackelberg followers grows. As a result, the differences between the Cournot, Stackelberg, and price-taking market structures shrink as the number of firms grows.

● APPLICATION

Deadweight Losses in the Food and Tobacco Industries

Bhuyan and Lopez (1998) and Bhuyan (2000) estimated the deadweight loss for various U.S. food and tobacco manufacturing oligopolies and monopolistically competitive markets. Most of these industries have deadweight losses that are a relatively small percentage of sales because their prices and quantities are close to competitive levels. However, a few industries, such as cereal and flour and grain mills, have deadweight losses that are a relatively large share of sales, as the last column of the table shows.

Industry	Loss, $ millions	Share of Sales, %
Cereal	2,192	33
Flour and grain mills	541	26
Poultry and eggs	1,183	8
Roasted coffee	440	7
Cigarettes	1,032	6
All food manufacturing	14,947	5

[14]Each firm's profit per passenger is price minus average cost, $p - AC$, so the firm's profit is $\pi = (p - AC)q$, where q is the number of passengers the firm flies. The monopoly price is $243 and the average cost is $147, so the monopoly profit is $\pi = (243 - 147) \times 96$ units per quarter = $9.216 million per quarter.

13.7   Bertrand Oligopoly Model

We have examined how oligopolistic firms set quantities to try to maximize their profits. However, many such firms set prices instead of quantities and allow consumers to decide how much to buy. The market equilibrium is different if firms set prices rather than quantities.

In monopolistic and competitive markets, the issue of whether firms set quantities or prices does not arise. Competitive firms have no choice: They cannot affect price and hence can choose only quantity (Chapter 8). The monopoly equilibrium is the same whether the monopoly sets price or quantity (Chapter 11).

In 1883, the French mathematician Joseph Bertrand argued that oligopolies set prices and then consumers decide how many units to buy. The resulting Nash equilibrium is called a **Bertrand equilibrium** or **Nash-Bertrand equilibrium** (or *Nash-in-prices equilibrium*): a set of prices such that no firm can obtain a higher profit by choosing a different price if the other firms continue to charge these prices.

Our analysis in this section shows that the price and quantity in a Nash-Bertrand equilibrium are different from those in a Cournot equilibrium. In addition, the properties of the Nash-Bertrand equilibrium depend on whether firms are producing identical or differentiated products.

BERTRAND EQUILIBRIUM WITH IDENTICAL PRODUCTS

We start by examining a price-setting oligopoly in which firms have identical costs and produce identical goods. The resulting Nash-Bertrand equilibrium price equals the marginal cost, as in the price-taking equilibrium. To show this result, we use best-response curves to determine the Nash-Bertrand equilibrium, as we did in the Nash-Cournot model.

Best-Response Curves. Suppose that each of the two price-setting oligopoly firms in a market produces an identical product and faces a constant marginal and average cost of $5 per unit. What is Firm 1's best response—what price should it set—if Firm 2 sets a price of $p_2 = \$10$? If Firm 1 charges more than $10, it makes no sales because consumers will buy from Firm 2. Firm 1 makes a profit of $5 on each unit it sells if it also charges $10 per unit. If the market demand is 200 units and both firms charge the same price, we would expect Firm 1 to make half the sales, so its profit is $500.

Suppose, however, that Firm 1 slightly undercuts its rival's price by charging $9.99. Because the products are identical, Firm 1 captures the entire market. Firm 1 makes a profit of $4.99 per unit and a total profit of $998. Thus Firm 1's profit is higher if it slightly undercuts its rival's price. By similar reasoning, if Firm 2 charges $8, Firm 1 also charges slightly less than Firm 2.

Now imagine that Firm 2 charges $p_2 = \$5$. If Firm 1 charges more than $5, it makes no sales. The firms split the market and make zero profit if Firm 1 charges $5. If Firm 1 undercuts its rival, it captures the entire market, but it makes a loss on each unit. Thus Firm 1 will undercut only if its rival's price is higher than Firm 1's marginal and average cost of $5. By similar reasoning, if Firm 2 charges less than $5, Firm 1 chooses not to produce.

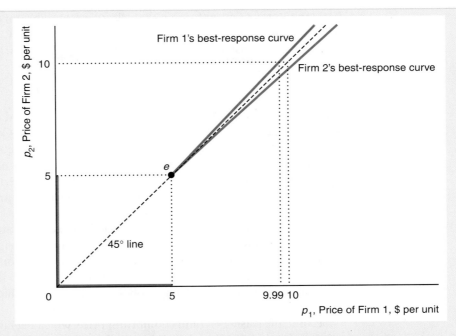

Figure 13.7 Bertrand Equilibrium with Identical Products. With identical products and constant marginal and average costs of $5, Firm 1's best-response curve starts at $5 and then lies slightly above the 45° line. That is, Firm 1 undercuts its rival's price as long as its price remains above $5. The best-response curves intersect at *e*, the Bertrand or Nash equilibrium, where both firms charge $5.

Figure 13.7 shows that Firm 1's best response is to produce nothing if Firm 2 charges less than $5. Firm 1's best response is $5 if Firm 2 charges $5. If Firm 2 sets its price above $5, Firm 1's best response is to undercut Firm 2's price slightly. Above $5, Firm 1's best-response curve is above the 45° line by the smallest amount possible. (The distance of the best-response curve from the 45° line is exaggerated in the figure for clarity.) By the same reasoning, Firm 2's best-response curve starts at $5 and lies slightly below the 45° line.

The two best-response functions intersect only at *e*, where each firm charges $5. It does not pay for either firm to change its price as long as the other charges $5, so *e* is a Nash-Bertrand equilibrium. In this equilibrium, each firm makes zero profit. Thus *the Nash-Bertrand equilibrium when firms produce identical products is the same as the price-taking, competitive equilibrium.*[15] This result remains the same for larger numbers of firms.

---

[15]This result depends heavily on the firms' facing a constant marginal cost. If firms face a binding capacity constraint so that the marginal cost eventually becomes large (infinite), the Nash-Bertrand equilibrium may be the same as the Nash-Cournot equilibrium (Kreps and Scheinkman, 1983).

Bertrand Versus Cournot. This Nash-Bertrand equilibrium differs substantially from the Nash-Cournot equilibrium. We can calculate the Nash-Cournot equilibrium price for firms with constant marginal costs of $5 per unit by rearranging Equation 13.10:

$$p = \frac{MC}{1 + 1/(n\varepsilon)} = \frac{\$5}{1 + 1/(n\varepsilon)}, \tag{13.34}$$

where n is the number of firms and ε is the market demand elasticity. For example, if the market demand elasticity is $\varepsilon = -1$ and $n = 2$, the Nash-Cournot equilibrium price is $\$5/(1 - \frac{1}{2}) = \$10$, which is double the Nash-Bertrand equilibrium price.

When firms produce identical products and have a constant marginal cost, the Nash-Cournot model is more plausible than the Nash-Bertrand model. The Nash-Bertrand model—unlike the Nash-Cournot model—appears inconsistent with real oligopoly markets in at least two ways.

First, the Nash-Bertrand model's "competitive" equilibrium price is implausible. In a market with few firms, why would the firms compete so vigorously that they would make no profit, as in the Nash-Bertrand equilibrium? In contrast, the Nash-Cournot equilibrium price with a small number of firms lies between the competitive price and the monopoly price. Because oligopolies typically charge a higher price than competitive firms, the Nash-Cournot equilibrium is more plausible.

Second, the Nash-Bertrand equilibrium price, which depends only on cost, is insensitive to demand conditions and the number of firms. In contrast, the Nash-Cournot equilibrium price, Equation 13.10, depends on demand conditions and the number of firms as well as on costs. In our last example, if the number of firms rises from two to three, the Cournot price falls from $10 to $\$5/(1 - \frac{1}{3}) = \$7.50$, but the Nash-Bertrand equilibrium price remains constant at $5. Again, the Cournot model is more plausible because we usually observe market price changing with the number of firms and demand conditions, not just with changes in costs. Thus for both of these reasons, economists are much more likely to use the Cournot model than the Bertrand model to study markets in which firms produce identical goods.

NASH-BERTRAND EQUILIBRIUM WITH DIFFERENTIATED PRODUCTS

Why don't they make mouse-flavored cat food? —Steven Wright

If most markets were characterized by firms producing homogeneous goods, the Bertrand model would probably have been forgotten. However, markets with differentiated goods—such as those for automobiles, stereos, computers, toothpaste, and spaghetti sauce—are extremely common, as is price setting by firms. In such markets, the Nash-Bertrand equilibrium is plausible, and the two "problems" of the homogeneous-goods model disappear. That is, firms set prices above marginal cost, and prices are sensitive to demand conditions.

Indeed, many economists believe that price-setting models are more plausible than quantity-setting models when goods are differentiated. If products are differentiated and firms set prices, then consumers determine quantities. In contrast, if firms set quantities, it is not clear how the prices of the differentiated goods are determined in the market.

The main reason the differentiated-goods Bertrand model differs from the undifferentiated-goods version is that one firm can charge more than another for a differentiated product without losing all its sales. For example, Coke and Pepsi produce similar but not identical products; many consumers prefer one to the other.[16] If the price of Pepsi were to fall slightly relative to that of Coke, most consumers who prefer Coke to Pepsi would not switch. Thus neither firm has to match its rival's price cut exactly to continue to sell cola.

Product differentiation allows a firm to charge a higher price because the differentiation causes its residual demand curve to become less elastic. That is, a given decrease in the price charged by a rival lowers the demand for this firm's product by *less,* the less substitutable the two goods. In contrast, if consumers view the goods as perfect substitutes, a small drop in the rival's price causes this firm to lose all its sales. For this reason, differentiation leads to higher equilibrium prices and profits in both the Bertrand and the Cournot models. As a result, a firm aggressively differentiates its products so as to raise its profit.[17]

General Demand Functions. We can use math to determine the Nash-Bertrand equilibrium for a duopoly. We derive equilibrium for general demand functions, and then we present the solution for the cola market. In both analyses, we first determine the best-response functions for each firm and then solve these best-response functions simultaneously for the equilibrium prices for the two firms.

Each firm's demand function depends on its own price and the other firm's price. The demand function for Firm 1 is $q_1 = q_1(p_1, p_2)$ and that of Firm 2 is $q_2 = q_2(p_1, p_2)$. For simplicity, we assume that marginal cost for both firms is constant, m, and neither has a fixed cost.

Firm 1's objective is to set its price so as to maximize its profit,

$$\max_{p_1} \pi_1(p_1, p_2) = (p_1 - m)q_1(p_1, p_2), \tag{13.35}$$

where $(p_1 - m)$ is the profit per unit. Firm 1 views p_2 as a constant. Firm 1's first-order condition is the derivative of its profit with respect to p_1 set equal to zero:

$$\frac{\partial \pi_1}{\partial p_1} = q_1(p_1, p_2) + (p_1 - m)\frac{\partial q_1(p_1, p_2)}{\partial p_1} = 0. \tag{13.36}$$

Equation 13.36 contains the information in Firm 1's best-response function: $p_1 = B_1(p_2)$.

Similarly, we can derive Firm 2's best-response function. Solving the best-response functions, Equations 13.35 and 13.36, simultaneously, we obtain the Nash-Bertrand equilibrium prices: p_1 and p_2. We illustrate this procedure for Coke and Pepsi.

---

[16]The critical issue is whether consumers believe products differ rather than whether the products physically differ because the consumers' beliefs affect their buying behavior. Although few consumers can reliably distinguish Coke from Pepsi in blind taste tests, many consumers strongly prefer buying one product over the other. I have run blind taste tests in my classes over the years involving literally thousands of students. Given a choice between Coke, Pepsi, and a generic cola, the share that can correctly identify the products does differ significantly from what one would expect from random guesses. People who do not regularly drink these products generally admit that they can't tell the difference. Apparently very few of the regular cola drinks can clearly distinguish among the brands.

[17]Chance that a British baby's first word is a brand name: 1 in 4.—*Harper's Index 2004.*

Cola Market. Because many consumers view Coke and Pepsi as imperfect substitutes, the demand for each good depends on both firms' prices. Gasmi, Laffont, and Vuong (1992) estimated the demand curve of Coke:[18]

$$q_C = 58 - 4p_C + 2p_P, \tag{13.37}$$

where q_C is the quantity of Coke demanded in tens of millions of cases (a case consists of 24 twelve-ounce cans) per quarter, p_C is the price of 10 cases of Coke, and p_P is the price of 10 cases of Pepsi. Partially differentiating Equation 13.37 with respect to p_C (that is, holding the price of Pepsi constant), we find that the change in quantity for every dollar change in price is $\partial q_C / \partial p_C = -4$, so a \$1-per-unit increase in the price of Coke causes the quantity of Coke demanded to fall by 4 units. Similarly, the demand for Coke rises by 2 units if the price of Pepsi rises by \$1, while the price of Coke remains constant: $\partial q_C / \partial p_P = 2$.

If Coke faces a constant marginal and average cost of m per unit, its profit is

$$\pi_C(p_C) = (p_C - m)q_C = (p_C - m)(58 - 4p_C + 2p_P). \tag{13.38}$$

To determine Coke's profit-maximizing price given that Pepsi's price is held constant, we set the partial derivative of the profit function, Equation 13.38, with respect to the price of Coke equal to zero,

$$\frac{\partial \pi_C}{\partial p_C} = q_C + (p_C - m)\frac{\partial q_C}{\partial p_C} = q_C - 4(p_C - m) = 0, \tag{13.39}$$

and solve for p_C as a function of p_P and m to find Coke's best-response function:

$$p_C = 7.25 + 0.25p_P + 0.5m. \tag{13.40}$$

Coke's best-response function tells us the price Coke charges that maximizes its profit as a function of the price Pepsi charges. Equation 13.40 shows that Coke's best-response price is 25¢ higher for every extra dollar that Pepsi charges and 50¢ higher for every extra dollar of Coke's marginal cost. Figure 13.8 plots Coke's best-response curve given that Coke's average and marginal cost of production is \$5 per unit, so its best-response function is

$$p_C = 9.75 + 0.25p_P. \tag{13.41}$$

If $p_P = \$13$, then Coke's best response is to set p_C at \$13.

Pepsi's demand curve is

$$q_P = 63.2 - 4p_P + 1.6p_C. \tag{13.42}$$

Using the same approach as we used for Coke, we find that Pepsi's best-response function (for $m = \$5$) is

$$p_P = 10.4 + 0.2p_C. \tag{13.43}$$

Thus neither firm's best-response curve in Figure 13.8 lies along a 45° line through the origin. The Bertrand best-response curves have different slopes than the Cournot best-response curves in Figure 13.3. The Cournot best-response curves—which plot

---

[18]Their estimated model allows the firms to set both prices and advertising. We assume that the firms' advertising is held constant. The Coke equation is the authors' estimates (with slight rounding). The Pepsi demand equation reported below is rescaled so that the equilibrium prices of Coke and Pepsi are equal. Prices (to retailers) and costs are in real 1982 dollars per 10 cases.

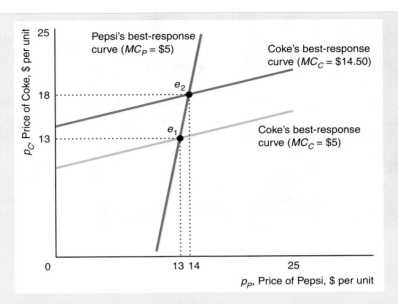

Figure 13.8 Bertrand Equilibrium with Differentiated Products. If both firms have a constant marginal cost of $5, the best-response curves of Coke and Pepsi intersect at e_1, where each sets a price of $13 per unit. If Coke's marginal cost rises to $14.50, its best-response function shifts upward. In the new equilibrium, e_2, Coke charges a higher price, $18, than Pepsi, $14.

relationships between quantities—slope downward, showing that a firm produces less the more it expects its rival to produce.[19] In Figure 13.8, the Bertrand best-response curves—which plot relationships between prices—slope upward, indicating that a firm charges a higher price the higher the price the firm expects its rival to charge.

The intersection of Coke's and Pepsi's best-response functions, Equations 13.41 and 13.43, determines the Nash equilibrium. By substituting Pepsi's best-response function, Equation 13.43, for p_P in Coke's best-response function, Equation 13.41, we find that

$$p_C = 9.75 + 0.25(10.4 + 0.2p_C).$$

The solution to this equation is that p_C—the equilibrium price of Coke—is $13. Substituting $p_C = $13 into Equation 13.43, we discover that the equilibrium price of Pepsi is also $13, as Figure 13.8 illustrates.

In this Nash-Bertrand equilibrium, each firm sets its best-response price *given the price the other firm is charging*. Neither firm wants to change its price because neither firm can increase its profit by so doing.

Product Differentiation and Welfare. We've just seen that prices are likely to be higher when products are differentiated than when they are identical, all else the same. We also know that welfare falls as the gap between price and marginal cost rises.

---

[19]Even for differentiated goods, Cournot best-response functions slope down—see the best-response functions in Solved Problem 13.2.

Does it follow that differentiating products lowers welfare? Not necessarily. Although differentiation leads to higher prices, which harm consumers, differentiation is desirable in its own right. Consumers value having a choice, and some may greatly prefer a new brand to existing ones.

One way to illustrate the importance of this second effect is to consider what the value is of introducing a new, differentiated product. This value reflects how much extra income consumers would require to be as well off without the good as with it.

APPLICATION

Welfare Gain from Greater Toilet Paper Variety

An article in the *Economist* asked, "Why does it cost more to wipe your bottom in Britain than in any other country in the European Union?" The answer given was that British consumers are "extremely fussy" in demanding a soft, luxurious texture—in contrast to barbarians elsewhere. As a consequence, they pay twice as much for toilet paper as the Germans and French, and nearly 2.5 times as much as Americans.

Probably completely uninfluenced by this important cross-country research, Hausman and Leonard (2002) used U.S. data to measure the price effect and the extra consumer surplus from greater variety resulting from Kimberly-Clark's introduction of Kleenex Bath Tissue (KBT). Bath tissue products are divided into premium, economy, and private labels, with premium receiving more than 70% of revenue. Before KBT's entry, the major premium brands were Angel Soft, Charmin, Cottonelle, and Northern. ScotTissue was the leading economy brand.

Firms incur a sizable fixed cost from capital investments. The marginal cost depends primarily on the price of wood pulp, which varies cyclically. Because KBT was rolled out in various cities at different times, Hausman and Leonard could compare the effects of entry at various times and control for variations in cost and other factors.

The prices of all rival brands fell after KBT entered; the price of the leading brand, Charmin, dropped by 3.5%, while Cottonelle's price plummeted 8.2%. In contrast, the price of ScotTissue, an economy brand, decreased by only 0.6%.

Hausman and Leonard calculated that the additional consumer surplus due to extra variety was $33.4 million, or 3.5% of sales. When they included the gains due to lower prices, the total consumer surplus increase was $69.2 million, or 7.3% of sales. Thus the gains to consumers were roughly equally divided between the price effect and the benefit from extra variety.

13.8 Monopolistic Competition

So far, we've concentrated on oligopoly firms—firms whose number is fixed because of barriers to entry. We've seen that these oligopoly firms (such as the airlines in our example) may earn economic profits. We now consider firms in monopolistically competitive markets in which there are no barriers to entry, so firms enter the market until no more firms can enter profitably.

If both competitive and monopolistically competitive firms make zero profits, what distinguishes these two market structures? Competitive firms face horizontal residual demand curves and charge prices equal to marginal cost. In contrast, monopolistically competitive firms face downward-sloping residual demand curves and thus charge prices above marginal cost. Monopolistically competitive firms face downward-sloping residual demand because (unlike competitive firms) they have relatively few rivals or sell differentiated products.

The fewer monopolistically competitive firms, the less elastic the residual demand curve each firm faces. As we saw, the elasticity of demand for an individual Cournot firm is $n\varepsilon$, where n is the number of firms and ε is the market elasticity. Thus the fewer the firms in a market, the less elastic the residual demand curve.

When monopolistically competitive firms benefit from economies of scale at high levels of output (the average cost curve is downward sloping), so that each firm is relatively large in comparison to market demand, there is room in the market for only a few firms. In the short run, if fixed costs are large and marginal costs are constant or diminishing, firms have economies of scale (Chapter 7) at all output levels, so there are relatively few firms in the market. In an extreme case with substantial enough economies of scale, the market may have room for only one firm: a natural monopoly (Chapter 11). The number of firms in equilibrium is smaller the greater the economies of scale and the farther to the left the market demand curve.

Monopolistically competitive firms also face downward-sloping residual demand curves if each firm differentiates its product so that at least some consumers believe that product is superior to other brands. If some consumers believe that Tide laundry detergent is better than Cheer and other brands, Tide won't lose all its sales even if Tide has a slightly higher price than Cheer. Thus Tide faces a downward-sloping demand curve—not a horizontal one.

MONOPOLISTICALLY COMPETITIVE EQUILIBRIUM

In a monopolistically competitive market, each firm tries to maximize its profit, but each makes zero economic profit due to entry. Two conditions hold in a monopolistically competitive equilibrium: *marginal revenue equals marginal cost* because firms set output to maximize profit, and *price equals average cost* because firms enter until no further profitable entry is possible.

Figure 13.9 shows a monopolistically competitive market equilibrium. A typical monopolistically competitive firm faces a residual demand curve D^r. To maximize its profit, the firm sets its output, q, where its marginal revenue curve corresponding to the residual demand curve intersects its marginal cost curve: $MR^r = MC$. At that quantity, the firm's average cost curve, AC, is tangent to its residual demand curve. Because the height of the residual demand curve is the price, at the tangency point price equals average cost, $p = AC$, and the firm makes zero profit.

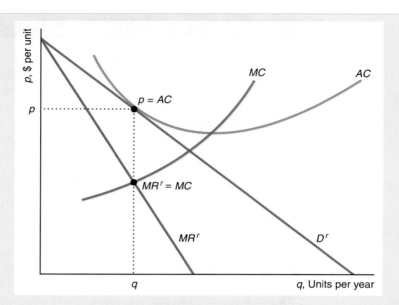

Figure 13.9 Monopolistically Competitive Equilibrium. A monopolistically competitive firm, facing residual demand curve D^r, sets its output where its marginal revenue equals its marginal cost: $MR^r = MC$. Because firms can enter this market, the profit of the firm is driven to zero, so price equals the firm's average cost: $p = AC$.

If the average cost were less than price at that quantity, firms would make positive profits and entrants would be attracted. If average cost were above price, firms would lose money, so firms would exit until the marginal firm was breaking even.

The smallest quantity at which the average cost curve reaches its minimum is referred to as *full capacity* or **minimum efficient scale.** The firm's full capacity or minimum efficient scale is the quantity at which the firm no longer benefits from economies of scale. Because a monopolistically competitive equilibrium occurs in the downward-sloping section of the average cost curve (where the average cost curve is tangent to the downward-sloping demand curve), a monopolistically competitive firm operates at less than full capacity in the long run.

FIXED COSTS AND THE NUMBER OF FIRMS

The number of firms in a monopolistically competitive equilibrium depends on firms' costs. The larger each firm's fixed cost, the smaller the number of monopolistically competitive firms in the market equilibrium.

Although entry is free, if the fixed costs are high, few firms may enter. In the automobile industry, just to develop a new fender costs $8 to $10 million.[20] Developing a new pharmaceutical drug may cost $350 million or more.

We can illustrate this relationship using the airline example, where we now modify our assumptions about entry and fixed costs. Recall that American and United are the only

---

[20]James B. Treece ("Sometimes, You Gotta Have Size," *Business Week*, Enterprise 1993:200–1) illustrates the importance of fixed costs on entry in the following anecdote: "In 1946, steel magnate Henry J. Kaiser boasted to a Detroit dinner gathering that two recent stock offerings had raised a huge $50 million to invest in his budding car company. Suddenly, a voice from the back of the room shot out: 'Give that man one white chip.'"

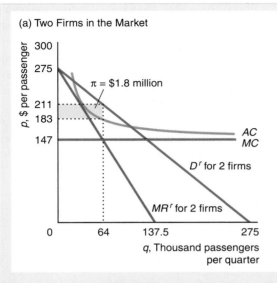

(a) Two Firms in the Market

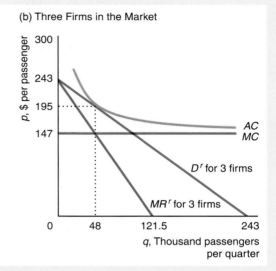

(b) Three Firms in the Market

Figure 13.10 Monopolistic Competition Among Airlines. (a) If each identical airline has a fixed cost of $2.3 million and there are two firms in the market, each firm flies $q = 64$ units (thousands of passengers) per quarter at a price of $p = \$211$ per passenger and makes a profit of $1.8 million. This profit attracts entry. (b) After a third firm enters, the residual demand curve shifts, so each firm flies $q = 48$ units at $p = \$195$ and makes zero profit, which is the monopolistically competitive equilibrium.

airlines providing service on the Chicago–Los Angeles route. Until now, we have assumed that a barrier to entry—such as an inability to obtain landing rights at both airports—prevented entry and that the firms had no fixed costs. If fixed cost is zero and marginal cost is constant at $147 per passenger, average cost is also constant at $147 per passenger. As we showed earlier, each firm in this oligopolistic market flies $q = 64$ thousand passengers per quarter at a price of $p = \$211$ and makes a profit of $4.1 million per quarter.

Now suppose that there are no barriers to entry and each airline firm incurs a fixed cost, F, due to airport fees, capital expenditure, or other factors. Each firm's marginal cost remains $147 per passenger, but its average cost,

$$AC = 147 + \frac{F}{q},$$

falls as the number of passengers rises, as panels a and b of Figure 13.10 illustrate for $F = \$2.3$ million.

If there are only two firms in a monopolistically competitive market, what must the fixed costs be so that the two firms earn zero profit? We know that these firms each receive a profit of $4.1 million in the absence of fixed costs. As a result, the fixed cost must be $4.1 million per firm for the firms to earn zero profit. With this fixed cost, the monopolistically competitive price and quantity are the same as they are in the oligopolistic equilibrium, $q = 64$ and $p = \$211$, and the number of firms is the same, but now each firm's profit is zero.

If the fixed cost is only $2.3 million and there are only two firms in the market, each firm makes a profit, as panel a shows. Each duopoly firm faces a residual demand curve (labeled "D^r for 2 firms"), which is the market demand minus its rival's Cournot equilibrium quantity, $q = 64$. Given this residual demand, each firm produces $q = 64$, which equates its marginal revenue, MR^r, and its marginal cost, MC. At $q = 64$, the firm's average cost is $AC = \$147 + (\$2.3 \text{ million})/(64 \text{ units}) \approx \$183$, so each firm makes a profit of $\pi = (p - AC)q \approx (\$211 - \$183) \times 64$ units per quarter $\approx \$1.8$ million per quarter.

This substantial economic profit attracts an entrant. The entry of a third firm causes the residual demand for any one firm to shift to the left in panel b. In the new equilibrium, each firm sets $q = 48$ and charges $p = \$195$. At this quantity, each firm's average cost is $195, so the firms break even. No other firms enter because if another one did, the residual demand curve would shift even farther to the left and all the firms would lose money. Thus if the fixed cost is $2.3 million, there are three firms in the monopolistically competitive equilibrium. This example illustrates a general result: *The lower the fixed costs, the more firms there are in the monopolistically competitive equilibrium.*

SOLVED PROBLEM   13.4

What is the monopolistically competitive airline equilibrium if each firm has a fixed cost of $3 million?

Answer

1. *Determine the number of firms:* We already know that the monopolistically competitive equilibrium has two firms if the fixed cost is $4.1 million and three firms if the fixed cost is $2.3 million. With a fixed cost of $3 million, if there are only two firms in the market, each makes a profit of $1.1 (= $4.1 − 3) million. If another firm enters, though, each firm's loss is −$0.7 (= $2.3 − 3) million. Thus the monopolistically competitive equilibrium has two firms, each of which earns a positive profit that is too small to attract another firm. This outcome is a monopolistically competitive equilibrium because no other firm wants to enter.

2. *Determine the equilibrium quantities and prices:* We already know that each duopoly firm produces $q = 64$, so $Q = 128$ and $p = \$211$.

Summary

1. **Market Structures:** Prices, profits, and quantities in a market equilibrium depend on the market's structure. Because profit-maximizing firms set marginal revenue equal to marginal cost, price is above marginal revenue—and hence marginal cost—only if firms face downward-sloping demand curves. In monopoly, oligopoly, and monopolistically competitive markets, firms face downward-sloping demand curves, in contrast to firms in a competitive market. When entry is blocked, as with a monopoly or an oligopoly, firms may earn positive profits; however, when entry is free, as in competition or monopolistic competition, profits are driven toward zero. Noncooperative oligopoly and monopolistically competitive firms, in contrast to competitive and monopoly firms, must pay attention to their rivals.

2. **Cartels:** If firms successfully collude, they produce the monopoly output and collectively earn the monopoly level of profit. Although their collective profits rise if all firms collude, each individual firm has an incentive to cheat on the cartel arrangement so as to raise its own profit even higher. For cartel prices to remain high, cartel members must be able to detect and prevent cheating, and noncartel firms must not be able to supply very much output. When antitrust laws or competition policies prevent firms from colluding, firms may try to merge if permitted by law.

3. **Noncooperative Oligopoly:** If oligopoly firms act independently, equilibrium output, price, and total firm profit lie between those of competition and cartel (monopoly). The market outcome depends on the characteristics of the market such as the number of firms, whether the firms produce differentiated products, and whether the firms act simultaneously or sequentially.

4. **Cournot Oligopoly Model:** If oligopoly firms act independently, market output and firms' profits lie between the competitive and monopoly levels. In a Cournot model, each oligopoly firm sets its output at the same time. In the Cournot (Nash) equilibrium, each firm

produces its best-response output—the output that maximizes its profit—given the output its rival produces. As the number of Cournot firms increases, the Cournot equilibrium price, quantity, and profits approach the price-taking levels.

5. **Stackelberg Oligopoly Model:** If one firm, the Stackelberg leader, chooses its output before its rivals, the Stackelberg followers, the leader produces more and earns a higher profit than each identical-cost follower firm. A government may subsidize a domestic oligopoly firm so that the firm produces the Stackelberg leader quantity, which it sells in an international market. For a given number of firms, the Stackelberg equilibrium output is less than the efficient (competitive market) level but exceeds that of the Cournot equilibrium, which exceeds that of the collusive equilibrium (which is the same as a monopoly produces). Correspondingly, the Stackelberg price is more than marginal cost but less than the Cournot price, which is less than the collusive or monopoly price.

6. **Comparison of Collusive, Cournot, Stackelberg, and Competitive Equilibria:** Total market output is maximized and price is minimized under competition. For a given number of firms, the Stackelberg equilibrium output exceeds that of the Cournot equilibrium, which is greater than that of the collusive or monopoly equilibrium. Correspondingly, the Stackelberg price is less than the Cournot price, which is less than the collusive or monopoly price.

7. **Bertrand Oligopoly Model:** In many oligopolistic or monopolistically competitive markets, firms set prices instead of quantities. If the product is homogeneous and firms set prices, the Bertrand equilibrium price equals marginal cost (which is lower than the Cournot quantity-setting equilibrium price). If the products are differentiated, the Bertrand equilibrium price is above marginal cost. Typically, the markup of price over marginal cost is greater the more the goods are differentiated.

8. **Monopolistic Competition:** In monopolistically competitive markets after all profitable entry occurs, there are few enough firms such that each firm faces a downward-sloping demand curve. Consequently, the firms charge prices above marginal cost. These markets are not perfectly competitive because there are relatively few firms—possibly because of high fixed costs or economies of scale that are large relative to market demand—or because the firms sell differentiated products.

Questions

* = *answer at the back of this book;* **W** = *audio-slide show answers by James Dearden at* **www.aw-bc.com/perloff**

1. At each Organization of Petroleum Exporting Countries (OPEC) meeting, Saudi Arabia, the largest oil producer, argues that the cartel should cut production. The Saudis complain that most OPEC countries, including Saudi Arabia (but not Indonesia or Venezuela), produce more oil than they are allotted under their cartel agreement (Simon Romero, "Saudis Push Plan for Cut in Production by OPEC," *New York Times,* March 31, 2004). Use a graph and words to explain why cartel members would produce more than the allotted amount given that they know that overproduction will drive down the price of their product.

*2. Your college is considering renting space in the student union to one or two commercial textbook stores. The rent the college can charge per square foot of space depends on the profit (before rent) of the firms and hence on whether there is a monopoly or a duopoly. Which number of stores is better for the college in terms of rent? Which is better for students? Why?

3. In the "Bail Bonds" application, the price tends to fall as the number of firms rises above 2, but prices are higher in New Haven (8 firms) and Bridgeport (10 firms) than in Norwalk (3 firms). Give possible explanations for this pattern.

4. The application "Deadweight Losses in the Food and Tobacco Industries" shows that the deadweight loss as a fraction of sales varies substantially across industries. One possible explanation is that the number of firms (degree of competition) varies across industries. Using Table 13.2, show how the deadweight loss varies in the airline market as the number of firms increases from one to three.

5. Southwest Airlines' cost to fly one seat 1 mile is 7.38¢ compared to 15.20¢ for USAir (*New York Times,* August 20, 2002:C4). Assuming that Southwest and USAir compete on a route, use a graph to show that their equilibrium quantities differ. (*Hint:* See Solved Problem 13.1.)

6. In 2005, the prices for 36 prescription painkillers shot up as much as 15% since Merck yanked its once-popular arthritis drug Vioxx from the market due to fears that it caused heart problems ("Prices Climb as Much as 15% for Some Painkillers," *Los Angeles Times,* June 3, 2005: C3). Can this product's exit be the cause of the price increases if the prices reflect a Cournot equilibrium? Explain.

7. Plot the best-response curve of the second firm in Solved Problem 13.1 if its marginal cost is m and if it is $m + x$. Add the first firm's best-response curve and show how the

Nash-Cournot equilibrium changes as its marginal cost increases.

8. What is the effect of a government subsidy that reduces the fixed cost of each firm in an industry in a Cournot monopolistic competition equilibrium?

9. In the monopolistically competitive airlines model, what is the equilibrium if firms face no fixed costs?

10. In a monopolistically competitive market, the government applies a specific tax of $1 per unit of output. What happens to the profit of a typical firm in this market? Does the number of firms in the market change? Why?

11. Does an oligopoly or a monopolistically competitive firm have a supply curve? Why or why not? (*Hint:* See the discussion in Chapter 11 of whether a monopoly has a supply curve.)

12. In the Coke and Pepsi example, what is the effect of a specific tax, τ, on the equilibrium prices? (*Hint:* What does the tax do to the firm's marginal cost? You do not have to use math to answer this problem.)

13. In 1998, California became the first state to adopt rules requiring many sport-utility vehicles, pickups, and minivans to meet the same pollution standards as regular cars, effective in 2004. As the deadline drew near, a business group (which may have an incentive to exaggerate) estimated that using the new technology to reduce pollution would increase vehicle prices by as much as $7,000. A spokesperson for the California Air Resources Board, which imposed the mandate, said that the additional materials cost is only about $70 to $270 per vehicle. Suppose that the two major producers are Toyota and Ford, and these firms are price setters with differentiated products. Show the effect of the new regulation. Is it possible that the price for these vehicles would rise by substantially more than the marginal cost would? Explain your answer.

14. What happens to the homogeneous-good Bertrand equilibrium price if the number of firms increases? Why?

*15. Will price be lower if duopoly firms set price or if they set quantity? Under what conditions can you give a definitive answer to this question?

*16. Why does differentiating its product allow an oligopoly to charge a higher price?

17. In the initial Bertrand equilibrium, two firms with differentiated products charge the same equilibrium prices. A consumer testing agency praises the product of one firm, causing its demand curve to shift to the right as new customers start buying the product. (The demand curve of the other product is not substantially affected.) Use a graph to illustrate how this new information affects the Bertrand equilibrium. What happens to the equilibrium prices of the two firms?

Problems

18. How would the Cournot equilibrium change in the airline example if United Airlines' marginal cost were $100 and American's were $200?

19. In the initial Cournot oligopoly equilibrium, both firms have constant marginal costs, m, and no fixed costs, and there is a barrier to entry. Use calculus to show what happens to the best-response function of firms if both firms now face a fixed cost of F.

20. A duopoly faces a market demand of $p = 120 - Q$. Firm 1 has a constant marginal cost of $MC^1 = 20$. Firm 2's constant marginal cost is $MC^2 = 40$. Calculate the output of each firm, market output, and price if there is (a) a collusive equilibrium or (b) a Cournot equilibrium.

*21. What is the duopoly Cournot equilibrium if the market demand function is $Q = 1,000 - 1,000p$ and each firm's marginal cost is $0.28 per unit?

22. What is the equilibrium in this chapter's airline example if both American and United receive a subsidy of $48 per passenger?

*23. The demand that duopoly quantity-setting firms face is $p = 90 - 2q_1 - 2q_2$. Firm 1 has no marginal cost of production, but Firm 2 has a marginal cost of $30. How much does each firm produce if they move simultaneously? What is the equilibrium price?

24. Determine the Stackelberg equilibrium with one leader firm and two follower firms if the market demand curve is linear and each firm faces a constant marginal cost, m, and no fixed cost.

*25. Suppose that identical duopoly firms have constant marginal costs of $10 per unit. Firm 1 faces a demand function of $q_1 = 100 - 2p_1 + p_2$, where q_1 is Firm 1's output, p_1 is Firm 1's price, and p_2 is Firm 2's price. Similarly, the demand Firm 2 faces is $q_2 = 100 - 2p_2 + p_1$. Solve for the Bertrand equilibrium.

26. Solve for the Bertrand equilibrium for the firms described in Problem 25 if both firms have a marginal cost of $0 per unit.

27. Solve for the Bertrand equilibrium for the firms described in Problem 25 if Firm 1's marginal cost is $30 per unit and Firm 2's marginal cost is $10 per unit.

*28. The viatical settlement industry enables terminally ill consumers, typically HIV patients, to borrow against equity in their existing life insurance contracts to finance their consumption and medical expenses. The introduction and dissemination of effective anti-HIV medication in 1996 reduced AIDS mortality, extending patients' lives and hence delaying when the viatical settlement industry would receive the insurance payments. However, viatical settlement payments (what patients can borrow) fell more than can be explained by greater life expectancy. The number of viatical settlement firms dropped from 44 in 1995 to 24 in 2001. Sood et al. (2005) found that an increase in market power of viatical settlement firms reduced the value of life insurance holdings of HIV-positive persons by about $1 billion. When marginal cost rises and the number of firms falls, what happens to the Cournot equilibrium price? Use graphs or math to illustrate your answer. (*Hint:* If you use math, it may be helpful to assume that the market demand curve has a constant elasticity throughout.)

29. Firms in some industries with a small number of competitors earn normal economic profit. The *Wall Street Journal* (Lee Gomes, "Competition Lives On in Just One PC Sector," March 17, 2003, B1) reports that the computer graphics chips industry is one such market. Two chip manufacturers, nVidia and ATI, "both face the prospect of razor-thin profits, largely on account of the other's existence."

   a. Consider the Bertrand model in which each firm has a positive fixed and sunk cost and a zero marginal cost. What are the Nash equilibrium prices? What are the Nash equilibrium profits?

   b. Does this "razor-thin" profit result imply that the two manufacturers necessarily produce chips that are nearly perfect substitutes? Explain.

   c. Assume that nVidia and ATI produce differentiated products and are Bertrand competitors. The demand for nVidia's chip is $q_V = \alpha - \beta p_V + \gamma p_A$; the demand for ATI's chip is $q_A = \alpha - \beta p_A + \gamma p_V$, where p_V is nVidia's price, p_A is ATI's price, and α, β, and γ are coefficients of the demand function. Suppose each manufacturer's marginal cost is a constant, m. What are the values of α, β, and γ for which the equilibrium profit of each chip manufacturer is zero? In answering this question, show that despite differentiated products, duopolists may earn zero economic profit. **W**

30. At a busy intersection on Route 309 in Quakertown, Pennsylvania, the convenience store and gasoline station, Wawa, competes with the service and gasoline station, Fred's Sunoco. In the Bertrand equilibrium with product differentiation competition for gasoline sales, the demand for Wawa's gas is $q_W = 680 - 500p_W + 400p_S$, and the demand for Fred's gas is $q_W = 680 - 500p_S + 400p_W$. Assume that the marginal cost of each gallon of gasoline is $m = \$2.00$. The gasoline retailers simultaneously set their prices.

   a. What is the Nash equilibrium?

   b. Suppose that for each gallon of gasoline sold, Wawa earns a profit of 25¢ from its sale of salty snacks to its gasoline customers. Fred sells no products that are related to the consumption of his gasoline. What is the Nash equilibrium? **W**

31. On an early Saturday morning in mid-July, each of three farmers–Abel, Bess, and Charles–decides how many sweet peppers to bring to the Perkasie, Pennsylvania, farmers' market. Each farmer has exactly 50 pounds of peppers to sell at either the farmers' market or at each farmer's home roadside stand. Each farmer's roadside stand is in a remote area of Bucks County, Pennsylvania, and, accordingly, is a monopoly. The inverse demand to Farmer i, $i = A$, B, or C, of selling q_{ih} peppers at his or her home roadside stand is $R_i = (5 - q_{ih}/10)q_{ih}$. In the market, the farmers are Cournot competitors. The inverse demand for peppers at the farmers' market is $10 - 0.1(q_{Am} + q_{Bm} + q_{Cm})$, where q_{im} is the amount each Farmer i sells at the market. What are the Nash-Cournot equilibrium quantities? What are the market and roadside stand prices? **W**

32. Acura and Volvo offer warranties on their automobiles, where w_A is the number of years of an Acura warranty and w_V is the number of years of a Volvo warranty. The revenue for Firm i, $i = A$ for Acura and V for Volvo, is $R_i = 32{,}000w_i/(w_A + w_V)$. Its cost of providing the warranty is $C_i = 2{,}000w_i$. Acura and Volvo simultaneously set warranties.

   a. What is the profit function for each firm?

   b. What are the Nash equilibrium warranties?

   c. Suppose that Acura and Volvo collude in setting warranties. What warranties do they set? **W**

33. In October 2002, the European Union fined Sotheby's auction house more than 20 million euros for operating (along with rival auction house Christie's) a price-fixing cartel (see **www.aw-bc.com/perloff**, Chapter 13, "The Art of Price Fixing"). The two auction houses were jointly setting the commission rates sellers must pay. Let r denote the jointly set auction commission rate, $D_i(r)$ represent the demand for auction house i's services by sellers of auctioned items, p denote the average price of auctioned items, F represent an auction house's fixed cost, and v denote its average variable cost of auctioning an object. At the agreed-upon commission rate r, the profit of an auction house i is $\pi_i = rpD_i(r) - [F + vD_i(r)]$.

   a. What is the sum of the profits of auction houses i and j?

   b. Characterize the commission rate that maximizes the sum of profits. That is, show that the commission rate that maximizes the sum of profits satisfies an equation that looks something like the monopoly's Lerner Index profit-maximizing condition, Equation 11.11.

   c. Do the auction houses have an incentive to cheat on their agreement? If Christie's does so while Sotheby's continues to charge r, what will happen to their individual and collective profits? **W**

34. In February 2005, the U.S. Federal Trade Commission (FTC) went to court to undo the January 2000 takeover of Highland Park Hospital by Evanston Northwestern Healthcare Corp. The FTC accused Evanston Northwestern of antitrust violations by using its postmerger market power in the Evanston hospital market to impose 40% to 60% price increases (Bernard Wysocki, Jr., "FTC Targets Hospital Merger in Antitrust Case," *Wall Street Journal*, January 17, 2005, A1). Hospitals, even within the same community, are geographically differentiated as well as possibly quality differentiated. The demand for an appendectomy at Highland Park Hospital is a function of the price of the procedure at Highland Park and Evanston Northwestern Hospital: $q_H = 50 - 0.01p_H + 0.005p_N$. The comparable demand function at Evanston Northwestern is $q_N = 500 - 0.01p_N + 0.005p_H$. At each hospital, the fixed cost of the procedure is $20,000 and the marginal cost is $2,000.

    a. Use the product-differentiated Bertrand model to analyze the prices the hospitals set before the merger. Find the Nash equilibrium prices of the procedure at the two hospitals.
    b. After the merger, find the profit-maximizing monopoly prices of the procedure at each hospital. Include the effect of each hospital's price on the profit of the other hospital.
    c. Does the merger result in increased prices? Explain. **W**

*35. To examine the trade-off between efficiency and market power from a merger, consider a market with two firms that sell identical products. Firm 1 has a constant marginal cost of 1, and Firm 2 has a constant marginal cost of 2. The market demand is $Q = 15 - p$.

    a. Solve for the Cournot equilibrium price, quantities, profits, consumer surplus, and deadweight loss.
    b. If the firms merge and produce at the lower marginal cost, how do the equilibrium values change?
    c. Discuss the change in efficiency (average cost of producing the output) and welfare—consumer surplus, producer surplus (or profit), and deadweight loss.

*36. Duopoly quantity-setting firms face the market demand

$$p = 150 - q_1 - q_2.$$

Each firm has a marginal cost of $60 per unit.

    a. What is the Cournot equilibrium?
    b. What is the Stackelberg equilibrium when Firm 1 moves first?

*37. An incumbent firm, Firm 1, faces a potential entrant, Firm 2, that has a lower marginal cost. The market demand curve is $p = 120 - q_1 - q_2$. Firm 1 has a constant marginal cost of $20, while Firm 2's is $10.

    a. What are the Cournot equilibrium price, quantities, and profits if there is no government intervention?
    b. To block entry, the incumbent appeals to the government to require that the entrant incur extra costs. What happens to the Cournot equilibrium if the legal requirement causes the marginal cost of the second firm to rise to that of the first firm, $20?
    c. Now suppose that the barrier leaves the marginal cost alone but imposes a fixed cost. What is the minimal fixed cost that will prevent entry?

38. Two firms, each in a different country, sell homogeneous output in a third country. Government 1 subsidizes its domestic firm by s per unit. The other government does not react. In the absence of government intervention, the market has a Cournot equilibrium. Suppose demand is linear, $p = 1 - q_1 - q_2$, and each firm's marginal and average costs of production are constant at m. Government 1 maximizes net national income (it does not care about transfers between the government and the firm, so it maximizes the firm's profit net of the transfers). Show that Government 1's optimal s results in its firm producing the Stackelberg leader quantity and the other firm producing the Stackelberg follower quantity in equilibrium.

39. Referring to Solved Problem 13.3, show the effect of a subsidy on Firm 1's best-response function if the firm faces a general demand function $p(Q)$.

40. Consider the Cournot model with n firms. The inverse linear market demand function is $p = a - bQ$. Each of the n identical firms has the same cost function $C(q_i) = \beta q_i + (\gamma/2)q_i^2$, where $a > \beta$. In terms of n, what is each firm's Nash equilibrium output and profit and the equilibrium price? As n gets very large (i.e., approaches infinity), does each firm's equilibrium profit approach zero? Why? **W**

Chapter 14

Game Theory

A camper awakens to the growl of a hungry bear and sees his friend putting on a pair of running shoes. "You can't outrun a bear," scoffs the camper. His friend coolly replies, "I don't have to. I only have to outrun you!"

In deciding how to price its video game controller, Nintendo takes into account the pricing of its rivals, Microsoft and Sony. When a small number of people or firms interact, they know that their actions significantly affect each other's welfare or profit, so they consider those actions carefully.

Firms compete on many fronts beyond setting quantity or price. To gain an edge over rivals, a firm makes many decisions, such as how much to advertise, whether to act to discourage a new firm from entering its market, how to differentiate its product, and whether to invest in new equipment. A firm with few rivals takes its rivals' behavior into account in determining how to act.

Over the last half-dozen years, French tire maker Michelin SCA and its Japanese competitor, Bridgestone Corp., have competed for bragging rights that they produce the world's fastest Formula One racing tires. They pour huge amounts of money into racing—$70 million a year for Michelin and $100 million for Bridgestone—so that the winner can claim in their advertising that they produce the fastest tires.[1]

Since 1999, when Westin Hotels and Resorts introduced the Heavenly Bed, the major hotel chains have been engaging in a "bed war." Marriott International, like virtually every rival chain, recently upgraded its bedding to feature 300-thread-count sheets, a feathered mattress topper, stylish pillow shams, a decorative bed scarf, and extra pillows. In 2006, Hilton Hotels announced a $1 billion effort that included the addition of its branded Serenity Bed to many of its properties, with its signature mattress pads, down pillows, linens, decorative bed pillows, and bolsters.[2] A hotel that won't compete in the bed war will lose customers.

And it's not just firms that have to consider the actions of others. When deciding how and when to bid on eBay for that 1957 Mickey Mantle baseball card or those cow-shaped salt and pepper shakers, you have to think about how other bidders are likely to behave.

In this chapter, we use game theory (von Neumann and Morgenstern, 1944) to examine how a small number of firms or individuals interact. **Game theory** is a set of tools that economists, political scientists, military analysts, and others use to analyze players' strategic decision making. This chapter introduces the basic concepts of game theory.[3] *Games* are competitions between players, such as individuals or firms, in which each player is aware that the outcome depends on the actions of all players.

Game theory has many practical applications. It is useful for analyzing oligopolistic firms' price and quantity setting, as well as their advertising; for bargaining between

---

[1]Jo Wrighton, and Jathon Sapsford, "For Tire Makers, An Expensive Battle at the Racetrack," *Wall Street Journal,* October 27, 2005:A1.

[2]Christopher Elliot, "Détente in the Hotel Bed Wars," *New York Times,* January 31, 2006.

[3]For more details, see for example Fudenberg and Tirole (1991) or Gibbons (1992).

unions and management or between employers and employees; for interactions between polluters and those harmed by pollution; for transactions between the buyers and sellers of homes; for negotiations between parties with information (such as between car owners and auto mechanics) and those with limited information; for bidding in auctions; and many other economic interactions. Game theory is used by economists and firms to study economic games, by political scientists and military planners to plan for avoiding or fighting wars, and by many others.

<table>
<tr>
<td>In this chapter, we examine four main topics</td>
<td>

1. **An Overview of Game Theory:** Game theory formally describes games and predicts their outcome conditional on the rules of the game, the information that players have, and other factors.

2. **Static Games:** A static game is played once by players who act simultaneously and hence do not know how other players will act at the time they must make a decision.

3. **Dynamic Games:** In a dynamic game, players may have perfect information about previous moves but imperfect information about current moves if players act simultaneously within each period.

4. **Auctions:** An auction is a game where bidders have incomplete information about the value that other bidders place on the auctioned good or service.

</td>
</tr>
</table>

14.1   An Overview of Game Theory

A **game** is any competition between players (such as individuals or firms) in which strategic behavior plays a major role. An **action** is a move that a player makes at a specified stage of a game, such as how much output a firm produces in the current period. A **strategy** is a battle plan that specifies the action that a player will make conditional on the information available at each move and for any possible contingency. For example, a firm may use a simple business strategy where it produces 100 units of output regardless of what any rival does. Or the firm may choose a more complex strategy in which it produces a small quantity as long as its rival produced a small amount last period, and a large quantity otherwise. The **payoffs** of a game are the players' valuation of the outcome of the game, such as profits for firms or utilities for individuals.

Strategic behavior is a set of actions a player takes to increase his or her payoff, taking into account the possible actions of other players. For example, a firm may set an output level, act to discourage potential firms from entering a market, or choose to employ a technology. Conflicts frequently arise among firms because the actions of each profit-maximizing firm affect the profits of other firms. Although we call conflicts between firms or individuals games, those involved do not view this competition as frivolous. These games are serious business. Each player wants to achieve the largest possible payoff at the end of the game.

We maintain two assumptions throughout our analyses. First, we assume that players are interested in maximizing their payoffs. Second, we assume that all players have **common knowledge** about the rules of the game, that each player's payoff depends on actions taken by all players, and that all players want to maximize their payoffs; all players know that all players know the payoffs and that their opponents are payoff maximizing; and so on.

Economists use game theory when a player's optimal strategy depends on the actions of others, which is called **strategic interdependence.** For example, oligopolistic cola manufacturers such as Coca-Cola and Pepsi carefully monitor each other's behavior. Because relatively few firms compete in such a market, each firm can influence the price, and hence the payoffs, of rival firms. The need to consider the behavior of rival firms makes each firm's profit maximization decision more difficult than that of a monopoly or a competitive firm. A monopoly has no rivals, and a competitive firm ignores the behavior of individual rivals—it considers only the market price and its own costs in choosing its profit-maximizing output. Thus we use game theory to study oligopolistic behavior but not competitive or monopolistic behavior.

Game theory tries to answer two questions: how to describe a game and how to predict the game's outcome. A game is described in terms of the players; its rules; the outcome (for example, who wins an auction); the payoffs to players corresponding to each possible outcome; and the information that players have about their rivals' moves. The **rules of the game** determine the *timing* of players' moves and the *actions* that players can make at each move.

For each game, a *payoff function* determines any player's payoff given the combination of actions by all players. We start by examining games with **complete information,** where the payoff function is common knowledge among all players. Each player knows the payoffs to all the players in the game for any possible combination of strategies. An example of a static game with complete information is the Cournot model (Chapter 13), where firms know the profit functions of all firms.

Game theorists distinguish between *complete information* and **perfect information,** where the player who is about to move knows the full history of the play of the game to this point, and that information is updated with each subsequent action. The *information* each player has about rivals' actions often turns on whether the players act simultaneously or sequentially. If the players move simultaneously, then they have *imperfect information* because they do not know how other players will act.

We start by examining a **static game** is one in which each player acts only once and the players act simultaneously (or, at least, each player acts without knowing rivals' actions). In these games, firms have complete information about the payoff functions but imperfect information about rivals' moves.

We then turn to a **dynamic game,** where players move either sequentially or repeatedly. Players have complete information about the payoff functions, and, at each move, players have perfect information about the previous moves by all players. We first look at *sequential move* dynamic games such as chess, in which a player knows the full history of prior moves. Similarly in the Stackelberg model (Chapter 13), after the leader firm chooses an output level, the follower firm has perfect information about the leader's output level at the time the follower must move.

We then analyze dynamic games in which players move simultaneously in each period and the game is repeated over a number of periods. For example, American Airlines and United Airlines play the same simultaneous-move, Cournot game, quarter after quarter. In repeated games, players have perfect information about moves in previous periods but imperfect information about the simultaneous moves they must make in the current period.

Finally, we turn to games of *incomplete information,* in which some player is uncertain about other players' payoff function. An example is an auction where one bidder's willingness to pay for a good is unknown to other bidders.

14.2   Static Games

We begin by examining static games, in which the players choose their actions simultaneously, have complete information about the payoff function, and play the game once. Examples include teenagers' game of "chicken" in cars, the duel between Aaron Burr and Alexander Hamilton in 1804, an employer's negotiations with a potential employee, street vendors' choice of locations and prices outside the Super Bowl, and the Cournot and Bertrand models. In this section, we show how to represent these static games in a table and how to predict their outcomes.

NORMAL-FORM GAMES

We examine a **normal-form** representation of a static game of complete information, which specifies the players in the game, their possible strategies, and the payoff function that specifies the players' payoffs for each combination of strategies.

Our first example is a two-player game in which the players have two possible actions. It is based on Chapter 13's United and American Airlines' duopoly competition on the Los Angeles–Chicago route as estimated by Brander and Zhang (1990). For simplicity, suppose that each airline can take only one of two possible actions: Each can fly either 64 or 48 thousand passengers between Chicago and Los Angeles per quarter. The normal-form representation of this static game is the *payoff matrix* (*profit matrix*) in Table 14.1. This payoff matrix shows the profits for each of the four possible combinations of the strategies that the firms may choose. For example, if American chooses a large quantity, $q_A = 64$ units per quarter, and United chooses a small quantity, $q_U = 48$ units per quarter, the firms' profits are in the cell in the lower left-hand corner of the profit matrix. That cell shows that American's profit (upper-right number) is $5.1 million per quarter, and United's profit (bottom-left number) is $3.8 million per quarter.

Because the firms choose their strategies simultaneously, each firm selects a strategy that maximizes its profit *given what it believes the other firm will do*. The firms are playing a *noncooperative game of imperfect information* in which each firm must choose an action before observing the simultaneous action by its rival. Thus while the players have complete information about all players' payoffs, they have imperfect information about how the other will act.

TABLE 14.1   **Profit Matrix for a Quantity-Setting Game: Dominant Strategy**

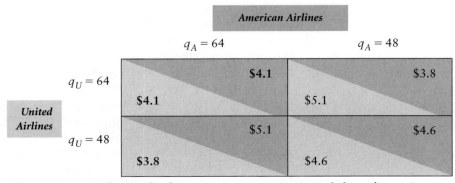

Note: Quantities are in thousands of passengers per quarter; (rounded) profits are in millions of dollars per quarter.

PREDICTING A GAME'S OUTCOME

> *[W]hen you have eliminated the impossible, whatever remains, however improbable,*
> *must be the truth.* —Sherlock Holmes (Sir Arthur Conan Doyle)

We can predict the outcome of some games by using the insight that rational players will avoid strategies that are *dominated* by other strategies. However, for many other games, this approach alone does not allow us precisely to predict the outcome. A broader class of games can be precisely predicted based on each player's choosing a *best response* to the other players' actions—the response that produces the largest possible payoff.

Dominant Strategies. We can precisely predict the outcome of any game in which every player has a **dominant strategy:** a strategy that produces a higher payoff than any other strategy the player can use for every possible combination of its rivals' strategies. When a firm has a dominant strategy, there is no belief that a firm could hold about its rivals' choice of strategies that would cause it to choose one of its other, strictly dominated strategies.

Although firms do not always have dominant strategies, they have them in our airline game. American's managers can determine its dominant strategy using the following reasoning:

- *If United chooses the high-output strategy ($q_U = 64$), American's high-output strategy maximizes its profit:* Given United's strategy, American's profit is $4.1 million (top-right number in the upper-left cell) with its high-output strategy ($q_A = 64$) and only $3.8 million (top-right number in the upper-right cell) with its low-output strategy ($q_A = 48$). Thus American is better off using a high-output strategy if United chooses its high-output strategy.
- *If United chooses the low-output strategy ($q_U = 48$), American's high-output strategy maximizes its profit:* Given United's strategy, American's profit is $5.1 million with its high-output strategy and only $4.6 million with its low-output strategy.
- *Thus the high-output strategy is American's dominant strategy:* Whichever strategy United uses, American's profit is higher if it uses its high-output strategy.

By the same type of reasoning, United's high-output strategy is also a dominant strategy. Because the high-output strategy is a dominant strategy for both firms, we can predict that the outcome of this game is the pair of high-output strategies, $q_A = q_U = 64$. (The corresponding payoffs appear in bold in Table 14.1.)

A striking feature of this game is that the players choose strategies that do not maximize their joint profit. Each firm earns $4.6 million if $q_A = q_U = 48$ rather than the $4.1 million they actually earn by setting $q_A = q_U = 64$. In this type of game—called a **prisoners' dilemma** game—all players have dominant strategies that lead to a profit (or another payoff) that is inferior to what they could achieve if they cooperated and pursued alternative strategies.

The prisoners' dilemma crops up in virtually every cops-and-robbers show you've seen. The cops arrest Larry and Duncan and put them in separate rooms so that they cannot talk to each other. An assistant district attorney tells Larry, "We have enough evidence to convict you both of a relatively minor crime for which you'll serve a year in prison. If you'll squeal on your partner and he stays silent, we can convict him of a major crime for which he'll serve five years and you'll go free. If you both confess, you'll each get two years." Meanwhile, another assistant district attorney is making Duncan the identical offer. By the same reasoning as in the airline example, both Larry and Duncan confess even though they are better off if they both keep quiet (see Question 2 at the end of the chapter).

Iterated Elimination of Strictly Dominated Strategies. In games where not all players have a dominant strategy, we cannot precisely identify the outcome of the game from what we know so far. Table 14.2 shows the normal-form representation of the game between United and American Airlines where they can each choose between three possible actions: fly 96, 64, or 48 thousand passengers per quarter between Chicago and Los Angeles.

Neither firm has a strictly dominant strategy in this game. As we showed before, if United chooses $q_U = 64$ or 48, American's profit is highest if it sets $q_A = 64$. However, if United selects $q_U = 96$, American's best action is to set $q_A = 48$.[4] Thus none of American's strategies is a dominant strategy: a single strategy that always produces the highest profit regardless of United's actions. Rather, the strategy that maximizes American's payoff depends on United's action.

Nonetheless, we can determine the outcome of this game by generalizing our earlier logic. Because we know that a firm will not use a strategy that is strictly dominated by another strategy, we can eliminate any strictly dominated strategy. By eliminating such strategies repeatedly, we can predict a unique set of strategies.

In Table 14.2, American's strategy of $q_A = 96$ is strictly dominated by its alternative strategy of $q_A = 64$. Regardless of which strategy United uses, $q_A = 64$ produces a higher profit for American than does $q_A = 96$. Similarly, United's strategy of $q_U = 96$ is strictly dominated by its $q_U = 64$ strategy. Consequently, we draw a red line through the $q_A = 96$ column and through the $q_U = 96$ row to show that the firms will not use these strictly dominated strategies.

TABLE 14.2   **Profit Matrix for a Quantity-Setting Game: Iterated Dominance**

		American Airlines				
		$q_A = 96$		$q_A = 64$		$q_A = 48$
United Airlines	$q_U = 96$	(United $0)	American $0	(United $3.1)	American $2.0	(United $4.6) American $2.3
	$q_U = 64$	(United $2.0)	American $3.1	(United $4.1)	American $4.1	(United $5.1) American $3.8
	$q_U = 48$	(United $2.3)	American $4.6	(United $3.8)	American $5.1	(United $4.6) American $4.6

Note: Quantities are in thousands of passengers per quarter; (rounded) profits are in millions of dollars per quarter.

---

[4]Given that $q_U = 96$, American's profit is \$2.3 million if $q_A = 48$, \$2.0 million if $q_A = 64$, and \$0 if $q_A = 96$.

After we eliminate these strategies, the remaining payoff matrix is the same 2×2 matrix as in Table 14.1: The firms choose to fly either 64 or 48 thousand passengers per quarter. From our previous analysis, we know that choosing 48 is strictly dominated by the strategy of choosing 64, so we draw a green line through the dominated strategies within the 2×2 matrix. By this *iterated elimination of strictly dominated strategies,* we again predict that the firms will each choose to fly 64 thousand passengers per quarter.

The dominant strategy approach is a special case of the iterated elimination of strictly dominated strategies, because the dominant strategy was determined by eliminating all inferior strategies. The iterated approach is based on the belief that players will not choose strictly dominated strategies. However, to rely on this approach, we have to assume that the players possess common knowledge that they are payoff maximizing, that the players know that the other players are payoff maximizing, and that the players know that all the players know that the other players are payoff maximizing, and so forth.

Even given that we are willing to make these strong assumptions about common knowledge, iterative elimination of strictly dominated strategies does not always allow us to make precise predictions about the outcome of a game. In many games, we cannot eliminate all but one strategy for each player.

Best Response and Nash Equilibrium. When iterative elimination of strictly dominated strategies fails to predict a unique outcome, we can use a related concept. For any given set of strategies chosen by rivals, a player wants to use its **best response:** the strategy that maximizes a player's payoff given its beliefs about its rivals' strategies. A dominant strategy is one that is a best response to all possible strategies that a rival might use. However, a particular strategy might be a best response for some rival strategies but not for others. Given that firms always choose a best response, we can accurately forecast the outcome of many games that we cannot precisely predict using the iterated elimination of strictly dominated strategies.

Economists usually rely on a solution concept introduced by John Nash (1951) that is based on the belief that players use their best responses. Formally, a set of strategies is a **Nash equilibrium** if, when all other players use these strategies, no player can obtain a higher payoff by choosing a different strategy.[5] An appealing property of the Nash equilibrium is that it is self-enforcing. If each player uses a Nash equilibrium strategy, then no player wants to deviate by choosing another strategy.

The Nash equilibrium is a stronger solution conception than the iterated elimination of strictly dominated strategies. Not all Nash equilibria can be determined using the iterated elimination of strictly dominated strategies. However, if the iterated elimination of strictly dominated strategies produces a solution consisting of a single pair of strategies, then that combination of strategies is the unique Nash equilibrium in that game.

We can use the profit matrix in Table 14.1 to illustrate that the pair of strategies we choose using iterated elimination of strictly dominated strategies is a Nash equilibrium. By eliminating strictly dominated strategies, we concluded that both firms want to set output at 64. Would either firm want to deviate from that proposed outcome? If American knew that United would set $q_U = 64$, American would not switch to $q_A = 48$,

---

[5]In Chapter 13, we used a special case of this definition of a Nash equilibrium in which we referred to actions instead of strategies. An action and a strategy are the same if the players can move only once; however, later in this chapter, we will consider games that last for many periods and hence we need a definition based on strategies.

because its profit would fall from \$4.1 million to \$3.8 million. By the same reasoning, United would not want change strategies either. That is, given that the other firm chooses 64, the strategy of 64 is a firm's best response. Because neither firm wants to change its strategy given that the other firm is playing its Nash equilibrium strategy, the pair of strategies $q_A = q_U = 64$ is a Nash equilibrium.

Moreover, for any other combination of strategies, one or the other firm would want to change its behavior; hence none of the other strategy pairs is a Nash equilibrium. At $q_A = q_U = 48$, either firm could raise its profit from \$4.6 to \$5.1 million by increasing its output to 64. At $q_A = 48$ and $q_U = 64$, American can raise its profit from \$3.8 to \$4.1 million by increasing its quantity to $q_A = 64$. Similarly, United would want to increase its output when $q_A = 64$ and $q_U = 48$.

A similar analysis applies to the more general Cournot model (Chapter 13), where firms can pick any output they desire. That model can be presented as a normal-form game with n players (firms), a choice of strategies (any real-number, nonnegative quantity), and a payoff function that is common knowledge (that is, all firms know the profit function of each firm). We derived the Nash equilibrium to that game by finding those quantities that were best responses for all the firms. It is possible to obtain that Nash equilibrium in a linear, duopoly Cournot model by iterative elimination of strictly dominated strategies. With three or more firms, iterative elimination provides only the imprecise observation that each firm's quantity will not exceed the monopoly quantity (Gibbons, 1992). In Chapter 13, we showed that we could obtain the Nash equilibrium using best-response functions with three or more firms.

In games where iterated elimination of strictly dominated strategies does not determine a single pair of strategies, there may be a single Nash equilibrium (such as the Cournot model with three or more firms), multiple Nash equilibria, or no Nash equilibrium. We now provide examples of the latter two possibilities.

MULTIPLE NASH EQUILIBRIA, NO NASH EQUILIBRIUM, AND MIXED STRATEGIES

> *In accordance with our principles of free enterprise and healthy competition,*
> *I'm going to ask you two to fight to the death for it.*   —Monty Python

In each of the games we have considered so far, there is only one Nash equilibrium, and the firms use a **pure strategy:** Each player chooses a single action. We now turn to an entry game that has more than one Nash equilibrium in pure strategies. Moreover, in addition to using a pure strategy, a firm in this entry game may employ a **mixed strategy** in which the player chooses among possible actions according to probabilities it assigns. A pure strategy assigns a probability of 1 to a single action, whereas a mixed strategy is a probability distribution over actions. That is, a pure strategy is a rule telling the player what action to take, whereas a mixed strategy is a rule telling the player which dice to throw, coin to flip, or other device to use to choose an action.

An entry game has both pure and mixed-strategy Nash equilibria. Suppose that two firms are considering opening gas stations at a highway rest stop that has no gas stations. There's enough physical space for at most two gas stations. The profit matrix in Table 14.3 shows that there is enough demand for only one station to operate profitably. If both firms enter, each loses \$1 (hundred thousand). Neither firm has a dominant strategy. Each firm's best action depends on what the other firm does.

TABLE 14.3   **Simultaneous Entry Game**

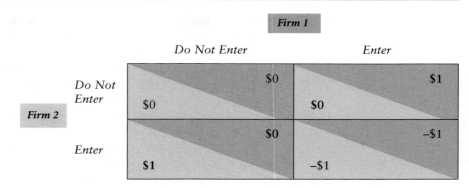

		Firm 1	
		Do Not Enter	*Enter*
Firm 2	*Do Not Enter*	$0 / $0	$0 / $1
	Enter	$1 / $0	−$1 / −$1

Pure Strategies. This game has two Nash equilibria in pure strategies: Firm 1 *enters* and Firm 2 *does not enter*, or Firm 2 *enters* and Firm 1 *does not enter*. The equilibrium in which only Firm 1 enters is Nash because neither firm wants to change its behavior. Given that Firm 2 does not enter, Firm 1 does not want to change its strategy from entering to staying out of the market. If it changed its behavior, it would go from earning $1 to earning nothing. Similarly, given that Firm 1 enters, Firm 2 does not want to switch its behavior and enter because it would lose $1 instead of making $0. Where only Firm 2 enters is also a Nash equilibrium by the same type of reasoning.

How do the players know which (if any) Nash equilibrium will result? They *don't* know. It is difficult to see how the firms choose strategies unless they collude and can enforce their agreement. For example, the firm that enters could pay the other firm to stay out of the market. Without an enforceable collusive agreement, even discussions between the firms before decisions are made are unlikely to help. These pure Nash equilibria are unappealing because they call for identical firms to use different strategies.

Mixed Strategies. Both firms may use the same mixed strategy. When both firms enter with a probability of one-half—say, if a flipped coin comes up heads—there is a Nash equilibrium in mixed strategies because neither firm wants to change its strategy, given that the other firm uses its Nash equilibrium mixed strategy.

If both firms use this mixed strategy, each of the four outcomes in the payoff matrix in Table 14.3 is equally likely. Firm 1 has a one-fourth chance of earning $1 (upper-right cell), a one-fourth chance of losing $1 (lower-right cell), and a one-half chance of earning $0 (upper-left and lower-left cells).[6] Thus Firm 1's expected profit—the firm's profit in each possible outcome times the probability of that outcome—is

$$\left(\$1 \times \frac{1}{4} \right) + \left(-\$1 \times \frac{1}{4} \right) + \left(\$0 \times \frac{1}{2} \right) = \$0.$$

[6]The probability that the outcome in a particular cell of the matrix occurs is the product of the probabilities that each player chooses the relevant action. The probability that a player chooses a given action is $\frac{1}{2}$, so the probability that both players will choose the relevant actions is $\frac{1}{2} \times \frac{1}{2} = \frac{1}{4}$.

Given that Firm 1 uses this mixed strategy, Firm 2 cannot achieve a higher expected profit by using a pure strategy. If Firm 2 uses the pure strategy of entering with probability 1, it earns $1 half the time and loses $1 the other half, so its expected profit is $0. If it stays out with certainty, Firm 2 earns $0 with certainty.

If Firm 2 believes that Firm 1 will use its equilibrium mixed strategy, Firm 2 is indifferent as to which pure strategy it uses (of the strategies that have a positive probability in that firm's mixed strategy). Suppose to the contrary that one of the actions in the equilibrium mixed strategy had a higher expected payoff than some other action. Then it would pay to increase the probability that Firm 2 takes the action with the higher expected payoff. However, if all of the pure strategies that have positive probability in a mixed strategy have the same expected payoff, then the expected payoff of the mixed strategy must also have that expected payoff. Thus Firm 2 is indifferent as to whether it uses any of these pure strategies or any mixed strategy over these pure strategies.

In our example, why would a firm pick a mixed strategy where its probability of entering is one-half? In a symmetric game such as this one, we know that both players have the same probability of entering, θ. Moreover, for Firm 2 to use a mixed strategy, it must be indifferent between entering or not entering if Firm 1 enters with probability θ. Firm 2's payoff from entering is $[\theta \times (-1)] + [(1 - \theta) \times 1] = 1 - 2\theta$. Its payoff from not entering is $[\theta \times 0] + [(1 - \theta) \times 0] = 0$. Equating these two expected profits, $1 - 2\theta = 0$, and solving, we find that $\theta = 1/2$. Thus both firms using a mixed strategy where they enter with a probability of one-half is a Nash equilibrium.[7]

Possible Equilibria. This game has two pure-strategy Nash equilibria—one firm employing the pure strategy of entering and the other firm pursuing the pure strategy of not entering—and a mixed-strategy Nash equilibrium. If Firm 1 decides to *enter* with a probability of one-half, Firm 2 is indifferent between choosing to enter with probability of 1 (the pure strategy of *enter*), 0 (the pure strategy of *do not enter*), or any fraction in between these extremes. However, for the firms' strategies to constitute a mixed-strategy Nash equilibrium, both firms must choose to enter with a probability of one-half.

One important reason for introducing the concept of a mixed strategy is that some games have no pure-strategy Nash equilibria (see Solved Problem 14.1). However, Nash (1950) proved that every static game with a finite number of players and a finite number of actions has at least one Nash equilibrium, which may involve mixed strategies.

Some game theorists argue that mixed strategies are implausible because firms do not flip coins to choose strategies. One response is that firms may only appear to be unpredictable. In this game with no dominant strategies, neither firm has a strong reason to believe that the other will choose a pure strategy. It may think about its rival's behavior as random. However, in actual games, a firm may use some information or reasoning that its rival does not observe in choosing a pure strategy. Another response is that a mixed strategy may be appealing in some games, such as the entry game or the similar game of chicken, where a random strategy and symmetry between players are plausible.

---

[7]The appendix to this chapter presents an alternative method for solving this mixed-strategy equilibrium using calculus.

Chicken

Two cars simultaneously approach an intersection that has no stop signs or traffic lights. Which driver stops? Or do the cars collide?

This game is rarely played at U.S. intersections, where stop signs or traffic lights are common. Moreover, at U.S. intersections without traffic signs or signals, the traffic rule is that if two cars arrive simultaneously at the intersection, the car to the left yields to the car approaching from the first car's right. France also uses that rule, called priorité de droite.

In contrast, Belgium, which has few traffic signs or signals, does not currently use a yield-to-the-right rule. Even worse, a driver in Belgium who stops to look both ways at an intersection loses the legal right to proceed first. A driver who merely taps his brakes can find that his pause has sent a dangerous signal to other drivers: Any sign of hesitation often spurs other drivers to hit the gas in a race to get through the crossing first. The result is a game of chicken, where to slow down is to "show weakness," according to Belgian traffic court lawyer Virginie Delannoy.[8] Neither driver wants to lose the game, Delannoy says, adding: "And then, bam!" Formally, chicken is the same as the entry game: Disaster occurs if both players enter the intersection at the same time. Strangely, proposals to put signs at crossroads or to adopt the yield-to-the-right rule are very unpopular in Belgium.

The absence of signs and rules may explain the usually high accident rate in Belgium. Failing to yield is the cause of more than two-thirds of the accidents at unmarked Belgian intersections that result in bodily injury. Last year, there were 11.2 deaths per 100,000 Belgians. In bordering countries with more stop signs and traffic lights and explicit rules about yielding right of way, the rate is much lower: only 4.6 per 100,000 in the Netherlands, 6.1 in Germany, and 8.7 in France.

SOLVED PROBLEM 14.1

Mimi wants to support her son Jeff if he looks for work but not otherwise. Jeff wants to try to find a job only if Mimi will not support his life of indolence. Their payoff matrix is

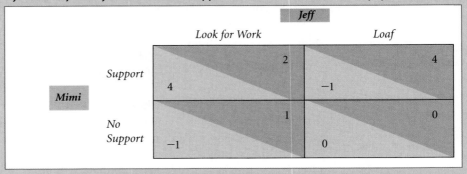

If they choose actions simultaneously, what are the pure- or mixed-strategy equilibria?

---

[8]Bertrand Russell observed that nuclear brinksmanship is essentially a game of chicken.

Answer

1. *Check whether any of the four possible pairs of pure strategies is a Nash equilibrium:* The four possible pure-strategy equilibria are support-look, support-loaf, no support-look, and no support-loaf. None of these pairs of pure strategies is a Nash equilibrium because one or the other player would want to change his or her strategy. The pair of strategies support-look is not a Nash equilibrium because, given that Mimi provides support, Jeff would have a higher payoff loafing, 4, than looking for work, 2. Support-loaf is not a Nash equilibrium because Mimi prefers not to support the bum, 0, to providing support, −1. We can reject no support-loaf because Jeff would prefer to search for work, 1, out of desperation rather than loaf, 0. Finally, no support-look is not a Nash equilibrium because Mimi would prefer to support her wonderful son, 4, rather than to feel guilty about not rewarding his search efforts, −1.

2. *By equating expected payoffs, determine the mixed-strategy equilibrium:* If Mimi provides support with probability θ_M, Jeff's expected payoff from looking for work is $2\theta_M + [1 \times (1 - \theta_M)] = 1 + \theta_M$, and his expected payoff from loafing is $4\theta_M + [0 \times (1 - \theta_M)] = 4\theta_M$. Thus his expected payoffs are equal if $1 + \theta_M = 4\theta_M$, or $\theta_M = \frac{1}{3}$. Similarly, if Jeff looks for work with probability θ_J, then Mimi's expected payoff from supporting him is $4\theta_J + [(-1) \times (1 - \theta_J)] = 5\theta_J - 1$, and her expected payoff from not supporting him is $-\theta_J + [0 \times (1 - \theta_J)] = -\theta_J$. By equating her expected payoffs, $5\theta_J - 1 = -\theta_J$, we determine that his mixed-strategy probability is $\theta_J = \frac{1}{6}$.

Comment: Although this game has no pure-strategy Nash equilibria, it does have a mixed-strategy Nash equilibrium.

COOPERATION

Whether players cooperate in a static game depends on the payoff function. Table 14.4 shows an advertising game in which each firm can choose to advertise or not, with two possible payoff functions. The unique Nash equilibrium maximizes the collective payoff to the players in the second game, but the unique Nash equilibrium in the first game is not the cooperative outcome.

The game in panel a is a prisoners' dilemma game similar to the airline game in Table 14.1. Each firm has a dominant strategy: to advertise. In this Nash equilibrium, each firm earns $1 million, which is less than the $2 million it would make if neither firm advertised. Thus *the sum of the firms' profits is not maximized in this simultaneous-choice one-period game.*

Many people are surprised the first time they hear this result. Why don't the firms cooperate and use the individually and jointly more profitable low-output strategies, by which each earns a profit of $2 million instead of the $1 million in the Nash equilibrium? The reason they don't cooperate is a lack of trust. Each firm uses the no-advertising strategy only if the firms have a binding (enforceable) agreement. The reason they do not trust each other is that each firm knows it is in the other firm's best interest to deviate from the actions that would maximize joint profits.

Table 14.4 Advertising Game

(a) Advertising Only Takes Customers from Rivals

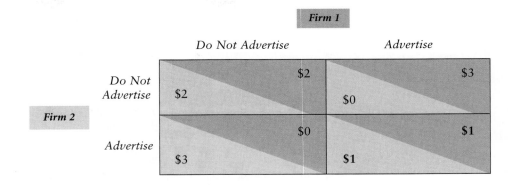

(b) Advertising Attracts New Customers to the Market

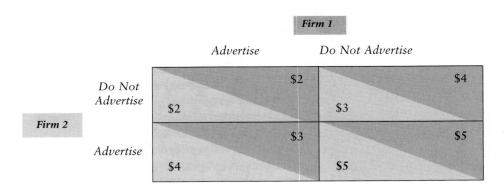

Suppose the two firms meet in advance and agree not to advertise. If the firms are going to engage in this game only once, each has an incentive to cheat on the agreement. If Firm 1 believes that Firm 2 will stick to the agreement and not advertise, Firm 1 can increase its profit from $2 million to $3 million by violating the agreement and advertising. Moreover, if Firm 1 thinks that Firm 2 will cheat on the agreement by advertising, Firm 1 wants to advertise (so that it will earn $1 million rather than $0). By this reasoning, each firm has a substantial profit incentive to cheat on the agreement. In this game, all else the same, if one firm advertises, its sales increase so that its profit rises, but its rival loses customers and hence the rival's profit falls.

In contrast, in panel b, when either firm advertises, the promotion attracts new customers to both firms. If neither firm advertises, both earn $2 (million). If only one firm advertises, its profit rises to $4, which is more than the $3 that the other firm makes. If both advertise, they are better off than if only one advertises or neither advertises. Again, advertising is a dominant strategy for both firms (as you are asked to prove in Question 1 at the end of the chapter). In the Nash equilibrium, both firms advertise.

Both firms advertise in the games in panel a and panel b. The distinction is that the Nash equilibrium in which both advertise is the same as the collusive equilibrium in panel b where advertising increases the market size, but it is not the collusive equilibrium in panel a. When advertising cannibalizes the sales of other firms in the market in panel a, the payoffs are lower in the equilibrium in which they advertise.

Strategic Advertising

A firm may advertise to inform consumers about a new use for its product. Its advertising may cause the quantity demanded for its own *and* rival brands to rise.

Toothpaste ads provide an example. Before World War I, only 26% of Americans brushed their teeth. By 1926, in part because of ads like those in Ipana's "pink toothbrush" campaign, which detailed the perils of bleeding gums, the share of Americans who brushed rose to 40%. Ipana's advertising helped all manufacturers of toothbrushes and toothpaste.

Although it's difficult to believe, starting in the 1970s, Wisk liquid detergent claimed that it solved a major social problem: ring around the collar (**www.youtube. com/watch?v=H5ro68Xs4Lc**). Presumably, some consumers—even among those who were gullible enough to find this ad compelling—could generalize that applying other liquid detergents would work equally well.

Alternatively, a firm's advertising may increase demand for its product by taking customers away from other firms. A firm may use advertising to differentiate its products from those of rivals. The advertising may describe actual physical differences in the products or try to convince customers that essentially identical products differ. If a firm succeeds with this latter type of advertising, the products are sometimes described as *spuriously* differentiated.

A firm can raise its profit if it can convince consumers that its product is superior to other brands. From the 1930s through the early 1970s, *secret ingredients* were a mainstay of consumer advertising. These ingredients were given names combining letters and numbers to suggest that they were cooked up in laboratories rather than by Madison Avenue. Dial soap boasted that it contained AT-7. Rinso detergent had solium; Comet included chlorinol; and Bufferin had di-alminate. Among the toothpastes, Colgate had Gardol, Gleem had GL-70, Crest had fluoristan, and Ipana had hexachlorophene and Durenamel.

About 30 years ago, secret ingredient claims fell out of favor, and manufacturers asserted that their brands contained *natural ingredients* such as baking soda and aloe. In the last few years, however, the secret ingredient approach has been reintroduced to differentiate brand names from cheaper competitors. Ads remind us that Clorets breath-freshening gum and mints contain Actizol. Cheer detergent touts an enzyme called Color Guard; Shade UVA Guard sunscreen lotion has Parasol 1789 and oxybenzone sun block agents; and Pond's Dramatic Results Skin Smoothing Capsules have Nutrium, "a miraculous oil-free complex."

Empirical evidence indicates that the impact of a firm's advertising on other firms varies across industries. At one extreme is cigarette advertising. Roberts and Samuelson (1988) found that cigarette advertising is cooperative in the sense that it increases the size of the market but does not change market shares substantially.[9] At the other extreme is cola advertising. Gasmi, Laffont, and Vuong (1992) reported that each firm's gain from advertising comes at the expense of its rivals; however, cola advertising has almost no effect on total market demand. Slade (1995) found results for saltine crackers that lie between these extremes.

If these empirical results are correct, cola firms would be delighted to have their advertising banned, but cigarette firms would oppose an advertising ban. In a more general model in which firms set the amount of advertising (rather than just decide whether to advertise or not), the amount of advertising depends critically on whether advertising increases the market size or only steals customers from rivals.

14.3 Dynamic Games

In static, normal-form games, players have imperfect information about how other players will act because everyone moves simultaneously and only once. In contrast, in *dynamic games* players move sequentially or move simultaneously repeatedly over time, so a player has perfect information about other players' previous moves. In this section, we show how to represent these static games diagrammatically and how to predict their outcomes.

Rather than use the normal form, economists analyze dynamic games in their **extensive form,** which specifies the *n* players, the sequence in which they make their moves, the actions they can take at each move, the information that each player has about players' previous moves, and the payoff function over all possible strategies. In this section, we assume that players not only have complete information about the payoff function but also have perfect information about the play of the game to this point.

We consider two types of dynamic games. We start with a *two-stage game,* which is played once and hence can be said to occur in a "single period." In the first stage, Player 1 moves. In the second stage, Player 2 moves and the game ends with the players' receiving payoffs based on their actions. An example of such a game is the Stackelberg model.

We then examine a *repeated* or *multiperiod* game in which a single-period, simultaneous-move game, such as the airline prisoners' dilemma game, is repeated at least twice and possibly many times. Although the players move simultaneously in each period, they know about their rivals' moves in previous periods, so a rival's previous move may affect a player's current action. As a result, it is a dynamic game.

In games where players move sequentially, we have to clearly distinguish between an action and a strategy. An action is a move that a player makes at a specified point, such as how much output a firm produces this period. A strategy is a battle plan that specifies the action that a player will make conditional on the information available at each

---

[9]However, evidence produced by the Centers for Disease Control and Prevention suggests that advertising may shift the brand loyalty of youths.

move. For example, American's strategy might state that it will fly 64 thousand passengers between Chicago and Los Angeles this quarter if United flew 64 thousand last quarter, but that it will fly only 48 thousand this quarter if United flew 48 thousand last quarter. This distinction between an action and a strategy is moot in a simultaneous-move, static game, where an action and a strategy are effectively the same.

SEQUENTIAL GAME

In solving a problem of this sort, the grand thing is to be able to reason backward.
—Sherlock Holmes (Sir Arthur Conan Doyle)

We illustrate a sequential-move or two-stage game using the Stackelberg airline model (Chapter 13), where American chooses its output level before United does. For simplicity, we assume that American and United Airlines can choose only output levels of 96, 64, and 48 million passengers per quarter.

Game Tree. The normal-form representation of this game, Table 14.2, does not capture the sequential nature of the firms' moves. To demonstrate the role of sequential moves, we use an *extensive-form diagram* or *game tree*, Figure 14.1, which shows the order of the firms' moves, each firm's possible actions at the time of its move, and the resulting profits at the end of the game.

In the figure, each box is a point of decision by one of the firms, called a *decision node*. The name in the decision node box indicates that it is that player's turn to

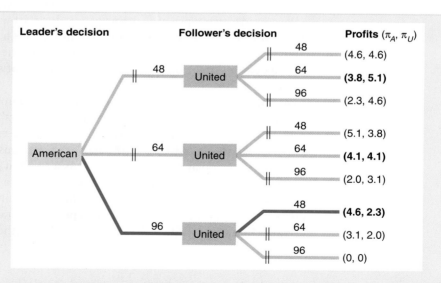

Figure 14.1 Stackelberg Game Tree. American, the leader firm, chooses its output level first. Given American's choice, United, the follower, picks an output level. The firms' profits that result from these decisions are shown on the right-hand side of the figure. Two lines through an action line show that the firm rejects that action.

move. The lines or *branches* extending out of the box represent a complete list of the possible actions that the player can make at that point of the game. On the left side of the figure, American, the leader, starts by picking one of the three output levels. In the middle of the figure, United, the follower, chooses one of the three quantities after learning the output level American chose. The right side of the figure shows the profits that American and United earn, given that they sequentially took the actions to reach this final branch. For instance, if American selects 64 and then United chooses 96, American earns $2.0 million profit per quarter and United earns $3.1 million.

Within this game are *subgames*. At a given stage, a subgame consists of all the subsequent decisions that players may make given the actions already taken. In the second stage where United makes a choice, there are three possible subgames. In Figure 14.1, if in the first stage American chooses $q_A = 48$, the relevant subgame is the top node in the second stage and its three branches. This game has four subgames. There are three subgames at the second stage where United makes a decision given each of American's three possible first-stage actions. There is an additional subgame at the time of the first-stage decision, which is the entire game.

Subgame Perfect Nash Equilibrium.   To predict the outcome of this sequential game, we introduce a stronger version of the Nash equilibrium concept. A set of strategies forms a **subgame perfect Nash equilibrium** if the players' strategies are a Nash equilibrium in every subgame. As the entire dynamic game is a subgame, a subgame perfect Nash equilibrium is also a Nash equilibrium. In contrast, in a simultaneous-move game such as the static prisoners' dilemma, the only subgame is the game itself, so there is no important distinction between the Nash equilibrium and the subgame perfect Nash equilibrium.

Table 14.2 shows the normal-form representation of this game in which the Nash equilibrium to the simultaneous-move game is for each firm to choose 64. However, if the firms move sequentially, the subgame perfect Nash equilibrium results in a different outcome.

We can solve for the subgame perfect Nash equilibrium using **backward induction,** where we first determine the best response by the last player to move, next determine the best response for the player who made the next-to-last move, and then repeat the process until we reach the move at the beginning of the game. In our example, we work backward from the decision by the follower, United, to the decision by the leader, American, moving from the right to the left side of the game tree.

How should American, the leader, select its output in the first stage? For each possible quantity it can produce, American predicts what United will do and picks the output level that maximizes its own profit. Thus to predict American's action in the first stage, American determines what United, the follower, will do in the second stage, given each possible output choice by American in the first stage. Using its conclusions about United's second-stage reaction, American makes its first-stage decision.

United, the follower, does not have a dominant strategy. The amount it chooses to produce depends on the quantity that American chose. If American chose 96, United's profit is $2.3 million if its output is 48, $2.0 million if it produces 64, and $0 if it picks a quantity of 96. Thus if American chose 96, United's best response is 48. The double lines through the other two action lines show that United will not choose those actions.

Using the same reasoning, American determines how United will respond to each of American's possible actions, as the right-hand side of the figure illustrates. American predicts that

- If American chooses 48, United will sell 64, so American's profit will be $3.8 million.
- If American chooses 64, United will sell 64, so American's profit will be $4.1 million.
- If American chooses 96, United will sell 48, so American's profit will be $4.6 million.

Thus to maximize its profit, American chooses 96 in the first stage. United's strategy is to make its best response to American's first-stage action: United selects 64 if American chooses 48 or 64, and United picks 48 if American chooses 96. Thus United responds in the second stage by selecting 48. In this subgame perfect Nash equilibrium, neither firm wants to change its strategy. Given that American Airlines sets its output at 96, United is using a strategy that maximizes its profit, $q_U = 48$, so it doesn't want to change. Similarly, given how United will respond to each possible American output level, American cannot make more profit than if it sells 96.

The subgame perfect Nash equilibrium requires players to believe that their opponents will act optimally—in their own best interests. No player has an incentive to deviate from the equilibrium strategies. The reason for adding the requirement of subgame perfection is that we want to explain what will happen if a player does not follow the equilibrium path. For example, if American does not choose its equilibrium output in the first stage, subgame perfection requires that United will still follow the strategy that maximizes its profit in the second stage conditional on American's actual output choice.

Not all Nash equilibria are subgame perfect Nash equilibria. For example, suppose that American's strategy is to pick 96 in the first stage, and United's strategy is to choose 96 if American selects 48 or 64, and 48 if American chooses 96. The outcome is the same as the subgame perfect Nash equilibrium we just derived because American selects 96, United chooses 48, and neither firm wants to deviate.[10] Thus this set of strategies is a Nash equilibrium. However, this set of strategies is not a subgame perfect Nash equilibrium. Although this Nash equilibrium has the same equilibrium path as the subgame perfect Nash equilibrium, United's strategy differs out of the equilibrium path. If American had selected 48 (or 64), United's strategy would not result in a Nash equilibrium. United would receive a higher profit if it produced 64 rather than the 96 that this strategy requires. Therefore this Nash equilibrium is not subgame perfect.

This subgame perfect Nash equilibrium, or Stackelberg equilibrium, differs from the simultaneous-move, Nash-Cournot equilibrium. American, the Stackelberg leader, sells 50% more than the Cournot quantity, 64, and earns $4.6 million, which is 15% more than the Cournot level of profit, $4.1 million. United, the Stackelberg follower, sells a quantity, 48, and earns a profit, $2.3 million, both of which are less than the Cournot levels. Thus although United has more information in the Stackelberg equilibrium than it does in the Cournot model—it knows American's output level—it is worse off than if both firms chose their actions simultaneously.

---

[10]Given United's strategy, American does not have any incentive to deviate. If American chooses 48 it will get $2.3 and if it chooses 64 it will get $2.0, both of which are less than $4.6 if chooses 96. And given American's strategy, no change in United's strategy would raise its profit.

Credibility. Why do the simultaneous-move and sequential-move games have different outcomes? Given the option to act first, American chooses a large output level to make it in United's best interest to pick a relatively small output level, 48. American benefits from moving first and choosing the Stackelberg leader quantity.

In the simultaneous-move game, why doesn't American announce that it will produce the Stackelberg leader's output to induce United to produce the Stackelberg follower's output level? The answer is that when the firms move simultaneously, United doesn't believe American's warning that it will produce a large quantity, because it is not in American's best interest to produce that large a quantity of output. For a firm's announced strategy to be a **credible threat,** rivals must believe that the firm's strategy is rational in the sense that it is in the firm's best interest to use it.[11] If American produced the leader's level of output and United produced the Cournot level, American's profit would be lower than if it too produced the Cournot level. Because American cannot be sure that United will believe its threat and reduce its output in the simultaneous-move game, American produces the Cournot output level. In contrast, in the sequential-move game, because American moves first, its commitment to produce a large quantity is credible.

The intuition for why commitment makes a threat credible is that of "burning bridges." If the general burns the bridge behind the army so that the troops can only advance and not retreat, the army becomes a more fearsome foe—like a cornered animal. Similarly, by limiting its future options, a firm makes itself stronger.[12]

Not all firms can make credible threats, however, because not all firms can make commitments. Typically, for a threat to succeed, a firm must have an advantage that allows it to harm the other firm before that firm can retaliate. Identical firms that act simultaneously cannot credibly threaten each other. However, a firm may be able to make its threatened behavior believable if firms differ. An important difference is the ability of one firm to act before the other. For example, an incumbent firm could lobby for the passage of a law that forbids further entry.

Dynamic Entry Game. We can illustrate the use of laws as a form of commitment by using the entry game. One gas station, the incumbent, is already operating at a highway rest stop that has room for at most two gas stations. The incumbent decides whether to pay b dollars to the rest stop's landlord for the *exclusive right* to be the only gas station at the rest stop. If this amount is paid, the landlord will rent the remaining land only to a restaurant or some other business that does not sell gasoline. The incumbent's profit, π_i, is the monopoly profit, π_m, minus b. If the incumbent does not

---

[11]No doubt you've been in a restaurant and listened to an exasperated father trying to control his brat with such extreme threats as "If you don't behave, you'll have to sit in the car while we eat dinner" or "If you don't behave, you'll never see television again." The kid, of course, does not view such threats as credible and continues to terrorize the restaurant—proving that the kid is a better game theorist than the father.

[12]Some psychologists use the idea of commitment to treat behavioral problems. A psychologist may advise an author with writer's block to set up an irreversible procedure whereby if the author's book is not finished by a certain date, the author's check for $10,000 will be sent to the group the author hates most in the world—be it the Nazi Party, the Ku Klux Klan, or the National Save the Skeets Foundation. Such an irreversible commitment helps the author get the project done by raising the cost of failure. (We can imagine the author playing a game against the author's own better self.)

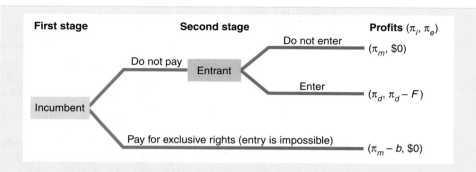

Figure 14.2 Game Tree: Whether an Incumbent Pays to Prevent Entry. If the potential entrant stays out of the market, it makes no profit, $\pi_e = 0$, and the incumbent firm makes the monopoly profit, $\pi_i = \pi_m$. If the potential entrant enters the market, the incumbent earns π_d and the entrant makes $\pi_d - F$. If the duopoly profit, π_d, is less than F, entry does not occur. Otherwise, entry occurs unless the incumbent acts to *deter* entry by paying for exclusive rights to be the only firm at the rest stop. The incumbent pays the landlord only if $\pi_m - b > \pi_d$.

act to prevent entry, the potential entrant decides whether or not to enter. If entry does not occur, the incumbent's profit, π_i, equals the monopoly profit, π_m, and the other firm's profit, π_e, is zero. If entry occurs, both firms receive the duopoly profit, π_d, but the entrant's profit, π_e, is $\pi_d - F$ after paying the fixed cost, F, to build a station. Using a game tree, we can show that the subgame perfect Nash equilibrium depends on the values of the parameters π_m, π_d, b, and F.

To draw the extensive-form diagram, we need to determine which firm acts at each stage of the game, what options a firm has at each stage, and the payoffs contingent on the firm's actions, and use that information to draw the extensive-form game tree. In the first stage, the incumbent decides whether to incur b so as to prevent entry. In the second stage, the potential entrant decides whether to enter. Figure 14.2 shows the extensive-form game tree. If the incumbent incurs b, $\pi_i = \pi_m - b$ and $\pi_e = 0$. If the incumbent does not incur b but the second firm chooses not to enter, $\pi_i = \pi_m$ and $\pi_e = 0$. Finally, if the incumbent does not incur b and the second firm enters, $\pi_i = \pi_d$ and $\pi_e = \pi_d - F$.

To solve for the subgame perfect Nash equilibrium, we use backward induction. If the incumbent acts to prevent entry by paying b, the entrant has no possible action, so the payoffs are $\pi_i = \pi_m - b$ and $\pi_e = 0$. If the incumbent does not pay the landlord to prevent entry, in the resulting subgame the potential entrant either enters and earns $\pi_e = \pi_d - F$ or it does not enter and earns $\pi_e = 0$. The potential entrant decides to enter if $\pi_d - F \geq 0$ (assuming that it enters if it breaks even), and otherwise it stays out of the market. Thus there are three possible subgame perfect Nash equilibria, depending on the parameters of the problem, π_m, π_d, b, and F:

■ If $\pi_d - F < 0$, the potential entrant stays out of the market, the incumbent does not spend b, so $\pi_i = \pi_m$ and $\pi_e = 0$ (top line).

■ If $\pi_d - F \geq 0$, then the potential entrant will enter unless the incumbent pays b. If $\pi_m - b \leq \pi_d$, the incumbent does not pay b, the other firm enters, and the payoffs are $\pi_i = \pi_d$ and $\pi_e = \pi_d - F$ (middle line).

■ If $\pi_d - F < 0$ and $\pi_m - b \geq \pi_d$, the incumbent pays b so that the other firm stays out of the market, and the payoffs are $\pi_i = \pi_m - b$ and $\pi_e = 0$ (bottom line).

Solved Problem 14.2 makes use of all the methods that we've covered to this point. It first assumes that the players are engaged in a simultaneous-move game and solves for the pure and mixed strategies. It then assumes that they play a sequential-move game and solves for the subgame perfect Nash equilibrium.

SOLVED PROBLEM 14.2

Currently, two groups of firms are fighting to determine the standard for the next generation of DVD players, which feature six-times-longer playing time and sharper images than previous models. A group led by Toshiba and NEC, with software from Microsoft, produce HD DVD discs. They are opposed by a group led by Sony that includes Dell, Hewlett-Packard, Panasonic, Samsung, and Sharp, which champions Blu-ray technology. According to its proponents, the Microsoft-Toshiba approach is easier to use and cheaper and maintains continuity with the legacy standard, while Blu-ray technology stores more data and produces sharper images. Each group apparently believes that its product will be more successful if all DVD players can handle its format, but each group wants to choose its own format. Suppose that the payoff matrix is[13]

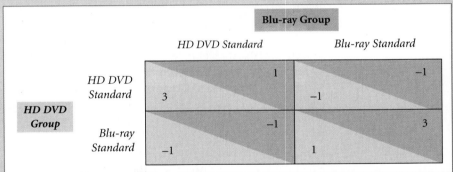

What are the pure- and mixed-strategy Nash equilibria if the firms must set their standards simultaneously?[14] If the HD DVD group could have committed to a standard before the Blu-ray group chose, what would the Nash equilibrium have been?

Answer

1. *Determine the pure-strategy Nash equilibria if the firms decide simultaneously:* There are two Nash equilibria in which both groups choose the same standard. If both choose the HD DVD standard, neither group would change its strategy if

---

[13]This game is of the same form as the game called *the battle of the sexes*. In that game, the husband likes to go to the mountains on vacation, and the wife prefers the ocean, but they both prefer to take their vacations together.

[14]In 2005, Toshiba and its Blu-ray rivals met to try to reach a compromise on the next-generation DVD standard. These efforts failed, and each side went ahead with its plans to produce a separate format, which started hitting the market in 2006. However, other firms quickly announced systems and discs that could handle both formats (Richard Siklos, "New Disc May Sway DVD Wars," *New York Times*, January 4, 2007).

it knew that the other was using the HD DVD standard. The HD DVD group's profit falls from 3 to −1 if it changes its strategy from the HD DVD to the Blu-ray standard, whereas the Blu-ray group's profit falls from 1 to −1 if it makes that change. Similarly, neither group would change its strategy from the Blu-ray standard if it believed that the other group would use the Blu-ray standard.

2. Determine the mixed-strategy Nash equilibria if the firms decide simultaneously: If the Blu-ray group chooses the HD DVD standard with a probability of θ_B, the HD DVD group's expected profit is $(3 \times \theta_B) + (-1 \times [1 - \theta_B]) = 4\theta_B - 1$ if it chooses the HD DVD standard and $(-1 \times \theta_B) + (1 \times [1 - \theta_B]) = 1 - 2\theta_B$ if it chooses the Blu-ray standard. For the HD DVD group to be indifferent between these two actions, its expected profits must be equal: $4\theta_B - 1 = 1 - 2\theta_B$. That is, if $\theta_B = \frac{1}{3}$, the HD DVD group is indifferent between choosing either standard. Similarly, if the HD DVD group selects the HD DVD standard with a probability of $\theta_H = \frac{2}{3}$, the Blu-ray group is indifferent between choosing either of the two standards.

3. Determine the Nash equilibrium if the HD DVD group could commit to a strategy first: The figure shows the extensive-form diagram given that the HD DVD group moves first. If it could commit first, the HD DVD group would choose the HD DVD standard. The HD DVD group knows that because the Blu-ray group realizes that the HD DVD group is using the HD DVD standard, the Blu-ray group will choose the HD DVD standard because it makes more (1) than if it chooses its own standard (−1). Thus with a first-mover advantage, the HD DVD group would choose its own standard, which its rival accepts.

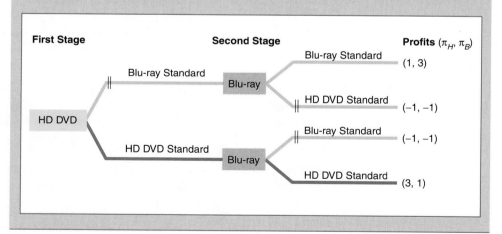

APPLICATION

Advantages and Disadvantages of Moving First

We've seen how a firm that enters the market first gains an advantage over potential rivals by moving first. The first-mover firm may prevent entry by building a reputation, committing to a large plant, raising costs to potential entrants, or getting an early start on learning by doing.

Toshiba, the main proponent of HD DVD, spent great sums of money to be the first to produce a next-generation DVD. In 2006, it started selling its format before any of its Blu-ray rivals. It sold its initial HD DVD player, which apparently contains nearly $700 worth of components, for $499. Presumably Toshiba was willing to lose $200 per unit to reinforce its first-to-market advantage by permeating the market with HD DVD units.

The downsides of entering early are that the cost of entering quickly is higher, the odds of miscalculating demand are greater, and later entrants may build on the pioneer's research to produce a superior product. As the first of a new class of anti-ulcer drugs, Tagamet was extremely successful when it was introduced. However, the second entrant, Zantac, rapidly took the lion's share of the market. Zantac works similarly to Tagamet but has fewer side effects, could be taken less frequently when it was first introduced, and was promoted more effectively.

However, such examples of domination by second entrants are unusual. Urban, Carter, and Gaskin (1986) examined 129 successful consumer products and found that the second entrant gained, on average, only three-quarters of the market share of the pioneer and that later entrants captured even smaller shares.

REPEATED GAME

We now turn to static games that are repeated. In each period, there is a single stage: Both players move simultaneously. However, these are dynamic games because Player 1's move in period t precedes Player 2's move in period $t + 1$; hence the earlier action may affect the later one. Such a repeated game is a *game of almost perfect information*: The players know all the moves from previous periods, but they do not know each other's moves within any one period because they all move simultaneously.

We showed that if American and United Airlines engage in a single-period prisoners' dilemma game, the two firms produce more than they would if they colluded. Yet cartels do form. What's wrong with this theory, which says that cartels won't occur? One explanation is that markets last for many periods, and collusion is more likely in a multiperiod game than in a single-period game.

In a single-period game, one firm cannot punish the other firm for cheating on a cartel agreement. But if the firms meet period after period, a wayward firm can be punished by the other.

Suppose now that the airlines' single-period prisoners' dilemma game is repeated quarter after quarter. If they play a single-period game, each firm takes its rival's strategy as a given and assumes that it cannot affect that strategy. When the same game is played repeatedly, the firms may devise strategies for this period that depend on rivals' actions in previous periods. For example, a firm may set a low output level this period only if its rival set a low output level in the previous period.

In a repeated game, a firm can influence its rival's behavior by *signaling* and *threatening to punish*. For example, one airline firm could use a low-quantity strategy for a couple of periods to signal to the other firm its desire that the two firms cooperate and produce that low quantity in the future. If the other firm does not respond by lowering its output in future periods, the first firm suffers lower profits for only a couple of periods. However, if the other firm responds to this signal and lowers its quantity, both firms can profitably produce at the low quantity thereafter.

In addition to or instead of signaling, a firm can threaten to punish a rival for not restricting output. The profit matrix in Table 14.1 illustrates how firms can punish rivals to ensure collusion. Suppose that American announces or somehow indicates to United that it will use the following two-part strategy:

- American will produce the smaller quantity each period as long as United does the same.
- If United produces the larger quantity in period t, American will produce the larger quantity in period $t + 1$ and all subsequent periods.

If United believes that American will follow this strategy, United knows that it will make $4.6 million each period if it produces the lower quantity. Although United can make a higher profit, $5.1 million, in period t by producing the larger quantity, by doing so it lowers its potential profit to $4.1 million in each following period. Thus United's best policy is to produce the lower quantity in each period unless it cares greatly about current profit and little about future profits. If United values future profits nearly as much as current ones, the one-period gain from deviating from the collusive output level will not compensate for the losses from reduced profits in future periods, which is the punishment American will impose. United may take this threat by American seriously because American's best response is to produce the larger quantity if it believes it can't trust United to produce the smaller quantity.[15] Thus if firms play the same game *indefinitely*, they should find it easier to collude.

Yet playing the same game many times does not necessarily help the firms cooperate. Suppose, for example, that the firms know that they are going to play the game for T periods. In the last period, they know that they're not going to play again, so they know they can cheat—produce a large quantity—without fear of punishment. As a result, the last period is like a single-period game, and both firms produce the large quantity. That makes the $T - 1$ period the last interesting period. By the same reasoning, the firms will cheat in $T - 1$ because they know that they will both cheat in the last period and hence no additional punishment can be imposed. Continuing this type of argument, we conclude that maintaining an agreement to produce the small quantity will be difficult if the game has a known stopping point. If the players know that the game will end but aren't sure when, cheating is less likely to occur. Cooperation is therefore more likely in a game that will continue forever or one that will end at an uncertain time.

14.4   Auctions

To this point, we have examined games in which players have complete information about payoff functions. We now turn to an important game, the auction, in which players devise bidding strategies without knowing other players' payoff functions.

An **auction** is a sale in which a good or service is sold to the highest bidder. A substantial amount of exchange takes place through auctions. Government contracts are typically awarded using procurement auctions. In recent years, governments have

---

[15]American does not have to punish United forever to induce it to cooperate. All it has to do is punish it for enough periods that it does not pay for United to deviate from the low-quantity strategy in any period.

auctioned portions of the airwaves for radio stations, mobile phones, and wireless Internet access and have used auctions to set up electricity and transport markets. Other goods commonly sold at auction are natural resources such as timber, as well as houses, cars, agricultural produce, horses, antiques, and art. In this section, we first consider the various types of auctions and then investigate how the rules of the auction influence buyers' strategies.

ELEMENTS OF AUCTIONS

Before deciding what strategy to use when bidding in an auction, one needs to know the rules of the game. Auctions have three key components: the number of units being sold, the format of the bidding, and the value that potential bidders place on the good.

Number of Units. Auctions can be used to sell one or many units of a good. In 2004, Google auctioned its initial public offering of many identical shares of stock at one time. In many other auctions, a single good—such as an original painting—is sold. For simplicity in this discussion, we concentrate on auctions where a single, indivisible item is sold.

Format. How auctions are conducted varies greatly. However, most approaches are variants of the *English auction*, the *Dutch auction*, or the *sealed-bid auction*.

- **English auction:** In the United States and Britain, almost everyone has seen an *English* or *ascending-bid auction*, at least in the movies. The auctioneer starts the bidding at the lowest price that is acceptable to the seller and then repeatedly encourages potential buyers to bid more than the previous highest bidder. The auction ends when no one is willing to bid more than the current highest bid: "Going, going, gone!" The good is sold to the last bidder for the highest bid. Sotheby's and Christie's use English auctions to sell art and antiques.
- **Dutch auction:** A *Dutch auction* or *descending-bid auction* ends dramatically with the first "bid." The seller starts by asking if anyone wants to buy at that price. The seller reduces the price by given increments until someone accepts the offered price and then buys at that price. Variants of Dutch auctions are often used to sell multiple goods at once, such as in Google's initial public offering auction and the U.S. Treasury's sales of Treasury bills.
- **Sealed-bid auction:** In a *sealed-bid auction*, everyone submits a bid simultaneously without seeing anyone else's bid (for example, by submitting each bid in a sealed envelope), and the highest bidder wins. The price the winner pays depends on whether it is a first-price auction or a second-price auction. In a *first-price auction*, the winner pays its own, highest bid. Governments often use this type of auction. In a *second-price auction*, the winner pays the amount bid by the second-highest bidder. Many computer auction houses use a variant of the second-price auction.

For example, you bid on eBay by specifying the maximum amount you are willing to bid. If your maximum is greater than the maximum bid of other participants, eBay's computer places a bid on your behalf that is a small increment above the maximum bid of the second-highest bidder. This system differs from the traditional sealed-bid auction in that people can continue to bid until the official end-time of the auction, and potential bidders know the current bid price (but not the maximum that the highest bidder is willing to pay). Thus eBay has some of the characteristics of an English

Value. Auctioned goods are normally described as having a *private value* or a *common value.* Typically, this distinction turns on whether the good is unique.

- **Private value:** If each potential bidder places a different personal value on the good, we say that the good has a *private value.* Individual bidders know how much the good is worth to them but not how much other bidders value it. The archetypical example is an original work of art about which people differ greatly as to how much they value it.
- **Common value:** Many auctions involve a good that has the same fundamental value to everyone, but no buyer knows exactly what that *common value* is. For example, in a timber auction, firms bid on all the trees in a given area. All firms know what the current price of lumber is; however, they do not know exactly how many board feet of lumber are contained in the trees.

In many actual auctions, goods have both private value and common value. For example, in the tree auction, bidding firms may differ not only in their estimates of the amount of lumber in the trees (common value), but also in their costs of harvesting (private value).

BIDDING STRATEGIES IN PRIVATE-VALUE AUCTIONS

A potential buyer's optimal strategy depends on the number of units, the format, and the type of values in an auction. For specificity, we examine auctions in which each bidder places a different private value on a single, indivisible good.

Second-Price Auction Strategies. According to eBay, if you choose to bid on an item in its second-price auction, you should "enter the maximum amount you are willing to spend" (**pages.ebay.com/education/gettingstarted/researching.html**). Is eBay's advice correct?

In a traditional sealed-bid, second-price auction, bidding your highest value *weakly dominates* all other bidding strategies: The strategy of bidding your maximum value leaves you *as well off* as, *or better off* than, bidding any other value. The amount that you bid affects whether you win, but it does not affect how much you pay if you win, which equals the second-highest bid.

Suppose that you value a folk art carving at $100. If the highest amount that any other participant is willing to bid is $85 and you place a bid greater than $85, you will buy the carving for $85 and receive $15 (= $100 − $85) of consumer surplus. Other bidders pay nothing and gain no consumer surplus.

Should you ever bid more than your value? Suppose that you bid $120. There are three possibilities. First, if the highest bid of your rivals is greater than $120, then you do not buy the good and receive no consumer surplus. This outcome is the same as what you would have received if you had bid $100, so bidding higher than $100 does not benefit you.

Second, if the highest alternative bid is less than $100, then you win and receive the same consumer surplus that you would have received had you bid $100. Again, bidding higher does not affect the outcome.

Third, if the highest bid by a rival were an amount between $100 and $120—say, $110—then bidding more than your maximum value causes you to win, but you purchase the good for more than you value it, so you receive negative consumer surplus: −$10 (= $100 − $110). In contrast, if you had bid your maximum value, you would not have won, and your consumer surplus would have been zero—which is better than losing $10. Thus bidding more than your maximum value can never make you better off than bidding your maximum value, and you may suffer.

Should you ever bid less than your maximum value, say, $90? No, because you only lower the odds of winning without affecting the price that you pay if you do win. If the highest alternative bid is less than $90 or greater than your value, you receive the same consumer surplus by bidding $90 as you would by bidding $100. However, if the highest alternative bid lies between $90 and $100, you will lose the auction and give up positive consumer surplus by underbidding.

Thus you do as well or better by bidding your value than by over- or underbidding. This argument does not turn on whether or not you know other bidders' valuation. If you know your own value but not other bidders' values, bidding your value is your best strategy. If everyone follows this strategy, the person who places the highest value on the good will win and will pay the second-highest value.

● APPLICATION

Who Bids Optimally?

We've seen that bidding one's value is the dominant strategy in a sealed-bid, second-price auction. Economics professors conducting experimental sealed-bid, second-price auctions under "laboratory" settings using college students as subjects have been surprised to observe many overbids—bids that exceed the bidder's value—and few underbids. Garratt et al. (2005) provided an explanation. The students participating in these experiments had little prior experience bidding in auctions. Would experienced bidders use better strategies?

Garratt et al. repeated the experiment using people with extensive experience in eBay auctions. Auctions on eBay are second-price auctions that occur over time rather than sealed-bid auctions. The researchers found that even these experienced bidders did not always bid their values. However, unlike the inexperienced subjects, these bidders did not exhibit a systematic bias: They were just as likely to underbid as to overbid.

English Auction Strategy. Suppose instead that the seller uses an English auction to sell the carving to bidders with various private values. Your best strategy is to raise the current highest bid as long as your bid is less than the value you place on the good, $100. If the current bid is $85, you should increase your bid by the smallest permitted amount, say, $86, which is less than your value. If no one raises the bid further, you win and receive a positive surplus of $14. By the same reasoning, it always pays to increase your bid up to $100, where you receive zero surplus if you win.

However, it never pays to bid more than $100. The best outcome that you can hope for is to lose and receive zero surplus. Were you to win, you would have negative surplus.

If all participants bid up to their value, the winner will pay slightly more than the value of the second-highest bidder. Thus the outcome is essentially the same as in the sealed-bid, second-price auction.

Equivalence of Auction Outcomes. For Dutch or first-price sealed-bid auctions, one can show that participants will *shave* their bids to less than their value. The basic intuition is that you do not know the values of the other bidders. Reducing your bid reduces the probability that you win but increases your consumer surplus if you win.

Your optimal bid, which balances these two effects, is lower than your actual value. Your bid depends on your beliefs about the strategies of your rivals. It can be shown that the best strategy is to bid an amount that is equal to or slightly greater than what you expect will be the second-highest bid, given that your value is the highest.

Thus the expected outcome is the same under each format for private-value auctions: The winner is the person with the highest value, and the winner pays roughly the second-highest value. According to the Revenue Equivalence Theorem (Klemperer, 2004), under certain plausible conditions we would expect the same revenue from any auction in which the winner is the person who places the highest value on the good.

WINNER'S CURSE

A phenomenon occurs in common-value auctions that does not occur in private-value auctions. The **winner's curse** is that the auction winner's bid exceeds the common-value item's value. The overbidding occurs when there is uncertainty about the true value of the good.

When the government auctions off timber on a plot of land, potential bidders may differ in their estimates of how many board feet of lumber are available on that land. The higher one's estimate, the more likely that one will make the winning bid. If the average bid is accurate, then the high bid is probably excessive. Thus the winner's curse is paying too much.

I can minimize the likelihood of falling prey to the winner's curse by *shading* my bid: reducing the bid below my estimate. I know that if I win, I am probably overestimating the value of the good. The amount by which I should shade my bid depends on the number of other bidders, because the more bidders, the more likely that the winning bid is an overestimate.

Because intelligent bidders shade their bids, sellers can do better with an English auction than with a sealed-bid auction. In an English auction, bidders revise their views about the object's value as they watch others bid.

Summary

1. **An Overview of Game Theory:** The set of tools that economists use to analyze conflict and cooperation among players (such as firms) is called game theory. Each player adopts a strategy or battle plan to compete with other firms. Economists typically assume that players have *common knowledge* about the rules of the game, the payoff functions, and other players' knowledge about these issues. In many games, players have *complete information* about how payoffs depend on the strategies of all players. In some games, players have *perfect information* about players' previous moves.

2. **Static Games:** In a static game, such as in the Cournot model or the prisoners' dilemma game, players each make one move simultaneously. Economists use a normal-form representation or payoff matrix to analyze a static game. Typically, economists study static games in which players have complete information about the payoff function—the payoff to any player conditional on the actions all

players take—but imperfect information about how their rivals behave because they act simultaneously. The set of players' strategies is a Nash equilibrium if, given that all other players use these strategies, no player can obtain a higher payoff by choosing a different strategy. Both pure-strategy and mixed-strategy Nash equilibria are possible in static games, and there may be multiple Nash equilibria for a given game. There is no guarantee that Nash equilibria in static games maximize the joint payoffs of all the players.

3. **Dynamic Games:** In dynamic games, a player takes the other players' previous moves into account when choosing a move. In sequential-move games, one player moves before the other player. Economists typical study sequential games of complete information about payoffs and perfect information about previous moves. The first mover may have an advantage over the second mover, such as in a Stackelberg game. An incumbent with first-mover advantage prevents entry by making a *credible*

threat. For example, in a Stackelberg game, the leader *commits* to producing so much output that it is in the follower's best interest to produce a relatively small amount of output. In a repeated game, players replay a static game in which they move simultaneously within a period. The players have perfect information about other players' moves in previous periods but imperfect information within a period because the players move simultaneously. The best-known solution of a dynamic game is a subgame perfect Nash equilibrium, where the players' strategies are a Nash equilibrium in every subgame—the remaining game following a particular junction in the game. Players may use more complex strategies in dynamic games than in static games. Moreover, it is easier for players to maximize their joint payoff in a repeated game than in a single-period game.

4. **Auctions:** Auctions are games of incomplete information because bidders do not know the valuation others place on a good. Buyers' optimal strategies depend on the characteristics of an auction. Under fairly general conditions, if the auction rules result in a win by the person placing the highest value on a good that various bidders value differently, the expected price is the same in all auctions. For example, the expected price in various types of private-value auctions is the value of the good to the person who values it second-highest. In auctions where everyone values the good the same, though they may differ in their estimates of that value, the successful bidder may suffer from the winner's curse—paying too much—unless bidders shade their bids to compensate for their overoptimistic estimation of the good's value.

Questions

* = answer at the back of this book; **W** = audio-slide show answers by James Dearden at **www.aw-bc.com/perloff**

1. Show that advertising is a dominant strategy for both firms in both panels of Table 14.4. Explain why that set of strategies is a Nash equilibrium.

*2. Show the payoff matrix and explain the reasoning in the prisoners' dilemma example where Larry and Duncan, possible criminals, will get one year in prison if neither talks; if one talks, one goes free and the other gets five years; and if both talk, both get two years. (*Note:* The payoffs are negative because they represent years in jail, which is a bad.)

3. Lori employs Max. She wants him to work hard rather than to loaf. She considers offering him a bonus or not giving him one. All else the same, Max prefers to loaf.

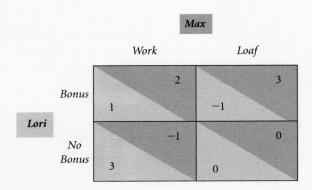

If they choose actions simultaneously, what are their strategies?

4. Two firms are planning to sell 10 or 20 units of their goods and face the following payoff matrix:

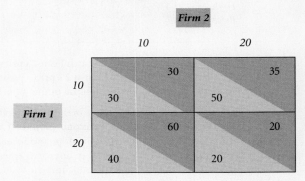

a. What is the Nash equilibrium or equilibria if both firms make their decisions simultaneously? Why? (What strategy does each firm use?)

b. Suppose that Firm 1 can decide first. What is the outcome? Why?

c. Suppose that Firm 2 can decide first. What is the outcome? Why?

5. Suppose that Panasonic and Zenith are the only two firms that can produce a new type of high-definition television. The payoffs (in millions of dollars) from entering this product market are shown in the following payoff matrix:

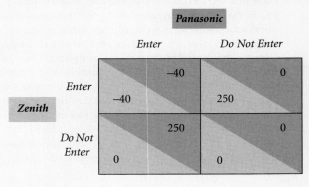

a. If both firms move simultaneously, does either firm have a dominant strategy? Explain.

b. What are the Nash equilibria given that both firms move simultaneously?

c. The U.S. government commits to paying Zenith a lump-sum subsidy of $50 million if it enters this market. What is the Nash equilibrium?

d. If Zenith does not receive a subsidy but has a head start over Panasonic, what is the Nash equilibrium?

6. Suppose that two firms face the following payoff matrix:

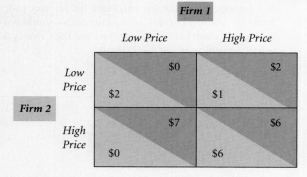

Firm 1

	Low Price	*High Price*
Low Price	$0 / $2	$2 / $1
High Price	$7 / $0	$6 / $6

Firm 2

Given these payoffs, Firm 2 wants to match Firm 1's price, but Firm 1 does not want to match Firm 2's price. What, if any, are the pure-strategy Nash equilibria of this game?

7. The more an incumbent firm produces in the first period, the lower its marginal cost in the second period. If a potential entrant expects the incumbent to produce a large quantity in the second period, it does not enter. Draw a game tree to illustrate why an incumbent would produce more in the first period than the single-period profit-maximizing level. Now change the payoffs in the tree to show a situation in which the firm does not increase production in the first period.

8. From the ninth century B.C. until the proliferation of gunpowder in the fifteenth century A.D., the ultimate weapon of mass destruction was the catapult (John Noble Wilford, "How Catapults Married Science, Politics and War," *New York Times*, February 24, 2004: D3). Hero of Alexandria pointed out in the first century A.D. that it was not enough to have catapults. You needed your potential enemies to know that you had catapults so that they would not attack you in the first place. As early as the fourth century B.C., rulers set up what were essentially research and development laboratories to support military technology. However, unlike today, there was a conspicuous lack of secrecy. According to Alex Roland, a historian of technology at Duke University, "Rulers seemed to promote the technology for immediate payoff for themselves and had not yet worked through the notion that you ought to protect your investment with secrecy and restrictions. So engineers shopped their wares around, and information circulated freely among countries." Given this information,

describe a ruler's optimal strategy with respect to catapult research, development, deployment, and public announcements. Should the strategy depend upon the country's wealth or size? What role does credibility of announcements play?

9. A thug wants the contents of a safe and is threatening the owner, the only person who knows the code, to open the safe. "I will kill you if you don't open the safe, and let you live if you do." Should the information holder believe the threat and open the safe? The table shows the value that each person places on the various possible outcomes.

	Thug	Safe's Owner
Open the safe, thug does not kill	4	3
Open the safe, thug kills	2	1
Do not open, thug kills	1	2
Do not open, thug does not kill	3	4

Such a game appears in many films, including *Die Hard*, *Crimson Tide*, and *The Maltese Falcon*.

a. Draw the game tree. Who moves first?

b. What is the equilibrium?

c. Does the safe's owner believe the thug's threat?

d. Does the safe's owner open the safe?   **W**

10. The *Wall Street Journal* (John Lippman, "The Producers: 'The Terminator' Is Back," March 8, 2002, A1) reports that Warner Bros. agreed to pay $50 million for its U.S. distribution rights, plus an additional $50 million in marketing costs, so that it could release *Terminator 3* (*T-3*) in the summer of 2003. It paid this large sum because it did not want anyone else to release *T-3* on the same weekend in 2003 that Warner Bros. released its movie *Matrix 2*. Suppose that Warner Bros. has not purchased the distribution rights to *T-3* and that the film's producer retains the rights. Warner Bros. decides whether to release *Matrix 2* on the July 4 weekend or on the July 18 weekend. Simultaneously, *T-3*'s producer decides which of those two weekends to release its film. The payoff matrix (in millions of dollars) of the simultaneous-moves game is:

Warner Bros.

	July 4	*July 18*
July 4	50 / 50	35 / 80
July 18	90 / 30	20 / 20

T-3 Producer

a. What is the Nash equilibrium to this simultaneous-moves game?

b. Which release dates maximize the sum of the profits? Explain.

c. What is the greatest price Warner Bros. is willing to pay to purchase the distribution rights to *T-3*? What is the lowest price that *T-3*'s producer is willing to accept to sell the rights? Are there mutually beneficial prices at which the trade takes place?

d. If Warner Bros. purchases the distribution rights of *T-3*, when does it release the film and when does it release *Matrix 2*? Explain. **W**

11. In 2003, Microsoft spent $150 million on an advertising campaign to promote its latest version of Microsoft Office (Nat Ives, "Advertising," *New York Times,* October 21, 2003: C6). That amount was five times as much as it spent promoting an upgrade in 2001. What are the possible explanations for its increase in expenditures? Does its action necessarily imply that Microsoft fears its competitors more than in previous years? Explain.

12. In Solved Problem 14.1, suppose that Mimi can move first. What are the equilibria, and why? Now repeat your analysis if Jeff can move first.

13. Takashi Hashiyama, president of the Japanese electronics firm Maspro Denkoh Corporation, was torn between having Christie's or Sotheby's auction the company's $20 million art collection, which included a van Gogh, a Cézanne, and an early Picasso (Carol Vogel, "Rock, Paper, Payoff," *New York Times,* April 29, 2005: A1, A24). He resolved the issue by having the two auction houses' representatives compete in the playground game of rock-paper-scissors. A rock (fist) breaks scissors (two fingers sticking out), scissors cut paper (flat hand), and paper smothers rock (**mediapickle.com/new/?p=content_template2&idb=458**). At stake were several million dollars in commissions. Christie's won: scissors beat paper.

a. Show the profit or payoff matrix for this rock-paper-scissors game. (*Hint:* You may assume that the payoff is –1 if you lose, 0 if you tie, and 1 if you win.)

b. Sotheby's expert in Impressionist and modern art said, "[T]his is a game of chance, so we didn't really give it much thought. We had no strategy in mind." In contrast, the president of Christie's in Japan researched the psychology of the game and consulted with the 11-year-old twin daughters of the director of the Impressionist and modern art department. One of these girls said, "Everybody knows you always start with scissors. Rock is way too obvious, and scissors beats paper." The other opined, "Since they were beginners, scissors was definitely the safest." Evaluate these comments on strategy. What strategy would you recommend if you knew that your rival was consulting with 11-year-old girls? In general, what pure or mixed strategy would you have recommended, and why?

14. Two firms are planning to sell 10 or 20 units of their goods and face the following payoff matrix:

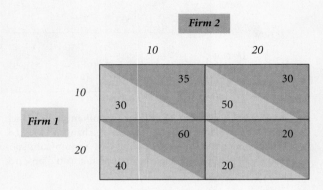

a. What is the Nash equilibrium if both firms make their decisions simultaneously? Why? (What strategy does each firm use?)

b. Suppose that Firm 1 can decide first. What is the outcome? Why?

c. Suppose that Firm 2 can decide first. What is the outcome? Why?

15. Two guys suffering from testosterone poisoning drive toward each other in the middle of a road. As they approach the impact point, each has the option of continuing to drive down the middle of the road or to swerve. Both believe that if only one driver swerves, that driver loses face (payoff = 0) and the other gains in self-esteem (payoff = 2). If neither swerves, they are maimed or killed (payoff = –10). If both swerve, no harm is done to either (payoff = 1). Show the payoff matrix for the two drivers engaged in this game of chicken. Determine the Nash equilibria for this game.

16. In 2007, Italy announced that an Italian journalist who had been held hostage for 15 days by the Taliban in Afghanistan had been ransomed for five Taliban prisoners. Governments in many nations denounced the act as a bad idea because it rewarded terrorism and encouraged more abductions. Use an extensive-form game tree to analyze the basic arguments. Can you draw any hard and fast conclusions about whether the Italians' actions were a good or bad idea? (*Hint:* Does your answer depend on the relative weight one puts on future costs and benefits relative to those today?)

*17. Suppose that Toyota and GM are considering entering a new market for electric automobiles and that their profits (in millions of dollars) from entering or staying out of the market are

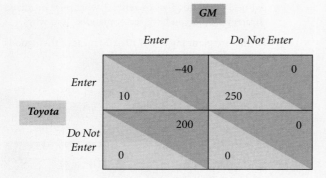

GM

	Enter	Do Not Enter
Enter	10 / −40	250 / 0
Do Not Enter	0 / 200	0 / 0

Toyota

If the firms make their decisions simultaneously, which firms enter? How would your answer change if the U.S. government committed to paying GM a lump-sum subsidy of $50 million on the condition that it would produce this new type of car?

18. Suppose the previous question were modified so that GM has no subsidy but does have a head start over Toyota and can move first. What is the Nash equilibrium? Explain.

19. In the repeated-game airline example, what happens if the game is played forever but one or both firms care only about current profit?

*20. A monopoly manufacturing plant currently uses many workers to pack its product into boxes. It can replace these workers with an expensive set of robotic arms. Although the robotic arms raise the monopoly's fixed cost substantially, they lower its marginal cost because it no longer has to hire as many workers. Buying the robotic arms raises its total cost: The monopoly can't sell enough boxes to make the machine pay for itself, given the market demand curve. Suppose the incumbent does not invest. If its rival does not enter, it earns $0 and the incumbent earns $900. If the rival enters, it earns $300 and the incumbent earns $400. Alternatively, the incumbent invests. If the rival does not enter, it earns $0 and the incumbent earns $500. If the rival enters, the rival loses $36 and the incumbent makes $132. Show the game tree. Should the monopoly buy the machine anyway?

*21. Suppose that an incumbent can commit to producing a large quantity of output before the potential entrant decides whether to enter. The incumbent chooses whether to commit to produce a small quantity, q_i, or a large quantity. The rival then decides whether to enter. If the incumbent commits to the small output level and if the rival does not enter, the rival makes $0 and the incumbent makes $900. If it does enter, the rival makes $125 and the incumbent earns $450. If the incumbent commits to producing the large quantity, and the potential entrant stays out of the market, the potential entrant makes $0 and the incumbent makes $800. If the rival enters, the best the entrant can make is $0, the same amount it would earn if it didn't enter, but the incumbent earns only $400. Show the game tree. What is the subgame perfect Nash equilibrium?

*22. Before entry, the incumbent earns a monopoly profit of $\pi_m = \$10$ (million). If entry occurs, the incumbent and entrant each earn the duopoly profit, $\pi_d = \$3$. Suppose that the incumbent can induce the government to require all firms to install pollution-control devices that cost each firm $4. Show the game tree. Should the incumbent urge the government to require pollution-control devices? Why or why not?

Problems

23. Suppose that you and a friend play a "matching pennies" game in which each of you uncovers a penny. If both pennies show heads or both show tails, you keep both. If one shows heads and the other shows tails, your friend keeps them. Show the payoff matrix. What, if any, is the pure-strategy Nash equilibrium to this game? Is there a mixed-strategy Nash equilibrium? If so, what is it?

24. Modify the payoff matrix in the game of chicken in Question 15 so that the payoff is −2 if neither driver swerves. How does the equilibrium change?

*25. What is the mixed-strategy Nash equilibrium for the game in Question 6?

26. What are the Nash equilibria to the battle of the sexes game in footnote 13? Discuss whether this game and the equilibrium concept make sense for analyzing a couple's decisions. How might you change the game's rules so that it makes more sense?

27. The town of Perkasie, Pennsylvania, has two diners: Emil's Diner and Bobby Ray's Diner. Both sell only chicken pies. Everyone who considers eating at the diners is aware that they sell the same chicken pies and knows the prices that they charge (p_E, p_{BR}). At precisely 5 P.M., each diner (simultaneously) sets its price of chicken pie for that evening. The market demand function for chicken pie is $Q = 120 - 20p$, where p is the lower of the two diners' prices. If there is a lower-priced diner, then people eat chicken pie at only that diner and the diner sells $120 - 20p$ chicken pies. If the two diners post the same price, then each sells to one-half of the market: $1/2(100 - 20p)$.

Suppose that prices can be quoted in dollar units only (0, 1, 2, 3, 4, 5, or 6). Each diner's marginal cost is $2 and the fixed cost is $0.

a. Create a 7×7 payoff matrix and fill in the diners' profits.
b. Identify all Nash equilibria.
c. Suppose that Bobby Ray's Diner is out of business and that Emil's is a monopoly. Find Emil's profit-maximizing price.
d. Now return to the Emil's-versus-Bobby Ray's game. Pick one of the Nash equilibria that you identified in part b. Could Emil's and Bobby Ray's collude—set prices different from the particular Nash equilibrium prices and increase both diners' profits? **W**

28. Acura and Volvo offer warranties on their automobiles, where w_A is the number of years of an Acura warranty and w_V is the number of years of a Volvo warranty. The revenue for Firm i, $i = A$ for Acura and V for Volvo, is $R_i = 27,000w_i/(w_A + w_V)$. Its cost of providing the warranty is $C_i = 2,000w_i$. Acura and Volvo participate in a warranty-setting game in which they simultaneously set warranties.

a. What is the profit function for each firm?
b. Suppose Acura and Volvo can set warranties in year lengths only, with a maximum of five years. Fill in a 5×5 payoff matrix with Acura's and Volvo's profits.
c. Determine the Nash equilibrium warranties.
d. Compare the Nash equilibrium warranties. If the two manufacturers offer the same warranty, explain why. If they offer different warranties, explain why.
e. Suppose Acura and Volvo collude in setting warranties. What warranties do they set?
f. Suppose Acura's cost of offering warranties decreases to $C_V = 1,000w_V$. What is the new Nash equilibrium? Explain the effect of the decrease in Volvo's cost function on the equilibrium warranties. **W**

29. In the competition to attract athletes and produce champion teams, universities increased their spending on college athletics four times faster than overall university spending from 2001 through 2003. Schools have poured money into athletic programs even though studies show that this practice does not increase winning rates or alumni donations ("Review & Outlook," *Wall Street Journal*, May 27, 2005, W15). Nonetheless, suppose that money does matter in producing championships. University A spends m_A on its football team and University B spends m_B. The fraction of the time that University A wins is $w_A = m_A/(m_A + m_B)$, and the fraction that B wins is $w_B = 1 - w_A = m_B/(m_A + m_B)$. Suppose that each university wants to maximize its profit from having sports teams. The expected profit of University i, $i = A, B$, is $\pi_i = v_i m_i/(m_A + m_B)$, where v_i is the value to University i of winning a game.

a. Show that if $v_A = v_B$ in the Nash equilibrium, each school wins one-half of its games.

b. Show that if $v_A = v_B$ increases, each school spends more on its teams but continues to win one-half of its games.
c. Explain the result that schools are spending more on sports without affecting their win-loss ratios. **W**

30. In their study of cigarette advertising, Roberts and Samuelson (1988) found that the advertising of a particular brand affects overall market demand for cigarettes but does not affect the brand's share of market sales. Suppose the demand for brand i is $q_i = a + b(A_i + A_j)^{1/2}$, where A_i is brand i's advertising expenditure. Brand i's profit function is $\pi_i = p_i(a + b(A_i + A_j)^{1/2}) - A_i$.

a. Does brand B's advertising expenditure affect A's market share, $q_A/(q_A + q_B)$?
b. In terms of a and b, what are the Nash equilibrium advertising expenditures? How does an increase in b affect the equilibrium expenditures? **W**

31. Two stars—the 100-meter gold medalist and the 200-meter gold medalist—from the last recent Olympic Games have agreed to a 150-meter duel. Before the race, each athlete decides whether to improve his performance by taking anabolic steroids. Each athlete's payoff is 20 from winning the race, 10 from tying, and 0 from losing. Furthermore, each athlete's utility of taking steroids is −6. Model this scenario as a game in which the players simultaneously decide whether to take steroids.

a. What is the Nash equilibrium? Is the game a prisoners' dilemma? Explain.
b. Suppose that one athlete's utility of taking steroids is −12, while the other's remains −6. What is the Nash equilibrium? Is the game a prisoners' dilemma? **W**

32. In the novel and film *The Princess Bride*, the villain Vizzini kidnaps the princess. In an attempt to rescue her, the hero, Westley, challenges Vizzini to a battle of wits. Consider this variation on the actual plot. (I do not want to reveal the actual story.) In the battle, Westley puts two identical glasses of wine behind his back, out of Vizzini's view, and adds iocane powder to only one glass. Iocane is "odorless, tasteless, dissolves instantly in liquid, and is among the more deadly poisons known to man." Westley decides which glass to put on a table in front of Vizzini and which to put on the table in front of himself. Then, with Westley's back turned so that he cannot observe Vizzini's move, Vizzini decides whether to switch the two glasses. Assume the two simultaneously drink all the wine in their respective wine glasses. Assume also that each player's payoff from drinking the poisoned wine is −3 and the payoff from drinking the safe wine is +1. Write the payoff matrix for this simultaneous-moves game. Specify the possible Nash equilibria. Is there a pure-strategy Nash equilibrium? Is there a mixed-strategy Nash equilibrium? **W**

33. Xavier and Ying are partners in a course project. Xavier is the project leader and thus is the first to decide how many

hours, h_X, to put into the project. After observing the amount of time that Xavier contributes, Ying decides how many hours, h_Y, to contribute. Xavier's utility function is $U_X = 18(h_X + h_Y)^{1/2} - h_X$, and Ying's utility function is $U_Y = 18(h_X + h_Y)^{1/2} - h_Y$. Ying threatens not to work on the project. For Ying's threat to be credible, what is the smallest number of hours that Xavier must contribute to the project? How much time does Xavier contribute? Does Ying work on the project? **W**

34. Suppose that Anna, Bill, and Cameron are the only three people interested in the paintings of the Bucks County artist Walter Emerson Baum. His painting *Sellers Mill* is being auctioned by a second-price sealed-bid auction. Suppose Anna's value of the painting is $20,000, Bill's is $18,500, and Cameron's is $16,800. Each bidder's consumer surplus is $v_i - p$ if he or she wins the auction and 0 if he or she loses. The values are private. What is each bidder's optimal bid? Who wins the auction, and what price does he or she pay? **W**

35. In the AFC championship game between the Indianapolis Colts and the New England Patriots in 2007, the Colts had a fourth down and inches play. Rather than punt the ball and turn it over to their opponent, the Colts decided to go for a first down. Suppose the Colts have two play options: a fullback running up the middle or a screen pass to a wide receiver. The Patriots also have two play options: setting up to defend against the run or setting up to defend against the screen pass. The coaches of the two teams simultaneously choose their plays. If the Colts run the ball and the Patriots set up to defend against the run, then the Colts' payoff is −1 and the Patriots' payoff is 1. If the Colts pass and the Patriots set up to defend against the pass, then the Colts' payoff is −2 and the Patriots receive 2. If the Colts run and the Patriots set up to defend against the pass, the Colts' payoff is 6 and the Patriots' is −6. If the Colts pass and the Patriots set up to defend against the run, the Colts' payoff is 10 and the Patriots' is −10.

a. Show the payoff matrix for this simultaneous-moves game. What is the Nash equilibrium? Is it a pure- or mixed-strategies Nash equilibrium?

b. Now suppose instead that if the Colts pass and the Patriots set up to defend against the run, the Colts' payoff is 8 and the Patriots' is −8. Write the payoff matrix for this simultaneous-moves game. What is the Nash equilibrium? Does this Nash equilibrium involve pure or mixed strategies? **W**

Solving for Mixed Strategies Using Calculus

We can solve for the mixed strategy in Table 14.4 using calculus. Suppose that Firm 1 enters with probability θ_1. If Firm 2 enters, it expects to earn

$$[1 \times \theta_1] + [(-1) \times (1 - \theta_1)] = 2\theta_1 - 1.$$

That is, it earns a dollar if Firm 1 fails to enter, which occurs with a probability of $1 - \theta_1$, and Firm 2 loses a dollar if Firm 1 enters, which it does with a probability of θ_2. Similarly, if Firm 2 does not enter, then Firm 2 expects to earn $[0 \times (1 - \theta_2)] + [0 \times \theta_2] = 0$.

Using these expectations that are conditional on Firm 1's entering with probability θ_1, if Firm 2 enters with probability θ_2, Firm 2's expected payoff is

$$\theta_2(2\theta_1 - 1) + (1 - \theta_2)0 = 2\theta_1\theta_2 - \theta_2. \tag{14A.1}$$

The first term on the left-hand side of Equation 14A.1 is the product of the probability that Firm 2 enters, θ_2, times Firm 2's expected earnings if it enters, $2\theta_1 - 1$; and the second term is the probability that Firm 2 does not enter, $1 - \theta_2$, times Firms 2's expected earnings if it does not enter, 0.

For what strategy of Firm 1, θ_1, is Firm 2's expected profit maximized? To answer this question, we choose θ_2 to maximize Firm 2's expected profit. That is, we set the derivative of Firm 2's expected payoff, Equation 14A.1, with respect to θ_2 equal to zero, to obtain the first-order condition

$$2\theta_1 - 1 = 0.$$

Thus in the mixed-strategy equilibrium, Firm 2's expected profit is maximized if Firm 1 picks the entry strategy with a probability of one-half: $\theta_1 = 1/2$.

We now assert that $\theta_1 = 1/2$ is Firm 1's mixed strategy. Why do we obtain Firm 1's strategy by choosing it to maximize Firm 2's expected profit? Given that an optimal mixed strategy exists for Firm 2, if Firm 1 chooses to enter with a lower probability than one-half, Firm 2 would always enter. Similarly, if Firm 1's probability of entering is greater than one-half, Firm 2 would not enter. Thus if a mixed strategy is to be optimal for Firm 2, Firm 1 must enter with a probability equal to 0.5 exactly.

Given the symmetry of the problem, Firm 2's strategy is the same as Firm 1's. Firm 2 enters with a probability of one-half. (In nonsymmetric games, firms may have different mixed strategies.)

Chapter 15

Factor Markets

Work is of two kinds: first, altering the position of matter at or near the earth's surface relative to other matter; second, telling other people to do so. — Bertrand Russell

To manufacture cell phones, Nokia has to decide how many workers to hire, how much equipment it needs, and whether to invest in a new factory. Its decisions depend on wages, the rental price of capital, and interest rates.

In this chapter, we show that the labor and capital factor market equilibrium prices — wages and the rental cost of capital — depend on the structure of factor markets and the output market. We first look at competitive factor and output markets and then examine the effect of a monopoly in either or both markets.

Next we consider markets in which there is a **monopsony**: the only buyer of a good in a market. A monopsony is the mirror image of a monopoly. Whereas a monopoly sells at a price higher than what a competitive industry would charge, a monopsony buys at a lower price than a competitive industry would.

Our analysis to this point applies to *nondurable* services such as one hour of work by an engineer or the use of a rental truck for a day. Nondurable services are those that are consumed when they are purchased or soon thereafter. Additional analytical complications arise when the input is *capital* or other *durable goods*: products that are usable for years. Firms use durable goods — such as manufacturing plants, machines, and trucks — to produce and distribute goods and services. Consumers spend one in every eight of their dollars on durable goods such as houses, cars, and refrigerators.

If a firm rents a durable good by the week, it faces a decision similar to its decision in buying a nondurable good or service. If the capital good must be bought or built rather than rented, the firm cannot apply this rule on the basis of current costs and benefits alone. (There are many types of specialized capital, such as a custom-built factory or a specially made piece of equipment, that a firm *cannot* rent.)

Does it pay for the firm to pay $1 million for a shop in downtown Topeka that it will rent for $6,000 a month indefinitely? To answer this question, we need to extend our analysis in two ways. First, we must develop a method of comparing the *future* flow of rental payments to the *current* cost of the building, as we do in this chapter. Second, we must consider the role of uncertainty about the future (can the firm rent all the apartments each month?), a subject we examine in Chapter 16.

In this chapter, we examine five main topics	
	1. **Competitive Factor Market:** The intersection of the factor supply curve and the factor demand curve (which depends on firms' production functions and on the market price for output) determines the equilibrium in a competitive factor market.
	2. **Noncompetitive Factor Market:** If firms exercise market power in either factor or output markets, the quantities of inputs and outputs sold fall.
	3. **Monopsony:** A monopsony — a single buyer — maximizes its profit by paying a price below the competitive level, which creates a deadweight loss for society.

4. **Capital Markets and Investing:** Investing money in a project pays if the return from that investment is greater than that from the best alternative when both returns are expressed on a comparable basis.

5. **Exhaustible Resources:** Scarcity, rising costs of extraction, and positive interest rates may cause the price of exhaustible resources such as coal and gold to rise exponentially over time.

15.1 Competitive Factor Market

Virtually all firms rely on factor markets for at least some inputs. The firms that buy factors may be competitive price takers or noncompetitive price setters, such as a monopsony firm. Competitive, monopolistically competitive, oligopolistic, and monopolistic firms sell factors. In this section, we examine factor markets in which firms that buy and sell are competitive price takers. In Section 15.2 we consider noncompetitive factor markets.

Factor markets are competitive when there are many small sellers and buyers. The flower auction in Amsterdam that the Verenigde Bloemenveilingen Aalsmeer cooperative holds daily (Chapter 8) typifies such a competitive market with many sellers and buyers. The sellers supply inputs—flowers in bulk—to buyers, who sell outputs—trimmed flowers in vases and wrapped bouquets—at retail to final customers.

Our earlier analysis of the competitive supply curve applies to factor markets. Chapter 5 derives the supply curve of labor by examining how individuals' choices between labor and leisure depend on tastes and the wage rate. Chapter 8 determines the competitive supply curves of firms in general, including those that produce factors for other firms. Given that we know the supply curve, once we determine the factor's demand curve, we can analyze a competitive factor.

A firm chooses inputs so as to maximize its profit. We illustrate this decision for a firm that combines labor, L, and capital, K, to produce output, q, where its production function is $q = q(L, K)$.[1] Using the theory of the firm (Chapters 6 and 7), we show how the amount of each input that the firm demands depends on the prices of the factors and the price of the final output. We begin by considering the firm's short-run problem when the firm can adjust only labor because capital is fixed. We then examine its long-run problem when both inputs are variable.

FIRM'S SHORT-RUN FACTOR DEMAND

In the short run, the firm's capital is fixed at $\overline{K}$, so the firm can increase its output only by using more labor. That is, the short-run production function might be written as $q = \widetilde{q}(L, \overline{K}) = q(L)$ to show that it is solely a function of labor.

The firm chooses how many workers to hire to maximize its profit. The firm is a price taker in the labor markets, so it can hire as many workers as it wants at the market

---

[1]In Chapters 6 and 7, we wrote the production function as $q = f(L, K)$. Here, for notational simplicity, we write the function as $q(L, K)$.

wage, w. Thus the firm's short-run cost is $C = wL + F$, where F is the fixed cost. The firm's revenue function is $R(q(L))$.

The firm's profit function is its revenue function minus its cost function. The firm's objective is to maximize its profit through its labor choice:

$$\max_{L} \pi = R(q(L)) - wL - F. \tag{15.1}$$

We use the chain rule to derive the firm's first-order condition for a profit maximum:[2]

$$\frac{d\pi}{dL} = \frac{dR}{dq}\frac{dq}{dL} - w = 0,$$

hence

$$\frac{dR}{dq}\frac{dq}{dL} = w. \tag{15.2}$$

According to Equation 15.2, a profit-maximizing firm chooses L so that the additional revenue it receives from employing the last worker equals the wage it must pay for the last worker. The additional revenue from the last unit of labor, $(dR/dq)(dq/dL)$, is called the **marginal revenue product of labor** (MRP_L).

The marginal revenue product of labor is the marginal revenue from the last unit of output, $MR = dR/dq$, times the marginal product of labor, $MP_L = dq/dL$, which is the extra output produced by the last unit of labor (Chapter 6):

$$MRP_L = MR \times MP_L.$$

A competitive firm faces an infinitely elastic demand for its output at the market price, p, so its marginal revenue is p (Chapter 8), and its marginal revenue product of labor is

$$MRP_L = p\frac{dq}{dL} = pMP_L.$$

The marginal revenue product for a competitive firm is also called the *value of the marginal product* because the marginal revenue product equals the market price or value times the marginal product of labor, which is the market value of the extra output. Thus for a competitive firm, Equation 15.2 is

$$MRP_L = pMP_L = w. \tag{15.3}$$

Equation 15.3 is the firm's short-run labor demand function. It shows that the marginal revenue product of labor curve is the firm's demand curve for labor when capital is fixed. One interpretation of Equation 15.3 is that the MRP_L determines the maximum wage a firm is willing to pay to hire a given number of workers (or vice versa). Dividing both sides of Equation 15.3 by p, we find that the marginal product of labor depends on the ratio of the wage to the output price: $MP_L = dq(L)/dL = w/p$. Because the marginal product of labor is a function of labor, this expression can be restated so that the quantity of labor demanded by a competitive firm is a function of the wage-price ratio: $L = L(w/p)$.

---

[2]We assume that the second-order condition, $(dR/dq)(d^2q/dL^2) < 0$, holds and that the firm does not want to shut down.

A Thread Mill's Short-Run Labor Demand Function. We can illustrate these calculations using an estimated (Baldwin and Gorecki, 1986) Cobb-Douglas production function for a Canadian thread mill: $q = L^{0.6}K^{0.2}$. If in the short run the firm's capital is fixed at $\overline{K} = 32$ units, its short-run production function is $q = L^{0.6}32^{0.2} = 2L^{0.6}$. The firm's marginal product of labor is $MP_L = d(2L^{0.6})/dL = 1.2L^{-0.4}$. As a result, Equation 15.3 becomes

$$MRP_L = 1.2pL^{-0.4} = w. \tag{15.4}$$

If the firm faces a price of $p = \$50$ per unit and a wage of $w = \$15$ an hour, Equation 15.4 becomes $MRP_L = 60L^{-0.4} = 15$, so the firm should employ $L = 32$ workers. More generally, when we solve Equation 15.4 for L in terms of p and w, the thread mill's demand for labor function is

$$L = \left(\frac{1}{1.2}\frac{w}{p}\right)^{1/[-0.4]} \approx 1.577\left(\frac{w}{p}\right)^{-2.5}. \tag{15.5}$$

Figure 15.1 plots the thread mill's MRP_L or labor supply curve when $p = \$50$. The wage line at $w = 15$ is the supply curve of labor that the firm faces. The firm can hire as many workers as it wants at a constant wage of \$15. The marginal revenue product of labor curve, MRP_L, is the firm's demand curve for labor when other inputs are fixed. The MRP_L shows the maximum wage that a firm is willing to pay to hire a given number of workers. Thus the intersection of the supply curve of labor facing the firm and the firm's demand curve for labor determines the profit-maximizing number of workers.

Change in the Wage. What happens to the short-run demand for labor if the wage increases or decreases? The firm's labor demand curve is usually downward sloping

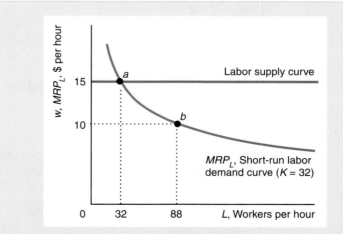

Figure 15.1 Short-Run Labor Demand of a Thread Mill. In the short run, capital is fixed at 32 units. If the market price is \$50 per unit and the wage is $w = \$15$ per hour, a Canadian thread mill hires 32 workers at point *a*, where the labor supply curve intersects the mill's short-run labor demand curve. If the wage falls to \$10, the mill hires 88 workers at point *b*.

because of the law of diminishing marginal returns (Chapter 6). The marginal product from extra workers, MP_L, of a firm with fixed capital eventually falls as the firm increases the amount of labor it uses. Because the marginal product of labor declines as more workers are hired, the marginal revenue product of labor (which equals a constant price times the marginal product of labor) or the demand curve must slope downward as well.

According to Equation 15.3, the firm hires labor until the value of its marginal product of labor equals the wage: $pMP_L = w$. If w increases and p remains constant, the only way for the firm to maintain this equality is to adjust its labor force so as to cause its marginal product of labor to rise. If the firm operates where the production function exhibits diminishing marginal returns to labor, its marginal product of labor rises when it reduces its labor force. Thus the firm's demand curve for labor is downward sloping.

We can confirm this reasoning using a formal comparative static analysis. Because Equation 15.3 is an identity, it must hold for all values of w; hence we can write the amount of labor demanded as an implicit function of the wage: $L(w)$. To show how labor demand varies with the wage, we differentiate Equation 15.3 with respect to w:

$$p \frac{dMP_L}{dL} \frac{dL}{dw} = 1.$$

Rearranging terms,

$$\frac{dL}{dw} = \frac{1}{p \dfrac{dMP_L}{dL}}. \tag{15.6}$$

Thus if the firm is operating where the production function exhibits diminishing marginal product of labor, $dMP_L/dL = d^2q/dL^2 < 0$, $dL/dw < 0$, and the demand curve for labor slopes downward.

Figure 15.1 shows that the thread mill's short-run labor demand curve is downward sloping: The quantity of labor services demanded rises from 32 to 88 workers if the wage falls from $15 to $10. The reason the firm's demand curve is downward sloping is that its marginal product of labor, $MP_L = 1.2L^{-0.4}$, falls as the firm uses more labor: $dMP_L/dL = -0.48L^{-1.4} < 0$. Indeed, because this inequality holds for any L, the production function exhibits diminishing marginal product of labor at any quantity of labor, and hence the mill's labor demand curve slopes downward everywhere.

SOLVED PROBLEM   15.1

How does a competitive firm adjust its short-run demand for labor if the local government collects a specific tax of τ on each unit of output, where this tax does not affect other firms in the market (because they are located in other communities)?

Answer

1. *Give intuition:* Because the tax is applied to only one competitive firm, it does not affect p or w measurably. Because the specific tax lowers the after-tax price per unit that the firm receives, we can apply the same type of analysis that we would use to show the comparative statics effect of a change in the output price. For a given amount of labor, the marginal revenue product of labor falls from

$pMP_L(L)$ to $(p - \tau)MP_L(L)$. The marginal revenue product of labor curve—the labor demand curve—shifts downward until it is only $(p - \tau)/p$ as high as the original labor demand curve at any quantity of labor, so the firm demands less labor at any given wage. We now use calculus to derive this result formally.

2. Differentiate the profit-maximizing condition with respect to the tax: The firm's profit-maximizing condition, Equation 15.3, is $(p - \tau)MP_L = w$ (which we evaluate at $\tau = 0$ before the tax is imposed). Given that this identity holds for all τ, the labor demanded is an implicit function of the tax: $L(\tau)$. Differentiating this identity with respect to τ, we find that

$$-MP_L + (p - \tau)\frac{dMP_L}{dL}\frac{dL}{d\tau} = 0,$$

where the right-hand side of the equation is zero because w does not vary with τ. Rearranging terms,

$$\frac{dL}{d\tau} = \frac{MP_L}{(p - \tau)\dfrac{dMP_L}{dL}}.$$

Because MP_L and $(p - \tau)$ are positive, the sign of this expression is the same as that of dMP_L/dL. Thus if the production process exhibits diminishing marginal product of labor, the quantity of labor demanded falls with the tax: $dL/d\tau < 0$.

FIRM'S LONG-RUN FACTOR DEMANDS

In the long run, the firm is free to vary all of its inputs. Thus in the long run, if the wage of labor rises, the firm adjusts both labor and capital. As a result, the short-run marginal revenue product of labor curve that holds capital fixed is not the firm's long-run labor demand curve. The long-run labor demand curve takes account of changes in the firm's use of capital as the wage rises.

Choice of Inputs. In the long run, the firm chooses both labor and capital so as to maximize its profit. If the firm is a price taker in these factor markets, then the firm's cost is $C = wL + rK$, where w is the wage and r is the rental cost of capital. Because the firm's production process is $q = q(L, K)$, its revenue function is $R(q(L, K))$.

The firm's profit function is its revenue function minus its costs. The firm's objective is to maximize its profit through its choice of inputs:

$$\max_{L, K} \pi = R(q(L, K)) - wL - rK. \tag{15.7}$$

The firm's first-order conditions for a profit maximum are:

$$\frac{\partial \pi}{\partial L} = \frac{\partial R}{\partial q}\frac{\partial q}{\partial L} - w = 0,$$

$$\frac{\partial \pi}{\partial K} = \frac{\partial R}{\partial q}\frac{\partial q}{\partial K} - r = 0.$$

These first-order conditions are closely analogous to the short-run profit-maximizing condition. They show that the firm sets its marginal revenue product of labor equal to the wage and its marginal revenue product of capital equal to the rental price of capital:

$$MRP_L = MR \times MP_L = \frac{\partial R}{\partial q}\frac{\partial q}{\partial L} = w, \tag{15.8}$$

$$MRP_K = MR \times MP_K = \frac{\partial R}{\partial q}\frac{\partial q}{\partial K} = r. \tag{15.9}$$

Again, if the firm is competitive, $MR = p$, these conditions are

$$MRP_L = pMP_L = p\frac{\partial q}{\partial L} = w, \tag{15.10}$$

$$MRP_K = pMP_K = p\frac{\partial q}{\partial K} = r. \tag{15.11}$$

That is, the value of the marginal product of each input equals its factor price. Equations 15.10 and 15.11 are the competitive firm's long-run factor demand equations.

Cobb-Douglas Factor Demand Functions. For example, if the production function is Cobb-Douglas, $q = AL^aK^b$, then Equations 15.10 and 15.11 are

$$paAL^{a-1}K^b = w,$$

$$pbAL^aK^{b-1} = r.$$

Solving these equations for L and K, we find that the factor demand functions are

$$L = \left(\frac{a}{w}\right)^{(1-b)/d}\left(\frac{b}{r}\right)^{b/d}(Ap)^{1/d}, \tag{15.12}$$

$$K = \left(\frac{a}{w}\right)^{a/d}\left(\frac{b}{r}\right)^{(1-a)/d}(Ap)^{1/d}, \tag{15.13}$$

where $d = 1 - a - b$.[3] By differentiating the input demand equation 15.12 and 15.13, we can show that the demand for each factor decreases with respect to its own factor price, w or r, and increases with p. Given the parameters for the Canadian thread mill, $a = 0.6$, $b = 0.2$, and $A = 1$, the long-run labor demand equation 15.12 is $L = (0.6/w)^4(0.2/r)p^5$, and the long-run capital demand equation 15.13 is $K = (0.6/w)^3(0.2/r)^2p^5$.

The shares of its total revenue that a competitive firm pays to labor and to capital do not vary with factor or output prices if the firm has a Cobb-Douglas production function, $q = AL^aK^b$. A competitive firm with a Cobb-Douglas production function pays its labor the value of its marginal product, $w = pMP_L = apAL^{a-1}K^b = apq/L$. As a result, the share of the firm's revenues that it pays to labor is $\omega_L = wL/(pq) = a$. Similarly, $\omega_K = rK/(pq) = b$. (Solved Problem 3.5 makes a similar point about the properties of the Cobb-Douglas utility functions.) Thus with a Cobb-Douglas production function, the payment shares to labor and to capital are fixed and independent of prices.

---

[3]If the Cobb-Douglas production function has constant returns to scale, $d = 0$, then Equations 15.12 and 15.13 are not helpful. The problem with constant returns to scale is that a competitive firm does not care how much it produces (and hence how many inputs it uses) as long as the market price and input prices are consistent with zero profit.

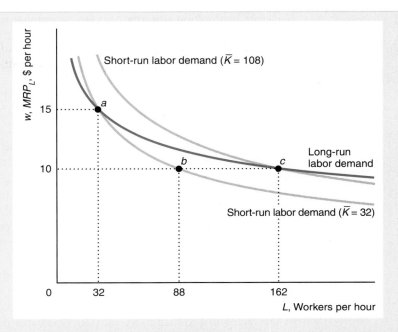

Figure 15.2 Labor Demand Curves of a Thread Mill. If the long-run market price is $50 per unit, the rental rate of capital services is $r = \$5$, and the wage is $w = \$15$ per hour, a Canadian thread mill hires 32 workers (and uses 32 units of capital) at point *a* on its long-run labor demand curve. In the short run, if capital is fixed at $\overline{K} = 32$, the firm still hires 32 workers per hour at point *a* on its short-run labor demand curve. If the wage drops to $10 and capital remains fixed at $\overline{K} = 32$, the firm would hire 88 workers, point *b* on the short-run labor demand curve. In the long run, however, it would increase its capital to $K = 108$ and hire 162 workers, point *c* on the long-run labor demand curve and on the short-run labor demand curve with $\overline{K} = 108$.

Comparing Short-Run and Long-Run Labor Demand Curves. In both the short run and the long run, the labor demand curve is the marginal revenue product curve of labor. In the short run, the firm cannot vary capital, so the short-run MP_L curve and hence the short-run MRP_L curves are relatively steep. In the long run, when the firm can vary all inputs, its long-run MP_L curve and MRP_L curves are flatter.

Figure 15.2 illustrates this difference for the Canadian thread mill, where $p = \$50$ per unit and $r = \$5$ per hour. On the short-run labor demand curve where capital is fixed at $\overline{K} = 32$, where $w = \$15$, the firm hires 32 workers per hour. Using 32 workers and 32 units of capital is profit maximizing in the long run, so point *a* is also on the firm's long-run labor demand curve. The short-run labor demand curve is steeper than the long-run curve at point *a*.[4]

In the short run, if the wage fell to $10, the firm could not increase its capital, so it would hire 88 workers, point *b* on the short-run labor demand curve, where $\overline{K} = 32$.

---

[4]If $p = \$50$, the Canadian thread mill's short-run labor demand equation is $L \approx 27{,}885.48w^{-2.5}$. In contrast, if $r = \$5$, its long-run labor demand equation is $L = 1{,}620{,}000w^{-4}$. At $w = \$15$, the two curves intersect at $L = 32$, as Figure 15.2 shows. At that point, the change in labor with respect to a change in the wage on the short-run labor demand curve is $dL/dw \approx -2.5(27{,}885.48)w^{-1.5} \approx -1{,}200$, and the corresponding derivative along the long-run curve is $dL/dw = -4(1{,}620{,}000) \times w^{-3} = -1{,}920$. Thus the slope of the short-run labor demand curve, dw/dL, is steeper than that of the long-run curve.

However, in the long run, the firm would employ more capital and even more labor (because it can sell as much output as it wants at the market price). It would hire 162 workers and use 108 units of capital, which is point c on both the long-run labor demand curve and the short-run labor demand curve for $\overline{K} = 108$.

FACTOR MARKET DEMAND

A factor market demand curve is the sum of the factor demand curves of the various firms that use the input. Determining a factor market demand curve is more difficult than deriving consumers' market demand for a final good. When horizontally summing the demand curves for individual consumers in Chapter 2, we were concerned with only a single market. Inputs such as labor and capital are used in many output markets, however. Thus to derive the labor market demand curve, we first determine the labor demand curve for each output market and then sum across output markets to obtain the factor market demand curve.

Earlier we derived the factor demand of a competitive firm that took the output market price as given. However, the output market price depends on the factor's price. As the factor's price falls, each firm, taking the original market price as given, uses more of the factor to produce more output. This extra production by all the firms in the market causes the market price to fall. As the market price falls, each firm reduces its output and hence its demand for the input. Thus a fall in an input price causes less of an increase in factor demand than would occur if the market price remained constant, as Figure 15.3 illustrates.

At the initial output market price of $9 per unit, the competitive firm's labor demand curve (panel a of Figure 15.3) is $MRP_L(p = \$9) = \$9 \times MP_L$. When the wage is $25 per hour, the firm hires 50 workers: point a. The 10 firms in the market (panel b) demand 500 hours of work: point A on the demand curve $D(p = \$9) = 100 \times \$9 \times MP_L$. If the wage falls to $10 while the market price remains fixed at $9, each firm hires 90 workers, point c, and all the firms in the market would hire 900 workers, point C. However, the extra output drives the price down to $7, so each firm hires 70 workers, point b, and the firms collectively demand 700 workers, point B. The market labor demand curve for this output market that takes price adjustments into account, D(price varies), goes through points A and B. Thus the market's demand for labor is steeper than it would be if output prices were fixed.

COMPETITIVE FACTOR MARKET EQUILIBRIUM

The intersection of the factor market demand curve and the factor market supply curve determines the competitive factor market equilibrium. We've just derived the factor market demand curve. There's nothing unusual about the factor market supply curve. The long-run factor supply curve for each firm is its marginal cost curve above the minimum of its average cost curve, and the factor market supply curve is the horizontal sum of the firms' supply curves. Because we've already analyzed competitive market equilibria for markets in general in Chapters 2, 8, and 9, there's no point in repeating the analysis. Been there. Done that.

Chapter 10 shows that factor prices are equalized across markets. For example, if wages were higher in one industry than in another, workers would shift from the low-wage industry to the high-wage industry until the wages were equalized.

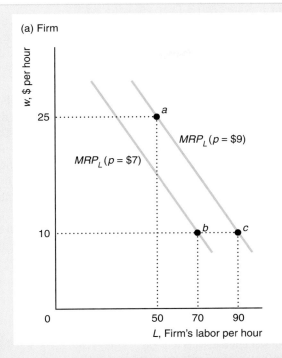

(a) Firm

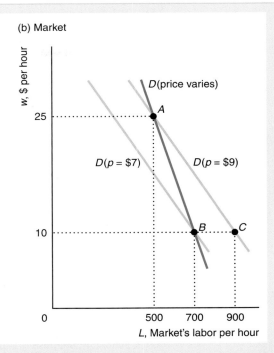

(b) Market

Figure 15.3 Firm and Market Demand for Labor.
When the output price is $p = \$9$, the individual competitive firm's labor demand curve is $MRP_L(p = \$9)$. If $w = \$25$ per hour, the firm hires 50 workers, point a in panel a, and the 10 firms in the market demand 500 workers, point A on the labor demand curve $D(p = \$9)$ in panel b. When the wage falls to $10, each firm would hire 90 workers, point c, if the market price stayed fixed at $9. The extra output, however, drives the price down to $7, so each firm hires 70 workers, point b. The market's demand for labor that takes price adjustments into account, D(price varies), goes through points A and B.

Black Death Raises Wages

The Black Death—bubonic plague—wiped out between a third and a half of the population of medieval Western Europe, resulting in a large increase in the real wage and sizable drops in the real rents on land and capital. Why?

The plague is characterized by large, dark lumps in the groin or armpits followed by livid black spots on the arms, thighs, and other parts of the body. In virtually all its victims, the Black Death led to a horrible demise within one to three days.

In England, the plague struck in 1348–1349, 1360–1361, 1369, and 1375. According to one historian, the population fell from 3.76 million in 1348 to 3.13 million in 1348–1350, 2.75 million in 1360, 2.45 million in 1369, and 2.25 million in 1374.

English nominal wages rose in the second half of the fourteenth century compared to the first half: Thatchers earned

35% more, thatcher's helpers 105%, carpenters 40%, masons 48%, mowers 24%, oat threshers 73%, and oat reapers 61%. Adjusting for output price changes (at a medieval consumer price index), the average real wage rose by about 25%. In Pistoia, Italy, rents in kind on land fell by about 40%, and the rate of return on capital fell by about the same proportion.

Because the plague wiped out one-half to two-thirds of the labor force, labor became scarce relative to capital and land, which, of course, were unaffected by the disease. The scarcity of labor caused the marginal product of labor, MP_L, to rise: The remaining workers had lots of capital and land to use and hence were very productive. In competitive markets, workers are paid a wage equal to the value of their marginal product (marginal revenue product), $w = pMP_L$. If we rearrange this expression, the real wage (the wage relative to the price level), w/p, equals the marginal product of labor—$w/p = MP_L$—hence a large increase in the marginal product of labor causes a comparable increase in the real wage. Similarly, the fall in labor reduced the marginal products of capital and land, resulting in a drop in the real prices that these factors of production received.

SOLVED PROBLEM 15.2

For simplicity, suppose that medieval England was a single, large, price-taking firm that produced one type of output with a constant-returns-to-scale Cobb-Douglas production function, $q = L^a K^{1-a}$. Labor and capital have inelastic supplies (everyone works and all capital is used). The Black Death killed $(1 - \theta)$ workers, causing the number of workers to fall from L to $L^* = \theta L$. Show how much the wage, w, rose. If p is normalized to 1, a is $\frac{1}{2}$, K is 100, and $\theta = \frac{1}{4}$, calculate the changes in the factor prices.

Answer

1. *Show how output falls due to a reduction in labor:* When labor falls from L to $L^* = \theta L$, output falls from $Q = L^a K^{1-a}$ to $Q^* = (\theta L)^a K^{1-a} = \theta^a L^a K^{1-a} = \theta^a Q$. That is, when labor falls to θ times its original level, output falls less than in proportion to θ^a times its initial level. (In our example, $\theta = 1/4$ and $a = 1/2$, so $\theta^a = 1/2$.)

2. *Given the effect of the plague on output, show how the marginal product of labor changed and hence how the wage changed:* We know that the marginal product of labor for a Cobb-Douglas production function is $MP_L = aQ/L$. The output-to-labor ratio changes from Q/L to $\theta^a Q/(\theta L) = \theta^{a-1} Q/L > Q/L$. Consequently, the marginal product of labor rose from $MP_L = \alpha Q/L$ to $MP_L^* = \theta^{a-1} aQ/L = \theta^{a-1} MP_L$. The competitive labor demand equation is determined by equating the marginal product of labor to the real wage, $MP_L = w/p$. (We refer to w/p as the real wage because there is only one price, p.) For this equation to hold when the marginal product of labor rose, the real wage of labor, $w^*/p = MP_L^*$, had to rise in proportion to MP_L^*.

3. *Show the corresponding effect on capital:* Because output fell and capital remained the same, the marginal product of capital fell from $MP_K = (1 - a)Q/K$ to $MP_K^* = \theta^a (1 - a)Q/K = \theta^a MP_K$. Consequently, the real price of capital, $r^*/p = MP_K$, dropped.

> 4. *Calculate the changes in wages and the rental price of capital using the specified parameters:* With the given parameters, initial output was $Q = L^a K^{1-a} = 100^{1/2}100^{1/2} = 100$. The marginal product of labor was $MP_L = aQ/L = 1/2(100/100) = 1/2$, so the real wage was $w/p = 1/2$, given that $p = 1$. Similarly, the marginal product of capital was $MP_K = (1 - a)Q/K = 1/2$, and the real price of capital was $r/p = 1/2$. After the plague, the labor force fell to $L^* = \theta \times 100 = 25$, and output dropped to $Q = 25^{1/2}100^{1/2} = 50$. Consequently, the marginal product of labor rose to $MP_L^* = 1/2(50/25) = 1$, so the real wage rose to $w^*/p = 1$. Similarly, the marginal product of capital and the real price of capital fell to $MP_K^* = 1/2(50/100) = 1/4 = r^*/p$. Thus the real wage doubled and the real rental rate on capital dropped by half.

15.2 Noncompetitive Factor Market

Having examined the factor market equilibrium where competitive firms sell a factor to a competitive output market, we now survey the effects of market power on factor market equilibrium. If firms in the output market *or* in the factor market exercise market power by setting price above marginal cost, less of a factor is sold than would be sold if all firms were competitive.

Factor demand curves vary with market power. As we saw in Chapter 11, the marginal revenue of profit-maximizing Firm i, $MR = p(1 + 1/\varepsilon_i)$, is a function of the elasticity of demand, ε_i, facing the firm and of the market price, p. Thus the firm's marginal revenue product of labor function is

$$MRP_L = p\left(1 + \frac{1}{\varepsilon_i}\right)MP_L.$$

The labor demand curve is $p \times MP_L$ for a competitive firm because it faces an infinitely elastic demand at the market price, so its marginal revenue equals the market price.

A monopoly operates in the elastic section of its downward-sloping market demand curve (Chapter 11), so its demand elasticity is less than -1 and finite: $-\infty < \varepsilon \leq -1$. As a result, at any given price, the monopoly's labor demand, $p(1 + 1/\varepsilon)MP_L$, lies below the labor demand curve, pMP_L, of a competitive firm with an identical marginal product of labor curve.

A Cournot firm faces an elasticity of demand of $n\varepsilon$, where n is the number of identical firms and ε is the market elasticity of demand (Chapter 13). If the market has a constant elasticity demand curve with an elasticity of ε, the demand elasticity faced by a duopoly Cournot firm is twice that, 2ε, of a monopoly. Consequently, a Cournot duopoly firm's labor demand curve, $p[1 + 1/(2\varepsilon)]MP_L$, lies above that of a monopoly but below that of a competitive firm. Figure 15.4 shows the short-run market labor demand curve for an actual competitive thread mill and the corresponding curves if the firm was one of two identical Cournot quantity-setting firms or a monopoly.[5]

---

[5]In the short run, the thread mill's marginal product function is $MP_L = 1.2L^{-0.4}$. The labor demand is $p \times 1.2L^{-0.4}$ for a competitive firm, $p[1 + 1/(2\varepsilon)] \times 1.2L^{-0.4}$ for one of two identical Cournot duopoly firms, and $p(1 + 1/\varepsilon) \times 1.2L^{-0.4}$ for a monopoly. In the figure, we assume that $\varepsilon = 2$.

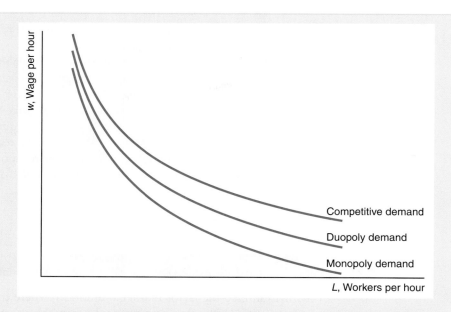

Figure 15.4 How Thread Mill Labor Demand Varies with Market Structure. For all profit-maximizing firms, the labor demand curve is the marginal revenue product of labor: $MRP_L = MR \times MP_L$. Because marginal revenue differs with market structure, so does the MRP_L. At a given wage, a competitive thread firm demands more workers than a Cournot duopoly firm, which demands more workers than a monopoly.

15.3   Monopsony

In Chapter 11, we saw that a *monopoly,* a single *seller,* picks a point—a price and a quantity combination—on the market *demand curve* that maximizes its profit. A *monopsony,* a single *buyer* in a market, chooses a price-quantity combination from the industry *supply curve* that maximizes its profit. A monopsony is the mirror image of monopoly, and it exercises its market power by buying at a price *below* the price that competitive buyers would pay.

Because an American manufacturer of state-of-the-art weapon systems can legally sell only to the federal government, the government is a monopsony. U.S. professional baseball teams, which act collectively, are the only U.S. firms that hire professional baseball players.[6] In many fisheries there is only one, monopsonistic buyer of fish (or at most a small number of buyers, an *oligopsony*).

MONOPSONY PROFIT MAXIMIZATION

Suppose that a firm is the sole employer in town—a monopsony in the local labor market. The firm uses only one factor, labor (L), to produce a final good. The value that the firm places on the last worker it hires is the marginal revenue product of that

---

[6]Baseball players belong to a union that acts collectively, like a monopoly, in an attempt to offset the monopsony market power of the baseball teams.

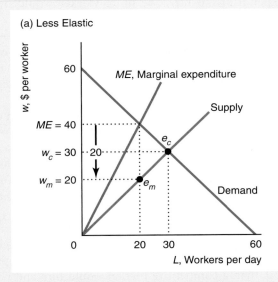
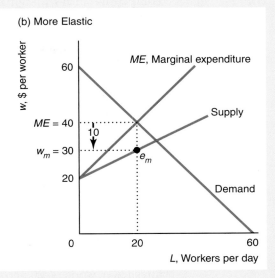

Figure 15.5 Monopsony. (a) The marginal expenditure curve—the monopsony's marginal cost of buying one more unit—lies above the upward-sloping market supply curve. The monopsony equilibrium, e_m, occurs where the marginal expenditure curve intersects the monopsony's demand curve. The monopsony buys fewer units at a lower price, $w_m = \$20$, than a competitive market, $w_c = \$30$, would. (b) The supply curve is more elastic at the optimum than in (a), so the value that the monopsony places on the last unit (which equals the marginal expenditure of \$40) exceeds the price the monopsony pays, $w_m = \$30$, by less than in (a).

worker—the value of the extra output the worker produces—which is the height of the firm's labor demand curve for the number of workers the firm employs.

The firm has a downward-sloping demand curve in panel a of Figure 15.5. The firm faces an upward-sloping supply curve of labor: The higher its daily wage, w, the more people want to work for the firm. The firm's *marginal expenditure*—the additional cost of hiring one more worker—depends on the shape of the supply curve.

The supply curve shows the average expenditure, or wage, that the monopsony pays to hire a certain number of workers. For example, the monopsony's average expenditure or wage is \$20 if it hires $L = 20$ workers per day. If the monopsony wants to obtain one more worker, it must raise its wage because the supply curve is upward sloping. Because it pays all workers the same wage, the monopsony must also pay more to each worker that it was already employing. Thus the monopsony's marginal expenditure on the last worker is greater than that worker's wage.

The monopsony's total expenditure is $E = w(L)L$, where $w(L)$ is the wage given by the market labor supply curve. Its marginal expenditure is

$$ME = w(L) + \frac{dw}{dL}L, \tag{15.14}$$

where $w(L)$ is the wage paid the last worker and $L[dw(L)/dL]$ is the extra amount the monopsony pays the workers it was already employing. Because the supply curve is upward sloping, $dw(L)/dL > 0$, the marginal expenditure, ME, is greater than the average expenditure, $w(L)$.

In contrast, if the firm were a competitive price taker in the labor market, it would face a supply curve that was horizontal at the market wage. Consequently, such a competitive firm's marginal expenditure to hire one more worker would be the market wage.

Any profit-maximizing firm—a monopsony and a competitive firm alike—*buys labor services up to the point at which the marginal value of the last unit of a factor equals the firm's marginal expenditure.* If the last unit is worth more to the buyer than its marginal expenditure, the buyer purchases another unit. Similarly, if the last unit is less valuable than its marginal expenditure, the buyer purchases one less unit.

In the figure, the monopsony employs 20 units of the factor. The intersection of its marginal expenditure curve and its demand curve determines the monopsony equilibrium, e_m. The monopsony values the labor services of the last worker at \$40 (the height of its demand curve), and its marginal expenditure at that unit (the height of its marginal expenditure curve) is \$40. It pays only \$20 (the height of the supply curve). In other words, the monopsony values the last unit at \$20 more than it actually has to pay.

If the market in Figure 15.5 were competitive, the intersection of the market demand curve and the market supply curve would determine the competitive equilibrium at e_c, where buyers purchase 30 units at $p_c = \$30$ per unit. Thus the monopsony hires fewer workers, 20 versus 30, than a competitive market would hire and pays a lower wage, \$20 versus \$30.

We can also use calculus to analyze the labor monopsony's behavior. For simplicity, we assume that the firm is a price taker in the output market. It chooses how much labor to hire to maximize its profit,

$$\pi = pQ(L) - w(L)L,$$

where $Q(L)$ is the production function, the amount of output produced using L hours of labor. The firm maximizes its profit by setting the derivative of profit with respect to labor equal to zero (assuming that the second-order condition holds):

$$p\frac{dQ}{dL} - w(L) - \frac{dw}{dL}L = 0,$$

or

$$MRP_L = p\frac{dQ}{dL} = w(L) + \frac{dw}{dL}L = ME. \tag{15.15}$$

That is, the monopsony hires labor up to the point where the marginal revenue product of labor—the value of the output produced by the last worker, $p(dQ/dL)$—equals the marginal expenditure on the last worker, $ME = w + (dw/dL)L$.

Monopsony power is the ability of a single buyer to pay less than the competitive price profitably. The size of the gap between the value the monopsony places on the last worker (the height of its demand curve) and the wage it pays (the height of the supply curve) depends on the elasticity of supply of labor, η, at the monopsony optimum. Using algebra, we can express the marginal expenditure, Equation 15.14, in terms of the elasticity of supply of labor:

$$ME = w(L) + \frac{dw}{dL}L = w(L)\left(1 + \frac{dw}{dL}\frac{L}{w}\right) = w(L)\left(1 + \frac{1}{\eta}\right), \tag{15.16}$$

The markup of the marginal expenditure (which equals the value to the monopsony) over the wage is inversely proportional to the elasticity of supply at the optimum:

By rearranging the terms in Equation 15.16, we derive an expression analogous to the Lerner Index:

$$\frac{ME - w}{w} = \frac{1}{\eta}. \tag{15.17}$$

Equation 15.17 shows that the percentage markup of the marginal expenditure (and the value to the monopsony) to the wage, $(ME - w)/w$, is inversely proportional to the elasticity of the supply of labor. Only if the firm is a price taker, so that η is infinite, does the wage equal the marginal expenditure.

By comparing panels a and b in Figure 15.5, we see that the less elastic the supply curve at the optimum, the greater the gap between marginal expenditure and the wage. At the monopsony optimum, the supply curve in panel b of Figure 15.5 is more elastic than the supply curve in panel a.[7] The gap between marginal expenditure and wage is greater in panel a, $ME - w = \$20$, than in panel b, $ME - w = \$10$. Similarly, the markup in panel a, $(ME - w)/w = 20/20 = 1$, is much greater than that in panel b, $(ME - w)/w = 10/30 = \frac{1}{3}$.

APPLICATION

Company Towns

Most firms cannot act as a monopsony, paying low wages to their workers, because their employees could move to higher-paying firms. The only exception occurs when workers live in an isolated area with a single employer (or have jobs in an occupation with only one nearby employer).

Company towns—small communities where a single firm is the only major employer—were relatively common in the United States from the late 1800s through the early 1900s. Typically, a company-town firm not only provided employment but also served as the purveyor of goods, the major landlord, the garbage collector, and the employer of police—the firm dispensed "justice."

Company towns were common in the coal mining industry in certain parts of the country. In the early 1920s, 65% to 80% of miners in southern Appalachia and in the Rocky Mountains lived in company towns, compared to 10% to 20% in most of the Midwest, 25% in Ohio, and 50% in Pennsylvania. Well-known examples are the Homestead Steel Mill in Homestead,

---

[7]The supply curve in panel a is $w = L$, while that in panel b is $w = 20 + 1/2L$. The elasticity of supply, $\eta = (dL/dw)(w/L)$, at the optimum is $w/L = 20/20 = 1$ in panel a and $2w/L = 2 \times 30/20 = 3$ in panel b. Consequently, the supply curve at the optimum is three times as elastic in panel b as in panel a.

Pennsylvania, and the Pullman Company that produced railroad cars in Pullman, Illinois.

The company town largely died out as automobiles and modern highways made workers more mobile. However, as the table shows, some company towns still exist. These modern-day firms can exercise monopsony power only if their workers cannot easily move to other jobs (possibly in other towns).

Company	Town	Local Employees	Population	Employees as a Percentage of Population
Lands' End (catalog retailer)	Dodgeville, WI	4,354	4,220	103
Wal-Mart (retail stores)	Bentonville, AK	20,000	19,730	101
L. L. Bean (catalog retailer)	Freeport, ME	1,600	1,813	88
Smithfield Foods (pork)	Smithfield, VA	4,511	6,324	71
Adelphia Communications (cable TV)	Coudersport, PA	1,500	2,650	57
Corning (optical fiber and cable)	Corning, NY	5,200	10,842	48
Hershey Foods (candy)	Hershey, PA	6,200	12,771	49
Pella (windows and doors)	Pella, IA	3,000	9,832	31
Maytag (appliances)	Newton, IA	4,000	15,579	26
Mohawk Industries (carpets)	Calhoun, GA	2,793	10,667	26
Whirlpool (appliances)	Benton Harbor, MI	2,700	11,182	24
Leggett & Platt (industrial materials)	Carthage, MO	2,169	12,668	17
Dow Chemical (chemicals)	Midland, MI	6,000	41,685	14
Timberland (boots and clothing)	Stratham, NH	730	5,810	13

SOLVED PROBLEM   15.3

How does the equilibrium in a labor market with a monopsony employer change if a minimum wage is set at the competitive level?

Answer

1. *Determine the original monopsony equilibrium:* Given the supply curve in the graph, the marginal expenditure curve is ME^1. The intersection of ME^1 and the demand curve determines the monopsony equilibrium, e_1. The monopsony hires L_1 workers at a wage of w_1.

2. *Determine the effect of the minimum wage on the marginal expenditure curve:* The minimum wage makes the supply curve, as viewed by the monopsony, flat in the range where the minimum wage is above the original supply curve (fewer

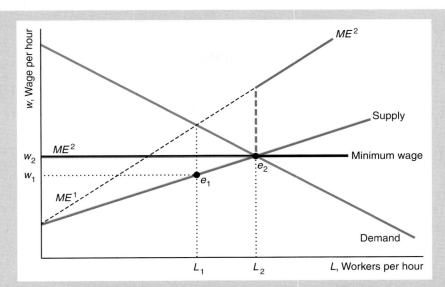

than L_2 workers). The new marginal expenditure curve, ME^2, is flat where the supply curve is flat. Where the supply curve is upward sloping, ME^2 is the same as ME^1.

3. *Determine the post-minimum-wage equilibrium:* The monopsony operates where its new marginal expenditure curve, ME^2, intersects the demand curve. With the minimum wage, the demand curve crosses the ME^2 curve at the end of the flat section. Thus at the new equilibrium, e_2, the monopsony pays the minimum wage, w_2, and employs L_2 workers.

4. *Compare the equilibria:* The post-minimum-wage equilibrium is the same as the competitive equilibrium determined by the intersection of the demand and supply curves. Workers receive a higher wage, and more are employed than in the monopsony equilibrium. Thus imposing the minimum wage helps workers and hurts the monopsony.

WELFARE EFFECTS OF MONOPSONY

By creating a wedge between the value to the monopsony and the value to the suppliers, the monopsony causes a welfare loss in comparison to a competitive market. In Figure 15.6, sellers lose producer surplus, $D + E$, because the monopsony price, p_m, for a good is below the competitive price, p_c. Area D is a transfer from the sellers to the monopsony and represents the savings of $p_c - p_m$ on the Q_m units the monopsony buys. The monopsony loses C because suppliers sell it less output, Q_m instead of Q_c, at the low price. Thus the deadweight loss of monopsony is $C + E$. This loss is due to the wedge between the value the monopsony places on the Q_m units, the monopoly expenditure ME in the figure, and the price it pays, p_m. The greater the difference between Q_c and Q_m and the larger the gap between ME and p_m, the greater the deadweight loss.

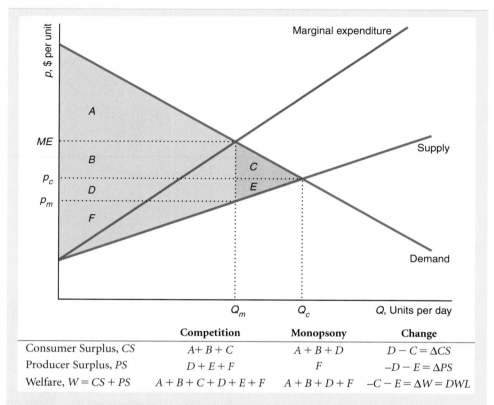

	Competition	Monopsony	Change
Consumer Surplus, CS	$A + B + C$	$A + B + D$	$D - C = \Delta CS$
Producer Surplus, PS	$D + E + F$	F	$-D - E = \Delta PS$
Welfare, $W = CS + PS$	$A + B + C + D + E + F$	$A + B + D + F$	$-C - E = \Delta W = DWL$

Figure 15.6　Welfare Effects of Monopsony. By setting a price, p_m, below the competitive level, p_c, a monopsony causes too little to be sold by the supplying market, thereby reducing welfare.

15.4　Capital Markets and Investing

If a firm rents a durable good by the week, it faces a decision similar to the one it encounters when buying a nondurable good or service. A firm demands workers' services (or other nondurable input) up to the point at which its *current* marginal cost (the wage) equals its *current* marginal benefit (the marginal revenue product of the workers' services). A firm that rents a durable good, such as a truck, by the week can use the same rule to decide how many trucks to rent per week. The firm rents trucks up to the point at which the *current* marginal rental cost equals its *current* marginal benefit—the marginal revenue product of the trucks.

If the capital good must be bought or built rather than rented, the firm cannot apply this rule on the basis of current costs and benefits alone. (There are many types of specialized capital, such as a factory or a customized piece of equipment, that a firm *cannot* rent.) In deciding whether to build a factory that will last for many years, a firm must compare the *current* cost of the capital to the *future* higher profits it will make over time from using the plant.

Such comparisons may involve both *stocks* and *flows*. A **stock** is a quantity or value that is measured independently of time. Because a durable good lasts for many periods, its stock is discussed without reference to its use within a particular time period. We say that a firm owns "an apartment building *this* year" (not "an apartment building *per* year"). If a firm buys the apartment building for $5 million, we say that it has a capital stock worth $5 million today.

A **flow** is a quantity or value that is measured per unit of time. The consumption of nondurable goods, such as the number of ice-cream cones you eat per week, is a flow. Similarly, the stock of a durable good provides a flow of services. A firm's apartment building—its capital stock—provides a flow of housing services (apartments rented per month or year) to tenants. In exchange for these housing services, the firm receives a flow of rental payments from the tenants. If the capital good or *asset* provides a monetary flow, it is called a *financial asset*.

Does it pay for a firm to buy an apartment building? To answer this question, we need to extend our analysis in two ways. First, we must compare a flow of dollars in the future to a dollar today, which we do in this chapter. Second, we need to consider the role of uncertainty about the future (can the firm rent all the apartments each month?), a subject taken up in Chapter 16.

We start by showing how we can use interest rates to compare money in the future to money today. We next show how we can use interest rates to compare streams of payments or streams of returns from investment over time to money today. Then we use these means of comparison to analyze how a firm chooses between two investments.

INTEREST RATES

Because virtually everyone values having a dollar today more than having a dollar in the future, you would not loan a bank a dollar today (that is, place money in a savings account) unless the bank agreed to pay back more than a dollar in the future. How much more you must be paid in the future is specified by an **interest rate:** the percentage more that must be repaid to borrow money for a fixed period of time.[8] In the following discussion, we assume that there is no inflation and concentrate on real interest rates.

If you invest a *present value* of PV dollars this year and the bank pays *i* percent interest per year, the bank will return a *future value* of $PV \times (1 + i)$ next year. If you leave your money in the bank for many years, you will earn interest in later years on the interest paid in the earlier years, which is called *compounded interest*. Thus if you deposit PV dollars in the bank today and allow the interest to compound for *t* years, the future value FV is

$$FV = PV \times (1 + i)^t. \tag{15.18}$$

Equivalently, we can ask what the *present value* is of an investment that pays FV next year. At an interest rate of *i*, the present value is $PV = FV/(1 + i)$. By rearranging Equation 15.18, we find that the amount of money that you would have to put in the bank today to get FV in *t* years at an interest rate of *i* is

$$PV = \frac{FV}{(1 + i)^t}. \tag{15.19}$$

---

[8]For simplicity, we refer to *the* interest rate, but in most economies there are many interest rates. For example, a bank charges a higher interest rate to loan you money than the interest rate it pays you to borrow your money. (See **www.aw-bc.com/perloff,** Chapter 15, "Usury," for a discussion of ancient people's opposition to paying interest, and current restrictions on Islamic banks.)

DISCOUNT RATE

You may value future consumption more or less than other members of society value it. If you knew you had a fatal disease that would kill you within two years, you would place less value on payments three or more years in the future than most other people would. We call an individual's personal "interest" rate that person's **discount rate:** a rate reflecting the relative value an individual places on future consumption compared to current consumption.

A person's willingness to borrow or lend depends on whether his or her discount rate is greater or less than the market interest rate. If your discount rate is nearly zero— you view current and future consumption as equally desirable—you would gladly loan money in exchange for a positive interest rate. Similarly, if your discount rate is high— current consumption is much more valuable to you than future consumption—you would be willing to borrow at a lower interest rate. In the following discussion, we assume for simplicity that an individual's discount rate is the same as the market interest rate unless we explicitly state otherwise.

STREAM OF PAYMENTS

Sometimes people pay a certain amount each month over time for their purchases. These payments are flow measures—in contrast to a present value and a future value, which are stock measures. For example, a firm may pay for a new factory by making monthly mortgage payments. In deciding whether to purchase the factory, the firm compares the present value of the stock (the factory) to a flow of payments over time.

One way to make such an evaluation is to determine the present value of the stream of payments and compare this value directly to the present value of the factory. The present value of the stream of payments is the sum of the present value of each future payment. Thus if the firm makes a *future payment* of f per year for t years at an interest rate of i, the present value (stock) of this flow of payments is

$$PV = f\left[\frac{1}{(1 + i)^1} + \frac{1}{(1 + i)^2} + \cdots + \frac{1}{(1 + i)^t}\right]. \tag{15.20}$$

If these payments must be made at the end of each year forever, the present value formula is easier to calculate than Equation 15.20. If the firm invests PV dollars into a bank account earning an interest rate of i, it receives interest or future payment of $f = i \times PV$ at the end of each year. Dividing both sides of this expression by i, we find that to get a payment of f each year forever, the firm would have to put

$$PV = \frac{f}{i} \tag{15.21}$$

in the bank.[9]

---

[9]In Equation 15.20, if the number of periods is infinite, the present value is

$$PV = \frac{f}{1 + i} + \frac{f}{(1 + i)^2} + \frac{f}{(1 + i)^3} + \cdots.$$

We can factor $1/(1 + i)$ out of the right-hand side and rewrite the equation as

$$PV = \frac{1}{1 + i}\left[f + \frac{f}{1 + i} + \frac{f}{(1 + i)^2} + \frac{f}{(1 + i)^3} + \cdots\right] = \frac{1}{1 + i}(f + PV).$$

Rearranging terms, we obtain Equation 15.21.

This payment-in-perpetuity formula, Equation 15.21, provides a good approximation of a payment for a large but finite number of years. At a 5% interest rate, the present value of a payment of $10 a year for 100 years, $198, is close to the present value of a permanent stream of payments, $200. At higher interest rates, this approximation is nearly perfect. At 10%, the present value of payments for 100 years is $99.9927 compared to $100 for perpetual payments. The reason this approximation works better at high rates is that a dollar paid more than 50 or 100 years from now is essentially worthless today.

We just calculated the present value of a stream of payments. This type of computation can help a firm decide whether to buy something today that it will pay for over time. Alternatively, the firm may want to know the future value of a bank account if it invests f each year. At the end of t years, the account has[10]

$$FV = f[1 + (1 + i)^1 + (1 + i)^2 + \cdots + (1 + i)^{t-1}]. \qquad (15.22)$$

APPLICATION

Saving for Retirement

If all goes well, you'll live long enough to retire. Will you live like royalty off your savings, or will you have to depend on Social Security to provide enough income so that you can avoid having to eat dog food to stay alive? (When I retire, I'm going to be a Velcro farmer.)

You almost certainly don't want to hear this, but it isn't too early to think about saving for retirement. Thanks to the power of compounding (earning interest on interest), if you start saving when you're young, you don't have to save as much per year as you would if you start saving when you're middle aged.

Suppose that you plan to work full time from age 22 until you retire at 70 and that you can earn 7% on your retirement savings account. Let's consider two approaches to savings:

- **Early bird:** You save $3,000 a year for the first 15 years of your working life and then let your savings accumulate interest until you retire.
- **Late bloomer:** After not saving for the first 15 years, you save $3,000 a year for the next 33 years until retirement.

Which scenario leads to a bigger retirement nest egg? To answer this question, we calculate the future value at retirement of each of these streams of investments.

The early bird adds $3,000 each year for 15 years into a retirement account. Using Equation 15.22, we calculate that the account has

$$\$3,000(1 + 1.07^1 + 1.07^2 + \cdots + 1.07^{14}) = \$75,387$$

---

[10]This equation can be written as $FV = f[(1 + i)^0 + (1 + i)^1 + (1 + i)^2 + \cdots + (1 + i)^{t-1}]$ because $(1 + i)^0 = 1$.

at the end of 15 years. Leaving this amount in the retirement account for the next 33 years increases the fund about 9.3 times, to

$$\$75,387.07 \times 1.07^{33} = \$703,010.$$

The late bloomer makes no investments for 15 years and then invests \$3,000 a year until retirement. Again using Equation 15.22, we calculate that the funds at retirement are

$$\$3,000(1 + 1.07 + 1.07^2 + \cdots + 1.07^{32}) = \$356,800.$$

Thus even though the late bloomer contributes to the account for more than twice as long as the early bird, the late bloomer has saved only about half as much at retirement. Indeed, to have roughly the same amount at retirement as the early bird, the late bloomer would have to save nearly \$6,000 a year for the 33 years. (By the way, someone who saved \$3,000 each year for all 48 years would have \$703,010 + \$356,800 = \$1,059,810 salted away by retirement.)

INVESTING

Frequently, firms must choose between two or more investments that have different streams of payments and streams of returns. MGM, a conglomerate, decides whether to produce a movie starring a muscle-bound hero who solves the pollution problem by beating up an evil capitalist, build a new hotel in Reno, buy a television studio, or put money in a long-term savings account.

For simplicity, we start by analyzing a firm's choice between two financial assets with no uncertainty and no inflation. In such a scenario, all assets must have the same rate of return, because no one would invest in any asset that had less than the highest available rate of return.

Just as you would not loan money to a bank unless it agreed to pay you interest, a firm will not make an investment—tie up its funds for a while—in either a financial asset or a piece of capital unless it expects a payoff greater than its initial investment. The *rate of return on an investment* is the payoff from that investment expressed as a percentage per time period. For example, a bond might pay a 5% rate of return per year.

One possible investment is to put \$1 (or \$1 million) in a bank and earn interest of i per year. For example, i might be 4%. The value of this investment next year is $1 + i$. A second possible investment is that the firm can buy an asset this year at \$1 and sell it with certainty next year for FV, the future value of the asset. The firm is indifferent between these two investments only if $FV = 1 + i$.

We now consider more complex investments. As a general rule, a firm makes an investment if the expected return from the investment is greater than the opportunity cost (Chapter 7). The opportunity cost is the best alternative use of its money, which is what it would earn in the next best use of the money.

Thus to decide whether to make an investment, the firm needs to compare the potential outlay of money to the firm's best alternative. One possibility is that its best alternative is to put the money that it would otherwise spend on this investment in an interest-bearing bank account. We consider two methods for making this comparison: the *net present value* approach and the *internal rate of return* approach.

Net Present Value Approach. A firm has to decide whether to buy a truck for $20,000. Because the opportunity cost is $20,000, the firm should make the investment only if the present value of expected future returns from the truck is greater than $20,000.

More generally, *a firm should make an investment only if the present value of the expected return exceeds the present value of the costs.* If R is the present value of the expected returns to an investment and C is the present value of the costs of the investment, the firm should make the investment if $R > C$.[11]

This rule is often restated in terms of the net present value, $NPV = R - C$, which is the difference between the present value of the returns, R, and the present value of the costs, C. *A firm should make an investment only if the net present value is positive:*

$$NPV = R - C > 0.$$

Assume that the initial year is $t = 0$, the firm's revenue in year t is R_t, and its cost in year t is C_t. If the last year in which either revenue or cost is nonzero is T, the net present value rule holds that the firm should invest if

$$NPV = R - C$$
$$= \left[R_0 + \frac{R_1}{(1 + i)^1} + \frac{R_2}{(1 + i)^2} + \cdots + \frac{R_T}{(1 + i)^T} \right]$$
$$- \left[C_0 + \frac{C_1}{(1 + i)^1} + \frac{C_2}{(1 + i)^2} + \cdots + \frac{C_T}{(1 + i)^T} \right] > 0.$$

Instead of comparing the present values of the returns and costs, we can examine whether the present value of the *cash flow* in each year (loosely, the annual *profit*), $\pi_t = R_t - C_t$, is positive. By rearranging the terms in the previous expression, we can rewrite the net present value rule as

$$NPV = (R_0 - C_0) + \frac{R_1 - C_1}{(1 + i)^1} + \frac{R_2 - C_2}{(1 + i)^2} + \cdots + \frac{R_T - C_T}{(1 + i)^T}$$
$$= \pi_0 + \frac{\pi_1}{(1 + i)^1} + \frac{\pi_2}{(1 + i)^2} + \cdots + \frac{\pi_T}{(1 + i)^T} > 0. \qquad (15.23)$$

This rule does not restrict the firm to making investments only where its cash flow is positive each year. For example, a firm buys a piece of equipment for $100 and spends the first year learning how to use it, so it makes no revenues from the machine and has a negative cash flow that year: $\pi_0 = -100$. The next year, its revenue is $350

---

[11]This rule holds when future costs and returns are known with certainty and investments can be reversed but cannot be delayed (Dixit and Pindyck, 1994).

and the machine's maintenance cost is \$50, so its second year's cash flow is $\pi_1 = \$300$. At the end of that year, the machine wears out, so the annual cash flow from this investment is zero thereafter. Using Equation 15.23, the firm calculates the investment's net present value at $i = 5\%$ as

$$NPV = -100 + 300/1.05 \approx \$185.71.$$

Because this net present value is positive, the firm makes the investment.

SOLVED PROBLEM   15.4

Lewis Wolff and his investment group bought the Oakland A's baseball team for \$180 million in 2005. *Forbes* magazine estimated their net income for 2005 as \$5.9 million. If the new owners believed that they would continue to earn this annual profit (after adjusting for inflation), $f = \$5.9$ million, forever, was this investment more lucrative than putting the \$180 million in a savings account that pays a real interest rate of $i = 3\%$?

Answer

Determine the net present value of the team: The net present value of buying the A's is positive if the present value of the expected returns, \$5.9 million/0.04 $\approx$ \$196.7 million, minus the present value of the cost, which is the purchase price of \$180 million, is positive:

$$NPV = \$196.7 \text{ million} - \$180 \text{ million} = \$16.7 \text{ million} > 0.$$

Thus it paid for the investors to buy the A's if their best alternative investment paid 3%.

Internal Rate of Return Approach. Whether the net present value of an investment is positive depends on the interest rate. In Solved Problem 15.4, the investors buy the baseball team, given an interest rate of 3%. However, if the interest rate were 10%, the net present value would be \$5.9 million/0.1 $-$ \$180 million $= -\$121$ million, and the investors would not buy the team.

At what discount rate (rate of return) is a firm indifferent between making an investment and not doing so? The **internal rate of return** (*irr*) is the discount rate such that the net present value of an investment is zero. Replacing the interest rate, *i*, in Equation 15.23 with *irr* and setting the *NPV* equal to zero, we implicitly determine the internal rate of return by solving

$$NPV = \pi_0 + \frac{\pi_1}{1 + irr} + \frac{\pi_2}{(1 + irr)^2} + \cdots + \frac{\pi_T}{(1 + irr)^T} = 0$$

for *irr*.

It is easier to calculate *irr* when the investment pays a steady stream of profit, *f*, forever and when the cost of the investment is *PV*. The investment's rate of return is found by rearranging Equation 15.21 and replacing *i* with *irr*:

$$irr = \frac{f}{PV}. \tag{15.24}$$

Instead of using the net present value rule, we can decide whether to invest by comparing the internal rate of return to the interest rate. If the firm is borrowing money to make the investment, *it pays for the firm to borrow to make the investment if the internal rate of return on that investment exceeds that of the next best alternative* (which we assume is the interest rate):[12]

$$irr > i.$$

SOLVED PROBLEM   15.5

A group of investors can buy the Oakland A's baseball team for $PV = \$180$ million. They expect an annual real flow of payments (profits) of $f = \$5.9$ million forever. If the interest rate is 3%, do they buy the team?

Answer

Determine the internal rate of return to this investment and compare it to the interest rate: Using Equation 15.24, we calculate that the internal rate of return from buying the A's is

$$irr = \frac{f}{PV} = \frac{\$5.9 \text{ million}}{\$180 \text{ million}} \approx 3.3\%.$$

Because this rate of return, 3.3%, is greater than the interest rate, 3%, the investors buy the team.

DURABILITY

Many firms must decide how durable to make the products they sell or those they produce for their own use. Should they make long-lasting products at a relatively high cost or less durable goods at a lower cost?

Suppose that the company can vary the quality of a factor (a machine) that it uses in its own production process. If it needs exactly one machine, it must replace the machine when it wears out. Thus *the firm should pick the durability level for the machine that minimizes the present discounted cost of having a machine forever.*

● APPLICATION

Durability of Telephone Poles

Pacific Gas & Electric (PG&E), a western power utility, must decide how durable to make its 132 million wooden utility poles. The poles are a capital stock for PG&E, which uses them to provide a flow of services: supporting power and phone lines year after year. A wooden utility pole provides the same services each year for T years under normal use. After T years, the pole breaks and is replaced because it can't be repaired, but the flow of services must be maintained. Until recently, PG&E used poles with a life span of $T = 25$ years.

---

[12]The net present value approach always works. The internal rate of return method is inapplicable if *irr* is not unique. In Solved Problem 15.5, *irr* is unique, and using this approach gives the same answer as the net present value approach.

The constant marginal cost of manufacturing and installing the poles depends on how long they last, $m(T)$. For an additional cost, the firm can extend the life span of a pole by treating it with chemicals to prevent bug infestations and rot, reinforcing it with metal bands, varying its thickness, or using higher-quality materials. Because the marginal cost increases with the pole's expected life span, a pole that lasts 50 years costs more than one that lasts 25 years: $m(50) > m(25)$.

The replacement cost of a pole that lasts 25 years is $m(25) = \$1,500$. Thus replacing all of PG&E's poles today would come to $198 billion—which is more than the cost of many giant power plants.

PG&E believes that it can save money by switching to a longer-lasting pole. The firm picks the duration, T, that minimizes its cost of maintaining its forest of poles. Because the utility keeps the same number of poles in place every year, after a pole wears out at T years, the firm incurs an expense of $m(T)$ to replace it. The present value of providing each pole is the cost of producing it today, $m(T)$, plus the discounted cost of producing another one in T years, $m(T)/(1 + i)^T$, plus the discounted cost of producing another one in $2T$ years, $m(T)/(1 + i)^{2T}$, and so on.

The table shows the present value of the cost of maintaining one pole for the next 100 years given that the utility faces an interest rate of 5%. Because the cost of producing a pole that lasts for 25 years is $m(25) = \$1,500$, the present value of the cost of providing a pole for the next 100 years is $2,112 (column 2). If the cost of a pole that lasts 50 years were $m(50) = \$1,943$ (column 4), the present value would be the same as that for the 25-year pole. If so, the utility would be indifferent between using poles that last 25 years and poles that last 50 years.

	25-Year Pole		50-Year Pole
Marginal Cost, $m(T)$:	$1,500	$1,650	$1,943
Year			
0	$1,500	$1,650	$1,943
25	443	0	0
50	131	$144	169
75	39	0	0
Present value of the cost of providing a pole for 100 years:	$2,112	$1,794	$2,112

Note: Column 2 does not add to the present value due to rounding.

Thus PG&E will not use 50-year poles if the extra cost is greater than $443 = \$1,943 - \$1,500$ but will use them if the difference in cost is less than that. The actual extra cost is less than $150, so $m(50) = \$1,650$. Thus the present value of the cost of a 50-year pole is only about $1,794 (column 3 of the table). Because using the 50-year poles reduces the present value by $318, or about 15% per pole, the utility wants to use the longer-lasting poles. By so doing, PG&E cuts the present value of the cost of maintaining all its poles for 100 years by about $42 billion. Thus the length of time one maintains a durable good depends on the alternatives and the rate of interest.

HUMAN CAPITAL

If a man is after money, he's money mad; if he keeps it, he's a capitalist; if he spends it, he's a playboy; if he doesn't get it, he's a ne'er-do-well; if he doesn't try to get it, he lacks ambition. If he gets it without working for it, he's a parasite; and if he accumulates it after a lifetime of hard work, people call him a fool who never got anything out of life. —Vic Oliver

Just as a firm considers whether or not to invest in physical capital, individuals decide whether to invest in their own *human capital*. Where a firm chooses the durability of a piece of equipment, some people invest in lengthening their expected life spans by exercising or purchasing medical care. Where a firm buys machinery and other capital to produce more output and increase its future profits, individuals invest in education to raise their productivity and their future earnings.

One of the most important human capital decisions you've had to make is whether to attend college. If you opted to go to college solely for the purpose of increasing your lifetime earnings, have you made a good investment?[13]

Let's look back at your last year of high school. During that year, you have to decide whether to invest in a college education or go directly into the job market. If you venture straight into the job market, we assume that you work from age 18 until you retire at age 70.

If your motivation for attending college is to increase your lifetime earnings, you should start college upon finishing high school so that you can earn a higher salary for as long as possible. Let's assume that you graduate from college in four years, during which time you do not work and you spend $12,000 a year on tuition and other schooling expenses such as books and fees. When you graduate from college, you work from ages 22 to 70. Thus the opportunity cost of a college education includes the tuition payments plus the four years of forgone earnings for someone with a high school diploma. The expected benefit is the stream of higher earnings in the future.

Figure 15.7 shows how much the typical person earns with a high school diploma and with a college degree at each age.[14] At age 22, a typical person earns $34,300 with a college degree but only $25,600 with a high school diploma. The college grad's earnings peak at 50 years of age, at $47,500. A high school grad's earnings reach a maximum at 50 years, at $35,400.[15]

If one stream of earnings is higher than the other at every age, we would pick the higher stream. Because these streams of earnings cross at age 22, we cannot use that

---

[13]"I have often thought that if there had been a good rap group around in those days, I would have chosen a career in music instead of politics." —Richard Nixon

[14]Our figures are based on a statistical analysis of full-time weekly earnings from the March 2004 U.S. *Current Population Survey*, where we have adjusted for an individual's work experience, education, and demographic characteristics (but not innate ability, which we do not observe). We assume that people are paid for 52 weeks per year and that wages increase at the same rate as inflation, so real earnings are constant over time. No adjustment is made for the greater incidence of unemployment among high school graduates.

[15]For some employers, the extra amount that a worker earns due to advanced degrees is explicitly stated. In Santa Cruz, California, a firefighter earns $240 more per month above the base salary with a master's degree, $180 more with a bachelor's degree, and $120 more with an associate's degree. (Shanna McCord, "Fire Department One of First to Pass Policy on Web Degrees," *San Francisco Chronicle*, December 3, 2006.)

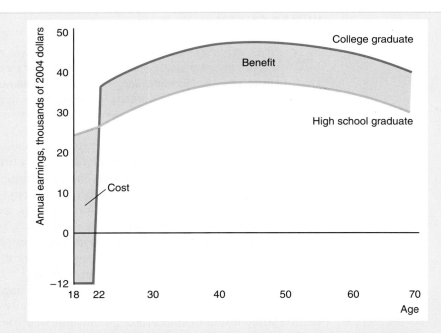

Figure 15.7 Annual Earnings of High School and College Graduates. On the basis of a statistical analysis, the earnings of high school and college graduates vary by age. The cost of getting a college education is four years of forgone earnings (at the rate high school graduates earn) and tuition, which is assumed to be $12,000 a year. The benefit is that the college graduate earns more each year thereafter than a high school graduate does.

method. One way to decide whether investing in a college education pays is to compare the present values at age 18 of the two earnings streams. The present values depend on the interest rate used, as Table 15.1 shows.

TABLE 15.1   Present Value of Earnings

	Present Value, Thousands of 2004 Dollars	
Discount Rate, %	High School	College
0	2,088	2,583
1	1,506	1,807
2	1,126	1,302
3	871	965
4	694	733
5	568	569
5.1	560	560
6	475	450
7	406	362
8	352	295
9	310	243
10	276	202

If potential college students can borrow money at an interest rate of 0%, money in the future is worth as much as money today, so the present value equals the sum of earnings over time. According to the table, the sum of a college graduate's earnings (including the initial negative earnings) is $2.58 million, which is about 24% more than the earnings of a high school grad. Thus it pays to go to college. Figure 15.7 also illustrates that attending college pays at a 0% discount rate because the sum of the (negative) cost and (positive) benefit areas—the difference in earnings between going to college and going to work after high school—is positive.

Table 15.1 demonstrates that the present value of earnings for a college grad is greater than that of a high school grad for any interest rate below 5.1%. That is, the average internal rate of return from a college education is 5.1%. Thus income-maximizing people with average characteristics go to college if the real interest rate at which they can borrow or invest is less than 5.1%.[16]

Making a decision about whether to go to college is more complex for people for whom education has a consumption component. Somebody who loves school may go to college even if alternative investments pay more. Someone who hates going to school invests in a college education only if the financial rewards are much higher than those for alternative investments.

● APPLICATION

Returns to Studying Economics

Black et al. (2003) estimated the returns to majoring in economics relative to those of other fields. Among undergraduates who did not go on to get graduate degrees, majors in other social sciences earned at least 13% less than economics majors; philosophy and theology majors made 48% less; music majors, 37% less; and business administration majors, 11% less. Only some types of engineering majors earned statistically significantly more than economics majors.

Nearly 45% of economics majors go on to earn graduate degrees. Of those undergraduates who went on to get a business (MBA) or law (JD) degree, economics majors earned substantially more than those with other undergraduate majors, including engineers. MBAs with an undergraduate degree in biology earned 22% less, mechanical engineers made 17% less, a business major made at least 14% less, and a history major received 30% less than someone with an economics degree. Lawyers with an undergraduate business administration major earned almost 24% less, those with a history or an English major earned 16% less, and those with a sociology major earned 30% less than lawyers with an economics major. Thus if you are interested in maximizing your income and don't find studying economics more taxing than majoring in sociology or history, your optimal investment decision is easy: Major in economics!

---

[16]In 2002, the nominal interest rate on federal Stafford loans, the most common type of educational loan, dropped to 4.06%, the lowest rate in its 37-year history. As of July 1, 2006, the rate was 6.8%. (New legislation in 2007 may cut that rate in half.) Real interest rates at which college students can loan money to a bank and the rates at which they can borrow using government loan programs are almost always lower than 5.1%. However, the commercial rates at which they can borrow money from banks may be higher than 5.1%. Some poor people who cannot borrow to pay for college at all—effectively, they face extremely high interest rates—do not go to college, unlike wealthier people with comparable abilities.

TIME-VARYING DISCOUNTING

Hard work pays off in the future. Laziness pays off now. —Steven Wright

People want immediate gratification.[17] We want rewards now and costs delayed until later: "Rain, rain, go away; come again some other day; we want to go out and play; come again some other day."

Time Consistency. So far in this chapter, we have explained such impatience by assuming that people discount future costs or benefits by using *exponential discounting,* as in Equation 15.19: The present value is the future value divided by $(1 + i)^t$, where t is the exponent and the discount rate, i, is constant over time. If people use this approach, their preferences are *time consistent:* They will discount an event that occurs a decade from the time they're asked by the same amount today as they will one year from now.

However, many of us indulge in immediate gratification in a manner that is inconsistent with our long-term preferences: Our "long-run self" disapproves of the lack of discipline of our "short-run self." Even though we plan today not to overeat tomorrow, tomorrow we may overindulge. We have *present-biased preferences:* When considering the trade-off between two future moments, we put more weight on the earlier moment as it gets closer. For example, if you are offered $100 in 10 years or $200 in 10 years and a day, you will almost certainly choose the larger amount one day later. After all, what's the cost of waiting one extra day a decade from now? However, if you are offered $100 today or $200 tomorrow, you may choose the smaller amount today because an extra day is an appreciable delay when your planning horizon is short.

Behavioral Economics. One explanation that behavioral economists (see Chapter 11) give for procrastination and other time-inconsistent behavior is that people's personal discount rates are smaller in the far future than in the near future. For example, suppose you know that you can mow your lawn today in two hours, but if you wait until next week, it will take you two-and-a-quarter hours because the grass will be longer. Your displeasure (negative utility) from spending two hours mowing is -20 and from spending 2.25 hours mowing is -22.5. The present value of mowing next week is $-22.5/(1 + i)$, where i is your personal discount rate for a week. If today your discount rate is $i = 0.25$, then your present value of mowing in a week is $-22.5/1.25 = -18$, which is not as bad as -20, so you delay mowing. However, if you were asked six months in advance, your discount rate might be much smaller, say $i = 0.1$. At that interest rate, the present value is $-22.5/1.1 \approx -20.45$, which is worse than -20, so you would plan to mow on the first of the two dates. Thus falling discount rates may explain this type of time-inconsistent behavior.

Falling Discount Rates and the Environment. A social discount rate that declines over time may be useful in planning for global warming or other future environmental disasters (Karp, 2005). Suppose that the harmful effects of greenhouse gases will not be felt for a century and that society used traditional, exponential discounting. We would be willing to invest at most 37¢ today to avoid a dollar's worth of damages in a century if society's constant discount rate is 1%, and only 1.8¢ if the discount rate is 4%. Thus even a modest discount rate makes us callous toward our distant descendants: We are unwilling to incur even moderate costs today to avoid large damages far in the future.

---

[17]This section draws heavily on Rabin (1988), O'Donoghue and Rabin (1999), and Karp (2005).

One alternative is for society to use a declining discount rate, although doing so will make our decisions time inconsistent. Parents today may care more about their existing children than about their (not-yet-seen) grandchildren, and therefore may be willing to significantly discount the welfare of their grandchildren relative to that of their children. They probably have a smaller difference in their relative emotional attachment to the tenth future generation relative to the eleventh generation. If society agrees with such reasoning, our future social discount rate should be lower than our current rate. By reducing the discount rate over time, we are saying that the weights we place on the welfare of any two successive generations in the distant future are more similar than the weights on two successive generations in the near future.

15.5 Exhaustible Resources

The meek shall inherit the earth, but not the mineral rights. —J. Paul Getty

Discounting plays an important role in decision making about how fast to consume oil, gold, copper, uranium, and other **exhaustible resources:** nonrenewable natural assets that cannot be increased, only depleted. An owner of an exhaustible resource decides when to extract and sell it so as to maximize the present value of the resource. Scarcity of the resource, mining costs, and market structure affect whether the price of such a resource rises or falls over time.

WHEN TO SELL AN EXHAUSTIBLE RESOURCE

Suppose that you own a coal mine. In what year do you mine the coal, and in what year do you sell it to maximize the present value of your coal? To illustrate how to answer these questions, we assume that there is no inflation or uncertainty and that you can sell the coal only this year or next in a competitive market, that the interest rate is i, and that the cost of mining each pound of coal, m, stays constant over time.

Given the last two of these assumptions, the present value of mining a pound of coal is m if you mine this year and $m/(1 + i)$ if you mine next year. As a result, if you're going to sell the coal next year, you're better off mining it next year because you postpone incurring the cost of mining. You mine the coal this year only if you plan to sell it this year.

Now that you have a rule that tells you when to mine the coal—at the last possible moment—your remaining problem is when to sell it. That decision depends on how the price of a pound of coal changes from one year to the next. Suppose that you know that the price of coal will increase from p_1 this year to p_2 next year.

To decide in which year to sell, you compare the present value of selling today to that of selling next year. The present value of your profit per pound of coal is $p_1 - m$ if you sell your coal this year and $(p_2 - m)/(1 + i)$ if you sell it next year. Thus to maximize the present value from selling your coal:

- *You sell all the coal this year* if the present value of selling this year is greater than the present value of selling next year: $p_1 - m > (p_2 - m)/(1 + i)$.
- *You sell all the coal next year* if $p_1 - m < (p_2 - m)/(1 + i)$.
- *You sell the coal in either year* if $p_1 - m = (p_2 - m)/(1 + i)$.

The intuition behind these rules is that storing coal in the ground is like keeping money in the bank. You can sell a pound of coal today, netting $p_1 - m$, invest the money in the bank, and have $(p_1 - m)(1 + i)$ next year. Alternatively, you can keep the coal in the ground for a year and then sell it. If the amount you'll get next year, $p_2 - m$, is less than what you can earn from selling now and keeping the money in a bank account, you sell the coal now. In contrast, if the price of coal is rising so rapidly that the coal will be worth more in the future than the wealth left in a bank, you leave your wealth in the mine.

PRICE OF A SCARCE EXHAUSTIBLE RESOURCE

This two-period analysis generalizes to many time periods (Hotelling, 1931). We use a multiperiod analysis to show how the price of an exhaustible resource changes over time.

The resource is sold both this year, year t, and next year, $t + 1$, only if the present value of a pound sold now is the same as the present value of a pound sold next year: $p_t - m = (p_{t+1} - m)/(1 + i)$, where the price is p_t in year t and is p_{t+1} in the following year. Using algebra to rearrange this equation, we obtain an expression that tells us how price changes from one year to the next:

$$p_{t+1} = p_t + i(p_t - m). \qquad (15.25)$$

If you're willing to sell the coal in both years, the price next year must exceed the price this year by $i(p_t - m)$, which is the interest payment you'd receive if you sold a pound of coal this year and put the profit in a bank that paid interest at rate i.

The gap between the price and the constant marginal cost of mining grows over time, as Figure 15.8 shows. To see why, we subtract p_t from both sides of Equation 15.25 to obtain an expression for the change in the price from one year to the next:

$$\Delta p \equiv p_{t+1} - p_t = i(p_t - m).$$

This equation shows that the gap between this year's price and next year's price widens as your cash flow this year, $p_t - m$, increases. Thus the price rises over time, and the gap

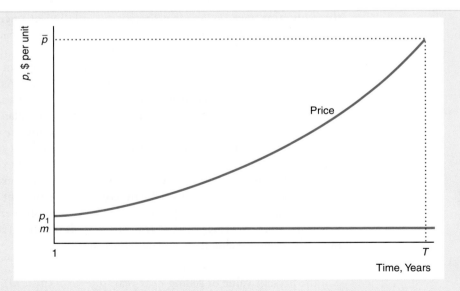

Figure 15.8 Price of an Exhaustible Resource. The price of an exhaustible resource in year $t + 1$ is higher than the price in year t by the interest rate times the difference between the price in year t and the marginal cost of mining, $i(p_t - m)$. Thus the gap between the price line and the marginal cost line, $p_t - m$, grows exponentially with the interest rate.

between the price line and the flat marginal cost of mining line grows, as the figure illustrates.

Although we now understand how price changes over time, we need more information to determine the price in the first year and hence in each subsequent year. Suppose mine owners know that the government will ban the use of coal in year T (or that a superior substitute will become available that year). They want to price the coal so that all of it is sold by year T, because any resource that is unsold by then is worthless. The restriction that all the coal is used up by T and Equation 15.25 determine the price in the first year and the increase in the price thereafter.

Price in a Two-Period Example. To illustrate how the price is determined in each year, we assume that there are many identical competitive mines, that no more coal will be sold after the second year because of a government ban, and that the marginal cost of mining is zero in each period. Setting $m = 0$ in Equation 15.25, we learn that the price in the second year equals the price in the first year plus the interest rate times the first-year price:

$$p_2 = p_1 + (i \times p_1) = p_1(1 + i). \tag{15.26}$$

Thus the price increases with the interest rate from the first year to the second year.

The mine owners face a resource constraint: They can't sell more coal than they have in their mines. The coal they sell in the first year, Q_1, plus the coal they sell in the second year, Q_2, equals the total amount of coal in the mines, Q. The mine owners want to sell all their coal within these two years because any coal they don't sell does them no good.

Suppose that the demand curve for coal is $Q_t = 200 - p_t$ in each year t. If the amount of coal in the ground is less than would be demanded at a zero price, the sum of the amount demanded in both years equals the total amount of coal in the ground:

$$Q_1 + Q_2 = (200 - p_1) + (200 - p_2) = Q.$$

Substituting the expression for p_2 from Equation 15.26 into this resource constraint to obtain $(200 - p_1) + [200 - p_1(1 + i)] = Q$ and rearranging terms, we find that

$$p_t = (400 - Q)/(2 + i). \tag{15.27}$$

Thus the first-year price depends on the amount of coal in the ground and the interest rate.

If the mines initially contain $Q = 169$ pounds of coal, then p_1 is $110 at a 10% interest rate and only $105 at a 20% interest rate, as Table 15.2 shows. At the lower interest rate,

TABLE 15.2 **Price and Quantity of Coal Reflecting the Amount of Coal and the Interest Rate**

	$Q = 169$		$Q = 400$
	$I = 10\%$	$i = 20\%$	Any i
$p_1 = (400 - Q)/(2 + i)$	$110	$105	$0
$p_2 = p_1(1 + i)$	$121	$126	$0
$\Delta p \equiv p_2 - p_1 = I \times p_1$	11	21	0
$Q_1 = 200 - p_1$	90	95	200
$Q_2 = 200 - p_2$	79	74	200
Share sold in Year 2	47%	44%	50%

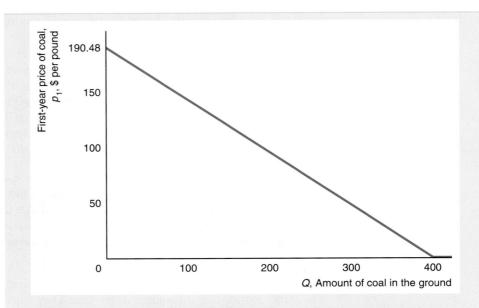

Figure 15.9 **First-Year Price in a Two-Period Model.** In a two-period model, the price of coal in the first year, p_1, falls as the amount of coal in the ground initially, Q, increases. This figure is based on an interest rate of 10%.

the difference between the first- and the second-year price is smaller ($11 versus $21), so relatively more of the original stock of coal is sold in the second year (47% versus 44%).

Rents. If coal is a scarce good, its competitive price is above the marginal cost of mining the coal ($m = 0$ in our example). How can we reconcile this result with our earlier finding that price equals marginal cost in a competitive market? The answer is that when coal is scarce, it earns a *rent:* a payment to the owner of an input beyond the minimum necessary for the input to be supplied (Chapter 9).

The owner of the coal need not be the same person who mines the coal. A miner could pay the owner for the right to take the coal out of the mine. After incurring the marginal cost of mining the coal, m, the miner earns $p_1 - m$. However, the owner of the mine charges that amount in rent for the right to mine this scarce resource, rather than giving any of this profit to the miner. Even if the owner of the coal and the miner are the same person, the amount beyond the marginal mining cost is a rent to scarcity.

If the coal were not scarce, no rent would be paid, and the price would equal the marginal cost of mining. Given the demand curve in the example, the most coal that anyone would buy in a year is 200 pounds, which is the amount demanded at a price of zero. If there are 400 pounds of coal in the ground initially—enough to provide 200 pounds in each year—the coal is not scarce, so the price of coal in both years is zero, as Table 15.2 illustrates.[18] As Figure 15.9 shows, the less coal in the ground initially, Q, the higher the initial price of coal.

---

[18]Equation 15.27 holds only when coal is scarce: $Q \le 400$. According to this equation, $p_1 = 0$ when $Q = 400$. If the quantity of coal in the ground is even greater, $Q > 400$, coal is not scarce—people don't want all the coal even if the price is zero—so the price in the first year equals the marginal mining cost of zero. That is, the price is not negative, as Equation 15.27 would imply if it held for quantities greater than 400.

Rising Prices. Thus according to our theory, the price of an exhaustible resource rises if the resource (1) is scarce, (2) can be mined at a marginal cost that remains constant over time, and (3) is sold in a competitive market. The price of old-growth redwood trees rose is predicted by this theory.

Redwood Trees

Many of the majestic old-growth redwood trees in America's western forests are several hundred to several thousand years old. If a mature redwood is cut, young redwoods will not grow to a comparable size within our lifetime. Thus an old-growth redwood forest, like fossil fuels, is effectively a nonrenewable resource, even though new redwoods are being created (very slowly). In contrast, many other types of trees, such as those grown as Christmas trees, are quickly replenished and therefore are renewable resources like fish.

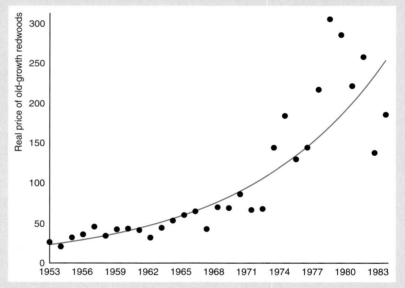

The exponential trend line on the graph shows that the real price of redwoods rose from 1953 to 1983 at an average rate of 8% a year. By the end of this period, virtually no redwood trees were available for sale. The trees either had been harvested or were growing in protected forests. The last remaining privately owned stand was purchased by the U.S. government and the state of California from the Maxxam Corporation in 1996.

The unusually high prices observed in the late 1960s through the 1970s were in large part due to actions of the federal government, which used its power of eminent domain to buy, at the market price, a considerable fraction of all remaining old-growth redwoods for the Redwood National Park. The government bought 1.7 million million-board feet (MBF) in 1968 and 1.4 million MBF in 1978. The latter purchase represented about two-and-a-quarter years of cutting at previous rates. These two government purchases combined equaled 43% of private holdings in 1978 of about 7.3 million MBF. Thus the government purchases were so large that they moved up the time of exhaustion of privately held redwoods by several years, causing the price to jump to the level it would have reached several years later.

WHY PRICE MAY BE CONSTANT OR FALL

If any one of the three conditions we've been assuming—*scarcity, constant marginal mining costs,* and *competition*—is not met, the price of an exhaustible resource may remain steady or fall.[19] Most exhaustible resources, such as aluminum, coal, lead, natural gas, silver, and zinc, have had decades-long periods of falling or constant real prices. Indeed, the real price of each major mineral and metal was lower in 2007 than it was in 1948.

Abundance. As we've already seen, the initial price is set at essentially the marginal cost of mining if the exhaustible resource is not scarce. The gap between the price and the marginal cost grows with the interest rate. If the good is so abundant that the initial gap is zero, the gap does not grow and the price stays constant at the marginal cost. Further, if the gap is initially very small, it has to grow for a long time before the increase becomes noticeable.

Because of abundance, the real prices for many exhaustible resources have remained relatively constant for decades. Moreover, the price falls when the discovery of a large deposit of the resource is announced.

The amount of a resource that can be profitably recovered using current technology is called a *reserve*. Known reserves of some resources are enormous; others are more limited.[20] We have enough silicon (from sand) and magnesium to last virtually forever at 2007 rates of extraction. Known reserves of zinc will last 46 years; lead, 42 years; gold, 36 years; and silver, 29 years. Known reserves of aluminum (bauxite) will last 185 years, and additional reserves are constantly being discovered. Because of this abundance, the real price of aluminum has remained virtually constant for the past 50 years.

Technical Progress. Steady technical progress over many years has reduced the marginal cost of mining and thereby lowered the price of many natural resources. A large enough drop in the marginal mining cost may more than offset the increase in the price due to the interest rate, so the price falls from one year to the next.[21]

Many advances in mining occurred in the years spanning the end of the nineteenth century and the beginning of the twentieth century. As a result of technical progress and discoveries of new supplies, the real prices of many exhaustible resources fell. For example, the real price of aluminum in 1945 was only 12% of the price 50 years earlier. Eventually, as mines play out, prospectors have to dig ever deeper to find resources, causing marginal costs to increase and prices to rise faster than they would with constant marginal costs.

---

[19]The following discussion of why prices of exhaustible resources might not rise and the accompanying examples are based on Berck and Roberts (1996) and additional data supplied by these authors. Their paper also shows that pollution controls and other environmental controls can keep resource prices from rising. Additional data are from Brown and Wolk (2000).

[20]Data are from **minerals.usgs.gov/minerals/pubs/mcs/2007/mcs2007.pdf**.

[21]When the marginal cost of mining is constant at m, Equation 15.25 shows that $p_{t+1} = p_t + i(p_t - m)$, so p_{t+1} must be above p_t. If we allow mining costs to vary from year to year, then

$$p_{t+1} = p_t + i(p_t - m_t) + (m_{t+1} - m_t).$$

Thus if the drop in the mining costs, $m_{t+1} - m_t$, is greater than $i(p_t - m)$, p_{t+1} is less than p_t.

Changing Market Power. Changes in market structure can result in either a rise or a fall in the price of an exhaustible resource. The real price of oil remained virtually constant from 1880 through 1972. But when the Organization of Petroleum Exporting Countries (OPEC) started to act as a cartel in 1973, the price of oil climbed rapidly. At its peak in 1981, the real price of oil was nearly five times higher than its nearly constant level during the period 1880–1972. When Iran and Iraq went to war in 1980, the OPEC cartel began to fall apart, and the real price of oil sank to traditional levels, where it remained through the 1990s. Since then, wars have caused the price to fluctuate substantially.

Summary

1. **Competitive Factor Market:** Any firm maximizes its profit by choosing the quantity of a factor such that the marginal revenue product (*MRP*) of that factor—the marginal revenue times the marginal product of the factor—equals the factor price. The *MRP* is the firm's factor demand. A competitive firm's marginal revenue is the market price, so its *MRP* is the market price times the marginal product. The firm's long-run factor demand is usually flatter than its short-run demand because the firm can adjust more factors, and thus benefit from more flexibility. The market demand for a factor reflects how changes in factor prices affect output prices and hence output levels in product markets.

2. **Noncompetitive Factor Market:** If firms exercise market power to raise price above marginal cost in an output market or a factor market, the quantity demanded by consumers falls. Because the quantity of output and the quantity of inputs are closely related, a reduction in the quantity of an input reduces output, and a reduction in output reduces the demand for inputs.

3. **Monopsony:** A profit-maximizing monopsony—a single buyer—sets its price so that the marginal value to the monopsony equals the firm's marginal expenditure. Because the monopsony pays a price below the competitive level, fewer units are sold than in a competitive market, producers of factors are worse off, the monopsony earns higher profits than it would if it were a price taker,

and society suffers a deadweight loss. A monopsony may also price discriminate.

4. **Capital Markets and Investing:** Inflation aside, most people value money in the future less than money today. An interest rate reflects how much more people value a dollar today than a dollar in the future. To compare a payment made in the future to one made today, we can express the future value in terms of current dollars—its present value—by discounting the future payment using the interest rate. Similarly, a flow of payments over time is related to the present or future value of these payments by the interest rate. A firm may choose between two options with different cash flows over time by picking the one with the higher present value. Similarly, a firm invests in a project if its net present value is positive or its internal rate of return is greater than the interest rate.

5. **Exhaustible Resources:** Nonrenewable resources such as coal, gold, and oil are used up over time and cannot be replenished. If these resources are scarce, the marginal cost of mining them is constant or increasing, and the market structure remains unchanged, their prices rise rapidly over time because of positive interest rates. However, if the resources are abundant, the marginal cost of mining falls over time, or the market becomes more competitive, nonrenewable resource prices may remain constant or fall over time.

Questions

* = answer at the back of this book; **W** *= audio-slide show answers by James Dearden at* **www.aw-bc.com/perloff**

1. What does a competitive firm's labor demand curve look like at quantities of labor such that the marginal product of labor is negative? Why?

**2. What effect does an *ad valorem* tax of α on the revenue of a competitive firm have on that firm's demand for labor?

3. How does a fall in the rental price of capital affect a firm's demand for labor in the long run?

4. How does a monopoly's demand for labor shift if a second firm enters its output market and the result is a Cournot duopoly equilibrium?

5. Does a shift in the supply curve of labor have a greater effect on wages if the output market is competitive or if it is monopolistic? Explain your answer.

6. What is a monopoly's demand for labor if it uses a fixed-proportions production function in which each unit of output takes one unit of labor and one unit of capital?

7. Suppose that the original labor supply curve, S^1, for a monopsony shifts to the right to S^2 if the firm spends $1,000 in advertising. Under what condition should the monopsony engage in this advertising? (*Hint:* See the analysis of monopoly advertising in Chapter 12.)

8. What happens to the monopsony equilibrium if the minimum wage is set slightly above or below the competitive wage?

9. Can a monopsony exercise monopsony power—that is, profitably set its price below the competitive level—if the supply curve it faces is horizontal? Why or why not?

10. What effect does a price support have on a monopsony? In particular, describe the equilibrium if the price support is set at the price where the supply curve intersects the demand curve.

11. Suppose that a modern plague (AIDS, SARS, Ebola hemorrhagic fever, avian flu) wipes out or incapacitates a major share of a small country's workforce. This country's labor market is monopsonistic. What effect will this disaster have on wages in this country?

12. U.S. logging companies employ Canadian loggers to cut Maine trees. When the federal government restricted the number of temporary workers permitted in the United States, the logging companies had to use fewer Canadian loggers. Unable to find U.S. workers willing to cut trees, the logging companies had to lay off workers in complementary operations—for example, truck drivers. Suppose that a logging company needs exactly one truck driver for each six loggers it employs. Each truck driver and team of six loggers can cut and transport 80 thousand tons of wood per day. What is the marginal revenue product function for truckers, and how does the function depend on the number of loggers employed? Show that with a decrease in the number of loggers, a logging company would hire fewer truckers. **W**

13. Oil companies, prompted by improvements in technology and increases in oil prices, are drilling in deeper and deeper water. Using a marginal revenue product and marginal cost diagram of drilling in deep water, show how improvements in drilling technology and increases in oil prices result in more deep-water drilling. **W**

14. Georges, the owner of Maison d'Ail, earned his coveted Michelin star by smothering his dishes in freshly minced garlic. Georges knows that he can save labor costs by using less garlic, albeit with a reduction in quality. If Georges puts g garlic cloves in a dish, the dish's quality, z, is $z = 1/2g^{0.5}$. Georges always fills his restaurant to its capacity, 250 seats. He knows that he can raise the price of each dish by 40¢ for each unit increase in quality and continue to fill his restaurant. Jacqueline, who earns $10 per hour, minces Georges's garlic at a rate of 120 garlic cloves per hour.

   a. What is Jacqueline's value of marginal revenue product?
   b. How many hours per afternoon (while the kitchen prep work is being done) does Jacqueline work?
   c. How many minced cloves of fresh garlic does Georges put in each dish? **W**

*15. How does an individual with a zero discount rate compare current and future consumption? How does your answer change if the discount rate is infinite?

16. If the interest rate is near zero, should an individual go to college, given the information in Figure 15.7? State a simple rule, in terms of the areas labeled "Benefit" and "Cost" in the figure, for determining whether this individual should go to college.

17. Discussing the $350 price of a ticket for one of her concerts, Barbra Streisand said, "If you amortize the money over 28 years, it's $12.50 a year. So is it worth $12.50 a year to see me sing? To hear me sing live?"[22] Under what condition is it useful for an individual to apply Ms. Streisand's rule to decide whether to go to the concert? What do we know about the discount rate of a person who makes such a purchase?

---

[22]"In Other Words . . ." *San Francisco Chronicle*, January 1, 1995: Sunday Section, p. 3. She divided the $350 ticket price by 28 years to get $12.50 as the payment per year.

Problems

18. If you spend $4 a day on a latte (in real dollars) for the rest of your life (essentially forever), what is your present discounted value at a 3% interest rate?

19. Show that the quantity of labor or capital that a firm demands decreases with a factor's own factor price and increases with the output price when the curves are Cobb-Douglas as in Equation 15.12 and 15.13.

20. The Cobb-Douglas production function for a U.S. tobacco products firm is $q = L^{0.2}K^{0.3}$ ("Returns to Scale in U.S. Manufacturing" application, Chapter 6). Derive the marginal revenue product of labor for this firm.

*21. A competitive firm's production function is $q = L + 2LK + K$, and the firm operates where it uses both capital and labor. What is its marginal revenue product of labor?

22. Suppose that a firm's production function is $q = L + K$. Can it be a competitive firm? Explain.

23. A monopoly with a Cobb-Douglas production function, $Q = AL^aK^b$, faces a constant elasticity demand curve. What is its marginal revenue product of labor?

24. A monopsony faces a supply curve of $p = 10 + Q$. What is its marginal expenditure curve?

25. If the monopsony in Problem 24 has a demand curve of $p = 50 - Q$, what are the equilibrium quantity and price? How does this equilibrium differ from the competitive equilibrium?

*26. For general functions, solve for the monopsony's first-order condition if it is also a monopoly in the product market.

27. If you buy a car for $100 down and $100 a year for two more years, what is the present value of these payments at a 5% rate of interest?

28. How much money do you have to put into a bank account that pays 10% interest compounded annually to receive annual payments of $200?

29. What is the present value of $100 paid a year from now and another $100 paid two years from now if the interest rate is i?

30. At a 10% interest rate, do you prefer to buy a phone for $100 or to rent the same phone for $10 a year? Does your answer depend on how long you think the phone will last?

31. Pacific Gas and Electric sent its customers a comparison showing that a person could save $80 per year in gas, water, and detergent expenses by replacing a traditional clothes washer with a new tumble-action washer. Suppose that the interest rate is 5%. You expect your current washer to die in five years. If the cost of a new tumble-action washer is $800, should you replace your washer now or in five years? Explain.

32. You plan to buy a used refrigerator this year for $200 and to sell it when you graduate in two years. Assuming that you can get $100 for the refrigerator at that time, there is no inflation, and the interest rate is 5%, what is the true cost (your current outlay minus the resale value in current terms) of the refrigerator to you?

33. You want to buy a room air conditioner. The price of one machine is $200. It costs $20 a year to operate. The price of the other air conditioner is $300, but it costs only $10 a year to operate. Assuming that both machines last 10 years, which is a better deal? (Do you need to do extensive calculations to answer this question?)

*34. A firm is considering an investment in which its cash flow is $\pi_1 = \$1$ (million), $\pi_2 = -\$12$, $\pi_3 = \$20$, and $\pi_t = 0$ for all other t. The interest rate is 7%. Use the net present

value rule to determine whether the firm should make the investment. Can the firm use the internal rate of return rule to make this decision?

35. You have a barrel of oil that you can sell today for p dollars. Assuming no inflation and no storage cost, how high would the price have to be next year for you to sell the oil next year rather than now?

36. If all the coal in the ground, Q, is to be consumed in two years and the demand for coal is $Q_t = A(p_t)^\varepsilon$ in each year t where ε is a constant demand elasticity, what is the price of coal each year?

37. With the end of the Cold War, the U.S. government decided to "downsize" the military. Along with a pink slip, the government offered ex-military personnel their choice of $8,000 a year for 30 years or a lump sum payment of $50,000 immediately. The lump-sum option was chosen by 92% of enlisted personnel and 51% of officers (Warner and Pleeter, 2001). What is the break-even personal discount rate at which someone would be indifferent between the two options? What can you conclude about the personal discount rates of the enlisted personnel and officers?

38. In 2002, Dell Computer made its suppliers wait 37 days on average to be paid for their goods; however, Dell was paid by its customers immediately. Thus Dell earned interest on this *float*, the money that it was implicitly borrowing. If Dell can earn an annual interest rate of 4%, what is this float worth to Dell per dollar spent on inputs?

39. Many retirement funds charge an administrative fee equal to 0.25% on managed assets. Suppose that Alexx and Spenser each invest $5,000 in the same stock this year. Alexx invests directly and earns 5% a year. Spenser uses a retirement fund and earns 4.75%. After 30 years, how much more will Alexx have than Spenser?

*40. Your gas-guzzling car gets only 10 miles to the gallon and has no resale value, but you are sure that it will last five years. You know that you can always buy a used car for $8,000 that gets 20 miles to the gallon. A gallon of gas costs $2 and you drive 6,000 miles a year. If the interest rate is 5% and you are interested only in saving money, should you buy a car now rather than wait until your current car dies? Would you make the same decision if you faced a 10% interest rate?

41. As discussed in Solved Problem 15.4, Lewis Wolff and his investment group bought the Oakland A's baseball team for $180 million in 2005. Reportedly, Hall-of-Famer Reggie Jackson offered $25 million more but was rebuffed (*Forbes*, 2005). How would the calculations in Solved Problem 15.4 change if the sales price had been $205 million?

42. To virtually everyone's surprise, the new Washington Nationals baseball team apparently earned a pretax profit

of $20 million in 2005, compared to a $10 million loss when the team was the Montreal Expos in 2004 (Thomas Heath, "Nationals' Expected '05 Profit Is $20 Million," *Washington Post,* June 21, 2005: A1). Major League Baseball, which bought the franchise for $120 million in 2002, received eight bids of between $300 million and $400 million for the team. Reportedly, most baseball teams sell for between two and three times their revenue, so given that the Nationals' projected revenue was $129 million in 2005, an offer of $400 million would be typical. If the Nationals were expected to earn $20 million each year in the future, what is the internal rate of return on a $400 million investment for this club?

*43. Two different teams offer a professional basketball player contracts for playing this year. Both contracts are guaranteed, and payments will be made even if the athlete is injured and cannot play. Team A's contract would pay him $1 million today. Team B's contract would pay him $500,000 today and $2 million 10 years from now. Assuming that there is no inflation, that our pro is concerned only about which contract has the highest present value, and that his personal discount rate is 5%, which contract does he accept? Does the answer change if the discount rate is 20%?

44. An economic consultant explaining the effect on labor demand of increasing health care costs, interviewed for the *Wall Street Journal*'s Capital column (David Wessel, "Health-Care Costs Blamed for Hiring Gap," March 11, 2004, A2), states, "Medical costs are rising more rapidly than anything else in the economy—more than prices, wages or profits. It isn't only current medical costs, but also the present value of the stream of endlessly high cost increases that retards hiring."

   a. Why does the present value of the stream of health care costs, and not just the current health care costs, affect a firm's decision whether to create a new position?

   b. Why should an employer discount future health care costs in deciding whether to create a new position? **W**

45. You are buying a new $20,000 car and have the option to pay for the car with a 0% loan or to receive $500 cash back at the time of the purchase. With the loan, you pay $5,000 down when you purchase the car and then make three $5,000 payments, one at the end of each year of the loan. You currently have $50,000 in your savings account.

   a. The rate of interest on your savings account is 4% and will remain so for the next three years. Which payment method should you choose?

   b. What interest rate, i, makes you indifferent between the two payment methods? **W**

46. A resident of New York City, you are considering purchasing a new Toyota Prius. The Prius sells for $20,000. Your annual expense of owning and driving the car is $3,000 (most of which is the cost of parking the car in a Manhattan garage). If you do not purchase the car, you will spend $5,000 per year on public transportation and rental cars. The interest rate is 4%. What is the lowest number of years that you must own the car for the discounted cost of owning the car to be less than the discounted cost of the alternative? **W**

47. Trees, wine, and cattle become more valuable over time and then possibly decrease in value. Draw a figure with present value on the vertical axis and years (age) on the horizontal axis and show this relationship. Show in what year the owner should "harvest" such a good assuming that there is no cost to harvesting. [*Hint:* If the good's present value is P_0 and we take that money and invest it at interest rate i (a small number such as 0.02 or 0.04), then its value in year t is $P_0(1 + i)^t$; or if we allow continuous compounding, $P_0 e^{it}$. Such a curve increases exponentially over time and looks like the curve labeled "Price" in Figure 15.8. Draw curves with different possible present values. Use those curves to choose the optimal harvest time.] How would your answer change if the interest rate were zero? Show in a figure.

48. The Canadian thread mill has an estimated production function of $q = L^{0.6} K^{0.2}$. Suppose the firm's capital is fixed at 30 units, it has monopsony power in hiring workers, and the inverse supply function of the number of workers employed by the thread mill is $w = 2L$.

   a. What is the marginal revenue product of labor function?

   b. What is the marginal expenditure on labor function?

   c. As a function of the price p of the firm's output, what is the optimal number of workers for the mill to employ? **W**

Chapter 16

Uncertainty

*We must believe in luck. For how else can we explain the success of those
we don't like?*
— Jean Cocteau

Life's a series of gambles. Will you receive Social Security when you retire? Will you win the lottery tomorrow? Will your stock increase in value? Will you avoid disease, earthquakes, and fire? In this chapter, we extend the model of decision making by individuals and firms to include uncertainty. We look at how uncertainty affects consumption decisions (Chapters 3–5), such as how much insurance to buy, as well as investment decisions (Chapter 15).

When making decisions about investments and other matters, you consider the possible *outcomes* under various circumstances, or *states of nature*. When deciding whether to carry a new type of doll, a toy store owner considers how many dolls will be sold if the doll is popular and, conversely, if it is unpopular—two possible outcomes—and how likely these two states of nature are.

Although we cannot know with certainty what a future outcome will be, we may know that some outcomes are more likely than others. When uncertainty can be quantified, it is sometimes called **risk:** the situation in which the likelihood of each possible outcome is known or can be estimated, and no single possible outcome is certain to occur. All the examples in this chapter concern quantifiable or risky situations.[1]

Consumers and firms modify their decisions about consumption and investment as the degree of risk varies. Indeed, most people are willing to spend money to reduce risk by buying insurance or taking preventive measures. Moreover, most people will choose a riskier investment over a less risky one only if they expect a higher return from the riskier investment.

1. **Degree of Risk:** Probabilities are used to measure the degree of risk and the likely profit from a risky undertaking.

2. **Decision Making Under Uncertainty:** Whether people choose a risky option over a nonrisky option depends on their attitudes toward risk and on the expected payoffs of each option.

3. **Avoiding Risk:** People try to reduce their overall risk by not making risky choices, taking actions to lower the likelihood of a disaster, combining offsetting risks, and insuring.

4. **Investing Under Uncertainty:** Whether people make an investment depends on the riskiness of the payoff, the expected return, their attitudes toward risk, the interest rate, and whether it is profitable to alter the likelihood of a good outcome.

In this chapter, we examine four main topics

---

[1]*Jargon alert:* Many people do not distinguish between the terms *risk* and *uncertainty*. Henceforth, we will use these terms interchangeably.

16.1 Degree of Risk

In America, anyone can be president. That's one of the risks you take. —Adlai Stevenson

You are thinking about buying lunch at a new restaurant. There are two possible outcomes: The lunch will or will not taste good to you. Knowing the likelihood of each of these outcomes would help you decide whether to try this new restaurant.

Before we can analyze decision making under uncertainty, we need a way to describe and quantify risk. A particular event—such as eating lunch at a new restaurant—has a number of possible outcomes—say, an enjoyable meal or an unenjoyable meal. Because you don't know whether you will enjoy the meal, eating at this new restaurant is risky. To describe how risky this activity is, we need to quantify the likelihood that each possible outcome will occur.

We can use our estimate of how risky each outcome is to estimate the most likely outcome. We then present measures of risk that reflect how much *actual* outcomes deviate from the *most* likely outcome.

PROBABILITY

A *probability* is a number between 0 and 1 that indicates the likelihood that a particular outcome will occur. For example, you might have a 25% probability—a 1 in 4 chance—of enjoying the meal at the restaurant. How do we estimate a probability?

Frequency. If we know the history of the outcomes for an event, we can use the frequency with which a particular outcome occurred as our estimate of the probability. Let n be the number of times that one particular outcome occurred during the N total number of times an event occurred. We set our estimate of the probability, θ (theta), equal to the frequency:

$$\theta = \frac{n}{N}.$$

A house either burns or does not burn. If $n = 13$ similar houses burned in your neighborhood of $N = 1,000$ homes last year, you might estimate the probability that your house will burn this year as $\theta = 13/1,000 = 1.3\%$.

Subjective Probability. Often we don't have a history that allows us to calculate the frequency. We use whatever information we have to form a *subjective probability,* which is our best estimate of the likelihood that an outcome will occur. We may use all available information—even information that is not based on a conscious, scientific estimation procedure.

How do you derive a subjective probability about the likelihood that you'll like the new restaurant? You might know that your friend liked the restaurant but that your economics professor did not. If you're not sure whether either of these people likes the same food you do, you may estimate the probability that you'll like the restaurant at 50%. However, if you know that your friend usually likes the same type of food you do but are less sure about whether your professor likes the same type of food, you might

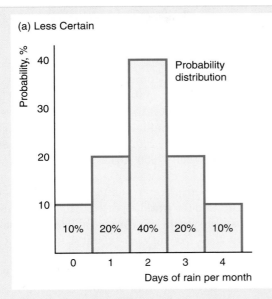
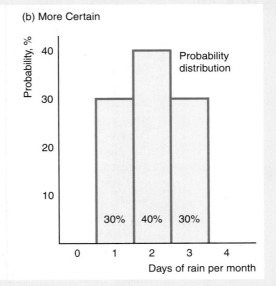

Figure 16.1 Probability Distribution. The probability distribution shows the probability of occurrence for each of the mutually exclusive outcomes. Panel a shows five possible mutually exclusive outcomes. The probability that it rains exactly two days per month is 40%. The probability that it rains five or more days per month is 0%. The probability distributions in panels a and b have the same mean. The variance is smaller in panel b, where the probability distribution is more concentrated around the mean than the distribution in panel a.

put more weight on your friend's report and estimate the probability that you'll like the restaurant as a number greater than 50%.[2]

Probability Distribution. A *probability distribution* relates the probability of occurrence to each possible outcome. Panel a of Figure 16.1 shows a probability distribution over five possible outcomes: zero to four days of rain per month in a relatively dry city. The probability that it rains no days during the month is 10%, as is the probability of exactly four days of rain. The chance of two rainy days is 40%, and the chance of one or three rainy days is 20% each. The probability that it rains five or more days a month is 0%.

These weather outcomes are *mutually exclusive*—only one of these outcomes can occur at a given time—and *exhaustive*—no other outcomes than those listed are possible. Where outcomes are mutually exclusive and exhaustive, exactly one of these outcomes will occur with certainty, and the probabilities must add up to 100%. For simplicity, we concentrate on situations in which there are only two possible outcomes.

---

[2]When events are repeated, we can compare our subjective probabilities to observed frequencies. Your subjective probability (guess) that it rains 50% of the days in January can be compared to the frequency of rain in January during the recorded history for your city. If an event is not going to be repeated, however, it may not be possible to check whether your subjective probability is reasonable or accurate by comparing it to a frequency. You might believe that there's a 75% chance of dry weather tomorrow. If it does rain tomorrow, that doesn't mean you were wrong. Only if you believed that the probability of rain was 0% would observing rain tomorrow prove you wrong.

Biased Estimates?

Do newspaper stories, television, and movies cause people to overestimate relatively rare events and underestimate relatively common ones? Newspapers are more likely to publish "man bites dog" stories than the more common "dog bites man" reports. For example, Indian papers recently published two stories on strange cases of men biting snakes; one was headlined, "Cobra Dies after Biting Priest of Snake Temple!" (*Express India,* July 11, 2005), while the other reported that Neeranjan Bhaskar has eaten more than 4,000 snakes (*Calcutta Telegraph,* August 1, 2005).

If you have seen the movie *Jaws,* you can't help but think about sharks before wading into the ocean. Newspapers around the world reported that an unfortunate 14-year-old girl was killed by a shark in waters off Florida in 2005 and that an Australian man survived an attack in 2007. Do you worry about shark attacks? You really shouldn't.

Only 12 people were killed by sharks in U.S. waters from 1990 through 2006: an average of 0.71 a year. You're just as likely to die from beanbag chair suffocation, more than twice as likely to die from being crushed by a soda machine toppling on you, and 10 times more likely to meet your maker in a roller skating accident. A typical American's chance of dying this year from a shark attack is 1 in 350 million; a bee sting, 1 in 6 million; falling into a hole, 1 in 2.8 million; a handgun, 1 in 1.9 million; excessive cold, 1 in 643,000; lightning, 1 in 600,000; homicide, 1 in 15,000; flu, 1 in 3,025; cancer, 1 in 514; heart disease, 1 in 384; and any cause, 1 in 117.

Benjamin et al. (2001) reported that, when asked to estimate the frequency of deaths from various causes for the entire population, people overestimate the number of deaths from infrequent causes and underestimate those from more common causes. In contrast, if they are asked to estimate the number of deaths among their own age group from a variety of causes, their estimates are almost completely unbiased. That is not to say that people know the true probabilities—only that their mistakes are not systematic. (However, you should know that, despite the widespread warnings issued every Christmas season, poinsettias are not poisonous.)

EXPECTED VALUE

> *One of the common denominators I have found is that expectations rise*
> *above that which is expected.*   —George W. Bush

Gregg, a promoter, schedules an outdoor concert for tomorrow.[3] How much money he'll make depends on the weather. If it doesn't rain, his profit or value from the concert is $V = \$15$. (If it will make you happier—and it will certainly make Gregg happier—you can think of the profits in this example as $150,000 instead of $15.) If it rains, he'll have to cancel the concert and he'll lose $V = -\$5$, which he must pay the band. Although Gregg does not know with certainty what the weather will be, he knows that the weather bureau forecasts a 50% chance of rain.

---

[3]My brother Gregg, a successful concert promoter, wants me to inform you that the hero of the following story is some other Gregg who is a concert promoter.

The amount Gregg expects to earn is called his *expected* value (here, his *expected profit*). The expected value, *EV*, is the value of each possible outcome times the probability of that outcome:

$$EV = [Pr(\text{no rain}) \times \text{Value(no rain)}] + [Pr(\text{rain}) \times \text{Value(rain)}]$$

$$= \left(\frac{1}{2} \times \$15\right) + \left[\frac{1}{2} \times (-\$5)\right] = \$5,$$

where *Pr* is the probability of an outcome, so *Pr*(rain) is the "probability that rain occurs."

The expected value is the amount that Gregg would earn on average if the event were repeated many times. If he puts on outdoor concerts many times over the years and the weather follows historical patterns, he will earn \$15 for the half of the concerts without rain, and he will get soaked for −\$5 for the half of the concerts that are rained out. Thus he'll earn an average of \$5 per concert over a long period of time. More generally, if there are *n* possible outcomes—*states of nature*—with payoffs or values V_i, $i = 1, \ldots, n$, and associated probabilities θ_i, then the expected value is

$$EV = \sum_{i=1}^{n} \theta_i V_i . \tag{16.1}$$

SOLVED PROBLEM 16.1

How much more would Gregg expect to earn if he knew far enough before the concert that he would obtain perfect information about the probability of rain and could book the band only if needed? How much does he expect to gain from having this perfect information?

Answer

1. *Determine how much Gregg would earn if he had perfect information in each state of nature:* If Gregg knew with certainty that it would rain at the time of the concert, he would not book the band, so he would make no loss or profit. If Gregg knew that it would not rain, he would hold the concert and make \$15.

2. *Determine how much Gregg would expect to earn before he learns with certainty what the weather will be:* Gregg knows that he'll make \$15 with a 50% probability and \$0 with a 50% probability, so his expected value, given that he'll receive perfect information in time to act on it, is

$$\left(\frac{1}{2} \times \$15\right) + \left(\frac{1}{2} \times \$0\right) = \$7.50.$$

3. *His expected gain from perfect information is the difference between his expected earnings with perfect information and his expected earnings with imperfect information:* Gregg expects to earn \$2.50 = \$7.50 − \$5 more with perfect information than with imperfect information. This answer can be reached more directly: Perfect weather information is valuable to him because he can avoid hiring the band unnecessarily when it rains. (Having information has no value if it doesn't alter behavior.) The *value of this information* is his expected savings from not hiring the band when it rains: $\frac{1}{2} \times \$5 = \$2.50$.

VARIANCE AND STANDARD DEVIATION

If Gregg would earn the same amount—the expected value—whether it rained or not, he would face no risk. We can measure the risk he faces in many different ways. One approach is to look at the degree by which actual outcomes vary from the expected value, *EV*.

The *difference* between his actual earnings and his expected earnings if it does not rain is $10 = $15 − $5. The difference if it does rain is −$10 = −$5 − $5. Because there are two differences—one difference for each state of nature—it is convenient to combine them in a single measure of risk.

One such measure of risk is the *variance*, which measures the spread of the probability distribution. For example, the variance in panel a of Figure 16.1, where the probability distribution ranges from zero to four days of rain per month, is greater than the variance in panel b, where the probability distribution ranges from one to three days of rain per month.

Formally, the variance is the probability-weighted average of the squares of the differences between the observed outcome and the expected value. If there are n possible outcomes with an expected value of EV, the value of outcome i is V_i, and the probability of that outcome is θ_i, then the variance is

$$\text{Variance} = \sum_{i=1}^{n} \theta_i (V_i - EV)^2. \tag{16.2}$$

The variance puts more weight on large deviations from the expected value than on smaller ones. Instead of describing risk using the variance, economists and businesspeople often report the *standard deviation*, which is the square root of the variance. The usual symbol for the standard deviation is σ (sigma), so the symbol for variance is σ^2.

Gregg faces the probability $\theta_1 = \frac{1}{2}$ if there is no rain and $\theta_2 = \frac{1}{2}$ if there is rain. The value of the concert is $V_1 = 15 if there is no rain and $V_2 = −$5$ if it rains. Thus the variance of the value that Gregg obtains from the outdoor concert is

$$\sigma^2 = [\theta_1 \times (V_1 - EV)^2] + [\theta_2 \times (V_2 - EV)^2]$$
$$= \left[\frac{1}{2} \times (\$15 - \$5)^2 \right] + \left[\frac{1}{2} \times (-\$5 - \$5)^2 \right]$$
$$= \left[\frac{1}{2} \times (\$10)^2 \right] + \left[\frac{1}{2} \times (-\$10)^2 \right] = \$100.$$

Because the variance of the payoff from the outdoor concert is $\sigma^2 = 100, the standard deviation is $\sigma = 10.

Holding the expected value constant, the smaller the standard deviation (or variance), the smaller the risk. Suppose that Gregg's expected value of profit is the same if he stages the concert indoors, but that the standard deviation of his profit is less. The indoor theater does not hold as many people as the outdoor venue, so the most that Gregg can earn if it does not rain is $10. Rain discourages attendance even at the indoor theater, so he just breaks even, earning $0. The expected value of the indoor concert,

$$EV = \left(\frac{1}{2} \times \$10 \right) + \left(\frac{1}{2} \times \$0 \right) = \$5,$$

is the same as that of the outdoor concert. Staging the concert indoors involves less risk, however. The variance of his earnings from the indoor concert is

$$\sigma^2 = \left[\frac{1}{2} \times (\$10 - \$5)^2 \right] + \left[\frac{1}{2} \times (\$0 - \$5)^2 \right]$$
$$= \left[\frac{1}{2} \times (\$5)^2 \right] + \left[\frac{1}{2} \times (-\$5)^2 \right] = \$25,$$

which is only a quarter of his variance if he holds the event outside.

16.2   Decision Making Under Uncertainty

Will Gregg stage an indoor or an outdoor concert? To answer such a question, we need to know his attitude toward bearing risk.

Although the indoor and outdoor concerts have the same expected value, the outdoor concert involves more risk. Gregg will earn more with good weather or lose more with bad weather by holding his concert outdoors instead of indoors. He'll book an outdoor concert only if he likes to gamble.

Even if he dislikes risk, Gregg may prefer a riskier option if it has a higher expected value. Suppose that he strikes a new agreement with the band by which he pays it only if the weather is good and the concert is held. Gregg's expected value is $7.50, the variance is $56.25, and the standard deviation is $7.50.[4] By holding the concert outdoors instead of inside, Gregg's expected value is higher ($7.50 instead of $5), and the standard deviation is higher ($7.50 instead of $5). He earns the same, $0, from both types of concerts in bad weather. In good weather, he earns more from the outdoor concert. Because he always does as well with an outdoor concert as with an indoor show, Gregg clearly prefers the riskier outdoor concert with its higher expected value.

If he dislikes risk, Gregg won't necessarily stage the concert with the higher expected value. Suppose that his choice is between the indoor concert and an outdoor concert from which he earns $100,015.50 if it doesn't rain and loses $100,005 if it rains. His expected value is greater with the outside concert, $5.25 instead of $5, but he faces much more risk. The standard deviation of the outdoor concert is $100,010.25 compared to $5. Gregg might reasonably opt for the indoor concert with the lower expected value if he dislikes risk. After all, he may be loath to risk losing $100,005 with a 50% probability.

EXPECTED UTILITY

We can formalize this type of reasoning by extending our model of utility maximization (Chapters 3–5) to show how people's taste for risk affects their choice among options (investments, career choices, consumption bundles) that differ in both value and risk. If people made choices to maximize expected value, they would always choose the option with the highest expected value regardless of the risks involved. However, most people care about risk in addition to the expected value. Indeed, most people are *risk averse*—they dislike risk—and will choose a bundle with higher risk only if its expected value is substantially higher than that of a less-risky bundle.

In Chapter 3, we noted that we can describe an individual's preferences over various bundles of goods by using a utility function. John von Neumann and Oskar Morgenstern (1944) suggested an extension of this standard utility-maximizing model that includes risk.[5] They did so by treating utility as a cardinal measure rather than an ordinal measure as we did in Chapters 3–5. In von Neumann's and Morgenstern's

---

[4]The expected value is the same as in Solved Problem 16.1: $(\frac{1}{2} \times \$15) + (\frac{1}{2} \times \$0) = \$7.50$. The variance is $\frac{1}{2} \times (\$15 - \$7.50)^2 + \frac{1}{2} \times (\$0 - \$7.50)^2 = \$56.25$, so the standard deviation is $7.50.

[5]This approach to handling choice under uncertainty is the most commonly used method. Schoemaker (1982) discusses the logic underlying this approach, the evidence for it, and several variants. Machina (1989) discusses a number of alternative methods.

reformulation, a rational person maximizes *expected utility*. Expected utility, *EU*, is the probability-weighted average of the utility, $U(\cdot)$, from each possible outcome:

$$EU = \sum_{i=1}^{n} \theta_i U(V_i). \qquad (16.3)$$

For example, Gregg's expected utility, *EU*, from the outdoor concert is

$$EU = \left[\theta_1 \times U(V_1) \right] + \left[\theta_2 \times U(V_2) \right]$$

$$= \left[\frac{1}{2} \times U(\$15) \right] + \left[\frac{1}{2} \times U(-\$5) \right],$$

where his utility function, *U*, depends on his earnings. For example, $U(\$15)$ is the amount of utility Gregg gets from $15. (People have preferences over the goods they consume. However, for simplicity we'll say that a person receives utility from earnings or wealth, which can be spent on consumption goods.)

In short, the expected utility calculation is similar to the expected value calculation. Both are weighted averages in which the weights are the probabilities that the state of nature will occur. The difference is that the expected value is the probability-weighted average of the monetary value, whereas the expected utility is the probability-weighted average of the utility from the monetary value.

ATTITUDES TOWARD RISK

If we know how an individual's utility increases with wealth, we can determine how that person reacts to risky propositions. We can classify people in terms of their willingness to make a **fair bet:** a wager with an expected value of zero. An example of a fair bet is one in which you pay a dollar if a flipped coin comes up heads and receive a dollar if it comes up tails. Because you expect to win half the time and lose half the time, the expected value of this bet is zero:

$$\left[\frac{1}{2} \times (-\$1) \right] + \left[\frac{1}{2} \times \$1 \right] = 0.$$

In contrast, a bet in which you pay $1 if you lose the coin flip and receive $2 if you win is an unfair bet that favors you, with an expected value of

$$\left[\frac{1}{2} \times (-\$1) \right] + \left[\frac{1}{2} \times \$2 \right] = 50¢.$$

Someone who is unwilling to make a fair bet is **risk averse.** A person who is indifferent about making a fair bet is **risk neutral.** A person who is **risk preferring** will make a fair bet.

Risk Aversion. We can use our expected utility model to examine how Irma, who is risk averse, makes a choice under uncertainty. Figure 16.2 shows Irma's utility function. The utility function is concave to the wealth axis, indicating that Irma's

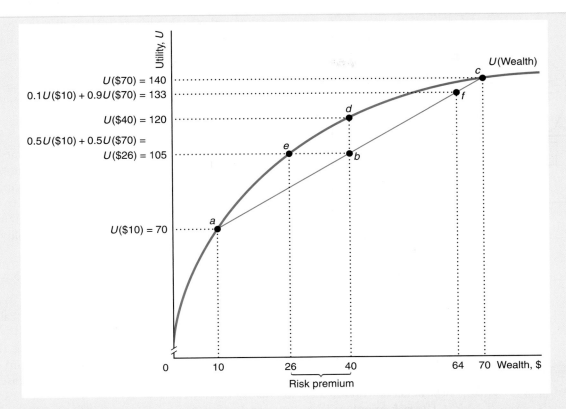

Figure 16.2 Risk Aversion. Initially, Irma's wealth is $40, so her utility is $U(\$40) = 120$, point *d*. If she buys the vase and it's a Ming, she is at point *c*, where her utility is $U(\$70) = 140$. If the purchased vase is an imitation, she is at point *a*, where $U(\$10) = 70$. If her subjective probability that the vase is a Ming is 50%, her expected utility from buying the vase, point *b*, is $\frac{1}{2}U(\$10) + \frac{1}{2}U(\$70) = 105$, which is less than her utility with a certain wealth of $40, $U(\$40) = 120$. Thus she does not buy the vase. If Irma's subjective probability that the vase is a Ming is 90%, her expected utility from buying the vase is $0.1U(\$10) + 0.9U(\$70) = 133$, point *f*, which is more than her utility with a certain wealth of $40, $U(\$40) = 120$, point *d*, so she buys the vase.

utility rises with wealth but at a diminishing rate. Irma's utility from wealth W is $U(W)$. She has positive marginal utility from extra wealth, $dU(W)/dW > 0$; however, her utility increases with wealth at a diminishing rate, $d^2U(W)/dW^2 < 0$. That is, she has *diminishing marginal utility of wealth:* The extra pleasure she gets from each extra dollar of wealth is smaller than the pleasure she gets from the previous dollar. An individual whose utility function is concave to the wealth axis is risk averse, as we now illustrate.

A person whose utility function is concave picks the less-risky choice if both choices have the same expected value. Suppose that Irma has an initial wealth of $40 and two options. One option is to do nothing and keep the $40, so her utility is $U(\$40) = 120$ (point *d* in Figure 16.2) with certainty.

Her other option is to buy a vase. Her wealth is $70 if the vase is a Ming and $10 if it is an imitation. Irma's subjective probability is 50% that it is a genuine Ming vase. Her expected value or wealth remains

$$\$40 = \left(\frac{1}{2} \times \$10\right) + \left(\frac{1}{2} \times \$70\right).$$

Thus buying the vase is a fair bet because she has the same expected wealth whether she purchases the vase or not.

Irma prefers the certain wealth from not buying the vase because that option carries less risk. Her utility if the vase is a Ming is $U(\$70) = 140$, point c. If it's an imitation, her utility is $U(\$10) = 70$, point a. Thus her expected utility is

$$\left[\frac{1}{2} \times U(\$10)\right] + \left[\frac{1}{2} \times U(\$70)\right] = \left(\frac{1}{2} \times 70\right) + \left(\frac{1}{2} \times 140\right) = 105.$$

Figure 16.2 shows that her expected utility is point b, the midpoint of a line (called a *chord*) between a and c.[6]

Because Irma's utility function is concave, her utility from certain wealth, 120 at point d, is greater than her expected utility from the risky activity, 105 at point b. As a result, she does not buy the vase. Buying this vase, which is a fair bet, increases the risk she faces without changing her expected wealth.

The **risk premium** is the amount that a risk-averse person would pay to avoid taking a risk. For example, an individual may buy insurance to avoid risk. Figure 16.2 shows how much Irma would be willing to pay to avoid this risk. Her certain utility from having a wealth of $26, $U(\$26) = 105$, is the same as her expected utility if she buys the vase. Thus Irma would be indifferent between buying the vase and having $26 with certainty. Irma would be willing to pay a risk premium of $14 = \$40 - \$26$ to avoid bearing the risk from buying the vase.

A risk-averse person chooses a riskier option only if it has a sufficiently higher expected value. If Irma were much more confident that the vase were a Ming, her expected value would rise and she'd buy the vase, as Solved Problem 16.2 shows.[7] Solved Problem 16.3 illustrates how to calculate the risk premium if we know the explicit functional form of the utility function.

---

[6]The chord represents all the possible weighted averages of the utility at point a and the utility at point c. When the probabilities of the two outcomes are equal, the expected value is the midpoint. If the probability that the vase is a Ming is greater than $\frac{1}{2}$, the expected value is closer to point c, as Solved Problem 16.2 illustrates.

[7]My colleague Irma Adelman visited an antique store and was offered a vase for $10. In addition to being an outstanding economist, she's an art expert. At first glance, she thought that the vase was a Ming. Turning it over, she found marks on the bottom that convinced her that it was a Ming (I think it said, "Made in China"). Because her subjective probability that the vase was a genuine Ming was very high, she bought it, even though she is risk averse. This lovely Ming vase graced her home until her !#@$! cat broke it.

SOLVED PROBLEM 16.2

Suppose that Irma's subjective probability is 90% that the vase is a Ming. What is her expected wealth if she buys the vase? What is her expected utility? Does she buy the vase?

Answer

1. *Calculate Irma's expected wealth:* Her expected value or wealth is 10% times her wealth if the vase is not a Ming plus 90% times her wealth if the vase is a Ming:

$$(0.1 \times \$10) + (0.9 \times \$70) = \$64.$$

In Figure 16.2, $64 is the distance along the wealth axis corresponding to point *f*.

2. *Calculate Irma's expected utility:* Her expected utility is the probability-weighted average of her utility under the two outcomes:

$$[0.1 \times U(\$10)] + [0.9 \times U(\$70)] = (0.1 \times 70) + (0.9 \times 140) = 133.$$

Her expected utility is the height on the utility axis of point *f*. Point *f* is nine-tenths of the distance along the line connecting point *a* to point *c*.

3. *Compare Irma's expected utility to her certain utility if she does not buy the vase:* Irma's expected utility from buying the vase, 133 (point *f*), is greater than her certain utility, 120 (point *d*), if she does not. Thus if Irma is this confident that the vase is a Ming, she buys it. Although the risk is greater from buying than from not buying, her expected wealth is higher enough ($64 instead of $40) that it's worth it to her to take the chance.

SOLVED PROBLEM 16.3

Jen has a concave utility function of $U(W) = \sqrt{W}$.[8] Her only major asset is shares in an Internet start-up company. Tomorrow she will find out her stock's value. She believes that it is worth $144 with probability 2/3 and $225 with probability 1/3. What is her expected utility? What risk premium, *P*, would she pay to avoid bearing this risk?

Answer

1. *Calculate Jen's expected wealth and her expected utility:* Her expected wealth is

$$EW = (2/3 \times 144) + (1/3 \times 225) = 96 + 75 = 171.$$

Her expected utility is

$$\begin{aligned} EU &= [2/3 \times U(144)] + [1/3 \times U(225)] \\ &= [2/3 \times \sqrt{144}] + [1/3 \times \sqrt{225}] \\ &= [2/3 \times 12] + [1/3 \times 15] = 13. \end{aligned}$$

---

[8]In Question 1, you are asked to plot this utility function to illustrate that it is concave and hence that Jen is risk averse.

2. *Solve for P such that her expected utility equals her utility from her expected wealth minus P:* Jen would pay up to an amount *P* to avoid bearing the risk, where $U(EW - P)$ equals her expected utility from the risky stock, *EU*. That is,

$$U(EW - P) = U(171 - P) = \sqrt{171 - P} = 13 = EU.$$

Squaring both sides, we find that $171 - P = 169$, or $P = 2$. That is, Jen would accept an offer for her stock today of $169 (or more), which reflects a risk premium of $2.

Risk Neutrality. Someone who is risk neutral has a constant marginal utility of wealth: Each extra dollar of wealth raises that person's utility by the same amount as the previous dollar. With constant marginal utility of wealth, the utility curve is a straight line in a utility and wealth graph.

Suppose that Irma is risk neutral and has the straight-line utility curve in panel a of Figure 16.3. She would be indifferent between buying the vase and not buying it if her

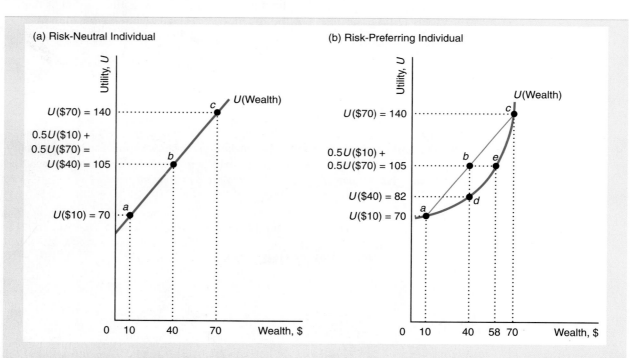

Figure 16.3 Risk Neutrality and Risk Preference. (a) If Irma's utility curve is a straight line, she is risk neutral and is indifferent as to whether or not to make a fair bet. Her expected utility from buying the vase, 105 at point *b*, is the same as from a certain wealth of $40 at point *b*. (b) If Irma's utility curve is convex to the horizontal axis, Irma has increasing marginal utility to wealth and is risk preferring. She buys the vase because her expected utility from buying the vase, 105 at point *b*, is higher than her utility from a certain wealth of $40, 82 at point *d*.

subjective probability is 50% that it is a Ming. Her expected utility from buying the vase is the average of her utility at points a ($10) and c ($70):

$$\left[\frac{1}{2} \times U(\$10) \right] + \left[\frac{1}{2} \times U(\$70) \right] = \left(\frac{1}{2} \times 70 \right) + \left(\frac{1}{2} \times 140 \right) = 105.$$

Her expected utility exactly equals her utility with certain wealth of $40 (point b) because the line connecting points a and c lies on the utility function and point b is the midpoint between a and c.

Here Irma is indifferent between buying and not buying the vase, a fair bet, because she doesn't care how much risk she faces. Because the expected wealth from both options is $40, she is indifferent between them.

In general, *a risk-neutral person chooses the option with the highest expected value because maximizing expected value maximizes utility.* A risk-neutral person chooses the riskier option if it has even a slightly higher expected value than the less-risky option. Equivalently, the risk premium for a risk-neutral person is zero.

Risk Preference. An individual with an increasing marginal utility of wealth is risk preferring: that is, willing to take a fair bet. If Irma has the utility curve in panel b of Figure 16.3, she is risk preferring. Her expected utility from buying the vase, 105 at point b, is higher than her certain utility if she does not buy the vase, 82 at point d. Therefore, she buys the vase.

A risk-preferring person is willing to pay for the right to make a fair bet (a negative risk premium). As the figure shows, Irma's expected utility from buying the vase is the same as the utility from a certain wealth of $58. Given her initial wealth of $40, if you offer her the opportunity to buy the vase or offer to give her $18, she is indifferent. With any payment smaller than $18, she prefers to buy the vase.

⬤ **APPLICATION**

Gambling

> *Horse sense is the thing a horse has which keeps it from betting on people.*
> —W. C. Fields

If you ask them, most people say that they don't like bearing risk. Consistent with such statements, they reduce the risk they face by buying insurance. Nonetheless, many of these people engage in games of chance from time to time. Not only do they gamble, but they make unfair bets, in which the expected value of the gamble is negative. That is, if they play the game repeatedly, they are likely to lose money in the long run.

Estimated worldwide Internet gambling was $12 billion in 2005 (though perhaps $6.5 billion of this amount was eliminated when the U.S. Congress voted to ban Internet gambling in 2006). In 2005, Americans spent about $29 billion in casinos, $45 billion on state lotteries, and at least $6 billion on online gambling. By some estimates, worldwide gambling has reached $245 billion. Half of the countries in the

world have lotteries with annual combined ticket sales of over $115 billion (Garrett, 2001).

These bets are unfair. For example, the British government keeps half of the total money bet on its lottery. Americans lose at least $50 billion, or 7% of the legal bets. A casino's *hold percentage*—the money the casino retains as a percentage of the amount of chips bought—for roulette wheels runs slightly over 20%; for the wheel of fortune about 45%; and for keno, nearly 30%.

Theories on Why People Gamble. Why do people take unfair bets? Some people gamble because they are risk preferring or because they have a compulsion to gamble (by one estimate, 2.3% of Australians suffer from a gambling compulsion, the highest rate in the world). However, neither of these observations is likely to explain noncompulsive gambling by most people who exhibit risk-averse behavior in the other aspects of their lives (such as buying insurance). Risk-averse people may make unfair bets for three reasons: They enjoy the game, they have a utility curve with both risk-averse and risk-preferring regions, or they falsely believe that the gamble favors them.

The first explanation is that gambling provides entertainment as well as risk. Risk-averse people insure their property, such as their houses, because there's nothing enjoyable about bearing the risk of theft, flooding, and fire. However, these same people may play poker or bet on horse races because they get enough pleasure from playing those games to put up with the financial risk and the expected loss.

The second explanation also involves tastes. Friedman and Savage (1948) suggested that gamblers place a high value on the chance to increase their wealth greatly.

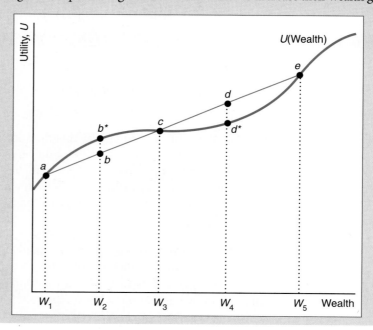

The graph shows Sylvia's utility curve, which has the shape that Friedman and Savage described. Sylvia is risk averse with respect to small gambles but risk preferring with respect to bets that allow for large potential winnings. Sylvia prefers receiving W_2 with certainty to engaging in a bet with an expected value of W_2, where she has an equal probability of receiving wealth W_1 or W_3. Sylvia chooses the certain wealth because her certain utility at b^* is above the expected utility at b. On the other hand, Sylvia prefers a bet with an equal chance of W_3 and W_5 to the certain wealth of W_4, which is the expected value of the bet, because the expected utility at d from the bet is greater than the certain utility at d^*.

The third explanation is that people make mistakes. Either people do not know the true probabilities or they cannot properly calculate expected values, so they do not realize that they are participating in an unfair bet.

These three explanations are not mutually exclusive. A person could get entertainment value from gambling *and* have a Friedman-Savage utility *and* be unable to calculate odds correctly.[9]

Evidence for Why People Gamble. Evidence supports all three explanations to some degree. People definitely like games of chance. One survey found that 65% of Americans say that they engage in games of chance even when the games award no money or only trivial sums (Brunk, 1981). That is, they play because they enjoy the games.[10]

Brunk indirectly examined whether the Friedman-Savage explanation or the love of the game explains bets. He asked people whether they were dissatisfied with their current income. Presumably, their answers would indicate whether they have increasing marginal utilities of wealth, at least over certain ranges of wealth. Brunk argued that, if the Friedman-Savage explanation is correct, people who were dissatisfied with their incomes would be more likely to buy lottery tickets, after controlling for other individual differences such as education. He expected that this factor would not be an important explanation for social gambling activities such as bingo, which people play because they enjoy the

---

[9]Economists, knowing how to calculate expected values and deriving most of their excitement from economic models, apparently are less likely to gamble than are real people. A number of years ago, a meeting of economists was held in Reno, Nevada. Reno hotels charged low room rates on the assumption that they'd make plenty from guests' gambling losses. However, the economists gambled so little that they were asked pointedly not to return.

[10]When I was an undergraduate at the University of Chicago, I lived in a dorm and saw overwhelming evidence that the "love of the game" is a powerful force. Because the neighborhood provided few forms of entertainment, the dorm's denizens regularly watched the man from the vending company refill the candy machine with fresh candy. He took the old, stale, unpopular bars that remained in the machine and placed them in the "mystery candy" bin. Thanks to our careful study of stocking techniques, we all knew that buying the mystery candy was not a fair bet—who would want unpopular, stale candy bars at the same price as a fresh, popular bar? Nonetheless, one of the dorm dwellers always bought the mystery candy. When asked why, he responded, "I love the excitement of not knowing what'll come out." Life was very boring indeed on the South Side of Chicago.

game. He found that people who were dissatisfied with their income were more likely than others to buy lottery tickets but not to engage in social gambling. This evidence is consistent with the Friedman-Savage explanation. Garrett and Sobel (1999) found that the utility functions of people who gamble on the lottery have the shape predicted by Friedman and Savage.

A number of studies show that many people have biased estimates of probabilities and cannot calculate expected values. For example, Golec and Tamarkin (1995) concluded that football bettors tend to make low-probability bets because they are overconfident.

Golec and Tamarkin found that bettors greatly overestimate their probabilities of winning certain types of exotic football bets (an *exotic bet* depends on the outcome of more than one game). In a small survey, gamblers estimated their chance of winning a particular bet at 45% when the objective probability was 20%. Of course, these people may also place exotic bets because they enjoy them more than simple bets.

DEGREE OF RISK AVERSION

Figures 16.2 and 16.3 illustrate that whether Irma is risk averse depends on the shape of her utility function over wealth, $U(W)$. Economists sometimes use quantitative measures of the curvature of the utility function to describe how risk averse an individual is.

Arrow-Pratt Measure of Risk Aversion. One of the most commonly used measures is the Arrow-Pratt measure of risk aversion (Pratt, 1964):

$$\rho(W) = -\frac{d^2U(W)/dW^2}{dU(W)/dW}. \tag{16.4}$$

Because Irma's marginal utility of wealth is positive, $dU(W)/dW > 0$, $\rho(W)$ has the opposite sign of $d^2U(W)/dW^2$. Irma is risk averse if her utility function is concave to the horizontal axis, so she has diminishing marginal utility of wealth, $d^2U(W)/dW^2 < 0$. Thus if she is risk averse, the Arrow-Pratt measure is positive.

If Irma has the concave utility function $U(W) = \ln W$, then $dU(W)/dW = 1/W$ and $d^2U(W)/dW^2 = -1/W^2$, so her Arrow-Pratt measure is $\rho(W) = 1/W > 0$. Her degree of risk aversion falls with wealth. In contrast, if she has an exponential utility function, $U(W) = -e^{-aW}$, where $a > 0$, her Arrow-Pratt measure is $\rho(W) = -(-a^2e^{-aW})/(ae^{-aW}) = a$, so her measure of risk aversion is constant over all possible values of wealth.

The Arrow-Pratt measure is zero if Irma is risk neutral. For example, if her utility function is $U(W) = aW$, then $dU(W)/dW = a$, $d^2U(W)/dW^2 = 0$, and her Arrow-Pratt risk aversion measure is $\rho(W) = -0/a = 0$. The Arrow-Pratt measure is negative if Irma is risk preferring.

Arrow-Pratt Measure and the Willingness to Gamble. We can show that the larger the Arrow-Pratt measure of risk aversion, the more small gambles that an individual will take. Suppose Ryan's house is currently worth W. He considers painting it bright orange, which he believes will lower its value by A with probability θ and raise it by B with probability $1 - \theta$. He will engage in this "gamble" if his expected utility is at least as high as his certain utility when he does not gamble: $\theta U(W - A) + (1 - \theta)U(W + B) \geq U(W)$. Let $B(A)$ show how large B must be for a given value of A such that Ryan's expected utility equals his certain utility:

$$\theta U(W - A) + (1 - \theta)U[W + B(A)] = U(W). \tag{16.5}$$

From Equation 16.5, if $A = 0$, $B(0) = 0$. Given that A is initially 0, how much does B change as we slightly increase A? That is, how much does the house's value have to rise in the good state of nature to offset the drop in value in the bad state such that Ryan is willing to take the gamble on painting his house? To answer these questions, we differentiate Equation 16.5 with respect to A,

$$-\theta\frac{dU(W - A)}{dA} + (1 - \theta)\frac{dU(W + B(A))}{dA}\frac{dB(A)}{dA} = 0, \tag{16.6}$$

and evaluate at $A = 0$:

$$-\theta\frac{dU(W)}{dA} + (1 - \theta)\frac{dU(W)}{dA}\frac{dB(0)}{dA} = 0.$$

Rearranging this last expression, we learn that

$$\frac{dB(0)}{dA} = \frac{\theta}{1 - \theta}. \tag{16.7}$$

That is, Ryan will be willing to engage in this gamble if the increase in B in response to an increase in A equals the odds $\theta/(1 - \theta)$.

For a given θ, A, and B, Ryan is more likely to take this gamble, the less risk averse he is. How risk averse he is depends on the curvature of his utility function, which is reflected by the second derivative of his utility function. Differentiating the identity 16.6 again with respect to A and evaluating at $A = 0$, we discover that

$$\theta\frac{d^2U(W)}{dA^2} + (1 - \theta)\frac{d^2U(W)}{dA^2}\left[\frac{dB(0)}{dA}\right]^2 + (1 - \theta)\frac{dU(W)}{dA}\frac{d^2B(0)}{dA^2} = 0. \tag{16.8}$$

Substituting Equation 16.7 into Equation 16.8, rearranging terms, and finally substituting in the definition 16.4, we obtain

$$\frac{d^2B(0)}{dA^2} = \frac{\theta}{(1 - \theta)^2}\left[-\frac{d^2U(W)/dA^2}{dU(W)/dA}\right] = \frac{\theta}{(1 - \theta)^2}\rho(W).$$

That is, $d^2B(0)/dA^2$ is proportional to the Arrow-Pratt risk-aversion measure. The larger d^2B/dA^2, the greater the rate that B must increase as A increases for Ryan to be willing to gamble. Thus for a given θ, A, and B, he is more likely to take the gamble, the smaller his Arrow-Pratt measure.

SOLVED PROBLEM   16.4

Jen's utility function is $U(W) = W^{0.5}$, while Ryan's is $U(W) = W^{0.25}$. Use the Arrow-Pratt measure to show that Ryan is more risk averse. Next suppose that each owns a home worth 100 and is considering painting it orange. If each does so, each house is worth 81 with probability $\frac{1}{2}$ or 121 with probability $\frac{1}{2}$. Will either take this gamble?

Answer

1. *Calculate their Arrow-Pratt measures using Equation 16.4:* Differentiating Jen's utility function, $U(W) = W^{0.5}$, with respect to W, we find that $dU/dW = 0.5W^{-0.5}$. Differentiating again, we learn that $d^2U/dW^2 = -0.25W^{-1.5}$. Thus her Arrow-Pratt risk measure is $\rho = -(d^2U/dW^2)/(dU/dW) = 0.25W^{-1.5}/0.5W^{-0.5} = 0.5/W$. Ryan's utility function is $U(W) = W^{0.25}$, so $dU/dW = 0.25W^{-0.75}$, $d^2U/dW^2 = -0.1875W^{-1.75}$, and his Arrow-Pratt risk measure is $\rho = 0.1875W^{-1.75}/0.25W^{-0.75} = 0.75/W$. Thus Ryan is more risk averse than Jen.

2. *By comparing their expected utility with the gamble to their utility without the gamble, determine if either is willing to take the gamble:* Without the gamble, Jen's utility is $U(100) = 100^{0.5} = 10$. With the gamble, her expected utility is $0.5U(81) + 0.5U(121) = (0.5 \times 9) + (0.5 \times 11) = 10$. Consequently, she is (barely) willing to take the gamble. Ryan's certain utility is $U(100) = 100^{0.25} \approx 3.1623$. With the gamble, his expected utility is $0.5U(81) + 0.5U(121) \approx (0.5 \times 3) + (0.5 \times 3.3166) = 3.1583$, which is less than 3.1623, so he is unwilling to take the gamble. Thus Jen will take this gamble, unlike Ryan, who is more risk averse.

16.3   Avoiding Risk

> *If 75% of all accidents happen within 5 miles of home, why not move 10 miles away?*
> —Steven Wright

Risk-averse people want to eliminate or reduce risk whether the bet is fair or biased against them. Risk-neutral people avoid unfair bets, and even risk-preferring people avoid very unfair bets.

Individuals can avoid optional risky activities, but they often can't escape risk altogether. Property owners, for instance, always face the possibility that their property will be damaged or stolen or will burn. They may be able to reduce the probability that bad states of nature occur, however.

JUST SAY NO

The simplest way to avoid risk is to abstain from optional risky activities. No one forces you to bet on the lottery, go into a high-risk occupation, or buy stock in a start-up biotech firm. If one brand of a product that you use comes with a warranty and an otherwise comparable brand does not, you lower your risk by buying the guaranteed product.

Even when you can't avoid risk altogether, you can take precautions to reduce the probability of bad states of nature happening or the magnitude of any loss that might occur. For example, by maintaining your car as the manufacturer recommends, you can reduce the probability that it will break down. By locking your apartment door, you lower the chance that your television will be stolen. Getting rid of your four-year-old collection of newspapers lessens the likelihood that your house will burn. Not only do these actions reduce your risk, but they also raise the expected value of your assets.

● APPLICATION

Harry Potter's Magic

Harry Potter protects his young fans from traumatic injuries on weekends. Stephen Gwilym of the John Radcliffe Hospital in Oxford and his colleagues found that only half as many 7- to 15-year-old children came to the emergency department on the weekends immediately after J. K. Rowling's books were released, compared to other summer weekends from 2003 to 2005. (Apparently, your mom was trying to maim you when she said, "Stop reading and go outside and play on this lovely summer day!")

OBTAIN INFORMATION

Collecting accurate information before acting is one of the most important ways in which people can reduce risk and increase expected value and expected utility, as Solved Problem 16.1 illustrates. Armed with information, you may avoid making a risky choice, or you may be able to take actions that reduce the probability of a disaster or the size of the loss.

Before buying a car or refrigerator, many people read *Consumer Reports* to determine how frequently a particular brand is likely to need repairs. By collecting such information before buying, they can reduce the likelihood of making a costly mistake.[11]

DIVERSIFY

Although it may sound paradoxical, individuals and firms often reduce their overall risk by making many risky investments instead of only one. This practice is called *risk pooling* or *diversifying*. As your grandparents may have told you, "Don't put all your eggs in one basket."[12]

Correlation and Diversification. The extent to which diversification reduces risk depends on the degree to which various events are correlated over states of nature. The degree of correlation ranges from negatively correlated to uncorrelated to positively

---

[11]See **www.aw-bc.com/perloff**, Chapter 16, "Bond Ratings," for a discussion of how the riskiness of bonds is expressed.

[12]Unlike the supermarket manager who left all his baskets in one exit, where they were smashed by a car.

correlated.[13] If you know that the first event occurs, you know that the probability that the second event will occur is lower if the events are *negatively correlated* and higher if the events are *positively correlated*. The outcomes are *independent* or *uncorrelated* if knowing whether the first event occurs tells you nothing about the probability that the second event will occur.

Diversification can eliminate risk if two events are perfectly negatively correlated. Suppose that two firms are competing for a government contract and have an equal chance of winning. Because only one firm can win, the other must lose, so the two events are *perfectly negatively correlated*. You can buy a share of stock in either firm for $20. The stock of the firm that wins the contract will be worth $40, whereas the stock of the loser will be worth $10. If you buy two shares of stock from the same company, your shares are going to be worth either $80 or $20 after the contract is awarded. Thus their expected value is

$$\$50 = \left(\frac{1}{2} \times \$80\right) + \left(\frac{1}{2} \times \$20\right)$$

with a variance of

$$\$900 = \left[\frac{1}{2} \times (\$80 - \$50)^2\right] + \left[\frac{1}{2} \times (\$20 - \$50)^2\right].$$

However, if you buy one share of each firm, your two shares will be worth $50 no matter which firm wins, and the variance is zero.

Diversification reduces risk even if the two events are imperfectly negatively correlated, uncorrelated, or imperfectly positively correlated. *The more negatively correlated two events are, the more diversification reduces risk.*

Now suppose that the values of the two stocks are uncorrelated. Each of the two firms has a 50% chance of getting a government contract, and whether one firm gets a contract does *not* affect whether the other firm wins one. Because of this independence, the chance that each firm's share is worth $40 is $\frac{1}{4}$, the chance that one is worth $40 and the other is worth $10 is $\frac{1}{2}$, and the chance that each is worth $10 is $\frac{1}{4}$. If you buy one share of each firm, the expected value of these two shares is

$$\$50 = \left(\frac{1}{4} \times \$80\right) + \left(\frac{1}{2} \times \$50\right) + \left(\frac{1}{2} \times \$20\right),$$

and the variance is

$$\$450 = \left[\frac{1}{4} \times (\$80 - \$50)^2\right] + \left[\frac{1}{2} \times (\$50 - \$50)^2\right] + \left[\frac{1}{2} \times (\$20 - \$50)^2\right].$$

The expected value is the same as when buying two shares in one firm, but the variance is only half as large. Thus diversification lowers risk when the values are uncorrelated.

In contrast, *diversification does not reduce risk if two events are perfectly positively correlated*. If the government will award contracts either to both firms or to neither firm, the risks are perfectly positively correlated. The expected value of the stocks and the variance are the same whether you buy two shares of one firm or one share of each firm.

---

[13]A measure of the *correlation* between two random variables x and y is

$$\rho = E\left(\frac{x - \bar{x}}{\sigma_x} \frac{y - \bar{y}}{\sigma_y}\right)$$

where the $E(\cdot)$ means "take the expectation" of the term in parentheses, $\bar{x}$ and $\bar{y}$ are the means, and σ_x and σ_y are the standard deviations of x and y. The two events are said to be uncorrelated if $\rho = 0$.

Mutual Funds Individual investors usually do not have the benefit of such detailed information about correlations. They know, however, that the value of the stock of most firms is not perfectly positively correlated with the value of other stocks, so buying stock in several companies tends to reduce risk. Many of these people effectively own shares in a number of companies at once by buying shares in a *mutual fund* of stocks. A mutual fund share is issued by a company that buys stocks in many other companies.

The *Standard & Poor's Composite Index of 500 Stocks* (S&P 500) is a value-weighted average of 500 large firms' stocks, most of which are listed on the New York Stock Exchange (NYSE), though some are on the American Stock Exchange or are traded over the counter. The S&P 500 companies constitute only about 7% of all publicly traded firms in the United States, but they represent approximately 80% of the total value of the U.S. stock market. The *New York Stock Exchange Composite Index* includes more than 1,500 common stocks traded on the NYSE. A number of "total market" funds have been introduced, such as the *Wilshire 5000 Index Portfolio,* which initially covered 5,000 stocks but now includes more than 7,200—virtually all of the U.S. stock market in terms of value. The retail assets in total market funds are relatively small: $11.1 billion versus $116.3 billion in S&P 500 index funds. Some other mutual funds are based on bonds or on a mixture of stocks, bonds, and other types of investments.[14]

Mutual funds allow you to reduce the risk associated with uncorrelated price movements across stocks. Suppose that two companies look very similar on the basis of everything you know about them. You have no reason to think that the stock of one firm will increase more in value or be riskier than the stock of the other firm. However, luck may cause one stock to do better than the other. You can reduce this type of random, unsystematic risk by diversifying and buying stock in both firms.

A stock mutual fund does have a systematic risk, however. The prices of all stocks tend to rise when the economy is expanding and to fall when the economy is contracting. Buying a diversified mutual stock fund does not eliminate the systematic risks associated with shifts in the economy that affect all stocks at once.

INSURE

> *I detest life-insurance agents; they always argue that I shall some day die, which is not so.*
> —Stephen Leacock

As we've already seen, a risk-averse person is willing to pay money—a risk premium— to avoid risk. The demand for risk reduction is met by insurance companies, which

---

[14]Norway refuses to invest its $300 billion from oil exports in Wal-Mart, Boeing, and other firms that it believes have ethical failings (Mark Landler, "Norway Keeps Nest Egg From Some U.S. Companies," *New York Times,* May 4, 2007). The Calvert, Domini Social Investments, Pax World Funds, and at least 200 other funds have portfolios consisting of only socially responsible firms (by the funds' own criteria). However, their investors must be willing to accept a lower return. Over the five years ending February 2007, the total return of the Domini 400 index averaged 4.8% a year compared to Standard & Poor's 500-stock index average of 6.81% (Alina Tugend, "Picking Stocks that Don't Sin," *New York Times,* March 17, 2007). If instead you want to invest in vice, go to **www.vicefund.com**.

bear the risk for anyone who buys an insurance policy. Many risk-averse individuals and firms buy insurance; global insurance premiums were $3.4 trillion in 2005.

How Much Insurance Individuals Want. The way insurance works is that a risk-averse person or firm gives money to an insurance company in the good state of nature, and the insurance company transfers money to the policyholder in the bad state of nature. This transaction allows the risk-averse person or firm to shift some or all of the risk to the insurance company.

Because Scott is risk averse, he wants to insure his house, which is worth $80 (thousand). There is a 25% probability that his house will burn down next year. If a fire occurs, the house will be worth only $40 (thousand).

With no insurance, the expected value of his house is

$$\left(\frac{1}{4} \times \$40\right) + \left(\frac{3}{4} \times \$80\right) = \$70.$$

Scott faces substantial risk: The variance of the value of his house is

$$\left[\frac{1}{4} \times (\$40 - \$70)^2\right] + \left[\frac{3}{4} \times (\$80 - \$70)^2\right] = \$300.$$

Now suppose that an insurance company offers him a *fair bet*, or **fair insurance:** a bet between an insurer and a policyholder in which the value of the bet to the policyholder is zero. The insurance company offers to let Scott trade $1 in the good state of nature (no fire) for $3 in the bad state of nature (fire).[15] This insurance is fair because the expected value of this insurance to Scott is zero:

$$\left(\frac{1}{4} \times \$3\right) + \left[\frac{3}{4} \times (-\$1)\right] = \$0.$$

Because Scott is risk averse, he *fully insures* by buying enough insurance to eliminate his risk altogether. With this amount of insurance, he has the same amount of wealth in either state of nature.

Scott pays the insurance company $10 in the good state of nature and receives $30 in the bad state. In the good state, he has a house worth $80 minus the $10 he pays the insurance company, for a net wealth of $70. If the fire occurs, he has a house worth $40 plus a $30 payment from the insurance company, for a net wealth, again, of $70.

Scott's expected value with fair insurance, $70, is the same as his expected value without insurance. However, the variance he faces drops from $300 without insurance to $0 with insurance. Scott is better off with insurance because he has the same expected value and faces no risk.

---

[15]As a practical matter, the insurance company collects money up front. If the fire doesn't occur, the company keeps the money. If the fire occurs, it gives back the amount paid originally plus additional funds. Scott's insurance company charges him $1 up front for every $4 it will pay him in the bad state. Thus Scott effectively pays $1 in the good state of nature and receives a net payment of $3 in the bad state.

SOLVED PROBLEM 16.5

The local government assesses a property tax of $4 (thousand) on Scott's house. If the tax is collected whether or not Scott's house burns down, how much fair insurance does Scott buy? If the tax is collected only if the house does not burn, how much fair insurance does Scott buy?

Answer

1. *Determine the after-tax expected value of the house without insurance:* The expected value of the house is

$$\$66 = \left(\frac{1}{4} \times \$36\right) + \left(\frac{3}{4} \times \$76\right)$$

if the tax is always collected and

$$\$67 = \left(\frac{1}{4} \times \$40\right) + \left(\frac{3}{4} \times \$76\right)$$

if the tax is collected only in the good state of nature.

2. *Calculate the amount of fair insurance Scott buys if the tax is always collected:* Because Scott is risk averse, he wants to be fully insured so that the after-tax value of his house is the same in both states of nature. If the tax is always collected, Scott pays the insurance company $10 in the good state of nature, so he has $76 − $10 = $66, and receives $30 in the bad state, so he has $36 + $30 = $66. That is, he buys the same amount of insurance as he would without any taxes. The tax has no effect on his insurance decision because he owes that amount regardless of the state of nature.

3. *Calculate the amount of fair insurance Scott buys if the tax is collected only if there is no fire:* If the tax is collected only in the good state of nature, Scott pays the insurance company $9 in the good state ($76 − $9 = $67) and receives $27 in the bad state ($40 + $27 = $67). Thus he has the same after-tax income in both states of nature. Effectively, Scott is partially insured by the tax system, so he purchases less insurance than he otherwise would.

Fairness and Insurance. When fair insurance is offered, risk-averse people fully insure. If insurance companies charge more than the fair-insurance price, individuals buy less insurance.[16]

Because insurance companies never offer fair insurance, most people do not fully insure. An insurance company could not stay in business if it offered fair insurance. With fair insurance, the insurance company's expected payments would equal the amount the insurance company collects. Because the insurance company has operating expenses—costs of maintaining offices, printing forms, hiring sales agents, and so forth—an insurance firm providing fair insurance would lose money. Insurance companies' rates must be high enough to cover their operating expenses, so the insurance is less than fair to policyholders.

How much can insurance companies charge for insurance? A monopoly insurance company could charge an amount up to the risk premium that a person is willing to

---

[16]As Solved Problem 16.3 shows, tax laws may act to offset this problem, so some insurance may be fair or more than fair after tax.

pay to avoid risk. For example, in Figure 16.2, Irma would be willing to pay up to $14 for an insurance policy that would compensate her if her vase were not a Ming. The more risk averse an individual is, the more a monopoly insurance company can charge. In a market with many insurance companies, the price of an insurance policy is less than the maximum that risk-averse individuals are willing to pay, but still high enough that the firms cover their operating expenses.

● APPLICATION

Air Insurance

If flying is so safe, why do they call the airport the terminal?

Insure America (IA) has brochures at many airports offering flight insurance. If I pay them $12 and die on a scheduled commercial flight, IA will pay my family $200,000. (IA also offers much larger amounts of insurance, but I figure there's no point in making myself worth more to my family dead than alive.)

If θ is my probability of dying on a flight, my family's expected value from this bet with IA is

$$(\theta \times \$200{,}000) + [(1 - \theta) \times (-\$12)].$$

For this insurance to be fair, the expected value must be zero, which it is if $\theta \approx$ 0.00006, or one out of every 16,668 passengers dies. I'm not tempted by IA's offer because its insurance is not at all close to being fair. The chance that I'll die on a flight is much, much less than 0.00006.

How great *is* my danger of being in a fatal commercial airline crash? According to the National Transportation Safety Board, there were no fatalities on scheduled U.S. commercial airline flights in 1993, 1998, and 2002. In 2005, when 20 passengers died, the probability that a passenger had a fatal accident was 0.00000027, or about one in 3.7 million. In 2004, the probability that a passenger died was 0.00000018, or 1 in 5.6 million. In 2001, the probability was much higher than average for the decade because of the deaths from the terrorist hijackings on September 11 and the subsequent sharp reduction in the number of flights. However, even in 2001, the probability was 0.00000086, or 1 in 1.1 million—still much lower than the probability that makes IA's insurance a fair bet.

Given the average rate for the last 10 years, 0.00000017, if I randomly choose a seat on a flight each day for 10 years, the probability of my *not* being in a fatal accident is 99.7%. If I fly each day for 100 years, the probability of my not being in a fatal accident is 99.4%. Indeed, only by flying every day for over 10,000 years would the probability of my being in a fatal crash rise as high as 50%. (The greatest risk of an airplane trip for many people is the drive to and from the airport. Indeed, twice as many people are killed in vehicle-deer collisions than in plane crashes.)

Given that the chance of being in a fatal crash is 0.00000017, the fair rate to pay for $200,000 of flight insurance is about 3.4¢. IA is offering to charge me 353 times more than the fair rate for this insurance.

I'd have to be incredibly risk averse to be tempted by this offer. Indeed, I would not buy this insurance even if I were that risk averse. Instead, I'd buy general life insurance, which is much less expensive than flight insurance and covers me for death from all types of accidents and diseases.

Insurance Only for Diversifiable Risks. Why is an insurance company willing to sell policies and take on risk? By pooling the risks of many people, the insurance company can lower its risk much below that of any individual. If the probability that one car is stolen is independent of whether other cars are stolen, the risk to an insurance company of insuring one person against car theft is much greater than the average risk of insuring many people.

An insurance company sells policies only for risks that it can diversify. If the risks from disasters to its policyholders are highly positively correlated, an insurance company is not well diversified by insuring many policyholders. A war affects all policyholders, so the outcomes that they face are perfectly correlated. Because wars are *nondiversifiable risks*, insurance companies do not offer policies insuring against wars.

● APPLICATION

No Insurance for Natural Disasters

In recent years, many insurance companies have started viewing some major natural disasters as nondiversifiable risks because such catastrophic events cause many insured people to suffer losses at the same time. As more homes have been built in parts of the country where damage from storms or earthquakes is likely, the size of the potential losses to insurers from nondiversifiable risks has grown.

According to some estimates, Hurricane Katrina in 2005 caused $100 to $200 billion worth of damage (not to mention the loss of life). Hurricane Andrew in 1992 inflicted $43.67 billion (in 2004 dollars) worth of damage. In 2004, Hurricanes Charley and Ivan caused $15 billion and $14.2 billion worth of harm, respectively.

Insurers paid out $12.5 billion in claims to residential homeowners after the 1994 Los Angeles earthquake. Farmers Insurance Group reported that it paid out three times as much for the Los Angeles earthquake as it collected in earthquake premiums over 30 years.

Insurance companies now refuse to offer hurricane or earthquake insurance in many parts of the country for these relatively nondiversifiable risks. When Nationwide Insurance Company announced in 1996 that it was sharply curtailing sales of new policies along the Gulf of Mexico and the eastern seaboard from Texas to Maine, a company official explained, "Prudence requires us to diligently manage our exposure to catastrophic losses."

In some of these areas, state-run insurance pools—such as the Florida Joint Underwriting Association and the California Earthquake Authority—provide households with insurance. However, not only do these policies provide less protection, but their rates are often three times more expensive than the previously available commercial rates, and they require large deductibles.

16.4 Investing Under Uncertainty

> *Don't invest money with any brokerage firm in which one of the partners is named Frenchy.*
> —Woody Allen

In Chapter 15, we ignored uncertainty when we analyzed how firms take account of discounting when making investment decisions. We now investigate how uncertainty affects the investment decision. In particular, we examine how attitudes toward risk affect individuals' willingness to invest, how people evaluate risky investments that last for many periods, and how investors pay to alter their probabilities of success.

In the following examples, the owner of a monopoly decides whether to open a new retail outlet. Because the firm is a monopoly, the owner's return from the investment does not depend on the actions of other firms. As a result, the owner faces no strategic considerations. The owner knows the cost of the investment but is unsure about how many people will patronize the new store; hence the profits are uncertain.

HOW INVESTING DEPENDS ON ATTITUDES TOWARD RISK

We start by considering a potential investment by the monopoly's owner that has an uncertain payoff this year. The owner must take risk into account but can ignore discounting. Whether the owner invests depends on how risk averse he or she is and on the risks involved.

Risk-Neutral Investing. Chris, the owner of a monopoly, is risk neutral. She maximizes her expected utility by making the investment only if the expected value of the return from the investment is positive.

To determine whether to invest, Chris uses the *decision tree* in panel a of Figure 16.4. The rectangle, called a *decision node,* indicates that she must make a decision about whether to invest or not. The circle, a *chance node,* denotes that a random process

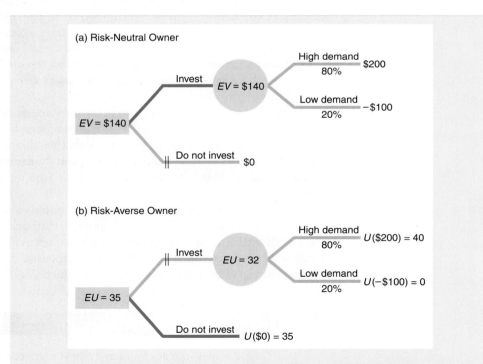

Figure 16.4 Investment Decision Tree with Risk Aversion. The owner of a monopoly must decide whether to invest in a new store. (a) The expected value is $140, so it pays for a risk-neutral owner to invest. (b) The utility from not investing for this risk-averse owner is greater than the expected utility from investing, so the owner does not invest.

determines the outcome (consistent with the given probabilities). If Chris does not open the new store, she makes $0. If she does open the new store, she expects to make $200 with 80% probability and to lose $100 with 20% probability. The expected value from a new store (see the circle in panel a) is

$$EV = (0.8 \times \$200) + [0.2 \times (-\$100)] = \$140.$$

Because she is risk neutral, she prefers an expected value of $140 to a certain one of $0, so she invests. Thus her expected value in the rectangle is $140.

Risk-Averse Investing. Ken, who is risk averse, faces the same decision as Chris. Ken invests in the new store if his expected utility from investing is greater than his certain utility from not investing. Panel b of Figure 16.4 shows the decision tree for a particular risk-averse utility function. The circle shows that Ken's expected utility from the investment is

$$EU = [0.2 \times U(-\$100)] + [0.8 \times U(\$200)]$$
$$= (0.2 \times 0) + (0.8 \times 40) = 32.$$

The certain utility from not investing is $U(\$0) = 35$. Thus Ken does not invest. As a result, his expected utility (here, certain utility) in the rectangle is 35.

● **APPLICATION**

Risk Premium

Risk-averse people will make risky investments only if these investments have an expected return that is sufficiently higher than that of a nonrisky investment such as a U.S. government bond, as Figure 16.2 illustrates.[17] Because most people are risk averse, they will make risky investments only if *the expected rate of return on a risky investment exceeds the rate of return on a nonrisky investment by a risk premium.*

Most stock funds have more nondiversifiable risks—as reflected by a higher standard deviation in returns—than bond funds, even junk bond funds. The historical standard deviation varies substantially across a number of diversified stock and bond funds.

Because stocks are riskier than bonds, the rates of return on stocks exceed those on bonds over long periods of time. Of course, given the greater risk associated with equities, they may perform worse than bonds in any given period. For example, the S&P 500 had negative returns of −12% in 2001 and −22% in 2002, unlike bonds. Nonetheless, we expect equities to have a higher rate of return over a longer period. For the 20 years from March 1987 to March 2007, the average annual real rates of return (after adjusting for inflation, taxes, and expenses) were 9.92% on the S&P 500, 10.44% on the Dow Jones Industrial Average, 4.48% on U.S. Treasury bills, 4.06% on municipal bonds, and 1.15% on single-family homes.

---

[17]The Tappet brothers (the hosts of National Public Radio's *Car Talk*) offer a risk-free investment. Their Capital Depreciation Fund guarantees a 50% return. You send them $100 and they send you back $50.

INVESTING WITH UNCERTAINTY AND DISCOUNTING

Now suppose that the uncertain returns or costs from an investment are spread out over time. In Chapter 15, we derived an investment rule by which we know future costs and returns with certainty. We concluded that an investment pays if its *net present value* (calculated by discounting the difference between the return and the cost in each future period) is positive.

How does this rule change if the returns are uncertain? A risk-neutral person chooses to invest if the *expected net present value* is positive. We calculate the expected net present value by discounting the difference between expected return and expected cost in each future period.

Sam is risk neutral. His decision tree, Figure 16.5, shows that his cost of investing is $C = \$25$ this year. Next year, he receives uncertain revenues from the investment of $125 with 80% probability or $50 with 20% probability. Thus the expected value of the revenues next year is

$$EV = (0.8 \times \$125) + (0.2 \times \$50) = \$110.$$

With a real interest rate of 10%, the expected present value of the revenues is

$$EPV = \$110/1.1 = \$100.$$

Subtracting the $25 cost incurred this year, Sam determines that his expected net present value is $ENPV = \$75$. As a result, he invests.

INVESTING WITH ALTERED PROBABILITIES

We have been assuming that nature dictates the probabilities of various states of nature. Sometimes, however, we can alter the probabilities, though usually at some expense.

Gautam, who is risk neutral, is considering whether to invest in a new store, as Figure 16.6 shows. After investing, he can increase the probability that demand will be high at the new store by advertising at a cost of $50.

If he makes the investment but does not advertise, he has a 40% probability of making $100 and a 60% probability of losing $100. His expected value without advertising is

$$(0.4 \times \$100) + [0.6 \times (-\$100)] = -\$20.$$

Thus if he could not advertise, he would not make this investment.

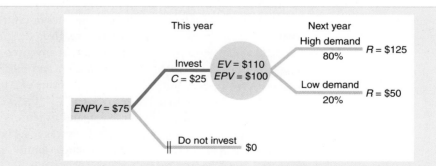

Figure 16.5 Investment Decision Tree with Uncertainty and Discounting. The risk-neutral owner invests if the expected net present value is positive. The expected value, *EV*, of the revenue from the investment next year is $110. With an interest rate of 10%, the expected present value, *EPV*, of the revenue is $100. The expected net present value, *ENPV*, is $EPV = \$100$ minus the $25 cost of the investment this year, which is $75. The owner therefore invests.

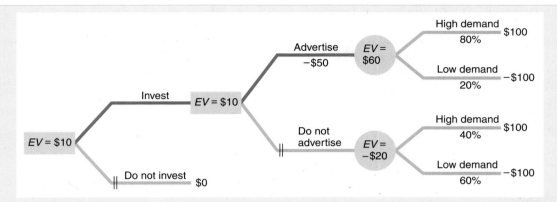

Figure 16.6 Investment Decision Tree with Advertising. By advertising, Gautam, a risk-neutral owner, can alter the probability of high demand. The expected value of the investment is −$20 without advertising and $60 with advertising. Because the cost of advertising is $50, the expected value of investing and advertising is $10 (= $60 − $50). Gautam therefore invests and advertises.

With advertising, the probability of his making $100 rises to 80%, so his expected value is

$$(0.8 \times \$100) + [0.2 \times (-\$100)] = \$60.$$

His expected value net of the cost of advertising is $10 (= $60 − $50). Thus he is better off investing and advertising than not investing at all or investing without advertising.

Summary

1. **Degree of Risk:** A probability measures the likelihood that a particular state of nature will occur. People may use historical frequencies, if available, to calculate a probability. Lacking detailed information, people form subjective estimates of the probability on the basis of available information. The expected value is the probability-weighted average of the values in each state of nature. One widely used measure of risk is the variance (or the standard deviation, which is the square root of the variance). The variance is the probability-weighted average of the squared difference of the value in each state of nature and the expected value.

2. **Decision Making Under Uncertainty:** Whether people choose a risky option over a nonrisky one depends on their attitudes toward risk and the expected payoffs of the various options. Most people are *risk averse* and will choose a riskier option only if its expected value is substantially higher than that of a less-risky option. *Risk-neutral* people choose whichever option has the higher rate of return because they do not care about risk. *Risk-preferring* people may choose the riskier option even if it has a lower rate of return. An individual's utility function reflects that person's attitude toward risk. People choose the option that provides the highest expected utility. Expected utility is the probability-weighted average of the utilities from the outcomes in the various states of nature. The larger someone's Arrow-Pratt measure of risk aversion, the less likely it is that the person is willing to make a small gamble.

3. **Avoiding Risk:** People try in several ways to reduce the risks they face. They avoid some optional risks and take actions that lower the probabilities of bad events or reduce the harm from those events. By collecting information before acting, investors can make better choices. People can further reduce risk by pooling their risky investments, a strategy called diversification. Unless returns are perfectly positively correlated, diversification reduces risk. Insurance companies offer policies for risks that they can diversify by pooling risks across many individuals. Risk-averse people fully insure if they are offered fair insurance, from which the expected return to the policyholder is zero. They may buy some insurance even if the insurance is not fair. When buying unfair insurance,

they exchange the risk of a large loss with the certainty of a smaller loss.

4. **Investing Under Uncertainty:** Whether a person makes an investment depends on the uncertainty of the payoff, the expected return, the individual's attitudes toward risk, the interest rate, and the cost of altering the likelihood of a good outcome. For a risk-neutral person, an investment pays if the expected net present value is positive. A risk-averse person invests only if that person's expected utility is higher after investing. Thus risk-averse people make risky investments if those investments pay higher rates of return than safer investments pay. If an investment takes place over time, a risk-neutral investor uses a real interest rate to discount expected future values and invests if the expected net present value is positive. People pay to alter the probabilities of various outcomes from an investment if doing so raises their expected utility.

Questions

*= answer at the back of this book; **W** = audio-slide show answers by James Dearden at **www.aw-bc.com/perloff**

1. Jen's utility function with respect to wealth is $U(W) = \sqrt{W}$. Plot this utility function and illustrate in your figure why Jen is risk averse.

2. Suppose that Irma's utility function with respect to wealth is $U(W) = \ln W$. Plot this utility function and illustrate in your figure why Irma is risk averse.

*3. Given the information in Solved Problem 16.2, Irma prefers to buy the vase. Show graphically how high her certain income would have to be for her to choose not to buy the vase.

4. A risk-averse individual has to choose between $100 with certainty and a risky option with two equally likely outcomes, $100 − x$ and $100 + x$. Use a graph (or math) to show that this person's risk premium is smaller, the smaller x is (the less variable the gamble is).

*5. To discourage people from breaking traffic laws, society can increase the probability that someone exceeding the speed limit will be caught and punished, or it can increase the size of the fine for speeding. Explain why either method can be used to discourage speeding. Which approach is a government likely to prefer, and why?

6. If criminals are rational, crime is deterred by large expected punishments, which are the product of the fine or the sentence given that the criminal is convicted and the probability of being caught and convicted. Thus one can raise the expected value of the punishment by raising either the penalty or the odds of capture and conviction. Is the following argument logical? "I propose executing one or two spammers. That way, even if we don't catch and convict many, the penalty will have a substantial deterrent effect. Because the cost of executing them is much less than the cost of catching them, it is cost effective to increase the punishment rather than the odds of capture and conviction." Explain your answer.

7. Use a decision tree to illustrate how a kidney patient would decide whether to have a transplant operation. The patient currently uses a dialysis machine, which lowers her utility. If the operation is successful, her utility will return to its level before the onset of her kidney problems. However, there is a 5% probability that she will die if she has the operation. (If it will help, make up utility numbers to illustrate your answer.)

8. Use a decision tree to illustrate how a risk-neutral plaintiff in a lawsuit decides whether to settle a claim or go to trial. The defendants offer $50,000 to settle now. If the plaintiff does not settle, the plaintiff believes that the probability of winning at trial is 60%. If the plaintiff wins, the amount awarded will be X. How large can X be before the plaintiff refuses to settle? How does the plaintiff's attitude toward risk affect this decision?

9. Would risk-neutral people ever buy insurance that was not fair (that was biased against them)? Explain.

10. After Hurricane Katrina in 2005, the government offered subsidies to people whose houses were destroyed. How would such subsidies affect the probability that, in the future, people who live in these areas will buy insurance and how much insurance they will buy? Use a utility curve for a risk-averse person to illustrate your answer.

11. Use a supply-and-demand analysis to show the effects on consumer loans of usury laws, which set a price ceiling on the interest rate that lenders can charge. (*Hint:* Draw supply curves and demand curves for a group of individuals who have a high probability of defaulting on their loans.)

12. Draw an individual's utility curve to illustrate that the person is risk averse with respect to a loss but is risk preferring with respect to a gain.

13. What is the difference—if any—between an individual's gambling at a casino and an individual's buying a stock? What is the difference for society?

Problems

14. What is the risk premium if, in Solved Problem 16.3, Jen's utility function were $\ln(W)$?

15 Suppose that Irma's utility function with respect to wealth is $U(W) = 100 + 100W - W^2$. Show that for $W < 10$, Irma's Arrow-Pratt risk-aversion measure increases with her wealth.

*16. Andy and Kim live together. Andy might invest $10,000 (possibly by taking on an extra job to earn the additional money) in Kim's education this year. This investment will raise the present value (see Chapter 15) of Kim's future earnings by $24,000. If they stay together, they will share the benefit from the additional earnings. However, the probability is 1/2 that they will split up in the future. If they were married (or in a civil union) and then split, Andy would get half of Kim's additional earnings. If they were living together without any legal ties and they split, Andy would get nothing. Suppose that Andy is risk neutral. Will Andy invest in Kim's education? Does your answer depend on the couple's legal status?

17. After her final exam this semester, Sylvia must drive from her school in Philadelphia to her home in upstate New York, and she has two possible routes for her trip: through Pennsylvania or through New Jersey. Sylvia drives over the speed limit. In choosing her route, Sylvia's only concern is the probability that she will receive a speeding ticket and the amount of the fine on a given route. Prior to the trip, Sylvia's wealth is $Y = \$300$. Sylvia's utility of wealth function is $U(Y) = Y^{1/2}$. Sylvia has a probability of 1/2 of receiving a $200 speeding ticket on the Pennsylvania route and a probability of 1/4 of receiving a $300 fine on the New Jersey route.

   a. What are Sylvia's expected fine, expected wealth, and expected utility if she travels through New Jersey?
   b. What are Sylvia's expected fine, expected wealth, and expected utility if she travels through Pennsylvania?
   c. Compare Sylvia's expected wealth and compare her expected utilities on the two routes. Comment on the comparison. **W**

18. An insurance agent (interviewed in Jonathan Clements, "Dare to Live Dangerously: Passing on Some Insurance Can Pay Off," *Wall Street Journal*, July 23, 2005, D1) states, "On paper, it never makes sense to have a policy with low deductibles or carry collision on an old car." But the agent notes that raising deductibles and dropping collision coverage can be a tough decision for people with a low income or little savings. Collision insurance is the coverage on a policyholder's own car for accidents in which another driver is not at fault.

   a. Suppose that the loss is $4,000 if an old car is in an accident. During the six-month coverage period, the probability that the insured person is found at fault in an accident is 1/36. Suppose that the price of the coverage is $150. Should a wealthy person purchase the coverage? Should a poor person purchase the coverage? Do your answers depend on the policyholder's degree of risk aversion? Does the policyholder's degree of risk aversion depend on his or her wealth?
   b. The agent advises wealthy people not to purchase insurance to protect against possible small losses. Why? **W**

19. DVD retailers choose how many copies of a movie to purchase from a studio and to stock. The retailers have the right to return all unsold copies to the studio for a full refund, but the retailer pays the shipping costs for returned copies. A small mom-and-pop retailer will sell 1, 2, 3, or 4 copies of a DVD with probabilities 0.2, 0.3, 0.3, and 0.2, respectively. Suppose that the retail market price of the DVD is $15 and that the retailer must pay the studio $8 for each copy. The studio's marginal cost is $1. The retailer's marginal profit is $7 for selling each copy, and the studio's marginal profit is $7 for each unreturned copy sold to the retailer. The cost of shipping each DVD back to the studio is $2. The studio and retailer are risk neutral.

   a. How many copies of the DVD will the retailer order from the studio? What is the studio's expected profit-maximizing number of copies for the retailer to order?
   b. Alternatively, suppose that the studio pays the shipping costs to return an unsold DVD. How many copies would the retailer order?
   c. Does the number of copies that the retailer orders depend on which party pays the shipping costs? Why? **W**

20. Hal is considering applying to Duke's law school. In light of Duke's reported information about acceptances and rejections based on GPAs (G) and LSAT scores (L), Hal estimates that his probability of being accepted, which is his utility, is a function:

$$U = \frac{1}{400}G^{0.36}L^{0.64}.$$

In this function, for example, a GPA of 4.00 is written as 400 and a GPA of 3.25 is written as 325. Hal calculates that for each one-point increase in his GPA (for example, from 350 to 351), he must study an additional eight minutes per week. So the opportunity cost or price (in minutes studied per week) of a unit increase in his GPA is $p_G = 8$. Similarly, the price of a unit increase in his LSAT score is $p_L = 32$. Hal has 8,650 minutes per week to study for either his classes or the LSATs.

   a. Graph Hal's budget constraint.
   b. Graph Hal's indifference curve for $U = 0.9$.
   c. What is Hal's optimal ratio, G/L?
   d. What is Hal's optimal choice, (G^*, L^*)?

e. What is Hal's equilibrium probability of being accepted by Duke?

f. If Hal has fewer than 8,650 minutes per week to study, will his probability of being accepted by Duke decrease? **W**

21. Farrel et al. (2000) estimate that the elasticity of demand for lottery tickets is about −1. If the U.K. National Lottery, which gets a percentage of the total revenues, is running its game to maximize how much it earns, is it running the lottery optimally? Explain your answer.

*22. Asa buys a painting. There is a 20% probability that the artist will become famous and the painting will be worth $1,000. There is a 10% probability that the painting will be destroyed by fire or some other disaster. If the painting is not destroyed and the artist does not become famous, it will be worth $500. What is the expected value of the painting?

23. Suppose that most people will not speed if the expected fine is at least $500. The actual fine for speeding is $800. How high must the probability of being caught and convicted be to discourage speeding?

24. Lori, who is risk averse, has two pieces of jewelry, each worth $1,000. She wants to send them to her sister in Thailand. She is concerned about the safety of shipping them. She believes that the probability that the jewelry won't arrive is θ. Is her expected utility higher if she sends the articles together or in two separate shipments? Explain.

25. Suppose that Mary's utility function is $U(W) = W^{1/3}$, where W is wealth. Is she risk averse? Why or why not?

26. Suppose that Mary (from Problem 25) has an initial wealth of $27,000. How much of a risk premium would she require to participate in a gamble that has a 50% probability of raising her wealth to $29,791 and a 50% probability of lowering her wealth to $24,389?

27. First answer the following two questions about your preferences:

a. You are given $5,000 and offered a choice between receiving an extra $2,500 with certainty or flipping a coin and getting $5,000 if it lands heads or $0 if it lands tails. Which option do you prefer?

b. You are given $10,000 if you make the following choice: return $2,500 or flip a coin and return $5,000 if it lands heads and $0 if it lands tails. Which option do you prefer?

Most people choose the sure $2,500 in the first case but flip the coin in the second. Explain why this behavior is not consistent. What do you conclude about how people make decisions concerning uncertain events?

28. Lisa just inherited a vineyard from a distant relative. In good years (when there is no rain or frost during harvest season), she earns $100,000 from the sale of grapes from the vineyard. If the weather is poor, she loses $20,000. Lisa's estimate of the probability of good weather is 60%.

a. Calculate the expected value and the variance of Lisa's income from the vineyard.

b. Lisa is risk averse. Ethan, a grape buyer, offers Lisa a guaranteed payment of $70,000 each year in exchange for her entire harvest. Will Lisa accept this offer? Explain.

c. Why might Ethan make such an offer? Give three reasons, and explain each. One of these reasons should refer to his attitude toward risk. Illustrate this reason using a diagram that shows the general shape of Ethan's utility function over income.

29. Carolyn and Sanjay are neighbors. Each owns a car valued at $10,000. Neither has comprehensive insurance (which covers losses due to theft). Carolyn's wealth, including the value of her car is $80,000. Sanjay's wealth, including the value of his car is $20,000. Carolyn and Sanjay have identical utility of wealth functions, $U(W) = W^{0.4}$. Carolyn and Sanjay can park their cars on the street or in a rented garage. In their neighborhood, the probability that a street-parked car is stolen is $\frac{1}{2}$ over a one-year period. A garage-parked car will not be stolen.

a. What is the largest amount that Carolyn is willing to pay for a garage? What is the maximum amount that Sanjay is willing to pay?

b. Compare Carolyn's willingness-to-pay to Sanjay's. Why do they differ? Include a comparison of their Arrow-Pratt measures of risk aversion. **W**

30. DVD retailers choose how many copies of a movie to purchase from a studio for potential resale. The retailers have the right to return all unsold copies to the studio for a full refund, but the retailer pays the costs of shipping when copies are returned. A small retailer is considering purchasing copies of the action film *Die Hard* and the film noir *Sunset Boulevard*. To simplify the problem, suppose the retailer has one client. While the retailer does not know the preferences of his client, he calculates correctly that his client is either an action film fan or a film noir fan, and not a fan of both. With probability 0.5, his client is an action movie fan; and with probability 0.5, she is a film noir fan. Suppose that the retail market price of the DVD is $15 and that the retailer must pay the studio $*p* for each copy. The cost of shipping each DVD back to the studio is $2 per disk. The retailer's utility function is $U(W) = W^{0.5}$ and his initial wealth is $10.

a. If the retailer's option is to purchase one copy of *Die Hard* from the studio or purchase no DVDs, what is the greatest amount the retailer is willing to pay to stock a copy of *Die Hard*?

b. Suppose the retailer's option is to purchase one copy of each movie or purchase no DVDs, what is the greatest amount the retailer is willing to pay per film to purchase the two copies? Discuss how the retailer's ability to diversify when purchasing two copies affects his willingness-to-pay. **W**

Chapter 17

Externalities, Open Access, and Public Goods

There's so much pollution in the air now that if it weren't for our lungs there'd be no place to put it all.
—Robert Orben

In 2007, former U.S. Vice President Al Gore won an Academy Award for his documentary movie, *An Inconvenient Truth,* which discusses the dangers of global warming from greenhouse gas emissions. A report at the UN-sponsored Intergovernmental Panel on Climate Change predicted catastrophic consequences—droughts, rising sea levels, heat waves, and disease—from pollution-created global warming. California's Republican Governor Arnold Schwarzenegger backed legislation to combat global warming by regulating emissions into the atmosphere. A hundred physicians and public health scientists wrote a letter urging the U.S. Environmental Protection Agency (EPA) to set more restrictive standards for ground-level ozone, as the EPA's own formal science advisers recommended. All the major Democratic and some Republican presidential candidates and most of the congressional Democrats called for much stiffer controls on pollution. However, President George W. Bush and many congressional Republicans argued that these proposals go too far and will impose excessive costs on firms. Canadian Conservative leaders called for a continent-wide environmental policy. Japan's Prime Minister called for cutting world emissions in half by 2050. European and U.S. leaders debated carbon credits. Clearly, pollution control will be one of the major issues debated throughout the world for the foreseeable future.

This chapter examines why unregulated markets do not adequately control pollution and other externalities. An *externality* occurs when someone's consumption or production activities hurt or help others outside a market. For example, a manufacturing plant produces noxious fumes as a by-product of its production process. The emission of these fumes creates an externality that harms people in surrounding areas. If the government does not intervene, the firm is uninterested in the fumes—it cannot sell the fumes, and it does not have to pay for the harm they cause. Because the firm has no financial incentive to reduce its level of pollution and it would be costly to do so, the firm pollutes excessively.

We start by examining externalities that arise as a by-product of production, such as water pollution from a factory, and consumption, such as air pollution from a car. We find that a competitive market produces more pollution than a market that is optimally regulated by the government and that a monopoly may not create as much of a pollution problem as a competitive market. Next we show that externalities are caused by a lack of clearly defined *property rights* that allow owners to prevent others from using their resources.

We then turn to other issues arising from externalities. Externalities create problems for a **common property,** which is a resource available to anyone, such as a city park. Each person using the park causes an externality by crowding other people. Because no one has a property right to exclude others, such common property is overused.

When externalities benefit others, too little of the externality may be produced. A *public good*—a commodity or service whose consumption by one person does not preclude others from also consuming it—provides a positive externality if no one can be excluded from consuming it. National defense is an example of such a public good. Private firms cannot profitably charge people to provide national defense because people who did not pay would also benefit from it. Supplying anyone with a public good makes it available to others, so public goods provide a positive externality. Either markets for public goods do not exist or such markets undersupply the good.

When an externality problem arises, government intervention may be necessary. A government may directly regulate an externality such as pollution or may provide a public good. Alternatively, a government may indirectly control an externality through taxation or laws that make polluters liable for the damage they cause.

In this chapter, we examine seven main topics	

1. **Externalities:** By-products of consumption and production may benefit or harm other people.

2. **The Inefficiency of Competition with Externalities:** A competitive market produces too much of a harmful externality.

3. **Regulating Externalities:** Overproduction of pollution and other externalities can be prevented through taxation or regulation.

4. **Market Structure and Externalities:** With a harmful externality, a noncompetitive market equilibrium may be closer to the socially optimal level than a competitive equilibrium.

5. **Allocating Property Rights to Reduce Externalities:** Clearly assigning property rights allows exchanges that reduce or eliminate externality problems.

6. **Open-Access Common Property:** People overexploit resources when property rights are not clearly defined.

7. **Public Goods:** Private markets supply too few public goods, and governments have difficulty determining their optimal levels.

17.1   Externalities

> *Tragedy is when I cut my finger. Comedy is when you walk into an open sewer and die.*
> —Mel Brooks

An **externality** occurs when a person's well-being or a firm's production capability is directly affected by the actions of other consumers or firms rather than indirectly through changes in prices. A firm whose production process generates fumes that harm its neighbors is creating an externality for which there is no market. In contrast, the firm is not causing an externality when it harms a rival by selling extra output that lowers the market price.

Externalities may either help or harm others. An externality that harms others is called a *negative externality*. For example, a chemical plant spoils a lake's beauty when it dumps its waste products into the water and in so doing also harms a firm that rents boats for use on that waterway. Government officials in Sydney, Australia, used loud Barry Manilow music to drive away late-night revelers from a suburban park—and in the process drove local residents out of their minds.[1]

---

[1]www.cnn.com/2006/WORLD/asiapcf/07/17/australia.manilow.ap/index.html, July 17, 2006.

A *positive externality* benefits others. By installing attractive shrubs and outdoor sculptures around its store, a firm provides a positive externality to its neighbors.

A single action may confer positive externalities on some people and negative externalities on others. Some people think that their wind chimes please their neighbors, but anyone with an ounce of sense would realize that those chimes make us want to strangle those people! It was reported that the efforts to clean up the air in Los Angeles, while helping people breathe more easily, also caused radiation levels to increase far more rapidly than if the air had remained dirty.

APPLICATION

Negative Externality: SUVs Kill

U.S. drivers have set off an "arms race" by buying increasingly heavy vehicles such as sport-utility vehicles (SUVs) and other light trucks. The replacement of cars with heavier vehicles might have two offsetting effects. First, people feel better protected in larger, heavier vehicles [although Anderson (2006) finds that they are not safer]. Second, a more massive vehicle may inflict greater harm—a negative externality—on the occupants of smaller vehicles, pedestrians, and bicyclists.

White (2004) concludes that light trucks and SUVs kill. For each 1 million light trucks that replace cars, between 34 and 93 additional car occupants, pedestrians, bicyclists, or motorcyclists are killed per year. That is, any safety gain to SUV and light truck owners comes at a very high cost: Each fatal crash that occupants of large vehicles avoid costs at least 4.3 additional fatal crashes involving others.

Similarly, Anderson (2006) finds that the doubling of the share of light trucks from 1980 to 2004 greatly increased deaths. A one-percentage-point increase in light trucks' share raises annual traffic fatalities by 0.41%, or 172 deaths per year. Two-thirds to three-quarters of these deaths involve occupants of other vehicles and pedestrians. Friends don't let friends drive SUVs and light trucks.

APPLICATION

Positive Externality: Michael Jordan

When Michael Jordan played for the Chicago Bulls, he raised sales throughout the National Basketball Association (NBA), creating positive externalities. Controlling for team records, Hausman and Leonard (1997) showed that Jordan's presence increased ticket revenues at away games throughout the league by $2.5 million during the 1991–1992 regular season. (Jordan didn't affect gate receipts for playoff games because those games would have sold out even without him.) Local television advertising revenues also rose by $2.4 million for these games. These increased ticket and local television advertising receipts reflected a positive externality because they went to the home team rather than to Jordan's employer, the Bulls.

Jordan's presence increased national television advertising by $6.6 million during the regular season and by $13.9 million during the playoffs. From 1990 through 2001, NBA television ratings in the finals were 27% higher during the years in which he played than in his retirement years. Jordan also boosted the earnings of NBA Properties, which licenses NBA paraphernalia such as clothing and videos, by $15.1 million. National television revenues and NBA Properties' earnings are shared equally by all teams, so most of this increase was a positive externality for other teams.

Hausman and Leonard estimated the total value of Jordan's positive externalities at $40.3 million for the 1991–1992 season. (Perhaps less precisely, *Fortune* magazine estimated that Jordan's NBA career contributed $10 billion to the U.S. economy before his last comeback.)

When Michael Jordan returned from his second retirement to play for the lowly Washington Wizards in 2001–2002 and 2002–2003, he again was the single biggest draw at away games. By various estimates, his return increased ticket sales by about 7% throughout the league, or about $8.2 million, and generated $20 million overall for the league.

17.2 The Inefficiency of Competition with Externalities

I shot an arrow in the air and it stuck.

Competitive firms and consumers do not have to pay for the harms of their negative externalities, so they create excessive amounts. Similarly, because producers are not compensated for the benefits of a positive externality, too little of such externalities is produced.

To illustrate why externalities lead to nonoptimal production, we examine a (hypothetical) competitive market in which firms produce paper and by-products of the production process—such as air and water pollution—that harm people who live near paper mills. We'll call the pollution *gunk*. Each ton of paper that is produced increases the amount of gunk by one unit, and the only way to decrease the volume of gunk is to reduce the amount of paper manufactured. No less-polluting technologies are available, and it is not possible to locate plants where the gunk bothers no one.

Paper firms do not have to pay for the harm from the pollution they cause. As a result, each firm's **private cost**—the cost of production only, not including externalities—includes its direct costs of labor, energy, and wood pulp but not the indirect costs of the harm from gunk. The true **social cost** is the private cost plus the cost of the harms from externalities.

SUPPLY-AND-DEMAND ANALYSIS

The paper industry is the major industrial source of water pollution. We use a supply-and-demand diagram for the paper market in Figure 17.1 to illustrate that *a competitive market produces excessive pollution because each firm's private cost is less than the social cost*. In the competitive equilibrium, the firms consider only their private costs in making decisions and ignore the harms of the pollution externality they inflict on others. The market supply curve is the aggregate *private marginal cost* curve, MC^p, which is the horizontal sum of the private marginal cost curves of each of the paper manufacturing plants.

The competitive equilibrium, e_c, is determined by the intersection of the market demand curve and the inverse market supply curve for paper. The inverse market demand function in the figure is $p = 450 - 2Q$. The inverse market supply function—the

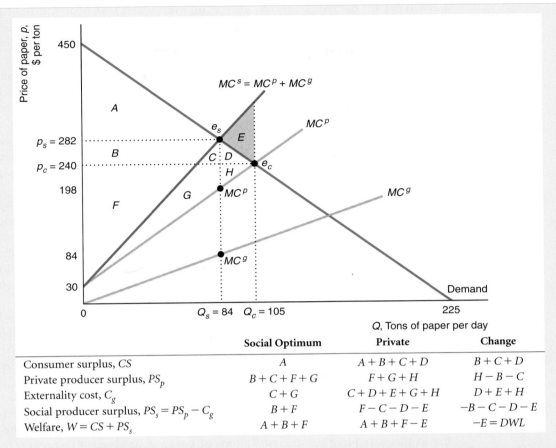

	Social Optimum	Private	Change
Consumer surplus, CS	A	$A+B+C+D$	$B+C+D$
Private producer surplus, PS_p	$B+C+F+G$	$F+G+H$	$H-B-C$
Externality cost, C_g	$C+G$	$C+D+E+G+H$	$D+E+H$
Social producer surplus, $PS_s = PS_p - C_g$	$B+F$	$F-C-D-E$	$-B-C-D-E$
Welfare, $W = CS + PS_s$	$A+B+F$	$A+B+F-E$	$-E=DWL$

Figure 17.1 Welfare Effects of Pollution in a Competitive Market. The competitive equilibrium, e_c, is determined by the intersection of the demand curve and the competitive supply or private marginal cost curve, MC^p, which ignores the cost of pollution. The social optimum, e_s, is at the intersection of the demand curve and the social marginal cost curve, $MC^s = MC^p + MC^g$, where MC^g is the marginal cost of the pollution (gunk). Private producer surplus is based on the MC^p curve, and social producer surplus is based on the MC^s curve.

sum of the private marginal cost curves of the individual firms—is $MC^p = 30 + 2Q$. Equating these functions and solving (or looking at the figure), we find that the competitive equilibrium quantity is $Q_c = 105$ tons per day, and the competitive equilibrium price is $p_c = \$240$ per ton.

The firms' *private producer surplus* is the producer surplus of the paper mills based on their *private marginal cost* curve: the area $F + G + H$, which is below the market price and above MC^p up to the competitive equilibrium quantity, 105. The competitive equilibrium maximizes the sum of consumer surplus and private producer surplus (Chapter 9). If there were no externality, the sum of consumer surplus and private producer surplus would equal welfare, so competition would maximize welfare.

Because of the pollution externality, however, the competitive equilibrium does *not* maximize welfare. Competitive firms produce too much gunk because they do not have to pay for the harm from the gunk. This *market failure* (Chapter 9) results from competitive forces that equalize the price and *private marginal cost* rather than *social marginal cost,* which includes both the private costs of production and the externality damage.

For a given amount of paper production, the full cost of one more ton of paper to society, the *social marginal cost* (MC^s), is the cost to the paper firms of manufacturing one more ton of paper plus the additional externality damage to people in the community from producing this last ton of paper. Thus the height of the social marginal cost curve, MC^s, at any given quantity equals the vertical sum of the height of the MC^p curve (the private marginal cost of producing another ton of paper) plus the height of the marginal externality damages curve, $MC^g = Q$ (the marginal harm from the gunk) at that quantity: $MC^s(Q) = MC^p(Q) + MC^g(Q) = (30 + 2Q) + Q = 30 + 3Q$.

The social marginal cost curve intersects the demand curve at the socially optimal quantity, $Q_s = 84$, and price $p_s = 282$. At smaller quantities, the price—the value consumers place on the last unit of the good sold—is higher than the full social marginal cost. There the gain to consumers of paper exceeds the cost of producing an extra unit of output (and hence an extra unit of gunk). At larger quantities, the price is below the social marginal cost, so the gain to consumers is less than the cost of producing an extra unit.

Welfare is the sum of consumer surplus and *social producer surplus,* which is based on the *social marginal cost* curve rather than the *private marginal cost* curve. *Welfare is maximized where price equals social marginal cost.* At the social optimum, e_s, welfare equals $A + B + F$: the area between the demand curve and the MC^s curve up to the optimal quantity, 84 tons of paper.

Welfare at the competitive equilibrium, e_c, is lower: $A + B + F - E$, the area between the demand curve and the MC^s curve up to 105 tons of paper. The area between these curves from 84 to 105, $-E$, is a deadweight loss because the social cost exceeds the value that consumers place on the last 21 tons of paper. *A deadweight loss results because the competitive market equates price with private marginal cost instead of with social marginal cost.*

Welfare is higher at the social optimum than at the competitive equilibrium because the gain from reducing pollution from the competitive to the socially optimal level more than offsets the loss to consumers and producers of the paper. The cost of the pollution to people who live near the factories is the area under the MC^g curve between zero and the quantity produced. By construction, this area is the same as the area between the MC^p and the MC^s curves. The total damage from the gunk is $-C - D - E - G - H$ at the competitive equilibrium and only $-C - G$ at the social optimum. Consequently, the extra pollution damage from producing the competitive output rather than the socially optimal quantity is $-D - E - H$.

The main beneficiaries from producing at the competitive output level rather than at the socially optimal level are the paper buyers, who pay $240 rather than $282 for a ton of paper. Their consumer surplus rises from A to $A + B + C + D$. The corresponding change in private producer surplus is $H - B - C$, which is negative in this figure.

The figure illustrates two main results with respect to negative externalities. First, *a competitive market produces excessive negative externalities.* Because the price of the pollution to the firms is zero, which is less than the marginal cost that the last unit of pollution imposes on society, an unregulated competitive market produces more pollution than is socially optimal. Second, *the optimal amount of pollution is greater than zero.* Even though pollution is harmful and we'd like to have none of it, we cannot wipe it out without eliminating virtually all production and consumption. Making paper, dishwashers, and televisions creates air and water pollution. Fertilizers used in farming pollute the water supply. Delivery people pollute the air by driving to your home.

COST-BENEFIT ANALYSIS

We've used a supply-and-demand analysis to show that *a competitive market produces too much pollution because the price of output equals the marginal private cost rather than the marginal social cost.* By using a cost-benefit analysis, we obtain another interpretation of the pollution problem in terms of the marginal cost and benefit of the pollution itself.

Let $H = \overline{G} - G$ be the amount that gunk, G, is reduced from the competitive level, $\overline{G}$. Let $B(H)$ be the benefit to society of reducing the units of gunk produced by H, and $C(H)$ be the associated social cost due to the forgone consumption of the good so as to reduce gunk. Society wants to maximize welfare, which is defined as the benefit net of the cost: $W = B(H) - C(H)$. To find the optimal amount of gunk to remove to maximize this measure of welfare, we set the derivative of welfare with respect to H equal to zero:

$$\frac{dW(H)}{dH} = \frac{dB(H)}{dH} - \frac{dC(H)}{dH} = 0.$$

Thus welfare is maximized when marginal benefit, $dB(H)/dH$, equals marginal cost, $dC(H)/dH$.

In the cost-benefit diagram, panel a of Figure 17.2 (which corresponds to Figure 17.1), the quantity on the horizontal axis starts at the competitive level, 105 tons, and *decreases to the right.* That is, H is zero at the origin of the axis and increases as G diminishes. Thus a movement to the right indicates a reduction in paper and gunk.

The benefit of reducing output is the reduced damage from gunk. At any given quantity, the height of the benefit curve in panel a is the difference between the pollution harm at that quantity and the harm at the competitive quantity. The cost of reducing output is that the consumer surplus and private producer surplus fall. The height of the cost curve at a given quantity is the sum of consumer surplus and private producer surplus at that quantity minus the corresponding value at the competitive quantity.

If society reduced output to 63 tons, the quantity at which the total benefit equals the total cost, society would be no better off than it is in the competitive equilibrium. To maximize welfare, we want to set output at 84 tons, the quantity at which the gap between the total benefit and total cost is greatest. At that quantity, the slope of the benefit curve, the marginal benefit, *MB*, equals the slope of the cost curve, the marginal cost, *MC*, as panel b of the figure shows.[2] Thus *welfare is maximized by reducing output and pollution until the marginal benefit from less pollution equals the marginal cost of less output.* See **www.aw-bc.com/perloff**, Chapter 17, "Emissions Standards for Ozone."

---

[2]This marginal cost curve, *MC*, reflects the social cost of removing the last unit of paper (gunk), whereas the social marginal cost curve, *MC*^{s} in Figure 17.1 captures the extra cost to society from the last unit of paper (or gunk).

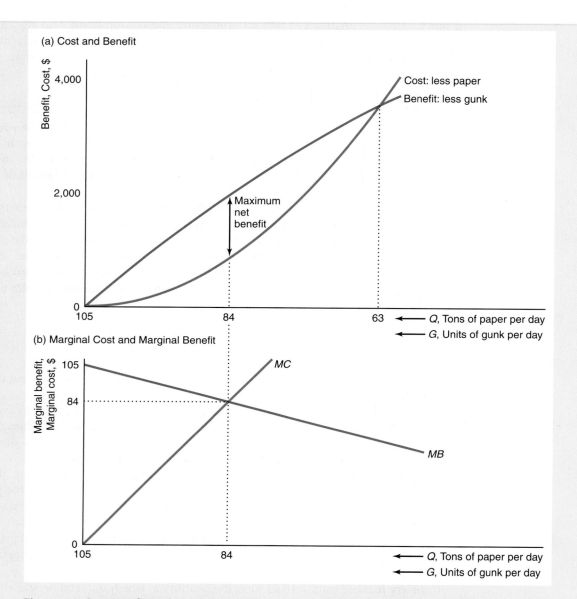

Figure 17.2 Cost-Benefit Analysis of Pollution.
(a) The benefit curve reflects the reduction in harm from pollution as the amount of gunk falls from the competitive level. The cost of reducing the amount of gunk is the fall in output, which reduces consumer surplus and private producer surplus. Welfare is maximized at 84 tons of paper and 84 units of gunk, the quantities at which the difference between the benefit and cost curves, the net benefit, is greatest. (b) The net benefit is maximized where the marginal benefit, *MB*, which is the slope of the benefit curve, equals the marginal cost, *MC*, the slope of the cost curve.

17.3   Regulating Externalities

Because competitive markets produce too many negative externalities, government intervention may provide a social gain. Half a century ago in 1952, London suffered from a thick "peasouper" fog—pollution so dense that people had trouble finding their way home—that killed an estimated 4,000 to 12,000 people. Those dark days prompted the British government to pass its first Clean Air Act, in 1956. The United States passed a Clean Air Act in 1970.

Carbon dioxide (CO_2), which is primarily produced by burning fossil fuels, is a major contributor to global warming, damages marine life, and causes other harms. Rich countries tend to produce more CO_2 from energy consumption than do poorer countries, as Table 17.1 shows. The United States produces nearly a quarter of the world's CO_2, one of the world's highest rates of CO_2 per capita, and a relatively high rate per thousand dollars of gross domestic product (GDP). The last column of the table shows that most countries have greatly increased their production of CO_2 relative to GDP since 1990. Only a few countries, such as Britain, have decreased their total CO_2 production since 1990.

Developing countries spend little on controlling pollution, while many developed countries' public expenditures on regulating pollution have fallen in recent years. In response, various protests have erupted, as in 2005 when thousands of rioters in a southeastern Chinese village protested against pollution from nearby factories.

In 1992, representatives from more than 150 countries began negotiating an international emissions reduction policy. An agreement was reached in Kyoto, Japan, in December 1997 that required most industrialized nations to reduce emissions by an average of 5.2% below 1990 levels by 2008–2012. To achieve this goal, the United States, Europe, and Japan needed to curb their CO_2 emissions by 31%, 22%, and 35%, respectively, from the levels that would have been attained in the absence of a reduction policy. The Bush administration rejected this agreement.

If a government has sufficient knowledge about pollution damage, the demand curve, costs, and the production technology, it can force a competitive market to produce the social optimum. The government might control pollution directly by restricting the amount of pollution that firms may produce or by taxing them for pollution they create. A governmental limit on the amount of air or water pollution that may be released is called an *emissions standard*. A tax on air pollution is called an *emissions fee*, and a tax on discharges into the air or waterways is an *effluent charge*.

TABLE 17.1 Industrial CO_2 Emissions, 2003

	Metric Tons of CO_2			
	Per Capita	Total	Per Thousand U.S. Dollars of GDP	Percentage Change Since 1990
United States	19.8	5,799	0.53	20
Australia	18.0	355	0.68	30
Canada	17.9	567	0.68	36
Russian Federation	10.3	1,496	3.45	NA
Germany	9.8	807	0.34	NA
Japan	9.7	1,234	0.29	12
United Kingdom	9.4	560	0.31	−2
France	6.2	375	0.21	3
Mexico	4.0	417	0.67	11
China	3.2	4,151	2.94	73
World	4.9	25,168		

Source: **mdgs.un.org/unsd/mdg/Data.aspx** as of 2007.

Frequently, however, a government controls pollution indirectly, through quantity restrictions or taxes on outputs or inputs. Whether the government restricts or taxes outputs or inputs may depend on the nature of the production process. It is generally better to regulate pollution directly than to regulate output, because direct regulation of pollution encourages firms to adopt efficient, new technologies to control pollution (a possibility we ignore in our example).

Emissions Standard. We can use the paper mill gunk example in Figure 17.1 to illustrate how a government may use an *emissions standard* to reduce pollution. Here the government can achieve the social optimum by forcing the paper mills to produce no more than 84 units of paper per day. (Because output and pollution move together in this example, regulating either reduces pollution in the same way.)

Unfortunately, the government usually does not know enough to regulate optimally. To set quantity restrictions on output optimally, the government must know how the marginal social cost curve, the demand for paper curve, and pollution vary with output. The ease with which the government can monitor output and pollution may determine whether it sets an output restriction or a pollution standard.

Even if the government knows enough to set the optimal regulation, it must enforce this regulation to achieve the social optimum. Although the U.S. Environmental Protection Agency (EPA) sets federal smog standards, it identified 474 counties in 31 states, home to 159 million people, as having excessive ozone (smog) in 2004. Most of these counties still have not met the new ozone standard of 0.085 parts per million, which replaced the older standard of 0.12 parts per million, set in 1979.[3]

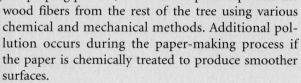

APPLICATION

Pulp and Paper Mill Pollution and Regulation

Pulp and paper mills are major sources of air and water pollution. Air pollution is generated primarily during the pulping process, in which the plant separates the

wood fibers from the rest of the tree using various chemical and mechanical methods. Additional pollution occurs during the paper-making process if the paper is chemically treated to produce smoother surfaces.

For simplicity in our example, we assume that pollution is emitted in fixed ratio to output. However, in actuality, firms can choose less-polluting technologies, use additional pollution-controlling capital, and take other actions to lower the amount of pollution per unit of output.

Shadbegian and Gray (2003) found significantly lower air pollution emissions per unit of paper in plants using more capital designed to fight air pollution; specifically, a 10% increase in pollution-reducing capital reduces emissions by 6.9%. Each dollar spent on extra capital stock provides an annual return of about 75¢ in pollution-reduction benefits.

[3]See **www.scorecard.org** for details on the environmental risks in your area.

Gray and Shadbegian (2004) found that the plants in areas where the perceived payoff to controlling pollution is greater produce less pollution, all else the same. They found that plants near communities with more kids, more elderly people, and fewer poor people emit less pollution. Similarly, plants in areas with politically active, environmentally conscious populations emit less pollution.

The lower levels of pollution in these areas were achieved through more stringent regulation. Under the 1977 amendments to the 1970 Clean Air Act, U.S. counties are designated annually as being in *attainment* (meeting ambient air quality standards) or in *nonattainment* (violating ambient air quality standards) for each of several criteria pollutants. Because plants in nonattainment counties are substantially more stringently regulated than those in attainment counties, they have 43% lower emissions.

Emissions Fee. The government may impose costs on polluters by taxing their output or the amount of pollution produced. (Similarly, a law could make a polluter liable in a court for damages.) In our paper mill example, taxing output works as well as taxing the pollution directly because the relationship between output and pollution is fixed. However, if firms can vary the output-pollution relationship by varying inputs or adding pollution-control devices, then the government should tax pollution.

In our paper mill example, if the government knows the marginal cost of the gunk, MC^g, it can set the output tax equal to this marginal cost curve, $t(Q) = MC^g$, so that the tax varies with output, Q. Figure 17.3 illustrates the manufacturers' after-tax marginal cost, $MC^s = MC^p + t(Q)$.

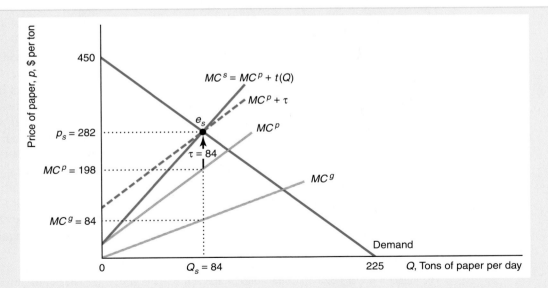

Figure 17.3 Taxes to Control Pollution. Placing a tax on firms equal to the harm from the gunk, $t(Q) = MC^g$, causes them to internalize the externality, so their private marginal cost is the same as the social marginal cost, MC^s. As a result, the competitive after-tax equilibrium is the same as the social optimum, e_s. Alternatively, applying a specific tax of $\tau = \$84$ per ton of paper, which is the marginal harm from the gunk at $Q_s = 84$, also results in the social optimum.

The output tax causes a manufacturer to **internalize the externality:** to bear the cost of the harm that one inflicts on others (or to capture the benefit that one provides to others). The after-tax private marginal cost or supply curve is the same as the social marginal cost curve. As a result, the after-tax competitive equilibrium is the social optimum.

Usually, the government sets a specific tax rather than a tax that varies with the amount of pollution, as MC^g does. As Solved Problem 17.1 shows, applying an appropriate specific tax results in the socially optimal level of production.

SOLVED PROBLEM   17.1

For the market with pollution in Figure 17.1, what constant, specific tax, τ, on output could the government set to maximize welfare?

Answer

Set the specific tax equal to the marginal harm of pollution at the socially optimal quantity: At the socially optimal quantity, $Q_s = 84$, the marginal harm from the gunk is $84, as Figure 17.3 shows. If the specific tax is $\tau = \$84$, the after-tax private marginal cost (the after-tax competitive supply curve), $MC_p + \tau$, equals the social marginal cost at the socially optimal quantity. As a consequence, the after-tax competitive supply curve intersects the demand curve at the socially optimal quantity. By paying this specific tax, the firms internalize the cost of the externality at the social optimum. All that is required for optimal production is that the tax equals the marginal cost of pollution at the optimum quantity; the tax need not equal the marginal cost of pollution at other quantities.

● APPLICATION

Sobering Drunk Drivers

Levitt and Porter (2001) estimated that drivers with alcohol in their blood are 7 times more likely to cause a fatal two-car crash and that legally drunk drivers are 13 times more likely to do so than are sober drivers.[4] Presumably, drunks have willingly accepted the increased risk, but they impose negative externalities on others. Levitt and Porter estimated that drunk drivers kill about 3,000 other people in two-car crashes. Given a conservative estimate of the value of a human life of $3 million, they calculated that a drunk driver imposes an externality of 30¢ per mile driven. They concluded that, at current arrest rates for drunk driving, the fine (or a comparably valued license suspension or a jail sentence) that internalizes this externality is at least $8,000 per arrest.[5]

Whether you are comfortable with making calculations based on the value of human life or not, current U.S. penalties are almost certainly inadequate.

---

[4]The higher a driver's blood alcohol concentration (BAC), the greater the odds of the driver's being killed. Compared to a sober driver, one with a BAC of 0.02 is 3 to 5 times more likely to die, and one who has a BAC of 0.05 is 6 to 17 times more likely ("Legal Not Always Safe," *San Francisco Chronicle,* August 31, 2002: A17). At the legal limit of 0.08, a driver is 11 to 52 times more likely to die. At higher levels, the odds are even more horrifying: 29 to 241 times more at 0.10 (the old legal limit), and 382 to 15,560 times more at 0.15.

[5]Analogously, Anderson (2006) estimated that the appropriate tax on SUVs and other light trucks is about $4,650 (see the application "Negative Externality: SUVs Kill").

A first-misdemeanor driving-while-intoxicated offense in California is likely to result in probation, a fine of $390–$1,000, and a brief assignment to treatment. Several states have no possibility of a license suspension for the first offense.

U.S. penalties pale compared to those in other countries. In Canada, the first offense has a $600–$2,000 (Canadian) fine, up to 12 to 36 months' prohibition on driving, and 0 to 6 months of jail time. However, a drunk driver who causes a death faces a loss of his or her license for 36 months to life and up to lifetime imprisonment. Japan imposes a $1,000–$5,000 fine or imprisonment for 6 months to 5 years. On the Australian island of Tasmania, a drunk driver can receive a $6,000 fine, 6 years' license disqualification, and up to 24 months in jail. In South Africa, the maximums are a $120,000 fine and 6 years' imprisonment. Sweden's maximum penalty for severe and repeated offenses is 2 years (6 years if the driver killed someone). Turkey suspends licenses for 6 months to 2 years and requires psychological treatment by a medical doctor after a third offense. A drunk driver in the United Kingdom faces a minimum 12 months' license disqualification and other penalties. El Salvador has no set punishment but has executed some drunk drivers.

EMISSIONS FEES VERSUS STANDARDS UNDER UNCERTAINTY

Is it better to tax emissions or to set standards? We have seen that the government can induce a firm to produce efficiently if it sets either a fee or a standard optimally. However, if the government is uncertain about the cost of pollution abatement, which approach produces more welfare depends on the shape of the marginal benefit and marginal cost curves for abating pollution (Weitzman, 1974).

Figure 17.4 shows the government's knowledge about the shape and location of the marginal benefit (MB) curve of reducing gunk, a pollutant, and the marginal cost (MC) of abatement of gunk. We assume that the government knows the MB curve but is uncertain about the MC curve. It believes that it is equally likely that the true marginal cost of abatement curve is MC^1 or MC^2.

To start our analysis, we ask how the government would regulate if it was certain that the MC curve equaled the expected marginal cost of abatement curve, shown in the figure, to set an emissions standard, s, on emissions (gunk) or an emissions fee, f per unit. Using its expected marginal cost of abatement curve, the government sets an emissions standard at $s = 100$ units or an emissions fee at $f = \$70$ per unit.

Although either regulation would be optimal in a world of certainty, these regulations are not optimal if the actual marginal cost curve is higher or lower than the expected curve. For example, if the true marginal cost of abatement curve is MC^1, which is higher than the expected marginal cost curve, the optimal standard is $s_1 = 70$ and the optimal fee is $f_1 = \$85$. Thus if the government uses the expected MC curve, it sets the emissions standard too high and the fee too low. In this example, the deadweight loss from too high an emissions standard, DWL_s^1, is greater than the deadweight loss from too low a fee, DWL_f^1, as the figure illustrates.

If the true marginal cost is less than expected, MC^2, the government has set the standard too low and the fee too high. Again, the deadweight loss from the wrong standard, DWL_s^2, is greater than that from the wrong fee, DWL_f^2. Consequently, given how this figure is drawn, if the government is uncertain about the marginal cost curve, it should use the fee.

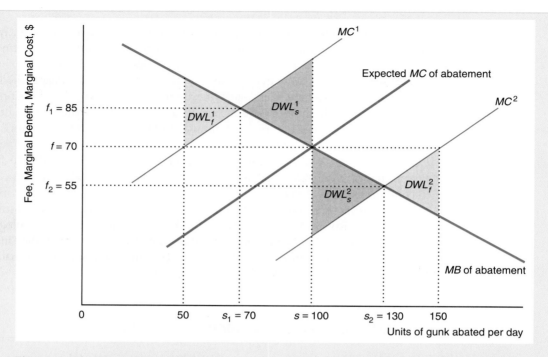

Figure 17.4 Fees Versus Standards Under Uncertainty. The government knows the marginal benefit curve but is uncertain about the marginal cost curve from abating gunk. If the government uses the expected marginal cost curve to set a fee of $70 or a standard of 100, the deadweight loss from the fee will be smaller than the deadweight loss from the standard regardless of whether the actual marginal cost curve is MC^1 or MC^2.

However, if we redraw the figure with a much steeper marginal benefit curve, the deadweight loss from the fee will be greater than that from the standard. Thus whether it is optimal to use fees or standards depends on the government's degree of uncertainty and the shape of the marginal benefit and marginal cost curves.

● APPLICATION

U.S. and EU Approaches to Regulating Pollution

The U.S. and EU governments apparently have different beliefs about how to regulate pollution under uncertainty. Usually, the U.S. government sets emissions standards, whereas European governments tax emissions or inputs. These differences are illustrated by how these governments are regulating automobiles and industrial pollution.

Because cars that get more miles to the gallon tend to produce less pollution per mile driven, the U.S. government mandates fuel-efficiency standards (Corporate Average Fuel Economy, CAFE) that require a manufacturer's cars to average 27.5 miles per gallon (this number was expected to increase annually starting in 2007). Compared to other countries, the United States sets relatively low gasoline taxes. Europe and Japan rarely set fuel-economy standards but impose gasoline taxes that are 5 to 10 times as high as U.S. federal and state taxes combined.

European countries also impose environmental taxes to reduce carbon dioxide, sulfur dioxide, and other air pollutants, and some of these countries similarly use taxes to limit the size of landfills. The taxes are returned to the economy by lowering personal income or Social Security taxes. Although the U.S. federal government occasionally takes an emissions fee–like approach to controlling sulfur dioxide, it generally sets standards on emissions and landfills.

17.4 Market Structure and Externalities

Two of the main results concerning competitive markets and negative externalities— that too much pollution is produced and that a tax equal to the marginal social cost of the externality solves the problem—do not hold for other market structures. Although a competitive market always produces too many negative externalities, a noncompetitive market may produce more or less than the optimal level of output and pollution. If a tax is set so that firms internalize the externalities, a competitive market produces the social optimum, whereas a noncompetitive market does not.

MONOPOLY AND EXTERNALITIES

We use the paper-gunk example to illustrate these results. In Figure 17.5, the monopoly equilibrium, e_m, is determined by the intersection of the marginal revenue, MR, and private marginal cost, MC^p, curves. Like the competitive firms, the monopoly ignores the harm its pollution causes, so it considers just its direct, private costs in making decisions.

Output is only 70 tons in the monopoly equilibrium, e_m, which is less than the 84 tons at the social optimum, e_s.[6] Thus this figure illustrates that *the monopoly outcome may be less than the social optimum even with an externality.*

Although the competitive market with an externality always produces more output than the social optimum, a monopoly may produce more than, the same as, or less than the social optimum. The reason that a monopoly may produce too little or too much is that it faces two offsetting effects. The monopoly tends to produce too little output because it sets its price above its marginal cost. But the monopoly tends to produce too much output because its decisions depend on its private marginal cost instead of the social marginal cost.

Which effect dominates depends on the elasticity of demand for the output and on the extent of the marginal damage the pollution causes. If the demand curve is very elastic, the monopoly markup is small. As a result, the monopoly equilibrium is close to the competitive equilibrium, e_c, and is greater than the social optimum, e_s. If extra pollution causes little additional harm—when MC^g is close to zero at the equilibrium— the social marginal cost essentially equals the private marginal cost, and the monopoly produces less than the social optimum.

---

[6]Given that the inverse demand function is $p = 450 - 2Q$, the monopoly's revenue function is $R = 450Q - 2Q^2$, so its marginal revenue function is $MR = 450 - 4Q$. If the monopoly is unregulated, its equilibrium is found by equating its marginal revenue function and its private marginal cost function, $MC^p = 30 + 2Q$, and solving: $Q_m = 70$ and (using the inverse demand function) $p_m = 310$.

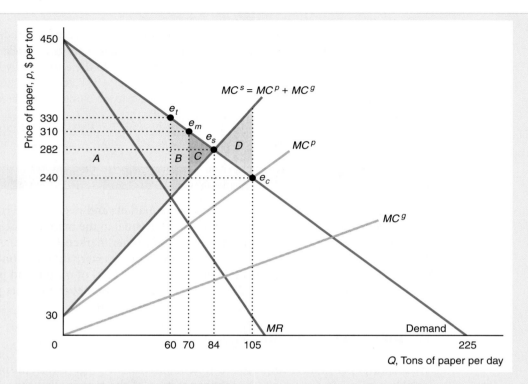

Figure 17.5 Monopoly, Competition, and Social Optimum with Pollution. At the competitive equilibrium, e_c, more is produced than at the social optimum, e_s. As a result, the deadweight loss in the competitive market is D. The monopoly equilibrium, e_m, quantity, 70, is deter-mined by the intersection of the marginal revenue and the private marginal cost, MC^p, curves. The social welfare (based on the marginal social cost, MC^s, curve) under monopoly is $A + B$. Here the deadweight loss of monopoly, C, is less than the deadweight loss under competition, D.

MONOPOLY VERSUS COMPETITIVE WELFARE WITH EXTERNALITIES

In the absence of externalities, welfare is greater under competition than under an unregulated monopoly (Chapter 11). However, with an externality, welfare may be greater with a monopoly than with competition.[7]

If both monopoly and competitive outputs are greater than the social optimum, welfare must be greater under monopoly because the competitive output is larger than the monopoly output. If the monopoly produces less than the social optimum, we need to check which distortion is greater: the monopoly's producing too little or the competitive market's producing too much.

Welfare is lower at monopoly equilibrium, area $A + B$, than at the social optimum, $A + B + C$, in Figure 17.5. The deadweight loss of monopoly, C, results from the monopoly's producing less output than is socially optimal.

---

[7]Several states, among them Pennsylvania and North Carolina, have created state monopolies to sell liquor. One possible purpose is to control the externalities created by alcohol consumption, such as drunk driving.

In the figure, the deadweight loss from monopoly, C, is less than the deadweight loss from competition, D, so welfare is greater under monopoly. The monopoly produces only slightly too little output, whereas competition produces excessive output—and hence far too much gunk.

SOLVED PROBLEM 17.2

In Figure 17.5, what is the effect on output, price, and welfare of taxing the monopoly an amount equal to the marginal harm of the externality?

Answer

1. *Show how the monopoly equilibrium shifts if the firm is taxed:* A tax equal to the marginal cost of the pollution causes the monopoly to internalize the externality and to view the social marginal cost as its private cost. The intersection of the marginal revenue, MR, curve and the social marginal cost, MC^s, curve determines the taxed-monopoly equilibrium, e_t. The tax causes the equilibrium quantity to fall from 70 to 60 and the equilibrium price to rise from \$310 to \$330.

2. *Determine how this shift affects the deadweight loss of monopoly:* The sum of consumer and producer surplus is only A after the tax, compared to $A + B$ before the tax. Thus welfare falls. The difference between A and welfare at the social optimum, $A + B + C$, is $-(B + C)$, which is the deadweight loss from the taxed monopoly. The tax exacerbates the monopoly's tendency to produce too little output. The deadweight loss increases from C to $B + C$. The monopoly produced too little before the tax; the taxed monopoly produces even less.

TAXING EXTERNALITIES IN NONCOMPETITIVE MARKETS

Many people argue that the government should tax firms an amount equal to the marginal harm of pollution on the grounds that such a tax achieves the social optimum in a competitive market. Solved Problem 17.2 shows that such a tax may lower welfare if applied to a monopoly. The tax definitely lowers welfare if the untaxed monopoly produces less than the social optimum. If the untaxed monopoly was originally producing more than the social optimum, a tax may cause welfare to increase.

If the government has enough information to determine the social optimum, it can force either a monopolized or a competitive market to produce the social optimum. If the social optimum is greater than the unregulated monopoly output, however, the government has to subsidize (rather than tax) the monopoly to get it to produce as much output as is desired.

In short, trying to solve a negative externality problem is more complex in a noncompetitive market than it is in a competitive market. To achieve a social optimum in a competitive market, the government only has to reduce the externality, possibly by decreasing output. In a noncompetitive market, the government must eliminate problems arising from both externalities *and* the exercise of market power. Thus the government needs more information to regulate a noncompetitive market optimally and may also require more tools, such as a subsidy. To the degree that the problems arising from market power and pollution are offsetting, however, the failure to regulate a noncompetitive market is less harmful than the failure to regulate a competitive market.

17.5   Allocating Property Rights to Reduce Externalities

Instead of controlling externalities directly through emissions fees and emissions standards, the government may take an indirect approach by assigning a **property right:** an exclusive privilege to use an asset. By owning this textbook, you have a property right to read it and to stop others from reading or taking it.

If no one holds a property right for a good or a bad, the good or bad is unlikely to have a price. If you had a property right that assured you of the right to be free from noise pollution, you could get the courts to stop your neighbor from playing loud music. Or you could sell your right, permitting your neighbor to play the music. If you did not have this property right, no one would be willing to pay you a positive price for it.

In earlier chapters, we implicitly assumed that property rights are clearly defined and that no harmful by-products are created, so externalities do not arise. In those chapters, all goods had prices. But for many bads, such as pollution, and for some goods, property rights are not clearly defined. No one has exclusive property rights to the air we breathe. Because of this lack of a price, a polluter's private marginal cost of production is less than the full social marginal cost.

COASE THEOREM

According to the *Coase Theorem* (Coase, 1960), the optimal levels of pollution and output can result from bargaining between polluters and their victims if property rights are clearly defined. Coase's contribution is not so much a practical solution to the pollution problem as a demonstration that a lack of clearly defined property rights is the root of the externality problem.

To illustrate the Coase Theorem, we consider two firms, a chemical plant and a boat rental company, that share a small lake. The chemical manufacturer dumps its waste by-products, which smell bad but are otherwise harmless, into the lake. The chemical company can reduce pollution only by restricting its output; it has no other outlet for this waste. The resulting pollution damages the boat rental firm's business. There are other lakes nearby where people can rent boats. Therefore, because they dislike the smell of the chemicals, people rent from this firm only if it charges a low enough price to compensate them fully for the smell.

No Property Rights. These two firms won't negotiate with each other unless property rights are clearly defined. After all, why would the manufacturer reduce its pollution if the boat rental firm has no legal right to clean water? Why would the boat rental firm pay the chemical company not to pollute if the courts may declare that the rental company has a right to be free from pollution?

If the firms do not negotiate, the chemical firm produces the output level that maximizes its profit, ignoring the effect on the boat rental firm. The profit matrix in panel a of Table 17.2 shows that the chemical firm makes $0 if it produces nothing, $10 if it produces 1 ton, and $15 if it produces 2 tons regardless of what the boat rental firm does. Thus the chemical company has a dominant strategy: It produces 2 tons. Knowing that the chemical company will produce 2 tons, the boat rental firm maximizes its profit with 1 boat.

TABLE 17.2   Property Rights and Bargaining

(a) No Property Rights

Chemical Firm: Tons per Day	Boat Rental Firm: Boats Rented per Day		
	0	**1**	**2**
0	$0 / $0	$14 / $0	$15 / $0
1	$0 / $10	$10 / $10	$5 / $10
2	$0 / $15	$2 / $15	–$3 / $15

(b) Boat Rental Firm Has Property Right: *Chemical company pays the boat rental firm $7 per ton for the right to dump*

Chemical Firm: Tons per Day	Boat Rental Firm: Boats Rented per Day		
	0	**1**	**2**
0	$0 / $0	$14 / $0	$15 / $0
1	$7 / $3	$17 / $3	$12 / $3
2	$14 / $1	$16 / $1	$11 / $1

(c) Chemical Company Has Property Right: *Boat rental firm pays the chemical company $6 for each ton by which it reduces its production below 2 tons*

Chemical Firm: Tons per Day	Boat Rental Firm: Boats Rented per Day		
	0	**1**	**2**
0	–$12 / $12	$2 / $12	$3 / $12
1	–$6 / $16	$4 / $16	–$1 / $16
2	$0 / $15	$2 / $15	–$3 / $15

Because nobody else is directly affected by this pollution, we call an outcome *efficient* if it maximizes the sum of the profits of the two firms.[8] The firms maximize their joint profits at $20 when the chemical company produces 1 ton and the boat rental firm rents 1 boat. Thus the no-property-rights equilibrium, with joint profits of $17, is inefficient: Too much pollution is produced.

Property Right to Be Free of Pollution. If a court or the government grants the boat rental firm the property right to be free of pollution, the firm can prevent the chemical company from dumping at all. With no pollution, the boat company rents 2 boats and makes $15. Rather than shut down, the chemical company offers to pay the boat company for the right to dump. The boat rental firm is willing to permit dumping only if

---

[8]Because people who want to rent boats pay sufficiently less as compensation for putting up with the chemicals, they are not harmed by the pollution. Only the boat rental firm is harmed through lower prices.

it makes at least $15, and it may hold out for more. The largest "bribe" the chemical company is willing to offer for the right to dump is one that leaves it with a positive profit. Panel b of Table 17.2 shows one possible compensation agreement: The chemical company offers the boat rental firm $7 per ton for the right to dump. If the firms agree to this deal, the chemical company's dominant strategy is to produce 1 ton, so the boat rental firm chooses to rent 1 boat. Both firms benefit. Indeed, in this equilibrium, their joint profits are maximized at $20.

In general, the chemical firm pays the boat rental firm between $5 and $10. The boat rental firm wants at least $5 so that its profit when both produce 1 unit is at least $15—the amount that it makes with no pollution. Any payment larger than $10 would leave the chemical company with a negative profit, so that's the most it is willing to pay. The exact payment outcome depends on the firms' bargaining skills. Because both parties benefit from a deal, they should be able to reach an agreement if transaction costs are low enough that it pays to negotiate.

Property Right to Pollute. Now suppose that the chemical company has the property right to dump in the lake (for example, by paying a pollution tax). Unless the boat rental company pays the chemical company not to pollute, the chemical company produces 2 tons, as in panel a of the table. The boat rental firm may bribe the chemical company to reduce its output so that both firms benefit. Again, the exact deal that is struck depends on their bargaining skills.

Panel c of Table 17.2 shows what happens if the boat rental firm pays the chemical company $6 per ton for each ton less than 2 that it produces. The chemical company's dominant strategy is to produce 1 ton, and the boat rental firm rents 1 boat. The equilibrium is efficient as in the previous case. Now, however, the boat rental firm compensates the chemical company rather than the other way around.

To summarize the results from the Coase Theorem:

- If there are no impediments to bargaining, *assigning property rights results in the efficient outcome* at which joint profits are maximized.
- *Efficiency is achieved regardless of who receives the property rights.*
- Who gets the property rights affects the income distribution. *The property rights are valuable.* The party with the property rights may be compensated by the other party.

Problems with the Coase Approach. To achieve the efficient outcome, the two sides must bargain successfully with each other. However, the parties may not be able to bargain successfully for at least three important reasons (Polinsky, 1979).

First, if transaction costs are very high, it might not pay for the two sides to meet. For example, if a manufacturing plant pollutes the air, thousands or even millions of people may be affected. The cost of getting them all together to bargain is prohibitive.

Second, if firms engage in strategic bargaining behavior, an agreement may not be reached. For instance, if one party says, "Give me everything I want" and will not budge, reaching an agreement may be impossible.

Third, if either side lacks information about the costs or benefits of reducing pollution, a nonefficient outcome may occur. It is difficult to know how much to offer the other party and to reach an agreement if you do not know how the polluting activity affects the other party.

For these reasons, Coasian bargaining is likely to occur in relatively few situations. Where bargaining cannot occur, the allocation of property rights affects the amount of pollution.

MARKETS FOR POLLUTION

If high transaction costs preclude bargaining, society may be able to overcome this problem by using a market, which facilitates exchanges between individuals. Starting in the early 1980s, the federal and some state governments experimented with issuing permits to pollute that could be exchanged in a market, often by means of an auction. Consequently, today many firms can buy the right to pollute—much as sinners bought indulgences in the Middle Ages. Under this *cap-and-trade* system, the government gives firms permits, each of which confers the right to create a certain amount of pollution. Each firm may use its permits or may sell them to other firms.

Firms whose products are worth a lot relative to the harm from pollution they create buy rights from firms that have less valuable products. Suppose that the cost in terms of forgone output from eliminating each ton of pollution is $200 at one plant and $300 at another. If the government tells both plants to reduce pollution by 1 ton, the total cost is $500. With tradable permits, the first plant can reduce its pollution by 2 tons and sell its allowance to the second plant, so the total social cost is only $400. The trading maximizes the value of the output for a given amount of pollution damage, thus increasing efficiency.

If the government knew enough, it could assign the optimal amount of pollution to each firm, and no trading would be necessary. By using a market, the government does not have to collect this type of detailed information to achieve efficiency. Its only decision concerns what total amount of pollution to allow.

APPLICATION

Selling the Right to Pollute

The Acid Rain Program under the 1990 U.S. Clean Air Act was designed to reduce 10 million tons of sulfur dioxide (SO_2) and 2 million tons of nitrogen oxides (NOx), the primary components of acid rain. Under the law, the EPA issues SO_2 permits, each of which allows a firm to produce 1 ton of emissions of SO_2 annually, equal to the aggregate emission cap. A firm that exceeds its pollution limit is fined $2,000 per ton of emissions above its allowance. But at the end of a year, if a company's emissions are less than its allowance, it may sell the remaining allowance to another firm, thus providing the firm with an incentive to reduce emissions. The EPA holds an annual spot auction for permits that may be used in the current year and an advanced auction for permits effective in seven years. Anyone can purchase allowances. Some environmental groups, such as the Acid Rain Retirement Fund, have purchased permits and withheld them from firms to reduce pollution further. (You can see the outcome of the auctions at **www.epa. gov/airmarkets/auctions**.)

Currently, power plants are responsible for 69% of SO_2 emissions, according to the EPA. By tightening limits on pollution, SO_2 emissions from power plants in 2006 were nearly 40% lower than in 1990. Schmalensee et al. (1998) estimated that, in the mid-1990s, the pollution reduction under the market program cost about a quarter to a third less than it would have cost if permits had not been tradable—a savings on the order of $225 to $375 million per year.

Permits are now traded in many countries around the world. The European Union Greenhouse Gas Emission Trading Scheme, started in 2005, is the largest multinational CO_2 emissions trading program in the world, covering all 25 member states of the European Union. To prepare for the Kyoto Treaty restrictions that commence in 2008, 12 thousand industrial plants across Europe now face limits on their carbon dioxide emissions. By some estimates, the new market's permits are worth about €35 billion per year.

17.6 Open-Access Common Property

So far we've examined externalities that arise as an undesired by-product of a production or consumption activity. Another important externality arises with **open-access common property:** resources to which everyone has free access and an equal right to exploit. Unlike private property, for which the owner can *exclude* others from using the property, open-access common property is not subject to such exclusion. For example, anyone can freely enter and enjoy urban parks such as Central Park in New York, Hyde Park in London, and the Boston Common.

OVERUSE OF OPEN-ACCESS COMMON PROPERTY

Because people do not have to pay to use open-access common property resources, these resources are overused. Parks with free entry often become crowded, an outcome that reduces everyone's enjoyment. Similarly, in less-developed economies, the sharing of public lands for hunting, grazing, or growing crops results in the overuse of common property. Other examples of common property problems are common pools, the Internet, roads, and fisheries.

Common Pools. Petroleum, water, and other fluids and gases are often extracted from a common pool. Owners of wells drawing from a common pool compete to remove the substance most rapidly, thereby gaining ownership of the good. This competition creates an externality by lowering fluid pressure, which makes further pumping more difficult. Iraq justified its invasion of Kuwait, which led to the Persian Gulf War in 1991, on the grounds that Kuwait was overexploiting common pools of oil underlying both countries.

The Internet. An important problem—one that may be inconveniencing you—is overcrowding on the Internet. If many people try to access a single Web site at one time, congestion may slow traffic to a crawl.

Roads. If you own a car, you have a property right to drive that car. But because you lack an exclusive property right to the highway on which you drive, you cannot exclude others from driving on the highway—you must share it with them. However, each driver claims a temporary property right in a portion of the highway by occupying it (thereby preventing others from occupying the same space). Competition for space on the highway leads to congestion (a negative externality), which slows up every driver.

Fisheries. Many fisheries have common access such that anyone can fish and no one has a property right to a fish until it is caught. Each fisher wants to land a fish before others do to gain the property right to that fish. The lack of clearly defined property rights leads to overfishing. Fishers have an incentive to catch more fish than they would if the fishery were private property.

Suppose that each fisher owns a private lake. Because the property rights are clearly defined, there is no externality. Each owner is careful not to overfish in any one year so as to maintain the stock (or number) of fish in future years.[9]

In contrast, most ocean fisheries are open-access common property. Like polluting manufacturers, ocean fishers look only at their private costs. In calculating these costs, fishers include the cost of boats, other equipment, a crew, and supplies. They do not include the cost that they impose on future generations by decreasing the stock of fish today, which reduces the number of fish in the sea next year. The fewer fish there are, the harder it is to catch any, so reducing the population today raises the cost of catching fish in the future. As a result, fishers do not forgo fishing now to leave fish for the future. The social cost is the private cost plus the externality cost from reduced future populations of fish.

● APPLICATION

Emptying the Seas

Ratio of fishing subsidies to the value of the fishing trade worldwide: 1:4.
—Harper's Index 2004

The tendency to overfish has dramatically diminished many fish populations because the rate at which fish are being born is lower than the rate at which they are being caught. A combination of free entry and foolish government subsidies is largely to blame.

A 2005 Pew study found that the stock of predatory fish populations, including shark, tuna, and North Atlantic cod, had fallen substantially, with many species dropping 90% or more in the last half-century. The 2004 U.S. Commission on Ocean Policy concluded that one-fifth of the 267 major U.S. fish populations are overfished, experiencing overfishing, or approaching an overfished condition.

A 2005 study of the UN Food and Agriculture Organization found an increasing trend in the proportion of over-exploited and depleted stocks, from about 10% in the mid-1970s to close to 25% today, with 70% of species being fished close to, at, or beyond their capacity. The top 10 species account for about 30% of the world fisheries' catch. Of these, seven have stocks that are fully exploited or overexploited (anchoveta, Chilean jack mackerel, Alaskan pollock, Japanese anchovy, blue whiting, capelin, and Atlantic herring).

In 2006, Mexico introduced a cap-and-trade approach to regulating its red snapper fishery. President Bush has advocated a similar plan for U.S. fisheries.

SOLVING THE COMMONS PROBLEM

There are two approaches to ameliorating the open-access commons problem. The first is direct government regulation through either taxation or restriction of access. The second is by clearly defining property rights.

---

[9]"There's a fine line between fishing and standing on the shore looking like an idiot." —Steven Wright

Overuse of a common resource occurs because individuals do not bear the full social cost. However, by applying a tax or fee equal to the externality harm that each individual imposes on others, a government forces each person to internalize the externality. For example, governments often charge an entrance fee to a park or a museum. However, if a government sets a fee that is less than the marginal externality harm, it reduces but does not eliminate the externality problem.

Instead of using a tax or fee, the government can restrict access to the commons. One typical approach is to grant access on a first-come, first-served basis. With quotas, people who arrive early gain access. In contrast, with taxes or fees, people who most heavily value the resource gain access. (See **www.aw-bc.com/perloff**, Chapter 17, "For Whom the Bell Tolls.")

An alternative approach to resolving the commons problem is to assign private property rights. Converting common-access property to private property removes the incentive to overuse it. (See **www.aw-bc.com/perloff**, Chapter 17, "Claiming Lobster Fisheries," for an example.)

In developing countries over the past century, common agricultural land has been broken up into smaller, private farms. Similarly, fish farming on private land is increasingly used as common-access fisheries are depleted.

17.7   Public Goods

We have seen that a competitive market produces too much output when a by-product creates a negative externality or when anyone can use a common property. That same competitive market may produce too little of a good in the presence of a positive externality. Too little production may occur when producers cannot restrict access to a **public good:** a commodity or service whose consumption by one person does not preclude others from also consuming it.

TYPES OF GOODS

Previous chapters discussed only *private goods. Private goods have the properties of rivalry and exclusion. Rivalry* means that only one person can consume the good: The good is used up in consumption—it is *depletable*. If you eat a candy bar, no one else can eat that particular candy bar. *Exclusion* means that others can be prevented from consuming the good. Only the person who owns a candy bar may eat it.

Other types of goods lack rivalry or exclusion or both, as Table 17.3 shows. *Public goods lack rivalry.* Your consumption of a public good does not preclude others from also consuming it. There is no need to ration a public good—everyone can consume it. Indeed, excluding someone from consuming it harms that person without helping other consumers.

All public goods lack rivalry, but only some lack exclusion. Major problems occur when no one can be prevented from consuming a public good. National defense is an important example of a nonexclusive public good. The cost of protecting an extra person is literally zero when all people are protected (no rivalry), and no one in the country can be left unprotected (no exclusion). Clean air is also a public good without exclusion (and air pollution is a *public bad*). If the air is clean, we all benefit. If we clean up the air, we cannot prevent others who live nearby from benefiting from this

TABLE 17.3   Rivalry and Exclusion

	Exclusion	No Exclusion
Rivalry	*Private good:* candy bar, pencil, aluminum foil	*Open-access common property:* fishery, hunting, highway
No Rivalry	*Public good with exclusion:* cable television, *club good* (concert, tennis club)	*Public good without exclusion:* national defense, aerial spraying of pesticide, clean air

improvement. A *public good produces a positive externality*, and *excluding anyone from consuming a public good is inefficient.*

Other public goods are exclusive but lack rivalry in consumption. Security guards prevent people who don't have a ticket from entering a concert hall. Until the concert hall is filled, the cost of providing the concert to one extra person is zero. Thus a concert in a hall that is not filled has elements of both a private good (exclusion) and a public good (no rivalry).

Such a concert is a special type of public good, called a *club good*. Although the marginal cost of providing the concert to one more person is zero as long as attendance is less than the seating capacity of the hall, adding another person creates congestion or other externalities that harm concertgoers once the concert hall is filled. Similarly, allowing more people to join a swim club doesn't inflict extra costs until members start getting in each other's way.

In addition to private goods, nonexclusive public goods, and club goods, there are resources with rivalry but without exclusion, such as an open-access common property resource. In an open-access fishery, anyone can fish (no exclusion), but once a fish is caught, no one else can catch it (rivalry).

Many goods differ in the degree to which they have rivalry and exclusion. Many goods are hybrids, with properties of both private and public goods. Telling your friend about something that you learned in a textbook provides a positive externality. A textbook is often viewed as a private good; however, the information in it is a public good. Because the cost of excluding people from a toll road is less than that of excluding people from an ocean fishery, a toll road may more closely resemble a private good than a fishery does.

MARKETS FOR PUBLIC GOODS

Markets for public goods exist only if nonpurchasers can be excluded from consuming them. Thus markets do not exist for nonexclusive public goods. Usually, if the government does not provide a nonexclusive public good, no one provides it.

Because computer software use is nonrivalrous, computer software is virtually a public good. At almost no extra cost, a copy of the software program that you use can be supplied to another consumer. In countries where exclusion is impossible, computer software is pirated and widely shared, so it is not profitable to produce and sell software. In countries where intellectual property rights to software are protected by preventing piracy, a company such as Microsoft can sell software (very) profitably.

Microsoft makes a fortune by selling its software at a price that is well above its marginal cost, so too few units are sold. Markets tend to produce too little of an exclusive public good because of the lack of rivalry. In the absence of rivalry, the marginal cost of providing a public good to one extra person is (essentially) zero. Firms have no incentive to produce at a zero price. If firms set a price of a public good above zero, consumers buy too little of it.

Demand for Public Goods. The demand for a private good is different from that for a public good. The social marginal benefit of a private good is the same as the marginal benefit to the individual who consumes that good. The market demand, which is the social marginal benefit curve, for private goods is the *horizontal* sum of the demand curves of each individual (Chapter 2).

In contrast, the social marginal benefit of a public good is the sum of the marginal benefit to each person who consumes the good. Because a public good lacks rivalry, many people can get pleasure from the same unit of output. As a consequence, the *social demand curve* or *willingness-to-pay curve* for a public good is the *vertical* sum of the demand curves of each individual.

We illustrate this vertical summing by deriving the demand for guard services by stores in a mall that want to discourage theft. Guards patrolling the mall provide a service without rivalry: All the stores in the mall are simultaneously protected. Each store's demand for guards reflects its marginal benefit from a reduction in thefts due to the guards. The demand curve for the television store, which stands to lose a lot if thieves strike, is D^1 in Figure 17.6. The ice-cream parlor, which loses less from a theft, demands fewer guards at any given price, D^2.

Because a guard patrolling the mall protects both stores at once, the marginal benefit to society of an additional guard is the sum of the benefit to each store. The social marginal benefit of a fifth guard, $10, is the sum of the marginal benefit to the television store, $8 (the height of D^1 at five guards per hour), and the marginal benefit to the ice-cream store, $2 (the height of D^2 at five guards per hour). Thus the social demand is the vertical sum of the individual demand curves.

A competitive market supplies as many guards as the stores want at $10 per hour per guard. At that price, the ice-cream store would not hire any guards on its own. The television store would hire four. If the stores act independently, four guards are hired at the private equilibrium, e_p. The sum of the marginal benefit to the two stores from four guards is $13, which is greater than the $10 marginal cost of an additional guard. If a fifth guard is hired, the social marginal benefit, $10, equals the marginal cost of the last guard. Thus the social equilibrium, e_s, has five guards.

The ice-cream store can get guard services without paying because the guard service is a public good. Acting alone, the television store hires fewer guards than are socially optimal because it ignores the positive externality provided to the ice-cream store, which the television store does not capture. Thus the competitive market for guard services provides too little of this public good.

Optimal Provision of a Public Good. To illustrate how to determine the socially optimal level of public goods, we use an example of a society consisting of two people with given incomes Y_1 and Y_2. For simplicity, there is one public good and one price good, and a unit of each can be purchased for $1. Each Person i contributes an amount A_i toward a public good, $A = A_1 + A_2$, and spends the remaining income on a private good, $B_i = Y_i - A_i$. Person i's utility is a function of the public good and the person's private good: $U_i(A, B_i) = U_i(A_1 + A_2, Y_i - A_i)$.

We use the Pareto concept to evaluate society's optimal policy (Chapter 10). Any reallocation that increases one person's utility while holding the other person's utility constant is Pareto superior. Thus to allocate resources efficiently, society chooses A_1

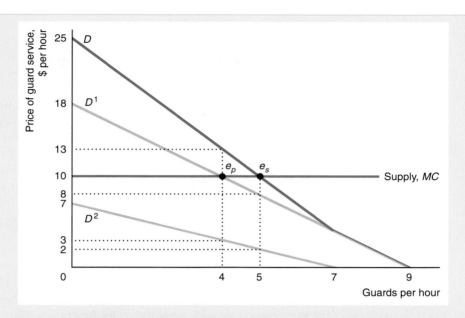

Figure 17.6 Inadequate Provision of a Public Good. Security guards protect both tenants of the mall. If each guard costs $10 per hour, the television store, with demand D^1, is willing to hire four guards per hour. The ice-cream parlor, with demand D^2, is not willing to hire any guards. Thus if everyone acts independently, the equilibrium is e_p. The social demand for this public good is the vertical sum of the individual demand curves, D. Thus the social optimum is e_s, at which five guards are hired.

and A_2 to maximize Person 1's utility while holding Person 2's utility at a given level, $\overline{U}_2$ (or vice versa). The corresponding Lagrangian expression is

$$\mathscr{L} = U_1(A, B_1) + \lambda\left[U_2(A, B_2) - \overline{U}_2\right], \tag{17.1}$$

where λ is the Lagrangian multiplier. The first-order conditions are

$$\begin{aligned}
\frac{\partial \mathscr{L}}{\partial A_1} &= \frac{\partial U_1}{\partial A}\frac{\mathrm{d}A}{\mathrm{d}A_1} + \frac{\partial U_1}{\partial B_1}\frac{\mathrm{d}B_1}{\mathrm{d}A_1} + \lambda\frac{\partial U_2}{\partial A}\frac{\mathrm{d}A}{\mathrm{d}A_1} \\
&= \frac{\partial U_1}{\partial A} - \frac{\partial U_1}{\partial B_1} + \lambda\frac{\partial U_2}{\partial A} = 0,
\end{aligned} \tag{17.2}$$

and

$$\frac{\partial \mathscr{L}}{\partial A_2} = \frac{\partial U_1}{\partial A} + \lambda\frac{\partial U_2}{\partial A} - \lambda\frac{\partial U_2}{\partial B_2} = 0. \tag{17.3}$$

By subtracting Equation 17.3 from Equation 17.2, we learn that $\partial U_1/\partial B_1 = \lambda\partial U_2/\partial B_2$. Dividing Equation 17.2 by $\partial U_1/\partial B_1$ and substituting in this result, we find that

$$\frac{\partial U_1/\partial A}{\partial U_1/\partial B_1} + \frac{\partial U_2/\partial A}{\partial U_2/\partial B_2} = 1, \tag{17.4}$$

or

$$MRS_1 + MRS_2 = 1. \tag{17.5}$$

That is, the sum of the marginal rates of substitution of all the members of society equals one.

In Chapter 3, we learned that an individual chooses a bundle of two goods so as to equate the consumer's marginal rate of substitution between the goods with the marginal rate of transformation in the market. Here the marginal rate of transformation between the public good and a private good is one: You can trade one unit of the public good for one unit of the private good. With a public good, instead of equating one person's marginal rate of substitution with the marginal rate of transformation, we equate the sum of the marginal rates of substitution for the two people with the marginal rate of transformation. Because both people suffer if one person contributes less to the public good, society's marginal rate of substitution must reflect how much of the public good all members of society are willing to give up for one more unit of the private good.

In general, there are many combinations of A, B_1, and B_2 that are consistent with Equation 17.5. However, for one utility function, we can solve for a unique quantity of the public good. If each person's utility function is $U_i(A) + B_i$, then Equation 17.5 becomes $\partial U_1(A)/\partial A + \partial U_2(A)/\partial A = 1$. Here the optimal amount of the public good is independent of the level of the private good, and consequently, we can solve this expression for a unique quantity of A independent of the private goods.

FREE RIDING

Unfortunately, society can rarely get individuals to contribute the optimal amounts toward a public good. Many people are unwilling to pay for their share of a public good. They try to get others to pay for it so that they can **free ride**: benefit from the actions of others without paying. That is, they want to benefit from a positive externality.

To illustrate the problem of free riding, we examine a game between two stores in a mall that are deciding whether to hire one guard or none. (For now, we assume that hiring two guards does no more good than hiring one.) The cost of hiring a guard is $10 per hour. The benefit to each store is $8. Because the collective benefit, $16, is greater than the cost of hiring a guard, the optimal solution is to hire the guard.

If the stores act independently, however, they do not achieve this optimal solution. Table 17.4 shows two games. In panel a, each store acts independently and pays $10 to hire a guard on its own or does not hire a guard. If both decide to hire a guard, two guards are hired, but the benefit is still only $8 per store.

In panel b, the stores split the cost of a guard if both firms agree to hire one. If only one firm wants to hire the guard, it must bear the full cost.

In each of these games, the Nash equilibrium is for neither store to hire a guard because of free riding. Each store has a dominant strategy. Regardless of what the other store does, each store is always as well off or better off not to hire a guard. The nonoptimal outcome occurs for the same reason as in other prisoners' dilemma games (Chapter 14): When the stores act independently, they don't do what is best for them collectively.

TABLE 17.4   Private Payments for a Public Good

(a) Stores Decide Independently Whether to Hire a Guard

		Television Store			
		Hire		Do Not Hire	
Stereo Store	Hire	−$2	−$2	−$2	$8
	Do Not Hire	$8	−$2	$0	$0

(b) Stores Voting to Hire a Guard Split the Cost

		Television Store			
		Hire		Do Not Hire	
Stereo Store	Hire	$3	$3	−$2	$8
	Do Not Hire	$8	−$2	$0	$0

Free Riding on Water

Water is a private good for most households in Perth, Australia: They can consume it only if they pay the price for each unit. Others can be excluded from consuming the water because each household's consumption is individually metered. However, about 10% of households share meters with one or more other households. Households in duplexes or apartments are likely to share meters. Perth's 20,545 flats have 1,800 meters between them, so on average, 11 households share each meter. Most group-metered households apportion the total bill equally among households.

How would you expect water consumption to vary between individually and collectively metered households? Because of free riding, you might expect households with individual meters to consume less water than households that draw from a common pool. Each member of the common pool has an incentive to free ride on the remaining members. As the household consumes a little more water, it receives all of the marginal benefits but has to pay only $1/n$ fraction of the marginal cost, where there are n households on a meter.

Moreover, you might expect that the incentive to free ride increases with the number of households sharing a meter. Not only is each household's share of the marginal cost smaller, but each household faces less effective social pressure to keep its free riding under control.

Grossman, Pirozzi, and Pope (1993) confirmed these predictions. They found that collectively metered households consume 17% more water on average than households with private meters do.

The extra water consumption rises with the number of households sharing a meter. A household in a two-family duplex consumes only 0.05 kiloliter more per year than an individually metered household. Even a household in a block of 10 housing units consumes only 1.3 kiloliters more. However, when the number in a housing block reaches 222 members (the largest in the sample), an extra household averages 640 extra kiloliters of water consumption.

REDUCING FREE RIDING

Governmental or other collective actions can reduce free riding. Methods that might be used include social pressure, mergers, compulsion, and privatization.

Sometimes, especially when the group is small, *social pressure* eliminates free riding. Social pressure results in at least minimal provision of some public goods. Such pressure may cause most firms at a mall to contribute "voluntarily" to a fund to hire security guards.

A direct way to eliminate free riding by firms is for them to *merge* into a single firm and thereby internalize the positive externality. The sum of the benefit to the individual stores equals the benefit to the single merged firm, so an optimal decision is made to hire guards.

If the independent stores sign a contract that requires them to share the cost of the guards, they achieve the practical advantage from a merger. However, the question of why they would agree to sign the contract remains, given the prisoners' dilemma problem. One explanation is that firms are more likely to cooperate in a repeated prisoners' dilemma game (Chapter 14).

Another way to overcome free riding is through *compulsion*. Some outside entity such as the government may dictate a solution to a free-riding problem. For example, the management of a mall with many firms may require tenants to sign a rental contract committing them to pay "taxes" that are assessed through tenants' votes. If the majority votes to hire guards, all must share the cost. Although a firm might be unwilling to pay for the guard service if it has no guarantee that others will also pay, it may vote to assess everyone—including itself—to pay for the service.

With government enforcement—a form of compulsion—milk producers avoided free-rider problems by taxing themselves to produce the "Got Milk?" advertisements. In many cities, restaurants and hotels tax themselves (or are taxed by the government) to advertise that their city is a place tourists should visit. Thus actions by a group or government may overcome the free-rider problem so that a public service is provided.

Finally, privatization—exclusion—eliminates free riding. A good that would be a public good if anyone could use it becomes a private good if access to it is restricted. An example is water, the use of which is limited by individual meters.

● **APPLICATION**

What's Their Beef?

Under federal laws, firms in many agricultural industries can solve their public goods problems by forcing all industry members to contribute to collective activities if the majority agree. Under the Beef Promotion and Research Act, all beef producers must pay a $1-per-head fee on cattle sold in the United States. The $80 million thus raised finances research, education programs on mad cow disease, and collective advertising campaigns: "Beef: It's what's for dinner." Some farmers sued to end this program, arguing that they shouldn't have to pay for ads with which they disagreed. In 2005, the U.S. Supreme Court rejected their argument, allowing cattlemen to continue this approach to solving their public goods challenge. Supporters of collective advertising estimate that producers receive $5.67 in additional marginal revenue for every dollar they contribute.

VALUING PUBLIC GOODS

To ensure that a nonexclusive public good is provided, a government usually produces it or compels others to do so. Issues that a government faces in providing such a public good include whether to provide it at all and, if so, how much to provide. To grapple with these questions, the government needs to know the cost—usually the easy part—and the value of the public good to many individuals—the hard part.

The government may try to determine through surveys or voting results the value that consumers place on the public good. One major problem with these methods is that most people do not know how much a public good is worth to them. How much would you pay to maintain the National Archives? How much does reducing air pollution improve your health? How much better do you sleep at night knowing that the Army stands ready to protect you?

Even if people know how much they value a public good, they have an incentive to lie on a survey. Those who value the good greatly and want the government to provide it may exaggerate the value of the benefit. Similarly, people who place a low value on it may report too low a value—possibly even a negative one—to discourage government action.

Rather than relying on surveys, a government may have its citizens vote directly on public goods. Suppose that a separate, majority-rule vote is held on whether to install a traffic signal—a public good—at each of several street corners. If a signal is installed, all voters are taxed equally to pay for it. An individual will vote to install a signal if the value of the signal to that voter is at least as much as the tax that each voter must pay for the signal.

Whether the majority votes for the signal depends on the preferences of the *median voter:* the person with respect to whom half the populace values the project less and half values the project more. If the median voter wants to install a signal, then at least half the voters agree, so the vote carries. Similarly, if the median voter is against the project, at least half the voters are against it, so the vote fails.

It is *efficient* to install the signal if the value of the signal to society is at least as great as its cost. Does majority voting result in efficiency? The following examples illustrate that efficiency is not ensured.

Each signal costs $300 to install. There are three voters, so each individual votes for the signal only if that person thinks that the signal is worth at least $100, which is the tax each person pays if the signal is installed. Table 17.5 shows the value that each voter places on installing a signal at each of three intersections.

For each of the proposed signals, Hayley is the median voter, so her views "determine" the outcome. If Hayley, the median voter, likes the signal, then she and Asa, a majority, vote for it. Otherwise, Nancy and Hayley vote against it. The majority favors installing a signal at corners *A* and *C* and is against doing so at corner *B*.

TABLE 17.5   Voting on $300 Traffic Signals

Signal Location	Value to Each Voter, $			Value to Society, $	Outcome of Vote*
	Nancy	Hayley	Asa		
Corner A	50	100	150	300	Yes
Corner B	50	75	250	375	No
Corner C	50	100	110	260	Yes

*An individual votes to install a signal at a particular corner if and only if that person thinks the signal is worth at least $100, the tax that the individual must pay if the signal is installed.

It would be efficient to install the signal at corner A, where the social value is $300, and at corner B, where the social value is $375, because each value equals or exceeds the cost of $300.

At corner A, the citizens vote for the signal, and that outcome is efficient. The other two votes lead to inefficient outcomes. No signal is installed at corner B, where society values the signal at more than $300, but a signal is installed at corner C, where voters value the signal at less than $300.

The problem with yes-no votes is that they ignore the intensity of preferences. A voter indicates only whether or not the project is worth more or less than a certain amount. Thus such majority voting fails to value the public good fully and hence does not guarantee that the public good is efficiently provided.[10]

---

[10]Although voting does not reveal how much a public good is worth, Tideman and Tullock (1976) and other economists have devised taxing methods that can sometimes induce people to reveal their true valuations. However, these methods are rarely used.

Summary

1. **Externalities:** An externality occurs when a consumer's well-being or a firm's production capabilities are directly affected by the actions of other consumers or firms rather than indirectly affected through changes in prices. An externality that harms others is a negative externality, and one that helps others is a positive externality. Some externalities benefit one group while harming another.

2. **The Inefficiency of Competition with Externalities:** Because producers do not pay for a negative externality such as pollution, the private costs are less than the social costs. As a consequence, competitive markets produce more negative externalities than are optimal. If the only way to cut externalities is to decrease output, the optimal solution is to set output where the marginal benefit from reducing the externality equals the marginal cost to consumers and producers from less output. It is usually optimal to have some negative externalities, because eliminating all of them requires eliminating desirable outputs and consumption activities as well. If the government has

sufficient information about demand, production cost, and the harm from the externality, it can use taxes or quotas to force the competitive market to produce the social optimum. It may tax or limit the negative externality, or it may tax or limit output.

3. **Regulating Externalities:** Governments may use emissions fees (taxes) or emissions standards to control externalities. If the government has full knowledge, it can set a fee equal to the marginal harm of the externality that causes firms to internalize the externality and produce the socially optimal output. Similarly, the government can set a standard that achieves the social optimum. However, if the government lacks full information, whether it should use a tax or fee depends on a number of factors.

4. **Market Structure and Externalities:** Although a competitive market produces excessive output and negative externalities, a noncompetitive market may produce more or less than the optimal level. With a negative externality,

a noncompetitive equilibrium may be closer than a competitive equilibrium to the social optimum. Although a fee equal to the marginal social harm of a negative externality results in the social optimum when applied to a competitive market, such a fee may lower welfare when applied to a noncompetitive market.

5. **Allocating Property Rights to Reduce Externalities:** Externalities arise because property rights are not clearly defined. According to the Coase Theorem, allocating property rights to *either* of two parties results in an efficient outcome if the parties can bargain. However, the assignment of the property rights affects income distribution because the rights are valuable. Unfortunately, bargaining is usually not practical, especially when many people are involved. In such cases, using markets for permits to produce externalities may overcome the externality problem.

6. **Open-Access Common Property:** Externalities are a problem with open-access common property, which is a resource to which everyone has free access and an equal right to exploit. Such resources are overexploited. For example, if anyone can drive on a highway, too many people are likely to do so because they ignore the externality—delays due to congestion—that they impose on others. Taxes and quotas may reduce or eliminate overuse.

7. **Public Goods:** Public goods lack rivalry. Once a public good is provided to anyone, it can be provided to others at no additional cost. Excluding anyone from consuming a public good is inefficient. Markets provide too little of a nonexclusive public good. A government faces challenges in providing the optimal amount because it is difficult to determine how much people value the public good.

Questions

*= answer at the back of this book; **W** = audio-slide show answers by James Dearden at **www.aw-bc.com/perloff**

1. Why is zero pollution not the best solution for society? Can there be too little pollution? Why or why not?

2. In 2002, Northern Victoria Australia imposed a vomit tax on pubs in the Greater Shepparton area that remain open between 3:00 A.M. and 6:00 A.M. The tax is to be used to pay for cleaning up the mess left by drunks who get sick in the street. Pub owners objected that politicians assume that hotel drinkers are responsible for the mess. Discuss the pros and cons of using such a tax to deal with this externality.

*3. In the paper market example in this chapter, what are the optimal emissions fee and the optimal tax on output (assuming that only one fee or tax is applied)?

4. In Figure 17.3, the government may optimally regulate the paper market by taxing output. Suppose that a technological change drives down the private marginal cost of production. Discuss the welfare implications if the output tax is unchanged.

5. Suppose that the only way to reduce pollution from paper production is to reduce output. The government imposes a tax on the monopoly producer that is equal to the marginal harm from the pollution. Show that the tax may raise welfare.

*6. Which allocation of property rights leads to the highest possible welfare level if the firms in Table 17.2 cannot bargain with each other?

7. Are broadcast television and cable television public goods? Is exclusion possible? If either is a public good, why is it privately provided?

8. Do publishers sell the optimal number of intermediate microeconomics textbooks? Discuss in terms of public goods, rivalry, and exclusion.

9. Analyze the following extract. Is garbage a positive or a negative externality? Why is a market solution practical here?

   Since the turn of the twentieth century, hog farmers in New Jersey fed Philadelphia garbage to their pigs. Philadelphia saved $3 million a year and reduced its garbage mound by allowing New Jersey farmers to pick up leftover food scraps for their porcine recyclers. The city paid $1.9 million to the New Jersey pig farmers for picking up the waste each year, which was about $79 a ton. Otherwise, the city would have had to pay $125 a ton for curbside recycling of the same food waste.

10. The state of Connecticut announced that commercial fleet operators would get a tax break if they converted vehicles from ozone-producing gasoline to what the state said were cleaner fuels such as natural gas and electricity. For every dollar spent on converting their fleets or building alternative fueling stations, operators could deduct 50¢ from their corporate tax. Is this approach likely to be a cost-effective way to control pollution? Explain.

11. You and your roommate have a stack of dirty dishes in the sink. Either of you would wash the dishes if the decision were up to you; however, neither will do it, in the expectation

(hope?) that the other will deal with the mess. Explain how this example illustrates the problem of public goods and free riding.

12. According to the application "Negative Externality: SUVs Kill," SUVs place other drivers at greater risk. What possible actions could the government take to reduce the negative externality generated by SUVs? Explain.

13. According to the application "Positive Externality: Michael Jordan," other teams benefited financially from having one team employ Jordan. Do such positive externalities lower social welfare? If not, why not? If so, what could the teams do to solve that problem?

14. When *Star Wars Episode III: Revenge of the Sith* opened at 12:01 A.M., Thursday, May 19, 2005, the most fanatical *Star Wars* fans stayed up until 3:00 to 4:00 A.M. and paid $50 million for tickets. Businesses around the country, especially those tied to high-tech industries, suffered reduced productivity due to absent (suffering from Darth Vader flu) or groggy workers on Thursday and Friday. By one estimate, fan loyalty cost U.S. employers as much as $627 million (Josie Roberts, *Pittsburgh Tribune-Review,* May 19, 2005). On the other hand, this sum is chicken feed compared to the estimated $890 million lost during NCAA March Madness: 16 days of virtually nonstop college basketball games (James Paton, "Hooky and Hoops—March Rituals," *Rocky Mountain News,* March 19, 2005: 3C). Are these examples of a negative externality? Explain.

15. According to the "What's Their Beef?" application, collective generic advertising produces $5.67 in additional marginal revenue for every dollar contributed by producers. Is the industry advertising optimally (see Chapter 12)? Explain your answer.

16. Guards patrolling a mall protect the mall's two stores. The television store's demand curve for guards is strictly greater at all prices than that of the ice-cream parlor. The marginal cost of a guard is $10 per hour. Use a diagram to show the equilibrium, and compare that to the socially optimal equilibrium. Now suppose that the mall's owner will provide an s-per-hour-per-guard subsidy. Show in your graph the optimal s that leads to the socially optimal outcome for the two stores.

17. To the dismay of business travelers, airlines now discretely cater to families with young children who fly first class (Katherine Rosman, "Frequent Criers," *Wall Street Journal,* May 20, 2005, W1). Suppose a family's value is $4,500 from traveling in first class and $1,500 from traveling in coach. The total price of first-class tickets for the family is $4,000. Thus the family's net value of traveling in first class is $500 = $4,500 − $4,000. Because the total price of coach tickets for the family is $1,200, the family's net value of traveling in coach is $300 = $1,500 − $1,200. A seasoned and weary business traveler who prefers to travel first class observes that a family is about to purchase first-class tickets. The business traveler quickly considers whether to offer to pay the family to fly in coach instead.

a. Suppose that the business traveler knows the value that the family places on coach and first-class travel. What is the minimum price that the traveler can offer the family not to travel in first class?

b. Suppose the business traveler values peace and quiet at $600. Will the business traveler and family reach a mutually agreeable price for the family to move to coach?

c. If instead the business traveler values peace and quiet at $200, can the business traveler and family reach a mutually agreeable price for the family to move to coach? **W**

18. In 1998, the National Highway Traffic Safety Administration distributed the film *Without Helmet Laws, We All Pay the Price.* Two reasons for this title are that some injured motorcyclists are treated at public expense (Medicaid) and that the dependents of those killed in accidents also receive public assistance.

a. Does the purchase of a motorcycle by an individual who does not wear a helmet create a negative externality? Explain.

b. If so, how should government set a no-helmet tax that would lead to a socially desirable level of motorcycle sales? **W**

*19. Suppose that the government knows the marginal cost, *MC,* curve of reducing pollution but is uncertain about the marginal benefit, *MB,* curve. With equal probability, the government faces a relatively high or a relatively low *MB* curve, so its expected *MB* curve is the same as the one in Figure 17.4. Should the government use an emissions fee or an emissions standard to maximize expected welfare? Explain. (*Hint:* Use an analysis similar to that employed in Figure 17.4.)

Problems

20. Universal Studios and Legoland California, among other theme parks, sell day passes that include line-cutting privileges for about twice the price of regular admission. Those who do not purchase the line-cutting privileges, however, are negatively affected by those who do. Perhaps your school can institute a similar policy. Suppose, for example, that Alan, Ben, and Clara are the only students who want to speak with Professor X during her office

hours. All three show up at Professor X's door at the same time and must decide who goes first, second, and third. Alan's value of being first in line is $12; second is $5; and third is $0. Ben's values are $6, $3, and $0. Clara's values are $3, $2, and $0. Being clever, the three design a game to determine the order in which they speak with Professor X. The game has prices for the first two spaces in line: $6 for being first and $2 for being second. They decide to give the proceeds to Professor X. With these prices in place, each person announces, simultaneously with the others, a place in line. If only one person announces a given slot, that person receives the slot. If two or three announce the same slot, then these two or three are randomly assigned, with equal probability, to the desired slot and the unannounced slot(s), each paying the price of his or her randomly assigned slot.

a. What is the Nash equilibrium of this game? Who purchases the right to be first?

b. What is the marginal external cost of the purchase?

c. Are the prices of the line-cutting privileges similar to a tax on the negative externality of line cutting? Explain.

d. What is the sum of each person's value on his or her place in line in the Nash equilibrium? Is there any other line order with a greater sum of values? Explain. **W**

*21. Using the algebraic equations underlying Figure 17.1, determine the social optimum if the marginal harm of gunk is $MC_g = \$84$ (that is, constant). Is there a shortcut that would allow you to solve this problem without algebra?

22. Suppose that the inverse demand curve for paper is $p = 200 - Q$, the private marginal cost (unregulated competitive market supply) is $MC^p = 80 + Q$, and the marginal harm from gunk is $MC^g = Q$.

a. What is the unregulated competitive equilibrium?

b. What is the social optimum? What specific tax (per unit of output of gunk) results in the social optimum?

c. What is the unregulated monopoly equilibrium?

d. How would you optimally regulate the monopoly? What is the resulting equilibrium?

23. Let $H = \overline{G} - G$ be the amount that gunk, G, is reduced from the competitive level, $\overline{G}$. The benefit of reducing gunk is $B(H) = AH^\alpha$. The cost is $C(H) = H^\beta$. If the benefit is increasing but at a diminishing rate as H increases, and the cost is rising at an increasing rate, what are the possible ranges of values for A, α, and B?

24. Applying the model in Problem 23, use calculus to determine the optimal level of H.

25. Two tenants of a mall are protected by the guard service, q. The number of guards per hour demanded by the television store is $q_1 = a_1 + b_1 p$, where p is the price of one hour of guard services. The ice-cream store's demand is $q_2 = a_2 + b_2 p$. What is the social demand for this service?

26. In the analysis of the optimal level of a public good, suppose that each person's utility function is $U_i = A^{a_i} B_i$. Solve for the optimal G as a function of B_1 and B_2.

27. There are 240 automobile drivers per minute who are considering using the EZ Pass lanes of the Interstate 78 toll bridge over the Delaware River that connects Easton, Pennsylvania and Phillipsburg, New Jersey. With that many autos, and a 5 mph speed restriction through the EZ Pass sensors, there is congestion. We can divide the drivers of these cars into groups A, B, C, and D. Each group has 60 drivers. Each driver in Group i has the following value of crossing the bridge: v_i if 60 or fewer autos cross, $v_i - 1$ if between 61 and 120 autos cross, $v_i - 2$ if between 121 and 180 cross, and $v_i - 3$ if more than 180 cross. Suppose $v_A = \$4$, $v_B = \$3$, $v_C = \$2$ and $v_D = \$1$. The marginal cost of crossing the bridge, not including the marginal cost of congestion, is zero.

a. If the price of crossing equals a driver's marginal private cost—the price in a competitive market—how many cars per minute will cross? Which groups will cross?

b. In the social optimum, which groups of drivers will cross? That is, which collection of groups crossing will maximize the sum of the drivers' utilities? **W**

28. Anna and Bess are assigned to write a joint paper within a 24-hour period about the Pareto optimal provision of public goods. Let t_A denote the number of hours that Anna contributes to the project and t_B the number of hours that Bess contributes. The numeric grade that Anna and Bess earn is a function, $23 \ln(t_A + t_B)$, of the total number of hours that they contribute to the project. If Anna contributes t_A, then she has $(24 - t_A)$ hours in the day for leisure. Anna's utility function is $U_A = 23 \ln(t_A + t_B) + \ln(24 - t_A)$; and Bess's utility function is $U_B = 23 \ln(t_A + t_B) + \ln(24 - t_B)$. If they choose the hours to contribute simultaneously and independently, what is the Nash equilibrium number of hours that each will provide? What is the number of hours each should contribute to the project that maximizes the sum of their utilities? **W**

Chapter 18

Asymmetric Information

The buyer needs a hundred eyes, the seller not one. —George Herbert (1651)

So far we've examined models in which everyone is equally knowledgeable or equally ignorant. In the competitive model, everyone knows all relevant facts. In the uncertainty models in Chapter 16, the companies that sell insurance and the people who buy it are equally uncertain about future events. In contrast, in this chapter's models, people have **asymmetric information**: One party to a transaction knows a material fact that the other party does not. For example, the seller knows the quality of a product and the buyer does not.

The more-informed party may exploit the less-informed party. That is, the informed party may engage in **opportunistic behavior**: taking advantage of someone when circumstances permit. Such *opportunistic behavior* due to asymmetric information leads to market failures, and destroys many desirable properties of competitive markets. In a competitive market in which everyone has full information, consumers can buy whatever quality good they want at its marginal cost. In contrast, when firms have information that consumers lack—when information is asymmetric—firms may sell only the lowest-quality good, the price may be above marginal cost, or other problems may occur.

If consumers do not know the quality of a good they are considering buying, some firms may try to sell them a dud at the price of a superior good. However, knowing that the chance of buying schlock is high, consumers may be unwilling to pay much for goods of unknown quality. As a result, firms that make high-quality products may not be able to sell them at prices anywhere near their cost of production. In other words, *bad products drive good products out of the market*. The market failure is that the market for a good-quality product is reduced or eliminated, even though (knowledgeable) consumers value the high-quality product at more than the cost of producing it.

If consumers (unlike sellers) do not know how prices vary across firms, *firms may gain market power and set prices above marginal cost*. Suppose that you go to Store A to buy a television set. If you know that Store B is charging $299 for that set, you are willing to pay Store A at most $299 (or perhaps a little more to avoid having to go to Store B). *Knowledge is power*. However, if you don't know Store B's price for that set, Store A might sell you a television for much more than $299. *Ignorance costs*.

Market failures due to asymmetric information can be eliminated if consumers can inexpensively determine the quality of a product or learn the prices that various stores charge. In many markets, however, obtaining this information is prohibitively expensive.

In this chapter, we examine five main topics	
	1. **Problems Due to Asymmetric Information:** Informed people take advantage of uninformed people.
	2. **Responses to Adverse Selection:** To reduce the harms from adverse selection—an informed person's benefiting from trading with an uninformed person who does not know about a characteristic of the informed person—government actions or contracts

between involved parties may be used to prevent opportunistic behavior, or the information asymmetry may be reduced or eliminated.

3. **How Ignorance About Quality Drives Out High-Quality Goods:** If consumers cannot distinguish between good and bad products before purchase, it is possible that only bad products will be sold.

4. **Market Power from Price Ignorance:** Consumers' ignorance about the price that each firm charges gives firms market power.

5. **Problems Arising from Ignorance when Hiring:** Attempts to eliminate information asymmetries in hiring may raise or lower social welfare.

18.1 Problems Due to Asymmetric Information

When both parties to a transaction have equally limited information, neither has an advantage over the other. If a roadside vendor sells a box of oranges to a passing motorist and neither person knows the quality of the oranges, neither has an advantage because both are operating with equal uncertainty.

In contrast, asymmetric information leads to problems of *opportunism,* whereby the informed person benefits at the expense of the person with less information. If only the vendor knows that the oranges are of low quality, the vendor may allege that the oranges are of high quality and charge a premium price for them.

The two major types of opportunistic behavior are *adverse selection* and *moral hazard*. **Adverse selection** is opportunism characterized by an informed person's benefiting from trading or otherwise contracting with a less-informed person who does not know about an *unobserved characteristic* of the informed person. For example, people who buy life insurance policies are better informed about their own health than insurance companies are. If an insurance company offers to insure people against death for 10 years at a fixed rate, a disproportionately large share of unhealthy people will buy this policy. Because of this adverse selection, the insurance company will pay off on more policies than it would pay if healthy and unhealthy people bought the policy in proportion to their share in the population.

Similarly, if one firm starts offering an unusually generous maternity leave to mothers of newborn children, a disproportionate number of women planning to become mothers in the near future will apply for employment with that firm. The intention to have children is known to potential employees but not to the firm. As a result, the cost of this benefit is greater to the firm than its cost would be if the employees were a random sample of the entire population.

Adverse selection creates a market failure by reducing the size of a market or eliminating it, thereby preventing desirable transactions. Insurance companies have to charge higher rates for insurance due to adverse selection or choose not to offer insurance at all. Very few older people, regardless of their state of health, buy term life insurance, because the rates are extremely high due to adverse selection. A parental leave benefit's higher cost due to adverse selection may discourage firms from offering the benefit, a decision that hurts both employees who are new parents (because they lose the benefit) and the firm (because it cannot use a benefit that would otherwise allow it to pay a lower wage).

Moral hazard is opportunism characterized by an informed person's taking advantage of a less-informed person through an *unobserved action*. An employee may *shirk*—fail to fulfill job responsibilities—if not monitored by the employer. Similarly, insured people tend to take unobserved actions—engage in risky behaviors—that increase the probability of large claims against insurance companies, or they fail to take reasonable precautions that would reduce the likelihood of such claims. An insured homeowner may fail to remove fire hazards such as piles of old newspapers. Some insured motorists drive more recklessly than they would without insurance. Moral hazards such as shirking, failure to take care, and reckless behavior reduce output or increase accidents, which are market failures that harm society.

The distinction between adverse selection and moral hazard—between unobserved characteristics and unobserved actions—is not always simple. A life insurance company may face unusually high risks if it insures George and Marge, who, unknown to the company, skydive. George will skydive whether or not he has life insurance. Knowing the risks of skydiving, he's more likely to buy life insurance than other, similar people are. His unobserved characteristic—his love of plunging toward the earth at high speed—leads to adverse selection. Marge will skydive only if she has life insurance. Her unobserved action is a moral hazard for the insurance company.

This chapter focuses on adverse selection and unobserved characteristics. We identify the problems that arise from adverse selection and discuss how they can sometimes be solved. Chapter 19 concentrates on moral hazard problems due to unobserved actions and on the use of contracts to deal with them.

● APPLICATION

Removing Pounds or Dollars?

Many firms advertise that they can help people lose weight—lots and lots of weight. Often these firms all but promise certain results. If you go to the Web sites of some well-known diet plans, you'll "learn" that "Medifast helps you lose up to 20 pounds in one month without shopping, cooking or counting" and that Optifast's program has been the subject of "[o]ver 80 studies published in recognized medical journals" and that "follow-up studies five years after treatment show the majority of people who complete the program are able to keep enough weight off to improve their health long-term."

According to a 2005 study in the *Annals of Internal Medicine,* none of these cited studies is based on proper randomized trials, and losing weight in these diet programs is anything but ensured. The researchers concluded that, with the exception of Weight Watchers, no commercial program has published reliable data from randomized trials showing that people who used their services weighed less a few months later than people who did not participate. Moreover, in the Weight Watchers' study, people lost only 5% after three to six months of dieting, much of which they regained.

Most independent studies find that people on very-low-calorie diets weigh about the same a year later as people on conventional diets. In addition, the commercial firms have high dropout rates (nearly half quit Optifast within 26 weeks).

Presumably, if consumers knew as much as the firms know about their abysmal success rates, few would sign on the dotted line—particularly given how much many firms charge. Although Weight Watchers' rate for three months is only $167, Medifast charges $840, Jenny Craig's fee is $1,249, Optifast goes for $1,800–$2,000, and Health Management Resources charges $1,700–$2,100.

The weight-loss business is definitely one of buyer beware! The FTC brought approximately 90 enforcement actions for false or deceptive weight-loss advertisements or claims between 1990 and 2002 and apparently never lost a case. In early 2007, the FTC levied large fines against four diet pill firms for making undocumented claims of weight loss.

18.2 Responses to Adverse Selection

The two main methods for solving adverse selection problems are to *restrict opportunistic behavior* and to *equalize information*. Responses to adverse selection problems increase welfare in some markets, but they may do more harm than good in others.

CONTROLLING OPPORTUNISTIC BEHAVIOR THROUGH UNIVERSAL COVERAGE

Adverse selection can be prevented if informed people have no choice. For example, a government can avoid adverse selection by providing insurance to everyone or by mandating that everyone buy insurance. Many states require that every driver carry auto insurance. They thereby reduce the adverse selection that would arise from having a disproportionate number of bad drivers buy insurance.

Similarly, firms often provide mandatory health insurance to all employees as a benefit, rather than paying a higher wage and letting employees decide whether to buy such insurance on their own. By doing so, firms reduce adverse selection problems for their insurance carriers: Both healthy and unhealthy people are covered. As a result, firms can buy medical insurance for their workers at a lower cost per person than workers could obtain on their own (because relatively more unhealthy individuals buy insurance).

EQUALIZING INFORMATION

Either informed or uninformed parties can eliminate information asymmetries. **Screening** is an action taken by an uninformed person to determine the information possessed by informed people. For example, a buyer may test-drive (screen) several used cars to determine which one starts and handles the best. **Signaling** is an action taken by an informed person to send information to a less-informed person. A firm may send a signal—such as by widely distributing a favorable report on its product by an independent testing agency—to try to convince buyers that its product is of high quality. In some markets, government agencies or nonprofit organizations such as Consumers Union also provide consumers with information.

"Good—very good! You qualify for our dental plan with no deductible whatsoever!"

Screening. Uninformed people may try to eliminate their disadvantage by screening to gather information on the hidden characteristics of informed people. If the originally uninformed people obtain better information, they may refuse to sign a contract or insist on changes in contract clauses or in the price of a good.

Insurance companies try to reduce adverse selection problems by learning the health history of their potential customers—for example, by requiring medical exams. A life insurance company uses such information to better estimate the probability that it will have to pay off on a policy. The firm can then decide not to insure high-risk individuals or can charge high-risk people a higher premium as compensation for the extra risk.

It is costly to collect information on how healthy a person is and on whether that individual has dangerous habits (such as smoking or drinking). As a result, insurance companies collect information only up to the point at which the marginal benefit from extra information equals the marginal cost of obtaining it. Over time, insurance companies have increasingly concluded that it pays to collect information about whether individuals exercise, have a family history of dying young, or engage in potentially life-threatening activities. If individuals but not insurance companies know about these characteristics, individuals can better predict whether they'll die young, and adverse selection occurs.

APPLICATION

Risky Hobbies

To reduce the risk of adverse selection, life insurance companies no longer rely solely on information about age and general health in determining risk. They now

also look into individuals' smoking and drinking habits, occupations, and even their hobbies. Indeed, some hobbies or activities greatly affect the probability that an individual will die from an accident. Various sports add $100 to $2,500 in annual premiums for each $100,000 of life insurance.

Steve Potter, a 40-year-old managing director at an executive recruiting firm, prepared to climb Mount Everest by buying a $2 million life insurance policy. His firm took out an additional $1 million on his life. Although Prudential Insurance Company of America would offer a typical healthy 40-year-old a $1 million policy for $1,000, the company wanted $6,000 to cover the adventurous Mr. Potter.

Signaling. Signaling is used primarily by informed parties to try to eliminate adverse selection. If a buyer cannot tell a high-quality good or service from one of low quality, the buyer is unwilling to pay top dollar for the better good. Informed sellers of better goods and services may signal to potential buyers that their products are of high quality.

Likewise, potential employees use a variety of signals to convince firms of their abilities. For a job interview, serious candidates arrive on time, dress appropriately, don't chew gum, document their training and achievements, and show that they worked for long periods at other firms. Similarly, an applicant for life insurance could have a physical examination and then present an insurance company with a written statement from the doctor to signal the applicant's good health.

Only people who believe they can show that they are better than others want to send a signal. Moreover, signaling solves an information problem only if the signals are accurate. For example, if it is easy for people to find an unscrupulous doctor who will report falsely that they are in good health, insurance companies won't rely on such signals. Here screening may work better, and the insurance firms may require that potential customers go to a designated doctor for a checkup.

18.3 | How Ignorance About Quality Drives Out High-Quality Goods

We now examine markets in which asymmetric information causes major problems due to adverse selection. In most of these situations, buyers know less than sellers.

Consumers often have trouble determining the quality of goods and services. Most people don't know how to judge the abilities of a professional such as a doctor, a lawyer, a plumber, an electrician, or an economist. Many of us have no reliable information about whether the processed foods we eat are safe or whether it's safer to fly in a Boeing 747 or in an Airbus 380.

Consumer ignorance about quality leads to a less-efficient use of resources than would occur if everyone had perfect information. In this section, we first examine how limited consumer information leads to adverse selection. We demonstrate that adverse selection occurs whether or not a seller can alter the quality of the good. We then consider how to ameliorate—though not necessarily eliminate—the adverse selection problem.

LEMONS MARKET WITH FIXED QUALITY

Anagram for General Motors: or great lemons

When buyers cannot judge a product's quality before purchasing it, low-quality products—*lemons*—may drive high-quality products out of the market (Akerlof, 1970). This situation is common in used-car markets: Owners of lemons are more likely than owners of high-quality vehicles to sell their cars, creating an adverse selection problem.

Cars that appear to be identical on the outside often differ substantially in the number of repairs they will need. Cars that are lemons are cursed. They have a variety of insidious problems that become apparent to the owner only after the car has been driven for a while. In contrast, the seller of a used car knows from experience whether the car is a lemon. We assume that the seller cannot alter the quality of the used car—at least not practically.

Suppose that there are many potential buyers for used cars. All are willing to pay $1,000 for a lemon and $2,000 for a good used car: The demand curve for lemons, D^L, is horizontal at $1,000 in panel a of Figure 18.1, and the demand curve for good cars, D^G, is horizontal at $2,000 in panel b.

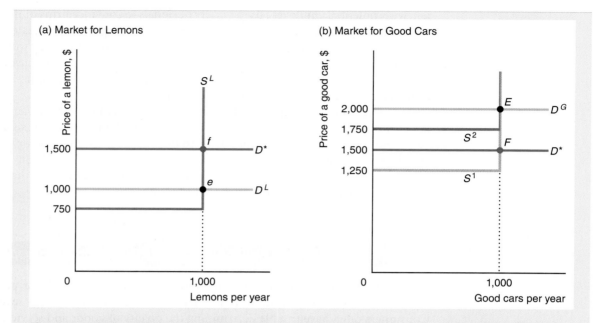

Figure 18.1 Markets for Lemons and Good Cars. If everyone has full information, the equilibrium in the lemons market is e (1,000 cars sold for $1,000 each), and the equilibrium in the good-car market is E (1,000 cars sold for $2,000 each). If buyers can't tell quality before buying but assume that equal numbers of the two types of cars are for sale, their demand in both markets is D^*, which is horizontal at $1,500. If the good car owners' reservation price is $1,250, the supply curve for good cars is S^1, and 1,000 good cars (point F) and 1,000 lemons (point f) sell for $1,500 each. If their reservation price is $1,750, the supply curve is S^2. No good cars are sold, but 1,000 lemons sell for $1,000 each (point e).

Although the number of potential buyers is virtually unlimited, only 1,000 owners of lemons and 1,000 owners of good cars are willing to sell. The *reservation price* of owners of lemons—the lowest price at which they will sell their cars—is $750. Consequently, the supply curve for lemons, S^L in panel a, is horizontal at $750 up to 1,000 cars, where it becomes vertical (no more cars are for sale at any price). The reservation price of owners of high-quality used cars is v, which is less than $2,000. Panel b shows two possible values of v. If $v = \$1,250$, the supply curve for good cars, S^1, is horizontal at $1,250 up to 1,000 cars and then becomes vertical. If $v = \$1,750$, the supply curve is S^2.

Symmetric Information. If both sellers and buyers know the quality of all used cars before any sales take place, all the cars are sold, and good cars sell for more than lemons. In panel a of Figure 18.1, the intersection of the lemons' demand curve D^L and the lemons' supply curve S^L determines the equilibrium at e in the lemons market, where 1,000 lemons sell for $1,000 each. Regardless of whether the supply curve for good cars is S^1 or S^2 in panel b, the equilibrium in the good-car market is E, where 1,000 good cars sell for $2,000 each.

This market is efficient because the goods go to the people who value them the most. All current owners, who value the cars less than the potential buyers, sell their cars.

More generally, all buyers and sellers may have symmetric information by being equally informed or equally uninformed. *All the cars are sold if everyone has the same information.* It does not matter whether they all have full information or all lack information—it's the equality of information that matters. However, *the amount of information they have affects the price at which the cars sell.* With full information, good cars sell for $2,000 and lemons sell for $1,000.

If no one can tell a lemon from a good car at the time of purchase, both types of cars sell for the same price. Suppose that everyone is risk neutral (Chapter 16) and that no one can identify the lemons: Buyers *and* sellers are equally ignorant. A buyer has an equal chance of buying a lemon or a good car. The expected value (Chapter 16) of a used car is

$$\$1,500 = (\tfrac{1}{2} \times \$1,000) + (\tfrac{1}{2} \times \$2,000).$$

A risk-neutral buyer would pay $1,500 for a car of unknown quality. Because sellers cannot distinguish between the cars either, sellers accept this amount and sell all the cars.[1] Thus this market is efficient because the cars go to people who value them more than their original owners did.

Sellers of good-quality cars are implicitly subsidizing sellers of lemons. If only lemons were sold, they would sell for $1,000. The presence of good-quality cars raises the price received by sellers of lemons. Similarly, if only good cars were sold, their owners would obtain $2,000. The presence of lemons lowers the price that sellers of good cars receive.

Asymmetric Information. If sellers know the quality but buyers do not, this market may be inefficient: The better-quality cars may not be sold even though buyers value good cars more than sellers do. The equilibrium in this market depends on whether the value that the owners of good cars place on their cars, v, is greater or less than the expected value of buyers, $1,500. *There are two possible equilibria: All cars sell at the average price, or only lemons sell for a price equal to the value that buyers place on lemons.*

Initially, we assume that the sellers of good cars value their cars at $v = \$1,250$, which is less than the buyers' expected value of the cars, so transactions can occur. The equilibrium in the good-car market is determined by the intersection of S^1 and D^* at point F, where 1,000 good cars sell at $1,500. Similarly, owners of lemons, who value their cars at only $750, are very happy to sell them for $1,500 each. The new equilibrium in the lemons market is f.

Thus all cars sell at the same price. Consequently, *asymmetric information does not cause an efficiency problem, but it does have equity implications.* Sellers of lemons benefit and sellers of good cars suffer from consumers' inability to distinguish quality. Consumers who buy the good cars get a bargain, and buyers of lemons are left with a sour taste in their mouths.

Now suppose that the sellers of good cars place a value of $v = \$1,750$ on their cars and thus are unwilling to sell them for $1,500. As a result, the *lemons drive good cars out of the market.* Buyers realize that, at any price lower than $1,750, they can buy only lemons. Consequently, in equilibrium, the 1,000 lemons sell for the expected (and

---

[1]Risk-neutral sellers place an expected value of $\left(\tfrac{1}{2} \times \$750\right) + \tfrac{1}{2}v = \$375 + \tfrac{1}{2}v < \$1,375$ (because $v < \$2,000$) on a car of unknown quality, so they are willing to sell their cars for $1,500.

actual) price of $1,000, and no good cars change hands. This equilibrium is inefficient because high-quality cars remain in the hands of people who value them less than potential buyers do.

In summary, if buyers have less information about product quality than sellers do, the result might be a lemons problem in which high-quality cars do not sell, even though potential buyers value the cars more than their current owners do. If so, the asymmetric information causes a competitive market to lose its desirable efficiency and welfare properties. However, if the information is symmetric, the lemons problem does not occur. That is, if buyers and sellers of used cars know the quality of the cars, each car sells for its true value in a perfectly competitive market. Moreover, if, as with new cars, neither buyers nor sellers can identify lemons, both good cars and lemons sell at a price equal to the expected value rather than at their (unknown) true values.

SOLVED PROBLEM   18.1

Suppose that everyone in our used-car example is risk neutral; potential car buyers value lemons at $1,000 and good used cars at $2,000; the reservation price of lemon owners is $750; and the reservation price of owners of high-quality used cars is $1,750. The share of current owners who have lemons is θ [in our previous example, the share was $\theta = \frac{1}{2} = 1,000/(1,000 + 1,000)$]. For what values of θ do all the potential sellers sell their used cars? Describe the equilibrium.

Answer

1. *Determine how much buyers are willing to pay if all cars are sold:* Because buyers are risk neutral, if they believe that the probability of getting a lemon is θ, the most they are willing to pay for a car of unknown quality is

$$p = [\$2,000 \times (1 - \theta)] + (\$1,000 \times \theta) = \$2,000 - (\$1,000 \times \theta). \quad (18.1)$$

For example, $p = \$1,500$ if $\theta = \frac{1}{2}$ and $p = \$1,750$ if $\theta = \frac{1}{4}$.

2. *Solve for the values of θ such that all the cars are sold, and describe the equilibrium:* All owners will sell if the market price equals or exceeds their reservation price, $1,750. Using Equation 18.1, we know that the market (equilibrium) price is $1,750 or more if a quarter or fewer of the used cars are lemons, $\theta \leq \frac{1}{4}$. Thus for $\theta \leq \frac{1}{4}$, all the cars are sold at the price given in Equation 18.1.

LEMONS MARKET WITH VARIABLE QUALITY

Many firms can vary the quality of their products. If consumers cannot identify high-quality goods before purchase, they pay the same for all goods regardless of quality. Because the price that firms receive for top-quality goods is the same as what they receive for schlock, they do not produce top-quality goods. Such an outcome is inefficient if consumers are willing to pay sufficiently more for top-quality goods.

This unwillingness to produce high-quality products is due to an externality: *A firm does not completely capture the benefits from raising the quality of its product.* By selling a better product than what other firms offer, a seller raises the average quality in the market, so buyers are willing to pay more for all products. As a result, the high-quality seller shares the benefits from its high-quality product with sellers of low-quality products by raising the average price of all products. *The social value of raising the quality*, as reflected by the increased revenues shared by all firms, *is greater than the private value*, which is the higher revenue received by only the firm with the good product.

Suppose that it costs $10 to produce a low-quality book bag and $20 to produce a high-quality bag; consumers cannot distinguish between the products before purchase; there are no repeat purchases; and consumers value the bags at their cost of production. The five firms in the market produce 100 bags each. A firm produces only high-quality or only low-quality bags.

If all five firms make a low-quality bag, consumers pay $10 per bag. If one firm makes a high-quality bag and all the others make low-quality bags, the expected value per bag to consumers is

$$\$12 = (\$10 \times \tfrac{4}{5}) + (\$20 \times \tfrac{1}{5}).$$

Thus if one firm raises the quality of its product, all firms benefit because the bags sell for $12 instead of $10. The high-quality firm receives only a fraction of the total benefit from raising quality. It gets $2 extra per high-quality bag sold, which is less than the extra $10 it costs to make the better bag. The other $8 is shared by the other firms. Because the high-quality firm incurs all the expenses of raising quality, $10 extra per bag, and reaps only a fraction, $2, of the benefits, it opts not to produce the high-quality bags. Thus *due to asymmetric information, the firms do not produce high-quality goods, even though consumers are willing to pay for the extra quality.*

LIMITING LEMONS

In some markets, it is possible to avoid problems stemming from consumer ignorance. Laws might provide protection against being sold a lemon, consumers might screen by collecting the information themselves, the government or another third party might supply reliable information, or sellers might send credible signals.

Laws to Prevent Opportunism. Product liability laws protect consumers from being stuck with nonfunctional or dangerous products. Moreover, many state supreme courts have concluded that products are sold with an implicit understanding that they will safely perform their intended functions. If they do not, consumers can sue the seller even in the absence of product liability laws. If consumers can rely on explicit or implicit product liability laws to force a manufacturer to make good on defective products, they need not worry about adverse selection.

An inherent problem with legal recourse, however, is that the transaction costs of going to court are very high. See **www.aw-bc.com/perloff**, Chapter 18, "Recycling Lemons," on laws in various countries that protect consumers with respect to cars that are lemons.

Consumer Screening. Consumers can avoid the lemons problem if they can obtain reliable information about quality (screen). When a consumer's cost of securing information is less than the private benefits, consumers obtain the information and markets function smoothly. However, if the cost exceeds the benefit, consumers do not gather the information and the market is inefficient. Consumers buy information from experts or infer product quality from sellers' reputations.

For many goods, consumers can buy reliable information from *objective experts*. For example, you can pay to have a mechanic appraise a used car. If the mechanic can reliably determine whether the car is a lemon, the information asymmetry is eliminated.

In some markets, consumers learn of a firm's *reputation* from other consumers or from observation. Consumers can avoid the adverse selection problem by buying only from firms that have reputations for providing high-quality goods. Consumers know that a used-car firm that expects repeat purchases has a strong incentive not to sell defective products.

Generally, in markets in which the same consumers and firms trade regularly, a reputation is easy to establish. In markets in which consumers buy a good only once, such as in tourist areas, firms cannot establish reputations as easily.

Third-Party Comparisons. Some nonprofit organizations, such as consumer groups, and for-profit firms publish expert comparisons of brands. To the degree that this information is credible, it may reduce adverse selection by enabling consumers to avoid buying low-quality goods.

If an outside organization is to provide believable information, it must convince consumers that it is trustworthy and is not deceiving them. Consumers Union, which publishes the product evaluation guide *Consumer Reports,* tries to establish its trustworthiness by refusing to accept advertising or other payments from firms.

Unfortunately, expert information is undersupplied because information is a *public good* (nonrivalrous and only sometimes exclusive—see Chapter 17). Consumers Union does not capture the full value of its information through sales of *Consumer Reports* because buyers lend their copies to friends, libraries stock the magazine, and newspapers report on its findings. As a result, Consumers Union conducts less research than is socially optimal.

Standards and Certification. The government, consumer groups, industry groups, and others provide information based on a **standard:** a metric or scale for evaluating the quality of a particular product. For example, the R-value of insulation—a standard—tells how effectively insulation works. Consumers learn of a brand's quality through **certification:** a report that a particular product meets or exceeds a given standard level.

Many industry groups set their own standards and get an outside group or firm, such as Underwriters' Laboratories (UL) or Factory Mutual Engineering Corporation (FMEC), to certify that their products meet specified standard levels. For example, setting standards for the size of the thread on a screw ensures that screws work in all products, regardless of the brand.

When standard and certification programs inexpensively and completely inform consumers about the relative quality of all goods in a market and do not restrict the goods available, the programs are socially desirable. However, some of these programs have harmful effects. Standard and certification programs that provide degraded information, for instance, may mislead consumers. Many standards use only a high- versus a low-quality rating, for example, even though quality varies continuously. Such standards encourage the manufacture of products that have either the lowest-possible quality (and cost of production) or the minimum quality level necessary to obtain the top rating.

If standard and certification programs restrict salable goods and services to those that are certified, such programs may also have anticompetitive effects. Many governments license only professionals and craftspeople who meet some minimum standards.

People without a license are not allowed to practice their profession or craft. In most states, dozens, if not hundreds, of categories of professionals, craftspeople, and others are licensed, including public school teachers, electricians, plumbers, dentists, psychologists, contractors, and beauticians.

The restrictions raise the average quality in the industry by eliminating low-quality goods and services. They drive up prices to consumers for two reasons. First, the number of people providing services is reduced because the restrictions eliminate some potential suppliers. Second, consumers are unable to obtain lower-quality and less-expensive goods or services. As a result, welfare may go up or down, depending on whether the increased-quality effect or the higher-price effect dominates. Whether such restrictions can be set properly and cost-effectively by government agencies is widely debated.

Moreover, licensing and mandatory standards and certification are often used for anticompetitive purposes such as erecting entry barriers to new firms and products. Doctors, lawyers, electricians, and other professionals establish their own licensing standards under government auspices. Frequently, these groups set standards that prevent the entry of professionals from other states or those who have just finished their education so as to keep the wages of currently licensed professionals high. Such licensing is socially harmful because it excludes qualified professionals and raises consumers' costs. (Unfortunately, economists have not been clever enough to get their profession licensed so that they can act anticompetitively to limit supply and raise their earnings.)

Signaling by Firms. Producers of high-quality goods often try to signal to consumers that their products are of better quality than their rivals' goods. If consumers believe these signals, the firms can charge higher prices for their goods. But if the signals are to be effective, they must be credible.

Firms use brand names as a signal of quality. For example, some farms brand their produce, while rivals sell their produce without labels. Shoppers may rely on this signal and choose only fruits and vegetables with brand labels. Presumably, a firm uses a brand name to enable buyers to identify its product only if the item's quality is better than that of a typical unbranded product.

Some firms provide guarantees or warranties as signals to convince consumers that their products are of high quality. Consumer durables such as cars and refrigerators commonly come with guarantees or warranties. Virtually all new cars have warranties. Moreover, one-third of used cars purchased from dealers include warranties (Genesove, 1993).

Signals prevent the adverse selection problem only when consumers view them as credible (only high-quality firms find their use profitable). Smart consumers may place little confidence in unsubstantiated claims by firms. Would you believe that a used car runs well just because an ad tells you so? Legally enforceable guarantees and warranties are more credible than advertising alone.

Signaling will not prevent an adverse selection problem if it is unprofitable for high-quality firms to signal or if both high- and low-quality firms send the same signal, thus making the signal worthless to consumers. For example, both low-quality and high-quality fruit and vegetable firms can use trademarks in tourist areas, where there are few repeat purchases. Similarly, all firms may provide guarantees for inexpensive goods, but transaction costs are usually too high for consumers to take advantage of guarantees. (See **www.aw-bc.com/perloff**, Chapter 18, "Wholesale Market for Cherries," for an example of how firms use sorting of their products to signal quality.)

Adverse Selection on eBay

When consumers buy over the Internet, they cannot directly observe quality, and shady sellers may misrepresent quality. In the worst-case lemons-market scenario, low-quality goods drive out high-quality ones. This adverse selection problem may be reduced or eliminated if warranties, brand names, and other means of establishing a reputation lower consumers' concerns about quality.

Philatelists can buy stamps at auctions on eBay or at a specialty stamps auction site, Michael Rogers, Inc. (MR). On eBay, a buyer has only the seller's description, possibly a photo, and the seller's eBay reputation, which is an index of the satisfaction of the previous trading partners. In contrast, MR takes possession of all stamps, inspects them, and provides standardized descriptions and photographic images. It also offers a 14-day refund guarantee on items if users were misled by inaccurate descriptions in their auction catalogs. Thus bidders at MR should have very little uncertainty about quality.

Dewan and Hsu (2004) compared prices on specific stamps at the two sites. They concluded that adverse selection fears reduce eBay prices by 10% to 15% of the value of the goods relative to MR. Without eBay's reputation index, the adverse selection discount would be greater. On average, a 10% increase in seller rating is associated with a 0.44% increase in auction price.

18.4   Market Power from Price Ignorance

We've just seen that consumer ignorance about quality can keep high-quality goods out of markets. We now illustrate that consumer ignorance about price variation across firms gives firms market power. As a result, firms have an incentive to make it difficult for consumers to collect information about prices. Because of this incentive, some stores won't quote prices over the phone.

In this section, we examine why asymmetric information about prices leads to non-competitive pricing in a market that would otherwise be competitive. Suppose that many stores in a town sell the same good. If consumers have *full information* about prices, all stores charge the full-information competitive price, p^*. If one store were to raise its price above p^*, the store would lose all its business. Each store faces a residual demand curve that is horizontal at the going market price and has no market power.

In contrast, if consumers have *limited information* about the price that firms charge for a product, one store can charge more than others and not lose all its customers. Customers who do not know that the product is available for less elsewhere keep buying from the high-price store.[2] Thus each store faces a downward-sloping residual demand curve and has some market power.

---

[2]A grave example concerns the ripping off of the dying and the survivors of the dead. A cremation arranged through a memorial society—which typically charges a nominal enrollment fee of $10 to $25—costs $400 to $600, compared with $1,500 to $2,000 for the same service when it is arranged through a mortuary. Consumers who know about memorial societies—which get competitive bids from mortuaries—can obtain a relatively low price. The less-knowledgeable people who deal directly with mortuaries pay more (Mary Rowland, "Shedding Light on a Dark Subject," *New York Times*, July 24, 1994:13).

TOURIST-TRAP MODEL

We now show that, if there is a single price in such a market, it is higher than p^*. Suppose you arrive in a small town near the site of the discovery of gold in California. Souvenir shops crowd the street. Wandering by one of these stores, you see that it sells the town's distinctive snowy: a plastic ball filled with water and imitation snow featuring a model of the Donner party. You instantly decide that you must buy at least one of these tasteful mementos—perhaps more if the price is low enough. Your bus will leave very soon, so you can't check the price at each shop to find the lowest price. Moreover, determining which shop has the lowest price won't be useful to you in the future because you do not intend to return anytime soon.

Let's assume that you and other tourists have a guidebook that reports how many souvenir shops charge each possible price for the snowy, but that the guidebook does not state the price at any particular shop.[3] There are many tourists in your position, each with an identical demand function.

It costs each tourist c in time and expenses to visit a shop to check the price or buy a snowy. Thus if the price is p, the cost of buying a snowy at the first shop you visit is $p + c$. If you go to two souvenir shops before buying at the second shop, the cost of the snowy is $p + 2c$.

When Price Is Not Competitive. Will all souvenir shops charge the same price? If so, what price will they charge? We start by considering whether each shop charges the full-information, competitive price, p^*.

The full-information, competitive price is the equilibrium price only if no firm has an incentive to charge a different price. No firm would charge less than p^*, which equals marginal cost, because it would lose money on each sale.

However, a shop could gain by charging a higher price than p^*, so p^* is *not* an equilibrium price. If all other shops charge p^*, a shop can profitably charge $p_1 = p^* + \varepsilon$, where ε, a small positive number, is the shop's price markup. Suppose that you walk into this shop and learn that it sells the snowy for p_1. You know from your guidebook that all the other souvenir shops charge only p^*. You say to yourself, "How unfortunate [or other words to that effect]! I've wandered into the only expensive shop in town." Annoyed, you consider going elsewhere. Nonetheless, you do not go to another shop if this first shop's markup, $\varepsilon = p_1 - p^*$, is less than c, the cost of going to another shop.

As a result, it pays for this shop to raise its price by an amount that is just slightly less than the cost of an additional search, thereby deviating from the proposed equilibrium where all other shops charge p^*. Thus *if consumers have limited information about price, an equilibrium in which all firms charge the full-information, competitive price is impossible.*

Monopoly Price. We've seen that the market price cannot be lower than or equal to the full-information, competitive price. Can there be an equilibrium in which all stores charge the same price and that price is higher than the competitive price? In particular, can we have an equilibrium when all shops charge $p_1 = p^* + \varepsilon$? No, because shops would deviate from this proposed equilibrium for the same reason that they deviated from charging the competitive price. A shop can profitably raise its price to $p_2 = p_1 + \varepsilon = p^* + 2\varepsilon$. Again, it does not pay for a tourist who is unlucky enough to enter that shop to go to another shop as long as $\varepsilon < c$. Thus p_1 is not the equilibrium price. By repeating this

---

[3]We make this assumption about the guidebook to keep the presentation as simple as possible. This assumption is not necessary to obtain the following result.

reasoning, we can reject other possible equilibrium prices that are above p^* and less than the monopoly price, p_m.

However, the monopoly price may be an equilibrium price. No firm wants to raise its price above the monopoly level because its profit would fall due to reduced sales. When tourists learn the price at a particular souvenir shop, they decide how many snowies to buy. If the price is set too high, the shop's lost sales more than offset the higher price, so its profit falls. Thus although the shop can charge a higher price without losing all its sales, it chooses not to do so.

The only remaining question is whether a shop would like to charge a lower price than p_m if all other shops charge that price. If not, p_m is an equilibrium price.

Should a shop reduce its price below p_m by less than c? If it does so, it does not pay for consumers to search for this low-price firm. The shop makes less on each sale, so its profits must fall. Thus a shop should not deviate by charging a price that is only slightly less than p_m.

Does it pay for a shop to drop its price below p_m by more than c? If there are few shops, consumers may search for this low-price shop. Although the shop makes less per sale than the high-price shops, its profits may be higher because of greater sales volume. If there are many shops, however, consumers do not search for the low-price shop because their chances of finding it are low. As a result, when the presence of a large number of shops makes searching for a low-price shop impractical, no firm lowers its price, so p_m is the equilibrium price. Thus *when consumers have asymmetric information and when search costs and the number of firms are large, the only possible single-price equilibrium is at the monopoly price.*

If the single-price equilibrium at p_m can be broken by a firm charging a low price, there is no single-price equilibrium. Either there is no equilibrium or there is an equilibrium in which prices vary across shops (see Stiglitz, 1979, or Carlton and Perloff, 2005). Multiple-price equilibria are common.

SOLVED PROBLEM 18.2

Initially, there are many souvenir shops, each of which charges p_m (because consumers do not know the shops' prices), and buyers' search costs are c. If the government pays for half of consumers' search costs, can there be a single-price equilibrium at a price less than p_m?

Answer

Show that the argument we used to reject a single-price equilibrium at any price except the monopoly price does not depend on the size of the search cost: If all other stores charge any single price p, where $p^* \le p < p_m$, a firm profits from raising its price. As long as it raises its price by no more than $c/2$ (the new cost of search to a consumer), unlucky consumers who stop at this deviant store will not search further. This profitable deviation shows that the proposed single-price equilibrium is not an equilibrium. Again, the only possible single-price equilibrium is at p_m.[4]

---

[4]If the search cost is low enough, however, the single-price equilibrium at p_m can be broken profitably by charging a low price so that only a multiple-price equilibrium is possible. If the search cost falls to zero, consumers have full information, so the only possible equilibrium is at the full-information, competitive price.

ADVERTISING AND PRICES

The U.S. Federal Trade Commission (FTC), a consumer protection agency, opposes groups that want to forbid price advertising; the FTC argues that advertising about price benefits consumers. If a firm informs consumers about its unusually low price, it may be able to gain enough extra customers to more than offset its loss from the lower price. If low-price stores advertise their prices and attract many customers, they can break the monopoly-price equilibrium that occurs when consumers must search store by store for low prices. The more successful the advertising, the larger these stores grow and the lower the average price in the market. If enough consumers become informed, all stores may charge the low price. Thus without advertising, no store may find it profitable to charge low prices, but with advertising, all stores may charge low prices. See **www.aw-bc.com/perloff**, Chapter 18, "Advertising Lowers Prices."

18.5   Problems Arising from Ignorance when Hiring

Asymmetric information is frequently a problem in labor markets. Prospective employees may have less information about working conditions than firms do. Firms may have less information about potential employees' abilities than the potential workers do.

Information asymmetries in labor markets lower welfare below the full-information level. Workers may signal and firms may screen to reduce the asymmetry in information about workers' abilities. Signaling and screening may raise or lower welfare, as we now consider.

INFORMATION ABOUT EMPLOYMENT RISKS

Firms typically have more information than workers do about job safety. This asymmetric information may lead to less-than-optimal levels of safety (Viscusi, 1979).

Prospective employees who do not know the injury rate at individual firms may know the average injury rates in an industry because these data are reported by the U.S. Bureau of Labor Statistics. People will work in a risky industry only if they are paid more than they would earn in less-risky industries.

Each firm must consider how safe to make its plant. Extra safety is costly. Safety investments—sprinkler systems, color-coded switches, fire extinguishers—made by one firm provide an externality to other firms: That firm's lower incidence of accidents reduces the wage that all firms in the industry must pay. *Because each firm bears the full cost of its safety investments but derives only some of the benefits, the firms underinvest in safety.*

The prisoners' dilemma game in Table 18.1, which is played by the only two firms in an industry, illustrates this result. In the Nash equilibrium (upper-left cell), neither firm invests and each earns $200.

An investment by only one firm raises safety levels at its plant. Workers in the industry do not know that safety has improved only at the plant of the investing firm. They realize only that it is safer to work in this industry, so both firms pay lower wages. The loss from the investment is greater than the wage savings, so the profit falls to $100 for the firm that invests. The wage savings causes its rival's profit to rise to $250.

If both firms invest (lower-right cell), both earn $225, which is more than they would earn in the Nash equilibrium. However, investment by both firms is not an equilibrium, as each firm has an incentive to deviate.

TABLE 18.1   Safety Investment Game

		Firm 2	
		No Investment	Investment
Firm 1	No Investment	$200 / $200	$250 / $100
	Investment	$100 / $250	$225 / $225

This prisoners' dilemma would not occur if workers knew how safe each firm was. Only the firm that invested in safety would be able to pay a lower wage if workers knew the accident rate of the firms. There would be no externality. Thus a firm that can credibly convince workers that it is a relatively safe place to work can overcome this asymmetric information problem.[5]

In this example, the underinvestment problem could be avoided if the government provided the information, if the government set safety standards that would force both firms to invest, or if unions effectively lobbied both firms for higher levels of safety. For the government or unions to provide these useful functions practically, however, their cost of gathering the necessary information would have to be relatively low.

CHEAP TALK

Honesty is the best policy—when there is money in it. —Mark Twain

We now consider situations in which workers have more information about their ability than firms do. We look first at inexpensive signals sent by workers, then at expensive signals sent by workers, and finally at screening by firms.

When an informed person voluntarily provides information to an uninformed person, the informed person engages in **cheap talk:** unsubstantiated claims or statements (see Farrell and Rabin, 1996). People use cheap talk to distinguish themselves or their attributes at low cost. Even though informed people may lie when it suits them, it is often in their and everyone else's best interest for them to tell the truth. Nothing stops me from advertising that I have a chimpanzee for sale, but doing so serves no purpose if I actually want to sell my DVD player. One advantage of cheap talk, if it is effective, is that it is a less-expensive method of signaling ability to a potential employer than paying to have that ability tested.

Suppose that a firm plans to hire Cyndi to do one of two jobs. The demanding job requires someone with high ability. The undemanding job can be done better by someone of low ability because the job bores more able people, who then perform poorly.

Cyndi knows whether her ability level is high or low, but the firm is unsure. It initially thinks that either level is equally likely. Panel a of Table 18.2 shows the payoffs to Cyndi and the firm under various possibilities.[6] If Cyndi has high ability, she enjoys the

---

[5]Because this information is a public good, others may obtain this information if the firm provides it to employees. The cost to the firm of having others, such as government regulators, obtain this information may exceed the lower-wage benefit from providing it to workers.

[6]Previously, we used a 2 × 2 matrix to show a simultaneous-move game (as in Table 18.1), in which both parties choose an action at the same time. In contrast, in Table 18.2, only the firm can make a move. Cyndi does not take an action, because she cannot choose her ability level.

TABLE 18.2 Employee-Employer Payoffs

(a) When Cheap Talk Works

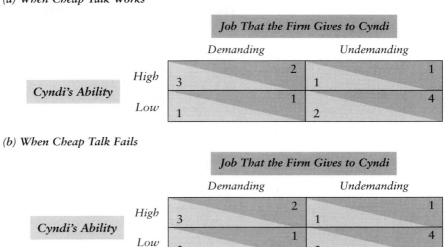

		Job That the Firm Gives to Cyndi	
		Demanding	*Undemanding*
Cyndi's Ability	*High*	3 / 2	1 / 1
	Low	1 / 1	2 / 4

(b) When Cheap Talk Fails

		Job That the Firm Gives to Cyndi	
		Demanding	*Undemanding*
Cyndi's Ability	*High*	3 / 2	1 / 1
	Low	3 / 1	2 / 4

demanding job: Her payoff is 3. If she has low ability, she finds the demanding job too stressful—her payoff is only 1—but she can handle the undemanding job. The payoff to the firm is greater if Cyndi is properly matched to the job: She is given the demanding job if she has high ability and the undemanding job if she has low ability.

We can view this example as a two-stage game. In the first stage, Cyndi tells the firm something. In the second stage, the firm decides which job she gets.

Cyndi could make many possible statements about her ability. For simplicity, though, we assume that she says either, "My ability is high" or "My ability is low." This two-stage game has an equilibrium in which Cyndi tells the truth and the firm, believing her, assigns her to the appropriate job. If she claims to have high ability, the firm gives her the demanding job.

If the firm reacts to her cheap talk in this manner, Cyndi has no incentive to lie. If she does lie, the firm would make a mistake, and a mistake would be bad for both parties. Cyndi and the firm want the same outcomes, so cheap talk works.

In many other situations, however, cheap talk does not work. Given the payoffs in panel b, Cyndi and the firm do not want the same outcomes. The firm still wants Cyndi in the demanding job if she has high ability and in the undemanding job otherwise. But Cyndi wants the demanding job regardless of her ability, so she claims to have high ability regardless of the truth. Knowing her incentives, the firm views her statement as meaningless babbling—her statement does not change the firm's view that her ability is equally likely to be high or low.

Given that belief, the firm gives her the undemanding job, for which its expected payoff is higher. The firm's expected payoff is $(\frac{1}{2} \times 1) + (\frac{1}{2} \times 4) = 2.5$ if it gives her the undemanding job and $(\frac{1}{2} \times 2) + (\frac{1}{2} \times 1) = 1.5$ if it assigns her to the demanding job. Thus given the firm's asymmetric information, the outcome is inefficient if Cyndi has high ability.

When the interests of the firm and the individual diverge, cheap talk does not provide a credible signal. Here, an individual has to send a more expensive signal to be believed. We now examine such a signal.

EDUCATION AS A SIGNAL

No doubt you've been told that one good reason to go to college is to get a good job. Going to college may get you a better job because you obtain valuable training. Another possibility is that a college degree may land you a good job because it serves as a signal to employers about your ability. If high-ability people are more likely to go to college than low-ability people, schooling signals ability to employers (Spence, 1974).

To illustrate how such signaling works, we'll make the extreme assumptions that graduating from an appropriate school serves as the signal and that schooling provides no training that is useful to firms (Stiglitz, 1975). High-ability workers are θ share of the workforce, and low-ability workers are $1 - \theta$ share. The value of output that a high-ability worker produces for a firm is worth w_h, and that of a low-ability worker is w_l (over their careers). If competitive employers knew workers' ability levels, they would pay this value of the marginal product to each worker, so a high-ability worker receives w_h and a low-ability worker earns w_l.

We assume that employers cannot directly determine a worker's skill level. For example, when production is a group effort—such as in an assembly line—a firm cannot determine the productivity of a single employee.

Two types of equilibria are possible, depending on whether or not employers can distinguish high-ability workers from others. If employers have no way of telling workers apart, the outcome is a **pooling equilibrium:** Dissimilar people are treated (paid) alike or behave alike. Employers pay all workers the average wage:

$$\overline{w} = \theta w_h + (1 - \theta)w_l. \tag{18.2}$$

Risk-neutral, competitive firms expect to break even because they underpay high-ability people by enough to offset the losses from overpaying low-ability workers.

We assume that high-ability individuals can get a degree by spending c to attend a school and that low-ability people cannot graduate from the school (or that the cost of doing so is prohibitively high). If high-ability people graduate and low-ability people do not, a degree is a signal of ability to employers. Given such a clear signal, the outcome is a **separating equilibrium:** One type of people takes actions (such as sending a signal) that allow them to be differentiated from other types of people. Here a successful signal causes high-ability workers to receive w_h and the others to receive w_l, so wages vary with ability.

We now examine whether a pooling or a separating equilibrium is possible. We consider whether anyone would want to change behavior in an equilibrium. If no one wants to change, the equilibrium is feasible.

Separating Equilibrium. In a separating equilibrium, high-ability people pay c to get a degree and are employed at a wage of w_h, while low-ability individuals do not get a degree and work for a wage of w_l. The low-ability people have no choice, because they can't get a degree. High-ability individuals have the option of not going to school. Without a degree, however, they are viewed as having low ability once they are hired, so they receive w_l. If they go to school, their net earnings are $w_h - c$. Thus it pays for a high-ability person to go to school if

$$w_h - c > w_l.$$

Rearranging terms in this expression, we find that a high-ability person chooses to get a degree if

$$w_h - w_l > c. \tag{18.3}$$

Equation 18.3 says that the benefit from graduating, the extra pay $w_h - w_l$, exceeds the cost of schooling, c. If Equation 18.3 holds, no worker wants to change behavior, so a separating equilibrium is feasible.

Suppose that $c = \$15,000$ and that high-ability workers are twice as productive as others: $w_h = \$40,000$ and $w_l = \$20,000$. Here the benefit to a high-ability worker from graduating, $w_h - w_l = \$20,000$, exceeds the cost by $\$5,000$. Thus no one wants to change behavior in this separating equilibrium.

Pooling Equilibrium. In a pooling equilibrium, all workers are paid the average wage from Equation 18.2, $\overline{w}$. Again, because low-ability people cannot graduate, they have no choice. A high-ability person must choose whether or not to go to school. Without a degree, that individual is paid the average wage. With a degree, the worker is paid w_h. It does not pay for the high-ability person to graduate if the benefit from graduating, the extra pay $w_h - \overline{w}$, is less than the cost of schooling:

$$w_h - \overline{w} < c. \tag{18.4}$$

Thus if Equation 18.4 holds, no worker wants to change behavior, so a pooling equilibrium persists.

For example, if $w_h = \$40,000$, $w_l = \$20,000$, and $\theta = \frac{1}{2}$, then

$$\overline{w} = (\tfrac{1}{2} \times \$40,000) + (\tfrac{1}{2} \times \$20,000) = \$30,000.$$

If the cost of going to school is $c = \$15,000$, the benefit to a high-ability person from graduating, $w_h - \overline{w} = \$10,000$, is less than the cost, so a high-ability individual does not want to go school. As a result, there is a pooling equilibrium.

SOLVED PROBLEM   18.3

If $c = \$15,000$, $w_h = \$40,000$, and $w_l = \$20,000$, for what values of θ is a pooling equilibrium possible?

Answer

1. *Determine the values of θ for which it pays for a high-ability person to go to school:* From Equation 18.4, we know that a high-ability individual does not go to school if $w_h - \overline{w} < c$. Using Equation 18.2, we substitute for $\overline{w}$ in Equation 18.4 and rearrange terms to find that high-ability people do not go to school if

$$w_h - [\theta w_h + (1 - \theta)w_l] < c,$$

or

$$\theta > 1 - \frac{c}{w_h - w_l}. \tag{18.5}$$

If almost everyone has high ability, so θ is large, a high-ability person does not go to school. The intuition is that, as the share of high-ability workers, θ, gets large (close to 1), the average wage approaches w_h (Equation 18.2), so there is little benefit, $w_h - \overline{w}$, in going to school.

2. *Solve for the possible values of* θ *for the specific parameters:* If we substitute $c =$ $15,000, $w_h =$ $40,000, and $w_l =$ $20,000 into Equation 18.5, we find that high-ability people do not go to school—that is, a pooling equilibrium is possible—when $\theta > \frac{1}{4}$.

Unique Equilibrium or Multiple Equilibria. Depending on differences in abilities, the cost of schooling, and the share of high-ability workers, only one type of equilibrium may be possible or both may be possible. In the following examples, using Figure 18.2, $w_h =$ $40,000 and $w_l =$ $20,000.

Only a pooling equilibrium is possible if schooling is very costly: $c > w_h - w_l =$ $20,000, so Equation 18.3 does not hold. The horizontal line in Figure 18.2 shows where $c = w_h - w_l =$ $20,000. Only a pooling equilibrium is feasible above that line, $c >$ $20,000, because it is not worthwhile for high-ability workers to go to school.

Equation 18.5 shows that, if there are few high-ability people (relative to the cost and earnings differential), only a separating equilibrium is possible. The figure shows a sloped line where $\theta = 1 - c/(w_h - w_l)$. Below that line, $\theta < 1 - c/(w_h - w_l)$, relatively few people have high ability, so the average wage, $\overline{w}$, is low. A pooling equilibrium is

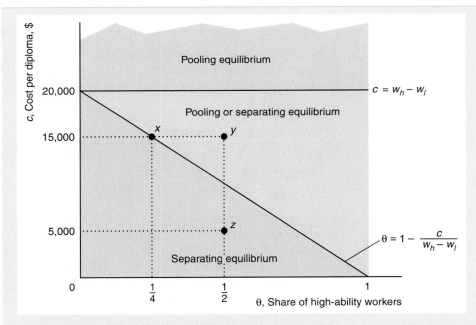

Figure 18.2 Pooling and Separating Equilibria. If firms know workers' abilities, high-ability workers are paid $w_h =$ $40,000 and low-ability workers get $w_l =$ $20,000. The type of equilibrium depends on the cost of schooling, c, and on the share of high-ability workers, θ. If $c >$ $20,000, only a pooling equilibrium, in which everyone gets the average wage, is possible. If there are relatively few high-ability people, $\theta < 1 - c/$20,000, only a separating equilibrium is possible. Between the horizontal and sloped lines, either type of equilibrium may occur.

not possible because high-ability workers would want to signal. Thus below this line, only a separating equilibrium is possible. Above this line, Equation 18.5 holds, so a pooling equilibrium is possible. (The answer to Solved Problem 18.3 shows that no one wants to change behavior in a pooling equilibrium if $c = \$15,000$ and $\theta > \frac{1}{4}$, which are points to the right of x in the figure, such as y.)

Below the horizontal line where the cost of signaling is less than $20,000 and above the sloped line where there are relatively many high-ability workers, either equilibrium may occur. For example at y, where $c = \$15,000$ and $\theta = \frac{1}{2}$, Equations 18.3 and 18.4 (or, equivalently, Equation 18.5) hold, so both a separating equilibrium and a pooling equilibrium are possible. In the pooling equilibrium, no one wants to change behavior, so that equilibrium is possible. Similarly, no one wants to change behavior in a separating equilibrium.

A government could ensure that one or the other of these equilibria occurs. It can achieve a pooling equilibrium by banning schooling (and other possible signals). Alternatively, the government can create a separating equilibrium by subsidizing schooling for some high-ability people. Once some individuals start to signal, so that firms pay either a low or a high wage (not a pooling wage), it is worthwhile for other high-ability people to signal.

Efficiency. In our example of a separating equilibrium, high-ability people get an otherwise useless education solely to show that they differ from low-ability people. An education is privately useful to the high-ability workers if it serves as a signal that gets them higher net pay. In our extreme example, education is socially inefficient because it is costly and provides no useful training.

Signaling changes the distribution of wages: Instead of everyone receiving the average wage, high-ability workers are paid more than low-ability workers. Nonetheless, the total amount that firms pay is the same, so firms make zero expected profits in both equilibria.[7] Moreover, everyone is employed in both the pooling and the screening equilibria, so total output is the same.

Nonetheless, everyone may be worse off in a separating equilibrium. At point y in Figure 18.2 ($w_h = \$40,000$, $w_l = \$20,000$, $c = \$15,000$, and $\theta = \frac{1}{2}$), either a pooling equilibrium or a separating equilibrium is possible. In the pooling equilibrium, each worker is paid $\overline{w} = \$30,000$ and there is no wasteful signaling. In the separating equilibrium, high-ability workers make $w_h - c = \$25,000$ and low-ability workers make $w_l = \$20,000$.

Here high-ability people earn less in the separating equilibrium, $25,000, than they would in a pooling equilibrium, $30,000. Nonetheless, if anyone signals, all the other high-ability workers will want to send a signal to prevent their wage from falling to that of a low-ability worker. The reason socially undesirable signaling happens is that the private return to signaling—high-ability workers net an extra $5,000 $[= (w_h - c) - w_l = \$25,000 - \$20,000]$—exceeds the net social return to signaling. The gross social return to the signal is zero because the signal changes only the distribution of wages. The net social return is negative because the signal is costly.

This inefficient expenditure on education is due to asymmetric information and the desire of high-ability workers to signal their ability. Here the government can increase

---

[7]Firms pay high-ability workers more than they pay low-ability workers in a separating equilibrium, but the average amount they pay per worker is $\overline{w}$, the same as in a pooling equilibrium.

total social wealth by banning wasteful signaling (that is, eliminating schooling). Both low-ability and high-ability people benefit from such a ban.

In other cases, however, high-ability people do not want a ban. At point z (where $\theta = \frac{1}{2}$ and $c = \$5,000$), only a separating equilibrium is possible without government intervention. In this equilibrium, high-ability workers earn $w_h - c = \$35,000$ and low-ability workers make $w_l = \$20,000$. If the government bans signaling, both types of workers earn $\$30,000$ in the resulting pooling equilibrium, so high-ability workers are harmed, losing $\$5,000$ each. Thus even though the ban raises efficiency by eliminating wasteful signaling, high-ability workers oppose the ban.

In this example, efficiency can always be increased by banning signaling because signaling is unproductive. However, some signaling is socially efficient because it increases total output. Education may raise output because its signal results in a better matching of workers and jobs or because it provides useful training as well as serving as a signal. Education also may make people better citizens. In conclusion, *total social output falls with signaling if signaling is socially unproductive but may rise with signaling if signaling also raises productivity or serves some other desirable purpose.*

Empirical evidence on the importance of signaling is mixed. For example, Tyler, Murnane, and Willett (2000) find that, for the least skilled high school dropouts, passing the General Educational Development (GED) equivalency credential (the equivalent of a high school diploma) increases white dropouts' earnings by 10% to 19% but has no statistically significant effect on minority dropouts. See **www.aw-bc.com/perloff**, Chapter 18, "Wages Rise with Education," for additional evidence that signaling raises wages.

SCREENING IN HIRING

Firms screen prospective workers in many ways. An employer may hire on the basis of a characteristic that the employer believes is correlated with ability, such as how a person dresses or speaks. Or a firm may use a test. Further, some employers engage in *statistical discrimination,* believing that an individual's gender, race, religion, or ethnicity is a proxy for ability.

Interviews and Tests. Most societies accept the use of interviews and tests by potential employers. Firms commonly use interviews and tests as screening devices to assess abilities. If such screening devices are accurate, the firm benefits by selecting superior workers and assigning them to appropriate tasks. However, as with signaling, these costly activities are inefficient if they do not increase output. In the United States, the use of hiring tests may be challenged and rejected by the courts if the employer cannot demonstrate that the tests accurately measure skills or abilities required on the job.

Statistical Discrimination. If employers think that people of a certain gender, race, religion, or ethnicity have higher ability than others on average, they may engage in *statistical discrimination* (Aigner and Cain, 1977) and hire only people with that characteristic. Employers may engage in this practice even if they know that the correlation between these factors and ability is imperfect.

Figure 18.3 illustrates one employer's belief that members of Race 1 have, on average, lower ability than members of Race 2: Much of the distribution curve for Race 2 lies to the right of the curve for Race 1. Nonetheless, the figure also shows that the employer believes that the highest skilled members of Race 1 have higher ability than

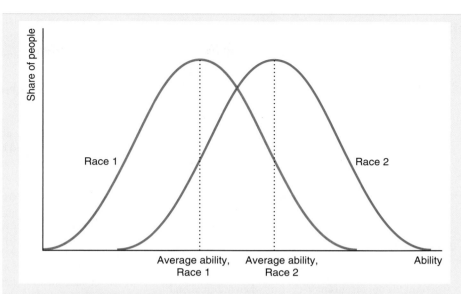

Figure 18.3 Statistical Discrimination. This figure shows the beliefs of an employer who thinks that people of Race 1 have less ability on average than people of Race 2. This employer hires only people of Race 2 even though the employer believes that some members of Race 1 have greater ability than some members of Race 2. Because this employer never employs members of Race 1, the employer may never learn that workers of both races have equal ability.

the lowest skilled members of Race 2: Part of the Race 1 curve lies to the right of part of the Race 2 curve. Still, because the employer believes that a group characteristic, race, is an (imperfect) indicator of individual ability, the employer hires only people of Race 2 if enough of them are available.

The employer may claim not to be prejudiced but to be concerned only with maximizing profit.[8] Nonetheless, this employer's actions harm members of Race 1 as much as they would if they were due to racial hatred.

It may be very difficult to eliminate statistical discrimination, even though ability distributions are identical across races. If all employers share the belief that members of Race 1 have such low ability that it is not worth hiring them, people of that race are never hired, so employers never learn that their beliefs are incorrect. Thus false beliefs can persist indefinitely. Such discrimination lowers social output if it keeps skilled members of Race 1 from performing certain jobs.

However, statistical discrimination may be based on true differences between groups. For example, insurance companies offer lower auto insurance rates to young women than to young men because young men are more likely, *on average,* to have an accident. The companies report that this practice lowers their costs of providing insurance by reducing moral hazard. Nonetheless, this practice penalizes young men who are unusually safe drivers, and benefits young women who are unusually reckless drivers.

---

[8]Not all employment discrimination is due to statistical discrimination. Other common sources of discrimination are prejudice (Becker, 1971) and the exercise of monopsony power (Madden, 1973).

Summary

1. **Problems Due to Asymmetric Information:** Asymmetric information causes market failures when informed parties engage in opportunistic behavior at the expense of uninformed parties. The resulting failures include the elimination of markets and pricing above marginal cost. Two types of problems, adverse selection and moral hazard, arise from opportunism. Adverse selection is opportunism whereby only informed parties who have an unobserved characteristic that allows them to benefit from a deal accept it, to the detriment of a less-informed party. In moral hazard, an informed party takes advantage of a less-informed party through an unobserved action.

2. **Responses to Adverse Selection:** Avoiding adverse selection problems requires restricting the opportunistic behavior or eliminating the information asymmetry. To prevent the opportunism that occurs when information is asymmetric, governments may intervene in markets, or the people involved may write contracts that restrict the behavior of informed people. To eliminate or reduce information asymmetries, uninformed people screen to determine the information of informed people, informed people send signals to uninformed people, or third parties such as the government provide information.

3. **How Ignorance About Quality Drives Out High-Quality Goods:** If consumers cannot distinguish between good and bad products before a purchase, bad products may drive good products out of the market. This lemons problem is due to adverse selection. Approaches to reducing the lemons problem include laws limiting opportunism; consumer screening (such as by using experts or relying on firms' reputations); the provision of information by third parties such as government agencies and consumer groups; and signaling by firms (including establishing brand names and providing guarantees or warranties).

4. **Market Power from Price Ignorance:** If consumers do not know how prices vary across firms, a firm can raise its price without losing all its customers. As a consequence, consumers' ignorance about price creates market power. In a market that would be competitive with full information, consumer ignorance about price may lead to a monopoly price or a distribution of prices.

5. **Problems Arising from Ignorance when Hiring:** Companies use signaling and screening to try to eliminate information asymmetries in hiring. Where prospective employees and firms share common interests—such as assigning the right worker to the right task—everyone benefits from eliminating the information asymmetry by having informed job candidates honestly tell the firms—through *cheap talk*—about their abilities. When the two parties do not share common interests, cheap talk does not work. Potential employees may inform employers about their abilities by using expensive signals such as a college degree. If these signals are unproductive (as when education serves only as a signal and provides no training), they may be privately beneficial but socially harmful. If the signals are productive (as when education provides training or leads to greater output due to more fitting job assignments), they may be both privately and socially beneficial. Firms may also screen. Job interviews, objective tests, and other screening devices that lead to a better matching of workers and jobs may be socially beneficial. Screening by statistical discrimination, however, is harmful to discriminated-against groups. Employers who discriminate on the basis of a particular group characteristic may never learn that their discrimination is based on false beliefs because they never test these beliefs.

Questions

*= answer at the back of this book; **W** = audio-slide show answers by James Dearden at **www.aw-bc.com/perloff**

1. Some states prohibit insurance companies from using car owners' home addresses to set auto insurance rates. Why do insurance companies use home addresses? What are the efficiency and equity implications of forbidding such practices?

*2. The state of California set up its own earthquake insurance program for homeowners in 1997. The rates vary by ZIP code, depending on the proximity of the nearest fault line. However, critics claim that the people who set the rates ignored soil type. Some houses rest on bedrock; others sit on unstable soil. What are the implications of such rate setting?

3. You want to determine whether there is a lemons problem in the market for single-engine airplanes. Can you use any of the following information to help answer this question? If so, how?

   a. Repair rates for original-owner planes versus planes that have been resold

   b. The fraction of planes resold in each year after purchase

4. If you buy a new car and try to sell it in the first year—indeed, in the first few days after you buy it—the price that you get is substantially less than the original price.

Use Akerlof's lemons model to give one explanation for this much-lower price.

5. Use Akerlof's lemons model to explain why restaurants that cater to tourists are likely to serve low-quality meals. Tourists will not return to the area, and they have no information about the relative quality of the food at various restaurants, but they can determine the relative price by looking at menus posted outside each restaurant.

*6. A firm advertises extensively to inform consumers of the brand name of its mushrooms. Should consumers conclude that its mushrooms are likely to be of higher quality than unbranded mushrooms? Why or why not?

7. Sometimes a firm sells the same product under two brand names. For example, the Chevy Tahoe and the GMC Yukon are virtually twins (although the Yukon sells for $490 more than the Tahoe). Give an asymmetric information explanation as to why the firm might use pairs of brand names and why one product might sell for more than the other.

8. In the signaling model, suppose that firms can pay c^* to have a worker's ability determined through a test. Does it pay for a firm to make this expenditure?

9. When is statistical discrimination privately inefficient? When is it socially inefficient? Does it always harm members of the discriminated-against group? Explain.

10. Certain universities do not give letter grades. One rationale is that eliminating the letter-grade system reduces pressure on students, thus enabling them to do better in school. Why might this policy help or hurt students?

11. Some firms are willing to hire only high school graduates. On the basis of past experience or statistical evidence, these companies believe that high school graduates perform better than nongraduates, on average. How does this hiring behavior compare to statistical discrimination by employers on the basis of race or gender? Discuss the equity and efficiency implications of this practice.

12. In the world of French high cuisine, a three-star rating from the Michelin Red Guide is a widely accepted indicator of gastronomic excellence. French consumers consider Gault Milleau, another restaurant guide, to be less authoritative than the Michelin guide because Gault Milleau, unlike Michelin, accepts advertising and its critics accept free meals (William Echikson, "Wish upon a Star," *Wall Street Journal*, February 28, 2003, A8).

   a. Why are guides' ratings important to restaurant owners and chefs? Discuss the effect of a restaurant's rating on the demand for the restaurant.
   b. Why do advertising and free meals taint the credibility of Gault Milleau? Discuss the moral hazard problem of Gault Milleau's ratings.
   c. If advertising and free meals taint the credibility of Gault Milleau, why does the guide accept advertising and free meals? **W**

Problems

13. Many wineries of the Napa region of California have strong reputations for producing high-quality wines and want to protect those reputations. Fred T. Franzia, the owner of Bronco Wine Co., sells Napa-brand wines that do not contain Napa grapes (Julia Flynn, "In Napa Valley, Winemaker's Brands Divide an Industry," *Wall Street Journal*, February 22, 2005, A1). Other Napa wineries are involved in legal disputes with Mr. Franzia, contending that his wines, made from lower-quality grapes, are damaging the reputation of the Napa wines. Use the analysis in Section 18.3 to answer the following questions. The wine market in this problem has 2,000 wineries, in which each chooses to sell one bottle of wine. One thousand of the wineries have Napa grapes and can choose to turn the grapes into wine, and 1,000 wineries have Central Valley grapes and can turn those grapes into wine. The marginal opportunity cost of selling a Napa wine is $20, and the marginal opportunity cost of selling a Central Valley wine is $5. A large number of risk-neutral consumers with identical tastes are willing to buy an unlimited number of bottles at their expected valuations. Each consumer values a wine made from Napa grapes at $25 and a wine made

from Central Valley grapes at $10. By looking at the bottles, the consumers cannot distinguish between the Napa and the Central Valley wines.

   a. If all of the wineries choose to sell wine, what is a consumer's expected value of the wine? If only the wineries with Central Valley grapes choose to sell wine, what is a consumer's expected value of the wine?
   b. What is the market equilibrium price? In the market equilibrium, which wineries choose to sell wine?
   c. Suppose that wine bottles clearly label where the grapes are grown. What are the equilibrium price and quantity of Napa wine? What are the equilibrium price and quantity of wine made from Central Valley grapes?
   d. Does the market equilibrium exhibit a lemons problem? Include an analysis of whether clearly labeling the origin of the grapes solves the lemons problem. **W**

14. While self-employed workers have the option to purchase private health insurance, many—especially younger—workers do not, due to adverse selection. Suppose that half the population is healthy and that the other half is

unhealthy. The cost of getting sick is $1,000 for healthy people and $10,000 for unhealthy people. In a given year, any one person (regardless of health) either becomes sick or does not become sick. The probability that any one person gets sick is 0.4. Each person's utility of wealth function is $U(Y) = Y^{1/2}$, where Y is the person's wealth. Each worker's initial wealth is $30,000. Although each person knows whether he or she is healthy, the insurance company does not know. The insurance company offers complete, actuarially fair insurance. Because the insurance company cannot determine whether a person is healthy or not, it must offer each person the same coverage at the same price. The only costs to the company are the medical expenses of the coverage. Under these conditions, the insurance company covers all the medical expenses of its policyholders, and its expected profit is zero.

a. If everyone purchases insurance, what is the price of the insurance?

b. At the price you determined in part a, do healthy people purchase the optimal amount of insurance?

c. If only unhealthy people purchase insurance, what is the price of the insurance?

d. At the price you determined in part c, do unhealthy people optimally purchase insurance?

e. Given that each person has the option to purchase insurance, which type actually purchases insurance? What is the price of the insurance? Discuss the adverse selection problem. **W**

*15. Many potential buyers value high-quality used cars at the full-information market price of p_1 and lemons at p_2. A limited number of potential sellers value high-quality cars at $v_1 \le p_1$ and lemons at $v_2 \le p_2$. Everyone is risk neutral. The share of lemons among all the used cars that might potentially be sold is θ. Under what conditions are all the cars sold? When are only lemons sold? Are there any conditions under which no cars are sold?

16. Suppose that the buyers in Problem 15 incur a transaction cost of $200 to purchase a car. This transaction cost is the value of their time to find a car. What is the equilibrium? Is it possible that no cars are sold?

17. Suppose that you are given w_h, w_l, and θ in the education signaling model. For what value of c are both a pooling equilibrium and a separating equilibrium possible? For what value of c are both types of equilibria possible, and do high-ability workers have higher net earnings in a separating equilibrium than in a pooling equilibrium?

18. Education is a continuous variable, where e_h is the years of schooling of a high-ability worker and e_l is the years of schooling of a low-ability worker. The cost per period of education for these types of workers is c_h and c_l, respectively, where $c_l > c_h$. The wages they receive if employers can tell them apart are w_h and w_l. Under what conditions is a separating equilibrium possible? How much education will each type of worker get?

19. In Problem 18, under what conditions is a pooling equilibrium possible?

20. In Problems 18 and 19, describe the equilibrium if $c_l \le c_h$.

21. Two restaurants in Bruges, Belgium—Oud Brugge and Den Dijver—engage in price competition. Oud Brugge is located on the central town square, which is the main tourist area. Den Dijver, located on a small side street, is recognized among beer lovers as being one of Belgium's top beer restaurants. Two types of diners patronize these restaurants: beer lovers, who are well-informed about both restaurants, and tourists, who know about Oud Brugge and may or may not know about Den Dijver. Suppose there are 100 beer lovers and 100 tourists. Beer lovers will not eat at Oud Brugge, and their demand function for meals at Den Dijver is $Q_D = 100\,(1 - \frac{1}{50}\,p_D)$. The tourists' demand function for Oud Brugge is $Q_B = n\,(\frac{1}{3} - \frac{1}{25}\,p_B + \frac{1}{50}\,p_D) + (100 - n)$ $(1 - \frac{1}{50}\,p_B)$, where n is the number of tourists who know about both restaurants. The tourists' demand function for Den Dijver is $Q_D = n\,(\frac{2}{3} - \frac{1}{50}\,p_D + \frac{1}{100}\,p_B)$. The marginal cost of a meal at Den Dijver is 15 and the marginal cost of a meal at Oud Brugge is 10. Oud Brugge and Den Dijver simultaneously set prices. If $n = 0$, what is the Nash equilibrium in prices? If $n = 100$, what is the Nash equilibrium? What is the Nash equilibrium as a function of n? Show that as n increases, the price of the tourist restaurant decreases and the price of the other restaurant increases. **W**

Chapter 19

Contracts and Moral Hazards

The contracts of at least 33 major league baseball players have incentive clauses providing a bonus if that player is named the Most Valuable Player in a Division Series. Unfortunately, no such award is given for a Division Series.[1]

An employee cruises the Internet for jokes instead of working when the boss is not watching. A driver of a rental car takes it off the highway and ruins the suspension. The dentist caps your tooth, not because you need it, but because he wants a new high-definition, flat-screen TV.

Each of these examples illustrates an inefficient use of resources due to a *moral hazard,* whereby an informed person takes advantage of a less-informed person, often through an *unobserved action* (Chapter 18). In this chapter, we examine how to design contracts that *eliminate inefficiencies* due to moral hazard problems *without shifting risk to people who hate bearing risk*—or contracts that at least reach a good compromise between these two goals.

For example, insurance companies face a trade-off between reducing moral hazards and increasing the risk of insurance buyers. Because an insurance company pools risks, it acts as though it is risk neutral (Chapter 16). The firm offers insurance contracts to risk-averse homeowners so that they can reduce their exposure to risk. If homeowners can buy full insurance so that they will suffer no loss if a fire occurs, some of them fail to take reasonable precautions. They might store flammable liquids and old newspapers in their houses, increasing the chance of a catastrophic fire.

A contract that avoids this moral hazard problem specifies that the insurance company will not pay in the event of a fire if the company can show that the policyholders stored flammable materials in their home. If this approach is impractical, however, the insurance company might offer a contract that provides incomplete insurance, covering only a fraction of the damage from a fire. The less complete the coverage, the greater the incentive for policyholders to avoid dangerous activities but the greater the risk that the risk-averse homeowners must bear.

To illustrate methods of controlling moral hazards and the trade-off between moral hazards and risk, we focus in this chapter on contracts between a principal—such as an employer—and an agent—such as an employee. The *principal* contracts with the *agent* to take some *action* that benefits the principal. Until now, we have assumed that firms can produce efficiently. However, if a principal cannot practically monitor an agent all the time, the agent may steal, not work hard, or engage in other opportunistic behavior that lowers productivity.[2]

Opportunistic behavior by an informed agent harms a less-informed principal. Sometimes the losses are so great that both parties would be better off if both had full information and if opportunistic behavior were impossible.

---

[1]Tom FitzGerald, "Top of the Sixth," *San Francisco Chronicle,* January 31, 1997:C6.

[2]Sometimes the principal's problem is not so much one of monitoring as one of legally verifying that opportunistic behavior occurred. For example, an insurance company (principal) might be able to determine that the homeowner (agent) engaged in arson but might have trouble proving it.

In this chapter, we examine six main topics

1. **Principal-Agent Problem:** The way that an uninformed principal contracts with an informed agent determines whether moral hazards occur and how risks are shared.

2. **Production Efficiency:** The agent's output depends on the type of contract used and the ability of the principal to monitor the agent's actions.

3. **Trade-Off Between Efficiency in Production and in Risk Bearing:** A principal and an agent may agree to a contract that does not eliminate moral hazards or optimally share risk but strikes a balance between these two objectives.

4. **Payments Linked to Production or Profit:** Employees work harder if they are rewarded for greater individual or group productivity.

5. **Monitoring:** Employees work harder if an employer monitors their behavior and makes it worthwhile for them to keep from being fired.

6. **Contract Choice:** By observing which type of contract an agent picks when offered a choice, a principal may obtain enough information to reduce moral hazards.

19.1 Principal-Agent Problem

When you contract with people whose actions you cannot observe or evaluate, they may take advantage of you. If you pay someone by the hour to prepare your tax return, you do not know whether that person worked all the hours billed. If you retain a lawyer to represent you in a suit arising from an accident, you do not know whether the settlement that the lawyer recommends is in your best interest or the lawyer's.

Of course, many people behave honorably even if they have opportunities to exploit others. Many people also honestly believe that they are putting in a full day's work even when they are not working as hard as they might. Aiko, who manages Pat's Printing Shop, is paid an hourly wage. She works every hour she is supposed to, even though Pat rarely checks on her. Nonetheless, Aiko may not be spending her time as effectively as possible. She politely (but impersonally) asks everyone who enters the shop, "May I help you?" If she were to receive the appropriate financial incentives—say, a share of the shop's profit—she would memorize the names of her customers, greet them enthusiastically by name when they enter the store, and check with nearby businesses to find out whether they would be interested in new services.

A MODEL

We can describe many principal-agent interactions using the following model. This model stresses that the output or profit from this relationship and the risk borne by the two parties depend on the actions of the agent and the state of nature.

In a typical principal-agent relationship, the principal, Paul, owns some property, such as a firm, or has a property right such as the right to sue for damages from an injury. Paul hires or contracts with an agent, Amy, to take some action a that increases the value of his property or that produces profit, π, from using his property.

The principal and the agent need each other. If Paul hires Amy to run his ice-cream shop, Amy needs Paul's shop and Paul needs Amy's efforts to sell ice cream. The profit from the ice cream sold, π, depends on the number of hours, a, that Amy works. The profit may also depend on the outcome of θ, which represents the *state of nature:*

$$\pi = \pi(a, \theta).$$

For example, profit may depend on whether the ice-cream machine breaks, $\theta = 1$, or does not break, $\theta = 0$. Or it may depend on whether it is a hot day, $\theta =$ the temperature.

In extreme cases, the profit function depends only on the agent's actions or only on the state of nature. At one extreme, profit depends only on the agent's action, $\pi = \pi(a)$, if there is only one state of nature: no uncertainty due to random events. In our example, the profit function has this form if demand does not vary with weather and if the ice-cream machine is reliable.

At the other extreme, profit depends only on the state of nature, $\pi = \pi(\theta)$, such as in an insurance market in which profit or value depends only on the state of nature and not on the actions of an agent. For instance, a couple buys insurance against rain on the day of their wedding. The value they place on their outdoor wedding ceremony is $\pi(\theta)$, which depends only on the weather, θ, because no actions are involved.

TYPES OF CONTRACTS

> *A verbal contract isn't worth the paper it's written on.* —Samuel Goldwyn

When a formal market exists, the principal may deal impersonally with an anonymous agent by buying a good or service of known quality at the market price. There is no opportunity for opportunism. In this chapter, we focus on situations in which either a formal market does not exist or a principal and an agent agree on a customized contract that is designed to reduce opportunism.

A contract between a principal and an agent determines how the outcome of their partnership (such as the profit or output) is split between them. Three common types of contracts are fixed-fee, hire, and contingent contracts.

In a *fixed-fee contract,* the payment to the agent, F, is independent of the agent's actions, a, the state of nature, θ, or the outcome, π. The principal keeps the *residual profit,* $\pi(a, \theta) - F$. Alternatively, the principal may get a fixed amount and the agent may receive the residual profit. For example, the agent may pay a fixed rent for the right to use the principal's property.[3]

In a *hire contract,* the payment to the agent depends on the agent's actions as they are observed by the principal. Two common types of hire contracts pay employees an *hourly rate*—a wage per hour—or a *piece rate*—a payment per unit of output produced. If w is the wage per hour (or the price per piece of output) and Amy works a hours (or produces a units of output), then Paul pays Amy wa and keeps the residual profit $\pi(a, \theta) - wa$.

In a *contingent contract,* the payoff to each person depends on the state of nature, which may not be known to the parties at the time they write the contract. For example, Penn agrees to pay Alexis a higher amount to fix his roof if it is raining than if it is not.

---

[3]Jefferson Hope says in the Sherlock Holmes mystery *A Study in Scarlet,* "I applied at a cab-owner's office, and soon got employment. I was to bring a certain sum a week to the owner, and whatever was over that I might keep for myself."

One type of contingent contract is a *splitting* or *sharing contract,* where the payoff to each person is a fraction of the total profit (which is observable). Alain sells Pamela's house for her for $\pi(a, \theta)$ and receives a commission of 7% on the sales price. He receives $0.07\pi(a, \theta)$, and she keeps $0.93\pi(a, \theta)$.

EFFICIENCY

The type of contract selected depends on what the parties can observe. A principal is more likely to use a hire contract if the principal can easily monitor the agent's actions. A contingent contract may be chosen if the state of nature can be observed after the work is completed. A fixed-fee contract does not depend on observing anything, so it can always be used.

Ideally, the principal and agent agree to an **efficient contract:** an agreement with provisions that ensure that no party can be made better off without harming the other party. Using an efficient contract results in *efficiency in production* and *efficiency in risk sharing.*

Efficiency in production requires that the principal's and the agent's combined value (profits, payoffs), π, is maximized. We say that production is efficient if Amy manages Paul's firm so that the sum of their profits cannot be increased. In our examples, the moral hazard hurts the principal more than it helps the agent, so total profit falls. Thus achieving efficiency in production requires preventing the moral hazard.

Efficiency in risk bearing requires that risk sharing is optimal in that the person who least minds facing risk—the risk-neutral or less-risk-averse person—bears more of the risk. In Chapter 16 we saw that risk-averse people are willing to pay a risk premium to avoid risk, whereas risk-neutral people do not care if they face fair risk or not. Suppose that Arlene is risk averse and is willing to pay a risk premium of $100 to avoid a particular risk. Peter is risk neutral and would bear the risk without a premium. Arlene and Peter can strike a deal whereby Peter agrees to bear *all* of Arlene's risk in exchange for a payment between $0 and $100. For simplicity, we concentrate on situations in which one party is risk averse and the other is risk neutral. (Generally, if both parties are risk averse, with one more risk averse than the other, both can be made better off if the less-risk-averse person bears more but not all of the risk.)

If everyone has full information—there is no uncertainty and no asymmetric information—efficiency can be achieved. The principal contracts with the agent to perform a task for some specified reward and observes whether the agent completes the task properly before paying, so no moral hazard problem arises.

Throughout the rest of this chapter, we examine what happens when the parties do not have full information. Production inefficiency is more likely when either the agent has more information than the principal or both parties are uncertain about the state of nature.

When the agent has more information than the principal and there is no risk because there is only one state of nature, contracts are used to achieve efficiency in production by conveying adequate information to the principal to eliminate moral hazard problems. Alternatively, incentives in the contract may discourage the informed person from engaging in opportunistic behavior. The contracts do not have to address efficiency in risk bearing because there is no risk.

Given that they face both asymmetric information and risk, the parties try to contract to achieve efficiency in production and efficiency in risk bearing. Often, however, both objectives cannot be achieved, so the parties must trade off between them.

19.2 Production Efficiency

The type of contract that an agent and principal use affects production efficiency. In the following example, production efficiency is achieved by maximizing *total* or *joint profit:* the sum of the principal's and the agent's individual profits. To isolate the production issues from risk bearing, we initially assume that there is only one state of nature, so the parties face no risk due to random events: Total profit, $\pi(a)$, is solely a function of the agent's action, a.

EFFICIENT CONTRACT

To be efficient and to maximize joint profit, the contract that a principal offers to an agent must have two properties. First, the contract must provide a large enough payoff that the agent is willing to *participate* in the contract. We know that the principal's payoff is adequate to ensure the principal's participation because the principal offers the contract.

Second, the contract must be **incentive compatible** in that it provides inducements such that the agent wants to perform the assigned task rather than engage in opportunistic behavior. That is, it is in the agent's best interest to take an action that maximizes joint profit. If the contract is not incentive compatible—so the agent tries to maximize personal profit rather than joint profit—efficiency can be achieved only if the principal monitors the agent and forces the agent to act so as to maximize joint profit.

We use an example to illustrate why some types of contracts lead to efficiency and others do not. Paula, the principal, owns a store called Buy-A-Duck (located near a canal) that sells wood carvings of ducks. Arthur, the agent, manages the store. Paula and Arthur's joint profit is

$$\pi(a) = R(a) - ma, \tag{19.1}$$

where $R(a)$ is the sales revenue from selling a carvings, and ma is the cost of the carvings. Arthur has a constant marginal cost m to obtain and sell each duck, including the amount he pays a local carver and the opportunity value (best alternative use) of his time.

Because Arthur bears the full marginal cost of selling one more carving, he wants to sell the joint-profit-maximizing output only if he also gets the full marginal benefit from selling one more duck. To determine the joint-profit-maximizing solution, we can ask what Arthur would do if he owned the shop and received all the profit, giving him an incentive to maximize total profit.

How many ducks must Arthur sell to maximize the parties' joint profit, Equation 19.1? To obtain the first-order condition to maximize profit, we set the derivative of Equation 19.1 equal to zero:

$$\frac{d\pi(a)}{da} = \frac{dR(a)}{da} - m = 0. \tag{19.2}$$

According to Equation 19.2, joint profit is maximized by choosing the number of ducks to sell, a, such that marginal revenue, $dR(a)/da$, equals marginal cost, m.

Suppose, for example, that $m = 12$, the inverse demand curve they face is $p = 24 - \frac{1}{2}a$, and hence the revenue function is $R(a) = 24a - \frac{1}{2}a^2$. The marginal revenue function is $MR(a) = dR(a)/da = 24 - a$. Substituting the marginal revenue function and the marginal cost into Equation 19.2, we find that $MR = 24 - a = 12 = m = MC$, or $a = 12$. Panel a of Figure 19.1 illustrates this result: The marginal revenue curve, MR, intersects

Figure 19.1 Maximizing Joint Profit when the Agent Gets the Residual Profit.
(a) If the agent, Arthur, gets all the joint profit, π, he maximizes his profit by selling 12 carvings at e, where the marginal revenue curve intersects his marginal cost curve: $MR = MC = 12$. If he pays the principal, Paula, a fixed rent of $48, he maximizes his profit by selling 12 carvings. (A fixed rent does not affect either his marginal revenue or his marginal cost.)
(b) Joint profit at 12 carvings is $72, point E. If Arthur pays a rent of $48 to Paula, Arthur's profit is $\pi - \$48$. By selling 12 carvings and maximizing joint profit, Arthur also maximizes his profit.

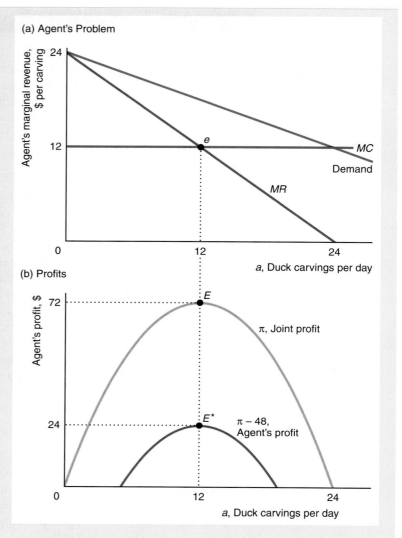

the marginal cost curve, $MC = m = \$12$, at the equilibrium point e. Panel b shows that total profit, π, reaches a maximum of $72 at point E.

Which types of contracts lead to production efficiency? To answer this question, we first examine which contracts yield that outcome when both parties have full information and then consider which contracts bring the desired result when the principal is relatively uninformed. It is important to remember that we are considering a special case: Contracts that work here may not work in some other settings, whereas contracts that do not work here may be effective elsewhere.

FULL INFORMATION

Suppose that both Paula and Arthur have full information. Each knows the actions Arthur takes—the number of carvings sold—and the effect of those actions on profit. Because she has full information, Paula can dictate exactly what Arthur is to do.

Are there incentive-compatible contracts that do not require such monitoring and supervision? To answer this question, we consider four kinds of contracts: a fixed-fee rental contract, a hire contract, and two types of contingent contracts.

Fixed-Fee Rental Contract. If Arthur contracts to rent the store from Paula for a fixed fee, F, joint profit is maximized. Arthur earns a residual profit equal to the joint profit minus the fixed rent he pays Paula, $\pi(a) - F$. Because the amount that Paula makes is fixed, Arthur gets the entire marginal profit from selling one more duck. As a consequence, the amount, a, that maximizes Arthur's profit,

$$\pi(a) - F = R(a) - ma - F, \tag{19.3}$$

also maximizes joint profit, $\pi(a)$. To show this result, we note that his first-order condition based on Equation 19.3,

$$\frac{d[\pi(a) - F]}{da} = \frac{dR(a)}{da} - m - \frac{dF}{da} = \frac{dR(a)}{da} - m = 0, \tag{19.4}$$

is identical to the first-order condition in Equation 19.2.

This result is illustrated in Figure 19.1, where Arthur pays Paula $F = \$48$ rent. This fixed payment does not affect his marginal cost. As a result, he maximizes his profit after paying the rent, $\pi - \$48$, by equating his marginal revenue to his marginal cost: $MR = MC = 12$ at point e in panel a.

Because Arthur pays the same fixed rent no matter how many units he sells, the agent's profit curve in panel b lies $\$48$ below the joint-profit curve at every quantity. As a result, Arthur's net-profit curve peaks (at point E^*) at the same quantity, 12, where the joint-profit curve peaks (at E). Thus the fixed-fee rental contract is incentive compatible. Arthur participates in this contract because he earns $\$24$ after paying for the rent and the carvings (point E^*).

Hire Contract. Now suppose that Paula contracts to pay Arthur for each carving he sells. If she pays him $\$12$ per carving, Arthur just breaks even on each sale. He is indifferent between participating and not. Even if he chooses to participate, he does not sell the joint-profit-maximizing number of carvings unless Paula supervises him. If she does supervise him, she instructs him to sell 12 carvings, and she gets all the joint profit of $\$72$.

For Arthur to want to participate and to sell carvings without supervision, he must receive more than $\$12$ per carving. If Paula pays Arthur $\$14$ per carving, for example, he makes a profit of $\$2$ per carving. He now has an incentive to sell as many carvings as he can (even if the price is less than the cost of the carving), which does not maximize joint profit, so this contract is not incentive compatible.

Even if the Paula can control how many carvings he sells, joint profit is not maximized. Paula keeps the revenue minus what she pays Arthur, $\$14$ times the number of carvings,

$$R(a) - 14a.$$

Thus her objective differs from the joint-profit-maximizing objective, $\pi(a) = R(a) - 12a$. Joint profit is maximized when marginal revenue equals the marginal cost of $\$12$. Because Paula's marginal cost, $\$14$, is larger, she directs Arthur to sell fewer than the optimal number of carvings. Paula maximizes $R - 14a = (24a - \frac{1}{2}a^2) - 14a = 10a - \frac{1}{2}a^2$. Given her first-order condition, where the derivative of Paula's profit with respect to a equals zero, $10 - a = 0$, she maximizes her profit by selling 10 carvings. Joint profit is only $\$70$ at 10 carvings, compared to $\$72$ at the optimal 12 carvings.

Revenue-Sharing Contract. If Paula and Arthur use a *contingent contract* whereby they share the *revenue,* joint profit is not maximized. Suppose that Arthur receives three-quarters of the revenue, $\frac{3}{4}R$, and Paula gets the rest, $\frac{1}{4}R$. Panel a of Figure 19.2 shows the marginal revenue that Arthur obtains from selling an extra carving, $MR^\star = \frac{3}{4}MR$. He maximizes his profit at $24 by selling 8 carvings, for which $MR^\star = MC$ at $e^\star$. Paula gets the remaining profit of $40, which is the difference between their total profit from selling 8 ducks per day, $\pi = \$64$, and Arthur's profit.

Thus their joint profit in panel b at $a = 8$ is $64, which is $8 less than the maximum possible profit of $72 (point E). Arthur has an incentive to sell fewer than the optimal number of ducks because he bears the full marginal cost of each carving he sells, $12, but gets only three-quarters of the marginal revenue.

Even if Paula controls how many carvings are sold, joint profit is not maximized. Because the amount she makes, $\frac{1}{4}R$, depends only on revenue and not on the cost of obtaining the carvings, she wants the revenue-maximizing quantity sold. Revenue is

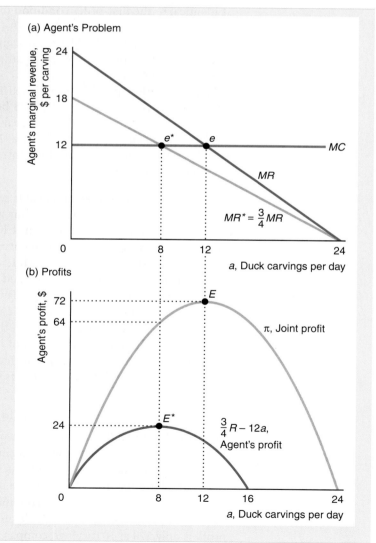

Figure 19.2 Why Revenue Sharing Reduces Agent's Efforts. (a) Joint profit is maximized at 12 carvings, where $MR = MC = 12$ at equilibrium point e. If Arthur gets three-quarters of the revenue and Paula gets the rest, Arthur maximizes his profit by selling 8 carvings, where his new marginal revenue curve, $MR^\star = \frac{3}{4}MR$, equals his marginal cost at point $e^\star$. (b) Joint profit reaches a maximum of $72 at E, where they sell 12 carvings per day. If they split the revenue, Arthur sells 8 ducks per day and gets $24 at $E^\star$, and Paula receives the residual, $40 (= $64 − $24).

maximized where marginal revenue is zero at $a = 24$ (panel a). Arthur would not participate if the contract granted him only three-quarters of the revenue but required him to sell 24 carvings, because he would lose money.

SOLVED PROBLEM 19.1

Use calculus to show that, if Arthur receives three-quarters of the revenue, $\frac{3}{4}R$, and Paula gets the rest, he does not sell the joint-profit-maximizing quantity.

Answer

1. *Write Arthur's profit function, calculate his first-order condition, and solve for his profit-maximizing output:* Arthur's profit is $\frac{3}{4}R(a) - 12a = \frac{3}{4}(24a - \frac{1}{2}a^2) - 12a$. To maximize his profit, he needs to choose a such that his marginal profit with respect to a equals zero: $\frac{3}{4}dR(a)/da - 12 = \frac{3}{4}(24 - a) - 12 = 0$. Thus the output that maximizes his profit is $a = 8$.

2. *Compare this solution to the joint-profit-maximizing output:* We know that the joint profit is maximized at 72, where $a = 12$. With revenue sharing, $a = 8$ and joint profits are only 64.

Comment: Arthur produces too little output because he bears the full marginal cost, 12, but earns only three-quarters of the marginal benefit (marginal revenue), $\frac{3}{4}(24 - a)$, from the joint-profit-maximizing problem, $24 - a$.

Profit-Sharing Contract. Paula and Arthur may instead use a *contingent contract* by which they divide the *economic profit*, π. If they can agree that the true marginal and average cost is $12 per carving (which includes Arthur's opportunity cost of time), the contract is incentive compatible because Arthur wants to sell the optimal number of carvings. Only by maximizing total profit can he maximize his share of profit. As Figure 19.3 illustrates, Arthur receives one-third of the joint profit and chooses to

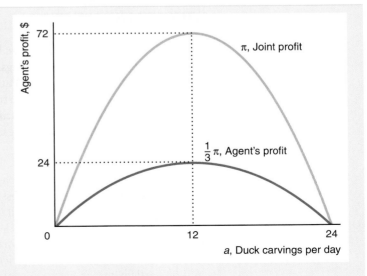

Figure 19.3 Why Profit Sharing Is Efficient. If the agent, Arthur, gets a third of the joint profit, he maximizes his profit, $\frac{1}{3}\pi$, by maximizing joint profit, π.

TABLE 19.1   **Production Efficiency and Moral Hazard Problems for Buy-A-Duck**

Contract	Full Information	Asymmetric Information	
	Production Efficiency	Production Efficiency	Moral Hazard Problem
Fixed-fee rental contract			
Rent (to principal)	Yes	Yes	No
Hire contract, per unit pay			
Pay equals marginal cost	No[a]	No[b]	Yes
Pay is greater than marginal cost	No[c]	No	Yes
Contingent contract			
Share revenue	No	No[b]	Yes
Share profit	Yes	No[b]	Yes

[a]The agent may not participate and has no incentive to sell the optimal number of carvings. Efficiency can be achieved only if the principal supervises.

[b]Unless the agent steals all the revenue (or profit) from an extra sale, inefficiency results.

[c]The agent sells too many or the principal directs the agent to sell too few carvings.

produce the level of output, $a = 12$, that maximizes joint profit. Arthur gets one-third of profit, $\frac{1}{3}\pi = \frac{1}{3}(R - C) = \frac{1}{3}R - \frac{1}{3}C$, where R is revenue and C is cost. He maximizes his profit where $\frac{1}{3}MR = \frac{1}{3}MC$. Although he gets only one-third of the marginal revenue, $\frac{1}{3}MR$, he bears only one-third of the marginal cost. Dividing both sides of the equation by $\frac{1}{3}$, we find that this condition is the same as the one for maximizing total profit: $MR = MC$. Arthur earns $24, so he is willing to participate.

The second column of Table 19.1 summarizes our analysis. Whether efficiency in production is achieved depends on the type of contract that the principal and the agent use. If the principal has full information (knows the agent's actions), the principal achieves production efficiency without having to supervise by using one of the incentive-compatible contracts: fixed-fee rental or profit-sharing.

ASYMMETRIC INFORMATION

Now suppose that the principal, Paula, has less information than the agent, Arthur. She cannot observe the number of carvings he sells or the revenue. Due to this asymmetric information, Arthur can steal from Paula without her detecting the theft.

As Table 19.1 shows, with asymmetric information, *the only contract that results in production efficiency and no moral hazard problem is the one whereby the principal gets a fixed rent*. All the other contracts result in inefficiency, and Arthur has an opportunity to take advantage of Paula.

Fixed-Fee Rental Contract. Arthur pays Paula the fixed rent that she is due because Paula would know if she were paid less. Arthur receives the residual profit, joint profit minus the fixed rent, so he wants to sell the joint-profit-maximizing number of carvings.

Hire Contract. If Paula offers to pay Arthur the actual marginal cost of $12 per carving and he is honest, he may refuse to participate in the contract because he makes no profit. Even if he participates, he has no incentive to sell the optimal number of carvings.

If he is dishonest, he may underreport sales and pocket some of the extra revenue. Unless he can steal all the extra revenue from an additional sale, he sells less than the joint-profit-maximizing quantity.

If Paula pays him more than the actual marginal cost per carving, he has an incentive to sell too many carvings, whether or not he steals. If he also steals, he has an even greater incentive to sell too many carvings.

Revenue-Sharing Contract. Even with full information, the revenue-sharing contract is inefficient. Asymmetric information adds a moral hazard problem: The agent may steal from the principal. If Arthur can steal a larger share of the revenues than the contract specifies, he has less of an incentive to undersell than he does with full information. Indeed, if the agent can steal all the extra revenue from an additional sale, the agent acts efficiently to maximize joint profit, all of which the agent keeps.

Profit-Sharing Contract. If they use a contingent contract by which they agree to split the economic profit, Arthur has to report both the revenue and the cost to Paula so that they can calculate their shares. If he can overreport cost or underreport revenue, he has an incentive to produce a nonoptimal quantity. Only if Arthur can appropriate all the profit does he produce efficiently.

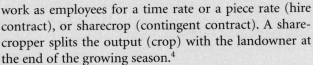

APPLICATION

Contracts and Productivity in Agriculture

In agriculture, landowners (principals) contract with farmers (agents) to work their land. Farmers may work on their own land (the principal and agent are the same person), work on land rented from a landowner (fixed-fee rental contract),

work as employees for a time rate or a piece rate (hire contract), or sharecrop (contingent contract). A sharecropper splits the output (crop) with the landowner at the end of the growing season.[4]

Our analysis tells us that farmers' willingness to work hard depends on the type of contract that is used. Farmers who keep all the marginal profit from additional work—those who own the land or rent it for a fixed fee—work hard and maximize (joint) profit. Sharecroppers, who bear the full marginal cost of working an extra hour and get only a fraction of the extra revenue, put in too little effort. Hired farmworkers who are paid by the hour may not work hard unless they are very carefully supervised. That is, they may engage in **shirking**: a moral hazard in which agents do not provide all the services they are paid to provide.

---

[4]If a farmer is someone who is out standing in his field, a sharecropper is someone who is out standing in someone else's field.

These predictions about contract type and agent effort were tested by using data on farmers in the Philippines. Foster and Rosenzweig (1994) could not directly monitor the work effort—any more than most landowners can. Rather, they ingeniously measured the effort indirectly. They contended that the harder people work, the more they eat and the more they use up body mass (defined as weight divided by height squared), holding calorie intake constant.

Foster and Rosenzweig estimated the effect of each compensation method on body mass and consumption (after adjusting for gender, age, type of activity, and other factors). They found that people who work for themselves or are paid by the piece use up 10% more body mass, holding calorie consumption constant, than time-rate workers and 13% more than sharecroppers. Foster and Rosenzweig also discovered that piece-rate workers consume 25% more calories per day and that people who work on their own farms consume 16% more than time-rate workers.

19.3   Trade-Off Between Efficiency in Production and in Risk Bearing

Writing an efficient contract is extremely difficult if the agent knows more than the principal, the principal never learns the truth, and both face risk. Usually, a contract does not achieve efficiency in production *and* in risk bearing. Contract clauses that increase efficiency in production may reduce efficiency in risk bearing, and vice versa. If these goals are incompatible, the parties may write imperfect contracts that reach a compromise between the two objectives. To illustrate the trade-offs involved, we consider a common situation in which it is difficult to achieve efficiency: contracting with an expert such as a lawyer.

We illustrate how contracts affect the outcome by using an example in which Pam, the principal, is injured in a traffic accident and is a plaintiff in a lawsuit, and Alfredo, the agent, is her lawyer. Pam faces uncertainty due to risk and to asymmetric information. The jury award at the conclusion of the trial, $\pi(a, \theta)$, depends on a, the number of hours Alfredo works before the trial, and θ, the state of nature due to the (unknown) attitudes of the jury. All else the same, the more time Alfredo spends working on the case, a, the larger the amount, π, that the jury is likely to award. Pam never learns the jury's attitudes, θ, so she cannot accurately judge Alfredo's efforts even after the trial. For example, if she loses the case, she won't know whether she lost because Alfredo didn't work hard (low a) or because the case was weak and the jury was prejudiced against her (bad θ).

CONTRACTS AND EFFICIENCY

How hard Alfredo works depends on his attitudes toward risk and his knowledge of the payoff for his trial preparations. For any hour that he does not devote to Pam's case, Alfredo can work on other cases. The most lucrative of these forgone opportunities is his marginal cost of working on Pam's case.

The beneficiary of the extra payoff that results if Alfredo works harder depends on his contract with Pam. If Alfredo is risk neutral and gets the entire marginal benefit from any extra work, he puts in the optimal number of hours that maximizes their

TABLE 19.2   **Efficiency of Client-Lawyer Contracts**

Type of Contract	Fixed Fee to Lawyer	Fixed Payment to Client	Lawyer Paid by the Hour	Contingent Contract
Lawyer's payoff	F	$\pi(a, \theta) - F$	wa	$\alpha\pi(a, \theta)$
Client's payoff	$\pi(a, \theta) - F$	F	$\pi(a, \theta) - wa$	$(1 - \alpha)\pi(a, \theta)$
Production efficiency?	No*	Yes	No*	No*
Who bears risk?	Client	Lawyer	Client	Shared

*Production efficiency is possible if the client can monitor and enforce optimal effort by the lawyer.

expected joint payoff. Alfredo collects the marginal benefit from the extra work and bears the marginal cost, so he sets his expected marginal benefit equal to his marginal cost, thus maximizing the expected joint payoff.

The choice of various possible contracts between Pam and Alfredo affects whether efficiency in production or in risk bearing is achieved. They choose among fixed-fee, hire (hourly wage), and contingent contracts. Table 19.2 summarizes the outcomes under each of these contracts.

Lawyer Gets a Fixed Fee. If Pam pays Alfredo a fixed fee, F, he gets paid the same no matter how much he works. Thus he has little incentive to work hard on this case, and his production is inefficient.[5] Production efficiency can be achieved only if Pam can monitor Alfredo and force him to act optimally. However, most individual plaintiffs cannot monitor a lawyer and thus cannot determine whether the lawyer is behaving appropriately.

Whether the fixed-fee contract leads to efficiency in risk bearing depends on the attitudes toward risk on the part of the principal and agent. Pam, the principal, bears all the risk. Alfredo's pay, F, is certain, while Pam's net payoff, $\pi(a, \theta) - F$, varies with the unknown state of nature, θ.

A lawyer who handles many similar cases may be less risk averse than an individual client whose financial future depends on a single case. If Alfredo has had many cases like Pam's and if Pam's future rests on the outcome of this suit, their choice of this type of contract leads to inefficiency in both production and risk bearing. Not only is Alfredo not working hard enough, but Pam bears the risk, even though she is more risk averse than Alfredo.

In contrast, suppose that Alfredo is a self-employed lawyer working on a major case for Pam, who runs a large insurance company with many similar cases. Alfredo is risk averse and Pam is risk neutral (because she is able to pool many similar cases). Here, having the principal bear all the risk is efficient. If the insurance company can monitor Alfredo's behavior, it is even possible to achieve production efficiency. Indeed, many insurance companies employ lawyers in this manner.

---

[5] His main incentive to work hard (other than honesty) is to establish a reputation as a good lawyer so as to attract future clients. For simplicity, we will ignore this effect, because it applies for all types of contracts.

Plaintiff Gets a Fixed Payment. Instead, the two parties could agree to a contract by which Alfredo could pay Pam a fixed amount of money, F, for the right to try the case and collect the entire verdict less the payment to Pam, $\pi(a, \theta) - F$. With such a contract, Alfredo has an incentive to put in the optimal number of hours. He works until his marginal cost—the opportunity cost of his time—equals the marginal benefit—the extra amount he gets if he wins at trial. Because he has already paid Pam, all extra amounts earned at trial go to Alfredo.

Under this contract, Alfredo bears all the risk related to the outcome of the trial. However, no matter how risk averse Pam is, she may hesitate to agree to such a contract. Because she is not an expert on the law, she cannot easily predict the jury's likely verdict. Thus she does not know how large a fixed fee she should insist on receiving. There is no practical way in which Alfredo's superior information about the likely outcome of the trial can be credibly revealed to her. She suspects that it is in his best interest to tell her that the likely payout is lower than he truly believes.[6]

Lawyer Is Hired by the Hour. In complicated cases, a lawyer's output is not easily measured, so it is not practical to pay the attorney by the piece. Pam could pay Alfredo a wage of w per hour for the a hours that he works. Doing so would create the potential for a serious moral hazard problem unless Pam could monitor Alfredo to determine how many hours he works. If she could not, Alfredo could bill her for more hours than he actually worked.[7] Even if Pam could observe how many hours he works, she would not know whether Alfredo worked effectively and whether the work was necessary. Thus it would be difficult, if not impossible, for Pam to monitor Alfredo's work.

Here Pam bears all the risk. Alfredo's earnings, wa, are determined before the outcome is known. Pam's return, $\pi(a, \theta) - wa$, varies with the state of nature and is unknown before the verdict.

Fee Is Contingent. Some lawyers offer plaintiffs a contract whereby the lawyer works for "free"—receiving no hourly payment—in exchange for splitting the compensation awarded in court or in a settlement before trial. The lawyer receives a **contingent fee:** a payment to a lawyer that is a share of the award in a court case (usually after legal expenses are deducted) if the client wins and nothing if the client loses. If the lawyer's share of the award is ω and the jury awards $\pi(a, \theta)$, the lawyer receives $\omega\pi(a, \theta)$ and the principal gets $(1 - \omega)\pi(a, \theta)$. This approach is attractive to many plaintiffs because they cannot monitor how hard the lawyer works and are unable or unwilling to make payments before the trial is completed.

How they split the award affects the amount of risk each bears. If Alfredo gets one-quarter of the award, $\omega = \frac{1}{4}$, and Pam gets three-quarters, Pam bears more risk than

---

[6]Alfredo may be hesitant to offer Pam a fixed fee. Their success in court depends on the merits of her case. Initially, Alfredo does not know how good a case she has, and she has an incentive to try to convince him that the case is very strong. Moreover, a lawyer may worry that if he pays the plaintiff a fixed fee, she will not fully cooperate in preparing the case (an issue that we've ignored in our example, in which only the actions of the lawyer matter).

[7]A lawyer dies in an accident and goes to heaven. A host of angels greet him with a banner that reads, "Welcome Oldest Man!" The lawyer is puzzled: "Why do you think I'm the oldest man who ever lived? I was only 47 when I died." One of the angels replied, "You can't fool us; you were at least 152 when you died. We saw how many hours you billed!"

Alfredo does. Suppose that the award is either 0 or 40 with equal probability. Alfredo receives either 0 or 10, so his average award is 5. His variance (Chapter 16) is

$$\sigma_a^2 = \frac{1}{2}(0 - 5)^2 + \frac{1}{2}(10 - 5)^2 = 25.$$

Pam makes either 0 or 30, so her average award is 15 and her variance is

$$\sigma_p^2 = \frac{1}{2}(0 - 15)^2 + \frac{1}{2}(30 - 15)^2 = 225.$$

Thus the variance in Pam's payoff is greater than Alfredo's.

Whether splitting the risk in this way is desirable depends on how risk averse each party is. If one is risk neutral and the other is risk averse, it is efficient for the risk-neutral person to bear all the risk. If they are equally risk averse, a splitting rule in which $\omega = \frac{1}{2}$ and they face equal risk may be optimal.[8]

A sharing contract encourages shirking: Alfredo is likely to put in too little effort. He bears the full cost of his labors—the forgone use of his time—but gets only ω share of the returns from this effort. Thus this contract results in production inefficiency and may or may not lead to inefficient risk bearing.

CHOOSING THE BEST CONTRACT

Which contract is best depends on the parties' attitudes toward risk, the degree of risk, the difficulty in monitoring, and other factors. If Alfredo is risk neutral, they can achieve both efficiency goals if Alfredo gives Pam a fixed fee. He has the incentive to put in the optimal amount of work and does not mind bearing the risk.

However, if Alfredo is risk averse and Pam is risk neutral, they may not be able to achieve both objectives. Contracts that provide Alfredo a fixed fee or a wage rate allocate all the risk to Pam and lead to inefficiency in production because Alfredo has too little incentive to work hard.

Often when the parties find that they cannot achieve both objectives, they choose a contract that attains neither goal. For example, they may use a contingent contract that fails to achieve efficiency in production and may not achieve efficiency in risk bearing. The contingent contract strikes a compromise between the two goals. Alfredo has more of an incentive to work if he splits the payoff than if he receives a fixed fee. He is less likely to work excessive hours with the contingent fee than if he were paid by the hour. Moreover, neither party has to bear all the risk—they share it under the contingent contract.

Lawyers usually work for a fixed fee only if the task or case is very simple, such as writing a will or handling an uncontested divorce. The client has some idea of whether the work is done satisfactorily, so monitoring is relatively easy and little risk is involved.

In riskier situations, the other types of contracts are more commonly used. When the lawyer is relatively risk averse or when the principal is very concerned that the lawyer works hard, an hourly wage may be used.

Contingent fee arrangements are particularly common for plaintiffs' lawyers who specialize in auto accidents, medical malpractice, product liability, and other *torts*: wrongful acts in which a person's body, property, or reputation is harmed and for which the injured party is entitled to compensation. Because these plaintiffs' lawyers can

---

[8]If Pam and Alfredo split the award equally and each receives either 0 or 20 with equal probability, each has a variance of $\frac{1}{2}(0 - 10)^2 + \frac{1}{2}(20 - 10)^2 = 100$.

typically pool risks across clients, they are less concerned than their clients are about risk. As a consequence, these attorneys are willing to accept contingent fees (and might agree to pay a fixed fee to the plaintiff). Moreover, accident victims often lack the resources to pay for a lawyer's time before winning at trial, so they often prefer contingent contracts.

● **APPLICATION**

Contingent Fees Versus Hourly Pay

Some jurisdictions restrict lawyers' contingent fees. California limits medical malpractice contingent fees to 40% of the first $50,000 of compensation, one-third of the next $50,000, 25% of the next $100,000, and 10% of anything over $200,000. All provinces of Canada except Ontario permit contingent fees, while most European countries ban them.

Historically, lawyers in personal injury cases have been paid a contingent fee. Increasingly, some states are banning or limiting such fees, and lawyers are paid hourly. One justification given for banning contingent fees is that they encourage "frivolous" lawsuits by lawyers looking for a big payout; however, this result is not obvious on the basis of economic theory. Helland and Tabarrok (2003) measured low-quality cases by the probability that the plaintiff dropped the case before a settlement or trial. They compared states that outlaw or severely limit contingent fees to those states that permit them. They also looked specifically at the record in Florida before and after a limit on contingent fees. They found that the use of hourly fees encourages lawyers to take poor cases and to delay the time to settle relative to what happens with contingent fees.

SOLVED PROBLEM   19.2

Gary's demand for medical services (visits to his doctor) depends on his health. Half the time his health is good and his demand is D^1 in the graph. When his health is less good, his demand is D^2. Without medical insurance, he pays $50 a visit. Because Gary is risk averse, he wants to buy medical insurance. With full insurance, Gary pays a fixed fee at the beginning of the year, and the insurance company pays the full cost of any visit. Alternatively, with a contingent contract, Gary pays a smaller premium at the beginning of the year, and the insurance company covers only $20 per visit, with Gary paying the remaining $30. How likely is a moral hazard problem to occur with each of these contracts? What is Gary's risk (variance of his medical costs) with no insurance and with each of the two types of insurance? Compare the contracts in terms of the trade-offs between risk and moral hazards.

Answer

1. *Describe the moral hazard for each demand curve for each contract:* If Gary's health is good, he increases from 1 visit, a_1, with no insurance (where he pays $50 a visit) to 6 visits, c_1, with full insurance (where he pays nothing per visit). Similarly, if his health is poor, he increases his visits from 5, a_2, to 10, c_2. Thus regardless of his health, he makes 5 extra visits a year with full insurance. These extra visits are the moral hazard. With a contingent contract whereby Gary pays $30 a visit, the moral hazard is less because he makes only 2 extra visits instead of 5 (the difference between the number of visits at b_1 and a_1 and between b_2 and a_2).

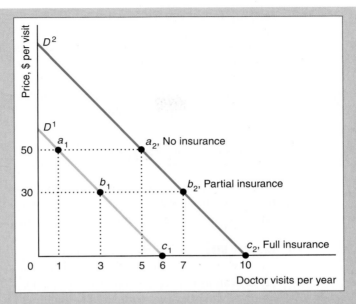

2. *Calculate the variance of Gary's medical expenses for no insurance and for the two insurance contracts:* Without insurance, his average number of visits is $3[= (\frac{1}{2} \times 1) + (\frac{1}{2} \times 5)]$, so his average annual medical cost is $150. Thus the variance of his medical expenses without insurance is

$$\sigma_n^2 = \tfrac{1}{2}[(1 \times \$50) - \$150]^2 + \tfrac{1}{2}[(5 \times 50) - \$150]^2$$
$$= \tfrac{1}{2}(\$50 - \$150)^2 + \tfrac{1}{2}(\$250 - \$150)^2$$
$$= \$10,000.$$

If he has full insurance, he makes a single fixed payment each year, so his payments do not vary with his health: His variance is $\sigma_f^2 = 0$. Finally, with partial insurance, he averages 5 visits with an average cost of $150, so his variance is

$$\sigma_p^2 = \tfrac{1}{2}(\$90 - \$150)^2 + \tfrac{1}{2}(\$210 - \$150)^2 = \$3,600.$$

Thus $\sigma_n^2 > \sigma_p^2 > \sigma_f^2$.

3. *Discuss the trade-offs:* Because Gary is risk averse, efficiency in risk bearing requires the insurance company to bear all the risk, as with full insurance. Full insurance, however, results in the largest moral hazard. Without insurance, there is no moral hazard, but Gary bears all the risk. The contingent contract is a compromise whereby both the moral hazard and the degree of risk lie between the extremes.

19.4   Payments Linked to Production or Profit

We now examine how additional clauses are added to a contract to eliminate or reduce moral hazards. For simplicity, we ignore risk bearing. We focus on employer-employee contracts. Under most such contracts, employees are paid by the hour or given a fixed salary. The problem with such agreements is that the workers are not directly rewarded for productive, profit-enhancing actions, so they tend to shirk. Here, rewarding agents for productive activities leads to greater efficiency.

There are two main ways to reward productive effort directly. One method is to link a worker's pay to his or her individual output. Another is to link a worker's pay to the firm's output or profitability. However, employers who cannot monitor workers do not use incentive-compatible contracts.

PIECE-RATE HIRE CONTRACTS

One direct approach to getting employees to work hard is to pay them by the *piece*—the output they produce—rather than by *time*—the number of hours they work. Piece rates are usually effective in increasing output, but they are not practical in all markets.

Greater Effort. Piece rates—by explicitly rewarding productivity—provide a greater incentive to employees to work hard than hourly wages do. For example, Billikopf (1995) found that employees who are paid by the piece prune a vineyard in only 19 hours of work per acre compared to 26 hours for employees paid by the hour. Shearer (2004) found that when tree planters were randomly assigned piece-rate pay or fixed hourly wages, they were 19% more productive when paid by the piece.

The increase in joint profit due to this greater productivity may be shared between the firm and the employees. Many workers, because they earn more with piece rates than they would earn with hourly pay, are pleased to be paid by the piece.

Problems with Piece Rates. Piece rates are not always practical, however. There are three chief difficulties with this system: measuring output, eliciting the desired behavior, and persuading workers to accept piece rates.

Paying piece rates is practical only if the employer can easily measure the output produced, such as the number of pieces of fruit picked or windshields installed. Employers do not use piece rates to compensate teachers, managers, and others whose output is difficult to measure. Thus piece rates are more common for blue-collar jobs than for white-collar jobs. Roughly 15% of the labor force receives pay based on individual productivity, but most piecework is concentrated in a handful of low-paying industries such as agriculture (in which about a third of workers are paid by the piece) and apparel manufacturing or is confined to sales personnel, individual contractors, and other similar occupations.

Piece rates backfire if they encourage undesirable behavior. Sears, Roebuck & Company used to reward auto shop employees on the basis of the size of customers' repair bills. This system apparently led to the overbilling of customers, which resulted in government actions and lawsuits.[9]

Some workers object to piece rates because they do not like to work hard or because they are concerned that firms will ratchet down workers' compensation after a while by lowering the pay per piece. In addition, piecework has a negative connotation in

---

[9]Buchholz, Barbara B., "The Bonus Isn't Reserved for Big Shots Anymore," *New York Times*, October 27, 1996.

many people's minds because of its association with sweatshops, where workers toil at repetitive tasks for 12 or more hours a day.

CONTINGENT CONTRACT REWARDS LINKED TO A FIRM'S SUCCESS

Although companies can use piece rates with workers who produce easily measured output, they need alternative incentive schemes for managers, corporate directors, and others whose productivity is difficult to quantify, especially those who work as part of a team. Such workers may be rewarded if their team or the firm does well in general. Frequently, year-end bonuses are based on increases in the firm's profit or the value of its stock.

A common type of incentive is a lump-sum year-end bonus based on the firm's performance or that of a group of workers within the firm. Another incentive is a stock option, which gives managers (and, increasingly, other workers) the option of buying a certain number of shares of stock in the firm at a prespecified *exercise price*. If the stock's market price exceeds the exercise price during that period, an employee can exercise the option—buy the stock—and then sell it at the market price, in this way making an immediate profit. But if the stock's price stays below the exercise price, the option is worthless. Beyond motivating employees to work hard, these incentives also act as *golden handcuffs*: a deterrent to taking a job at a competing firm and forfeiting the stock option. See **www.aw-bc.com/perloff**, Chapter 19, "Increasing Use of Incentives."

19.5 Monitoring

When a firm cannot use piece rates or reward workers for the firm's success, an employer usually pays fixed-fee salaries or hourly wages. Employees who are paid a fixed salary have little incentive to work hard if the employer cannot observe shirking. And if an employer pays employees by the hour but cannot observe how many hours they work, employees may inflate the number of hours they report working.

A firm can reduce such shirking by intensively supervising or monitoring its workers. Monitoring eliminates the asymmetric information problem: Both the employee and the employer know how hard the employee works. If the cost of monitoring workers is low enough, it pays to prevent shirking by carefully monitoring and firing employees who do not work hard.

Firms have experimented with various means of lowering the cost of monitoring. Requiring employees to punch a time clock or installing video cameras to record employees' work efforts are examples of firms' attempts to use capital to monitor job performance. Similarly, by installing assembly lines that force employees to work at a pace dictated by the firm, employers can control employees' work rate.

According to a recent survey by the American Management Association, nearly two-thirds of employers record employees' voice mail, e-mail, or phone calls; review their computer files; or videotape workers. A quarter of the firms that use surveillance don't tell their employees. The most common types of surveillance are tallying phone numbers called and recording the duration of the calls (37%), videotaping employees' work (16%), storing and reviewing e-mail (15%), storing and reviewing computer files (14%), and taping and reviewing phone conversations (10%). Monitoring and surveillance are most common in the financial sector, in which 81% of firms use these techniques. Rather than watching all employees all the time, companies usually monitor selected workers using spot checks.

For some jobs, however, monitoring is counterproductive or not cost effective. Monitoring may lower employees' morale, which in turn reduces productivity. Several years ago, Northwest Airlines took the doors off bathroom stalls to prevent workers from slacking off there. When new management eliminated this policy (and made many other changes as well), productivity increased.

It is usually impractical for firms to monitor how hard salespeople work if they spend most of their time away from the main office. As telecommuting increases, monitoring workers may become increasingly difficult.

When direct monitoring is very costly, firms may use various financial incentives, which we consider in the next section, to reduce the amount of monitoring that is necessary. Each of these incentives—bonding, deferred payments, and efficiency (unusually high) wages—acts as a *hostage* for good behavior (Williamson, 1983). Workers who are caught shirking or engaging in other undesirable acts not only lose their jobs but give up the hostage too. The more valuable the hostage, the less monitoring the firm needs to use to deter bad behavior.

BONDING

A direct approach to ensuring good behavior by agents is to require that they deposit funds guaranteeing their good behavior, just as a landlord requires tenants to post security deposits to ensure that they will not damage an apartment. An employer may require an employee to provide a performance *bond*, an amount of money that will be given to the principal if the agent fails to complete certain duties or achieve certain goals. Typically, the agent *posts* (leaves) this bond with the principal or another party, such as an insurance company, before starting the job.

Many couriers who transport valuable shipments (such as jewels) or guards who watch over them have to post bonds against theft and other moral hazards. Similarly, bonds may be used to keep employees from quitting immediately after receiving costly training (Salop and Salop, 1976). Most of the other approaches that we will examine as strategies for controlling shirking can be viewed as forms of bonding.

Bonding to Prevent Shirking.   Some employers require a worker to post a bond that is forfeited if the employee is discovered shirking. For example, a professional athlete faces a specified fine (the equivalent of a bond) for skipping a meeting or game. The higher the bond, the less frequently the employer needs to monitor to prevent shirking.

Suppose that the value a worker puts on the gain from taking it easy on the job is G dollars. If a worker's only potential punishment for shirking is dismissal if caught, some workers will shirk.

Suppose, however, that the worker must post a bond of B dollars that the worker forfeits if caught not working. Given the firm's level of monitoring, the probability that a worker is caught is θ. Thus a worker who shirks expects to lose θB.[10] A risk-neutral

---

[10]The expected penalty is $\theta B + (1 - \theta)0 = \theta B$, where the first term on the left-hand side is the probability of being caught times the fine of B and the second term is the probability of not being caught and facing no fine.

worker chooses not to shirk if the certain gain from shirking, G, is less than or equal to the expected penalty, θB, from forfeiting the bond if caught: $G \leq B$. Thus the minimum bond that discourages shirking is

$$B = \frac{G}{\theta}. \tag{19.5}$$

Equation 19.5 shows that the bond must be larger, the higher the value that the employee places on shirking and the lower the probability that the worker will be caught.

Trade-Off Between Bonds and Monitoring. Thus the larger the bond, the less monitoring is necessary to prevent shirking. Suppose that a worker places a value of $G = \$1,000$ a year on shirking. A bond that is large enough to discourage shirking is $1,000 if the probability of the worker's being caught is 100%, $2,000 at 50%, $5,000 at 20%, $10,000 at 10%, and $20,000 if the probability of being caught is only 5%.

SOLVED PROBLEM 19.3

Workers post bonds of B that are forfeited if they are caught stealing (but no other punishment is imposed). Each extra unit of monitoring, M, raises the probability that a firm catches a worker who steals, θ, by 5%. A unit of M costs $10. A worker can steal a piece of equipment and resell it for its full value of G dollars. What is the optimal M that the firm uses if it believes that workers are risk neutral? In particular, if $B = \$5,000$ and $G = \$500$, what is the optimal M?

Answer

1. *Determine how many units of monitoring are necessary to deter stealing:* The least amount of monitoring that deters stealing is the amount at which a worker's gain from stealing equals the worker's expected loss if caught. A worker is just deterred from stealing when the gain, G, equals the expected penalty, θB. Thus the worker is deterred when the probability of being caught is $\theta = G/B$. The number of units of monitoring effort is $M = \theta/0.05$, because each extra unit of monitoring raises θ by 5%.

2. *Determine whether monitoring is cost effective:* It pays for the firm to pay for M units of monitoring only if the expected benefit to the firm is greater than the cost of monitoring, $\$10 \times M$. The expected benefit if stealing is prevented is G, so monitoring pays if $G > \$10 \times M$, or $G/M > \$10$.

3. *Solve for the optimal monitoring in the special case:* The optimal level of monitoring is

$$M = \frac{\theta}{0.05} = \frac{G/B}{0.05} = \frac{500/5,000}{0.05} = \frac{0.1}{0.05} = 2.$$

It pays to engage in this level of monitoring because $G/M = \$500/2 = \$250 > \$10$.

Problems with Bonding. Employers like the bond-posting solution because it reduces the amount of employee monitoring that is necessary to discourage moral hazards such as shirking and thievery. Nonetheless, firms use explicit bonding only occasionally to prevent stealing, and they rarely use it to prevent shirking.

Two major problems are inherent in posting bonds. First, to capture a bond, an unscrupulous employer might falsely accuse an employee of stealing. An employee who fears such employer opportunism might be unwilling to post a bond. One possible solution to this problem is for the firm to develop a reputation for not behaving in this manner. Another possible approach is for the firm to make the grounds for forfeiture of the bond objective and thus verifiable by others.

A second problem with bonds is that workers may not have enough wealth to post them. In our example, if the worker could steal $10,000, and if the probability of being caught were only 5%, shirking would be deterred only if a risk-neutral worker were required to post a bond of at least $200,000.

Principals and agents use bonds when these two problems are avoidable. Bonds are more common in contracts between firms than in those between an employer and employees. Moreover, firms have fewer problems than typical employees do in raising funds to post bonds.

Construction contractors sometimes post bonds to guarantee that they will satisfactorily finish their work by a given date. It is easy to verify whether the contract has been completed on time, so there is relatively little chance of opportunistic behavior by the principal.

DEFERRED PAYMENTS

Effectively, firms can post bonds for their employees through the use of deferred payments. For example, a firm pays new workers a low wage for some initial period of employment. Then, over time, workers who are caught shirking are fired, and those who remain get higher wages. In another form of deferred wages, the firm provides a pension that rewards only hard workers who stay with the firm until their retirement. *Deferred payments serve the same function as bonds.* They raise the cost of being fired, so less monitoring is necessary to deter shirking.

Workers care about the present value (see Chapter 15) of their earnings stream over their lifetime. A firm may offer its workers one of two wage payment schemes. In the first, the firm pays w per year for each year that the worker is employed by the firm. In the second arrangement, the starting wage is less than w but rises over the years to a wage that exceeds w.

If employees can borrow against future earnings, those who work for one company their entire careers are indifferent between the two wage payment schemes if those plans have identical present values. The firm, however, prefers the second payment method because employees work harder to avoid being fired and losing the high future earnings.

Reduced shirking leads to greater output. If the employer and the employee share the extra output in the form of higher profit and lifetime earnings, both the firm and workers prefer the deferred-payment scheme that lowers incentives to shirk.

A drawback of the deferred-payment approach is that, like bond posting, it can encourage employers to engage in opportunistic behavior. For example, an employer might fire nonshirking senior workers to avoid paying their higher wages, and then replace them with less expensive junior workers. However, if the firm can establish a reputation for not firing senior workers unjustifiably, the deferred-payment system can help prevent shirking.

EFFICIENCY WAGES

As we've seen, the use of bonds and deferred payments discourages shirking by raising an employee's cost of losing a job. An alternative is for the firm to pay an **efficiency wage**: an unusually high wage that a firm pays workers as an incentive to avoid shirking.[11] If a worker who is fired for shirking can immediately go to another firm and earn the same wage, the worker risks nothing by shirking. However, a high wage payment raises the cost of getting fired, so it discourages shirking.[12]

How Efficiency Wages Act Like Bonds. Suppose that a firm pays each worker an efficiency wage w, which is more than the *going wage* $\underline{w}$ that an employee would earn elsewhere after being fired for shirking. We now show that the less frequently the firm monitors workers, the greater the wage differential must be between w and $\underline{w}$ to prevent shirking.

An efficiency wage acts like a bond to prevent shirking. A risk-neutral worker decides whether to shirk by comparing the expected loss of earnings from getting fired to the value, G, that the worker places on shirking. An employee who never shirks is not fired and earns the efficiency wage, w. A fired worker goes elsewhere and earns the lower, going wage, $\underline{w}$. Consequently, a shirking worker expects to lose $\theta(w - \underline{w})$, where θ is the probability that a shirking worker is caught and fired and where the term in parentheses is the lost earnings from being fired. Thus the expected value to a shirking employee is

$$\theta\underline{w} + (1 - \theta)w + G,$$

where the first term is the probability of being caught shirking, θ, times earnings elsewhere if caught and fired; the second term is the probability of not being caught times the efficiency wage; and the third term, G, is the value that a worker derives from shirking. The worker chooses not to shirk if the certain high wage from not shirking exceeds the expected return from shirking:

$$w \geq (1 - \theta)w + \theta\underline{w} + G.$$

Rearranging this expression, we find that a worker does not shirk if the expected loss from being fired is greater than or equal to the gain from shirking:

$$\theta(w - \underline{w}) \geq G. \tag{19.6}$$

The smallest amount by which w can exceed $\underline{w}$ and prevent shirking is determined when this expression holds with equality, $\theta(w - \underline{w}) = G$, or

$$w - \underline{w} = \frac{G}{\theta}. \tag{19.7}$$

The extra earnings, $w - \underline{w}$, in Equation 19.7 serve the same function as the bond, B, in Equation 19.5 in discouraging bad behavior.

---

[11]The discussion of efficiency wages is based on Yellen (1984), Stiglitz (1987), and especially Shapiro and Stiglitz (1984).

[12]There are other explanations for why efficiency wages lead to higher productivity. Some economists claim that in less-developed countries, employers pay an efficiency wage—more than they need to hire workers—to ensure that workers can afford to eat well enough that they can work hard. Other economists (Akerlof, 1982) and management experts contend that the higher wage acts like a gift, making workers feel beholden or loyal to the firm, so less (or no) monitoring is needed.

Suppose that the worker gets $G = \$1,000$ pleasure a year from not working hard and $\underline{w}$ is $20,000 a year. If the probability that a shirking worker is caught is $\theta = 20\%$, then the efficiency wage w must be at least $25,000 to prevent shirking. With greater monitoring, so that θ is 50%, the minimum w that prevents shirking is $22,000. From the possible pairs of monitoring levels and efficiency wages that deter shirking, the firm picks the combination that minimizes its labor cost.

AFTER-THE-FACT MONITORING

So far we've concentrated on monitoring by employers looking for bad behavior as it occurs. If shirking or other bad behavior is detected after the fact, the offending employee is fired or otherwise disciplined. This punishment discourages shirking in the future.

Punishment. It is often very difficult to detect bad behavior as it occurs but relatively easy to determine it after the fact. As long as a contract holds off payment until after the principal checks for bad behavior, after-the-fact monitoring discourages bad behavior. For example, an employer can check the quality of an employee's work. If it is substandard, the employer can force the employee to make it right.

Insurance companies frequently use this approach in contracts with their customers. Insurance firms try to avoid extreme moral hazard problems by offering contracts that do not cover spectacularly reckless, stupid, or malicious behavior. If an insurance company determines after the fact that a claim is based on reckless behavior rather than chance, the firm will refuse to pay.

For example, an insurance company will not pay damages for a traffic accident if the insured driver is shown to have been drunk at the time. A house insurance company disallows claims due to an explosion that is found to result from an illegal activity such as making methamphetamine. It will certainly disallow claims by arsonists who torch their own homes or businesses. Life insurance companies may refuse to pay benefits to the family of someone who commits suicide (as in the play *Death of a Salesman*).

APPLICATION

Abusing Leased Cars

Because drivers of fleet automobiles such as rental cars do not own them, they do not bear all the cost from neglecting or abusing the vehicles, resulting in a moral hazard problem. These vehicles are driven harder and farther and depreciate faster than owner-operated vehicles. In 2005, about 14% of car shoppers leased their vehicles.

Using data from sales at used-car auctions, Dunham (2003), after controlling for mileage, found that fleet vehicles (not including taxis or police cars) depreciate 10% to 13% more rapidly than owner-driven vehicles.[13] The average auction price for a Pontiac 6000 was $5,200 for a fleet car and $6,500 for a nonfleet car. This $1,300 difference, which was one-fourth of the fleet car's price, reflects the increased depreciation of fleet cars.

---

[13]According to National Public Radio's *Car Talk*—one of the world's most reliable sources of information—police cars have very few miles on them, but their engines are quickly shot because cops spend untold hours sitting in their cruisers in front of donut shops with the engine running and the air conditioner on high.

To deal with this moral hazard, an automobile-leasing firm commonly writes contracts—open-ended leases—in which the driver's final payment for the vehicle depends on the selling price of the car. In this way, the contract makes the leasing driver responsible for at least some of the harm done to the car, to encourage the lessee to take greater care of the vehicle. Given the difference in auction prices, however, such leases apparently are not the full solution to this moral hazard.

No Punishment. Finding out about moral hazards after they occur is too late if wrongdoers cannot be punished at that time. Indeed, there's no point in monitoring after the fact if punishment is then impossible or impractical. Although it's upsetting to find that you've been victimized, there's nothing you can do beyond trying to prevent the situation from happening again.

● APPLICATION

Mortgaging Our Future

Moral hazard played an important role in causing the bankruptcies of many savings and loans (S&Ls) in the late 1980s and early 1990s—and it threatens another disaster today. Individuals loan their money to an S&L because they know that federal or state agencies insure their deposits against an S&L failure. If the S&L defaults, the government must make good on lenders' losses.

To prevent S&L employees from engaging in moral hazards that lead to bankruptcies, government agencies traditionally required these institutions to invest primarily in relatively safe, local residential mortgage loans. However, in the early 1980s, the government changed its rules to allow S&Ls to invest more easily in other assets so that they could diversify their portfolios of investments. With this change, the percentage of investments in nontraditional assets by federally insured S&Ls increased from 11.5% in 1982 to 20.2% in 1985.

To keep S&L officers from engaging in extremely risky behavior or committing fraud, government agencies examined their records. Unfortunately, just when S&Ls were given greater latitude in investment, the number of examinations of S&Ls fell, from 3,210 in 1980 to 2,347 in 1984, and the examinations per billion dollars of assets dropped from 5.4 to 2.4.

After the rules changed, many S&L managers made extremely risky investments, reasoning that they would make a lot of money if these investments paid off, and believing—correctly—that if the S&L went bankrupt, they could walk away with impunity. They anticipated that the federal government would make good on the losses and not punish them (unless fraud was involved—and, apparently, not always even then). The combination of government insurance, greater freedom to invest, and slack monitoring created a moral hazard problem from bad investments.

The fastest-growing S&Ls tended to be those that took the largest risks. Whereas S&Ls that grew less than 15% in 1984 had 68% of their assets in traditional residential mortgages and mortgage-backed securities, S&Ls that were growing at more than 50% had only 53% in traditional assets. In 1985, shaky S&Ls had more commercial (rather than residential) mortgage loans, 13.4% versus 8.1%;

more land loans, 7.7% versus 1.2%; more commercial loans, 2.2% versus 1.3%; and more direct equity (stock) investments, 5.0% versus 1.7%. Many S&Ls that had invested heavily in these relatively risky investments went into bankruptcy when the investments failed.

To bail out the failed S&Ls, the federal government made huge payouts—much larger than those of earlier periods. In 1979, the federal government had had to dispose of only three failed S&Ls through liquidating their assets—about 0.1% of all S&L assets—or finding a new owner. By 1988, however, the federal government had to deal with 205 disposals, representing 7.45% of all S&L assets.

The present discounted value of the government's cost for 1988 alone was $38 billion. By 1990, a conservative estimate of the present value of costs for the financial disasters was about $150 billion, or nearly $600 for every man, woman, and child in the United States. The estimates of losses continue to rise, and taxpayers are still paying for cleaning up the losses created by moral hazards.

To minimize future moral hazard problems among S&Ls, government insurers raised the capital requirements that govern how much money the S&L owners and managers must provide. Now the owners and managers of S&Ls are investing more of their own money and less of account holders' money that is insured by the government. A capital requirement acts like an insurance deductible. It forces S&L managers and owners to put more of their own money (and less of account holders' money) at risk when making investments. As a consequence, the feds hoped that the S&L managers would invest more conservatively.

SOLVED PROBLEM   19.4

An S&L can make one of two types of loans. It can loan money on home mortgages, where it has a 75% probability of earning $100 million and a 25% probability of earning $80 million. Alternatively, it can loan money to oil speculators, where it has a 25% probability of earning $400 million and a 75% probability of losing $160 million (due to loan defaults by the speculators). The manager of the S&L, who will make the lending decision, receives 1% of the firm's earnings. He believes that if the S&L loses money, he can walk away from his job without repercussions, although without compensation. The manager and the shareholders of the company are risk neutral. What decision will the manager make if all he cares about is maximizing his personal expected earnings, and what decision do the stockholders prefer that he make?

Answer

1. *Determine the S&L's expected return on the two investments:* If the S&L makes home mortgage loans, its expected return is

$$(0.75 \times 100) + (0.25 \times 80) = 95$$

million dollars. Alternatively, if it loans to the oil speculators, its expected return is

$$(0.25 \times 400) + [0.75 \times (-160)] = -20$$

million dollars, an expected loss.

2. *Compare the S&L manager's expected profits on the two investments:* The manager expects to earn 1% of $95 million, or $950,000, from investing in mortgages. His take from investing in oil is 1% of $400 million, or $4 million, with a probability of 25% and no compensation with a probability of 75%. Thus he expects to earn

$$(0.25 \times 4) + (0.75 \times 0) = 1$$

million dollars from investing in oil. Because he is risk neutral and does not care a whit about anyone else, he invests in oil.

3. *Compare the shareholders' expected profits on the two investments:* The shareholders expect to receive 99% of the profit from the mortgages, or 0.99 × $95 million = $94.05 million. With the oil loans, they earn 99% of the $400 million, or $396 million, if the investment is good, and bear the full loss in the case of defaults, $160 million, so their expected profit (loss) is

$$(0.25 \times 396) + [0.75 \times (-160)] = -21$$

million dollars. Thus the shareholders would prefer that the S&L invest in mortgages.

Comment: Given that the manager has the wrong incentives (and no integrity), he makes the investment that is not in the shareholders' interest. One possible solution to the problem of their diverging interests is to change the manager's compensation scheme.

19.6 Contract Choice

We have examined how to construct a single contract so as to prevent moral hazards. Often, however, a principal gives an agent a choice of contracts. By observing the agent's choice, the principal obtains enough information to prevent agent opportunism.

Firms want to avoid hiring workers who will shirk. Employers know that not all workers shirk, even when given an opportunity to do so. So rather than focusing on stopping lazy workers from shirking, an employer may concentrate on hiring only industrious people. With this approach, the firm seeks to avoid *moral hazard* problems by preventing *adverse selection,* whereby lazy employees falsely assert that they are hardworking.

As discussed in Chapter 18, employees may *signal* to employers that they are productive. For example, if only nonshirking employees agree to work long hours, a commitment to working long hours serves as a reliable signal. In addition, employees can signal their productiveness by developing a reputation as hard workers. To the degree that employers can rely on this reputation, sorting is achieved.

When workers cannot credibly signal, firms may try to *screen out* bad workers. One way in which firms can determine which prospective employees will work hard and which will shirk is to give them a choice of contracts. Job candidates, by selecting a contingent contract in which their pay depends on how hard they work, signal that they are hard workers. In contrast, if job applicants choose a fixed-fee contract, they

TABLE 19.3   Firm's Spreadsheet

	Contingent Contract (30% of Sales), $	Fixed-Fee Contract ($25,000 Salary), $
Hard Worker		
Sales	100,000	100,000
− Salesperson's pay	−30,000	−25,000
= Firm's net revenue	70,000	75,000
− Office expenses	−50,000	−50,000
= Firm's profit	20,000	25,000
Lazy Worker		
Sales	60,000	60,000
− Salesperson's pay	−18,000	−25,000
= Firm's net revenue	42,000	35,000
− Office expenses	−50,000	−50,000
= Firm's profit	−8,000	−15,000

signal that they are lazy workers. Thus the firm can tell the applicants apart by their choices.

Suppose that a firm wants to hire a salesperson who will run its Cleveland office and that the potential employees are risk neutral. A hardworking salesperson can sell $100,000 worth of goods a year, but a lazy one can sell only $60,000 worth (see Table 19.3). A hard worker can earn $30,000 from other firms, so the firm considers using a contingent contract that pays a salesperson a 30% commission on sales.

If the firm succeeds in hiring a hard worker, the salesperson makes $30,000 = $100,000 × 0.30. The firm's share of sales is $70,000. The firm has no costs of production (for simplicity), but maintaining this branch office costs the firm $50,000 a year. The firm's profit is therefore $20,000. If the firm hires a lazy salesperson under the same contract, the salesperson makes $18,000, the firm's share of sales is $42,000, and the firm loses $8,000 after paying for the office.

Thus the firm wants to hire only a hard worker. Unfortunately, the firm does not know in advance whether a potential employee is a hard worker. To acquire this information, the firm offers a potential employee a choice of contracts:

- *Contingent contract:* No salary and 30% of sales
- *Fixed-fee contract:* Annual salary of $25,000, regardless of sales

A prospective employee who doesn't mind hard work would earn $5,000 more by choosing the contingent contract. In contrast, a lazy candidate would make $7,000 more from a salary than from commissions. If an applicant chooses the fixed-fee contract, the firm knows that the person does not intend to work hard and decides not to hire that person.

The firm learns what it needs to know by offering this contract choice as long as the lazy applicant does not pretend to be a hard worker and chooses the contingent contract. Under the contingent contract, the lazy person makes only $18,000, but that offer may dominate others available in the market. If this pair of contracts fails to sort workers, the firm may try different pairs. If all these choices fail to sort the potential employees, the firm must use other means to prevent shirking.

Summary

1. **Principal-Agent Problem:** A principal contracts with an agent to perform some task. The size of their joint profit depends on any assets that the principal contributes, the actions of the agent, and the state of nature. If the principal cannot observe the agent's actions, the agent may engage in opportunistic behavior. This moral hazard reduces the joint profit. An efficient contract leads to efficiency in production (joint profit is maximized by eliminating moral hazards) and efficiency in risk bearing (the less-risk-averse party bears more of the risk). Three common types of contracts are *fixed-fee contracts*, whereby one party pays the other a fixed fee and the other keeps the rest of the profits; *hire contracts*, in which the principal pays the agent a wage or by the piece of output produced; and *contingent contracts*, wherein the payoffs vary with the amount of output produced or in some other way. Because a contract that reduces the moral hazard may increase the risk for a relatively risk-averse person, a contract is chosen to achieve the best trade-off between the twin goals of efficiency in production and efficiency in risk bearing.

2. **Production Efficiency:** Whether efficiency in production is achieved depends on the type of contract that the principal and the agent use and on the degree to which their information is asymmetric. For the agent in our example to put forth the optimal level of effort, the agent must get the full marginal profit from that effort or the principal must monitor the agent. When the parties have full information, an agent with a fixed-fee rental or profit-sharing contract gets the entire marginal profit and produces optimally without being monitored. If the principal cannot monitor the agent or does not observe profit and cost, only a fixed-fee rental contract prevents moral hazard problems and achieves production efficiency.

3. **Trade-Off Between Efficiency in Production and in Risk Bearing:** A principal and an agent may agree to a contract that strikes a balance between reducing moral hazards and allocating risk optimally. Contracts that eliminate moral hazards require the agent to bear the risk. If the agent is more risk averse than the principal, the parties may trade off a reduction in production efficiency to lower risk for the agent.

4. **Payments Linked to Production or Profit:** To reduce shirking, employers may reward employees for greater individual or group productivity. Piece rates, which reward individuals who work unusually fast, are practical only when individual output can be easily measured and the quality of work is not critical. Bonuses and stock options that reward workers for increases in group effort provide less of an incentive than piece rates but still may reduce shirking.

5. **Monitoring:** Because of asymmetric information, an employer must normally monitor workers' efforts to prevent shirking. Less monitoring is necessary as the employee's interest in keeping the job increases. The employer may require the employee to post a large bond that is forfeited if the employee is caught shirking, stealing, or otherwise misbehaving. If an employee cannot afford to post a bond, the employer may use deferred payments or efficiency wages—unusually high wages—to make it worthwhile for the employee to keep the job. Employers may also be able to prevent shirking by engaging in after-the-fact monitoring. However, such monitoring works only if bad behavior can be punished after the fact.

6. **Contract Choice:** A principal may be able to prevent moral hazard problems from adverse selection by observing choices made by potential agents. For example, an employer may present potential employees with a choice of contracts, prompting hardworking job applicants to choose a contract that compensates the worker for working hard and lazy candidates to choose a different contract that provides a guaranteed salary.

Questions

*= answer at the back of this book; **W** = audio-slide show answers by James Dearden at **www.aw-bc.com/perloff**

*1. In the duck-carving example with full information (which the second column of Table 19.1 summarizes), is a contract efficient if it requires Paula to give Arthur a fixed-fee salary of $168 and leaves all the decisions to Arthur? If so, why? If not, are there additional steps that Paula can take to ensure that Arthur sells the optimal number of carvings?

2. The state of California set up its own earthquake insurance program in 1997. Because the state agency in charge has few staff members, it pays private insurance carriers to handle claims for earthquake damage. These insurance firms receive 9% of each approved claim. Is this compensation scheme likely to lead to opportunistic behavior by insurance companies? Explain. What would be a better way to handle the compensation?

3. Two students are given an assignment to produce a joint report for which they will receive the same grade. What problems, if any, are likely to arise?

4. In the duck-carving example with limited information (summarized in the third and fourth columns of Table 19.1), is a fixed-fee contract efficient? If so, why? If not,

are there additional steps that Paula can take to ensure efficiency?

5. A health insurance company tries to prevent the moral hazard of "excessive" dentist visits by limiting the number of visits each person can have per year. How does such a restriction affect moral hazard and risk bearing? Show in a graph.

*6. Some sellers offer to buy back a good later at some prespecified price. Why would a firm make such a commitment?

7. Traditionally, doctors have been paid on a fee-for-service basis. Now doctors are increasingly paid on a capitated basis: They get paid for treating a patient for a year, regardless of how much treatment is required. In this arrangement, doctors form a group and sign a capitation contract whereby they take turns seeing a given patient. What are the implications of this change in compensation for moral hazards and for risk bearing?

8. Fourteen states have laws that limit a franchisor's ability to terminate a franchise agreement. What effects do such laws have on production efficiency and risk bearing?

*9. A promoter arranges for many different restaurants to set up booths to sell Cajun-Creole food at a fair. Appropriate music and other entertainment are provided. Customers can buy food using only "Cajun Cash," which is scrip that has the same denominations as actual cash and is sold by the promoter at the fair. Why aren't the food booths allowed to sell food directly for cash?

10. Many law firms consist of partners who share profits. On being made a partner, a lawyer must post a bond, a large payment to the firm that will be forfeited on bad behavior. Why?

11. According to a flyer from Schwab's *Advisor-Source,* "Most personal investment managers base their fees on a percentage of assets managed. We believe this is in your best interest because your manager is paid for investment management, not solely on the basis of trading commissions charged to your account. You can be assured your manager's investment decisions are guided by one primary goal—increasing your assets." Is this policy in a customer's best interest? Why or why not?

12. Is shirking more likely to be a problem when employees are paid by the piece or by the hour? Explain.

*13. Zhihua and Pu are partners in a store in which they do all the work. They split the store's *business profit* equally (ignoring the opportunity cost of their own time in calculating this profit). Does their business profit-sharing contract give them an incentive to maximize their joint economic profit if neither can force the other to work? (*Hint:* Imagine Zhihua's thought process late one Saturday night when he is alone in the store, debating whether to keep the store open a little later or go out on the town.)

*14. When I was in graduate school, I shared an apartment with a fellow who was madly in love with a woman who lived in another city. They agreed to split the costs of their long-distance phone calls equally, regardless of who placed the calls. What is the implication of this fee-sharing arrangement on their total phone bill? Why?

15. In 2005, the co-founders of Google, Larry Page and Sergey Brin, asked that their annual pay be reduced to $1 (from $150,000 with bonuses of $206,556 in 2003, and $43,750 plus bonuses of $1,556 in 2004). Chief executive Eric Schmidt made the same request (Verne Kopytoff, "Google's Execs Paid $1 a Year," *San Francisco Chronicle,* April 9, 2005:C1, C2). Their compensation would be based on increases in the value of the vast amounts of Google stock that each owned (as of March 28, 2005, Page had 36.5 million Google shares; Brin, 36.4 million; and Schmidt, 13.9 million). How would you feel about this offer if you were a shareholder? What are the implications for moral hazard, efficiency, and risk sharing?

Problems

16. Book retailers can return unsold copies to publishers. Effectively, retailers pay for the books they order only after they sell the books. Dowell's Books believes that it will sell, with 1/2 probability each, either 0 or 1 copy of *The Fool's Handbook of Macroeconomics.* The bookstore also believes that it will sell, with 1/2 probability each, either 0 or 1 copy of *The Genius's Handbook of Microeconomics.* The retail price of each book is $25. Suppose that the marginal cost of manufacturing another copy of a book is $6. The publisher's value of a returned copy is zero. The *Microeconomics* publisher charges a $13 wholesale price and offers a full refund if an unsold book is returned. While the *Macroeconomics* publisher charges a low $10.50 wholesale price, it pays a retailer only $8 if it returns an unsold book. Dowell's places an order for one copy of each title. When the two books arrive, Dowell's has space to shelve only one. Which title does Dowell's return? Comment on how Dowell's decision about which title to return depends on the books' wholesale prices and on the compensation from the publishers for returned unsold books. **W**

17. In the National Basketball Association (NBA), the owners share revenue but not costs. Suppose that one team, the L.A. Clippers, sells only general-admission seats to a home

game with the visiting Philadelphia 76ers (Sixers). The inverse demand for the Clippers-Sixers tickets is $p = 100 - 0.004Q$. The Clippers' cost function of selling Q tickets and running the franchise is $C(Q) = 10Q$.

a. Find the Clippers' profit-maximizing number of tickets sold and the price if the Clippers must give 50% of their revenue to the Sixers. At the maximum, what are the Clippers' profit and the Sixers' share of the revenues?

b. Instead, suppose that the Sixers set the Clippers' ticket price based on the same revenue-sharing rule. What price will the Sixers set, how many tickets are sold, and what revenue payment will the Sixers receive? Explain why your answers to parts a and b differ.

c. Now suppose that the Clippers must share their profit rather than their revenue. The Clippers keep 45% of their profit and share 55% with the Sixers. The Clippers set the price. Find the Clippers' profit-maximizing price and determine how many tickets the team sells and its share of the profit.

d. Compare your answers to parts a and c using marginal revenue and marginal cost in your explanation. **W**

18. Warner Bros. Studios sells DVD copies of its films to Blockbuster, and the studio has revenue-sharing arrangements with the rental chain for VCR tapes of its films (Bruce Orwall, Martin Peers, and Ann Zimmerman, "DVD Gains on Tape, but Economics Have Hollywood in a Tizzy," *Wall Street Journal*, February 5, 2002, A1.) Suppose that Blockbuster is the only place where Perkasie, Pennsylvania, residents can rent videos and that the Saturday-night demand function to rent *L.A. Confidential* on either DVD or VHS is $p = 10 - Q/2$.

a. Suppose that the Perkasie Blockbuster purchased 10 copies of *L.A. Confidential* under the studio sales arrangement. What is Blockbuster's optimal rental price?

b. Suppose that Blockbuster pays the studio $2 per copy rented under the revenue-sharing arrangement, and that the store has 10 copies in stock. What is Blockbuster's optimal rental price?

c. Compare your answers to parts a and b. **W**

19. Suppose that a textbook author is paid a royalty of ω share of the revenue from sales, where the revenue is $R = pq$, p is the competitive market price for textbooks, and q is the number of sold copies of this textbook (which is similar to others on the market). The publisher's cost of printing and distributing the book is $C(q)$. Determine the equilib-

rium, and compare it to the outcome that maximizes the sum of the payment to the author plus the firm's profit. Answer using both math and a graph.

20. Suppose now that the textbook publisher in Problem 19 faces a downward-sloping demand curve. The revenue is $R(Q)$, and the publisher's cost of printing and distributing the book is $C(Q)$. Compare the equilibria for the following compensation methods in which the author receives the same total compensation from each method:

a. The author is paid a lump sum, $\mathcal{L}$.

b. The author is paid α share of the revenue.

c. The author receives a lump-sum payment and a share of the revenue.

Why do you think that authors are usually paid a share of the revenue?

*21. In Solved Problem 19.3, a firm calculated the optimal level of monitoring to prevent stealing. If $G = \$500$ and $\theta = 20\%$, what is the minimum bond that deters stealing?

22. In Problem 21, suppose that, for each extra $1,000 of bonding the firm requires a worker to post, the firm must pay that worker $10 more per period to get the worker to work for the firm. What is the minimum bond that deters stealing?

23. John manages Rachel's used CD music store. To provide John with the incentive to sell CDs, Rachel offers him 50% of the store's profit. John has the opportunity to misrepresent sales by fraudulently recording sales that actually did not take place. Let t represent his fraudulent profit. John's expected earnings from reporting the fraudulent profit is $0.5t$. Rachel tries to detect such frauds and either detects all or none of the fraud. The probability that Rachel detects the entire fraud is $t/(1 + t)$ and the probability that Rachel does not detect the fraud is $1 - t/(1 + t)$. Hence, Rachel's probability of detecting fraud is zero if John reports no fraudulent profit, increases with the amount of fraudulent profit he reports, and approaches 1 as the amount of fraud approaches infinity. If Rachel detects the fraud, then $x > 0.5$ is the fine that John pays Rachel per dollar of fraud. John's expected fine of reporting fraudulent profit t is $t^2x/(1 + t)$. In choosing the level of fraud, John's objective is to maximize his expected earnings from the fraud, $0.5t$, less his expected fine, $t^2x/(1 + t)$. As a function of x, what is John's optimal fraudulent profit? (*Hint*: check the second-order condition.) Show that $\partial t/\partial x < 0$. Also show that as $x \to \infty$, John's optimal reported fraudulent profit goes to zero. **W**

Calculus Appendix

In mathematics you don't understand things. You just get used to them.

—John von Neumann

This appendix reviews the basic tools from calculus and mathematics that we use throughout this book.[1] It emphasizes unconstrained and constrained maximization.

A.1 Functions

A *function* associates each member of a set with a single member of another set. In this section, we first examine *functions of a single variable* and then discuss *functions of several variables*.

FUNCTIONS OF A SINGLE VARIABLE

Suppose that we are interested in a variable x that is a member or an element of a set X. For example, the set X may be the nonnegative real numbers. A function f associates elements of the set X with elements of a set Y, which may be the same set as X. The function f is a *mapping* from X to Y, which we denote by $f: X \rightarrow Y$. The set X is the *domain* of the function f, while Y is the *range* of the function. In applying the mapping from an element of X to Y, we write $y = f(x)$.

We concentrate on real-number functions. Frequently, these functions map from the set of real numbers ($X = \mathbb{R}$) into the same set of real numbers ($Y = \mathbb{R}$). However, sometimes we consider functions with a domain that is an *interval* within the real numbers. For example, we might study a function that maps the numbers between zero and one. Such intervals are written as $[0, 1]$ if the interval includes zero and one, or as $(0, 1)$ if the endpoints of the interval are not included in the set. One can also use a parenthesis and a bracket, writing $(0, 1]$ for the interval of real numbers that are strictly greater than zero but less than or equal to one. By writing that $x \in (0, 1]$, we mean that the variable x can take on only a value that is greater than zero and less than or equal to one.

Some examples of functions of a single variable include the

- *Identity function:* $f(x) = x$ for all $x \in X$.
- *Zero function:* $f(x) = 0$ for all $x \in X$.
- *Square root function:* $f(x) = \sqrt{x}$ for all $x \geq 0$.
- *Hyperbolic function:* $f(x) = 1/x$, which is not defined when $x = 0$.

---

[1] Ethan Ligon is my co-author on this appendix.

These examples are called *explicit* functions because we can write them in the form $y = f(x)$. Some functions are *implicit* mappings between X and Y and are written in the form $g(x, y) = 0$. For example, $x^2 + y^2 - 1 = 0$ implicitly defines y in terms of x. We can always express an explicit function f in implicit form by defining $g(x, y) = y - f(x)$. However, it is not possible to express every implicit function explicitly. For example, the implicit function $g(x, y) = ay^5 + by^4 + cy^3 + dy^2 + ey + x = 0$ cannot generally be rewritten so that y is a closed-form expression of the variable x and the parameters a, b, c, d, and e.

FUNCTIONS OF SEVERAL VARIABLES

A function may depend on more than one variable. An example of such a function is $y = f(x_1, x_2)$, where $x \in X_1$ and $x_2 \in X_2$. Then the domain of the function is written as $X = X_1 \times X_2$, where the symbol $\times$ when applied to sets means to take all possible combinations of elements of the two sets. For example, the set $X = [0, 1] \times [0, 1]$ contains all the pairs of real numbers between zero and one, inclusive. The function f associates elements of the domain, the set $X = X_1 \times X_2$, with elements of the range, the set Y. That is, f is a mapping from X to Y, which may be denoted either by $f \colon X \to Y$ or by $f \colon X_1 \times X_2 \to Y$.

An example of mapping from a pair of variables to a single variable is the well-known measure of physical fitness, the *body mass index* (BMI), which is a function of weight (in kilograms) and height (in meters):

$$\text{BMI} = \frac{\text{weight}}{(\text{height})^2}.$$

If we let the variable z measure the BMI, w reflect the weight, and h denote the height, we can write this function more compactly as

$$z = f(w, h) = \frac{w}{h^2}.$$

Other examples of functions of two or more variables are the

- *Cobb-Douglas function with two variables:* $y = f(K, L) = 3L^{1/3}K^{2/3}$.
- *Cobb-Douglas function with two variables and two parameters:* $y = f(K, L) = AL^\alpha K^{1-\alpha}$, where A and α are parameters rather than variables—they represent unknown numbers rather than quantities that can change. The previous example is a special case, where $A = 3$ and $\alpha = 1/3$.
- *Cobb-Douglas function with n variables:* $y = f(x_1, x_2, x_3, \ldots, x_n) = Ax_1^{\alpha_1}x_2^{\alpha_2} \ldots x_n^{\alpha_n}$.

A.2 Properties of Functions

We make extensive use of several key properties that functions may possess. In this section, we start by discussing the main properties that we use, which are *monotonicity* (meaning that the graph of a function always goes up or always goes down), *continuity* (there are no breaks in the graph of the function), *concavity* and *convexity* (the function consistently curves upward or downward), and *homogeneity* (the function "scales" up or down in a consistent manner). After reviewing these properties, we list three properties of the logarithmic function that we use repeatedly.

MONOTONICITY

A monotonic function is one that is either always *increasing* or always *decreasing*. For example, the identity function, $f(x) = x$, is monotonically increasing. That is, as x increases, so does the value of the function $f(x)$. Some functions are monotonic only under certain conditions. For example, the function $f(x) = 1/x$ is monotonically decreasing when x is positive. The function $f(x) = x^2$ isn't monotonic; it is decreasing when x is negative and increasing when x is positive.

CONTINUITY

A function exhibits the property of *continuity* if a graph of the function has no jumps or breaks in it. A function can be continuous *at a point* if there are no jumps or breaks very near the point; if the function is continuous at all points, we say that the function is continuous. A sufficient condition for a function to be continuous at a point a is

$$\lim_{x \to a} f(x) = f(a),$$

which indicates that the limit of the function $f(x)$ as x approaches a is $f(a)$.[2]

CONCAVITY AND CONVEXITY

Economists make extensive use of the properties of concavity and convexity. We say that the function f is *concave* over a region A if the graph of the function $f(x)$ never goes below the line drawn between *any* pair of points in A. For example, in panel a of Figure A.1, we evaluate a function f with a domain X. Within this domain, we choose a subset A, and we evaluate f at two points x and x' within this subset A. This procedure gives us two points in the range of f, $f(x)$ and $f(x')$. The line connecting the points $(x, f(x))$ and $(x', f(x'))$ is below $f(x)$ for all x between x and x'.

This "never below the line" test reflects the intuition of concavity for functions of a single variable. But for functions of multiple variables and for testing the concavity of a function that we cannot easily draw, we have a better test. To illustrate this approach, we examine the concavity of a function of a pair of variables (x, y) that maps $f: X \times Y \to Z$. Again let A be a subset of the domain of f, $X \times Y$, and choose two points from the domain, (x, y) and (x', y'). The function f is concave over A if, for any value of θ such that $0 < \theta < 1$ and for any pair (x, y) and (x', y') in A,

$$f(\theta x + (1 - \theta)x', \theta y + (1 - \theta)y') \geq \theta f(x, y) + (1 - \theta)f(x', y'). \tag{A.1}$$

Equation A.1 is an extension of our "never below the line" test. If we let θ vary between zero and one, we can trace out all the values of the function f evaluated at points in A on the left-hand side of the inequality, while varying θ on the right-hand side of the

---

[2]If an infinite sequence tends toward some particular value as we progress through that sequence, that value is the limit of the sequence. For example, in the sequence $\{1, \frac{1}{2}, \frac{1}{3}, \frac{1}{4}, \ldots\}$, the nth element in the sequence equals $1/n$, where n is a positive whole number. As n gets larger, the value of $1/n$ tends to zero, so the limit of this sequence is zero (even though zero is not an element of the sequence).

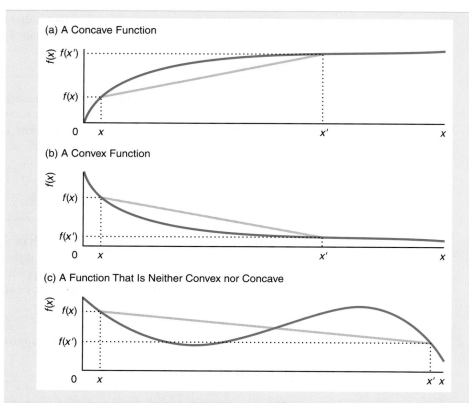

Figure A.1 Concave and Convex Functions. Some functions are convex, some concave, and some neither. (a) This function is convex because a straight line drawn between any two points never goes below the curve. (b) This function is concave because a straight line drawn between two points never goes below the curve. (c) This function violates both of these conditions and thus is neither convex nor concave.

expression traces out a line segment connecting the function f evaluated at (x, y) and at (x', y'). Thus this expression says that the function lies above the connecting line.

Sometimes a distinction is drawn between a function that is *weakly concave* or *strictly concave*. A *weakly concave* function f satisfies the requirement in Equation A.1, while a *strictly concave* function satisfies a replacement condition:

$$f(\theta x + (1 - \theta)x', \theta y + (1 - \theta)y') > \theta f(x, y) + (1 - \theta)f(x', y').$$

A function is *convex* over a region A if the opposite of the concavity condition holds. That is, the function never goes *above* a line connecting points on the function, as panel b of Figure A.1 illustrates. The mathematical requirement is same as the requirement for concavity with the inequality reversed: The function f is *weakly convex* over A if, for any value of θ such that $0 < \theta < 1$ and for any (x, y) and (x', y') in A,

$$f(\theta x + (1 - \theta)x', \theta y + (1 - \theta)y') \leq \theta f(x, y) + (1 - \theta)f(x', y').$$

The function is *strictly convex* if this expression holds with a strict inequality.

The function $f(x) = x^2$ is strictly convex. To demonstrate this convexity, we pick any two points on the real line x and x', and check that

$$f(\theta x + (1 - \theta)x') < \theta f(x) + (1 - \theta)f(x')$$

holds for this function. We substitute the actual function into this expression:

$$(\theta x + (1 - \theta)x')^2 < \theta x^2 + (1 - \theta)(x')^2, \text{ or}$$
$$\theta^2 x^2 + (1 - \theta)^2(x')^2 + 2\theta(1 - \theta)xx' < \theta x^2 + (1 - \theta)(x')^2.$$

Rearranging terms,

$$\theta(1 - \theta)x^2 + \theta(1 - \theta)(x')^2 - 2\theta(1 - \theta)xx' > 0, \text{ or}$$
$$x^2 + (x')^2 - 2xx' = (x - x')^2 > 0.$$

Thus this function is strictly convex.

In panel c of Figure A.1, the function x^3 is not concave or convex over the domain of real numbers: It is concave over the negative real numbers and convex over the positive real numbers. Finally, the Cobb-Douglas function $f(K, L) = AL^\alpha K^\beta$, where L and K are nonnegative real numbers, is concave if $\alpha + \beta \leq 1$.

HOMOGENEOUS FUNCTIONS

A function $f(x_1, x_2, \ldots, x_n)$ is said to be *homogeneous* of degree γ if

$$f(ax_1, ax_2, \ldots, ax_n) = a^\gamma f(x_1, x_2, \ldots, x_n)$$

for any constant $a > 0$. For example, suppose that f is a production function and the set $\{x_i\}$ consists of inputs to production. Given a particular set of inputs $(x_1, x_2, \ldots, x_n)$, the production function tells us how much output, $q = f(x_1, x_2, \ldots, x_n)$, the firm can produce. What happens to q if we double all the inputs so that $a = 2$? If for any set of inputs, output always doubles, then the production function is homogeneous of degree one. If output does not change at all, then it is homogeneous of degree zero. If it always quadruples, it is homogeneous of degree two, and so on. Some other examples are

- The function $f(x) = 1$ is homogeneous of degree zero because doubling x leaves $f(x)$ unchanged.
- The square root function $f(x_1, x_2) = \sqrt{x_1 + x_2}$ is homogeneous of degree one-half because doubling x_1 and x_2 causes the function to change to $\sqrt{2x_1 + 2x_2} = \sqrt{2}\sqrt{x_1 + x_2} = 2^{1/2}\sqrt{x_1 + x_2}$.
- The function $f(x_1, x_2) = \sqrt{x_1 x_2}$ is homogeneous of degree one because $\sqrt{(2x_1)(2x_2)} = 2\sqrt{x_1 x_2}$.
- The Cobb-Douglas function $f(L, K) = AL^\alpha K^\beta$ is homogeneous of degree $\alpha + \beta$ because $A(2L)^\alpha(2K)^\beta = 2^{\alpha + \beta}AL^\alpha K^\beta$.
- The functions $f(x) = x + 1$ and $f(x_1, x_2) = x_1 + \sqrt{x_2}$ are not homogeneous of any degree.

SPECIAL PROPERTIES OF LOGARITHMIC FUNCTIONS

Logarithms are wonderful, logarithms are fine.
Once you learn the rules of logs, you'll think they are sublime.

We use the logarithmic function repeatedly in this textbook because it has a number of desirable properties. For example, we can convert some multiplication problems into addition problems by using the logarithmic function. We always use the natural logarithm (or natural log) function of x, which we write as $\ln(x)$, where $x = e^{\ln(x)}$ for $x > 0$.

The key properties of logarithms that we use are

- The log of a product is equal to a sum of logs: $\ln(xz) = \ln(x) + \ln(z)$.
- The log of a number to a power is equal to the power times the log of the number: $\ln(x^b) = b \ln(x)$.
- It follows from this previous rule that the log of the reciprocal of x equals the negative of the log of x: $\ln(1/x) = \ln(x^{-1}) = -\ln(x)$.

A.3 Derivatives

We want a way to summarize how a function changes as its argument changes. One such measure is the slope. However, we generally use an alternative measure, the *derivative*, which is essentially the slope at a particular point. We illustrate the distinction between these two measures using a function of a single variable, $f: \mathbb{R} \to \mathbb{R}$.

The usual definition of a *slope* is "rise over run"—that is, the change in the value of a function when moving from point x_1 to another point x_2:

$$\text{Slope} = \frac{\text{rise}}{\text{run}} = \frac{f(x_2) - f(x_1)}{x_2 - x_1}.$$

This definition of a slope depends on comparing the function at *two* different points, x_1 and x_2. However, typically we want the slope of f at a point.

To determine the slope at a point, we first implicitly define the difference, h, between these points as $x_2 = x_1 + h$. Substituting this expression into our formula for the slope gives us

$$\frac{f(x_2) - f(x_1)}{x_2 - x_1} = \frac{f(x_1 + h) - f(x_1)}{h}.$$

The derivative of a real-value function $f: \mathbb{R} \to \mathbb{R}$ at a point x in $\mathbb{R}$ is

$$\frac{df(x)}{dx} = \lim_{h \to 0} \frac{f(x + h) - f(x)}{h}. \tag{A.2}$$

In this textbook, we use two different notational conventions to denote the derivative of a function. Here and in most places in the text, we write the derivative using the notation $df(x)/dx$. Sometimes for notational simplicity, we omit explicit reference to the argument of f, writing the derivative of f at x as df/dx where no ambiguity results.

The derivative has a graphical interpretation. The slope of a function between two points is equal to the slope of a straight line connecting those two points. The slope of such a straight line can be computed using the rise-over-run formula. In Figure A.2, the slope of a function between x_1 and x_2 is equal to the slope of a straight line connecting the two points $b = (x_1, f(x_1))$ and $(x_2, f(x_2))$. Now fix one of the points, b, and move the other point ever closer so that the run ($h = x_2 - x_1$) gets smaller and smaller. If the derivative exists, the rise, $f(x_2) - f(x_1) = f(x_1 + h) - f(x_1)$, will eventually get

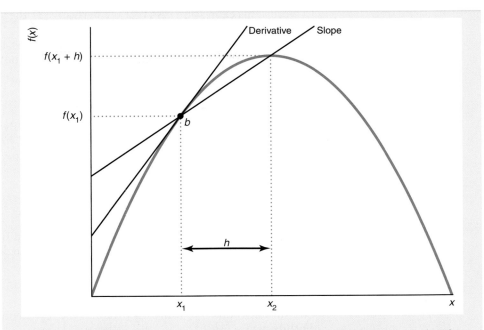

Figure A.2 Derivative and Slope. The slope of a function between x_1 and x_2 is equal to the slope (= rise over run) of a straight line connecting the two points $b = (x_1, f(x_1))$ and $(x_2, f(x_2))$. If we fix one of the points, b, and move the other point closer, then the run ($h = x_2 - x_1$) grows smaller and smaller. If the derivative exists, the rise, $f(x_2) - f(x_1) = f(x_1 + h) - f(x_1)$, will eventually get smaller as well, but typically at a different rate than the run. The limiting value of this slope is the derivative, which equals the slope of a line tangent to the function at b.

smaller and smaller as well, but typically at a different rate than the run. The limiting value of the ratio of the rise to the run will be the slope of an infinitesimally short line—the slope of the function at a point. The limiting value of this slope is the derivative, which equals the slope of a line tangent to the function at b.

If $df(x)/dx$ is positive, the function is *increasing* at x. That is, as x increases slightly, the function evaluated at x also increases. Similarly, if $df(x)/dx$ is negative, the function is said to be *decreasing* at x.

One problem with using derivatives instead of slopes is that in some circumstances, the derivative of a function may not be defined because the limit given in Equation A.2 does not exist. Discontinuous functions do not have derivatives at any point of discontinuity. For example, the derivative of the function $1/x$ does not exist at $x = 0$. The derivative also fails to exist for a continuous function at a kink, such as at $x = 0$ for the function $|x|$.

RULES FOR CALCULATING DERIVATIVES

This book repeatedly uses a few rules for calculating the derivatives of functions.

- *The addition rule:* If a function $f: \mathbb{R} \to \mathbb{R}$ can be written as the sum of two other functions, so that $f(x) = g(x) + h(x)$, then

$$\frac{df(x)}{dx} = \frac{dg(x)}{dx} + \frac{dh(x)}{dx}.$$

In words, this expression says that the derivative of the sum is equal to the sum of the derivatives.

- *The product rule:* If a function $f: \mathbb{R} \to \mathbb{R}$ can be written as the product of two other functions, so that $f(x) = g(x)h(x)$ where g and h are both differentiable at x, then

$$\frac{df(x)}{dx} = \frac{dg(x)}{dx}h(x) + g(x)\frac{dh(x)}{dx}.$$

An important special case occurs when $g(x)$ is a constant, say, b. Then $dg(x)/dx = 0$, so the product rule yields the result that $dbh(x)/dx = bdh(x)/dx$.

- *The power rule:* If $f(x) = ax^b$, then the derivative of f at x, provided that the derivative exists, is

$$\frac{df(x)}{dx} = abx^{b-1}.$$

For example, using the power rule, we can show that $d(bx^2)/dx = 2bx$. Applying this result and the product rule, we can determine the derivative $d(bx^3)/dx$:

$$\frac{dbx^3}{dx} = x\frac{dbx^2}{dx} + \frac{dx}{dx}bx^2 = x(2bx) + bx^2 = 3bx^2.$$

Continuing in this vein using the product rule repeatedly, we learn that in general, $dbx^n/dx = nbx^{n-1}$.

- *The polynomial rule:* A polynomial function is a function that takes the form

$$f(x) = b_0 + b_1x + b_2x^2 + \cdots + b_nx^n,$$

where n is a nonnegative whole number. The *order* of the polynomial is the largest exponent, n. Using the power rule repeatedly (as we just showed), the derivative of the polynomial $f(x)$ is

$$\frac{df(x)}{dx} = b_1 + 2b_2x + \cdots + nb_nx^{n-1}.$$

- *The reciprocal rule:* Using the power rule and the product rule, we can show that if $f(x) = 1/f(x)$, then

$$\frac{d[1/f(x)]}{dx} = -\frac{df(x)/dx}{[f(x)]^2}.$$

- *The quotient rule:* Using the reciprocal rule and the product rule, we can show that if $f(x) = g(x)/h(x)$, then

$$\frac{d[g(x)/h(x)]}{dx} = \frac{h(x)\dfrac{dg(x)}{dx} - g(x)\dfrac{dh(x)}{dx}}{[h(x)]^2}.$$

- *The chain rule:* We can compute the derivatives of functions such as $f(x) = g(h(x))$ by using all the previous rules,

$$\frac{df(x)}{dx} = \frac{dg(h(x))}{dx} = \frac{dg(h(x))}{dh(x)}\frac{dh(x)}{dx},$$

provided that h is differentiable at x and that g is differentiable at $h(x)$. As an example, let $h(x) = x^2$, and $g(z) = 2 + z^2$ so that $f(x) = g(h(x)) = 2 + x^4$. By direct differentiation, we know that $df(x)/dx = 4x^3$. We can derive the same result using the chain rule. First, we use the power rule to show that $dg(z)/dz = 2z$ and that $dh(x)/dx = 2x$. Second, we substitute $h(x)$ for z in the expression for $dg(z)/dz$, which gives us $dg(h(x))/dh(x)$, and apply the chain rule to obtain

$$\frac{dg(h(x))}{dx} = \frac{d[2 + h(x)]}{dh(x)}\frac{dh(x)}{dx} = (2x^2) \times (2x) = 4x^3.$$

■ *The exponential rule:* For any differentiable function $g(x)$,

$$\frac{de^{g(x)}}{dx} = \frac{dg(x)}{dx}e^{g(x)}.$$

An important special case of this rule is that

$$\frac{dae^{bx}}{dx} = abe^{bx}.$$

■ *The exponent rule:* An exponential function is one that can be written in the form $f(x) = a^x$, where a number a is raised to the power x. One can use the properties of logarithms together with the exponential rule and the chain rule to show that

$$\frac{da^x}{dx} = \frac{de^{\ln(a)x}}{dx} = \ln(a)a^x.$$

■ *The logarithm rule:* The derivative of the function $\ln(x)$ is

$$\frac{d\ln(x)}{dx} = \frac{1}{x}.$$

HIGHER-ORDER DERIVATIVES

If the derivative exists everywhere in the domain, we say that the function is *continuously differentiable*. For example, the function $f(x) = 1/x$ on the domain $(0, 1]$ is a continuously differentiable function. We can use the power rule to show that the ordinary derivative is

$$\frac{d[1/x]}{dx} = \frac{d[x^{-1}]}{dx} = -\frac{1}{x^2}.$$

This derivative is itself continuously differentiable on $(0, 1]$. Accordingly, we can use the power rule to differentiate this derivative a second time:

$$\frac{d[-1/x^2]}{dx} = \frac{d[-x^{-2}]}{dx} = \frac{2}{x^3}.$$

Rather than referring to this result as the "derivative of the derivative of $f(x)$," we call it the *second derivative of* $f(x)$, which we write as $d^2f(x)/dx^2$.

Higher-order derivatives are defined similarly. The derivative of the derivative of the derivative of $f(x)$, called the third derivative of $f(x)$, is written $d^3f(x)/dx^3$. In general, the nth order derivative of $f(x)$ is $d^nf(x)/dx^n$.

PARTIAL DERIVATIVES

When using a function of more than one variable, we want to know how the value of the function varies as we change one variable while holding the others constant. Consider a function of two real variables, $f: \mathbb{R}^2 \to \mathbb{R}$. The slope of this function at a point is a little

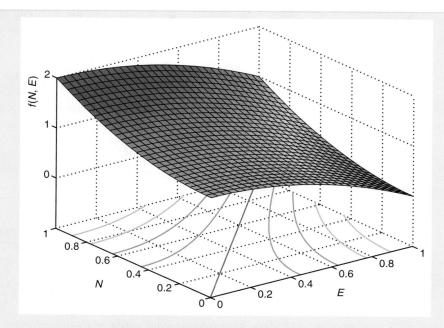

Figure A.3 Illustration of Partial Derivatives. The figure shows the surface and contour lines of the function $f(N, E) = N^2 - E^2 + 1$. If we move only in the N direction, the elevation rises at an increasing rate, whereas if we move only in the E direction, the elevation falls at the same increasing rate. The curves in the (N, E) plane are contour lines of the surface above the plane. The curves show that if E increases at the same rate as N, the elevation remains constant.

more complicated to define than the slope of a function with a single argument, because the slope of the function at a point now depends on direction. For example, let

$$f(N, E) = N^2 - E^2 + 1.$$

The variable names are chosen to evoke a map, where N reflects the latitude and E denotes the longitude. The value of the function f evaluated at a point on this map can then be thought of as corresponding to the altitude (height). Figure A.3 shows the surface and contour lines of this function.

This function takes the value of zero at the origin but changes in quite different ways as one moves away from the origin, depending on the direction of the move. If one were to move directly to the northeast, then N and E would increase at the same rate (hence their squares do, too). Thus if one moves directly to the northeast (or southwest), the altitude does not change. In the figure, the curves in the (N, E) plane are contour lines of the surface above the plane. The curves show that if E increases at the same rate as N, the elevation remains constant.

However, if one begins at the origin and heads directly north, then N increases while E remains fixed. One's altitude increases in this direction. If, on the other hand, one heads directly east, E increases while N remains fixed, and one heads downhill (after traveling E units, one attains an altitude of $1 - E^2$).

Going *just* north or *just* east gets at the idea behind the *partial derivative:* The idea is to vary the value of one variable while holding all the other variables fixed. This procedure also gives us an easy algorithm for computing the partial derivative of f with respect to, say, N: Just pretend that E is a constant, and compute the *ordinary* derivative. Thus we have the partial derivative of f with respect to N,

$$\frac{\partial f(N, E)}{\partial N} = \frac{\partial(N^2 - E^2)}{\partial N} = \frac{\partial N^2}{\partial N} = 2N,$$

and the partial derivative of f with respect to E,

$$\frac{\partial f(N, E)}{\partial E} = \frac{\partial(N^2 - E^2)}{\partial E} = -\frac{\partial E^2}{\partial E} = -2E.$$

In the special case in which f is a function of only a single variable, the partial derivative is exactly the same as the ordinary derivative:

$$\frac{\partial f(x)}{\partial x} = \frac{df(x)}{dx}.$$

In the general case in which the function $f: \mathbb{R}^m \to \mathbb{R}$ depends on several variables, one can think of the partial derivative of f with respect to, say, the first variable as measuring the *direct* effects of changes in the first variable on the value of the function, while neglecting the effects that changes in this variable might have on *other* variables that might influence the value of $f(x)$. Just as the ordinary derivative of an ordinary derivative is called a second (ordinary) derivative, there are also higher-order partial derivatives. For example, the partial derivative of $g(x_1, x_2)$ with respect to x_1 is written as $\partial g(x_1, x_2)/\partial x_1$; the *second* partial derivative of $g(x_1, x_2)$ with respect to x_1 is written $\partial^2 g(x_1, x_2)/\partial x_1^2$, while the second partial derivative of $g(x_1, x_2)$ with respect to x_2 is written as $\partial^2 g(x_1, x_2)/\partial x_2^2$.

We can derive second-order (or higher-order) derivatives that involve the repeated differentiation of the function with respect to more than one variable. For example, if we differentiate the partial derivative of our function $g(x_1, x_2)$ with respect to x_1, $\partial g(x_1, x_2)/\partial x_1$, with respect to x_2, we obtain the cross-partial derivative, $\partial^2 g(x_1, x_2)/(\partial x_1 \partial x_2)$. The order of differentiation doesn't matter for the functions we usually study. According to Young's Theorem, $\partial^2 f/(\partial x_1 \partial x_2) = \partial^2 f/(\partial x_2 \partial x_1)$ if the cross-partial derivatives $\partial^2 f/(\partial x_1 \partial x_2)$ and $\partial^2 f/(\partial x_2 \partial x_1)$ exist and are continuous. Similarly, $\partial^5 g(x_1, x_2)/(\partial x_1^2 \partial x_2^3)$ indicates partial differentiation of g with respect to x_1 twice and with respect to x_2 thrice, thus yielding a fifth-order partial derivative.

EULER'S HOMOGENEOUS FUNCTION THEOREM

A function $f: \mathbb{R}^n \to \mathbb{R}$ is *homogeneous* of degree γ if

$$f(tx_1, tx_2, \ldots, tx_n) = t^\gamma f(x_1, \ldots, x_n)$$

holds for all possible values of $x_1, x_2, \ldots, x_n$ and constant scalar t. That is, multiplying each of the arguments of the function by t increases the value of the function by t^γ. The degree need not be an integer. For example, the Cobb-Douglas function $A x_1^{\alpha_1} x_2^{\alpha_2} \ldots x_n^{\alpha_n}$ is homogeneous of degree $\alpha_1 + \alpha_2 + \cdots + \alpha_n$, where the α_i's may be fractions. Such a function satisfies Euler's homogeneous function theorem

$$\sum_{i=1}^{n} x_i \frac{\partial f(x_1, \ldots, x_n)}{\partial x_i} = \gamma f(x_1, \ldots, x_n).$$

A.4 Maximum and Minimum

Most microeconomic analysis concerns finding the maximum or minimum of a function. For example, a consumer chooses a bundle of goods to maximize utility, or a firm chooses inputs so as to minimize cost.

The problems of finding a maximum and finding a minimum may sound as though they are very different, but they are similar mathematically. We think of the problems of finding either *maxima* or *minima* as special cases of the more general problem of finding *extrema*.

LOCAL EXTREMA

Mathematicians and economists are sometimes interested in the *local* properties of a function, or, equivalently, the properties of a function within the *neighborhood* of a point x. A local property is one that holds within a neighborhood of x—that is, within some positive (but possibly very small) distance $\varepsilon > 0$ from the point x. For example, a function has a local maximum at x^* if there exists an $\varepsilon > 0$ such that $f(x^*) \geq f(x)$ for all $x \in (x^* - \varepsilon, x^* + \varepsilon)$—that is, in the neighborhood of x^*.

A *local* extremum of a function $f(x)$ is either a local minimum or a local maximum of the function f. If we move from the local extremum at x by an amount less than ε, the value of the function becomes less extreme. Figure A.4 graphs the function $f(x) = x \sin(6\pi x)$, which has many peaks and troughs. All the local extrema are indicated with bullets. Points a, b, and c are local maxima, while points d, e, and f are local minima. All these local maxima and local minima together compose the set of local extrema. Point a is a local maximum because if we either increase or decrease x just a little, the

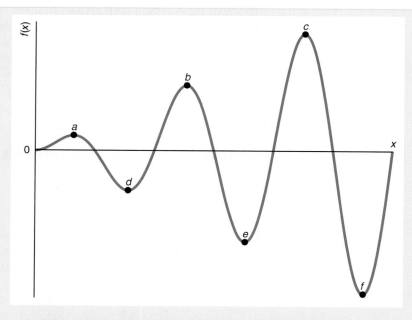

Figure A.4 Illustration of Local and Global Extrema. The bullets indicate the local extrema. Point c is the global maximum, and point f is the global minimum.

value of $f(x)$ decreases. Similarly, d is a local minimum because if we either increase or decrease x slightly, the value of $f(x)$ increases.

GLOBAL EXTREMA

The *global maximum* (usually referred to as the *maximum*) is the largest local maximum, and the *global minimum* (or *minimum*) is the smallest local minimum. In Figure A.4, the global maximum is point c and the global minimum is point f. If there are two local maxima that are both equally large and larger than all other points, we would say that there are *two* global maxima.

EXISTENCE OF EXTREMA

In economics, we often want to know if a function has a maximum or a minimum in the relevant domain. For example, we might examine whether there is a minimum for a function $f: [0,1] \rightarrow \mathbb{R}$; that is, f takes values from the interval between zero and one (inclusive) and maps them into the real line.

Not all such functions have a maximum or a minimum. Continuity of a function is a *sufficient* condition for the existence of both a maximum and a minimum. This result is a consequence of the *Extreme Value Theorem:* If the function f is continuous and defined on the closed interval $[a, b]$, there is at least one c in $[a, b]$ such that $f(c) \geq f(x)$ for all x in $[a, b]$, and there is at least one d in $[a, b]$ such that $f(d) \leq f(x)$ for all x in $[a, b]$. Functions that are not continuous *might* have minima and maxima—we just don't have a guarantee of that.

Figure A.5 illustrates several possibilities. Panel a shows a continuous function, $y = f(x) = 24x - 75x^2 + 50x^3$, with a single minimum and a single (local and global) maximum in $[0,1]$. In panel b, the continuous function $y = f(x) = 1$ has an infinite number of maxima and minima in $[0, 1]$. In panel c, the discontinuity in the function

$$y = \begin{cases} 24x - 75x^2 + 50x^3, & x < 0.8 \\ 24x - 75x^2 + 50x^3, & x > 0.8 \end{cases}$$

is shown as a hollow circle. Because of this missing point, there is a unique maximum, but there isn't a global minimum within $[0, 1]$. Finally, the discontinuous function plotted in panel d,

$$y = \begin{cases} 0, & x < 0.8 \\ 1, & x \geq 0.8, \end{cases}$$

has an infinite number of maxima and minima in $[0, 1]$.

UNIQUENESS OF EXTREMA

As panels b and d of Figure A.5 illustrate, even when a function has global maxima or global minima, there may be more than one maximum or minimum. We want to determine when the function will have a unique solution. There is a unique global maximum if the function f is strictly concave, and a unique global minimum if f is strictly convex. For example, in panel a of Figure A.5, when x is less than about 0.46, where the curve hits the horizontal axis, the function is concave, so there is a single global maximum. However, to the right of this point, the function is convex and has a single global minimum.

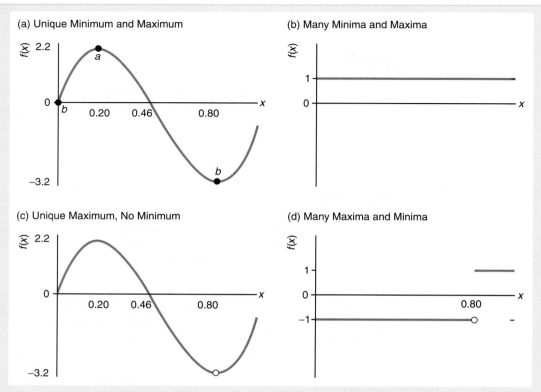

Figure A.5 Illustration of the Extreme Value Theorem. According to the Extreme Value Theorem, if a function is continuous and defined on the closed interval, it contains at least one minimum and at least one maximum. (a) This continuous function has a maximum at point *a* and a minimum at *b*. (b) This continuous function has an infinite number of max- ima and minima that equal one. (c) This functions is discontinuous at the point marked with a hollow point, so the theorem cannot be used to draw infer- ences about the existence of minima and maxima. For the domain (0, 1], the function has a maximum, but no minimum. (d) This discontinuous function has infinite maxima and minima.

INTERIOR EXTREMA

Often in the text we care whether the maximum or minimum is located in the interior of the range of *x* or at one of the end points. To illustrate this distinction, we consider the function $f(x) = -(x - \frac{1}{2})^2/2$, where *x* lies within [0, 1], as panel a of Figure A.6 shows. This function has a maximum at point *a* where $x^* = 0.5$, which we call an *interior* maximum because $x^* \in (0, 1)$ and it is not on the edge of the domain [0, 1]. That is, x^* is not zero or one. In contrast, in panel b, because the maximum of the function $g(x) = -x^2/2$ is zero at point *a*, which is on the edge or *corner* of the domain [0, 1], the maximum of this function is *not* interior.

A.5 Finding the Extrema of a Function

Because it is not always practical to plot functions and look for extrema, we use calcu- lus to find local extrema. The key insight is that for functions that are continuously differentiable, the *slope* of the function at any interior minimum or maximum is zero.

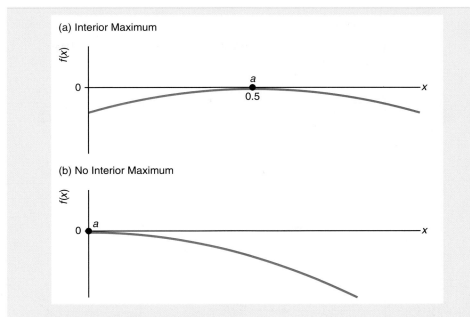

Figure A.6 Interior Extrema. In panel a, the maximum, point *a*, occurs at $x = 0.5$, which lies in the interior of the interval $[0, 1]$. In panel b, the maximum at *a* is at the corner—not in the interior of the domain.

Figure A.7 illustrates that the slope of the graph at every interior local minimum or maximum is zero.

Because derivatives can be thought of as the slope of a function, one way to find all the interior local extrema of a continuously differentiable function is to find where the partial derivatives of the function equal zero. Let's begin with a problem that has only a single independent variable and $f: [0, 1] \rightarrow \mathbb{R}$, where f is assumed to be continuously differentiable and strictly concave. What is the importance of these assumptions?

There are two important consequences of our assumption that f is continuously differentiable. First, because f is continuously differentiable, it must also be continuous, so we know that it has a maximum. Second, because it is continuously differentiable, we know that its derivative exists, and hence we can use this derivative to determine the local extrema.

Because f is assumed to be strictly concave, we know that it has a unique global maximum. Thus if we find a point x where $df(x)/dx = 0$, it follows that this point x is the unique global maximum of the function f over the interval $[0, 1]$.

The usual way to write the problem of finding a maximum of a function $f(x)$ is

$$\max_{x} f(x),$$

where *max* is called the *max operator,* the variable x that appears below the max operator is the *choice variable,* and f is the function to be maximized and is called the *objective function.*

Any x^* in $[0, 1]$ that solves $df(x^*)/dx = 0$ is a point at which the function $f(x)$ has a local maximum. The equation $df(x)/dx = 0$, in which we set the first-order derivative equal to zero, is called the *first-order condition.* The x^* that solves this equation,

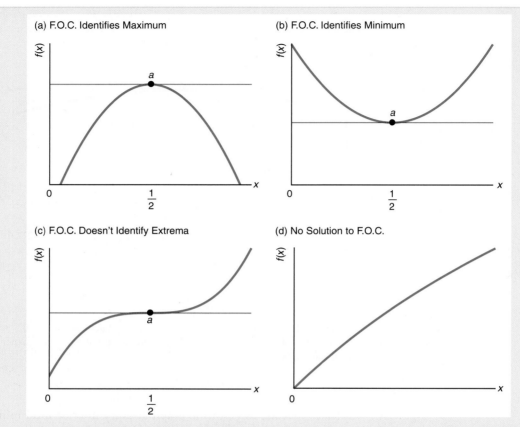

Figure A.7 Extrema and the First-Order Condition (F.O.C.). If a function is continuously differentiable and concave, it must have a unique maximum. Further, if the F.O.C. has a solution (that is, the function has a point where its slope is zero), the F.O.C. characterizes the unique maximum. (a) This function is continuously differentiable and concave, so the F.O.C. identifies a unique maximum (at point *a*). (b) The function is continuously differentiable, so it has at least one maximum, but the function is not concave, so the maximum may not be unique (indeed, there are two maxima at the end points). The function is convex, so the F.O.C. characterizes a minimum. (c) The function is continuously differentiable, so it possesses a maximum in the interval [0, 1]. However, at point *a* where the F.O.C. holds, the function is neither concave nor convex, so *a* is neither a minimum nor a maximum—it is a saddle point. (d) The function is concave, so this maximum will be unique. However, the F.O.C. does not have a solution in the interval [0, 1]—there is no place where the function has a slope equal to zero—so the unique maximum is not characterized by the F.O.C.

$df(x^*)/dx$, is called a *critical value.* Given our assumptions that *f* is continuously differentiable and concave, we know that x^* is a unique global maximum.

So far, we've assumed that *f* is concave, as in panel a of Figure A.7. In practice, we need to check whether the function is concave. For example, if we falsely assume that the function is concave and it is convex, we may find a minimum rather than a maximum, as in panel b.

If $f(x^*)$ is at least twice-differentiable in a neighborhood of x^*, we can use the *second-order condition* to determine whether the function is concave in that neighborhood. The second-order condition for concavity is that the second derivative of $f(x^*)$

is negative, $d^2f(x^*)/dx^2 < 0$. If this condition holds, we know that the x^* that the first-order condition identified is a unique maximum in this neighborhood of x^*. In contrast, if the second derivative is positive, we know that the function is convex in this neighborhood and that we have found a minimum.

EXAMPLES

We can illustrate this approach using several examples where $f: [0, 1] \rightarrow \mathbb{R}$. Our first maximization problem is

$$\max_x -\frac{1}{2}\left(x - \frac{1}{2}\right)^2.$$

The first-order condition is $df(x)/dx = \frac{1}{2} - x = 0$, so $x^* = \frac{1}{2}$, as panel a of Figure A.7 shows. The second-order condition is $d^2f(x^*)/dx^2 = -1 < 0$, so $\frac{1}{2}$ is a maximum. One can demonstrate that this function f is continuously differentiable and concave throughout the domain, so $f(\frac{1}{2}) = 0$, point a, is the global maximum of this function.

Now consider the maximization problem

$$\max_x \frac{1}{2}\left(x - \frac{1}{2}\right)^2.$$

The first-order condition is $df(x)/dx = x - \frac{1}{2} = 0$, so this problem has the same critical value, $x = \frac{1}{2}$, as in the previous example. Because f is continuously differentiable, we know that it has a maximum and a minimum on $[0, 1]$. The second-order condition is $d^2f(\frac{1}{2})/dx^2 = 1 > 0$, so $x^* = \frac{1}{2}$ is a minimum, as panel b of Figure A.7 shows. There are two global maxima, which are not interior, at $x = 0$ and $x = 1$.

The maximization problem

$$\max_x \frac{1}{3}\left(x - \frac{1}{2}\right)^3$$

has a first-order condition $df(x)/dx = (x - \frac{1}{2})^2 = 0$, so the critical value is again at $x = \frac{1}{2}$. Because f is continuously differentiable, we know it has a maximum on $[0, 1]$, but as in the previous example, the maximum is not interior; instead, it occurs at $x = 1$. This function is neither concave nor convex at $x = \frac{1}{2}$, so $x^* = \frac{1}{2}$ is neither a minimum nor a maximum of f, as panel c of Figure A.7 illustrates. It is called a *saddle point*. We have a saddle point when the second-order condition is zero, as in this case: $d^2f(\frac{1}{2})/dx^2 = 2(x - \frac{1}{2}) = 2(\frac{1}{2} - \frac{1}{2}) = 0$. The sign of the second derivative changes from one side to the other of the saddle point.

Finally, the maximization problem

$$\max_x \ln(x + 1)$$

yields the first-order condition $1/(x + 1) = 0$. Here f is continuously differentiable and strictly concave, so we know that a unique global maximum exists. However, there is no value of x in the $[0, 1]$ interval that solves the first-order condition. Consequently, we know that the unique global maximum is *not* interior (in this case, it occurs where $x = 1$), as panel d of Figure A.7 illustrates.

More generally, we may want to find the maximum of a function of several variables, and hence several choice variables appear under the max operator. To use calculus to solve such a maximization problem, we compute the partial derivatives of the objective function with respect to each of the choice variables and then set these equal to zero. These equations, in which the first-order partial derivatives are set equal to zero, are called the *first-order conditions*.

For example, let $g : [0, 1] \times [0, 1] \rightarrow \mathbb{R}$, and assume that g is continuously differentiable and strictly concave. Then we know, as we did for f, that g has a unique global maximum. Accordingly, we can write the problem as

$$\max_{x_1, x_2} g(x_1, x_2),$$

which yields the pair of first-order conditions

$$\frac{\partial g(x_1, x_2)}{\partial x_1} = 0, \tag{A.3}$$

$$\frac{\partial g(x_1, x_2)}{\partial x_2} = 0. \tag{A.4}$$

The solution to this pair of equations A.3 and A.4 determines where the global maximum of g is located, if a solution exists. If a solution to these equations does not exist, then the maximum must lie on the boundary of the choice set $[0, 1] \times [0, 1]$, so either x_1 or x_2 (or both) must be equal to either zero or one at the maximum.

INDIRECT OBJECTIVE FUNCTIONS AND THE ENVELOPE THEOREM

Economic problems generally involve choice variables that are under the control of a person or a firm, such as how much of a good to buy or to produce. Economic problems may also depend on *exogenous* parameters that influence the decision maker's behavior but are not under the decision maker's direct control, such as the price at which the good can be bought or sold. We can add these exogenous parameters to the formulation of a maximization problem.

To illustrate this approach, we examine a function $g : [0, 1] \times [0, 1] \times \mathbb{R} \rightarrow \mathbb{R}$. We write this function and its arguments as $g(x_1, x_2, z)$, where the variables x_1 and x_2 are choice variables and z is an exogenous parameter. We assume that g is continuously differentiable in all three of its arguments and is strictly concave in the first two (the choice variables). Consequently, g has a unique global maximum (even if g is not concave in the exogenous parameters).

The decision maker's problem of choosing x_1 and x_2 to maximize g given z is written as

$$\max_{x_1, x_2} g(x_1, x_2, z).$$

The first-order conditions are

$$\frac{\partial g(x_1, x_2, z)}{\partial x_1} = 0,$$

$$\frac{\partial g(x_1, x_2, z)}{\partial x_2} = 0,$$

so the optimal choice of x_1 and x_2 typically depends on the value of z. Accordingly, the values of x_1 and x_2 that solve the optimization problem for a given z may be written as $x_1^*(z)$ and $x_2^*(z)$.

Given a solution to the maximization problem, the value of g at the maximum is $g(x_1^*(z), x_2^*(z), z)$. Given some value z, the act of maximization determines the optimal values of x_1^* and x_2^*. Accordingly, we may sometimes write the maximum as

$$V(z) = g(x_1^*(z), x_2^*(z), z) = \max_{x_1, x_2} g(x_1, x_2, z).$$

The function $V(z)$ is called the *value function* because it tells us what the value of z is to the decision maker. It is also called the *indirect objective function*, in contrast to $g(x_1, x_2, z)$, which is the *direct objective function*.

A natural question to ask is how the value function changes when z changes. At first glance, this problem is very complicated because (as we have seen) a change in z has a direct effect on the value of $g(x_1, x_2, z)$ and it *also* causes the decision maker to change x_1 and x_2 in what may be complicated ways. However, at least for *small* changes in z, an important shortcut to solving this problem exists. The *Envelope Theorem* tells us that the direct effect of small changes in z matter but that the indirect effects do not. That is, according to the Envelope Theorem, the solution to our particular problem is

$$\frac{\partial V(z)}{\partial z} = \frac{\partial g(x_1, x_2, z)}{\partial z}. \tag{A.5}$$

We offer another, more general statement of this theorem below when we talk about the solutions to constrained maximization problems, and offer a constructive proof there.

COMPARATIVE STATICS

Not only do we want to know how a change in the exogenous parameter affects the value function, we also want to know how this change in the exogenous parameter, z, affects the choice variables, x_1 and x_2. We can use our first-order conditions to answer this question because the first-order conditions show how the optimal choice of x_1 and x_2 depends on z. In our example, the first-order conditions are

$$\frac{\partial g(x_1^*(z), x_2^*(z), z)}{\partial x_1(z)} = 0,$$

$$\frac{\partial g(x_1^*(z), x_2^*(z), z)}{\partial x_2(z)} = 0.$$

Provided that the function g is twice continuously differentiable, we can then compute the derivatives of each of these first-order conditions with respect to the exogenous parameter:

$$\frac{\partial^2 g}{\partial x_1^2} \frac{dx_1^*(z)}{dz} + \frac{\partial^2 g}{\partial x_1 \partial x_2} \frac{dx_2^*(z)}{dz} + \frac{\partial g}{\partial z} = 0, \tag{A.6}$$

$$\frac{\partial^2 g}{\partial x_1 \partial x_2} \frac{dx_1^*(z)}{dz} + \frac{\partial^2 g}{\partial x_2^2} \frac{dx_2^*(z)}{dz} + \frac{\partial g}{\partial z} = 0, \tag{A.7}$$

where we omit the arguments to the function g for notational simplicity.

By treating the derivatives $dx_1^*(z)/dz$ and $dx_2^*(z)/dz$ as variables in the pair of linear equations A.6 and A.7 and the partial derivatives of g as coefficients, we can solve this system of equations to determine how the maximizing choice of x_1 and x_2 changes for small changes in z. That is, we can solve for $dx_1^*(z)/dz$ and $dx_2^*(z)/dz$.

A.6 Maximizing with Equality Constraints

Most questions in microeconomics involving maximizing or minimizing an objective function subject to one or more *constraints*. For example, consumers maximize their well-being subject to a budget constraint. A firm chooses the cost-minimizing bundle of inputs subject to a feasibility constraint that summarizes which combinations of inputs can produce a given amount of output.

There are two commonly used approaches to solving problems with equality constraints mathematically: the substitution method and Lagrange's method. To illustrate these two approaches, we consider the problem of maximizing the function $g(x_1, x_2)$ subject to the constraint that $h(x_1, x_2) = z$, where z is an exogenous parameter. We write the constraint in implicit function form as $z - h(x_1, x_2) = 0$. This *constrained* maximization problem is written

$$\max_{x_1, x_2} g(x_1, x_2)$$

$$\text{s.t. } z - h(x_1, x_2) = 0. \tag{A.8}$$

Conceptually, we need to find the set of all those x_1 and x_2 that satisfy the constraint $z - h(x_1, x_2) = 0$, and from only this set, we need to choose those values of x_1 and x_2 that maximize $g(x_1, x_2)$.

SUBSTITUTION METHOD

Sometimes we can solve a constrained maximization problem by substituting the constraint into the objective so that the problem becomes an unconstrained problem. We can rewrite the constraint as $x_1 = r(x_2, z)$. Because this solution for x_1 as a function of x_2 contains the information in the constraint, we can substitute it into our objective function and rewrite the problem as an unconstrained maximum:

$$\max_{x_2} g(r(x_2, z), x_2).$$

Because we wrote x_1 as a function of x_2, the unconstrained maximization problem has only one choice variable, x_2.

As with any unconstrained maximum problem, we use the first-order condition,

$$\frac{\partial g(r(x_2, z), x_2)}{\partial x_1} \frac{\partial r(x_2, z)}{\partial x_2} + \frac{\partial g(r(x_2, z), x_2)}{\partial x_2} = 0, \tag{A.9}$$

to find the critical value of the choice variable x_2. We solve the first-order equation, Equation A.9, for x_2^*, substitute this solution for x_2 into $x_1 = r(x_2, z)$ to obtain $x_1^* = r(x_2^*, z)$, and then substitute x_1^* and x_2^* into the objective function to determine the maximum.

The following illustrates this approach, where the objective function is $g(x_1, x_2) = x_1 x_2$ and the constraint is $z - h(x_1, x_2) = z - x_1 - x_2$, so the constrained maximization problem is

$$\max_{x_1, x_2} \ln(x_1 x_2)$$

$$\text{s.t. } z - x_1 - x_2 = 0. \tag{A.10}$$

Using the constraint to solve for x_1 in terms of x_2, we find that $x_1 = r(x_2, z) = z - x_2$. Substituting this function into the objective function, we obtain the corresponding unconstrained maximization problem:

$$\max_{x_2} \ln((z - x_2)x_2) = \ln(z - x_2) + \ln(x_2).$$

Because the first-order condition is $-1/(z - x_2) + 1/x_2 = 0$, the solution of the first-order condition is $x_2^* = 0.5z$. Substituting this expression into the formula for x_1, we find that $x_1^* = z - 0.5z = 0.5z$. Evaluating the objective function at the maximizing values x_1^* and x_2^*, we find that $g(x_1^*, x_2^*) = \ln(0.25z^2)$.

The problem with using this method is that writing x_1 as a function of x_2 and z may be very difficult. If we have many constraints, this approach will usually be infeasible or impractical.

LAGRANGE'S METHOD

Joseph Louis Lagrange developed an alternative method to solving a constrained maximization problem that works for a wider variety of problems than the substitution method. As with the substitution method, Lagrange's method converts a constrained maximization problem into an unconstrained maximization problem.

Solving a General Problem. The first step of Lagrange's method is to write the *Lagrangian function*, which is the sum of the original objective function, $g(x_1, x_2)$, and the left-hand side of the constraint, $z - h(x_1, x_2) = 0$, multiplied by a constant, λ, called the *Lagrange multiplier*:

$$\mathscr{L}(x_1, x_2, \lambda; z) = g(x_1, x_2) + \lambda[z - h(x_1, x_2)]. \tag{A.11}$$

If $\lambda = 0$ or the constraint holds, the Lagrangian function is identical to the original objective function.

The second step is to find the critical values of the (unconstrained) Lagrangian function, Equation A.11, where the choice variables are the original ones and λ:

$$\max_{x_1, x_2, \lambda} \mathscr{L}(x_1, x_2, \lambda; z) = g(x_1, x_2) + \lambda[z - h(x_1, x_2)]. \tag{A.12}$$

To do so, we use the first-order conditions:

$$\frac{\partial \mathscr{L}(x_1, x_2, \lambda; z)}{\partial x_1} = \frac{\partial g(x_1, x_2)}{\partial x_1} - \lambda \frac{\partial h(x_1, x_2)}{\partial x_1} = 0, \tag{A.13}$$

$$\frac{\partial \mathscr{L}(x_1, x_2, \lambda; z)}{\partial x_2} = \frac{\partial g(x_1, x_2)}{\partial x_2} - \lambda \frac{\partial h(x_1, x_2)}{\partial x_2} = 0, \tag{A.14}$$

$$\frac{\partial \mathscr{L}(x_1, x_2, \lambda; z)}{\partial \lambda} = z - h(x_1, x_2) = 0. \tag{A.15}$$

We simultaneously solve the first-order conditions, Equations A.13, A.14, and A.15, for the critical values of $x_1^*(z)$, $x_2^*(z)$, and $\lambda^*(z)$. We then substitute $x_1^*(z)$ and $x_2^*(z)$ into the original objective function to determine the maximum value, $g(x_1^*(z), x_2^*(z))$.

The key result of Lagrange's method is that the solution to this unconstrained problem, Equation A.12, also satisfies the original constrained problem, Equation A.8. Lagrange's method can be generalized to handle problems with more choice variables and more constraints. For each constraint, we need an additional Lagrange multiplier.

An Example.   To illustrate this method, we return to the problem A.10, where $g(x_1, x_2) = \ln(x_1 x_2)$ and the constraint is $z - h(x_1, x_2) = z - x_1 - x_2$. The Lagrangian problem is

$$\max_{x_1, x_2, \lambda} \mathcal{L}(x_1, x_2, z, \lambda) = \ln(x_1 x_2) + \lambda(z - x_1 - x_2).$$

The first-order conditions are

$$1/x_2 = \lambda,$$
$$1/x_1 = \lambda,$$
$$z - x_1 - x_2 = 0.$$

Solving these first-order conditions simultaneously, we find that

$$x_1^*(z) = 0.5z, \quad x_2^*(z) = 0.5z, \quad \text{and} \quad \lambda^*(z) = 2/z.$$

Because this solution is the same as the one we obtained using the substitution method, the maximum value of our original objective function is also the same: $g(x_1^*(z), x_2^*(z)) = \ln(0.25z^2)$.

Interpreting the Lagrange Multiplier.   The Lagrange multiplier not only helps us convert a constrained maximization problem to an unconstrained problem but also provides additional information that is often valuable in economic problems. The value of λ that solves the first-order conditions can be interpreted as the (marginal) cost of the constraint.

The change in the original objective function with respect to a change in z is

$$\frac{dg(x_1^*, x_2^*)}{dz} = \frac{\partial g}{\partial x_1} \frac{dx_1^*}{dz} + \frac{\partial g}{\partial x_2} \frac{dx_2^*}{dz}.$$

By substituting the first-order conditions for the original choice variables, Equations A.13 and A.14, into this expression, we obtain

$$\frac{dg(x_1^*, x_2^*)}{dz} = \lambda^* \frac{\partial h}{\partial x_1} \frac{dx_1^*}{dz} + \lambda^* \frac{\partial h}{\partial x_2} \frac{dx_2^*}{dz}. \tag{A.16}$$

Differentiating the first-order condition for the Lagrange multiplier, Equation A.15, we have the additional result that

$$\frac{\partial h}{\partial x_1} \frac{dx_1^*}{dz} + \frac{\partial h}{\partial x_2} \frac{dx_2^*}{dz} = 1. \tag{A.17}$$

Substituting Equation A.17 into Equation A.16, we find that

$$\frac{dg(x_1^*, x_2^*)}{dz} = \lambda^*. \tag{A.18}$$

Equation A.18 shows that the critical value of the Lagrange multiplier reflects the sensitivity of the original objective function to a change in the exogenous parameter, z. In our last example, a small increase in z changes the value of the objective function by a factor of $\lambda = 2/z$. The Lagrange multiplier shows the value of relaxing the constraint slightly.

A.7 | Maximizing with Inequality Constraints

The method of solving constrained extremum problems devised by Lagrange is appropriate if the constraints hold with strict equality. This method works even when the constraint need not hold with equality in general, as long as we know that it *will* hold

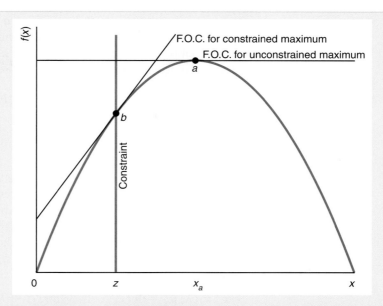

Figure A.8 Constrained and Unconstrained Maxima. In the absence of constraints, the maximum occurs at point *a*. However, if the choice variable, *x*, is constrained to be less than or equal to *z* (that is, it lies to the left of the constraint line), the constrained maximum is point *b*, where the line tangent to the curve at the constrained maximum is upward sloping.

with equality at the solution to the problem. For example, even if Lisa, who would always like to consume more goods, doesn't *have* to spend all of her money, we know that she will. However, if we do not know whether a constraint will be satisfied with equality, we need new tools.

Figure A.8 illustrates the distinction between an unconstrained maximum and a maximum for a concave objective function $f(x)$ subject to an inequality constraint. The unconstrained function reaches a maximum at its peak, point *a*, where a line tangent to the curve is horizontal. That is, the first-order condition requires that $df(x)/dx = 0$.

If *x* is constrained to be less than or equal to *z*, $x \le z$, then point *b* in the figure is the constrained maximum. It occurs where the vertical constraint line at *z* intersects the function. There the line tangent to the function, or first-order condition, is upward sloping, so $df(x)/dx > 0$.

An inequality constraint need not bind. If *z* is so large that it exceeds the *x* corresponding to point *a*, x_a, then the inequality constraint does not bind and the maximum remains at *a*, where the unconstrained-maximum first-order condition holds. We can solve these types of problems mathematically by using the Kuhn-Tucker method, named after its inventors, Harold Kuhn and Albert Tucker. We start by applying the method to a specific example and then use it on a general problem.

AN ILLUSTRATION OF THE KUHN-TUCKER METHOD

The Kuhn-Tucker approach closely resembles the Lagrange approach except that it permits the use of inequality ("greater-than-or-equal-to") constraints as well as equality constraints. To illustrate this method, we consider the problem of trying to maximize an objective function $a\ln(x_1) + b\ln(x_2)$, where a and b are positive, subject to the inequality constraints that $z - p_1x_1 - p_2x_2 \geq 0$ *and* $x_1 \geq 0$, where p_1, p_2, and z are all positive. It is possible that these constraints could hold with equality. For example, it is possible that the solution to this problem involves setting x_1 equal to zero. We write this problem as

$$\max_{x_1, x_2} a\ln(x_1 + 1) + b\ln(x_2)$$

$$\text{s.t.} \ z - p_1x_1 - p_2x_2 \geq 0, \tag{A.19}$$

$$x_1 \geq 0.$$

The collection of all the constraints on choice variables implicitly defines a set of "feasible" values for the choice variables. In the present example, the set of feasible values is defined by $\{(x_1, x_2) | z - p_1x_1 - p_2x_2 \geq 0 \text{ and } x_1 \geq 0\}$, called the *constraint set.*

We now formulate the Lagrangian function (the function is still named after Lagrange rather than after Kuhn and Tucker) by choosing some additional variables to multiply times the left-hand side of the constraints, and then adding these to the objective function,

$$\mathcal{L}(x_1, x_2; \lambda, \mu) = \ln(x_1 + 1) + \ln(x_2) + \lambda(y - p_1x_1 - p_2x_2) + \mu x_1,$$

where λ and μ are called the *Kuhn-Tucker multipliers* (or often simply *multipliers*).

Kuhn and Tucker showed that we can characterize the solution to problem A.19 using four conditions (two sets of two conditions each). The first two equations are the first-order conditions that are obtained by setting the partial derivatives of the Lagrangian function with respect to the original choice variables, x_1 and x_2, equal to zero:

$$\frac{\partial \mathcal{L}}{\partial x_1} = \frac{a}{x_1 + 1} - p_1\lambda + \mu = 0, \tag{A.20}$$

$$\frac{\partial \mathcal{L}}{\partial x_2} = \frac{b}{x_2} - p_2\lambda = 0. \tag{A.21}$$

The next two conditions, called *complementary slackness conditions*, state that the product of each multiplier and the left-hand side of the corresponding constraint equals zero:

$$\lambda(y - p_1x_1 - p_2x_2) = 0, \tag{A.22}$$

$$\mu x_1 = 0. \tag{A.23}$$

That is, either the constraint holds with equality or the multiplier is zero.

To find the solution to the problem A.19, we solve Equations A.20–A.23 in several steps. Combining the first-order conditions in Equations A.20 and A.21 with the complementary slackness conditions in Equations A.22 and A.23 gives us a system of equations that characterize any local extrema for the problem, provided that both objective function and constraints are all continuously differentiable in the choice variables.

Rearranging Equation A.21, we find that $\lambda = b/(p_2x_2)$, so because b and p_2 are positive, λ is strictly positive: $\lambda > 0$. Combining this result with the first-order condition for x_1, Equation A.22, we find that the first constraint holds with equality: $z - p_1x_1 - p_2x_2 = 0$. Moreover, by substituting this expression for λ into the first-order condition for x_2, Equation A.21, we obtain

$$\frac{a}{x_1 + 1} + \mu = b\frac{p_1}{p_2x_2}.$$

Multiplying both sides of this expression by $(x_1 + 1)$ yields

$$a + \mu x_1 + \mu = b(x_1 + 1)\frac{p_1}{p_2 x_2}.$$

However, $\mu x_1 = 0$ from Equation A.23, so we know that

$$(a + \mu)p_2 x_2 = bp_1(x_1 + 1). \tag{A.24}$$

Now we have two cases to consider. Either x_1 or μ must be zero if Equation A.23 is to be satisfied. If $\mu = 0$ and we substitute that value into Equation A.24, we find that

$$x_2 = \frac{p_1}{p_2}\frac{b}{a}(x + 1).$$

Substituting this expression into the complementary slackness condition for the first constraint, Equation A.22, and remembering that $\lambda > 0$, we find that

$$x_2 = \frac{b}{a + b}\frac{z}{p_2},$$

$$x_1 = \frac{a}{a + b}\frac{z}{p_1} - 1. \tag{A.25}$$

Now instead suppose that $x_1 = 0$, so Equation A.24 becomes

$$x_2 = \frac{p_1}{p_2}\frac{b}{a + \mu}.$$

Remembering that $\lambda > 0$ and substituting this expression into the complementary slackness condition for the first constraint, Equation A.22, we find that $\mu = p_1(b/y) - a$ and $x_2 = y/p_2$.

Thus we have two possible solutions. Either

$$x_1 = \frac{a}{a + b}\frac{z}{p_1} - 1, \quad x_2 = \frac{b}{a + b}\frac{z}{p_2}, \quad \text{and} \quad \mu = 0; \text{ or} \tag{A.26}$$

$$x_1 = 0, \quad x_2 = \frac{z}{p_2}, \quad \text{and} \quad \mu = p_1\frac{b}{z} - a. \tag{A.27}$$

This multiplicity of possible solutions, Equations A.26 and A.27, does *not* mean that both solve the maximization problem. Only one of these possible answers solves the maximization problem, and which one is the solution depends on the values of the parameters a, b, p_1, p_2, and y. There are several ways to check which is correct, conditional on these values. One way in this example is to substitute the actual values of a, b, y, and p_1 into the expression for x_1 in Equation A.25 and check whether it is positive. If not, $x_1 = 0$.

Conditions for Existence and Uniqueness.

Although the Kuhn-Tucker method gives us a general means of *formulating* problems of finding constrained extrema, there is no guarantee that a solution to the Kuhn-Tucker formulation exists. Even if a solution does exist, there is no guarantee that it is unique.

In Section A.4, we summarized the sufficient conditions that guarantee the existence and uniqueness of solutions to *unconstrained* extrema problems. Now we would like some simple conditions guaranteeing both the existence and the uniqueness of a solution to the Kuhn-Tucker formulation of a *constrained* extremum problem.

We want to specify these conditions for a general Kuhn-Tucker problem with n choice variables $x_1, x_2, \ldots, x_n$, where we want to maximize an objective function $f: \mathbb{R}^n \to \mathbb{R}$ subject to m constraints, $g_j(x_1, x_2, \ldots, x_n) \geq 0$, for $j = 1, 2, \ldots, m$:

$$\max_{x_1, x_2, \ldots, x_n} f(x_1, x_2, \ldots, x_n)$$

$$\text{s.t. } g_j(x_1, x_2, \ldots, x_n) \geq 0, \quad \text{for} \quad j = 1, 2, \ldots, m. \tag{A.28}$$

The *Slater condition* guarantees the existence of a solution to problem A.28. The Slater condition requires that the solution to the maximization problem is not determined entirely by the constraints for any of the choice variables: There exists a point $(x_1, x_2, \ldots, x_n)$ such that $g_j(x_1, x_2, \ldots, x_n) > 0$ for all $j = 1, 2, \ldots, m$. Because this condition holds with a strict inequality, the constraint set has a non-empty interior.

A local maximum exists if the objective function and constraints are continuously differentiable and if the Slater condition is satisfied. If $(x_1^*, \ldots, x_n^*)$ is a local maximum of the problem A.28, it is also global maximum if f is weakly concave and if g_j is weakly convex for all $j = 1, \ldots, m$. However, there could be more than one global maximum.

Sufficient conditions for a local maximum $(x_1^*, \ldots, x_n^*)$ to the problem A.28 to be a unique global maximum are that f is weakly concave; g_j is weakly convex for all $j = 1, 2, \ldots, m$; and one of two alternative conditions holds:

1. The objective function f is strictly concave; or
2. At least one of the constraints $g_j(x_1^*, \ldots, x_n^*) = 0$ and is strictly convex at $g_j(x_1^*, \ldots, x_n^*)$.

The Envelope Theorem.   We can state and prove a version of the Envelope Theorem that holds for constrained extremum problems. To facilitate this discussion, we use our previous formulation of the Kuhn-Tucker problem, but we explicitly add an exogenous parameter z so that z can have a direct effect on the objective function as well as a direct effect on any of the constraints g_j,[3]

$$V(z) = \max_{x_1, x_2, \ldots, x_n} f(x_1, x_2, \ldots, x_n, z)$$

$$\text{s.t. } g_j(x_1, x_2, \ldots, x_n, z) \geq 0, \quad \text{for} \quad j = 1, 2, \ldots, m, \tag{A.29}$$

where $V(z)$ is the maximized value of the objective function. The equivalent Lagrangian problem is

$$V(z) = \max_{x_1, x_2, \ldots, x_n} f(x_1, x_2, \ldots, x_n, z) + \sum_{j=1}^{m} \lambda_j g_j(x_1, x_2, \ldots, x_n, z), \tag{A.30}$$

where $\lambda_1, \lambda_2, \ldots, \lambda_m$ are the Kuhn-Tucker multipliers.

The first-order conditions are

$$\frac{\partial f}{\partial x_i} + \sum_{j=1}^{m} \lambda_j \frac{\partial g_j}{\partial x_i} = 0, \quad \text{for} \quad i = 1, \ldots, n \quad \text{and} \quad j = 1, \ldots, m, \tag{A.31}$$

and the complementary slackness conditions are

$$\lambda_j g(x_1, \ldots, x_n, z) = 0, \quad \text{for} \quad j = 1, \ldots, m. \tag{A.32}$$

---

[3]We could have added any finite number of such exogenous parameters; however, one is enough for our purposes.

The *Envelope Theorem* states that, if the constraints $g_j(x_1, x_2, \ldots, x_n, z)$ satisfy the Slater condition and if $x_i(z)$, $i = 1, 2, \ldots, n$, solve the first-order conditions, Equation A.31, and complementary slackness conditions, Equation A.32, then

$$\frac{\partial V(z)}{\partial z} = \frac{\partial f(x_1, \ldots, x_n, z)}{\partial z} + \sum_{j=1}^{m} \lambda_j \frac{\partial g_j}{\partial z}.$$

Proof. The value function $V(z) = f(x_1(z), \ldots, x_n(z), z) + \sum_{j=1}^{m} \lambda_j g_j(x_1, \ldots, x_n, z)$. Differentiating this expression with respect to z yields

$$\frac{\partial V(z)}{\partial z} = \frac{\partial f(x_1, \ldots, x_n, z)}{\partial z} + \sum_{i=1}^{n} \left[\frac{\partial f(x_1, \ldots, x_n, z)}{\partial x_i} \frac{\partial x_i(z)}{\partial z} + \sum_{j=1}^{m} \lambda_j \frac{\partial g_j(x_1, \ldots, x_n, z)}{\partial x_i} \frac{\partial x_i(z)}{\partial z} \right]$$
$$+ \sum_{j=1}^{m} \left[\frac{\partial \lambda_j(z)}{\partial z} g_j(x_1, \ldots, x_n, z) + \lambda_j(z) \frac{\partial g_j(x_1, \ldots, x_n, z)}{\partial z} \right].$$

Collecting terms, we can rewrite this equation as

$$\frac{\partial V(z)}{\partial z} = \frac{\partial f(x_1, \ldots, x_n, z)}{\partial z} + \sum_{j=1}^{m} \left[\frac{\partial \lambda_j(z)}{\partial z} g_j(x_1, \ldots, x_n, z) + \lambda_j(z) \frac{\partial g_j(x_1, \ldots, x_n, z)}{\partial z} \right]$$
$$+ \sum_{i=1}^{n} \left[\frac{\partial f(x_1, \ldots, x_n, z)}{\partial x_i} \frac{\partial x_i(z)}{\partial z} + \sum_{j=1}^{m} \lambda_j \frac{\partial g_j(x_1, \ldots, x_n, z)}{\partial x_i} \right] \frac{\partial x_i(z)}{\partial z}. \tag{A.33}$$

Using Equation A.31, the last bracketed expression in Equation A.33 equals zero. If we can show that the $\Sigma(\partial\lambda_j/\partial z)g_j$ expression in the other bracketed term is zero, we have proved the theorem. We know by the complementary slackness conditions that $\lambda_j g_j(x_1, x_2, \ldots, x_n, z) = 0$. If $g_j(x_1, x_2, \ldots, x_n, z) = 0$, then $(\partial\lambda_j/\partial z)g_j(x_1, x_2, \ldots, x_m) = 0$. Alternatively, if $g_j(x_1, x_2, \ldots, x_n, z) > 0$, so that $\lambda_j = 0$, the Slater condition implies that $\partial\lambda_j(z)/\partial z = 0$, thus proving the theorem.

Comparative Statics.   The method of comparative statics can often be applied when one is solving a problem with inequality constraints, but the matter is complicated by the need to keep track of which inequality constraints are binding. Let's return to our earlier problem A.19, where the Lagrangian function is $\mathcal{L} = a \ln(x_1 + 1) + b \ln(x_2) + \lambda(y - p_1 x_1 - p_2 x_2) + \mu x_1$ and has first-order conditions

$$\frac{a}{x_1 + 1} - \lambda p_1 + \mu = 0,$$

$$\frac{b}{x_2} - \lambda p_2 = 0,$$

and associated complementary slackness conditions

$$\lambda(y - p_1 x_1 - p_2 x_2) = 0, \tag{A.34}$$

$$\mu x_1 = 0. \tag{A.35}$$

These complementary slackness conditions complicate the comparative statics analysis. If a constraint is clearly binding, we don't have a problem, because we know how it affects the solution. Unfortunately, we do not always know if a constraint binds.

In this example, we may be confident that the first constraint binds, so we know that $\lambda > 0$. Consequently, we can divide both sides of Equation A.34 by λ to eliminate it from the complementary slackness conditions. However, we do not know whether the constraint $x_1 \geq 0$ is binding without knowing the actual parameters.

In one approach, we initially assume that all the constraints *are* binding, and then use this assumption to substitute the constraints into the first-order conditions and solve them. Here we assume that the constraint, Equation A.35, holds, $x_1 = 0$. Consequently, using Equation A.27, $x_2 = y/p_2$. Substituting these solutions into the first-order conditions, we have

$$a - \lambda p_1 + \mu = 0,$$
$$\frac{b}{y} - \lambda = 0,$$

or solving for μ and λ,

$$\mu = \frac{b}{y} p_1 - a,$$
$$\lambda = b/y.$$

Consequently, we've potentially solved the entire system, with proposed solutions for x_1, x_2, and both the multipliers. However, our initial assumption that $x_1 = 0$ implies that $\mu > 0$ or that $(b/y)p_1 > a$. This last inequality is exactly what we need to check. If it's satisfied, then we have the correct solution that we're at a *corner*. If it's not, then the maximum is in the interior and not at a corner, and the constraint $x_1 \geq 0$ does not bind. If it's not binding, then $\mu = 0$. Now we can go back and plug this condition into the first-order conditions, and solve. Given either set of these solutions, we can examine the effect of a change in a parameter.

RECIPE FOR FINDING THE CONSTRAINED EXTREMA OF A FUNCTION

The following is a step-by-step set of practical instructions for solving a constrained extrema problem. The focus of this section is very much on the mechanics of *how* rather than on the issues of *why*.

1. *Make the problem a maximization problem.* If the problem is to minimize $f(x_1, x_2, \ldots, x_n)$ subject to constraints, we can convert it into a maximization problem by maximizing *minus* the function subject to the same constraints.
2. *Rewrite any constraints so that they take the form of "greater than or equal to zero."* Here's a brief field guide to constraints and how to deal with them:
   a. *Greater than or equal to:* If the constraint is initially stated in the form of $g(x_1, x_2) \geq f(x_1, x_2)$, subtract the term $f(x_1, x_2)$ from both sides to obtain $g(x_1, x_2) - f(x_1, x_2) \geq 0$.
   b. *Less than or equal to:* Given an initial constraint of $g(x_1, x_2) \leq f(x_1, x_2)$, multiply both sides by -1, making it a greater-than-or-equal-to problem, and use the method in (a): $f(x_1, x_2) - g(x_1, x_2) \geq 0$.
   c. *Strictly greater than or strictly less than:* If your constraint is $g(x_1, x_2) > f(x_1, x_2)$ or $g(x_1, x_2) < f(x_1, x_2)$, you're in trouble! If this constraint has any effect on the problem, it will be to make it so that no solution exists. (Consider the problem of minimizing x such that $x > 0$ to see why this is a problem.) You have to reformulate your problem.
   d. *Equal to:* If it seems that the constraint truly has to hold with equality, put yourself in the shoes of the firm's manager, who is doing the maximizing. If the firm could somehow challenge the natural order of things and violate the

constraint, would the firm prefer a "less-than-or-equal-to" constraint or a "greater-than-or-equal-to" constraint? For example, a firm facing a constraint that required output q to be equal to a function $f(x)$ of inputs x would, if the firm could violate the laws of nature, prefer that output was greater than production, or that $q \geq f(x)$. Let's give the firm the opposite of what it would want, imposing the constraint $q \leq f(x)$. Multiply both sides by -1 and then move the terms on the right-hand side to the left to get a "greater-than-or-equal-to-zero" constraint: $f(x) - q \geq 0$. Think again about whether the constraint *really* has to be an equality constraint—in this case, could the firm throw some output away? If the answer is yes, then you're done. Otherwise, add *another* "greater-than-or-equal-to" constraint but with the opposite sign. So, in the example of our firm, we would have both constraints:

$$f(x) - q \geq 0, \tag{A.36}$$

$$q - f(x) \geq 0. \tag{A.37}$$

You can verify that these two inequality constraints imply a single equality constraint.

Now you've got all your constraints formulated in the "greater-than-or-equal-to" form. Take a moment to be sure you haven't neglected any. Are there some choice variables that can't be negative? If so, add a nonnegativity constraint requiring them to be greater than or equal to zero.

3. *Construct the Lagrangian function.* Assign a multiplier to each of your constraints (it's traditional to use Greek letters for these multipliers), which you multiply times the left-hand side of the corresponding constraint, and add the products to the objective function you formulated in the first step.

4. *Partially differentiate the Lagrangian function.* Beginning with the first of your choice variables, partially differentiate the Lagrangian function with respect to this variable. Repeat for each of the remaining choice variables. Set each of these expressions equal to zero, yielding a collection of first-order conditions.

5. *List the complementary slackness conditions.* Take each of the products of the "greater-than-or-equal-to" constraints with their corresponding multipliers and set them equal to zero, yielding the complementary slackness conditions.

7. *Solve the system of equations.* Simultaneously solve the collection of first-order conditions and the complementary slackness conditions to find the critical values. The set of values of the choice variables that satisfy this system solve the constrained maximization problem.[4]

A.8 Duality

There's a close connection between constrained maxima and minima called *duality*. The following proposition makes this connection: Let λ be a scalar greater than zero. If there exists a solution $x^*(z)$ to the *primal* problem

$$V(z) = \max_x f(x, z) + \lambda(C(z) - g(x, z)), \tag{A.38}$$

---

[4]We sometimes may be unable to find an explicit solution to these sets of equations, even if a solution exists. In such cases, we can use numerical techniques to find solutions (see Judd, 1998), or we can employ the method of comparative statics to try to understand the character of the solution.

then $x^*(z)$ also solves the *dual* problem

$$C(z) = \min_x g(x, z) + \frac{1}{\lambda}(V(z) - f(x, z)). \qquad (A.39)$$

Proof. We need to show that the maximization problem A.38 is equivalent to the minimization problem A.39 when $\lambda > 0$. Because a solution $x^*(z)$ exists, the function $V(z)$ exists. Subtracting $V(z)$ from both sides of Equation A.38 yields

$$0 = \max_x [f(x, z) - V(z)] + \lambda(C(z) - g(x, z)).$$

Then subtracting $\lambda C(z)$ from both sides gives us

$$-\lambda C(z) = \max_x [f(x, z) - V(z)] - \lambda g(x, z).$$

Multiplying both sides by -1 transforms the max operator into the min operator,

$$\lambda C(z) = \min_x [V(z) - f(x, z)] + \lambda g(x, z),$$

and dividing both sides by the positive constant λ yields the result in Equation A.39.

This result implies that when we solve a primal constrained maximization problem *and the constraint binds*, then a dual representation of the problem also exists. To see why, consider the constrained problem

$$\max_x f(x, z)$$

$$\text{s.t. } g(x, z) \leq C(z).$$

For example, a firm could face this problem when it is maximizing output $f(x, z)$ subject to keeping its cost $g(x, z)$ below some critical level $C(z)$. The Lagrangian function corresponding to this problem is $\mathcal{L}(x, z) = f(x, z) + \lambda(C(z) - g(x, z))$. The result implies that if the maximizing choice of x given z (which in our example maximizes output subject to keeping cost below some limit) makes the constraint bind, then this same choice also solves the *dual* problem of minimizing $g(x, z)$ subject to satisfying the constraint $f(x, z) \geq V(z)$ [or, in our example, minimizing costs subject to keeping output above $V(z)$]. Further, the value of the multiplier in the dual problem will be the reciprocal of the value of the multiplier in the primal problem.

This result does not rely on the differentiability or shape of the functions f and g, only on the existence of a solution to the primal maximization problem. However, if the solution to the primal problem satisfies its associated first-order conditions and the constraint is binding, then the same first-order conditions will characterize the dual problem.

Answers to Selected Problems

I know the answer! The answer lies within the heart of all mankind! The answer is twelve? I think I'm in the wrong building. —Charles Schultz

Chapter 2

1. The statement "Talk is cheap because supply exceeds demand" makes sense if we interpret it to mean that the *quantity supplied* of talk exceeds the *quantity demanded* at a price of zero. Imagine a downward-sloping demand curve that hits the horizontal, quantity axis to the left of where the upward-sloping supply curve hits the axis. (The correct aphorism is "Talk is cheap until you hire a lawyer.")

5. Shifts of both the U.S. supply and the U.S. demand curves affected the U.S. equilibrium. U.S. beef consumers' fear of mad cow disease caused their demand curve in the figure to shift slightly to the left from D^1 to D^2. In the short run, total U.S. production was essentially unchanged. Because of the ban on exports, beef that would have been sold in Japan and elsewhere was sold in the United States, causing the U.S. supply curve to shift to the right from S^1 to S^2. As a result, the U.S. equilibrium changed from e_1 (where S^1 intersects D^1) to e_2 (where S^2 intersects D^2). The U.S. price fell 15% from p_1 to $p_2 = 0.85p_1$, while the quantity rose 43% from Q_1 to $Q_2 = 1.43Q_1$. *Comment:* Depending on exactly how the U.S. supply and demand curves had shifted, it would have been possible for the U.S. price and quantity to have both fallen. For example, if D^2 had

For Problem 5

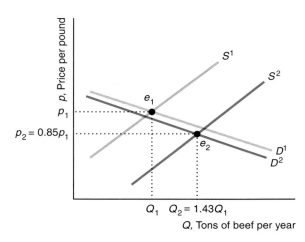

shifted far enough left, it could have intersected S^2 to the left of Q_1, and the equilibrium quantity would have fallen.

12. In the figure below, the no-quota total supply curve, S in panel c, is the horizontal sum of the U.S. domestic supply curve, S^d, and the no-quota foreign supply curve, S^f. At prices

For Problem 12

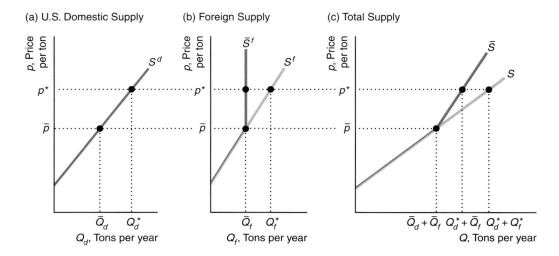

(a) U.S. Domestic Supply   (b) Foreign Supply   (c) Total Supply

less than $\bar{p}$, foreign suppliers want to supply quantities less than $\bar{p}$, foreign suppliers want to supply quantities less than $\bar{p}$. As a result, the foreign supply curve under the quota, $\bar{S}^f$, is the same as the no-quota foreign supply curve, S^f, for prices less than $\bar{p}$. At prices above $\bar{p}$, foreign suppliers want to supply more but are limited to $\bar{Q}$. Thus the foreign supply curve with a quota, $\bar{S}^f$, is vertical at $\bar{Q}$ for prices above $\bar{p}$. The total supply curve with the quota, $\bar{S}$, is the horizontal sum of S^d and $\bar{S}^f$. At any price above $\bar{p}$, the total supply equals the quota plus the domestic supply. For example at p^*, the domestic supply is Q_d^* and the foreign supply is $\bar{Q}_f$, so the total supply is $Q_d^* + \bar{Q}_f$. Above $\bar{p}$, $\bar{S}$ is the domestic supply curve shifted $\bar{Q}$ units to the right. As a result, the portion of $\bar{S}$ above $\bar{p}$ has the same slope as S^d. At prices less than or equal to $\bar{p}$, the same quantity is supplied with and without the quota, so $\bar{S}$ is the same as S. At prices above $\bar{p}$, less is supplied with the quota than without one, so $\bar{S}$ is steeper than S, indicating that a given increase in price raises the quantity supplied by less with a quota than without one.

13. The graph below reproduces the no-quota total American supply curve of steel, S, and the total supply curve under the quota, $\bar{S}$, which we derived in the answer to the previous question. At a price below $\bar{p}$, the two supply curves are identical because the quota is not binding: It is greater than the quantity foreign firms want to supply. Above $\bar{p}$, $\bar{S}$ lies to the left of S. Suppose that the American demand is relatively *low* at any given price so that the demand curve, D^l, intersects both the supply curves at a price below $\bar{p}$. The equilibria both before and after the quota is imposed are at e_1, where the equilibrium price, p_1, is less than $\bar{p}$. Thus if the demand curve lies near enough to the origin that the quota is not binding, the quota has no effect on the equilibrium. With a relatively *high* demand curve, D^h, the quota affects the equilibrium. The no-quota equilibrium is e_2, where D^h intersects the no-quota total supply curve, S.

After the quota is imposed, the equilibrium is e_3, where D^h intersects the total supply curve with the quota, $\bar{S}$. The quota raises the price of steel in the United States from p_2 to p_3 and reduces the quantity from Q_2 to Q_3.

21. We showed that, in a competitive market, the effect of a specific tax is the same whether it is placed on suppliers or demanders. Thus if the market for milk is competitive, consumers will pay the same price in equilibrium regardless of whether the government taxes consumers or stores.

22. The law would create a price ceiling (at 110% of the pre-emergency price). Because the supply curve shifts substantially to the left during the emergency, the price control will create a shortage: A smaller quantity will be supplied at the ceiling price than will be demanded.

23. The demand curve for pork is $Q = 171 - 20p + 20p_b + 3p_c + 2Y$. As a result, $\partial Q / \partial Y = 2$. A \$100 increase in income causes the quantity demanded to increase by 0.2 million kg per year.

24. $Q = Q_1 + Q_2 = (120 - p) + (60 - 1/2p)$
    $= 180 - 1.5p$.

28. Equating the right-hand sides of the tomato supply and demand functions and using algebra, we find that $\ln p = 3.2 + 0.2 \ln p_t$. We then set $p_t = 110$, solve for $\ln p$, and exponentiate $\ln p$ to obtain the equilibrium price, $p \approx$ \$61.62/ton. Substituting p into the supply curve and exponentiating, we determine the equilibrium quantity, $Q \approx 11.78$ million short tons/year.

30. The elasticity of demand is $(dQ/dp)(p/Q) = (-9.5$ thousand metric tons per year per cent$) \times (45¢/1,275$ thousand metric tons per year$) \approx -0.34$. That is, for every 1% fall in the price, a third of a percent more coconut oil is demanded. The cross-price elasticity of demand for

For Problem 13

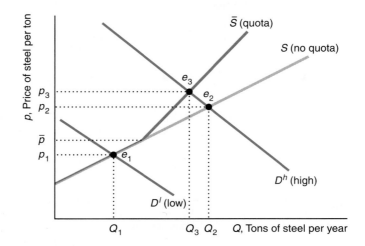

coconut oil with respect to the price of palm oil is $(dQ/dp_p)(p_p/Q) = 16.2 \times (31/1{,}275) \approx 0.39$.

39. Differentiating quantity, $Q(p(\tau))$, with respect to τ, we learn that the change in quantity as the tax changes is $(dQ/dp)(dp/d\tau)$. Multiplying and dividing this expression by p/Q, we find that the change in quantity as the tax changes is $\varepsilon(Q/p)(dp/d\tau)$. Thus the closer ε is to zero, the less the quantity falls, all else the same.

Because $R = p(\tau)Q(p(\tau))$, an increase in the tax rate changes revenues by

$$\frac{dR}{d\tau} = \frac{dp}{d\tau}Q + p\frac{dQ}{dp}\frac{dp}{d\tau},$$

using the chain rule. Using algebra, we can rewrite this expression as

$$\frac{dR}{d\tau} = \frac{dp}{d\tau}\left(Q + p\frac{dQ}{dp}\right) = \frac{dp}{d\tau}Q\left(1 + \frac{dQ}{dp}\frac{p}{Q}\right) = \frac{dp}{d\tau}Q(1 + \varepsilon).$$

Thus the effect of a change in τ on R depends on the elasticity of demand, ε. Revenue rises with the tax, given an inelastic demand $(0 > \varepsilon > -1)$, and falls with an elastic demand, $\varepsilon < -1$.

40. We can determine how the total wage payment, $W = wL(w)$, varies with respect to w by differentiating. We then use algebra to express this result in terms of an elasticity:

$$\frac{dW}{dw} = L + w\frac{dL}{dw} = L\left(1 + \frac{dL}{dw}\frac{w}{L}\right) = L(1 + \varepsilon),$$

where ε is the elasticity of demand of labor. The sign of dW/dw is the same as that of $1 + \varepsilon$. Thus total labor payment decreases as the minimum wage forces up the wage if labor demand is elastic, $\varepsilon < -1$, and increases if labor demand is inelastic, $\varepsilon > -1$.

Chapter 3

3. If the neutral product is on the vertical axis, the indifference curves are parallel vertical lines.

5. Sofia's indifference curves are right angles (as in panel b of Figure 3.4). Her utility function is $U = \min(H, W)$, where *min* means the minimum of the two arguments, H is the number of units of hot dogs, and W is the number of units of whipped cream.

8. See **www.aw-bc.com/perloff**, Chapter 3, Solved Problem.

9. In the figure at the top of the next column, the consumer can afford to buy up to 12 thousand gallons of water a week if not constrained. The opportunity set, area A and B, is bounded by the axes and the budget line. A vertical line at 10 thousand on the water axis indicates the quota.

For Problem 9

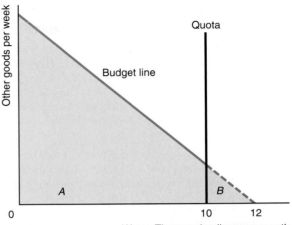

The new opportunity set, area A, is bounded by the axes, the budget line, and the quota line. Because of the rationing, the consumer loses part of the original opportunity set: the triangle B to the right of the 10-thousand-gallons quota line. The consumer has fewer opportunities because of rationing.

14. Suppose that Dale purchases two goods at prices p_1 and p_2. If her original income is Y, the intercept of the budget line on the Good 1 axis (where the consumer buys only Good 1) is Y/p_1. Similarly, the intercept is Y/p_2 on the Good 2 axis. A 50% income tax lowers income to half its original level, $Y/2$. As a result, the budget line shifts inward toward the origin. The intercepts on the Good 1 and Good 2 axes are $Y/(2p_1)$ and $Y/(2p_2)$, respectively. The opportunity set shrinks by the area between the original budget line and the new line.

18. Andy's marginal utility of apples divided by the price of apples is $3/2 = 1.5$. The marginal utility for kumquats is $5/4 = 1.2$. That is, a dollar spent on apples gives him more extra utils than a dollar spent on kumquats. Thus he maximizes his utility by spending all his money on apples and buying $40/2 = 20$ pounds of apples.

19. David's marginal utility of B is $\partial U/\partial B = \partial(B + 2Z)/\partial B = 1$ and his marginal utility of Z is 2. If we plot B on the vertical axis and Z on the horizontal axis, the slope of David's indifference curve is $-U_Z/U_B = -2$. The marginal utility from one extra unit of Z is twice that from one extra unit of B. Thus if the price of Z is less than twice that of B, David buys only Z (the optimal bundle is on the Z axis at Y/p_Z, where Y is his income and p_Z is the price of Z). If the price of Z is more than twice that of B, David buys only B. If the price of Z is exactly twice as much as that of B, he is

indifferent between buying any bundle along his budget line.

21. We can solve this problem by noting that Nadia determines her optimal bundle by equating the ratios of each good's marginal utility to its price.

   a. At the original prices, this condition is $U_R/10 = 2RC = 2R^2 = U_C/5$. Thus by dividing both sides of the middle equality by $2R$, we know that her optimal bundle has the property that $R = C$. Her budget constraint is $90 = 10R + 5C$. Substituting C for R, we find that $15C = 90$, or $C = 6 = R$.

   b. At the new price, the optimum condition requires that $U_R/10 = 2RC = R^2 = U_C/10$, or $2C = R$. By substituting this condition into her budget constraint, $90 = 10R + 10C$, and solving, we learn that $C = 3$ and $R = 6$. Thus as the price of chickens doubles, she cuts her consumption of chicken in half but does not change how many slabs of ribs she eats.

28. Given the original utility function, U, the consumer's marginal rate of substitution is $-U_1/U_2$. If $V(q_1, q_2) = F(U(q_1, q_2))$, the new marginal rate of substitution is $-V_1/V_2 = -[(dF/\underline{d}U)U_1]/[(dF/\underline{d}U)U_2] = -U_1/U_2$, which is the same as originally.

33. If we apply the transformation function $F(x) = x^\rho$ to the original utility function, we obtain the new utility function $V(q_1, q_2) = F(U(q_1, q_2)) = [(q_1^\rho + q_2^\rho)^{1/\rho}]^\rho = q_1^\rho + q_2^\rho$, which has the same preference properties as does the original function.

34. The marginal rate of substitution is

$$-U_1/U_2 = -\rho q_1^{\rho-1}/ (\rho q_2^{\rho-1}) = -(q_1/q_2)^{\rho-1}.$$

Chapter 4

1. An opera performance must be a normal good for Don because he views the only other good he buys as an inferior good. To show this result in a graph, draw a figure similar to Figure 4.3, but relabel the vertical "Housing" axis as "Opera performances." Don's equilibrium will be in the upper-left quadrant at a point like a in Figure 4.3.

4. The CPI accurately reflects the true cost of living because Alix does not substitute between the goods as the relative prices change.

6. On the graph, L^f is the budget line at the factory store and L^o is the constraint at the outlet store. At the factory store, the consumer maximum occurs at e_f on indifference curve I^f. Suppose that we increase the income of a consumer who shops at the outlet store to Y^* so that the resulting budget line L^* is tangent to the indifference curve I^f. The consumer would buy Bundle e^*. That is, the pure substitution effect (the movement from e_f to e^*) causes the consumer to buy relatively more firsts. The total effect

(the movement from e_f to e_o) reflects both the substitution effect (firsts are now relatively less expensive) and the income effect (the consumer is worse off after paying for shipping). Presumably the income effect is small because the budget share of plates is small.

21. The figure on the facing page shows that the price-consumption curve is horizontal. The demand for DVDs depends only on income and the own price, $q_2 = 0.4Y/p_2$, so it is unaffected by a change in p_1.

24. If the price of Coke, p_C, is greater than the price of Pepsi, p_P, Madeline buys only Pepsi. If the two prices are equal, $p_C = p_P = p$, she buys Y/p cans of either Coke or Pepsi. Finally, if $p_C < p_P$, she buys Y/p_C cans of Coke. Hence as the price approaches zero, her Coke demand curve approaches the quantity axis asymptotically, as the figure shows.

26. Jackie's demand for CDs is given by Equation 4.3, $q_1 = 0.6Y/p_1$. Consequently, her Engel curve is a straight line with a slope of $dq_1/dY = 0.6/p_1$.

Chapter 5

14. Parents who do not receive subsidies prefer that poor parents receive lump-sum payments rather than a subsidized hourly rate for child care. If the supply curve for day care services is upward sloping, by shifting the demand curve farther to the right, the price subsidy raises the price of day care for these other parents.

15. The government could give a smaller lump-sum subsidy that shifts the L^{LS} curve down so that it is parallel to the original curve but tangent to indifference curve I^2. This tangency point is to the left of e_2, so the parents would use fewer hours of child care than with the original lump-sum payment.

26. Yes. The tax system may exempt a fixed amount of income from taxes per person. Suppose that the first $10,000 of income is exempt and a flat 10% rate is charged on the remaining income. Someone who earns $20,000 has an average tax rate of 5%, whereas someone who earns $40,000 has an average tax rate of 7.5%.

27. As the marginal tax rate on income increases, people substitute away from work due to the pure substitution effect. However, the income effect can be either positive or negative, so the net effect of a tax increase is ambiguous. Also, because wage rates differ across countries, the initial level of income differs, again adding to the theoretical ambiguity. If we know that people work less as the marginal tax rate increases, we can infer that the substitution effect and the income effect go in the same direction or that the substitution effect is larger. However, Prescott's (2004) evidence alone about hours worked and marginal tax rates does not allow us to draw such an inference because U.S.

For Chapter 4, Problem 21

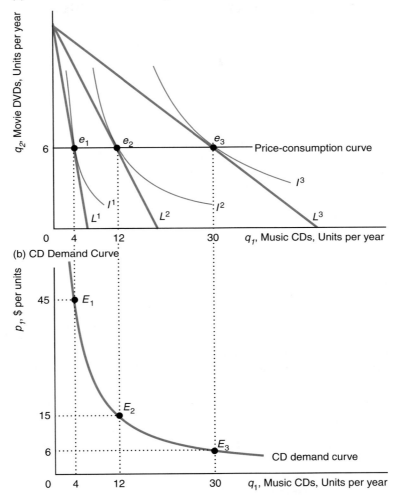

(a) Indifference Curves and Budget Constraints

(b) CD Demand Curve

and European workers may have different tastes and face different wages.

28. The figure on the next page shows Julia's original consumer equilibrium: Originally, Julia's budget constraint was a straight line, L^1 with a slope of $-w$, which was tangent to her indifference curve I^1 at e_1, so she worked 12 hours a day and consumed $Y_1 = 12w$ goods. The maximum-hours restriction creates a kink in Julia's new budget constraint, L^2. This constraint is the same as L^1 up to 8 hours of work, and is horizontal at $Y = 8w$ for more hours of work. The highest indifference curve that touches this constraint is I^2. Because of the restriction on the hours she can work, Julia chooses to work 8 hours a day and to consume $Y_2 = 8w$ goods, at e_2. (She will not choose to work fewer than 8 hours. For her to do so, her indifference curve I^2 would have to be tangent to the downward-sloping

section of the new budget constraint. However, such an indifference curve would have to cross the original indifference curve, I^1, which is impossible—see Chapter 3.) Thus forcing Julia to restrict her hours lowers her utility: I^2 must be below I^1. *Comment*: When I was in college, I was offered a summer job in California. My employer said, "You're lucky you're a male." He claimed that, in order to protect women (and children) from overwork, an archaic law required him to pay women, but not men, double overtime after eight hours of work. As a result, he offered overtime work only to his male employees. Such clearly discriminatory rules and behavior are now prohibited. Today, however, both females and males must be paid higher overtime wages—typically 1.5 times as much as the usual wage. As a consequence, many employers do not let employees work overtime.

For Chapter 5, Problem 28

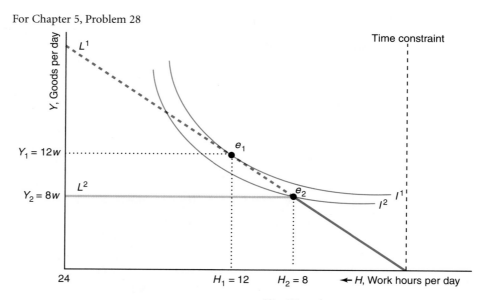

Chapter 6

1. One worker produces one unit of output, two workers produce two units of output, and n workers produce n units of output. Thus the total product of labor equals the number of workers: $q = L$. The total product of labor curve is a straight line with a slope of 1. Because we are told that each extra worker produces one more unit of output, we know that the marginal product of labor, dq/dL, is 1. By dividing both sides of the production function, $q = L$, by L, we find that the average product of labor, q/L, is 1.

6. The isoquant looks like the "right angle" ones in panel b of Figure 6.3 because the firm cannot substitute between discs and machines but must use them in equal proportions: one disc and one hour of machine services.

10. The isoquant for $q = 10$ is a straight line that hits the B axis at 10 and the G axis at 20. The marginal product of B is 1 everywhere along the isoquant. The marginal rate of technical substitution is 2 if B is on the horizontal axis.

19. Not enough information is given to answer this question. If we assume that Japanese and American firms have identical production functions and produce using the same ratio of factors during good times, Japanese firms will have a lower average product of labor during recessions because they are less likely to lay off workers. However, it is not clear how Japanese and American firms expand output during good times (do they hire the same number of extra workers?). As a result, we cannot predict which country has the higher average product of labor.

22. The production function is $q = L^{3/4}K^{1/4}$. (a) As a result, the average product of labor, holding capital fixed at $\overline{K}$, is $AP_L = q/L = L^{-1/4}\overline{K}^{1/4} = (\overline{K}/L)^{1/4}$. (b) The marginal product of labor is $MP_L = dq/dL = \frac{3}{4}(\overline{K}/L)^{1/4}$. (c) If we double both inputs, output doubles to $(2L)^{3/4}(2K)^{1/4} =$

$2L^{3/4}K^{1/4} = 2q$, where q is the original output level. Thus this production function has constant returns to scale.

24. Using Equation 6.7, we know that the marginal rate of technical substitution is $MRTS = MP_L/MP_K = \frac{2}{3}$.

27. The marginal product of labor of Firm 1 is only 90% of the marginal product of labor of Firm 2 for a particular level of inputs. Using calculus, we find that the MP_L of Firm 1 is $\partial q_1/\partial L = 0.9\partial f(L, K)/\partial L = 0.9\partial q_2/\partial L$.

29. This production function is a Cobb-Douglas. Even though it has three inputs instead of two, the same logic applies. Thus we can calculate the returns to scale as the sum of the exponents: $\gamma = 0.27 + 0.16 + 0.61 = 1.04$. Thus it has (nearly) constant returns to scale. The marginal product of material is $\partial q/\partial M = 0.61L^{0.27}K^{0.16}M^{-0.39} = 0.61q/M$.

Chapter 7

1. If the plane cannot be resold, its purchase price is a sunk cost, which is unaffected by the number of times the plane is flown. Consequently, the average cost per flight falls with the number of flights, but the total cost of owning and operating the plane rises because of extra consumption of gasoline and maintenance. Thus the more frequently someone has reason to fly, the more likely that flying one's own plane costs less per flight than a ticket on a commercial airline. However, by making extra ("unnecessary") trips, Mr. Agassi raises his total cost of owning and operating the airplane.

3. The total cost of building a 1-cubic-foot crate is $6. It costs four times as much to build an 8-cubic-foot crate, $24. In general, as the height of a cube increases, the total cost of building it rises with the square of the height, but the volume

increases with the cube of the height. Thus the cost per unit of volume falls.

4. You produce your output, exam points, using as inputs the time spent on Question 1, t_1, and the time spent on Question 2, t_2. If you have diminishing marginal returns to extra time on each problem, your isoquants have the usual shapes: They curve away from the origin. You face a constraint that you may spend no more than 60 minutes on the two questions: $60 = t_1 + t_2$. The slope of the 60-minute isocost curve is −1: For every extra minute you spend on Question 1, you have one less minute to spend on Question 2. To maximize your test score, given that you can spend no more than 60 minutes on the exam, you want to pick the highest isoquant that is tangent to your 60-minute isocost curve. At the tangency, the slope of your isocost curve, −1, equals the slope of your isoquant, $-MP_1/MP_2$. That is, your score on the exam is maximized when $MP_1 = MP_2$, where the last minute spent on Question 1 would increase your score by as much as spending it on Question 2 would. Therefore, you've allocated your time on the exam wisely if you are indifferent as to which question to work on during the last minute of the exam.

12. From the information given and assuming that there are no economies of scale in shipping baseballs, it appears that balls are produced using a constant returns to scale, fixed-proportion production function. The corresponding cost function is $C(q) = (w + s + m)q$, where w is the wage for the time period it takes to stitch one ball, s is the cost of shipping one ball, and m is the price of all material to produce a ball. Because the cost of all inputs other than labor and transportation are the same everywhere, the cost difference between Georgia and Costa Rica depends on $w + s$ in both locations. As firms choose to produce in Costa Rica, the extra shipping cost must be less than the labor savings in Costa Rica.

14. According to Equation 7.11, if the firm were minimizing its cost, the extra output it gets from the last dollar spent on labor, $MP_L/w = 50/200 = 0.25$, should equal the extra output it derives from the last dollar spent on capital, $MP_K/r = 200/1,000 = 0.2$. Thus the firm is not minimizing its costs. It would do better if it used relatively less capital and more labor, from which it gets more extra output from the last dollar spent.

19. If $-w/r$ is the same as the slope of the line segment connecting the wafer-handling stepper and the stepper technologies, then the isocost will lie on that line segment, and the firm will be indifferent between using either of the two technologies (or any combination of the two). In all the isocost lines in the figure, the cost of capital is the same, and the wage varies. The wage such that the firm is indifferent lies between the relatively high wage on the C^2 isocost line and the lower wage on the C^3 isocost line.

23. Let w be the cost of a unit of L and r be the cost of a unit of K. Because the two inputs are perfect substitutes in the production process, the firm uses only the less expensive of the two inputs. Therefore, the long-run cost function is $C(q) = wq$ if $w \leq r$; otherwise, it is $C(q) = rq$.

29. The average cost of producing one unit is α (regardless of the value of β). If $\beta = 0$, the average cost does not change with volume. If learning by doing increases with volume, $\beta < 0$, so the average cost falls with volume. Here the average cost falls exponentially (a smooth curve that asymptotically approaches the quantity axis).

34. The firm chooses its optimal labor-capital ratio using Equation 7.11: $MP_L/w = MP_K/r$. That is, $1/2q/(wL) = 1/2q/(rK)$, or $L/K = r/w$. In the United States where $w = r = 10$, the optimal $L/K = 1$, or $L = K$. The firm produces where $q = 100 = L^{1/2}K^{1/2} = K^{1/2}K^{1/2} = K$. Thus $q = K = L = 100$. The cost is $C = wL + rK = 10 \times 100 + 10 \times 100 = 2,000$. At its Asian plant, the optimal input ratio is $L^*/K^* = 1.1r/(w/1.1) = 11/(10/1.1) = 1.21$. That is, $L^* = 1.21K^*$. Thus $q = (1.21K^*)^{1/2}(K^*)^{1/2} = 1.1K^*$. So $K^* = 100/1.1$ and $L^* = 110$. The cost is $C^* = [(10/1.1) \times 110] + [11 \times (100/1.1)] = 2,000$. That is, the firm will use a different factor ratio in Asia, but the cost will be the same. If the firm could not substitute toward the less-expensive input, its cost in Asia would be $C^{**} = [(10/1.1) \times 100] + [11 \times 100] = 2,009.09$.

Chapter 8

2. How much the firm produces and whether it shuts down in the short run depend only on the firm's variable costs. (The firm picks its output level so that its marginal cost—which depends only on variable costs—equals the market price, and it shuts down only if market price is less than its minimum average variable cost.) Learning that the amount spent on the plant was greater than previously believed should not change the output level that the manager chooses. The change in the bookkeeper's valuation of the historical amount spent on the plant may affect the firm's short-run business profit but does not affect the firm's true economic profit. The economic profit is based on opportunity costs—the amount for which the firm could rent the plant to someone else—and not on historical payments.

3. Suppose that a U-shaped marginal cost curve cuts a competitive firm's demand curve (price line) from above at q_1 and from below at q_2. By increasing output to $q_2 + 1$, the firm earns extra profit because the last unit sells for price p, which is greater than the marginal cost of that last unit. Indeed, the price exceeds the marginal cost of all units between q_1 and q_2, so it is more profitable to produce q_2 than q_1. Thus the firm should either produce q_2 or shut down (if it is making a loss at q_2). We can derive this result using calculus. The second-order condition for a competitive firm

requires that marginal cost cut the demand line from below at q^*, the profit-maximizing quantity:

$$dMC(q^*)/dq > 0.$$

9. Some farmers did not pick apples so as to avoid incurring the variable cost of harvesting apples. These farmers left open the question of whether they would harvest in the future if the price rose above the shutdown level. Other, more pessimistic farmers did not expect price to rise anytime soon, so they bulldozed their trees, leaving the market for good. (Most farmers planted alternative apples such as Granny Smith and Gala, which are more popular with the public and sell at a price above the minimum average variable cost.)

25. The shutdown notice reduces the firm's flexibility, which matters in an uncertain market. If conditions suddenly change, the firm may have to operate at a loss for six months before it can shut down. This potential extra expense of shutting down may discourage some firms from entering the market initially.

33. The competitive firm's marginal cost function is found by differentiating its cost function with respect to quantity: $MC(q) = dC(q)/dq = b + 2cq + 3dq^2$. The firm's necessary profit-maximizing condition is $p = MC = b + 2cq + 3dq^2$. The firm solves this equation for q for a specific price to determine its profit-maximizing output.

35. Because the clinics are operating at minimum average cost, a lump-sum tax that causes the minimum average cost to rise by 10% would cause the market price of abortions to rise by 10%. Based on the estimated price elasticity of between -0.70 and -0.99, the number of abortions would fall to between 7% and 10%. A lump-sum tax shifts upward the average cost curve but does not affect the marginal cost curve. Consequently, the market supply curve, which is horizontal and the minimum of the average cost curve, shifts up in parallel.

36. To derive the expression for the elasticity of the residual or excess supply curve in Equation 8.17, we differentiate the residual supply curve, Equation 8.16, $S^r(p) = S(p) - D^o(p)$, with respect to p to obtain

$$\frac{dS^r}{dp} = \frac{dS}{dp} - \frac{dD^o}{dp}.$$

Let $Q_r = S^r(p)$, $Q = S(p)$, and $Q_o = D(p)$. We multiply both sides of the differentiated expression by p/Q_r, and for convenience, we also multiply the second term by $Q/Q = 1$ and the last term by $Q_o/Q_o = 1$:

$$\frac{dS^r}{dp}\frac{p}{Q_r} = \frac{dS}{dp}\frac{p}{Q_r}\frac{Q}{Q} - \frac{dD^o}{dp}\frac{p}{Q_r}\frac{Q_o}{Q_o}.$$

We can rewrite this expression as Equation 8.17 by noting that $\eta_r = (dS^r/dp)(p/Q_r)$ is the residual supply elasticity, $\eta = (dS/dp)(p/Q)$ is the market supply elasticity, $\varepsilon_o = (dD^o/dp)(p/Q_o)$ is the demand elasticity of the other

countries, and $\theta = Q_r/Q$ is the residual country's share of the world's output (hence $1 - \theta = Q_o/Q$ is the share of the rest of the world). If there are n countries with equal outputs, then $1/\theta = n$, so this equation can be rewritten as $\eta_r = n\eta - (n - 1)\,\varepsilon_o$.

37. See the text for details:

a. The incidence of the federal specific tax is shared equally between consumers and firms, whereas firms bear virtually none of the incidence of the state tax (they pass the tax on to consumers).

b. From Chapter 2, we know that the incidence of a tax that falls on consumers in a competitive market is approximately $\eta/(\eta - \varepsilon)$. Although the national elasticity of supply may be a relatively small number, the residual supply elasticity facing a particular state is very large. Using the analysis about residual supply curves, we can infer that the supply curve to a particular state is likely to be nearly horizontal—nearly perfectly elastic. For example, if the price rises even slightly in Maine relative to Vermont, suppliers in Vermont will be willing to shift up to their entire supply to Maine. Thus we expect the incidence on consumers to be nearly one from a state tax but less from a federal tax, consistent with the empirical evidence.

c. If all 50 states were identical, we could write the residual elasticity of supply, Equation 8.17, as $\eta_r = 50\eta - 49\varepsilon_o$. Given this equation, the residual supply elasticity to one state is at least 50 times larger than the national elasticity of supply, $\eta_r \geq 50\eta$, because $\varepsilon_o < 0$, so the $-49\varepsilon_o$ term is positive and increases the residual supply elasticity.

38. Each competitive firm wants to choose its output q to maximize its after-tax profit: $\pi = pq - C(q) - \mathcal{L}$. Its necessary condition to maximize profit is that price equals marginal cost: $p - dC(q)/dq = 0$. Industry supply is determined by entry, which occurs until profits are driven to zero (we ignore the problem of fractional firms and treat the number of firms, n, as a continuous variable): $pq - [C(q) + \mathcal{L}] = 0$. In equilibrium, each firm produces the same output, q, so market output is $Q = nq$, and the market inverse demand function is $p = p(Q) = p(nq)$. By substituting the market inverse demand function into the necessary and sufficient condition, we determine the market equilibrium (n^*, q^*) by the two conditions:

$$p(n^*q^*) - dC(q^*)/dq = 0,$$
$$p(n^*q^*)q^* - [C(q^*) + \mathcal{L}] = 0.$$

For notational simplicity, we henceforth leave off the asterisks. To determine how the equilibrium is affected by an increase in the lump-sum tax, we evaluate the comparative statics at $\mathcal{L} = 0$. We totally differentiate our two equilibrium equations with respect to the two endogenous variables, n and q, and the exogenous variable, $\mathcal{L}$:

$$dq(n[dp(nq)/dQ] - d^2C(q)/dq^2)$$
$$+ dn(q[dp(nq)/dQ]) + d\mathscr{L}(0) = 0,$$

$$dq(n[qdp(nq)/dQ] + p(nq) - dC/dq)$$
$$+ dn(q^2[dp(nq)/dQ]) - d\mathscr{L} = 0.$$

We can write these equations in matrix form (noting that $p - dC/dq = 0$ from the necessary condition) as

$$\begin{bmatrix} n\dfrac{dp}{dQ} - \dfrac{d^2C}{dq^2} & q\dfrac{dp}{dQ} \\ nq\dfrac{dp}{dQ} & q^2\dfrac{dp}{dQ} \end{bmatrix} \begin{bmatrix} dq \\ dn \end{bmatrix} = \begin{bmatrix} 0 \\ 1 \end{bmatrix} d\mathscr{L}.$$

There are several ways to solve these equations. One is to use Cramer's rule. Define

$$D = \begin{vmatrix} n\dfrac{dp}{dQ} - \dfrac{d^2C}{dq^2} & q\dfrac{dp}{dQ} \\ nq\dfrac{dp}{dQ} & q^2\dfrac{dp}{dQ} \end{vmatrix}$$

$$= \left(n\dfrac{dp}{dQ} - \dfrac{d^2C}{dq^2} \right) q^2\dfrac{dp}{dQ} - q\dfrac{dp}{dQ}\left(nq\dfrac{dp}{dQ} \right)$$

$$= -\dfrac{d^2C}{dq^2}q^2\dfrac{dp}{dQ} > 0,$$

where the inequality follows from each firm's sufficient condition. Using Cramer's rule:

$$\dfrac{dq}{d\mathscr{L}} = \dfrac{\begin{vmatrix} 0 & q\dfrac{dp}{dQ} \\ 1 & q^2\dfrac{dp}{dQ} \end{vmatrix}}{D} = \dfrac{-q\dfrac{dp}{dQ}}{D} > 0, \quad \text{and}$$

$$\dfrac{dn}{d\mathscr{L}} = \dfrac{\begin{vmatrix} n\dfrac{dp}{dQ} - \dfrac{d^2C}{dq^2} & 0 \\ nq\dfrac{dp}{dQ} & 1 \end{vmatrix}}{D}$$

$$= \dfrac{n\dfrac{dp}{dQ} - \dfrac{d^2C}{dq^2}}{D} < 0.$$

The change in price is

$$\dfrac{dp(nq)}{d\mathscr{L}} = \dfrac{dp}{dQ}\left[q\dfrac{dn}{d\mathscr{L}} + n\dfrac{dq}{d\mathscr{L}} \right]$$

$$= \dfrac{dp}{dQ}\left[\dfrac{\left(n\dfrac{dp}{dQ} - \dfrac{d^2C}{dq^2} \right)q}{D} - \dfrac{nq\dfrac{dp}{dQ}}{D} \right]$$

$$= \dfrac{dp}{dQ}\left(\dfrac{-\dfrac{d^2C}{dq^2}q}{D} \right) > 0.$$

Chapter 9

4. If the tax is based on *economic* profit, the tax has no long-run effect because the firms make zero economic profit. If the tax is based on *business* profit and business profit is greater than economic profit, the profit tax raises firms' after-tax costs and results in fewer firms in the market. The exact effect of the tax depends on why business profit is less than economic profit. For example, if the government ignores opportunity labor cost but includes all capital cost in computing profit, firms will substitute toward labor and away from capital.

7. Solved Problem 8.5 shows the long-run effect of a lump-sum tax in a competitive market. Consumer surplus falls by more than tax revenue increases, and producer surplus remains zero, so welfare falls.

29. The specific subsidy shifts the supply curve, S in the figure on the next page, down by $s = 11$¢, to the curve labeled $S - 11$¢. Consequently, the equilibrium shifts from e_1 to e_2, so the quantity sold increases (from 1.25 to 1.34 billion rose stems per year), the price that consumers pay falls (from 30¢ to 28¢ per stem), and the amount that suppliers receive, including the subsidy, rises (from 30¢ to 39¢), so that the differential between what the consumers pay and what the producers receive is 11¢. Consumers and producers of roses are delighted to be subsidized by other members of society. Because the price to customers drops, consumer surplus rises from $A + B$ to $A + B + D + E$. Because firms receive more per stem after the subsidy, producer surplus rises from $D + G$ to $B + C + D + G$ (the area under the price they receive and above the original supply curve). Because the government pays a subsidy of 11¢ per stem for each stem sold, the government's expenditures go from zero to the rectangle $B + C + D + E + F$. Thus the new welfare is the sum of the new consumer surplus and producer surplus minus the government's expenses. Welfare falls from $A + B + D + G$ to $A + B + D + G - F$. The deadweight loss, this drop in welfare $\Delta W = -F$, results from producing too much: The marginal cost to producers of the last stem, 39¢, exceeds the marginal benefit to consumers, 28¢.

30. The consumer surplus at a price of 30 is $\frac{1}{2}(30 \times 30) = 450$.

34. a. The initial equilibrium is determined by equating the quantity demanded to the quantity supplied: $100 - 10p = 10p$. That is, the equilibrium is $p = 5$ and $Q = 50$. At the support price, the quantity supplied is $Q_s = 60$. The market clearing price is $p = 4$. The deficiency payment was $D = (\underline{p} - p)Q_s = (6 - 4)60 = 120$.

For Chapter 9, Problem 29

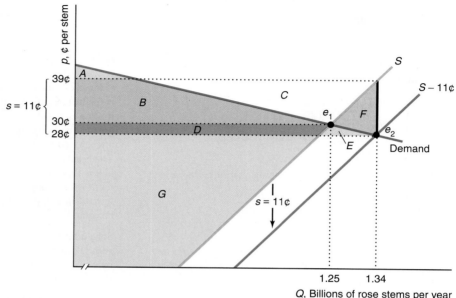

b. Consumer surplus rises from $CS_1 = \frac{1}{2}(10 - 5)50 = 125$ to $CS_2 = \frac{1}{2}(10 - 4)60 = 180$. Producer surplus rises from $PS_1 = \frac{1}{2}(5 - 0)50 = 125$ to $PS_2 = \frac{1}{2} \times (6 - 0)60 = 180$. Welfare falls from $CS_1 + PS_1 = 125 + 125 = 250$ to $CS_2 + PS_2 - D = 180 + 180 - 120 = 240$. Thus the deadweight loss is 10.

37. Without the tariff, the U.S. supply curve of oil is horizontal at a price of $14.70 ($S^1$ in Figure 9.9), and the equilibrium is determined by the intersection of this horizontal supply curve with the demand curve. With a new, small tariff of τ, the U.S. supply curve is horizontal at $14.70 + \tau$, and the new equilibrium quantity is determined by substituting $p = 14.70 + \tau$ into the demand function: $Q = 35.41(14.70 + \tau)p^{-0.37}$. Evaluated at $\tau = 0$, the equilibrium quantity remains at 13.1. The deadweight loss is the area to the right of the domestic supply curve and to the left of the demand curve between $14.70 and $14.70 + \tau$ (area $C + D + E$ in Figure 9.9) minus the tariff revenues (area D):

$$DWL = \int_{14.70}^{14.70+\tau} [D(p) - S(p)]dp - \tau[D(p + \tau) - S(p + \tau)]$$

$$= \int_{14.70}^{14.70+\tau} [3.54p^{-0.67} - 3.35p^{0.33}]dp$$

$$- \tau[3.54(p + \tau)^{-0.67} - 3.35(p + \tau)^{0.33}].$$

To see how a change in τ affects welfare, we differentiate DWL with respect to τ:

$$\frac{dDWL}{d\tau} = \frac{d}{d\tau}\left\{ \int_{14.70}^{14.70+\tau} [D(p) - S(p)]dp \right.$$

$$\left. - \tau[D(14.70 + \tau) - S(14.70 + \tau)] \right\}$$

$$= [D(14.70 + \tau) - S(14.70 + \tau)] - [D(14.70 + \tau)$$

$$- S(14.70 + \tau)] - \tau\left[\frac{dD(14.70 + \tau)}{d\tau} - \frac{dS(14.70 + \tau)}{d\tau} \right]$$

$$= -\tau\left[\frac{dD(14.70 + \tau)}{d\tau} - \frac{dS(14.70 + \tau)}{d\tau} \right].$$

If we evaluate this expression at $\tau = 0$, we find that $dDWL/d\tau = 0$. In short, applying a small tariff to the free-trade equilibrium has a negligible effect on quantity and deadweight loss. Only if the tariff is larger—as in Figure 9.9—do we see a measurable effect.

Chapter 10

1. A subsidy is a negative tax. Thus we can use the same analysis that we used in Solved Problem 10.1 to answer this question by reversing the signs of the effects.

11. As Chapter 4 shows, the slope of the budget constraint facing an individual equals the negative of that person's wage.

Panel a of the figure illustrates that Pat's budget constraint is steeper than Chris's because Pat's wage is larger than Chris's. Panel b shows their combined budget constraint after they marry. Before they marry, each spends some time in the marketplace earning money and other time at home cooking, cleaning, and consuming leisure. After they marry, one of them can specialize in earning money and the other at working at home. If they are both equally skilled at household work (or if Chris is better), then Pat has a comparative advantage (see Figure 10.5) in working in the marketplace, and Chris has a comparative advantage in working at home. Of course, if both enjoy consuming leisure, they may not fully specialize. As an example, suppose that, before they got married, Chris and Pat each spent 10 hours a day in sleep and leisure activities, 5 hours working in the marketplace, and 9 hours working at home. Because Chris earns $10 an hour and Pat earns $20, they collectively earned $150 a day and worked 18 hours a day at home. After they marry, they can benefit from specialization. If Chris works entirely at home and Pat works 10 hours in the marketplace and the rest at home, they collectively earn $200 a day (a one-third increase) and still have 18 hours of work at home. If they do not need to spend as much time working at home because of economies of scale, one or both could work more hours in the marketplace, and they will have even greater disposable income.

17. If you draw the convex production possibility frontier on Figure 10.5, you will see that it lies strictly inside the concave production possibility frontier. Thus more output can be obtained if Jane and Denise use the concave frontier. That is, each should specialize in producing the good for which she has a comparative advantage.

Chapter 11

5. Yes. As the "Electric Power Utilities" application illustrates, the demand curve could cut the average cost curve only in its downward-sloping section. Consequently, the average cost is strictly downward sloping in the relevant region.

22. For a general linear inverse demand function, $p(Q) = a - bQ$, $dQ/dp = -1/b$, so the elasticity is $\varepsilon = -p/(bQ)$. The demand curve hits the horizontal (quantity) axis at a/b. At half that quantity (the midpoint of the demand curve), the quantity is $a/(2b)$, and the price is $a/2$. Thus the elasticity of demand is $\varepsilon = -p/(bQ) = -(a/2)/[ab/(2b)] = -1$ at the midpoint of any linear demand curve. As the chapter shows, a monopoly will not operate in the inelastic section of its demand curve, so a monopoly will not operate in the right half of its linear demand curve.

32. See **www.aw-bc.com/perloff**, Chapter 11, "Humana Hospitals," for more examples. For saline solution, $p/MC \approx 55.4$ and the Lerner Index is $(p - MC)/p \approx 0.98$. From Equation 11.9, we know that $(p - MC)/p \approx 0.98 = -1/\varepsilon$, so $\varepsilon \approx 1.02$.

37. A profit tax (of less than 100%) has no effect on a firm's profit-maximizing behavior. Suppose the government's share of the profit is β. Then the firm wants to maximize its after-tax profit, which is $(1 - \gamma)\pi$. However, whatever choice of Q (or p) maximizes π will also maximize $(1 - \gamma)\pi$. Figure 19.3 gives a graphical example where $\gamma = 1/3$. Consequently, the tribe's behavior is unaffected by a change in the share that the government receives. We can also answer this problem using calculus. The before-tax profit is $\pi_B = R(Q) - C(Q)$, and the after-tax profit is $\pi_A = (1 - \gamma)[R(Q) - C(Q)]$. For both, the first-order condition is marginal revenue equals marginal cost: $dR(Q)/dQ = dC(Q)/dQ$.

For Chapter 10, Problem 11

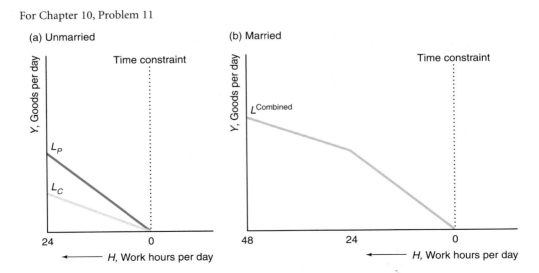

(a) Unmarried

(b) Married

41. Given the demand curve is $p = 10 - Q$, its marginal revenue curve is $MR = 10 - 2Q$. Thus the output that maximizes the monopoly's profit is determined by $MR = 10 - 2Q = 2 = MC$, or $Q^* = 4$. At that output level, its price is $p^* = 6$ and its profit is $\pi^* = 16$. If the monopoly chooses to sell 8 units in the first period (it has no incentive to sell more), its price is 2 and it makes no profit. Given that the firm sells 8 units in the first period, its demand curve in the second period is $p = 10 - Q/\beta$, so its marginal revenue function is $MR = 10 - 2Q/\beta$. The output that leads to its maximum profit is determined by $MR = 10 - 2Q/\beta = 2 = MC$, or its output is 4β. Thus its price is 6 and its profit is 16β. It pays for the firm to set a low price in the first period if the lost profit, 16, is less than the extra profit in the second period, which is $16(\beta - 1)$. Thus it pays to set a low price in the first period if $16 < 16(\beta - 1)$, or $2 < \beta$.

Chapter 12

2. This policy allows the firm to maximize its profit by price discriminating if people who put a lower value on their time (so are willing to drive to the store and move their purchases themselves) have a higher elasticity of demand than people who want to order over the phone and have the goods delivered.

3. The colleges may be providing scholarships as a form of charity, or they may be price discriminating by lowering the final price for less wealthy families (who presumably have higher elasticities of demand).

28. Equating the right-hand sides of the demand and supply functions, $100 - w = w - 20$, and solving, we find that $w = 60$. Substituting that into either the demand or supply function, we find that $H^* = 100 - 60 = 60 - 20 = 40$. To find w^*, we need to equate areas A and C in the figure in Solved Problem 12.1. We could integrate, but with a linear demand function, it is easier to calculate the area of triangles. The area of A is $\frac{1}{2}(100 - w^*)^2$ while the area of B is $\frac{1}{2}(w^* - 60)^2$. Equating these areas and solving, we find that $w^* = 80$. Substituting that into the demand function, we obtain $\overline{H} = 20$.

29. See **www.aw-bc.com/perloff**, Chapter 12, "Aibo," for more details. The two marginal revenue curves are $MR_J = 3,500 - Q_J$ and $MR_A = 4,500 - 2Q_A$. Equating the marginal revenues with the marginal cost of $500, we find that $Q_J = 3,000$ and $Q_A = 2,000$. Substituting these quantities into the inverse demand curves, we learn that $p_J = \$2,000$ and $p_A = \$2,500$. Rearranging Equation 11.9, we know that the elasticities of demand are $\varepsilon_J = p/(MC - p) = 2,000/(500 - 2,000) = -\frac{4}{3}$ and $\varepsilon_A = 2,500/(500 - 2,500) = -\frac{5}{4}$. Thus using Equation 12.3, we find that

$$\frac{p_J}{p_A} = \frac{2,000}{2,500} = 0.8 = \frac{1 + 1/\left(-\frac{5}{4}\right)}{1 + 1/\left(-\frac{4}{3}\right)} = \frac{1 + 1/\varepsilon_A}{1 + 1/\varepsilon_J}.$$

The profit in Japan is $(p_J - m)Q_J = (\$2,000 - \$500) \times 3,000 = \$4.5$ million, and the U.S. profit is $4 million. The deadweight loss is greater in Japan, $2.25 million ($= \frac{1}{2} \times \$1,500 \times 3,000$), than in the United States, $2 million ($= \frac{1}{2} \times \$2,000 \times 2,000$).

30. By differentiating, we find that the American marginal revenue function is $MR_A = 100 - 2Q_A$, and the Japanese one is $MR_J = 80 - 4Q_J$. To determine how many units to sell in the United States, the monopoly sets its American marginal revenue equal to its marginal cost, $MR_A = 100 - 2Q_A = 20$, and solves for the optimal quantity, $Q_A = 40$ units. Similarly, because $MR_J = 80 - 4Q_J = 20$, the optimal quantity is $Q_J = 15$ units in Japan. Substituting $Q_A = 40$ into the American demand function, we find that $p_A = 100 - 40 = \$60$. Similarly, substituting $Q_J = 15$ units into the Japanese demand function, we learn that $p_J = 80 - (2 \times 15) = \$50$. Thus the price-discriminating monopoly charges 20% more in the United States than in Japan. We can also show this result using elasticities. From Equation 2.22, we know that the elasticity of demand is $\varepsilon_A = -p_A/Q_A$ in the United States and $\varepsilon_J = -1/2p_J/Q_J$ in Japan. In the equilibrium, $\varepsilon_A = -60/40 = -3/2$ and $\varepsilon_J = -50/(2 \times 15) = -5/3$. As Equation 12.3 shows, the ratio of the prices depends on the relative elasticities of demand: $p_A/p_J = 60/50 = (1 + 1/\varepsilon_J)/(1 + 1/\varepsilon_A) = (1 - 3/5)/(1 - 2/3) = 6/5$.

32. From the problem, we know that the profit-maximizing Chinese price is $p = 3$ and that the quantity is $Q = 0.1$ (million). The marginal cost is $m = 1$. Using Equation 11.9, $(p_C - m)/p_C = (3 - 1)/3 = -1/\varepsilon_C$, so $\varepsilon_C = -3/2$. If the Chinese inverse demand curve is $p = a - bQ$, then the corresponding marginal revenue curve is $MR = a - 2bQ$. Warner maximizes its profit where $MR = a - 2bQ = m = 1$, so its optimal $Q = (a - 1)/(2b)$. Substituting this expression into the inverse demand curve, we find that its optimal $p = (a + 1)/2 = 3$, or $a = 5$. Substituting that result into the output equation, we have $Q = (5 - 1)/(2b) = 0.1$ (million). Thus $b = 20$, the inverse demand function is $p = 5 - 20Q$, and the marginal revenue function is $MR = 5 - 40Q$. Using this information, you can draw a figure similar to Figure 12.4.

Chapter 13

2. The monopoly will make more profit than the duopoly will, so the monopoly is willing to pay the college more rent. Although granting monopoly rights may be attractive to the college in terms of higher rent, students will suffer (lose consumer surplus) because of the higher textbook prices.

15. Given that the duopolies produce identical goods, the equilibrium price is lower if the duopolies set price rather than quantity. If the goods are heterogeneous, we cannot answer this question definitively.

16. By differentiating its product, a firm makes the residual demand curve it faces less elastic everywhere. For example, no consumer will buy from that firm if its rival charges less and the goods are homogeneous. In contrast, some consumers who prefer this firm's product to that of its rival will still buy from this firm even if its rival charges less. As the chapter shows, a firm sets a higher price the lower the elasticity of demand at the equilibrium.

21. The inverse demand curve is $p = 1 - 0.001Q$. The first firm's profit is $\pi_1 = [1 - 0.001(q_1 + q_2)]q_1 - 0.28q_1$. Its first-order condition is $d\pi_1/dq_1 = 1 - 0.001(2q_1 + q_2) - 0.28 = 0$. If we rearrange the terms, the first firm's best-response function is $q_1 = 360 - \frac{1}{2}q_2$. Similarly, the second firm's best-response function is $q_2 = 360 - \frac{1}{2}q_1$. By substituting one of these best-response functions into the other, we learn that the Nash-Cournot equilibrium occurs at $q_1 = q_2 = 240$, so the equilibrium price is 52¢.

23. See Solved Problem 13.1. The equilibrium quantities are $q_1 = (a - 2m_1 + m_2)/3b = (90 + 30)/6 = 20$ and $q_2 = (90 - 60)/6 = 5$. As a result, the equilibrium price is $p = 90 - 20 - 5 = 65$.

25. Firm 1 wants to maximize its profit:

$$\pi_1 = (p_1 - 10)q_1 = (p_1 - 10)(100 - 2p_1 + p_2).$$

Its first-order condition is $d\pi_1/dp_1 = 100 - 4p_1 + p_2 + 20 = 0$, so its best-response function is $p_1 = 30 + \frac{1}{4}p_2$. Similarly, Firm 2's best-response function is $p_2 = 30 + \frac{1}{4}p_1$. Solving, the Nash-Bertrand equilibrium prices are $p_1 = p_2 = 40$. Each firm produces 60 units.

28. One approach is to show that a rise in marginal cost or a fall in the number of firms tends to cause the price to rise. Solved Problem 13.3 shows the effect of a decrease in marginal cost due to a subsidy (the opposite effect). The section titled "The Cournot Equilibrium with Two or More Firms" shows that as the number of firms falls, market power increases and the markup of price over marginal cost increases. The two effects reinforce each other. Suppose that the market demand curve has a constant elasticity of ε. We can rewrite Equation 13.10 as $p = m/[1 + 1/(n\varepsilon)] = m\mu$, where $\mu = 1/[1 + 1/(n\varepsilon)]$ is the markup factor. Suppose that marginal cost increases to $(1 + \alpha)m$ and that the drop in the number of firms causes the markup factor to rise to $(1 + \beta)\mu$; then the change in price is $[(1 + \alpha)m \times (1 + \beta)\mu] - m\mu = (\alpha + \beta + \alpha\beta)m\mu$. That is, price increases by the fractional increase in the marginal cost, α, plus the fractional increase in the markup factor, β, plus the interaction of the two, $\alpha\beta$.

35. You can solve this problem using calculus or the formulas for the linear demand and constant marginal cost Cournot model from the chapter.

   a. For the duopoly, $q_1 = (15 - 2 + 2)/3 = 5$, $q_2 = (15 - 4 + 1)/3 = 4$, $p_d = 6$, $\pi_1 = (6 - 1)5 = 25$, $\pi_2 = (6 - 2)4 = 16$.

Total output is $Q_d = 5 + 4 = 9$. Total profit is $\pi_d = 25 + 16 = 41$. Consumer surplus is $CS_d = 1/2(15 - 6)9 = 81/2 = 40.5$. At the efficient price (equal to marginal cost of 1), the output is 14. The deadweight loss is $DWL_d = 1/2(6 - 1)(14 - 9) = 25/2 = 12.5$.

   b. A monopoly equates its marginal revenue and marginal cost: $MR = 15 - 2Q_m = 1 = MC$. Thus $Q_m = 7$, $p_m = 8$, $\pi_m = (8 - 1)7 = 49$. Consumer surplus is $CS_m = 1/2(15 - 8)7 = 49/2 = 24.5$. The deadweight loss is $DWL_m = 1/2(8 - 1)(14 - 7) = 49/2 = 24.5$.

   c. The average cost of production for the duopoly is $[(5 \times 1) + (4 \times 2)]/(5 + 4) = 1.44$, whereas the average cost of production for the monopoly is 1. The increase in market power effect swamps the efficiency gain, so consumer surplus falls while deadweight loss nearly doubles.

36. The answers are:

   a. In the Cournot equilibrium, $q_i = (a - m)/(3b) = (150 - 60)/3 = 30$, $Q = 60$, $p = 90$.

   b. In the Stackelberg equilibrium in which Firm 1 moves first, $q_1 = (a - m)/(2b) = (150 - 60)/2 = 45$, $q_2 = (a - m)/(4b) = (150 - 60)/4 = 22.5$, $Q = 67.5$, and $p = 82.5$.

37. The answers are:

   a. The Cournot equilibrium in the absence of government intervention is $q_1 = 30$, $q_2 = 40$, $p = 50$, $\pi_1 = 900$, and $\pi_2 = 1,600$.

   b. The Cournot equilibrium is now $q_1 = 33.3$, $q_2 = 33.3$, $p = 53.3$, $\pi_1 = 1,108.9$, and $\pi_2 = 1,108.9$.

   c. Because Firm 2's profit was 1,600 in part a, a fixed cost slightly greater than 1,600 will prevent entry.

Chapter 14

2. The payoff matrix in this prisoners' dilemma game is

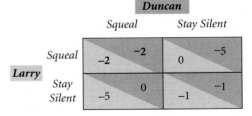

If Duncan stays silent, Larry gets 0 if he squeals and -1 (a year in jail) if he stays silent. If Duncan confesses, Larry gets -2 if he squeals and -5 if he does not. Thus Larry is better off squealing in either case, so squealing is his dominant strategy. By the same reasoning, squealing is also Duncan's dominant strategy. As a result, the Nash equilibrium is for both to confess.

17. We start by checking for dominant strategies. Given the payoff matrix, Toyota always does at least as well by entering the market. If GM enters, Toyota earns 10 by entering and 0 by staying out of the market. If GM does not enter, Toyota earns 250 if it enters and 0 otherwise. Thus entering is Toyota's dominant strategy. GM does not have a dominant strategy. It wants to enter if Toyota does not enter (earning 200 rather than 0), and it wants to stay out if Toyota enters (earning 0 rather than −40). Because GM knows that Toyota will enter (entering is Toyota's dominant strategy), GM stays out of the market. Toyota's entering and GM's not entering is a Nash equilibrium. Given the other firm's strategy, neither firm wants to change its strategy. Next we examine how the subsidy affects the payoff matrix and dominant strategies. The subsidy does not affect Toyota's payoff, so Toyota still has a dominant strategy: It enters the market. With the subsidy, GM's payoff if it enters increases by 50: GM earns 10 if both enter and 250 if it enters and Toyota does not. With the subsidy, entering is a dominant strategy for GM. Thus both firms' entering is a Nash equilibrium.

20. The game tree at the bottom of the page illustrates why the incumbent may install the robotic arms to discourage entry even though its total cost rises. If the incumbent fears that a rival is poised to enter, it invests to discourage entry. The incumbent can invest in equipment that lowers its marginal cost. With the lowered marginal cost, it is credible that the incumbent will produce larger quantities of output, which discourages entry. The incumbent's monopoly (no-entry) profit drops from $900 to $500 if it makes the investment because the investment raises its total cost. If the incumbent doesn't buy the robotic arms, the rival enters because it makes $300 by entering and nothing if it stays out of the market. With entry, the incumbent's profit is $400. With the investment, the rival loses $36 if it enters, so it stays out of the market, losing nothing. Because of the investment, the incumbent earns $500. Nonetheless, earning $500 is better than earning only $400, so the incumbent invests.

21. The incumbent firm has a *first-mover advantage*, as the game tree on the facing page illustrates. Moving first allows the incumbent or leader firm to *commit* to producing a relatively large quantity. If the incumbent does not make a commitment before its rival enters, entry occurs and the incumbent earns a relatively low profit. By committing to produce such a large output level that the potential entrant decides not to enter because it cannot make a positive profit, the incumbent's commitment discourages entry. Moving backward in time (moving to the left in the diagram), we examine the incumbent's choice. If the incumbent commits to the small quantity, its rival enters and the incumbent earns $450. If the incumbent commits to the larger quantity, its rival does not enter and the incumbent earns $800. Clearly, the incumbent should commit to the larger quantity because it earns a larger profit and the potential entrant chooses to stay out of the market. Their chosen paths are identified by the darker blue in the figure.

22. It is worth more to the monopoly to keep the potential entrant out than it is worth to the potential entrant to enter, as the figure on the facing page shows. Before the pollution-control device requirement, the entrant would pay up to $3 to enter, whereas the incumbent would pay up to $\pi_i - \pi_d = \$7$ to exclude the potential entrant. The incumbent's profit is $6 if entry does not occur, and it loses $1 if entry occurs. Because the new firm would lose $1 if it enters, it does not enter. Thus the incumbent has an incentive to raise costs by $4 to both firms. The incumbent's profit is $6 if it raises costs rather than $3 if it does not.

25. Let the probability that a firm sets a low price be θ_1 for Firm 1 and θ_2 for Firm 2. If the firms choose their prices independently, then $\theta_1\theta_2$ is the probability that both set a low price, $(1 - \theta_1)(1 - \theta_2)$ is the probability that both set a high price, $\theta_1(1 - \theta_2)$ is the probability that Firm 1 prices low and Firm 2 prices high, and $(1 - \theta_1)\theta_2$ is the probability that Firm 1 prices high and Firm 2 prices low. Firm 2's expected payoff is $E(\pi_2) = 2\theta_1\theta_2 + (0)\theta_1(1 - \theta_2) + (1 - \theta_1)\theta_2 + 6(1 - \theta_1)(1 - \theta_2) = (6 - 6\theta_1) - (5 - 7\theta_1)\theta_2$. Similarly, Firm 1's expected payoff is $E(\pi_1) = (0)\theta_1\theta_2 + 7\theta_1(1 - \theta_2) + 2(1 - \theta_1)\theta_2 + 6(1 - \theta_1)(1 - \theta_2) = (6 - 4\theta_2) - (1 - 3\theta_2)\theta_1$. Each firm forms a belief about its rival's behavior. For example, suppose that Firm 1 believes that Firm 2 will choose a low price with a probability $\hat{\theta}_2$. If $\hat{\theta}_2$

For Chapter 14, Problem 20

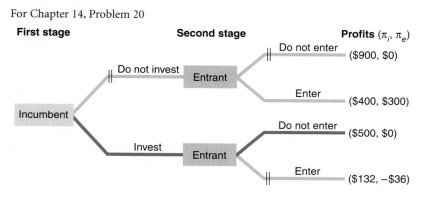

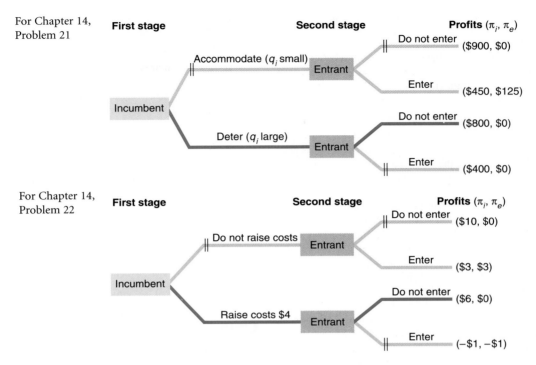

For Chapter 14, Problem 21

First stage   **Second stage**   **Profits** (π_i, π_e)

Incumbent

Accommodate (q_i small) — Entrant
- Do not enter ($900, $0)
- Enter ($450, $125)

Deter (q_i large) — Entrant
- Do not enter ($800, $0)
- Enter ($400, $0)

For Chapter 14, Problem 22

First stage   **Second stage**   **Profits** (π_i, π_e)

Incumbent

Do not raise costs — Entrant
- Do not enter ($10, $0)
- Enter ($3, $3)

Raise costs $4 — Entrant
- Do not enter ($6, $0)
- Enter (−$1, −$1)

is less than $\frac{1}{3}$ (Firm 2 is relatively unlikely to choose a low price), it pays for Firm 1 to choose the low price because the second term in $E(\pi_1)$,$(1 - 3\hat{\theta}_2)\theta_1$, is positive, so as θ_1 increases, $E(\pi_1)$ increases. Because the highest possible θ_1 is 1, Firm 1 chooses the low price with certainty. Similarly, if Firm 1 believes $\hat{\theta}_2$ is greater than $\frac{1}{3}$, it sets a high price with certainty ($\theta_1 = 0$).

If Firm 2 believes that Firm 1 thinks $\hat{\theta}_2$ is slightly below $\frac{1}{3}$, Firm 2 believes that Firm 1 will choose a low price with certainty, and hence Firm 2 will also choose a low price. That outcome, $\theta_2 = 1$, however, is not consistent with Firm 1's expectation that $\hat{\theta}_2$ is a fraction. Indeed, it is only rational for Firm 2 to believe that Firm 1 believes Firm 2 will use a mixed strategy if Firm 1's belief about Firm 2 makes Firm 1 unpredictable. That is, Firm 1 uses a mixed strategy only if it is *indifferent* between setting a high or a low price. It is indifferent only if it believes $\hat{\theta}_2$ is exactly $\frac{1}{3}$. By similar reasoning, Firm 2 will use a mixed strategy only if its belief is that Firm 1 chooses a low price with probability $\hat{\theta}_1 = \frac{5}{7}$. Thus the only possible Nash equilibrium is $\theta_1 = \frac{5}{7}$ and $\theta_2 = \frac{1}{3}$.

Chapter 15

2. Before the tax, the competitive firm's labor demand was $p \times MP_L$. After the tax, the firm's effective price is $(1 - \alpha)p$, so its labor demand becomes $(1 - \alpha)p \times MP_L$.

15. An individual with a zero discount rate views current and future consumption as equally attractive. An individual with an infinite discount rate cares only about current consumption and puts no value on future consumption.

21. The competitive firm's marginal revenue of labor is $MRP_L = p(1 + 2K)$.

26. If a firm has a monopoly in the output market and is a monopsony in the labor market, its profit is

$$\pi = p(Q(L))Q(L) - w(L)L,$$

where $Q(L)$ is the production function, $p(Q)Q$ is its revenue, and wL—the wage times the number of workers—is its cost of production. The firm maximizes its profit by setting the derivative of profit with respect to labor equal to zero (if the second-order condition holds):

$$\left(p + Q(L)\frac{dp}{dQ}\right)\frac{dQ}{dL} - w(L) - \frac{dw}{dL}L = 0.$$

Rearranging terms in the first-order condition, we find that the maximization condition is that the marginal revenue product of labor,

$$MRP_L = pMPL = \left(p + Q(L)\frac{dp}{dQ}\right)\frac{dQ}{dL} = p\left(1 + \frac{1}{\varepsilon}\right)\frac{dQ}{dL},$$

equals the marginal expenditure,

$$ME = w(L) + \frac{dw}{dL}L = w(L)\left(1 + \frac{w}{L}\frac{dw}{dL}\right)$$

$$= w(L)\left(1 + \frac{1}{\eta}\right),$$

where ε is the elasticity of demand in the output market and η is the supply elasticity of labor.

34. Solving for *irr*, we find that *irr* equals 1 or 9. This approach fails to give us a unique solution, so we should use the *NPV* approach instead. The $NPV = 1 - 12/1.07 + 20/1.07^2 \approx 7.254$, which is positive, so that the firm should invest.

40. Currently, you are buying 600 gallons of gas at a cost of $1,200 per year. With a more gas-efficient car, you would spend only $600 per year, saving $600 per year in gas payments. If we assume that these payments are made at the end of each year, the present value of these savings for five years is $2,580 at a 5% annual interest rate and $2,280 at 10%. The present value of the amount you must spend to buy the car in five years is $6,240 at 5% and $4,960 at 10%. Thus the present value of the additional cost of buying now rather than later is $1,760 (= $8,000 − $6,240) at 5% and $3,040 at 10%. The benefit from buying now is the present value of the reduced gas payments. The cost is the present value of the additional cost of buying the car sooner rather than later. At 5%, the benefit is $2,580 and the cost is $1,760, so you should buy now. However, at 10%, the benefit, $2,280, is less than the cost, $3,040, so you should buy later.

43. Because the first contract is paid immediately, its present value equals the contract payment of $1 million. Our pro can use Equation 15.19 and a calculator to determine the present value of the second contract (or hire you to do the job for him). The present value of a $2 million payment 10 years from now is $2,000,000/(1.05)^{10} \approx $1,227,827 at 5% and $2,000,000/(1.2)^{10} \approx $323,011 at 20%. Consequently, the present values are as shown in the table.

Payment	Present Value at 5%	Present Value at 20%
$500,000 today	$50,000	$500,000
$2 million in 10 years	$1,227,827	$323,011
Total	$1,727,827	$823,011

Thus at 5%, he should accept Contract B, with a present value of $1,727,827, which is much greater than the present value of Contract A, $1 million. At 20%, he should sign Contract A.

Chapter 16

3. As Figure 16.2 shows, Irma's expected utility of 133 at point *f* (where her expected wealth is $64) is the same as her utility from a certain wealth of Y.

5. The expected punishment for violating traffic laws is θV, where θ is the probability of being caught and fined and V is the fine. If people care only about the expected punishment (that is, there's no additional psychological pain from the experience), increasing the expected punishment by increasing θ or V works equally well in discouraging bad

behavior. The government prefers to increase the fine, V, which is costless, rather than to raise θ, which is costly due to the extra police, district attorneys, and courts required.

16. If they were married, Andy would receive half the potential earnings whether they stayed married or not. As a result, Andy will receive $12,000 in present-value terms from Kim's additional earnings. Because the returns to the investment exceed the cost, Andy will make this investment (unless a better investment is available). However, if they stay unmarried and split, Andy's expected return on the investment is the probability of their staying together, 1/2, times Kim's half of the returns if they stay together, $12,000. Thus Andy's expected return on the investment, $6,000, is less than the cost of the education, so Andy is unwilling to make that investment (regardless of other investment opportunities).

22. Assuming that the painting is not insured against fire, its expected value is

$$\$550 = (0.2 \times \$1,000) + (0.1 \times \$0) + (0.7 \times \$500).$$

Chapter 17

3. As Figure 17.3 shows, a specific tax of $84 per ton of output or per unit of emissions (gunk) leads to the social optimum.

6. Granting the chemical company the right to dump 1 ton per day results in that firm's dumping 1 ton and the boat rental company's maintaining one boat, which maximizes joint profit at $20.

19. As the figure on the facing page shows, the government uses its expected marginal benefit curve to set a standard at S or a fee at f. If the true marginal benefit curve is MB^1, the optimal standard is S_1 and the optimal fee is f_1. The deadweight loss from setting either the fee or the standard too high is the same, DWL_1. Similarly, if the true marginal benefit curve is MB^2, both the fee and the standard are set too low, but both have the same deadweight loss, DWL_2. Thus the deadweight loss from a mistaken belief about the marginal benefit does not depend on whether the government uses a fee or a standard. When the government sets an emissions fee or standard, the amount of gunk actually produced depends only on the marginal cost of abatement and not on the marginal benefit. Because the standard and fee lead to the same level of abatement at e, they cause the same deadweight loss.

21. We care only about the marginal harm of gunk at the social optimum, which we know is $MC^g = \$84$ (because it is the same at every level of output). Thus the social optimum is the same as in our graphical example (and no algebra is necessary). We can also solve the problem using algebra. Using the equations from the chapter, we set the inverse demand function, $p = 450 - 2Q$, equal to the new social marginal cost, $MC^s = MC^p + 84 = 30 + 2Q + 84 = 114 + 2Q$, and we find that the socially optimal quantity is $Q_s = (450 - 114)/(2 + 2) = 84$.

For Chapter 17, Problem 19

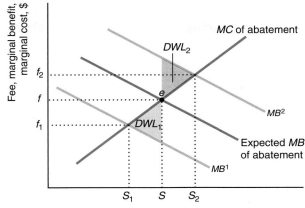

Units of gunk abated per day

Chapter 18

2. Because insurance costs do not vary with soil type, buying insurance is unattractive for houses on good soil and relatively attractive for houses on bad soil. These incentives create a moral hazard problem: Relatively more homeowners with houses on poor soil buy insurance, so the state insurance agency will face disproportionately many bad outcomes in the next earthquake.

6. Brand names allow consumers to identify a particular company's product in the future. If a mushroom company expects to remain in business over time, it would be foolish for it to brand its product if its mushrooms are of inferior quality. (Just ask Babar's grandfather.) Thus all else the same, we would expect branded mushrooms to be of higher quality than unbranded ones.

15. Because buyers are risk neutral, if they believe that the probability of getting a lemon is θ, the most they are willing to pay for a car of unknown quality is $p = p_1(1 - \theta) + p_2\theta$. If p is greater than both v_1 and v_2, all cars are sold. If $v_1 > p > v_2$, only lemons are sold. If p were less than both v_1 and v_2, no cars would be sold. However, we know that $v_2 < p_2$ and that $p_2 < p$, so owners of lemons are certainly willing to sell them. (If sellers bear a transaction cost of c and $p < v_2 + c$, no cars are sold.)

Chapter 19

1. If Paula pays Arthur a fixed-fee salary of $168, Arthur has no incentive to buy any carvings for resale, given that the $12 per carving cost comes out of his pocket. Thus Arthur sells no carvings if he receives a fixed salary and can sell as many or as few carvings as he wants. The contract is not incentive compatible. For Arthur to behave efficiently, this fixed-fee contract must be modified. For example, the contract could specify that Arthur gets a salary of $168 and that he must obtain and sell 12 carvings. Paula must monitor his behavior. (Paula's residual profit is the joint profit minus

$168, so she gets the marginal profit from each additional sale and wants to sell the joint-profit-maximizing number of carvings.) Arthur makes $24 = $168 − $144, so he is willing to participate. Joint profit is maximized at $72, and Paula gets the maximum possible residual profit of $48.

6. By making this commitment, the company may be trying to assure customers who cannot judge how quickly the product will deteriorate that the product is durable enough to maintain at least a certain value in the future. The firm is trying to eliminate asymmetric information to increase the demand for its product.

9. Presumably, the promoter collects a percentage of the revenue of each restaurant. If customers can pay cash, the restaurants may lie to the promoter about the amount of food they sold. The scrip makes such opportunistic behavior difficult.

13. A partner who works an extra hour bears the full opportunity cost of this extra hour but gets only half the marginal benefit from the extra business profit. The opportunity cost of extra time spent at the store is the partner's best alternative use of time. A partner could earn money working for someone else or use the time to have fun. Because a partner bears the full marginal cost but gets only half the marginal benefit (the extra business profit) from an extra hour of work, each partner works only up to the point at which the marginal cost equals half the marginal benefit. Thus each has an incentive to put in less effort than the level that maximizes their joint profit, where the marginal cost equals the marginal benefit.

14. This agreement led to very long conversations. Whichever of them was enjoying the call more apparently figured that he or she would get the full marginal benefit of one more minute of talking while having to pay only half the marginal cost. What I learned from this experience was not to open our phone bill so as to avoid being shocked by the amount due.

21. The minimum bond that deters stealing is $2,500.

Definitions

I hate definitions. —Benjamin Disraeli

action: a move that a player makes at a specified stage of a game, such as how much output a firm produces in the current period. (14)*

adverse selection: opportunism characterized by an informed person's benefiting from trading or otherwise contracting with a less-informed person who does not know about an *unobserved characteristic* of the informed person. (18)

asymmetric information: the situation in which one party to a transaction knows a material fact that the other party does not. (18)

auction: a sale in which a good or service is sold to the highest bidder. (14)

average cost (*AC*): the total cost divided by the units of output produced: $AC = C/q$. (7)

average fixed cost (*AFC*): the fixed cost divided by the units of output produced: $AFC = F/q$. (7)

average product of labor (*AP_L*): the ratio of output, q, to the number of workers, L, used to produce that output: $AP_L = q/L$. (6)

average variable cost (*AVC*): the variable cost divided by the units of output produced: $AVC = VC/q$. (7)

backward induction: a process in which we first determine the best response by the last player to move, next determine the best response for the player who made the next-to-last move, and then repeat the process until we reach the move at the beginning of the game. (14)

bad: something for which less is preferred to more, such as pollution. (3)

bandwagon effect: the situation in which a person places greater value on a good as more and more other people possess it. (11)

barrier to entry: an explicit restriction or a cost that applies only to potential new firms—existing firms are not subject to the restriction or do not bear the cost. (9)

Bertrand equilibrium (*Nash-Bertrand equilibrium* or *Nash-in-prices equilibrium*): a set of prices such that no firm can obtain a higher profit by choosing a different price if the other firms continue to charge these prices. (13)

best response: the strategy that maximizes a player's payoff given the player's beliefs about its rivals' strategies. (14)

budget line (or *budget constraint*): the bundles of goods that can be bought if the entire budget is spent on those goods at given prices. (3)

bundling (*package tie-in sale*): a type of tie-in sale in which two goods are combined so that customers cannot buy either good separately. (12)

cartel: a group of firms that explicitly agree (collude) to coordinate their activities. (13)

certification: a report that a particular product meets or exceeds a given standard level. (18)

cheap talk: unsubstantiated claims or statements. (18)

common knowledge: what all players know about the rules of the game, that each player's payoff depends on actions taken by all players, and that all players want to maximize their payoffs; all players know that all players know the payoffs and that their opponents are payoff maximizing; and so on. (14)

common property: a resource that is available to anyone. (17)

comparative advantage: the ability to produce a good at a lower opportunity cost than someone else. (10)

comparative statics: the method that economists use to analyze how variables controlled by consumers and firms react to a change in environmental variables. (2)

compensating variation (*CV*): the amount of money one would have to give a consumer to offset completely the harm from a price increase. (5)

complete information: the situation where the payoff function is common knowledge among all players. (14)

constant returns to scale (*CRS*): the property of a production function whereby when all inputs are increased by a certain percentage, output increases by that same percentage. (6)

consumer surplus (*CS*): the monetary difference between what a consumer is willing to pay for the quantity of the good purchased and what the good actually costs. (5)

contingent fee: a payment to a lawyer that is a share of the award in a court case (usually after legal expenses are deducted) if the client wins and nothing if the client loses. (19)

contract curve: the set of all Pareto-efficient bundles. (10)

cost (*total cost, C*): the sum of a firm's variable cost and fixed cost: $C = VC + F$. (7)

Cournot equilibrium (*Nash-Cournot equilibrium* or *Nash-in-quantities equilibrium*): a set of quantities chosen by firms such that, holding the quantities of all other firms constant, no firm can obtain a higher profit by choosing a different quantity. (13)

---

* Numbers refer to the chapter where the term is defined.

credible threat: an announcement that a firm will use a strategy harmful to its rivals that the rivals believe because the firm's strategy is rational in the sense that it is in the firm's best interest to use it. (14)

cross-price elasticity of demand: the percentage change in the quantity demanded in response to a given percentage change in the price of another good. (2)

deadweight loss (*DWL*): the net reduction in welfare from a loss of surplus by one group that is not offset by a gain to another group from an action that alters a market equilibrium. (9)

decreasing returns to scale (*DRS*): the property of a production function whereby output rises less than in proportion to an equal percentage increase in all inputs. (6)

demand curve: a plot of the demand function that shows the quantity demanded at each possible price, holding constant the other factors that influence purchases. (2)

demand function: the correspondence between the quantity demanded and price and other factors that influence purchases. (2)

discount rate: a rate reflecting the relative value an individual places on future consumption compared to current consumption. (15)

diseconomies of scale: the property of a cost function whereby the average cost of production rises when output increases. (7)

dominant strategy: a strategy that produces a higher payoff than any other strategy the player can use for every possible combination of its rivals' strategies. (14)

duopoly: an oligopoly with two firms. (13)

durable good: a product that is usable for years. (7)

dynamic game: game in which players move either sequentially or repeatedly. (14)

economic cost (*opportunity cost*): the value of the best alternative use of a resource. (7)

economic profit: revenue minus economic cost. (8)

economically efficient: minimizing the cost of producing a specified amount of output. (7)

economies of scale: the property of a cost function whereby the average cost of production falls as output expands. (7)

economies of scope: a situation in which it is less expensive to produce goods jointly than separately. (7)

efficiency in production: a situation in which the principal's and the agent's combined value (profits, payoffs), π, is maximized. (19)

efficiency in risk bearing: a situation in which risk sharing is optimal in that the person who least minds facing risk—the risk-neutral or less-risk-averse person—bears more of the risk. (19)

efficiency wage: an unusually high wage that a firm pays workers as an incentive to avoid shirking. (19)

efficient contract: an agreement with provisions that ensure that no party can be made better off without harming the other party. (19)

efficient production (*technological efficiency*): situation in which the current level of output cannot be produced

with fewer inputs, given existing knowledge about technology and the organization of production. (6)

elasticity: the percentage change in one variable in response to a given percentage change in another variable, holding all other relevant variables constant. (2)

elasticity of substitution (σ): the percentage change in the capital-labor ratio divided by the percentage change in the marginal rate of technical substitution (*MRTS*). (6)

endowment: an initial allocation of goods. (10)

Engel curve: the relationship between the quantity demanded of a single good and income, holding prices constant. (4)

equilibrium: a situation in which no one wants to change his or her behavior. (2)

equivalent variation (*EV*): the amount of money one would have to take from a consumer to harm the consumer by as much as the price increase. (5)

essential facility: a scarce resource that rivals need to use to survive. (11)

excess demand: the amount by which the quantity demanded exceeds the quantity supplied at a specified price. (2)

excess supply: the amount by which the quantity supplied is greater than the quantity demanded at a specified price. (2)

exhaustible resources: nonrenewable natural assets that cannot be increased, only depleted. (15)

expansion path: the cost-minimizing combination of labor and capital for each output level. (7)

expenditure function: the relationship showing the minimal expenditures necessary to achieve a specific utility level for a given set of prices. (3)

extensive form: specifies the *n* players, the sequence in which they make their moves, the actions they can take at each move, the information that each player has about players' previous moves, and the payoff function over all possible strategies. (14)

externality: occurs when a person's well-being or a firm's production capability is directly affected by the actions of other consumers or firms rather than indirectly through changes in prices. (17)

fair bet: a wager with an expected value of zero. (16)

fair insurance: a bet between an insurer and a policyholder in which the value of the bet to the policyholder is zero. (16)

firm: an organization that converts *inputs* such as labor, materials, energy, and capital into *outputs,* the goods and services that it sells. (6)

fixed cost (*F*): a production expense that does not vary with output. (7)

fixed input: a factor of production that cannot be varied practically in the short run. (6)

flow: a quantity or value that is measured per unit of time. (15)

free ride: to benefit from the actions of others without paying. (17)

game: any competition between players (such as individuals or firms) in which strategic behavior plays a major role. (14)

game theory: a set of tools that economists, political scientists, military analysts, and others use to analyze players' strategic decision making. (14)

general-equilibrium analysis: the study of how equilibrium is determined in all markets simultaneously. (10)

Giffen good: a commodity for which a decrease in its price causes the quantity demanded to fall. (4)

good: a commodity for which more is preferred to less, at least at some levels of consumption. (3)

incentive compatible: when a contract provides inducements such that the agent wants to perform the assigned task rather than engage in opportunistic behavior. (19)

incidence of a tax on consumers: the share of the tax that falls on consumers. (2)

income effect: the change in the quantity of a good a consumer demands because of a change in income, holding prices constant. (4)

income elasticity of demand (or *income elasticity*): the percentage change in the quantity demanded in response to a given percentage increase in income. (2)

increasing returns to scale (*IRS*): the property of a production function whereby output rises more than in proportion to an equal increase in all inputs. (6)

indifference curve: the set of all bundles of goods that a consumer views as being equally desirable. (3)

indifference map (or *preference map*): a complete set of indifference curves that summarize a consumer's tastes. (3)

inferior good: a commodity of which less is demanded as income rises. (4)

interest rate: the percentage more that must be repaid to borrow money for a fixed period of time. (15)

internal rate of return (*irr*): the discount rate such that the net present value of an investment is zero. (15)

internalize the externality: to bear the cost of the harm that one inflicts on others (or to capture the benefit that one provides to others). (17)

isocost line: all the combinations of inputs that require the same (*iso*) total expenditure (*cost*). (7)

isoquant: a curve that shows the efficient combinations of labor and capital that can produce a single (*iso*) level of output (*quantity*). (6)

Law of Demand: consumers demand more of a good the lower its price, holding constant tastes, the prices of other goods, and other factors that influence the amount they consume. (2)

learning by doing: the productive skills and knowledge of better ways to produce that workers and managers gain from experience. (7)

Lerner Index: the ratio of the difference between price and marginal cost to the price: $(p - MC)/p$. (11)

limited liability: condition whereby the personal assets of the corporate owners cannot be taken to pay a corporation's debts if it goes into bankruptcy. (6)

long run: a lengthy enough period of time that all inputs can be varied. (6)

marginal cost (*MC*): the amount by which a firm's cost changes if the firm produces one more unit of output: $MC = \Delta C/\Delta q$. (6)

marginal product of labor (*MP$_L$*): the change in output resulting from using an extra unit of labor, holding other factors (such as capital) constant: $MP_L = \Delta q/\Delta L$. (6)

marginal profit: the change in the profit a firm gets from selling one more unit of output. (8)

marginal rate of substitution (*MRS*): the maximum amount of one good that a consumer will sacrifice (trade) to obtain one more unit of another good. (3)

marginal rate of technical substitution: how many units of capital the firm can replace with an extra unit of labor while holding output constant. (6)

marginal rate of transformation (*MRT*): the trade-off the market imposes on the consumer in terms of the amount of one good the consumer must give up to obtain more of the other good. (3)

marginal revenue (*MR*): the change in revenue a firm gets from selling one more unit of output. (8)

marginal revenue product of labor (*MRP$_L$*): the additional revenue from the last unit of labor. (15)

marginal utility: the extra utility that a consumer gets from consuming the last unit of a good. (3)

market: an exchange mechanism that allows buyers to trade with sellers. (1)

market failure: inefficient production or consumption, often because a price exceeds marginal cost. (9)

market power: the ability of a firm to charge a price above marginal cost and earn a positive profit. (11)

market structure: the number of firms in the market, the ease with which firms can enter and leave the market, and the ability of firms to differentiate their products from those of their rivals. (8)

microeconomics: the study of how individuals and firms make themselves as well off as possible in a world of scarcity, and the consequences of those individual decisions for markets and the entire economy. (1)

minimum efficient scale (*full capacity*): the smallest quantity at which the average cost curve reaches its minimum. (13)

mixed strategy: a strategy in which the player chooses among possible actions according to probabilities the player assigns. (14)

model: a description of the relationship between two or more economic variables. (1)

monopolistic competition: a market structure in which firms have market power but no additional firm can enter and earn positive profits. (13)

monopoly: the only supplier of a good for which there is no close substitute. (11)

monopsony: the only buyer of a good in a market. (15)

moral hazard: opportunism characterized by an informed person's taking advantage of a less-informed person through an *unobserved action*. (18)

multimarket price discrimination (*third-degree price discrimination*): a situation in which a firm charges different groups of customers different prices but charges a given customer the same price for every unit of output sold. (12)

Nash equilibrium: a set of strategies such that, when all other players use these strategies, no player can obtain a higher payoff by choosing a different strategy. (14)

Nash-Bertrand equilibrium (*Bertrand equilibrium* or *Nash-in-prices equilibrium*): a set of prices chosen by firms such that no firm can obtain a higher profit by choosing a different price if the other firms continue to charge these prices. (13)

Nash-Cournot equilibrium (*Cournot equilibrium* or *Nash-in-quantities equilibrium*): a set of quantities chosen by firms such that, holding the quantities of all other firms constant, no firm can obtain a higher profit by choosing a different quantity. (13)

natural monopoly: a situation in which one firm can produce the total output of the market at lower cost than several firms could. (11)

network externality: the situation where one person's demand for a good depends on the consumption of the good by others. (11)

nonuniform pricing: charging consumers different prices for the same product or charging a single customer a price that depends on the number of units the customer buys. (12)

normal good: a commodity of which as much or more is demanded as income rises. (4)

normal form: a representation of a static game of complete information that specifies the players in the game, their possible strategies, and the payoff function that details the players' payoff for each combination of strategies. (14)

normative statement: a conclusion as to whether something is good or bad. (1)

oligopoly: a small group of firms in a market with substantial barriers to entry. (13)

open-access common property: resources to which everyone has free access and an equal right to exploit. (17)

opportunistic behavior: taking advantage of someone when circumstances permit. (18)

opportunity cost (*economic cost*): the value of the best alternative use of a resource. (7)

opportunity set: all the bundles a consumer can buy, including all the bundles inside the budget constraint and on the budget constraint. (3)

Pareto efficient: describing an allocation of goods or services such that any possible reallocation would harm at least one person. (10)

partial equilibrium analysis: an examination of equilibrium and changes in equilibrium in one market in isolation. (10)

patent: an exclusive right granted to the inventor to sell a new and useful product, process, substance, or design for a fixed period of time. (11)

payoffs (of a game): players' valuation of the outcome of the game, such as profits for firms or utilities for individuals. (14)

perfect complements: goods that a consumer is interested in consuming only in fixed proportions. (3)

perfect information: the situation where the player who is about to move knows the full history of the play of the game to this point, and that information is updated with each subsequent action. (14)

perfect price discrimination (*first-degree price discrimination*): the situation in which a firm sells each unit at the maximum amount any customer is willing to pay for it, so prices differ across customers, and a given customer may pay more for some units than for others. (12)

perfect substitutes: goods that a consumer is completely indifferent as to which to consume. (3)

pooling equilibrium: an equilibrium in which dissimilar people are treated (paid) alike or behave alike. (18)

positive statement: a testable hypothesis about cause and effect. (1)

price discrimination: the practice in which a firm charges consumers different prices for the same good. (12)

price elasticity of demand (or *demand elasticity* or *elasticity of demand*, ε): the percentage change in the quantity demanded in response to a given percentage change in the price. (2)

price elasticity of supply (or *supply elasticity*, η): the percentage change in the quantity supplied in response to a given percentage change in the price. (2)

prisoners' dilemma: a game in which all players have dominant strategies that lead to a profit (or another payoff) that is inferior to what they could achieve if they cooperated and pursued alternative strategies. (14)

private cost: the cost of production only, not including externalities. (17)

producer surplus (*PS*): the difference between the amount for which a good sells and the minimum amount necessary for the seller to be willing to produce the good. (9)

production function: the relationship between the quantities of inputs used and the *maximum* quantity of output that can be produced, given current knowledge about technology and organization. (6)

production possibility frontier: the maximum amount of outputs that can be produced from a fixed amount of input. (7)

profit (π): the difference between a firm's revenue, R, and its cost, C: $\pi = R - C$. (6)

property right: an exclusive privilege to use an asset. (17)

public good: a commodity or service whose consumption by one person does not preclude others from also consuming it. (17)

pure strategy: strategy in which each player chooses a single action. (14)

quantity demanded: the amount of a good that consumers are *willing* to buy at a given price during a specified time period, holding constant the other factors that influence purchases. (2)

quantity discrimination (*second-degree price discrimination*): the situation in which a firm charges a different price for large quantities than for small quantities, but all customers who buy a given quantity pay the same price. (12)

quantity supplied: the amount of a good that firms *want* to sell in a given time period at a given price, holding constant other factors that influence firms' supply decisions, such as costs and government actions. (2)

quota: the limit that a government sets on the quantity of a foreign-produced good that may be imported. (2)

rent: a payment to the owner of an input beyond the minimum necessary for the factor to be supplied. (9)

rent seeking: efforts and expenditures to gain a rent or a profit from government actions. (9)

requirement tie-in sale: a tie-in sale in which customers who buy one product from a firm are required to make all their purchases of another product from that firm. (12)

reservation price: the maximum amount a person would be willing to pay for a unit of output. (12)

residual demand curve: the market demand that is not met by other sellers at any given price. (8)

residual supply curve: the quantity that the market supplies that is not consumed by other demanders at any given price. (8)

risk: the situation in which the likelihood of each possible outcome is known or can be estimated, and no single possible outcome is certain to occur. (16)

risk averse: being unwilling to make a fair bet. (16)

risk neutral: being indifferent about making a fair bet. (16)

risk preferring: being willing to make a fair bet. (16)

risk premium: the amount that a risk-averse person would pay to avoid taking a risk. (16)

rules of the game: regulations that determine the timing of players' moves and the actions that players can make at each move. (14)

screening: an action taken by an uninformed person to determine the information possessed by informed people. (18)

separating equilibrium: an equilibrium in which one type of people takes actions (such as sending a signal) that allows them to be differentiated from other types of people. (18)

shirking: a moral hazard in which agents do not provide all the services they are paid to provide. (19)

short run: a period of time so brief that at least one factor of production cannot be varied practically. (6)

shortage: a persistent excess demand. (2)

signaling: an action taken by an informed person to send information to a less-informed person. (18)

snob effect: the situation in which a person places greater value on a good as fewer and fewer other people possess it. (11)

social cost: the private cost plus the cost of the harms from externalities. (17)

standard: a metric or scale for evaluating the quality of a particular product. (18)

static game: game in which each player acts only once and the players act simultaneously (or, at least, each player acts without knowing rivals' actions). (14)

stock: a quantity or value that is measured independently of time. (15)

strategic behavior: a set of actions a player takes to increase the player's payoff, taking into account the possible actions of other players. (14)

strategic interdependence: a player's optimal strategy depends on the actions of others. (14)

strategy: a battle plan that specifies the action that a player will make conditional on the information available at each move and for any possible contingency. (14)

subgame perfect Nash equilibrium: the situation in which players' strategies are a Nash equilibrium in every subgame. (14)

substitution effect: the change in the quantity of a good that a consumer demands when the good's price rises, holding other prices and the consumer's utility constant. (4)

sunk cost: an expenditure that cannot be recovered. (7)

supply curve: the quantity supplied at each possible price, holding constant the other factors that influence firms' supply decisions. (2)

supply function: the correspondence between the quantity supplied and the price and other factors that influence the number of units offered for sale. (2)

tariff (*duty*): a tax only on imported goods. (9)

technical progress: an advance in knowledge that allows more output to be produced with the same level of inputs. (6)

technological efficiency (*efficient production*): property of a production function such that the current level of output cannot be produced with fewer inputs, given existing knowledge about technology and the organization of production. (6)

tie-in sale: a type of nonlinear pricing in which customers can buy one product only if they agree to buy another product as well. (12)

total cost (*C*): the sum of a firm's variable cost and fixed cost: $C = VC + F$. (7)

total product of labor: the amount of output (or *total product*) that a given amount of labor can produce holding the quantity of other inputs fixed. (6)

transaction costs: the expenses of finding a trading partner and making a trade for a good or service other than the price paid for that good or service. (2)

two-part tariff: a pricing system in which the firm charges a consumer a lump-sum fee (the first tariff or price) for the right to buy as many units of the good as the consumer wants at a specified price (the second tariff). (12)

utility: a set of numerical values that reflect the relative rankings of various bundles of goods. (3)

utility function: the relationship between utility measures and every possible bundle of goods. (3)

variable cost (*VC*): a production expense that changes with the quantity of output produced. (7)

variable input: a factor of production whose quantity the firm can change readily during the relevant time period. (6)

winner's curse: auction winner's bid exceeds the common-value item's value. (14)

References

Adelaja, Adesoji O., "Price Changes, Supply Elasticities, Industry Organization, and Dairy Output Distribution," *American Journal of Agricultural Economics,* 73(1), February 1991:89–102.

Agcaoili-Sombilla, Mercedita C. "The World Rice Market: A Model of Imperfect Substitutes," Ph.D. Dissertation, University of Minnesota, 1991.

Aigner, Dennis J., and Glen G. Cain, "Statistical Theories of Discrimination in Labor Markets," *Industrial and Labor Relations Review,* 30(2), January 1977:175–187.

Akerlof, George A., "The Market for 'Lemons': Quality Uncertainty and the Market Mechanism," *Quarterly Journal of Economics,* 84(3), August 1970:488–500.

Akerlof, George A., "Labor Contacts as Partial Gift Exchanges," *Quarterly Journal of Economics,* 97(4), November 1982:543–569.

Alexander, Donald L., "Major League Baseball," *Journal of Sports Economics,* 2(4), November 2001:341–355.

Anderson, Keith B., and Michael R. Metzger, *Petroleum Tariffs as a Source of Government Revenues.* Washington, D.C.: Bureau of Economics, Federal Trade Commission, 1991.

Anderson, Michael, "Safety for Whom? The Effects of Light Trucks on Traffic Fatalities," U.C. Berkeley working paper, November 2006.

Arrow, Kenneth, *Social Choice and Individual Values,* New York: Wiley, 1951.

Ayres, Ian, and Joel Waldfogel, "A Market Test for Race Discrimination in Bail Setting," *Stanford Law Review,* 46(5), May 1994:987–1047.

Baldwin, John R., and Paul K. Gorecki, The Role of Scale in Canada/U.S. Productivity Differences in the Manufacturing Sector, 1970–1979. Toronto: University of Toronto Press, 1986.

Battalio, Raymond, John H. Kagel, and Carl Kogut, "Experimental Confirmation of the Existence of a Giffen Good," *American Economic Review,* 81(3), September 1991:961–970.

Becker, Gary S., *The Economics of Discrimination,* 2nd ed. Chicago: University of Chicago Press, 1971.

Benjamin, Daniel K., William R. Dougan, and David Buschena, *Journal of Risk and Uncertainty,* 22(1), January 2001:35–57.

Berck, Peter, and Michael Roberts, "Natural Resource Prices: Will They Ever Turn Up?" *Journal of Environmental Economics and Management,* 31(1), July 1996:65–78.

Besley, Timothy J., and Harvey S. Rosen, "Vertical Externalities in Tax Setting: Evidence from Gasoline and Cigarettes," *Journal of Public Economics,* 70(3), December 1998:383–398.

Bhuyan, Sanjib, "Corporate Political Activities and Oligopoly Welfare Loss," *Review of Industrial Organization,* 17(4), December 2000:411–426.

Bhuyan, Sanjib, and Rigoberto A. Lopez, "What Determines Welfare Losses from Oligopoly Power in the Food and Tobacco Industries?" *Agricultural and Resource Economics Review,* 27(2), October 1998:258–265.

Billikopf, Gregory Encina, "High Piece-Rate Wages Do Not Reduce Hours Worked," *California Agriculture,* 49(1), January–February 1995:17–18.

Bishai, David M., and Hui-Chu Lang, "The Willingness to Pay for Wait Reduction: The Disutility of Queues for Cataract Surgery in Canada, Denmark, and Spain," *Journal of Health Economics,* 19(2), March 2000:219–230.

Black, Dan A., Seth Sanders, and Lowell Taylor, "The Economic Rewards to Studying Economics," *Economic Inquiry,* 41(3), July 2003:365–377.

Blanciforti, Laura Ann, "The Almost Ideal Demand System Incorporating Habits: An Analysis of Expenditures on Food and Aggregate Commodity Groups," Ph.D. thesis, U.C. Davis, 1982.

Bordley, Robert F., and James B. McDonald, "Estimating Aggregate Automotive Income Elasticities from the Population Income-Share Elasticity," *Journal of Business and Economic Statistics,* 11(2), April 1993:209–214.

Borenstein, Severin, James Bushnell, and Matthew Lewis, "Market Power in California's Gasoline Market," University of California Energy Institute, CSEM WP 132, May 2004, **www.ucei.berkeley.edu/PDF/csemwp132.pdf**.

Borenstein, Severin, and Nancy L. Rose, "Competition and Price Dispersion in the U.S. Airline Industry," *Journal of Political Economy,* 102(4), August 1994:653–683.

Borjas, George J., "The Labor Demand Curve Is Downward Sloping: Reexamining the Impact of Immigration on the Labor Market," *Quarterly Journal of Economics,* 118(4), November 2003:1335–1374.

Boroski, John W., and Gerard C. S. Mildner, "An Economic Analysis of Taxicab Regulation in Portland, Oregon," Cascade Policy Institute, **www.cascadepolicy.org**, 1998.

Boskin, Michael J., Ellen R. Dulberger, Robert J. Gordon, Zvi Griliches, and Dale W. Jorgenson, "The CPI Commission: Findings and Recommendations," *American Economic Review,* 87(2), May 1997:78–93.

Boskin, Michael J., and Dale W. Jorgenson, "Implications of Overstating Inflation for Indexing Government Programs and Understanding Economic Progress," *American Economic Review,* 87(2), May 1997:89–93.

Brander, James A., and M. Scott Taylor, "The Simple Economics of Easter Island: A Ricardo-Malthus Model of Renewable Resource Use," *American Economic Review,* 88(1), March 1998:119–138.

Brander, James A., and Anming Zhang, "Market Conduct in the Airline Industry: An Empirical Investigation," *Rand Journal of Economics,* 21(4), Winter 1990:567–583.

Brown, Stephen P. A., and Daniel Wolk, "Natural Resource Scarcity and Technological Change," *Economic and Financial Review* (Federal Reserve Bank of Dallas), First Quarter 2000:2–13.

Brownlee, Oswald, and George Perry, "The Effects of the 1965 Federal Excise Tax Reductions on Prices." *National Tax Journal,* 20(3), September 1967:235–249.

Brozovic, Nicholas, David L. Sunding, and David Zilberman, "Prices and Quantities Reconsidered," University of California, Berkeley, working paper, 2002.

Brunk, Gregory G., "A Test of the Friedman-Savage Gambling Model," *Quarterly Journal of Economics,* 96(2), May 1981:341–348.

Busch, Susan H., Mireia Jofre-Bonet, Tracy Falba, and Jody Sindelar, "Burning a Hole in the Budget: Tobacco Spending and its Crowd-out of Other Goods," *Applied Health Economics and Policy,* 3(4), 2004:263–272.

Buschena, David E., and Jeffrey M. Perloff, "The Creation of Dominant Firm Market Power in the Coconut Oil Export Market," *American Journal of Agricultural Economics,* 73(4), November 1991:1000–1008.

Caputo, Michael R., and Quirino Paris, "An Atemporal Microeconomic Theory and an Empirical Test of Price-Induced Technical Progress," *Journal of Productivity Analysis,* 24(3), November 2005:259–281.

Card, David, and Alan B. Krueger, *Myth and Measurement: The New Economics of the Minimum Wage.* Princeton, N.J.: Princeton University Press, 1995.

Carlson, Steven, "An Overview of Food Stamp Cashout Research in the Food and Nutrition Service," in Nancy Fasciano, Darryl Hall, and Harold Beebout, eds., *New Directions in Food Stamp Policy Research.* Alexandria, Va.: U.S. Department of Agriculture, Food and Nutrition Service, 1993.

Carlton, Dennis W., and Jeffrey M. Perloff, *Modern Industrial Organization,* 4th ed. Reading, Mass.: Addison Wesley Longman, 2005.

Caves, Richard E., and David R. Barton, *Technical Efficiency in U.S. Manufacturing Industries.* Cambridge, Mass.: MIT Press, 1990.

Chouinard, Hayley H., David Davis, Jeffrey T. LaFrance, and Jeffrey M. Perloff, "The Effects of a Fat Tax on Dairy Products," *Forum for Health Economics & Policy,* forthcoming, 2007.

Chouinard, Hayley, and Jeffrey M. Perloff, "Incidence of Federal and State Gasoline Taxes," *Economic Letters,* 83(1), April 2004:55–60.

Christensen, Laurits R., and William H. Greene, "Economies of Scale in U.S. Electric Power Generation," *Journal of Political Economy,* 84(4, pt. 1), August 1976:655–676.

Chung, Sangho, "The Learning Curve and the Yield Factor: The Case of Korea's Semiconductor Industry," *Applied Economics,* 33(4), March 2001:472–483.

Coase, Ronald H., "The Problem of Social Cost," *Journal of Law and Economics,* 3, October 1960:1–44.

Connolly, Marie, and Alan B. Krueger, "Rockonomics: The Economics of Popular Music," NBER Working Paper 11282, **www.nber.org/papers/w11282,** 2005.

Crawford, David, John Del Roccili, and Richard Voith, "Comments on Proposed Tax Reforms," Econsult Corporation, June 9, 2004.

Cutler, David M., Edward L. Glaeser, and Jesse M. Shapiro, "Why Have Americans Become More Obese?" *Journal of Economic Perspectives,* 17(3), Summer 2003:93–118.

Deacon, Robert T., and Jon Sonstelie, "The Welfare Costs of Rationing by Waiting," *Economic Inquiry,* 27(2), April 1989:179–196.

Delipalla, Sophia, and Michael Keen, "The Comparison Between Ad Valorem and Specific Taxation Under Imperfect Competition," *Journal of Public Economics,* 49(3), December 1992:351–367.

de Melo, Jaime, and David Tarr, *A General Equilibrium Analysis of U.S. Foreign Trade Policy.* Cambridge, Mass.: MIT Press, 1992.

Dewan, Sanjeev, and Vernon Hsu, "Adverse Selection in Electronic Markets: Evidence from Online Stamp Auctions," *Journal of Industrial Economics,* LII(4), December 2004:497–516.

Diewert, W. Edwin, and Alice O. Nakamura, eds., *Essays in Index Number Theory,* Vol. 1. New York: North Holland, 1993.

Dixit, Avinash K., and Robert S. Pindyck, *Investment Under Uncertainty.* Princeton, N.J.: Princeton University Press, 1994.

Duffy-Deno, Kevin T., "Business Demand for Broadband Access Capacity," *Journal of Regulatory Economics,* 24(3), 2003:359–372.

Dunham, Wayne R., "Moral Hazard and the Market for Used Automobiles," *Review of Industrial Organization,* 23(1), August 2003:65–83

Dunn, L. F., "Quantifying Nonpecuniary Returns," *Journal of Human Resources,* 2(3), Summer 1977:347–359.

Dunn, L. F., "An Empirical Indifference Function for Income and Leisure," *Review of Economics and Statistics,* 60(4), November 1978:533–540.

Dunn, L. F., "Measurement of Internal Income-Leisure Tradeoffs," *Quarterly Journal of Economics,* 93(3), August 1979:373–393.

Eastwood, David B., and John A. Craven, "Food Demand and Savings in a Complete, Extended, Linear Expenditure System," *American Journal of Agricultural Economics,* 63(3), August 1981:544–549.

Economides, Nicholas, "The Economics of Networks," *International Journal of Industrial Organization,* 14(6), October 1996:673–699.

Econsult Corporation, *Choosing the Best Mix of Taxes for Philadelphia: An Econometric Analysis of the Impacts of Tax Rates on Tax Bases, Tax Revenue, and the Private Economy,* Report to the Philadelphia Tax Reform Commission, 2003.

Edell, Richard J., and Pravin P. Varaiya, "Providing Internet Access: What We Learn from the INDEX Trial," **www.index.berkeley. edu/reports/99-010W,** April 1999.

Farrell, Joseph, and Matthew Rabin, "Cheap Talk," *Journal of Economic Perspectives,* 10(3), Summer 1996:103–118.

Farrell, Lisa, Roger Hartley, Gauthier Lanot, and Ian Walker, "The Demand for Lotto," *Journal of Business & Economic Statistics,* 18(2), April 2000:228–241.

Fasciano, Nancy, Daryl Hall, and Harold Beebout, eds., *New Directions in Food Stamp Policy Research.* Alexandria, Va.: U.S. Department of Agriculture, Food and Nutrition Service, 1993.

Fisher, Franklin M., "The Social Cost of Monopoly and Regulation: Posner Reconsidered," *Journal of Political Economy,* 93(2), April 1985:410–416.

Foster, Andrew D., and Mark R. Rosenzweig, "A Test for Moral Hazard in the Labor Market: Contractual Arrangements, Effort, and Health," *Review of Economics and Statistics,* 76(2), May 1994:213–227.

Fraker, Thomas M., "The Effects of Food Stamps on Food Consumption: A Review of the Literature," in Nancy Fasciano, Darryl Hall, and Harold Beebout, eds., *Current Perspectives on Food Stamp Program Participation.* Alexandria, Va.: U.S. Department of Agriculture, Food and Nutrition Service, 1990.

Fraker, Tomas M., Alberto P. Martini, and James C. Ohls, "The Effect of Food Stamp Cashout on Food Expenditures: An Assessment of the Findings from Four Demonstrations," *Journal of Human Resources,* 30(4), Fall 1995:633–49.

Frech, H. E., III, and William C. Lee, "The Welfare Cost of Rationing-by-Queuing Across Markets: Theory and Estimates from the U.S. Gasoline Crisis," *Quarterly Journal of Economics,* 102(1), February 1987:97–108.

Friedlaender, Ann F., Clifford Winston, and Kung Wang, "Costs, Technology, and Productivity in the U.S. Automobile Industry," *Bell Journal of Economics and Management Science,* 14(1), Spring 1983:1–20.

Friedman, Milton, and Leonard J. Savage, "The Utility Analysis of Choices Involving Risk," *Journal of Political Economy,* 56(4), August 1948:279–304.

Fudenberg, Drew, and Jean Tirole, *Game Theory.* Cambridge, Mass and London: MIT Press, 1991.

Fullerton, Don, "On the Possibility of an Inverse Relationship Between Tax Rates and Government Revenues," *Journal of Public Economy,* 19(1), October 1982:3–22.

Fullerton, Don, and Li Gan, "A Simulation-Based Welfare Loss Calculation for Labor Taxes with Piecewise-Linear Budgets," *Journal of Public Economics,* 88(11), September 2004:2339–2359.

Gallini, Nancy T., "Demand for Gasoline in Canada," *Canadian Journal of Economics,* 16(2), May 1983:299–324.

Garratt, Rod, Mark Walker, and John Wooders, *"Behavior in Second-Price Auctions by Highly Experienced eBay Buyers and Sellers,"* University of California at Santa Barbara Economics Working Paper 1181, 2005.

Garrett, Thomas A., "An International Comparison and Analysis of Lotteries and the Distribution of Lottery Expenditures," *International Review of Applied Economics,* 15(20), April 2001:213–227.

Garrett, Thomas A., and Russell S. Sobel, "Gamblers Favor Skewness, Not Risk: Further Evidence from United States' Lottery Games," *Economics Letters,* 63(1), April 1999:85–90.

Gasmi, Farid, D., Mark Kennet, Jean-Jacques Laffont, and William W. Sharkey, *Cost Proxy Models and Telecommunications Policy.* Cambridge, MA: MIT Press, 2002.

Gasmi, Farid, Jean-Jacques Laffont, and Quang H. Vuong, "Econometric Analysis of Collusive Behavior in a Soft-Drink Market," *Journal of Economics and Management Strategy,* 1(2), Summer 1992, 277–311.

Genesove, David, "Adverse Selection in the Wholesale Used Car Market," *Journal of Political Economy,* 101(4), August 1993:644–665.

Gibbons, Robert, *Game Theory for Applied Economists.* Princeon, N.J.: Princeton University Press, 1992.

Golec, Joseph, and Maurry Tamarkin, "Do Bettors Prefer Long Shots Because They Are Risk Lovers, or Are They Just Overconfident?" *Journal of Risk and Uncertainty,* 11(1), July 1995:51–64.

Goolsbee, Austan, "What Happens When You Tax the Rich? Evidence from Executive Compensation," *Journal of Political Economy,* 108(2), April 2000:352–378.

Gray, Wayne B., and Ronald J. Shadbegian, "'Optimal' Pollution Abatement: Whose Benefits Matter, and How Much?" *Journal of Environmental Economics and Management,* 47(3), May 2004:510–534.

Green, Richard, Richard Howitt, and Carlo Russo, "Estimation of Supply and Demand Elasticities of California Commodities," manuscript, May 2005.

Grossman, Michael, and Frank Chaloupka, "Demand for Cocaine by Young Adults: A Rational Addiction Approach," *Journal of Health Economics,* 17(4), August 1998: 427–474.

Grossman, Philip J., Marco Pirozzi, and Jeff Pope, "An Empirical Test of Free-Rider Behaviour," *Australian Economic Papers,* 32(60), June 1993:152–160.

Gruber, Harald, "The Learning Curve in the Production of Semiconductor Memory Chips," *Applied Economics,* 24(8), August 1992:885–894.

Gruber, Jonathan, Anihdya Sen, and Mark Stabile, "Estimating Price Elasticities When There Is Smuggling: The Sensitivity of Smoking to Price in Canada," *Journal of Health Economics* 22(5), September 2003:821–842.

Hamilton, Stephen F., "The Comparative Efficiency of Ad Valorem and Specific Taxes Under Monopoly and Monopsony," *Economics Letters,* 63(2), May 1999:235–238.

Harkness, Joseph, and Sandra Newman, "The Interactive Effects of Housing Assistance and Food Stamps on Food Spending," *Journal of Housing Economics,* 12(3), September 2003:224–249.

Hausman, Jerry A., "Efficiency Effects on the U.S. Economy from Wireless Taxation," *National Tax Journal,* 52(3, part 2), September 2000:733–742.

Hausman, Jerry A., and Gregory K. Leonard, "Superstars in the NBA: Economic Value and Policy," *Journal of Labor Economics,* 14(4), October 1997:586–624.

Hausman, Jerry A., and Gregory K. Leonard, "The Competitive Effects of a New Product Introduction: A Case Study," *Journal of Industrial Economics,* 50(3), September 2002:237–263.

Hay, George A., and Daniel Kelley, "An Empirical Survey of Price-Fixing Conspiracies," *Journal of Law and Economics,* 17(1), April 1974:13–38.

Heijman, W. J. M., and J. A. C. van Ophem, *Journal of Socio-Economics,* 34(5), October 2005:714–723.

Helland, Eric, and Alexander Tabarrok, "Contingency Fees, Settlement Delay, and Low-Quality Litigation: Empirical Evidence from Two Datasets," *Journal of Law, Economics, and Organization,* 19(2), Special Issue, October 2003:517–542.

Henderson, Jason, "FAQs about Mad Cow Disease and Its Impacts," *The Main Street Economist,* December 2003.

Holt, Matthew, "A Multimarket Bounded Price Variation Model Under Rational Expectations: Corn and Soybeans in the United States," *American Journal of Agricultural Economics,* 74(1), February 1992:10–20.

Hotelling, Harold, "The Economics of Exhaustible Resources," *Journal of Political Economy,* 39(2), April 1931:137–175.

Houthakker, Hendrik S., "An International Comparison of Household Expenditures Patterns, Commemorating the Centenary of Engel's Law," *Econometrica,* 25(3), December 1957:532–551.

Hsieh, Wen-Jen, "Test of Variable Output and Scale Elasticities for 20 U.S. Manufacturing Industries," *Applied Economics Letters,* 2(8), August 1995:284–287.

Hummels, David, and Alexandre Skiba, "Shipping the Good Apples Out? An Empirical Confirmation of the Alchian-Allen Conjecture," *Journal of Political Economy,* 112(6), December 2004:1384–1402.

Ida, Takanori, and Tetsuya Kuwahara, "Yardstick Cost Comparison and Economies of Scale and Scope in Japan's Electric Power Industry," *Asian Economic Journal,* 18(4), December 2004:423–438.

Imbens, Guido W., Donald B. Rubin, and Bruce I. Sacerdote, "Estimating the Effect of Unearned Income on Labor Earnings, Savings, and Consumption: Evidence from a Survey of Lottery Players," *American Economic Review*, 91(4), September 2001:778–794.

Irwin, Douglas A., "The Welfare Cost of Autarky: Evidence from the Jeffersonian Trade Embargo, 1807-09," *Review of International Economics*, 13(4), September 2005:631–645.

Irwin, Douglas A., and Peter J. Klenow, "Learning-by-Doing Spillovers in the Semiconductor Industry," *Journal of Political Economy*, 102(6), December 1994:1200–1227.

Irwin, Douglas A., and Nina Pavcnik, "Airbus versus Boeing Revisited: International Competition in the Aircraft Market," *Journal of International Economics*, 64(2), December 2004:223–245.

Ito, Harumi, and Darin Lee, "Assessing the Impact of the September 11 Terrorist Attacks on U.S. Airline Demand," *Journal of Economics and Business*, 57(1), January-February 2005:75–95.

Jacobson, Michael F., and Kelly D. Brownell, "Small Taxes on Soft Drinks and Snack Foods to Promote Health," *American Journal of Public Health*, 90(6), June 2000:854–857.

Jagannathan, Ravi, Ellen R. McGrattan, and Anna Scherbina, "The Declining U.S. Equity Premium," *Quarterly Review* (Federal Reserve Bank of Minneapolis), Fall 2000:3–19.

Jetter, Karen M., James A. Chalfant, and David A. Sumner, "Does 5-a-Day Pay?" *AIC Issues Brief*, No. 27, August 2004.

Jha, Prabhat, and Frank J. Chaloupka, "The Economics of Global Tobacco Control," *BMJ*, **bmj.com**, 321, August 2000:358–361.

Johnson, Ronald N., and Charles J. Romeo, "The Impact of Self-Service Bans in the Retail Gasoline Market," *Review of Economics and Statistics*, 82(4), November 2000:625–633.

Judd, Kenneth L. *Numerical Methods in Economics*. Cambridge, Mass.: MIT Press, 1998.

Kakalik, J. S., and N. M. Pace, *Costs and Compensation Paid in Tort Litigation*. Santa Monica, Calif.: RAND Corporation, Institute for Civil Justice, 1986.

Kalirajan, K. P., and M. B. Obwona, "Frontier Production Function: The Stochastic Coefficient Approach," *Oxford Bulletin of Economics and Statistics*, 56(1), 1994:87–96.

Karp, Larry, "Global Warming and Hyperbolic Discounting," *Journal of Public Economics*, 89(2–3), February 2005:261–282.

Katz, Michael L., and Carl Shapiro, "Systems Competition and Network Effects," *Journal of Economic Perspectives*, 8(2), 1994:93–115.

Keeler, Theodore E., Teh-Wei Hu, Paul G. Barnett, and Willard G. Manning, "Taxation, Regulation, and Addiction: A Demand Function for Cigarettes Based on Time-Series Evidence," *Journal of Health Economics*, 12(1), April 1993:1–18.

Keeler, Theodore E., Teh-Wei Hu, Michael Ong, and Hai-Yen Sung, "The U.S. National Tobacco Settlement: The Effects of Advertising and Price Changes on Cigarette Consumption," *Applied Economics*, 36(15), August 2004:1623–1629.

Kennickell, Arthur B., "An Examination of the Changes in the Distribution of Wealth from 1989 to 1998: Evidence from the Survey of Consumer Finances," Federal Reserve, 2001.

Kennickell, Arthur B., "A Rolling Tide: Changes in the Distribution of Wealth in the U.S., 1989–2001," Federal Reserve Board, 2003, **www.federalreserve.gov/pubs/oss/oss2/papers/asa2003.7.pdf**.

Killingsworth, Mark R., *Labor Supply*. New York: Cambridge University Press, 1983.

Kim, H. Youn, "Economies of Scale and Scope in Multiproduct Firms: Evidence from U.S. Railroads," *Applied Economics*, 19(6), June 1987:733–741.

Klein, Lawrence R., "The Use of the Input–Output Tables to Estimate the Productivity of IT," *Journal of Policy Modeling*, 25(5), July 2003:471–475.

Klemperer, Paul, *Auctions: Theory and Practice*. Princeon, N.J.: Princeton University Press, 2004.

Kreps, David M., and Scheinkman, Jose A., "Quantity Precommitment and Bertrand Competition Yield Cournot Outcomes, *Bell Journal of Economics*, 14(2), Autumn 1983:326–337.

Kridel, D. J., P. N. Rappoport, and L. D. Taylor, "An Econometric Model of the Demand for Access to the Internet," in D. G. Loomis and L. D. Taylor, eds. *The Future of the Telecommunications Industry: Forecasting and Demand Analysis*. Boston, Mass.: Kluwer Academic Publishers, 1999.

Kridel, D. J., P. N. Rappoport, and L. D. Taylor, "An Econometric Model of the Demand for Access to the Internet by Cable Modem," in D. G. Loomis and L. D. Taylor, eds., *Forecasting the Internet: Understanding the Explosive Growth of Data Communications*. Boston, Mass.: Kluwer Academic Publishers, 2001.

Levedahl, J. William, "A Theoretical and Empirical Evaluation of the Functional Forms Used to Estimate the Food Expenditure Equation of Food Stamp Recipients: Reply," *American Journal of Agricultural Economics*, 84(4), November 2002:1161–1164.

Levin, Richard C., Alvin K. Klevorick, Richard R. Nelson, and Sidney G. Winter, "Appropriating the Returns from Industrial Research and Development," *Brookings Papers on Economic Activity*, 3(Special Issue on Microeconomics), 1987:783–820.

Levitt, Steven D., and Jack Porter, "How Dangerous Are Drinking Drivers?" *Journal of Political Economy*, 109(6), December 2001:1198–1237.

Levy, Douglas E., and Ellen Meara, "The Effect of the 1998 Master Settlement Agreement on Prenatal Smoking," NBER Working Paper 11176, March 2005, **www.nber.org/papers/w11176**.

Lewit, Eugene M., and Douglas Coate, "The Potential for Using Excise Taxes to Reduce Smoking," *Journal of Health Economics*, 1(2), January 1982:121–145.

Liebenstein, Harvey, "Bandwagon, Snob, and Veblen Effects in the Theory of Consumers' Demand," *Quarterly Journal of Economics*, 64(2), May 1950:183–207.

Lipsey, R.G., and Kelvin Lancaster, "The General Theory of Second Best," *Review of Economic Studies*, 24(1), October, 1956:11–32.

Lopez, Rigoberto A., and Emilio Pagoulatos, "Rent Seeking and the Welfare Cost of Trade Barriers," *Public Choice*, 79(1–2), April 1994:149–160.

MacAvoy, Paul W., "Tacit Collusion Under Regulation in the Pricing of Interstate Long-Distance Services," *Journal of Economics and Management Strategy*, 4(2), Summer 1995:147–185.

MacCrimmon, Kenneth R., and M. Toda, "The Experimental Determination of Indifference Curves," *Review of Economic Studies*, 56(3), July 1969:433–451.

Machina, Mark, "Dynamic Consistency and Non-Expected Utility Models of Choice Under Uncertainty," *Journal of Economic Literature*, 27(4), December 1989:1622–1668.

MacKie-Mason, Jeffrey K., and Robert S. Pindyck, "Cartel Theory and Cartel Experience in International Minerals Markets," in R. L. Gordon, H. D. Jacoby, and M. B. Zimmerman, eds., *Energy: Markets and Regulation: Essays in Honor of M. A. Adelman*. Cambridge, Mass.: MIT Press, 1986.

MaCurdy, Thomas, David Green, and Harry Paarsch, "Assessing Empirical Approaches for Analyzing Taxes and Labor Supply," *Journal of Human Resources,* 25(3), Summer 1990:415–490.

Madden, Janice F., *The Economics of Sex Discrimination.* Lexington, Mass.: Heath, 1973.

Marks, Steven V., "A Reassessment of Empirical Evidence on the U.S. Sugar Program," in S. V. Marks and K. Maskus, eds., *The Economics and Politics of World Sugar Policy.* Ann Arbor: University of Michigan Press, 1993.

Medoff, Marshall H., "A Pooled Time-Series Analysis of Abortion Demand," *Population Research and Policy Review,* 16(6), December 1997:597–605.

Moschini, Giancarlo, and Karl D. Meilke, "Production Subsidy and Countervailing Duties in Vertically Related Markets: The Hog-Pork Case Between Canada and the United States," *American Journal of Agricultural Economics,* 74(4), November 1992:951–961.

Nash, John F., "Equilibrium Points in *n*-Person Games," *Proceedings of the National Academy of Sciences,* 36, 1950:48–49.

Nash, John F., "Non-Cooperative Games," *Annals of Mathematics,* 54(2), July 1951:286–295.

O'Donoghue, Ted, and Matthew Rabin, "Doing It Now or Later," *American Economic Review,* 89(1), March 1999:103–124.

OECD (Organization for Economic Cooperation and Development), *Agricultural Policies In OECD Countries: Monitoring And Evaluation 2005,* 2005.

Oxfam, *Dumping Without Borders,* Oxfam Briefing Paper 50, 2003.

Panzar, John C., and Robert D. Willig, "Economies of Scale in Multi-Output Production," *Quarterly Journal of Economics,* 91(3), August 1977:481–493.

Panzar, John C., and Robert D. Willig, "Economies of Scope," *American Economic Review,* 71(2), May 1981:268–272.

Paszkiewicz, Laura. "From AFDC to TANF: Have the New Public Assistance Laws Affected Consumer Spending of Recipients?" Bureau of Labor Statistics, *Consumer Expenditure Survey Anthology,* 2005, **www.bls.gov/cex/csxanthol05.htm**.

Perry, Martin K., "Forward Integration by Alcoa:1888–1930," *Journal of Industrial Economics,* 29(1), September 1980:37–53.

Polinsky, A. Mitchell, "Controlling Externalities and Protecting Entitlements: Property Right, Liability Rule, and Tax-Subsidy Approaches," *Journal of Legal Studies,* 8(1), January 1979:1–48.

Pollak, Robert A., *The Theory of the Cost-of-Living Index.* New York: Oxford University Press, 1989.

Posner, Richard A., "The Social Cost of Monopoly and Regulation," *Journal of Political Economy,* 83(4), August 1975:807–827.

Pratt, John W. "Risk Aversion in the Small and in the Large," *Econometrica,* 32(1–2), January/April 1964):122–136.

Prescott, Edward C., "Why Do Americans Work So Much More Than Europeans?" *Federal Reserve Bank of Minneapolis Quarterly Review,* 28(1), July 2004:2–13.

Rabin, Matthew, "Psychology and Economics," *Journal of Economic Literature,* 36(1), March 1998:11–46.

Rappoport, P. N., D. J. Kridel, L. D. Taylor, and K. T. Duffy-Deno, "Residential Demand for Access to the Internet," in Gary Madden, ed., *The International Handbook of Telecommunications Economics,* vol. II. Chelthenham, U.K.: Edward Elgar, 2002.

Rawls, John, *A Theory of Justice.* New York: Oxford University Press, 1971.

Reimer, Jeffrey J., and Thomas W. Hertel, "International Cross Section Estimates of Demand for Use in the GTAP Model," Global Trade Analysis Project Technical Paper No. 23, 2004.

Richard, Oliver, "Flight Frequency and Mergers in Airline Markets," *International Journal of Industrial Organization,* 21(6), June 2003:907–922.

Rob, Rafael, and Joel Waldfogel, "Piracy on the High C's: Music Downloading, Sales Displacement, and Social Welfare in a Sample of College Students," NBER Working Paper 10874, 2004, **www.nber.org/papers/w10874**.

Roberts, Mark J., and Larry Samuelson, "An Empirical Analysis of Dynamic Nonprice Competition in an Oligopolistic Industry," *Rand Journal of Economics,* 19(2), Summer 1988:200–220.

Robidoux, Benoît, and John Lester, "Econometric Estimates of Scale Economies in Canadian Manufacturing," Working Paper No. 88–4, Canadian Department of Finance, 1988.

Robidoux, Benoît, and John Lester, "Econometric Estimates of Scale Economies in Canadian Manufacturing," *Applied Economics,* 24(1), January 1992:113–122.

Rohlfs, Jeffrey H., *Bandwagon Effects in High-Technology Industries.* Cambridge: MIT Press, 2001.

Rohlfs, Jeffrey H., "A Theory of Interdependent Demand for a Communications Service," *Bell Journal of Economics and Management Science,* 5(1), Spring 1974:16–37.

Rosenberg, Howard R., "Many Fewer Steps for Pickers—A Leap for Harvestkind? Emerging Change in Strawberry Harvest Technology," *Choices,* 1st Quarter 2004:5–11.

Rousseas, S. W., and A. G. Hart, "Experimental Verification of a Composite Indifference Map," *Journal of Political Economy,* 59(4), August 1951:288–318.

Ruffin, R. J., "Cournot Oligopoly and Competitive Behavior," *Review of Economic Studies,* 38(116), October 1971:493–502.

Salgado, Hugo, "A Dynamic Duopoly Model under Learning-by-doing in the Computer CPU Industry," Working paper, 2007.

Salop, Joanne, and Steven C. Salop, "Self-Selection and Turnover in the Labor Market," *Quarterly Journal of Economics,* 90(4), November 1976:619–627.

Salop, Steven C., "Practices That (Credibly) Facilitate Oligopoly Coordination," in Joseph E. Stiglitz and G. Frank Mathewson, eds., *New Developments in the Analysis of Market Structure.* Cambridge, Mass.: MIT Press, 1986.

Samuelson, Paul A., *Foundations of Economic Analysis.* Cambridge, Mass.: Harvard University Press, 1947.

Schaller Consulting, *The New York City Taxicab Fact Book,* 2004, **www.schallerconsult.com**.

Scherer, F. M., "An Early Application of the Average Total Cost Concept," *Journal of Economic Literature,* 39(3), September 2001:897–901.

Schmalensee, Richard, Paul L. Joskow, A. Denny Ellerman, Juan Pablo Montero, and Elizabeth M. Bailey, "An Interim Evaluation of Sulfur Dioxide Emissions Trading," *Journal of Economic Perspectives,* 12(3), Summer 1998:53–68.

Schoemaker, Paul J. H., "The Expected Utility Model: Its Variants, Purposes, Evidence and Limitation," *Journal of Economic Literature,* 20(2), June 1982:529–563.

Shadbegian, Ronald J., and Wayne B. Gray, "What Determines Environmental Performance at Paper Mills? The Roles of Abatement Spending, Regulation and Efficiency," *Topics in Economic Analysis and Policy,* 3(1), 2003.

Shapiro, Carl, and Joseph E. Stiglitz, "Equilibrium Unemployment as a Worker Discipline Device," *American Economic Review,* 74(3), June 1984:434–444.

Shapiro, Carl, and Hal R. Varian, *Information Rules: A Strategic Guide to the Network Economy.* Boston: Harvard Business School Press, 1999.

Shearer, Bruce, "Piece Rates, Fixed Wages and Incentives: Evidence from a Field Experiment," *Review of Economic Studies,* 71(2), April 2004:513–534.

Skeath, Susan E., and Gregory A. Trandel, "A Pareto Comparison of Ad Valorem and Unit Taxes in Noncompetitive Environments," *Journal of Public Economics,* 53(1), January 1994:53–71.

Slade, Margaret E., "Product Rivalry with Multiple Strategic Weapons: An Analysis of Price and Advertising Competition," *Journal of Economics and Management Strategy,"* 4(3), Fall 1995:224–276.

Sood, Neeraj, Abby Alpert, and Jay Bhattacharya, "Technology, Monopoly, and the Decline of the Viatical Settlements Industry," NBER Working Paper 11164, March 2005, **www.nber.org/papers/w11164**.

Spence, A. Michael, *Market Signaling.* Cambridge, Mass.: Harvard University Press, 1974.

Spencer, Barbara J., and James A. Brander, "International R&D Rivalry and Industrial Strategy," *Review of Economic Studies,* 50(4), October 1983:707–722.

Stiglitz, Joseph E., "The Theory of 'Screening,' Education, and the Distribution of Income," *American Economic Review,* 65(3), June 1975:283–300.

Stiglitz, Joseph E., "Equilibrium in Product Markets with Imperfect Information," *American Economic Review,* 69(2), May 1979:339–345.

Stiglitz, Joseph E., "The Causes and Consequences of the Dependence of Quality on Price," *Journal of Economic Literature,* 25(1), March 1987:1–48.

Stuart, Charles, "Welfare Costs per Dollar of Additional Tax Revenue in the United States," *American Economic Review,* 74(3), June 1984:352–362.

Sullivan, Ashley F., and Eunyoung Choi, "Hunger and Food Insecurity in the Fifty States:1998–2000," Center on Hunger and Poverty, Brandeis University, August 2002.

Swinton, John R., and Christopher R. Thomas, "Using Empirical Point Elasticities to Teach Tax Incidence," *Journal of Economic Education,* 32(4), Fall 2001:356–368.

Tian, Weiming, and Guang Hua Wan, "Technical Efficiency and Its Determinants in China's Grain Production," *Journal of Productivity Analysis* 13(2), 2000:159–174.

Tideman, T. Nicholaus, and Gordon Tullock, "A New and Superior Process for Making Social Choices," *Journal of Political Economy,* 84(6), December 1976:1145–1159.

Tullock, G., "The Welfare Cost of Tariffs, Monopolies, and Theft," *Western Economic Journal,* 5(3), June 1967:224–232.

Tyler, John H., Richard J. Murnane, and John B. Willett, "Estimating the Labor Market Signaling Value of the GED," *Quarterly Journal of Economics,* 115(2), May 2000:431–468.

Urban, Glen L., Theresa Carter, and Steven Gaskin, "Market Share Rewards to Pioneering Brands: An Empirical Analysis and Strategic Implications," *Management Science,* 32(6), June 1986:645–659.

Varian, Hal R., "Measuring the Deadweight Cost of DUP and Rent-Seeking Activities," *Economics and Politics,* 1(1), Spring 1989:81–95.

Varian, Hal R., "The Demand for Bandwidth," **www.sims.berkeley. edu/~hal/Papers/brookings.pdf**, February 2002.

Villegas, Daniel J., "The Impact of Usury Ceilings on Consumer Credit," *Southern Economic Journal,* 56(1), July 1989: 126–141.

Viscusi, W. Kip, *Employment Hazards.* Cambridge, Mass.: Harvard University Press, 1979.

Von Hippel, F. A., and W. F. Von Hippel, "Sex Drugs and Animal Parts: Will Viagra Save Threatened Species?" *Environmental Conservation,* 29(3), 2002:277–281.

Von Hippel, F. A., and W. F. Von Hippel, "Is Viagra a Viable Conservation Tool? Response to Hoover, 2003," *Environmental Conservation,* 31(1), 2004:4–6.

von Neumann, John, and Oskar Morgenstern, *Theory of Games and Economic Behavior.* Princeton, N.J.: Princeton University Press, 1944.

Waldfogel, Joel, "The Deadweight Loss of Christmas," *American Economic Review,* 83(5), December 1993:1328–1336.

Waldfogel, Joel, "Does Consumer Irrationality Trump Consumer Sovereignty?" working paper, 2004.

Warner, John T., and Saul Pleeter, "The Personal Discount Rate: Evidence from Military Downsizing Programs," *American Economic Review,* 91(1), March 2001:33–53.

Weiher, Jesse C., Robin C. Sickles, and Jeffrey M. Perloff, "Market Power in the U.S. Airline Industry," in D. J. Slottje, ed., *Economic Issues in Measuring Market Power, Contributions to Economic Analysis,* vol. 255. Elsevier 2002.

Weitzman, Martin L., "Prices vs. Quantities," *Review of Economic Studies,* 41(4), October 1974:477–491.

White, Michelle J., "The 'Arms Race' on American Roads," *Journal of Law and Economics,* 47(2), October 2004:333–355.

Whitmore, Diane, "What Are Food Stamps Worth?" Princeton University Working Paper #468, July, 2002, **www.irs.princeton.edu/pubs/pdfs/468.pdf**.

Williamson, Oliver E., "Credible Commitments: Using Hostages to Support Exchange," *American Economic Review,* 73(4), September 1983:519–540.

Willig, Robert D., "Consumer's Surplus without Apology," *American Economic Review,* 66(4), September 1976:589–597.

Willis, Robert D., "A New Approach to the Economic Theory of Fertility Behavior," *Journal of Political Economy,* 81(2, pt. 2), March–April 1973:S14–S64.

Winicki, Joshua, "Low-Income Families Participating in Fewer Assistance Programs," *Food Review,* May–August, 2001:38–44.

Womer, N. Keith, and J. Wayne Patterson, "Estimation and Testing of Learning Curves," *Journal of Business and Economic Statistics,* 1(4), October 1983:265–272.

Yellen, Janet L., "Efficiency Wage Models of Unemployment," *American Economic Review,* 74(2), May 1984:200–205.

Sources for Applications

Chapter 1

Addressing a Flu Vaccine Shortage: "State Accuses Lauderdale Firm of Price Gouging for Flu Vaccine," **sun-sentinel.com**, October 13, 2004; O'Neill, Patrick, "CDC Hopes to Inoculate against Recurrence of Flu-shot Shortage," *The Oregonian,* September 7, 2005; "Maine Health Officials Don't Foresee Flu Vaccine Shortage," **WMTW.com**, September 8, 2005; **www.cidrap.umn.edu/cidrap/content/influenza/general/news/mar0807asthma-jw.html**, 2007.

Twinkie Tax: Jacobson and Brownell (2000); Bartlett, Bruce, "The Big Food Tax," *National Review Online,* April 3, 2002; Lemieux, Pierre, "It's the Fat Police," *National Post,* April 6, 2002; Tobler, Helen, "Call for Tax War on Obesity," *Australian IT,* August 16, 2002; "Soda Pop to Be Banned in L.A. Schools," **CBSNEWS.com**, August 28, 2002; Chouniard et al. (2007).

Income Threshold Model and China: "Next in Line: Chinese Consumers," *Economist,* 326(7795), January 23, 1993:66–67; Pelline, Jeff, "U.S. Businesses Pour into China," *San Francisco Chronicle,* May 17, 1994: B1–B2; *China Statistical Yearbook* (Beijing: China Statistical Publishing House, 2000); **www.oecd.org/searchResult/0,2665,en_2825_293564_1_1_1_1_1,00.html; www.uschina.org/info/chops/2006/fdi.html.**

Chapter 2

Sideways Wine: ACNielsen Press Release, "ACNielsen Examines Sales Trends Since Popular Movie's Release," February 21, 2005; Kinssies, Richard, "On Wine: 'Sideways' Has Intoxicating Effect on Pinot Noir Sales, Some Say," *Seattle Post-Intelligencer,* February 23, 2005; Harlow, John, "Oscar Winner Knocks Sales of Merlot Wine Sideways," *The Sunday Times,* March 6, 2005.

Aggregating the Demand for Broadband Service: Duffy-Deno (2003).

Willingness to Surf: Edell and Varaiya (1999); Varian (2002); Ahmad, Nadia, "Internet Fees Alter Network Use," *Daily Californian,* May 21, 1999:1, 3; **www.index.berkeley.edu/reports/99-01w**; Kridel et al. (1999, 2001); Rappoport et al. (2002); Varian (2002); Duffy-Deno (2003).

Substitution May Save Endangered Species: Von Hippel and Von Hippel (2002, 2004).

Oil Drilling in the Arctic National Wildlife Refuge: Lee, Dwight, "To Drill or Not to Drill: Let the Environmentalists Decide," *The Independent Review,* Fall 2001, pp. 217–226; Energy Information Administration, "The Effects of Alaska Oil and Natural Gas Provisions of H.R. 4 and S. 1776 on U.S. Energy Markets," February 2002; United States Geological Survey, "Arctic National Wildlife Refuge, 1002 Area, Petroleum Assessment, 1998, Including Economic Analysis," **pubs.usgs.gov/fs/fs-0028-01/fs-0028-01.pdf**; "Oil Companies Could Benefit from Alaska Drilling," VNU Business Media, Inc.,November 22, 2004; Borenstein, Severin, "ANWR Oil and the Price of Gasoline," U.C. Energy Institute, *Energy Notes,* 3(2), June 2005.

Zimbabwe Price Controls: "Mugabe's Election Victory May Be Short-Lived," *The Daily News,* March 15, 2002; "Smuggling Results in Sugar Shortages in Zimbabwe," *Harare,* April 21, 2002; "Construction Industry Faces Bleak Future," *Zimbabwe Standard,* May 5, 2002; "Zimbabwe Raises Cement Prices to Ease Shortage," *Harare,* May 7, 2002; "Makoni Admits Price Controls to Blame for Thriving Black Market," *The Daily News,* May 10, 2002; "Supermarkets Adjust Price of Chicken," *The Daily News,* May 17, 2002; James, Stanley, "Bakeries Scale Down Operations," *The Independent,* September 6, 2002; "Zimbabwe Faces Food Shortages," **cnn.com**, May 24, 2005; "Zim Slaps Price Control on Food," News24, **finance24.com**, June 4, 2005; Jongwe, Fanuel, "Watchdog Unlikely to Get Teeth into Zimbabwe Inflation," *Business Report,* November 13, 2006, **www.busrep.co.za/index.php?fArticleId=3534401**.

Chapter 3

MRS Between Music CDs and Movie DVDs; Utility Maximization for Music CDs and Movie DVDs: We estimated the Cobb-Douglas utility function using budget share information (see Solved Problem 3.5) and obtained prices and quantities from **www.leesmovieinfo.net/Video-Sales.php, www.usatoday.com/life/music/news/2005-12-28-music-sales_x.htm, quickfacts.census.gov/qfd/states/00000.html, www.nytimes.com/2004/12/27/business/media/27music.html?ex=1261803600&en=49d1239df6399ffe&ei=5090&partner=rssuserland, bigpicture.typepad.com/comments/2004/12/music_industry_.html, www.ce.org/Press/CEA_Pubs/834.asp.**

Indifference Curves Between Food and Clothing: Eastwood and Craven (1981).

U.S. Versus EU SUVs: Power, Stephen, and Jo Wrighton, "In Europe, SUVs May Face Taxes Amid Drive to Penalize Emissions," *Wall Street Journal,* June 30, 2004; Harding, Gareth, "Europe's SUV Backlash Begins," *Washington Times,* July 8, 2004; Goldsmith, Rebecca, "In Europe, SUVs are Autos Non Grata," *San Francisco Chronicle,* September 28, 2004; Ford, Royal, "Resurgent Sedan Muscling Past SUV," *Boston Globe,* September 29, 2004:1; **www.selfemployedweb.com/suv-tax-deduction-changes.htm**; "SUV Tax Write-Offs Last Until End of Year," *Tulsa World,* December 15, 2004; "Tax-Law Change Real Cause of Drop in Sales of SUVs," *Palm Beach Post,* June 23, 2005:21A.

Chapter 4

Going Up in Smoke: Keeler, Hu, Barnett, and Manning (1993); "A Tax We Can Live With," University of California at Berkeley *Wellness Letter,* 9(9), June 1993:7; "In Canada, They're Cutting Sin Taxes," *Business Week,* February 21, 1994:44; Farrell, Christopher, "This Sin Tax Is Win-Win," *Business Week,* April 11, 1994:31; Grossman, Michael, "Health Economics," *NBER Reporter,* Winter 1998:1–5; **www.ash.org**; Besley and Rosen (1998); **tobaccofreekids.org** (2002);

ash.org/cigtaxfacts.html (2002); Gruber, Sen, and Stabile (2003); Jha and Chaloupka (2000); Levy and Meara (2005); Busch et al. (2004).

What to Do with Extra Income: U.S. Consumer Expenditure Survey; Reimer and Hertel (2004).

Shipping the Good Stuff Away: Hummels and Skiba (2004).

Fixing the CPI Substitution Bias: Hausman (1997); "Who's Afraid of the Big Bad Deficit?" *Economist,* 336(7934), September 30, 1995:25–26; Uchitelle, Louis, "Balancing Quantity, Quality and Inflation," *New York Times,* December 18, 1996: C1, C6; Marshall, Jonathan, "Figuring Inflation Is a Truly Tough Job," *San Francisco Chronicle,* December 9, 1996:C1, C2; Boskin et al. (1997); *Statistical Abstract of the United States* (Washington, D.C.: U.S. Bureau of the Census, 1999); White, Alan G., "Measurement Biases in Consumer Price Indexes," *International Statistical Review,* 67(3), December 1999:301–325; Boskin and Jorgenson (1997); symposium in *Journal of Economic Perspectives,* Winter 1998; **www.bls.gov/cpi/home.htm** (2002).

Chapter 5

Willingness to Pay on eBay: www.eBay.com.

Bruce Springsteen's Gift to His Fans: Johnson, Kevin C., "As Concert Tickets Rise Sharply, Attendance Falls Flat But Big-Name Acts May Yet Produce Record Profits for Industry," *St. Louis Post-Dispatch,* July 29, 2002:A1; Krueger, Alan B., "Economic Scene: Music Sales Slump, Concert Ticket Costs Jump and Rock Fans Pay the Price," *New York Times,* October 17, 2002: C2.

Compensating Variation for Television: Delsol, Michel, "Would You Give Up TV for a Million Bucks?" *TV Guide,* October 10, 1992:11; Aegis System Ltd., "Survey to Determine Consumers' Surplus Accruing TV Viewers and Radio Listeners," Prepared for the Radiocommunications Agency, October 2000.

Food Stamps: Moffitt (1989); Fraker (1990); Fasciano, Hall, and Beebout (1993); Carlson (1993); Winicki (2001); Whitmore (2002); "U.S. Converting Food Stamps into Debit-Card Benefits," *Chattanooga Times Free Press,* June 23, 2004.

Leisure-Income Choices of Textile Workers: Dunn (1977, 1978, 1979).

Winning the Good Life: Imbens et al. (2001).

Tax Revenues and Tax Cuts: Fullerton (1982); Stuart (1984); Goolsbee (2000); Fullerton and Gan (2004); Heijman and van Ophem (2005).

Chapter 6

Malthus and the Green Revolution: Tweeten, Luther, *Farm Policy Analysis* (Boulder, Colo.: Westview Press, 1989); Duvick, Donald N., "Genetic Contributions to Advances in Yield of U.S. Maize," *Maydica,* 37(1), 1992:69–79; Crossette, Barbara, "How to Fix a Crowded World: Add People," *New York Times,* November 2, 1997: sec. 4:1, 3; Brander and Taylor (1998); Phillips, Michael M., "Greenspan Credits New Technology for Helping Farmers Weather Crisis," *Wall Street Journal,* March 17, 1999; *Statistical Abstract of the United States* (Washington, D.C.: U.S. Bureau of the Census, 1999); *FAO Quarterly Bulletin of Statistics* (New York: United Nations, 1999); Barkema, Alan, "Ag

Biotech," *The Main Street Economist,* October 2000; Levy, Marc, "Robots Do the Milking at Some U.S. Dairy Farms," *San Francisco Chronicle,* March 4, 2002:E3; **www.unep.org/aeo/251.htm**; **www.fao.org/NEWS/2000/000704-e.htm**; Borlaug, Norman, "Nobel Lecture," December 11, 1970, **Nobelprize.org**; Easterbrook, Gregg, "Forgotten Benefactor of Humanity," *Atlantic Monthly,* February 1997; "Biotechnology and the Green Revolution: Interview with Norman Borlaug," November 2002, **ActionBioscience.org**.

A Semiconductor Integrated Circuit Isoquant: Nile Hatch, personal communications; Roy Mallory, personal communications; "PC Processor War Rages On," Deutsche Presse-Agentur, September 1, 2002.

Returns to Scale in U.S. Manufacturing: Hsieh (1995).

Dell Computer's Organizational Innovations: Songini, Marc L., "Just-In-Time Manufacturing," *Computerworld,* November 20, 2000; Perman, Stacy, "Automate or Die," *Business 2.0,* July 2001; Harrison, Crayton, "Innovative Manufacturing Gives Dell an Advantage," *Dallas Morning News,* July 24, 2002; Dignan, Larry, "Is Dell Hitting the Efficiency Wall?" *c/net* **News.Com,** July 29, 2002; Pletz, John, "Dell Turns Productivity Gains into Market Share," *Austin American Statesman,* August 26, 2002: D1; Rivlin, Gary, "Who's Afraid of China? How Dell Became the World's Most Efficient Computer Maker," *New York Times,* December 19, 2004:3:1 and 3:4; "Five Top Tips," *The Manufacturer,* March 8, 2005; *The Dell Effect,* Dell Computer Company, 2007, **www1.ap.dell.com/content/topics/global.aspx/corp/delleffect/en/index?c=au&l=en&s=corp.**

Chapter 7

Waiting for the Doctor: Bishai and Lang (2000); Moorhouse, Jamie, "Waiting Game," **www.chmonline.ca/issue/article.jsp?content=20020201_210080_9280**; Matthew Young, with Eamonn Butler, "Measuring How Long People Wait for NHS Treatment," Adam Smith Institute, 2002, **www.adamsmith.org/cissues/waiting-list.htm**; "NHS Waiting Time 'Underestimated,'" *BBC News,* May 27, 2004; "Waiting for Access," *CBC News,* September 10, 2004; Easton, Brian, "The Gains from Reducing Waiting Times," *Wellington Health Economist's Group,* April 21, 2005; Sachdave, Khushwant, "18 Months for a Brain Scan (or 2 Weeks Private)," *Daily Mail,* June 18, 2005; Esmail, Nadeem, and Michael A. Walker, "Waiting Your Turn: Hospital Waiting Lists in Canada, 16th Edition," The Fraser Institute, 2006; Department of Health, "Cancer Treatment Waiting Time Target Success," 2007, **www.dh.gov.uk/NewsHome/NewsArticle/fs/en? CONTENT_ID=4139467&chk=95FlSp.**

Swarthmore College's Cost of Capital: Passell, Peter, "One Top College's Price Tag: Why So Low, and So High?" *New York Times,* July 27, 1994:A1.

Short-Run Cost Curves for a Furniture Manufacturer: Hsieh (1995).

The Internet and Outsourcing: Richetel, Matt, "Outsourced All the Way," *San Francisco Chronicle,* June 21, 2005.

Innovations and Economies of Scale: Brown, Stuart F., "Robotic Assembly Lines Help Drive Tire Innovation," *New York Times,* January 13, 2007.

Choosing an Ink-Jet or a Laser Printer: Various advertisements.

Learning by Doing in Computer Chips: Gruber (1992); Irwin and Klenow (1994); Chung (2001).

Chapter 8

Breaking Even on Christmas Trees: "How They Do It: Breaking Even in a Seasonal Business," *New York Times,* December 25, 1993:21.

Oil Sands Shutdowns: Salpukas, Agis, "Low Prices Have Sapped Little Oil Producers," *New York Times,* April 3, 1999: B1, B4; Collier, Robert, "Oil's Dirty Future," *San Francisco Chronicle,* May 22, 2005:A1, A14, A15; Collier, Robert, "Coaxing Oil from Huge U.S. Shale Deposits," *San Francisco Chronicle,* September 4, 2006:A1.

Upward-Sloping Long-Run Supply Curve for Cotton: International Cotton Advisory Committee, *Survey of the Cost of Production of Raw Cotton,* September 1992:5; *Cotton: World Statistics,* April 1993:4–5. The figure shows the supply of the major producing countries for which we have cost information. The only large producers for whom cost data are missing are India and China.

Special Blends and Gasoline Supply Curves: Borenstein, Bushnell, and Lewis (2004); Baker, David R., "Rules Fuel Patchwork Quilt of Gas Blends Nationwide," *San Francisco Chronicle,* June 19, 2005:B1, B3.

Chapter 9

Deadweight Loss of Christmas: Waldfogel (1993); "Help! What Do We Do With All This Stuff? 'Regift,' of Course," *New York Times,* December 26, 2004:3.2.

Cab Fare: Fisher, Ian, "A Bumpier Ride for New York Taxis," *New York Times,* October 6, 1991:7; Marshall, Jonathan, "Cab Companies Haled into Court," *San Francisco Chronicle,* July 1, 1993:A1, A11; Fragin, Sheryl, "Taxi!" *Atlantic Monthly,* May 1994:30f; Yeh, Emerald, and Christine McMurry, "Are San Francisco Cabs a Bit Too Rare?" *San Francisco Chronicle,* September 15, 1996:4; Bowman, Catherine, "Why San Francisco Taxis Are Catch as Catch Can," *San Francisco Chronicle,* September 16, 1995:A1, A11; Harrington, Kathleen, "Bottom Line: 300 More Cabs Needed," *San Francisco Chronicle,* July 28, 1998:A19; Coliver, Victoria, "Taxi Turmoil," *San Francisco Examiner,* June 13, 1999:B1, B7; Epstein, Edward, "S.F. Tax Deal Rejected by Board of Supervisors," *San Francisco Chronicle,* April 13, 1999:A16; Boroski and Mildner (1998); Tharp, Pau, "He's Driven by Yellow Cabs," *New York Post,* June 30, 2002:31; Oberbeck, Steven, "Medallion Financial Looks to Utah to Expand Taxi Licenses," *Salt Lake Tribune,* August 13, 2002:B5; Schaller (2004); Berdik, Chris, "Fare Game," *Boston Globe,* 42(9) September 2004:98–105; Kim, Hansu, "Taxi Medallions—Why Give S.F. Assets Away?" *San Francisco Chronicle,* March 29, 2005:B7.

Deadweight Loss from Wireless Taxes: Hausman (2000).

Giving Money to Farmers: *Agricultural Policies in OECD Countries* (Geneva: Organization for Economic Cooperation and Development, 2006).

Chapter 10

Partial Versus General Equilibrium Analysis in Corn and Soy Markets: Holt (1992).

Urban Flight: Econsult (2003); Crawford et al. (2004).

Wealth Distribution in the United States: Nasar, Sylvia, "The Rich Get Richer, but Never the Same Way Twice," *New York Times,* August 16, 1992:3; Golan, Elise, and Mark Nord, "How Government Assistance Affects Income," *Food Review,* 21(1), January–April 1998:2–7; Johnston, David Cay, "Gap Between Rich and Poor Bigger than Ever," *San Francisco Examiner,* September 5, 1999:B4; "*Forbes*' List of the Wealthy Finds Richest Even Richer," *San Francisco Chronicle,* September 24, 1999:A2; Kennickell (2001, 2003); Johnston, David Cay, "Richest Are Leaving Even the Rich Far Behind," *New York Times,* June 5, 2005:A1, A17; Said, Carolyn, "Number of Millionaires Rises in Bay Area, U.S. and World," *San Francisco Chronicle,* June 10, 2005:C1, C5.

How You Vote Matters: "The Mathematics of Voting: Democratic Symmetry," *The Economist,* March 4, 2000:83.

Chapter 11

Cable Cars and Profit Maximization: Gordon, Rachel, "A Fare Too Steep?" *San Francisco Chronicle,* September 12, 2006:B-1.

Apple's iPod: "The History of Apple's iPod," **osviews.com/modules. php?op=modload&name=News&file=article&sid=4259**; Gibson, Brad, "First on TMO," **www.macobserver.com**, November 3, 2004, and May 4, 2005; "A Brief History of the iPod," **www.uberreview.com/ history.htm**, 2004–2005; **en.wikipedia.org/wiki/Ipod**, July 28, 2005; Betteridge, Ian, "iPod Market Share Falls to 87%," **www.pcmag.com/ default/0,2602,,00.asp**; "iPod Earns 72% Market Share in December," *iPodObserver.com,* January 17, 2007, **www.ipodobserver.com/story/ 29996**.

Electric Power Utilities: Christensen and Greene (1976).

Botox Patent Monopoly: Weiss, Mike, "For S.F. Doctor, Drug Botox Becomes a Real Eye-Opener," *San Francisco Chronicle,* April 14, 2002:A1, A19; Abelson, Reed, "F.D.A. Approves Allergan Drug for Fighting Wrinkles," *New York Times,* April 16, 2002; Tramer, Harriet, "Docs Detecting How to Boost Botox Profitability," *Crain's Cleveland Business,* March 7, 2005:17; Singer, Natasha, "Botox Plus: New Mixes for Plumping and Padding," *New York Times,* July 14, 2005; "The No-Knife Eye Lift," **magazines.ivillage.com/goodhousekeeping/archive/0,, 284598,00.html**, 2005. The graph shows an inverse linear demand curve of the form $p = a - bQ$. Such a linear demand curve has an elasticity of $\varepsilon = -(1/b)(p/Q)$. Given that the elasticity of demand is $-400/375 = -(1/b)(400/1)$, where Q is measured in millions of vials, then $b = 375$. Solving $p = 400 = a - 375 \times 1$, we find that $a = 775$. The height of triangle $A + B + C$ is $750 = \$775 - \$25$, and its length is 2 million vials, so its area is \$750 million.

Internet and Other Pirates: Protecting Intellectual Property Rights: Kahn, Joseph, "The Pinch of Piracy Wakes China Up On Copyright Issue," *New York Times,* November 1, 2002:C1, C5; Evangelista, Benny, and Nick Wingfield, "Online Swapping of Music Declines in Wake of Suits," *Wall Street Journal,* January 5, 2004:B4; Connolly and Krueger (2005); Wardell, Jane, "Software Piracy Rate Is Steady," *San Francisco Chronicle,* May 19, 2005; Kirby, Carrie, "Survey Shows Little Progress in Effort to Halt Pirated Software," *San Francisco Chronicle,* May 19, 2005; Charles, Deborah, "U.S. Court Rules against Grokster in File-Share Case," Reuters, June 27, 2005; Said, Carolyn, "Pay to Play—Or Else," *San Francisco Chronicle,* June 28, 2005; BSA, "Piracy Study," May 2006, **www.bsa.org/globalstudy/upload/2005%20Piracy% 20Study%20-%20Official%20Version.pdf**; "China Signs Anti-Piracy Deal with MPA," December 19, 2006, **www.businessofcinema. com/?file=story&id=2171**.

Creating and Destroying an Auto Monopoly: Heong, Chee Yoke, "Malaysia's Proton Struggles On," *Asia Times Online,* **www.atimes.com**, August 26, 2003; "Malaysian Government Buys Back Stake in Proton," *Mercury News,* January 12, 2005; Reuters, "Auto Sales Expected to Slow in Malaysia," **secure.detroitnewspapers.com**, January 26, 2005; Kamiso, Sidek, "Dr Mahathir: Proton Has to Raise Output," **thestar.com.my**, February 12, 2005.

Chapter 12

Disneyland Pricing: Disneyland, **www.disneyland.com**.

Amazon.com Is Watching You: Streitfeld, David, "Amazon Pays a Price for Marketing Test," *Los Angeles Times,* October 2, 2000:C1; Streitfeld, David, "Amazon Mystery: Pricing of Books," *Los Angeles Times,* January 2, 2007; **www.managingchange.com/dynamic/ survey/analysis.html**.

Botox Revisited: See Chapter 11 application "Botox Patent Monopoly."

Unions That Have It All: Sleeth, Peter, and Jim Lynch, "Lockout Disaster Averted," *Sunday Oregonian,* October 13, 2002:F1; Raine, George, "Port Talks Turn Positive," *San Francisco Chronicle,* November 2, 2002:A1, A16; Moberg, David, "What's Up on the Docks?" *These Times,* November 11, 2002:12; **www.ilwu.org**; Biers, Carl, and Marsha Niemeijer, "Members Angry Over Multi-Tier Wage and Benefit System," **www.labornotes.org**, June 2004; *Pacific Coast Longshore Contract Document,* July 1, 2002–July 1, 2008.

Smuggling Prescription Drugs into the United States: Harper, Tim, "Canada's Drugs 'Dangerous,'" *Toronto Star,* August 28, 2003:A12; Rowland, Christopher, "FDA Sting Targets Medicine Supplier Springfield," *Boston Globe,* August 28, 2003; Pugh, Tony, "Canadian Online Pharmacies Struggle to Find Suppliers," *San Diego Union-Tribune,* September 7, 2003:A-3; Harris, Gardiner, "U.S. Moves to Halt Import Of Drugs From Canada," *New York Times,* September 10, 2003:C2; Connolly, Ceci, "Hopefuls Back Drug Reimports," *Washington Post,* October 8, 2003:A6; Baldor, Lolita C., "FDA Questions Canada Drug Import Safety," *Associated Press Online,* December 23, 2003; "Survey: U.S. Families Struggle to Pay for Drugs," MSNBC News, February 23, 2004; Pear, Robert, "U.S. to Study Importing Canada Drugs," *New York Times,* February 26, 2004:A16; Colliver, Victoria, "U.S. Drug Prices 81% Higher than in 7 Western Nations," *San Francisco Chronicle,* October 29, 2004:C1, C6; Timmons, Heather, "Court Refuses To Hear Case on European Drug Pricing," *New York Times,* June 1, 2005:C7; Ridgeway, James, "Congress vs. Big Pharma: Let the Games Begin," *Mother Jones,* December 14 , 2006.

Consumers Pay for Lower Prices: Borenstein and Rose (1994); Varian, Hal, "Priceline's Magic Show," *Industry Standard,* April 17, 2000; "PMA Coupon Council Celebrates September as National Coupon Month," *PR Newswire,* September 3, 2002; **www.couponmonth. com/pages/ allabout.htm** (2005); **www.pmalink.org/about/press_releases/ release80.asp** (2005).

IBM: *IBM* v. *United States,* 298 U.S. 131 (1936).

Magazine Advertising: "Magazine Fund Ensures Canadian Presence," *Montreal Gazette,* May 24, 2002:B2; Carr, David, "Magazines: With Advertising in Deep Distress, Publishers Consider an End to the Era of Cheap Subscriptions," *New York Times,* October 28, 2002:C9; **www.pch.gc.ca/progs/ac-ca/progs/fcm-cmf/index_e.cfm**; "News Mags Drop in Circulation," **NewsMax.com**, August 16, 2005; *The Magazine*

Handbook 2005/2006, **www.magazines.org**; "Newsstand Circ Drops," **www.mediabuyerplanner.com/2006/08/22/newsstand_circ_drops/**, August 22, 2006; **www.magazine.org/content/Files/MPAHandbook06. pdf**; "Time Magazine to Raise Cover Price by $1," *Houston Chronicle,* November 9, 2006, **www.chron.com/disp/story.mpl/ap/fn/4324638. html**.

Chapter 13

Catwalk Cartel: Sherman, William, "Catwalk Rocked by Legal Catfight," *Daily News,* March 14, 2004; St. John, Warren, "Behind the Catwalk, Suspicion and Suits," *New York Times,* April 18, 2004:sec. 9:1, 12; Chandler, Neil, "Models in GBP 28m Wage Battle," *Daily Star,* June 6, 2004:8; *Carolyn Fears et al.* v. *Wilhelmina Model Agency, Inc., et al.,* 02 Civ. 4911 (HB), United States District Court For The Southern District Of New York, 2004 U.S. Dist. Lexis 4502; 2004–1 Trade Cas. (CCH) P74,351, March 23, 2004.

Bail Bonds: Ayres and Waldfogel (1994).

Airline Mergers: Market Power Versus Flight Frequency: Richard (2003).

Air Ticket Prices and Rivalry: Weiher, Sickles, and Perloff (2002).

Government Aircraft Subsidies: Irwin and Pavcnik (2004); Brand, Constant, "EU, Washington Resume Battle Over Boeing," *San Francisco Chronicle,* May 31, 2005.

Deadweight Losses in the Food and Tobacco Industries: Bhuyan and Lopez (1998).

Welfare Gain from Greater Toilet Paper Variety: "Going Soft?" *The Economist,* March 4, 2000:59; Hausman and Leonard (2002).

Chapter 14

Chicken: Jacoby, Mary, "As Cars Collide, Belgian Motorists Refuse to Yield," *Wall Street Journal,* September 25, 2006:A1.

Strategic Advertising: "50 Years Ago . . .," *Consumer Reports,* January 1986; Roberts and Samuelson (1988); Gasmi, Laffont, and Vuong (1992); Elliott, Stuart, "Advertising," *New York Times,* April 28, 1994:C7; Slade (1995).

Advantages and Disadvantages of Moving First: The cost estimates are based on an iSuppli "teardown" analysis: McGrath, Dylan, "'Teardown' Finds Toshiba Taking a Loss on HD DVD Player," *EE Times,* June 23, 2006, **www.eetimes.com/showArticle.jhtml? articleID=189600999**; Urban, Carter, and Gaskin (1986); McGrath, Dylan, "Analyst Predicts Stalemate in Next-Gen DVD War," *EE Times,* June 23, 2006, **www.eetimes.com/showArticle.jhtml? articleID= 189601178**.

Who Bids Optimally?: Garratt et al. (2005).

Chapter 15

Black Death Raises Wages: Wellington (1990); **www.history-magazine.com/black.html**; **www.historylearningsite.co.uk/black_death_ of_1348-to-1350.htm**; **www.bric.postech.ac.kr/science/97now/00_ 11now/ 001127a.html**.

Company Towns: Romanko, J. R., "The Big Business of Small Towns," *New York Times,* September 22, 2002:sec. 6:20; Boyd, Lawrence W., "The Company Town," **www.eh.net.**

Durability of Telephone Poles: Marshall, Jonathan, "PG&E Cultivates Its Forest," *San Francisco Chronicle,* May 5, 1995:D1.

Returns to Studying Economics: Black et al. (2003).

Redwood Trees: Berck, Peter, and William R. Bentley, "Hotelling's Theory, Enhancement, and the Taking of the Redwood National Park," *American Journal of Agricultural Economics,* 79(2), May 1997:287–298; Peter Berck, personal communications.

Chapter 16

Biased Estimates?: Benjamin et al. (2001); Wyman, Scott, "Fatal Shark Attack Highlights Need for Safety," **Sun-Sentinel.com,** June 27, 2005; International Shark Attack File, **www.flmnh.ufl.edu/fish/sharks/ isaf/graphs.htm,** 2005; **www.arthurhu.com/index/health/death. htm#deathrank; www.findarticles.com/p/articles/mi_m0GER/ is_2002_Fall/ai_93135768;** Taylor, Jerome, and Anne Giacomantonio, "Survival Stories," *The Independent,* January 27, 2007, **news.independent. co.uk/environment/article2190042.ece.**

Gambling: Friedman and Savage (1948); Brunk (1981); Golec and Tamarkin (1995); Gurdon, Meghan Cox, "British Accuse Their Lottery of Robbing the Poor to Give to the Rich," *San Francisco Chronicle,* November 25, 1995:D1; Coll, Steve, "Chances Are Brits Have Bet on It," *San Francisco Examiner,* July 10, 1994:4; Pollack, Andrew, "In the Gaming Industry, the House Can Have Bad Luck, Too," *New York Times,* July 25, 1999:Business, 4; Garrett and Sobel (1999); Will, George, "Government's Hand in Surge of Gambling," *San Francisco Chronicle,* June 28, 1999:A21; Garrett (2001); Walton, Marsha, "The Business of Gambling," **CNN.com,** July 6, 2005.

Harry Potter's Magic: Gardner, Amanda, "Harry Potter Books Keep Kids Safe," **www.healthday.com,** December 22, 2005; "Harry Potter and the Injury-Free Children," *San Francisco Chronicle,* December 27, 2005:A2.

Air Insurance: Insure America brochure; National Transportation Safety Board; "U.S. Airlines Getting Safer, Statistics Show," *St. Petersburg Times Online,* January 4, 2005; **www.airlines.org;** "The Day in Numbers: $6.5 Billion," *CNN.com,* October 3, 2006, **www.cnn. com/2006/BUSINESS/10/03/numbers.gambling/index.html.**

No Insurance for Natural Disasters: Treaster, Joseph B., "Insurer Curbing Sales of Policies in Storm Areas," *New York Times,* October 10, 1996:A1, C4; Treaster, Joseph B., "Headed for Trouble," *New York Times,* September 18, 1998:B1, B14; "The New Protection Game," *Consumer Reports,* January 1999:16–19; Treaster, Joseph B., "Why Insurers Shrink from Earthquake Risk," *New York Times,* November 21, 1999:sec. 3:1, 13; Abate, Tom, "Storm May Be Costliest Ever in U.S.," *San Francisco Chronicle,* August 31, 2005:C1; Sterngold, James, "Losses Could Total $100 Billion," *San Francisco Chronicle,* September 4, 2005:A7.

Risk Premium: "The Cost of Looking," *Economist,* 328(7828), September 11, 1993:74; Eaton, Leslie, "Assessing a Fund's Risk Is Part Math, Part Art," *New York Times,* April 2, 1995:sec. 3:9; Jagannathan, McGrattan, and Scherbina (2000); **www.standardandpoors.com;**
www.thornburginvestments.com/research/articles/ real_real_0705.asp (2005).

Chapter 17

Negative Externality: SUVs Kill: White (2004); Anderson (2006).

Positive Externality: Michael Jordan: Hausman and Leonard (1997); *Harper's Index,* 1999; Wise, Mike, "NBC Focuses on the Story Lines," *New York Times,* May 9, 1999; "Jordan Is No Slam Dunk," *CNNMoney,* September 28, 2001; "Old Man Wizard Keeps Rolling It In," *U.S. News & World Report,* October 8, 2001:10; Weinstein, Brad, "No-Frills Free Agents Foiled by Impending Tax," *San Francisco Chronicle,* August 4, 2002:B3.

Pulp and Paper Mill Pollution and Regulation: Gray and Shadbegian (2004); Shadbegian and Gray (2003).

Sobering Drunk Drivers: Levitt and Porter (2001); **www.drinking driving.net; www.ohsinc.com/drunk_driving_laws_blood_breath% 20_alcohol_limits_CHART.htm; www.aaa-calif.com/members/ corpinfo/duiguide.asp#sec4;** *Drinking and Driving Report 2003,* The Brewers of Europe, 2004, **www.brewersofeurope.org/uk/$$$members $$$/doc/others/publications/drink_drive_report_2003.pdf.**

U.S. and EU Approaches to Regulating Pollution: Becker, Gary S., "A High Gas Tax, Not Fuel Efficiency Rules, Will Get Drivers to Conserve," *Wisconsin State Journal,* June 21, 2002:A12; "The Invisible Green Hand," *The Economist,* July 6, 2002; "Can the 'Environmental Tax Shift' Really Help?" *Green Living Magazine,* November 28, 2002:E3; see Brozovic, Sunding, and Zilberman (2002) for an explanation of why real-world standards are more likely to dominate fees than this example suggests.

Selling the Right to Pollute: Burtraw, Dallas, "Trading Emissions to Clean the Air: Exchanges Few but Savings Many," *Resources,* 122, Winter 1996:3–6; Passell, Peter, "For Utilities, New Clean-Air Plan," *New York Times,* November 18, 1994:C1, C6; Wald, Matthew L., "Acid-Rain Pollution Credits Are Not Enticing Utilities," *New York Times,* June 5, 1995:C11; Passell, Peter, "Economic Scene," *New York Times,* January 4, 1996:C2; Rensberger, Boyce, "Clean Air Sale," *Washington Post,* August 8, 1999:W7; Schmalensee et al. (1998); "Trading in Pollution," *OECD Observer,* August 19, 2002; Reuters, "Brokers Blaze Trail for New Greenhouse Gas Market," *EVWorld,* August 28, 2002; **www.epa.gov/region09/air/reclaim/index.html; www.epa.gov/airmarkt/ progress/arpreport/acidrainprogress.pdf; www.emissionstrading. com; www.epa.com; www.wikipedia.com;** Bennhold, Katrin, "New Limits on Pollution Herald Change in Europe," *New York Times,* January 1, 2005:C2; EPA, "Clear Air Interstate Rule," March 2005.

Emptying the Seas: "The Economics of the Sea," *Economist,* 334(7906), March 18, 1995:48; Clifford, Frank, "Fishing Limits on Key Species Take Effect," *Los Angeles Times,* January 1, 1998:A29; "New England Fisherman Fear Catch Limits for Cod," *San Francisco Chronicle,* December 7, 1998:A4; Molyneaux, Paul, "Drastic Measures to Save Cod Are Discussed in New England," *New York Times,* March 7, 1999:35; "The Invisible Green Hand," *The Economist,* July 6, 2002; **www.grinningplanet.com/2005/06-07/overfishing-article.htm; www.fao.org/documents/show_cdr.asp?url_file=//DOCREP/007/y5 600e/y5600e05.htm@;** Freeman, Allison A., "Fisheries: Feds Try Cap-and-Trade Regs to Halt 'Race for Fish,'" **www.eenews.net/eenewspm/ print/2006/03/24/1.**

Free Riding on Water: Grossman, Pirozzi, and Pope (1993).

What's Their Beef?: Holland, Gina, "Top Court Considers Challenge to Beef Ads," *San Francisco Chronicle,* December 9, 2004:C1, C4; **www. extension.iastate.edu/agdm/articles/mceowen/McEowJuly05.htm**.

Chapter 18

Removing Pounds or Dollars?: *2004 Weight-Loss Advertising Survey,* Federal Trade Commission, April 2005; Kolata, Gina, "Diet and Lose Weight? Scientists Say 'Prove It!'" *New York Times,* January 4, 2005:D1, D6; **www.medifast1.com/index.asp?engine=adwords!2931&keyword= %28medifast+weight+loss%29&match_type=**; www.optifast.com/ at_a_glance.jsp.

Risky Hobbies: Cropper, Carol Marie, "Risk Takers Pay Dearly: It's the Danger of Living Fearlessly," *New York Times,* April 2, 1995:sec. 3:11.

Adverse Selection on eBay: Dewan and Hsu (2004).

Chapter 19

Contracts and Productivity in Agriculture: Foster and Rosenzweig (1994).

Contingent Fees Versus Hourly Pay: Kakalik and Pace (1986); Gravelle, Hugh, and Michael Waterson, "No Win, No Fee: Some Economics of Contingent Legal Fees," *Economic Journal,* 103(420), September 1993:1205–1220; Shearer (2004).

Abusing Leased Cars: Dunham (2003); *Car Talk,* National Public Radio, May 1997; Valdes-Dapena, Peter, "Car Leases are Back: Should You Bite?" *CNN/Money,* May 26, 2005.

Mortgaging Our Future: White, Lawrence J., *The S&L Debacle* (New York: Oxford University Press, 1991); Labaton, Stephen, "The Debacle That Buried Washington," *New York Times,* November 22, 1998:sec. 3:1, 12; Andrews, Edmund L., "A Hands-Off Policy on Mortgage Loans," *New York Times,* July 15, 2005.

Credits

Index